THE ROUTLEDGE HISTORY OF HUMAN RIGHTS

The Routledge History of Human Rights is an interdisciplinary collection that provides historical and global perspectives on a range of human rights themes of the past 150 years.

The volume is made up of 34 original contributions. It opens with the emergence of a "new internationalism" in the mid-nineteenth century, examines the interwar, League of Nations, and the United Nations eras of human rights and decolonization, and ends with the serious challenges for rights norms, laws, institutions, and multilateral cooperation in the national security world after 9/11. These essays provide a big picture of the strategic, political, and changing nature of human rights work in the past and into the present day, and reveal the contingent nature of historical developments. Highlighting local, national, and non-Western voices and struggles, the volume contributes to overcoming Eurocentric biases that burden human rights histories and studies of international law. It analyzes regions and organizations that are often overlooked. The volume thus offers readers a new and broader perspective on the subject.

International in coverage and containing cutting-edge interpretations, the volume provides an overview of major themes and suggestions for future research. This is the perfect book for those interested in social justice, grass roots activism, and international politics and society.

Jean H. Quataert is SUNY Distinguished Professor of History Emerita at Binghamton University, USA and co-editor of the *Journal of Women's History* (2010–20). She has published many books and articles, including *Advocating Dignity: Human Rights Mobilizations in Global Politics* (2009) and "A New Look at International Law: Gendering the Practices of Humanitarian Medicine in Europe's 'Small Wars,' 1879–1907," *Human Rights Quarterly*, 2018, vol. 40, no. 3, 547–69.

Lora Wildenthal is John Antony Weir Professor of History and Associate Dean of Humanities at Rice University in Houston, Texas, USA. She is the author of *German Women for Empire, 1884–1945* (2001) and *The Language of Human Rights in West Germany* (2013).

THE ROUTLEDGE HISTORIES

The Routledge Histories is a series of landmark books surveying some of the most important topics and themes in history today. Edited and written by an international team of world-renowned experts, they are the works against which all future books on their subjects will be judged.

THE ROUTLEDGE HISTORY OF THE RENAISSANCE
Edited by William Caferro

THE ROUTLEDGE HISTORY OF MADNESS AND MENTAL HEALTH
Edited by Greg Eghigian

THE ROUTLEDGE HISTORY OF DISABILITY
Edited by Roy Hanes, Ivan Brown, and Nancy E. Hansen

THE ROUTLEDGE HISTORY OF NINETEENTH-CENTURY AMERICA
Edited by Jonathan Daniel Wells

THE ROUTLEDGE HISTORY OF GENDER, WAR, AND THE U.S. MILITARY
Edited by Kara Dixon Vuic

THE ROUTLEDGE HISTORY OF THE AMERICAN SOUTH
Edited by Maggi M. Morehouse

THE ROUTLEDGE HISTORY OF ITALIAN AMERICANS
Edited by William J. Connell and Stanislao Pugliese

THE ROUTLEDGE HISTORY OF LATIN AMERICAN CULTURE
Edited by Carlos Manuel Salomon

THE ROUTLEDGE HISTORY OF GLOBAL WAR AND SOCIETY
Edited by Matthew S. Muehlbauer and David J. Ulbrich

THE ROUTLEDGE HISTORY OF TWENTIETH-CENTURY UNITED STATES
Edited by Jerald R. Podair and Darren Dochuk

THE ROUTLEDGE HISTORY OF WORLD PEACE SINCE 1750
Edited by Christian Philip Peterson, William M. Knoblauch, and Michael Loadenthal

THE ROUTLEDGE HISTORY OF MEDIEVAL MAGIC
Edited by Sophie Page and Catherine Rider

THE ROUTLEDGE HISTORY OF MONARCHY
Edited by Elena Woodacre, Lucinda H.S. Dean, Chris Jones, Russell E. Martin, and Zita Eva Rohr

THE ROUTLEDGE HISTORY OF EMOTIONS IN EUROPE, 1100–1700
Edited by Andrew Lynch and Susan Broomhall

THE ROUTLEDGE HISTORY OF HUMAN RIGHTS
Edited by Jean H. Quataert and Lora Wildenthal

For more information about this series, please visit:
www.routledge.com/Routledge-Histories/book-series/RHISTS

THE ROUTLEDGE HISTORY OF HUMAN RIGHTS

Edited by
Jean H. Quataert and Lora Wildenthal

Routledge
Taylor & Francis Group
LONDON AND NEW YORK

First published 2020
by Routledge
2 Park Square, Milton Park, Abingdon, Oxon OX14 4RN

and by Routledge
52 Vanderbilt Avenue, New York, NY 10017

Routledge is an imprint of the Taylor & Francis Group, an informa business

First issued in paperback 2021

British Library Cataloguing-in-Publication Data
A catalogue record for this book is available from the British Library

Library of Congress Cataloging-in-Publication Data
A catalog record has been requested for this book

ISBN: 978-1-138-78433-8 (hbk)
ISBN: 978-1-032-08966-9 (pbk)
ISBN: 978-0-429-32437-6 (ebk)

Typeset in Baskerville
by Swales & Willis, Exeter, Devon, UK

CONTENTS

List of illustrations x
List of contributors xi
Acknowledgments xviii

1 **Introduction: an open-ended and contingent history of human rights** 1
JEAN H. QUATAERT AND LORA WILDENTHAL

PART I
The new internationalism 19

2 **John Anderson – slave, refugee, and freedom fighter: a human rights campaign in the age of empire** 21
CAROLINE SHAW

3 **Investigating and ameliorating atrocities in the nineteenth century: international commissions of inquiry in the Balkans (1876–80)** 37
BENJAMIN E. BROCKMAN-HAWE

4 **Reclaiming Congo reform for the history of human rights** 57
MAIRI S. MACDONALD

5 **The Red Cross and the laws of war, 1863–1949: international rights activism before human rights** 75
KIMBERLY A. LOWE

PART II
The interwar era: the League of Nations 97

6 **United in their quest for peace? Transnational women activists between the World Wars** 99
MARIE SANDELL

7 **The "rights of man" and sex equality: international human rights discourses in the 1930s** 122
REGULA LUDI

PART III
The formative UN era
A. UN treaty-making 139

8 **Social and economic rights: the struggle for equivalent protection** 141
CLAIRE-MICHELLE SMYTH

9 **Islam and UN human rights treaty ratification in the Middle East: the impact of international law on diplomacy** 163
RACHEL A. GEORGE

10 **When the war came: the child rights convention and the conflation of human rights and the laws of war** 183
LINDE LINDKVIST

B. Decolonization 201

11 **"Why then call it the declaration of human rights?" The failures of universal human rights in colonial Africa's internationally supervised territories** 203
MEREDITH TERRETTA

12 **Decolonization, development, and identity: the evolution of the anticolonial human rights critique, 1948–78** 222
ROLAND BURKE

13 **"When you are weak, you have to stick to principles": Botswana and anticolonialism in human rights history** 241
JAMES CHRISTIAN KIRBY

C. Socialist and capitalist versions of human rights 257

14 **The International Labour Organization and the gender of economic rights** 259
EILEEN BORIS AND JILL JENSEN

15 **Human rights movements and the fall of the Berlin wall: explaining the peaceful revolution of 1989** 281
NED RICHARDSON-LITTLE

16 **Human rights in China: resisting orthodoxy** 298
PITMAN B. POTTER

17 **Continuity and change in US human rights policy** 316
SARAH B. SNYDER

PART IV
After formal empire and the Cold War: how human rights are practiced around the globe (1980s–2001) 335

18 **The universality of human rights: early NGO practices in the Arab world** 337
CATHERINE BAYLIN DURYEA

19 **How women become human: Chilean contributions to women's human rights from dictatorship to the twenty-first century** 354
JADWIGA E. PIEPER MOONEY

20 **The Mothers of the Plaza de Mayo: from dictatorship to democracy** 375
JENNIFER ADAIR

21 **Asma Jahangir: personifying the human rights debate in Pakistan** 392
AFIYA SHEHRBANO ZIA

PART V
The universal human rights pantheon in national contexts 413

22 **Freedom of religion and the new diversity: case studies from Canada** 415
LORI G. BEAMAN

23 **Indigenous activism for human rights: a case study from Australia** 432
RACHEL STANDFIELD AND LYNETTE RUSSELL

24 The international LGBT rights movement: an introductory history 448
LAURA A. BELMONTE

25 Rights in isolation: lessons on public health and human rights from leprosy and HIV in the Pacific Islands 467
ADAM R HOUSTON

PART VI
New forms of accountability in a national security world (2001 to the present) 487

26 Decentralization and public–private diplomacy in the business and human rights field 489
STEVEN S. NAM

27 The selectivity of universal jurisdiction: the history of transnational human rights prosecutions in Latin America and Spain 507
ULRIKE CAPDEPÓN

28 Militarized sexual violence and campaigns for redress 523
VERA MACKIE

29 Solidarity rights and the common heritage of humanity 542
ANCA CLAUDIA PRODAN

30 Intellectual property law and human rights 559
STEVEN WILF

31 Caged at the border: immigration detention and the denial of human rights to asylum seekers and other migrants 579
STEPHANIE J. SILVERMAN AND PETRA MOLNAR

PART VII
The transformative impact of human rights on knowledge 601

32 Archiving human rights in Latin America: transitional justice and shifting visions of political change 603
MICHELLE CARMODY

33 Emotion in the history of human rights: a case study of the Canadian Museum for Human Rights 621
CHRISTINE LAVRENCE

34 From the classroom to the public: engaging students in human rights history 638
JESSICA M. FRAZIER

Selected bibliography 650
Index 661

ILLUSTRATIONS

Figures

3.1	From *The Graphic*, 7 September 1878. The Commission is "busy at work at Gabrova, examining the victims of Russian brutality at Kushalar. Consul Fawcett is interrogating the unfortunates; and the remaining Europeans are the other members of the Commission"	41
3.2	Map of a portion of the Rhodope Mountains based on a sketch by Commissioner Fawcett, showing the locations of burned villages, abandoned villages, and repopulated villages	43
4.1	King Leopold II's Independent Congo State	59
9.1	Map of the MENA region, including the countries discussed in this essay	164
13.1	Southern Africa, ca. 1977	242
25.1	The Pacific Islands	468

Tables

9.1	MENA RUDs to CAT	169
9.2	MENA RUDs to CRC	169
9.3	MENA RUDs to CEDAW	171

CONTRIBUTORS

Jennifer Adair is Assistant Professor of History at Fairfield University. Her current research examines the restoration of democracy in Latin America following decades of military dictatorship and fiscal crisis. She is the author of *In Search of the Lost Decade: Everyday Rights in Post-Dictatorship Argentina*, forthcoming in 2019.

Lori G. Beaman, PhD, FRSC, is the Canada Research Chair in Religious Diversity and Social Change and Professor in the Department of Classics and Religious Studies at the University of Ottawa. She was Principal Investigator of the Religion and Diversity Project, a 37-member international research team whose focus was religion and diversity (www.religionanddiversity.ca). Recent books include *Deep Equality in an Era of Religious Diversity* (2017), and *Rethinking Reasonable Accommodation: Muslims and the Navigation and Negotiation of the Everyday* (2018), co-authored with Jennifer Selby and Amélie Barras. She has published numerous articles, including "Living Together v. Living Well Together: A Normative Examination of the SAS Case," *Social Inclusion*, 2017, vol. 4, no. 2, 3–13; "Recognize the New Religious Diversity," *Canadian Diversity*, 2017, vol. 14, no. 4, 17–19; and "Transcendence/Religion to Immanence/Nonreligion in Assisted Dying," *International Journal of Human Rights in Healthcare*, 2018, vol. 11, no. 2, 129–43, co-authored with Cory Steele. She is the 2017 recipient of the Social Sciences and Humanities Research Council of Canada's Impact Award in the Insight Category. Beaman also holds an Honorary Doctorate from Uppsala University.

Laura A. Belmonte is Dean of the College of Liberal Arts and Human Sciences at Virginia Polytechnic Institute and State University in Blacksburg, Virginia. A specialist in the history of US foreign relations, she is author of *Selling the American Way: US Propaganda and the Cold War* (2010) and co-author of *Global Americans: A History of the United States* (2017). Her new book, *The International LGBT Rights Movement: A History*, is forthcoming in 2020.

Eileen Boris is the Hull Professor and Distinguished Professor of Feminist Studies, History, Black Studies, and Global Studies at the University of California at Santa Barbara. She writes on the home as a workplace and on racialized gender and the state. Her books include the prizewinning monographs *Home to Work: Motherhood and the Politics of Industrial Homework in the United States* (1994) and *Caring for America: Home Health Workers in the Shadow of the Welfare State*, co-authored with Jennifer Klein (2012, rpt. 2015). She is co-editor with Rhacel Parreñas of *Intimate Labors: Cultures, Technologies, and the Politics of Care*

(2010) and co-editor with Dorothea Hoehtker and Susan Zimmermann of *Women's ILO: Transnational Networks, Global Labour Standards, and Gender Equity, 1919 to Present* (2018). Her latest book is *Making the Woman Worker: Precarious Labor and the Fight for Global Standards, 1919–2019* (2019). She is the President of the International Federation for Research in Women's History, 2015–20, and has served most recently on the advisory boards of the Global Labor Migration Network, Center for Global Migration Studies, University of Maryland, College Park, and on DomEQUAL: A Global Approach to Paid Domestic Work and Social Inequalities, Ca'Foscari, University of Venice.

Benjamin E. Brockman-Hawe received his JD from Boston University, where he graduated with honors in the concentration of International Law in 2008, and received his LLM from Columbia University in 2016.

Roland Burke is author of *Decolonization and the Evolution of International Human Rights* (2010) and Senior Lecturer in History at La Trobe University in Melbourne, Australia. His research is focused on international idealism, principally postwar human rights. His recent work has charted the changing meaning of the Universal Declaration of Human Rights (*Journal of Global History, International History Review, History & Memory*), economic and social rights (*Humanity*), and the recession of sentiment and emotion in human rights diplomacy and activism (*Human Rights Quarterly* and the *Journal of Human Rights*). He is currently revising a manuscript on challenges to the ideas set out in the 1948 Universal Declaration, *Human Rights in Eclipse.*

Ulrike Capdepón is currently Research Fellow with the "Reconstructing Memory in the City – Transnational and Local (European) Sites of Memory" Balzan Prize project with Professors Aleida Assmann and Jan Assmann at the University of Konstanz, Germany. She is also Lecturer in the Program in Latin American Studies (PLAS) at Princeton University. She holds a PhD in Political Science from the University of Hamburg, Germany (2011) and is Associate Researcher at the Institute of Latin American Studies (ILAS) of the German Institute of Global and Area Studies (GIGA). She has been a Marie Curie Fellow at the Spanish National Research Council (CSIC) in Madrid and a Postdoctoral Research Fellow in the European Research Council project "Narratives of Terror and Disappearance in Argentina" at the University of Konstanz. From 2014 to 2016, she was a Postdoctoral Research Scholar affiliated with the Institute for the Study of Human Rights (ISHR) at Columbia University in New York City. Her research interests include human rights, memory studies, and transitional justice processes in Latin America and Spain, as well as national and international prosecutions of human rights crimes and enforced disappearance.

Michelle Carmody is Lecturer in Latin American Studies at the University of Melbourne, Australia. Her book *Human Rights, Transitional Justice, and the Reconstruction of Political Order in Latin America* (2018) examines state-sponsored human rights policies in the period following the Cold War, while her research agenda more broadly considers how Latin Americans use the opportunities provided by human rights politics to transform their societies.

Catherine Baylin Duryea is Assistant Professor at St. Johns School of Law and a PhD Candidate in History at Stanford University. Her dissertation is titled *Practicing*

Human Rights in the Arab World: International Law in 20th-Century Advocacy. She earned a BA and JD from Stanford, and an MA from the American University in Cairo.

Jessica M. Frazier, PhD, is Assistant Professor in the Department of History, Gender and Women's Studies Program, and the Department of Marine Affairs at the University of Rhode Island, Kingston, Rhode Island. She is the author of *Women's Antiwar Diplomacy During the Vietnam War Era* (2017).

Rachel A. George is Senior Researcher in the Overseas Development Institute in London, where her research focuses on law, international relations, and the Middle East. Her research has been featured in blogs, books, and journals, including the *International Journal on Law and Interdisciplinary Legal Studies* and the volume *The Arab Gulf and the West: Perception and Realities – Opportunities and Perils* (2018). She holds a BA in Politics from Princeton University, an MA in Middle Eastern Studies from Harvard University, and a PhD in International Relations from the London School of Economics and Political Science.

Adam R Houston holds a JD, an MA in Global Development, and an LLM in Health Law. His research is on the intersection of health, human rights, and globalization. He has worked with organizations such as Avocats Sans Frontières Canada, the Pacific Islands AIDS Foundation, and the Institute for Justice & Democracy in Haiti. He has published in journals such as *Health & Human Rights Journal* and *Foreign Affairs*. He is currently a PhD candidate in Law at the University of Ottawa.

Jill Jensen is a Visiting Assistant Professor in the Department of Business Administration and Management, University of Redlands, in Redlands, California, where she teaches courses on the history of capitalism, workers in the global economy, and the history of work. Her research focuses on US policies regarding international labor standards, human rights, and the basic needs approach of the International Labour Organization (ILO) and wider UN. She is co-editor with Nelson Lichtenstein of *The ILO from Geneva to the Pacific Rim: West Meets East* (2016), and editor of a section on women and development that will be included in the Women and Social Movements Library (2020).

James Christian Kirby is a COFUND Junior Research Fellow in History at Durham University, Durham, UK. He completed his PhD at La Trobe University in Melbourne, Australia, under the supervision of Dr. Roland Burke, with a doctoral dissertation on the history of human rights and decolonization in Botswana. He has published articles in several peer-reviewed journals, including *International History Review, Journal of Imperial and Commonwealth History*, and *law&history*.

Christine Lavrence, PhD, is Associate Professor in the Department of Sociology at King's University College at Western University, in London, Ontario. Her research interests include memory and memorialization, culture, gender, and identity. Her work has been published in the *Canadian Review of Sociology, Oral History Review*, and *Space and Culture*, among other journals.

Linde Lindkvist is Senior Lecturer in Human Rights Studies at the School of Human Rights, Stockholm University College, Stockholm, Sweden. He specializes in questions of human rights history, the right to religious freedom, and children's rights. He is the author of *Religious Freedom and the Universal Declaration of Human Rights* (2017), which evolved out of his 2014 PhD thesis completed at Lund University. His ongoing postdoctoral project concerns the origins of the UN Convention on the Rights of the Child.

Kimberly A. Lowe is Assistant Professor of History at Lesley University in Cambridge, Massachusetts, USA. She received her PhD from Yale University and has held doctoral and postdoctoral fellowships at Amherst College (Amherst, Massachusetts), the Graduate Institute of International and Development Studies (Geneva, Switzerland), and the Albert-Ludwigs-Universität (Freiburg im Breisgau, Germany). Her research interests include the history of humanitarianism, international humanitarian law, transnational social movements, and intergovernmental organizations. Recent publications include "The League of Red Cross Societies and International Committee of the Red Cross: A Re-Evaluation of American Influence in Interwar Internationalism," *Moving the Social. Journal of Social History and the History of Social Movements*, 2017, vol. 57, 37–56 and "Humanitarianism and National Sovereignty: Red Cross Intervention on Behalf of Political Prisoners in Soviet Russia, 1921–3," *Journal of Contemporary History*, 2014, vol. 49, no. 4, 652–71.

Regula Ludi is Professor of Modern History at the University of Zurich and Research Director at the Interdisciplinary Center for Ethics and Human Rights of the University of Fribourg, Switzerland. Recent publications include *Reparations for Nazi Victims in Postwar Europe* (2012), *Zwang zur Freiheit. Krise und Neoliberalismus in der Schweiz*, co-edited with Matthias Ruoss and Leena Schmitter (2018), and articles in the *Journal of Women's History, Journal of Contemporary History*, and *Jewish Social Studies.*

Mairi S. MacDonald is an independent scholar and regulatory lawyer based in Toronto, Canada. In addition to her law degree, she holds a BA from Queen's University and PhD from the University of Toronto, both in history. Her writing and teaching interests include colonization, decolonization, and humanitarian intervention in Africa in the nineteenth and twentieth centuries and the importance of imperialism to the development of the normative and legal framework of international relations and human rights.

Vera Mackie is Senior Professor of Asian and International Studies and Director of the Centre for Critical Human Rights Research at the University of Wollongong, New South Wales, Australia. Publications include *Remembering Women's Activism*, co-authored with Sharon Crozier-De Rosa (2019) *Routledge Handbook of Sexuality Studies in East Asia*, co-edited with Mark McLelland (2015), and *Ways of Knowing about Human Rights in Asia* (2014).

Petra Molnar is a refugee and human rights lawyer in Toronto, Canada and a researcher at the International Human Rights Program, University of Toronto Faculty of Law. She focuses on immigration detention, health and human rights, new technologies in immigration, and the politics of refugee, immigration, and international law. She is co-author with Lex Gill, of *Bots at the Gate: A Human Rights Analysis of Automated Decision-Making in Canada's Refugee and Immigration System* (2018).

Steven S. Nam is Managing Editor of the *Stanford Journal of Blockchain Law & Policy*, a member of the Stanford CodeX Blockchain Group, and Law Steward (Advisor) for the

MIT Digital Currency Initiative. He earned a BA at Yale and an MA in Political Science and a JD at Columbia University, New York City.

Jadwiga E. Pieper Mooney is Associate Professor in the Department of History at the University of Arizona, USA. She is the author of *The Politics of Motherhood: Maternity and Women's Rights in Twentieth-Century Chile* (2009), co-editor with Fabio Lanza of *Decentering Cold War History: Local and Global Change* (2013), and co-editor with Tamara Chaplin of *The Global Sixties: Convention, Contest and Counterculture* (2017). She has written on forced sterilization campaigns and human rights violations in Peru and North Carolina, the experience of exile in the Cold War, reproductive rights, and transnational women's activism. Her research interests focus on Latin America and explore subjects of gender, human rights, feminisms, and the global politics of health and rights.

Pitman B. Potter is Professor of Law at Peter A. Allard School of Law at the University of British Columbia, Vancouver, British Columbia, Canada. He has authored many books about law in China, including most recently *Assessing Treaty Performance in China: Trade and Human Rights* (2014) and *The Legal System of the People's Republic of China* (2013). He is a Fellow of the Royal Society of Canada.

Anca Claudia Prodan, PhD, is Scientific Associate and Lecturer at the Brandenburg Technical University Cottbus-Senftenberg, Cottbus, Germany. She teaches, researches, and publishes on various subjects in the field of Heritage Studies. She is a corresponding member of the Sub-Committee for Education and Research of the UNESCO Memory of the World Programme, a member of the Editorial Advisory Board of the Heritage Studies Series published by Springer International Publishing, and a member of the International Association of World Heritage Professionals (IAWHP e.V.).

Jean H. Quataert is SUNY Distinguished Professor of History Emerita at Binghamton University and co-editor of the *Journal of Women's History* (2010–20). A pioneer in German women's history, over the last decade she has turned to transnational history, human rights, and international law. She has published many books and articles, including *Advocating Dignity: Human Rights Mobilizations in Global Politics* (2009) and "A New Look at International Law: Gendering the Practices of Humanitarian Medicine in Europe's 'Small Wars,' 1879–1907," *Human Rights Quarterly*, 2018, vol. 40, no. 3, 547–69.

Ned Richardson-Little is Principal Investigator of the "Transnational Crime and Deviant Globalization in 20th-Century Germany" research group at the University of Erfurt in Erfurt, Germany, supported by a Freigeist Fellowship from the Volkswagen Stiftung. Originally from Canada, he studied at McGill University in Montreal and completed his PhD at the University of North Carolina at Chapel Hill in 2013. His first book, *The Human Rights Dictatorship: East Germany, the Collapse of State Socialism and the Rise of Global Human Rights, 1945–1990*, will be published in 2019.

Lynette Russell is Professor of Indigenous Studies (History) at the Monash Indigenous Studies Centre at Monash University, Melbourne, Australia, and Deputy Director of the Australian Research Council's Centre of Excellence for Australian Biodiversity and Heritage. She is the author or editor of 12 books and specializes in Aboriginal history.

Marie Sandell holds a PhD from Royal Holloway, University of London. Her publications include *The Rise of Women's Transnational Activism: Identity and Sisterhood Between the World Wars* (2015) and articles in *International History Review* and *History of Education.* She teaches Modern History on the University of London International Programme.

Caroline Shaw is Associate Professor of Modern European History and a member of the European Studies Program at Bates College in Lewiston, Maine, USA. She received her BA from Johns Hopkins University and her MA and PhD from the University of California at Berkeley. Her first book, *Britannia's Embrace: Modern Humanitarianism and the Imperial Origins of Refugee Relief,* is a story of the development of humanitarian norms and liberalism on the global stage (2015). Shaw is currently investigating the peculiar status of reputation as a quasi-right in British legal culture. As with *Britannia's Embrace*, this project is concerned with the nature of people's responsibility to community, to nation and empire, and to abstract notions of justice.

Stephanie J. Silverman teaches Ethics, Society and Law at Trinity College in the University of Toronto in Toronto, Canada, and is a partner at the human rights consultancy Thinking Forward. Her research examines immigration detention and alternatives to detention programs among other topics. She is co-editor with Amy Nethery of *Immigration Detention: The Migration of a Policy and its Human Impact* (2015, rpt. 2017), and publishes peer-reviewed journal articles, government reports, book chapters, working papers, and items in the popular press. McGill-Queens University Press will publish her monograph *Demystifying Detention* in 2019. Stephanie received her DPhil from the University of Oxford in 2013, where she was a Commonwealth Scholar and associated with the Economic and Social Research Council (ESRC) Centre on Migration, Policy and Society, and in 2017 she completed her tenure as the Bora Laskin National Fellow in Human Rights Research, awarded by the Social Sciences and Humanities Research Council of Canada.

Claire-Michelle Smyth graduated with a PhD from Queens University Belfast. She is a Senior Lecturer in Law at the University of Brighton, Brighton, UK, where she researches and publishes widely in the area of social and economic rights. She is the author of *Social and Economic Rights in Ireland* (2017).

Sarah B. Snyder teaches in the School of International Service at American University, Washington, DC, USA. She is the author of *From Selma to Moscow: How Human Rights Activists Transformed U.S. Foreign Policy* (2018) and *Human Rights Activism and the End of the Cold War: A Transnational History of the Helsinki Network* (2011). She is co-editor with Nicolas Badalassi of *The CSCE and the End of the Cold War: Diplomacy, Societies and Human Rights, 1972–1990* (2018).

Rachel Standfield is Lecturer in the Monash Indigenous Studies Centre at Monash University, Melbourne, Australia. She is a historian of Indigenous societies and colonial histories in Australia and New Zealand, and has also worked in public policy and in support of Indigenous activism for human rights. She is editor of *Indigenous Mobilities: Across and Beyond the Antipodes* (2018), which opens new inquiries into travel and movement on Indigenous terms, and her monograph *Race and Identity in the Tasman World, 1769–1840* (2012) explores and extends regional histories of colonialism and Indigenous encounters.

Meredith Terretta holds the Gordon F. Henderson Research Chair in Human Rights and is Associate Professor of History at the University of Ottawa in Ottawa, Ontario, Canada. She specializes in African liberation movements, legal activism, histories of refuge-seeking, and human rights. She is co-editor with Iris Berger et al. of *African Asylum at a Crossroads: Activism, Expert Testimony, and Refugee Rights* (2015). Her most recent single-authored book is *Nation of Outlaws, State of Violence: Nationalism, Grassfields Tradition, and State-Building in Cameroon* (2014). Her articles have appeared in numerous journals including *Journal of Contemporary History, Politique Africaine, Journal of World History, Human Rights Quarterly*, and *Journal of African History*. She is currently working on a book tentatively entitled *Activism at the Fringes of Empire: Rogue Lawyers and Rights Activists in and out of 20th-Century Africa*.

Lora Wildenthal is John Antony Weir Professor of History and Associate Dean of Humanities at Rice University in Houston, Texas, USA. She is the author of *German Women for Empire, 1884–1945* (2001) and *The Language of Human Rights in West Germany* (2013). Currently she is interested in labor rights as human rights and the history of wages.

Steven Wilf is Anthony J. Smits Professor of Global Commerce at the University of Connecticut Law School. He received his PhD in History and JD from Yale University. Among his publications are *The Law Before the Law* (2008), *Law's Imagined Republic: Popular Politics and Criminal Justice in Revolutionary America* (2010), and is co-editor with Graeme Gooday of *Fashioning Global Patent Cultures: Diversity and Harmonization in Historical Perspective* (forthcoming). He is currently writing a history of intellectual property law for Cambridge University Press.

Afiya Shehrbano Zia holds a doctorate in Women and Gender Studies from the University of Toronto, Canada. She is author of *Faith and Feminism in Pakistan: Religious Agency or Secular Autonomy?* (2018) and *Sex Crime in the Islamic Context: Rape, Class and Gender in Pakistan* (1994). She has edited a series of books and authored a dozen peer-reviewed essays in scholarly publications. Afiya is an active member of Women's Action Forum, Pakistan. She has taught at the University of Toronto, Canada and currently teaches at Habib University in Karachi, Pakistan.

ACKNOWLEDGMENTS

The editors would like to thank the many individuals and institutions who made this volume possible. First of all, we thank Brad Simpson for his early engagement. It was his early and influential guidance that helped set the project in motion. At Routledge, Eve Setch gave early and steady support, and Zoe Thomson helped us in the final stages. Several scholars responded to our calls but for various reasons were unable to participate. Their comments and participation enriched the collective discussion. These people at Rice University arranged generous funding that allowed our globally dispersed group to meet in person and via Zoom in May and October 2017: Alida Metcalf, Chair of the Department of History; Farès el-Dahdah, Director of the Humanities Research Center; Marie Lynn Miranda, Provost of Rice University; and Yousif Shamoo, Vice-Provost for Research, who supported us through Rice University's Creative Ventures funding program. We could not have held our conferences without staff support in the Department of History, the Center for Languages and Intercultural Communication, and the School of Humanities: Special thanks to Erin Baezner, Eric Granquist, Beverly Konzem, and Chi-Liang Yu. Christina Gomez and James Myers, doctoral students in the Department of History, provided conference and editing assistance.

All translations are the authors' own unless otherwise stated.

1

INTRODUCTION

An open-ended and contingent history of human rights

Jean H. Quataert and Lora Wildenthal

This essay collection offers historical perspectives on an array of human rights themes. We have assembled it in order to provide a sampling of the state of the field in human rights history, to give teachers and students of human rights a useful resource, and to make our own distinct interventions into the historiography of human rights. Our authors are not all professionally located as historians; all, however, emphasize the importance of historical context to understanding a field that is urgent for both its intellectual and its practical importance.

We present here open-ended, contingent, non-linear and non-teleological histories of human rights. The very structure of the volume, which comprises essays that can stand alone as well as speak to each other (and, as e-chapters, are available for purchase both separately and in combination) helps to accomplish this task. It is important to us to avoid narratives of seemingly inevitable progress, and to avoid turns of phrase that imply that human rights are passed like a torch from generation to generation, that is, remain stable in content over time and across place. We do not seek to tell our readers one single story of human rights. Rather, we find manifold concepts and struggles and, like human rights themselves, these are often in tension with each other. Human rights are the stuff of contestation with no guarantees about the final result. Rights, after all, can be won and they can be lost; the cause of right alone cannot assure a just and fair outcome. While our collection provides no single or simple story, it is incumbent on scholars of human rights to help orient those who are new to this material. Our authors have ensured that their essays are comprehensible to those encountering the subject matter for the first time. We are mindful that human rights courses are often wide-ranging, while instructors (including ourselves) have necessarily limited areas of expertise – so we present this volume as a guide for both colleagues and students. Our volume refrains from folding these stories into a single formula, and therefore provides the necessary distance for a big picture of the strategic, political, and changing nature of human rights work.

The mutability and variety of political opportunities are revealed by a richly empirical, geographically and temporally diverse history of human rights. Our essays draw upon the settings of South America, North America, Australia, Africa, the Middle East, Europe, Asia, and the Pacific. They foreground institutions ranging from nineteenth-century international commissions of inquiry to the International Committee of the Red Cross (ICRC), the International Labour Organization (ILO), the UN treaty-making process, and the UN Trusteeship Council, among others.

Here we will outline the points of emphasis that have guided this project and indicate our historiographical intervention. We give a brief glimpse of each essay in the volume, and suggest ways that readers might group essays to explore themes and temporal periods.

Our collection emphasizes non-linear versions of history, law, and the voices of globally dispersed activists. Regarding non-linear versions of history, it is important to us not to foreclose the significance of particular episodes by folding them into a larger narrative that could reinscribe familiar understandings and power relations, or imply inevitability. This commitment means attention to specifics of time and place. Deeper understanding of difference cannot be intuited; it must grow out of confrontations with other times, places, and viewpoints. A deep grounding in historical specificity – what historians call "historicization" – helps to overcome simple linear narratives of historical change, which too readily reinforce Eurocentric biases of much human rights scholarship. In the absence of solid empirical research and documentation, particularly of less frequently studied countries and eras, it is all too easy to assume that abstracted and generalized European patterns are or were globally normative. Our authors are committed to foregrounding the local as well as the distinctly national, regional, and often non-Western voices, perspectives, and struggles in human rights histories. We hope the case studies open new avenues for future research. Our authors make linkages and comparisons, showing how human rights discourses develop at various times; they do not emphasize claims about origins. Power is central to all these stories, but cannot be allowed to impose assumptions about what is important in histories of human rights. This is because histories about human rights show how our perceptions of power and weakness can be very different depending on the chronological or geographical scale of the investigation.

With respect to law, we note that human rights discourse is a heavily legalized discourse as well as a moral and philosophical one. Efforts at legalization are common (though interestingly not universal) in human rights activity; they aim to translate rhetoric and ideological and political movements into something institutionalized. Those demanding and debating human rights often invoke existing international law, or seek new conventions and treaties, or use the law as a rhetorical device to express what should or should not exist. Invocations of law can lead people to perceive law as that which settles conflict, as something reified and powerful. In fact, however, international and even domestic law is mutable and multifaceted in its meanings and impacts. Law does not necessarily affirm rights. Moreover, because interpretation is the essence of any actor's invocation of law, its meaning derives precisely from competing interpretations. Law is the point of departure for debate, not a conversation stopper. A number of our authors are legal scholars conscious of their task of addressing non-lawyers. They explicate the workings of law in the context of human rights in a manner that emphasizes law's open-endedness and mutability. Several offer novel interpretations of international human rights laws.

We bring forward a variety of voices of globally dispersed activists, especially those located outside centers of power in their own countries or located in countries found outside the circle of great powers. Ordinary people's voices are vital to the history of human rights, which is in large part a history of social movements, and the essence of human rights is the challenge to authority. Moreover, the inclusion of voices from globally dispersed locations helps redress a Eurocentric and great power perspective that creeps into histories where states, not people, appear as the key human rights actors. Ideas alone, however alluring, are not self-executing; they need human interventions and agency to become real – that is, material, concrete, and institutionally and legally embodied.

These points of emphasis are important to us because unspoken expectations can govern how readers receive information about human rights. Human rights are highly politicized, which means that perceptions of them are partial and truncated at any given time and change considerably depending on the political moment. To gain a fuller understanding less constrained by our own political moment, it is important to take seriously contexts of past actions, advocacy, norms, and structures on their own terms. Moreover, the subject matter of human rights unleashes emotional responses in both authors and readers, and these emotional responses infuse understandings in ways we should be mindful of. The demand for impact and effectiveness in the area of human rights is high. Optimism and pessimism, frustration and empowerment swirl in the minds of activists, researchers, and readers, affecting how we analyze information in the domain of human rights. One result of human rights' emotional freight can be an insistence on optimism, even against good historical judgement. Indeed, human rights can, if taken at their own prescriptive word, imply a teleological narrative of progress. Another result can be pessimism, including a dismissal of the power of ideas or of the relevance of seemingly useless past efforts. Worse, we can oscillate between these moods, with unreflected optimism flipping over rapidly to an equally unreflected cynicism. Like all movements resting on a politics of morality, human rights require emotional staying power. It is vital to escape a narrow perspective driven by a political moment, a mood, or reliance on an inevitably limited common sense.

The historical study of human rights confronts us with material much more complicated than a hopeful story of progress or a dismal series of disappointments. It shows us multifarious stories that demonstrate the power and contingency of human rights ideas and action. The reward is not a definite answer or formula to apply to the problem of the day. Rather, the reward is more sophisticated thinking about the very nature of the interaction of ideas, institutions, and human interventions, an interaction that continually renews human rights opportunities. All the while, human rights activists must deal with the long-standing claims of states to sovereignty, national defense, and national security – the legal props of state autonomy and power that most notably infringe on individual and group rights.

Historians are latecomers to the scholarship on human rights. For decades, the academic study of human rights was dominated by what we might call presentist perspectives of the social sciences, specifically sociology, political science and anthropology, and law. Such presentism arises from understanding human rights as a matter of policy challenges, and it highlights what seems effective or usable in the moment. Attention to change over time, including in the very meaning of human rights keywords, seems less pertinent in that context. Legal scholarship has tended to claim or imply an objective and universally valid method for reading legal doctrines, authoritative decisions, and the law's structures and scope, independent of society. Such scholarship has taken the law too much at its own word by flattening time and space. These tendencies of legal scholars have limited historical inquiry and also the inquiry of students, who may well assume that if a law exists there must be no injustice.[1]

Historians' interest in human rights as a promising topic of research emerged around the 1990s. With the formal ending of the Cold War, the 1990s were simultaneously a high point of human rights nongovernmental organization (NGO) activities, which exploded across the globe, and an expression of sustained networks of global interconnections, which prompted new research on the historical foundations of transnational linkages. Both NGOs and intensified globalization challenged the centrality of the nation-state and led to experiments in transnational, international, and global histories.

The 1990s were a heady, optimistic time, and important early historical scholarship on human rights tended to present a story of unfolding progress and human rights as the self-evident fulfillment of the principles of human equality.[2] This literature presented a hoped-for usable past for activism in the form of human rights genealogies. However, these genealogies reflected some fallacies of historical interpretation. For example, all kinds of historical expressions of rights and moral principles were marshaled as forerunners of human rights, as if all those actors had somehow sought the same goal.[3] This produced linear histories, in which the assumed end result of developments shaped the narrative, such that, for example, the human rights system established formally in the United Nations (UN) in 1945 became the intentional and predetermined result of the facts the historian had chosen. A related approach saw human rights in cyclical terms, with the 1990s supposedly witnessing a "revival" or "rebirth" of European Enlightenment "rights talk" and humanitarian sentiments from the eighteenth century.[4] Here too, the past is used for the present, and Europe is situated as the prime locus of human rights thought. These publications contained many important insights, yet teleology and rebirth are flawed as frameworks for historical interpretation.

By the onset of the twenty-first century, an understanding of the paradoxes, unintended consequences, and ambiguities of human rights activism began to displace the early optimism. These phrases are now keywords of newer scholarship. This too reflects contemporary geopolitical transformations, which have led to a more sober assessment of the previous decade with its horrifying descent into wars, ethnic cleansing, and genocides, and also a mounting scholarly and activist critique of so-called humanitarian intervention and concern about the ease with which states have appropriated the language of human rights for invasion and occupation.[5] Our section on accountability in the post-9/11 world shows the complicated politics of human rights advocacy in this new global setting.

Ironically, the loss of optimism has been fruitful for opening up new areas of critical research. Human rights history entered a period of vibrant historiographical discussion and reflection. Research now critically examined human rights visions in international politics after World War II, their intersection with Cold War imperatives and the reshaping of domestic politics, and their resurgence in the 1970s and after the Cold War's end.[6] The UN-led humanitarian military interventions in the 1990s raised questions about historical forerunners, turning all manner of humanitarian expressions into compelling topics for historical investigation.[7] Other work analyzed women's and feminists' contributions to human rights visions, laws, and advocacy, bringing gender as an analytical method and a description of power relations and violations into play.[8] Critique of international law from within and without helped bring about new rapprochement by legal scholars with historians.[9] Influential works focused on the 1970s as "breakthrough decade" or new origin point for human rights.[10] This was salutary for its rejection of longer chronologies that had posed the above-mentioned problems of intentionality and oversimplification. However, this claim rested on Euro-American mass participation in new human rights causes since the 1970s, rather than a global view of that era. While the "breakthrough" thesis has generated exciting new research, as a new master chronology it would distort the history of human rights in the global South and foreshorten specific chronologies. This collection responds with more open time frames and a more global perspective. It places the study of human rights in a wider geopolitical and cultural context.

Our chronology extends from the mid-nineteenth century to the present day. We do not claim the mid-nineteenth century as the proper starting or origin point for a study of human rights movements, mobilizations, ideals, or histories. Rather, we draw attention to that moment because of a confluence of changes that collectively promoted new transnational identifications, sentiments, institutional networks, and border crossings. It was in the nineteenth century that the law of nations governing the relations among states took on many of its present-day characteristics, not least due to the truly global spread of imperial colonization. The older positive and customary law affecting war and peace, commerce and trade, among other critical arenas of interaction, came to be increasingly multilateral and to be increasingly written down as codes and rules, in the hope of strengthening its power and enforceability. These codifications were framed so as to invite future participation by additional sovereign states, and thus became lasting institutions that facilitated ever-denser global interconnections. These changes inaugurated a new era in legal history.[11] The expansion of international law's scope and of states' compliance became its own cause in the latter decades of the nineteenth century, both for the emerging profession of international lawyers and for a wide range of reformers and peace-minded men and women.

The volume's nineteenth-century starting point draws attention to entanglement and contradiction, an inevitable accompaniment to developments in rights and law when analyzed in the context of the geopolitical order. The nineteenth century marked the onset of what historians call the new imperialism (roughly 1870–1914). International law and European empire were mutually constitutive, to the point where international law still carries imperialist connotations and is suspect regarding both objectives and effects.[12] Law has had continuous ties to various iterations of empire, from formal colonial rule in the later nineteenth century to more recent neoliberal policies, and from corporate interests to great power politics and rivalries.[13] Rights language and its principle of nondiscrimination are not immune from co-optation and appropriation by these same forces and groups nationally and internationally. Human rights and international law both claim to adherence to universality, neutrality, and nonpartisan values, yet both are deeply entangled with power, imperial projects, national and elite self-interest, and the preservation of economic inequality. It is for this reason too that our story cannot simply be about progress. It is necessary to include the nineteenth century in critical histories of human rights in order to grasp the integration of international law, colonialism, and transnational reform movements. A prominent theme in this volume is the history of how those living under legacies of colonialism and in the midst of postcolonial predicaments have embraced, tested, and reformulated human rights ideas and ideals.

A big picture

The scholarly collaboration for this volume originated with open calls for participation that drew a diverse set of scholars.[14] Most were formally trained historians, a substantial number were legal scholars, and several more were social scientists and interdisciplinary scholars, including feminist and heritage studies scholars. We selected those who were actively researching in human rights materials (as opposed to summarizing the findings of others) – lending empirical richness to their work – and those who historicized their findings, while we also sought to preserve the geographical, temporal, and thematic range of responses to our calls. We could not have predicted that wide range, which reinforces our point about the contingency of human rights. We hosted two conferences where conversations revealed the historiographical priorities outlined above. We workshopped papers there in pairs and groups but, importantly, we have avoided any requirement for interpretive uniformity.

In what follows, we sketch out each essay's contribution to the volume. While we have arranged the essays in rough chronological order, it is important to note that a number of our authors challenge received chronological milestones as part of their argument, based on their own research in various global locations.

The volume's subject matter opens in the second half of the long nineteenth century (to 1914), a period that falls between two historical eras that have received more attention in the human rights literature: eighteenth-century Enlightenment with its "rights talk," and the World War II-era embrace of universal human rights by way of the 1945 UN Charter (which was binding treaty law) and the 1948 Universal Declaration of Human Rights (non-binding in its origin but later accepted as the authoritative statement of human rights mentioned in the Charter).[15] We label this latter part of the long nineteenth century the era of the "New Internationalism." It was simultaneously a time of heightened nationalism and of new internationalist visions comprised of nations as actors understood as the authentic voices of their respective populations. Law came to be seen as a vehicle for progressive international relations, that is, the legalization of international relations seemed to hold the promise of sustaining peace, progress, and national cooperation. Legal testimony gained new prominence, as international commissions of inquiry practiced interstate fact-finding procedures to develop evidence with which to respond to atrocities. Mairi MacDonald refers to this development as a new "practice of persuasion," and Benjamin Brockman-Hawe, Caroline Shaw, and Kimberly Lowe also focus on persuasive rhetorics as linkages between law and values.[16] Practices of persuasion remind us to consider who is attempting to persuade whom regarding what rights of which people – and to consider how one may develop one's own practices of persuasion. Nationalism bestowed new significance on ordinary people's voices, while literacy and media markets created broader reading publics. The legacy of the transnational antislavery movement's assertion of a common humanity is relevant here. The long nineteenth century also saw humanitarianism juxtaposed with human rights, a relationship that several later essays in the volume also examine.

In Part I, Caroline Shaw takes us to a transnational public drawn from the United States, Canada and Britain. She reveals a counterpoint between legal statutes and the moralizing public in Canada and Britain that produces an innovative legal outcome in the case of John Anderson, who had been enslaved in the United States and was now facing extradition from Canada as a fugitive. Benjamin Brockman-Hawe's setting is the Ottoman Empire, where he traces the efforts of multinational Commissions of Inquiry. These were new fact-finding institutions created in the absence of established international criminal law to respond to what had become known as atrocities, especially massacres and the suffering of refugees. The Commissions' difficulties typified those that hamper human rights inquiries to this day. Mairi MacDonald makes an argument about the nature and possibilities of legal innovation by examining how evidence is composed. She frames the story of Roger Casement's intervention into the atrocities of the Belgian

Congo as an exercise in a new methodology: she examines the very process of claiming and trying to enforce rights on behalf of distant human beings as a method for revealing linkages in the history of human rights. The way advocates select and report evidence can give strong indications of the strategies they pursue and the political outcomes they seek, and reveal correspondences to efforts in very different contexts. Because reformers like Casement did have access to a framework of international law (due to the internationalization of colonial rule), they were able to "restate the law in a way that could protect the natural rights of Congo's Indigenous peoples."[17] Kimberly Lowe addresses the distinctions between humanitarianism (e.g. an immediate focus on relieving suffering) and human rights law (legal norms concerning soldiers and civilians, especially refugees, that may or may not reduce suffering on the ground). Her account depicts the tension between humanitarianism and human rights in the International Red Cross movement from its inception in 1863 until 1949. All four of the essays in this section make the case for the importance of detailed investigations of human rights concepts and institutions located in the long nineteenth century and a careful focus on the workings of law. They work against the assumption that humanitarian sentiment gave rise to human rights law; rather, these elements remain, even up to today, in creative tension with each other.

Part II, "The Interwar Era: The League of Nations," holds a pivotal place in our volume. As scholars elsewhere have recently demonstrated, the League of Nations is key for a historical understanding of our subject matter.[18] Far from an episode of mere failure, it was a new era of intergovernmental organization with a new global center, Geneva, attracting all manner of state and non-state advocacy groups.[19] The League's various missions created openings for marginalized people, including women, to join a transnational public sphere. Men and women discussing reforms in League venues carried forward the nineteenth-century vision of legalizing international relations, this time with even greater urgency concerning the threat of yet more war. While the League failed, that does not mean that its emphases and findings were wrong. Marie Sandell shows the emergence of women's internationalist activism in the midst of World War I and recaptures a lost human rights language of pacifism. Regula Ludi demonstrates how partial and contingent the incorporation of women into discourses of law actually was, something hard to see at first given the seemingly simple statements of sex equality in the Charter and Universal Declaration of Human Rights. She argues for "conceptual linkages" when exploring political imagination over time and demonstrates why people's battle cries for justice in the 1930s were used after 1945 to deepen the human rights principle of nondiscrimination at the level of the UN. Hers is a contingent and not automatic story. Both Ludi's actors and the women internationalist pacifists spotlighted in Sandell's essay focused attention on discrimination. We mention here Kimberly Lowe's essay again as a reminder of how the essay topics push past established chronologies: Lowe's analysis is important for understanding the interwar era, as 1921 was the moment when the ICRC sought formally to make the major transition from focusing solely on its humanitarian mission for wounded soldiers to including civilians and refugees in its mission. The Red Cross was prescient in its appreciation of the blurring of military and civilian arenas in industrial warfare, civil strife, and terror tactics up to the present day. Together, the essays in this section demonstrate how critical the interwar era is for an understanding of human rights. Together with nineteenth-century ideas of human rights, these essays throw into the relief the improvised and incomplete nature of the post-World War II arrangements that are familiar to us.

Part III, "The Formative UN Era," takes up the first years of the iteration of human rights with which our readers are most familiar. In 1945, in the aftermath of the devastations of two World Wars fought in the heartland of the great powers rather than only on the colonial periphery, victors created a new, unprecedentedly strong institutional framework that, as later years were to show, was capable of further strengthening – especially regarding human rights investigation and sanctions.[20] In those early years there was broad-based support for universalism, even as there were also profound divides. The Cold War soon took hold, and decolonization struggles unfolded in that context. The UN understandably dominates this era, but in those years it was not yet representative of the entire political world. It is important to highlight globally dispersed voices at this time who seized on the universalist promise to add their visions of justice. Not everything significant about human rights at that time emanated from the UN, however. On the contrary: The UN's prominence in human rights developed because of the pressures people all over the world exerted on it to respond to their needs, leading to a human rights mission much greater than what the UN founders had anticipated.

Part III is comprised of three sections: "UN Treaty-Making," "Decolonization," and "Socialist and Capitalist Versions of Human Rights." In the first part, "UN Treaty-Making," Claire-Michelle Smyth illustrates Cold War divides as she undoes the ideological separation of rights into political on one hand and social and economic on the other. Her analysis of the actual impacts of relevant law shows that the divide originated in politics, rather than inhering in legal logic or practice. Rachel George examines the role of reservations in the human rights treaty-making process, which allows her to reveal some change over time and convergence among states parties around questions of religion (here, Islam) and universal human rights. By taking seriously the discussions recorded at the moment of signing human rights treaties, which reveal more common ground than one might expect, she shows the value of these sources for analyzing the major human rights problem of how to relate cultural specificity to universalism. Linde Lindkvist likewise examines the treaty-making process, in this case concerning a debate between the Red Cross and various NGOs on whether child soldiers should be protected through international humanitarian law or through human rights convention such as the UN Convention on the Rights of the Child. Like Lowe, Lindkvist offers a vivid account of the costs and controversies of blurring the boundary between humanitarianism and human rights.

The second section of Part III, "Decolonization," includes essays by Meredith Terretta, Roland Burke, and James Kirby that explore what happened when human rights were taken seriously in colonial contexts that inherently violate human rights. Meredith Terretta sees colonial Africa from the 1920s to the 1970s as a "pivotal site" for the emergence of transnational rights activism.[21] The visions of inhabitants of white-ruled territories of Africa concerning rights to self-determination, racial and economic equality, and education did not necessarily lead to positive international human rights innovations at the level of norm or treaty. Yet they show us how fertile the ground was for post-World War II debates about the meaning of human rights. Non-legal human rights ideas were advanced in the earlier years of those decades that did come to be legalized in the 1960s, 1970s, and later. Knowledge of these voices has been obscured by the simple lack of research – itself a major source of misguided argument in the history of human rights – and by NGOs from the global North whose institutionalized power in more recent years has selected among and disproportionately shaped possible meanings of human rights in Africa. Roland Burke observes that the well-known argument that human rights are imperialist has lacked grounding in historical research. He offers that research here, examining political debates about the relationship between development and human rights. He traces the argument that a country with a less developed economy should not be held accountable to the same human rights standards as a country with a more developed economy, an argument known as the "development exception." Burke shows how the "development exception" changed location and its very nature over time: While in the interwar and early post-World War II years colonial great powers invoked the development exception, claiming that their territories' lower level of development meant that human rights norms were not fully applicable, after decolonization it was postcolonial heads of state who invoked the exception. Meanwhile, the nature of the exception changed subtly, from one concerning passage through economic stages to an assertion of essential, permanent cultural difference. Lost in both versions were the demands of ordinary people for holding their political leadership accountable through democratic procedures. James Kirby tells a very different story equally vital to our knowledge of African voices in human rights. Kirby shows how Seretse Khama, the first president of the geographically vulnerable nation of Botswana, used international human rights as a mode of securing his country's national integrity against the pressures of its neighbor, apartheid South Africa, and also of the Organization of African Unity, which sought to draw it into African liberation struggles. It is an unusual story of how the embrace of international human rights served to augment state power. Neither cynical nor hypocritical, Seretse developed an effective recipe that is suggestive of how small countries can benefit in various ways from embracing international governance structures. Seretse's regime drew on notions of individual liberties as well as principles of national self-determination to defend independence and sovereignty.

"Socialist and Capitalist Versions of Human Rights" is the third section in Part III concerning the UN era. Eileen Boris and Jill Jensen examine the efforts of the International Labour Organization (ILO), an important yet often overlooked human rights institution, to integrate women workers' needs into international labor standards. Like Regula Ludi's essay, that by Boris and Jensen offers an account of the complexities of gendering abstract international norms, and like Claire-Michelle Smyth's essay, it is a substantial account of claiming economic rights as human rights. While in the interwar years it was capitalist member countries and activists who supported a "difference feminism" approach using protectionist measures for women, by the later Cold War years it was state socialists and non-aligned countries who argued for protections for women; subsequently capitalist countries tended to support gender-blind norms. These puzzles are with us still. Ned Richardson-Little recovers the well-elaborated human rights doctrines of the German Democratic Republic – important for a human rights historiography that continues to be too ignorant of socialist legacies in human rights thinking. His main contention is that it was East Germans' reception of the socialist language of human rights that planted the seeds of democratization leading to 1989 and the iconic fall of the Berlin Wall, more than East Germans' adoption of Western liberal human rights ideas. East Germany's failure to live up to its human rights promises, particularly regarding social and economic rights, undermined the regime's legitimacy among ordinary East Germans and even among members of the regime who had internalized the promises of socialist human rights. Examining socialist voices in international institutions such as the ILO and within socialist regimes is important for gaining a more accurate sense of the global discussion of social and economic rights. While Richardson-Little gives the reader a strong sense of the distinctiveness of socialist human rights, Pitman Potter's essay on the People's Republic of China today pulls in a different direction. Potter shows how the socialist regime's responses to challenges from human rights advocates actually fit into a long tradition of ideas of state sovereignty and authority. While the Chinese Communist Party (CCP), similar to its erstwhile East German counterpart, has participated in human rights covenants and has broadcast its achievements in the area of rights, the CCP also makes clear that those achievements are to be defined and enacted by the party-state, not by ordinary people outside the party-state's apparatus. When the latter do articulate claims, Potter argues, it is perhaps less the rights at issue that have led to controversy for officials than what party leaders see as the claimants' illegitimacy, their lack of standing in the party-state to speak out. Finally, Sarah Snyder takes readers to the United States, a great power, key architect of the UN system, and defender of capitalist freedoms. Her essay details official uses of human rights principles in the calculation of US foreign policy objectives. Snyder shows a surprisingly consistent pattern of deference to national interests over defense of rights across varied presidential administrations after 1945, with a few exceptions when pushed by congressional activism or human rights NGOs. In the George W. Bush administration, she notes soberly, it was US human rights abuses that became matters of serious international concern.

Part IV, "After Formal Empire and the Cold War: How Human Rights Are Practiced Around the Globe (1980s–2001)," highlights the era of NGO optimism, when human rights activism in NGOs seemed to herald the success of human rights politics and ordinary people's heroic actions. The essays here are studies of civil society activism at a time when the model of the human rights NGOs took hold around the world. These essays contextualize this advocacy work in specific settings and highlight the challenges it faced and still faces. Catherine Baylin Duryea introduces us to human rights NGOs in three environments that are not very hospitable to such work: the Palestinian West Bank, Morocco, and Kuwait. She shows how each NGO responded to its environment in order to sustain its work. In each case, activists turned to human rights and international law as a way to avoid the quagmire of local party politics; they embraced the human rights that were most relevant to their specific circumstances; and these were classic rights that their governments could not openly repudiate with ease. While these activists were often unsuccessful in bringing about major social change, and have not become well known outside their regions, their work shows that they did see the compatibility of international human rights and the specific problems they faced. Jadwiga Pieper Mooney's essay on Chilean women's activism under Pinochet makes a different argument: that Chile's high visibility in the UN human rights institutional setting in those years meant that women's activism there concerning gendering human rights became influential at a transnational level – which in turn helped to end dictatorship. Jennifer Adair takes up the Mothers of the Plaza de Mayo, an iconic human rights NGO, but with the unusual question of what happened after dictatorship's end. She examines how an NGO deals with what (at least initially) appears to be success. The Mothers, Adair shows, broadened their agenda beyond accountability for torture and murder to encompass social and economic rights that were under pressure in the post-dictatorship years of neoliberal reforms. They sustained their mix of pragmatic and idealistic work under more and less friendly regimes, seeking to avoid co-optation while also greeting long-denied fruits of their work with the ending of amnesty for past crimes. Adair, like Lavrence in the latter's examination of museum practice, raises the issue of how closeness to governments can co-opt human rights messages, or at least create the appearance of doing so. Afiya Shehrbano Zia provides a compelling account of one of Pakistan's most important human rights activists, Asma Jahangir, against a background of NGO activism that has brilliantly highlighted key legal issues of equality for minorities and for women. Jahangir and other activists have navigated a complex and shifting political environment of modernizing dictators, Islamist dictators, and so-called postsecular intellectuals by keeping their eye on the rule of law and by exploiting possibilities for legal innovation. As with several other essays in this book, here too we see the strong salience of international human rights norms for voices outside the global North. The studies of NGOs in this section show common patterns and problems emerging during those years of NGO "optimism," such as the influence of Western financial backing on the leadership structure of local NGOs, which could push them to respond more to donor priorities than pressing community needs.

Part V, "The Universal Human Rights Pantheon in National Contexts," showcases essays that examine how a major human rights principle has played out in one national setting – even as the theme pushes activism beyond state borders. This examination of mobilization around a specific cause over the long term in one national setting provides a grounding in the ramifications of that right and suggests to readers how they might develop research questions about the right in other contexts. Lori Beaman opens the section with her essay on the freedom of religion in Canada. Religion, an old indicator of human difference that has long been important for international relations, appears here in a survey encompassing centuries of colonial history as well as postcolonial and current issues. Such issues include the imperative of decentering Christianity; the rights of the non-religious; and the politics of redefining religion as culture in a self-consciously multicultural state. Rachel Standfield and Lynette Russell carry out a similarly structured survey of Indigenous rights in the setting of the state of Victoria in Australia. They highlight distinctive Aboriginal forms of social organization and kinship ties that have sustained the movement. They trace phases of Indigenous peoples' rights mobilizations from nineteenth-century struggles within the colonial authorities' "humanitarian" protection system to demands for full citizenship in the later twentieth century to more recent renewed land claims using UN and state-based networks. Indigenous struggles undergird notions of both collective and individual rights. Laura Belmonte surveys the rights of lesbians, gays, and other sexual minorities in US and European settings, highlighting the impacts of innovation and context on activism. Her long-term perspective provokes reflection on what has made the securing of rights possible and what continues to endanger activists. Adam R Houston takes up the right to health in the setting of the Pacific Islands, examining responses to leprosy and HIV there. He glosses the latter as the first illness to have emerged during the human rights era. Houston shows Pacific Islanders talking back to so-called outsider medical experts during both the colonial and postcolonial era, experts who often projected their own notions of isolation and illness onto the islands. The ensuing debate that he traces shows how ideas of the rights of the ill and the rights of surrounding society patterned debates about these illnesses.

Part VI, "New Forms of Accountability in a National Security World (2001–present)," encompasses essays on international law innovations in the difficult post-9/11 global context. Even as we observe a resurgence of state sovereignty, we also see deepening forces of economic globalization working against such political trends. In addition, we see the continued activist drive to transnationalize human rights, a drive that responds to and in some ways benefits from the processes of economic globalization.

The world of the 2000s up to today is very different from that of the 1990s. Activists' optimism about NGOs' ability to remake international relations has lessened, yet activism remains a powerful force for governments and for-profit corporations to reckon with. Steven S. Nam reviews the history of the principle of corporate (business) accountability since the Nuremberg Trials in the wake of World War II. While the US Alien Tort Statute once seemed a promising path for prosecution of corporate criminality, the United States and other states have stepped away from that legal instrument. Nam points to the promise of polycentric, public/private diplomatic negotiations as vehicles for accountability that include NGOs as voices of civil society. While this strategy lacks the promise of strong legal sanction that the Alien Tort Statute offered, in some cases it has proven more effective at bringing all affected parties to the table. Nam sees here an empirical basis for a viable new legal model of transnational corporate accountability. Ulrike Capdepón examines how the principle of universal jurisdiction has functioned in a transnational story of accountability connecting Chile, Spain, and Argentina. In each country, domestic political debates took hold whose actors had to answer to legal demands emanating from institutions located in other countries – and these demands were in turn responses to those internal political contexts. These countries' domestic political spaces became thereby linked. While impunity persisted, precedents concerning transnational justice strategies reverberated through all three national polities, constituting a new form of extraterritorial human rights prosecutions and memory politics. Vera Mackie examines accountability for gender violence, particularly in military settings, in East Asia and in the former Yugoslavia. In particular, she analyzes how sexual violence became a matter of international concern in the first place, in the wake of World War II and, subsequently, in the Balkans in the 1990s, and demonstrates how gender transforms the categories of violation in human rights norms. Anca Claudia Prodan traces the confluence of heritage law and international human rights in her study of how heritage rights have affected state behavior, including by serving to limit state sovereignty. Once more, we see that a focus on practice reveals that supposedly marked distinctions between individual rights and group rights can be blurred in actuality. This observation also holds in Steven Wilf's essay on the relationship between human rights and intellectual property rights since the late eighteenth century. Both of these legal domains, Wilf asserts, are critical to human flourishing: One protects the body, while the other asserts guardianship over the mind's artistic expression and technological invention. They have evolved through "wary" encounters.[22] Wilf examines how the various claims were asserted in different historical settings and adjudicated over time, which in turn lay a foundation for transnational governance. Finally, Stephanie Silverman and Petra Molnar offer a graphic and moving reading of immigration detention policies in liberal societies, using the United States, the United Kingdom, and Canada as their main examples. The practice of detention operates through opaque and discretionary administrative decision-making, and therefore challenges traditions of individual liberty and freedom from arbitrary arrest that have been enshrined as human rights and international law norms. The authors offer a historical overview of immigration detention, and show how the trend of criminalizing migration and mobilities accelerated after 9/11 in scope and breadth. The essay demonstrates the real-life dangers of sidelining human rights principles in favor of trumped-up, often meritless, national security concerns.

Finally, Part VII, "The Transformative Impact of Human Rights on Knowledge," includes essays that show how human rights thinking has implications for knowledge creation. Human rights ideas and activism have transformed both institutions shaping historical memory and academic subject matter. Michelle Carmody examines the emergence of human rights archives in the wake of dictatorships in Argentina and Paraguay. She shows the changing role of information about human rights violations in transitional justice efforts. Information had played a central role in transitional justice initiatives like truth commissions and trials during the 1980s and early 1990s. Those endeavors intersected with new ideas about justice beginning to circulate in the mid-1990s that emphasized memory rather than the law as the key to guaranteeing a stable, human rights-respecting order. This shift resulted in the creation of archives that were designed to facilitate the construction of memory from the perspective of the victims. In other words, changing ideas about the nature of justice have shaped human rights archives in post-dictatorship polities.

Christine Lavrence provides the reader with an up-close tour of the architecture and exhibits of a state-approved human rights museum in Canada, as she summarizes the original impetus for establishing the museum and the national debate that ensued. Canada's effort to create a national human rights museum was pioneering, and has raised the question (broached also in Adair's essay) of the unintended effects of state approval of human rights projects – namely, the perception and danger of co-optation. Lavrence analyzes the spaces and exhibits in terms of their goal of producing certain forms of empathy while foreclosing others – in effect, individualizing the emotional arc of learning about human violations while reassuring visitors that resolution is possible. Jessica M. Frazier gives our readers a vibrant example of how she teaches human rights as both mode and subject matter. That is, human rights principles have shaped her pedagogy as well as providing her with subject matter for her history course. Frazier teaches through published primary and secondary materials, uses documentaries, and ends the course with students producing their own videos. The essay is a valuable real-life example and guide for instructors of courses on human rights.

E-version flexibility: alternative themes and perspectives

Our commitment to integrating research and pedagogy distinguishes our collection from other edited volumes in the field.[23] The electronic version of this book allows for multiple uses and groupings according to themes. The innovative format of e-versions of each chapter aids in this endeavor. These e-chapters can be assigned to students singly or in any combination adapted to a particular course; similarly, any reader can order an e-chapter or any combination of chapters. We offer some possibilities here to assist those teaching and training in the new history of human rights. Below, we regroup essays according to the following themes: international law; colonialism and decolonization; gender and sexuality; and activism. Each of these themes are substantial components of international human rights.

The essays relevant to international law extend from the mid-nineteenth century to the present. These authors offer fine-grained accounts of legal development and change over 150 years. Human rights is largely about law, yet it is difficult to come to grips with law's dynamism and functions. As an operating system, international law offers rules and regulations that govern the behavior of states, individuals, corporations, and intergovernmental organizations in international society. Law opens up new frameworks for transnational cooperation and advocacy, yet at the same time sets powerful limits to effective action in international society. Indeed, at times, the law's structures can work to impede normative change and, thus, widen the gaps between shifting societal understandings of justice and fair play and the law's rules and doctrines.[24]

International law, while not necessarily foremost in popular understanding of rights struggles – not even for the community of activists themselves – has emerged as a decisive context for transnational rights advocacy. International law is both a prescriptive and a normative system, reflecting a set of values that help constitute human behaviors and not merely mirror them. Not surprisingly, then, over time international law has become increasingly infused with the transformative understandings of humanitarian and human rights sentiments – and in turn has worked to spread their messages. There is nothing abstract about the developments in international law. They are embedded in changing social norms and times and, as historian of human rights Samuel Moyn has recognized, speak to the "importance of social movements [for] legal priorities."[25] Put another way: The close ties between law and society mean that understandings of the law often turn on insights beyond the law itself.[26]

Readers interested in international law should turn to the essays by Caroline Shaw, Benjamin Brockman-Hawe, Mairi MacDonald, Claire-Michelle Smyth, Rachel George, Linde Lindkvist, Catherine Baylin Duryea, Steven Nam, Ulrike Capdepón, Anca Claudia Prodan, and Steven Wilf.

Our volume contends that the history of human rights requires an examination of colonial contexts and postcolonial politics. As noted above, the histories of international law and colonial rule have been intertwined. One major line of interpretation denies the compatibility of anticolonial movements with international human rights. Many of our authors contest this line of interpretation. Readers interested in the theme of colonialism and anticolonial politics in human rights should look at the essays by Mairi MacDonald, Meredith Terretta, Roland Burke, James Kirby, Lori Beaman, Rachel Standfield and Lynette Russell, Adam R Houston, and Christine Lavrence.

Women, gender, and sexuality are substantial components of this volume. In a number of our essays, women are prominent as activists and also as the intended objects of human rights norms. Feminist activism has led to entirely new protections for gender-specific violations, protections not foreseen by the original UN Charter's sex equality clause. Applying the norms to women has proven to be complex due to the masculine meanings of long-standing rights formulations. Here we recommend the essays by Marie Sandell, Regula Ludi, Eileen Boris and Jill Jensen, Rachel George, Jadwiga Pieper Mooney, Jennifer Adair, Laura Belmonte, Vera Mackie, and Afiya Shehrbano Zia.

We also claim that it is insufficient to focus on institutions, treaty-making, and legal norms as if they capture the full project of human rights. Human rights change has been driven by the pressures of often ordinary people. The recovery of their voices and the analysis of the mode and politics of their interventions and the barriers they faced continue to be research desiderata. Readers who wish to focus on activism, voluntary associations, and NGOs should turn to the essays by Caroline Shaw, Mairi MacDonald, Kimberly Lowe, Marie Sandell, Linde Lindkvist, Meredith Terretta, Catherine Baylin Duryea, Jadwiga Pieper Mooney, Jennifer Adair, Afiya Shehrbano Zia, Laura Belmonte, Vera Mackie, and Michelle Carmody.

The above thematic groupings do not provide definitive answers to human rights challenges, but they do offer empirical richness. They are designed to help readers pose their own questions.

The essays in this collection each reflect original research and offer a distinct methodological, theoretical, and interpretive contribution. Each is written to stand alone and yet also serves as part of the whole volume. Taken together, they show a long, complicated global story of struggle for emancipation, socio-economic and gender justice, and the affirmation of collective and individual selfhood, struggle that continues into the present day. We have presented our chronological framework, thematic groupings, and the reasons why these narratives are open and contingent, with no certainty about outcomes.

As a study of history, this book reflects its own historical present. We locate this book in our "post-NGO optimism" world. We live today in challenging times, where the sentiments and values, networks and laws, as well as multilateral institutional connections that are at the center of human rights history are partially eclipsed by rising intolerance, wars and civil strife, and a resurgence of illiberal regimes and of nationalist thinking and action. People still suffer at the hands of repressive governments, as well as at the hands of powerful state leaders and elites who stand idly by, indifferent or, worse, complicit. Economic inequality is increasing within and between states and peoples, given the constraints of present-day globalization. The once electrifying promise of "never again" rings more hollow today, not least because while inaction seemed to be part of the problem in the 1990s, in our own time militarized action has manifested itself as part of the problem as well.

Yet a multitude of obstacles were part of the historical record from the start of our chronology. Quite unexpectedly, ordinary people operating in ordinary and extraordinary times changed the global moral, legal, and institutional landscape, testing in various iterations new standards of conduct for states, intergovernmental organizations, corporations, and peoples. Historians are not in the business of prediction. We cannot say whether human rights as norms and laws will be a viable guide for the future. But we do hope that the empirically rich and historically specific lessons here about roadblocks and the possibilities for change will be incorporated widely into classroom instruction, so that the next human rights outcomes will be our readers' concerns as well.

Notes

1 Mainstream legal scholars claim that legal analysis offers an impartial authority that allows the practitioner to stand outside the social order to reflect on the world objectively. For an overview, see Richard Falk, Friedrich Kratochwil, and Saul H. Mendlovitz, *International Law: A Contemporary Perspective*, Boulder, CO: Westview Press, 1985. For feminist perspectives, see Hilary Charlesworth and Christine Chinkin, *The Boundaries of International Law: A Feminist Analysis*, Manchester: Manchester University Press, 2000, and Mary Jane Mossman, "Feminism and Legal Method: The Difference It Makes," *Australian Journal of Law and Society*, 1986, vol. 3, 30–52. For a historical assessment of law in practice see Jean H. Quataert, "A New Look at International Law: Gendering the Practices of Humanitarian Medicine in Europe's Small Wars, 1879–1907," *Human Rights Quarterly*, 2018, vol. 40, no. 3, 547–69.

2 See, in particular, Paul Gordon Lauren, *The Evolution of International Human Rights: Visions Seen*, Philadelphia: University of Pennsylvania Press, 1998. The book is cast globally and provides fascinating details of activism prior to 1945. Capturing a simplistic optimism in the field, Linda Kerber, president of the American Historical Association stated in 2006 that "we are all historians of human rights." Linda Kerber, *Perspectives on History. The Newsmagazine of the American Historical Association*, 2006, vol. 44, no. 7. Online. Available at www.historians.org/publications-and-directories/perspectives-on-history/october-2006/we-are-all-historians-of-human-rights (accessed 11 November 2018).

3 Reza Afshari, "On Historiography of Human Rights. Reflections on Paul Gordon Lauren's *The Evolution of International Human Rights: Visions Seen*," *Human Rights Quarterly*, 2007, vol. 29, no. 1, 1–67.

4 Micheline R. Ishay (ed.), *The Human Rights Reader: Major Political Essays, Speeches, and Documents from the Bible to the Present*, New York: Routledge, 1997; Lauren, *Evolution*; Jan Herman Burgers, "The Road to San Francisco: The Revival of the Human Rights Idea in the Twentieth

Century," *Human Rights Quarterly*, 1992, vol. 14, no. 4, 447–77; and, more recently, Lynn Hunt, *Inventing Human Rights: A History*, New York: W. W. Norton, 2007.

5 Many human rights and humanitarian NGOs supported the Security Council's new initiative of "humanitarian" military interventions sent to keep people safe in the civil strife and armed conflicts breaking out in the decade of the 1990s. Opinion shifted dramatically after the US invasion of Iraq in 2003, partly because authorities justified the war as a defense of human rights and promotion of women's rights. For critical assessments of humanitarianism, see Didier Fassin and Mariella Panolfi (eds.), *Contemporary States of Emergency: The Politics of Military and Humanitarian Interventions*, New York: Zone, 2010; and Eric D. Weitz, "From the Vienna to the Paris System: International Politics and the Entangled Histories of Human Rights, Forced Deportations, and Civilizing Missions," *American Historical Review*, 2008, vol. 113, no. 5, 1313–43.

6 Mark Mazower, *No Enchanted Palace: The End of Empire and the Ideological Origins of the United Nations*, Princeton, NJ: Princeton University Press, 2009; A. W. Brian Simpson, *Human Rights and the End of Empire: Britain and the Genesis of the European Convention*, Oxford: Oxford University Press, 2004; Roger Normand and Sarah Zaidi, *Human Rights at the UN: The Political History of Universal Justice*, Bloomington: Indiana University Press, 2008; Roland Burke, *Decolonization and the Evolution of International Human Rights*, Philadelphia: University of Pennsylvania Press, 2010; Mary Ann Glendon, *A World Made New: Eleanor Roosevelt and the Universal Declaration of Human Rights*, New York: Random House, 2002; Carol Anderson, *Eyes Off the Prize: The United Nations and the African American Struggle for Human Rights, 1944–1955*, New York: Cambridge University Press, 2003; and Sarah B. Snyder, *From Selma to Moscow: How Human Rights Activists Transformed US Foreign Policy*, New York: Columbia University Press, 2018. An essential resource is David P. Forsythe's massive *Encyclopedia of Human Rights*, 5 vols., New York: Oxford University Press, 2009. See also Kenneth Cmiel, "The Recent History of Human Rights," *American Historical Review*, 2004, vol. 109, no. 1, 117–35; Jeffrey N. Wasserstrom, Greg Grandin, Lynn Hunt, and Marilyn B. Young (eds.), *Human Rights and Revolutions*, Lanham, MD: Rowman & Littlefield, 2000; and Jean H. Quataert, *Advocating Dignity: Human Rights Mobilizations in Global Politics*, Philadelphia: University of Pennsylvania Press, 2010. An account from an activist's perspective is Aryeh Neier, *The International Human Rights Movement: A History*, Princeton, NJ: Princeton University Press, 2012.

7 This literature is large; see e.g. Michael Barnett, *Empire of Humanity: A History of Humanitarianism*, Ithaca, NY: Cornell University Press, 2011; Bruno Cabanes, *The Great War and the Origins of Humanitarianism, 1918–1922*, Cambridge, UK: Cambridge University Press, 2014; and Keith David Watenpaugh, "The League of Nations' Rescue of Armenian Genocide Survivors and the Making of Modern Humanitarianism, 1920–1927," *American Historical Review*, 2010, vol. 115, no. 5, 1315–39. See, for an aid perspective on the ground, David Rieff, *A Bed for the Night: Humanitarianism in Crisis*, New York: Simon & Schuster, 2002.

8 This literature is likewise large. See, among many other possible sources, "Human Rights, Global Conferences and the Making of Postwar Transnational Feminisms," a special issue edited by Jean H. Quataert and Benita Roth of the *Journal of Women's History*, 2012, vol. 24, no. 4; Amrita Basu (ed.), *Women's Movements in the Global Era: The Power of Local Feminisms*, Boulder, CO: Westview Press, 2010; Julie Peters and Andrea Wolper (eds.), *Women's Rights, Human Rights: International Feminist Perspectives*, New York: Routledge, 1995; and Bert B. Lockwood (ed.), *Women's Rights: A Human Rights Quarterly Reader*, Baltimore, MD: Johns Hopkins University Press, 2006. On how these debates challenge contemporary feminist theory and theorists, see Chandra Talpade Mohanty, *Feminism Without Borders: Decolonizing Theory, Practicing Solidarity*, Durham, NC: Duke University Press, 2003 and Brooke A. Ackerly, *Universal Human Rights in a World of Difference*, New York: Cambridge University Press, 2008.

9 See especially Martti Koskenniemi, *The Gentle Civilizer of Nations: The Rise and Fall of International Law*, Cambridge, UK: Cambridge University Press, 2001, p. 9. See also Jean H. Quataert, "International Law and Human Rights: Diverging and Converging Histories," *New Global Studies*, 2012, vol. 6, no. 3, 1–22.

10 Samuel Moyn, *The Last Utopia. Human Rights in History*, Cambridge, MA: Belknap Press at Harvard University Press, 2010; and Jan Eckel and Samuel Moyn (eds.), *The Breakthrough: Human Rights in the 1970s*, Philadelphia: University of Pennsylvania Press, 2013. Moyn has recently, in dialogue with Stefan-Ludwig Hoffmann, repositioned the debate to the 1990s. See Stefan-

Ludwig Hoffmann, "Viewpoint: Human Rights and History," *Past & Present*, 2016, no. 232, no. 1, 279–310, and Samuel Moyn, "The End of Human Rights History," *Past & Present*, 2016, vol. 233, no. 1, 307–22. For an alternative interpretation of the 1970s as a moment when neoliberal economists hijacked the human rights agenda, see Joseph Slaughter, *Human Rights, Inc.: The World Novel, Narrative Form, and International Law*, New York: Fordham University Press, 2007.

11 See Arthur Nussbaum, *A Concise History of the Law of Nations*, New York: Macmillan, 1950, pp. 191, 198. Nussbaum sees the mid-nineteenth century as the beginning of a "new era" in legal history. See also Koskenniemi, *Gentle Civilizer*, p. 6.

12 The "new imperialism" is a common designation for the period when many European states as well as the United States and Japan established formal colonial empires in Africa, Southeast Asia and parts of East Asia. The key study on the intertwining of colonialism and imperialism from the sixteenth century onwards is Antony Anghie, *Imperialism, Sovereignty and the Making of International Law*, Cambridge, UK: Cambridge University Press, 2005.

13 In addition to Anghie, *Imperialism*, see B. S. Chimni, "Third World Approaches to International Law: A Manifesto," *International Community Law Review*, 2006, vol. 8, 3–27.

14 For our call, see "Call for Chapter Proposals for Innovative Volume in the History of Human Rights." Online. Available at https://networks.h-net.org/node/73374/announcements/106760/call-chapter-proposals-innovative-volume-history-human-rights (accessed 11 November 2018).

15 On the place of the Universal Declaration of Human Rights in international law, see Hurst Hannum, "The Status of the Universal Declaration of Human Rights in National and International Law" *Georgia Journal of International and Comparative Law*, 1996, vol. 25, no. 287, 289–397, 317–35.

16 Mairi MacDonald, "Reclaiming Congo Reform for the History of Human Rights," p. 57, in this volume.

17 MacDonald, "Reclaiming," p. 71, in this volume.

18 Susan Pedersen, *The Guardians: The League of Nations and the Crisis of Empire*, Oxford: Oxford University Press, 2015; Carole Fink, *Defending the Rights of Others: The Great Powers, the Jews, and International Minority Protection, 1878–1938*, New York: Cambridge University Press, 2004; and more recently Marco Duranti, *The Conservative Human Rights Revolution. European Identity, Transnational Politics, and the Origins of the European Convention*, New York: Oxford University Press, 2017.

19 Carol Miller, "'Geneva – The Key to Equality': Inter-War Feminism and the League of Nations," *Women's History Review*, 1994, vol. 3, no. 2, 219–45.

20 See e.g. Mark Goodale (ed.), *Letters to the Contrary: A Curated History of the UNESCO Human Rights Survey*, Stanford, CA: Stanford University Press, 2018.

21 Meredith Terretta, "'Why Then Call It the Declaration of Human Rights?' The Failures of Universal Human Rights in Colonial Africa's Internationally Supervised Territories," p. 203, in this volume.

22 Steven Wilf, "Intellectual Property Law and Human Rights," p. 560, in this volume.

23 See e.g. Cynthia Soohoo, Catherine Albisa, and Martha Davis (eds.), *Bringing Human Rights Home: A History of Human Rights in the United States*, 3 vols., Philadelphia: University of Pennsylvania Press, 2009; Mark Philip Bradley and Patrice Petro (eds.), *Truth Claims: Representation and Human Rights*, New Brunswick, NJ: Rutgers University Press, 2002; Akira Iriye, Petra Goedde, and William I. Hitchcock (eds.), *The Human Rights Revolution: An International History*, New York: Oxford University Press, 2012; Stefan-Ludwig Hoffmann (ed.), *Human Rights in the Twentieth Century*, New York: Cambridge University Press, 2010; and Eckel and Moyn (eds.), *The Breakthrough.*

24 Charlotte Ku and Paul F. Diehl, "International Law as Operating and Normative Systems: An Overview," in Ku and Diehl (eds.), *International Law: Classic and Contemporary Readings*, 3rd ed., Boulder, CO: Lynne Rienner, 2009, pp. 1–18.

25 Moyn, *Last Utopia*, p. 180.

26 Quataert, *Advocating Dignity*, p. 13.

PART I

THE NEW INTERNATIONALISM

2

JOHN ANDERSON – SLAVE, REFUGEE, AND FREEDOM FIGHTER

A human rights campaign in the age of empire

Caroline Shaw

In October 1860, the US government requested the extradition of an alleged murderer from Canada. John Anderson had indeed killed a man in Missouri in 1853 and fled to Canada, where he first established himself in Windsor as a laborer under an assumed name. Canadian officials immediately arrested Anderson and began proceedings for Anderson's return under the terms of the reigning US–British extradition clauses of the 1842 Webster–Ashburton Treaty. The extradition of a suspected murderer for trial would not normally have attracted notice from public commentators or activists in Canada or in the United Kingdom. However, the difference of Anderson's case became readily apparent to officials and to activists on both sides of the Atlantic. The US secretary of state had failed to mention that John Anderson had been a slave in the American South.[1] Anderson had stabbed a man intent on returning him to bondage. Understood in this light, Anderson's return to the South would have made a mockery of justice. For those who rallied to Anderson's side, American slavery deprived men and women of "all human rights."[2] The demand that Britons become complicit in a system by returning a slave who had fought for his freedom added insult to injury. It was unfathomable, his lawyer proclaimed, that they would add to slavery's violation of "human rights" by further depriving this man of "the universally allowed natural prerogative of our species" for a person to "strike a justifiable blow in defense of his personal liberty."[3]

The unthinkable very nearly did happen, however, for the Webster–Ashburton Treaty's clauses on extradition contained no exemptions for fugitive slaves.[4] Moreover, injunctions against refusing refuge for any foreign refugees – though deeply embedded in British culture in this period – were not yet articulated in domestic, imperial, or international policy.[5] That Anderson was not extradited to the United States in the winter of 1861 was not a matter of a human rights regime, but rather a matter of the power of a moralizing public and antislavery activists to demand that the government act in accordance with shared commitment to a right to liberty and sense of public responsibility to uphold that right for persecuted foreigners as well as for themselves.

This essay uses John Anderson's story to explore the relationship between humanitarianism and popular and official discussions of universal rights and their incorporation into institutional norms in the nineteenth century. Scholars have tended to describe this relationship as a handoff from humanitarianism, on the one hand, to codified rights – policy and law – on the other.[6] Anderson's case helps us to move beyond this model, in favor of a more dynamic relationship between humanitarianism and human rights, joining newer scholarship in refugee history and international antislavery efforts that revises the chronology of human rights efforts.[7] I argue that Anderson's lawyers, the John Anderson Committee, public protests, and addresses to officials on either side of the Atlantic reveal an already deeply entrenched commitment to protecting individuals' right to liberty from unjust foreign laws in the century before our more modern human rights regime took root in international law. John Anderson's history was not the first time the wider public safeguarded the rights of foreigners, foreign slaves included. Indeed the Anderson case, seen in a wider context, is a successor to earlier public and official efforts to embed changing humanitarian norms in national, imperial, and international policy. These efforts bore fruit. While reluctant to impose universal norms on an independent Canadian judiciary and conscious of tense diplomacy with the United States, activists ensured the sanctity of that "universally allowed natural prerogative of our species," the right to liberty. Their language – their hopes for a more robust and just system of international justice and their fears of what this justice might spell for international peace – ought to be strikingly familiar to us today.[8]

The language of activism: key concepts at a critical crossroads

Anderson's case challenges scholars' tendency to downplay the nineteenth century in histories of human rights. This literature highlights the twentieth century as the matrix of the modern human rights regime. According to these scholars, the nineteenth century saw advances in civil rights, which are inherently local and particularistic, and humanitarian aid to outsiders, but not universal human rights. This scholarship makes it difficult to imagine a case like Anderson's, which is set in an era of empire and the rise of the nation-state, and features powerful, successful claims on behalf of a persecuted foreigner whose race and place of birth set him apart from those who would come to his aid.

According to this line of scholarship, civil rights are rooted in the age of revolutions, but human rights emerge as the product of international conventions since World War II. There were, of course, antecedents to this more recent provenance; scholars point to the Judeo-Christian tradition as well as the ethics of Islamic law and Confucianism.[9] To these cosmologies, one adds the language of natural rights that emerged in the eighteenth-century Enlightenment, one that drew upon the universalism of religious injunctions and the broader application of language of privilege that had formerly been accorded more narrowly to certain subjects of a monarch's realm.[10] Combined with a burgeoning print culture and political revolution, the formerly limited purview of rights became a "cascading logic" of human rights by the end of the eighteenth century, as historian Lynn Hunt explains.[11] Whether one focuses on the Enlightenment or the period after World War II, however, the nineteenth century seems retrograde. Nationalism and imperialism, both hallmarks of this period, emphasize citizenship and illiberal rule, respectively, rather than the liberal universalism that undergirds modern human rights movements.[12]

Contrary to expectations, then, officials and advocates in Anderson's case routinely alternated between languages of universalism and human rights on the one hand, and the particular rights valid on British soil and traditionally granted to subjects of the crown on the other. Britons' desire to protect Anderson expressed a combination of universal moral injunctions and a particularly British ability to intervene on his behalf. Anderson was, at some moments, seen as a British subject whose personal sovereignty his sovereign government was bound to uphold. At other moments, he was the quintessential persecuted foreigner, entitled to safe harbor and liberty on British soil because his own country would not protect him.

During the Anderson controversy, activists unashamedly blended together these claims – claims that scholars today tend to hold distinct. One might attribute this mixing of arguments to the novelty of modern rights claims during 1860s. There is, after all, something of a hybrid approach to argumentation at work here; those arguing on Anderson's behalf did not limit themselves to a single approach since they themselves did not know which appeals would be most effective. This makes sense in a period in which there was no codified process for determining asylum cases in circumstances like Anderson's. Officials and activists alike thus hoped to use Anderson's case as a means of establishing a firm legal precedent for safeguarding fugitive slaves who sought asylum on British soil.

In this respect, activists sought legal precedent as a means of institutionalizing what was already a robust British interest in the fate of foreign refugees. As I have argued elsewhere, the project of supporting foreign refugees was, for the British, an international projection of their liberal aspirations and burgeoning national and imperial identity. Calls for assistance for refugees extended from the radical left to the heights of the establishment. Failing to protect refugees was shameful and could be mobilized as a political weapon by the middle of the nineteenth century. Refugee slaves were very much part of this proud campaign to safeguard persecuted foreigners from their oppressors. Harriet Beecher Stowe's *Uncle Tom's Cabin*, published in the wake of the Fugitive Slave Act, was wildly popular in Britain as well as in America. Famous fugitive slaves and European revolutionary refugees toured Britain on speaking tours, their audiences becoming all the more likely to see the two sets of foreigners in the same light. Stowe herself had made the connection within her novel when she compared her fictional fugitive slave, George Harris, with Hungarian noblemen who similarly were forced to take up arms in their quest for liberty.[13] So entrenched was this public commitment to refugees, so impossible did it seem for Britons to renege on their moral responsibilities, that commentators by the middle of the nineteenth century assumed refuge was in fact a broad right and one whose defense was intimately tied to Britons' perceptions of themselves as the liberal superpower on the world stage.

Seen in this light, Anderson's champions would have thought of their wide-ranging arguments not as a new departure in the area of human rights, but as a restatement of a well-established British moral commitment to these freedom fighters. Activists had every reason to believe that they might be successful in attaining positive legal protections for foreign refugees. They could draw upon more than 50 years of national relief efforts foregrounding the needs of foreign refugees, dating to the French Revolution of the 1790s. Furthermore, by the 1810s, humanitarians had won the abolition of the international slave trade and the policing of the Atlantic by a special Royal Navy squadron.[14]

A few words of caution seem necessary here. Commitment to a human right to liberty and, in turn, to refugees, did not assume human equality. Nineteenth-century activists – even the most ardent of Anderson's supporters – were not free from the racial prejudices of their age. John Anderson himself would fall victim to racial anxieties; his most ardent benefactors assumed he would find it difficult to flourish in Canada or in Britain following his ordeal. They sent him to resettle in Liberia. Anderson's treatment fit a pattern; race, religion, and social class tended to shape the nature of long-term refuge under the British aegis. There is a tendency, though, among students and scholars alike to dismiss this imperial age wholesale and to see, in cases like Anderson's, a story of international posturing and diplomatic power-play rather than genuine humanitarianism or human rights advocacy. The hallmark of the genuinely universal is that it is free from politics and racism, so the argument goes.[15] I understand the inclination and the concern for purity of motives. Yet, dismissing the more overtly politicized and racialized activism of the past risks assuming that "we moderns" have overcome the seductiveness of imperialism, of nationalism, and of race that one sees so readily in the past, Anderson's case included.[16] One risks, too, missing the power of identity politics that undergirded efforts to safeguard persecuted foreigners. Refusing to protect Anderson portended deep international shame, more than just a blemish on the role Britons were so proud of as moral leaders at a time when most of the European Continent had been engulfed in revolution and American still held onto their "peculiar institution." Shame, pride, and a sense of exceptionalism could save lives – John Anderson's included.

Anderson's story: melodrama, empathy, and universal rights

By the time that Harper Twelvetrees, member of the British and Foreign Anti-Slavery Society and of the John Anderson Committee, published his *Story of the Life of John Anderson* in 1863, Anderson was himself a free man living in Liberia. This account of John Anderson's case, the most sustained one we have, congratulates activists for their successful efforts on Anderson's behalf. The book is dedicated to the hard work of George Thompson, recently a member of Parliament and an advocate for the "cause of freedom throughout the world."[17] The author deems the story useful, furnishing a primer on American slavery and cautioning defenders of freedom to remain vigilant. By Twelvetrees' publication date, Lincoln's Emancipation Proclamation had made it unlikely that the exact case would be repeated. Yet the Confederacy was still fighting hard for slavery and Anderson's predicament was also meant to stand in for the situation of slaves in "the empire of Brazil, and in the islands of the Gulf of Mexico," as Twelvetrees explained in the book's preface. Mirroring the tenor of the press reports published in the middle of Anderson's extradition hearings – indeed, Twelvetrees includes key passages from the press and from official correspondence in its pages – *The Story of the Life of John Anderson* captures well both Anderson's harrowing story and its nearly unhappy outcome.

Following a chapter on Missouri's recent history and the struggle over the status of slavery that ended in the Missouri Compromise, Twelvetrees embarked on an account of Anderson's childhood. His description harkened back to the preface, in which the author had not minced words over the impact of the slave system on enslaved families. The law, he highlighted, ignored the "natural rights, duties, or affections" of parents. It made the bond between mother and child significant only in determining legal ownership of the child by the mother's master.[18] Anderson's situation was no different. His father escaped slavery when Anderson was still a baby, driven by a desire for freedom that Twelvetrees judged reasonable given the havoc slavery wreaked on Africans' families.[19] At 7 years old, Anderson was "left an orphan," when his mother was sold to a trader who took her to market in New Orleans.[20]

In some respects, Anderson was, in fact, fortunate in his early life despite having been "deprived of his parents" so young; he was, from age 7, in the charge of a "mistress of a kind disposition, who supplied, in a great degree, the place of the parents."[21] Years later Anderson would recall this Mrs. Burton "in terms of gratitude and affection," and a childhood that, as Twelvetrees surmises "did not pass unhappily," often engaged in sport as well as in the labor of the farm.[22] An "expert in the all the duties of the farm," Anderson extended his ambit as he grew into a man by joining the Freewill Baptist Church and attending all of their meetings. Whether he met his future wife Maria Tomlin through the Freewill Baptists is unclear in Twelvetrees' account. The two remained close to the religious center Anderson had found, married by a minister of color and "pledging to live together as husband and wife and promising to be faithful to each other."[23] Maria, a recent widow at the time of their marriage, further requested that Anderson "act the part of father" to her older children.[24] They had a child of their own and, initially, lived only several miles apart with their respective masters' families.

As the reader is meant to surmise by this point, their promises and their early happiness would be impossible to maintain within the slave system. Sure enough, Anderson was soon sold to a master 30 miles distant. Not permitted to visit his wife and young son, he was "told to abandon and forget them, and take a new wife, or mistress, from amongst the slaves of his present owner." Twelvetrees made clear that Anderson understood well that his new master wanted the property that might issue from such a relationship.[25]

Unwilling to break his oaths to his family and surrender to his new master's will, Anderson fled in September 1853. He escaped first to his father-in-law's house and then to bid farewell to his family. A freeman himself, his father-in-law encouraged Anderson to run, and his wife had at marriage encouraged Anderson to seek his freedom and then his children's as well. Anderson met trouble almost immediately. While Anderson was still in Missouri, a man named Seneca Diggs saw Anderson traveling on his own. Suspecting a runaway, Diggs gave chase, exhorting three of his slaves to assist. Tired and cornered, Anderson

> struck a blow at Diggs and retired from the spot; but hearing him repeat his order that the slaves should take him dead or alive, and fearing that he had not inflicted sufficient injury to prevent pursuit, he returned and again struck Diggs, and effectually disarmed him.[26]

Twelvetrees' point was that Anderson fought in self-defense, had no intention of killing his attacker, and indeed had no knowledge that his attacker would die of these wounds several days later. After several more narrow escapes, Anderson finally crossed the Missouri River with a dollar and a half to his name. Anderson ran through Illinois, Indiana, and Michigan en route to Canada. Aided by a "good-hearted English settler" among other abolitionists, Anderson found himself be "beneath the British flag" about a month later.

By the time Anderson arrived in the fall of 1853, Canada, then a British colony, had been a promised land for American slaves for three-quarters of a century. Black Loyalists, promised their freedom in exchange for aid during the American Revolution and the War of 1812, escaped north after the close of each conflict, resettling there or in the British West Indies.[27] Enslaved persons also sought refuge on British soil. Those numbers increased after Congress passed the Fugitive Slave Act of 1850, making it a crime for Americans in free states to harbor those who attempted to escape. Someone like Anderson, then, could well have had trouble in finding refuge in Indiana, Illinois, or Michigan, free states along his escape route. Slave catchers like Diggs, emboldened by the 1850 law, pursued fugitives through the north, obtaining aid from officials, private individuals, and others whom they could bribe, as Diggs had the group of slave men who pursued Anderson in Missouri.

Though Canada beckoned like "an arc of freedom" for American slaves, the British colony was far from a paradise. As in the American North, blacks encountered deeply engrained racial prejudices and a harsh climate that contrasted sharply with that of the American South. With financial assistance from abolitionists in the United States, Canada, and Britain, refugee slaves established separate village settlements and integrated into the economic lives of the larger cities. Free blacks traveled from the northern states to set up churches and schools. While life was not easy, the strength of black institutions provided critical support and solace for the growing community of refugees.[28] Anderson seems to have fitted readily into this tableau, finding friendship and work enough to support him comfortably, first helping to lay the Windsor to Chatham railway and then, later, becoming a wood chopper and a mason. Eventually he saved enough of his wages to become a homeowner.

Anderson's life in Canada was to be disrupted more by slave catchers than by any want of entrepreneurial spirit of his own. Indeed, black settlements in Canada had been long harassed by American bounty hunters whose rare successes in kidnapping fugitive slaves inspired terror within the community.[29] Well aware of this threat, abolitionists had lobbied the foreign office during the Webster–Ashburton Treaty negotiations, fearful that the extradition article would leave slaves' status in jeopardy and embolden slave catchers to cross the border.[30] Foreign Secretary Lord Aberdeen sought to mollify their concerns even though the government was aware of the diplomatic tightrope they walked by protecting American fugitives. Early cases had, in fact, been decided in the slaves' favor, one in 1829 denying the US request for the return of fugitives who had been traveling with their master. The Canadian executive council had, however, ruled in terms that could haunt them in the later extradition treaty; slaves were not to be returned unless they had committed a crime recognized by local law.[31]

From the start, Anderson caught wind of rumors that slave catchers were targeting him, for instance by trying to lure him to Michigan. Seeking advice from a lawyer, Anderson moved and assumed different aliases, finding new employment and gaining new skills in each location until he settled more permanently in Caledonia. It was there that his past caught up with him. A supposed friend betrayed his true identity to a justice of the peace who, in turn, informed Diggs' family. In rapid order, officials in Missouri solicited the assistance of a detective in Michigan who was also a professional slave catcher, a point Twelvetrees carefully notes in order to highlight the impossibility of distinguishing between the formal justice system and the slave system in the United States.[32] On the basis of information from the United States about Anderson's seemingly dubious past, Canadian officials arrested him twice between April and September 1860 and released him twice, thanks to legal assistance he received. In October 1860, however, Anderson's case took a turn for the worse as the US government intervened, requesting his extradition on murder charges. Much to British officials' chagrin, the US secretary of state General Cass failed to mention that Anderson, a "man of color," had been a slave in Missouri.[33] It is possible that, had Anderson's legal status been known, his petition to be released would have been accepted unanimously and his extradition would have met a curt denial. This is not certain, however, given the initial decision of the Toronto court, which was made after his history was better known.

For officials and activists, Anderson's case was less a surprise than a long-anticipated opportunity to test British commitment to the cause of freedom as a broad right. Upon learning of Anderson's arrest, John Scoble of the Toronto branch of the British and Foreign Anti-Slavery Society set to action immediately trying to secure his release. Lawyer and antislavery sympathizer Samuel Freeman lobbied the Canadian government and then took up Anderson's cause in the extradition hearing before the court. The language of Freeman's initial petition on Anderson's behalf was muted, emphasizing primarily the sovereignty of British soil in the face of American importunity rather than the broader question of liberty.[34] But the significance of the extradition hearing for blacks in Canada was immediately apparent, a point that antislavery activists continued to hammer home. The announcement of the court's ruling itself garnered a large audience, including many men and women of color and some fugitive slaves. Evidently, court officials feared that violence would break out if Anderson were not freed; Twelvetrees mentions that authorities took weapons at the door.[35]

If Anderson's extradition hearing was a test for a universal human right to liberty, the men issuing the decision failed. Two of the three judges of the Queen's Bench in Toronto – Chief Justice Robinson and Justice Burns – dismissed Anderson's petition for release. Only Justice McLean found in Anderson's behalf. McLean's dissent was scathing, finding in the request for extradition, first, a willful blindness to the fact that Anderson's actions had defended his personal liberty in a moment of extreme danger; second, a perversion of the rights espoused in the American Declaration of Independence; and, finally, a violation of British law. McLean reiterated Anderson's history and the naturalness of fighting for one's freedom, especially in the context of slavery. He pointed out that America's own Declaration of Independence "proclaimed to the world that all men are born equal and possessed of certain inalienable rights, amongst which are life, liberty, and the pursuit of happiness." Only the strength of the white population in the United States had "deprived [slaves] of all human rights."[36] McLean was unwilling to bend British law to the perverse mockery of justice that could "convert into chattels a very large number of the human race." Rather, as McLean implied and others asserted immediately on Anderson's behalf, upstanding Britons would have to establish instead the "inviolability of British asylum – the proudest institution of the British Empire," as Twelvetrees put it in his rendition of the judges' dissent.[37]

Having hoped for a verdict more in line with McLean's opinion, public commentators in Canada and in Britain were aghast at the majority's decision. In Toronto, the *Globe* set out to defend Anderson with far more vigor than Freeman had before the court, emphasizing the evils of slavery and painting the decision of the court as a moral failing by then governor general Sir John MacDonald and his administration of Upper Canada.[38] Members of the British and Foreign Anti-Slavery Society organized a protest meeting presided over by John Scoble. His address to the crowds emphasized that the decision was a threat to liberty as well as to British officials' commitments to protecting slaves despite the Webster–Ashburton Treaty. To repudiate these promises was thus a much a violation of the government's commitments as it was a violation of Anderson's natural rights.[39] In Britain, newspapers followed suit, reprinting Justice McLean's dissenting opinion and carrying Anderson's story to a wide audience.[40] Few believed it possible that Anderson would be extradited to the United States; one article, published with minor variations in newspapers across the United

Kingdom, called even the hint that the British would surrender Anderson "a gross libel on the guardians of our national liberties."[41] John Plummer, a journalist then living in Kettering in the English Midlands, wrote a stirring poem about Anderson that was printed in the *Manchester Guardian* and reprinted as far distant as Jersey in the British Channel Islands:

> Give him up? Never! While Englishmen wear
> In their hearts the sign of the free.
> Give him up? Never! No Briton will dare
> A traitor to liberty be.
> Have we then liv'd in the land of our sires,
> Its pride and its glory to stain:
> To sit and dose by bright ruddy fires,
> Forgetting the slave and his chain?
> Are we as the serfs, who fain would forget
> The mem'ries that round them ee'r throng?
> No! England shall see her children can yet
> Be first in the battle'gainst wrong ...[42]

Personal sovereignty, national sovereignty, and intra-imperial politics

Anderson's supporters on both sides of the Atlantic had reason to believe that the language of national pride alongside universal rights and compassion for the persecuted would be powerful in making their case. International anti-slave-trade treaties had championed the right to liberty since the late 1810s, requiring both the liberation of illegally-trafficked slaves and their protection – their refuge – under the aegis of the signing powers. By statute, then, the British were responsible for protecting liberated Africans. While there was no similar statute regulating the treatment of slaves who fled slavery, as opposed to the illegal slave trade, courts more often than not maintained a "freedom principle" for those who fled across a border. The *Creole* case offered something of a case in point in recent memory, as did that of the *Amistad*.[43] In the *Amistad* case, even the slaveholding United States recognized the power of the turn to human rights. In his defense of the Africans on trial, John Quincy Adams appealed to "human rights" three times, a phrase echoed by other members of the Africans' counsel as well.[44]

Despite these powerful precedents, however, Anderson was dangerously close to being extradited to face murder changes per Secretary Cass' request. The British might commit themselves to the cause of liberty, but even in the nineteenth century, taking such a stand against the United States was not a step to take lightly. Saving John Anderson would entail a costly assertion of power in the service of humanitarianism and human rights, albeit one that commentators like journalist and poet John Plummer viewed as synonymous with Britishness itself.

Even in the broader history of British abolitionism, there were indications that a case like that of John Anderson's would not necessarily be decided in the slave's favor. From the start, Black Loyalists at the time of the Revolution and the War of 1812 were political tools in the struggle between America and Great Britain. While international tensions deescalated later in the nineteenth century, border disputes remained contentious for decades. British-Canadian officials disliked the incursions of American slave catchers on Canadian soil. Nevertheless, Anderson's case, like those of other fugitive slaves in times of peace between America and the British Empire, threatened to strain the newly friendly relations. In a sense, the Webster–Ashburton Treaty offered a means for Canadian justices to thread the needle, appeasing their neighbors to the south, while avoiding the larger moral question of slavery itself. Pointing to Anderson's crime and playing down his identity, the prosecution had emphasized that murder was murder and an extraditable crime. Justice Burns' decision emphasized the letter of the law as well. He recognized that a British audience would find the return of a fugitive slave despicable. However, officials – he found – must respect the laws of other nations.[45]

Anderson's advocates, by contrast, refused to accept that this was any ordinary murder or that the British were required to recognize the laws of another nation on their own territory. Neither members of Parliament nor commentators in the British press could believe that Anderson's killing of Diggs constituted a felonious murder. To them, it was clearly an act of self-defense in protection of his liberty. The prime minister himself underscored that, had Anderson been a freeman, committing the murder of Diggs would have been an extraditable offence. Since Anderson was a slave, however, Palmerston could not support his return to the United States.[46] The technical question of murder thus became a proxy for the larger moral question of complicity in American slavery.

More immediately, the British commentators seized on the ready comparison between refugee slaves and European revolutionaries, both groups that had sought protection on British soil from persecution in their homelands. British asylum was a matter of national identity and international pride. The point was made explicitly in the *Times* of London on 5 January 1861. Drawing on the language of both Stowe and of accounts of British support for European revolutionaries, the writer exclaimed:

> That we, who look with such scorn upon the little State of Saxony for delivering up a Hungarian nobleman who had trusted to her hospitality, should, in our strength and our grandeur, deliver up a wretched slave who had run for our soil as to the ark of freedom, may be argued as logical necessity in a court of law, but is an obvious impossibility as a fact.[47]

The *Times* further underscored the shame of violating asylum, recognizing the need to bolster what was then (as now) only a quasi-right to refuge, nowhere guaranteed in law. The *Times* article appeared in newspapers across the United Kingdom in the following days and the media continued to draw parallels between Anderson and the plight of refugee European revolutionaries.[48] News of Anderson's case that highlighted the oppressiveness of American slavery routinely appeared in print next to accounts of Continental despotism, as it did in the journal *Once a Week*, for example, which railed against French emperor Louis Napoleon's attempts to stymie the popular cause of Italian nationalism.[49] The timing of the article – and of the case itself – could not have been more appropriate. South Carolina had seceded from the Union on 20 December 1860. The question of slavery was fast drawing the United States to a moment of crisis. British newspaper audiences were well aware of these developments early in 1861.

In this context, Anderson's supporters hoped, with reason, that officials would intercede on his behalf. The British public's humanitarian advocacy of foreign refugees had elicited government support and parliamentary action from the start. The secretary of state for foreign affairs and the Colonial Office had promised abolitionists in 1842 that they would never surrender a fugitive slave. There were more recent examples, as well. Just three years prior to Anderson's case, the British had refused extradition for Dr. Simon Bernard, a Frenchman living in Birmingham who was reported to have aided in Felice Orsini's attempted assassination of French emperor Louis Napoleon. Activists successfully advocated his protection in a state trial in London. Barrister and Member of Parliament Edwin James framed his defense of Bernard as Britons' commitment to a broad right to asylum for foreign refugees and the moral impossibility of surrendering them to face persecution overseas.[50] In the winter of 1861, this same Edwin James argued Anderson's case before the queen's lawyers in London, as I will discuss below. If Bernard had been spared extradition for the far more odious offence of conspiring against the life of neighboring ruler, Anderson's safety ought, one would think, to have been confirmed without question. Indeed, the radical weekly journal the *National Reformer* made the parallel explicit by comparing Anderson with Orsini. Whereas the British might begrudgingly admit that the likes of an Orsini could receive refuge in Britain,[51] the editors of the *National Reformer* emphasized that by comparison Anderson was blameless for the blood on his hands.

This line of defense of Anderson threatened to antagonize the United States, an otherwise friendly nation. Yet there was a subtle though critical subtext in the argument that offered something of a cushion for officials in making their decision. Commentators described Anderson as an American fugitive slave, of course, but also labeled him a Canadian resident or, more frequently, a British subject. Twelvetrees announced in his prefatory remarks on the case as a whole the degree to which the extradition request was a "foul wrong attempted to be perpetuated on a subject of the British Crown."[52] The point that Anderson was a British subject by virtue of his residence in Canada featured in the legal proceedings as well. Lawyers and judges considered whether they could intervene on behalf of a subject in Canada, not whether Anderson was entitled to that status. Louis Chamerovzow, secretary of the British and Foreign Anti-Slavery Society, used this construction in his affidavit to the Queen's Bench in London on Anderson's behalf.[53] In the course of the deliberations, Edwin James adopted it and Lord Chief Justice Cockburn, citing William Blackstone, again comfortably assumed that Anderson was indeed a subject of the Crown.[54] To call Anderson a British subject was a claim that supporters routinely made to improve his standing before judges who might balk at taking an officially hostile stance toward American slavery.

Such a broad application of subject status belies the supposed temper of the era. It offers a stark contrast to the simultaneous emphases on citizenship, as set out, for example, in the French Constitutions. Scholars assume that the nineteenth century was a period in which concern for state sovereignty and civic rights predominated. Such nationally specific phenomena seem to preclude the possibility of rights more broadly construed. However, Anderson's situation demonstrates both a fluidity of subject status in the British context and legal authorities' willingness to draw upon the language of subjecthood on behalf of a foreign slave.

It was not a given that they would do so, or even that they needed to do so in this era. Subject status was an important vehicle for holding and transmitting property but was not a prerequisite for the protection of personal liberties by British officials or courts.[55] In this way, the power of universal liberty from slavery was – at least theoretically – about being on British soil, not about being British. It is rare in the archives to find refugees seeking official British subject status. Indeed, even after a longer residence, refugees' foreignness mattered rhetorically. Their rescue from persecution – something presumptively impossible within liberal Britain – was the critical element. Second, it is interesting that British advocates used the language of subject status in Anderson's case so readily, because it was not a given that he would have received it if he had formally applied. Imperial subjecthood was a broad and fluid category in this period. Following the *Calvin* case of 1608, subject status belonged to those born within the territory of the sovereign. While still influential in the nineteenth century, the alignment of subject status with place of birth became strained during the imperial expansion of the later eighteenth century.[56] The growth of empire drew in new populations who had not been affiliated with British territory at birth; the loss of the American colonies had the same impact, only in reverse. In an era of great flux, then, allegiance became as important as birth as a mode of acquiring imperial subject status.[57] For American fugitive slaves, assertions of loyalty were critical in gaining freedom in British hands. Black Loyalists joined the British army in both the Revolutionary War and the War of 1812 as a means of gaining their freedom.[58] In times of relative peace, the need to expand colonial populations similarly made officials more receptive to oaths of allegiance as an avenue of naturalization as British subjects.[59] However, officials did not necessarily accept just any assertion of loyalty. As Bradley Miller has shown, American fugitive slaves petitioned the Canadian government in the 1830s claiming their allegiance to the crown as a means of gaining protection against extradition, but the effort did not work.[60] So far as I have found, Anderson took no oath of allegiance.

Why, then, were claims about Anderson's subject status so routinely made on his behalf? Future researchers should undertake a more systemic examination of the fluidity of subject status across the imperial world at this height of empire.[61] In Anderson's case, I would suggest that claims to subject status were made because they were rhetorically powerful, establishing universal rights principles more firmly by making a claim upon the host state. By underscoring Anderson's Britishness, his supporters implied that it was even more necessary for officials to issue a writ of habeas corpus, a demand that he be brought to London to appeal his case before the Court of the Queen's Bench. In Britain, they assumed, it would be easier for the court to reverse the decision of the Canadian judges and free Anderson. As a British subject, Anderson's legal claims would seem to transcend any competing claims that Canadian officials might make on their own. However, between the signing of the Webster–Ashburton Treaty and 1860 the relationship between Britain and Canada had changed. Having worked assiduously for greater institutional independence, Canada was now on the path toward a home rule that would be fully in place by 1867. Home rule did not mean complete independence; Britain retained (until 1931) control over foreign affairs. However, by the 1860s the courts were meant to be independent. Officials were, however, not certain what that independence meant for appellate decisions in Canadian court cases. Could they be remanded to Britain by writ of habeas corpus? Since extradition was a matter of foreign policy, did the decision-making power lie in London anyway? The case threatened to pit mother country and colony against one another during a time of heightened sensitivity about sovereignty. Did the Queen's Bench then have a right to intervene in the matter? Even if it did, would intervention be politically wise? In this respect, calling Anderson a British subject became an argument in favor of intervention. But the argument would not be won so easily.

The judges of the Queen's Bench in London assessed these demands for British protection of Anderson. Drawing upon precedents from the seventeenth and eighteenth centuries, the Justices determined that the Queen's Bench had a legal right to intercede, though the political desirability of doing so gave them pause.[62] Lord Chief Justice Cockburn's decision to issue the writ despite these reservations maintained the older precedents in this case.

The decision elicited an immediate reaction on both sides of the Atlantic, making onlookers, even some of Anderson's supporters, anxious over the assertion of imperial authority. In Britain, the legal community was not unified behind Cockburn's decision, questioning Whitehall's jurisdiction while fretting that the Queen's Bench was setting the stage for a second War for Independence in the Americas.[63] Though legal experts in Canada were less hyperbolic, they admitted that the writ likely gave birth "to a feeling of resistance, which will not in all probability slumber till the assumed jurisdiction of the English court is tested and defeated on national grounds."[64]

After issuing the writ, officials in London never executed it. On 1 February 1861, the Canadian Court of Common Pleas, under Chief Justice Draper, issued its own writ of habeas corpus and, within a week, commenced hearings under its jurisdiction. On 16 February the court freed John Anderson. We will never know whether the decision was in response to public outrage over the initial court decision, the pending writ of habeas corpus, or a combination thereof. Draper's ruling was not based in a claim about asylum, slavery, humanitarian intervention, or human rights; it hinged instead on a technicality. The warrant for his arrest had stated that Anderson was accused of "felonious homicide," not murder. Only crimes of murder fell under the auspices of the extradition treaty.[65] Greatly relieved on all accounts, Anderson's supporters swiftly brought the freed man to Britain lest the United States attempt extradition once more. There, he, like other high-profile American fugitive slaves, toured the UK, retelling his tale of persecution, escape, and rescue from re-enslavement to rapt audiences before moving to Liberia a year later.

Conclusion: making universal rights stick

Those looking for the origin of human rights history in big moral victories would be surprised, even upset, by the outcome in the Anderson case. The final decision in the case pointedly eschewed broad moral claims, and the outbreak of the Civil War within months meant that the same question would never again be posed to British and Canadian authorities over an American fugitive slave. In this respect, the case fits a pattern in imperial jurisprudence, which had long been closely attentive to local context and geopolitical exigencies.[66]

Yet a case like Anderson's also demonstrated the power of public pressure and the normative assumptions held by members of the establishment. Officials were as unwilling to see a refugee extradited as were members of the public in Canada and in the United Kingdom. Over the next 40 years, British activists succeeded in maintaining – as they had for John Anderson – the primacy of the right to life and liberty for bona fide refugees regardless of race, politics, or creed. Protection for political offenders was written into Briton's new extradition treaties from 1870 and even into the restrictive Aliens Act of 1905, which aimed to reduce the number of destitute migrants to Britain but contained an exemption for those who were being persecuted in "hot blood."[67] Emphasis on supporting only bona fide refugees had the effect of subjecting individuals to new and sometimes stricter tests, especially in times of heightened public or political fear. As in the Anderson case, public pressure remains critical to maintaining protections for subjects, citizens, and foreigners alike.

In this respect, the Anderson case should warn us against placing too much emphasis on a singular "hand-off" between an era of humanitarianism to one of modern human rights. Progress then, as progress now, was uneven, entailing several steps backward for every movement forward. As Mairi MacDonald writes in her essay on atrocities in the Congo in this volume, to understand human rights better we must view it as a "a practice of persuasion," an effort that has a far longer history than the more recent one of a human rights regime and that better emphasizes the instability of those rights both then and now.[68] The relationship between activist, humanitarian movements and the pursuit and maintenance of rights is thus a dynamic one, a point future researchers would do well to incorporate into studies of cases ranging from the eighteenth and nineteenth centuries through the twenty-first.[69] Persuasion remains to this day critical to asylum seekers' ability to find a safe haven. Still only guaranteed the right to an "asylum-seeking process," by reigning international convention, refugees' protection, as in the case of John Anderson more than 150 years ago, depends on eliciting the sympathy of the would-be hosts.

Notes

1 Harper Twelvetrees, *The Story of the Life of John Anderson*, London: William Tweedie, 1863, 26; Great Britain, House of Commons, *Parliamentary Papers* (hereafter *Parliamentary Papers*), (1861 [2813]), "Correspondence Respecting the Case of Fugitive Slave, Anderson," Correspondence Between Irvine and Russell, 8 October 1860, no. 1 and enclosure 1, p. 1; Lord Lyons to Lord John Russell, 8 April 1861, no. 20, p. 46. It would be another three months before Anderson was referred to as a "fugitive slave" in a letter from Downing Street dated 9 January 1861. See p. 2.

2 Twelvetrees, *Story of the Life of John Anderson*, p. 35.

3 Twelvetrees, *Story of the Life of John Anderson*, p. 40.

4 See Article 10 of the treaty. The text of the treaty is online. Available at http://avalon.law.yale.edu/subject_menus/br1842m.asp (accessed 18 December 2018).

5 A right to refuge first appeared in British law in the 1870 Extradition Act, which exempted the political offender from the operation of the treaty. The treaty became the baseline model for international law in the decades that followed. Further British policies followed suit to grapple with the question of fugitive slaves in the Indian Ocean world (1876) and a further protection of foreigners escaping political or religious persecution (1905). See Caroline Shaw, *Britannia's Embrace: Modern Humanitarianism and the Imperial Origins of Refugee Relief*, New York: Oxford University Press, 2015, pp. 147–235.

6 Samuel Moyn rejects the idea that campaigns prior to the 1940s were human rights campaigns, for example. Samuel Moyn, *The Last Utopia: Human Rights in History*, Cambridge, MA: Belknap Press at Harvard University Press, 2010. Michael Barnett, for example, describes human rights as vested in "legal discourses and frameworks" and the "long-term goal of eliminating the causes of suffering," whereas humanitarianism focuses attention on "moral codes and sentiments" as well as the immediate need of "keeping people alive." These are the very distinctions Barnett applies to two threads of humanitarianism. However, his history of humanitarianism distinguishes between an "emergency branch that focuses on symptoms, and an alchemical variety that adds the ambition of eliminating the root causes of suffering." Michael Barnett, *Empires of Humanity: A History of Humanitarianism*, Ithaca, NY: Cornell University Press, pp. 16 and 10.

7 See the essays by Mairi MacDonald and Meredith Terretta in this volume. See also Jenny S. Martinez, *The Slave Trade and the Origins of International Human Rights Law*, Oxford: Oxford University Press, 2012; Shaw, *Britannia's Embrace*, pp. 41–70 and 98–123; and Brian E. Vick, *The Congress of Vienna: Power and Politics after Napoleon*, Cambridge, MA: Harvard University Press, 2014, pp. 193–232. This new trend offers an important counterbalance to Moyn's suggestion that antislavery and anticolonialism, for example, were not human rights issues.

8 This essay is an expanded version of the exploration of the Anderson case initially published as a portion of chapter 5 in Shaw, *Britannia's Embrace*. Anderson's case receives regular mention in histories of American fugitive slaves. It is the core of Patrick Brode's well-researched 1989

narrative of Anderson's ordeal for the Osgoode Legal Society of Toronto, Canada. Patrick Brode, *The Odyssey of John Anderson*, Toronto: University of Toronto Press, 1989. More recently, Bradley Miller has focused on it, in his chapter on refugees. Bradley Miller, *Borderline Crime: Fugitive Criminals and the Challenge of the Border, 1819–1914*, Toronto: Osgoode Society for Canadian Legal History and University of Toronto Press, 2016, pp. 114–52. Legal historian Paul Halliday draws upon the case at the close of his examination of the jurisdiction of writs of habeas corpus in the early modern era. Paul Halliday, *Habeas Corpus: From England to Empire*, Cambridge, MA: Belknap Press at Harvard University Press, 2010, pp. 299–301.

9 See, among others, Micheline Ishay, *The History of Human Rights from Ancient Times to the Globalization Era*, Berkeley: University of California Press, 2004, and Paul Gordon Lauren, *The Evolution of International Human Rights Visions Seen*, 3rd ed., Philadelphia: University of Pennsylvania Press, 2011.

10 For subject status and the mixing of the language of rights and privileges, see Hannah Weiss Muller, *Subjects and Sovereign: Bonds of Belonging in the Eighteenth-Century British Empire*, New York: Oxford University Press, 2017.

11 Lynn Hunt, *Inventing Human Rights*, New York: W. W. Norton, 2008, pp. 176–214.

12 Hunt, *Inventing Human Rights*, pp. 160–7; Moyn, *Last Utopia*, p. 32.

13 Harriet Beecher Stowe, *Uncle Tom's Cabin, or Life Among the Lowly*, Philadelphia: Henry Altemus, 1900, pp. 281–2. See Shaw, *Britannia's Embrace*, pp. 71–97. For more on the culture of antislavery in the middle of the nineteenth century, see Richard Huzzey, *Freedom Burning: Anti-Slavery and Empire in Victorian Britain*, Ithaca, NY: Cornell University Press, 2012.

14 Slave trade treaties contained clauses to provide refuge to those deemed illegally trafficked. Shaw, *Britannia's Embrace*, pp. 48, 56–7.

15 This is the crux of a debate among scholars over the campaigns against the slave trade. Whereas Martinez, among others, have seen in them the first articulation of international human rights, others – notably Philip Alston – have dismissed this claim. Alston points to the conditions of liberated Africans as evidence that there could not have been a genuine belief in a right to human liberty. Philip Alston, "Does the Past Matter? On the Origin of Human Rights," *Harvard Law Review*, 2013, vol. 126, no. 1, 2054–5. Liberated Africans' conditions were abominable; more often than not they became indentured servants. But as scholars on theories of labor have noted, what is distinctly unfree to us seemed free in the early nineteenth century – crucially, contractual and distinct from the violence of the slave traffic. A generation later, activists, missionaries, and officials highlighted concerns about the nature of freedom in these cases.

16 This should make us uncomfortable. As Stefan-Ludwig Hoffmann noted in an essay on human rights historiography, if we do not look to the longer history we will not "be able to understand the latency of concepts, the trapdoors that rights claims based on equality as well as difference might entail." Hoffmann, "Human Rights and History," *Past and Present*, 2016, vol. 232, no. 1, 31.

17 Twelvetrees, *Story of the Life of John Anderson*, dedication page.

18 Twelvetrees, *Story of the Life of John Anderson*, p. viii.

19 Twelvetrees, *Story of the Life of John Anderson*, pp. vii, 9.

20 Twelvetrees, *Story of the Life of John Anderson*, p. 9.

21 Twelvetrees, *Story of the Life of John Anderson*, p. 9.

22 Twelvetrees, *Story of the Life of John Anderson*, p. 10.

23 Twelvetrees, *Story of the Life of John Anderson*, p. 10.

24 Twelvetrees, *Story of the Life of John Anderson*, p. 11.

25 Twelvetrees, *Story of the Life of John Anderson*, pp. 11–12.

26 Twelvetrees, *Story of the Life of John Anderson*, p. 16.

27 Among other works on the Black Loyalists, see Cassandra Pybus, *Epic Journeys of Freedom: Runaway Slaves of the American Revolution and their Global Quest for Liberty*, Boston: Beacon Press, 2006, and Maya Jasanoff, *Liberty's Exiles: American Loyalists in the Revolutionary World*, New York: Vintage Books, 2011.

28 Jason Silverman, *Unwelcome Guests: Canada West's Response to American Fugitive Slaves, 1800–1865*, New York: Associated Faculty Press, 1985; Robin Winks, *The Blacks in Canada*, 2nd ed., Montreal and Kingston, ON: McGill-Queen's University Press.

29 Winks, *Blacks in Canada*, p. 168.

30 Rhodes House Special Collections, Oxford, Archives of the British and Foreign Anti-Slavery Society, E 2/19 Memorials and Petitions, "On the Extradition Clause of the Treaty of Washington," Memorial addressed to Aberdeen, 13 February 1843, f. 193.
31 Winks, *Blacks in Canada*, p. 168.
32 Twelvetrees, *Story of the Life of John Anderson*, p. 25.
33 Twelvetrees, *Story of the Life of John Anderson*, p. 26; *Parliamentary Papers* (1861 [2813]), Correspondence Between Irvine and Russell, 8 October 1860, no. 1 and enclosure 1; Correspondence Respecting the Case of Fugitive Slave, Anderson, 1; Lyons to Russell, 8 April 1861, no. 20, p. 46.
34 Twelvetrees, *Story of the Life of John Anderson*, pp. 29–30; Brode, *Odyssey of John Anderson*, p. 31.
35 Twelvetrees, *Story of the Life of John Anderson*, p. 36; Brode, *Odyssey of John Anderson*, p. 47.
36 Twelvetrees, *Story of the Life of John Anderson*, p. 40.
37 Twelvetrees, *Story of the Life of John Anderson* p. 41.
38 As Brode explains, the case emphasized the split between liberal-reformists – here, George Brown of the *Globe* – and MacDonald's more conservative branch of the liberal party. Brode, *Odyssey of John Anderson*, pp. 32–5.
39 Twelvetrees, *Story of the Life of John Anderson*, pp. 45–7.
40 For example, an article in London's *Morning Chronicle* (4 January 1861, 3) appeared in provincial newspapers across the United Kingdom. The same coverage, including extended discussion of McLean's dissent thus appeared, for example, in Dublin's *Evening Freeman* (4 January 1861, 3), London's *The Morning Advertiser* (4 January 1861, 6), and the *Portsmouth Times and Naval Gazette* (5 January 1861, 4).
41 "Fugitive Slaves in Canada: Are They to be Given Up?" *Bradford Observer*, 10 January 1861, 6. The same comment about "gross libel" appeared in seven papers in early January 1861.
42 John Plummer, "John Anderson, The Fugitive Slave." Reprinted in *Jersey Independent and Daily Telegraph*, 19 January 1861, 4; Ken Stewart, "Plummer, John (1831–1914)," *Australian Dictionary of National Biography*, Melbourne: Melbourne University Press, 1988. Online. Available athttp://adb.anu.edu.au/biography/plummer-john-8066/text14075 (accessed 18 December 2018).
43 The *Amistad* was a Spanish ship bringing newly purchased slaves from Sierra Leone to Cuba in 1839 when the Africans successfully took control of the ship. Recaptured by an American vessel, the Africans were brought to the United States where they stood trial for extradition. The Supreme Court decided in their favor in 1841. That same year, American slaves on board the *Creole* gained control of the ship, steering it to port in the British Bahamas. There, they claimed their freedom. Charged with piracy, they won in court on the grounds that they had fought only for their liberty. Local officials agreed. In Anderson's case, his lawyer had used the *Creole* unsuccessfully in his defense of Anderson at the extradition hearing. Brode, *Odyssey of John Anderson*, pp. 43, 93. My hunch is that this precedent would not have been helpful to Anderson, given the violence of the earlier case. Indeed, as I return to below, abolitionists curried favor for Anderson by contrasting him favorably with violent political refugees like Felice Orsini.
44 Christopher McCrudden, "Human Rights Histories," *Oxford Journal of Legal Studies*, 2015, vol. 35, no. 1, 179 n. 113.
45 *Parliamentary Papers*, 1861, vol. 64, p. 33, Correspondence Respecting the Case of the Fugitive Slave, Anderson.
46 "Last Week," *Once a Week*, [London] 1861, vol. 4, 26 January 1861, 138–40.
47 Twelvetrees, *Story of the Life of John Anderson*, p. 67, citing the *Times*, 5 January 1861.
48 For example, see reprint of *Times* article "Fugitive Slaves in Canada: Are They to Be Given Up?" *Bradford Observer*, 10 January 1861, 6.
49 "Last Week," 139; see also: "London, Thursday, 2 January 1861," *Morning Post*, 3 January 1861, 4.
50 *The Speech of Edwin James, Esq., One of Her Majesty's Counsel, in Defense of Dr. Simon Bernard, Delivered at the Central Criminal Court, on Friday, the 16 of April, 1858*, London: Effingham Wilson, 1858.
51 "Orsini and John Anderson the Fugitive Slave," *National Reformer*, 2 February 1861. The question of whether to provide refuge or to extradite terrorists would become a live question by the end of the 1860s in the wake of the rise of Anarchism and violent Irish Fenianism. See Shaw, *Britannia's Embrace*, pp. 147–75.

52 Twelvetrees, *Story of the Life of John Anderson*, pp. v–vi.
53 Twelvetrees, *Story of the Life of John Anderson*, p. 56.
54 Speeches and opinions as cited in Twelvetrees, *Story of the Life of John Anderson*, pp. 58, 63.
55 Alexander Cockburn, *Nationality: Or, the Law Relating to Subjects and Aliens, Considered with a View to Future Legislation*, London: W. Ridgway, 1869, pp. 138 and 149.
56 For the eighteenth century, see Muller, *Subject and Sovereign*, and, for a useful examination of the literature as a whole, Hannah Weiss Muller, "Subjecthood in the Atlantic World," *Oxford Bibliographies in Atlantic History*, New York: Oxford University Press, 2017. Online. Available at www.oxfordbibliographies.com/view/document/obo-9780199730414/obo-9780199730414-0143.xml (accessed 18 December 2018).
57 Caitlin Anderson, "Old Subjects, New Subjects, and Non-Subjects: Silences and Subjecthood," in Jane Rendall, Nicholas Guyatt, and Richard Bessel (eds.) *War, Empire, and Slavery, 1770–1830*, New York: Palgrave, 2010, pp. 201–17; Christopher L. Brown, "From Slaves to Subjects: Envisioning an Empire Without Slavery, 1772–1834," in Philip D. Morgan and Sean Hawkins (eds.) *Black Experience and the Empire*, New York: Oxford University Press, 2004, pp. 111–40.
58 Maya Jasanoff, *Liberty's Exiles: American Loyalists in the Revolutionary World*, New York: Knopf, 2011.
59 Reiko Karatani, *Defining British Citizenship: Empire, Commonwealth and Modern Britain*, London: Frank Cass, 2003, pp. 55–6.
60 Miller, *Borderline Crime*, p. 122. Nor, for example, did claims to subject status work consistently in the South Asian context. See Sudipta Sen, "Imperial Subjects on Trial: On the Legal Identity of Britons in Late Eighteenth-Century India," *Journal of British* Studies, 2006, vol. 45, no. 3, 532–55.
61 Studies of this nature have focused on the eighteenth and early nineteenth century. We do not yet have similar accounts of the later nineteenth century or of the twentieth century. Such work would be of critical importance in thinking about the nature of community, as well as of what I suspect remains a fairly fluid category of subjecthood and responsibility. In the twentieth century, this area of research is important regarding changing imperial relations during struggles for and on the eve of independence.
62 The question of the courts' jurisdiction on this matter, while given new life in the process of devolving colonial powers, had a long history with regards to semi-autonomous legal systems across the hybrid empire. See Halliday, *Habeas Corpus*.
63 Thomas Tapping, "Art. III. The Case of Anderson, the Fugitive Slave. The Application for the Writ of habeas corpus and Judgment Considered," *Law Magazine and Law Review*, 1861, no. 21, 60–3.
64 "The Case of John Anderson, Fugitive Slave," *Upper Canada Law Journal*, 1861, appended to Tapping, "Art. III," 64. Indeed, the issue remained a tense one even after the Anderson case concluded. As late as the 1980s there still seems to have been simmering resentment. Brode calls the *Toronto Globe*'s enthusiasm for intervention in the case "reckless." Brode, *Odyssey of John Anderson*, p. 48.

"The Case of John Anderson, Fugitive Slave," 64.

65 Twelvetrees, *Story of the Life of John Anderson*, p. 77.
66 Lauren Benton and Lisa Ford, *Rage for Order: The British Empire and the Origins of International Law, 1800–1850*, Cambridge, MA: Harvard University Press, 2016.
67 Shaw, *Britannia's Embrace*, p. 228. There would be no stand-alone international laws about refugees in the nineteenth century. The securities provided for refugees appeared as caveats carved out within the later extradition treaties and, in the British context, in restrictive immigration acts and guiding governmental policy positions. Shaw, *Britannia's Embrace*, pp. 205–35.
68 Mairi MacDonald, "Reclaiming Congo Reform for the History of Human Rights," p. 57, in this volume.
69 Future researchers might productively continue to probe the language of refuge in former settler colonies like Canada. At the time of Anderson's case, supporters drew upon a history of British refuge and imperial pride in advancing his case, as I have highlighted. Already rife with tension for a colony on the eve of home rule, such a rhetorical strategy presumably shifted in the decades thereafter. The story would presumably tell us much about developing universal rights campaigns as well as the changing visions of international community and post-imperial commonwealth identity formation.

3

INVESTIGATING AND AMELIORATING ATROCITIES IN THE NINETEENTH CENTURY

International commissions of inquiry in the Balkans (1876–80)

Benjamin E. Brockman-Hawe

In recent decades, international institutions authorized to assign responsibility for serious and widespread human rights violations have become ubiquitous. Prosecutions for acts of genocide, war crimes, or crimes against humanity before international or internationalized criminal courts are routine; the dockets of regional human rights courts have exploded with filings related to large-scale rights violations; and dozens of international fact-finding commissions have been established under the auspices of the United Nations (or one of its organs), regional organizations, and independent groups of states with the ultimate goal of producing an authoritative statement explaining "what happened" and identifying what will, should, or can be done to rectify the harm. These institutions have become hallmarks of the contemporary legal order and influential reconstructive forces in societies riven by violence.

Despite their prominence as a feature of the contemporary human rights landscape, and the existence of a rich scholarly literature that debates their *raison d'être* and practices, to date our understanding of the historical pedigree of international human rights fact-finding remains slight. This is to be lamented, as nineteenth-century bodies matching this description – typically identified at the time as a "European Commission" or "International Commission" – are extremely interesting objects of study. International Commissions were natural focal points for international energies, as Commissions fostered negotiations and debate between representatives of numerous countries about the purpose, scope, and consequences of their investigative enterprise. But their international bona fides went beyond simply counting among their membership agents drawn from around Europe. Commissions sometimes transcended the nation-states that created them, as when they placed the ultimate responsibility for a humanitarian crisis on one of their establishing states or expressed international human rights values. On another front, in the absence of clearly codified international human rights law, these institutions and their work product occupied a central place in the public consciousness, drawing international attention to suffering and serving as visible symbols of a transnational commitment to its remediation. Thus, in their genesis, functioning, and perception, Commissions served as a point of emergence and convergence for the transnational human rights community, as well as serving as instruments of propagation that expanded the influence of that community and the values it espoused.

The story of these Commissions also illustrates the limitations and weaknesses of nineteenth-century human rights fact-finding. As will be seen in this essay, many of the same problems that plague human rights inquiry today existed then. Commissions predictably aroused opposition from those whom the Commissions sought to make accountable, and this opposition was not always overcome, as the effort required was not always deemed to be worth making. Moreover, the considerations of "humanity" that animated the investigative work, for all their pretensions to urgent activity and universalism, were often selective, sometimes half-hearted, Janus-faced, or overridden by other political and social priorities. Nor did it escape notice that it was powerful Western states with their own record of human rights abuses that were often pushing for inquiry.

The story of human rights fact-finding is as much a story of triumphs as it is one of failures, with the line between the two not always clear. For that reason, it is important to study both the Commissions that were formed and those that never made it past the drawing board. While a comprehensive or definitive history of these institutions would require full exploration of widely scattered archives and other secondary materials in at least six languages, my goal for this essay is more modest: to provide a brief survey of the situations in which international commissions were pursued between 1876 and 1880. This was a period of unusually intense activity in the field of international human rights fact-finding due to the "Great Eastern Crisis" in the Ottoman Balkans and the Russo-Turkish War (1877–8). These conflicts were inherently pan-European dramas, as they played out against the background of the decades-long "Eastern Question" – the perception of the terminal decline of the Ottoman Empire and the diplomatic and strategic dilemmas this posed for all of Europe's Great Powers: Great Britain, France, Germany, Austria-Hungary, Italy, and Russia.

During this five-year period, several acts of (to use the common parlance of the era) "massacre," "barbarity," "outrage," and "atrocity" captured European imagination. This essay briefly examines the events that triggered official efforts to make known by international investigation the status of victims and causes of their oppression; details the remit and composition of each investigative commission; traces some of the legal and political maneuvers of the individual commissioners and the states they represented as they completed their work; and explores the results of their efforts.

Proposed international commissions in the early stages of the "Great Eastern Crisis" (1876)

In the mid-1870s a series of Christian uprisings in Montenegro, Serbia, Bosnia, Herzegovina, and Bulgaria threatened the Ottoman Empire with complete collapse of its authority in the Balkans. The Great Powers were at first reluctant to intervene, but exaggerated newspaper accounts of mass slaughter of Christians particularly at Batak (in Bulgaria), where it was reported that between 10,000 and 15,000 innocent Christian men, women, and children had been killed by Turkish irregulars (bashi-bazouks), galvanized the public and eroded sympathy for the Ottoman cause across Europe.[1] In Russia, substantial fundraising activities for the victims were undertaken and thousands of men departed for the Balkans to fight alongside Orthodox forces.[2] In Great Britain, where the official policy since the Crimean War had been to support the Porte (the Ottoman government) and curtail Russia's regional ambitions, a new anti-Turk attitude swept the country as popular polemics like former prime minister Gladstone's *Bulgarian Horrors and the Question of the East* laid responsibility for the "barest and blackest outrages upon record within the present century" at the feet of both the ruling Conservative party and the Turkish government.[3] Britain's Conservative government, fearful of the destabilizing consequences for the international balance of power in Europe of either an Ottoman victory or an Ottoman loss in the Balkans, appalled at the growing calls for the elimination of Turkish authority in the Balkans that might if heeded provoke a general European war, and mindful of the need to deny their political rivals ammunition by appearing callous in the face of so-called "Bulgarian atrocities," pushed for a negotiated settlement between the belligerents.[4] A conference of the Great Powers and Turkey was accordingly convened at Constantinople in the final weeks of 1876.[5]

On 21 December 1876 the Powers shared their vision of the future organization of the Balkans with the Porte. What they aimed for was quasi-autonomy for Montenegro and Bosnia-Herzegovina, and a complete overhaul of the political, financial, and judicial systems of both territories. This audacious plan of administrative reform in Bosnia-Herzegovina and Bulgaria was to be overseen by international commissions with broad authorization to "superintend" the new regulations, directly enforce their decisions through an international gendarmerie, and investigate claims brought against local Ottoman authorities. To ensure that the full extent of Muslim depredations were known and that appropriate punitive and compensatory measures were taken in response, the commissioners would inter alia "find out the culprits, … superintend the examinations, and … insure punishment" of "the perpetrators of the massacres and other excesses," revise sentences against guilty parties that had already been announced by Ottoman authorities, estimate losses suffered by Christians, determine an appropriate indemnity, and "seek for means generally to assist a population fallen into misery."[6]

None of the European proposals were adopted. The appointment of an international commission was anathema to the Porte, which protested the idea as "derogatory to the dignity, the authority, the prestige, and the independence of the Sovereign."[7] Moreover, in a stunning *coup de théâtre*, the Ottoman minister of foreign affairs Safavet Pasha announced at the first official session of the conference that his government had just promulgated a Constitution (the passage of which, Safavet explained, accounted for the rounds of festive cannon fire that were periodically interrupting the delegates) that modernized the administration of the Balkans, and he insisted that the European Powers give his government due opportunity to implement it.[8] When the European negotiators argued that the new Constitution provided neither reparations nor guarantees for the future security of Christians in the Balkans, the Ottomans reminded their counterparts of their own struggles with religious plurality, specifically the massacre of Calvinist Protestants by French Catholics in 1572.[9] By 20 January 1877 it had become clear to all that the negotiations had reached an impasse, and the conference was dissolved.[10]

A European commission in the wake of the Russo-Turkish War: the Commission for Mt. Rhodope (1878)

The failure of the Constantinople Congress was felt particularly acutely in Russia, where Tsar Alexander II had cleared the way for thousands of Russians to volunteer in the fight for Balkan independence and staked his national reputation on delivering the

Christian populations of Ottoman Europe from alleged Turkish depredations.[11] A favorable international climate – threats to the integrity of Ottoman Turkey elicited little sympathy from the European public or its diplomatic classes, and Austria agreed to remain neutral in the event of a Russo-Turkish war in exchange for Russian acceptance of Austrian annexation of Bosnia-Herzegovina – coupled with a surge in nationalist sentiment at home prompted a Russian declaration of war against Turkey on 24 April 1877.[12]

The Russian army advanced southward across Bulgaria and by mid-February 1878 had captured San Stefano, an outer suburb of Constantinople.[13] The Russian terms of peace were severe: the imposition on the Porte of a crippling indemnity, transfer of certain Ottoman territories to Russia, independence and enlargement of Serbia and Montenegro, independence of Roumania, and the creation of a Christian-governed Bulgaria encompassing the current Bulgarian territory, most of Macedonia, and Eastern Roumelia.[14] Although the Porte assented to these terms on 3 March 1878, the elimination of an official Turkish presence from such a large swath of Europe was too much for Great Britain and Austria-Hungary to accept, and a Congress was convened in Berlin to revise the bilateral agreement and determine the future of the Balkans, Caucasus, and Middle East.[15]

The fortunes of the belligerents and course of the Berlin negotiations were not the only aspects of the war closely followed by the public. Once war broke out, tales of Turkish, Russian, and Bulgarian abuses, and the tidal wave of suffering refugees these abuses produced, appeared with regularity in the papers. The representatives at Berlin were neither insulated from these stories nor without heart, and on 11 July the plenipotentiaries, "concerned by the reports which have reached some of them on the present sufferings of the populations of the Rhodope [a range of mountains mostly located in what is today southern Bulgaria] and neighboring countries," jointly adopted a resolution tasking their representatives in Constantinople with forming a "European Commission" that was to include the Porte in order to "verify the gravity of the situation and seek to remedy it as far as possible."[16]

An active conversation thus began in Constantinople among the representatives of the Great Powers over how best to carry out this directive. Russian ambassador Prince Aleksey Lobanov-Rostovsky was particularly active in this debate, but he ultimately failed to convince his counterparts that the Commission's inquiries should not extend into Russian-occupied territory, and that Muslim refugees from the Mt. Rhodope area should not be permitted to return in any numbers to those areas.[17] The instructions ultimately issued to the commissioners provided for Russian cooperation, anticipated repatriation, and included a broad mandate to

> estimate, as far as possible, the number of these refugees … endeavor to ascertain the places from whence they come, their race, their religion, the motives which have compelled them to leave their country, and which still prevent their return … ascertain what measures can be taken for the immediate relief of their sufferings, and for continuing such relief until these refugees can be repatriated and restored to their homes with every security for their existence.[18]

The members of the Commission – M. Fawcett (British consul-general); Colonel R. Raab (Austrian military attaché); M. Challet (French consul at Constantinople); M. Basily (first secretary at the Russian Embassy); M. Graziani (second dragoman of the Italian Embassy); M. Müller (German vice consul); M. Naşit Paşa (former governor of the vilayet of Syria); and M. Rıza Bey (former ambassador to Russia) – began meeting in mid-July.[19] Relations between the Russian commissioner and his counterparts broke down almost as soon as the Commission commenced its work. As the commissioners heard testimony in Xanthi – a city located to the south of the Rhodope Mountains that had hosted approximately 60,000 refugees, mostly Turkish Muslims, before measures were put in place to send nearly 50,000 of them to other Ottoman territories[20] – from refugee-delegates representing the various districts that the exiled population had fled, Basily made several objections to the Commission's information-gathering procedures. Before any testimonies had even been heard, he protested the appearance of district representatives, proposing that refugees should be "made to appear in groups composed of individuals" from the same village. He also proposed that the Commission, and not the refugees, should be responsible for appointing refugee spokespersons. The other commissioners outvoted Basily on both counts.[21] Basily fulminated as numerous testimonies implicating Russian troops in various acts of murder, pillage, theft, and rape were taken, and eventually he threatened to abandon the Commission unless its members confined

Figure 3.1 From *The Graphic*, 7 September 1878. The Commission is "busy at work at Gabrova, examining the victims of Russian brutality at Kushalar. Consul Fawcett is interrogating the unfortunates; and the remaining Europeans are the other members of the Commission."

themselves to "receiving general statements, without entering into details of facts."[22] The matter was tabled, and the Commission spent the rest of the day hearing from refugees that blamed Russian troops for their current condition.

Basily expanded on his objection at the next session, complaining that the method of inquiry was unnecessarily retrospective and meticulous (and therefore in contravention of instructions), and was inefficient and dilatory.[23] He insisted that the refugees who had been heard from were coached and that there was no truth to their "odious calumnies," going so far as to claim that he had acquired intelligence to the effect that one of the men who had been heard from the day before was himself responsible for the massacre that had been testified to.[24] The Commission, he complained, had altogether taken on too much the flavor of a "judicial inquiry," with its "[examination] of individuals with regard to a series of personal facts" and its "[entry] into the [*procès-verbaux*] details of all sorts."[25] Ultimately, however, only Müller sided with the Russian representative. The other commissioners voted to carry on as before unless instructed to do otherwise by their respective governments, and continued holding meetings in anticipation that such a corrective would not be issued. Indeed none was, as the majority were directed by their superiors in Constantinople to persist in their approach so long as their method had the backing of a preponderance of the commissioners.[26]

Over the course of the next 19 sessions (27 July through 14 August) the Commission heard from hundreds of refugees, including widows and orphans. Their testimonies (even the versions recorded in the Commission's protocols, which were sanitized to preserve, in the words of Raab, the Commission's "impartiality") were heart-wrenching and largely consistent: Turks of any age who encountered Russian troops were subject to mutilation, slaughter, and rape; Turkish property was stolen or burnt; relations between Christian Bulgarians and Muslim Turks were fine until the Russians arrived; to return home was unthinkable in light of the occupation. Christian Bulgarians were sometimes implicated in crimes against the refugees, but were more frequently described as having acted to protect them and eager to see their neighbors return home.[27]

The tensions between the Russian (and to a lesser extent, the German) commissioners with their colleagues came to a boil as the final report took shape. M. Leschine, who replaced Basily after the latter fell ill, quit the Commission after a draft report was presented that cast Russian troops in a negative light, reiterating the latter's objections and protesting the inclusion of "details … quite foreign to the object of the Commission" in the draft report.[28] A revised draft report was still too recriminatory and one-sided for Müller, who reminded his colleagues that the Commission was intended to look ahead, not back, and that refugees who had given their testimony were, as victims, naturally "partial and unjust."[29] The Austrian representative, Colonel Raab, pled illness to explain his failure to attend the Commission's final meetings and he did not sign the revised draft, but had privately admitted a few days before that his ambassador, Count Zichy, was pressuring him to act in a manner that preserved Russian honor.[30] Ultimately, the final report was presented individually by the delegates of England, Turkey, Italy, and France to their respective ambassadors.[31]

Per the final report, approximately 200,000 refugees were living in the Mt. Rhodope area, all of whom were Muslim and from territories occupied by the Russians. The refugees had fled advancing Russian troops, who butchered and raped Muslims in their path and destroyed their houses and places of worship. Victim testimonies had not been exaggerated; the commissioners had tested their evidence against their own observations of

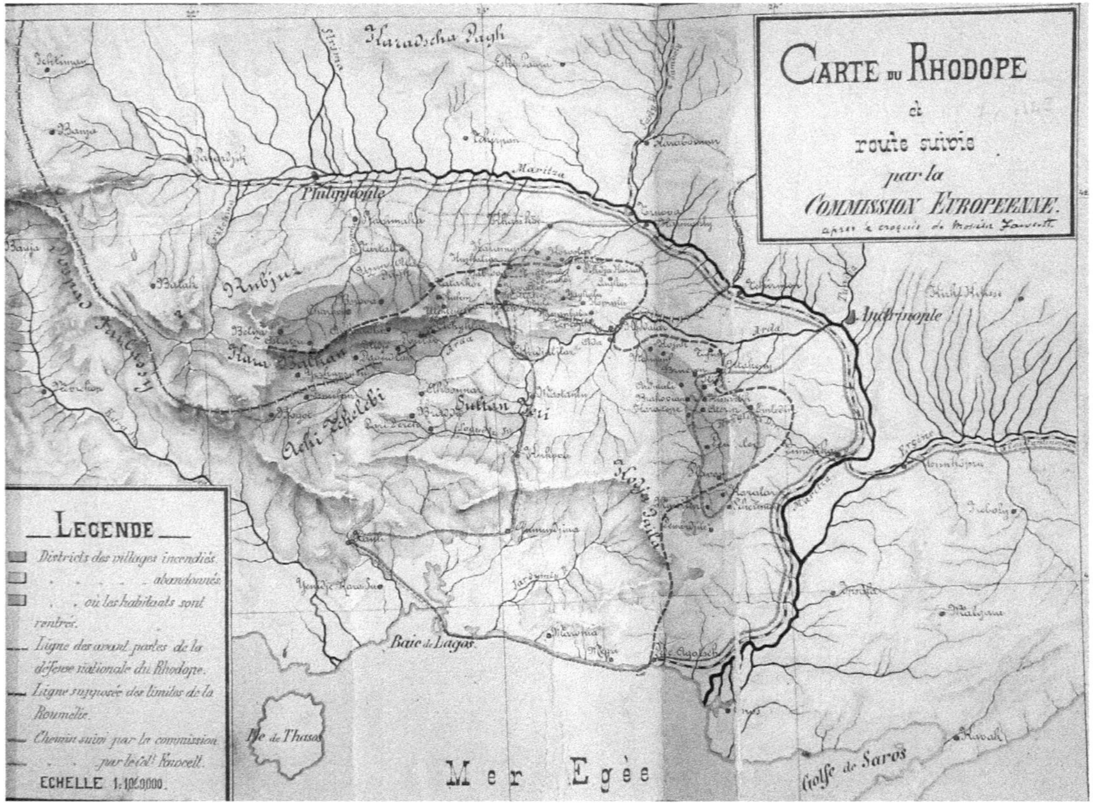

Figure 3.2 Map of a portion of the Rhodope Mountains based on a sketch by Commissioner Fawcett, showing the locations of burned villages (lightly shaded), abandoned villages (light horizontal lines), and repopulated villages (light vertical lines). TNA FO 78/2797, enclosure in no. 1046, Layard to Salisbury, 20 August 1878.

"ruins blackened by the traces of conflagration" behind Russian lines. The refugees themselves were in a sorry state:

> Conceive a long line of human beings, for the most part in rags, broken down by fatigue, privation, grief, and sickness, stretching from the first spurs of the Rhodope towards Philippopolis and Adrianople, and ceasing only at the borders of the pestilential marshes of the plain ... struggling in vain against all kinds of sickness, without any other assistance than a little barley bread parsimoniously distributed by the authorities or the inhabitants ... in a word, decimated by certain death, which mows down their ranks.[32]

Although the Russians and Bulgarians had in some cases collaborated in their acts of destruction, the refugees bore no ill will toward the Bulgarians, but attributed their misfortunes almost exclusively to the Russians, and were accordingly of the view that they could not return home until the Turkish government once against exercised its authority in the area.[33]

The four commissioners closed with an arresting call for European action:

> [I]f in the opinion of Europe justice requires that the Mussulmans of Roumelia should be reinstated in their properties, she will accomplish a duty to humanity in substituting her protection for that of a Power which itself acknowledges that this task is beyond its strength.

This was coupled with additional recommendations intended to restore tranquility and economic prosperity to the decimated areas in the event that Europe assumed this ambitious task, including the establishment of a new Commission to deal with restitution of property and a mixed police force.[34]

The issuance of the report registered in the press, but had little constructive impact on the geopolitical status quo.[35] Lobanov stubbornly refused to meet with his colleagues in Constantinople to discuss or even "take notice" of the report, taking the position that the terms of the Berlin Congress' mandate had been fulfilled and that it was for the commissioners, not the ambassadors, to determine how to relieve and repatriate the refugees.[36] Appeals for remedial action from the Sultan to the Tsar directly were met with dissimulation and bromides, as Alexander affected ignorance of the true state of affairs in Rhodope and confidence in the fair-mindedness of his troops.[37] In the Mt. Rhodope district, epicenter of the refugee crisis, commander of the Russian forces Prince Dondoukoff played at brinksmanship with the British, telling their representative that everything that had come out of the Berlin Congress (including the Rhodope Commission) added up to mere "comedies, bouffonades [the work of a jester], [and] bouffonneries [tomfoolery]."[38]

Of Europe's diplomatic luminaries, only British Foreign Secretary Robert Cecil, the Marquess of Salisbury, showed any initiative in holding the Russians to account. Before Fawcett's final report had even crossed his desk, he repeatedly complained to his Russian counterpart, Nikolai Giers, of the conduct of the Russian occupiers, and had gone as far as to float the idea of a "Consular Commission" to hear "complaints of the Mussulman population in Bulgaria and to protect them when injured or menaced" to M. Plunkett, Her Majesty's chargé d'affaires in Russia.[39] Giers bristled at the idea, replying that

Russia was "at home [in Bulgaria], and such a Commission … would be an insult to the Russian Army."[40] It was impossible to imagine, he averred, that Russian commanders would permit outrages of the sort described.[41] The evidence on which the Report was based was dismissed as "without any serious proof or foundation, and founded on evidence of obvious partiality," and the Russian army's reputation defended as "too well established for such calumnies to hold the slightest attraction."[42]

In the absence of coordinated, firm, and public condemnations of Russian practices from Italy, France, Great Britain, and Turkey, refugees were left in a worse position than if inquiry had never been made at all. The Commission had inspired hope among some of the refugees, prompting them to leave their comparatively secure positions and exhaust their meager resources in a futile bid to return to their homes.[43] Meanwhile, East Roumelia's Christian ethnic Bulgarians had learned that the Powers other than Russia and the Porte were paper tigers, and that little therefore stood between them and their dream of an independent Christian Bulgaria.[44]

Atrocities in the new state of Eastern Roumelia: the Aidos and Kirdjali commissions of inquiry (1880)

The Berlin Congress resulted in more than the creation of a European Commission of Inquiry into the Mt. Rhodope district. Through the Berlin Treaty, the Powers established two semi-autonomous provinces in the region that today encompasses Bulgaria. The Principality of Bulgaria, although it remained a nominal suzerain of the Porte, was established as a constitutional monarchy governed by a Christian prince who was to be both elected by the citizens and vetted by the signatory powers of the Berlin treaty.[45] Eastern Roumelia, in theory at least, remained more directly under the control of the Sultan, who retained the authority to appoint a Christian governor-general to administer the region and to garrison troops along the its land and sea frontiers. However, the Sultan was only to appoint a governor-general who met with the approval of the other treaty signatories, was to station Ottoman troops within the province only if the governor-general summoned them, and was not to employ irregular troops along the borders.[46] In addition to these treaty-based limits, the Sultan's freedom of action in Eastern Roumelia was curtailed by the political realities associated with having recently lost a war to Russia and survived only with the intercession of other powerful states.[47]

The withdrawal of Russian troops from both regions in mid-1879 marked the end of the first stage in the restoration of international tranquility, but the situation remained on a knife edge as growing religious and nationalist tensions threatened the integrity of the new states, and by extension the balance among European powers that had been struck in Berlin.[48] Roumelia's Muslims, the favorite target of Russian forces, were now beset by "Gymnasts" – Christian ethnic Bulgarians who belonged to so-called Secret Societies that received weapons and training from the Russian Army and who openly worked towards the goal of uniting Bulgaria and Eastern Roumelia and cleansing the region of Greeks and Muslims – as well as by opportunistic Bulgarians covetous of Muslim land, property, and women.[49] Meanwhile, the Roumelian National Assembly, which was overwhelmingly dominated by Bulgarians despite the fact that Muslims comprised at least 20 percent of the population, relegated the latter's pleas for assistance, in the words of British consul Michell, "to confinement in an official pigeon-hole."[50] The British archives are rife with stories of crimes against Muslims and a Roumelian government that "by its negligence, and partly by its connivance, [was] greatly instrumental in placing a large section of [the Muslim] population on the verge of death."[51] In short, the Muslims' oppressors were well armed, cruel, persistent, and operating with de facto official sanction.

In the sprawling Rhodope Mountains, dozens of predominantly Muslim villages rejected the rule of the Treaty-sanctioned Plovdiv- (Philippopolis) based national government and effectively established independent republics.[52] The situation became critical in February 1880, when gendarmes dispatched to restore Roumelian state authority in the Kirdjali district cooperated with local Gymnasts in a campaign of widespread murder, rape, and destruction.

The abuses triggered diplomatic action in favor of international inquiry. On receiving the news, the Ottoman minister of foreign affairs Sawas Pasha reached out to British ambassador Constantinople Austen Layard to inform him that it was the Ottoman government's intention to send a Commission to investigate. Presuming that Sawas "would wish that it should be a Mixed or International one," Layard threw his weight behind the suggestion and attempted to bring Salisbury on board. Layard presented it as an opportunity to prove to the Sultan that Europe remonstrated against all acts of oppression regardless of whether the victim or perpetrator was Muslim or Christian, and to smooth over enduring resentments caused by the imposition of the Treaty of Berlin, which had effectively removed the victims from the Sultan's direct protection. The European interest in a Commission, he claimed, lay in the opportunity to gain a moral victory and demonstrate a commitment to the integrity of the fledgling statelet: "Surely Europe cannot have established a free Eastern Roumelia in order that one part of its population, however greatly in the majority, should use its freedom in persecuting and shamefully oppressing the remainder."[53] Michell, for his part, more modestly suggested to Salisbury that he, the Porte, and the Austrians (who had also received verified intelligence confirming the violence) collaborate on an inquiry in order to "reassure the suffering villagers."[54] But the Austrians could not be brought on board, as Austrian foreign minister Baron Haymerle explained that "a Consular investigation would be more likely to add to them than to calm the exasperation of the two parties."[55]

As international efforts stalled, Governor-General Aleko Pasha (Alexander Bogoridi) dispatched a Commission of his own to investigate the crimes. It is not clear what prompted Aleko, a Greek-educated Bulgarian who took every opportunity to dismiss Muslim complaints and depress Muslim morale, to move so swiftly in this case.[56] Michell suggested that Bulgaria's political class was anxious that the attacks on Muslim and Greek communities were reaching such a pitch that they risked condemnation and action by the Powers or the Porte if they failed to show initiative.[57] A savvy political operative with years of experience in the Ottoman administration, it is likely that Aleko was acting in the hopes of preempting a more searching and independent international and Turkish inquiry.

Aleko's first Commission was composed of "notable Muslims of the country," and its mission was to identify anyone involved in the atrocities, bring them to trial, and draft a comprehensive report on the events.[58] The reports sent back by this Commission, however, were deemed to be at such variance with the victims' petitions for damages and intervention submitted to the national government, as well as those documents sent by the local governors, that Aleko sent a second Commission "to ascertain on the spot the acts committed, to listen to the complaints of the inhabitants, and to investigate the crimes committed by soldiers of the militia."[59] Upon reaching Kirdjali the two

Commissions were combined, and the final report was ultimately signed by nine commissioners, including two foreigners working for the Roumelian government: Baron de Toustain (a French lieutenant colonel and chief of staff in the Roumelian military), and George Colville Borthwick (an Englishman employed as a colonel-inspector of the Roumelian Gendarmerie).[60]

The Commission's final report was issued in late May. The first section was given to describing in detail the recent history of the Kirdjali district, a region marked since the Russian occupation of 1877 by open pro-Turkish insurrection, first against occupying Russians, and later against Roumelian authorities, as well as a high incidence of banditry and violence. The commissioners described the immediate aftermath of the decision of at least 12 Kirdjali villages to declare independence from Roumelia – "like a rosary breaking apart" in the words of one of the rebellion's ringleaders – in early February 1880, as well as the decision by local Bulgarian officials to send Roumelian gendarmes to pacify the area.[61]

The second section dealt primarily with the details of this operation, during which the Muslims had suffered. The commissioners were highly critical of Captain Yacheroff, the Russian commander of the Roumelian army, who had made an error "from a political point of view" by instructing his column chiefs to mobilize local Gymnasts and requisition food from the villages. Moreover, the general, who had received orders to avoid bloodshed as much as possible, had at the beginning of the deployment directed his Bulgarian troops to emulate the notoriously "generous" and "courageous" conduct of the Russian Army that had until recently occupied the country, inflaming passions and transforming "a simple action into an expedition of war."[62]

The commissioners also noted that in many cases villagers had exaggerated their harms in their petitions to the government and to the press. Many women, according to the Commission, embellished or fabricated their claims of rape, numerous bodies of persons purportedly murdered by government troops were discovered in remote locations, as opposed to in the villages themselves, or had injuries consistent with weapons in use by local brigands, and many claims for physical damage to property were disavowed once the Commission arrived.[63] But even accounting for these cases, Colonel Borthwick wrote to the British ambassador at Constantinople, it was "only too painfully evident that in several instances people had been most brutally and wantonly murdered," and that despite the difficulties in verifying the occurrence of rapes so long after the events, many had certainly occurred and circumstantial evidence "[laid] the crime indisputably at the door of the militia [gendarmes]."[64] The commissioners largely acquitted the Gymnasts as a group, concluding that "the Bulgarian population, suddenly called to arms, attenuated Captain Yacheroff's irresponsibility with its innate discipline."[65]

The theme of harms suffered was continued in the third section of the report, in which the commissioners briefly described the injuries sustained in each of the 23 villages that participated in the inquiry, separately noting the basic circumstances accompanying the arrival of the gendarmes to each town (including fighting, or more commonly, the retreat of all but the women, children, or elderly from the area), the number of rapes and murders, physical damage to property, and the amount requested by the villagers in compensation. The nature of the evidence, physical or testimonial, that had been offered in proof of the claims, and whether any contradictory evidence existed, was also recorded.[66]

In the fourth and final section of their report, the commissioners reiterated that the Roumelian government was forced by circumstances to deploy troops, but nevertheless identified certain individuals who had "gone beyond the limits" and committed "unpardonable crimes." Yacheroff was cleared of direct participation (though the Commission noted in a footnote the conflicting testimonies that the commander had killed two elderly Turks) but was deemed to be morally responsible for the "lightness of command" that had allowed his troops to act without restraint. Four low-ranking officers (three Russians and one Bulgarian) were cited for a handful of acts of murder, violence, incendiarism, and theft, and two Bulgarian gendarmes were accused of rape. Despite the favorable comments towards the Gymnasts in the second section, 26 Bulgarian villagers were accused of theft, incendiarism (two cases), and brigandage (one case).[67]

In mid-May 1880, before the Kirdjali Commission's report was issued, word reached Plovdiv of a second series of outrages in the northeastern canton of Anchialou. Local Roumelian authorities were accused of collaborating with troops from the Bulgarian Principality and members of the local Gymnast Societies in "barbarous proceedings" against Muslim villages.[68] In what Michell described as a "striking illustration" of Governor-General Aleko Pasha's method of either "deceiving himself or attempt[ing] to deceive others as to the real state of affairs," Aleko dismissed British and Austrian reports of atrocities as "intentionally malevolent."[69] By June, however, his denialism had run its course, and he had once again decided to dispatch a Commission to investigate the incidents. He later explained to British consul Stephen, Michell's temporary replacement, that it was from the start his priority to appoint a Commission with a "European element" to investigate the matter. Indeed, his first proposals called for an inquiry by four Bulgarians, two Turks, and three foreigners in the Roumelian service, including M. Baraczi, a Hungarian serving as the governor-general's private secretary; M. Mrachek, an Austrian in the service of the Roumelian government as the procurer of Bourgas; and Borthwick.[70] The Permanent Committee (the main organ of the legislative branch), however, only approved funds for a five-member body, reducing the number of foreign nationals from three to two in the process. This provoked a confrontation with the small community of foreign nationals in Plovdiv who sought a more internationalized inquiry. Baraczi promptly resigned from his post, seething at what he called the conspiracy "to influence … the ultimate verdict of the Commission and to understate the importance of what had taken place."[71] Stephen met with various Bulgarian officials, including the governor-general, to explain that by including a "strong European element" on the Commission they could preempt allegations that they had attempted to conceal the facts and that "there had been inequality in the formation of the Commission."[72] Borthwick, for his part, refused to participate in any Commission that did not include Baraczi.[73] Aleko relented, but as the Hungarian secretary had become ill and was no longer available the parties remained at an impasse, with Aleko complaining to Stephen that he could only nominate members, not cure them. Ultimately, Borthwick and Stephen accepted that two international representatives would sit on the Commission, and that Mrachek would take the place of the incapacitated Barcazi.[74] The Commission was thus ultimately composed of three Bulgarians (including Zlataroff of the Kirdjali Commission), two Europeans, and one Turk (Pehlivanoglou) who, it was rumored, harbored Bulgarian sympathies.[75]

Aleko Pasha's commissioners were instructed to

> travel to the scene of the events to investigate them, seek the perpetrators of the burning and pillage of the villagers in order to hand them over to justice, and make a fair estimate of the burned houses and destroyed effects.[76]

Their final report summarized the course events had taken in the region, explaining how certain villages, including some that straddled the border separating Eastern Roumelia from Bulgaria, had for years mistakenly paid their taxes to the former, much to the annoyance of the latter. Upon being notified of its proper status as a Bulgarian town, the mayor of one of those villages, Belovo, prepared to receive the Principality's troops. He was not, however, informed of the date of their arrival, and fighting occurred when local Muslims mistook some Principality irregulars without uniforms for brigands, and continued when the irregulars were replaced by state troops. As the Principality's troops advanced through the region (and into Roumelian territory) they passively stood by while anti-Turk Gymnasts burned and plundered Muslim property. In a few cases, Roumelian gendarmes themselves took advantage of the opportunities for pillage. But the majority of the responsibility for the atrocities was placed at the feet of the highest-ranking Roumelian officials and commanders of the canton, who had called the Gymnast forces into action, refused to send gendarmes to protect Muslim citizens, and exacerbated the chaos by abandoning their posts as thousands of Muslim refugees in search of aid and security scattered throughout the region.[77]

The commissioners specifically recommended against collective punishment of local Bulgarians, and suggested that 23 villagers be tried for a few acts of murder and numerous acts of pillage, five gendarmes for various acts of looting, corruption and dereliction of duty, their commander for failing to deploy his men to restore public order, and two local officials for various negligent acts that exacerbated the conflict.[78] The commissioners also recommended that indemnities be paid to the villagers whose properties and places of worship had been destroyed.[79]

The Great Powers had not sat idly by as the Muslims in Kirdjali and Aidos were attacked and as the Roumelian inquiries proceeded, but the possibility of joint investigative action was dealt a fatal blow by the replacement of Disraeli's Conservatives with William Gladstone's Liberal party in the April 1880 general election in Great Britain. Gladstone had spent the campaign delivering impassioned broadsides against the Conservative government for, among other things, antagonizing Russia, favoring unilateral over collective Great Power action, and coddling the Porte.[80] As prime minister, he proved to be every bit as committed to reversing these policies as one would have expected.

That is not to say that the new administration was immune to the humanitarian problem of Muslim suffering in Roumelia. Gladstone's new foreign minister, George Gower, Earl Granville, wasted no time in attempting to find an appropriate solution to the humanitarian crisis in Eastern Roumelia: one of his first instructions to the newly appointed ambassador to the Porte, George Goschen, was to consult with colleagues "as to the best means of ascertaining the truth of the reports respecting the destruction of Turkish villages, and making representations at Philippopolis which may secure the punishment of the offenders and future adequate protection for the Mussulman inhabitants."[81] But in practical terms, the new course plotted by Gladstone meant that

Russia (or indeed, any of the Powers) could single-handedly stymie even the most dedicated British efforts to undertake an international inquiry.

For about a month, the possibility of appointing an International Commission to investigate and remediate was discussed among the Great Powers, with Goschen (enthusiastically), British ambassador to Russia Frederick Hamilton Temple-Blackwood, First Marquess of Dufferin (enthusiastically), and Granville (half-heartedly) trying to shepherd the idea to fruition.[82] The Italians, Austrians, Germans, and French were each amenable to collective inquiry, but shared Gladstone's view that it should only be undertaken if Russia could be brought on board.[83] But Russia, predictably, would not budge. Russian representatives, among their objections, professed that the events in Roumelia did not warrant the label of "massacre" and that such deaths were simply a feature of life in the Orient; that sending a Turkish commissioner as part of a notional Commission would weaken the authority of the largely independent Roumelian government; that fictitious evidence would be presented; that the investigation might foment hatred between Roumelia's ethnic groups; and that the investigation might "be perverted into an instrument for discrediting the Russian Army" in the event ("though this is unlikely," according to Russian foreign minister de Giers) it were to catch "in its net a few" misbehaving Russian officers.[84] Between Russia's intransigence, Aleko Pasha's decision to conduct his own inquiries, the reshuffling of Great Britain's priorities to favor rapprochement with Russia and collective action, and the failure of any other Great Power to seize the initiative, the possibility of collective investigative action was eliminated.[85]

There is no indication in the British archives that any of the persons referred for trial by the Aidos Commission were prosecuted or punished, but the prefect of Aidos resigned a few months after the attacks.[86] Of the four Russian officers implicated in the Kirdjali attacks, the three lowest-ranking officers were discreetly dismissed from service in the Roumelian gendarmerie; no appeal was made to the Russian consulate for their punishment and no announcement of their release was published in the local papers.[87] Captain Yacheroff was treated even more leniently, being granted special permission to publish a defense of his conduct and given two months' "leave of absence" to travel to Russia, a trip from which it was expected he would not return.[88] Charges were dropped in almost all of the other cases recommended for prosecution.[89] Only one of the two "incendiares" was found guilty; his punishment was eight days' imprisonment for negligence. Around half of the Gymnasts accused of theft were found guilty, and most of them received sentences of no more than a few weeks in prison.[90]

Concluding thoughts

What this essay's examination of 1876–80 makes clear is that the road of international human rights fact-finding was a rocky one. The fact that international commissions were considered or formed at all in response to reports of mass violence, when the practice was entirely absent from earlier centuries, suggests a significant shift in thinking had taken place across Europe by the latter half of the nineteenth century. By 1876 advocates, pamphleteers, and journalists throughout Europe would have recognized among each other a widely shared belief that states must be held to minimum standards of conduct, and that massacre demanded not merely individual state-to-state remonstrances, but extraordinary explication and condign correction. The diplomatic record reveals that this vision was often professed by the political class of each of Europe's Great Powers as well. Moreover, the anti-massacre sentiments that animated lay and official actions arose in response to violence against Muslims and Christians alike, giving the inquisitorial interventions of this period a veneer of ethnic and religious even-handedness that still resonates as laudable. A word of caution is due however; this essay has only cracked open the door to the history of international human rights inquiry. The questions of how deep and pure this vein of equal opportunity empathy ran in the public and in policy-makers, how it interacted with the ever-shifting realpolitik considerations and cultural preconceptions that framed interstate relations, as well as the question of the cause and effect relationship between activism and political outcome, will only be answerable after additional research.

These expressions of a Great Power movement towards joint human rights inquiry are interesting, but it is this new model's limitations and the attempts to resist it that stand out in the three stories told in this essay. Great Power efforts to inquire and remediate could rouse strong opposition in their targets, as illustrated by the failure to secure Commissions in response to reported Ottoman abuses in Bosnia-Herzegovina and Bulgaria in 1876. The chief objection then raised by the Porte, that the proposed inquiry would infringe on its sovereignty, is one that persists today among states targeted by inquiry.

For states secure in their sovereignty but sensitive to a loss of international status, the offensive quality of the new mode of inquiry was its inherently public nature. Even where an international Commission seemed well launched – as with the Mt. Rhodope inquiry of 1878 – the merest hint that one of the inquiring states would be embarrassed before the world by being named as a cause of the crisis could result in a Commission cut off at the knees. Russia's fierce objections that the Mt. Rhodope Commission had been led astray in Roumelia, and that the reputation of the Russian army alone was enough to exonerate its troops, rang hollow in 1878, but successfully deprived the body of its exceptional quality of jointness that lent its commissioner's findings a sense of momentum, that is, a sense that their suggestions were of the highest quality and the expectation that they would be seriously discussed. In the case of Russia, the experience with the Mt. Rhodope Commission left such a bad aftertaste that it spoiled the possibility of a Great Power-led effort to inquire into and remediate the attacks on Muslims that marred Roumelia two years later.

One of the most interesting counter-thrusts to the trend of international inquiry was the decision of Governor-General Aleko Pasha to convene two Commissions of his own, and effectively internationalize them by including non-Roumelian nationals among the commissioners. There is no reason to believe that foreigners like Borthwick actively assisted the Roumelian government in covering up its crimes but as the commissioner's employer, Governor-General Aleko Pasha was in an excellent position to exercise a subtle influence over his staffer.[91] At any rate, Aleko retained the power to select the non-foreign commissioners, control the scope and timing of the inquiries, and shape his government's "humanitarian" and public relations response to their recommendations – all circumstances that certainly call into question the accuracy of their reports.

The scope of this essay is too narrow to produce broad generalizations about international human rights fact-finding in the nineteenth century. It does, however, remind us to pause and appreciate the tremendous gains that have been made since then. True, international fact-finding may even today be delegitimized, defied, or deflected by states, but not nearly so casually as between 1876 and 1880. That fact alone, and the victory over the forces of impunity it represents, should serve as a source of inspiration for our generation's ongoing efforts to perfect the science and art of human rights fact-finding.

Notes

1 Alexander Macfie, *The Eastern Question 1774–1923*, London: Routledge, 1996, pp. 35–6; Richard Millman, "The Bulgarian Massacres Reconsidered," *East European Review*, 1980, vol. 58, no. 2, 218–31.
2 James Phillips, "The Eastern Crisis, 1875–1878, in British and Russian Press and Society," University of Nottingham, PhD thesis, 2012, pp. 129–36.
3 William Gladstone, *Bulgarian Horrors and the Question of the East*, London: J. Murray, 1876, p. 8. See generally Jeremy Black, *The Tory World*, London: Routledge, 2016, pp. 160–5, p. 179.
4 George Buckle, *The Life of Benjamin Disraeli, Earl of Beaconsfield*, vol. 6, London: John Murray, 1920, pp. 60–6.
5 Buckle, *Benjamin Disraeli*, pp. 84–7.
6 The National Archives (London), Foreign Office (hereafter TNA FO) 424/37, annexes 2, 3, 4, and 5 to enclosure 4 in no. 126, Salisbury to Derby, 23 December 1876.
7 TNA FO 424/37, enclosure 1 in no. 230, Salisbury to Derby, 22 January 1877.
8 Sinan Kuneralp (ed.), *Temoignages Diplomatiques Français sur la Conference de Constantinople Decembre 1876–Janvier 1877*, Istanbul: Isis Press, 2013, p. 39. Count Charles de Moüy, secretary of the French Embassy, wrote in his memoirs that on receiving this news, the European plenipotentiaries simply "kept a deep silence … then, without any compliment, and as if nothing had happened, presented their general considerations on the object of their meeting." Count Charles de Moüy, *Souvenirs et Causeries d'un Diplomate*, Paris: PlonNourrit, 1909, p. 51.
9 Kuneralp, *Temoignages*, p. 43.
10 TNA FO 424/37, enclosure 3 in no. 223, Salisbury to Derby, 22 January 1877.
11 A. J. Rieber, "Alexander II: A Revisionist View," *Journal of Modern History*, 1971, vol. 43, no. 1, 57; Quentin Barry, *War in the East. A Military History of the Russo-Turkish War 1877–78*, London: Helion, 2012, p. 47; David MacKenzie, *The Serbs and Russian Pan-Slavism, 1875–1878*, New York: Cornell University Press, 1967, pp. 121–6.
12 MacKenzie, *The Serbs*, pp. 189, 195.
13 Mesut Uyar and Edward Erickson, *A Military History of the Ottomans. From Osman to Ataturk*, Santa Barbara, CA: ABC-CLIO, 2009, p. 193.
14 Barry, *War in the East*, p. 430.
15 William Medlicott, *The Congress of Berlin and After. A Diplomatic History of the Near Eastern Settlement, 1878–1880*, London: Frank Cass, 1963, pp. 1–34.
16 TNA FO 78/2900, attachment to no. 103, Salisbury to Secretary of State, 12 July 1878.
17 *Turkey. No. 49 (1878) – Correspondence Respecting the Proceedings of the International Commission Sent to the Mount Rhodope District*, London: Harrison, 1878 (hereafter *Turkey No. 49*), p. 48, no. 1, Layard to Salisbury, 18 July 1878.
18 *Turkey No. 49*, enclosure in no. 1.
19 *Turkey No. 49*, enclosure in no. 1.
20 *Turkey No. 49*, enclosure 1 in no. 6, Layard to Salisbury, 5 August 1878.
21 *Turkey No. 49*, enclosure 2 in no. 6, Layard to Salisbury, 5 August 1878.
22 *Turkey No. 49*, enclosure 2 in no. 6, Layard to Salisbury, 5 August 1878.
23 *Turkey No. 49*, enclosure 3 in no. 6, Layard to Salisbury, 5 August 1878.
24 *Turkey No. 49*, enclosure 3 in no. 6, Layard to Salisbury, 5 August 1878.
25 *Turkey No. 49*, enclosure 3 in no. 6, Layard to Salisbury, 5 August 1878.
26 *Turkey No. 45 (1878) – Further Correspondence Respecting the Affairs of Turkey*, London: Harrison, 1878, p. 56, no. 15, Layard to Salisbury, 29 July 1878.
27 *Turkey No. 52 (1878) – Further Correspondence Respecting the Proceedings of the International Commission Sent to the Mount Rhodope District*, London: Harrison, 1878, p. 6, "Report of the Austrian Military Attaché, Colonel Ritter von Raab, to Count Zichy, in Constantinople."
28 *Turkey No. 49*, enclosure 2 in no. 10, Layard to Salisbury, 20 August 1878; annex to Procès--Verbal no. 28 in enclosure 6 in no. 12, Layard to Salisbury, 1 September 1878.

29 *Turkey No. 49*, enclosure 6 in no. 12.

30 TNA FO 78/2796, Fawcett to Layard, 2 August 1878. Raab was hopeful that British ambassador to Constantinople Austen Layard would be able counteract whatever influences held sway over the Austro-Hungarian ambassador. During a subsequent conversation between Zichy and Layard, the Austrian ambassador admitted that he was convinced of the truth of the allegations against Russia, but he believed that only a new "International Commission for the protection of the Mussulmans of Roumelia" could check "the ill treatment and outrages" of the Russians, and that nothing would be accomplished in this direction unless the question of causes was avoided entirely. TNA FO 78/2798, no. 1088, Layard to Salisbury, 1 September 1878.

31 *Turkey No. 49*, enclosure 7 in no. 10.

32 *Turkey No. 49*, enclosure 1 in no. 13, Layard to Salisbury, 28 August 1878.

33 *Turkey No. 49*, enclosure 1 in no. 13, Layard to Salisbury, 28 August 1878.

34 *Turkey No. 49*, enclosure 1 in no. 13, Layard to Salisbury, 28 August 1878.

35 Russian newspapers decried the actions of the Commission as an attack on Russian troops and a deviation from the instructions given by the Congress. TNA FO 65/1076, no. 814, Plunkett to Marquis of Salisbury, 25 September 1878; TNA FO 65/1077, no. 848, Lord Loftus to Salisbury, 9 October 1878; no. 854, Loftus to Salisbury, 16 October 1878. The report received a mixed reception in the British press. Papers like *The Essex Standard* took the report at face value, declaring that "nothing in the experience of mankind in the darkest passages of its history exceeds in fiendish barbarity the deeds which this document reveals." *The Essex Standard, West Suffolk Gazette, and Eastern Counties' Advertiser*, 31 August 1878, 2. Others criticized the commissioners for the absence of efforts to verify the claims of the refugees through steps as basic as cross-examination and considered it unlikely that a fighting force as widely respected as the Russian would stoop to the level of conduct described in the Report. The Rhodope Commission, *Spectator*, 16 November 1878, 9.

36 *Turkey No. 49*, no. 11, Layard to Salisbury, 1 September 1878; no. 15, Layard to Salisbury, 29 September 1878.

37 TNA FO 65/1006, no. 788, Plunkett to Salisbury, 17 September 1878.

38 *Turkey No. 54*, enclosure in no. 30, Wolff to Salisbury, 24 September 1878.

39 TNA FO 65/1006, no. 730, Plunkett to Salisbury, 22 August 1878.

40 TNA FO 65/1006, no. 730, Plunkett to Salisbury, 22 August 1878.

41 TNA FO 65/1006, no. 730, Plunkett to Salisbury, 22 August 1878.

42 TNA FO 181/632, no. 110, Giers to Plunkett, 10 September 1871. Curiously, I have not found any evidence that Salisbury lodged a protest once the final report was placed before him in early September. Perhaps he felt there was little to be gained from another remonstration destined to fall on deaf ears.

43 *Turkey No. 54*, enclosure 2 in no. 235, Layard to Marquis of Salisbury, 9 November 1878.

44 *Turkey No. 54*, enclosure 6 in no. 176, Layard to the Marquis of Salisbury, 25 October 1878. "[W]e see by the example of the Rhodope Commission that the Great Powers will never be able to pull together, whilst Russia is the only one amongst them which will stand up for us, and from whom we can hope to obtain our just rights," said one Bulgarian member of the district government at Bourgas to a British vice consul.

45 R. J. Crampton, *Bulgaria*, Oxford: Oxford University Press, 2008, p. 94. William Miller, *The Ottoman Empire and its Successors, 1801–1927*, New York: Routledge, 2012, p. 389.

46 Crampton, *Bulgaria*, p. 95.

47 For example, although the Treaty of Berlin allowed the Sultan to do so, as of 1880 he had not garrisoned troops along Roumelia's borders. Medlicott, *Congress of Berlin*, pp. 360–3 (speculating as to the political, financial, and tactical reasons for this decision). In 1880 the Russian ambassador at Constantinople confessed to his British counterpart that Russia had only agreed to allow Turkey to occupy the Roumelian frontier to satisfy public opinion, but that if Ottoman troops had been stationed there Russia would have retaliated. TNA FO 78/3084, no. 410, Layard to Ball, 20 April 1880.

48 Medlicott, *Congress of Berlin*, p. 359.

49 Ömer Turan, *The Turkish Minority in Bulgaria, 1878–1908*, Ankara: Türk Tarih Kurumu Basımevi, 1998, p. 67; TNA FO 424/96, enclosure 1 in no. 150, Michell to Salisbury, 29 February 1880; Justin McCarthy, *Death and Exile: The Ethnic Cleansing of Ottoman Muslims, 1821–1922*,

Princeton, NJ: Darwin Press, 1995, pp. 72–4 (discussing the persecution of Muslims by Bulgarians in the context of the 1876–1877 war).

50 TNA FO 424/94, no. 65, Michell to Salisbury, 8 December 1879; Turan, *Turkish Minority*, p. 253.

51 TNA FO 424/94, no. 31, Michell to Salisbury, 20 December 1879. See also TNA FO 424/94, enclosure in no. 65, Michell to Salisbury, 28 December 1870; TNA FO 424/94, enclosures in no. 66, Michell to Salisbury, 28 December 1879; TNA FO 424/95, enclosures in no. 232, Layard to Salisbury, 10 January 1880; TNA FO 424/96, enclosure in no. 298, Michell to Salisbury, 12 March 1880.

52 TNA FO 424/96, no. 39, Michell to Salisbury, 22 February 1880. Bernard Lory, "Ahmed Aga Tämräsljata: The Last Derebey of the Rhodopes," in Kemal H. Karpat (ed.) *The Turks of Bulgaria: The History, Culture and Political Fate of a Minority*, Istanbul: Isis, 1990, pp. 194–6.

53 TNA FO 424/97, Layard to Salisbury, 31 March 1880. He sent a follow-up message a few days later enclosing a translated copy of a newspaper article alleging hypocrisy on the part of the European Powers that had been so quick to decry outrages perpetrated by Muslims at Batak and elsewhere. TNA FO, 78/3084, no. 388, Layard to Salisbury, 6 April 1880.

54 TNA FO 424/96, no. 325, Michell to Salisbury, 26 March 1880.

55 TNA FO 424/97, no. 56, Elliot to Salisbury, 29 March 1880.

56 TNA FO 78/3121, no. 54, Michell to Salisbury, 13 February 1880 (Aleko delayed distributing government order declaring Gymnastic Societies illegal to provincial authorities, allowing their drilling and intimidation to continue). TNA FO 424/95, no. 334, Michell to Salisbury, 13 February 1880 (Aleko criticizes Borthwick of "meddling in political affairs" when the latter complains that civilians are being drilled in contravention of suppression order); TNA FO 424/96, no. 23, Michell to Salisbury, 3 March 1880 (Aleko "in no rush to move against secret societies").

57 TNA FO 424/97, no. 251, Michell to Salisbury, 10 April 1880.

58 *Commission d'Enquete du Kirdjali, Annexes au Rapport*, Philippopolis: Imprimerie Centrale, 1880, p. 167 (reproducing the "Order of the Governor-General of Eastern Roumelia" of 28 February 1880, translation on file with author).

59 *Turkey No. 10 – Report of the Commission Appointed to Inquire into the Occurrences in the Kirdjali District*, London: Harrison, 1880 (hereafter *Kirdjali Report*), pp. 1, 12 n. 2.

60 *Kirdjali Report*, p. 19; TNA FO 78/3124, no. 239, Michell to Earl Granville, 4 May 1880.

61 *Kirdjali Report*, pp. 2–8.

62 *Kirdjali Report*, pp. 7–9 (identifying culpable conduct and querying whether it could not be assumed "that the soldiers, hearing such language in the mouth of their chief, would no longer see the inhabitants of Kirdjali as those who had been led astray, but as an enemy they had to fight?"). Yacheroff, in his written testimony, stated that he had activated the Gymnasts to "make a moral impression on the rebels." *Commission d'Enquete du Kirdjali, Annexes au Rapport*, p. 101.

63 *Kirdjali Report*, pp. 11–12. It does not seem to have occurred to the commissioners that some families or individuals might wish to conceal a rape to preserve family or personal honor, or out of fear of reprisals.

64 *Kirdjali Report*, pp. 11–12.

65 *Kirdjali Report*, p. 9.

66 *Kirdjali Report*, pp. 12–18.

67 *Kirdjali Report*, pp. 18–19; TNA FO 424/101, no. 200, Stephen to Granville, 31 July 1880.

68 TNA FO 424/98, no. 233, Layard to Granville, 11 May 1880; TNA FO 78/3124, no. 260, Michell to Granville, 22 May 1880; TNA FO 78/3124, no. 261, Michell to Granville, 22 May 1880 (attaching report by Austrian vice consul). The violence was widely reported to have occurred in the district of Aidos, but in fact it had occurred in the neighboring canton of d'Anchialou-Messemvria, a fact noted by the commissioners in their report. *Turkey No. 14 – Despatch from Her Majesty's Consul-General at Philippopolis forwarding the Report of the Aidos Commission*, London: Harrison, 1880 (hereafter *Aidos Report*), p. 2. The Commission was nevertheless widely referred to as the "Aidos Commission."

69 TNA FO 424/99, no. 3, Michell to Granville, 22 May 1880; TNA FO 424/99, enclosure 1 in no. 189, Michell to Granville, 29 May 1880 (illustrating how Aleko misrepresented the extent

of the harms suffered by Muslims and the identity of the perpetrators in his messages to the Porte).

70 TNA FO 195/1320, Michell to Goschen, 8 June 1880; TNA FO 424/99, no. 615, Stephen to Granville, 16 June 1880.

71 TNA FO 424/99, no. 615, Stephen to Granville, 16 June 1880. As noted there, Baraczi privately communicated to Stephen that "many Bulgarians" were opposed to his appointment, as he had already visited the district in response to the outrages and provided the governor-general with a report incriminating their "compatriots." When he also learned that the number of commissioners was reduced in number, he was so disgusted that he abandoned his efforts to sit on the Commission.

72 TNA FO 424/99, no. 615, Stephen to Granville, 16 June 1880; TNA FO 424/99, no. 618, Stephen to Granville, 19 June 1880.

73 TNA FO 424/99, no. 618, Stephen to Granville, 19 June 1880.

74 TNA FO 424/99, no. 618, Stephen to Granville, 19 June 1880. As noted there, Aleko also promised Stephen that he would inquire whether Toustain could also return as a third European commissioner, but he apparently could not be spared.

75 *Aidos Report*, p. 8; TNA FO 424/99, no. 615, Stephen to Granville, 16 June 1880.

76 *Aidos Report*, p. 3.

77 *Aidos Report*, pp. 2–6.

78 *Aidos Report*, pp. 7–8.

79 *Aidos Report*, pp. 7–8. Villages on both sides of the Bulgarian-Roumelia border had been victimized, but the commissioners refrained from reporting on acts of destruction that occurred in Bulgarian territory. TNA FO 424/101, no. 71, Goschen to Granville, 28 July 1880.

80 William Ewart Gladstone, *Political Speeches in Scotland – March and April 1880 – by the Right Hon. W. E. Gladstone, M.P.*, vol. 2, Edinburgh: Andrew Elliot, 1880, pp. 208–21 (13th Midlothian speech, delivered 22 March 1880) and p. 320 (17th Midlothian speech, delivered 30 March 1880).

81 TNA FO 424/98, no. 395, Granville to Goschen, 25 May 1880.

82 TNA FO 424/99, Dufferin to Granville, 5 June 1880; TNA FO 424/99, no. 100, Granville to Goschen, 5 June 1880 (instructing Goschen not to press the point if there was difficulty in getting all the representatives in Constantinople to agree to joint action). TNA FO 424/99, no. 180, Granville to Elliot, 8 June 1880; TNA FO 424/99, no. 293, Granville to Goschen, 14 June 1880; TNA FO 424/99, no. 294, Granville to Paget, 14 June 1880; TNA FO 424/99, no. 114, Granville to Dufferin, 6 June 1880; TNA FO 424/99, no. 364, Goschen to Granville, 17 June 1880; TNA FO 424/99, no. 376, Granville to Dufferin, 18 June 1880; TNA FO 424/99, no. 655, Lyons to Granville, 29 June 1880.

83 TNA FO 424/99, no. 270, Elliot to Granville, 9 June 1880; TNA FO 424/99, no. 306, Goschen to Granville, 8 June 1880; TNA FO 424/99, no. 279, Russell to Granville, 7 June 1880; TNA FO 424/99, no. 438, Granville to Lyons, 21 June 1880; TNA FO 424/99, no. 352, Goschen to Granville, 18 June 1880.

84 TNA FO 424/99, no. 156, Goschen to Granville, 31 May 1880.

85 TNA FO 424/99, no. 293, Granville to Goschen, 14 June 1880 ("Until the Commission appointed by Aleko Pasha to inquire into the burning of the Turkish villages in the Aidos district shall have made its report, it would not be desirable to institute a separate Consular inquiry into that matter."); TNA FO 424/99, no. 402, Granville to Dufferin, 19 June 1880 (expressing satisfaction at receiving Russian support for proposal to settle frontier line between Turkey and Greece); TNA FO 424/99, no. 529, Granville to Lyons, 24 June 1880 (abandoning the idea "as the Russian government seemed to be so strongly opposed to anything having the character of an international inquiry"); TNA FO 424/99, no. 532, Goschen to Granville, 18 June 1880 (reporting that from the perspective of the ambassadors, there could be "no question that, in view of the Commission having made a Report, which clearly must be accepted under the circumstances, and in view of a Commission having been appointed to inquire into the Aidos outrages," a collective inquiry "could not take place").

86 TNA FO 78/3126, no. 332, Stephen to Granville, 5 September 1880.

87 TNA FO 78/3125, no. 314, Stephen to Granville, 31 July 1880.

88 TNA FO 78/3125, no. 314, Stephen to Granville, 31 July 1880; TNA FO 78/3126, no. 365, Stephen to Granville, 16 November 1880. Yacheroff's defense can be found at TNA FO 78/3125, no. 298, Stephen to Granville, 26 June 1880.

89 TNA FO 78/3125, no. 314, Stephen to Granville, 31 July 1880.

90 *Turkey No. 19*, enclosure in no. 134, Stephen to Granville, 31 July 1880. At least one punishment of two years was handed out, but it is not clear from the records which crime this was in response to. TNA FO 424/105, no. 159, Stephen to Granville, 3 December 1880.

91 The jury is out. Borthwick was quite able to stand up to the Gymnasts in Aleko Pasha's inner circle, and in a private communication to Michell or Goschen he freely admitted that he had no faith in the "medical knowledge or political honesty" of the doctor who had accompanied the Kirdjali Commission to examine exhumed bodies and women alleging rape. TNA FO 424/97, enclosures in no. 10, Michell to Salisbury, 19 March 1880; TNA FO 424/99, enclosure 2 in Goschen, no. 532. Michell, however, noted a number of inconsistencies between the final report and Borthwick's earlier letters to him, as well as the overall weak tone of the final report. Enclosure 3 in Goschen, no. 532.

4

RECLAIMING CONGO REFORM FOR THE HISTORY OF HUMAN RIGHTS

Mairi S. MacDonald

In 1903, British consul Roger Casement traveled up the Congo River to gather evidence about the devastation the Independent Congo State (ICS) was inflicting on its indigenous population. Casement's report was not the first news Britain's government or people heard about the atrocities committed in Congo in the name of, and with the knowledge, of Leopold II, king of the Belgians and king-sovereign of the ICS. Nor did Casement's report have an immediate impact. But the report was the central event in a long process of persuading one state to take effective action against another in response to a humanitarian catastrophe – a process that built upon a vague sense that even Congo's indigenous people had rights that should be protected.

Where does the international movement to reform the administration of the Congo fit into the history of human rights? If we exclude from that history any humanitarian advocacy that does not explicitly demand respect for the innate rights of human beings, we have a simple answer: Congo reform cannot have been about human rights, because none of its advocates wrote of the "human rights" of the people of the Congo. Yet the argument that convinced the British government to act against the administration of Belgium's king Leopold II in his central African domain did ultimately rest on the principle that the Congo State was violating rights that colonized Africans must enjoy by virtue of their humanity. Moreover, in acting against Leopold, Britain's Foreign Office relied on evidence of atrocity and indifference to human life that Casement collected and presented with a clear eye to making a case that would withstand legal challenge. The consul's method, "meticulously documented and narrated testimony" based wherever possible on the direct accounts of the people affected, still dominates investigations of human rights claims more than a century later.[1] His principal finding, of a "great reduction observable everywhere in native life," relied on demographics as evidence of humanitarian catastrophe – a practice that finds present-day echoes in the study of population epidemiology.[2] Both in substance and in process, therefore, Casement and the movement for Congo reform must have a place in the history of human rights.

In this essay, I argue that in order to understand the contribution that the Congo reform movement made to the history of human rights, we must develop a new analytical approach that focuses on human rights advocacy as a practice of persuasion. This differs from an approach that traces the language of rights. One prominent example of a language-focused approach is Lynn Hunt's argument that the history of human rights dates to the late eighteenth century, when, she says, the idea of claiming human rights first gained political salience, that is, when human rights "came to make sense in societies where they had not done so previously."[3] It also differs from an approach that tracks the scope and scale of institutional organization on behalf of rights. Samuel Moyn's contentious argument that human rights "as a powerful transnational ideal and movement" date from the United States of America in the 1970s – not the 1770s – is an example of this kind of an operational approach.[4]

Analyzing human rights advocacy as a practice of persuasion requires us to think about the substance of the rights the advocate claims on behalf of others, rather than the language used to describe them. We then look to the process by which advocates persuade decision-makers to act. It would have been outlandish, and ineffective, for advocates for Congo reform to claim that the human rights of Africans were being violated by Leopold. International law and European (and American) societies alike legitimized his brutality in the Congo, like that of the other European powers engaged in the Scramble for Africa, as a necessary part of "assuring to that vast continent the benefits of peace and civilization."[5] It was not enough either to stir public opinion to outrage at the atrocities committed in Leopold's name, as did missionaries, the British and Foreign Anti-Slavery Society, the Aborigines' Protection Society, and the Congo Reform Association that journalist E. D. Morel founded with Casement's help. Public outrage alone could not force the British government to act in this period when states considered sovereignty to be the exclusive preserve of "civilized" peoples and guarded it closely.[6] The Foreign Office needed to know that it was on solid legal ground in pressing Leopold for change, and here Casement and Morel were instrumental.

The essay begins with the evidence that Casement gathered and presented to the Foreign Office. Casement, a British consul, knew from his experience in Congo that to force change he needed to persuade his government, and through it other colonial powers, to look beyond the state's apparently adequate legal protection of its indigenous population to the brutal reality on the ground. I then move from the facts to the law, exploring why the official British case against Leopold rested on rights to trade that were guaranteed by international law. The campaigners had to rely on a weak connection between free trade and humanitarian objectives so they could base their claim in the safest source of international law available: treaties. That, in turn, helped them create and maintain a united front and implicate Britain in the enforcement of those treaties. The third section examines why Leopold's defense crumbled in the face of an international inquiry that verified the gap between laws on paper and facts on Congolese soil. I return in the conclusion to the idea of human rights advocacy as a practice of persuasion and suggest how this analysis might shine a new light on the history of human rights generally.

"Their lives were useless to them": Roger Casement prepares the evidence

When Roger Casement reported to the Foreign Office that he had returned from a journey of investigation into conditions on the Upper Congo, he was clearly proud of his work. His notes, he wrote, "constitute an extraordinary case for inquiry, seeing that I have been away from Stanley Pool only since the 2 July 1903, and in the regions where atrocities are very profitable not more than six weeks."[7] The consul's accomplishment was undeniable. In this brief period, Casement covered over 1,600 miles, collecting evidence from Congolese people, European and American missionaries, company employees, and Congo government officials he met along the way. Casement planned his trip so that it would retrace a path he had followed 16 years earlier. He could therefore complement the depositions he heard with his own recollections of conditions on the previous trip. His final report, together with the many dispatches, memoranda, and letters he wrote to share additional evidence with his colleagues in the Foreign Office, amount to careful, vivid documentation of how a European king had effectively enslaved the African population of an area eight times the size of his own country.

Casement's overwhelming impression of the Upper Congo River region was its depopulation. "The most striking change observed during my journey into the interior was the great reduction observable everywhere in native life. Communities I had formerly known as large and flourishing centres of population are to-day entirely gone, or … unrecognizable." To explain the collapse of Congo's population, the British consul

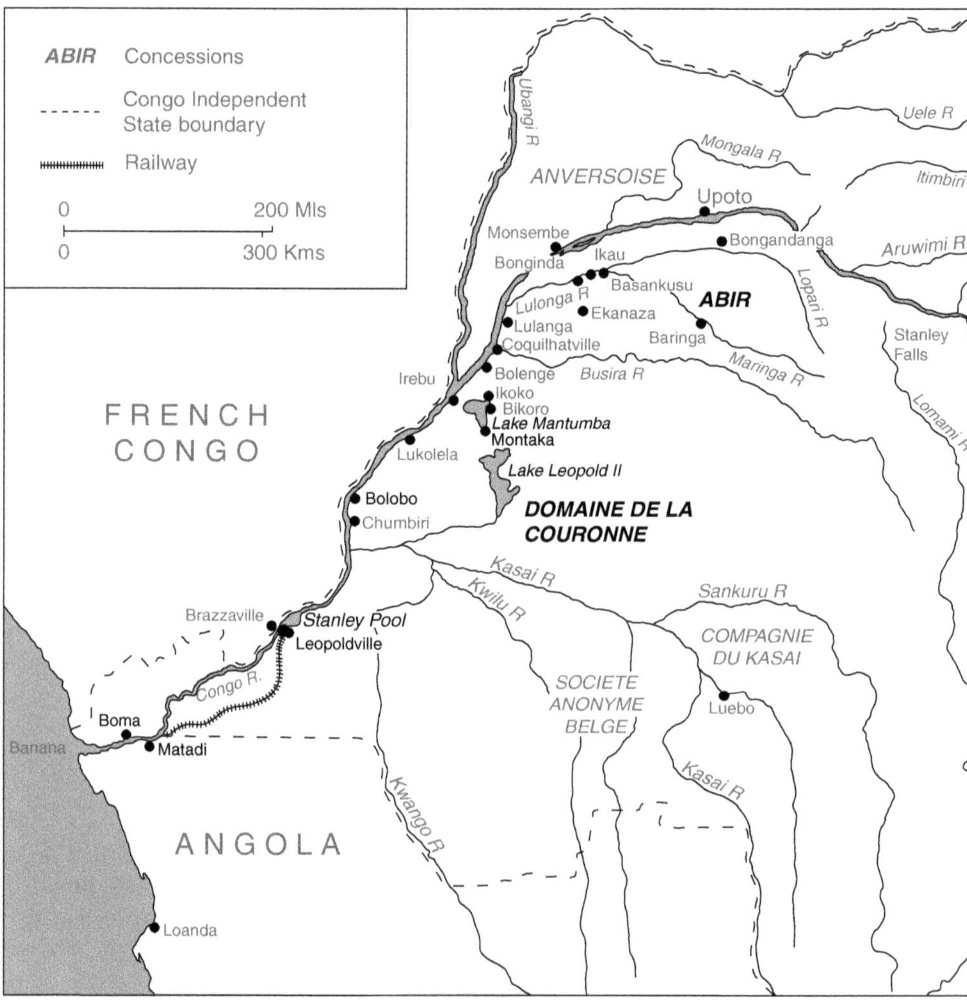

Figure 4.1 King Leopold II's Independent Congo State.

assigned "a prominent place" to sleeping sickness (trypanosomiasis), a disease endemic to the Lower Congo that was "all too rapidly eating its way into the heart of Africa," noting that the indigenous people themselves attributed "their alarming death-rate" in part to the disease. Crucially, though, Casement focused his investigation on the Congolese people's own attribution – he thought "principally" – of "their rapid decrease in numbers to other causes as well."[8]

What could trigger depopulation on a scale he estimated as 60 percent in less than two decades? In addition to disease, Casement heard about the emigration of entire villages, most often across the Congo River to the adjacent French colony, and the murders and mutilations of both living and dead bodies for which Congo was already infamous in Britain and other parts of Europe. He heard of women, including many who were pregnant and nursing, imprisoned as hostages to force their husbands to meet impossible quotas to deliver natural rubber, food and building materials to white men and their African intermediaries. He heard of children sold into slavery so that their villages could pay fines imposed because they had failed to meet those quotas. He saw ample evidence of slower forms of violence, as well, notably mass starvation. He noticed that few villagers had any livestock left with which to feed themselves; when he asked where all the sheep, goats, and fowl that he had noticed on his earlier trip had gone, villagers pointed to Congo's colonial administration: "Bula Matadi [*sic*] has taken them."[9] Even *kwanga*, a staple food preparation based on cassava root, was in short supply. Everywhere he went, the consul discovered that the local people were required to deliver enormous quantities of it to the representatives of the State or its authorized companies, leaving little to be traded in local markets. The markets themselves were few and poor, and indigenous people did much less trading than in earlier times. In short, Roger Casement documented a humanitarian catastrophe consisting of an extraordinarily rapid population decline whose survivors were reduced to "lives [that] were useless to them."[10]

At first glance, Casement's report seems to be a grim travelogue. He notes the date he arrived in each place on his trajectory up the Congo, then compares his first impressions with what he had seen in the same district on his earlier voyage as an employee of the Sanford Exploring Expedition.[11] He alludes to the conditions of his travel from place to place. He traveled from Matadi to Léopoldville on 5–6 June 1903 by way of the "excellently constructed" and "most efficient" railway through the "generally unproductive and … sterile" land of the cataract region. After a month at Léopoldville, though, he was reduced to begging passage on one of the few nongovernment steamships permitted to carry passengers. After another lengthy delay, Casement records having secured "a small steam-launch … for my private use" on which he continued his journey beyond Bolobo early in August.[12] The report carefully documents the amount of time he spent in each town or village, noting when transportation difficulties prolonged his stay. It then summarizes the testimony he heard from the people in each place: missionaries, local chiefs and other villagers, and local agents for the State and the largely Belgian-owned companies the State permitted to operate in each place.

A deeper look, however, shows that Casement took as much care in constructing his report as he had in planning his journey. He investigated and documented all the permutations of the economic system that Congo's king-sovereign had implemented to make his investment profitable. At each stage of his report on a journey that, coincidentally or not, mirrored Marlow's journey in Joseph Conrad's 1899 novella *Heart of Darkness*, Casement juxtaposes observed reality against the legal and institutional arrangements Leopold used to insulate his system from the criticisms of Belgians and other Europeans.[13] It was a system designed to extract maximum profit with minimum investment. The system forced Congo's indigenous people to gather their most profitable commodities, ivory and rubber, and deliver them to chartered companies and other entities that were in turn required to hand over the lion's share of the profit to the State and its sovereign. Casement's journey took him to, or near, areas under the State's direct governance as well as districts subject to all three of the major systems of land ownership and exploitation to be found in Congo: the Domaine de la Couronne, personally owned by Leopold, and operated for his direct profit; the Domaine Privé, or state-owned lands, from which rubber was extracted by partially state-owned companies operating under concession (in this case, the Anglo-Belgian India Rubber Company known as ABIR); and a region "regarded as one of the free-trading districts wherein no exclusive right to the products of the soil is recognized," and yet where a single private company, the La Lulonga Company, operated the same type of extraction system that the king's own forces and the concession companies did. Casement even observed conditions on a plantation, one of the few in existence despite Leopold's frequent promises to turn his Congolese possession to more long-term productive use.[14]

Though Casement's report summarizes the legal distinctions among these exploitation models, in practice he found little to differentiate them. He was not able to learn much about the Domaine de la Couronne directly, but he did take evidence from a large number of Basengili people who had fled their own lands near Lac Léopold II, in the king's personal domain. He interviewed several groups of these "industrious blacksmiths and brass-workers," and heard them explain that they had left because

> they had endured such ill-treatment at the hands of the Government officials and the Government soldiers in their own country that life had become intolerable, that nothing had remained for them at home but to be killed for failure to bring in a certain amount of rubber or to die from starvation or exposure in their attempts to satisfy the demands made upon them.

Dubious at first, Casement sought and received confirmation from other Basengili that he met two days' journey further up the river. Their stories were also confirmed by a missionary, A. E. Scrivener, who embarked on a fact-finding expedition of his own and who reported his own observations as well as the statements of the "present Government officer in charge of the district."[15]

Casement heard versions of the Basengili story wherever he went. Whatever industry or trade the Congolese had carried on before the advent of the Congo State, with its *force publique* (military-cum-police) and private companies, local people were now spending all their energies on supplying the invaders with food, supplies, and marketable commodities (mostly rubber, and gum-copal where the rubber had been tapped out or had never been plentiful). Europe counted the elimination of the Congolese trade in slaves as a humanitarian advance in itself, and Casement was careful to give credit to the ICS for reducing – though not eliminating – this practice. Casement argued, though, that its replacement could not really be considered trade, since the locals could not market what they harvested: they had to turn these products over for the exclusive use and profit of the local company and through it, the state.

Casement also found that any differences in the quality of native life in the Domaine de la Couronne, the Domaine Privé, and the so-called free-trade zone were of degree, not kind, despite divergences in the applicable laws. The law specified rates of pay for goods delivered, both for sustenance and for the export market. In practice, when indigenous gatherers were paid, it was either with brass rods, a currency whose length and hence value European officials could easily manipulate from one district to the next, or in substitute goods such as cloth that were either largely worthless to the local people or, when they were useful, destroyed the local market by flooding it.[16] The ABIR, as a concession company in the Domaine Privé, enjoyed "*droits de police*" (the right to employ armed men) whereas the La Lulonga Company legally did not. In practice, both firms employed and armed "sentinels" or "forest guards" who were Africans, usually from distant parts of Congo, charged with enforcing the delivery quotas by any means necessary. These guards were not responsible for all the murder, mutilation, hostage-taking, flogging, and other excesses of force that took place. Casement heard about plenty of brutality meted out directly by white officials and traders, both on his journey and in his regular work as British consul at Boma. The sentinels, however, were held responsible for ensuring that deliveries met the quotas set by white supervisors, and those supervisors showed little or no interest in constraining the means by which the sentinels achieved their task.

In a passage that reads like the record of a cross-examination, the report explains how Casement tried and failed to elicit a coherent explanation of the system from the ABIR's local employees. To their claim that concession company employees had to be armed to protect European establishments, Casement objected by asking why so many armed guards were stationed in native villages and acted aggressively rather than defensively. They answered that this was necessary in order to enforce the collection of "impositions" or taxes that were required by law. This made no sense either, for the official statistics recorded what was being collected as the "outcome of commercial dealings with the natives" – profit for the companies, not taxes destined for government coffers. Casement put to the ABIR's representatives the explanation he had heard from the Congolese: the sentries were armed to force the people to produce commodities for the companies' benefit. Again, the company men denied this. All they were doing was trading with the indigenous Congolese, since after all they did pay for the goods they delivered. In that case, said Casement, are you not paying the Congolese for goods you already own, since the State, which by decree owned the soil and its produce, had turned over that ownership to the concession company? Again, this was not correct: they were only paying the Africans for their labor to collect "our produce on our land." If so, said Casement, where was the contract of employment? No contract was required, they answered, because Congolese were performing these services "as a public duty required of [them] by [their] Government."[17] The laborer was free, living on his own land, in effect paying his taxes by working to deliver the company's commodities from its land. Casement tried again: did this not, in effect, mean that the company owned both land and laborer? Again, that was not correct: the concession company did not own its poorly paid, compelled labor force. As Casement noted, "there was not an explanation offered to me that was not at once contradicted by the next."[18]

It all added up to an economic system based on the forced labor of local people, subject to unpredictable and often onerous demands in the best cases, and to lethal violence in the worst. ABIR employees attempted to justify it as "forced labour conceived in the true interest of the native, who, if not controlled in this way, would spend his days in idleness, unprofitable to himself and the general community." But the consequences of this system – at least from the perspective of Casement, the missionaries, and the Congolese they interviewed – were so starkly at odds with the interest of the natives that Casement summed up the companies' explanations as "true alternatives of excuse … so obviously untrue, that they could not be admitted as having any real relation to the things which came before me."[19]

Writing to Henry Farnall, head of the Foreign Office's African department, Casement summed up his thesis about what was responsible for the collapse of Congo's indigenous population. It stemmed from "disease, bad government, and the dreadful excesses of the past (which I find on closer view were minimized [by company and state officials])."[20] The key to his argument was, in his phrase, bad government. To improve its government, the Independent Congo State would have to be forced to adopt the "changed measures, entirely changed" Casement thought necessary to avoid further destruction. But how were the concerned citizens of one sovereign state to convince a sovereign government to change its ways?

"Measures … to abate the evils prevalent in that state": framing the law

We need to consider the international legal framework for the Scramble generally and for Leopold's claim to the Congo in particular in order to understand how crucial Casement's report was to the process of persuading the British Foreign Office to translate growing public outrage into effective, albeit cautious, diplomatic action. That framework was unusual in many respects. For one thing, it was explicit. It consisted of two multilateral treaties, signed in Berlin in 1885 and Brussels in 1890, and the interpretation that a small group of international jurists accorded them. For another thing, the primary objective of these treaties was to prevent clashes over African soil from developing into wars in Europe. The more usual route was to resolve imperial claims in the wake of a war between European powers. A third unusual feature was the explicitly humanitarian justification the signatories attached to their appropriation of African land – a cause they espoused without input from the people of Africa themselves. The challenge for Congo reformers was to convince the Foreign Office that this framework of international law permitted a signatory to invoke this humanitarian language to protect the rights of people whom neither the treaties nor jurists recognized as being civilized and therefore able to invoke the law on their own behalf.

Reformers scored a major victory when they forced the House of Commons to debate the Congo issue on 20 May 1903. Calling on the government to make good on

> the boast of this country, not only that our own native subjects were governed on principles of justice, but that, ever since the days of Wilberforce, England had been the leader in all movements on behalf of the backward races of the earth,

opposition M. P. Herbert Samuel succeeded in getting the House to ask the government "to confer with the other Powers, signatories of the Berlin General Act by virtue of which the Congo Free State exists, in order that measures may be adopted to abate the evils prevalent in that State."[21]

The next victory was that the Foreign Office authorized Casement's investigation. The foreign secretary Marquess of Lansdowne proceeded to the next step after that in early August 1903. Even as his consul Casement was taking evidence near Lake Mantumba, Lansdowne wrote a dispatch to Britain's ambassadors in the capitals of the other states that had signed the Berlin Act, asking them to forward it to the local minister of foreign affairs. Lansdowne's dispatch began with an almost apologetic explanation of this extraordinary intervention. Philanthropic societies, commercial bodies, the public press, and "despatches from His Majesty's consuls" had "repeatedly" called attention over the past several years to "alleged cases of ill-treatment of natives and ... the existence of trade monopolies in the Independent State of the Congo." Although the government would not take a position on the extent to which the accusations were true, they were so widely believed "that it is no longer possible to ignore them."

> The question has now arisen whether the Congo State can be considered to have fulfilled the special pledges, given under the Berlin Act, to watch over the preservation of the native tribes, and to care for their moral and material advancement.

Thus, he said, Britain had decided "the time has come when the Powers parties to the Berlin Act should consider whether the system of trade now prevailing in the Independent State is in harmony with the provisions of the Act."[22]

Lansdowne's dispatch recounted many of the allegations made in the Commons debate.[23] Yet it was a far cry from Samuel's appeal for humanitarian action in Britain's tradition of antislavery diplomacy. Lansdowne distinguished between "isolated acts of cruelty committed by individuals, whether in the service of the State or not, and a system of administration involving and accompanied by systematic cruelty or oppression." The most serious of the allegations amounted to the latter accusation – what Casement would call "bad government." However, the only question the foreign secretary was prepared to bring to Britain's fellow signatories was that of free trade:

> whether the system of making grants of vast areas of territory is permissible under the [Berlin] Act if the effect of such grants is in practice to create a monopoly of trade by excluding all persons other than the concession-holder from trading with the natives in that area.

Lansdowne ignored Samuel's appeal for humanitarian intervention, which would have risked opening Britain's treatment of its own subjects to international scrutiny. Instead, the foreign secretary proposed to discuss at the international level only whether Congo was guilty of violating the Berlin Act by creating trade monopolies.

Lansdowne's decision to channel public sentiment about Congo's atrocities into a narrower discussion of trade law reflected the Foreign Office's hesitation about stepping into a new area of diplomacy: non-military humanitarian intervention in a sovereign state. The connection between free trade and humanitarian objectives might have been weak, but it did permit the Congo State's opponents to frame their objections broadly enough to achieve several vital purposes. First, it offered a means of uniting what might otherwise have been disparate voices. Colonialism's often divergent missions of Christianity, commerce and civilization could join here in a single appeal, voiced by missionaries, philanthropists, chambers of commerce, and, crucially, the British government itself. Second, making the case that Congo's atrocities arose naturally from its economic system allowed the campaigners to ground their appeal in positive, treaty-based international law. This was an easier case to make than one relying on more ambiguous ideas about the "natural" law of nations and peoples, let alone ideas justifying state action on the basis of human sympathy for strangers. Third, it implicated the British government as a signatory of the Berlin and Brussels treaties. Indeed, Britain was the prime mover behind the Brussels treaty, and it was that treaty which had cemented the logic that gave Leopold free rein in Congo in the interests of Africa's peoples.[24] Without a united front, a strong basis in positive international law, and the ability to rouse Britain's government to action, humanitarian sentiment could not have achieved what it did.

Leopold's counterattack proved that all three elements were necessary. The king's message came through the usual diplomatic channel: Edmund van Eetvelde, whom the king had made a baron for his long and faithful service to the Congo State, met with the United Kingdom's minister to Belgium, Sir E. Constantine Phipps, early in February 1904. Phipps believed that van Eetvelde was using Leopold's own "very uncompromising" language to convey the king's displeasure. The baron began his tirade with its only new element: a complaint about Casement's journey, which he said had had the objective of "stirring up the natives to opposition against the organized Government or Administration," and that thus elevated Congo's complaint to the highest level as "an unheard-of point of departure in the history of international relations with a friendly State." Van Eetvelde then suggested that Britain's government was losing control to domestic radicals: the campaign against the Congo was the work of Protestant missionaries seeking to have Britain expropriate the Belgian king's territory, and "the Liverpool merchants who had found their pecuniary interests injured by the comprehensive scheme of exploitation organized in the interest of civilization by the Sovereign." Even a unified Britain would not succeed in raising other Berlin signatories against Congo's administration, warned van Eetvelde. In any case, "no foreign intervention was necessary to make the Congo government recognize its obligations towards humanity, or could induce it to alter the system which it was fully justified in pursuing."[25]

Phipps addressed the first necessary element of the campaign – unity – as he defended his government's motives against van Eetvelde's implication that it was trying to gain the other powers' sanction for a British takeover by escalating the matter to the international level. Members of his government "were animated by no covert aims whatever," he protested:

> [T]heir action had been prompted by public opinion, to which expression had been given in the House of Commons, and which could not be resisted in a constitutional country. They were simply desirous that the conditions under which the Congo régime had been inaugurated should be maintained to the benefit of the natives under the Administration.

Casement's trip was no violation of international relations, either. The consul had made no secret of his mission, Phipps had no doubt the ICS would avail itself of every means of refuting "any unfair statements" the consul might make, and in any case, it was "an unquestionable fact" that Casement "had been in a position to glean serious evidence of abuses."[26]

Phipps did not engage van Eetvelde on the substance of the ICS' self-defense: that it was fully justified in law and in the interests of civilization in operating its "comprehensive scheme of exploitation." The question here was whether, to what extent, and how the sovereignty of the ICS was limited by the terms of the Berlin and Brussels treaties. Nigerian writer Wole Soyinka created an indelible image of the European colonial powers at the 1884–5 Berlin Conference acting like "demented tailors" as they cut up and stitched the African continent among themselves. Yet in reality the Conference did create a set of rules. These were intended to prevent European disputes about African territory from escalating into war in Europe.[27] Leopold's sovereignty over the Congo basin came to be recognized through a "side event" to the Conference: a series of bilateral agreements, beginning with the United States even before the Conference opened, and followed by other powers gathered in Berlin.[28] These side agreements left international jurists and Foreign Office officials alike in some doubt as to whether the Independent Congo State was actually "called into existence" by the international treaty and therefore, implicitly, capable of being disbanded by the parties to the same treaty.[29] Either way, though, the new State had adhered to the treaty upon its creation in July 1885, and claimed that all its laws were consistent with its international obligations. Now the issue was whether or not this was true.

The Berlin Act set out fundamental principles that should apply to the river and the territory that surrounded it, in the interests, according to its preamble, of "regulat[ing] the conditions most favourable to the development of trade and civilization in certain regions of Africa." Its first article defined the basin and stated bluntly: "The trade of all nations shall enjoy complete freedom" within it. Article V was equally unequivocal: "No Power which exercises or shall exercise sovereign rights in the above-mentioned regions shall be allowed to grant therein a monopoly or favour of any kind in matters of trade." The powers also declared the territories of the Congo basin to be subject to the rules governing neutrality, explicitly "in order to give a new guarantee of security to trade and industry, and to encourage, by the maintenance of peace, the development of civilization" in those lands. By contrast, the powers used vague language to define the obligations of the Congo basin's new governors towards the people already living in the area. They bound themselves "to watch over the preservation of the native tribes, and to care for the improvement of the conditions of their moral and material well-being, and to help in suppressing slavery, and especially the slave trade." They would also "protect and favour" institutions "which aim at … bringing home to [the natives] the blessings of civilization."[30]

The second treaty, the Brussels Act, seemed to offer more precise direction to colonial powers advancing the humanitarian objective of introducing "civilization" throughout the interior of Africa. In fact, it resulted in Leopold gaining even more latitude in the Congo State. The preamble of the Brussels Act describes a treaty that seeks ways to achieve international purposes that have already been agreed upon:

> Equally animated by the firm intention of putting an end to the crimes and devastations engendered by the traffic in African slaves, of effectively protecting the aboriginal populations of Africa, and of assuring to that vast continent the benefits of peace and civilization;
>
> Wishing to give a fresh sanction to the decisions already taken in the same sense and at different periods by the Powers; to complete the results obtained by them; and to draw up a collection of measures guaranteeing the accomplishment of the work which is the object of their common solicitude…

The "collection of measures" amounted, in effect, to European cooperation in the military conquest of the rest of the continent. The treaty justified the instruments of European colonial rule – "administrative, judicial, religious, and military services," fortified stations in the interior to protect against and repress "manhunts," roads, railways, steamers on waterways supported by fortified stations, telegraph lines, expeditions and flying columns, and restrictions on the import of firearms – as means by which to end a slave trade focused on the Indian Ocean and Red Sea in which European traders no longer played a significant role. The treaty also justified fortified stations as means to protect indigenous people and "raise them to civilization" and to "give aid and protection to commercial undertakings," "watch over their legality," and facilitate "the foundation of permanent centres of cultivation and of commercial establishments." There is no further explicit reference to commerce in the Brussels Act.[31] The treaty took it as given that free trade would play a "civilizing" role. The international community was signaling its support for the idea that whatever Leopold's forces did in Congo, they did in the name of civilization.

Yet international lawyers trying to make sense of the treaties were not completely confident about this assumption. One controversial issue was whether a "civilizing" colonial power, asserting territorial sovereignty over African land on the basis of the positive law the treaties contained, really extinguished all the pre-existing rights of the land's inhabitants, including those considered to be part of "natural" international law. In 1888, members of the Institute of International Law (Institut de Droit International, IDI) debated whether to endorse the proposal that "all regions, whether or not they are inhabited, be regarded as *territorium nullius*." It rejected it by a narrow margin. The IDI concluded that the proposal would give European sovereigns arbitrary powers over private property. True, the lawyers were concerned with the limits of European sovereignty, not the rights of Africans. Nevertheless, this debate revealed a narrow gap in the wall of international law justifying their exploitation of Africa that the signatories of Berlin and Brussels had been building.[32]

That narrow gap was the idea that Africans could not arbitrarily be deprived of their property rights in their land, and it remained open despite Leopold's best efforts to seal it up.[33] When the House of Commons debate forced the British government to take up the issue in 1903, John Westlake, Britain's foremost authority on international law, wrote to the Foreign Office on the issue of whether the ICS was violating the Berlin Act's prohibition against monopolies. Westlake conceded that indigenous Congolese might enjoy some kind of rights that were likely being violated by Leopold's regime. Like France, which operated a similar system of exploitation across the Congo River, the ICS defended its operations by claiming

> the undisputed right which a State has to make a grant of land … or to assume for itself the private property in land within its territory. This being done, the rubber produced becomes private property along with the land which produces it, and its sale by the owner is no more a monopoly than the sale of anything else that one may own.

However, the sheer scale of the Congo State's appropriation of land and produce seemed abnormal: "one feels that the stipulation against monopolies has been infringed in spirit." What was different? "It has occurred to me," said Westlake, "that a sufficient distinction might possibly be found in the rights of the natives, which would have to be bought out or compensated in a State grant of land, but which cannot have been sufficiently considered in giving such rights." The crux of his argument was this:

> [I]t may be said that the conditions under which European sovereignty was acquired [over Congo] precluded any restriction of the freedom of that trade with the natives, at least with the freedom of trade with each native person or tribe, for the rubber produced on land to be fairly deemed to belong to that person or tribe. And the argument would be completed by saying that what has been done has been a mere fizzle for obscuring that issue.

Westlake would not commit himself to an opinion as to how the International Court of Arbitration might rule on such an argument. However, he thought that a claim founded on the spirit of the Berlin Act would likely do better in an international court than in a domestic one. An international court could draw upon convention, which was in turn based on ideas about natural law, to redress Congo's "abnormal" and extreme interpretation of the treaties, because they extinguished indigenous people's natural rights to trade.[34]

This was the idea that would permit Britain to object to the legality of Leopold's "comprehensive scheme of exploitation." If the Berlin Act did anything, it decreed that the Congo basin, as defined, should be a free trade zone. And if the rationale enunciated in both the Berlin and Brussels Acts of protecting and improving the lives of Congo's indigenous people meant anything, surely those rights to trade freely must extend to them, too. When Lansdowne wrote to the other Berlin signatories to solicit their suggestions about how to deal with the Congo, he sought to square the circle of sovereign and indigenous rights:

> His Majesty's Government in no way deny either that the State has the right to partition the State lands among *bona fide* occupants, or that the natives will, as the land is so divided out among *bona fide* occupants, lose their right of roaming over it and collecting the natural fruits which it produces; but His Majesty's Government maintain that until unoccupied land is reduced into individual occupation, and so long as the produce can only be collected by the native, *the native should be free to dispose of that produce as he pleases* [emphasis added].[35]

At a time when Britain, France and Germany were enthusiastically competing for rights of territorial sovereignty over African land, joining older imperial powers such as Portugal and Spain, this was as far as the Foreign Office could go. The unusual circumstance that positive international law – treaties – authorized Leopold's operations in Congo created the opening for Lansdowne to ask "whether the system of trade now prevailing in the Independent State is in harmony with the provisions of the [Berlin] Act." The argument that that system was violating indigenous rights helped Britain to weld the disparate components of the public outcry against the Congo atrocities into a unified front that, based in positive international law, enabled one or more signatories to a treaty to call into question the actions of another.

Confronting the evidence: Leopold's international inquiry

By the time the British Foreign Office released an edited version of Roger Casement's report to the public and to the ministers of foreign affairs of the co-signatories of the Berlin Act in early 1904, apologists for Leopold's Independent Congo State had their defense well rehearsed. Edmund van Eetvelde's conversation with Phipps was just the beginning of the backlash against the British consul. The growing unanimity in Belgium in favor of its king's African ventures seemed to make the attack even bolder than usual.[36] The ICS issued a press communiqué on 15 February 1904 that attacked Casement's report as having been "conceived in the least benevolent spirit" and impugning Casement's findings as "based in large part upon the unverified allegations of natives."[37] A few weeks later, van Eetvelde expanded on these themes, now alleging that Casement's evidence was unreliable because it was based on the testimony of people he called "unreasoning beings" whom Casement had stirred up against the government. In any case, nothing about the administration of Congo was out of line with what Britain itself was doing in the parts of Africa that it controlled.[38]

Buried in the Congo State's counterattack was a key concession: Casement's evidence was sufficiently worrisome that the Congo had decided to call its own inquiry to counter it. The Foreign Office now focused on the process through which the Congo State was proposing to defend its record. In his response to the State's attack on Casement, Lansdowne complimented the ICS on its decision to undertake "a searching and impartial inquiry" into the allegations. He also pushed for measures to strengthen the inquiry's independence. Lansdowne refused Congo's request for the particulars on the basis of Casement's view that it was not safe to disclose his full report. Although Britain was willing to help the proposed inquiry, it would identify Casement's witnesses only on condition that

> the Congo Government ... accept full responsibility for the manner in which the information thus furnished is used [and] communicate to His Majesty's Government the measures which they are prepared to adopt and enforce in order to protect the witnesses, both European and native, from any violence or acts of retaliation on the part of those against whom they have given evidence.[39]

In a second response Lansdowne returned to these themes and went further: Britain would only disclose "all the information [it possessed] respecting the position of affairs in the Congo" to an inquiry "composed of members of well-established reputation and in part, at least, of persons unconnected with the Congo State."[40]

The ICS caviled. Belgium's minister of foreign affairs, Paul de Favereau, told Phipps that the king would never agree to "a commission in which there should be foreign officials," seeing it as "an abdication of sovereign rights," but Leopold surprised them by giving in.[41] The king named a Commission of Inquiry composed of Edmond Janssens, advocate-general of the Brussels Court of Appeal; Giacomo Nisco, president of Congo's court of appeal at Boma; and a Swiss magistrate, Edmond de Schumacher. The Commission began hearing evidence in Congo in November 1904 and delivered its report the next autumn. As Phipps summarized the report, "[i]n spite of the reserved and dignified tone which pervades the whole Report, it contains the most scathing criticisms of the policy pursued in the Congo State." The three jurists disputed Casement's evidence on two points. First, it found that mutilation had been "voluntarily inflicted on living natives" in only two cases. Second, with respect to depopulation, it found only "small-pox and sleeping sickness" to be unequivocal primary causes. "The causes put forward by the missionaries [*sic*] are declared to be difficult to establish, and to be secondary ones," Phipps noted. Otherwise, Leopold's Commission of Inquiry vindicated the British consul and even went further than Casement did in some important respects. On the fundamental legal question of the impact of Congo's economic system on indigenous rights, Phipps ably summarized the Commission of Inquiry report:

> Whilst not contesting the legality of the appropriation by the State of vacant lands, it is pointed out that in practice the State has monopolized the entire fruits of the soil, and has interfered with the whole evolution of native existence. It has failed to give a liberal and wide interpretation to [its own] Laws of 1885 and 1886, which conferred on the native population the free enjoyment of the zones of territory adjoining their huts under the authority of the Chiefs, enabling them to trade in the produce of such zones. This Law has become a dead letter.[42]

The report of the Commission of Inquiry removed the last vestiges of credibility from the ICS' argument that its system was contributing to the "civilization" of Congo's people. Leopold's legalistic defense collapsed in the face of irrefutable evidence. However, it would take another three years before Leopold II turned over his Independent Congo State to the control of democratic Belgium, a move that the king's domestic critics had been advocating since at least 1892. It would take a further four years – until 1913 – before Britain would officially recognize the move, declaring itself to be satisfied

> that the transfer of the Congo to Belgium has been attended by the happiest results, both as regards the condition of the natives in which all the [Berlin] Powers have taken so warm an interest, and as regards the security to be enjoyed by British subjects in the exercise of their commercial and other rights.[43]

Conclusions: human rights advocacy as a practice of persuasion

The British push to reform Leopold's Congo was an international intervention motivated by outrage at the human cost of the Belgian king's rapacity and conducted by diplomatic means. It was mounted on behalf of people whom international politics and international law conspired to deprive of a voice as well as all material means of defending themselves. The success of the Congo reform movement turned on its successful assertion that even those whom international law treated as uncivilized enjoyed some substantive rights. To the Foreign Office, as well as to the international jurists who had articulated their unease with the implications of an international law that governed only the so-called civilized and in effect protected even their most inhumane behavior, what mattered was that the people of the Congo retained some rights to their land and its products. A much broader concern rested on those narrow rights, however: that African subjects of colonial rule must be able to benefit from what civilization was supposed to bring them, including the "free" trade and "free" labor with which Britain justified its own colonial adventures to domestic audiences and co-signatories of international treaties alike.[44] This essay has attended closely to how reformers used the law that was available to them to halt a humanitarian catastrophe. It shows us that Congo reform belongs to the history of human rights, and also suggests a new way to identify links in that history: by tracing efforts to persuade people with power that what was at stake in a situation was no more nor less than the right not to be made a victim. I suggest that this practice of persuasion is a recurring characteristic of human rights advocacy.

In labeling Casement and Morel's effort on behalf of the rights of the Congolese a practice of persuasion, I draw from two insights. The first relates to how advocates must present the evidence they gather. Lora Wildenthal has identified the essence of human rights in the post-1948 period: they are "ahistorical and decontextualized." To assert a human right is to "persuade others to see [the] situation in isolation from its historical context and usual justifications."[45] Yet to succeed in this act of persuasion, the advocate needs to understand that context – and how to get beyond it to undermine those "usual justifications." This is exactly what Casement did by showing the powers that "where a law beneficial to a [Congo] native comes into conflict to-day with the so-called interests of the State, i.e., the rubber or ivory return of a given district, neither law nor native stand a chance."[46]

The second insight concerns the nature of law and, in particular, the task the advocate takes on when making the argument that the law protects people whom those behind that law would rather ignore. Duncan Kennedy once observed that "there is a lot more play in the [legal] system than lawyers and judges pretend there is" – and, by extension, than most historians and students of history and law believe there to be. Kennedy defines legal argument as "the process of *creating* the field of law through restatement rather than rule application."[47] Using legal rights to trade as the opening through which to advocate for humane treatment of Congo's people was just such a process. In providing the evidence to flesh out Westlake's feeling that the law "was being violated in spirit," Casement's report supported an argument to restate the law in a way that could protect the natural rights of Congo's indigenous people.

As these two insights suggest, there is more to the history of human rights than a series of ideas that accumulate to produce our present-day understanding of what people can claim as inherent in their humanity. There is also something more than a history of substantive international or domestic law, whether lawyers accept that law as precedent or consider it irrelevant or inapplicable. Both approaches suggest a teleology that is easily disproven. The history of both human rights and humanitarian intervention is paradoxical: although initiatives on behalf of others are "fragmentary and conditional," our records of them also show their "persistence … over a very long time."[48] Moreover, both of these approaches focus on ideas and so can overlook the actors involved – the people whose rights were violated, the people who took up that cause and framed it in a persuasive way, and the people who finally convinced themselves to press the advantage of the power they possessed for the benefit of others. Thinking about human rights activism as a practice of persuasion focuses on those actors. In thinking about who they were, what they did, and why it worked, we can perhaps begin to see the flaws in our assumptions about how best to intervene on behalf of others.

We noted at the outset, for instance, that human rights nongovernmental organizations (NGOs) still practice Casement's method today. Those who observe that the reality of persecution reveals how far the theory and rhetoric of protection fall short are still considered more credible if they are impartial and secular, as Casement tried to be. They still focus on documenting the gap between those who used to live in a place, and how, and those who live there after genocide, ethnic cleansing, or other crime against humanity has taken place. Advocates must still be able to raise popular outrage and compassion about how people are being treated, and find a way to channel that compassion into a case that those people are being deprived of a specific, often much narrower, right that they should enjoy. To effect change in another place, advocates still rely on the idea that Congo reformers pioneered, that the international community bears some responsibility to police its members' actions even inside those members' own jurisdictions.

Thinking about Congo reform as a practice of persuasion also helps us to recognize its limitations. Casement's own status played a central role in authenticating his report. He was a European, a man, and a trained, professional representative of the diplomatic service of Europe's foremost power. Because of his status, it was harder for the ICS' apologists to dismiss the evidence he gathered and presented as the exaggerations of a troublemaker.[49] Status, and the perception that the fact-finder must be impartial (and international) to be believed, also made it possible for jurists on the Commission of Inquiry called by Leopold himself to uphold Casement's evidence.

The status of the evidence-gatherer and advocate still matters, more than a century after Casement's death. The international community still finds it too easy to dismiss survivors' testimony as the word of the "unreasoning beings" that Belgian Baron Edmund van Eetvelde thought them to be. The International Criminal Court transgresses this expectation by giving victims their day in court. It is also important to be aware of prejudices like the "standard of civilization." In recent years, African leaders in the dock have claimed that the Court is still imposing that "standard of civilization" on them long after the formal colonialism of the Berlin and Brussels Act has ended. The practice of persuasion must rely on, interact with, and sometimes challenge those prejudices. Persuasion is at the center of human rights advocacy. It is vital to capture crucial aspects of how the process works so that advocates can continue to persuade in even the most challenging environments and times.

Notes

1 Steven L. B. Jensen and Roland Burke, "From the Normative to the Transnational: Methods in the Study of Human Rights History," in Bård-Anders Andreassen, Hans-Otto Sano, and Siobhán McInerny-Langford (eds.) *Research Methods in Human Rights: A Handbook*, Cheltenham, MA: Edward Elgar, 2017, p. 126.

2 Roger D. Casement, "The Congo Report," in Séamas Ó Síocháin and Michael O'Sullivan (eds.) *The Eyes of Another Race: Roger Casement's Congo Report and 1903 Diary*, Dublin: University College Dublin Press, 2003, pp. 49–50. I am indebted to Courtland Robinson for connecting Casement's methodology to the current practice of population epidemiology.

3 Lynn Hunt, *Inventing Human Rights: A History*, New York: Norton, 2007; Hunt, "Response to Viewpoint: The Long and the Short of the History of Human Rights," *Past & Present*, 2016, no. 233, 329.

4 Samuel Moyn, *The Last Utopia: Human Rights in History* (Cambridge, MA: Belknap Press at Harvard University Press, 2010, and Samuel Moyn, *Human Rights and the Uses of History*, London: Verso, 2014.

5 "General Act of the Brussels Conference relative to the African Slave Trade, etc. Signed at Brussels, 2 July 1890," reproduced in Sir Edward Hertslet et al., *The Map of Africa by Treaty*,

2nd rev. ed., London: HMSO, 1896, p. 49 (Preamble). The term "Scramble" was coined by a columnist for *The Times* of London.

6 The story of Leopold's Congo, and of the public outrage and action it evoked in Britain, has been told many times. See, in particular, Adam Hochschild, *King Leopold's Ghost: A Story of Greed, Terror, and Heroism in Colonial Africa*, Boston: Houghton Mifflin, 1998; Wm. Roger Louis and Jean Stengers, *E. D. Morel's History of the Congo Reform Movement*, Oxford: Clarendon, 1968; and Dean Pavlakis, *British Humanitarianism and the Congo Reform Movement, 1896–1913*, London and New York: Routledge, 2016.

7 The National Archives (London), Foreign Office (TNA FO) 403/338, Casement to Secretary of State (Lansdowne), 15–16 September 1903, "No. 34, Africa."

8 Casement, "The Congo Report," pp. 49–50.

9 TNA FO 403/351, Casement to Lansdowne, 19 January 1904. On Bula Matari, which means "he who crushes rocks," as a local nickname for the Congo's colonial administration see for instance Crawford Young, "Constructing Bula Matari," in Crawford Young, *The African Colonial State in Comparative Perspective*, New Haven, CT: Yale University Press, 1994, pp. 77–140.

10 Casement, "Report," p. 84.

11 Séamas Ó Síocháin and Michael O'Sullivan, "Introduction," in Ó Síocháin and O'Sullivan, *The Eyes of Another Race*, p. 8.

12 Casement, "Report," pp. 50, 63.

13 Joseph Conrad's *Heart of Darkness* was first published in serial form in 1899 and as a book in 1902.

14 Casement, "Report," pp. 90, 64.

15 Casement, "Report," pp. 62–3.

16 Casement, "Report," p. 52.

17 Casement, "Report," pp. 91–2.

18 Casement, "Report," p. 92.

19 Casement, "Report," pp. 91–2.

20 TNA FO 403/338, Casement to Farnall, 5 August 1903. On some of the "dreadful excesses" to which Casement refers, and how both the Congo State and Britain played them down in the 1890s, see Mairi S. MacDonald, "Lord Vivian's Tears: The Moral Hazards of Humanitarian Intervention," in Fabian Klose (ed.) *The Emergence of Humanitarian Intervention: Ideas and Practice from the Nineteenth Century to the Present*, Cambridge, UK: Cambridge University Press, 2016, pp. 121–41.

21 Herbert Samuel, *House of Commons Debates*, 20 May 1903, vol. 122, cols. 1289–332.

22 TNA FO 403/338, Lansdowne to Monson et al., 8 August 1903.

23 Many of the allegations were drawn from a pamphlet published by E. D. Morel called "The British Case Against the Congo." On British antislavery, see Richard Huzzey, *Freedom Burning: Anti-Slavery and Empire in Victorian Britain*, Ithaca, NY: Cornell University Press, 2012, and Suzanne Miers, *Britain and the Ending of the Slave Trade*, London: Longman, 1975.

24 On Britain's role in bringing about the Brussels Conference, see MacDonald, "Lord Vivian's Tears."

25 TNA FO 443/351, Phipps to Lansdowne, "No. 7, Africa Confidential," 5 February 1904.

26 TNA FO 443/351, Phipps to Lansdowne, "No. 7, Africa Confidential," 5 February 1904.

27 Wole Soyinka, 15 May 1994, quoted in Dakas C. J. Dakas, "The Role of International Law in the Colonization of Africa: A Review in Light of Recent Calls for Re-Colonization," *African Yearbook of International Law*, 1999, vol. 7, 105.

28 Matthew Craven, "Between Law and History: The Berlin Conference of 1884–1885 and the Logic of Free Trade," *London Review of International Law*, 2015, vol. 3, no. 1, 32; Wm. Roger Louis, "The Berlin Congo Conference and the (non-)Partition of Africa, 1884–1885," in Wm. Roger Louis, *Ends of British Imperialism: The Scramble for Empire, Suez and Decolonization*, London: I. B. Tauris, 2006, pp. 75–126.

29 Compare these two memoranda: TNA FO 403/351, Villiers memorandum, 6 June 1904 and FO 403/338, Atkinson memorandum, 28 December 1903.

30 "General Act of the Conference of Berlin, relative to the Development of Trade and Civilization in Africa; the free Navigation of the Rivers Congo, Niger, &c.; the Suppression of the Slave Trade by Sea and Land; the occupation of Territory on the African Coasts, &c. Signed

at Berlin, 26 February 1885," reproduced in Hertslet et al., *The Map of Africa by Treaty*, pp. 468–87, the "Berlin Act," Articles I, V, X, and VI.

31 "General Act of the Brussels Conference relative to the African Slave Trade, etc. Signed at Brussels, 2 July 1890," reproduced in Sir Edward Hertslet et al., *The Map of Africa by Treaty*, pp. 48–87; preamble at 49.

32 Martti Koskenniemi, *The Gentle Civilizer of Nations: The Rise and Fall of International Law, 1870–1960*, Cambridge, UK: Cambridge University Press, 2002, 137–40; Andrew Fitzmaurice, "Liberalism and Empire in Nineteenth-Century International Law," *American Historical Review*, 2012, vol. 117, no. 1, 130–3; Fitzmaurice, *Sovereignty, Property and Empire, 1500–1800*, Cambridge, UK: Cambridge University Press, 2015, pp. 271–300.

33 Members of the IDI continued to debate the issues in journals, notably the *Revue de Droit International et de legislation comparée* and the *Annuaire de l'Institut de droit international.* French jurist Charles Salomon stated the case at length in *L'Occupation des terres sans maîtres: Étude de droit international*, Paris: A. Giard, 1889. The debate erupted in 1892 in Brussels when Leopold II appropriated most of Congo's land as the ICS' private domain. The king won the political contest, but failed to extinguish the legal objection.

34 TNA FO 403/338, Westlake to Foreign Office, 26 June 1903.

35 TNA FO 403/338, Lansdowne to Monson et al., 8 August 1903.

36 For instance, Phipps noted a July 1903 debate about Congo in Belgium's parliament, where in response to growing criticism from abroad "the country has rallied round the Sovereign" and his Congo policy. TNA FO 403/338, Phipps to Lansdowne, 4 July 1903.

37 TNA FO 403/351, Phipps to Lansdowne, 15 February 1904.

38 TNA FO 403/351, Phipps to Lansdowne, 5 February 1903; "Notes on the Report of Mr. Casement, Consul of His Britannic Majesty, of the 11 December 1903," 12 March 1904.

39 TNA FO 403/351, Lansdowne to Phipps, "No. 52 Africa," 19 April 1904.

40 TNA FO 403/351, Lansdowne to Phipps, "No. 72 Africa," 6 June 1904.

41 TNA FO 403/351, Phipps to Lansdowne, "No. 68 Africa," 11 June 1904.

42 *Bulletin officiel de l'État Indépendant du Congo*, no. 9–10, 1905, "Rapport au Roi-Souverain." Online. Available atwww.droitcongolais.info/files/rapport-d-enquete-Leopold-II-l-EIC-et-le-genocide.pdf (accessed 5 January 2019); TNA FO 403/364, Phipps to Lansdowne, "No. 102 Africa," 7 November 1905.

43 TNA FO 403/443, Sir Edward Grey to Count de Lalaing, 27 June 1913.

44 On the connections among free trade, free labor, and colonial rule, see Huzzey, *Freedom Burning.* On the centrality of antislavery to Britain's self-image as a just imperial power, see Christopher Leslie Brown, *Moral Capital: Foundations of British Abolitionism*, Chapel Hill: University of North Carolina Press, 2006.

45 Lora Wildenthal, "Rudolf Laun and the Human Rights of Germans in Occupied and Early West Germany," in Stefan-Ludwig Hoffmann (ed.) *Human Rights in the Twentieth Century*, Cambridge, UK: Cambridge University Press, 2011, p. 125.

46 TNA FO 403/304, Casement to Gosselin, 30 September 1900.

47 Duncan Kennedy, "Are Lawyers Really Necessary?" *Barrister*, 1987, vol. 14, no. 4, 11–16, 37. Online. Available at www.duncankennedy.net/documents/Photo%20articles/Are%20lawyers%20really%20necessary.pdf (accessed 5 January 2019); Duncan Kennedy, "Freedom and Constraint in Adjudication: A Critical Phenomenology," in James Boyle (ed.) *Critical Legal Studies*, New York: New York University Press, 1992, p. 562.

48 Michael Geyer, "Humanitarianism and Human Rights: A Troubled Rapport," in Klose, *The Emergence of Humanitarian Intervention*, p. 34.

49 The British government systematically undermined Casement's status in order to influence public opinion to permit him to be hanged as a traitor in 1916. See Séamas Ó Síocháin, *Roger Casement: Imperialist, Rebel, Revolutionary*, Dublin: Lilliput, 2008.

5

THE RED CROSS AND THE LAWS OF WAR, 1863–1949

International rights activism before human rights

Kimberly A. Lowe

Is the history of international humanitarian law and aid to war victims part of the history of human rights? The purpose of this essay is to explain how and why the Red Cross and Red Crescent movement developed a radical new stance towards the rights of war victims, which combined the language of humanitarianism with the language of human rights. I argue that in 1921 the Red Cross/Red Crescent abandoned its previous understanding that war victims' rights were limited and contingent, and adopted the belief that these rights were equal, universal, and inalienable. The movement declared that combatant and noncombatant war victims possessed equal rights to medical care and humane conditions of incarceration. In doing so, they rejected the long-standing legal distinction between combatant wounded soldiers and prisoners of war (POWs), and noncombatant civilian internees and refugees. The movement also declared that the rights of war victims applied universally to all armed conflicts, both international and internal (e.g. civil wars, revolutions, rebellions). Finally, these rights were guaranteed by a moral code that transcended reciprocal agreements among states, and therefore must be respected even if the enemy failed to abide by the laws of war. After declaring these rights, the movement sought to secure them through the direct provision of aid to victims of armed conflict and indirect revision of international humanitarian law. Many of these efforts failed, but in 1949 four greatly expanded Geneva Conventions provided a legal basis for the rights of both civilians and victims of non-international armed conflicts for the first time.

Scholars are divided over whether humanitarianism and human rights belong to a shared history of efforts to protect the human person or are conceptually and historically distinct. International humanitarian law, also known as the laws of war or the law of armed conflict (*jus in bello*[1]), seeks to outline standards of "humane conduct" during war, including prohibiting attacks on noncombatants and requiring medical aid to wounded enemy soldiers and POWs. The international Red Cross and Red Crescent movement was founded to alleviate the suffering created by war by providing food and medical care to wounded soldiers and lobbying for protections under international law. Do these efforts to provide aid to those in need have any relationship to the work of human rights activists? In *The Last Utopia*, Samuel Moyn argues that humanitarianism, with its focus on religious sentiment and support for the hierarchical "civilizing mission" of European empires, was a historical discourse distinct from human rights, which he defines as grass-roots advocacy for the protection of individuals against the state.[2] The International Committee of the Red Cross (hereafter ICRC) itself stated in the 1970s that although the concepts of humanitarianism and human rights share a common goal of protecting the human person, they are legally and historically distinct.[3] Scholars such as Jan Eckel, Philippe Ryfman, Davide Rodogno, and Michael Barnett similarly argue that because of the conceptual divide between voluntary moral action and universal rights claims, these histories are separate.[4]

Other scholars, such as Paul Gordon Lauren, David Forsythe, Gary Bass, Brendan Simms, Amanda Moniz, Ian Tyrell, Bruno Cabanes, Stephen Hopgood, and Lasse Heerten argue that the eighteenth- and nineteenth-century humanitarian movements made an important impact on human rights activists during the twentieth century.[5] For these authors, the discourses of humanitarianism and human rights overlapped and intersected. During the 1960s, the early leaders of the London-based human rights organization Amnesty International identified the Red Cross as a model for their own activism.[6] In 1968, the United Nations Conference on Human Rights in Tehran explicitly connected human rights to international humanitarian law.[7] That same year, activists concerned with the Biafran War used the language of humanitarianism, human rights, self-determination, and genocide to advocate on behalf of Biafrans.[8] From the 1980s onward, the New York-based non-governmental organization Human Rights Watch justified its activism through the principles of international humanitarian law.[9] Further research is needed to develop a comprehensive picture of how, when, and why activists chose to draw upon humanitarianism, human rights, or both discourses simultaneously.

Not all humanitarian activities relied on a discourse of rights, but those of the Red Cross/ Red Crescent did. The history of this movement and its efforts to revise the law of armed conflict provides an opportunity to study the interaction among the codification of international positive law by sovereign states, a transnational social movement, and a discourse of universal rights, during a period of time when the language of humanitarianism had more salience than the language of human rights (namely, before the 1970s or even 1948).

From the second half of the nineteenth century to the present, the Geneva Convention (1864, revised in 1906, 1929, and 1949) and Hague Convention (1899, revised in 1907) comprised one of the most extensive bodies of positive international law outlining constraints on state behavior. The Geneva and Hague Conventions are noteworthy not only for their content, but also for their widespread ratification. Accepting the conventions was a prestigious symbol of membership in the exclusive "international society of civilized states," and most states ratified them sooner or later.[10] The conventions gave combatant victims of war – wounded soldiers and POWs – international rights to medical care and humane conditions of incarceration. The Hague Convention was built on a fundamental distinction between combatants and noncombatants, designed to ensure that noncombatants did not become victims of war. Noncombatants were not considered legitimate military targets, and military occupation authorities were prohibited from exploiting civilian populations under their control.

Sovereign states were the only entities with the power to make international humanitarian law, but the Red Cross and Red Crescent movement has helped develop and implement the Geneva Convention since the former's inception in 1863. The movement consists of three different parts, each of which has had different forms of influence vis-à-vis sovereign states. One part is the ICRC, a small private organization founded in 1863 and based in Geneva, Switzerland. It utilized private diplomatic contacts and the patronage of the Swiss government to influence intergovernmental revisions of the Geneva Convention. The second part comprises the various national Red Cross and Red

Crescent societies. The national societies, limited to one official relief organization per country, have had a broad-based membership, the patronage of their respective national governments, and domestic prestige. During World War I the membership of these societies reached into the millions. This made the Red Cross and Red Crescent the largest global humanitarian network in existence, both during World War I and into the present. The third part is a federation, which sought to facilitate cooperation among the national societies. The federation was founded in 1919 as the League of Red Cross Societies, and renamed the International Federation of Red Cross and Red Crescent Societies in 1991. The guiding principles of the movement are decided at international conferences that include delegates from each national society, the ICRC, governments party to the Geneva Convention, and other private organizations invited to participate.

This essay focuses on the development of the Red Cross/Red Crescent and international humanitarian law from 1863 to 1949. Both the positive law of armed conflict and the movement grew exponentially between 1863 and 1921. However, during this period governments considered the rights of war victims to be limited and contingent on contractual agreements among sovereign states – not natural or universal, transcending the sovereignty of the state. The national Red Cross and Red Crescent societies, far from fighting for a more inclusive definition of war victims' rights, embraced the policy of their respective governments. The rights of wounded combatants and POWs, and the prohibition on violence against civilians, were legally confined to international wars between states party to the convention. Only so-called "civilized" nations were permitted to ratify the conventions. Victims of civil wars, revolutions, colonial wars, or other internal conflicts had no rights under the laws of war. Governments party to the conventions also interpreted these agreements as contingent on the behavior of the enemy. If the enemy violated the laws of war, states considered violent reprisals against wounded soldiers, POWs, or civilians to be legally justified. During World War I this justification fueled a brutal cycle of reciprocal violence against vulnerable populations.

After World War I, the Red Cross/Red Crescent movement rejected its previous understanding of war victims' rights as limited and contingent. The Tenth International Conference of the Red Cross in 1921 stated in clear terms that combatant and civilian victims of war, in international and internal conflicts, possessed equal, inalienable, and universal rights. Consistent with their traditions of humanitarian aid, the movement focused on two rights: the right to medical care and the right to humane conditions of incarceration. They did not address other political, civil, social, or economic rights that we might consider human rights today. Finally, the 1921 conference called on each national society to establish autonomy from their respective government. Independence was a crucial component of the planned mechanism to safeguard victims' rights from violations by the state. The national societies were to use their broad-based membership to exert public pressure on domestic governments to respect these newly proclaimed rights of soldiers, civilians, political prisoners, and victims of internal conflicts.

From 1921 to 1939, the ICRC sought to implement these new principles through legal revisions to the law of armed conflict and extra-legal aid to political prisoners. Their efforts failed, however, because independence did not materialize. The Red Cross and Red Crescent societies did not mobilize to create public pressure on national governments to respect the rights of war victims or revise international law. Only in 1949 – after a majority of continental European populations had experienced brutal occupation by the Third Reich – would the laws of war be revised in keeping with the Red Cross and Red Crescent's resolutions of 1921.

Absolute obedience to the state, 1863–1914

During the second half of the nineteenth century, two developments regarding the rights of war victims overlapped. First, governments codified the customary practices of Western warfare into positive law through the Geneva Convention of 1864 and Hague Convention of 1899. In doing so, states voluntarily accepted international obligations to provide medical care for wounded friendly and enemy soldiers and humane conditions of captivity for POWs. Second, the Red Cross movement began in 1863, with the purpose of creating voluntary societies devoted to the alleviation of wartime suffering through the care of wounded soldiers. The rhetoric accompanying both these developments made reference to a universal moral duty to address the needs of strangers, and to a belief in common humanity. Yet in reality the codification of the laws of war and growth of the Red Cross movement established that the rights of combatants and noncombatants in war were limited in scope and contingent on the reciprocal agreements of governments in "civilized" nations.

European governments' decision to establish the Geneva and Hague Conventions was heavily influenced by their national publics' growing concern over the treatment of citizen-soldiers. Over the course of the nineteenth century, many continental European nations revised their laws regarding military conscription, creating an expanded obligation for military service that in some cases included all male citizens. At the same time, advances in communication technologies, such as the telegraph, allowed news from the battle front to be immediately conveyed to soldiers' families at home. During the Crimean War (1853–6) reports of unsanitary medical conditions in both the British and French armies, conveyed by telegraph, produced a public outcry. Governments now faced the prospect that soldiers' mistreatment could threaten domestic stability and undermine support for an ongoing war effort.

The idea that governments had a duty to care for their soldiers was not new, but only in the nineteenth century did a broad cross-section of the European and North American population begin to pressure their respective governments to adopt the policy. Reformers in the eighteenth century had sought government provision of medical care to enemy soldiers, but these proposals never gained traction with established authorities. In the 1850s, a growing transnational coalition of prominent individuals publicly argued that men who were forced to fight for the state had a right to humane treatment from that state. Dr. Jean-Charles Chenu, a prominent military surgeon who had directed the French military medical operations during the Crimean War, described the issue this way: "[T]he whole question, I believe, is in the assessment of the duties of a government and the rights of the soldier."[11] Dr. Chenu, the British nurse Florence Nightingale, and Swiss philanthropist Henry Dunant (whose *A Memory of Solferino* is often credited with originating the idea of the Red Cross) were just three of many individuals calling for the improvement of military medical services and neutralization of medical personnel.[12] European governments had to confront the broad-based conviction among their own citizens that soldiers forced to fight in defense of the state had a right to medical care from their governments. The issue was domestic: the duty of a government to treat its own citizens humanely.

The Geneva and Hague Conventions were an international effort by governments to address this domestic conviction. An international convention would provide reciprocal assurances that one's own soldiers would not be mistreated by the enemy. In 1864, at the invitation of the Swiss Federal Council, 16 European states sent delegates to a conference that concluded with the signing of the Convention for the Amelioration of the Condition of the Wounded in Armies in the Field (known as the Geneva Convention). The 57 states that eventually ratified the convention bound themselves to respect the following principles during wartime: (1) relief to the wounded would be provided without any distinction as to nationality; (2) the neutrality of medical personnel and establishments would be respected at all times; and (3) a red cross on a white background would be used by all belligerents to indicate the noncombatant status of medical personnel, ambulances, and hospitals. In 1899, at the proposal of Russian Tsar Nicholas II, 26 state delegates from Europe, the United States, and Mexico met in The Hague, Netherlands to codify customs governing the conduct of war. Section I, Chapter II of the resulting Hague Convention included 20 articles defining the humane treatment of POWs. These included food, living quarters, and clothing commensurate with the treatment of the captor governments' troops, as well as the ability to correspond with the outside world and receive charitable assistance from relief societies. A fundamental principle of the Hague Convention was a distinction between combatants and noncombatants; the latter were not considered legitimate military targets. Section III outlined the duties of a military authority in occupied enemy territory, including prohibiting forced civilian labor or confiscation of civilians' private property.

By ratifying the Geneva and Hague Conventions, a state was agreeing to restrict wartime aggression towards enemy medical personnel, wounded soldiers, POWs, and civilians. However, these restrictions were not universal. Both the restrictions and protections applied only to combatants and noncombatants in signatory states. Like all other international legal agreements at this time, only governments belonging to the "international society of civilized states" were permitted to sign the conventions. European states, who dominated this exclusive club, regularly used this distinction to further their own imperial incursions, much to the displeasure of the Ottoman Empire, Japan, and other non-Western states. The choice of the red cross as the mark of neutrality underscored the assumed relationship between civilization and Christendom. The red crescent was provisionally accepted as a marker only after extensive protest from the Ottoman Empire during the Russo-Turkish War (1877–8). After fighting began, the Russian Tsar Alexander II agreed to provisionally recognize the neutrality of personnel bearing the emblem of the Ottoman Red Crescent Society, if the Ottoman army reciprocated in kind. This decision was not without controversy, however, and only in 1929 did the Geneva Convention recognize the red crescent as an official emblem.[13]

Soldiers' rights to medical care and humane conditions of incarceration, and civilians' status as noncombatants, were also not absolute. While there was a common expectation that state parties would apply the conventions in "good faith," the agreements themselves did not state whether or not these restrictions applied at all times. The result is that signatory states interpreted their adherence to the laws of war as contingent on contextual factors, namely the behavior of the enemy or the needs of the armed forces to achieve their military objectives. For example, the United States, France, and Great Britain all interpreted the Geneva and Hague Conventions as binding only on the condition of reciprocity. If the enemy failed to abide by the conventions, these states considered themselves legally justified in resorting to brutal reprisals against enemy soldiers and civilians.[14] Jurists in Germany took contingency one step further, arguing that actions taken for reasons of military necessity did not constitute violations of the laws of war.[15]

Signatory states agreed that certain conditions created a legal justification for violent acts otherwise condemned by the laws of war, even if they did not agree on what those conditions were.

The Red Cross/Red Crescent, far from arguing that soldiers' rights applied in all circumstances, supported national governments' interpretation of the law of armed conflict. As the movement grew in strength, increasing official ties to the government, professionalization, and the deepening of gender hierarchy resulted in a definition of war victims' rights as limited and contingent. The rapid growth of the Red Cross/Red Crescent movement from 1863 to 1914 should not be interpreted as a public embrace of moral duty but rather of growing state loyalty.

Two founders of the Red Cross, Louis Appia and Gustave Moynier, wrote in 1867 of a transcendent "universal duty imposed by Christian civilization on all peoples" to aid wounded soldiers. Their original goal was not only to humanize the conduct of war, but also contribute to the "disarmament of nations" by sensitizing domestic publics to the horrors of the battlefield.[16] The language of universal duty was correlated with a voluntary ideal focused on Christian charity and feminine virtue as a force for peace. Wealthy and aristocratic women served as early patrons and founders of many national societies, while middle-class women formed the volunteer backbone of the national societies' membership.

At the same time, most governments refused to officially recognize the national societies in the first two decades of their existence. Proponents of medical care for wounded soldiers such as Chenu and Nightingale argued that volunteers would only hinder the state's official medical care. The argument against voluntary aid gained even more salience after the Franco-Prussian War (1870–1). The activities of voluntary societies created disorder for the French military, while Prussian volunteers were placed under the strict control of army officers. In the wake of France's humiliating defeat, the Red Cross movement began a decisive shift away from voluntarism and towards subservience to the sovereign state.[17]

By the 1880s, the Red Cross/Red Crescent had abandoned the language of universal duty, and any expectation that voluntary humanitarian aid to wounded soldiers would lead to fewer wars. At its 1884 international conference, the movement officially endorsed the principle of "sympathy and deference towards the military authority in times of peace; absolute obedience in times of war."[18] In return for this loyalty, the state offered legal recognition and special privileges. By the turn of the twentieth century, the national societies had become official auxiliaries to armies of their states, valued for their ability to increase the patriotic engagement of civilians during war. The revised Geneva Convention of 1906 gave them official status under international law for the first time.

Agreements with national militaries also promoted professionalization over voluntary charity. In keeping with existing gender hierarchies that defined the armed forces as a male domain, men took control over female volunteers, who were relegated to supporting roles. In the American Red Cross, for example, an increasingly official relationship with the US government from 1905 onward resulted in the transfer of leadership from women to men.[19] The leadership of the ICRC was also entirely male, until Marguerite Frick-Cramer became the first female member in 1918. Women's charitable and professional energies were secured in a consolidating hierarchy whose apex was male. Deeper official ties, professionalization, and predominantly male leadership produced a twentieth-century movement with both broad public influence and an absolute commitment to serving the needs of the state.

The movement's understanding of soldiers' rights as limited and contingent and of fealty to state power can be seen most clearly in its rejection of any attempt to grant rights to victims of civil wars, be they combatants or noncombatants. In 1863, the five male founders of the Red Cross decided "first and foremost ... no action should be contemplated during civil wars."[20] They correctly discerned that governments would view this as unwarranted interference in the internal affairs of a sovereign state. For the first 50 years of the movement's existence, no attempt was made to contest the idea that only soldiers in international wars between "civilized" states had a right to medical care or humane conditions of incarceration.

No debate over the issue would take place until 1912, at the Ninth International Conference of the Red Cross in Washington, DC. Both the American and Cuban Red Cross societies submitted reports arguing for the creation of a new international convention governing civil wars. This would ensure that the neutrality of medical personnel was respected and that aid would be distributed on an impartial basis, irrespective of the political divisions within the country at war.[21]

The American and Cuban reports were informed by three arguments about civil wars. First, these reports reflected the Cuban and American argument that the Cuban war of independence against Spain (1895–8) had been a legitimate struggle for national liberation.[22] Second, the American delegate argued that the American Civil War (1861–5) served as a historic precedent for detaching the rights of wounded combatants to medical relief from the recognition of a rebel group as a legitimate, sovereign power. During the American Civil War, US president Abraham Lincoln's declaration of a blockade of Confederate ports in April 1861 resulted in a de facto recognition of belligerent status for the Confederacy, but no recognition of sovereignty.[23] This meant that Confederate soldiers were treated as official POWs with rights under the laws of war. Even Union Army General William T. Sherman, infamous for his reprisal violence in Georgia and the Carolinas, respected this status.[24] The conclusion of the American Red Cross in 1912 was that soldiers in a domestic insurrection could still be granted rights under the laws of war. Third, the American delegate argued that there was a "universal duty" to alleviate suffering that was determined by a shared humanity, not by legal distinctions between official combatants and rebels.[25]

In 1912, the other delegates vehemently rejected these arguments. In their view, providing food or medical aid to rebels was synonymous with recognizing them as a legitimate government. Aid to rebels was therefore treason. The delegate of the Russian Empire declared that his government could not consider insurgents or revolutionaries as anything but "criminals," and therefore

> all offer of services, direct or indirect from the Red Cross societies to insurgents or revolutionaries could not be considered as anything but a violation of friendly relations, as an "unfriendly act," tending to encourage and to foment rebellion in a country.

Only the delegate from Uruguay was prepared to offer his "complete, enthusiastic, radical" support of their proposals.[26] All others agreed that aid to civilian and combatant victims in civil wars could never be separated from the sovereign status of the conflicting parties. They further agreed that the Red Cross/Red Crescent should do nothing unless their governments gave official recognition to civil wars under the laws of war (a legal revision they deemed highly unlikely). In short, for both signatory states and the majority of Red Cross and Red Crescent delegates, the rights of combatants and noncombatants were the result of positive legal agreements between sovereign powers, not a natural or universal moral code. These same rights were limited and contingent, reserved for populations of "civilized states" engaged in international wars.

Violence against wounded soldiers, POWs, and civilians, 1914–21

From 1914 to 1918, World War I produced both unprecedented outpourings of humanitarian aid and unprecedented reprisal violence against vulnerable populations that alarmed neutral states and the ICRC. In all the belligerent countries, membership in the Red Cross and Red Crescent societies increased, as did the scope of their activities in service to the national war effort. The national societies, in partnership with their governments, initiated aid campaigns of unprecedented size and scope. Yet aid was always directed in keeping with the military priorities of the government. For example, when news reached the British and French governments that their captured soldiers were starving in camps in Germany and Austria-Hungary, they began a massive operation to send food parcels to these men. Parcels were distributed along strictly national lines. Governments realized that the starvation of their citizen-soldiers would damage domestic support for the war effort. By 1916, French, British, and Belgian prisoners were living off of food parcels they received from their home governments. POWs of those nationalities that did not receive regular parcels from their home governments, such as Italians and Romanians, died of malnutrition.[27] The American Red Cross introduced a unique set of programs designed to aid foreign civilians – the first of their kind. At the same time, these activities were designed to further US foreign policy. The sites of American Red Cross operations were carefully planned to align with US president Woodrow Wilson's strategic objective of fostering peace in the Allied nations of Europe.[28]

In keeping with prewar interpretations of the Geneva and Hague conventions as contingent on reciprocity or military necessity, wounded soldiers, POWs, and civilians all suffered from wartime violence. Quickly setting aside the Hague Convention's fundamental principle that noncombatants were not a legitimate target of hostilities, all belligerents interned foreign civilians as a security measure. For some civilians, this internment lasted a full four years, in conditions less sanitary than those of POW camps. Real and imagined mistreatment of POWs became a source of outrage for national publics and belligerent governments, and fueled a dangerous cycle of reciprocal violence.[29] POWs in the hands of both the Allied and Central Powers faced inadequate food and lodging that led to death from malnutrition and disease, forced labor in dangerous occupations such as mine removal on the front lines, and other violations of the Hague Convention. Whether intentional or the result of inadequate resources, mistreatment of POWs led to reciprocal mistreatment. Wounded and imprisoned soldiers suffered physical harm from both official reprisals and spontaneous acts of hostility from British, French, and German Red Cross volunteers.[30] Whether or not these were violations of the laws of war depended on belligerents' differing interpretations of which contextual factors provided legal justification for acts that were otherwise prohibited by the Geneva and Hague Conventions. On this point the belligerents did not agree, which fueled accusations of wartime atrocities against both the Allied and Central Powers.[31]

The ICRC considered this violence against wounded soldiers, POWs, and civilians a violation of at least the principles of "humane conduct" in war, if not the law itself. The ease and frequency with which belligerents justified violence in the name of reprisals alarmed the ICRC and neutral states, such as the Vatican. Neutral states and the ICRC created an ad hoc system of camp inspections and bilateral agreements for prisoner exchanges in the hopes of ending the cycle of reprisals. The war ended, however, before these could make a substantial impact. ICRC delegates were also painfully aware that civilians, once interned, had even fewer legal protections than POWs. The ICRC sought to monitor the welfare of these civilian internees through its International Prisoners of War Agency. However, its efforts to collect information about interned civilians to share with family members and to distribute aid to internees were entirely dependent on the voluntary cooperation of the captor authorities.[32]

Violence against wounded soldiers, POWs and civilians did not end in 1918. Rather, it spread through conflicts that historians Peter Gatrell and Robert Gerwarth have termed the "wars after the war."[33] The dissolution of the Russian, Austro-Hungarian, Ottoman, and German empires led to a series of revolutions, civil wars, border disputes, and inter-ethnic conflicts. From 1918 to 1923, these wars killed at least 4 million people and created many more refugees and expellees throughout Central and Eastern Europe, Central Asia, the Balkans and the Middle East. The national Red Cross and Red Crescent societies, once loyal servants to empires that were now defunct, found themselves ill-equipped to address the suffering caused by these conflicts. Communist revolutionaries and nationalist independence fighters viewed the national societies with suspicion, making it impossible for societies' members to deliver aid to all parties in the conflict. After the Bolsheviks took power in Russia, they violently dissolved the Russian Red Cross, confiscated its property, arrested its leaders, and rebuilt the society from the ground up as an instrument of the revolutionary government.[34]

The experiences of World War I and "wars after the war" prompted the Red Cross and Red Crescent movement to reevaluate its principles concerning the limited and contingent rights of war victims and subservience to the state. Violent reprisals against POWs and wounded soldiers demonstrated the need to declare that prohibitions against mistreatment were binding at all times, irrespective of the behavior of the enemy. The large number of civilians interned without adequate food or medical care highlighted that the Hague's blanket prohibition on violence against noncombatants was out of step with the realities of modern war. The victims of revolutions and civil wars highlighted the need to establish protections for victims of internal conflicts. Finally, the dissolution of national societies revealed that reliance on government patronage could seriously impair the ability of the movement to provide humanitarian assistance.

The superior laws of humanity, 1921

The ICRC began planning for major changes in the movement at least by 1918, but the Paris Peace Conference and continued unrest in Central/Eastern Europe caused repeated delays. It was not until 1921 that the Tenth International Conference of the Red Cross met in Geneva. The delegates at the 1921 conference passed a series of resolutions declaring that civilian victims of war possessed rights equal to those of wounded soldiers and POWs. These rights were guaranteed by the immutable moral principles of humanity, not reciprocal agreements between states. They also applied to all armed conflicts: civil war, revolution, and insurrection as well as international conflicts. For the first time, the Red Cross and Red Crescent movement formally declared that the rights to medical care and humane conditions of captivity were universal, equal, and inalienable. This dramatic break with previous policies is worthy of a detailed analysis.

The 1921 resolutions asserted that all prisoners, whether combatant or civilian, had equal rights during wartime. The delegates based their assertion on the belief that the prisoner "has the right to the respect due to every human being," and that it is the responsibility of both the home state and captor state to protect that right.[35] Wartime prisoners had been found guilty of no crime, deserved no punishment, and could only be held in order to weaken the combat power of the enemy state. Therefore, violent reprisals against POWs, mass deportations of civilians, and taking hostages from the civilian population should be expressly forbidden under all circumstances. If military necessity required the internment of certain civilians, they were to be treated at least as humanely as POWs. To secure these rights for POWs, deportees, evacuees, and refugees, the delegates resolved that governments should modify the Hague Convention as soon as possible.

The delegates further declared that the rights of war victims applied universally to all conflicts: "all victims of civil war or any [revolutionary disturbance], without exception, have the right to be rescued according to the general principles of the Red Cross."[36] They also passed a resolution stating that political prisoners must be treated according to the principles of the Hague Convention. Giovanni Ciraolo, the president of the Italian Red Cross, wrote that neutral aid

> must be extended to all human conflicts, because a man who suffers or is in peril has the right to be rescued wherever he is found, regardless of the cause of his suffering or danger. It is an incontestable right that the man who suffers has to the pity of another man.[37]

Ciraolo invoked the language of humanitarian sentiment and combined it with a declaration that suffering created a universal right to medical care, food, and other humanitarian aid. In 1921 the delegates embraced the idea of a universal right based on a shared humanity, accepting the very argument that had been vehemently rejected in 1912.

The delegates of the 1921 conference took great pains to separate the rights of war victims from the recognition of revolutionaries, rebels, or insurgents as sovereign powers. There was no consensus among the delegates regarding the sovereign legitimacy of these different struggles. In fact, the comments of US Army Colonel Robert Olds prompted a contentious debate over whether a "real civil war," such as that experienced by the United States, should have the same legal status as rebellions and revolutions, such as those fomented by the Bolsheviks throughout Eastern Europe. This question was never resolved.[38] Instead, the delegates deliberately used the word "authority" instead of government to avoid the question of sovereign recognition. Their goal was to allow for humanitarian assistance to war victims when the established government denied them permission to work yet an insurgent "authority" with de facto control over territory was asking for their help.[39] The only criterion that would exclude a party from receiving aid, they decided, would be a flagrant violation of humanitarian principles, such as the massacre of medical personnel.

The 1921 conference resolutions declared that war victims' rights transcended the sovereignty of the state. In their official resolution, the delegates drew the attention of

> all governments and of all political parties, national or otherwise, to the fact that the state of civil war cannot justify the violation of the law of nations [*droit des gens*], and that this law must be safeguarded at all cost.[40]

The Ottoman Red Crescent, in its report on civil wars, argued that "the sovereignty of the State does not confer to it the right or privilege to violate the superior laws of humanity." The report reasoned that since the "most elementary duty of a government is to safeguard the life and property of its subjects," no government "truly worthy of the name" could justify denying insurgents or rebels the same care that an enemy soldier in an international war would receive.[41] For decades states designated by European governments as "uncivilized" had been denied the right to sign the international conventions that would provide protection for their populations during war. In contrast, the Ottoman Red Crescent report envisioned sovereignty as something determined by respect for the inalienable rights granted by the "superior laws of humanity." This assertion inverted the nineteenth-century relationship between positive law and international recognition of a government as fully sovereign.

It was not only war victims' rights that were now to transcend state sovereignty. So too did the Red Cross and Red Crescent's right and duty to intervene on behalf of war victims, even if the established government refused them entry into their territory.[42] In practice, however, the right to intervene meant protest, not forced entry. If a country were to deny the ICRC permission to enter its territory, the response planned in 1921 was a public protest by the national societies. The weakness of this plan was not lost on those at the conference. The Georgian Red Cross delegate, painfully aware that his country was losing an ongoing war with the Soviet Red Army, disdainfully characterized it as "nothing." Jacques Chenevière of the ICRC agreed, but he also pointed out that "the Red Cross cannot do anything other than submit infractions to moral disapproval … The Red Cross does not have an army to go punish a government that refuses its help."[43] Moral disapproval meant mobilizing the broad-based membership of the national societies to pressure their own government or a foreign government into allowing the ICRC to work in its territory.

The right to intervene therefore necessitated a final new principle: independence. The reports of the German Red Cross and the "old" Russian Red Cross (an exile group, not the newly rebuilt Bolshevik society) noted that the dissolution of national societies after revolutions demonstrated that the Red Cross must not be dependent on an established government.[44] The delegates called on all national societies to foster independence, educate their membership, and prepare for mobilizing public opinion against governments who failed to uphold humanitarian principles.[45]

The absence of sacred respect, 1922–39

None of the Red Cross/Red Crescent's 1921 program could be realized without significant changes to both the law of armed conflict and the structure of the movement. The 1921 conference called for the existing rights of POWs under the Hague Convention to be included in the Geneva Convention, and for reprisal violence to be prohibited under all circumstances. The conference also called for a new international diplomatic convention that would specify the rights of interned civilians, refugees, deportees, and evacuees.

Finally, the delegates expressed the hope that the rights of victims in civil wars would be codified at a future date.[46] In the meantime, the delegates gave the ICRC a mandate to undertake immediate relief work on behalf of political prisoners.

The success of these legal revisions and practical interventions depended on the transformation of the national societies from military auxiliaries into independent influencers of public opinion. The ICRC, an organization with 16 Swiss members at the end of World War I, could not on its own transform national or international public opinion. The 1921 resolutions recognized that only the national societies had the broad-based membership needed to pressure states into changing their behavior. The Geneva Convention of 1864 had been a governmental response to changing societal norms regarding the rights of soldiers vis-à-vis their governments. For rights to be expanded for civilians and victims of internal conflicts, a similar broad-based conviction would need to take hold. In other words, without pressure from concerned citizens for compliance, neither positive law nor moral pronouncements would influence states' behavior.

Delegates within the movement recognized that the revision of international humanitarian law, itself a difficult task, could not guarantee the rights of war victims. At the Eleventh International Conference of the Red Cross in 1923, the delegates explicitly discussed the fact that the real source of violence against POWs, wounded soldiers, and civilians during World War I was not the absence of positive law, but of "sacred respect ... without which no civilization is worthy of the name."[47] The ease with which governments found legal justification for brutal reprisals indicated a lack of respect for the humanitarian principles behind the legal articles. For example, the Dutch Red Cross representative pointed out that the Hague Convention's fundamental distinction between combatants and noncombatants already prohibited taking civilians as prisoners. The very notion of a civilian prisoner was "a conception generally condemned by the law of nations."[48] The French Red Cross delegate agreed that mistreatment was not the result of "insufficient regulations." It was not the law, but "the spirit that matters; without it all work is useless."[49] He argued that fostering a public opinion that would require governments to uphold both their agreements and the principles behind them was more important than legal changes.

Paul Des Gouttes, vice president of the ICRC, agreed with the national delegates. Yet the ICRC was at a loss for how to create this sacred respect. Its only hope was that clearer legal provisions would strengthen public protests against government violations. Des Gouttes believed that "public opinion judges severely those who have signed an obligation and do not hold to it."[50] Between 1922 and 1939 he was to be severely disappointed. Public moral approbation and an independent Red Cross/Red Crescent movement did not materialize during the interwar years. National societies defended their governments, rather than aiding ICRC efforts. As a result, efforts to implement the new program were seriously compromised from the start. Without the support of the national societies' broad-based membership, the ICRC struggled to find an incentive for governments to allow a neutral party access to political prisoners or to revise international humanitarian law.

It is important to note that the ICRC's interwar designation of political prisoner (*prisonnier politique*) or political detainee (*détenue politique*) was much broader than today's usage, which typically refers to someone imprisoned by their government for their beliefs. The ICRC's interwar usage encompassed any prisoners who did not meet the definition of

POWs, as defined by the Hague Convention. Such prisoners included victims of government repression, but also civilians taken as hostages during internal or international conflicts, combatants captured in internal conflicts, and combatant or civilian prisoners retained as hostages after the end of hostilities. After 1921 the ICRC sought to intervene on behalf of all these types of political prisoners. Established governments did not welcome its efforts. They did not recognize the ICRC's mandate and viewed its interventions as unwarranted interference in the internal affairs of a state.

The ICRC had the most success gaining access to political prisoners when two states had imprisoned one another's citizens. These governments had a reciprocal interest in exchanging prisoners in order to repatriate their own citizens. The ICRC successfully arranged for exchanges of political prisoners between Greece and Turkey (1923) and Ukraine and Czechoslovakia (1925). It was unsuccessful in arranging a general prisoner exchange between Poland and Lithuania from 1924 to 1929, but the negotiations did have a secondary effect of giving ICRC delegates access to prisons, improving the conditions of incarceration, and liberating some prisoners.[51]

The ICRC found it much more difficult to obtain government cooperation in cases where the state was maltreating its own citizens. Over the course of two decades, only the Kingdom of Serbs, Croats, and Slovenes allowed the ICRC to visit political prisoners without restrictions.[52] The ICRC argued that governments had no reason to refuse them authorization to inspect detention centers where political prisoners were being held if the governments were doing no wrong.[53] However, no public protests or broad-based moral disapproval accompanied their requests for access. Unlike citizen-soldiers, domestically unpopular victims – often from ethnic, religious, or political minorities – elicited little popular pressure. In other cases, repressive governments had little concern for domestic or international public opinion. The Soviet Union, for example, refused to allow any intervention. From 1921 to 1923, the ICRC sought to use economic investment from Western European governments as an incentive for Soviet authorities to allow its delegates access to political prisoners. These efforts fell apart when that foreign investment failed to materialize.[54] The Soviet government and Soviet Russian Red Cross summarily rejected additional requests in 1924, 1925, and 1927.[55]

Other governments permitted ICRC inspections, but only with conditions that all but guaranteed a positive report. The ICRC had to choose between gaining access to prisoners or insisting on a free and neutral inspection. They chose access. For example, in 1923 two ICRC delegates, Raymond Schlemmer and Rudolph Haccius, investigated reports that the Irish Free State government was summarily executing prisoners from the Irish Republican Army who refused to recognize the legitimacy of the Free State government.[56] The Irish Red Cross society refused to cooperate with the mission. Upon arriving in Dublin, Schlemmer and Haccius were informed by Desmond Fitzgerald, the minister for external affairs, that his government did not recognize the ICRC's "right of intervention in the case of civil war." Fitzgerald viewed the prisoners in question as ordinary criminals. As a "courtesy," Fitzgerald allowed the delegates access to three detention camps and one prison, but with significant restrictions. The delegates were not permitted to speak to any of the detainees.[57] They also could not visit any of the specific detainment camps in which abuse had been reported. Based on what they did see, the delegates' final report concluded that the complaints of mistreatment had been exaggerated, and that the Irish Free State upheld the principles of the 1921 conference. The ICRC published a truncated version of this report but did not make public the fact that the delegates had only limited access to prisoners. Unfortunately, this had the effect of quieting public concern about conditions in the prison without holding the Irish Free State government accountable.

Efforts to expand the rights of civilian victims of war under international law also met with fierce resistance during the 1920s. In 1923 the ICRC drafted both a new convention for POWs and a convention for civilians. The head of Switzerland's Federal Department of Foreign Affairs, Paul Dinichert, predicted that governments would not create a civilian convention because they had no reciprocal interest or domestic pressure to do so.[58] Dinichert was right. He approached the French and British governments about revising the Geneva Convention, but both were adamant that there should be no discussion about applying the rights of POWs to civilians.[59] The Swiss government only included the draft convention for POWs on the agenda for the diplomatic convention to revise the Geneva Convention in 1929. This elicited objections from countries in which civilians had recently suffered from civil war, revolution, or border disputes. The governments of Egypt, Greece, and the Kingdom of Serbs, Croats, and Slovenes all explicitly requested that a convention for civilians be included.[60] However, the French and British position prevailed.

The successful revision of the Geneva Convention in 1929 accepted both the new convention for POWs and a blanket prohibition on reprisals against POWs. A real or alleged violation of the laws of war by the enemy could no longer justify reciprocal violence against POWs. This marked an important shift towards viewing the rights of POWs as inalienable.[61] The rights of civilian war victims, in contrast, were still confined to the Hague Convention's existing distinction between combatants and noncombatants. Not only did the conference fail to consider the ICRC's draft convention for civilians; the delegates deleted the one reference to civilian prisoners in the draft of the POW code presented by the ICRC in 1929. Ignoring the many civilian victims of World War I, the majority of delegations insisted that the Hague Convention was sufficient protection for civilians, who, as noncombatants, should never become targets of violence.[62] The only concession to the issue of civilian victims was the request, in the Final Act of the conference, that a study be made to consider the possibility of a new convention.

The 1930s further highlighted the vulnerability of political prisoners and of civilians, and the inability and unwillingness of the Red Cross and Red Crescent movement to protect them. Victims of government repression in fascist Italy and Nazi Germany, civilian victims of Italian war crimes during the Italo-Ethiopian War (1935–6), and prisoners held during the Spanish Civil War (1936–9) found little protection. In most countries the national Red Cross societies became even more closely tied to their governments. The ICRC was also increasingly reliant on the Swiss government for funding, which curtailed its independence of action. The ICRC did not condone these flagrant violations of the 1921 resolutions, but neither did it denounce them.

During the second Italo-Abyssinian (Ethiopian) War, the ICRC sought to protect both civilians and POWs. Abyssinia had not ratified the new POW convention, but it had ratified the Geneva Convention of 1929 for the protection of wounded soldiers and the Geneva Protocol of 1925, which prohibited the use of chemical weapons. Italy had also ratified both conventions. The law of armed conflict therefore applied to the war, but the ICRC could do little to force the cooperation of the belligerents. The Italian army used chemical weapons against Ethiopian civilians and bombed neutral Red Cross hospitals. The ICRC privately protested to Mussolini, which made no impact. No public denunciations of Italian war crimes followed, either from the ICRC, the Italian Red Cross, or the League of Nations.[63]

During the Spanish Civil War, the law of armed conflict did not officially apply. However, both the Republican and Nationalist armies initially agreed to respect the principles of the Geneva and Hague Conventions and condemned the taking of civilian hostages. Both sides also accepted the ICRC offer to provide neutral medical care for the wounded, aid civilian victims of the war, and monitor POWs. Yet, in practice both parties imprisoned civilians who had not taken part in the hostilities. The detaining authorities did not distinguish between combatants bearing arms openly, and prisoners accused of espionage. This meant that multiple types of prisoners were all treated as spies guilty of treason, leading to the summary execution of many. Both sides refused to provide accurate lists of those taken captive and denied ICRC delegates access to prisoners. Over three years of conflict, prolonged negotiations over an exchange of prisoners resulted in the release of fewer than a hundred men.[64]

Victims of government repression fared no better. Faced with the unenviable choice of a public protest without domestic or international support, silent disapproval, or compromised access to prisoners, the ICRC most often chose the latter two. In 1931, the ICRC declined to visit political prisoners in Italy because ICRC president Max Huber feared the visit would be used as pro-fascist propaganda. The Italian Red Cross conducted the inspection instead, and its positive report was published by the ICRC.[65] In 1935, the ICRC formed a Political Detainees Commission (*Commission des détenues politiques*) to help deal with the growing number of political prisoners in Europe, but the policy of choosing access over protest did not change.

That same year, with the help of the vice president of the German Red Cross, the ICRC received authorization for Carl J. Burckhardt to visit the concentration camps of Lichtenburg, Esterwegen, and Dachau. His report criticized the fact that political prisoners were not separated from common criminals, and that the length of their sentences was at the discretion of the Gestapo. The ICRC did not publish the report. The following year the German Red Cross, on Hitler's orders and in preparation for improving Germany's reputation during the Berlin Olympics, invited the ICRC for another visit. Burckhardt noted with approval the separation of political prisoners from common criminals, the creation of aid organizations for detainees, and the liberation of prisoners. His positive account of the camps was published in the ICRC's General Report in 1938.[66] Just four months later, the ICRC reacted in shock to the violence against Jews on Kristallnacht on 9 November 1938. It tried to investigate the Buchenwald concentration camp again, but its requests were denied. The ICRC made no public protest against the Third Reich's refusal to cooperate.[67]

That same year, the ICRC made a final attempt to organize a legal revision. It asked the delegates of the Sixteenth International Conference of the Red Cross to approve a draft convention that created specific rights for victims of civil wars and political prisoners. This draft included a recognition of the ICRC's right to offer its services during internal conflicts, known in contemporary legal terms as the "right of initiative."[68] The delegates declined to approve the proposal because it was deemed too explosive given the political climate.[69] The following year, the ICRC convinced the Swiss government to convene a diplomatic conference to discuss a code for civilians drafted in 1934.[70] Yet events were outstripping the slow process of legal change. By September 1939 war had begun in Europe.

International legal revisions, 1945–9

World War II provided further evidence of the vulnerability of both civilian victims of war and victims of internal conflicts. The brutal occupation policies of both Germany and Japan, and the Nazi genocide produced more civilian than combatant deaths. While the Allies vigorously denounced these atrocities, the German and Japanese Red Cross societies grew more, not less, loyal during the war. The Allies' strategic bombing of civilian targets drew little domestic protest. The national societies in belligerent states remained divided by patriotic loyalties.

The ICRC's pattern of silence was repeated when, in 1942, it chose not to issue a public denunciation and appeal concerning the Third Reich's massacre of Jews, mass deportation of Jews to death camps in occupied Poland and the Soviet Union, the Allied expansion of air raids targeting civilians, and German mistreatment of Soviet POWs, (whose government had never signed the Geneva Convention of 1929). The ICRC debated launching this appeal on 14 October 1942. Those opposed to the appeal feared, not without reason, that it would endanger the ICRC's ongoing work on behalf of officially recognized POWs. The Swiss Federal Councillor Philip Etter also sought to prevent the ICRC from taking an action that might endanger Switzerland's precarious neutrality and lead to a German occupation of the country.[71] The four female members of the 23-person International Committee – Suzanne Ferrière, Marguerite Frick-Cramer, Lucie Odier, and Renée Bordier – argued passionately in favor of an appeal, even though they recognized that it would likely change nothing.[72] In hindsight, the ICRC has declared this failure to publicly denounce the Third Reich's policy of genocide to be its "greatest failure."[73]

In the aftermath of World War II, states undertook a major revision of the Geneva Convention. The Hague Convention was incorporated into four greatly expanded Geneva Conventions. Common Article 7 (Article 8 in the Fourth Convention) stated that the rights of protected persons were inalienable; "no circumstances" could result in the renunciation of an individual's rights under the conventions. Protected persons included civilians under occupation by the enemy. The Fourth Convention prohibited the imprisonment, forced transport, and rape of civilian populations. The conventions also addressed internal conflicts for the first time. Common Article 3, which was included in all four of the Geneva Conventions, banned "violence to life and person," "outrages upon dignity," and torture during "non-international armed conflicts." It also recognized the ICRC's "right of initiative" to protect victims in these conflicts.[74] In sum, the Geneva Conventions of 1949 began to incorporate legal changes first called for the Tenth International Conference of the Red Cross in 1921.

What was responsible for states' willingness to revise the Geneva Convention in ways that they had vigorously opposed for decades? Scholars have identified some key factors, but further research is needed to fully understand the many national perspectives represented at the international diplomatic convention. As this essay has shown, from 1921 onward the ICRC sought to make the Geneva Convention universally applicable to all victims of conflict. Throughout the 1920s and 1930s they used private diplomacy to encourage revisions of the convention. Most states, especially France and Great Britain, opposed their efforts. Only Egypt, Greece, and the Kingdom of Serbs, Croats, and Slovenes supported a convention for civilians in 1929.

By 1949, the direct experience of occupation and resistance gave rise to increasing domestic pressures to expand protections to civilians and internal conflicts. The experience of brutal occupation throughout continental Europe during World War II, combined with civil wars in Spain, China, and beyond, created a critical mass of states willing to support the ICRC's position, as stated in its proposed preamble in 1949: "respect for the personality and dignity of human beings constitutes a universal principle that is binding even in the absence of any contractual undertaking."[75] In addition to the preamble, the ICRC's draft gave combatants and civilians in international and civil wars full and equal rights in all four expanded conventions.

Continental European states that had endured direct German occupation supported the ICRC's draft convention. Britain, Australia, and the United States, concerned with the growth of anticolonial independence movements, fought against the application of the convention to civil wars. They also opposed the reference to a universal principle included in the ICRC's preamble. The four revised Geneva Conventions of 1949, with the limited protections created by Common Article 3, and without the proposed preamble, were a compromise between these two blocks of states.[76]

This compromise was the most substantial revision of the laws of war seen since 1864. However, the Geneva Conventions of 1949 still did not recognize that all victims of conflict possessed universal, equal, or inalienable rights. Most rights still applied only to civilians or combatants in international conflicts. The rights of victims in "non-international armed conflicts" were limited to the general prohibitions mentioned by Common Article 3. Perhaps most importantly, over the next three decades national liberation movements and established governments would bitterly disagree over whether anticolonial wars for independence qualified as non-international armed conflicts.[77]

Conclusion

How and when does the history of international humanitarian law and the Red Cross/Red Crescent intersect with the history of human rights? Until 1921, there is little evidence to suggest that either states or the Red Cross and Red Crescent movement considered the rights of war victims to be inalienable, equal, or universal. These rights were not equal because the rights of wounded soldiers and POWs were more extensive than those of civilians. They were not universal, because they applied only to international conflicts between "civilized" states. Finally, they were not inalienable, because governments considered themselves bound to uphold the conventions only if their enemy did so as well. National societies supported the view of their respective national governments. The Red Cross and Red Crescent movement avoided any consideration of the rights of war victims in internal conflicts, which national governments viewed as an unwarranted interference in their internal affairs. During the nineteenth century, the rights of wounded soldiers, POWs, and civilians were limited and contingent on reciprocal agreements among "civilized" states.

The violence perpetrated against these vulnerable populations during World War I and "wars after the war" caused the Red Cross and Red Crescent movement to reconsider both its principles concerning the rights of war victims and its relationship to the state. In 1921, it declared that combatants and civilians possessed equal rights and that these rights applied to both international and internal conflicts. They further declared that the rights of war victims were not dependent on the behavior of the enemy. They were inalienable – guaranteed by the "superior laws of humanity" – and valid in all circumstances. The 1921 resolutions also recognized that the protection of war victims, especially during civil wars and internal conflicts, required independence from established governments. At the same time, the Red Cross and Red Crescent movement advocated only two universal rights: the right to medical care and the right to humane conditions of incarceration. These two rights reflected the movement's humanitarian focus during the nineteenth century, even as national societies like the Ottoman Red Crescent sought to use rights discourse to upend humanitarianism's imperial past. The humanitarian principles outlined by the 1921 conference represent a crucial instance in which the language of humanitarian charity and language of universal rights overlapped.

From 1921 to 1949, the ICRC sought both legal revisions and humanitarian interventions in keeping with its 1921 program. However, these efforts could not be realized without an independent public opinion willing to pressure governments to respect the rights of war victims. This failed to materialize. National societies continued to prioritize their official role as military auxiliaries. This had tragic consequences for the willingness and ability of the movement to protect war victims from abuses by established governments during World War II. Only after the war did the Geneva Conventions of 1949 begin to reflect an understanding of war victims' rights as inalienable, equal, and universal.

The 1949 revision of international humanitarian law was the culmination of over two decades of work. Yet, the mechanism to enforce war victims' rights remained a key problem. Both World War I and the interwar years had made it clear that neither moral declarations nor positive law were sufficient to protect individuals from state abuse. Broad-based domestic concern was also necessary. Further research is needed to understand the dynamic between domestic publics and national policies towards the rights of war victims as well as the dynamic among official ties, codification, professionalization, gender, and the exclusion of noncombatants from legal purview. In 1863, governments' perception of reciprocal interest was shaped by a broad-based domestic outcry over the treatment of citizen-soldiers. A similar dynamic seems to have been at work in 1949. During the interwar years, by contrast, the Red Cross and Red Crescent societies failed to develop the independence necessary to apply broad-based public pressure on governments to change their behavior. After 1949, in spite of the changes in international law, the problem of how to foster a spirit of respect – or at least incentives for compliance – has remained an ongoing challenge for both advocates of human rights and international humanitarian law.

Notes

1 The phrase "laws of war" includes both laws regulating the conduct of parties engaged in an armed conflict (*jus in bello*, "right conduct in war") and laws regulating when it is permissible/legal to engage in war (*jus ad bellum*, or "right to go to war"). *Jus in bello* can also be referred to as the "law of armed conflict" or "International Humanitarian Law" (IHL). The laws of war included both the Geneva and Hague Conventions and widely accepted customs of military conduct.

2 Samuel Moyn, *The Last Utopia: Human Rights in History*, Cambridge, MA: Belknap Press of Harvard University Press, 2010, p. 220.

3 Dietrich Schindler, "Le Comité International de la Croix-Rouge et les Droits de l'Homme," *Revue Internationale de la Croix-Rouge* 61, no. 715, 1979, 3–15.

4 See Jan Eckel, "The Rebirth of Politics from the Spirit of Morality: Explaining the Human Rights Revolution of the 1970s," in Jan Eckel and Samuel Moyn (eds.) *The Breakthrough: Human Rights in the 1970s*, Philadelphia: University of Pennsylvania Press, 2013, pp. 226–60; Philippe Ryfman, *Une histoire de l'humanitaire*, Paris: La Découverte, 2016; Davide Rodogno, *Against Massacre: Humanitarian Interventions in the Ottoman Empire* 1815–1914, Princeton, NJ: Princeton University Press, 2011; Michael Barnett, *Empire of Humanity: A History of Humanitarianism*, Ithaca, NY: Cornell University Press, 2011.

5 These scholars do not agree on when and how this transformation occurred. Paul Gordon Lauren, *The Evolution of International Human Rights: Visions Seen*, Philadelphia: University of Pennsylvania Press, 2011; David P. Forsythe, *The Internationalization of Human Rights*, Lexington, KY: Lexington Books, 1991; Gary J. Bass, *Freedom's Battle: The Origins of Humanitarian Intervention*, New York: Vintage, 2009; Brendan Simms and D. J. B. Trim (eds.), *Humanitarian Intervention: A History*, Cambridge, UK: Cambridge University Press, 2011; Bruno Cabanes, *The Great War and the Origins of Humanitarianism, 1918–1924*, Cambridge, UK: Cambridge University Press, 2014; Lasse Heerten, *The Biafran War and Postcolonial Humanitarianism: Spectacles of Suffering*, Cambridge, UK: Cambridge University Press, 2017; Amanda B. Moniz, *From Empire to Humanity*, Oxford: Oxford University Press, 2016; Ian Tyrell, *Reforming the World: The Creation of America's Moral Empire*, Princeton, NJ: Princeton University Press, 2010.

6 Stephen Hopgood, *Keepers of the Flame: Understanding Amnesty International*, Ithaca, NY: Cornell University Press, 2006, pp. 68–9.

7 *Final Act of the International Conference on Human Rights, Tehran, 22 April to 13 May 1968*, New York: United Nations, 1968, p. 18. Online. Available at http://legal.un.org/avl/pdf/ha/fatchr/Final_Act_of_TehranConf.pdf (accessed 15 December 2018).

8 Heerten, *The Biafran War*, p. 7.

9 Stephen Hopgood, *The Endtimes of Human Rights*, Ithaca, NY: Cornell University Press, 2013, pp. 120–1. See also Emily Crawford, "Convergence of Norms Across the Spectrum of Armed Conflicts: International Humanitarian and Human Rights Law," in Gregory Rose and Bruce Oswald (eds.) *Detention of Non-State Actors Engaged in Hostilities: The Future Law*, Leiden: Brill/Nijhoff, 2016, pp. 7–22.

10 All conventions and states party to the convention can be found online. Available at https://ihl-databases.icrc.org (accessed 15 December 2018). There is an extensive literature on international law and the "international society of civilized states," including Antony Anghie, *Imperialism, Sovereignty, and the Making of International Law*, Cambridge, UK: Cambridge University Press, 2005; Gerrit W. Gong, *The Standard of "Civilization" in International Society*, Oxford: Oxford University Press, 1984; Martti Koskenniemi, *The Gentle Civilizer of Nations: The Rise and Fall of International Law, 1870–1960*, Cambridge, UK: Cambridge University Press, 2002.

11 Jean-Charles Chenu, *Rapport au Conseil de Santé des Armées sur les Résultats du Service Médico-chirurgical aux Ambulances de Crimée et aux Hopitaux Militaires Français en Turquie pendant la Campagne D'Orient en 1854–1955–1956*, Paris: Victor Masson et Fils, 1865, p. 689.

12 John F. Hutchinson, *Champions of Charity: War and the Rise of the Red Cross*, Boulder, CO: Westview Press, 1996, pp. 26–7.

13 Hutchinson, *Champions of Charity*, pp. 140–7.

14 For the US interpretation, see John Fabian Witt, *Lincoln's Code: The Laws of War in American History*, New York: Simon & Schuster, 2012. The French considered any violation of the conventions by the enemy to justify reprisal violence. See Robert Jacomet, *Les Lois de la Guerre Continentale*, Paris: L. Fournier, 1913, p. 26. The British manual argued that reprisal violence was justified in the face of "repeated violations" by the enemy. See Colonel James E. Edmonds and Lassa Oppenheim, *Land Warfare: An Exposition of the Laws and Usages of War on Land, for the Guidance of Officers of His Majesty's Army*, London: H. M. Stationery Office, 1912, p. 25.

15 Isabel V. Hull, *A Scrap of Paper: Breaking and Making International Law During the Great War*, Ithaca, NY: Cornell University Press, 2014.

16 Gustave Moynier and Louis P. A. Appia, *La Guerre et la Charité: Traité Théorique et Pratique de Philanthropie Appliquée aux Armées en Campagne*, Genève: Cherbuliez, 1867, pp. 63–4, 134.

17 Hutchinson, *Champions of Charity*, pp. 105–49.

18 *Troisième Conférence Internationale des Sociétés de la Croix-Rouge, tenue à Genève du 1er au 6 Septembre 1884: Compte Rendu*, Geneva: Comité International de la Croix-Rouge, 1885, pp. 139–40.
19 Julia F. Irwin, *Making the World Safe: The American Red Cross and a Nation's Humanitarian Awakening*, Oxford: Oxford University Press, 2013, pp. 30–4.
20 Quoted in André Durand, *The International Committee of the Red Cross*, Geneva: International Committee of the Red Cross, 1983, p. 11.
21 *Neuvième Conférence Internationale de la Croix-Rouge, tenue à Washington du 7 au 17 Mai 1912: Compte Rendu*, Washington, DC: American Red Cross, 1912, pp. 45–9.
22 American support for Cuban nationalists resulted not only in the Spanish-American War (1898) but also private and governmental humanitarian aid. See Tyrell, *Reforming the World*, p. 100.
23 See opinion of the US Supreme Court in: Robert Cooper Grier and Supreme Court of the United States, *US Reports: Prize Cases, 67 US 2 Black 635. 862*. Available at www.loc.gov/item/usrep067635 (accessed 21 November 2018). See also Howard Jones, *Blue and Gray Diplomacy: A History of Union and Confederate Foreign Relations*, Chapel Hill: University of North Carolina Press, 2010, pp. 47–82, and Don H. Doyle, *The Cause of All Nations: An International History of the American Civil War*, New York: Basic Books, pp. 27–49.
24 For an analysis of General Sherman's campaigns and their relationship to the issue of reprisals, see Witt, *Lincoln's Code*, pp. 250–84.
25 *Neuvième Conférence Internationale de la Croix-Rouge*, p. 203.
26 Archives du Comité Internationale de la Croix-Rouge, Geneva (hereafter ACICR), CR 22–1, 32, Commission chargée de préciser les fonctions de la Croix-Rouge en cas de guerre civile, Minutes, 10 May 1912.
27 Heather Jones, "International or Transnational? Humanitarian Action During the First World War," *European Review of* History, 2009, vol. 16, no. 5, 697–713, here 698, and Giovanna Procacci, *Soldati e Prigionieri Italiani nella Grande Guerra: Con una Raccolta di Lettere Inedite*, Rome: Editori Riuniti, 1993, pp. 174–5.
28 Irwin, *Making the World Safe*, pp. 72–3.
29 Heather Jones, "The German Spring Reprisals of 1917: Prisoners of War and the Violence of the Western Front," *German History*, 2008, vol. 26, no. 3, 335–56.
30 Jones, "International or Transnational?"
31 For an extensive discussion of these disputes, see Hull, *A Scrap of Paper*.
32 Comité International de la Croix-Rouge (hereafter CICR), *Rapport Général du Comité International de la Croix-Rouge sur son Activité de 1912 à 1920*, Geneva: CICR, 1921, pp. 75, 129–73.
33 Robert Gerwarth, "The Continuum of Violence," in Jay Winter (ed.) *The Cambridge History of the First World War. Vol. 2. The State*, Cambridge. UK: Cambridge University Press, 2014, pp. 638–62; Peter Gatrell, "War After the War: Conflicts, 1919–1923," in John Horne (ed.) *A Companion to World War I*, London: Blackwell, 2010, pp. 558–75.
34 Jiří Toman, *La Russie et la Croix-Rouge, 1917–1945: La Croix-Rouge dans un État Révolutionnaire et l'action du CICR en Russie après la Révolution d'Octobre 1917*, Geneva: Institut Henry-Dunant, 1997.
35 *Dixième Conférence Internationale de la Croix-Rouge, tenue à Genève du 30 Mars au 7 Avril 1921: Compte Rendu*, Genève: Albert Renaud, 1921, p. 218.
36 *Dixième Conférence Internationale*, p. 217.
37 Bibliothèque du Comité international de la Croix-Rouge, Geneva, Switzerland (hereafter BCICR), Croix-Rouge Italienne, *La Croix-Rouge Internationale dans la Guerre Civile*, Geneva: Journal de Genève, 1921, p. 11.
38 Bibliotheque du Comité Internationale de la Croix-Rouge, *Commissions I–VII de la Xe Conférence Internationale de la Croix-Rouge, 1921: Procès-Verbaux et Documents*, (hereafter *Commissions 1921*), Third Commission, minutes, 31 March 1921, pp. 7–8. In the French minutes Olds' phrase is recorded as "*veritable guerre civile.*"
39 *Commissions 1921*, Third Commission, minutes, 4 April 1921, p. 13.
40 *Dixième Conférence Internationale*, p. 218.
41 BCICR, Croissant-Rouge Ottoman, *Croix-Rouge Internationale dans la Guerre Civile*, Geneva: Journal de Genève, 1921, p. 7.
42 *Commissions 1921*, Third Commission, minutes, 31 March 1921, p. 6.
43 *Commissions 1921*, Third Commission, minutes, 4 April 1921, p. 14.

44 BCICR, Deutsches Rotes Kreuz, *La Croix-Rouge et la Guerre Civile*, Berlin, 1921, p. 1; BCICR, Ancienne Croix-Rouge Russe, *La Croix-Rouge dans la Guerre Civile*, Geneva, 1921, p. 5.
45 *Dixième Conférence Internationale*, p. 218.
46 *Commissions 1921*, Third Commission, minutes, 1 April 1921, p. 3.
47 ACICR, CR 119–7, "Question des civils, evacués, et deportés," notes of a meeting between the ICRC and P. Dinichert, 15 December 1923.
48 ACICR, CR 119–2/173, *Extraits des procés-verbaux de la conference diplomatique (Juillet 1929) relatifs aux prisonniers civils*, 22 July 1929. The Belgian Red Cross delegate similarly insisted that the real problem facing the movement was how to obligate states to respect legal agreements, when the "sentiments of altruism and justice … are not respected by all." See ACICR, CR 119–7, *Procès-verbal de la 4ème commission de la Onzième Conférénce Internationale de la Croix-Rouge*, 29 August 1923.
49 "Question des civils, evacués, et deportés."
50 "Question des civils, evacués, et deportés."
51 CICR, *Rapport Général du Comité International de la Croix-Rouge sur son Activité de 1921 à 1923*, Geneva: CICR, 1923, pp. 55–8; CICR, *Rapport Général du Comité International de la Croix-Rouge sur son Activité de 1923 à 1925*, Geneva: CICR, 1925, pp. 12–13, 48–9; CICR, *Rapport Général du Comité International de la Croix-Rouge sur son Activité de 1925 à 1928*, Geneva: CICR, 1928, pp. 17–23; CICR, *Rapport Général du Comité International de la Croix-Rouge sur son Activité de 1928 à 1930*, Geneva: CICR, 1930, pp. 21–2.
52 CICR, *Rapport Général … 1923 à 1925*, p. 13.
53 CICR, *Rapport Général … 1925 à 1928*, p. 24.
54 Kimberly A. Lowe, "Humanitarianism and National Sovereignty: Red Cross Intervention on Behalf of Political Prisoners in Soviet Russia, 1921–3," *Journal of Contemporary History*, 2014, vol. 49, no. 4, 652–74.
55 CICR, *Rapport Général … 1925 à 1928*, pp. 24–5.
56 In 1921 the Anglo-Irish Treaty officially ended the Irish War of Independence (1919–21). The Irish Free State became a self-governing dominion of the British Empire. In 1922, members of the Irish Republican Army who opposed the treaty began a guerrilla war against the National Army of the Irish Free State government.
57 ACICR, CR 22–11/134, Rapport General de Mr. R. Haccius, délégué en Irlande, à CICR (Commission des Missions).
58 "Question des civils, evacués, et deportés."
59 National Archives, London, UK, Memoranda 42–62, CAB 16/66, Doc. 52, 28 May 1929, Red Cross Convention of 1906 (Geneva), Revision of, and Preparation of Conventions for the Treatment of POWs and for Civil Populations in Enemy Hands. ACICR, CR 119–7, "Prisonniers civils: visite de MM. Cramer & Drachenfels à M. Dinichert le 30 Juillet 1925."
60 National Archives, London, UK, Memoranda 42–62, CAB 16/66, Doc. 51, 14 May 1929, Red Cross Convention of 1906 (Geneva), Revision of, and Preparation of Conventions for the Treatment of POWs and for Civil Populations in Enemy Hands.
61 Neville Wylie, "The 1929 Prisoner of War Convention and the Building of the Inter-War Prisoner of War Regime," in Sibylle Scheipers (ed.) *Prisoners in War*, Oxford: Oxford University Press, 2010, p. 97.
62 BCICR, *Actes de la conférence diplomatique de Genève de 1929*, Geneva: Journal de Genève, 1930, pp. 436, 510, 555; *Procès-verbaux de la sous-commission I et de la Commission II*, minutes, 11 July 1929, p. 1.
63 Rainer Baudendistel, *Between Bombs and Good Intentions: The International Committee of the Red Cross (ICRC) and the Italo-Ethiopian War, 1935–1936*, New York: Berghahn, 2006.
64 CICR, *Rapport Général du Comité International de la Croix-Rouge sur son Activité d'Août 1934 à Mars 1938*, Geneva: CICR, 1938, pp. 119, 121–4.
65 Gerald Steinacher, *Humanitarians at War: The Red Cross in the Shadow of the Holocaust*, Oxford: Oxford University Press, 2017, 22. Jean-Claude Favez, with the collaboration of Geneviève Billeter, *Une Mission Impossible? Le CICR, les Déportations et les Camps de Concentration Nazis*, Lausanne: Payot, 1988, p. 31.
66 CICR, *Rapport Général … 1934 à Mars 1938*, p. 39.

67 Jean-Claude Favez, *The Red Cross and the Holocaust*, Cambridge, UK: Cambridge University Press, 1999, p. 20.
68 ICRC, *Role and Activities of the Red Cross in Time of Civil War*, Geneva: CICR 1938, p. 7.
69 *XVIth International Red Cross Conference, London, June, 1938: Report*, Geneva: ICRC, 1938, pp. 82–3.
70 ACICR, CR 22–1/39, Giuseppe Motta to Max Huber, letter, 6 February 1939.
71 Favez, *The Red Cross and the Holocaust*, pp. 279–82; Sébastien Farré, "The ICRC and the Detainees in Nazi Concentration Camps (1942–1945)," *International Review of the Red Cross*, 2012, vol. 94, no. 888, 1–28.
72 Steinacher, *Humanitarians at War*, p. 44. Both before and during the war the female members of the ICRC advocated for stronger policies regarding civilians and political prisoners.
73 ICRC, "Commemorating the Liberation of Auschwitz," 27 January 2005. Online. Available at www.icrc.org/eng/resources/documents/statement/68zeb2.htm (accessed 15 August 2017). See also François Bugnion, "Dialogue with the Past: The ICRC and the Nazi Death Camps," 5 November 2002 (ICRC statement). Online. Available at www.icrc.org/eng/resources/documents/misc/6ayg86.htm (accessed 21 November 2018); Peter Maurer, "Remembering the Shoah: The ICRC and the International Community's Efforts in Responding to Genocide," 28 April 2015 (speech by ICRC president). Online. Available at www.icrc.org/en/document/remembering-shoah-icrc-and-international-communitys-efforts-responding-genocide-and (accessed 15 August 2017). Historians continue to debate the extent to which anti-Semitism within the ICRC shaped their response to Nazi persecutions. See Favez, *The Red Cross and the Holocaust*; Farré, "The ICRC and the Detainees"; and Steinacher, *Humanitarians at War*.
74 *The Geneva Conventions of 12 August 1949*, Geneva: ICRC, 1995.
75 Quoted in J. Pictet (ed.), *Commentary on the Second Geneva Convention*, Geneva: ICRC, 1960, pp. 21–2.
76 William I. Hitchcock, "Human Rights and the Laws of War: The Geneva Conventions of 1949," in Petra Goedde, William I. Hitchcock, and Akira Iriye (eds.) *The Human Rights Revolution: An International History*, New York: Oxford University Press, 2012, pp. 97, 104–5.
77 In 1977, when postcolonial states had achieved a numerical majority at intergovernmental conferences, the Additional Protocols clearly defined the rights of combatants engaged in struggles against colonial or racist regimes. See Giovanni Mantilla, "The Origins and Development of the 1949 Geneva Conventions and 1977 Additional Protocols," in Matthew Evangelista and Nina Tannenwald (eds.) *Do the Geneva Conventions Matter?* Oxford: Oxford University Press, 2017, pp. 35–68.

PART II

THE INTERWAR ERA

The League of Nations

6

UNITED IN THEIR QUEST FOR PEACE?

Transnational women activists between the World Wars

Marie Sandell

Women activists emerged from World War I with a renewed determination to work to improve women's situation worldwide. Even though the war had disrupted women's international movements, board members of associations such as the International Council of Women and the International Woman Suffrage Alliance made efforts to keep in contact with one another and their members during the war years.[1] And indeed a new organization, the Women's International League for Peace and Freedom was established during the war, in 1915. Even in wartime, then, international ties helped set the stage for women's postwar activism. Alongside significant victories for many national women's movements in the aftermath of the war, notably in terms of suffrage, women's advocacy flourished. Many activists believed that further work was needed to end other inequalities (for example, better educational and employment opportunities for girls and women and legal rights for married women), and they coupled this belief with a strong desire for a true and lasting peace. These commitments translated into a renewed effort to forge transnational cooperation following the war.

Women were of course not alone in their commitment to internationalism in the interwar era. They found themselves operating in a broader context of increased belief in and practical application of transnational activism.[2] Yet, as the historians Glenda Sluga and Patricia Clavin, among others, point out, women often had more to gain from this internationalism because in most national contexts they were politically marginalized. Women activists looked to intergovernmental organizations for ways to expand their political opportunities and represent their concerns.[3] They drew on a long tradition of organizing in movements and associations with transnational links: temperance, prostitution, and peace were areas of earlier reform efforts with such links.[4] Many of these women believed that they, as women, had a special inclination for international issues such as peace, justice, and tolerance.[5] Some believed that this inclination belonged to mothers in particular, who sought to ensure that their children would grow up without war.[6] In the interwar period, the issue of peace served to unite very different groups of women. This was a time when international women's organizations expanded their membership into countries beyond Europe, North America, Australia, and New Zealand and expanded their agendas beyond specific rights for women to the pressing humanitarian issues of the day. These humanitarian issues often centered on strengthening more traditional and less contentious women's roles, and so could be seen as relevant for larger and more disparate groups of women.

This essay focuses on women's international peace activism in the interwar period. It will examine the increased prominence given to peace by the three major international women's organizations of the day: the International Council of Women (ICW, formed in 1888), the International Woman Suffrage Alliance (IWSA, formed in 1904; later known as the International Alliance of Women for Suffrage and Equal Citizenship or simply International Alliance of Women, IAW), and the Women's International League for Peace and Freedom (WILPF, formed in 1915). These three organizations were closely related: historian Leila Rupp has suggested that they be viewed as "grandmother, mother and daughter," as one in effect gave birth to another.[7] All three were secular, had no particular political affiliation, and, from the outset welcomed female members from around the world. Integral to all their activities was the belief that women could and should organize across national borders and racial and language differences, because women in all societies were subordinated to men and denied their rights. This was something that they shared with other women's organizations of the same vintage, as notions of gender difference and shared female characteristics lay firmly at the heart of the broader women's movements that had begun to take shape towards the end of the nineteenth century. Their disappointment at responses to their demands at the national level led these women to see new opportunities for pursuing equality and peace at the international level, with the platform provided by the League of Nations, the new intergovernmental organization. They recognized that the League provided opportunities for their work precisely because it gave them access to a wider international audience. They believed that any resolution passed there would automatically have international impact, thanks to the involvement of governments around the world.

This essay explores these organizations' focus on peace and disarmament during a time of a deteriorating geopolitical climate, and how the delicate matters of war and peace caused both disagreements among and resulted in greater collobaration between female activists, for example, through the establishment of new associations and ways of organizing. The peace question resulted in new commitments to what we can in hindsight describe as humanism, understood as the care for all humanity and everyone's right to determine their own goals and values, and a renewed focus on rights, which laid important foundations for future debates and developments regarding human rights, particularly women's human rights. This essay therefore aims to contribute to the gender analysis of internationalisms, something that is still often absent in international history.[8] It aims to show how women contributed to the development of human rights in this period, which, as the historiography increasingly indicates, emerged as an idea before the establishment of the United Nations.[9]

The essay opens in wartime with the establishment of WILPF, and then examines the optimism and expansion surrounding the development of women's activism in the 1920s. It then explores the challenges that the political and economic instabilities of the 1930s posed for transnational feminist activism, and shows how this challenging environment increasingly led women activists to leave their separate organizations and enter more fully into the international arena provided by the League of Nations.

The wartime gathering of women at The Hague and the creation of the Women's International League for Peace and Freedom

World War I disrupted the activities and developments of international women's organizations such as the International Council of Women (ICW) and the International Woman Suffrage Alliance (IWSA). Yet the war also produced a new association: the

Women's International League for Peace and Freedom (WILPF). WILPF was a product of the challenges posed to the women's movement by World War I. It grew out of the conference held in The Hague by the Dutch section of the IWSA in 1915, although it failed to get an official blessing from that organization.[10] Participants viewed The Hague congress as "a remarkable wartime gathering of women from the neutral and belligerent countries."[11] In the words of British delegate Emmeline Pethick-Lawrence, "The Congress did much more than pass resolutions. It brought into friendly association the women from belligerent countries and made them realize that their fundamental interests were one and the same."[12]

Interwar international women's organizations such as the ICW, IAW, and WILPF had firmly nineteenth-century origins. Dissatisfaction with women's subordinate roles in society had led to the emergence of international women's movements by the end of the nineteenth century. The main pattern to note in the growth of these movements was that American women were the forerunners. Many countries in western and northern Europe witnessed similar developments, as did countries outside the West, albeit a little later. The outbreak of World War I disrupted these developments. During the war years, the ICW and the IWSA held no conferences and no new societies were affiliated, although ICW board members did try to maintain contact with each other. The IWSA was able to keep publishing its journal, *Jus Suffragii*. Its editor, Mary Sheepshanks, deliberately included news from the two opposing sides with the aim of putting a human face on the enemy.

It was Sheepshanks who published Dr. Aletta Jacobs' "Call to the Women of All Nations" on the subject of holding an international conference in The Hague. Jacobs was a physician, senior member of the IWSA, and leader of the Dutch national section of the IWSA. Fellow suffragists criticized Jacobs' call because it fell outside the organization's and publication's aim of suffrage. Just as disagreement over the issue of suffrage within the ICW (which sought to remain neutral on the issue) had earlier produced the IWSA, so did disagreement within the IWSA over the issue of peace activism at the start of the war lead directly to the formation of the WILPF.[13] The reason for ICW's cautious stand on suffrage was that it had set out to be a general women's organization – in its own words a "Women's League of Nations" – that was to be all-embracing and open to all types of women's groups, ranging from literary clubs to labor groups.[14] The IWSA was likewise cautious about its Dutch section's divisive call to the international conference at The Hague in 1915. The IWSA did not sanction the conference and none of the national suffrage societies of states then at war sent delegates. Yet several leading personalities from the women's movements gave their support to the conference at The Hague. These included Jane Addams (American suffragist, peace activist, and pioneering social worker), Emily Greene Balch (American peace activist and Nobel Peace Prize recipient in 1946), Lida Gustava Heymann (German pacifist and women's rights activist), Anita Augspurg (German pacifist and women's rights activist), Rosika Schwimmer (Hungarian feminist and internationalist), Maude Royden (British women's rights and peace activist with strong religious convictions), Charlotte Despard (British suffragist and socialist), and Mary Sheepshanks (British suffragist and social reformer).[15]

The conference in The Hague was significant for bringing together women from countries in the rival Entente and Central Powers alliances during the war, even as many governments tried to stop them. The choice of the imposing Hague Peace Palace for their conference was also significant, as it connected them with a "new internationalism" – the promotion of international law, international institutions, and international publications.[16] The Peace Palace had been built in the wake of the 1899 and 1907 Hague conferences. Those conferences had been attended by European states in response to imperial powers' escalating militarization. While women had lacked formal roles at either of those gatherings, they had lobbied at both, including the high-profile Austrian pacifist Bertha von Suttner, who was on the Standing Committee on Peace and Arbitration organized by the ICW at both the 1899 and 1907 meetings.[17]

WILPF was established with the express purpose of securing disarmament, social and economic justice, and an end to all wars. In contrast to the ICW and the IAW, it started life with a functioning international structure, but it had to build national sections. At its inception, it had 13 national sections attached to it: those of Austria, Belgium, Canada, Denmark, France, Germany, Great Britain, Hungary, Italy, Netherlands, Norway, Sweden, and the United States. Australia, Bulgaria, Finland, Ireland, Poland, and Switzerland joined shortly after the war, in 1919. Like its predecessors, WILPF was an all-female separatist organization, even though some of its members called for uniting forces with men from the outset and it wrestled with the question of male collaboration, as they saw the concentration of all forces, female and males, as necessary when working for peace.[18] Nonetheless, WILPF remained a women-only organization. Following its first meeting, it held its second gathering in conjunction with World War I peace talks in Paris in 1919. WILPF subsequently organized its conferences in many different locations. However, the importance of The Hague was again evident in 1922, when it assembled an emergency conference in the same city where the organization had been founded, to consider "A New Peace" and to urge a revision of the peace treaties and reparations of World War I.[19] Likewise, it was Geneva's importance for the new internationalism of this era that prompted WILPF to use this city for its headquearters following the end of the war:

> This has made it easy for leading members of the League to stay in Geneva, work with the secretary, and confer and cooperate with other internationalists in Geneva. By delegations, petitions and informal contacts, fruitful relations are established with League of Nations circles and with other official and unofficial personages.[20]

Peace as a unifying goal in the 1920s

The 1920s was a period of expansion and optimism for many of the major international women's organizations. World War I, rather than breaking the bonds formed in the prewar period among women in different countries, served to unite these international groups of women and renewed their resolve to work internationally.[21] There were of course other groups of women whose definition of internationalism differed from those of liberal groups such as ICW and IAW, notably socialist women. Socialist women's internationalism was marked as much by their membership of a particular socialist party, in which the language of "comradeship" rather than "sisterhood" was the orthodoxy, as by gender. Moreover, unlike the women in liberal international women's organizations, socialist women's transnational activities took place in mixed-sex organizations and forums.[22] What liberal and socialist women had in common, however, was that for historical reasons their prewar international gatherings tended to be dominated by participants from countries in Europe and North America. It is important to know that this limitation was about to change in the 1920s.

In the 1920s liberal international women organizations' unity of determination to prevent conflicts came to extend far beyond the cooperation of only European and North American women, in contrast to before the war. The major organizations followed this pattern of expansion: Having set out with memberships and affiliations predominately drawn from western Europe and North America, they expanded membership into Australia, New Zealand, southern and eastern Europe, and then South America, Asia, and the Middle East in the 1920s and 1930s.[23] During these years the number of their national affiliations grew substantially, and included for the first time members from countries outside Europe, North America, Australia, and New Zealand.[24] For example, the number of national councils affiliated with the ICW rose from 8 in 1899 to 39 in 1925. Some 11 new national councils, of which the majority were from eastern Europe and South America, joined following the 1920 conference in Kristiania (now Oslo), Norway, alone. Between 1923 and 1929, the IWSA (soon to be renamed the International Alliance of Women, IAW) likewise gained affiliates from countries outside western Europe and North America, including Brazil, Egypt, India, Jamaica, Japan, Palestine, Lithuania, Ukraine, Bermuda, Cuba, Peru, Puerto Rico, Turkey, Ceylon, the Dutch East Indies, Syria, and Rhodesia. By the end of the 1920s, the IAW possessed 52 member societies, of which half had joined during the 1920s.[25]

The Women's International League for Peace and Freedom (WILPF), which had only recently formed, also expanded markedly over the 1920s. By the end of the 1920s, it had acquired affiliates in 26 countries. The slower growth of WILPF can be explained by the fact that it was formed later than the ICW and IAW, and started with an international structure and then had to build national sections. Its growth may also have been affected by its more radical and outspoken agenda on issues such as peace, disarmament, and colonialism.

The geographical expansion of these organizations meant that women from all over the world now congregated in greater numbers at international women's conferences. Geneva was of course a key meeting place, but they also congregated elsewhere in Europe and North America. The ICW held conferences in Kristiania in 1920 and Washington in 1925, while the IAW held congresses in Geneva (1920), Rome (1923), Paris (1926), and Berlin (1929). WILPF, following its founding conference in 1915 in The Hague, organized a conference in conjunction with the peace talks in Paris in 1919, and then in Vienna (1921), Washington (1924), Dublin (1926), and Prague (1929). It also organized an international conference in The Hague in 1922 that attracted delegates from 111 international and national women's organizations, and held international summer schools at which prominent WILPF members and academics gave lectures on topics related to peace, disarmament, and international cooperation.

The rapid expansion of international women's organizations in the difficult interwar period is not widely known, and an investigation into women's activism at this time reveals that more countries were represented and more delegates, especially from outside Europe and North America, attended conferences than in previous decades. A total of 36 countries were represented at the IAW's first conference after the war in Geneva in 1920. For the first time, women from the so-called East (i.e. Asia) attended. Ten delegates represented India and two represented Japan; at the conference as a whole there was an average of 12 delegates per nation.[26] The conference in Rome in 1923 was even more international than its predecessor: women from 43 different countries attended, including Egypt, China, India, Japan, and Brazil.[27] In addition, it was reported that hundreds from Rome itself flocked to the evening meetings.[28] The IAW's expansion continued at its subsequent conferences in Paris in 1926 and Berlin in 1929.[29] The size of the delegations from non-Western countries was also larger at Paris and Berlin: for example, the Egyptian delegation comprised five women at Paris and eight in Berlin, while it had numbered three at Rome.[30]

Some 30 countries were represented at WILPF's 1921 Vienna conference, including Japan, China, Mexico, and the Ukraine. In addition, some 300 women and men attended its first summer school, including from China, India, Japan, Mexico, and the Ukraine. WILPF continued to expand at its conference in Washington in 1924, when four new national sections were admitted, including those of Haiti and Japan. In addition to the 85 delegates representing national sections, there were also fraternal delegates and visitors, including representatives from governments, organizations, and universities as well as women visitors from different parts of Asia, Africa, and Latin America. Thus, the 1924 WILPF conference proved to be as international as the conferences of the IAW described above. A total of 150 delegates and 8 fraternal delegates attended the conference in Dublin in 1926, and 20 out of 24 national sections were represented.[31]

What stands out with regards to the topics covered at conferences during the 1920s is the new focus on peace. For example, the programme of the IAW conference in Paris in 1926 included two meetings dedicated to "women of all nations" and "women of all nations for peace." Likewise, WILPF organized a mass meeting for young people, "Youth for Peace," at its 1924 Washington conference. At its Dublin Congress in 1926, Tano Jodai of Japan spoke on "Economic Imperialism," and the Prague congress of 1929 featured a session on the political, racial, and international aspects of the settlement of internal disputes, with contributions from Miss Paranjpye and Mrs. Chattopadhyaya of India, and from Irene Ho Tung of China.[32]

Women from all over the world now congregated in greater numbers at international women's conferences. Non-Western participants still constituted a minority with their delegations, often comprising just two women. Yet their presence was significantly greater than in the prewar period, and contemporary conference reports are replete with references to the international unity and sisterhood symbolized by their involvement.

Disagreements over methods of peace activism

The international peace movement comprised many different groups, including socialists, religious groups, and women's organizations. While united in their quest for a long-lasting peace, they differed over how to achieve this. Some favored more radical methods, such as strikes and protests, while others proposed a more moderate approach, such as working closely with the newly established League of Nations.[33] The women's movements also showed this pattern, with the ICW standing for the moderate line and WILPF for the radical line. However, what is important to know is that all liberal international women's organizations shared a common belief in women's special affinity with peace, justice, and tolerance, as essential female qualities. This belief stemmed both from the gendered expectations attached to the role of "woman," especially the implied qualities of nurturing, caring, and protecting, and from the experiences that they accumulated working on these issues. For example, the IAW's declaration of principles stated: "The barbarism of war, torture and famine threatens to engulf the world. It is for the woman's movement to awaken and strengthen sanity, compassion, wisdom and foresight, which are the gifts of womanhood."[34]

The question of what course of action to take in activism was a delicate matter that caused disagreement and division between and within organizations. Within WILPF, there were disagreements over principles, ideology, and tactics that became more pronounced in the 1930s. Catherine Foster highlights organizational infighting that coincided with fascism coming to power in Italy and Germany. Some members called repeatedly for economic sanctions such as trade boycotts and oil embargoes, yet the organization as a whole never focused on such proposals. As a result, some members criticized WILPF for not being pacifist enough. Others thought it was too pacifist. As a result, its membership declined in the 1930s.[35] In 1936 at an executive committee meeting in Paris some national sections expressed opposition to WILPF's objectives as adopted at its 1924 Washington congress: The American, British, Polish, Danish, Norweigan, and Swedish sections considered the 1924 wording that stated that WILPF opposed all war including "defensive war" to be too strong, as that position made it impossible for members to support the use of "military sanctions" by the League of Nations, as was permitted by the Geneva Convention. The League of Nations' idea of "defensive war" meant that an attack on a member nation was to be seen as an attack on all member nations. This was tested in 1935 when Italy invaded Abyssinia (now Ethiopia). Both were members of the League, which resulted in sanctions against Italy, and later the League came to Abyssinia's aid militarily. Yet the intervention was slow and ineffective and was not able to stop Mussolini.[36] This type of military action was thus something that many WILPF members condoned, while others remained opposed due to their absolute pacifism.

The Scandinavian sections proposed a compromise, to the effect that WILPF should accept as members those who were "interested in" pacifism but not necessarily prepared to support all the WILPF's principles.[37] This debate continued in WILPF's journal *Pax*, where members joined with the Scandinavian sections in arguing for greater flexibility regarding new admissions, partly to be achieved by providing education on peace questions upon affiliation. Other members stressed the importance of holding to WILPF's original role of attracting women who were determined to fight peace, internationalism, and social justice under all circumstances. Strength in numbers, they believed was an illusion, if it came at the price of weakening the organization's position in such a way that it no longer differed greatly from that of numerous other pacifist organizations – organizations that, they claimed, kept silent and even supported their war-prone governments at the moment of crisis.[38] Among the opponents of "softening" WILPF's objectives in order to increase membership were prominent members such as Dr. Aletta Jacobs, one of WILPF's founders.[39] Despite these differences of opinion among its members, WILPF managed to avoid a split.

Other organizations also had internal disagreements among members. However, an analysis of women's interwar activism reveals that their organizational records downplayed these and sought to present a united front. This is not surprising, given that such records had been collected and passed on to the organization's headquarters.[40] These organizations were conscious of the historical value of their documents, as demonstrated by the careful way in which they recorded their activities in conference reports, executive meeting reports, journals, and other publications.[41] Their records allowed them to have a voice and make claims, and thereby to exert extensive power over their own history.[42] Frank and partisan passages in private letters sometimes contrast sharply with official accounts, and so provide alternative insights into the nature of women's international cooperation, offering a window into the thoughts and feelings of women engaged in international cooperation. However, private accounts in letters represent the views of only a minority of members of international women's organizations. Interpretation of both organizational records and private correspondence must therefore be careful.

At least outwardly, then, organizations' reports displayed a heightened sense of optimism and belief in international cooperation in the interwar period. At that time, the identity of the international women's movement was based on a collective sense among women, for the important reason that women's lack of political power continued to divide the sexes.[43] After all, these organizations focused on inequalities between women and men (in particular, on political rights and legislation), rather than inequalities that may have divided women themselves. These organizations' message of equality, justice, and above all peace resonated with many women and enabled good collaboration among women's organizations and with the League of Nations. It is important to know that despite differences of opinion about goals and tactics, the women's movements continued to be driven by women's marginalization, and marginalization united like-minded women on a scale far more international in the 1920s and 1930s than in previous decades. While the organizations continued to differ in their campaigns and methods, they were united as women and united by their renewed focus on international peace following World War I.

Cooperation for peace and disarmament: toward a new vision of humanism

As one historian summed up the interwar situation, "If peace was to be preserved, the world had to disarm – and it was up to the League [of Nations] to achieve this."[44] International women's organizations were keen to cooperate with the League of Nations, and were central to its disarmament campaigns that followed World War I. In the 1920s and early 1930s the importance of the League's work was self-evident to many organizations around the world. Yet, while the pursuit of international disarmament was the greatest crusade of the League of Nations, it was also its greatest disappointment.[45]

Deteriorating international relations during the 1930s directed these international women's organizations more firmly towards peace work, and in particular, the question of disarmament. Conference reports, journals, and correspondence from the period are replete with references to the pursuit of peace as opposed to separatist feminist concerns. Reflecting this is an "Appeal to the World's Statesmen" that several international women's organizations, including the ICW, the IAW, and WILPF, jointly issued in 1930:

> We declare the work for peace to be the most urgent task before the world today. We appeal, therefore, to every right-thinking person and, in particular to women, who pay the first cost of human life, to realize their responsibility and power.[46]

What is significant to remember is that this new commitment to peace placed the interests of all humans and the preservation of the dignity of all people above all else. Many female activists believed that they were particularly suited to push this agenda of peace and humanism because of their special ability regarding justice and tolerance as mothers, and because of their extensive previous experience with transnational collaboration. Indeed, the urgency of the situation led to new ways of interaction: greater collaboration between organizations and even talk of fusion; widening of regional cooperation, and more and stronger liaisons with the League of Nations. While these organizations had cooperated with each other in the past, in the 1930s their work on peace and disarmament united them more closely. Increasingly, they left their separate conferences to join with each other, and also entered more fully into the intergovernmental arena provided by the League of Nations.

During the 1930s, however, the practical organization of peace activism became more difficult for WILPF and other international women's organizations. Most international women's organizations in Europe were badly affected, with Italy, Germany, and Austria losing sections. Italy's totalitarian regime closed down women's associations and forbade women to attend international conferences. German branches of international women's organizations were ordered to submit unconditionally to the Führer, recognize the special tasks that the Nazi state assigned to women (mainly racialized social welfare), expel Jewish members from their national boards as well as from the boards of affiliates and local councils, and accept the imposed appointment of Nazi women to leading positions. Spain's and Czechoslovakia's associations became practically inoperative. In Japan too, women's organizations working for peace experienced difficulties.[47] Nevertheless, as we have seen, six women's international organizations joined forces to present the "Appeal of Women to the World's Statesmen" to the League of Nations in 1930, declaring women's urgent concern for the future and the need for peace work. The same year, at the London Naval Conference, a delegation of American, British, French, and Japanese women urged substantial reductions in naval armaments.

Disarmament became the main focus of the 1930s peace activism. Disarmament was part of broader agenda for peace, yet it was a campaign theme in itself. It had an advantage over more general calls for "peace" in that it called equally on all parties to pull back from an arms race. The upsurge in cooperation across organizations is well demonstrated by the disarmament campaign initiated by WILPF in the early 1930s. WILPF initiated a petition that was translated into 18 languages, published, and discussed around the world. Due to the growing size of the campaign and the public opinion in favor of disarmament, the campaign was taken over by the Disarmament Committee of the Women's International Organizations (DCWIO), formed in 1931 as a special committee of the Liaison Committee of Women's International Organizations (LCWIO). The Disarmament Committee was composed of 14 international organizations and one powerful national federal organization. The Disarmament Committee announced its creation as follows:

> In spite of the popular allegation that women do not know how to work together, actually the largest women's international organisations which represent over forty million women and cover every organised sphere of women's activity in all parts of the globe, have joined forces for the first time and have created the Disarmament Committee.[48]

WILPF'S disarmament petition combined with similar efforts carried out by other organizations. It enjoyed the backing of prominent peace activists such as Mohandas (Mahatma) Gandhi, who was using peaceful and nonviolent methods in his work to achieve independence from the British Empire for India. WILPF was also keen to include and gain help from those who they regarded as most interested in disarmament: the laboring masses of all countries. Representatives of women's organizations from 56 countries, together with other organizations representing Catholic women and young people and representatives from the Labour Organization of the Second International and the League for the Rights of Man (forerunner of the International League for Human Rights), presented millions of signatures of women and men from around the world to the Conference for the Reduction and Limitation of Armaments (also known as the World Conference on Disarmament), which began in Geneva in 1932. Japan alone contributed 173,000 signatures, and impressive numbers of signatures also came from England, Switzerland, Denmark, Sweden, and Czechoslovakia.[49] At the conference Mary Dingman declared: "To us women, as mothers, the thought of what another great war would mean for our children is the strongest incentive impelling us to spend ourselves in the endeavour to make their lives secure from such a disastrous fate."[50]

Despite the failure of the disarmament campaign and the eruption of a new war, the international peace movement demonstrated how the League helped drive the creation of international solidarity. The disarmament negotiations, attended by states, groups, and individuals who operated transnationally, likewise showed that these occasions could function as mechanisms of global governance.[51] The League itself was keen to encourage greater involvement of women in its work, as reflected in a resolution introduced by Spain and passed by the assembly of the League in 1931 regarding collaboration with Women's International Organizations:

> The Assembly, convinced of the great value of the contribution of women to the work of peace and the friendly relations between the peoples which is the principal aim of the League, requests the Council to examine the possibility of increasing the collaboration of women in the work of the League of Nations.[52]

The League dispatched its own representatives to international women's conferences, in an attempt on its part to bolster support at a time when the popularity of the League of Nations was declining.[53] However, members of international women's organizations differed in their views of the League: some were supporters and others were critics. At the level of organizations, the ICW was the most enthusiastic about the League of Nations. The IAW was largely positive towards the League; for example, its Declaration of Principles at its 1935 Congress included references to supporting the League of Nations and peace.[54] WILPF was the most critical. Yet WILPF's British section continued to support the League. Moreover, WILPF did make use of the 1933 and 1938 League of Nations conventions on refugees (on legal protection and residence rights) in their November 1939 newsletter that announced its appeal to President Franklin D. Roosevelt to uphold standards of civilization at the Conference on Refugees he was soon to host.[55]

Organizational affiliation was only one factor influencing women's commitment to the League of Nations. For example, historian Christine Bolt argues that the fact that the United States remained outside the League meant that some American feminists felt themselves to be outsiders in Geneva, while British women, whose state belonged to the League, enjoyed a sense of insider status.[56] It is important to know that the League of Nations definitely offered an important and distinctively new space to operate for the international women's organizations. The League shared the women's concerns with peace and humanism and provided them with new ways of cooperating.

Broadening agendas and working for "human rights"

During the difficult decade of the 1930s, the major international women's organizations under scrutiny here broadened their agendas and moved toward a new and supposedly less radical feminism compared to the egalitarian feminism that had dominated some organizations previously. While still pursuing women's rights, this was now often done within a larger and less gender-specific peace and disarmament agenda. Indeed, some organizations and indivuduals chose to speak of "humanism" rather than "feminism," and through this touched on issues of human rights and social justice. This change in focus was also evident closer to home, in national and local settings, where debates took place between these new feminists, also sometimes referred to as social and welfare feminists, and egalitarian feminists, also known as equalitarian and even old feminists.[57] As the broader view of feminism and turn to humanism came to dominate many of the major international women's organizations at this time, some egalitarian feminists decided to break away and form new associations that continued to focus primarily on obtaining equal rights for women.

The 1920s had already witnessed the growing influence of so-called new feminism that emphasized women's difference from men, women's rights for women as a distinct group, and women's distinctive contributions to society. This 1920s new feminism had made demands for change based on women's traditional spheres, unlike the more established egalitarian feminism that downplayed differences between the sexes, rejected socially constructed gender roles, and demanded women's equality with men.[58] Whether it was really new at all has been debated,[59] yet it did emerge with a new rigor following the war. This movement fit well with these organizations' shift toward humanism and their focus on the question of peace, which, like new feminism, emphasized women's difference from men because of their special inclination for this issue.

An investigation into women's peace activism in the troubled 1930s reveals how activists in international women's organizations came to view peace and disarmament as prerequisites for achieving other rights. Their commitment to disarmament above all else demonstrates that they regarded this as a precondition for improvements for women in all other areas. While these women, working alongside other groups and associations, were drawing attention to issues that we would today label "human rights," they rarely used that term.[60] However, they did use the term humanism, which was part of the broader view of feminism that focused less on achieving legal equalities for women and instead on liberty and respect for all humans.[61] The turn to humanism and new feminism were thus linked, and was in part the result of the difficult circumstances in which female activists operated in the 1930s. The outcome was that at least some of these organizations adopted a broader agenda that was capable of attracting a wider, more diverse membership. The ICW, for instance, added concerns with such varied issues as nutrition, women in radio programming and broadcasting, children's libraries, more equitable distribution of the world's resources, and the technical training of disabled children to its existing work on slavery, prostitution, the nationality of married women, and equal working conditions for women and men. Of the three organizations, the IAW remained the most obviously committed to women's equality, despite changes to its agenda, as it continued to work for women's suffrage, equal moral standards, maternity rights, and the legal status of women. The two different conceptions of equality in these organizations in the 1930s continued to generate disagreement on issues such as protective legislation for women workers and women's civil status and nationality. However, the international organizations explored here all aimed to be as all-encompassing as possible. Inclusiveness, that is, opening their doors as wide as possible to a range of women from different national backgrounds, became a priority. Strength in numbers was obviously important, and for organizations that operated transnationally by expanding their horizons beyond Europe and North America, so too was the aim of becoming truly international, as they themselves described it. Broader agendas were required to encompass differences in objectives and forms of development in various national and local women's movements. This changed focus was also evident closer to home, in debates between so-called "old" or egalitarian feminists and "new," social or welfare feminists. While the former had been dominant, the latter emerged as the stronger in the 1920s. The latter moved beyond the egalitarian feminist agenda by for instance taking up the issue of endowments for married women who stayed outside the paid workforce. Thus, "new" feminism appealed to women from a wider range of backgrounds, including women who did not respond to a feminism focused on equality in the political and professional spheres.[62]

Some women, as their contemporary reports attest, were prepared to describe as "feminist" any individual or institution that they believed was working to improve the status of women. Other organizations, such as the ICW, were much less willing to apply the term "feminist" to their own activities, even when they used that term in relation to others' work.[63] For ICW, then, the term "feminist" meant egalitarian feminism and it, and other international organizations, clearly saw a need to downplay any overt connection to egalitarian feminism in order to be acceptable to a wider cross-section of women and to society at large. The newer organization WILPF also lost its strong feminist focus in the interwar period. According to Catherine Foster, WILPF pioneers' linkage of feminism, and in particular suffrage, to peace loosened as WILPF leaders realized that the advent of women's suffrage did not bring about the desired changes. WILPF increasingly concentrated its work on peace and international relations and decreased its attention to women's rights. In the 1930s there were even discussions of dropping the word "Women's" from the organization's title. Yet WILPF did remain an organization of women that continued to stress women's special responsibility for peace work.[64]

It is important to note that this broadening and more inclusive agenda of new feminism and humanism did not go unchallenged in any of these major international women's organizations. The renewed emphasis on peace unsettled some members of international women's organizations, including Carrie Chapman Catt, former president of the IAW. Catt declared in a 1935 letter to Rosa Manus:

> I feel a sense of disappointment whenever I think of the absence of progress concerning the enfranchisement of women in Switzerland and the rather slow progress being made in France. I do not mind other countries so much. I would think that the Alliance might very well come to an end now were it not for the possibility it has to do some good in the peace movement.[65]

Disagreements over the new focus on peace by these organizations also appeared in their publications. For example, IAW's journal *Jus Suffragii* published a debate over the terms "feminist" and "humanist." Proponents of the former viewed the new focus on humanism as a betrayal and a move away from their feminist commitment by working for peace. Others, including the IAW president Margery Corbett Ashby, saw no problem with combining the two, and argued that they needed to be not only feminists, but humanists as well.[66] Indeed, the IAW's increased focus on peace work and social reform meant that female activists previously associated with it were now attracted to new equal rights organizations such as Open Door International (ODI) and Equal Rights International (ERI).[67] Leading British feminists, including the British suffragist and women's equal rights campaigner Lady Rhondda, formed ODI in 1929.[68] ODI targeted the International Labour Organization (ILO), seeking to prevent the adoption of protective legislation for women workers, which ODI members believed would restrict women's equality and choice.[69] ERI was established a year later, in 1930, with the goal of an international equal rights treaty.[70] WILPF's increased focus on peace work likewise displeased some of its own members, including the committed feminists and pacifists Lida Gustava Heymann and Anita Augspurg, who wanted to retain WILPF's emphasis on women's rights.[71]

It was not only the broadening of these organizations' agendas and work for peace that caused disagreements among members, but also what methods and course of action that were most suitable for this struggle. While WILPF boldly declared at its 1937 Congress that it sought a "New International Order" far different from the existing situation characterized by disorder and chaos, one in which not only individuals but states would behave according to moral laws,[72] members continued to disagree on what action to take. While some members wanted to make bold statements, others preferred taking more prudent steps. As pointed out by Catherine Foster, the German and French sections, whose members were feeling the brunt of Nazi politics earlier and more directly than the British, Scandinavian, and North American sections, favored intense action through an alliance with radical movements and even the Soviet regime.[73] Even though WILPF managed to avoid a split, internal disagreement weakened it during the interwar period. The Women's Peace Crusade, a British umbrella organization that included the British section of WILPF and affiliates of other international women's associations,[74] also faced divisions over whether or not to take political action, over closer cooperation with radical left-wing movements, and over direct action tactics such as strikes and violent demonstrations. The latter, it was feared, would reduce their public appeal and the number of potential collaborators among other organizations.[75] The ICW also faced this dilemma, as its leading members hesitated to join the disarmament campaign, given that the ICW constitution prevented the organization from proclaiming its views of political issues. The fact that the ICW did eventually join the disarmament campaign highlights the organization's flexibility in the context of the severe instability facing Europe in the 1930s.

This turn to working for humanism and human rights was thus closely linked to the deteriorating situation in Europe. As Christine Bolt notes, women activists in Europe felt that their societies were moving backwards in the 1930s, not just with regard to feminism, but also core values such as liberty, democracy, political tolerance, and international cooperation. The Spanish Civil War (1936–9) manifested this backward movement more than anything else, they felt. Just as the disarmament campaign had united diverse organizations, both women's and male-dominated, so also the Spanish Civil War saw women organizing across political and national boundaries and together with men, holding, for example, several anti-fascist conferences in the 1930s.[76] Despite disagreements within and between these international organizations, it is important to note that they all agreed that international cooperation was crucial in this period. Women, they believed, had a special talent for international cooperation, and they also believed that working for peace and disarmament was prerequisite to achievements in other areas, including equality for women.

Strengthening equal rights through peace

Peace and humanism were thought to go hand in hand with improved rights of women, whose presence in intergovernmental organizations was seen as necessary to achieve the desired changes to women's status. While peace and disarmament were priorities during the interwar period, women's groups related these to their equal rights campaign by arguing that women's full equality would unleash a powerful social force in favor of peace and disarmament. Women's groups realized that the League of Nations provided opportunities for their work precisely because of its international membership of states. Any resolution passed by the League, they believed, would have an impact on those states' governments across the world.

International women's organizations used the international platform provided by the League of Nations to work for peace and disarmament, and also to lobby for change on so-called "women's rights" issues. This work had started already in the 1920s, but greatly intensified in the 1930s and they perceived greater success in their lobbying in the 1930s. The ICW used their political networks at the 1919 Peace Congress to demand women's self-determination as a complement of national self-determination. Yet core countries such as the United States, Britain, Japan, and France insisted that women's political status within each state was not a legitimate concern.[77] According to Carol Miller, women's organizations made the decision to turn to the international arena that the League of Nations provided in order to counter regressive changes taking place inside many countries.

A successful example of this type of campaigning was the establishment of the Women's Consultative Committee on Nationality by the League of Nations in the early 1930s. The League did so in direct response to pressure from women's organizations, in particular international coalitions of these, such as the Liaison Committee of Women's International Organizations (LCWIO). The Women's Consultative Committee on Nationality began its campaign for wives' independent nationality status in 1930, in connection with a legal conference at The Hague sponsored by the League of Nations. This conference, the Codification Conference, met to establish worldwide standards of law on three issues: maritime law; states' responsibilities for actions against foreigners; and universal, non-conflicting rules on nationality. This last was of concern to women activists, for as historian Ellen DuBois explains, the drive for independent nationality for married women combined two main feminist concerns: establishing full and equal citizenship for women, and undoing women's marital disabilities (women who married foreign men lost their own nationality).[78] Women were largely excluded from the official proceedings of the legal conference, as only two women had full delegate status, so women activists had to lobby from the outside, something they were used to doing. A group combining members from the IAW and the ICW organized an elaborate demonstration for the conference's evening opening ceremonies. In response, the chairman of the Codification Conference, former Dutch prime minister Theodorus Heemskerk, reluctantly agreed to receive a small deputation of the women the next day at the Peace Palace and accept a copy of their requests.[79] As nothing came of the meeting, their hopes were now with a second group of women, this time from the United States and South American countries, who made another attempt to influence the Codification Conference. According to DuBois, these women were more familiar with activism in mixed-sex settings and also were bolder in their requests. Yet, despite their intense lobbying efforts, and the decision by the United States to vote against the recommendations by The Hague conference, the report favoring minimal changes in the law of married women's nationality was passed on to Geneva for eventual ratification by member nations.

This meant that the feminist nationality campaign now moved to the League of Nations itself and feminist activists descended on Geneva to try and halt ratification of the findings with respect to nationality of The Hague Codification Conference.[80] WILPF placed a room at its Maison Internationale at the disposal of the Women's Consultative Committee on Nationality[81] and its members lobbied national delegates about the inadequacies of The Hague recommendations.[82] Lillian von Matsch, chair of the Sub-Committee for Propaganda of the Women's Consultative Committee on Nationality, noted that "There was a noticeable increase in the recognition of the seriousness of the dissatisfaction of women with The Hague Nationality Convention, on the part of the delegates to the 1932 Assembly."[83] Indeed, at the vote in the plenary session of the Assembly, nine countries – Chile, China, Colombia, Czechoslovakia, Guatemala, Mexico, Poland, and Turkey – abstained and in this way registered their protest against The Hague Nationality Convention. Yet the League adopted the Convention, and it was eventually ratified by the entire League in 1937. Disappointed that the changes did not extend as far as to grant women independent nationality rights, many of the US and South American activists, including prominent feminists such as Marta Vergara of Chile, decided to cease collaborating with the League.[84]

Nevertheless, the 1930s witnessed continued efforts on the part of women's organizations to secure an Equal Rights Treaty via the League. Lobbying for this had begun in the mid-1920s, reflecting their belief in the common problems facing women worldwide. By the late 1930s it had become a vigorous campaign to demand a convention in which women's civil, political, and legal status would be based on the equality of the sexes. In preparation for such a convention, and following a proposal by the president of the Swedish National Council of Women, Kerstin Hesselgren, in 1937 the League established a committee of experts. Women comprised the majority of the members of this committee, and it was charged with studying the national laws on which the status of women was based. However, the success of this effort, according to Carol Miller, was hampered by tensions among women stemming from their divergent conceptions of equality, that is, whether equality was to be achieved by giving women the same rights as men or by taking into account women's differences.

Such frictions did not dampen the belief of many of these women that their organizations were important. Although the League of Nations repeatedly rejected the demand for a Woman's Charter and a separate body for Women's Questions, the League's Covenant did work toward gender equality by making positions in the League secretariat open to both sexes. This resulted in an important minority of highly qualified women inside the League administration, albeit in "second divisions"[85] and occupying positions with less influence than their male counterparts. An example is Dame Rachel Crowdy, who held the highest post of any woman in the League bureaucracy, as the administrator of its Social Section. This department was allegedly seen as being in charge of matters of "soft politics," such as protection of children and trafficking of women. Moreover, Crowdy was never given the title of director, a rank bestowed on her male replacement in 1930.[86] Women were also eligible to serve as their countries' delegates to the League, or as experts on its advisory commissions. Over two decades of League of Nations activity, 17 women served as delegates to the League General Assembly. Indeed, individual women's footholds in intergovernmental politics and the activism of women's international organizations were both important characteristics of the interwar period.[87] Other successes for women's activism included the League's decision in the mid-1930s to view the regulation of vice as an exceptional measure against women and to condemn it. The IAW was happy to take credit for this League decision, claiming it in its 1935 congress report.[88] It is important to note that these women placed their faith in twentieth-century international law, institutions, and practice as the way to improve their collective gender status, as well as to achieve peace, humanitarianism, and social justice.[89] These female activists gained invaluable experience through their work with the League of Nations. Indeed, their various campaigns during the interwar period, ranging from disarmament to equal nationality to men, were essentially about human rights. These campaigns laid the foundations for the establishment of human rights and women's rights in later decades, through a new organization: the United Nations. An examination of women's activism in the interwar period shows that United Nations-era work for women's rights, including the Convention Eliminating All Forms of Discrimination against Women (1979), were foreshadowed in the campaigns by these interwar international female activists.[90]

Challenges to internationalisms

While internationalisms clearly enjoyed support from diverse groups of people and gained ground in the interwar period, it was nationalisms that reigned supreme.[91] By the late 1930s, the factors working against internationalism and pacifism were stronger than those working in favor, and the League of Nations remained unrepresentative and without much power.[92] Male politicians' and the public's – and even women's – mixed responses to women's active roles in the 1930s peace movements reflected that larger context. While women activists' extensive work for peace through disarmament during the 1930s received recognition and individual women were publicly honored in a range of ways, some viewed these women's commitment to internationalism as naive and even unpatriotic.

Newspapers at the time highlighted how women occupied center stage at the League of Nations' disarmament conference. The appointment of IAW president Margery Corbett Ashby as substitute member of the British delegation to the disarmament conference was covered extensively in the press. WILPF president Jane Addams received the ultimate accolade, the Nobel Peace Prize, in 1931, to great public attention. Yet while women's activity was much noted in the press at the time, few histories of the League of Nations credit women's contributions to the disarmament campaign and the 1931 Geneva Conference. Some statesmen of the period, such as British prime minister at the time Ramsay MacDonald, were interested in women's work for peace, yet also suggested that the women were naive in their quest for peace. Of course, opinions were sharply divided on the best course of action for dealing with the instabilities of the interwar years. WILPF was from its inception committed to uprooting the fundamental causes of war, including inequality, oppression, and exploitation, and it stood out among peace organizations for its political (but not party-political) approach to peace. Often attacked for its positions and activism, in the United States WILPF was targeted as "red" and "unpatriotic."

Domestic attitudes such as these, in addition to the already difficult international political climate, made WILPF's work for peace especially challenging in the 1930s. There were disappointments at the failure of the Disarmament Conferences. Margery Corbett Ashby resigned from the British committee in 1935, claiming that "My two years as UK substitute delegate to this conference were the most miserable of my life."[93] Towards the end of the 1930s, a contributor to *Pax* described disappointment at the lack of an "international spirit" inside WILPF. Even though there was no shortage of international organizations and conferences, this contributor claimed, the spirit of international "preparedness" was hollow and had become "degraded to national interests" compared with 20 or 30 years ago.[94] It is true that the impact of the disarmament campaign was limited, the League of Nations was inefficient in dealing with the Manchurian, Ethiopian, and Spanish crises,[95] and the international political and economic situation deteriorated further towards the end of the decade.

At the same time as Europe's collapse into another war began to seem inevitable, demands for national independence elsewhere were destabilizing Western empires. These demands challenged many non-Western women's commitment to international feminism. The 1930s therefore saw an increase in regional cooperation among women outside the parameters of Europe, in the context of growing resentment of colonialism. An All-Asian Women's Conference was held in Lahore in 1931, for example, and similar gatherings were also organized in Damascus and Tehran by Middle Eastern feminists.[96] Meanwhile, most major international women's organizations remained silent on the issue of colonial empire, a choice shaped by the organizations' non-political stance as well as the fact that Western women continued to dominate the organizations. WILPF stood apart with its markedly "progressive" stance on international relations and inequalities. Nonetheless, even WILPF's peace work and international expansion were affected by conflicts and disputes in colonies, and those prevented local female activists from making full commitments to WILPF's principle of opposing every kind of war.

Conclusion

Women from many different backgrounds joined in action following the Great War to prevent another one. This broad movement for peace and humanism was truly international in character. During the 1930s in particular, disarmament became an urgent concern, and many different groups came together in fighting for this cause above all else. International women's organizations took the lead in this campaign. This meant that work for disarmament and peace was often prioritized over work for women's equality, such as the activism concerning women's legal status in marriage or equal employment rights that had preoccupied earlier activists.

In the aftermath of World War I, major international women's organizations such as the ICW, IAW, and WILPF all expanded. They shared a growing interest in non-Western regions of the world and a desire to establish new affiliations where none had previously existed. Conferences took on a more visibly international character and became an ideal place in which to forge connections and establish friendships that crossed national borders. Such gatherings reinforced the belief that the similarities among women outweighed any differences separating them. For these women, it was their marginalization that united them, and also their strong belief that international cooperation would solve the most pressing issues of the time.

International women's organizations started to work with the League of Nations very soon after its creation in 1920. Their cooperation with the League intensified during the 1930s, largely because the League provided them with a new international platform that allowed them to reach a larger audience with their concerns about peace and women's rights. While the cause of peace had been a unifying force already in the 1920s, peace became considerably more urgent in the 1930s due to the serious world situation. As the 1930s progressed, the agendas of these international women's organizations converged. The similarities among their programmes allowed for greater collaboration and increased the significance of internationalism and coalitions between different international organizations.

While women were united in their quest for peace and disarmament, they did not agree on the methods to reach those goals. Many chose to prioritize peace above all else, moving away from their focus on women's rights, while others continued to pursue both agendas side by side. There were also those who did not wish to cooperate with intergovernmental organizations such as the League of Nations, as they saw them working against women, as illustrated, for example, by their disappointment with the nationality campaign. These activists believed that differences between men and women were socially constructed and stressed similarities between the sexes, and believed that more radical change was required to combat these institutionalized inequalities. Moreover, the cooperation among women was never really that of straightforwardly equal partners. These organizations comprised women with diverse ideas and aims and were hierarchical.

These international women's organizations' commitment to transnational cooperation among women and to the League of Nations persisted in the face of the complexities of the interwar period. The main aim of this cooperation was an end to all wars, and also, for many women, to establish equality between the sexes. Indeed, these international women's organizations had different ideas about what feminism signified and how useful it was for their campaigns. Yet all of these organizations were united in their desire to improve the lives and status of women wherever they lived in the world. And despite their varied foci on political, social, educational, and/or legal rights, and their debates over emphasizing "equality" or "difference," it could be argued that the international organizations under scrutiny here all moved, to varying degrees, toward broader definitions of feminism, and humanism with an emphasis on peace during the difficult interwar period. The peace question resulted in new commitments to what we can in hindsight describe as humanism, understood as the care for all humanity and everyone's right to determine their own goals and values.

As another war approached and eventually engulfed Europe, these organizations' contribution to peace work took on a practical and humanitarian dimension that was nonetheless international: assistance to refugees. The solidarity that stemmed from women's continued marginalization and their firm commitment to internationalism and humanism continued to unite many of them in activism, not only during the challenging 1930s decade but during World War II itself and beyond.

Notes

1 This was arranged by distributing articles via neutral countries such as Sweden, Denmark, the Netherlands, and Switzerland. See Sybil Oldfield, "Mary Sheepshank Edits an International Suffrage Monthly in Wartime: *Jus Suffragii* 1914–19," *Women's History Review*, 2003, vol. 12, no. 1, 119–34.

2 Glenda Sluga and Patricia Clavin, "Rethinking the History of Internationalism," in Glenda Sluga and Patricia Clavin (eds.) *Internationalisms: A Twentieth-Century History*, Cambridge, UK: Cambridge University Press, 2017, p. 9.

3 Sluga and Clavin, "Rethinking," p. 10.

4 For example, one of the earliest and most influential women's temperance organizations was the Woman's Christian Temperance Union (WCTU), established in 1874 in the United States. The WCTU fought against alcohol, which they blamed for many social ills, including immorality, as well as against war. They embraced Christian and family values as well as advocating social reform and women's emancipation. From its inception, the WCTU advocated internationalism and organized world conventions from the 1870s onwards. See Ian Tyrrell, *Woman's World, Woman's Empire: The Woman's Christian Temperance Union in International Perspective, 1880–1930*, Chapel Hill: University of North Carolina Press, 1991.

5 International Alliance of Women for Suffrage and Equal Citizenship (IAWSEC), *Report of the Twelfth Congress, Istanbul, 18–24 April 1935*, London: IAWSEC, 1935; International Alliance of Women for Suffrage and Equal Citizenship (IAWSEC), *Report of the Thirteenth Congress, Copenhagen, 8–14 July 1939*, Ashford, Kent: IAWSEC, 1939.

6 At the 1932 Disarmament Conference, Dingman stressed that their greatest determination came to them as mothers, for women wanted to ensure that their children's lives would be free from war. *Disarmament Committee of the Women's International Organizations* (DCWIO), *Official Record of the Declarations and Petitions Presented by the Disarmament Committee of the Women's International Organizations to the Disarmament Conference Geneva 1932*, Geneva: DCWIO, 1932, pp. 31–2.

7 Leila J. Rupp, *Worlds of Women: The Making of an International Women's Movement*, Princeton, NJ: Princeton University Press, 1997, p. 13.

8 As pointed out in Sluga and Clavin, "Rethinking," p. 62.

9 See for example Roland Burke, "The Internationalism of Human Rights," in Sluga and Clavin, *Internationalisms*, pp. 287–314.

10 Catherine Foster, *Women for All Seasons: The Story of the Women's International League for Peace and Freedom*, Athens: University of Georgia Press, 1989, pp. 7–11.

11 Rupp, *Worlds of Women*, p. 27.

12 Foster, *Women for All Seasons*, p. 12.

13 Sybil Oldfield (ed.), *International Woman Suffrage*: Ius suffragii, *1913–1920*, London: Routledge, 2003, pp. 15–17, 119–34; Rupp, *Worlds of Women*, p. 26.

14 Rupp, *Worlds of Women*, pp. 15–21.

15 Oldfield, *International Woman Suffrage*, p. 15; Foster, *Women for All Seasons*, p. 7; Rupp, *Worlds of Women*, pp. 19, 27, 90–1.

16 Glenda Sluga, "Women, Feminism and Twentieth-Century Internationalism," in Sluga and Clavin, *Internationalisms*, p. 65.

17 Sluga, "Women, Feminism and Twentieth-Century Internationalism," p. 65.

18 Rupp, *Worlds of Women*, pp. 90–1.

19 WILPF, *Women's International League for Peace and Freedom 1915–1938: A Venture in Internationalism*, Geneva: Women's International League, 1938.

20 WILPF, *Women's International League for Peace and Freedom 1915–1938: A Venture*, p. 12.

21 Rebecca Sherrick, "Toward Universal Sisterhood," *Women's Studies International Forum*, 1982, vol. 5, no. 9, 656.

22 Karen Hunt, "'The Immense Meaning of it All': The Challenges of Internationalism for British Socialist Women before the First World War," *Socialist History*, 2000, vol. 17, 22–42. See also June Hannam and Karen Hunt, *Socialist Women: Britain, 1880s to 1920s*, London: Routledge, 2002.

23 ICW, *Combined Third and Fourth Annual Report of the Seventh Quinquennial Period, 1922–1924*, compiled by Fru Anna Backer, Hon. Corresponding Secretary, n.p.: ICW, 1924; ICW, *Report of the Quinquennial Meeting. Washington, 1925*, Marchioness of Aberdeen and Temair, President of the ICW (ed.) London: ICW, 1926; IAWSEC, *Report of the Tenth Congress, La Sorbonne, Paris, France,*

30 May–6 June 1926, London: London Caledonian Press, 1926; Women's International League for Peace and Freedom (WILPF), *Report of the Third International Congress of Women, Vienna, 10–17 July 1921*, Geneva and Vienna: WILPF, 1921; WILPF, *Report of the Fourth Congress, Washington, 1–7 May 1924*, Washington and Geneva: WILPF US Section, 1924; WILPF, *Report of the Fifth Congress, Dublin, 8–15 July 1926*, Washington and Geneva: WILPF, 1926; WILPF, *Report of the Sixth Congress, Prague, 24–28 August 1929*, Geneva: WILPF, 1929.

24 The exceptions were Argentina (joined ICW in 1901) and China (society affiliated with IWSA in 1913). However, Chinese women did not attend the congress in Budapest in 1913 nor the one in Geneva in 1920, arriving late due to travel difficulties. See IWSA, *Report of the Eighth Congress, Geneva, Switzerland, 6–12 June 1920*, Manchester: Percy Brothers, 1920, p. 22; Rupp, *Worlds of Women*, p. 16.

25 ICW, *Report of the Quinquennial Meeting. Washington, 1925*. IWSA, *Report of the Ninth Congress, Rome, Italy, 12–19 May 1923*, Dresden: B. G. Teubner, 1923. IAWSEC, *Report of the Tenth Congress, La Sorbonne, Paris, France, 30 May–6 June 1926*, London: London Caledonian Press; IAWSEC, *Report of the Eleventh Congress, Berlin, 17–22 June 1929*, London: IAWSEC, 1929.

26 IWSA, *Report of the Eighth Congress, Geneva, Switzerland, 6–12 June 1920*.

27 IWSA, *Report of the Ninth Congress, Rome, Italy, 12–19 May 1923*.

28 Adele Schreiber and Margaret Mathieson, *Journey Towards Freedom. Written for the Golden Jubilee of the International Alliance of Women*, Copenhagen: IAW, 1955, p. 34.

29 IAWSEC, *Report of the Tenth Congress, La Sorbonne, Paris, France, 30 May–6 June 1926*; IAWSEC, *Report of the Eleventh Congress, Berlin, 17–22 June 1929*. More than one society per country was allowed to affiliate.

30 IAWSEC, *Report of the Tenth Congress, La Sorbonne, Paris, France, 30 May–6 June 1926*; Huda Shaarawi, *Harem Years: The Memoirs of an Egyptian Feminist (1879–1924)*, Margot Badran (ed. and trans.), New York: Feminist Press, 1986.

31 WILPF, *Report of the Internaitonal Congress of Women in Zurich, 1919*, Geneva: WILPF, 1919; WILPF, *Report of the Third International Congress of Women, Vienna, 10–17 July 1921*; WILPF, *Report of the International Conference of Women at The Hague, 7–9 December 1922. Organized by WILPF*, London and Geneva, 1922; WILPF, *Report of the Fourth Congress, Washington, 1–7 May 1924*; WILPF, *Report of the Fifth Congress, Dublin, 8–15 July 1926*; WILPF, *Report of the Sixth Congress, Prague, 24–28 August 1929*.

32 WILPF, *Report of the Fourth Congress, Washington, 1–7 May 1924*; WILPF, *Report of the Fifth Congress, Dublin, 8–15 July 1926*; "Prague Congress," *Pax International*, 1929, vol. 4, no. 10.

33 Karl Holl, "History of Peace Movements," in *International Encyclopedia of the Social and Behavioral Sciences*, Amsterdam: Elsevier, 2001, 11147–51.

34 IAWSEC, *Report of the Thirteenth Congress, Copenhagen, 8–14 July 1939*, Ashford, UK: IAWSEC, 1939.

35 Foster, *Women for All Seasons*, p. 22.

36 See George W. Baer, "Sanctions and Security: The League of Nations and the Italian-Ethiopian War, 1935–36," *International Organization*, 1973, vol. 27, no. 2, 165–79.

37 Gothenburg University Library, Gothenburg, Sweden, Kvinnohistoriska Samlingarna (hereafter GUL-KS), Internationella kvinnoförbundet för fred och frihet (IKFF), EI: 2, Utländska brev 1920-talet.

38 Gabrielle Duchêne, "The League Must Not Go Backward" and Marguerite Gobat, "The Danger of Crystalization," *Pax International*, 1926, vol. 1, no. 7.

39 GUL-KS, IKFF, EI: 2, Utländska brev 1920-talet.

40 Richard Olney has pointed out that formal manuscript records such as committee meetings might have been "constructively" written to record what should have been said rather than what was actually discussed. See Richard J. Olney, *Manuscript Sources for British History: Their Nature, Location and Use*, London: Institute of Historical Research, 1995.

41 In 1935 the International Archives for the Women's Movement (Internationaal Archief voor de Vrouwenbeweging, IAV) was set up in Amsterdam. One of the cofounders was Rosa Manus, long-term vice president of the IAW and also active in other international women's organizations. The official goal of the IAV was "to further the knowledge and scientific study of the women's movement in the broadest sense of the world." It enjoyed support from women like Carrie Chapman Catt and Margery Corbett Ashby (IAW presidents 1904–23 and

1923–46 respectively). In 1940, the IAV was closed by German officials and much of its material disappeared. However, it reopened in 1947 and in 2003 some of the lost material, which had ended up in Moscow, was returned to the Netherlands. See Francisca de Haan, "Getting to the Source: A 'Truly International' Archive for the Women's Movement (IAV, now IIAV): From its Foundation in Amsterdam in 1935 to the Return of its Looted Archives in 2003," *Journal of Women's History*, 2004, vol. 16, no. 4, 148–72.

42 This discussion has been influenced by Jane Martin's "Feminist Teachers and Social Action: The Case of City Politics" and Jane McDermid's "A Public Life: Grace Paterson, Educationalist and Suffragist," research papers presented at the 15th Annual Conference of the Women's History Network, "Thinking Women: Education, Culture and Society," 1–3 September 2006, Collingwood College, University of Durham.

43 See Leila J. Rupp and Verta Taylor, "Forging Feminist Identity in an International Movement: A Collective Identity Approach to Twentieth-Century Feminism," *Signs: Journal of Women in Culture and Society*, 1999, vol. 24, no. 2, 376, 380–1.

44 Andrew Webster, "The League of Nations, Disarmament and Internationalism," in Sluga and Clavin, *Internationalisms*, p. 140.

45 Webster, "The League of Nations," pp. 140, 145.

46 "Appeal of Women to the World's Statesmen," signed by Ishbel Aberdeen and Temair (ICW), Jane Addams (WILFP), C.M. van Asch van Wyck (WYWCA), M. I. Corbett Ashby (IAWSEC), Clara Guthrie D'Arcis (WUWIC), and Winifred Cullis (IFUW), *Pax International*, 1930, vol. 5, no. 11.

47 Schreiber and and Mathieson, *Journey Towards Freedom*, p. 51; WILPF, *Report of the Seventh Congress, Grenoble, 15–19 May 1932*, Geneva: WILPF, 1932; WILPF, *Report of the Ninth Congress, Luhacovice, Czechoslovakia, 27–31 July 1937*, Geneva: WILPF, 1937; Marie-Hélène Lefaucheux, *Women in a Changing World: The Dynamic Story of the International Council of Women Since 1888*, London: Routledge & Kegan Paul, 1966, pp. 64–70; Mary Grey Peck, *Carrie Chapman Catt: A Biography*, New York: H. W. Wilson, 1944, p. 454; IAWSEC, *Report of the Twelfth Congress, Istanbul, 18–24 April 1935; International Council of Women Bulletin*, 1934, vol. 13, no. 1; Fusae Ichikawa Memorial Association Library, Tokyo, Japan, Japanese Women's Suffrage Movement Collection I 1918–46, document no. 0213–14: Katherine Bompas (IAWSEC headquarters secretary) to Fusae Ichikawa; ICW, *Report on the Quinquennial Meeting, Vienna, 1930*, Marchioness of Aberdeen and Temair, President of the ICW (ed.), Tarland: ICW, 1930.

48 London School of Economics and Political Science, London, Women's Library (hereafter LSE-WL), Margery Corbett Ashby Papers (hereafter MCA Papers), Disarmament Conference Correspondence 1931–5, Disarmament Committee of the Women's International Organisations, "Appeal."

49 WILPF, *Report of the Seventh Congress, Grenoble, 15–19 May 1932.*

50 *Disarmament Committee of the Women's International Organizations, Official Record of the Declarations and Petitions presented by the Disarmament Committee of the Women's International Organizations to the Disarmament Conference*, Geneva: DCWIO, 1932, pp. 31–2.

51 Webster, "The League of Nations," pp. 144–5.

52 League of Nations, *Conference for the Reduction and Limitations of Armaments, Collaboration of Women in the Organisation of Peace, Geneva, February 12th, 1932.* Series IX. Disarmament, Geneva: League of Nations, 1932.

53 Carol Miller, "'Geneva – The Key to Equality': Interwar Feminists and the League of Nations," *Women's History Review*, 1994, vol. 3, no. 2, 219–45.

54 IAWSEC, *Report of the Twelfth Congress, Istanbul, 18–24 April 1935.*

55 *WILPF Newsletter*, 1939, vol. 14, no. 8, 5.

56 Christine Bolt, *Sisterhood Questioned? Race, Class and Internationalism in the American and British Women's Movements, c.1880s–1970s*, London: Routledge, 2004, pp. 69–75.

57 Maria DiCenzo and Alexis Motuz, "Politicizing the Home: Welfare Feminism and the Feminist Press in Interwar Britain," *Women: A Cultural Review*, 2016, vol. 27, no. 4, 378–96.

58 Most scholars use the terms "new feminism" and "equalitarian" or "egalitarian feminism." See for example Cheryl Law, *Suffrage and Power: The Women's Movement, 1918–1928*, London: I. B. Tauris, 2000 and Susan Kingsley Kent, "The Politics of Sexual Difference: World War I and the Demise of British Feminism," *Journal of British Studies*, 1988, vol. 27, no. 3, 232–53. Karen Offen has reworked this terminology in favor of "relational" and "individualist"

feminism: Karen Offen, "Defining Feminism: A Comparative Historical Approach," *Signs: Journal of Women in Culture and Society*, 1988, vol. 14, no. 1, 119–57. For further discussion of these terms, see Wendy Sarvasy, "Beyond the Difference versus Equality Policy Debate: Postsuffrage Feminism, Citizenship, and the Quest for a Feminist Welfare State," *Signs: Journal of Women in Culture and Society*, 1992, vol. 17, no. 2, 329–62.

59 According to Offen, who refers to it as "relational feminism," it had been the dominant line of argument in much of the West prior to the twentieth century, while "individualist feminism" arguments had characterized specifically Anglo-American feminism. Offen, "Defining Feminism."

60 During the interwar period several organizations and individuals tried to draw attention to what we today view as human rights violations. They did not use this term themselves. See David Weissbrodt, Fionnuala D. Ní Aoláin, and Mary Rumsey, *The Development of International Human Rights Law*, vol. 1, Farnham: Ashgate, 2014, pp. 3–56.

61 Rupp, *Worlds of Women*, p. 133.

62 DiCenzo and Motuz, "Politicizing the Home."

63 This supports Catriona Beaumont's findings. She has shown how so-called mainstream women's organizations in interwar Britain preferred to employ the terminology of "citizenship" rather than "feminism" to argue for enhancing women's status in society, as they believed that the latter was unpopular at that time. Catriona Beaumont, "Citizens not Feminists: The Boundary Negotiated between Citizenship and Feminism by Mainstream Women's Organizations in England, 1928–39," *Women's History Review*, 2000, vol. 9, no. 2, 415.

64 Foster, *Women for All Seasons*, pp. 17–18.

65 Carrie Chapman Catt to Rosa Manus, 17 July 1935, in Mineke Bosch with Annemarie Kloosterman (eds.) *Politics and Friendship: Letters from the International Woman Suffrage Alliance, 1902–1942*, Columbus: Ohio State University Press, 1990, p. 234.

66 Rupp, *Worlds of Women*, p. 133.

67 Miller, "Geneva – The Key to Equality," 224.

68 Lady Rhondda was an active member of the Women's Social and Political Union, the Women's Freedom League, and was founder of both the Six Point Group and Open Door International. See Elisabeth Crawford, *The Women's Suffrage Movement: A Reference Guide 1866–1928*, London: UCL Press, 1999, pp. 211, 256, and Angela V. John, *Turning the Tide: The Life of Lady Rhondda*, Cardigan, Wales: Partian, 2013.

69 See the essay by Eileen Boris and Jane Jensen in this volume.

70 Deborah Stienstra, *Women's Movements and International Organizations*, London: Macmillan, 1994, p. 66.

71 Foster, *Women for All Seasons*, p. 18.

72 WILPF, *Report of the Ninth Congress, Luhacovice, Czechoslovakia, 27–31 July 1937*, Geneva: WILPF, 1937; "The Grenoble Congress," *Pax International*, 1932, vol. 7, no. 7.

73 Foster, *Women for All Seasons*, pp. 21–2.

74 Among others: British Commonwealth League, British Women's Temperance Association, Scottish Christian Union, National Council for Equal Citizenship, Standing Joint Committee of Industrial Women's Organizations, and Union of Jewish Women. Smith College, Northampton, Massachusetts, Sophia Smith Collection of Women's History (hereafter SC-SSC), Josephine Schain Papers (hereafter JS Papers), Women's Peace Crusade, Box 11, File 3.

75 SC-SSC, JS Papers, Women's Peace Crusade Correspondence, Courtney, Kathleen, 1929–40, Kathleen Courtney to Josephine Schain, 14 March 1936.

76 Bolt, *Sisterhood Questioned?* p. 140.

77 Sluga, "Women, Feminism and Twentieth-Century Internationalism," p. 67.

78 Ellen C. DuBois, "Storming The Hague: The 1930 Campaign for Independent Nationality for Women Regardless of Marital Status," *Tijdschrift voor Genderstudies*, 2013, vol.16, no. 4, 18.

79 DuBois, "Storming The Hague," 20–2.

80 DuBois, "Storming The Hague," 24–5.

81 Women's Consultative Committee on Nationality and 1932 League Assembly, *Final Report by Lillian von Matsch, Chairman of Sub-Committee for Propaganda of the Women's Consultative Committee on Nationality, Created by the League of Nations*. Reprinted in *Equal Rights*, 10 December 1932.

82 Ellen C. DuBois, "Storming The Hague," 25.

83 Women's Consultative Committee on Nationality and 1932 League Assembly, *Final Report by Lillian von Matsch.*
84 Ellen C. DuBois, "Storming The Hague," 26–7.
85 Sluga, "Women, Feminism and Twentieth-Century Internationalism," p. 68.
86 Sluga, "Women, Feminism and Twentieth-Century Internationalism," pp. 68–9. "Soft politics" is mentioned on p. 68.
87 Sluga, "Women, Feminism and Twentieth-Century Internationalism," pp. 68–70.
88 IAWSEC, *Report of the Twelfth Congress, Istanbul, 18–24 April 1935.*
89 Sluga, "Women, Feminism and Twentieth-Century Internationalism," p. 84.
90 Ellen C. DuBois, "Storming The Hague," 27–8.
91 Glenda Sluga, *Internationalism in an Era of Nationalism*, Philadelphia: University of Pennsylvania Press, 2013.
92 Bolt, *Sisterhood Questioned?* p. 142.
93 LSE-WL, MCA Papers, Disarmament Conference Correspondence, "Disarmament Conference in Geneva 1932/33."
94 L. G. H., "International Community – World Citizenship," *Pax International*, 1939, vol. 14, no. 2.
95 Bolt, *Sisterhood Questioned?* p. 142.
96 See SC-SSC, Countries Collection, All-Asian Women's Conference Box 3, File 1, *All-Asian Women's Conference, First Session, Lahore 19–25 January 1931*, Bombay: Times of India Press, 1931 and Charlotte Weber, "Between Nationalism and Feminism: The Eastern Women's Congresses of 1930 and 1932," *Journal of Middle East Women's Studies*, 2008, vol. 4, no. 1, 83–106.

7

THE "RIGHTS OF MAN" AND SEX EQUALITY

International human rights discourses in the 1930s

Regula Ludi

The United Nations (UN) Charter is the first legal document to recognize individual freedom and equality as a cornerstone of the international order. In its preamble, it famously affirms "faith in the fundamental human rights, in the dignity and worth of the human person, in the equal rights of men and women" and specifically emphasizes the principle of nondiscrimination by expressing respect "for human rights and fundamental freedoms for all without distinction as to race, sex, language, or religion."[1] These often-cited phrases institutionalized new language in international relations and shaped the ways in which future UN bodies would conceive of provisions for the protection of individuals. At the same time, they strikingly echoed legal terminology of the interwar era, such as the guarantee of equality for all citizens "without distinction as to language, race and religion," which had been included in the minority treaties of 1919–20.[2] In borrowing such vocabulary, the architects of the emerging UN system in 1945 tied international human rights to interwar struggles and organized them around a concept of equality specified as nondiscrimination. Yet they also made an important amendment: they added "sex" to the list of inadmissible reasons for legal distinctions.

Though groundbreaking, this innovation has not attracted much attention in human rights historiography.[3] Perhaps, adding equal rights for men and women to the human rights catalogue was just too obvious to require further explanation – "natural enough," as Dorothy Kenyon, the first US delegate to the newly created UN Commission on the Status of Women, in 1947 suggested. Betraying her own uncertainty, however, Kenyon continued by claiming that it was clear that "women are people, that they are human beings with human rights like every other human being, and that it is hardly possible to promote human rights without promoting women's rights as well."[4] Why this explication? Was it maybe not as obvious that "women's rights are human rights" as Kenyon tried to make her audience believe?[5]

There was indeed disagreement in 1945 as to whether sex equality qualified as a human rights norm. Hersh Lauterpacht, a highly respected authority in the field, denied that discrimination against women was a problem that could be solved "within the framework of a general international instrument" because it was "intimately connected with the legal tradition, the social conditions, and the state of public opinion on this subject in various countries."[6] His voice was by no means an isolated one. Research shows that the recognition of sex equality in the UN Charter required concerted lobbying efforts by female delegates and civil society activists present at the San

Francisco Conference.[7] Similarly, the use of gender-neutral language and the consideration of women's claims were anything but self-evident in the subsequent drafting of the Universal Declaration of Human Rights.[8]

The apparent discrepancy between these two viewpoints – the supposed evidence of the claim to universal equality blazoned by Kenyon on the one hand and the social rootedness informing Lauterpacht's reservations on the other – signified that the insertion of gender equality in the human rights catalogue was indeed revolutionary, marking a discontinuity in the conception of international obligations and entitlements.[9] On the other hand, considering equal rights for men and women "natural" implied that these claims smoothly fit in the dominant way of talking about equality as nondiscrimination. In other words, the human rights revolution of 1945 drew on a discourse about rights and international responsibilities that had unfolded in previous decades and spawned a political imagery that permitted the articulation of new connections between normative concepts. How did this relationship emerge? And in what ways did interwar discourses frame the imaginary associated with human rights?

In revisiting the interwar era, this essay aims to fill a gap. Most of the recent literature dealing with the international breakthrough of human rights has paid little attention to events preceding World War II. In their efforts to underline discontinuity, authors tend to draw a sharp line between international obligations under the League of Nations, such as minority protection, and later innovations of the emerging UN system favoring individuals. They focus their explanations for the sudden rise of human rights on the prospective benefits key players expected from endorsing the new norms.[10] Human rights, of course, did not exist as international law guarantees before 1945. Nor did interwar debates provide direct precedents for the emerging UN system, as some of the older literature has suggested.[11] But human rights were nonetheless present. They constituted a political language that shaped claims and organized debate by framing the relationship between the individual and the collective and between state power and the international community. This language was premised on ontological assumptions about human nature and agency. It also carried unspoken beliefs about the essence of civilization that were fraught with the contradictions of interwar internationalism and its entanglement with empire.[12]

This essay is accordingly based on the methodological premise that the human rights revolution was very much about language, the political imagery of words, and the manner in which concepts resonated with different constituencies. Each of the key phrases in the UN Charter, such as "equal rights," "fundamental freedom," and "the dignity and worth of the human person," was reminiscent of previous political struggles and intellectual traditions.[13] And each of them was saturated with meaning intimately linked to its history as an ideal or battle cry in people's quest for justice. To explore the shifts in the imagery flowing from such concepts and the reshaping of human rights, I will first address the international emergence of the "rights of man" in the late 1920s and that concept's role in framing the notion of nondiscrimination. Second, I will examine the new significance these claims attained in 1933–4 in response to the Nazis' rise to power in Germany. The last section of this essay is dedicated to the formative impact that feminist campaigns of the 1930s had on the concept of equality that ensued. The literature up to the present day entertains the assumption that women's rights and human rights were two separate issues and, until 1945, followed their own routes, each guided by its own logic. Taking a fresh look at these events will shed new light on the interconnections between human rights advocacy and feminist campaigns while also illuminating continuities between interwar internationalism and the UN system that have been long recognized by the literature on transnational feminism.[14]

The focus on conceptual history requires some remarks on terminology. The concept of gender, of course, did not exist in the period covered by this essay. Instead, authors would generally use the term "sex" no matter what ideas they had about the origins and significance of gender difference. I will therefore use sex when referring to the period's usage. Similar considerations apply to the term "human rights." In English and French documents of the 1920s and 1930s, the generic term was "rights of man" or "*droits de l'homme*" respectively. Unlike "*Menschenrechte*" in German, these expressions were not gender-neutral; they had a male bias and required specification. Such definition, however, always engendered the risk of inadvertently stressing the aspect of difference, a dilemma that has haunted women's engagement with human rights ever since Olympe de Gouges' "Déclaration des Droits de la Femme et de la Citoyenne" of 1791.[15]

The international declaration of the rights of man: a conversation among experts

> A future historian of our era will pay full attention to one aspect epitomizing legal consciousness of the postwar period, that is the idea of the international significance of human rights and the belief that their protection lies within the authority of international law.[16]

Informed readers would not be surprised to find such an observation in documents of the late 1940s. But the remark dates from an article of 1930, written by Boris Mirkine-Guetzevitch, a Russian emigrant specializing in comparative law and referring to trends of the previous decade. In hindsight, this vision may appear naively optimistic. However, its positive outlook was a fair reflection of opinions about the progressive potential of international law that many of Mirkine-Guetzevitch's colleagues shared. They were convinced they would witness the imminent breakthrough and consolidation of individual rights in international affairs.[17] Maurice Bourquin, for example, a Belgian professor of international law, predicted in 1931 that the current evolution "is pushing us toward the international recognition of human rights."[18]

Such optimism did not lack justification. Even skeptics at that time admitted that the importance of the individual in international relations had tremendously swelled since the Great War, being "one of the most discussed [issues] in our discipline," according to Jean Spiropoulos, another professor of international law.[19] Humanitarian action had identified diverse groups of people as worthy of international attention: Minority treaties, though fraught with countless difficulties when it came to their implementation, recognized the rights of collectives as well as those of individuals. The 1926 Slavery Convention and the 1921 Convention for the Suppression of Traffic in Women and Children outlawed practices inimical to personal freedom and established rudimentary machinery for international cooperation in fighting such abuses. Various refugee conventions, finally, protected selected groups of persons forced out of their home countries by events of persecution and civil war. Based on that record, André Mandelstam, a former Russian diplomat living in exile, concluded that "when it comes to the universal recognition of human rights, we are facing a great transformation in international affairs, a complete reassessment of the relationship between the state and the human being."[20]

In reality, none of the cited examples constituted anything comparable to full-fledged human rights guarantees. Some conventions, such as the anti-slavery and anti-trafficking norms, imposed more or less binding obligations on the ratifying states. They also engendered an international language to talk about abuses in the idiom of innate rights. But except for specific provisions in the minority treaties none of these documents codified rights of the individual. And despite the predictions of leading scholars at the time, they failed to bring about a lasting pattern. The League of Nations' humanitarian regime was designed to be transient and, as the historian Bruno Cabanes argues, established no rights and no universal claims. Instead, international assistance benefited only narrowly defined groups of vulnerable people and was meant to phase out once the humanitarian crises had ebbed.[21]

The creation of the League of Nations filled international law specialists with a new sense of mission. It animated their faith in international law as a means for promoting individual welfare and encouraging progressive reform. This movement was spearheaded by the International Law Institute (ILI), founded in 1873 in Ghent as an offspring of the period's liberal internationalism and uniting academics and diplomats from Europe, the Americas, and Japan in the interwar period.[22] In the 1920s, individual members of the ILI started propagating the guarantee of individual rights as a remedy for agonizing problems in international relations such as the situations of minorities and the stateless. Both grievances resulted from the territorial changes at the end of World War I and the Versailles settlement, which imposed the obligation to protect minorities in states that emerged from the collapse of multiethnic empires in central and eastern Europe. The League of Nations was charged with the supervision of these treaties. The League of Nations minority regime quickly morphed into a source of endless complaints. Governments liable to treaty obligations resented the attached restrictions on their national sovereignty, and starting in the early 1920s they strove unsuccessfully for a revision of the system. For minorities, on the other hand, the emerging practice was a mixed blessing, as it was toothless when it came to rectifying injuries and often counterproductive when it exposed particularly vulnerable groups to new prejudice.[23]

As early as 1921, the ILI formed a special commission to tackle these challenges. Headed by André Mandelstam, this committee reached the conclusion that minority protection was caught in an impasse and that international human rights would be the most elegant way to overcome this predicament. Mandelstam prepared a draft declaration designed to kill two birds with one stone, that is, to enhance the position of individuals and at the same time to silence the governments liable to treaty obligations. According to Mandelstam such a document would constitute a compromise that guaranteed a minimal standard by universalizing the individual rights that were already contained in the minority treaties.[24] Portraying human rights as an extension of the logic guiding minority protection – a frequent selling point – was obviously meant to dispel the impression of any break with previous state practice.[25] At the same time, human rights could be characterized as a pragmatic remedy that would be the "smaller evil" than many other proposals for reform of the minority regime.[26]

The ILI adopted Mandelstam's draft, entitled "Déclaration des Droits Internationaux de l'Homme," in October 1929 at its annual session in Briarcliff Manor, New York.[27] Often referred to as the New York Declaration, this document subscribed to the constitutional tradition of the eighteenth-century Atlantic revolutions and, according to its preamble, aimed to protect the individual "against all encroachment on the part of the state." It contained no more than six articles, with its first article stating every individual's equal right to life, liberty, and property "without any distinction as to nationality, sex, race, language, or religion." The second article addressed religious freedom, the third provided for the free use of language, and the fourth article required state authorities to grant their nationals equal civil and political rights and access to public education, professions, and economic activity without any restrictions based on "the distinction of sex, race, language and religion." Article 5 fleshed out the nondiscrimination principle by stating that the envisaged equality may not be merely formal; it was to be "effective. It excludes any direct or indirect discrimination." Article 6 prohibited states from depriving individuals of their citizenship for reasons of "sex, race, language and religion."[28]

The rights of man enshrined in the New York Declaration may appear to be a list of seemingly timeless commandments of universal ethics, but in fact they were devised as a solution for specific problems of the day such as minority protection and statelessness. They reflected historical experiences and pertinent power relations through their careful phrasing chosen not to offend colonial powers or not to impose on states burdensome obligations of social and economic rights, although some of the period's more ambitious projects did include those.[29] The rights of man could be boiled down to an idea of equality modeled on the minority treaties and defined by the principle of nondiscrimination. No fewer than three of the declaration's six articles almost literally quoted from the provision included in the minority treaties according to which all citizens "shall be equal before the law and shall enjoy the same civil and political rights without distinction as to race, language or religion."[30]

For obvious reasons, members of the ILI celebrated the New York Declaration as a "remarkable" document that was "epoch-making" and initiated a "revolutionary" turn in international law.[31] It did not resonate beyond the small circle of academics and reach a larger public, however. It is true that in the early 1930s a number of transnational organizations such as the Académie Diplomatique Internationale, the International Federation of League of Nations Societies, and the Fédération Internationale des Ligues des Droits de l'Homme expressed their support, mostly at the instigation of André Mandelstam, and of other protagonists of international guarantees for individual rights such as Boris Mirkine-Guetzevitch and Antoine Frangulis.[32] Also, it happened under new conditions that would be critical for propelling the rights of man into the international arena.

A cry of desperation: human rights entering the international arena

In 1933, as the New York Declaration made its way into the League of Nations, a series of disastrous developments dispelled the optimistic mood of previous years. The industrialized world suffered from surging unemployment in the wake of the Great Depression. Governments' preference for austerity and protectionism failed to revive the economy and fueled social tensions. In international relations, the failure to settle the Manchurian crisis was eroding confidence in the League of Nations' capacity for conflict resolution. In early 1933, Hitler's rise to power in Germany further destabilized an already fragile international situation. The new regime's anti-Semitism and brutal crackdown on its political opponents drove tens of thousands of Germans, both Jewish and non-Jewish, into exile. Under those dismal conditions, the appeal to international human rights was no longer a move of progressive imagination but rather an expression of utter desperation and a last resort for Jews in Germany who were left with no defense against state-sponsored abuse.[33]

In the spring of 1933, Jewish organizations filed the famous Bernheim petition. Their move relied on unique provisions of the Upper Silesia Treaty, which permitted non-state actors to put the plight of German Jews on the League of Nations' agenda and frame their grievances as a matter of international concern.[34] Occasionally interpreted as a proto-human rights claim, the petition in fact aimed at expanding minority protection and forcing the Nazi regime to recognize its Jewish citizens as a group entitled to international guarantees. But chances were faint for the petition to find the approval of the international community, let alone the consent of the Third Reich, then still a member of the League of Nations. Since the Nazis' rise to power, the German government had made a rapid about-face from having once been an ardent supporter of minority protection to being a rigid defender of domestic jurisdiction over against foreign intervention. The German government loudly denounced international criticism of its treatment of Jews as impermissible meddling in internal affairs.[35] Thus the strategy deployed with the Bernheim petition was a hopeless cause, although it did mobilize public opinion by providing democratic governments a welcome opportunity to condemn Nazi persecution in the League of Nations without any pressure to act upon their proclamations, first in May 1933 in the League Council, and then in the fall of 1933 during the fourteenth session of the General Assembly.[36]

In the midst of that debate, Antoine Frangulis, a former Greek diplomat acting as the delegate of Haiti, filed a draft resolution demanding an international bill of the rights of man. The petition referred to the New York Declaration, but its phrasing relied on an earlier draft and placed its main emphasis on the requirement that all citizens of any given state be treated equally before the law "without any distinction as to race, language and religion."[37] In his speech, Frangulis, who was known as "the human rights delegate" in Geneva's diplomatic circles, stressed that "the rights of men as individuals should no longer be subject to the arbitrary authority of the state." He deemed the ensuing equality of rights "one of the greatest boons which can be conferred on humanity as a whole" and reminded fellow delegates that "it would be fatal for the League of Nations to shut out the vivifying breath of new ideas and new institutions."[38]

Under the prevailing circumstances, there was no doubt that Frangulis' demand targeted the German political situation, and indeed it was widely understood as a maneuver to encourage sharp condemnation of Nazi anti-Semitism.[39] Particularly in France, where the League of the Rights of Man (Ligue des Droits de l'Homme) was at its height in the 1930s, it struck a chord with public opinion.[40] But in the League of Nations few delegates were ready to delve into the matter and even fewer to endorse the demand. The Greek foreign minister Nikolaos Politis, a former professor of international law and member of the ILI, who aired his support, and the Swiss delegate William Rappard, another academic of international distinction, who similarly displayed sympathy, were among the rare exceptions.[41] Germany's subsequent withdrawal from the League of Nations did not facilitate matters. In 1934, Poland resubmitted its previous demand for universalizing minority protection so that the same standards would apply to all League members but added the threat to terminate its obligations if the League were to refuse. Raising the issue of an international bill of the rights of man under these new conditions no longer served as a gambit to criticize the Nazi regime, and instead steered the debate right back into the deadlock over reforming the minority regime. However, Frangulis renewed his demand by insisting that the League abandon the existing "bad system" of minority protection and overhaul it entirely "from the angle of the jurisdictional guarantee of the rights possessed by men as such, irrespective of whether they belong to a minority or a majority."[42] Again, Frangulis agitated public opinion, particularly in France, but failed to find understanding from fellow delegates. The only government ready to endorse "a convention to universalize those sacred rights of the individual which should not be taken from him under any pretext by any majority whatever," was Ireland, a young state with its own Catholic human rights ethos and a fresh memory of violence dating from its recent struggle for independence.[43]

The rights of man subsequently remained a marginal subject in the international arena. Politically meaningless, the idea of the rights of man failed to overcome the deadlock of minority protection or prevent the demise of the minority regime once Poland canceled its cooperation.[44] Though exposing fateful deficits in international law, as Jewish commentators registered with heightened alarm, neither the Bernheim petition nor the subsequent call for the international recognition of universal rights were capable of stopping state-sponsored abuse or defending its victims against further harm. The international debate was nonetheless consequential, insofar as it reshaped the significance of human rights. Emerging as a potentially viable alternative to the obviously dysfunctional system of minority protection, the rights of man, after being introduced in the international arena as a shield against racial discrimination, became almost interchangeable with legal equality and the protection of the individual against the abuse of state power, an interpretation that resonated with the public reception of transnational human rights advocacy and the debates in the League Assembly.[45] In the following years, parallel feminist engagement with international law not only reinforced the emphasis on equality but also changed and widened the meaning of nondiscrimination.

Whose rights are the rights of man? Sex equality and expanding the definition of nondiscrimination

It did not escape informed observers that the draft resolution Frangulis put on the League's agenda differed from the New York Declaration in one important point: it did not list "sex" among the inadmissible categories of legal distinction. When asked about the reasons for this omission, Frangulis admitted it happened "in view of the need of arriving at an immediate solution of a more urgent problem."[46] In fact, he had built his proposal on an earlier draft of the New York Declaration, probably in anticipation of warnings similar to those several speakers had voiced during the ILI's 1929 session not to antagonize with a strong commitment to sex equality those countries where women had not yet gained the vote.[47] Against this backdrop, it seems all the more surprising that the New York Declaration was explicit in banning discrimination on the grounds of "sex" in three of its six articles. Even in the eyes of its main protagonists, this was groundbreaking. James Brown Scott, for instance, the eminent legal scholar from the United States who presided over the ILI's 1929 session, celebrated the declaration as the first truly universal human rights document because it applied to all human beings, "man, woman, or child, in the state as well as the international community." According to him, it also amounted to the special "glory" of the declaration that it united "the two sexes … in complete legal equality" as a tribute to modern life.[48]

Scott's praise, however, could barely conceal that before 1929 including sex equality in the declaration had been anything but obvious. It had actually happened at a late stage of the drafting process and, as involved scholars conceded, only upon the intervention of feminists from the United States. That intervention was probably instigated by the circle around Alice Paul and Doris Stevens, two leading members of the National Woman's Party who had been pushing for the international recognition of equal rights since the 1920s and who were also in close contact to James Brown Scott.[49] In exposing the ambiguity of human rights language, the British feminist Winifred Mayo later also recalled that it was the insistence of American colleagues that guaranteed "that 'Rights of Man' was to be read as meaning 'Rights' for both sexes."[50] Women also intervened to this end with various private organizations that were about to pass resolutions endorsing the rights of man, capitalizing on their connections with members of the political establishment and influential internationalists sympathetic to their cause such as Edvard Beneš, the foreign minister of Czechoslovakia, and the conservative British politician Lord Robert Cecil, a leading member of the British League of Nations Union and the International Federation of League of Nations Societies. As several transnational associations in 1933 considered endorsing Frangulis' demand for an international human rights convention, the Briton Helen Archdale and other members of Equal Rights International urged Cecil to ensure that any resolution supporting the "'Rights of Man' included also 'Rights of Women.'"[51] The resolution passed by the International Federation at its 1934 Montreux gathering did not include "sex" but, unlike the proposal Frangulis submitted to the League of Nations, it satisfied equal rights advocates by using gender-neutral language and stating that "every individual ... has an equal right to life, to material existence, and to liberty ... without any discrimination whatsoever."[52]

In general, however, feminists remained distrustful of the rights of man project. Based on the experience that the recognition of their own claims was contingent on political expediency and other twists of fate, they suspected that the rights of man could easily eclipse and supplant their demands. "I feel that although we must give some attention to the Rights of Man convention," Helen Archdale surmised in her private correspondence,

> it must only be as secondary to our real demand for sex equality. It must by no means be allowed to supersede or in any way replace our demand. There is a danger that people might use the rather chimerical Rights of Man convention as an excuse to drop our much more practical equality of the sexes convention.[53]

These apprehensions were not unfounded. In 1935, the Belgian delegate to the League Assembly, for instance, proposed that the question of legal equality between men and women "can advantageously be examined by the League of Nations when the latter has before it the question of the rights of man and of the citizen."[54] At that point there was little doubt about the true intentions behind the suggestion of binding women's claims to the obviously hopeless proposition for international human rights. The same speaker made this fairly clear in a later statement by pointing out if "the League had to deal with the question of discrimination of status, it could do so more usefully on the basis of race, language and religion."[55]

In brief, if any linkage existed in the 1930s between sex equality and human rights, it was certainly weak or could easily be exploited to invert feminist demands. For the women's movement, endorsing human rights implied the risk of shelving their own interests, a prospect that was particularly unattractive in view of the considerable headway feminists had made in the League of Nations and other international bodies. Since the early 1930s, advocates of equal rights for men and women had been swamping international organizations with their requests, and in 1934 they succeeded, with the help of Latin American states, to put "the entire status of women" on the agenda of the League of Nations. This was "indeed a marvelous triumph for women everywhere," Emma Wold, a member of the National Woman's Party and previously a technical advisor to the US delegation at the International Codification Conference at the Hague, observed.[56]

Recognition of the status of women as an international affair was first and foremost a victory of the egalitarian wing of the transnational women's movement. Its campaign, often associated with the "left wing" of international feminism (not to be confused with socialist feminists), had roots dating back to the 1920s.[57] For example, their work drew upon a then-new strategy devised by Alice Paul and Doris Stevens for leveraging the Equal Rights Amendment to the US constitution in domestic lawmaking. They lobbied the Pan-American Union to pass a binding statement on equal rights for men and women, hoping that its adoption would put national legislation under pressure to comply with international standards. Latin American feminists joined the efforts, and they scored their first success in 1928, when the Pan-American Union recognized their claim by appointing a new agency, the Inter-American Commission of Women, to concern itself exclusively with women's rights. Upon the request of this commission, the Pan-American Union in 1933 approved an equal rights treaty drafted by Alice Paul, and Latin American governments subsequently submitted it to the League of Nations for adoption.[58]

A parallel campaign for the repeal of the policy pursued by the International Labour Organization (ILO) was an additional source for radicalizing egalitarianism. Since 1919, several conventions of the ILO had erected a system of international regulations aimed at shielding women, specifically mothers, from labor-related health risks. This legislation entailed differential treatment of men and women at the workplace, including a ban on night work for women in manufacturing; standards regarding maternity leave; and provisions targeting pregnant women. While the majority of feminist organizations including socialist women supported this legislation, radical egalitarians, many of whom were well-educated professionals with an academic background, identified special protection as a new source of sex discrimination in the labor market. Their fight against the ILO policy intensified with the Great Depression and the backlash that women suffered in many industrialized countries due to new restrictions on married women's employment.[59]

The Conference for the Codification of International Law in 1930 was a third influence, and it propelled the radical egalitarians into action. The Conference passed an agreement entitled "Convention on Certain Questions Relating to the Conflict of Nationality Laws," which was designed to harmonize citizenship legislation so as to remove causes for statelessness. Disregarding feminist claims, this convention expressly condoned the widespread practice of requiring women who married men of foreign citizenship to give up their own original citizenship. This decision by the Conference stirred a storm of protest from women's organizations. Feminists tried to block the ratification of the convention and called for its immediate revision. In response to these demands, the League of Nations set up a semi-official committee of representatives from women's organizations. The committee issued several statements condemning the convention as a dangerous precedent in international law for being "founded upon the theory of the subjection of women."[60]

In the early 1930s, these different campaigns coalesced around the draft of an equal rights treaty. In 1929, the British Six Point Group was the first feminist organization to use that draft to lobby diplomats in Geneva, and was soon joined by others, such as Equal Rights International.[61] By scheduling debate on the equal rights treaty in the fall of 1935, the League of Nations signaled that the inferior status of women constituted a political problem of international range and, therefore, a legitimate matter for the world organization to be concerned with and to collect information on from states and women's organizations. This decision opened the floodgates. It offered feminist organizations an opportunity to display their expertise and to claim authority in defining problems related to discrimination against women. As the League circulated its reports together with the responses from governments, it was in a position to shape the discourse by stressing equality as the standard of comparison. The League's semi-official Women's Consultative Committee on Nationality, for instance, which was dominated by radical egalitarians, maintained that "countries which are held to be most civilized and progressive are those countries where some measure of equality has been given [to women]."[62]

In the League Assembly's public debates, speakers sympathizing with the feminist cause successfully linked women's rights to social progress, reinforcing sex equality as a standard of global modernity. The Danish delegate Anna Westergaard, for instance, declared that the

> progress of a country depended to a great extent on its willingness to free itself from prejudices regarding the status of women and to loosen the shackles which, in so many States, still bound women so that they were unable to make their full contribution to the future development of the world.[63]

As a novel parameter of international comparison, sex equality provided governments with the opportunity to present themselves as trailblazers of modernity by displaying the advancement of their female citizens, while also shaming those governments that could not produce a brilliant record or that were unwilling to abide by the new rules. The frustration voiced by the latter testified to a sea change in the manner in which the international community broached gender relations. One speaker, for instance, complained about the new tendency "to divide the states into two categories – the so-called progressive states and the others, the latter being regarded more or less as culprits" with respect to women's advancement.[64]

In short, by the mid-1930s, the discourse in the international arena leaned towards the endorsement of sex equality as a universal goal and as a self-evident standard that no longer required justification. In 1937, the Swedish delegate Kerstin Hesselgren spoke for many feminists who sensed "a growing process of evolution" geared "towards complete emancipation of women."[65] In 1938, these efforts culminated in the appointment of an expert committee by the League to perform a worldwide study on the legal status of women.

At first sight these activities had no direct relationship to human rights advocacy. As Jean Quataert has summed up the situation, women's rights were not "yet framed in the explicit language of *human* rights."[66] But the League's engagement with feminist demands was in fact instrumental in establishing an ever-stronger bond between the rights of man and gender equality. By making sex equality a standard of international comparison, the League infused it with implicitness and universal validity, thereby preparing the ground for its recognition as an intrinsic and constitutive element of human rights. Moreover, on closer examination connections between feminist campaigns and the rights of man were more frequent at that time than generally assumed. Human rights language molded opposition to the nationality convention, and the New York Declaration served as a yardstick to condemn the nationality convention's provisions regarding married women, for instance in resolutions of the ILI. This legislation, being "based upon the principle of masculine superiority" and disadvantaging "women in [*sic*] behalf of men in express terms," this legislation constituted a clear case of "discrimination in the matter of sex," according to James Brown Scott.[67]

Networks of radical egalitarians used human rights language not only to invoke the natural rights legacy it carried but increasingly also to advance new legal concepts and to highlight the universal character of their demands. This was the strategy Open Door International for the Emancipation of the Woman Worker (ODI), a group founded in 1929, applied in its struggle against special protection legislation. According to ODI it was the "aim of feminism" that "a woman should enjoy the same human rights as a man in all spheres of life," meaning that a "woman should not be classified with a child or a young person … [and] the natural function of motherhood is not a reason for restricting the woman in any of her rights as a human being."[68] Exposing the dominant tendency of taking the male standard for the norm, the association argued that differential treatment of men and women actually amounted to denying women basic rights. "In every community," ODI stated in 1935,

> it is the status of the man which is taken as the normal. His rights are accepted as those pertaining to the human being. To the woman are always denied some of these human rights … In many countries, marriage itself deprives women of human rights. There is no country in which … the woman is not denied by reason of sex or marriage or childbirth some of the normal human rights enjoyed by the male worker.[69]

As an early testimony to an unflinching identification of sex equality as human rights claim, this line of argument also bespoke a wider conception of human rights than the one guiding the New York Declaration. It indicated a shift in the significance of human rights language, a new connection that explains why the association of women's rights with human rights would appear increasingly obvious in the following decades.

With the looming collapse of the international order and the mounting reports on state-sponsored abuses, women's organizations often used human rights language to present their struggle as a general concern about the fate of humanity. Feminist demands merged with the call for guarantees to protect "human values and individual liberty … without regard to sex, race or religion," as the International Alliance of Women for Suffrage and Equal Citizenship proclaimed at its 1939 congress.[70] And in March 1941, a draft resolution of international women's organizations expressed their expectation that a postwar settlement be built on "the inviolable right of the individual to life and bodily integrity, the right to worship and to earn, to contract, to possess and use property … irrespective of sex, race, creed or class."[71] This was just a few months before the Atlantic Charter of August 1941 was to set off an international avalanche of human rights demands.

Conclusion

It is true that the call for human rights fell on deaf ears in the interwar period to a great extent, and failed, except in France, to mobilize public support on a wider scale. Does this conclusion confirm Hannah Arendt's scathing judgment that the rights of man were but lofty ideals harbored "by a few international jurists without political experience or professional philanthropists supported by the uncertain sentiments of professional idealists"? Does it corroborate her conclusion that their declarations "showed an uncanny similarity in language and composition to that of societies for the prevention of cruelty to animals"?[72]

For people exposed to persecution and deprived of all other means of protection, it might well be thus. For them human rights were at best ideals inspired by the faith in universal moral values to which they would appeal in the last resort. Beyond that, human rights were likely to be, for them, empty words, legally and politically toothless. Yet this conclusion should not be taken to imply that interwar human rights advocacy had no further significance. The struggles against the differential treatment of religious and national minorities, women, and refugees exposed the grievances of these groups as discrimination and injustice. By prioritizing equality – according to Hersh Lauterpacht "the most fundamental of all of the rights of man" – over other claims while conflating it with nondiscrimination, these campaigns informed the human rights revolution with its emphasis on the equal worth of all human beings.[73]

At the same time, they catalyzed new language for condemning legal inequities. and this new language came to be amalgamated with the New World predilection for freedom, as in FDR's Four Freedoms and the Atlantic Charter.[74] Political scientist Philip Quincy Wright gave an example of such a new pairing in 1942, when he wrote:

> Particularly important in international experience has been the freedom from inequality of opportunity because of race, religion, nationality or other classifications ... Reasonable equality of treatment and security against unreasonable discriminations is doubtless to be implied from the very conception of human freedom and the integrity of the human personality asserted by the four freedoms.[75]

The interwar discourse of equality blended with the individualistic rhetoric of the postwar settlement. It helped to bring about and disseminate a political imagery that reverberated internationally and that has infused claims such as gender and racial equality with credibility and evidence.

Notes

1 Preamble and Article 1(3), United Nations Charter, 1945. Online. Available at www.un.org/en/charter-united-nations/ (accessed 26 December 2018).

2 "Minorities Treaty Between the Principal Allied and Associated Powers ... and Poland, Signed at Versailles, 28 June 1919." Online. Available at www.forost.ungarisches-institut.de/pdf/19190628-3.pdf (accessed 26 December 2018).

3 One of the very few surveys mentioning the amendment is Johannes Morsink, *The Universal Declaration of Human Rights. Origins, Drafting, and Intent*, Philadelphia: University of Pennsylvania Press, 1999. See pp. 116–20.

4 Dorothy Kenyon, "United Nations Commission on Status of Women," *Women Lawyers' Journal*, 1947, vol. 33, 38.

5 Dorothy Kenyon, "Victories on the International Front," *Annals of the American Academy of Political and Social Science*, 1947, vol. 251, no. 1, 19.
6 Hersch Lauterpacht, *An International Bill of the Rights of Man*, New York: Columbia University Press, 1945, p. 119.
7 Ellen DuBois and Lauren Derby, "The Strange Case of Minerva Bernardino: Pan American and United Nations Womens Rights Activist," *Women's Studies International Forum*, 2009, vol. 32, 43–50; Jean Quataert and Benita Roth, "Guest Editorial Note: Human Rights, Global Conferences, and the Making of Postwar Transnational Feminisms," *Journal of Women's History*, 2012, vol. 24, no. 4, 15.
8 Allida Black, "Are Women 'Human'? The UN and the Struggle to Recognize Women's Rights as Human Rights," in Akira Iriye, Petra Goedde, and William I. Hitchcock (eds.) *The Human Rights Revolution. An International History*, New York: Oxford University Press, 2012, pp. 138–41; Johannes Morsink, "Women's Rights in the Universal Declaration," *Human Rights Quarterly*, 1991, vol. 13, 229–56.
9 Among the rapidly growing literature emphasizing that 1945 marks a moment of discontinuity in the history of international law, see Jean H. Quataert, *Advocating Dignity: Human Rights Mobilizations in Global Politics*, Philadelphia: University of Pennsylvania Press, 2009; Samuel Moyn, *The Last Utopia. Human Rights in History*, Cambridge, MA: Belknap Press at Harvard University Press, 2010; and Jan Eckel, *Die Ambivalenz des Guten. Menschenrechte in der internationalen Politik seit den 1940er Jahren*, Göttingen: Vandenhoeck & Ruprecht, 2014.
10 There are diverging interpretations. Mark Mazower, "The Strange Triumph of Human Rights 1933–1950," *Historical Journal*, 2004, vol. 47, no. 2, 379–98, emphasizes the opportunistic rationale behind the big powers' postwar support for lofty human rights principles to replace the onerous obligations of the interwar minority regime. G. Daniel Cohen, "The Holocaust and the 'Human Rights Revolution': A Reassessment," in Iriye et al., *The Human Rights Revolution*, stresses the significance of the Jewish genocide for key human rights advocates. Marco Duranti, *The Conservative Human Rights Revolution: European Identity, Transnational Politics and the Origins of the European Convention*, Oxford: Oxford University Press, 2017, and Lora Wildenthal, *The Language of Human Rights in West Germany*, Philadelphia: University of Pennsylvania Press, 2013, shed light on the role conservative and reactionary circles and politically compromised individuals played in promoting the European human rights regime after World War II, as they recognized the value of international guarantees for advancing such diverse causes as religious education and amnesties for war criminals and collaborationists.
11 Jan Herman Burgers, "The Road to San Francisco: The Revival of the Human Rights Idea in the Twentieth Century," *Human Rights Quarterly*, 1992, vol. 14, no. 4, 447–77. Also Paul Gordon Lauren, *The Evolution of International Human Rights. Visions Seen*, 1st ed., Philadelphia: University of Pennsylvania Press, 1998. Rehabilitating the notion of certain continuities: Pamela Slotte and Miia Halme-Tuomisaari (eds.), *Revisiting the Origins of Human Rights*, Cambridge, UK: Cambridge University Press, 2015.
12 Susan Pedersen, *The Guardians: The League of Nations and the Crisis of Empire*, Oxford: Oxford University Press, 2015; Antony Anghie, *Imperialism, Sovereignty, and the Making of International Law*, Cambridge, UK: Cambridge University Press, 2005.
13 On the disparate origins of "human dignity" and "human person," see Samuel Moyn, *Christian Human Rights*, Philadelphia: University of Pennsylvania Press, 2015.
14 See, for instance, Marilyn Lake, "From Self-Determination via Protection to Equality via Non-Discrimination: Defining Women's Rights at the League of Nations and the United Nations," in Patricia Grimshaw, Katie Holmes, and Marilyn Lake (eds.) *Women's Rights and Human Rights. International Historical Perspectives*, Basingstoke, UK: Palgrave, 2001, pp. 254–71; Karen Offen, *European Feminisms 1700–1950: A Political* History, Stanford, CA: Stanford University Press, 2000; Karen Garner, *Shaping a Global Women's Agenda: Women's NGOs and Global Governance, 1925–1985*, Manchester: Manchester University Press, 2010. Emphasizing the role of individuals, such as Dorothy Kenyon: Jaci Eisenberg, "The Status of Women: A Bridge from the League of Nations to the United Nations," *Journal of International Organizations*, 2013, vol. 4, no. 2, 8–24.
15 Joan Scott, *Only Paradoxes to Offer. French Feminists and the Rights of Man*, Cambridge, MA: Harvard University Press, 1996.

16 Boris Mirkine-Guetzevitch, "Das Menschenrecht der Heimatlosen," *Die Friedens-Warte*, 1930, vol. 30, no. 7–8, 213. On the author, see Dzovinar Kévonian, "Les juristes juifs russes en France et l'action internationale dans les années vingt," *Archives Juives*, 2001, vol. 34, no. 2, 72–94.

17 For an early testimony, see Philip Marshall Brown, "The Individual and International Law," *American Journal of International Law*, 1924, vol. 18, no. 3, 532–6.

18 Maurice Bourquin, "Règles générales du droit de la paix," *Recueil des cours de l'Académie de droit international*, 1931, vol. 35, no. 1, 172.

19 Jean Spiropoulos, "L'individu et le droit international," *Recueil des cours de l'Académie de droit international*, 1929, vol. 30, no. 5, 195. Similarly Charles Dupuis, "Règles générales du droit de la paix," *Recueil des cours de l'Académie de droit international*, 1930, vol. 32, no. 2, 50; Hersch Lauterpacht, "Règles générales du droit de la paix," *Recueil des cours de l'Académie de droit international*, 1937, vol. 62, no. 4, 207–9.

20 André N. Mandelstam, "Der internationale Schutz der Menschenrechte und die New-Yorker Erklärung des Instituts für Völkerrecht," *Zeitschrift für ausländisches öffentliches Recht und Völkerrecht*, 1931, vol. 2, no. 1, 366. Mandelstam interpreted most of the League's social and humanitarian work through the lens of human rights. He also praised the League's mandate system for erecting "true strongholds of human rights" in the territories under its supervision as part of its civilizing mission. Historical research is less positive regarding the achievements of the mandate system. See Pedersen, *The Guardians*; Michael D. Callahan, *Mandates and Empire. The League of Nations and Africa, 1914–1931*, Brighton, UK: Sussex Academic Press, 1999.

21 Bruno Cabanes, *The Great War and the Origins of Humanitarianism, 1918–1924*, Cambridge, UK: Cambridge University Press, 2014. For a more affirmative interpretation, see Barbara Metzger, "Towards an International Human Rights Regime during the Inter-War Years: The League of Nations' Combat of Traffic in Women and Children," in Kevin Grant, Philippa Levine, and Frank Trentmann (eds.) *Beyond Sovereignty: Britain, Empire and Transnationalism, c.1880–1950*, Basingstoke, UK: Palgrave Macmillan, 2007, pp. 54–79.

22 Martti Koskenniemi, *The Gentle Civilizer of Nations. The Rise and Fall of International Law 1870–1960*, Cambridge, UK: Cambridge University Press, 2005.

23 For an overview, see Carole Fink, *Defending the Rights of Others: The Great Powers, the Jews, and International Minority Protection, 1878–1938*, Cambridge, UK: Cambridge University Press, 2004, pp. 267–304.

24 André N. Mandelstam, "Question méthodologique: La généralisation du droit des minorités par rapport à la généralisation du droit de l'homme et du citoyen," *Annuaire de l'Institut de Droit International*, Brussels: Institut de Droit International, 1928, pp. 284–5. Similarly Robert Redslob, "Le principe des nationalités," *Recueil des cours de l'Académie de droit international*, 1931, vol. 37, no. 3, 60. On Mandelstam, see Dzovinar Kévonian, "André Mandelstam and the Internationalization of Human Rights (1869–1949)," in Slotte et al., *Revisiting the Origins of Human Rights*, pp. 239–66. Also Rainer Huhle, "Vom Minderheitenrecht zum Menschenrecht. André Mandelstam und die Entwicklung des menschenrechtlichen Völkerrechts," *Europa Ethnica*, 2013, no. 1–2.

25 André N. Mandelstam, "Das Problem der Menschen- und Bürgerrechte im 'Institut de Droit International,'" *Die Friedens-Warte*, 1928, vol. 28, no. 12; André N. Mandelstam, "La généralisation de la protection internationale des droits de l'homme," *Revue de droit international et de la législation comparée*, 1930, vol. 11; "Les dernières phases du mouvement pour la protection internationale des droits de l'homme," *Revue du droit internationale et de la législation comparée*, 1934, vol. 13.

26 Wilhelm G. Hertz, "Die Menschenrechte," *Die Friedens-Warte*, 1934, vol. 34, no. 5, p. 226. Similarly Alfred Berl, "La Déclaration des Droits Internationaux de l'homme et le judaïsme," *Paix et droit. Organe de l'Alliance israélite universelle*, 1930, vol. 10, no. 6, 2.

27 "Déclaration des droits internationaux de l'homme," 1929. Online. Available at www.idi-iil.org/app/uploads/2017/06/1929_nyork_03_fr.pdf (accessed 26 December 2018). The translation is my own.

28 "Déclaration des droits internationaux de l'homme," *Annuaire de l'Institut de Droit International*, 1929, vol. 2, 125–6. Hans Wehberg, "Probleme der rechtlichen Organisation der Welt," *Die Friedens-Warte*, 1929, vol. 29, no. 12, 356.

29 "La Session de Cambridge de l'Institut de Droit International," *Revue de Droit International*, 1931, vol. 5, no. 8, 301–8; James Brown Scott, "The Two Institutes of International Law," *American Journal of International Law*, 1932, vol. 26, no. 1, 93. On the period's more ambitious projects

that also included social, cultural, and economic rights, see Emmanuel Naquet, "L'action de la Fédération Internationale des Ligues des droits de l'Homme (FIDH) entre les deux guerres," *Matériaux pour l'Histoire de Notre Temps*, 2009, vol. 95, 61–2.

30 Article 7, "Minorities Treaty Between the Principal Allied and Associated Powers ... and Poland, Signed at Versailles, 28 June 1919."

31 "bemerkenswert" in Wehberg, "Probleme der rechtlichen Organisation der Welt," 357; "epoch-making" in Scott, "Two Institutes," 93; "revolutionary" in Philip Marshall Brown, "The New York Session of the Institut de Droit International," *American Journal of International Law*, 1930, vol. 24, no. 1, 127.

32 "Le Congrès international des Ligues des droits de l'homme," *Les Cahiers des Droits de l'Homme* 1933, vol. 33, no. 2, 33–7.

33 See Zara Steiner, *The Triumph of the Dark. European International History 1933–1939*, Oxford: Oxford University Press, 2011. With different emphasis: Marc Matera and Susan Kingsley Kent, *The Global 1930s: The International Decade*, New York: Routledge, 2017.

34 On the following, see Philipp Graf, *Die Bernheim-Petition 1933: Jüdische Politik in der Zwischenkriegszeit*, Göttingen: Vandenhoeck & Ruprecht, 2008. In his detailed examination, Graf has revised previous interpretations that depicted the Bernheim petition as an early attempt to internationalize human rights. For such views, see Dorothy V. Jones, *Toward a Just World: The Critical Years in the Search for International Justice*, Chicago: University of Chicago Press, 2002, pp. 119–32; Lauren, *The Evolution of International Human Rights*, pp. 126–34.

35 Fink, *Defending the Rights of Others*, pp. 328–35.

36 Both debates were public. See the proceedings in League of Nations (hereafter LoN), *Official Journal*, 1933, vol. 14, no. 7, 838–44; 929–35 (Council); LoN, *Official Journal. Special Supplement No. 120, Records of the Fourteenth Ordinary Session of the Assembly. Minutes of the Sixth Committee*, 1933, 22–59.

37 For the draft resolution, see LoN, *Official Journal. Special Supplement No. 115: Plenary Meetings*, 1933, 50.

38 LoN, *Official Journal. Special Supplement No. 120*, 32, 34. "Les droits de l'homme et du citoyen devant la 14e Assemblée de la S.D.N.," in *La Revue Diplomatique*, 1922, no. 56, 6–7.

39 "Die Generaldebatte in der Völkerbundsversammlung," in *Neue Zürcher Zeitung*, 1 October 1933.

40 For the most extensive coverage in the French press, see Alfred Berl, "Racisme ou droit humain?" *Paix et Droit*, 1933, vol. 13, no. 7–8, 1–3. On the *Ligue des Droits de l'Homme*, see William D. Irvine, *Between Justice and Politics. The Ligue des Droits de l'Homme 1898–1945*, Stanford, CA: Stanford University Press, 2007.

41 LoN, *Official Journal, Special Supplement No. 120*, 52 (Politis), 53 (Rappard).

42 LoN, *Official Journal, Special Supplement No. 130: Records of the Fifteenth Ordinary Session of the Assembly. Minutes of the Sixth Committee*, 1934, 44.

43 LoN, *Official Journal, Special Supplement No. 130: Records of the Fifteenth Ordinary Session of the Assembly. Minutes of the Sixth Committee*, 1934, 63 (Eamon de Valera). For the reception in France, see *Le Temps*, 21 September 1934, 6 and *Le Journal*, 21 September 1934, 3. On de Valera's notion of human rights, see Moyn, *Christian Human Rights*, pp. 40–4.

44 On the demise of minority protection, see Fink, *Defending the Rights of Others*, pp. 338–43.

45 See, for instance, the report on the Assembly debate in *Le Petit Journal*, 1 October 1933, 3.

46 LoN, *Official Journal, Special Supplement No. 139: Records of the Sixteenth Ordinary Session of the Assembly. Minutes of the First Committee*, 1935, 38.

47 "Déclaration des droits internationaux de l'homme," *Annuaire de l'Institut de Droit International*, 1929, vol. 2, 124–7.

48 James Brown Scott, "La Déclaration Internationale des Droits de l'Homme," *Revue de droit international*, 1930, vol. 4, no. 5, 79–80, 99.

49 See, for instance, Wehberg, "Probleme der rechtlichen Organisation der Welt," 357. Referring to Alice Paul and Doris Stevens, see Scott, "Two Institutes," 100–1.

50 "Minutes of the Liaison Committee of Women's International Organizations," 19 February 1934, in Thomas Dublin and Kathryn Sklar (eds.) *Women and Social Movements, International: 1840 to Present*, Alexander Street/ProQuest, 2012. Online. Available through subscribing libraries at https://proquest.libguides.com/WASI (accessed 21 December 2017).

51 Women's Library, London (hereafter WL), 5ERI, Box FL330, "Report of the Honorary Secretary 1934."

52 "Report of the Honorary Secretary 1934."
53 WL, 5ERI, Box FL331, Helen Archdale to K. Malinkova Popprova, 23 December 1933. See also Lake, "From Self-Determination," pp. 263–4.
54 LoN, *Official Journal, Special Supplement No. 139*, 35.
55 LoN, *Official Journal, Special Supplement No. 139*, 49.
56 Emma Wold, "League of Nations to Consider Status of Women," *Women Lawyers' Journal*, 1934–5, vol. 21, 9.
57 Helen Archdale, "International Developments in the Woman's Movement," *Current History*, 1928, vol. 29, no. 1, 51. Also Carol Miller, "'Geneva – the Key to Equality': Inter-War Feminists and the League of Nations," *Women's History Review*, 1994, vol. 3, no. 2, 219–45.
58 See Beatrice McKenzie, "The Power of International Positioning: The National Woman's Party, International Law and Diplomacy, 1928–34," *Gender & History*, 2011, vol. 23, no. 1, 130–46; Ann Towns, "The Inter-American Commission of Women and Women's Suffrage 1920–1945," *Journal of Latin American Studies*, 2010, vol. 42, 779–807; Patricia Ward D'Itri, *Cross Currents in the International Women's Movement 1848–1948*, Bowling Green, OH: Bowling Green State University Popular Press, 1999, pp. 153–8.
59 Eliane Gubin, "Pour le droit de travail: entre protection et égalité," in Eliane Gubin et al. (eds.) *Le siècle des féminismes*, Paris: Les Éditions de l'Atelier, 2004, pp. 163–78. See also the essay by Eileen Boris and Jane Jensen in this volume.
60 LoN Archive, "V. Legal 1932. Proposals of the Committee of Representatives of Women's International Organizations," 6 July 1931, p. 8. On the feminist campaign: Paula F. Pfeffer, "'A Whisper in the Assembly of Nations.' United States' Participation in the International Movement for Women's Rights from the League of Nations to the United Nations," *Women's Studies International Forum*, 1985, vol. 8, no. 5, 459–71; Ellen C. DuBois, "Internationalizing Married Women's Nationality: The Hague Campaign of 1930," in Karen Offen (ed.) *Globalizing Feminisms, 1789–1945*, London: Routledge, 2010, pp. 204–16.
61 WL, 5ERI, Box FL330, "Minutes of the Meeting of the Equal Rights International Council," 8 September 1931.
62 League of Nations and United Nations Office at Geneva Archives (hereafter LoN Archive), "A.19.1935.V. Nationality and Status of Women," p. 28.
63 LoN, *Official Journal, Special Supplement No. 139*, 27.
64 LoN, *Official Journal, Special Supplement No. 139*, 19.
65 LoN Archive, "A.54.1937.V. Status of Women. Report Submitted by the First Committee to the Assembly," 25 September 1937, p. 3.
66 Jean H. Quataert, *The Gendering of Human Rights in the International Systems of Law in the Twentieth Century*, Washington, DC: American Historical Association, 2006, p. 15 (emphasis in the original).
67 James Brown Scott, "Editorial Comment: Nationality," *American Journal of International Law*, 1930, vol. 24, no. 3, 558–60. Also Scott, "Two Institutes," 94 (referring to the resolutions of the ILI).
68 Open Door International for the Emancipation of the Woman Worker, *Report of the Conference Held in Berlin, June 15th and 16th, 1929*, London: Open Door International, pp. 7–8, 45–6.
69 LoN Archive, "A.19.1935. V. Nationality and Status of Women, Statements Presented by International Women's Organizations," p. 41.
70 International Alliance of Women, *Report of the Thirteenth Congress 1939*, London: International Alliance of Women, 1939, pp. 18–19.
71 "Minutes of the Liaison Committee," 6 March 1941, in Dublin and Sklar, *Women and Social Movements*.
72 Hannah Arendt, *The Origins of Totalitarianism. New Edition with Added Prefaces*, Orlando: Harcourt, 1985, p. 292.
73 Lauterpacht, *An International Bill of the Rights of Man*, p. 115.
74 See Elizabeth Borgwardt, *A New Deal for the World. America's Vision for Human Rights*, Cambridge, MA: Belknap Press at Harvard University Press, 2005.
75 Quincy Wright, "Human Rights and the World Order," *International Conciliation*, 1942–3, vol. 21, 256.

PART III

THE FORMATIVE UN ERA

A. UN treaty-making

8

SOCIAL AND ECONOMIC RIGHTS

The struggle for equivalent protection

Claire-Michelle Smyth

Introduction

Social and economic rights, broadly defined, are those necessary to sustain life, including housing, food, clothing, water, health care, social security, and an adequate standard of living. These rights could be described as the most fundamental of human rights, as they are essential for continued survival. However, they are not afforded the same legal status and protection as civil and political rights in international, regional and domestic systems. They are often seen as subordinate to civil and political rights, and it has been argued that they should not be justiciable, meaning that they should not be enforceable in a court of law.

This essay charts the development of social and economic rights in international law, from the creation of the International Covenant on Economic, Social and Cultural Rights (ICESCR) and its legacy to contemporary debates on the legal status of these rights. This essay takes a legalistic approach towards the protection of rights. The legalistic approach to human rights affirms that rights are meaningless unless they can be enforced in a court of law. While not dismissing or diminishing the impact that policy and grassroots movements can have on the furtherance of all human rights, as a lawyer I believe that the safety net of justiciability is vital for the effective protection of human rights. To that end, the focus of this essay is on illustrating the positive impact that courts have had when they have deigned to intervene. If social and economic rights are not elevated to the purview of the judiciary, they will continue to be perceived as less important than their civil and political counterparts. To illustrate this point, this essay examines moves towards justiciability at international, regional, and domestic levels, and the resulting positive impacts.

The International Covenant on Economic, Social and Cultural Rights

In the aftermath of World War II and the failed League of Nations, the Charter establishing the United Nations (UN) entered into force on 24 October 1945.[1] The primary purpose of this new institution, the United Nations, was twofold: to maintain international peace and stability, and to protect human rights. On 10 December 1948 the UN General Assembly adopted the Universal Declaration of Human Rights (UDHR), which provided a comprehensive catalog of human rights for the first time and encouraged their protection by the rule of law.

The UDHR makes no distinction between civil and political rights and social and economic rights; rather, the document is a thorough account of the rights that states ought to strive to protect. This indicates that at the commencement of the modern human rights movement social and economic rights were recognized as being as important as civil and political rights, at least theoretically. It can therefore be argued that international law does not support a division of rights, and that such a division is grounded in national law perspectives that cling to a negative model of human rights. Political and civil rights are negative rights in the sense that they restrain the actions of states, whereas economic and social rights require positive investments by states. In other words, if the state merely has to avoid interfering with your rights (for example, not kill you) then this will not have significant budgetary implications, whereas if the state is required to provide you with healthcare or housing, that will be costly. Unfortunately, the UDHR was not a legally binding document. It did not require that any of the rights mentioned be transposed into national law. Negotiations in the UN began in 1949 to transpose the rights in the UDHR into legally binding obligations, but in the context of Cold War tensions, the discussions devolved into polemics and the attempts to create a single legally binding document were abandoned.[2]

There have been recent disputes about which moment was the pivotal one for human rights in international law. Samuel Moyn argues that the 1970s are a turning point for international human rights law, as that was when the first UN human rights treaties came into force,[3] while Steven Jensen contends that the anticolonial movements of the 1960s had a significant, though often overlooked, impact on the development of international human rights.[4] Jensen's position has considerable merit because, although negotiations to transpose the UDHR began in 1949, it was during the 1960s that these efforts resulted in binding treaties, which, however, did establish in international law a persistent divide between the two sets of fundamental rights: civil and political on the one hand, and social and economic on the other.

Although the UN has maintained an official position that all of the rights at issue are universal, interdependent, interrelated, and indivisible,[5] there has been a long-running and deep disagreement regarding the proper status of social and economic rights, and each side has adopted extreme and discordant views. On one side is the position that social and economic rights are superior to civil and political rights in chronological terms, meaning that without the fulfillment of social and economic rights, civil and political rights cannot be realized. The other side claims that social and economic rights are not rights in the traditional and classic sense of the term, and that to treat them as such undermines individual freedoms and distorts the free market. The Western states, led by the United States, expressed concern about the scope of obligations and opposed the inclusion of social and economic rights, while many eastern European and emerging Third World nations strongly advocated their inclusion. The European states that at the time still held colonies were concerned about the cost of securing social and economic rights opposed their exclusion. The outcome of these debates was that the rights were split between two distinct documents. The International Covenant on Civil and Political Rights (ICCPR),[6] which contained civil and political rights, and the International Covenant on Economic Social and Cultural Rights (ICESCR),[7] consisting of social and economic rights, were both adopted by the General Assembly in 1966.

The effect of this compromise cannot be overstated. Rights were cemented into two categories and set on divergent paths, with different importance ascribed to each. Given the geopolitical balance of power, social and economic rights were relegated to a subordinate status,[8] which created difficulties for their propagation and for the degree of force accorded to these rights in international, regional, and domestic contexts. Social and economic rights were to be realized progressively, subject to available resources[9]– a - "programmatic"[10] approach not applied to civil and political rights. The absence of immediate and concrete obligations in the ICESCR, coupled with the lack of a complaints mechanism,[11] contributed powerfully to continued violations and compounded the inferior status of these rights at the international level.[12] The ICCPR, by contrast, contains more compulsory wording, such as that "all peoples have the right," and that states must "ensure" these rights.[13]

Under the ICESCR, the state has three core obligations: to respect, to protect, and to fulfill the rights contained therein.[14] The duty to respect is a passive obligation and requires the state to avoid interfering, by law or conduct, with the enjoyment of the rights contained within the Covenant. The duty to protect is more active in nature, requiring the state to take positive steps to protect against violations by third parties. For example, states are to put in place, by way of legislation or policy, effective measures to prevent abuses of individuals by powerful actors such as landlords or banks. The duty to fulfill is the most contentious of the three, as it requires the state to provide for those who cannot support themselves, either by ensuring access to existing services or by directly providing services where access through existing structures is unavailable.

The Committee on Economic, Social and Cultural Rights was established in 1985 in order to monitor state compliance with the ICESCR, in 1985.[15] Its primary functions and objectives are to develop the normative content of the rights, develop state benchmarks, and hold states accountable for failure to implement. In addition, the Committee produces general comments that clarify the contents of rights and direct their interpretation. These general comments are nonbinding, so they do not create enforceable obligations; they are merely authoritative interpretations that set out what steps should be taken. They are published with a view to assisting each state in its implementation of the ICESCR.

Each state must submit periodic reports to the Committee, which the Committee considers along with a so-called shadow report that is normally produced by independent nongovernmental organizations (NGOs) from the state in question. The Committee then raises a list of issues and poses specific questions to the state; the state and the organizations that compiled the shadow report then submit their replies. The Committee makes its concluding remarks, which note areas of good practice, recommendations concerning further implementation, and areas where the state is considered to be failing. The Committee has no power to enforce its recommendations. Given that the obligation is to realize rights progressively, it is difficult for the Committee to determine whether a state has breached its obligations at all. The Maastricht Guidelines of 1997 clarify that a state is in breach of its obligations if it fails to allocate the maximum of its resources to the realization of human rights.[16] Following this principle, the Committee issued a 2007 statement entitled "An Evaluation of the Obligation to Take Steps to the Maximum of Available Resources Under an Optional Protocol to the Covenant," which regrettably did not define what constituted "available resources."[17]

The concept of progressive realization imposes a continuing obligation of states to take steps towards full realization while introducing an element of flexibility into that obligation. There are three main elements to progressive realization. First, there must be immediate and tangible progress towards the agreed end. In other words, the element of flexibility does not mean that the state can postpone implementation.[18] Second, the state cannot pursue regressive measures, meaning that the state cannot reduce existing minimum levels of support. Such reductions are justified only where they can be demonstrated to be necessary for achieving equity in the realization of a right, or to create a more sustainable basis for realization.[19] The state is likely to be held to a high standard here, as the Committee examines whether:

> (a) there was reasonable justification for the action (b) alternatives were comprehensively examined (c) there was genuine participation of affected groups in examining the proposed measures and alternatives (d) the measures were directly or indirectly discriminatory (e) the measures have a sustained impact on the realisation of the right and (f) whether there as an independent review of the measure at national level.[20]

The Committee offers little guidance, however. At times, it will criticize a measure without identifying whether the measure did in fact breach the state's obligation. This is problematic particularly during times of austerity measures.[21] The third element of progressive realization is that special measures are to be implemented for particularly vulnerable and disadvantaged groups. This requires the state to take positive steps to reduce structural inequality and give preferential treatment to these groups.

The steps to be taken toward progressive realization vary depending on the resources of the state. The minimum core approach sets out that there is a minimum level that the state must ensure. In other words, the obligation to implement minimum core rights is an immediate obligation, while the general application of the Covenant is an obligation to be met by progressive realization subject to state resources. As noted above, one of the Committee's functions is to define, through its general comments, the content and scope of rights. The greatest challenges for the Committee have arisen when it has been tasked with articulating these in terms of a state's minimum core obligations. Committee members seek to establish a minimum content, asserting that people are entitled to a minimum standard and that it is unacceptable for individuals to live in conditions of extreme poverty and deprivation that fall below the minimum standard. The general comments, while useful as elaborations of the content of rights, fail to define adequately what the minimum core of each right is.[22] General Comment No. 3 states that:

> a minimum core obligation to ensure the satisfaction of, at the very least minimum essential levels of each of the rights is incumbent upon every state party. Thus, for example, a state party in which any significant number of individuals is deprived of essential foodstuffs, of essential primary health care, of basic shelter and housing, or of the most basic forms of education is, prima facie, failing to discharge its obligations under the Covenant.[23]

However, this statement is partially qualified, as the ICESCR states a number of conditions that must be present before a state can be said to have breached its minimum core obligations. Originally, there had to be a significant number of people suffering from the particular deprivation. As that significant number seemed impossible to quantify, the Committee subsequently clarified that minimum core obligations apply as an individual right – thereby effectively obviating the original requirement.[24] Moreover, "any assessment as to whether a state has discharged its minimum core obligations must also take account of resource constraints applying within the country concerned."[25]

Benchmarks for progressively meeting social and economic rights have not been clearly defined, nor has the content of minimum core rights been cataloged. Given this situation, legal academic Katherine Young identifies three distinct approaches to understanding the minimum core rights and obligations.[26] First, the essence approach seeks to establish the essential minimum of the right: "it is the absolute, inalienable and universal crux, an unrelinquishable nucleus that is the *raison d'etre* of the basic legal norm, essential to its definition."[27] Here, then, the minimum core is the satisfaction of the basic needs of the individual – the essentials for survival and life, as interpreted by the Committee.[28] Such an approach can be problematic, however, as it can deteriorate into an exercise in defining the minimum requirements for humans' biological survival. A value-based approach focuses, by contrast, on the dignity of the person, a concept that has flourished since the UDHR.[29] This approach also creates difficulties, however, in that dignity can be measured either objectively or subjectively, which hampers a precise definition of the minimum core of the right.[30] The second approach identified by Young is the consensus approach. Here the focus is on identifying where a consensus has been reached, rather than on defining the normative content of the minimum core. The idea is that evidence of a consensus can emerge from an examination of jurisprudence, and that consensus can be used to in turn to develop the normative content of the right. Indeed, the Committee has been able to ascertain a consensus, or an emerging consensus, from state reports, in spite of the lack of justiciability in many national jurisdictions. The focus on consensus, arguably, augments the legitimacy of the outcome. Young's third approach is the minimum obligation approach. It focuses on the duties required to implement the minimum core right. While it is helpful for establishing the steps states should be taking to implement the right, it does little in the way of establishing normative content.

The difficulty of determining the minimum core of a given right has played out in practice in the South African Constitutional Court. In the case of *Government of the Republic of South Africa v. Grootboom*, the court considered the right to adequate housing, and felt that it was impossible to say what the minimum threshold was without identifying need, which in turn would depend on factors such as income, employment, and availability of land. The court therefore preferred to examine the case based on the reasonableness of steps taken. Similarly, in the *Treatment Action Campaign* case, the South African Constitutional Court maintained that the minimum core right is subject to resource constraints, specifically rejecting arguments to the contrary. These cases are considered in more detail below.

The concepts of progressive realization and minimum core rights have done much to curtail the development of social and economic rights. The steps required of states may be minimal and subject to resource constraints. While the Committee has been strongly critical of regressive measures, the global financial crisis since 2008 nevertheless resulted in fewer available resources, and austerity has had a significant impact on the enjoyment of rights protected by the ICESCR. Moreover, the failure to meet the minimum core content of each right can be due to the imprecise and contested nature of that content. Given that the role of the Committee has primarily been as a monitoring body, the introduction of the optional protocol of the ICESCR, intended to allow the court to deliver opinions and decisions on particular cases, may serve to clarify these areas. The optional protocol, in force since 2013, is also considered in more detail below.

Objections to justiciability

The main difference between social and economic rights on the one hand and civil and political rights on the other has been, and continues to be, the ability to enforce them legally, that is, their justiciability. Early arguments against the justiciability of social and economic rights centered on whether they could even be properly classified as rights, due to the then current understanding that they carried positive and resource-heavy obligations. This debate has been concluded for the most part by the general acceptance of their status as human rights. Arguments now focus on which branch of the state should be responsible for their protection and vindication: the judiciary, the executive branch, or even the legislature.

Overall, objections to the legalization of social and economic rights can be categorized under three headings: characterization, legitimacy, and institutional capacity.[31] To briefly summarize these objections: Characterization refers to the content, obligation, and cost of the right. The objection here is twofold; first, that the content of the right itself is vague, and that therefore a court cannot make a determination, and second, that social and economic rights necessarily carry positive (and therefore expensive) obligations. This objection is easily countered: Civil and political rights have also been vague and imprecise historically, and through court intervention the parameters and scope of those rights have been better defined. Furthermore, all rights contain an amalgam of both positive and negative obligations. For example, it can be costly to ensure the right to a fair trial, as that requires an effective police force, an impartial judiciary, adequate representation, etc.

The second kind of objection is legitimacy, and is related to the cost argument. This objection holds that, as these rights will cost the state, only the government has the power to decide how to allocate state resources, and that if the court were to determine these issues, it would be breaching the separation of powers. Again, all rights contain both positive and negative obligations. Moreover, to relegate an entire category of rights to a position beyond the scrutiny of the courts arguably creates a situation that the separation of powers was designed to prevent, for it places all of the power over them within one branch of the state, with no oversight.

The third kind of objection centers on institutional capacity. It contends that courts do not have the capability to handle cases involving social and economic rights, due primarily to the polycentric or far-reaching effects of claims arising in such cases.[32] This is possibly the least persuasive of the objections, as the vast majority of decisions have an impact on people beyond those who were party to the case, particularly if the case was brought against the state or an organ thereof. Judges often find themselves inserted into controversies that lie beyond their expertise, such as financial accounting, aviation, marine biology, etc. To overcome this deficiency, experts in the field are brought in to explain; the same could be done in cases concerning social and economic rights. In sum, objections to justiciability are misplaced. The next section further supports this conclusion by showing a clear trend toward court intervention and, more importantly, by showing that judicial intervention enhances protection.

Moving towards justiciability

International law: the optional protocol to the ICESCR

In 1990 the Committee began calling for the introduction of an optional protocol that would establish an individual complaints mechanism. An individual complaints mechanism, it was argued, would empower the Committee to offer more effective protection in instances of concrete abuse, to issue more definitive guidance on the interpretation of rights, and to increase the stature of the ICESCR.[33] Ongoing opposition to justiciability was apparent at the outset of negotiations on the optional protocol.[34] Delegates argued that a complaints mechanism would be impractical due to the imprecise nature of the rights, and would undermine the democratic process in policy and budgetary matters.[35] Despite such objections, the Human Rights Council approved the protocol in June 2008, the General Assembly adopted it, it was opened for signature in December 2008, and it entered into force in 2013.[36] Numerous admissibility criteria must be met in order to address the Committee with a complaint, including the exhaustion of domestic remedies, a time limitation of one year, and the requirement that the claim must not be anonymous, vexatious, or an abuse of the right to petition.[37] The Committee has jurisdiction only to hear claims in which the breach occurred or continued after the protocol came into effect, which confirms the principle of non-retrospectivity.[38] It does, however, have the power to request interim measures to protect against continuing and ongoing violations.[39]

The optional protocol has two main weaknesses. First, the treaty's wording remains the same: Rights are to be realized progressively, subject to resources, rather than as matters of immediate obligation. Again, this makes it difficult to prove that a state has breached its obligations.[40] There is currently no jurisprudence from the Committee that could indicate how it will interpret state obligations or how influential the General Comments will be in defining state obligations. Legal analysts anticipate that this ambiguity will decline once the Committee begins to deliver opinions. The weak wording of the optional protocol, a result of political rather than legal considerations, is also a matter of concern. Extensive admissibility criteria were added in order to assuage fears of opening the floodgates. To my mind, that suggests that the Committee is aware of the vast and significant violations of these rights. The optional protocol also requires the Committee to take account of the "reasonableness" of any steps that the state has taken.[41] The interpretation of reasonableness may have a considerable impact on the efficacy of the optional protocol, which in turn could influence interpretation in regional and domestic systems. If the Committee interprets reasonableness minimally, so too will the individual states.[42] A second weakness of the optional protocol relates to the Committee's enforcement and sanction powers. These extend to making recommendations only. The Committee has no authority to enforce its decisions or to impose sanctions on the offending state. The only requirement is that the State Party give due consideration to the Committee's views.

Despite these inherent weaknesses, the optional protocol is a significant step toward approximating the treatment of all rights without regard to derivation or classification. By providing a forum in which violations of rights can be voiced and adjudicated, albeit in a nonenforceable manner, the optional protocol elevates social and economic rights to a level comparable to civil and political rights in international law.[43] This marks a considerable advancement of these rights and indeed categorically affirms their status as rights.

Regional developments

The Council of Europe was established in the wake of World War II as a sister institution to the European Economic Community (which developed into what we know today as the European Union). While the European Union and its antecedent institutions have been charged with ensuring economic stability, the Council of Europe has had responsibility for protecting human rights. Disappointed at the delays in transposing the UDHR, the Council of Europe set about creating the European Convention on Human Rights, which entered into force in 1953. Here too the same arguments arose regarding the status of social and economic rights. In order to ensure that the convention could enter into force as quickly as possible, members agreed that only those rights would be included that were readily accepted by all.

The text of the European Convention on Human Rights protects only civil and political rights. From its very early cases, however, the European Court of Human Rights found that there could be no watertight division of rights. At the same time, the Court was fairly stagnant for many years regarding developing that line of judicial reasoning.[44] In the last decade or so, the Court has shown considerable activism regarding reading social and economic rights into the Convention. Its approach is that where violations of social and economic rights are such that the enjoyment of civil or political rights is materially affected, it will adjudicate. The following examples of case law illustrate this. The Court has primarily considered cases concerning housing, health, and social assistance, and initially it placed negative obligations on the state. In the case of *Moldovan v. Romania*, the Court determined that while the state does not have to provide housing for all homeless, the state may have a positive obligation if it has been complicit in creating that homelessness.[45] In *Connors v. UK*[46] and *Yordanova v. Bulgaria*,[47] the Court affirmed that the state cannot arbitrarily evict without adequate safeguards, and that while the state does not have to provide benefits, where it does it must do so without discrimination.[48] The Court moreover questioned whether the state can deport those with medical conditions.[49] In recent cases, more positive obligations have been placed on the state. In *Soares de Melo v. Portugal*, a complex case involving removal of the applicant's children for neglect due to poverty-stricken conditions, the court found such action to be a breach of the right to family life.[50] This case is of particular note in that the court was critical of the fact that the state had knowledge of the applicant's living conditions yet had not intervened to ameliorate the situation.

The European Court of Human Rights is not the only court that has displayed this approach of adjudicating violations of social and economic rights where they affect the enjoyment of civil or political rights. Paralleling the above account of the UDHR, the American Declaration of the Rights and Duties of Man (1948)[51] encompasses social and economic rights, such as the right to health, education, rest and leisure, and the right to social security, but these were not integrated into the judicially enforceable American Convention on Human Rights that entered into force in 1969.[52] However, even in the absence of specified protection, the Inter-American Court has interpreted civil and political rights, in particular the right to life, in a manner that renders social and economic rights justiciable through them.[53] One of the first of its cases dealing with social and economic rights, known as the *Street Children* case,[54] involved the plight of children living on the streets of Guatemala. The Inter-American Court reasoned that the right to live a dignified existence was implicit in the right to life.[55]

An additional protocol of the American Convention on Human Rights that concerns social and economic rights, commonly referred to as the Protocol of San Salvador, entered into force in 1999.[56] Through application of the American Convention on Human Rights in a manner harmonious with this additional protocol, the notion of a decent and dignified life has come to encompass social and economic rights, particularly the right to health.[57] The interpretation of the American Convention on Human Rights as an integral part of a system of human rights documents, rather than as a stand-alone document, has in effect made social and economic rights justiciable.

In the context of this essay, both the manner in which the Inter-American Court has encompassed social and economic rights jurisprudence and the remedies it has awarded are important. The court does not only award damages where a breach has occurred; it has also developed the practice of ordering positive obligations at the interim stage. In other words, the court has ordered immediate measures to prevent violations of rights, rather than waiting for a violation to occur and responding reactively. These measures have so far primarily involved ordering medical treatment and improved living conditions for those under the care or control of the state.[58] However, it is fair to expect the extension of this precedent to those dependent on state resources. The Inter-American Court has indirectly given effect to social and economic rights through its expansive interpretation of the civil and political rights contained in the Convention, and has thereby confirmed the indivisibility and interdependence of the two sets of rights in a manner that was "always intuitive."[59]

Domestic jurisprudence

Turning to domestic legal systems, it should be noted that recent national constitutions contain explicit protections for social and economic rights.[60] The Croatian Constitution,[61] the Charter of Fundamental Rights and Freedoms of the Czech Republic (justiciable under the Constitution of the Czech Republic),[62] the Constitution of Finland,[63] the Constitution of Moldova,[64] the Constitution of Hungary,[65] the Constitution of Poland,[66] the Constitution of Serbia,[67] and the Swiss Constitution[68] all provide express protections for various social and economic rights and for their judicial enforcement. South Africa provides the foremost example of a domestic system that enshrines social and economic rights within its Constitution[69] and confers full justiciability on them.[70] Rights such as housing, healthcare, food, social security, and shelter[71] are of a rank and dignity equal to civil and political rights, a measure intended to transform the post-apartheid nation.[72]

The first substantive case[73] on the issue of social and economic rights to come before the South African Constitutional Court was *Soobramoney v. Minister for Health, KwaZulu-Natal*, which challenged the denial of dialysis treatment to prolong the life of a terminally ill patient.[74] The applicant relied on the provision that "no one may be refused emergency medical treatment,"[75] which the court rejected. The court determined that the provision could not be extended to prolonging the life of a terminally ill patient, as the right had to be weighed against the limited resources of the state,[76] and it held that the state was justified in restricting this treatment to non-terminal patients. The decision caused concern about the future of social and economic rights jurisprudence, as it appeared to defer excessively to the executive.[77]

The case of *Government of the Republic of South Africa v. Grootboom*, noted above and decided two years after *Soobramoney*, gave fresh hope.[78] This case sought to enforce the right to housing under Section 26 of the constitution.[79] The applicant and several hundred other residents of an informal settlement had left that area, due to dismal living conditions, and had settled on private land. A court granted an eviction order, and during its enforcement the residents' temporary shelters and possessions were destroyed, forcing them to return to the original informal settlement. A High Court found that the Constitution did not confer an enforceable individual right to a minimum entitlement to temporary shelter. It also found, however, that where parents were unable to provide basic shelter, Section 28 imposed an obligation on the state to provide "tents, portable latrines and a regular supply of water,"[80] and made declaratory orders in that regard, requiring the respondents to provide temporary accommodation particularly for the children within three months.[81] The Constitutional Court upheld the decision, but found that the state was in breach of Section 26(2), as its housing plan failed to provide reasonable measures "to provide for relief for people who have no access to land, no roof over their heads, and who are living in intolerable conditions or crisis situations,"[82] and that "it is essential that a reasonable part of the national housing budget be devoted to the homeless."[83] However, it merely granted declaratory orders, and did not state what measures would satisfy this reasonableness test.

The limits of enforceability for social and economic rights remained in question following this judgment.[84] Its paramount significance, however, is that it confirmed that social and economic rights contain both negative and positive dimensions and obligations. With regard to negative obligations, a number of cases that involved evictions[85] showed that the courts, while not stating a positive duty to provide for housing, did strike down legislation and procedures that allowed for arguably arbitrary eviction. This approach has not been confined to housing cases; in *Khosa v. Minister for Social Development* the court found unconstitutional the exclusion of permanent residents from certain social assistance benefits.[86]

While the court in *Grootboom* did not elaborate on the specifics of the positive obligations, it did confirm that the Constitution placed a duty on the state to ameliorate lamentable living conditions,[87] and the court reserves the ability to enforce that by way of mandatory orders. The High Court did grant these mandatory orders in the *Treatment Action Campaign* case.[88] This case challenged a policy that restricted the drug Nevirapine to certain pilot areas.[89] In the first instance, the High Court ordered that the drug be made available to all infected mothers giving birth in state institutions, and that the state develop a comprehensive plan and report back to the court within three months in relation to its development and implementation.[90] On appeal to the Constitutional Court, the ruling of the High Court was upheld in that the Constitutional Court affirmed the state's duty to remove restrictions. However, in terms of the obligation to develop and implement the plan, the court preferred to grant declaratory relief with no time frame for completion.[91]

This deference toward defendants in cases of social and economic rights can also be seen in the *Mazibuko* case, which involved a challenge to the introduction of prepaid water meters in the poverty-stricken area of Soweto.[92] The applicants argued that the water meters breached their constitutional right to adequate access to water.[93] In the High Court, Justice Tsoka held that the installation of prepaid water meters constituted a violation of the right to water in that "To deny the applicants a right to water is to deny them the right to lead a dignified human existence."[94] The case was appealed to the Supreme Court of Appeal, which upheld the order of the High Court, stating that the city had no authority to install prepaid meters and, *a fortiori*, that the discontinuation of water when the free limit had been reached was unlawful.[95] The case was appealed once more to the Constitutional Court, which overturned the High Court's and Supreme

Court of Appeal's previous orders. The Constitutional Court determined that the installation of meters did not breach any rights, and further refused to declare what amount of water was a sufficient daily allowance.[96] The example of South Africa indicates that even when social and economic rights are placed in the text of a country's constitution, that does not mean that they will be upheld in every case. Rather, they will be subject to the same balancing and tests that are applied to all other rights. Of particular note, the availability of resources has proven to be a paramount concern for the court.

India is a contrasting case, in that it has been the most assiduous in reading social and economic rights into its constitution. It has done so through an expansive interpretation of the right to life. The pivotal moment was the expansion of Article 21 to make the Directive Principles of State Policy justiciable. That initiated the era of social and economic rights jurisprudence in India.[97]The first case to test the position of social and economic rights in the Indian Constitution was *Olga Tellis v. Bombay*, which concerned housing and shelter.[98] This public interest litigation was brought on behalf of pavement dwellers against eviction without notice or compensation to the outskirts of the city. They argued that this eviction deprived them of their livelihood, and that this displacement from their source of income infringed their right to life under Article 21 of the Constitution. Chief Justice Chandrachud observed that it would be "sheer pedantry to exclude the right to livelihood from the content of the right to life."[99] In *Shantistar Builders v. Narayan Khimalal Totame* the court entrenched its position, observing that the right to food, clothing, and reasonable accommodation were encompassed in the right to life,[100] which it interpreted as the right to live with dignity and to flourish intellectually and materially.[101] The theme of protecting poverty-stricken and vulnerable parts of society with regard to housing issues continued in *Chameli Singh v. State of Uttar Pradesh*. Here the court upheld a policy that infringed on the rights of the privileged for the benefit of the marginalized.[102]

The court also expanded the parameters of the right to life in order to guarantee the right to health. In *Consumer Education and Research Centre v. Union of India*, the court held that the right to health and medical care was an integral part of the right to life.[103] This ruling established the foundations of a positive obligation on the part of the state to ensure certain standards of good health.[104] In *Parmanand Katara v. Union of India*, the court addressed emergency medical care as an iteration of the right to life.[105] Here it ordered the removal of legal impediments that prevented some hospitals from treating medico-legal cases, following the death of a traffic accident victim who had been refused admission to such a hospital. The court further ordered that its decision be publicized in order to creating general awareness of the state's responsibility to provide emergency medical care.[106] In *Paschim Banga Khet Mazdoor Samity v. State of West Bengal*, the court reiterated the duty to provide emergency medical care as an integral part of the preservation of life.[107] Undeterred by the significant cost implications, it ordered that equipment and facilities be provided to ensure the preservation of life in emergency medical situations.[108] However, the court has also accepted resource limitations as a legitimate reason to restrict access in certain circumstances. Faced with the question of whether a reduction in the reimbursement for medical expenses to which one was entitled was a breach of Article 21, the court accepted the state's contention that the reduction was necessary due to financial constraints.[109] This outcome may have been different if the reimbursement benefit was to have been removed entirely, rather than reduced, as medical care must be affordable in order to be within the reach of all.[110]

The case of *Laxmi Mandal v. Deen Dayal Harinagar Hospital* expanded on the *Paschim Banga* judgment.[111] The case was brought on behalf of a woman who died as a result of carrying a dead fetus in her womb. It was the first case worldwide to recognize preventable maternal mortality as a human rights violation.[112] She had been refused access to emergency maternal care because her husband was unable to show a valid ration card for medical services, a card to which he was in fact entitled. The High Court of Delhi found that there had been systematic failure on the part of the state. Declaring that it was the responsibility of the state to ensure that valid ration cards were circulated, the court ordered an overhaul of that system. The overhaul included the requirement for the state to seek out those in need of ration cards. The court also mandated the establishment of monitoring systems to ensure that its orders were being fully implemented. Since that judgment, a plethora of cases involving maternal healthcare have come before the court.[113] It is noteworthy that the court's initial activism in this area has not diminished. In 2010, on its own motion, the court brought a case against the Union of India following reports of a destitute woman who died several days after giving birth on the street.[114] After a preliminary hearing, the court ordered the government of Delhi to open five homes exclusively for pregnant or lactating destitute women, establish a helpline to promote the homes, make food and medical care available 24 hours a day in the shelters, disseminate information about the shelters, host awareness camps, mobilize medical units to bring women to the shelters, and involve NGOs. The state took issue with the expansive nature of the orders and filed objections to this effect. Nevertheless, and pending final determination of the appeals process, they were ordered to implement immediately two of the shelters with food and medical care. In 2013, the conditions of those shelters were brought before the court following the death of a baby.[115] Following an inspection of the facility and a finding of unsatisfactory conditions,[116] the court ordered several remedial measures, including a supplemental nutrition, adequate hot water, heating in winter, and dedicated space for prenatal checkups.[117]

It is even more interesting that such extensive measures in relation to emergency medical care and maternity care do have precedents. The ongoing public interest litigation in the case of *People's Union for Civil Liberties* illustrates the dramatic measures taken to protect social and economic rights.[118] This case, instigated in 2001, initially sought an order to compel the government to release food stocks on behalf of those dying of starvation in the state of Rajasthan. Over a number of years, the open case was establishing the principle of an intrinsic link between the right to food and the constitutionally protected right to life. The litigation continued until the subject matter was overtaken by legislation, and during that time the Supreme Court issued a plethora of orders regarding grain allocation, a midday meal scheme in schools, ration cards for those living below the poverty line, and the operation of ration shops. Orders were also issued for a price-setting mechanism for grain, for the doubling of the grain allocation in a work-for-food scheme, and for the increase of financial assistance for these schemes. Some criticized this activism, arguing that the court was acting outside of its mandate, breaching the separation of powers, and pursuing its own political agenda. The efficacy of the court's orders has been scrutinized and found wanting in many instances. Nevertheless, the court has had an impact on the implementation of law and policy through its directive principles, in a system rife with corruption.

With regard to developing the justiciability of social and economic rights, Canada falls more or less midway between South Africa and India. The main instrument protecting human rights in Canada is the Charter of Rights and Freedoms (1982),[119] which incorporates seven classes of rights and freedoms.[120] There is no explicit provision for social and economic rights, but section 7, ensuring life, liberty, and security of the person, and section 15, guaranteeing equality,[121] have been interpreted as encompassing social and economic rights, and this possibility was apparent even in the earliest cases.

A defining case for social and economic rights in Canada was *Victoria City v. Adams*, which challenged the constitutionality of a bylaw that had been enacted to prohibit temporary shelters in public parks.[122] In seeking to enforce the bylaw and remove the temporary shelters that had been erected by homeless people, the city argued that this was a justified measure to prevent damage to the park. Evidence of the lack of availability and overcrowding in the city's homeless shelters was adduced.[123] The British Columbia Supreme Court held that sleep and shelter were necessary preconditions to life and rejected the contention that Charter rights could not be engaged without positive action from the state.[124] It therefore struck down the bylaw as breaching section 7 of the Charter. While this judgment does not impose positive obligations on the state to provide adequate shelter, it does impose negative obligations.[125] The court did not order the provision of more spaces in homeless shelters, nor did it require that the park dwellers be housed in public housing. Rather, where these were not available, the state could not arbitrarily remove the temporary shelters, as they were deemed to be essential to life. For that matter, early cases in which applicants sought state-funded healthcare under section 7 of the Charter were unsuccessful: The court held that the provision did not include a guarantee to enhance life, liberty, or security of the person.[126] However, restrictions on access to healthcare were struck down. For example, criminal restrictions on therapeutic abortions came to be regarded as unconstitutional,[127] and the denial of sign language support in medical care was found impermissibly to impede access to healthcare.[128]

The Canadian Supreme Court case of *PHS Community Services v. Canada*, also known as the *Insite* case, has entrenched the status of the social and economic rights within the Charter.[129] The case related to a drug consumption room that had been established as a harm reduction mechanism, due to a widespread addiction problem in the city. The facility, called Insite, operated under an exemption to the criminal law for an initial three years, which was then extended by 15 months. Following a change in government, plans were announced to discontinue the exemption and close the facility.[130] Insite brought a claim to the British Columbia Supreme Court that the state would be in breach of section 7 of the Charter if the exemption were terminated and the facility closed.[131] That court found that, given that the staff managed and prevented the spread of disease and provided services that amounted to healthcare,[132] the withdrawal of the exemption would prevent access to healthcare and therefore engage the right to life and section 7. The British Columbia Court of Appeal upheld the ruling, determining that the right to life was engaged, as the service prevented death by overdose, and, further, that the injection of drugs without medical supervision posed a risk to life.[133] On final appeal to the Canadian Supreme Court, the removal of the exemption was unanimously held to breach Charter rights. Chief Justice McLachlin stated that "where the law creates a risk to health by preventing access to health care, a deprivation of the right to security of the person is made out."[134]

To date, the Canadian courts have not declared positive obligations in respect of social and economic rights, although such an outcome is possible. In *Gosselin v. Quebec*, then-justice McLachlin felt that the Charter should be allowed to develop incrementally and that its content should not be constricted by previous cases,[135] and the court's language in *Insite* is indicative of future possibilities.[136] However, a recent attempt to impose positive obligations was rejected without a hearing. The case, named *Tanudjaja v. Canada*, was brought by a group of housing activists who alleged that the Ontario government's legislative and policy changes had resulted in inadequate housing and increased homelessness.[137] In essence, they were asking the court to determine whether sections 7 and 15 of the Charter carried a positive obligation to be housed. The petition was initially rejected and the Court of Appeal upheld that determination, as the challenge pointed to a complex matrix of policies rather than any specific offending law. The majority on the Court of Appeal agreed with the lower court's decision, so there was no further discussion of whether positive obligations regarding homelessness could be placed on the state. In a dissenting judgment, however, Justice Feldman opined that it was too early to decide whether this case contained circumstances that could merit the court imposing positive obligations, and she strongly advocated hearing the case.[138] Leave to appeal the case to the Supreme Court was rejected in 2015. Nevertheless, Canada has shown that it is possible to protect social and economic rights adequately without imposing excessively burdensome positive obligations.

Conclusion

As social and economic rights continue to lack protection equivalent to that of civil and political rights, judicial intervention is a necessary step in the approximation of rights. Without this oversight or enforcement, social and economic rights remain overlooked, neglected, or even denied by governments. As the jurisprudence shows, justiciability enhances accountability, which in turn makes a significant difference to the protection and vindication of these most fundamental of human rights.

Notes

1 United Nations, Charter of the United Nations, 24 October 1945 UN Document 1 UNTSXVI. Online. Available athttps://treaties.un.org/pages/ViewDetails.aspx?src=IND&mtdsg_no=I-1&chapter=1&clang=_en (accessed 29 December 2018).
2 This was primarily due to pressure from the Western-dominated Commission on Human Rights. See UN Document A2929 (1955) 7. Online. Available at https://documents-dds-ny.un.org/doc/UNDOC/GEN/N55/173/02/PDF/N5517302.pdf?OpenElement (accessed 29 December 2018).
3 Samuel Moyn, *The Last Utopia*, Cambridge, MA: Belknap Press at Harvard University Press, 2010.
4 Steven L. B. Jensen, *The Making of International Human Rights Law: The 1960s, Decolonization, and the Reconstruction of Global Values*, Cambridge, UK: Cambridge University Press, 2017.
5 World Conference on Human Rights, "Vienna Declaration and Programme of Action," 1993, §5. Online. Available at www.ohchr.org/en/professionalinterest/pages/vienna.aspx (accessed 29 December 2018).
6 United Nations, "International Covenant on Civil and Political Rights" (ICCPR), adopted on 16 December 1966 and entered into force on 23 March 1976. See UN Document 999 UNTS 171. Online. Available at https://treaties.un.org/pages/showdetails.aspx?objid=0800000280004bf5. See also UN Document 1057 UNTS 407/[1980] ATS 23/6 ILM 368 (1967). Online. Available at https://treaties.un.org/doc/publication/unts/volume%20999/volume-999-i-14668-english.pdf (both accessed 29 December 2018).
7 United Nations, "International Covenant on Economic Social and Cultural Rights" (ICESCR), adopted on 16 December 1966 and entered into force on 3 January 1976. See

UN Document 993 UNTS 3/[1976] ATS 5/6 ILM 360 (1967). Online. Available at https://treaties.un.org/Pages/ViewDetails.aspx?src=IND&mtdsg_no=IV-3&chapter=4&lang=en (accessed 29 December 2018).

8 Daniel J. Whelan and Jack Donnelly, "The West, Economic and Social Rights, and the Global Human Rights Regime: Setting the Record Straight," *Human Rights Quarterly*, 2007, vol. 29, no. 4, 931.

9 ICESCR, Part II, Article 2(1).

10 Henry Steiner, Ryan Goodman, and Philip Alston, *International Human Rights Law in Context: Law Politics Morals*, 3rd ed., Oxford: Oxford University Press, 2007, p. 284.

11 In contrast to the ICESCR, the ICCPR contained within its first optional protocol an individual complaints mechanism to the Human Rights Committee. See UN Document 999 UNTS 171 (see n. 6).

12 Catarina de Albuquerque, "Chronicle of an Announced Birth: The Coming into Life of the Optional Protocol to the International Covenant on Economic Social and Cultural Rights – The Missing Piece of the International Bill of Human Rights," *Human Rights Quarterly*, 2010, vol. 32, 144.

13 ICCPR, Article 2(3).

14 "Maastricht Guidelines on Violations of Economic, Social and Cultural Rights," 26 January 1997, Article 6. Online. Available at http://hrlibrary.umn.edu/instree/Maastrichtguidelines_.html (accessed 29 December 2018).

15 Office of the High Commissioner for Human Rights, "Review of the Composition, Organization and Administrative Arrangements of the Sessional Working Group of Governmental Experts on the Implementation of the International Covenant on Economic, Social and Cultural Rights," 28 May 1985. Economic and Social Council (ECOSOC) resolution 1985/17. Online. Available at https://digitallibrary.un.org/record/58615/files/E_C.12_1989_4-EN.pdf (accessed 29 December 2018).

16 "Maastricht Guidelines."

17 United Nations Economic and Social Council, "An Evaluation of the Obligation to Take Steps to the Maximum of Available Resources under an Optional Protocol to the Covenant," 2007. UN Document E/C.12/2007/1. Online. Available at https://documents-dds-ny.un.org/doc/UNDOC/GEN/G07/441/63/PDF/G0744163.pdf?OpenElement (accessed 29 December 2018).

18 Limburg Principles on the Implementation of the ICESCR, Annex, §21. UN Document E/CN4/1987/17. Online. Available at www.refworld.org/docid/48abd5790.html (accessed 29 December 2018).

19 Sandra Liebenberg, *Socio-Economic Rights: Adjudication Under a Transformative Constitution*, Cape Town: Juta Academic, 2010, p. 190.

20 United Nations Committee on Economic, Social and Cultural Rights, "General Comment No. 19 The Right to Social Security (Article 9 of the Covenant)," adopted 23 November 2007, §42. UN Document E/C.12/GC/19. Online. Available at www.refworld.org/docid/47b17b5b39c.html (accessed 29 December 2018).

21 Colm O'Cinneide, "Austerity and the Faded Dream of a Social Europe," in Aoife Nolan (ed.) *Economic Social and Cultural Rights after the Global Financial Crisis*, Cambridge, UK: Cambridge University Press, 2014, p. 21.

22 Mesenbet Assefa, "Defining Minimum Core Conundrums in International Human Rights Law and Lessons from the Constitutional Court of South Africa," *Mekelle University Law Journal*, 2010, vol. 1, no. 1, 50.

23 United Nations Committee on Economic, Social and Cultural Rights, "General Comment No. 3 The Nature of States Parties' Obligations (Article 2, Paragraph 1, of the Covenant)," §10. UN Document E/1991/23. Online. Available at www.refworld.org/docid/4538838e10.html (accessed 29 December 2018).

24 United Nations Committee on Economic, Social and Cultural Rights, "General Comment No. 15: The Right to Water (Arts. 11 and 12 of the Covenant)," §44. UN Document E/C.12/2002/11. Online. Available at www.refworld.org/docid/4538838d11.html (accessed 29 December 2018).

25 "General Comment No. 3," §10.

26 Katharine G. Young, "The Minimum Core of Social and Economic Rights: A Concept in Search of Content," *Yale Journal of International Law*, 2008, vol. 33, 113.

27 Young, "The Minimum Core of Social and Economic Rights," 126.
28 "General Comment No. 3," §10.
29 E.g. in *Khosa v. Minister of Social Development* 2004 (6) SA 505 (CC), the South African Constitutional Court emphasized the connection between dignity and social assistance. Online. Available at https://collections.concourt.org.za/handle/20.500.12144/17376>. See also *Social and Economic Rights Action Centre v. Nigeria*, Comm No. 155/96 2001–2. The African Commission held that the right to food is inseparably linked to dignity. Online. Available at www.achpr.org/communications/decision/155.96/ (both accessed 29 December 2018).
30 Oscar Schachter, "Human Dignity as a Normative Concept," *American Journal of International Law*, 1983, vol. 77, 848.
31 For a full analysis of these, see Claire-Michelle Smyth, "Social and Economic Rights in a Post Neo-Liberal Society," in Claire-Michelle Smyth and Richard Lang (eds.) *The Future of Human Rights in the UK*, Cambridge, UK: Cambridge Scholars Publishing, 2017.
32 Lon Fuller, "The Forms and Limits of Adjudication," *Harvard Law Review*, 1978, vol. 92, 353; J. W. F. Allison, "Fuller's Analysis of Polycentric Disputes and the Limits of Adjudication," *Cambridge Law Journal*, 1994, vol. 53, 367.
33 Tara Melish, "Introductory Note to the Optional Protocol to the International Covenant on Economic Social and Cultural Rights," *International Legal Materials*, 2009, vol. 48, 256.
34 For an overview of the main arguments used in negotiations, see Malcolm Langford, "Closing the Gap? – An Introduction to the Optional Protocol to the International Covenant on Economic Social and Cultural Rights," *Nordic Journal of Human Rights*, 2009, vol. 27, no. 1, 9–18.
35 UN Economic and Social Council, "Report of First Session," 15 March 2004, p. 7. UN Document E/CN.4/2004/44. Online. Available at https://documents-dds-ny.un.org/doc/UNDOC/GEN/G04/120/29/PDF/G0412029.pdf?OpenElement. UN Economic and Social Council, "Report of Fourth Session," 30 August 2007, 5. UN Document A/HRC/6/8. Online. Available at https://documents-dds-ny.un.org/doc/UNDOC/GEN/G07/138/89/PDF/G0713889.pdf?OpenElement (both accessed 29 December 2018).
36 United Nations, "Optional Protocol to the International Covenant on Economic, Social and Cultural Rights." UN Document. A/RES/63/117. Online. Available at www2.ohchr.org/english/bodies/cescr/docs/A-RES-63-117.pdf (accessed 29 December 2018). For a detailed analysis of the background to the optional protocol's drafting, see Claire Mahon, "Progress at the Front: The Draft Optional Protocol to the International Covenant on Economic Social and Cultural Rights," *Human Rights Law Review*, 2008, vol. 8, 617–46.
37 United Nations, "Optional Protocol," Articles 3(1) and 3(2).
38 United Nations, "Optional Protocol," Article 3(2b).
39 United Nations, "Optional Protocol," Article 5.
40 Claire-Michelle Smyth, "The Optional Protocol to the International Covenant on Economic Social and Cultural Rights in Ireland: Will It Make a Difference?" *Socio-Legal Studies Review*, 2013, vol. 2, 1–22.
41 United Nations, "Optional Protocol," Article 8(4). Brian Griffey, "The Reasonableness Test: Assessing Violations of State Obligations under the Optional Protocol to the International Covenant on Economic Social and Cultural Rights," *Human Rights Law Review*, 2011, vol. 11, no. 2, 291–304.
42 Bruce Porter, "The Reasonableness of Article 8(4) – Adjudicating Claims from the Margin," *Nordic Journal of Human Rights*, 2009, vol. 27, no. 1, 39–40.
43 De Albuquerque, "Chronicle of an Announced Birth," 177.
44 European Court of Human Rights (ECtHR), "Case of *Airey v. Ireland*. Judgement," 1979. 2 EHRR 305. Online. Available at http://hudoc.echr.coe.int/eng?i=001-57420 (accessed 29 December 2018).
45 ECtHR, "Case of *Moldovan v. Romania*," Judgements No. 1 and 2, 2005. ECHR 458. Online. Available at http://hudoc.echr.coe.int/eng?i=001-69610 (Judgement No. 1) and http://hudoc.echr.coe.int/eng?i=001-69670 (Judgement No. 2) (accessed 29 December 2018).
46 ECtHR, "Case of *Connors v. United Kingdom*, Judgement," 2004. ECHR 223. Online. Available at http://hudoc.echr.coe.int/eng?i=001-61795 (accessed 29 December 2018).
47 ECtHR, "Case of *Yordanova and others v. Bulgaria*," 2012. Application No. 25446/06. Online. Available athttp://hudoc.echr.coe.int/eng?i=001-110449 (accessed 29 December 2018).

48 ECtHR, "Case of *Petrovic v. Austria*," 1998. Application No. 20458/92. Online. Available at http://hudoc.echr.coe.int/eng?i=001-58146 (accessed 29 December 2018).

49 ECtHR, "Case of *D v. UK*," 1997. EHRR 423. Online. Available at www.refworld.org/cases,ECHR,46deb3452.html. ECtHR, "Case of *N v. UK*," 2008, Application No. 26565/05. Online. Available at http://hudoc.echr.coe.int/eng?i=001-86490. ECHR, "Case of *S. J. v. Belgium*," 2015. ECHR 543. Online. Available at http://hudoc.echr.coe.int/eng?i=001-153361. ECtHR, "Case of *Paposhvili v. Belgium*," 2016. Application No. 41738/10. Online. Available at http://hudoc.echr.coe.int/eng?i=001-169662 (all accessed 29 December 2018).

50 ECtHR, "Affaire *Soares de Melo c. Portugal*," 2016. Application No. 72850/14. Online. Available at http://hudoc.echr.coe.int/eng?i=001-160938 (accessed 29 December 2018).

51 Organization of American States (OAS), "American Declaration of the Rights and Duties of Man," adopted by the Ninth International Conference of American States, 1948. Online. Available at www.oas.org/dil/access_to_information_human_right_American_Declaration_of_the_Rights_and_Duties_of_Man.pdf (accessed 29 December 2018). See Philip Alston and Ryan Goodman, *International Human Rights: The Successor to International Human Rights in Context*, Oxford: Oxford University Press 2013, p. 978. See Articles XI, XII, XV, XVI.

52 OAS, "American Convention on Human Rights. Adopted at the Inter-American Specialized Conference on Human Rights, San José, Costa Rica, 22 November 1969." Entered into force on 22 November 1969. Also known as the Pact of San Jose. Online. Available at www.cidh.oas.org/basicos/english/basic3.american%20convention.htm (accessed 29 December 2018).

53 For a full discussion see Tara Melish, *Protecting Economic Social and Cultural Rights in the Inter-American Human Rights System. A Manual on Presenting Claims*, Quito and New Haven: Centro de Derechos Económicos y Sociales and Orville H. Schell, Jr. Center for International Human Rights at Yale Law School, 2002, pp. 233–332.

54 Inter-American Court of Human Rights (IACHR), "Case of the *'Street Children' (Villagran-Morales et al.) v. Guatemala*. Judgment," 1999. Online. Available at www.refworld.org/cases,IACRTHR,4b17bc442.html (accessed 29 December 2018).

55 Monica Feria Tinta, "Justiciability of Economic, Social and Cultural Rights in the Inter-American System of Protection of Human Rights: Beyond Traditional Paradigms and Notions," *Human Rights Quarterly*, 2007, vol. 29, 446.

56 OAS, "Additional Protocol to the American Convention on Human Rights in the Area of Economic Social and Cultural Rights," 1999. Also known as the Protocol of San Salvador. Online. Available at www.oas.org/juridico/english/treaties/a-52.html (accessed 29 December 2018).

57 IACHR, "Juridical Condition and Human Rights of the Child. Advisory Opinion OC-17/2002 of 28 August 2002, Requested by the Inter-American Commission on Human Rights," 2002. Online. Available at www.corteidh.or.cr/docs/opiniones/seriea_17_ing.pdf (accessed 29 December 2018).

58 The court ordered the provision of proper medical treatment for a detainee with heart disease in the *Cesti-Hurtado* and *Mendoza Prison* cases. See IACHR, "Case of *Cesti-Hurtado v. Peru*. Judgment," 1999. Online. Available at www.corteidh.or.cr/docs/casos/articulos/seriec_56_ing.pdf and IACHR, "Case of *Mendoza et al. v. Argentina*. Judgement," 2013. Online. Available at www.corteidh.or.cr/docs/casos/articulos/seriec_260_ing.pdf. In the *Febem Prison* case, the court made orders in relation to overcrowding, sanitation and nutrition to ensure conditions for detainees and workers compatible with their dignity. See IACHR, "Order of the Inter-American Court of Human Rights of 4 July 2006. Provisional Measures and Request for Extension of Provisional Measures Regarding the Federative Republic of Brazil. Matter of Children and Adolescents Deprived of Liberty in the 'Complexo do Tatuapé' of Febem," 2006. Online. Available at www.corteidh.or.cr/docs/medidas/febem_se_03_ing.pdf (all accessed 29 December 2018).

59 Colm O'Cinneide, "The Constitutionalization of Social and Economic Rights," in Helena Alviar Garcia, Karl Klare, and Lucy A. Williams (eds.) *Social and Economic Rights in Theory and in Practice: Critical Enquiries*, London: Routledge, 2014, p. 268.

60 Identification of these provisions was made by way of a search of world constitutions using the Constitute website. Online. Available at www.constituteproject.org/ (accessed 29 December 2018).

61 The constitution of Croatia entered into force on 22 December 1990 and protects the right to social assistance (Article 58), the right to healthcare (Articles 59 and 70) and the right to

education (Article 66). Online. Available at www.constituteproject.org/constitution/Croatia_2013?lang=en (accessed 29 December 2018).

62 The constitution of the Czech Republic entered into force 1 January 1993 and protects the right to social assistance (Article 30), the right to health (Article 31) and the right to education (Article 33). Online. Available at www.constituteproject.org/constitution/Czech_Republic_2013?lang=en (accessed 29 December 2018). The Charter is online. Available at www.usoud.cz/fileadmin/user_upload/ustavni_soud_www/Pravni_uprava/AJ/Listina_English_version.pdf.

63 The constitution of Finland entered into force 1 March 2000 and protects the right to social security and housing assistance (§19) and the right to education (§16). Online. Available at www.constituteproject.org/constitution/Finland_2011?lang=en(accessed 29 December 2018).

64 The constitution of Moldova entered into force 29 July 1994 and protects the right to education (Article 35), the right of health security (Article 36), the right to live in a healthy environment (Article 37), and the right to social assistance, including food, clothing, shelter and medical care (Article 47). Online. Available at www.constituteproject.org/constitution/Moldova_2016?lang=en (accessed 29 December 2018).

65 The constitution of Hungary entered into force 25 April 2011 and protects the right to education (Article XI), social security (Article XIX), the right to health (Article XX), and the right to decent housing conditions (Article XXII). Online. Available at www.constituteproject.org/constitution/Hungary_2016?lang=en (accessed 29 December 2018).

66 The constitution of Poland entered into force 2 April 1997 and protects the right to health (Article 68). Online. Available at www.constituteproject.org/constitution/Poland_2009?lang=en (accessed 29 December 2018).

67 The constitution of Serbia entered into force 8 November 2006 and protects the right to health (Article 68), the right to education (Article 71), and social protection (Article 69). Online. Available at www.constituteproject.org/constitution/Serbia_2006?lang=en (accessed 29 December 2018).

68 The constitution of Switzerland entered into force 18 April 1999 and protects the right to social assistance (Article 12) and the right to basic education (Article 19). Online. Available at www.constituteproject.org/constitution/Switzerland_2014?lang=en (accessed 29 December 2018).

69 The constitution of the Republic of South Africa was approved by the Constitutional Court on 4 December 1996 and entered into force on 4 February 1997. Online. Available at www.constituteproject.org/constitution/South_Africa_2012?lang=en (accessed 29 December 2018).

70 For an in-depth analysis of the debate on constitutionalizing social and economic rights in the South African constitution, see Craig Scott and Patrick Macklem, "Constitutional Ropes of Sand or Justiciable Guarantees? Social Rights in a New South African Constitution," *University of Pennsylvania Law Review*, 1992, vol. 141, 1–148 and Liebenberg, *Socio-Economic Rights*.

71 See the constitution of the Republic of South Africa, §26 (housing), §27 (healthcare, food, social security), and §28 shelter (with respect to children).

72 Marius Pieterse, "Beyond the Welfare State: Globalisation of Neo-Liberal Culture and the Constitutional Protection of Social and Economic Rights in South Africa," *Stellenbosch Law Review*, 2003, vol. 14, no. 3, 9.

73 The first case, regarding *Certification of the Constitution of the Republic of South Africa*, 1996 (CCT 23/96) [1996] ZACC 26; 1996 (4) SA 744 (CC); 1996 (10) BCLR 1253 (CC) (6 September 1996), found that the inclusion of social and economic rights in the Constitution did not breach the separation of powers and was Constitutional. See Jeremy Sarkin, "The Drafting of South Africa's Final Constitution from a Human Rights Perspective," *American Journal of Comparative Law*, 1999, vol. 47, 67.

74 Constitutional Court, South Africa, *Soobramoney v. Minister of Health (Kwazulu-Natal)* (CCT32/97) [1997] ZACC 17; 1998 (1) SA 765 (CC); 1997 (12) BCLR 1696 (27 November 1997). Online. Available at www.saflii.org/za/cases/ZACC/1997/17.html (accessed 29 December 2018).

75 Constitution of the Republic of South Africa, §27(3).

76 This is expressly provided for in §27(2) of the Constitution of the Republic of South Africa: "the state must take reasonable legislative and other measures, within its available resources to achieve progressive realisation."

77 Eric C. Christiansen, "Adjudicating Non-Justiciable Rights: Socio-Economic Rights and the South African Constitution," *Columbia Human Rights Law Review*, 2007, vol. 38, 321.
78 Case of *Government of the Republic of South Africa and Others v. Grootboom and Others* (CCT11/00) [2000] ZACC 19; 2001 (1) SA 46; 2000 (11) BCLR 1169 (4 October 2000). Online. Available at www.saflii.org/za/cases/ZACC/2000/19.pdf (accessed 29 December 2018).
79 Constitution of the Republic of South Africa: "Everyone has the right to have access to adequate housing," §26(1); "The state must take reasonable legislative and other measures, within its available resources to achieve the progressive realization of this right," §26(2); "No one may be evicted from their home or have their home demolished without an order of the court made after considering all the relevant circumstances. No legislation may permit arbitrary evictions," §26(3).
80 The High Court Judgment of Justice Davis is referred to in the case of *Government of the Republic of South Africa and Others v. Grootboom and Others*, on pp. 3–4. See n. 78.
81 For a full history of the case, see Rosalind Dixon, "Creating Dialogue about Socio-Economic Rights: Strong-Form versus Weak-Form Judicial Review Revisited," *International Journal of Constitutional Law*, 2007, vol. 5, 391.
82 This is referred to in the case of *Government of the Republic of South Africa and Others v. Grootboom and Others*, on p. 149. See n. 78.
83 This is referred to in the case of *Government of the Republic of South Africa and Others v. Grootboom and Others*, on p. 149. See n. 78.
84 Marius Pieterse, "Coming to Terms with Judicial Enforcement of Socio-Economic Rights," *South African Journal of Human Rights*, 2004, vol. 20, 383.
85 These cases are the following: *Jaftha v. Schoeman and Others, Van Rooyen v. Stoltz and Others* (CCT74/03) [2004] ZACC 25; 2005 (2) SA 140 (CC); 2005 (1) BCLR 78 (CC) (8 October 2004). Online. Available at www.saflii.org/za/cases/ZACC/2004/25.html. *City of Johannesburg v. Rand Properties (Pty) Ltd* (253/06) [2007] ZASCA 25; [2007] 2 All SA 459 (SCA); 2007 (6) SA 417 (SCA); 2007 (6) BCLR 643 (SCA) (26 March 2007). Online. Available at www.saflii.org/za/cases/ZASCA/2007/25.html. *Abahlali Basemjondolo Movement SA and Another v. Premier of the Province of Kwazulu-Natal and Others* (CCT12/09) [2009] ZACC 31; 2010 (2) BCLR 99 (CC) (14 October 2009). Online. Available at www.saflii.org/za/cases/ZACC/2009/31.html (all accessed 29 December 2018).
86 *Khosa and Others v. Minister of Social Development and Others, Mahlaule and Another v. Minister of Social Development* (CCT 13/03, CCT 12/03) [2004] ZACC 11; 2004 (6) SA 505 (CC); 2004 (6) BCLR 569 (CC) (4 March 2004). Online. Available at www.saflii.org/za/cases/ZACC/2004/11.html (accessed 29 December 2018).
87 *Government of the Republic of South Africa and Others v. Grootboom and Others*, on p. #. See n. 78.
88 *Minister of Health and Others v. Treatment Action Campaign and Others* (No 1) (CCT9/02) [2002] ZACC 16; 2002 (5) SA 703; 2002 (10) BCLR 1075 (5 July 2002). Online. Available at www.saflii.org/za/cases/ZACC/2002/16.html (accessed 29 December 2018).
89 This drug dramatically reduces the chance of infection of the child with HIV during birth. At this time South Africa was in the midst of a HIV epidemic and manufacturers had agreed to provide the drug freely to the state for five years.
90 *Minister of Health and Another v. New Clicks South Africa (Pty) Ltd and Others* (CCT59/04A) [2005] ZACC 25; 2006 (8) BCLR 872 (CC) (30 September 2005). The High Court's orders are referred to at items 85–87. Online. Available at www.saflii.org/za/cases/ZACC/2005/25.html (accessed 29 December 2018).
91 *Minister of Health and Others v. Treatment Action Campaign and Others* (No 2) (CCT8/02) [2002] ZACC 15; 2002 (5) SA 721; 2002 (10) BCLR 1033 (5 July 2002). Orders at §135. Online. Available at www.saflii.org/za/cases/ZACC/2002/15.html (accessed 29 December 2018).
92 *Mazibuko and Others v. City of Johannesburg and Others* (06/13865) [2008] ZAGPHC 491; [2008] 4 All SA 471 (W) (30 April 2008). Case No. 06/13865. Online. Available at www.saflii.org/za/cases/ZAGPHC/2008/491.html (accessed 29 December 2018).
93 Constitution of the Republic of South Africa, §27(1)(b) states that "everyone has the right to have access to sufficient food and water."
94 *Mazibuko and Others v. City of Johannesburg and Others*, §160.

95 *City of Johannesburg and Others v. Mazibuko and Others* (489/08) [2009] ZASCA 20; 2009 (3) SA 592 (SCA); 2009 (8) BCLR 791 (SCA); [2009] 3 All SA 202 (SCA) (25 March 2009). Online. Available at www.saflii.org/za/cases/ZASCA/2009/20.pdf (accessed 29 December 2018).

96 *Mazibuko and Others v. City of Johannesburg and Others* (CCT 39/09) [2009] ZACC 28; 2010 (3) BCLR 239 (CC); 2010 (4) SA 1 (CC) (8 October 2009). See §9 and §56. Online. Available at www.saflii.org/za/cases/ZACC/2009/28.pdf (accessed 29 December 2018).

97 The court had previously engaged the right to life to determine cases involving bail in the case of *Maneka Gandhi v. Union of India* AIR 1978 SC 597). Online. Available at www.sci.gov.in/jonew/judis/5154.pdf (accessed 29 December 2018). It had engaged the issue of treatment in custody in the case of *Mullin v. Union Territory of Delhi* AIR 1981 SC 746. Online. Available at www.sci.gov.in/jonew/judis/10150.pdf (accessed 29 December 2018).

98 Case of *Olga Tellis v. Bombay* AIR 1986 SC 180. Online. Available at www.sci.gov.in/jonew/judis/9246.pdf (accessed 29 December 2018).

99 Case of *Olga Tellis v. Bombay*, §2.2.

100 Case of *Shantistar Builders v. Narayan Khimalal Totame*, Civil Appeal No. 2598/1989 (1990) 1 SCC 520. Online. Available at www.sci.gov.in/jonew/judis/10314.pdf (accessed 29 December 2018).

101 Jessie Hohmann, "Mumbai: The Struggle for the Right to Housing," *Yale Human Rights and Development Law Journal*, 2013, vol. 13, 135.

102 Case of *Chameli Singh v. State of Uttar Pradesh* (1996) 2 SCC 549. See Hohmann, "Mumbai," 140.

103 Case of *Consumer Education and Research Centre v. Union of India* (1995) 3 SCC 42. Online. Available at www.sci.gov.in/jonew/judis/10927.pdf (accessed 29 December 2018).

104 Sheetal B. Shah, "Illuminating the Possible in the Developing World: Guaranteeing the Human Right to Health in India," *Vanderbilt Journal of Transnational Law*, 1999, vol. 32, 435.

105 Case of *Pt. Parmanand Katara v. Union of India*, AIR 1989 SC 2039. Online. Available at www.sci.gov.in/jonew/judis/7839.pdf (accessed 29 December 2018).

106 Sarvepelli Radhakrishnan, "Development of Human Rights in an Indian Context," *International Journal of Legal Information*, 2008, vol. 36, 303–15.

107 Case of *Paschim Banga Khet Mazdoor Samity v. State of West Bengal* 1996 3 SCJ 25. Online. Available at www.sci.gov.in/jonew/judis/15597.pdf (accessed 29 December 2018).

108 Jennifer Sellin, "Justiciability of the Right to Health – Access to Medicines – The South African and Indian Experience," *Erasmus Law Review*, 2009, vol. 2, no. 4, 445–62.

109 Case of *State of Punjab v. Ram Lubhaya Bagga* (1998) 4 SCC 117. Online. Available at www.sci.gov.in/jonew/judis/13394.pdf (accessed 29 December 2018).

110 Case of *Vincent Panikurlangara v. Union of India* (1987) 2 SCC 165. Online. Available at www.sci.gov.in/jonew/judis/8787.pdf (accessed 29 December 2018).

111 Case of *Laxmi Mandal v. Deen Dayal Harinagar Hospital & Ors* WP (C) 8853/2008. Online. Available at http://lobis.nic.in/ddir/dhc/SMD/judgement/04-06-2010/SMD04062010CW88532008.pdf (accessed 29 December 2018).

112 Sukti Dhital and Jayshree Satpute, "Claiming the Right to Safe Motherhood through Litigation: The Indian Story," in Garcia et al., *Social and Economic Rights in Theory and in Practice*, p. 159.

113 Twenty-five cases were lodged between 2010 and 2013. Dhital and Satpute, "Claiming the Right to Safe Motherhood."

114 Case of *Court on its own Motion v. Union of India* (WP 5913/2010). Online. Available at http://lobis.nic.in/ddir/dhc/DMA/judgement/12-01-2011/DMA12012011CW59132010.pdf (accessed 29 December 2018).

115 Case of *Priya Kale v. Govt. of NCT of Delhi & Ors* WP (C) 641/2013. Online. Available at http://delhihighcourt.nic.in/dhcqrydisp_O.asp?pn=21117&yr=2013 (accessed 2018).

116 "Follow Up Fact-Finding Report: Priya Kale v. GNCT of Delhi and Ors," 25 May 2016. Online. Available at http://reproductiverights.hrln.org/follow-up-fact-finding-report-priya-kale-vs-gnct-of-delhi-and-ors/ (accessed 29 December 2018).

117 Dhital and Satpute, "Claiming the Right to Safe Motherhood," p. 165. The order is online. Available at https://hrln.org/wp-content/uploads/2017/12/Priya-Kale-Order-01022013.pdf (accessed 29 December 2018).

118 *People's Union for Civil Liberties & Ors v. India* Writ No 196 of 2001. It has been overtaken by legislation (the National Food Security Act of 2013). See "Office Report," 31 January 2017. Online. Available at www.sci.gov.in/jonew/ropor/or/or/all/191780.pdf (accessed 29 December 2018).

119 Canada, "Charter of Rights and Freedoms," Part I of the "Constitution Act, 1982." Enacted as Schedule B to the Canada Act 1982 (UK), 1982, c. 11. Online. Available at https://laws-lois.justice.gc.ca/eng/const/page-15.html (accessed 29 December 2018). See Patrick Macklem, "Social Rights in Canada," in Daphne Barak-Erez and Eyal M. Gross (eds.) *Exploring Social Rights: Between Theory and Practice*, Oxford: Hart, 2007, pp. 213–42.

120 Canada, "Charter of Rights and Freedoms," §2 (fundamental freedoms), §3 to §5 (democratic rights), §6 (mobility rights), §7 to §14 (legal rights), §15 and §28 (equality rights), §16 to §22 (language rights), and §23 (minority language education rights).

121 Canada, "Charter of Rights and Freedoms," §7 ("everyone has the right to life, liberty and security of the person and the right not to be deprived thereof except in accordance with the principles of fundamental justice") and §15(1) ("every individual is equal before the law and has the right to equal protection and equal benefit of the law without discrimination and, in particular, without discrimination based on race, national or ethnic origin, colour, religion, sex, age or mental or physical disability").

122 Case of *Victoria City v. Adams* 2008 BCSC 1363. Online. Available at www.courts.gov.bc.ca/Jdb-txt/SC/08/13/2008BCSC1363.htm (accessed 29 December 2018).

123 The case of *Chaoulli v. Quebec (Attorney General)* [2005] 1 SCR 791 was relied upon in this regard. The Supreme Court struck down a provision that prohibited individuals from obtaining private health care. Evidence of long delays in accessing medical care was adduced and the court found that the provision engaged the right to life. While the court did not require the state to provide the care, it found that the state could not prevent the procurement of private treatment. See generally Christopher P. Manfredi and Antonia Maioni, "The Last Line of Defence for the Citizen: Litigating Private Health Insurance in *Chaoulli v. Quebec*," *Osgoode Hall Law Journal*, 2006, vol. 44, no. 2, 249–71; Thomas M. J. Bateman, "Legal Modesty and Political Boldness: The Supreme Court of Canada's Decision in *Chaoulli v. Quebec*," *Review of Constitutional Studies*, 2006, vol. 11, no. 2, 317–43; and Jamie Cameron, "From the MRV to *Chaoulli v. Canada*: The Road Not Taken and the Future of Section 7," *Supreme Court Law Review*, 2006, vol. 34, 105–68.

124 *Victoria City v. Adams* 2008 BCSC 1363, §39, where the Attorney General claimed that the deprivation must arise from state action, and, since the government did not cause the homelessness, the Charter could not be invoked.

125 Margot E. Young, "Rights, the Homeless and Social Change: Reflections on *Victoria City v. Adams* (BCSC)," *British Columbia Studies*, 2009, vol. 164, 103–13.

126 *Brown v. British Columbia (Minister for Health)* (1990) 6 DLR (4th) 444 BCSC.

127 *R. v. Morgentaler* [1988] 1 SCR 30. Online. Available at https://scc-csc.lexum.com/scc-csc/scc-csc/en/item/288/index.do (accessed 29 December 2018). The restriction required a woman to obtain the approval from a committee of an approved hospital. Failure to do so could result in criminal prosecution.

128 *Eldridge v. British Columbia* (1997)151 DLR (4th) 577 (SCC). Online. Available at https://scc-csc.lexum.com/scc-csc/scc-csc/en/item/1552/index.do (accessed 29 December 2018). See also Isabel Grant and Judith Mossof, "Hearing Claims of Inequality – Eldridge v. British Columbia," *Canadian Journal of Women and Law*, 1998, vol. 10, 229–43.

129 *PHS Community Services v. Canada* 2011 SCC 44. Online. Available at https://scc-csc.lexum.com/scc-csc/scc-csc/en/item/7960/index.do (accessed 29 December 2018).

130 For detailed background to the case, see Margot E. Young, "Context, Choice, and Rights: PHS Community Services v. Canada (Attorney General)," *University of British Columbia Law Review*, 2011, vol. 44, 221–54; Claire-Michelle Smyth and Siobhan Kelly, "Drug Consumption Rooms: Towards the Right to Health for Addicts," *Irish Law Times*, 2013, vol. 31, 197.

131 *PHS Community Services Ltd v. Canada (Attorney General)* [2008] BCSC 661. Online. Available at www.courts.gov.bc.ca/Jdb-txt/SC/08/06/2008BCSC0661err1.htm (accessed 29 December 2018).

132 These services included prenatal classes for pregnant women, who may not have received them otherwise due to their addictions.

133 2010 BCCA 15, 314 DLR (4th) 209. Online. Available at www.courts.gov.bc.ca/jdb-txt/CA/10/00/2010BCCA0015cor1.htm (accessed 29 December 2018).

134 Case of *Canada (Attorney General) v. PHS Community Services Society*, 2011 SCC 44 §93. Online. Available at https://scc-csc.lexum.com/scc-csc/scc-csc/en/item/7960/index.do (accessed 29 December 2018).

135 Case of *Gosselin v. Quebec*, [2002] SCC 42 §79. Online. Available at https://scc-csc.lexum.com/scc-csc/scc-csc/en/item/2027/index.do (accessed 29 December 2018).
136 Matthew Rottier Voell, "*PHS Community Services Society v. Canada (Attorney General)*: Positive Health Rights, Health Care Policy, and Section 7 of the Charter," *Windsor Review of Legal and Social Issues*, 2011, vol. 31, 41–56.
137 Case of *Tanudjaja v. Canada*, 2014 ONCA 852. Online. Available at www.ontariocourts.ca/decisions/2014/2014ONCA0852.htm (accessed 29 December 2018).
138 Case of *Tanudjaja v. Canada*, 2014 ONCA 852 §49.

9

ISLAM AND UN HUMAN RIGHTS TREATY RATIFICATION IN THE MIDDLE EAST

The impact of international law on diplomacy

Rachel A. George

When the Universal Declaration of Human Rights was first introduced at the United Nations (UN) in 1948, Lebanese politician and UN representative Charles Habib Malik proclaimed that the Declaration was a "potent ideological weapon" that "if wielded in complete goodwill, sincerity and truth, can prove most significant in the history of the spirit."[1] The hope was that the Declaration, in solidifying and enshrining common understandings of the human rights, would help secure their recognition and observance in every country, regardless of social and cultural differences.[2]

Most scholars today agree that this view was overly optimistic. International human rights agreements, though very numerous and also wide in scope, are often violated without consequence. By most measures, the impact of international human rights law on improving states' human rights records has been modest, at best. And, although international human rights declarations and treaties enjoy widespread support and purport to represent international consensus regarding the meanings of human rights, conceptualizations of the vision remain disputed and heterogeneous across countries and cultures.

Some of today's pessimism is misguided. International human rights law does have influence, although it is often subtle. To understand the power of international law, scholars would benefit from closer consideration of the impact of UN human rights treaty ratification in cases such as those in the Middle East where compliance has been minimal, but engagement with international human rights law has helped frame and influence the ways in which Middle Eastern actors communicate ideas about human rights.

This essay explores the impact of UN human rights treaties in the Middle East and North Africa (MENA) by examining diplomatic discourses relating to three core UN human rights treaties: the Convention on the Elimination of all forms of Discrimination Against Women (CEDAW), the Convention on the Rights of the Child (CRC) and the Convention Against Torture (CAT). All three conventions were widely ratified across MENA in the 1990s and 2000s.[3] First, the essay will establish the broad landscape in which Islam and human rights were discussed principally by government representatives, as well as other lawyers, activists, and diplomats in the MENA region over time. The essay will then go on to analyze the content and nature of the Reservations,

Understandings and Declarations (RUDs) concerning Islam that MENA states have submitted upon commitment to these human rights conventions. Next, the essay will analyze resulting diplomatic dialogues surrounding Islam and ratification taking place within international treaty committees as part of regular reporting procedures, and will consider the impact on broader dialogue between diplomats and MENA civil society groups. Finally, the essay offers conclusions regarding my observations of the convergence demonstrated by MENA actors' increasing use of UN human rights concepts as understood through an Islamic perspective.

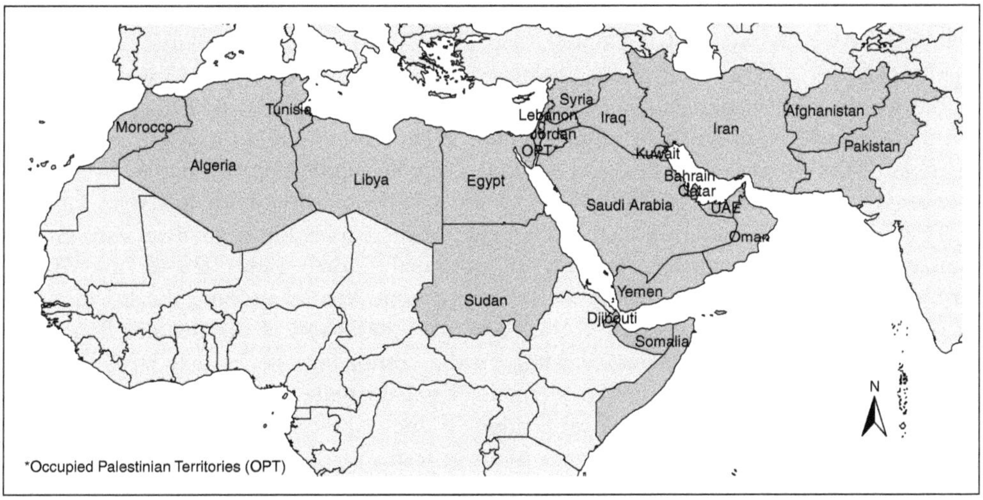

Figure 9.1 Map of the MENA region, including the countries discussed in this essay.

The essay shows that there is a great diversity in the ways in which MENA states communicate concerns about compatibility between Islam and international law during UN meetings. It also demonstrates that ratification of the three conventions has helped stimulate discussions that underscore the similarities and differences in understandings about Islam and human rights within the region. MENA states are engaging in balancing conservative Muslim principles with this modern language of human rights in different ways. The essay highlights such variation. Beyond this, it also contributes to a growing convergence in the vocabulary used by MENA actors around UN human rights concepts. I argue that a diverse and evolving diplomatic discourse about Islam and human rights in MENA has resulted from UN human rights treaty ratification. A deeper understanding of such discourses can provide a clearer picture of the limits and potential for human rights activism in the Middle East.

Theoretical puzzles

Because the international system lacks direct enforcement mechanisms, the status of these laws as "law" at all has been challenged.[4] There is little to no correlation between human rights treaty ratification and human rights compliance in practice.[5] This has led some leading scholars to claim that "the world's idealists have thrown too much law at problems of human rights" without offering effective solutions to the world's human rights problems.[6]

The MENA region is case in point. MENA states ratified most human rights treaties throughout the 1980s, 1990s, and 2000s, but there is little evidence this step has made a difference in improving human rights practices as a result of ratification. MENA states rate consistently poorly in various international human rights monitoring rankings (for example, despite widespread ratification of UN human rights treaties, the US-based non-governmental organization (NGO) Freedom House, which conducts research and provides annual reports on democracy, political freedom, and human rights, ranks the category of "Middle East and North Africa" in its 2016 global freedom rankings as 5 percent free.[7] And, in the Global Gender Gap index's most current rankings, the Middle East and North Africa region ranks consistently poorly, with only Israel listed as having a "gender gap" of 30 percent or below).[8] For this reason, the region is often ignored in existing scholarly work on international human rights law. Some write it off as a blanket example of the futility of the treaties, without providing any account for the diverse and evolving ways that MENA states have interacted with human rights treaties over time.

There is a need for international human rights law scholarship to analyze with greater subtlety the growing engagement with international human rights law in the Middle East. Here I demonstrate the value of a different approach, examining the discourse on Islam and human rights emerging in the 1990s and 2000s out of the region's diplomatic responses to human rights laws, regardless of the compliance issues that have followed. This essay focuses on one particular element of engagement: discussions among MENA and UN diplomats as a result of ratification of the core human rights treaties in the region over time. Scholars often discuss Islam in terms of so-called issues of "incompatibility" between Islam and international human rights laws.[9] While focusing on Islam, and, particularly, the ways in which it is discussed in diplomatic discourses related to UN human rights treaties is just one lens through which to consider MENA engagement with the diplomats and stakeholders participating in UN human rights committees, this focus offers insights into how arguments about human rights among MENA diplomats have developed as a result of engagement with UN human rights law.

Islam and human rights in MENA

Since the early expansion of the Islamic empire from the seventh century, law in the Middle East has been traditionally "anchored to religious institutions and personnel."[10] Law in the region was seen as derived from divine origin, based on the Quran and the sayings of the Prophet. In reality, however, Islamic law has been far from static, and instead highly dynamic and evolving. Far from being anchored in some unmoving divine authority, sacred law has been closely intertwined with the social and political context in which it was interpreted throughout history. Islamic law can be seen, as historian Noel Coulson writes, as "an evolving legal system."[11] Sharia was invoked broadly in early Islamic history by clerics (*'ulama*) and interpreted to regulate a wide range of affairs, from civil transactions, taxation, penal law, to most other areas of criminal and social and family law. Islamic legal scholar Sami Zubaida argues,

> There is a common view that the Shari'a is fixed and clearly discernible from its sacred sources … Shar'ia is a product of articulations of legal discourses and

> institutions to varying patterns of society and politics. The holy law has co-existed and interacted with statute laws issued by rulers, as well as customary conduct, sometimes extending its vocabulary and concepts to cover these existing practices.[12]

In addition to a lasting influence of Islam in legal systems across the Middle East, Western secular legal traditions have had also had a strong influence on modern Middle Eastern legal systems. Starting with the Ottoman system of the nineteenth century the modern state (the extensive modernizing reform of during the *tanzimat* era, 1839–76), legal systems across the Middle East were highly influenced by European law, among other influences.[13] The processes of modernization and reform in the Ottoman lands led to upheavals in legal systems, including widespread changes of legal and institutional systems across the region in which laws moved away from traditional and divine understandings to include those informed by a secular state.[14] Even when the *Shari'a* was the formal source of legislation, as in the Ottoman civil law codification of the 1860s known as the *Majalla,* these elements largely reflected European understandings of law.[15]

Islamic legal historian Noel Coulson observes that there is a constant push between the basic principles in contemporary Islamic law of practical necessity and religious principles:

> During the first stage of legal modernism these two influences had produced a clear-cut dichotomy in the law. Western law was directly adopted in the field of crime and civil transactions generally, while traditional Shari'a doctrine continued to govern the sphere of personal status.[16]

Indeed by 1900, religious Sharia law in the Middle East had reduced in scope to mainly concern finite areas of personal status such as child custody, marriage, and inheritance, and dominated less in areas of criminal law.[17] Colonial Europe "promoted the idea that personal law was sacred to Muslims and that, out of sensitivity and respect, colonial powers left it alone."[18] As family law emerged as a foothold for Islamic identity, it represented a "last fortress of the Shari'a to survive the ravages of modernization."[19] However, conservative interpretations of Islamic Law remained on the books in some Middle East states in areas of criminal law for example in Saudi Arabia, Yemen, and the United Arab Emirates (UAE) where, for example, harsh punishments are on the books for apostasy and blasphemy. These punishments, however, were more commonly imparted by political rulers than by Sharia courts themselves. This was a political rather than purely religious issue, as "Shari'a judges historically tended to be sparing in the application of corporal punishments of amputations and executions. These were undertaken more freely by the rulers."[20]

Lasting elements of the Islamic legal system across the Middle East today reflect a special – at times politicized – meaning attributed by states to religious law in the region, particularly in the areas of morality and justice. Law in the Middle East is not just "law" in the modern sense, but "a total discourse of religion, morality and justice. As such it is always exploited as a medium of contest."[21] The legal relevance of Sharia today is strongest and most pervasive in the legal systems of Iran and the Arab Gulf states. In Saudi Arabia, in particular, Islamic law has remained in a much more traditional and conservative form than in other states of the Middle East. This is what Islamic legal scholar Zubaida calls the "Saudi Exception,"[22] saying,

> The Kingdom of Saudi Arabia is the one major country in the region which has not followed the general pattern of the codification and etatization of law. Saudi courts and *qadis* (judges) rule in accordance with Hanbali *fiqh* (jurisprudence), which is not codified as state law but formally left largely to the discretion and *ijtihad* (reason) of the qadi … the ulama remain the main legislators.[23]

In Saudi Arabia, strong adherence to conservative principles in Islamic law have also resulted from the monarchy's quest for legitimacy. Zubaida argues that the political importance of Sharia is strong in bolstering the Saudi monarchy, saying,

> Religious legitimacy and its agents have been crucial for the defence of the [Saudi] dynasty against modernist political opposition of nationalism, constitutionalism and democracy, as well as against the Islamic opposition from various quarters, mainly centered on the dependence of the dynasty on US power, as well as the perceived hypocrisy and corruption of the royal house and its circles.[24]

Given this context, it is important to view Islam as a moving and dynamic topic influencing law, society, and power in the Middle East. Of course, the region is not monolithic, and these dynamics play out in varied ways in each country. The ways in which Islam is discussed at the UN, however, reflect certain patterns and commonalities across the region, as well as a heterogeneity in understandings concerning Islam. The era of the proliferation of UN human rights treaties has helped stimulate a unique and evolving discourse on Islam and human rights among MENA state representatives at meetings with UN human rights committees. The nature and content of these discourses among MENA and UN diplomats over time since ratification is the focus of the following section.

Islam and MENA RUDs to human rights treaties

As UN human rights treaties proliferated on the international stage, most MENA countries have today ratified most UN human rights conventions. Although there are significant exceptions,[25] there is an assumption that UN human rights law, in general, represents certain "universal" understandings of human rights – and the large number of countries ratifying these conventions serves as key evidence for this.[26] Widespread ratification of the women's (CEDAW), children's (CRC), and torture (CAT) conventions in the Middle East reflect this idea that UN human rights law, despite important exceptions, is embraced across the world.

Still, MENA commitments to these UN human rights treaties have often been met with great controversy from global human rights monitors and other UN states. A particular area of controversy has been MENA states' widespread use of "reservations," or statements of exception, issued upon a government's ratification. Under the 1969 Vienna Convention on the Law of Treaties (VCLT), states can enter statements upon treaty ratification clarifying commitment in "Reservations, Understandings and

Declarations" (RUDS) so long as the statement does not "defeat the object and purpose of a treaty prior to its entry into force."[27] The practice is common – and, although not all states submit RUDs, those that do submit a variety of types of statements, from sweeping and broad clarifying statements to detailed points about application of specific issues, including countries praised for relatively strong human rights practices. MENA states most commonly enter reservations upon commitment to UN human rights treaties, and these concerns oftentimes (but, importantly, not all the time) refer to possible potential incompatibility with Islam.[28] These RUDs referring to Islamic exceptions are accepted by the UN, but have often been met with criticism from other UN states that claim these reservations lack specificity and are not in line with the general spirit of each convention. While the RUDs are clearly informed by various societal and political factors, perhaps shaped by Islamic elites and intellectuals contributing to interpretations of Islam in each country context, the RUD is submitted by the state as a statement about Islam without citing Islamic texts or Islamic thinkers that might inform these interpretations in each country context. The following section discusses the ratification process, exploring the ways in which Islam has been referenced in RUDs to the CAT, CRC, and CEDAW by various MENA governments. Following this section, the next explores the ensuing negotiations between MENA government diplomats at the relevant human rights committees, as part of the official international human rights review process, which have taken place primarily over the 1990s, 2000s, and 2010s in the decades since ratification.

The 1984 UN Convention Against Torture (CAT), initially introduced as a response to the widespread use of torture during the Cold War "dirty wars" in Latin America, has been widely ratified across MENA, with many states ratifying after some delay in the 1990s and 2000s. Notably, Islam was not a common concern voiced by MENA states upon ratification of the torture convention. Only one MENA state, Qatar, mentioned Islam in RUDs to the CAT in 2000 – reserving commitment to the CAT with the exception of "Any interpretation of the provisions of the Convention that is incompatible with the precepts of Islamic law and the Islamic religion." Qatar did not at this time clarify where Islamic law and religion might be incompatible with UN law on torture. And, in 2011, Qatar withdrew the general reservation about Islam entirely. During this period Qatar instituted a number of so-called "liberal" political reforms, also doing the same with its reservations to the CRC. Qatar's removal of its CAT reservation about Islam must be explained as part of a broader process in which Qatar has pursued a more "modern" image promoting its reputation as a "good global citizen" on the international stage.[29] Other MENA states, including those with conservative interpretations of Sharia law in criminal laws, concerns in RUDs that were entirely unrelated to Islam, and most commonly in relation to the competence of the CAT committee.

By contrast, Islam was raised as a central concern by many MENA states in RUDs submitted to the children's (CRC) convention. The CRC is the most widely ratified convention in MENA (it has been universally accepted there) and is the most popular UN human rights treaty globally. Most MENA states mentioned possible conflict with Islam in RUDs to the CRC, some making sweeping statements about any conflict possible between the treaty and Islam, others focusing on specific issues – such as Islam's position on adoption or the religion of children raised in an Islamic household.

While Afghanistan entered a sweeping reservation in 1994 to the CRC to "all provisions of the convention that are incompatible with the laws of Islamic Shari'a and the local legislation in effect," other MENA states offered more specific claims about

Table 9.1 MENA RUDs to CAT (* indicates withdrawn)

Mention of Islam	1	Qatar*
Article 20 (competence of CAT committee investigations)	3	Saudi Arabia, Syria, Kuwait
Article 30 (competence of the ICJ for referral)	5	Afghanistan, Bahrain, Morocco, Saudi Arabia, UAE
Other reservation	2	Turkey, Tunisia*
No reservation	5	Egypt, Iraq, Jordan, Yemen, Lebanon

Source: Author's observation from the state party reservations published in the UN Treaty database for the CAT, "Chapter IV: Human Rights, 9. Convention Against Torture and Other Cruel, Inhuman or Degrading Treatment or Punishment." Online. Available at https://treaties.un.org/pages/viewdetails.aspx?src=treaty&mtdsg_no=iv-9&chapter=4&lang=en (accessed 10 November 2018).

Table 9.2 MENA RUDs to CRC (* indicates withdrawn)

Mention of Islam	11	Afghanistan, Algeria, Iran, Iraq, Jordan, Kuwait, Morocco, UAE, Saudi Arabia, Qatar*
Article 14 (Freedom of conscience and religion)	7	Algeria, Iraq, Jordan, Morocco, Oman, UAE, Qatar*
Article 21 (Adoption)	3	Jordan, Kuwait, UAE
No reservation	3	Egypt, Bahrain, Libya

Source: Author's observation from the state party reservations published in the UN Treaty database for the CRC, "Chapter IV: Human Rights, 11. Convention on the Rights of the Child." Online. Available at https://treaties.un.org/pages/ViewDetails.aspx?src=IND&mtdsg_no=IV-11&chapter=4&lang=en (accessed 10 November 2018).

potential conflict with Islam. For example, Jordan in 1991 reserved specifically about Articles 14, 20, and 21 concerning adoption, claiming that these violated Islam, saying it took issue with clauses "which grant the child the right to freedom of choice of religion and concern the question of adoption, since they are at variance with the precepts of the tolerant Islamic Shariah." Notably, although legal adoption was an uncommon practice in most MENA states, only three (Jordan, Kuwait, and the UAE) mentioned Islam as in conflict with CRC principles about adoption in their RUDs. Kuwait in 1990 expressed upon signature "[Kuwait expresses] reservations on all provisions of the Convention that are incompatible with the laws of Islamic Shari'a and the local statutes in effect." But specified, upon ratification in 1991, "Article 21: the State of Kuwait, as it adheres to the provisions of the Islamic Shariah as the main source of legislation, strictly bans abandoning the Islamic religion and does not therefore approve adoption." Similarly, the UAE reserved upon ratification in 1997, noting that

> Since, given its commitment to the principles of Islamic law, the United Arab Emirates does not permit the system of adoption, it has reservations with respect to this article and does not deem it necessary to be bound by its provisions.

Here, adoption stood as the only clear reflections of shared understandings of Islam that are viewed in the region as standing in conflict with the UN document.

Other states offered similarly specific reservations but discussed entirely different topics, in several cases concerned instead with the concept of freedom of religion. For example, Oman in 1996 stated as its reservation "The Sultanate of Oman is not committed to the contents of Article (14) of the Convention, which gives the child the right to freedom of religion until he reaches the age of maturity." That same year in 1996 Saudi Arabia entered a sweeping, non-specific reservation to the CRC similar to Afghanistan's, saying, simply, "The Government of Saudi Arabia enters reservations with respect to all such articles as are in conflict with the provisions of Islamic Law." These illustrations of MENA RUDs demonstrate furthermore important heterogeneity among statements about Islam entered to the CRC showing that Islam is by no means monolithic but shaped by political dimensions as to which states interpret and express their concerns about Islam in different ways.

Gender has arisen as a key fault line in the politics between MENA states and the UN, as elsewhere in the world. MENA RUDs most frequently raise Islam in RUDs to the women's convention (CEDAW). Notably, Iran has not ratified the CEDAW, with authorities citing incompatibility with national laws including Sharia law.[30]

More often, as was the case in the CRC debates, MENA states mentioned Islam in RUDs to the CEDAW but specified these concerns – many entered RUDs concerning Islamic positions on marriage, nationality, and freedom of movement, for example. Egypt was one of the first in the region to ratify CEDAW in 1981, and upon ratification entered a lengthy statement describing specifically how a CEDAW clause concerning equality in marriage violates interpretations of Sharia law, saying,

> Reservation to the text of Article 16 concerning the equality of men and women in all matters relating to marriage and family relations during the marriage and upon its dissolution, without prejudice to the Islamic *Sharia's* provisions whereby women are accorded rights equivalent to those of their spouses so as to ensure a just balance between them. This is out of respect for the sacrosanct nature of the firm religious beliefs which govern marital relations in Egypt.[31]

Kuwait ratified the treaty a few years later in 1984 and also entered a specific reservation about Islam, stating,

> The Government of the State of Kuwait declares that it does not consider itself bound by the provision contained in Article 16(f) [concerning equal rights in marriage] inasmuch as it conflicts with the provisions of the *Islamic Shariah*, Islam being the official religion of the State.

Tunisia, ratifying a year later, entered a reservation that did not specifically mention Islam by name. Its declaration, however, may be read to suggest a similar concern, as it stated, "The Tunisian Government declares that it shall not take any organizational or legislative decision in conformity with the requirements of this Convention where such a decision would conflict with the provisions of Chapter I of the Tunisian Constitution." (Chapter 1 of the Tunisian Constitution at the time stated, "Tunisia is a free, independent and sovereign state. Its religion is Islam, its language is Arabic and its type of government is the Republic.")

Arab Gulf states, Kuwait (ratified in 1992), Bahrain (ratified in 2002), and UAE (ratified in 2004) all entered more specific reservations to CEDAW than Saudi Arabia with mentioning Article 16 (concerning equal rights in marriage), but, in each case, the specific wording differed. Kuwait's reservation referenced Article 16 (f) and stated:

> The Government of the State of Kuwait declares that it does not consider itself bound by the provision contained in Article 16(f) inasmuch as it conflicts with the provisions of the *Islamic Shariah,* Islam being the official religion of the State.

Bahrain reserved regarding Sharia both to Article 2 and 16, promising to comply only "within the bounds" of Sharia, saying,

> The Kingdom of Bahrain makes reservations with respect to the following provisions of the Convention: Article 2, in order to ensure its implementation within the bounds of the provisions of the Islamic Shariah … Article 16, in so far as it is incompatible with the provisions of the Islamic Shariah.

The UAE reserved more generally to Article 16 concerning marriage, saying, "Article 16 The United Arab Emirates will abide by the provisions of this article insofar as they are not in conflict with the principles of the Shariah." Saudi Arabia, a state that was relatively late to accede to the women's convention, reserved in 2000 "in case of contradiction between any term of the Convention and the norms of Islamic law, the Kingdom is not under obligation to observe the contradictory terms of the Convention." This statement clearly suggests that the regime sees Islam as potentially incompatible with UN law, without going further to specify any areas that might be of particular concern.

When considered together, MENA RUDs to the CAT, CRC, and CEDAW offer, on the one hand, evidence that Islam is a concern often voiced in the region in relation to human rights treaties – most commonly to the CRC and the CEDAW and rarely (although in one case, later removed) in the case of the CAT. Notably, the states of the

Table 9.3 MENA RUDs to CEDAW (* indicates withdrawn)

Mention of Islam	11	Bahrain, Egypt, Iraq, Kuwait, Libya, Morocco, Oman, Saudi Arabia, Syria, Qatar, UAE
Article 9 (concerning equal right to nationality)	7	Bahrain, Jordan, Kuwait, Lebanon, Oman, Qatar, Saudi Arabia
Article 15 (concerning freedom of movement/residence)	7	Algeria, Bahrain, Morocco, Oman, Syria, UAE, Turkey*
Article 16 (concerning equal rights in marriage)	12	Algeria, Bahrain, Egypt, Iraq, Jordan, Kuwait, Lebanon, Oman, Qatar, Syria, UAE, Turkey*
Article 29 (concerning referral to the ICJ)	9	Algeria, Bahrain, Egypt, Iraq, Kuwait, Morocco, Oman, Qatar, Turkey*

Source: Author's observation from the state party reservations published in the UN Treaty database for the CEDAW, "Chapter IV: Human Rights, 8. Convention on the Elimination of All Forms of Discrimination Against Women." Online. Available at https://treaties.un.org/Pages/ViewDetails.aspx?src=IND&mtdsg_no=IV-8&chapter=4&lang=en (accessed 10 November 2018).

Arab Gulf with conservative interpretations of Sharia law (these include Qatar, UAE, Bahrain, Kuwait, Oman, and Saudi Arabia) in particular most often cite Islam in their RUDs. However, the debates in the region show considerable diversity in the ways in which Islam is raised upon initial ratification. Where Saudi Arabia offers vague, sweeping statements about Islam upon ratification, the UAE and Kuwait more often enter specific statements detailing with more practical detail concerning potential incompatibility, and these points of detail are not identical among these Arab Gulf states that have ratified the same convention.

There is a need to better understand the motivations behind these RUDs as they vary between MENA regimes. The particular substance of the RUDs submitted is perhaps the result of the "vagaries of domestic politics" (as Goldsmith and Posner have suggested) – however, they indicate important trends, which are explored in the section that follows on resulting UN–MENA state dialogues.[32] In interviews with UN human rights committees and human rights activists in the Arab Gulf, respondents have suggested that the regimes craft their RUDs not only for the UN and international audiences, but also for a domestic audience to signify that they are "serious" about Islam and eager to push back against the UN. These motivations behind certain regimes' arguments made in RUDs, as well as behind lifting the reservations, are key areas for future research.

MENA diplomatic dialogues with UN human rights treaty committees

In the wake of RUDs, MENA state representatives, who are a set of nominated government officials, are obliged to participate in regular reporting dialogues with the international convention committees, established UN bodies with official oversight and regular review procedures over state parties to treaties. These dialogues have helped capture a vast catalogue of arguments about Islam and human rights, which can be analyzed in the records of these diplomatic dialogues taking place across the years since ratification. MENA states, like all states, are required to submit regular reports to the UN committee and participate in summary meetings. The representatives participating in these meetings change year to year, and are often professional civil servants who represent their governments in UN human rights meetings. As was the case with initial RUDs, these statements are publicly recorded, and are diverse in their nature and content although they, too, reflect certain patterns allowing readers of these dialogue reports to glean an understanding of the nature of debates on human rights in the region.

Islam, MENA, and the CAT committee proceedings

Even though Islam was not commonly referenced in MENA RUDs to the torture (CAT) convention, resulting dialogues between the UN CAT committee and participating MENA state party representatives brought the topic to the fore in relation to Islamic religious *hadd* punishments (offenses said to violate divine authority and prescribed specific punishments in the Quran). For example, although Saudi Arabia did not mention Islam in its RUDs submitted to the CAT, discussions between Saudi diplomats and the CAT committee after ratification quickly turned to the topic of Islamic *hadd* punishments, the Saudi regime claiming that such practices were not incompatible with the convention and, importantly, permitted under Islam. For example, the committee pressed Saudi Arabia about certain punishments including flogging and amputation in a 2002 meeting following Saudi Arabia's ratification of the CAT. Saudi Arabia quickly defended these practices not necessarily as constituting "torture" but crucially as sanctioned under Islam, saying,

> [Mr. Al-Hogail] said that Saudi Arabia was an Islamic State that applied the dictates of the Holy Koran. The Koran set out specific sanctions such as amputation, flogging (whipping) and stoning for certain crimes. Those sanctions could neither be abrogated, nor amended since they emanated from God ... The Saudi Arabian Code of Criminal Procedure prohibited the infliction of any punishment other than that prescribed by the Shariah or the law.

Here Saudi interaction with the CAT provided a particular platform for the Saudi regime to make public statements about Saudi interpretations of Islam and its centrality in guiding certain areas of criminal punishment in the Kingdom. In response to tense interactions between Saudi delegates and CAT in 2001 and 2002, Saudi Arabia's Grand Mufti Abdu'l Aziz al-Sheikh made a statement criticizing the UN committee in the newspaper *Daily Okaz*, saying UN claims that Saudi Arabia was in violation of the international accord were based on "lies, jealousy, and ignorance of Islamic Law."[33]

However, after this initial Saudi affirmation of the "right" to flog under Islamic Law and the failure of the CAT committee to express sensitivity to such religious practices, there was a measurable change over a decade later in 2015 CAT–Saudi Arabia meetings. Saudi Arabian diplomats stepped back from defending flogging and, instead, said such practices were not commonly "condoned" by the government. In a 2015 CAT meeting, the Saudi Arabian representative responded to an inquiry about the flogging of activists and bloggers including the 2013 flogging of prominent Saudi human rights blogger Raif Badawi:

> Mr. Al-Shahrani (Saudi Arabia) said that the report referred to by Ms. Belmir was incorrect. The sentence had not yet been carried out. Committee members would do well to rely on credible sources of information rather than on what appeared to be little other than baseless slander ... International instruments to which Saudi Arabia was a party had the force of law in the country. The provisions of those instruments could therefore be invoked in domestic proceedings. As a rule, Saudi law did not condone flogging.[34]

The final sentence in Mr. Al-Shahrani's statement that "Saudi law did not condone flogging" is a noticeable step-change occurring over the decade from previous statements from Saudi representatives defending flogging as allowable (and indeed, sometimes even necessary) under Islam. This change over time is indicative of a degree of "norm diffusion" indicating some change over time stimulated, among other factors, by these kinds of dialogues.

Like Saudi Arabia's representations, the Qatari delegation also at first defended practices such as stoning and amputation under religious claims. They further justified the use of such tactics as by claiming that these practices were few in number. After ratifying the CAT in 2000, Qatar's initial report assured the committee of legal protections against torture in the

Kingdom under Sharia law, writing, "The Islamic sharia totally prohibits acts of torture and other forms of ill-treatment, since such acts are an affront to human dignity, which the religion enjoins us to respect and protect."[35] Qatari delegates responded to further concern voiced by the CAT committee by claiming such practices were being reformed, and also that the use of certain Sharia laws for punishment of Muslims' crimes were defensible under international legal standards because they were rarely practiced:

> A bill had been drawn up to abolish the penalties of flogging and stoning. Article 1 of the Penal Code stipulated that Islamic sharia applied to the crimes of theft, banditry, adultery, apostasy and alcohol consumption, when the perpetrators or victims were Muslims. Under the same article, stoning and amputation concerned only a very small number of offences and were hardly ever put into practice.[36]

A similar process is visible in Kuwait, with growing convergence in the vocabulary and concepts used with UN human rights concepts invoked to address Islam and punishment as CAT meetings progress. After ratifying the CAT in 1994, Kuwaiti representatives defended the right to maintain laws that allow for capital punishment under Islam; however, in these defenses the practices were framed in their first CAT review meeting in 2011 as necessarily *legal* under Kuwait's commitment to Islam, but extreme and rare, saying,

> Mr. Razzooqi (Kuwait), It was difficult to abolish capital punishment because it formed part of the Islamic Sharia. However, the conditions to be met for its imposition were so exacting that it was scarcely ever imposed. Nobody had been executed for more than four or five years. He had never heard of any case in which an accused had been sentenced to amputation of his or her hands or feet. Such sentences did not exist in Kuwait.[37]

Kuwaiti delegates in CAT meetings also responded to criticisms of the committee members by invoking the concept of judicial independence in an effort to appear modern and in conformity with other UN states. Replying to a list of issues raised by the CAT committee in 2015 about unfair trials, Kuwaiti delegates responded by defending Kuwaiti law with reference to these modern concepts, saying,

> Within the context of the principle of the separation of powers, the constitutional provision governing the relationship between the country's Amir and the judicial power is worded differently from that governing his relationship with the executive and legislative powers. Hence, under Articles 51 and 52 of the Constitution, the legislative and executive powers are vested in the Amir, the Council of Ministers, ministers and the National Assembly (Parliament) whereas, under Article 53, the judicial power is vested in the courts, which exercise it in the name of the Amir within the limits prescribed in the Constitution. The work of judges is periodically appraised in order to ensure the proper administration of justice and completion of cases. Such appraisals are carried out by the Justice Inspectorate, which comprises qualified and experienced judges.[38]

Here, the practices of Islamic punishments are still defended as a religious duty, but the justifications from Kuwait's representatives shifted as the meetings progressed in 2015 to also include justification beyond pure religious claims, invoking concepts of judicial independence and judicial fairness.

Overall MENA interaction with the CAT committee evidences an evolving dialogue about Islam and punishment. Even where Islam was not a focus of initial RUDs, Islam has become prominent in ongoing engagement with the UN. In this way, ratification has captured the ways in which MENA countries have justified certain practices over time, with a continual desire to portray Islam as against "torture" and generally in-line with UN standards by complying with a range of UN concepts about rights and fairness in justice.

Islam, MENA, and the CEDAW committee proceedings

Mentions of Islam were more commonplace in MENA RUDs to the women's CEDAW convention, as noted earlier. Islam also subsequently was central in CEDAW committee dialogues with MENA states, but went far beyond the focus on certain areas contained in the RUDs (of marriage and nationality, for example) to discussions of a range of topics from the weight of women's legal testimony to civil and political rights of women. Even in cases where MENA states entered similar RUDs, subsequent committee dialogues about Islam and women's rights varied widely between MENA states.

For example, where statements from Saudi delegations focused heavily during CEDAW committee proceedings on Islamic exceptions to compatibility with international standards based on Sharia law, statements from Tunisian and Jordanian delegations focused heavily on Islam's harmonious place with international women's rights standards. When pressed by CEDAW committee members on Islamic incompatibility with Tunisia's commitment to the CEDAW, delegates suggested that the two were indeed fully compatible, reflecting that such dialogues were possibly helping stimulate, or, at a minimum reflecting, a new approach to incorporating "women's rights" into a distinctly Tunisian context. The delegates stated,

> Islam is unfairly accused of thwarting progress, but is in fact the quintessential religion of progress … In Tunisia's new era, the main thrust of its modernist philosophy lies in its determination to bring women's status into harmony with a state of law, of democratic freedoms and human rights.[39]

Not only did dialogue focus on compatibility between Islam and international human rights, it also, by extension, further bolstered the claim that UN conceptions of women's rights (and other concepts like "modernity" and "progress") were concepts Tunisia itself was spearheading. Engagement with the treaties, whether prompting, or reflecting, this sense of shared purpose, was, at the minimum, acknowledging compatibility. Cementing this sense of "change" in a "new era" of human rights thinking and leadership in defense of "women's rights," Tunisia made the decision in 2014 to withdraw its RUDs on Islamic concerns about women's role in marriage, after elections in that year in Tunisia brought a plurality in parliament won by Nidaa Tounnes, a wide-ranging secular political party.

Jordan's interactions with the CEDAW committee similarly reflect a desire to portray Islam as in accordance with international women's rights standards. In a 2001 initial meeting with the CEDAW committee, Jordan submitted assurances not only that Jordanian law generally upheld international standards on women's rights about the equality of men and women under the law, but also assured that the country was engaging in reform efforts, saying,

> In addition to a number of amendments to other laws concerning pension rights for women, nationality, health insurance and a wife's separate financial identity, the Government was currently studying a new draft Civil Status Code that underscored the rights Islam granted to women.[40]

In reply to criticisms from the CEDAW committee regarding lack of equality in marriage law, as Jordanian law for example gives men but not women an absolute right to divorce at will, Jordanian representatives highlighted the fact that women enjoy "equality" in the law, and can specify conditions in marriage contracts (a right not commonly used but progressive in the sense that it can favor a woman who wishes to ensure her financial and personal well-being before entering marriage with certain legal protections, and a process that is not available in all other Muslim majority countries).[41]

Jordanian representatives in 2001 told the CEDAW committee,

> Jordanian women enjoyed full equality with men under the law in all civil matters, including contracts, property management and commercial transactions; any impediments were attributable to social mores. In the area of family life, Jordan subscribed to the principles of the Islamic Shariah. Although women had the right to specify their own conditions in marriage contracts, few did so. Non-governmental organizations had launched legal literacy campaigns to educate women about their entitlements.[42]

The language and concepts used by Jordanian diplomats in these statements, while not addressing an intention necessarily to remove gender discriminatory laws around divorce, nonetheless reflect the overall effort to describe Islam as favoring gender "equality" and holding a degree of flexibility and adaptability in favor of women's rights. The effort is to advertise Jordanian law as in support of the protection of women under the law, which however leaves open to further criticism the question why, if the government favored the principle of equality so strongly, it would not amend unequal rights between males and females in divorce.

An important feature of UN human rights treaty ratification includes "shadow reporting" where local individuals and organizations are welcomed to submit reports to the UN human rights committees. A group of anonymous Saudi women submitted a shadow report to the CEDAW committee in 2007 contesting the government's report to the committee, saying,

> The reservations of SA on the CEDAW are mainly about "all what controvert Islamic law," i.e. that SA will follow just what conforms to Islamic laws. This concept is very obscure and inaccurate, which was, thankfully, commented on by the CEDAW committee to the government. It is important to note that Islam

> incorporates many schools of thought that adopt different stands according to their interpretation of the sacred text in regard to women and other social issues.[43]

Here Saudi Arabia's ratification of CEDAW has prompted local voices to contribute to intra-cultural dialogues at the UN women's rights committee, even if anonymously, resulting in further contestation of the topic of Islam and women's rights communicated and catalogued at the UN over time.

CEDAW ratification has helped stimulate and frame diplomatic dialogue between MENA states and UN committee members concerning conceptions of gender in Islam. Resulting dialogues helped frame issues concerning marriage and equality. In this way ratification has provoked a number of statements from government representatives at the UN, however cosmetic, concerning a commitment to gender equality in law in each country. And "shadow reports" continue to push the matter further.

Islam, MENA, and the CRC committee proceedings

MENA interactions with the CRC committee also capture an important and evolving dialogue about Islam and human rights. In some meetings, the topic of Islam related to children's rights was not discussed. For example, at Oman's meeting with the CRC committee in November 2006, the topic of Islam or Sharia law was not mentioned at all, despite Oman not advancing policies in line with the CRC's freedom of religion for children clause. In the case of the UAE, although the similar incompatibility of Emirati law with the CRC principle of freedom of religion was not raised at all in the UAE's RUDs to the CRC, the topic of the freedom of children's religion and belief was central in meetings with the UAE, in a November 2006 meeting that same month, where the UAE expressly claimed that the CRC principles of children's rights in this area conflict with Sharia law, saying,

> The State expressed a reservation to Article 14 of the Convention concerning freedom of thought and religion, because the article conflicts with the principles of the Islamic sharia. Freedom to profess a religion and to worship is available to all. No child in the United Arab Emirates is subject to any discrimination because of the child's religion or creed.[44]

In the same report, UAE officials defended reservations concerning adoption, claiming that for Islamic reasons of maintaining names solely based on blood-line, adoption could not take place in the Kingdom. However, this stance was later clarified in the document alongside more progressive ideas about the rights of the children with "unknown parentage" to be protected and assisted by the State.

> The State expressed a reservation to Article 21 on the right to adopt a child. Islam, which is the official religion and main source of legislation of the United Arab Emirates, does not permit the adoption method. However, this does not deny the rights of children of unknown lineage or parentage. The State provides for an appropriate role for the care and upbringing of such children and acts to provide all their needs. It has also established rules for

> alternative families. Children of unknown parentage obtain social assistance under the Social Security Act.[45]

The UAE's statements here to the CRC reflect a common dual character of UN human rights committee dialogue with MENA states, where oftentimes Islam is raised in a defensive way pushing back against the UN's imposition of values upon local interpretations of religious law and custom, all the while expressing that Islam is fully compatible with UN ideals of "freedom," "rights," and "non-discrimination."

Saudi Arabia's dialogues with the CRC committee also focused substantially on Islam's compatibility with CRC provisions. Saudi Arabia's 2014 report specifically attributes special protection for children to the country's system of Islamic law, claiming that Islamic legal principles actively contribute to "modern" human rights ideas such as the protection and encouragement of child development, saying, "The Kingdom of Saudi Arabia has derived its regulations concerning child welfare from these divinely revealed teachings of Islam which are in harmony with, and even surpass, the provisions of the Convention."[46] Moroccan dialogues with the CAT committee illustrate a similar effort to demonstrate in UN meetings Islam's special role in protecting the rights of children. In initial 1996 meetings, the Moroccan representative claimed this special protection dates back 1,400 years in its history as an Islamic country:

> Mr. Moslih (Morocco) said that children's rights had been protected in Morocco well before the adoption of the Convention in 1989. Morocco had been an Islamic country for the past 1,400 years and, during that time, a wide range of children's rights had been recognized and protected under the Koran, Shariya law and various subsequent writings on those and other texts. He himself was engaged in preparing a detailed review of the various texts covering the rights of the child under Moroccan law, which would be made available to the Committee in due course.[47]

Beyond these efforts to claim compatibility (if not superiority) of Islamic law in protecting children under CRC definitions of children's rights, the key area of contestation in many MENA–CRC dialogues concerned the rights of freedom of religion. Like a number of MENA countries, Moroccan representatives claimed that Muslim apostasy laws did not violate the CRC, saying,

> In response to Mr. Hammarberg's question on Article 14 of the convention, he said that the Moroccan Constitution stipulated that the religion of the State was Islam, but guaranteed freedom of religion to all citizens without reserve. Both Christians and Jews were free to practise their religion in their own places of worship throughout the country and did in fact do so.[48]

And, seven years later in 2003 Morocco's meetings with the CRC committee, another Moroccan representative reiterated this same stance, suggesting that Moroccan children who left Islam were not guaranteed a right to freedom of religion. However, the same statements seemed to contradict this point when they appealed to the principle of "freedom of expression," suggesting that the government might be further pressed to explain this inconsistency in the rights of Muslim children.

> Mr. Mediani (Morocco) said that Morocco's reservation to Article 14 of the Convention did not affect the right of followers of other religions to freedom of thought, conscience and religion, a right that was guaranteed by the Constitution, even though the official religion of Morocco was Islam. A number of measures had been taken to enhance the right to freedom of expression. For example, a new law had been adopted to facilitate the work of journalists. Another law had been adopted to allow the establishment of associations serving a public interest.[49]

These excerpts demonstrate a growing incorporation of human rights language contained in the CRC by MENA states articulating an Islamic perspective. Although there remain areas of dispute, for example, related to freedom of religion and the practice of adoption, the language of rights invoked by MENA states and UN representatives is becoming increasingly similar.

Conclusions: Islam and UN human rights treaty ratification in MENA – progress and limitations

While Islam is an important topic and indeed often central to MENA interactions with many UN human rights conventions and their relevant committees, it is by no means a clear area of so-called "conflict" related to engagement with these UN instruments that can be broadly understood and accounted for in the same way regionally. Ratification and ensuing negotiations with international convention committees alternate between universalism and relativism. Even in such cases as the CEDAW where concerns about compatibility with Islam have been central to MENA engagement with the women's convention, the ways in which these concerns have been communicated over time and in each country context have varied widely. In this way, it is important for international human rights literature to look beyond so-called issues of compatibility with Islam across the region as a whole in a broad sense and to consider how each individual country in MENA engages with the UN instruments individually and over time. Engagement is not simply reduced to the religio-philosophical dimensions; there are broader legal, political, and social issues at play.

Still, the patterns are clear that most MENA states have made some effort to assert a claim about Islamic exceptions to UN human rights conceptions in their ratification of these UN human rights instruments, all while insisting that any conflict is minor. The burden of justifying practices and explaining religion resulting from voluntary engagement with these UN human rights treaty instruments stemming from ratification across the region has created a unique space in which language and concepts about Islam and human rights are being negotiated. As a result, MENA engagement with UN human rights conventions has revealed a certain dynamism and evolution in the way these ideas have been communicated by governments that is worthy of further study and deeper understanding, particularly by those working to make international human rights efforts more effective.

In a discussion with the author, one prominent human rights activist from the UAE described the use of Islam as an exception to CEDAW commitments as "a pretext" – attempting to appeal to citizens to suggest the government cares about Islam, while implying that organizations like the UN were "against Islam."[50] In his opinion, it is not important how Islam is brought up, simply *that* it is brought up in the context of the UN meetings. The ways in which government arguments about Islam are used as a political tool in this international context should continue to be studied and critiqued.

International relations scholar Jack Donnelly has argued that a broad global consensus has been achieved today regarding human rights. "In the contemporary world differences with respect to human rights largely concern matters of detail rather than basic norms," he writes.[51] Therefore, he claims, the process of argumentation can be much more important than the substance. "Anything that even hints of imposing Western values," Donnelly writes, "is likely to be met with understandable suspicion, even resistance. How arguments of universalism and arguments of relativism are advanced may sometimes be as important as the substance of those arguments."[52] The cases of MENA ratification of the CAT, CEDAW, and CRC offer evidence for part of Donnelly's claims in that they reveal large areas of consensus (at least in rhetoric) over concepts of "equality" and "non-discrimination" exemplified by ratification. Still, key areas of contention remain, particularly surrounding ideas about gender equality in marriage. The way arguments are crafted in dialogues and reporting proceedings (about flexibility in Islam, for example) can be more revealing than the substance of the arguments put forward at the UN (such as the substance of RUDs). Statements from MENA states to the human rights committees over time support Donnelly's argument about a degree of consensus about human rights in the broadest sense, in terms of the language and concepts used, while demonstrating that human rights terminology can still be an empty shell for deeper debate over disagreements.

The focus on compliance in the existing scholarship leads us to overlook the dynamics of engagement playing out in cases like MENA, where engagement is high but policy progress measured in liberal human rights reforms has been minimal. This fails to account for the impact on discourse on Islam and human rights that is resulting from ratification. This impact on dialogue is a form of norm diffusion as a nascent "first step" in a complex process. Discourse is simply discourse – it does not directly change law and practices. The growing convergence in the use of UN concepts in the context of Islamic understandings of human rights in MENA could have negative consequences, as states become more brazen in making human rights promises that are not fulfilled. However, law and practices are less likely to liberalize without a liberal discourse framing understandings of human rights more closely alongside international human rights vocabulary and concepts. As more and more states demonstrate they are willing – if not compelled – to dance to a diplomatic tune using a vocabulary of human rights, there is a rich record emerging in which statements about the harmony between Islam and UN human rights concepts are developing. If scholars and policymakers develop a deeper understanding of the ways that UN human rights treaty ratification can move discourses about human rights in these cases, a clearer understanding of UN human rights treaties will be achieved, with the possibility that international law will become more realistic and effective.

Notes

1 Susan Muaddi Darraj, *The Universal Declaration of Human Rights*, New York: Infobase Publishing, 2010, p. 83.
2 Mary Ann Glendon, *A World Made New: Eleanor Roosevelt and the Universal Declaration of Human Rights*, New York: Random House, 2001, p. 8.
3 Notably, the United States has only ratified the UN Convention Against Torture (CAT) in 1998 and has not ratified the children's (CRC) or women's (CEDAW) conventions.
4 See, for example, critiques in Anthony D'Amato, "Is International Law Really Law?" Northwestern School of Law: Faculty Working Papers, 2010, Online. Available at http://anthonydamato.

law.northwestern.edu/Adobefiles/A853.pdf (accessed 4 September 2017). For critiques of effectiveness across categories of international law as compared with domestic law see Jack Goldsmith and Eric Posner, *The Limits of International Law*, Oxford: Oxford University Press, 2005.

5 See this study of human rights treaty compliance: Emilie M. Hafner-Burton, Kiyoteru Tsutsui, and John W. Meyer, "Repressive States and Human Rights Treaties: International Human Rights Law and the Politics of Legitimation," *International Sociology*, 2008, vol. 23, 115. "Formal agreements by national governments intended to improve human rights practices have not only done little to achieve the goal, but also seem to have sometimes resulted in worse practices." Hafner-Burton et al., "Repressive States," 116. Also, Goldsmith and Posner, *The Limits of International Law*.

6 As argued by Beth Simmons, *Mobilizing for Human Rights*, Cambridge, UK: Cambridge University Press, 2009, p. 7.

7 "Freedom in the Middle East and North Africa," Freedom House. Online. Available at https://freedomhouse.org/regions/middle-east-and-north-africa (accessed 2 September 2017).

8 A gender gap of 0 percent indicates gender equality. "Global Gender Gap Report 2015," World Economic Forum. Available at http://reports.weforum.org/global-gender-gap-report-2015/the-global-gender-gap-index-results-in-2015/ (accessed 31 August 2017).

9 See, for example, R. Javaid, "Islam and Human Rights: Is Compatibility Achievable between the Sharia and Human Rights Law?" 2 January 2014. Online. Available at http://ssrn.com/abstract=2373930</URI (accessed 31 August 2017).

10 Sami Zubaida "Islam and Secularization," *Asian Journal of Social Science*, 2005, vol. 33, no. 3, 2005, pp. 438–48, 440.

11 Noel James Coulson, *A History of Islamic Law*, Edinburgh: Edinburgh University Press.1964, p. 4.

12 Sami Zubaida, *Law and Power in the Islamic World*, New York: I. B. Tauris, 2004, p. 1.

13 The origins of legal changes are contested in newer literature, for example, Kent Schull identifies once ignored influence of Islamic criminal law on changes in reforms in Turkish prisons in the late Ottoman Empire. See K. Schull, *Prisons in the Late Ottoman Empire: Microcosms of Modernity*, Edinburgh: Edinburgh University Press, 2014.

14 Zubaida, *Law and Power*, p. 4.

15 Zubaida, *Law and Power*, pp. 130–5 as in S. Zubaida, "Islam and Secularization," p. 440.

16 Coulson, *A History of Islamic Law*, p. 218.

17 Wael Hallaq, *Introduction to Islamic Law*, Cambridge, UK: Cambridge University Press, 2011, p. 115.

18 Hallaq, *Introduction*, p. 115. This was, of course, controversial among emerging "feminists" in the Middle East. See Elizabeth Thompson, *Colonial Citizens*, New York: Columbia University Press, 1999.

19 Hallaq, *Introduction*, p. 115

20 Sami Zubaida, *Law and Power*, p. 200.

21 Zubaida, *Law and Power*, p. 4.

22 Zubaida, *Law and Power*, p. 153.

23 Zubaida, *Law and Power*, p. 153.

24 Zubaida, *Law and Power*, p. 155.

25 Although most MENA states have ratified most UN human rights conventions, key exceptions include, for example, Iran's standing rejection of the CEDAW, Oman's rejection of the CAT, and Saudi Arabia's ongoing refusal to accede to the ICCPR.

26 The most popular UN human rights convention is the CRC, which holds 196 state parties and has been ratified by all eligible UN states, with the exception of the United States.

27 Vienna Convention on the Law of Treaties, 1969. Online. Available at https://treaties.un.org/doc/Publication/UNTS/Volume%201155/volume-1155-I-18232-English.pdf (accessed 10 November 2018).

28 Religious exceptions for example of Catholic-majority countries are also reflected in RUDs, for example, the Holy See explicitly states in RUDs in reference to its ratification of the CRC, "[The Holy See] interprets the phrase 'Family planning education and services' in Article 24.2, to mean only those methods of family planning which it considers morally acceptable, that is, the natural methods of family planning." Online. Available at www.vatican.va/roman_curia/secretariat_state/2014/documents/rc-seg-st-20140205_concluding-observations-rights-child_en.html#_ftn3 (accessed 10 November 2018).

29 This is the EU-EEAS/GCC diplomat's point in an interview, 28 April 2017, by phone.
30 Women's Committee of the National Council of Resistance of Iran, "CEDAW: Why the Iranian Regime Does Not Join the CEDAW," March 2016. Available at https://women.ncr-iran.org/images/documents/CEDAW-NCRI%20Womens%20Committee-March2016.pdf (accessed 11 November 2018). One should note that a number of other states have not ratified CEDAW, including the United States and the Holy See.
31 United Nations. Reservations and Declarations. Online. Available at https://treaties.un.org/Pages/Declarations.aspx?index=Egypt&lang=_en&chapter=4&treaty=330 (accessed 10 September 2017).
32 Goldsmith and Posner, *The Limits of International Law.*
33 "Top Islamic Cleric Criticizes UN Watchdog for Accusing Saudi Arabia of Flawed Torture Record," *Ghandchi*, 23 May. Online. Available at http://iona.ghandchi.com/Saudi/abdulaziz.htm (accessed 30 August 2017).
34 CAT/C/SR.1402, Summary record of the 1402nd meeting, 57th session, Committee Against Torture, Palais Wilson, Geneva, Chair: Mr. Modvig, 22 April 2016, p. 2.
35 CAT/C/58/Add.1/47. "Consideration of reports submitted by states parties under article 19 of the convention, Initial reports of states parties due in 2000," Qatar, Committee Against Torture, 5 October 2005.
36 CAT/C/58/Add.1. Qatar Addendum to the Initial Report, Summary Records, Geneva, 25 July 2006.
37 CAT/C/SR.989. "Examen des rapports soumis par les Etats parties en application de l'article 19 de la Convention" (Kuwait Second Periodic Report), 31 May 2012, p. 2.
38 CAT/C/KWT/3. "Consideration of reports submitted by States parties under article 19 of the Convention pursuant to the optional reporting procedure," Third periodic reports of States parties due in 2015, Kuwait, 17 August 2015, p. 7.
39 CEDAW/C/TUN/1–2. "Consideration of reports submitted by states parties under Article 18 of the Convention," Combined initial and second reports of State parties, Tunisia, 12 April 1994.
40 CEDAW/C/SR.448. "Consideration of reports submitted by States parties under article 18 of the Convention," Initial and second periodic reports of Jordan, Summary record of the 448th meeting, 27 July 2001.
41 A. El-Azhary Sonbol, *Women of Jordan: Islam, Labor, & the Law*, Syracuse, NY: Syracuse University Press, 2003.
42 CEDAW/C/SR.448 27 July 2001.
43 "The Shadow Report for CEDAW Prepared by 'Saudi Women for Reform' Saudi Arabia." Office of the High Commissioner for Human Rights. Online. Available at www2.ohchr.org/english/bodies/cedaw/docs/ngos/womenreform40.pdf (accessed 30 August 2017).
44 CRC/C/ARE/2. "Consideration of reports submitted by States parties under Article 44 of the Convention," Second periodic reports of States parties due in 2004, United Arab Emirates, 3 November 2014.
45 "Consideration of reports submitted by States parties under Article 44 of the Convention," Second periodic reports of States parties due in 2004, United Arab Emirates, 3 November 2014.
46 CRC/C/61/Add.2, "Consideration of reports submitted by states parties under Article 44 of the Convention," Initial report of Saudi Arabia due in 1998, 29 March 2000, p. 8.
47 CRC/C/SR.317. "Consideration of reports of states parties: Initial report of Morocco," Summary record of the 317th meeting, 24 September 1996.
48 CRC/C/SR.317. "Consideration of reports of states parties: Initial report of Morocco," Summary record of the 317th meeting, 24 September 1996, p. 4.
49 CRC/C/SR.882. "Consideration of reports of states parties," Summary record of the 882nd meeting, second periodic report of Morocco, 2 June 2003.
50 Telephone interview with a prominent UAE human rights activist. 14 June 2016.
51 Jack Donnelly, "Human Rights and the Dialogue Among Civilizations," unpublished paper, Online. Available at https://mysite.du.edu/~jdonnell/papers/dialogue.pdf (accessed 30 August 2017).
52 Jack Donnelly, "The Relative Universality of Human Rights," *Human Rights Quarterly*, 2007, vol. 29, 281–306.

10

WHEN THE WAR CAME

The child rights convention and the conflation of human rights and the laws of war

Linde Lindkvist

The UN Convention on the Rights of the Child (UNCRC) is widely regarded as a milestone in the development of international human rights law after 1945. The Convention has so far been ratified by 196 states (far more than any other human rights treaty) and now functions as the normative frame for myriad state and non-state actors working to promote the human rights of children. Against this backdrop, it should come as no surprise that the Convention's emergence has already been the subject of a number of drafting histories, which retrace the text's evolution from the initial 1978 draft to the final version, which was promulgated by the UN General Assembly on 20 November 1989.[1] In recent years, the UNCRC's genesis has also generated interest among historians of childhood, offering crucial insights into how the drafting related to changing conceptions of the child in twentieth-century politics and law.[2] Yet, in spite of the Convention's present-day significance for the international human rights project, it has so far generated little interest among historians of human rights. Even if many of the fine-grained contextual accounts of late have encouraged us to center our attention on the alleged global "breakthrough" of human rights between the mid-1970s and mid-1990s, they have not helped to shed more light on one of the most significant human rights instruments that came out of this period.[3]

In this essay, I propose one way of bringing the making of the UNCRC into the wider history of international human rights. This essay is informed by a view of the drafting of international human rights treaties as staging grounds for ideological contestations on the meaning and scope of human rights as a concept and as a political and legal enterprise, a view that is inspired by insights from both international history and the history of political thought.[4] In the case of the child rights convention, the most obvious ideological debate concerned the question of to what extent children should have the same human rights as adults (including, for instance, the right to freedom of expression and the freedom of religion). Yet like earlier, concurrent, and ensuing processes of codifying human rights in international law, the drafting of the UNCRC also actualized broader questions of what norms actually should count as human rights, how these should be articulated and under what circumstances they should apply. In what follows, I will highlight one specific category of norms that had not been recognized as part of human rights law until they were included in the UNCRC, namely the protection of civilians in times of armed conflict. More specifically, this essay highlights the making of UNCRC's Article 38 on Children in Armed Conflict, which focuses on the duty of states to protect children from military recruitment and direct participation in warfare:

1. States Parties undertake to respect and to ensure respect for rules of international humanitarian law to them in armed conflicts which are relevant to the child.
2. States Parties shall take all feasible measures to ensure that persons who have not attained the age of fifteen years do not take a direct part in hostilities.
3. States Parties shall refrain from recruiting any person who has not attained the age of fifteen years into their armed forces. In recruiting among those persons who have attained the age of fifteen years but who have not attained the age of eighteen years, States Parties shall endeavour to give priority to those who are oldest.
4. In accordance with their obligations under international humanitarian law to protect the civilian population in armed conflicts, States Parties shall take all feasible measures to ensure protection and care of children who are affected by an armed conflict.[5]

It may come as a surprise that this Article – couched as it is in the characteristically vague format of international human rights law – is widely characterized as one of the UNCRC's most glaring imperfections. The principal reason for this is its second and third paragraphs, which define 15 years as the minimum age for military recruitment and direct participation in armed conflict. These paragraphs were adopted in spite of overwhelming support for an alternative text setting the age limit at 18 years, which at that point also had been defined as the upper limit of childhood in the Convention's opening clause. But because the drafting group worked with a strict consensus principle, and because the United States and the USSR opposed calls for a higher age limit, the final version of Article 38 was, as one early commentator put it, "the most disappointing part of the Convention."[6]

Most drafting accounts portray the making of Article 38 as one of the most vexed issues that surfaced in the negotiations on the UNCRC and suggest that this was mainly because of the US insistence on protecting their domestic practice of recruiting adolescents into the armed forces.[7] There is no reason to call this interpretation into question if we want to account for the failed campaign to raise the age limit for recruitment and participation. But what the available accounts tend to disregard is how the years of negotiations leading up to the finalization of Article 38 did not just revolve around questions of age, but also actualized more principled questions concerning the relation between human rights law and humanitarian law (the latter being international laws regulating the conduct of war). In this essay, I claim that the fundamental issue at stake in the making of Article 38 was whether it was legitimate at all for a UN human rights treaty to be concerned with the protection of civilians in armed conflict.

For present-day human rights practitioners, it may seem strange to think that there ever was a time when human rights were not about protecting civilians from the scourge of war. But when the UNCRC was being negotiated, it was common for international lawyers to hold that human rights and humanitarian law were distinct legal fields with different institutional affiliations and areas of application. Whereas human rights law was linked to the UN system and was premised on an understanding of wars as strictly speaking illegal, humanitarian law was institutionally affiliated with the International Committee of the Red Cross (ICRC) and rested on a realization that wars sometimes do occur, but that the conduct in war could and should be regulated. Some even maintained that human rights law ends where humanitarian law begins so that the former system was only fully applicable in times of peace whereas the latter was activated only in times of war.[8]

The drafting of the UNCRC was not the first time that this division between human rights and the laws of war was being called into question. In the 1960s, for example, the ICRC had failed to garner sufficient support for a comprehensive set of draft rules concerning the protection of civilians in times of war, which was intended to supplement the more general rules concerning the protection of civilians contained in the Geneva Conventions of 1949. The ensuing deadlock in the evolution of humanitarian law occurred at the same time as the UN human rights system experienced a significant upswing with the finalization of two core human rights covenants of 1966.[9] At the end of the decade, these developments, together with a growing demand for new humanitarian law standards in the wake of the wars in Algeria, Biafra, and Vietnam, meant that the protection of civilians in armed conflict was momentarily transformed into an issue of UN human rights politics.[10]

In 1968, the International Conference on Human Rights in Teheran adopted both a general resolution on "Human Rights in Armed Conflict" and a specific resolution calling on Israel to respect both human rights and humanitarian standards in the territories occupied after the Six Day War. These texts were followed by a series of UN General Assembly resolution and UN secretary-general reports, all calling for improved protection of civilians in times of war. In the early 1970s, the ICRC responded to these calls by effectively reclaiming the development of humanitarian law from the UN. It convened a series of diplomatic conferences and compiled two draft texts on international and non-international conflicts respectively – which after some diplomatic wrangling were adopted as the two 1977 Additional Protocols of the Geneva Conventions.[11] The two protocols were drafted to apply to international and non-international conflicts respectively. Among their many detailed provisions were clauses that drew directly on the content of international human rights law (e.g. non-discrimination, due-process rights, right to life, and physical integrity in Article 75 of Additional Protocol I). Because of such substantial overlaps, it was fully possible to interpret the Protocols as attempts to bridge the gap between human rights and humanitarian law. But the Protocols also marked a return to an earlier division of labor between the UN and the ICRC, with the former being concerned with human rights and the latter with the laws of armed conflict.

At the dawn of the 1980s, there was growing recognition among scholars that human rights and humanitarian law were closely related fields, which sometimes covered similar issues (e.g. torture, extrajudicial killings, and enforced disappearances).[12] There was also a growing tendency of human rights organizations (such as Americas Watch/Human Rights Watch) to use humanitarian law, and not just principles of human rights, to monitor violations in times of armed conflict.[13] What was not clear, however, was whether it was possible for human rights treaties (and their accompanying bodies for overseeing state compliance) to be openly concerned with the protection of civilians in times of war. It was as an intervention in this broader ideological debate on the reach of the international human rights project that UNCRC's Article 38 acquired its significance. By including substantial provisions concerning the treatment of children in armed conflict, the UNCRC marked a definite break with a previous understanding of the relation between human rights and the laws of war. It helped to change our understanding of the international human rights system in that it, as Fiona Ang puts it, proved the "reconcilability of IHL [international humanitarian law] and human rights."[14]

In what follows, I draw on the official UN transcripts and previously unexplored archival sources to recount the many twists and turns that led to the finalization of Article 38. In the conclusion, I note how the frustrated negotiations on this Article helped to trigger a massive international movement against the use of child soldiers in the 1990s and early 2000s. But I also suggest that the drafting of Article 38 encourages us to pause and reflect on two indirect consequences of incorporating humanitarian law standards in the framework of international human rights law. The first such consequence has to do with the language of rights. Drawing on the protectionist language of the Geneva Conventions and its Additional Protocols, Article 38 construed children as passive objects in need of protection, rather than subjects capable of claiming their rights. The second has to do with the more general orientation of the international human rights project. It is my impression that Article 38 manifested (and to some extent helped to reinforce) a shift from a previous understanding of international human rights as a forward-looking project aimed at addressing the causes of war, to a more pragmatic project aimed at alleviating wartime suffering of civilians. Revisiting the drafting of the UNCRC and its Article 38 invites us to see how this shift was the product of historical contingency and decision. And it encourages us to reflect on the potential costs and benefits that were involved in the process of remaking international human rights into a project of regulating the conduct of wars, rather than a project of charting a path to a world without wars.

The long road to a weak article

Negotiations on a binding UN treaty on children's rights began in March 1978 as Poland submitted a draft convention to the annual session of the Commission on Human Rights.[15] The initial aim was to have the text – which was nearly identical in content to a nonbinding UN declaration from 1959 – adopted before the end of 1979, which two years earlier had been designated as the International Year of the Child. Mainstream accounts present the initiative as a reflection of Poland's long-standing commitment to defend the needs of children in international forums, a commitment that is said to have been powered by the "suffering of its younger generations" as well as the legacy of the country's child rights pioneers (e.g. Janusz Korczak).[16] Others have suggested that the initiative marked a mere revival of a humanitarian child rights discourse that crystallized in the interwar period and influenced two ILO conventions on child labor of 1919 and, more famously, the League of Nations' 1924 Declaration on the Rights of the Child, a document that is strongly associated with what Susan Pedersen refers to as the "humanitarian entrepreneurialism" of Eglantyne Jebb and the Save the Children Fund. In either case, we are told that the idea of a binding instrument on children's rights was only a natural consequence of initiatives that had emerged in the first half of the twentieth century.[17]

While these accounts contain a kernel of truth, they gloss over how the Polish draft played out in the more immediate context of UN human rights politics of the late 1970s. In fact, in 1978 many regarded the proposal of drafting a treaty on children's rights as an inadvertent attempt to delay what was then the main project of the UN Commission on Human Rights: the finalization of the UN Convention Against Torture.[18] It is true that the Commission agreed to set up an open-ended working group on children's rights, but for the first few years, the negotiations in this forum led nowhere. This was partly due to the employment of a strict consensus principle and the fact that it only met for a week of formal sessions each year, but also due to the tendency of states to allocate their limited resources (including expertise on human rights and juvenile law) to other areas. Nor did it help that the project was associated with one of the Commission's least credible members. At the same time as the Polish representatives were trying to make headway with the Convention, they had to face criticism of the government's crackdown on civil and political rights after the imposition of martial law in December 1981. The Commission even adopted a Canadian-sponsored resolution expressing deep concern with the Polish government's human rights record.

Apart from such external constraints, there was also some concern with the content of the Polish draft. Canon Joseph Moerman of the International Catholic Child Bureau (and the principal architect of the International Year of the Child) argued that a hurried drafting process was likely to interfere with the many studies and workshops being planned for 1979. He suggested that the UN await the results of these efforts before taking on the task of codifying the rights of children. The few states that cared to respond to the Polish draft also argued that it was unwise to use the 1959 Declaration as the raw material for a binding treaty since it had been vaguely formulated and did not, as the Dutch delegate put it, "reflect the social, economic and cultural developments and changes" of the past two decades. The prime concern was that the 1959 instrument focused too much on the "special safeguards and care" that stemmed from the child's "physical and mental immaturity." This meant – as the Nordic countries also pointed out – that the text was not only out of touch with the current realities of children, but also did not reflect the changing geographies of international human rights law and politics in the postcolonial era.[19]

There were also critics who expressed unease with the draft Convention's implications for the protection of children in armed conflicts. Although the text – just like its 1959 antecedent – never mentioned children in war, it did carry a clause specifying that, "The Child shall *in all circumstances* be among the first to receive protection and relief" (Article VII, emphasis added). This formulation caught the eye of the ICRC, which replied that a human rights convention using the terminology "in all circumstances" would, albeit unintentionally, trespass on the territory of international humanitarian law. The principal fear was that this general terminology could be interpreted in ways that would allow states to sidestep the more detailed rules on the wartime protection of children laid down in the Geneva conventions and their additional protocols:

> We are confronted, on the one hand, by a draft convention characterized by the general and global nature of both its scope and its provisions and, on the other, by the provisions of the Geneva instruments, which are more precise and which apply only in times of armed conflict.[20]

There is no evidence suggesting that this triggered any further debate in the drafting group. But as Poland submitted a revised draft a year later, it responded to the ICRC's remarks on the need to distinguish between human rights and the laws of war by removing Article VII in its entirety.[21] At this point, there was nothing to suggest that a future convention on children's rights would confront the situation of children in armed conflict, and another seven years passed before the first version of what is now Article 38 was folded into the convention text.

This did not mean that there were no voices calling for an instrument that would highlight the suffering and exploitation of children in war. In 1980, the Friends World Committee for Consultation (the Quakers) circulated a draft aiming to ban the participation of children in military training and action. It also cited reports suggesting that children of at least ten countries were currently "taking part in civil wars, in resistance movements, in wars of liberation from colonial powers, and in international conflicts."[22] These efforts appear to have originated in an individual petition by a member of the Swiss Quaker community, Dorothy Woods, who in the late 1970s urged the organization to define child soldiers as one of its central concerns for the International Year of the Child. According to Rachel Brett, the question was then relatively quickly established as an ideal case for the Quakers' UN office, not least since it was located "at the interface of peace/war and human rights," and thereby served as a bridge between the movement's traditional areas of interest.[23]

About the same time, Rädda Barnen (Swedish Save the Children) began to take an active interest in making the issue of children in armed conflict into a matter of children's rights. Having recently set up its own Geneva office to escape internal tensions within umbrella organizations like the International Union of Child Welfare and Save the Children Alliance, it began to follow the debates on the child rights convention in the early 1980s. In 1981, it circulated its own, alternative bill on children's rights, *Carta Infantium*, to UN member states and nongovernmental groups. This covered similar areas as the Polish draft of the UNCRC, but also contained language on children in armed conflict suggesting that states should be responsible to "prevent any act of war or other political violence especially directed towards children," and to "ensure that the child will not be permitted or compelled to engage in military service or actions."[24]

It is important to note that these were largely non-coordinated attempts. In the early 1980s, few nongovernmental organizations (NGOs) participated actively in the drafting process, and there is little to suggest that the ones who did exercised any actual influence. All of this began to change in 1983 when Rädda Barnen, the International Catholic Child Bureau and Defence for Children International (with some financial backing from UNICEF) succeeded in gathering 15 NGOs in Geneva to discuss different issues relating to the drafting process and the possibility of joint NGO amendments. The group – which sailed under the impossible name the NGO Ad Hoc Group on the Drafting of the Convention of the Rights of the Child (henceforth the NGO Group) – would later be celebrated as one of the first successful attempts at civil society cooperation in UN human rights politics, showing that by "combining their skill and expertise, NGOs can have an important, constructive impact on the UN treaty-making process."[25]

Together with the finalization of the UN Convention on Torture in 1984 and a more general thaw in international human rights politics after Soviet premier Mikhail Gorbachev's 1985 policy of *glasnost* or openness, the NGO Group was one of the main reasons why state interest in a treaty on children's rights surged in the mid-1980s. The final outcome would bear many imprints of the group's internal deliberations and lobbying efforts, including language on "harmful traditional practices" (code for female genital mutilation), sexual exploitation, and juvenile justice.[26] What is rarely recognized, however, is that one of the first questions around which the NGOs came together was that of children in armed conflicts.

Some of these organizations could show clear links between their work in Geneva and the relief work they carried out in war zones. For instance, Rädda Barnen, which in the 1980s became one of Sweden's most prolific aid groups with some 90,000 members, ran an extensive program in Lebanon, which included training for personnel in orphanages as well as fact-finding missions in the Palestinian refugee camps Sabra and Shatila after the massacres in September 1982.[27] Defence for Children International – which functioned as the coordinator and administrative office of the NGO group – also ran several relevant field projects, including investigative missions to El Salvador and Guatemala and a school close to Baghdad for Iranian child soldiers captured by the Iraqi army.[28] They were also able to draw on a growing of body of literature documenting the hardships of children in war, including Roger Rosenblatt's award-winning 1983 book, *Children of War*, which was based on encounters with children in Northern Ireland, Israel, Palestine, Lebanon, Cambodia, and Vietnam.[29]

Yet it seems that the more immediate and pedestrian reason why the NGOs came together to pen a joint text on children in armed conflict was their dissatisfaction with an Algerian draft amendment of 1983. This proposal had suggested the inclusion of a clause denouncing all forms of colonialism, foreign aggression, apartheid, and racial discrimination, and spelled out that children should always, "and especially during armed conflicts," enjoy protection from "attacks, acts of violence, bombardments and other inhuman practices which impair their moral and physical integrity."[30]

In a letter to Rädda Barnen's representative Simone Ek, Valerie Clements of the Quakers argued that the Algerian proposal was deficient since it did not address "the question of children bearing arms and being involved in armed conflict," including the treatment of child prisoners of war.[31] After some internal deliberation at its first round of meetings in the spring and summer of 1983, the NGO Group issued a draft demanding that states "refrain from recruiting children into the armed forces" and "take all measures to ensure that children do not take part in hostilities." It also proposed an additional clause on the duty to "prevent all children from being subjected to any form of physical or psychological violation," and to ensure that children are "always among the first to receive protection and care."[32]

The initial response to the NGO Group's proposal was either lukewarm or hostile. Some states apparently came out against the idea of singling out children as prioritized receivers of protection and care because this could create situations in which children were effectively separated from their families.[33] Again, the strongest pushback came from the ICRC. In a 1984 memo to the members of the NGO Group, it claimed that an article along the lines of the NGO proposal would interfere with international humanitarian laws concerning children, and perhaps even impair their implementation. The NGO draft was problematic, not least because it singled out the issues of recruitment, participation and protection from direct violence, while disregarding other areas addressed by the Geneva instruments (including identification, the right to communicate with family members, education and the freedom of religious practice) and the more general interdependence of the many different rules concerning the protection of civilians in times of war.[34]

As the guardian of the Geneva Conventions, the ICRC was no doubt a significant authority in this field. But in the mid-1980s, it also became more and more isolated as some Western European states embraced the idea of advocating clauses on the rights of children in armed conflict in the child rights convention.[35] The single most important context for this growing interest appears to have been the protracted war between Iraq and Iran, and, more specifically, reports of the high number of adolescents serving in the Iranian armed forces.

In the spring of 1984, major international news outlets ran chilling accounts of how children aged between 12 and 17 were regularly recruited by Iranian clerics, received "intensive indoctrination in the Shiite tradition of martyrdom," and then sent weaponless into the heat of battle, equipped only with metal keys that would help them unlock the gates to heaven. "Often bound together in groups of 20 by ropes to prevent the fainthearted from deserting," Terence Smith noted in a graphic, almost apocalyptic, account for the *New York Times Magazine*, "they hurl themselves on barbed wire or march into Iraqi mine fields in the face of withering machine-gun fire to clear the way for Iranian tanks."[36]

The previous year, Iran's use of child soldiers had been brought up for discussion in the UN Sub-Commission on Prevention of Discrimination and Protection of Minorities. Responding to critical remarks from the Anti-Slavery Society, the Iranian delegate retorted that,

> It was an honor for their country that these young people had become sufficiently mature to understand the seriousness of their country's situation. Their heroism and enthusiasm were based on the nation of martyrdom, which materialists were unable to understand.[37]

A resolution was immediately put together calling on Iran to abide by international standards and "cease immediately the use of children in the Armed Forces."[38] This statement was later adopted by the UN Commission on Human Rights at its 1984 session.[39]

One of the main players behind these resolutions was the Netherlands. In her meticulous study on human rights in Dutch foreign policy, Hilde Reiding reveals how this stance was in part triggered by calls from NGOs (including Defence for Children International) but also by a realization that child soldiers constituted a relatively risk-free area from a standpoint of domestic politics. In the fall of 1984, Dutch and Swedish diplomats met to devise a joint draft Article for the UNCRC.[40] The Dutch-Swedish draft made a general reference to "respect for rules of international humanitarian law" and emphasized that this required states to refrain from "recruiting children into the armed forces" and to take "all feasible measures to ensure that children do not take part in hostilities." The importance of the Iran–Iraq War was also visible in so far as the Working Group was presented with competing draft articles from both Iran (focusing on chemical and bacteriological weapons) and Iraq (focusing on child soldiers). An intense but fairly short debate followed in the 1986 session of the drafting group, a debate that centered on the question of whether to include specific age limits on recruitment and participation. Some argued that this was unnecessary, not least since no age limit had been defined in other instances of the convention, such as the article on child labor. Algeria and Venezuela called for an 18-year limit, since that would be most consistent with the upper limit of childhood defined in the convention's Article 1. Others, including Bangladesh, Canada, and Norway, called for a 15-year limit for recruitment because that was most consistent with Additional Protocol I to the Geneva Conventions.[41] Eventually, the drafting group came out in support of the last of these three alternatives, and adopted the text as follows:

1. The States Parties to the present Convention undertake to respect and to ensure respect for rules of international humanitarian law applicable to them in armed conflicts which are relevant to the child.
2. States Parties to the present Convention shall take all feasible measures to ensure that no child takes a direct part in hostilities and that they shall refrain in particular

from recruiting any child who has not attained the age of fifteen years into their armed forces.

3. In accordance with their obligation under international humanitarian law to protect the civilian population in armed conflicts, States Parties to this Convention shall take all feasible measures to ensure protection and care of children who are affected by an armed conflict.[42]

It is striking to note just how easily the drafters were able to reach a consensus on this text. While it was clear that there were many different views on what constituted the optimal formula, the 1986 session also displayed a strong and widespread willingness to compromise for the benefit of moving the negotiations forward. This stood in sharp contrast to the complete deadlock that had characterized the work a few years earlier. Yet what was even more remarkable was that this was not the end. What soon became clear was that the 1986 text did precisely what the ICRC had feared all along: by extending the child rights convention to the protection of children in war, the text would create standards that could be interpreted as a lowering of protection already granted to children under international humanitarian law.

Correcting the drafting mistake

In its technical but fierce review of the 1986 text, the ICRC argued that it not only conveyed a false "impression of addressing the entire question" of children in armed conflict, but also marked "a step backwards in relation to existing instruments of international law." The pressing issue was that the text only contained a specific age limit on recruitment (15 years), but not on participation. ICRC noted that the word "child" in the first part of paragraph 2 (see above), was to be read in light of the Convention's Article 1, which defined the child as "every human being to the age of 18 years *unless, under the law of his State, he has attained his age of majority earlier*" (emphasis added). This flexibility in the Convention's understanding of childhood effectively meant that the draft's provisions did not apply to situations where persons under the age of 15 years took part in battle, as long as they had reached the locally defined age of majority. The ICRC pointed to some "Islamic countries" where this age "is reached by boys between 12 and 15 years of age and by girls at 17 years of age" and to a 1982 Angolan law setting the age of majority at 14 years. It was because of such contextual variations that the drafters of the Additional Protocols had agreed on 15 years as a minimum age for both recruitment and participation in both international and non-international conflicts. This solution, which had represented "some progress while remaining realistic," was now being jeopardized by the attempts to incorporate humanitarian law into the UNCRC.[43]

In academic forums, ICRC experts continued to question the value of developing more instruments on children in armed conflict, arguing that problem was not the content of the Geneva instruments but the general lack of knowledge of these standards and the political will to abide by them.[44] Yet at this point, we can also discern an increased interest in the UNCRC among different actors within the Red Cross and Red Crescent society. In October 1986, the International Conference of the Red Cross adopted a resolution submitted by the Swedish and Finnish Red Cross Committees, which expressed support for the drafting of the UNCRC's provisions on children in armed conflict, while also underscoring that the protection offered should at least be equal to that of the Geneva instruments.[45] The objective of using a human rights instrument to address the situation of children in times of war was increasingly seen, as ICRC lawyer Françoise Krill also suggested in a piece for the Norwegian human rights journal *Mennesker og Rettigheter* (Humans and Rights), as entirely legitimate. Some even viewed it as an opportunity to address the shortcomings of the Additional Protocols (including the narrow concern with the child's "direct" participation, which failed to cover the many indirect roles children can and often do play in military operations). But this, Krill suggested, would require greater awareness of the integrity of humanitarian law, and, above all, that the drafters of the UNCRC decide to undo the mistakes of the version adopted in 1986.[46]

In these calls for revising the text, the ICRC found a staunch ally in Rädda Barnen, which from 1987 onwards would make the rights of children in armed conflicts into the main concern of its Geneva office. In an official communication to the Working Group, the organization's secretary-general, Thomas Hammarberg – who had recently joined the organization from a previous job as secretary-general of Amnesty International – reiterated the ICRC's main point that the 1986 text was not an improvement on the Geneva instruments:

> This in itself is disappointing, as, during the decade since protocols were agreed, the real situation in this area has deteriorated seriously. In recent years a large number of children have been pushed into taking part in warfare itself, even in combative roles. Stricter rules in this field are required.

He further recalled a suggestion made by the Brazilian delegate to the negotiations on the 1977 protocols on setting the age limit for both recruitment and participation at "18 full stop." "This," Hammarberg concluded, "is the decent position."[47]

One of Rädda Barnen's central points was that the need for new international standards found its principal motivation in the recent experiences of modern warfare, where there are "no clear-cut front lines" and where the lines between war and peace themselves are increasingly blurred. Rädda Barnen cited the open breaches of humanitarian law in the international conflict between Iran and Iraq, but also pointed to the recruitment of teenagers into the armed forces of Afghanistan, Angola, and Mozambique, as well as by local militias like the Contras in Nicaragua. "These cannot be written off as mistakes," Hammarberg argued in a 1987 op-ed for the *International Herald Tribune*, adding that NGOs, states, and international organizations must intensify their efforts to spread awareness of the existing standards, but also create more robust international laws that take into account the complexities of modern warfare. The underlying point was that in a context where the distinction between war and peace could not be sustained, it was also difficult to insist on there being clear boundaries between human rights (as norms of peace) and humanitarian law (as the laws of war).[48]

In 1987, the ICRC, Rädda Barnen, and the Quakers succeeded in convincing the Netherlands, Sweden, Switzerland, and Venezuela to support the demand to reopen the negotiations on the article on children in armed conflict. This irritated the Working Group's chairman, Adam Lopatka, who pointed out that they had all been present when the previous version was negotiated without raising any of these concerns.[49] But the supporters of a stronger text refused to back down. Instead, they initiated an intense and variegated campaign that included numerous informal meetings with state representatives, public events in many countries (including a seminal UNICEF workshop in Nairobi in the summer of 1987), as well as a public appeal that was handed over to the UN secretary-general Javier Pérez de Cuéllar in November 1987.[50] Lopatka eventually gave in and agreed to consider new versions of the Article at the extra session (the so-called Second Reading) that was scheduled for the fall of 1988.[51]

In preparing for this final showdown, a drafting committee headed by Sweden proposed a text specifying that states were responsible for banning direct participation in armed conflict by children below 15 years, and to "endeavor to prevent" those under 18 years from taking "direct part in hostilities." In what would prove to be a fateful decision, it also included a weaker text, which required states to "take all feasible measures" to keep children under 15 years from participating in hostilities.[52]

On the eve of the final debate, the *New York Times* reported that there was a broad coalition in favor of the stronger text. It also noted that the main stumbling block would probably be the United States. The piece cited American diplomats saying that the UN Commission on Human Rights was not authorized to create new humanitarian law. If states wanted to do so, they should instead turn to "other international forums, such as a conference to negotiate new protocols to the Geneva Conventions, where experts on military law would be present."[53] There was great uncertainty as to what motivated this separatist stance on the relation between human rights and humanitarian law. One thing that was clear was that it contrasted with US policies of the late 1960s. Back then, US officials – concerned with the maltreatment of captured American soldiers in Vietnam – had voiced strong support for an increased attention by UN human rights bodies to the suffering caused by armed conflicts.[54] The NGOs pushing for a higher age limit in the UNCRC were also baffled by the US rhetorical use of the Geneva instruments, which they viewed as an attempt to disguise the government's real concern of protecting the practice of recruiting 17-year-olds with parental consent into the American military.

What followed was one of the most bewildering chapters of the negotiation process. Before the states began their discussions, Lopatka invited the chairman of the youth section of the Swedish Red Cross Society, Lars Pettersson, to address the drafting group. Pettersson's organization launched a massive appeal against child soldiers and for revising the text that (partly due to input from the Swedish Red Cross Committee and Rädda Barnen) had been initiated in the summer of 1988. The appeal – which also showcases the decentralized nature of the Red Cross and Red Crescent movements – was signed by some 650 youth organizations, including the youth sections of about 70 Red Cross and Red Crescent societies.[55] This was one of the few occasions in the decade of negotiations where some of the UNCRC's intended beneficiaries actually addressed the members of the Working Group. The handing over of the long list of signatories made for an excellent photo-op. But the protocols offer no evidence suggesting that the plea was ever picked up in the ensuing diplomatic debate (a fact showcasing the difficulties of writing children's agency into the history of the UNCRC's emergence).

As the debates began, it soon became clear that there was wide support for the stronger text. Australia, for instance, suggested that "our mandate here is to improve international law with respect to children, not to defend the status quo." But an overwhelming majority was not enough in a forum operating with a consensus principle. It also became clear that the United States had no intention of abandoning its position that this was the wrong forum for developing new humanitarian law. The very same point was made by the Soviet delegate, who also favored the weaker text: "My impression is that we are trying to do more than we can with this Article. We don't have a mandate to review and improve international humanitarian law."[56]

The discussions then moved on to the question of how to handle the lack of consensus. Some states tried to work out last-minute compromises, while others suggested that it might be best to simply remove the entire paragraph 2 on participation in armed conflict. These proposals were rejected by Lopatka, who thought it was too late for new ideas. Instead, he temporarily defused the issue by turning the Working Group's attention to the article's paragraph 3. After this clause had been adopted without debate, Lopatka hurried back to paragraph 2 and simply declared that the weaker version of the text (which only involved a 15-year limit) had been adopted. The protocol from this part of the debate is well worth quoting at length because it showcases how the article on children in armed conflict was finalized in a state of total confusion:

Chairman: Then we should consider paragraph 2, the second (weaker) bracketed version … Is there opposition? No? Then it is adopted.

USSR: Excuse me, Mr. Chairman. But could you please repeat which version of paragraph 2 we have adopted?

Chairman: It was the second one. The second bracketed version. And now, before adjourning, I have some announcements to make. (The chair went on to make series of administrative announcements).

Italy: I have just received specific instructions from my government and I must declare that I cannot join the consensus on Article 20 as it was adopted. I was forced to leave the proceedings to receive these instructions concerning the second (weaker) bracketed paragraph 2 and have just returned only to find out it has been adopted. Since my government opposes this version, I cannot join the consensus. [Netherlands, Sweden, Finland, Austria, Australia, and Switzerland likewise declared that they could not be part of the consensus on paragraph 2.]

Chairman: But this is a ridiculous situation!

Norway: We need clarification. Does this mean that consensus on paragraph 2 has been broken?

Chairman: My understanding is that the consensus is not broken. The remarks are only to be entered. The meeting is adjourned![57]

It was in the midst of such chaos and frustration that the final version of what is now Article 38 was adopted. A rumor circulating at the time suggested that Lopatka had rushed to close the meeting in order to catch a flight from Geneva to New York, where he was slated to receive the UN Prize in the Field of Human Rights in connection to the 40th anniversary of the Universal Declaration of Human Rights.[58]

Some supporters of a stronger text thought that this was a battle that had to be won for the convention to mark any progress in the protection of children, and were thinking about trying once again to renegotiate the text as the draft Convention moved up the hierarchy of the UN system over the year of 1989. Swedish diplomats also met with Soviet officials in Moscow, who stated that the USSR had no substantial objections to a stronger text, but explained that they read the whole campaign as an illegitimate attempt to use a human rights treaty to modify the content of international humanitarian law. Swedish officials held similar consultations with high-level officials of the US State

Department, who confirmed that Pentagon was responsible for the assessment that a stronger version of Article 38 would "interfere negatively with US practices," while also reiterating the point that the UN Commission on Human Rights had no authority to create new standards for the protection of civilians in times of war. In its report, the Swedish Embassy in Washington also noted that the timing of these kinds of lobbying efforts was particularly bad. It was unlikely that the United States would change positions during the administrative shift that followed on the recent inauguration of George H. W. Bush.[59]

At this point, there was also a growing resistance to the idea of trying to create a more ambitious text. To the dismay of the Nordic delegations and Rädda Barnen, the ICRC changed its strategy to damage control. When the Convention was brought up for debate in the Commission on Human Rights in the Spring of 1989, the ICRC joined with the United States in suggesting an amendment that would effectively remove most of Article 38, except a general reference to the responsibility of states to abide by humanitarian law. There were also increased concerns that attempts to remake Article 38 would put the whole Convention at risk. The United States, for instance, floated ideas of revising the clause on religious freedom, since it did not go as far as the Convention on Civil and Political Rights in terms of protecting the free choice of religion. For many, the primary goal was now to meet what was known as "Target 89," and to have the Convention (with all its imperfections) adopted by the General Assembly the following November. The struggle for increased protection of children in armed conflict had to move to other settings.

Conclusions and suggestions for further research

The negotiations on Article 38 marked only the starting point of what would soon evolve into a broad international movement against the use of child soldiers. As Rachel Brett shows, what happened after 1989 was essentially that the proponents of a higher age limit "refused to let the matter drop." One of the most the concrete developments that gave this movement momentum was the appointment of Thomas Hammarberg – then secretary-general of Rädda Barnen – to one of the seats of the UN Committee on the Rights of the Child. From its first meetings in 1991, the Committee used the full range of its mandate to keep the issue on the UN agenda, requesting both a broad UN study on children in armed conflict and the development of an Optional Protocol that would amend the shortcomings of Article 38.[60]

The first of these calls triggered the landmark 1996 report by the former Mozambican minister of education and culture, Graça Machel. The report helped to frame the issue of children in armed conflicts as a challenge of existential proportions, claiming that "more and more of the world is being sucked into a desolate moral vacuum" in which children are subjected to extreme brutality and starvation and are "exploited as soldiers." The report still stands as a model for an effective UN study, not only because of its impressive geographical reach and underlying sense of urgency, but also because of the way it drew on a mix of normative sources (including human rights, humanitarian law, and refugee law) in documenting the involvement of children in armed conflicts. In justifying this mix of human rights and humanitarian law, Machel pointed to the wording of Article 38, citing the UNCRC as "one of the most important bridges linking two bodies of law whose complementarity is increasingly recognized."[61]

The CRC committee's second request – also reiterated by the Machel study – resulted in the Optional Protocol on Children in Armed Conflict of May 2000, which went further than UNCRC in so far as it required states and non-state actors to ensure that persons under 18 years were not subjected to compulsory recruitment or allowed to take direct part in hostilities.[62] One of the great ironies here is that while the United States had blocked further progress on Article 38 and remains the only UN member state yet to ratify the UNCRC, the Clinton administration succeeded in getting the US Senate's consent for ratification of the Optional Protocol (along with a different one on trafficking, prostitution, and child pornography). This was preceded by several years of negotiations between the White House and Pentagon, which concluded only when it became clear that ratification would affect only about 3,000 persons in uniform.[63]

The finalization of the Optional Protocol was also encouraged by developments in other forums. The first of these was the African Charter on the Rights and Welfare of the Child of 1990, which included a strict 18-year limit on both recruitment and participation. This was followed by the ILO Convention 182 of 1999, which included a strict ban on compulsory recruitment of persons under 18 years for participation in armed conflicts. The most famous instrument, however, was the Rome Statute on the International Criminal Court of 1998, which defined conscription and military use of children (albeit only under the age of 15) as an international crime. Several of the cases that have so far come before the ICC have also focused on the use of child soldiers.

Looking back, the debates on Article 38 form an interesting backdrop to these later normative developments for a number of reasons. It is, for one, striking how the broad question of children in armed conflict was gradually boiled down to a dispute on age limits for recruitment and participation. As I have shown here, it was far from self-evident that the UNCRC would even mention the rights of children in armed conflict, let alone spotlight the specific issue of child soldiers. It was also relatively late in the negotiations that the question of age became a matter of dispute. Even the most ardent supporters of an 18-year limit did not make this a priority before the first version of Article 38 had been adopted in 1986. And even then, their main argument for a higher age limit had less to do with any claims about the difference in maturity between 15- and 18-year-olds than with the integrity of the UNCRC and the risk of lowering existing humanitarian standards.

Many of the developments since 1989 have been already subjected to academic scrutiny, including several critical accounts that contrast the development of ever-stricter international standards on child soldiering with the findings of studies on the complex local settings in which children become participants in armed conflicts, and so call into the question the notion of the "victimized child-soldier."[64] There have also been significant studies suggesting that the strong movement to counter the participation of children in armed conflicts has emerged at the expense of sustained political efforts to advance the basic rights and social status of former child soldiers.[65] What we are still lacking, though, are serious efforts to connect the emergence of the movement against child soldiers to the broader developments in international human rights politics after 1989. By my lights, this is symptomatic of a more general tendency among scholars to treat children's rights as a distinct international project, which unfolds in isolation from the more general field of international human rights.

The main point of this essay has been to demonstrate that the drafting of the UNCRC and its Article 38 was an important step in a more general process of blurring the boundaries between human rights and humanitarian law. The 1980s saw a growing appreciation among international lawyers that these were overlapping fields, which shared the same goal of protecting the dignity of the human person. There was also a growing recognition of how human rights ideas had influenced, if not the Geneva Conventions of 1949, then at least the Additional Protocols of 1977 and the subsequent evolution of international custom.[66] That said, it was still possible to insist that these were distinct legal fields that applied to different situations and involved different mechanisms for oversight. Article 38 was significant in that it marked the first time that humanitarian law standards were directly infused into the body of human rights law.

It is easy to fall into the temptation of reading this as a step toward greater cohesion of the international framework for the protection of children in armed conflict, or, more broadly, toward the emergence of a so-called "humanity's law" – a minimalist morality underlying the contemporary international legal order, which is said to be constituted by the shared humanitarian norms of human rights law, humanitarian law, and international criminal law.[67] But there are at least two aspects that give us reason to resist such temptation, aspects that have to do with what happens when a human rights treaty adopts the language of humanitarian law.

The first of these has to do with the very notion of rights. Although Article 38 was part of a human rights treaty, it also marked a complete embrace of the protectionist language of humanitarian law. This can be seen in the way Article 38 outlines the duty of states to protect children in armed conflicts, while stopping short from recognizing children as bearers of rights. In keeping with the predominant discourse of humanitarian law, Article 38 imagines children as objects of protection, but not as subjects who are capable of claiming their own rights. To the extent that the UNCRC is now celebrated as an affirmation of the view that children are full human beings, and not just human beings in the making, this does not apply to its novel section on children in armed conflicts. Here, the child is rendered only as a passive, vulnerable, and helpless victim in need of outside protection.[68]

The debates in Article 38 can also be read as manifestations of a deeper change in the orientation of the UN human rights project. In the Universal Declaration of Human Rights of 1948 and the follow-on treaties of 1966, we search in vain for references to the protection of human rights in situations of armed conflict. In fact, when the so-called derogation clauses of the 1966 treaties were being negotiated, the drafters made a conscious decision not to mention armed conflicts among the situations in which rights can be restricted. The reason for this, one commentator remarked, was that the covenants should "not envisage, not even by implication, the possibility of war," since that would go against the general prohibition on warfare in the UN Charter.[69] But there was also a more principled argument for why human rights should be unconcerned with situations of armed conflict. Some historians have suggested that if there was anything that united advocates of international human rights in the first decades after 1945, it was an understanding of human rights as a forward-looking project, which was designed to address the root causes of armed conflict. In this era, human rights advocacy often rested on an analysis suggesting that if states violated the rights of their citizens, they would also be more inclined to engage in aggressive warfare.[70] While it is vital to stress the heterogeneity of human rights activism in the 1940s and beyond, it is clear that for seminal figures like René Cassin and O. Frederick Nolde, a fundamental rationale for the codification of international human rights law was the promise that such standards would help to chart the path to a world of peace.[71]

By the 1980s, the discussions in international human rights forums had taken a more realist turn. If the human rights project in the 1940s was centered on the objective of safeguarding rights for the sake of world peace, it was now more concerned with the goal of mitigating the most destructive aspects of war. This shift was clearly manifested in the UNCRC and its Article 38 on children in armed conflict. This was also recognized by one the Convention's early critics, the renowned journalist and UNICEF executive, Varindra Tarzie Vittachi. "One of the main defects of the Convention on the Rights of the Child," he noted in 1993, "is its failure to denounce war as one of the taproots of children's sufferings." "Couched in the characteristic weasel-words of international diplomacy," he added, the Convention's provisions "provide a legal basis for taking action to mitigate the trauma suffered by children in war," but does little to eradicate war itself.[72]

In a landmark 2010 piece on human rights mainstreaming, Martti Koskenniemi remarked: "One cannot be a revolutionary and participate in the regular management of things without some cost to both of these projects."[73] This would suggest that the gradual conflation of human rights and the laws of war (to which I think the struggle for the rights of children in armed conflicts strongly contributed) was not merely a step toward a more cohesive, humanity-centered international legal order, but a process that involved real costs and meant that alternative understandings of both projects were pushed aside. It remains an open question what these trade-offs actually were, and to what extent the rapprochement between human rights and humanitarian law "narrowed or eclipsed the broader aspirations of the human rights movement," as some thinkers have recently suggested.[74] At the very least, the kind of microscopic account I have proposed here allows us to grasp how such shifts are never inevitable, but products of historical contingency and decision.

Notes

1 Sharon Detrick (ed.), *The UN Convention on the Rights of the Child: A Guide to the Travaux Préparatoires*, Dordrecht: Martinus Nijhoff, 1992; Lawrence LeBlanc, *The Convention on the Rights of the Child*, Lincoln: University of Nebraska Press, 1995.

2 Paula Fass, "A Historical Context for the United Nations Convention on the Rights of the Child," *Annals of the American Academy of Political and Social Science*, 2011, vol. 633, 17–29; Zoe Moody, *Les Droits de l'Enfant: Genèse, Institutionnalisation et Diffusion (1924–1989)*, Neuchâtel: Éditions Alphil-Presses Universitaires Suisses, 2016. For the surest guide to the field, see Anna Holzscheiter, *Children's Rights in International Politics*, Basingstoke, UK: Palgrave Macmillan, 2010.

3 For a notable exception, see Kelly J. Shannon, "The Right to Bodily Integrity. Women's Rights as Human Rights and the International Movement to End Female Genital Mutilation, 1970s–1990s," in Akira Iriye, Petra Goedde, and William I. Hitchcock (eds.) *The Human Rights Revolution*, New York: Oxford University Press, 2012, pp. 285–310.

4 See also Linde Lindkvist, *Religious Freedom and the Universal Declaration of Human Rights*, New York: Cambridge University Press, 2017.

5 United Nations, *Convention on the Rights of the Child*. Online. Available at www.ohchr.org/en/professionalinterest/pages/crc.aspx (accessed 14 December 2018).

6 Thomas Hammarberg, "The UN Convention on the Rights of the Child – and How to Make It Work," *Human Rights Quarterly*, 1990, vol. 12, no. 1, 101.

7 Simone Ek, *Självklart barnets rättigheter*, Stockholm: Rädda barnen, 2009, p. 138.

8 For a 1985 discussion of this distinction, see Göran Melander, "International Humanitarian Law and Human Rights," *Scandinavian Studies in Law*, 1985, vol. 29, 137–48.

9 R. R. Baxter, "Humanitarian Law or Humanitarian Politics?" *Harvard International Law Journal*, 1975, vol. 16, 3.
10 René Provost, *International Human Rights and Humanitarian Law*, New York: Cambridge University Press, 2004, pp. 2–3.
11 Baxter, "Humanitarian Law or Humanitarian Politics?" 6.
12 Asbjørn Eide, "Gråsonen mellom krigens rett og menneskerettigheter," *Mennesker og Rettigheter*, 1986, vol. 19, 19–22.
13 Aryeh Neier, *The International Human Rights Movement: A History*, Princeton, NJ: Princeton University Press, 2012, pp. 131, 210.
14 Fiona Ang, "Article 38. Children in Armed Conflicts," in André Alen, Johan Vande Lanotte, Eugeen Verhellen, Fiona Ang, Eva Berghmans, and Mieke Verheyde (eds.) *A Commentary on the United Nations Convention on the Rights of the Child*, Leiden: Martinus Nijhoff, 2005, pp. 3–4, 13.
15 UN Doc. E/CN.4/L.1366/Rev.1 (1978).
16 Adam Lopatka, "Introduction," in United Nations High Commissioner of Human Rights (ed.) *Legislative History of the Convention on the Rights of the Child. Vol. 1*, New York and Geneva: United Nations, 2007, p. 37.
17 Susan Pedersen, "Back to the League of Nations: Review Essay," *American Historical Review*, 2007, vol. 112, no. 4, 1111; Zoe Moody, "Transnational Treaties on Children's Rights: Norm Building and Circulation in the Twentieth Century," *Paedagogica Historica*, 2014, vol. 50, no. 1–2, 155–6.
18 Hilde Reiding, *The Netherlands and the Development of International Human Rights Instruments*, Cambridge, UK: Intersentia, 2007, p. 251.
19 For the full list of answers, see UN Doc. E/CN.4/1324 (1978).
20 UN Doc. E/CN.4/1324 (1978), 27.
21 UN Doc. E/CN.4/1349 (1979).
22 UN Doc. E/CN.4/NGO/265 (1980); UN Doc. E/CN.4/NGO/295 (1981).
23 Rachel Brett, *Snakes and Ladders*, London: Quaker Books, 2012, pp. 24, 49.
24 Rädda Barnen, *Carta Infantium*, Stockholm: Rädda Barnen, 1981, Article IX.
25 Cynthia Price Cohen, "The Role of Nongovernmental Organizations in the Drafting of the Convention on the Rights of the Child," *Human Rights Quarterly*, 1990, vol. 12, no. 1, 147.
26 Cohen, "The Role of Nongovernmental Organizations," 143–4.
27 Rädda Barnen, *Barnen och vi: Rädda barnens årsrapport 1982*, Stockholm: Rädda Barnen, 1983, p. 29.
28 Archives of Rädda Barnen, Stockholm, F1 fd 2, RBI – NGO Committee on UNICEF, 1987–9. Defence for Children International, "Activity Report of the International Secretariat (1986)."
29 Roger Rosenblatt, *Children of War*, Garden City, NY: Anchor Press, 1983.
30 UN Doc. E/CN.4/1983/WG.1/WP.27 (1983).
31 Letter from Valerie Clement to Simone Ek, 27 April 1983. Archives of Defence for Children International, Geneva, PRO-CRC, 1983–84.
32 UN Doc. E/CN.4/1985/WG.1/WP.1 (1985).
33 Ek, *Självklart barnets rättigheter*, p. 127.
34 Letter from Michel Veuthey to Nigel Cantwell, 16 May 1984. Archives of Defence for Children International, Geneva, PRO-CRC, 1983–84.
35 See drafts submitted by Canada and Iran in UN Doc. E/CN.4/1984/71, annex II (1984).
36 Terence Smith, "Iran: Five Years of Fanaticism," *New York Times Magazine*, 12 February 1984.
37 UN Doc. E/CN.4/Sub.3/1983/SR.12 (1983)
38 UN Doc. E/CN. 4/Sub.2/1983/43 (1983), 7; Howard Mann, "International Law and the Child Soldier," *International and Comparative Law Quarterly*, 1987, vol. 36, no. 1, 54.
39 UN Doc. E/CN.4/1984/77 (1984), 72–3.
40 Reiding, *The Netherlands*, pp. 296–7.
41 UN Doc. E/CN.4/1986/39 (1986), 124–45.
42 UN Doc. E/CN.4/1986/39 (1986), annex I.
43 UN Doc. E/CN.4/1987/WG.1/WP.4 (1987), 17.

44 See, e.g., Sarah Singer "La protection des enfants dans les conflits armés," *Revue Internationale de la Croix-Rouge*, 1986, vol. 68, no. 759, 171.
45 International Committee of the Red Cross, *Twenty-Fifth International Conference of the Red Cross, Geneva, 23–31 October 1986. Report*, Berne: Swiss Red Cross, 1987, p. 137.
46 Françoise Krill, "The United Nations Convention on the Rights of the Child and His [*sic*] Protection in Armed Conflict," *Mennesker og Rettigheter*, 1986, vol. 4, no. 3, 39–45.
47 UN Doc. E/CN.4/1987/WG.1/WP.3.
48 Thomas Hammarberg, "Children Shouldn't Pay the Costs of Adults' Wars," *International Herald Tribune*, 23 January 1987.
49 Ek, *Självklart barnets rättigheter*, pp. 132–3; UN Doc. E/CN.4/1987/25 (1987), paragraphs 160–5.
50 Archives of Rädda Barnen, F1 fd 2, RBI – NGO Committee on UNICEF, 1987–9. Report by Working Group on Implementation of UNICEF resolutions related to NGOs, 20 April 1988.
51 Reiding, *The Netherlands*, p. 302.
52 UN Doc. E/CN.4/1989/WG.1/WP.65 (1989)
53 "US Opposes Raising Minimum Combat Age to 18," *New York Times*, 1 December 1988.
54 "Until mankind was able to abolish war," US representative Jean Picker stated in a major 1968 address before the UN General Assembly, "it must take every effort to reduce as far as possible the suffering which accompanied it." UN Doc. A/C.3/L.1634 (1968).
55 Archives of Defence for Children International, Geneva, PRO-CRC, 1987–9. "Protection of Children in Armed Conflict," Excerpt from unnamed ICRC publication, 1989. On the decentralized nature of the Red Cross, see Kimberly Lowe's essay in this volume.
56 Protocol of the Debate of the Working Group, Article 20, 7 December 1988. Archives of the Swedish UN Delegation in Geneva, Stockholm, Vol. F1C:4, HP48, mål 4/3, del 1.
57 Protocol of the Debate of the Working Group, Article 20, 7 December 1988.
58 Reiding, *The Netherlands*, 305.
59 Archives of the Swedish UN Delegation in New York, Stockholm, Vol. F2: a 84–5, HP48, mål K/B, del 71. Letter from Amb. Rönnquist to Swedish UN-delegation, 18 January 1988; Letters from Swedish Embassy, Washington DC, January 1988.
60 Rachel Brett, "Child Soldiers: Law, Politics and Practice," *International Journal of Children's Rights*, 1996, vol. 4, 119.
61 UN Doc. A/51/306 (1996), paras 209–10.
62 UN Doc. A/RES/54/263 (2000).
63 "Clinton Signs International Agreements to Help Protect Children," *New York Times*, 6 July 2000.
64 Karl Hanson, "International Children's Rights and Armed Conflict," *Human Rights and International Legal Discourse*, 2011, vol. 5, 40–63; Mark A. Drumbl, *Reimagining Child Soldiers in International Law and Policy*, New York: Oxford University Press, 2012; David M. Rosen, *Child Soldiers in the Western Imagination: From Patriots to Victims*, New Brunswick, NJ: Rutgers University Press, 2015.
65 Jacqueline Bhabha, *Child Migration and Human Rights in a Global Age*, Princeton, NJ: Princeton University Press, 2014, p. 178.
66 The legal literature on the relationship between human rights and humanitarian law is vast. For a recent overview, see Gerd Oberleitner, *Human Rights in Armed Conflict: Law, Practice, Policy*, New York: Cambridge University Press, 2015.
67 Ruti G. Teitel, *Humanity's Law*, New York: Oxford University Press, 2011.
68 Provost, *International Human Rights and Humanitarian Law*, p. 34.
69 W. E. Hewitt, "Respect for Human Rights in Armed Conflicts," *New York University Journal of International Law and Politics*, 1971, vol. 4, 42.
70 Jay Winter and Antoine Prost, *René Cassin and Human Rights*, New York: Cambridge University Press, 2013, p. 352.
71 O. Frederick Nolde, *Power for Peace*, Philadelphia, PA: Muhlenberg Press, 1946.
72 Varindra Tarzie Vittachi, *Between the Guns*, London: Hodder & Stoughton, 1993, p. 103.
73 Martti Koskenniemi, "Human Rights Mainstreaming as a Strategy for Institutional Power," *Humanity*, 2010, vol. 1 no. 1, 58.
74 Bronwyn Leebaw, "Justice, Charity, or Alibi? Humanitarianism, Human Rights, and 'Humanity Law,'" *Humanity*, 2014, vol. 5, no. 2, 269.

PART III

THE FORMATIVE UN ERA

B. Decolonization

11

"WHY THEN CALL IT THE DECLARATION OF HUMAN RIGHTS?"

The failures of universal human rights in colonial Africa's internationally supervised territories

Meredith Terretta

Rights claims emanating from twentieth-century colonial Africa belong at the center of the resurgence of history-writing from an internationalist perspective, of human rights as a field of historical inquiry, and of the current turn to history in international law. The archival data pertaining to rights claims from mid-twentieth-century Africa shed light on two crucial questions about the history of human rights in Africa. First, how did activists from various imperially dominated territories connect with lawyers trained in metropolitan centers and practicing across empires to influence the debates taking place at the League of Nations and, later, the United Nations (UN)?[1] Second, how did activists in non-self-governing territories – whether mandates, colonies, trusteeships, or protectorates – leverage multiples systems of law to claim their collective or individual rights and advance arguments against foreign rule? This essay probes these questions by analyzing historical evidence in petitions to the League of Nations and UN and in administrative and nongovernmental organization (NGO) archives. It presents Africa's League of Nations mandate territories and UN Trust Territories as pivotal sites for the conception, definition, and grassroots popularization of claiming rights and articulating legal arguments against colonialism, from the interwar period through the postwar period. It considers the practice of rights-claiming as feeding universal human rights as an ideal. The essay's aim is to understand the ways that Africans residing far away from Geneva and New York engaged with evolving metropolitan, territorial, and international systems of law to articulate rights claims in legal terms and broadcast them on a world stage.

My historical approach to understanding rights claims in colonial-era Africa reorders an assumed and fallacious causality characterizing human rights scholarship. Human rights historian Steven L. B. Jensen, for instance, argues that human rights first had to become a recognized "international language" and then legally binding standards in international law before they could be broadcast through activism, institutional infrastructure, and policy.[2] However, the empirical data referenced in this essay demonstrate that activism preceded a universal language of rights, international law, and the emergence of an institutional infrastructure supporting human rights. In colonial and imperial settings, long before the Universal Declaration of Human Rights (UDHR) and the Covenants that made that Declaration implementable and enforceable in international law, rights claimants, activists, and their advocates viewed colonialism – which made it legal to assign colonial subjects fewer rights than metropolitan citizens – as a primary cause of twentieth-century rightlessness. The evidence in petitions, colonial surveillance records, correspondence, league and associations' archives, lawyers' case files, and oral interviews demonstrates that from the early twentieth century, colonial subjects found ways to claim basic rights in situations where, legally, they had few to none. In so doing, they contested colonialism on legal grounds even when they lacked the political right to do so.

Rights activism issuing from Africa from about the 1920s and into the 1970s varied from one colonial setting to another and evolved from one decade to the next. Despite its contingent variability, it comprised a formula of common elements. First, claimants and their advocates formed networks that crossed imperial boundaries and within which European and African activists converged. Second, activists and their advocates leveraged colonial law, customary law, metropolitan law, and international law in the legally plural colonial settings where they practiced in order to advance their claims in multiple jurisdictions ranging from the local to the international.[3] The formula of rights activism worked most effectively to challenge imperial authority in those territories where jurisdictional status mitigated a colonial power's sovereignty, as in the cases of internationally mandated and trusteeship territories.

Legalism in Africa's internationally mandated territories

In colonies, foreign rulers claimed possession of a territory and brought it under total administrative and political control on behalf of a faraway imperial center.[4] Nineteenth- and twentieth-century international law and its less standardized precursor, *jus gentium*, recognized the sovereignty of the colonizing power over the territory. However, after World War I, the League of Nations established a new international system to monitor the recognized administering authorities of mandate territories in Africa, the Middle East, and Oceania that the Germans, the Ottomans, and the Japanese lost to Allied powers during the war.[5] The League's Permanent Mandates Commission convened regularly to ensure the protection of the 14 mandate territories, 8 of which were in Africa, which they sought to do by promoting open-door trade policies and preventing settler colonialism (with the exception of British administered Palestine). The Permanent Mandates Commission further aimed to abolish forced labor, military conscription, slavery, and corporal punishment.[6]

Despite these gestures towards reform, many critics of empire viewed the mandates system of the League of Nations as cover for an internationally justified expansion of great power imperialism. Caribbean Pan-Africanist and anti-imperialist thinker George Padmore even called it a "huge fraud" masking imperial annexation.[7] Where administering authorities ignored League of Nations principles, petitioners from the mandate territories could address the League of Nations through the colonial office of a given administering authority. Historian Susan Pedersen has read the petitions and the Permanent Mandates Commission's responses to them as resulting in the League's curtailment of imperial powers' legal sovereignty in mandate territories.[8] To rights claimants and their legal advocates in Africa's mandate territories, the shifting legal terrain offered an ideal platform for reclaiming territorial sovereignty, exposing the rights abuses suffered under British, French, Belgian and South African rule, and advancing legal arguments against European rule. These claims cited Article 22 of the League's covenant, which proclaimed that "mandatory governments" would govern mandate territories as "a sacred trust of civilization," and in the best interest of their inhabitants.[9] Mandate agreements set administrative guidelines and listed the responsibilities of governing authorities for each particular territory. Legal historian Natasha Wheatley portrays Palestinian petitioners as deliberately pitting the League's principles against the policies of administering authorities.[10] A similar strategy can be read in petitions issuing from mandate territories in Africa.

Activist lawyers led the way in transmitting the earliest rights claims from colonial Africa. Until World War II, most anticolonialist activist lawyers practicing in Africa came, not from metropolitan Europe, but rather from the Caribbean, Oceania, Asia, or Africa. They integrated political cause and profession, placing their professional and activist networks in the service of their legal clients.[11] They were lawyers from territories under European rule, schooled in metropolitan systems of law, who then set about reforming the law in Africa's colonial territories, mandates, and protectorates. With the populations they represented, they articulated legal arguments against colonialism, its arbitrariness as an aberration to twentieth-century notions of rule of law, and the judicial irregularities characteristic of colonial governance. Colonial administrators, fearing the tendency of these activist lawyers to agitate as a feature of their legal practice, painted them as rogue lawyers, Garveyists, and communists. French administrators conceived antirevolutionary colonial policies to curtail and to counteract their influence.[12]

Perhaps galvanized by the proliferation of legalism and an increase in political trials that characterized the age, rights claims became prevalent in the interwar period. Often but not always working with activist lawyers, inhabitants of League of Nations mandate territories filed petitions with the Permanent Mandates Commission seated in Geneva. Denouncing racial discrimination and imposed legislation, the petitions expressed grievances against corporal punishment of laborers, made claims for the restoration of traditional nobility titles, and protested unjust taxation or expropriation of land. Some advanced legal arguments for the restoration of their national sovereignty, as did the Duala, a coastal population of French Cameroon who called into question the French right to administer them, given their history as first, a German protectorate, and then, a League of Nations Mandate territory.[13] Petitioners who tapped into interterritorial advocacy networks had greater success in reaching the Permanent Mandates Commission. Guyanese anticolonialist Vincent Ganty's organization, the Defense of Negro Cameroonian Citizens, retained Paris-based Antillean lawyer Maître P. Jean-Baptiste[14] and supported Duala petitioners.

Similarly, in South West Africa, the Rehoboth Basters[15] hired a lawyer to ensure that their protests against South African infringement on their right to self-government reached the League of Nations. They began to petition the League in 1924, two years after the South Africans forcefully crushed the Bondelswart Rebellion of 1922. That South African aggression was committed against inhabitants of a mandate territory whom the League of Nations covenant promised to protect in "sacred trust."[16] In petitions sent over the next years, the Basters approached the League directly to invoke its Covenant and to insist that the international body protect their rights as an "independent people."[17]

Although few cases brought before the League were settled in favor of the claimants, the petitions represent an effort on the part of colonial subjects – whom colonialism mostly excluded from civil, political, and legal rights – to claim political subjectivity as they defined for themselves the rights delineated in League of Nations mandate agreements.[18] Further, such claims signaled a new and growing tendency among populations whom colonial and colonial settler states administered to call for the League's supranational intervention in territorial affairs. In other words, petitions to the League and references to Wilsonian self-determination indicated a spreading awareness that mandate territories had a jurisdictional status different from that of colonies proper. That, in turn, could foster an international awareness of local affairs, no matter how unwanted international attention might be to mandate territory administrators.[19]

Rights claims from colonial Africa during the interwar period did not issue only from mandate territories under international oversight. Indeed, some campaigns for rights expanded within the boundaries for a given empire. For example, in Madagascar, Malagasy war veterans collaborated with Antillean lawyers to launch a campaign claiming French citizenship. They did so after the first African deputy to sit in the French National Assembly, Blaise Diagne of Senegal, lobbied with Antillean deputy Gratien Candace for French African soldiers' access to French citizenship. Their efforts paid off in a decree passed to that effect on 14 January 1918. The Malagasy citizenship movement began as a veterans' rights movement after the war before reaching its peak in a petition and mass rally for collective citizenship for all Malagasies in 1929.[20] The movement failed when its primary leaders were arrested and their publications censored by the French administration. However, its leaders recast it as a call for independence from France as early as 1931.[21]

It is interesting for the human rights historian that many petitioners and agitators, whether Malagasy, African, or Antillean, had held memberships in various local sections of larger associations, such as Leagues and Defense Committees. These included the the League of the Rights of Man (Ligue des Droits de l'Homme, LDH) founded in France in 1898. Africans founded local chapters of the LDH, such as Joseph Deemin of Gabon.[22] The LDH supported a number of petitioners to the League of Nations. From the early twentieth century, the LDH assisted at times those claiming French citizenship or protesting the abuses of the *indigénat*, the legal code of exception applied to colonial subjects. Another important rights association in this period was the League of the Defense of the Negro Race, founded by Tiemoko Kouyate. Kouyate not only sought to mobilize local chapters throughout Africa, but was also in correspondence with activists throughout Europe and the United States, including Roger Baldwin, a key founder of the American Civil Liberties Union (ACLU), and W. E. B. Du Bois, the Pan-Africanist anticolonialist who, in 1900, declared the color line to be the problem of the twentieth century.[23] The ideas that Kouyate shared with Du Bois about the importance of building transatlantic connections reached beyond race to the notion of international equality: "We are very attached to the very humane ideal of fraternal harmony and collaboration between the races. But we believe that this ideal is conditional on our national liberty and international equality."[24]

In British Africa, an emergent African elite contested colonial expropriation of land. While local courts and imperial courts of appeal most often ruled in favor of colonial interests, in such cases apparently privileging "customary communal rights" over individual property rights, the Judicial Committee of the Privy Council, an institution that existed before, during, and after the League of Nations, overturned these rulings, as in the Apapa Land Case of 1921 in Lagos, Nigeria.[25] In the wake of the Privy Council's ruling that the colonial government of Nigeria was to compensate the Apapa community of Lagos in full for the government's compulsory acquisition of land that the Apapa claimed as rightfully theirs, the indigenous elite came to view the Privy Council as a custodian of African liberties.[26]

As the interwar years progressed, African lawyers appealed to both the Privy Council and the court of public opinion to defend the standing of traditional authorities vis-à-vis the colonial government, as in the case of Chief Eshugbayi Eleko, paramount ruler of Lagos.[27] The colonial government of Nigeria had first suspended, then deposed and ordered the deportation of Chief Eleko for having refused to implement a new tax in 1915, for having independently made political appointments in 1919, and for having refused to apologize for statements made by African journalist Herbert Macaulay in London regarding the Apapa land case before Privy Council.[28] Chief Eleko's lawyers, Eric Moore and J. Egerton-Shyngle, petitioned the Supreme Court in 1926 for a writ of habeas corpus to overturn the chief's deportation. The Supreme Court dismissed the appeal and Chief Eleko's lawyers appealed to the Privy Council, which upheld the chief's right to apply for a writ of habeas corpus. Again, the Nigerian courts tied the chief's appeals up in procedure until his lawyers again appealed to the Privy Council in 1931. The Privy Council ruled in favor of the chief's right to habeas corpus and further specified how the Nigerian courts were to hear the case resulting in what historian Bonny Ibhawoh categorizes as a clear "indictment of both the Nigerian government and judiciary."[29] Chief Eleko's deportation case was only resolved when the British governor appointed to Nigeria in 1931 decided to stop pursuing it in the courts and withdrew the deportation order against Chief Eleko. The protracted legal battle received abundant coverage in British West African newspapers and Macaulay succeeded in rallying a few British members of parliament to the chief's cause. Like the Apapa land case that preceded it, Chief Eleko's deportation case offered a compelling illustration to West Africans that British rule in the colonies could be legally contested before the Privy Council as a strategy of reclaiming expropriated land.

Whether through claiming self-determination, compensation, or a writ of habeas corpus, African and Africa-descended elite modeled strategies of claiming rights both at home and in metropolitan and international political arenas. In the interwar period the components of early rights activism included long-distance advocacy reaching from colonial territories to metropolitan or international centers of governance, the involvement of activist lawyers who instrumentalized the law to change the status quo, public opinion campaigns launched through the press, and the use of petition or appeal in lieu of political processes such voting, or political party membership. Thinking historically about these components of rights activism enables us to read them as precursors to the 1948 expression of rights as the UDHR.

Comparative literature scholar Lydia Liu reviewed the debates and conceptual differences among authors of the UDHR, and locates a contradiction between the articulation of universal human rights as a document in 1948 and the classical nineteenth-century standard of civilization in international law. There was a widespread European assumption that that "standard of civilization" did not apply to colonized populations. Liu argues that it was "shadows of universalism" that gave definition to the nascent concept of universal human rights at the UN.[30] These shadows included the effort to expand the universal beyond its specifically Western conceptual framework undertaken by figures such as P. C. Chang, a Chinese representative to the UN who, with John Humphrey and Eleanor Roosevelt, composed a preliminary draft of an international bill of human rights in 1947. Another shadow was the defeat in the UN General Assembly on 2 November 1950 of the "colonial clause." Britain, France, Belgium, and the Netherlands proposed to exclude colonial and non-self-governing territories from application of the universal human rights covenants under preparation.[31] The following week, Arab, African, and Asian states unanimously supported a draft resolution to include self-determination as a human right in those universal human rights covenants. The draft resolution helped lead to the defeat of the colonial clause. Nevertheless, colonial powers continued to exclude their subjects from human rights protections until after empire's end.[32] The colonial powers' reluctance to apply human rights universally was a major reason why the legally binding Human Rights Covenants were not adopted until 1966. Liu refutes the revisionist human rights historians' conviction that "anticolonialism wasn't a human rights movement,"[33] writing that such a position could only derive from "a disavowal of universalism as a political problem in human rights" at the time of the Declaration's adoption "rather than from any meaningful corroboration by the events on the ground between 1945 and 1950."[34]

Historical discussions of the tensions among universal human rights, colonialism and self-determination, such as Lydia Liu's and Samuel Moyn's, focus most often on the period after World War II. Yet, as the previous section of this essay showed, colonial subjects experienced colonialism as generative of racially ordered rights abuses long before the postwar conception of the UDHR. Even before the UN launched political discussions about universal human rights in the late 1940s and 1950s, many activists, advocates, claimants, and petitioners advancing rights claims in twentieth-century Africa understood the contradiction between the laws regulating rights in colonial settings and the notion of a common or a universal humanity. Legal scholar Martti Koskenniemi explains how law historically structured the forms of government that Europeans imposed on non-European territories and their inhabitants during four centuries of conquest and settlement. The hybridity of colonial law – made up of international law (public law) and domestic, administrative law – served to protect colonial rule from being held to international criteria.[35] This, in turn, enabled colonial powers to treat colonial populations by standards that were different from those applied to citizens of the colonizing country. By the nineteenth century, as international law began to achieve normative power, empire's legal standard stripped subject populations of political and civil rights and categorically excluded them from the political structures governing them. Colonial subjects were rightless in the way that Hannah Arendt, who examined the paradox of universal rights in her early postwar works, described the stateless flooding Europe after the war: They lacked the civil and political rights that were "supposed to embody and spell out in the form of tangible laws the eternal Rights of Man."[36] Although Arendt, like most European thinkers at the time, did not consider colonial populations stateless, they posed a quandary for universal human rights in the same terms that she outlined for Europe's refugees. The widespread European assumption that the concept of human rights did not apply to colonized populations actually underscored Arendt's insistence that "independent of citizenship and nationality,"[37] the notion of inalienable rights was meaningless.

Five years before Arendt published her seminal piece "'The Rights of Man': What are They?"[38] W. E. B. Du Bois arrived at the political problems of the concept of the universal by focusing on not the displaced refugees in Europe, but rather those subject to racial hierarchies in governance within the states to which they ostensibly belonged as second-class citizens. Du Bois' correspondence in 1944 and 1945 reveals his understanding of colonialism as a world system underwriting legally sanctioned racial discrimination in the Allied, "United" nations' systems of governance and his realization that many white and Jewish human rights thinkers at the time remained blind to the human rights dilemma that racial segregation and racially contingent legal rights presented. In October 1944, as lobbyists prepared the road to the San Francisco signing of the UN Charter, Du Bois received a letter from Judge Joseph Proskauer of the American Jewish Committee asking him to add his signature to the committee's draft of a "Declaration of Human Rights." Proskauer wrote, "On the eve of liberation, we feel a particular urgency for all men of peace and goodwill to emphasize and reaffirm the godly concept of the dignity of the individual man."[39] Proskauer imagined Du Bois would readily sign and return a copy of the Declaration in the self-addressed envelope provided. Du Bois had decried the persecution of Jews in Europe in many of his writings and referred to their systematic extermination as the "supertragedy" of European civilization.[40] But Du Bois did not sign. Instead, he responded by explaining how Proskauer's declaration fell short:

> Under paragraph five you appeal for sympathy for persons driven from the land of their birth; but how about American Negroes, Africans, and Indians who have not been driven from their land of birth but are nonetheless deprived of their rights? Under paragraph six you want redress for those who wander the earth but how about those who do not wander and nevertheless are deprived of their fundamental human rights? In other words, this declaration of rights has apparently no thought of the rights of Negroes, Indians and South Sea Islanders. Why then call it the declaration of human rights?[41]

Soon after his response to Proskauer, Du Bois prepared a proposal for the UN Conference in San Francisco. In it, he stated that "the first statute of international law" should read:

> The colonial system of government, however deeply rooted in history and custom, is today undemocratic, socially dangerous, and a main cause of wars [and] at the earliest practice moment no nation or group shall be deprived of effective voice in its own government and enjoyment of the four freedoms.[42]

Du Bois focused on colonialism, rather than statelessness, as a cause of rightlessness. So too did the activists and their advocates, who, decades before 1948, had formed strategic networks to claim rights for themselves and others as the previous section of this essay shows. Rights activism continued after the legally binding UN Trusteeship Agreements were signed into law in territories under UN supervision, 7 out of 11 of which were located in Africa, and trust territory inhabitants claimed human rights in ways that exposed racism as the structuring feature of European administration of Africans.

Universal human rights claims from Africa's UN trust territories

After World War II, the UN replaced the League of Nations and the mandates became trust territories. The primary architect of the UN trusteeship system, the African American statesman Ralph Bunche, conceived significant changes to the League's mandate system. Bunche was informed by his doctoral research for a PhD in political science at Harvard University in the late 1920s and early 1930s.[43] Having compared the French colony of Dahomey with the neighboring mandate territory of French Togo, Bunche found that despite the difference in jurisdictional status, the social, economic, and political conditions for inhabitants of the two territories were nearly identical.[44]

To deliver on the promise of self-governance, Bunche ushered procedural changes into the UN trusteeship system. These changes required administering authorities to prepare trusteeships for self-governance, ensured direct communication between trust territory inhabitants and the UN Trusteeship Council, and increased supranational oversight.[45] In Article 76, the UN Charter specified that trust territories were to become self-governing and that legally binding Trusteeship Agreements spelling out how administering authorities would facilitate self-determination were to be signed and ratified in due haste. In order to enable petitioners' direct access to the UN, petitions could now be sent directly to the Trusteeship Council in any language rather than, as the League had required, in the language of the administering authority. Responsibility for translating henceforth fell upon the UN. Petitioners could now travel to New York to address orally the UN Trusteeship Council and the Fourth Committee of the General Assembly. Every three years, beginning in 1948, UN Visiting Missions inspected conditions on the ground and distributed copies, in local languages, of the UDHR, the trusteeship agreements and the UN Charter. As a result of these changes, trust territory inhabitants became the first in the world accorded the right to petition the UN directly. They did so to denounce injustices and administrators' violations of the UN Charter and Trusteeship Agreements.[46] The trusteeship system thus offered even more opportunity for rights claimants and their advocates to expose the injustices of imperial rule, at the same time that the UN gave expression to the concept of universal human rights.

Given Ralph Bunche's role in reforming the international supervisory system prevailing in the UN trust territories, it is perhaps not coincidental that the first oral petitioner to address the UN, Sylvanus Olympio, was from French Togo – the site of Bunche's interwar PhD research. When limited political rights began to be conferred to African elite subjects of British and French rule, Olympio emerged as the leader of the nationalist Committee of Togolese Unity, and at Togolese independence in 1960 he became the first president of the independent Republic of Togo.

Although their voices were prominent at the UN, political leaders were not the only trust territory inhabitants to make use of the world's first international petitioning system. Thousands wrote from Africa's seven UN trust territories, calling for an end to racial discrimination in commerce, education, the development of infrastructure, and access to land. Others used the petitioning process to reclaim the lands of which they had been dispossessed. More still complained of the administering authorities' suppression of the civil and political liberties – freedom of speech, freedom of assembly, free mobility, and the right to fair justice and legal defense – that the legally binding UN Trusteeship Agreements and the UN Charter specifically conferred on trust territory inhabitants whom the governing administrations were obliged, by international law, to prepare for self-determination. The petitions comprise a voluminous documentary corpus, but the following paragraphs provide examples of the characteristics of claims from inhabitants of the various African trusteeships.

Racial discrimination

From the perspective of a number of petitioners, racial discrimination was a major obstacle to the administering authorities' proper implementation of the rights and principles defined in the UN Charter and the Trusteeship Agreements. The racism of colonial policies permeated civil rights, commerce, education, land ownership, distribution, and usufruct, and undergirded racially hierarchized economic inequalities in the trust territories.

In 1948, Ahmed Ishak, a Muslim of Pakistani origin, told the UN Visiting Mission at Usumbura that Belgian administrators enforced the segregation of Asian and African Muslims on feast days.[47] In 1949, the Women's Committee of the Union of the Populations of Cameroon (UPC) denounced policies of racial discrimination that affected the daily lives of Cameroonian women, who "have no right to get served ... before white women and their servants in the shops."[48] Tanganyikan petitioners belonging to the Government Employees Association directly referenced the UDHR in claiming a "decent wage" for "equal work," thus implying that racial discrimination oriented remuneration in the territory, contra trusteeship principles.[49]

Other petitioners took up the issue of education. The Women's Committee of the UPC stated, in 1949, that the "lack of education constitutes a serious obstacle to the prospects" of women taking "part in the work of emancipating our country."[50] When the Union of the Democratic Women of Cameroon (UDEFEC), the women's party affiliated with the UPC, formed in 1952, the first petition on record stated that the lack of schools in the territory of French Cameroon caused over half the children of school age to go without schooling.[51] In 1954, Marthe Penda insisted that an education curriculum that included "subjects relating to our country, language, history, and dances" must be designed to replace one that taught children only "the history of distant countries so that a child who can recite details of the map of France does not know the name of a river flowing through his own village."[52] Writing from Kampala, Uganda in 1955, Augustine Mutabaruka addressed the Trusteeship Council to deplore the lack of educational opportunities for non-Catholic children in the territory of Ruanda-Urundi. His parents had found themselves obliged to send him to the neighboring protectorate of Uganda to complete secondary school. Mutabaruka expressed dismay that, unlike in Uganda and Tanganyika, where students obtained scholarships, not a single student from Ruanda-Urundi had ever been sent to study overseas. He found that "the absence of highly educated people has kept our country lagging behind our neighbouring countries in progress."[53]

Many petitioners stressed obstacles to economic equality posed by a lack of development. The people of Babimbi, a region only 70 kilometers from the major port city of Douala in French Cameroon, wrote to the UN in September 1954, just days after a ferry capsized while crossing the Sanaga river from Songmbengu to Sakbayeme – the sole route connecting them to Douala – causing 50 casualties.[54] The petition criticized the lack of infrastructure that had already led to accidents on the Sanaga in 1936, 1948, and 1952. The lack of roads, hospitals, and schools indicated the French administration's negligence and misuse of people's taxes.[55] Further, Babimbi's infrastructural isolation caused the region to stagnate in comparison with regions east and west of it.[56]

In the same vein of racial discrimination's impact on economic rights, petitioners homed in on the economic inequalities that the colonial system imposed on trust territory inhabitants. A group of women bread sellers from French Togo wrote to expose the privileges the French administration accorded to French bakers in the territory: "They have obtained lower price for flour from the government, which allows them to sell their bread more inexpensively. Since we do not benefit from this favour, our merchandise goes unsold." They asked the UN to put a stop to the price fixing and added that "Our Togo is a country under trusteeship and we desire our independence."[57]

Writing in 1948 to expose the white privilege underwritten by the Belgian administration in the trust territory of Ruanda-Urundi, François Rukeba of Cyato Hill, Shangugu Territory and president of the Rwanda National Union (UNAR),[58] protested against policies that prevented African inhabitants from freely participating in commerce; rendered credit accessible only to whites, Arabs, and Indians; prohibited African merchants from opening shops in European trading centers; and privileged European investment in land while withholding authorization from Africans to purchase and exploit their land.[59] Five years later, on 30 October 1953, the words of Abdullahi Issa, representative of the Somali Youth League, which were addressed to the chairman of the Fourth Committee (Trusteeship Council) at the UN General Assembly's Eighth Session, echoed Rukeba's concerns. Issa described the Italian administration's discriminatory policies that subsidized Italian commercial activity and excluded Somalis. Issa requested credit facilities for Somalis in urban areas involved in fishing and small business (retail, grocery markets, coffee shops, trucking, and transport). Specifically, Issa urged "that Somali traders be given the same opportunities as the non-Somalis who are entitled to receive loans and other credit facilities from the local banks."[60]

Reclaiming expropriated lands

Inhabitants of UN trusteeships seized the opportunity afforded by petitioning to attempt to right the European expropriation of land that they deemed unjust. In 1948 the Chagga Council of Chiefs in Tanganyika forwarded a request for the government to hand back all "alienated lands *gratis*."[61] Rukeba's 1948 petition, mentioned above and written in kiSwahili, contained a series of questions that were especially prescient regarding the question of landholding for the purpose of mining the mineral-rich soils of Rwanda:

> Why are Europeans who want to buy land authorized to occupy such land, and thus to compel the occupants to leave their land and seek another? The natives cannot buy back lands sold to Europeans where there are deposits of gold, cassiterite [*sic*], sand or clay for brick-making; if the Europeans looking for land and mines increase in number and the natives have no right to refuse to give up their land to them, where shall we go? The number of Europeans in the country is increasing, and we do not know how many will be authorized to settle in Ruanda.[62]

In 1951, a group of Somali farmers at Goluen, petitioned the UN Advisory Council of Somalia to claim that an Italian settler with the "help of the authorities has wrongfully taken possession of our agricultural farms which we inherited from our fathers and which were cultivated by our ancestors and by ourselves and of which we were the lawful possessors."[63] The petitioners added another alarming claim: "When we apply to the authorities of Merca for justice, we are threatened and sometimes imprisoned," and that "the people of Goluen were … struggling for their rights." In the petitioners' words, "the administering authorities are endeavouring to despoil our rights in favour of Italians," and they asked the UN advisory council to "examine our complaint with spirit of humanity."[64]

The issue of unjust land expropriation gained the Trusteeship Council's full attention with a case that some 3,000 displaced Meru inhabitants of Tanganyika brought before the UN in 1952 with the Bermudan-born lawyer Earle Edward Seaton as their legal representative. Seaton, appearing before the Trusteeship Council with Kirilo Japhet, secretary of the Arusha Branch of the Tanganyika African Association (TAA), argued that their displacement was a violation of the legally binding Trusteeship Agreement that the British had signed with the UN.[65] Although the British government upheld the displacement and advised Meru farmers to accept the compensation offered to them rather than demand the return of their land, the case spread public awareness of the significance of the jurisdictional status of trusteeship as one affording inhabitants the right to be heard on the UN's supranational stage, and one requiring administering authorities to account for the grievances that petitioners brought before it.

Although claims to retrieve rightful ownership of alienated land were often made collectively, the individual claim sent by Mrs. Lydia Dopo, a cultivator and widow based in the Mungo region of French Cameroon, exposed the French administrators' transgression of trusteeship terms and showed the administration's failure to respect individual property rights:

> On 12 February 1954, a European Official of the Water and Forestry Service asked me to ... show him the boundaries of my plantation ... He refused to accept the boundaries I showed him, and ... he cut off a large part of my plantation, which was under cultivation, for classification in the private domain. From time to time this European Official ... tells me that he will send me to prison ... *if I persist in claiming my rights.*[66]

Civil and political liberties

Many petitioners requested greater protection of civil and political liberties essential to democratic political processes. The Central Committee of the Somali Youth League (SYL) subtitled a section of a petition sent on 21 April 1951 "Discrimination, 'Divide and Rule' and Lack of Human Rights." The petition stated that although "the Italian Administration has accepted, as a standard of achievement for the Territory, the Universal Declaration of Human Rights," Italian police routinely arrested Somalis in general and SYL supporters in particular.[67] In custody "they undergo unhuman [*sic*] ill-treatments and are – in most of the cases – released after a detention of weeks or even months without being informed of the reasons of their arrest."[68] Another petition, prepared by leaders of JUVENTO, a youth party in French Togo and sent in January 1953, began this way:

> It is with heartfelt regret that we, young Togolese, imbued with the principles listed in the Universal Declaration Human Rights and in the Atlantic Charter, have the honor of submitting to your attention, in chronological order, the abuses and assaults carried out by police agents against the peaceful people of Lomé.[69]

Specific references to the UDHR in conjunction with complaints regarding the administering authorities' violation of civil and political liberties became prevalent in French Cameroon also. Petitioners began to include specific details, such as names, dates, locations, and even the time at which particular rights violations occurred, as though memorializing events in such a way as to compel the UN to respond beyond the usual form of letters citing resolutions passed in the Trusteeship Council or General Assembly. In December 1956, Geneviève Magapgo of French Cameroon wrote: "To be found in possession of a book issued by the UN is regarded as a crime in our Trust Territory" and described the arrest of Mr. Sipoufo Kemga Gaspard "in a train at 4:40 pm on 5 August 1956 by Gérard Prestat, Chief Subdivision Officer of Mbanga."[70]

A number of petitioners addressed judicial irregularities that ran contrary to the Trusteeship Agreements that administering authorities had signed with the UN. Writing from Ruanda-Urundi in 1948, Rukeba expressed his concern regarding the lack of an independent judiciary by questioning whether the *Mwami* (king) should rule the highest court of the land. Once the *Mwami* meted out judgment, Rukeba wrote, there was no further appeal:

> We know that in other countries, both European and African, the king has no judicial functions because that is not his task ... Why is the *Mwami* judge of Rwanda? Justice is not done in the country ... What does a litigant do if he is injured by a decision of the *Mwami*?[71]

In 1951, the Central Committee of the Somali Youth League addressed the lack of an independent judiciary by quoting from Article 7 of the Trusteeship Agreement regulating the administration of Italian Somaliland that stipulated that:

> The Administering Authority shall have full powers of legislation, administration and jurisdiction in the Territory, *subject to the provisions of the Charter of the United Nations, of this Agreement and of the annex attached hereto and shall have power to apply to the territory, TEMPORARILY and with such MODIFICATIONS as are considered necessary, such Italian laws as are APPROPRIATE to the CONDITIONS and NEEDS of the territory and as are not INCOMPATIBLE with the ATTAINMENT of its INDEPENDENCE.*[72]

Article 7 further specified that the administering authority was to "establish a judicial system" and to ensure the "absolute independence of the judiciary."[73] Yet, contrary to the agreement, only the Italian Penal Code was used in the courts of the territory and, in the view of the petitioners, was completely dependent upon the Italian administration and police.

Other petitions took oral narrative forms such as songs, showing that the act of petitioning, once instigated, spread into rural areas where nonliterate populations accessed it with the assistance of local scribes rather than lawyers. In 1956, Chrestine Emachoua, a farmer from Bafang, French Cameroon, sent the following petition to the UN Trusteeship Council:

> Sir: When I left for Bafang with a bundle of wood,
> they beat me and took my wood away from me without reason.
> They did the same when I had a basket of cassava.
> They beat me and took away a basket of cassava meal without reason.
> When I was carrying a basket of macabo, they sent the police, beat me, and took away the macabo.
> When I had a basket of taro, they sent it to the police and it was the same story.
> When I fell sick. I was taken to the dispensary, where I was given no treatment.
> When a woman gives birth at the dispensary, they give the baby an injection to kill it.
> I haven't much to tell you.
> Long live the United Nations!
> Long live a unified and independent
> Cameroons!
> Emachoua Chrestine[74]

Emachoua's petition must have sounded strange to members of the Trusteeship Council, and unlike other petitioners, she did not use the word "rights" although she describes rights violations. The petition succinctly expressed Emachoua's perception of a colonial order that preyed upon her daily existence, robbing her of the fruits of her labor and taking away her means of supporting herself and her family. She suspected that the available medical treatment caused further misfortune. Writing at a time when villagers and pro-independence chiefs in the Bamileke region of French Cameroon were launching a tax boycott, Mrs. Emachoua told of an administration that stripped her of her means of subsistence and offered nothing in return. Her petition denounces an administration taxing her productive labor while threatening reproduction.

Rights claimants in the interwar period relied most often on lawyers to transmit their grievances across long distances to where they would be heard. Activist lawyers were likewise often involved in the formulation of claims in the postwar period. In the early 1950s, French activist lawyer Maître Sylvestre Alcandre of Guadeloupe, who had been a founding lawyer of the African Democratic Rally (*Rassemblement démocratique africain*, RDA),[75] provided legal counsel and representation to JUVENTO, the youth party writing to the UN from Lomé, French Togo.[76] At the very time that Mrs. Dopo was petitioning for the return of her land, Maître Yves Henry Louisia, a French activist lawyer from Martinique, maintained an office near her plantation, in the town of Nkongsamba, French Cameroon.[77] In cases such as that of the displaced Meru farmers who were arguing for the return of their land, lawyers traveled to the UN to represent petitioners. However, as the examples above demonstrate, many trust territory inhabitants also petitioned without legal assistance. Knowingly or not, they benefited from long-distance advocacy networks, particularly that created by the International League of the Rights of Man, which ensured that their petitions did not go unnoticed.

In New York, Roger Baldwin, who had helped found the American Civil Liberties Union at the end of World War I, was now chairman of the International League of the Rights of Man (ILRM). In 1947 the ILRM became the first self-designated human rights NGO to gain consultative status with the UN. It organized support and used Baldwin's associational and UN contacts to lobby the UN on behalf of the trusteeship petitioners. Baldwin viewed the trust territories as the best legal and political opening through which to address the human rights abuses of colonial rule.[78] He encouraged African political leaders to found local sections of the ILRM, just as LDH leaders had done in the interwar period, and he worked with lawyers to ensure the petitioners were able to procure exit permits and visas to travel to New York in order to address the UN. He mobilized existing anticolonial networks such as the UK-based Movement for Colonial Freedom and facilitated the emergence of other such networks, including the American Committee on Africa in the United States. Baldwin and other international advocates learned immeasurably from petitioners about in-territory conditions, local politics, administrators' violations of trusteeship agreements, and how human rights could best be defined to bring about colonialism's demise. Rights claims voiced in the era of Africa's decolonization were comprised of international advocacy, legal activism, an increased use of media to shape public opinion, petitioning, and an engagement with the UN – specifically the UN Charter, the trusteeship agreements, and the UDHR.

The outcome of the petitions that trust territory inhabitants sent to the UN is difficult to measure in contemporary human rights terms. Even at the time, African political leaders had their doubts about the trusteeship system's usefulness in supporting claims and grievances. Speaking as an oral petitioner before the UN, the Cameroonian nationalist leader Ruben Um Nyobé stated that the

> Trusteeship Council, in examining the petitions from populations of these territories, which bring up important problems, limits itself in most cases either to referencing the resolutions previously adopted, or to drawing the petitioners' attention to statements made by the administering authority.[79]

Yet petitioners deliberately voiced rights claims in terms that should have required the UN's intervention, and in some cases did. A UN Advisory Council for Somaliland operated in Italian Somaliland from 1949 to 1958. A plebiscite was held, under the Trusteeship Council's supervision, in British Togoland in 1956, and a UN Commission supervised elections in Togo in 1958. Upon a resolution of the General Assembly, the French government had to produce inventories accounting for every political prisoner in French Cameroon before the Trusteeship could be lifted on 1 January 1960. The UN organized a referendum in British Cameroons in 1961.

Although the immediate and long-term outcome of these supervisory measures remains ambiguous, the archival record shows that human rights became a feature of people's protests against the racially discriminatory policies under mandate and trusteeship administration that structured their daily lives. In joining rights groups such as the Malagasy citizenship campaign, the LDH, or the Defense of Negro Cameroonian Citizens, engaging lawyers to represent their claims as did the Rehoboth Basters of South West Africa, and petitioning the League of Nations and UN, African colonial subjects claimed their "right to have rights."[80] In so doing they claimed their political subjectivity and shaped, however briefly, the evolving definition of universal human rights in the early Cold War period.

Following political theorists Vicki Squire and Jonathan Darling, this archivally researched history analyzes human rights claims issuing from African territories as they emerged at the periphery, far from the New York-based UN, where universal human rights were conceptualized.[81] This essay has emphasized human rights practice over theory, and the stories it has showcased reveal African claims to have rights to be significant insofar as these claims question the definitions and limitations of institutionalized human rights. It also shows how African petitioners highlighted the failure of universal human rights to recognize and denounce racial discrimination as a primary cause of human rights abuses, socioeconomic inequality, and injustice under colonialism.

As the human rights movement became institutionalized in the late 1970s, the rights activism formula examined here changed in significant and paradoxical ways. Although further study of this period must be undertaken to assess the impact on rights activism issuing from Africa of the shift from long-distance networks of activists to the new institutional NGO model, the effects discussed by historian Gregory Mann were undoubtedly paradigmatic in scale and import.[82] Perhaps most significantly, the institutionalization of human rights and humanitarian activism in NGOs based in the global North served to move activism's points of origin from sites on the African continent to the West and North, and to transform it from a counterbalanced collaboration to asymmetrical broadcasting and distribution from North to South.

The institutionalization of human rights activism coincided with the emergence of a human rights movement striving for consensus in the global North. Consensus-seeking rights activists have sought definitive answers to questions that human rights activists across political spectra had debated during previous decades. Collective rights such as calls for self-determination, economic equality, the return of communal lands, infrastructural development, and better education, all of which coexisted with calls for individual rights protections in the trust territory petitions, gave way to a human rights emphasis on individual rights. Political and civil liberties took center stage, crowding out an examination of economic injustices underwritten by racial hierarchies on a geopolitical scale as causes of human rights crises.[83] Personal relationships between in-country activists and their international advocates gave way to Amnesty International's "own-country-rule" forbidding activists to work for political prisoners in their homeland.[84]

Since the publication of Samuel Moyn's *The Last Utopia* in 2010, revisionist historians have spilt a lot of ink about the human rights breakthrough of the late 1970s.[85] Empirically based research on the emergence of rights claims and human rights activism on the African continent leads us to consider that what broke through in the late 1970s was not human rights activism, but rather, the institutionalization of human rights NGOs and human rights as a matter of foreign policy in the global North. Histories of human rights that track outside the Anglo-American global North offer alternative genealogies to the revisionist late 1970s "breakthrough."[86] Arguably the human rights "breakthrough" of the late 1970s signaled a narrowing, rather than a broadening, of understandings of common humanity and of universal human rights. Students and scholars of human rights are in need of a greater historical understanding of the effects of human rights' rapid institutionalization and consensus building on the heterogeneous and contested human rights activist networks that predated them. Following these activists and their advocates into the shadows of today's concept of human rights can reveal parts of their history that may light the way to alternative futures.[87]

Human rights have evolved as historically contingent, as humans grappled with the particular ways they experienced the causes and the perplexities of rightlessness. This essay shows how human rights practices emerged from rights activism in places where people experienced rightlessness as a result of racially hierarchical colonial governance that privileged white Europe-descended settlers over indigenous inhabitants and brown migrants from elsewhere. Historical inquiry enables us to know what continuities, ruptures, struggles, and innovations have been contained in people's experiences of rightlessness, opens these past understandings and practices of human rights to productive reinterpretations, and makes human rights history a potential source of innovation[88] for thinking about the tensions between the universal and the particular that continue to be part of the concept and practice of human rights.

Notes

1 Historians have approached this topic mostly from a top-down internationalist perspective in recent years. See, for example, Susan Pedersen, *The Guardians: The League of Nations and the Crisis of Empire*, New York: Oxford University Press, 2015; Sandrine Kott, "Organizing World Peace. The International Labour Organization from the Second to the Cold War," in Stefan-Ludwig Hoffmann et al. (eds.) *Seeking Peace in the Wake of War: Europe, 1943–1947*, Amsterdam: Amsterdam University Press, 2015, pp. 299–316; and Steven L. B. Jensen, *The Making of International Human Rights: The 1960s, Decolonization, and the Reconstruction of Global Values*, New York: Cambridge University Press, 2016.

2 Jensen, *Making of International Human Rights*, pp. 13–14.

3 Martti Koskenniemi argues that colonial law emerged as a hybrid between "public (international) law and domestic (administrative) law. He emphasizes the haphazard nature of colonial law, which evolved as a system to apply "different laws to different human groups and activities" that were characteristic of the heterogeneous context of imperial peripheries. See his

"Colonial Laws: Sources, Strategies and Lessons?" *Journal of the History of International Law*, 2016, vol. 18, 248–77.

4 Jürgen Osterhammel, *Colonialism: A Theoretical Overview* (Shelley L. Frisch trans.) Princeton, NJ: Markus Wiener, 2005, p. 10.

5 Michael D. Callahan, *Mandates and Empire: The League of Nations and Africa, 1914–1931*, Brighton, UK: Sussex Academic Press, 2008.

6 The authoritative account of the work of the Permanent Mandates Commission is Pedersen, *The Guardians*.

7 Susan Pedersen, "Settler Colonialism at the Bar of the League of Nations," in Caroline Elkins and Susan Pedersen (eds.) *Settler Colonialism in the Twentieth Century*, New York: Routledge, 2005, p. 113.

8 Pedersen, *The Guardians*, pp. 204–88. See also Susan Pedersen, "Samoa on the World Stage: Petitions and Peoples before the Mandates Commission of the League of Nations," *Journal of Imperial and Commonwealth History*, 2012, vol. 40, 231–61.

9 "Covenant of the League of Nations," 1919, Article 22. Online. Available at http://avalon.law.yale.edu/20th_century/leagcov.asp (accessed 2 January 2019).

10 Natasha Wheatley, "Mandatory Interpretation: Legal Hermeneutics and the New International Order in Arab and Jewish Petitions to the League of Nations," *Past and Present*, 2015, vol. 227, no. 1, 205–48.

11 Marcel Willard trained young lawyers in the legal strategies advocating for communist oppositionists and defending trade unionists and workers' rights in the 1930s through the Association Juridique Internationale's political school. Willard credited Lenin with the politico-legal strategy he promoted. See Sylvie Thénault, "Défendre les nationalistes algériens en lutte pour l'indépendance. La 'défense de rupture' en question," *Le Mouvement Social*, 2012, no. 240, 121–35.

12 Meredith Terretta, "'In the Colonies, Black Lives Don't Matter.' Legalism and Rights Claims across the Interwar French Empire," *Journal of Contemporary History*, 2018, vol. 53, 12–37.

13 See Ralph A. Austen and Jonathan Derrick, *Middlemen of the Cameroons Rivers: The Duala and their Hinterland c.1600–c.1960*, Cambridge, UK: Cambridge University Press, 1999, 144–59.

14 Archives nationales d'outre-mer, Aix-en-Provence, France (hereafter ANOM), 3 Slotfom 34, Founding documents, Groupe-Ganty de Défense des Citoyens Nègres Camerounais et Ami des Nègres, Paris, 20 March 1931.

15 Descendants of Khoekhoe and seventeenth-century Dutch settlers at the Cape, the Rehoboth Basters served as intermediaries between indigenous Africans and white settlers in the nineteenth century. German administrators of German South West Africa viewed them as superior and granted them greater privileges relative to other indigenous inhabitants of the territory. Despite this, during World War I Rehoboth Basters refused to comply with German orders to guard South African prisoners of war, provoking a German attack. See Tilman Dedering, "Petitioning Geneva: Transnational Aspects of Protest and Resistance in South West Africa/Namibia after the First World War," *Journal of Southern African Studies*, 2009, vol. 35, 785–801, and George Steinmetz, *The Devil's Handwriting: Precoloniality and the German Colonial State in Quingdao, Samoa and Southwest Africa*, Chicago: University of Chicago Press, 2007, pp. 216–31.

16 For details concerning the League's and others' reactions to the Bondelswart massacre see Dedering, "Petitioning," 792.

17 Petition of Rehoboth Council to Hertzog, 8 November 1924, as quoted in Dedering, "Petitioning," 796. Similar claims to sovereignty issued from populations under colonial rule elsewhere. For instance, in Canada the Iroquois Chief Deskaheh petitioned the League of Nations to admit the Six Iroquois Nations as member states in order to enable the League to mediate the Nations' claims to territory against the Canadian government's position. See Emmanuelle Sibeud, "Entre Geste Impériale et Cause Internationale: Défendre les Indigènes à Genève dans les Années 1920," *Mondes*, 2014, vol. 6, 23–43.

18 On the importance of claiming rights to claim political subjectivity, see Jacques Rancière, "Who Is the Subject of the Rights of Man?" *South Atlantic Quarterly*, 2004, vol. 103, 297–301.

19 On this point as it pertained to Jewish and Arab petitioners of former Ottoman territories see Wheatley, "Mandatory Interpretation," 206.

20 On the movement for citizenship for all Malagasies, see Michael Goebel, *Anti-Imperial Metropolis: Interwar Paris and the Seeds of Third World Nationalism*, Cambridge, UK: Cambridge University Press, 2015, pp. 178–94, and Terretta, "'Black Lives Don't Matter.'"

21 See Jonathan Derrick, *Africa's Agitators: Militant Anti-Colonialism in Africa and the West, 1918–1939*, New York: Oxford University Press, 2008, pp. 235–6.
22 La Contemporaine, formerly Bibliothèque de Documentation Internationale Contemporaine, Nanterre, France (hereafter BDIC), Archives Ligue des Droits de l'Homme, F Delta rés. 0798/90, President of the French League for the Defense of the Rights of Man and the Citizen to the Minister of the Colonies, 3 January 1920; Congo français-Gabon, Deemin Claim, 15 July 1918; Assistant Secretary-General LDH to President LDH, 21 August 1919; Joseph Deemin to President of the LDH, 1 June 1919; Councilor of State, Ministry of Colonies to President of the LDH, 17 April 1920; Claim filed with the Prosecutor of the Republic, Libreville, 3 October 1918. On the LDH in Gabon, see Jeremy Rich, "Gabonese Men for French Decency: The Rise and Fall of the Gabonese Chapter of the Ligue des Droits de l'Homme, 1916–1939," *French Colonial History*, 2012, vol. 13, 23–53.
23 On Roger Baldwin, see Robert Cotrell, *Roger Nash Baldwin and the American Civil Liberties Union*, New York: Columbia University Press, 2000; on the ACLU's interwar evolution, see Laura Weinrib, *The Taming of Free Speech: America's Civil Liberties Compromise*, Cambridge, MA: Harvard University Press, 2016.
24 ANOM, 3 Slotfom 111, Kouyate to W. E. B. Du Bois, 29 April 1929.
25 Bonny Ibhawoh, *Imperial Justice: Africans in Empire's Court*, Oxford: Oxford University Press, 2013, pp. 124–39.
26 Ibhawoh, *Imperial Justice*, p. 141.
27 Ibhawoh, *Imperial Justice*, pp. 139–46.
28 On Macaulay's profession as a journalist in Nigeria, see Wale Adebanwi, "Colonial Modernity and Tradition: Herbert Macaulay, the Newspaper Press and the (Re)Production of Engaged Publics in Colonial Lagos," in Derek Peterson, Steph Newell, and Emma Hunter (eds.) *African Print Cultures*, Ann Arbor: University of Michigan Press, 2016, pp. 125–48.
29 Ibhawoh, *Imperial Justice*, p. 144.
30 Lydia Liu, "Shadows of Universalism: The Untold Story of Human Rights Around 1948," *Critical Inquiry*, 2014, vol. 40, 385–417.
31 On colonial clause debates see Roland Burke, *Decolonization and the Evolution of Human Rights*, Philadelphia: Pennsylvania University Press, 2010, pp. 39–44.
32 On UN debates on self-determination as a human right, see Jensen, *Making of International Human Rights*, pp. 43–4.
33 See Samuel Moyn, *The Last Utopia: Human Rights in History*, Cambridge, MA: Harvard University Press, 2010, pp. 84–119 and Jan Eckel, "Human Rights and Decolonization: New Perspectives and Open Questions," *Humanity: An International Journal of Human Rights, Humanitarianism, and Development*, 2010, vol. 1, 111–35.
34 Liu, "Shadows," 388.
35 Koskenniemi, "Colonial Laws."
36 Hannah Arendt, *The Origins of Totalitarianism*, New York: Mariner Books, 2001, p. 295. Originally published 1951.
37 Arendt, *Origins of Totalitarianism*, p. 295.
38 Hannah Arendt, "'The Rights of Man': What Are They?" *Modern Review*, 1949, vol. 3, 25–37.
39 Proskauer to Du Bois, October 1944, as quoted in Randall Williams, *The Divided World: Human Rights and Its Violence*, Minneapolis: University of Minnesota Press, 2010, p. xiii.
40 Williams, *Divided World*, p. xiii.
41 Du Bois to Proskauer, November 1944, as quoted in Williams, *Divided World*, p. xiii.
42 As quoted in Williams, *Divided World*, p. xiv.
43 On Bunche's role at the UN, see Robert A. Hill and Edmond J. Keller (eds.), *Trustee for the Human Community: Ralph J. Bunche and the Decolonization of Africa*, Athens: Ohio University Press, 2010.
44 On this point as well as for Bunche's role in American international relations, see Robert Vitalis, *White World Order, Black Power Politics: The Birth of American International Relations*, Ithaca, NY: Cornell University Press, 2015, p. 77. On Bunche's contributions to African studies see Pearl Robinson, "Ralph Bunche and African Studies: Reflections on the Politics of Knowledge," *African Studies Review*, 2008, vol. 51, 1–16.

45 On these changes and Bunche's role in overseeing their enactment, see Neta C. Crawford, "Decolonization through Trusteeship: The Legacy of Ralph Bunche," in Hill and Keller, *Trustee*, pp. 93–115.
46 Not until the mid-1960s would the UN institutionalize the reception of human rights complaints for the rest of the world, through its Third Committee. I take up the significance of this genealogy of petitioning the UN in Meredith Terretta, "'We Had Been Fooled into Thinking that the UN Watches Over the Entire World': Human Rights, UN Trust Territories, and Africa's Decolonization," *Human Rights Quarterly*, 2012, vol. 34, 329–60.
47 United Nations, United Nations Dag Hammarskjöld Library, New York City (hereafter UNTC), United Nations Trusteeship Council (UNTC), T/PET.3/3, Ahmed Ishak to the UNTC, 22 July 1948.
48 UNTC, T/PET.4/32, Petition from the Women's Committee of the UPC concerning the Cameroons under French and British administration, 20 November 1949.
49 UNTC, T/PET.2/102, Petition from the Government Employees Association, 10 August 1951.
50 UNTC, T/PET.2/102, Petition from the Government Employees Association, 10 August 1951.
51 UDEFEC, Petition remise à la Mission d'enquête du Conseil de Tutelle en visite au Cameroun, 1 November 1952, Douala. Personal archives of Marie-Irène Ngapeth-Biyong. This petition does not appear in the UNTC records.
52 UNTC, T/PET.5/409, Petition from Marthe Penda, Secretary of the Babimbi branch of UDEFEC, 13 December 1954.
53 UNTC, T/PET.3/83, Augustine Mutabaruka to The President [*sic*], UN, 10 June 1955.
54 UNTC, T/PET.5/322, Petition from the Babimbi People Concerning the Cameroons under French Administration, 29 September 1954.
55 Petition from the Babimbi People Concerning the Cameroons Under French Administration, 29 September 1954.
56 Richard Joseph, *Radical Nationalism in Cameroon: Social Origins of the UPC Rebellion*, Oxford: Clarendon Press, 1977, pp. 111–14, 136–9.
57 UNTC, T/PET.7/344, Petition from Béatrice Coudjoe, President of the Group of Bread Sellers, Lomé, 20 September 1953.
58 The UNAR was an interethnic nationalist movement that rejected collaboration with the Belgian administering authority of Ruanda-Urundi.
59 UNTC, T/PET.3/9, Petition from Francis Rukeba, 3 August 1948.
60 New York Public Library, New York City, International League of the Rights of Man (hereafter ILRM), Box 12, Abdullahi Issa, Representative of the Somali Youth League to the Chairman of the Fourth Committee, UN General Assembly, Eighth Session, 30 October 1953.
61 UNTC, T/PET.2/59, Petition from the Chagga Council of Chiefs, 10 September 1948.
62 UNTC, T/PET.3/9, Petition from Francis Rukeba, 3 August 1948.
63 UNTC, Idris Omar Gude, Mahi Hassa Mohamed, Yunus Hassno Libah of Goluen in the District of Merca to the UN Advisory Council of Somalia, 15 April 1951.
64 Yunus Hassno Libah of Goluen in the District of Merca to the UN Advisory Council of Somalia, 15 April 1951.
65 UNTC, T/PET.2/99, Petition from Munya Lengoroi, Maasa Makyia, M. S. Isak, waMeru Tribe Representatives, 23 August 1951. For the context of the Meru land case at the UN, see Ullrich Lohrmann, *Voices from Tanganyika: Great Britain, the United Nations and the Decolonization of a Trust Territory, 1946–1961*, Berlin: LIT Verlag, 2007, and Thomas Spear, *Mountain Farmers: Moral Economies of Land and Agricultural Development in Arusha and Meru*, Berkeley: University of California Press, 1997, pp. 228–30.
66 UNTC, T/PET.5/400, Copy, Lydia Dopo to the High Commissioner of the French Republic in the Cameroons, 28 February 1954.
67 UNTC, T/PET.11/40, Somali Youth League to the Trusteeship Council, UN, 14 April 1951.
68 Somali Youth League to the Trusteeship Council, UN, 14 April 1951.
69 UNTC, T/Pet.7/325, Copy, President of the JUVENTO National Committee to the Governor of Overseas France, Commissioner of the Republic of Togo, 20 January 1953.
70 UNTC, T/PET.5/L.320, Petition from Mrs. Geneviève Magapgo concerning the Cameroons under French Administration: Magapgo Geneviève, Housewife, Babété, Mbouda, Bamileke

Region, c/o Central Council of UDEFEC, Kumba, Kamerun [*sic*] under British Administration, 3 December 1956.

71 UNTC, T/PET.3/9, Petition from Francis Rukeba, 3 August 1948.

72 UNTC, T/PET.11/40, Somali Youth League to the Trusteeship Council, UN, 14 April 1951. Emphasis and capitalization in the original.

73 Somali Youth League to the Trusteeship Council, UN, 14 April 1951.

74 UNTC, T/PET.5/1112, Petition from Mrs. Chrestine Emachoua concerning the Cameroons under French administration, Baboucha, 13 December 1956.

75 ANOM, 1 AffPol 2263, "Investigation into the African Independence Movement," Secret communiqué to the High Commissioner of Côte-d'Ivoire, 21 October 1946.

76 Archives Départementales de la Seine-Saint-Denis, Bobigny, France, Kaldor Papers, Box 27. These papers were not yet cataloged at the time that I researched them. Therefore the reference is subject to change.

77 Louisia was expelled from the territory in October 1957. See ANOM, 1 Affpol 3283/2, High Commissioner of the French Republic of Cameroon to Minister of Overseas France, 25 October 1957 and Pierre Messmer to Maître Meignie, President of the National Association of Lawyers, Paris, 28 January 1958.

78 See Terretta, "'We Had Been Fooled.'"

79 Ruben Um Nyobé, "Objectifs immédiats du mouvement national camerounais," in Joseph-Achille Mbembe (ed.) *Le problème national kamerunais*, Paris: L'Harmattan, 1984, p. 111.

80 Arendt, "'The Rights of Man.'"

81 Squire and Darling consider how the political practices of sanctuary contest the limits of citizenship, and posit those practices as politically significant for the ways they contest rights institutionalized and conferred by states and expose the injustices that citizenship involves. Vicki Squire and Jonathan Darling, "The 'Minor' Politics of Rightful Presence: Justice and Relationality in *City of Sanctuary*," *International Political Sociology*, 2013, vol. 7, 59–74, 65.

82 A regionally focused historical analysis of this shift can be found in Gregory Mann, *From Empires to NGOs in the West African Sahel*, Cambridge, UK: Cambridge University Press, 2015.

83 On the dialectical tension between "the global equality of individuals and the global equality of races" that was present as universal human rights were expressed in the UDHR, see Siep Stuurman, *The Invention of Humanity: Equality and Cultural Difference in World History*, Cambridge, MA: Harvard University Press, 2017, p. 487.

84 Stephen Hopgood, *Keepers of the Flame: Understanding Amnesty International*, Ithaca, NY: Cornell University Press, 2013, pp. 97–101.

85 Moyn, *Last Utopia*; Jan Eckel and Samuel Moyn (eds.), *The Breakthrough: Human Rights in the 1970s*, Philadelphia: Pennsylvania University Press, 2014; Sarah B. Snyder, *Human Rights Activism and the End of the Cold War: A Transnational History of the Helsinki Network*, New York: Cambridge University Press, 2011.

86 See, among others, Jensen, *Making of International Human Rights*; Bonny Ibhawoh, *Imperialism and Human Rights: Colonial Discourses of Rights and Liberties in African History*, Albany, SUNY Press, 2008; Luis van Isschot, *The Social Origins of Human Rights: Protesting Political Violence in Colombia's Oil Capital, 1919–2010*, Madison: University of Wisconsin Press, 2015; Keith David Watenpaugh, *Bread from Stones: The Middle East and the Making of Modern Humanitarianism*, Berkeley: University of California Press, 2015; and Liu, "Shadows."

87 Ben Golder, "Beyond Redemption? Problematising the Critique of Human Rights in Contemporary International Thought," *London Review of International Law*, 2014, vol. 2, 1–38.

88 On human rights history as a source of innovation, see Robert Brier, "Beyond the Quest for a 'Breakthrough': Reflections on the Recent Historiography on Human Rights," in Sarah Panter (ed.) *Mobility and Biography*, Berlin: De Gruyter, 2015, pp. 155–74, 173.

12

DECOLONIZATION, DEVELOPMENT, AND IDENTITY

The evolution of the anticolonial human rights critique, 1948–78

Roland Burke

Almost four decades after publication of arguably the most forthright postcolonial broadside against universal human rights, *Human Rights: Cultural and Ideological Perspectives*, this strand of human rights critique remains a phenomenon only weakly historicized.[1] The 1979 collection prepared by American scholars Adamantia Pollis and Peter Schwab sparked much debate. Very little of it has been historical.[2] Philosophical, anthropological, and social scientific contests about the validity of postcolonial arguments against universal human rights are abundant, and now represent a durable feature of rights scholarship.[3] Yet the origins, provenance, and evolution of the various types of dissent to universal human rights have been, for the most part, neglected in these works, invoked only insofar as they are aligned to present day disquisitions on universalism.

Whatever the merits of these postcolonial arguments in the abstract, they sit uneasily with the course of anti-imperialism as it was enacted on the ground. In the peak years of the anticolonial movement, human rights were embraced as a language integral to opposing empire. Liberal nationalist movements that, in the late 1940s through early 1960s, were the principal force for decolonization, saw their own aspirations in the precepts of the 1948 Universal Declaration of Human Rights (UDHR). Universalistic, promising the full swathe of freedoms – civil and political, economic and social – human rights were at once the answer to patronizing imperial claims of civilizational tutelage, the foremost weapon against colonial authoritarianism, and the most fundamental rejoinder to racial discrimination.

For around a decade, harmony prevailed between anticolonial nationalism and the form of human rights enunciated in the postwar period, which presumed the properly constituted sovereign state as the premier guarantor of freedom. If anything, the main dissenters to the incipient global human rights order were the European imperial powers, who guarded their own sovereign prerogative across overseas territories, and in a more elemental sense, the moral legitimacy of colonial rule. The dissolution of this alliance between human rights and anti-imperialism has complex origins, and the strain was evident by 1958. Initially, these anticolonial critiques were limited in extent, and only episodically florid in expression. Nevertheless, by the mid-1960s, human rights, as they were understood in the late 1940s and early 1950s, were the subject of growing skepticism and even outright hostility from post-independence governments and a number of African, Asian, Arab, and Western intellectuals. Emphatic on the urgency of national mobilizations, the equilibrium between individual and state agreed at in 1948 no longer seemed sufficient for many in this later generation of anticolonial voices.

With the radical expansion of the human rights nongovernmental organization (NGO) movement in the 1970s, with its center of gravity firmly within the political West, anticolonialism and the new transnational human rights movement drew further apart. Human rights NGOs that ascended to prominence in this breakthrough moment, Amnesty and Human Rights Watch in particular, championed a quite different interpretation of human rights even to that posited in 1948. Their "human rights" were avowedly anti-statist in inflexion – at precisely the moment when strengthening the state was the priority concern of the Third World. Stung by the more confrontational style of the 1970s NGOs, post-independence governments began to issue strident defensive critique to specific, condemnatory NGO reports, notably those from Amnesty International.[4] Alongside the usual dissembling characteristic of most governments indicted by an NGO denunciation, Third World states now began to repudiate key elements of universalism, and advanced subversive, particularistic schemes of regional, religious, and traditionalist redefinition. In their rejections of NGO scrutiny, Third World governments denounced the authority of Western activists, which formed much of the early transnational human rights movement. Yet these states – and numerous others, notably apartheid South Africa – went further than debating substantive merit of NGO criticisms: they began to attack those concepts of universality, indivisibility, and inherence, the very features that had subtended the power of human rights as an anti-imperial discourse. In the rhetoric of many postcolonial regimes, human rights scrutiny was increasingly dismissed as a new mode of imperialism.

This essay will survey and contextualize this overlooked transformation and characterize the features of the dissents that emerged from the Third World. The majority of its attention is on the emergence and growing acceptance of pleas for a temporary exception – an allowance for the exigencies of development, which were often an extension of imperial pleas for gradualism. These calls, which had once been treated – properly – with scorn when recited by British and French legations – were the first wave of anticolonial arguments against universality in the mid-to-late 1950s advanced by new national leaders. By the later 1960s, these arguments for a caveated and deferred universality had migrated to the center of international human rights conversation. Invoking very real imperatives for economic development, this wave of critique opened the first major, sustained breach in the conceptual foundation of the UDHR. Tension between state mobilization for material well-being, and individual civil and political freedoms, was a latent site of rupture from the late 1940s. Differences in capacity between the developed and underdeveloped had been raised repeatedly during the formulation of the UDHR, and a principal factor in the division of the human rights covenant that followed it. Given the scope and expense of the rights envisaged, much of this represented a realistic engagement with the challenge.

However, the radicalization of these arguments, typically from the wave of repressive rulers that arrived after the first hopeful moment of independence, turned good faith recognition of a problem into a bold dismissal of universal human rights in any practical sense. Conditions themselves also altered the terrain of the debate – the sheer duration of the Third World's economic misery obscured any appreciable difference between transient and reluctant variation of an accepted norm – and transmuted into a permanent assertion of essential difference. The later accretion of cultural and traditionalist identity particularism, which were grafted on to the original core of developmental claims, further foreclosed the sweeping universality of 1948.

The essay argues that the divergence between anticolonialism and human rights was mutual – the former changed dramatically in character, and the latter acquired a narrower set of emphases in the 1970s. While there were doubtlessly areas of radical transformation that cut across this dynamic, exemplified by a revivified international women's rights movement, the most prominent human rights NGOs had built much of their campaign on a sparing set of priority concerns. Their human rights minimalism – which devoted much effort to the most primordial subjects, torture and extra-judicial killing – was a language of limited capacity to inspire. The more radical transformations envisaged in the 1940s and 1950s, of economic sovereignty, the welfare state, and a redistribution of global power, which had been at least part of the appeal of human rights for anticolonial movements, were much less readily set in this new architecture. A logic of the least worst, and the most that could be hoped, which often seemed a breviary of the philosophy under which groups like Amnesty International operated, was a world away from revolutionary promises of a New International Economic Order.[5] This conflict produced a deep confusion in the language, and an erosion of its normative power, as numerous hostile species of human rights proliferated.[6] Human rights, for a substantial bloc of postcolonial states, became commingled with another project, the augmentation and development of their own states, and a repartitioning of global economic power along more equitable lines. For many Western NGOs, the state, once recognized as a vital pillar for realizing an ambitious vision of human rights, was recast as the prime enemy of a much more austere set of freedoms.[7] Both had departed from the UDHR, while simultaneously proclaiming their fealty to it. Each variant of "human rights" was deployed to attack the other. Human rights critique was, by the 1980s, almost always conducted in the name of another "human rights."

Sincere aspiration or the armament of expediency? Human rights against and after empire

An apparent normative consensus around the UDHR was literally written into foundational stones of the Third World. The UDHR was explicitly cited as a notional lodestar for national purpose in scores of independence constitutions, and in the Final Communique of the 1955 Asian–African Conference.[8] For historians, this celebration of human rights as a concept of first recourse against imperial abuses – and empire itself – is a much-debated phenomenon. Even if there is rough acceptance that human rights were a common part of the anticolonial lexicon, the meaning and significance of this proliferation of rights verbiage is much more contested. Solemn intonations of support for the UDHR, and passionate invocations of its articles, were almost always paired with a single instrumental purpose, anticolonial agitation. As in 1776, another anticolonial touchstone, rights operated as the mode for expressing legitimate grievance, and were coupled to a very specific remedy, sovereignty.

The rapid failure of postcolonial leaders to govern in ways even remotely consistent with their philosophy once sovereignty was secured has invited considerable skepticism as to sincerity. According to leading exponents of the skeptical view, foremost the persuasive triumvirate of A. W. B. Simpson, Reza Afshari, and Samuel Moyn, any serious affinity between contemporary human rights and anticolonial agitation was illusory.[9] Human rights were never much more than a weapon of convenience – part of the armamentarium to wrest power, with their purpose fully expended the day after the hand-over pageantry concluded. As Tricolors and Union Jacks were carefully folded away, so too were the handbills that professed full faith in those universal human rights that had once served as exquisite tools for eroding empire's moral claim to rule.[10]

Yet even as the substantive commitment to human rights disintegrated with alarming speed in the first few years of independence, professions of acceptance of the concept as a normative ambition remained mostly unchanged. Predominantly, the rhetorical approach taken by newly independent governments was that of adjustment at the margins, as opposed to open normative insurrection. Ideologically, the scope for critique was slender; the guideposts of postwar human rights were much the same as those that had underwritten the moral claims of anticolonialism. The cohort of leaders themselves were typically fluent in the language of democratic nationalism, social reform, and individual liberty. There was not, yet, a readily available, distinctive, mode of anti- or postcolonial dissent that found wide appeal. For most, candid rejection was not a salable project on the international stage. Internally and regionally, however, the norms were already under assault.

"Somebody else's book of rules": the rise of development as a human rights exception, 1953–61

Rejectionist counsels for developmental dictatorship over any concept of human rights had been authored and circulated in the 1950s, and actually preceded the majority of independence transitions. The issue at stake here is less the invention of a developmentalist repudiation of universality, but, rather, its appeal and persuasiveness. In the context of a contest against empire, such arguments, which often implied repressions even worse than those of imperialism, were dissonant with the mood of the moment. The fanatical advocacy of those who authored them did little to raise their respectability. An especially striking early exposition developmental dictatorship was authored by Nigerian Chike Obi in October 1953. Before liberal and social democratic methods had even been attempted in Africa, Obi argued for totalitarian mobilization to remove inherited colonial disadvantage. Reminiscent of Tsarist modernizers and the labor regimentation proposed by Leon Trotsky, he lauded fascist models, and praised National Socialism. Obi, an academic in mathematics, and future member of the Federal parliament, articulated a blueprint for development that rested solely on repression and total mobilization.

His vision was populated with a pantheon of autocrats, old and new, left and right. Obi drew inspiration from Emperor Meiji, Ali Pasha, Peter the Great, Mustafa Kemal, Prussian General von Moltke (the Elder), the *British Army Field Service Manual*, Stalin, Hitler, and Mussolini.[11] He dismissed democracy and individual freedom in wholesale terms for colonial peoples.

> What holds good for Nigeria holds good *mutatis mutandis* for Gold Coast, Tanganyika Territory, the West Indies and indeed any colonial territory peopled by backward people whatever be their race … Colonial nationalists should no longer allow themselves to be deceived by inflated emphasis on those flimsy traces of democracy in their respective countries.[12]

This modernization was not defined in terms of benefit for individual citizens – it was a crusade for "collective equality with the advanced peoples of the world," European and Soviet. Obi spoke in terms of a "collective freedom," of a world order not of human rights, but of ethnically defined peoples, in which "every race has the right to exist and to determine its mode of existence."[13] Individuals would purchase this "collective freedom" via a transaction denominated "in the special currency of the personal restraint and personal discipline," and thereby surrender their rights to the state.[14]

The surprisingly polemical mathematician held liberal anticolonialists in contempt and described their moderation in the most vituperative terms. Nigeria, Obi asserted, was "not ripe for parliamentary democratic self-government now or in 1956 or in the near future."[15] Those that argued otherwise were "parasitical democrats in Houses of Assembly," a collection "of illiterate and semi-educated lackeys."[16] He railed against "the rantings of uninformed and ostrich-like" voices who spoke out "against regimentation, dictatorship, totalitarianism," and defended "freedom of speech." These, he protested were "the fools who would rather die for their 'democratic freedom of speech,'" than to "help in 'paying the price,'" through requisite "discipline for the upliftment of their backward RACE and for the guarantee of REAL DEMOCRATIC FREEDOM for their descendants."[17]

Mobilization and sacrifice, and the deferral of freedom to the future were his prescription, the "trade-off" argument that Singapore's Lee Kuan Yew would later articulate in more measured form.[18] "Total conscription" was, Obi proclaimed, "the only specific remedy for backwardness," and he warned that "a backward country," his Nigeria, "must take it."[19] With an animated civil society, and a comparatively liberal political culture, Nigeria's citizenry was not enamored with his formula, which reduced their lives to feedstock for national modernization. Praising the fascism of Hitler and Mussolini, for "raising the standards of living of their peoples," and Stalin's Soviet Union for "mobilizing or conscripting all their resources," Obi embraced a symmetry between totalitarianisms: the complete instrumentalization of the individual.[20]

Still under British rule, Nigeria did not pursue Obi's prescriptions – that was left to another member of the African vanguard, and near neighbor, Ghana.[21] Nkrumah's new nation was the first of the British African postcolonial states, and one of the earliest pioneers of postcolonial economic modernization in the authoritarian mode. While the road to authoritarianism owed much to Nkrumah himself, it had some ancestry in the wider Pan-Africanist diaspora. Much of Nkrumah's approach had been advised even before Ghana's accession to statehood, by the famous author Richard Wright, a giant of African American literature.

Best known for his celebrated account of Bandung, Wright set out a program of authoritarian state building in his open letter to Nkrumah on the eve of independence in 1954.

> There will be no way to avoid a degree of suffering … but you have within your power the means to make this suffering of your people meaningful … None but Africans can perform this for Africa. And, as you launch your bold programmes, as you call on your people for sacrifices, you can be confident that there are free men beyond the continent of Africa who see deeply enough into life to know and understand what you *must* do, what you *must* impose.[22]

Even at this early stage, Wright seemed to recognize that such a program would meet resistance on the basis of human rights concerns. These were objections that he dismissed in sneering phrase, and a concluding warning against moderation.

> Kwame, they are going to come at you with words about democracy; you are going to be pinned to the wall and warned about decency; plump-faced men will mumble academic phrases about "sound" development; gentlemen of the cloth will speak unctuously of values and standards; in short, a barrage of concentrated arguments will be hurled at you to persuade you to temper the pace and drive of your movement.[23]

Authoritarianism would impose a redemptive repression, and the misery of African individuals would secure "Africa."

By 1963, and the inauguration of the development plan, Nkrumah had begun to apply this counsel with rigor.[24] Wright's letter framed Nkrumah's mournful and embittered 1968 memoir, written in exile in Sekou Touré's Guinea. Printed on the first inset page, the deposed Pan-Africanist icon found explanation for his predicament in Wright's correspondence. His failure was to embark on an authoritarian modernization that was both too late and too restrained.

> A once dependent territory if it is to survive in the modern world must try to accomplish in a single generation what it has taken developed nations 300 years or more to achieve ... There can be no place for slackers or saboteurs.[25]

Centralization of power into a single party, as Nkrumah had undertaken in 1964, remained an unshakeable belief. Modernization and state building was ample justification, "maximum unity and effort was vital," Nkrumah wrote, "if my government was successfully to carry out its mandate of reconstruction and development."[26] It was a line of reasoning that became the one constant feature in the rapid procession of Ghanaian dictatorships, which arrived at its ultimate refinement in February 1972, in the figure of Colonel Julius Acheamphong, who distilled an entire philosophy for developmental dictatorship into a 19-word aphorism: "One Man, One Vote is meaningless unless it is linked up with the principles of One Man, One Bread."[27]

Nkrumah's new home, Guinea, had elaborated the rationale for modernizing dictatorship earlier than most, with barely any pause between independence and full-scale autocratic mobilization. Then president-elect Sekou Touré, the trade unionist who led the march to independence, proclaimed his enthusiasm for coercive economic mobilization in 1958. Forced labor, an oft-cited grievance against French administration, was now embraced "for the benefit of those who are going to work" for their own nation. "We shall be," Sekou Touré boasted, "the first African government to institute forced labor."[28]

The new president launched a campaign against economic crimes in 1959, in conjunction with his pursuit of "a new society for the greatest happiness of man."[29] With political self-determination secured, the next task, stipulated in the Third National Congress of the Democratic Party of Guinea (PDG), was the pursuit of "total economic freedom."[30] A January 1962 address, to welcome the New Year, was an opportunity to redouble the urgency of national mobilization, to enhance "revolutionary firmness," against "the bourgeoisie of merchants" as well as associated enemies "segregationists, opportunists, and social parasites."[31] There was no ambiguity, the president explained that he had "already affirmed, with no misunderstanding, that the Party wanted to apply dictatorship," which required that "the individual whatever his personality ... must withdraw himself for the benefit of the political, human social personality of our people."[32] Guineans would be subordinated to the construction of the new Guinea.

A month earlier, in December 1961, as the United Nations' (UN) First Development Decade opened, Julius Nyerere had begun to gesture toward a similar subordination of the individual to the state.[33] In a lengthy article for *Transition*, the leading journal for African intellectuals, he mapped out the future of Tanganyika under the ominous title, "One Party Government." Nyerere asserted the "supreme task" that confronted the government was "the building up of the country's economy so as to raise the living standards of the people."[34] He reiterated what had become a postcolonial orthodoxy, which drew upon at least a century of social democratic and Marxist thought: "freedom alone is not enough; there can be a freedom which is merely the freedom to starve."[35] The manifesto included a sharp condemnation of the "irresponsible individuals" that constituted the political opposition. Political opponents, Nyerere charged, "exploit the very privileges of democracy – freedom of the press, freedom of association, freedom to criticize in order to deflect the government from its responsibilities to the people."[36]

This was a project that demanded full mobilization. Securing a developed state, "no less than the struggle against colonialism, calls for the maximum united effort by the whole country if it is to succeed." Desperation underwrote a suspension of democratic standards. "In Western democracies," the Tanzanian president explained, "in times of emergency opposition parties sink their differences" for a unity government, a recognition that in those circumstances, there was "no room for difference or division." He continued, "This our time of emergency, and until our war against poverty, ignorance and disease has been won-we should not let our unity be destroyed by a desire to follow somebody else's book of rules."[37] Whether the "book of rules" included the UDHR was, at this stage, unclear. Nyerere had passionately invoked that document, and human rights, in the preceding years.

Anticolonial human rights renovation in the 1960s: a more perfect universalism?

Notwithstanding the growing set of dissents in national and regional forums, the developmentalist critique found much more timorous expression in the international realm. At the interface between national and international, the primary response to discussion of human rights was less to repudiate than to renovate the framework of the late 1940s and early 1950s.[38] Divergences were presented less as philosophical ripostes to universalism, but practical revisions to realize its contents. These renovations were not unique to anticolonial voices: the reasoning was almost generic. In the main, the rationale rested upon claims of exceptional circumstances, often citing Western precedents of national emergency (as Nyerere had), as opposed to intrinsic features that invalidated universalism in perpetuity.[39] Although the gradations between prolonged exception, renovation, altered priority, and fundamental rejection are an imperfect demarcation, the difference between the inflexion of these departures from the scheme of the UDHR, and those that would emerge in the later 1960s and across the 1970s, was clear enough.

Developmental exceptionalism, already finding foothold in Africa, was the claim around which most international critique of human rights universality would orbit in the early to mid-1960s.[40] This was, in terms of its normative implications, initially a self-limited threat to the UDHR, at least in an abstract sense. It presumed that human rights were – eventually – universally valid. In a period when the horizons for economic development were thought visible, if distant, the sorts of variations that were needed, and their duration, was less alarming. Above all, the main line of developmentalist critique was, at this stage, not one that rejected universalism and interdependence as the ideal: it disputed the order, emphasis, and immediate feasibility. Until the second half of the 1960s, whenever exhibited to international audience, be they NGO or UN, the arguments themselves were typically framed in pragmatism, and advocated by a cohort of more specialist personnel. Reservations were mostly pinned to specified items, and rarely drifted into general dissent. Bound by the material circumstances of the moment, the remedy was understanding and time. Harmonization with 1948's "common standard of achievement," a reasonably forgiving task given its imprecision, was no problem with adequate patience and resources. The UDHR remained secure as an aspirational norm – the plea, in short, was to be made universalists, just not yet.

As one of the few human rights NGOs with global reach, the International Commission of Jurists (ICJ) had been the earliest to engage the "New States," as part of its established mission to promote the rule of law and democratic constitutionalism worldwide. It was amongst the first to encounter this developmentalist exception. From 1955 onward, at its Congress in Athens, the ICJ had begun to examine and dissect the relationship between rights, the postcolonial state, and the problems of development.[41] At that point, with postcolonial democracy shaky and dysfunctional, but very much alive, the efflorescence of hope had not yet faded. The manifest tensions between urgent questions of poverty alleviation, entrenched foreign economic interest, democracy, and an independent judicial system could be navigated without major compromise to established liberal and social democratic models. That option was receding rapidly by January 1959, when the ICJ sortied to New Delhi, for a dedicated study of how individual freedoms might be preserved in an increasingly unpromising Third World. From the moment the delegates checked in at the Hotel Janpath, the ICJ wrestled with the eroding status of human rights in many postcolonial states. In barely 12 months, a large swathe of these new nations had traversed from fragile democracy to frankly authoritarian, including Sudan, Burma, Pakistan, Iraq, Guinea, and Ghana.[42] Pakistan's new military regime, led by General Mohammed Ayub Khan, explicitly justified its rule, and massive diminution of political freedoms, on the pressing need for development.[43]

Convened in the wake of the coups and democratic collapses of 1958, and the emergence of an imposing catalogue of new dictatorships, the tripartite balance between individual freedom, state power, and simple subsistence was the motif of the proceedings. The inaugural speech, from Prime Minister Jawaharlal Nehru, edged toward confirming the authoritarian tendency of postcolonialism, which many within the ICJ, and its close counterpart NGO, the International League for the Rights of Man, had begun to identify. After a series of anodyne observations about the dynamism of society and the need for a similarly dynamic notion of law, Nehru made the case for greater executive privilege. Rapid development meant that "the judge may be left a little behind by the changes" and "may not quite represent that mood which happens to be the mood of society."[44] In such circumstances, the prime minister postulated that "it may even be that the executive" that was suited "much more for the moment."[45] The rule of law had to be reconciled with "the rule of life."[46]

This "rule of life" was taken to mean, by the consensus of the Asian and African participants and Western conveners, a focus on the economic and social side of interdependence written into the UDHR. Although much of human rights centered on the "individual in a free society," it was "also concerned with the establishment by the State of social, economic, educational and cultural conditions under which man's legitimate aspirations and dignity may be realized." Large tracts of universality were temporarily ceded, "freedom of expression," was "meaningless to an illiterate," so too suffrage, which might "be perverted into an instrument of tyranny" in the setting of "an unenlightened electorate." Restraints on the state "must not spell freedom to starve." One side of the UDHR's indivisibility and interdependence was now being placed in the foreground, and New Delhi adopted a more plastic notion of universality. Given "ever changing conditions of human existence," there was a need to depart from "static notions," and hew closer to the flexible approach exemplified by India.[47] Vivian Bose, a future leader of the ICJ, echoed this modified universalism. Bose urged "close and sympathetic consideration of the problems special to those countries" that were emerging from colonialism. There was, he insisted, a vital requirement for "understanding the plight of those that accept our principles and ideals but who, whether they be right or wrong, feel it their duty temporarily to reject certain of the matters in which they also have ultimate faith." It was not a surrender, but a tactical retreat so "the things in which they believe and we believe can be preserved and ultimately restored in a cleaner and newer form."[48]

Two year later, with dozens of additional states now independent, the ICJ Conference in Lagos, held in January 1961, was among the last gasps of a liberal anticolonialism close to exhaustion.[49] Drawn from a catchment of liberal African jurists and intellectuals generally inclined toward the precepts of universal human rights, its local participants were increasingly anomalous in the context of the continent.[50] From Senegal, there was Abdoulaye Wade, lecturer in law at the University of Dakar. In the 1970s, he would become a central figure in Senegal's transition to multi-party rule as leader of the opposition Parti Démocratique Sénégalais, and a prime example of the "third" liberation of Africa – from President Leopold Senghor's creeping authoritarianism.[51]

Wade was joined by a more senior colleague, Keba M'Baye from Senegal's Supreme Court, a graduate from the elite École normale supérieure in Paris. M'Baye was already a rising star in human rights academe, who would reach international prominence in the early 1970s. From Sudan, there was the head Supreme Court justice, Mohammed Abu Rannat. He would help to secure the fledgling mechanism for studying individual complaints when serving on the expert sub-commission at the UN in the late 1960s. Joseph Danquah, leader of the opposition to President Nkrumah, attended. Author of the Nigerian constitution, Chief Justice Taslim Olawele Elias delivered an impressive paper defending the rule of law. They were joined by leading and emerging figures from the West, notably UN Division Chief, and co-architect of the UDHR, John Humphrey, and his European colleague, Karel Vasak.[52]

Replete with a formal dinner with archetypal anticolonial liberal, Nigerian leader Nnamdi Azikiwe, an address from Humphrey, and a ceremonial ball, it was a grand occasion by the frugal standards of international human rights activism. With the subsequent unwinding of almost all optimism, Lagos would serve as the closing moment of a hopeful era. The hope was not so much in the trends themselves, which were all portents for the coming disastrous disintegration of democracy, but in the fact that the grave risk had been identified. Across the working papers, committees, and plenary debate, there was a sense of an impending disaster. Whether it could be forestalled was unclear. Elias and Wade appeared almost resigned, preparing eloquent taxonomies of the authoritarian logic of postcolonial nationalism, and the basis for its seduction of the Third World.

Not all agreed with the principle of a universal human rights metric, with several speakers arguing for adjustments, allowances, and other special case exceptions beyond those in the UDHR. At the plenary discussion on 6 January 1961, the final full day of the conference, the chair, Gabriel d'Arboussier, intervened with his appraisal of the situation in the new countries. After a period serving in the Chamber of Deputies of the French Fourth Republic, d'Arboussier had helped to create the Rassemblement Démocraqitue Africain, a pan-Francophone African nationalist party. In his then-current capacity, as Senegal's minister of justice, he argued that "together with the principle of universal legality" were "also principles of legality specific to Africa and corresponding to the African requirements of independence, unity, democracy and economic development."[53] He stated, cautiously, that his propositions "may come in conflict with certain ready-made ideas," and "certain classic concepts of democracy, socialism or liberalism."[54] Pragmatic modification of the standards was implied. "Reality," he warned, "does not forgive errors of doctrine and we must attempt to face all the African realities."[55]

D'Arboussier found an ally in Dashwood Wilson, Liberia's Chief Justice, who echoed the call for a level of postcolonial exception. Although the concepts were perhaps valid, Wilson reminded his colleagues that "unlike advanced nations, we face complex problems not generally experienced in other parts of the world."[56] Newly emergent states were, he pleaded, "entitled to the sympathetic consideration of those advanced nations."[57] Beset by challenges, a relaxation of standards was necessary from the Western world, because "measuring us by their own yardstick would be premature and unjustified."[58] This was a less than auspicious note on which to terminate the conference.

Bad advice? Postcolonial critique of human rights arrives at the UN

As the 1960s progressed, the authoritarian turn in the Third World consolidated. The next senior ICJ excursion to Africa, from Secretary-General Leslie Munro, promptly ended when he was refused entry to Ghana in 1962. By 1963, the ICJ was salvaging its purpose in the mere fact of sustaining the struggle, as opposed to any perceptible result for its effort. The International League for the Rights of Man was devoting increasing effort to Ghana, and a growing list of former colonial territories. Among the modest selection of human rights NGOs operational in the 1950s and 1960s, postcolonial reservations and adjustments received a fairly charitable hearing. Only a handful of situations, Iraq, and Ghana, aroused visible outrage, mostly from British figures, many of whom had been ardent champions of decolonization, and in the case of Ghana, on personal terms with President Kwame Nkrumah.[59] This would change dramatically, but the clash between Third World renovated universality, and human rights NGO advocacy, was not yet a dominant feature of the global human rights dynamic. Dissents from universality remained mostly unspectacular before the epochal World Conference on Human Rights in 1968, and were usually aired at lower level regional forums.[60]

At the UN, the numerical advantage of the new states was an incontrovertible fact by the close of 1960. Third World priorities, which had been inscribed into the human rights agenda much earlier via the opportunities opened up by Western lassitude, became annual mainstays. Racial discrimination, most grotesquely in the form of apartheid, along with residual colonialism, dominated the proceedings of the General Assembly and the Commission on Human Rights, with economic development a near-peer competitor for attention. A relentless focus on the first two priorities posed no mortal threat to the philosophical integrity of the UDHR. Much as they deformed the balance of scrutiny and annexed most of the available energy in human rights forums, the standard by which apartheid and colonialism were attacked was the opening article, and a defining principle, of 1948. Development, conversely, was different. Unlike the early expositions of the developmental exception in national and NGO realms, at the UN, an environment where there was already a strong constituency for autocratic modernization in the Soviet bloc, the exception cascaded across the mid- and late-1960s. It would eventually crystallize into a de facto revision of the UDHR's indivisibility, a position consecrated at the 1968 conference.[61] By 1968–70, the philosophical obliquity that had mostly characterized preceding criticisms of universality had transitioned to something both less equivocal, and less avowedly temporary.

Initial airing of skepticism about universality occurred in the assorted special UN seminars on human rights in the developing world, held under the auspices of the educational Advisory Services Program. Inaugurated at Kabul in 1964 and followed by sequel conferences in Dakar (1966) and Nicosia (1969); and derivatives at Cairo (1969), Lusaka (1970), and Dar es Salaam (1973), the meetings had decidedly heterodox advice. At Kabul, then amidst the ambitious "New Democracy" reforms of Zahir Shah's government, the tenor was moderate – with the special case of the developing world not so special as to be a *sui generis* that lived outside the UDHR.[62] Nine years later, at Dar es Salaam, there were arguments that the standards themselves had only the most marginal application to begin with. "On the whole," recorded the Dar es Salaam report, the UN's human rights treaties "were alien to African reality."[63]

The first open clash on universality was the second of the seminars, held in Dakar in February 1966.[64] For the first time at the UN, the UDHR's legitimacy for Africa was challenged beyond minor reservation.[65] For the first time, a cultural identity element was interlaced with the developmental exception – adding a philosophical layer, with implied permanence, to the pragmatic rationales of urgent modernization. For the last time until the late 1980s, there remained enough African support to keep a residual quantum of faith in the UDHR as the best consensus position for the continent, but with little margin for further decline. Despite a more promising third seminar, that in Nicosia, the trend was now firmly away from optimistic universalism. After a welcoming address from iconic Cypriot nationalist leader, Archbishop Makarios, the last of the seminars began its work in the famous Ledra Palace Hotel, a symbol of the divided island. Held between 26 June and 9 July 1969, the debates themselves were temperate with questions on the balance between development and the individual, the nature of property, and the legitimacy of restrictions on human rights investigated in detail. Paeans to single-party regimes and total social mobilization were met by vigorous defense of a liberal approach.[66] There were, however, clear notes of pessimism registered in the final report, which reflected dissents from any meaningful realization of universality in the near term. Given the "great disparity of economic development and cultural traditions among States," the report surmised, "it might be a long time" before any universal implementation might be secured.[67]

Towards a universal particularism: identity, community, and tradition

Critiques of universality that invoked tradition, culture, and identity had been, prior to the 1970s, relatively scarce in the main UN forums. They were not a strong feature of 1960s dissents, which were overwhelming devoted to state building. One major exception, traditional conceptions of the right to property, was raised sporadically in discussions of African conditions in the 1960s, being a prominent item at Dakar in 1966. Property was among the anthropologically stronger areas for an exception – and already established as among the more caveated and contested human rights. Any adamantine version of the right to individual property was also seen as an impediment to almost any feasible scheme of the land reform required for development. It mostly operated as a bounded zone of human rights variation that never posed much threat to the wider architecture of universality. Similarly, plenty of counterexamples were elaborated whenever historical custom appeared to endorse repression. Throughout the early and mid-1960s, tradition was marshaled to demonstrate values consonant with much of the UDHR, prefiguring the transient 1990s enthusiasm for a cross-cultural rebasing of universality.

More profound criticisms of the very pretense of universalist norms, which had been voiced since at least 1947, in the famous American Anthropological Association Statement, and in Saudi Arabia's later abstention on the UDHR, were initially cast to the margins of postcolonial rhetoric.[68] Inside the UN, cultural relativism outright was not a popular critique across the 1950s and 1960s.[69] At best, it was an objection made rarely, for questions on family law, and typically viewed with distaste by the Third World representatives. Association of the essentialist reasoning that underpinned cultural relativism and identity with unpalatable sponsors, both South Africa, and the former imperial powers, effaced the provenance of the discourse as one with anti-imperial origins. Cynical colonial deployment of "native custom," and the more proximate outrages of "multi-nationalism" and "Separate Development" then being peddled by the South African National Party were poor advertisements for "culturalist" argument.[70]

However, by 1969 faith in universality was wandering further away. Realization of rights began to retreat into regional and national forms, which would serve as an intermediary system connecting state to globe. These institutions, while notionally based on universal human rights, were also predicated on the need to create a more spacious canopy for difference. In the early case of the 1950 European Convention on Human Rights, regional coherence allowed for a subset of rights to be subject to exceptionally intrusive enforcement procedure. Some of this hope was evident in the renascent regionalism of late 1960s. Yet it was also impelled by the waning of faith in rights universalism. A particularistic basis for migration to regionalist human rights institutions was reflected in the September 1969 meeting on a regional system for Africa, held in Cairo.

Among the assortment of rationales for regionalism was an unveiled objection to the pretension of universality in the UDHR. "There was," the Cairo report stated, "a basic lack of confidence in the fundamental texts on human rights." The reason was straightforward, the human rights canon, "failed to reflect non-European civilizations and traditions."

> Even the Universal Declaration of Human Rights, in some respects, was regarded as falling short of containing "common standards" which were valid universally, since at the time of the adoption of the Universal Declaration there

> were fifty-two States Members of the United Nations, having mostly white populations with largely European and Christian traditions. Most of the Afro-Asian countries were not independent at the time, and therefore the hopes of those countries and their peoples were not fully reflected in that document.

From this premise, it followed that an African system of rights was "highly desirable." When Africa was decoupled from the wider norms of the UDHR, "the tenets and traditions of African peoples would surely be taken duly into consideration."[71] The genesis of "cultural rights" as a privileged part of the program a year earlier only expedited the path to human rights particularism.[72]

Within scholarship, the era of postwar universalism, with its faith in technocratic schemes of development and government, and assumption of a shared destiny and humanity, was thoroughly routed by the close of the 1960s. Verities of liberal progressivism were shredded by the scions of the New Left and the rise of "identity." Most of the radical scholarship of the 1960s, New Left, *tiers-mondiste* (Third-Worldist), and others – did not directly engage human rights. Yet its authors generally operated with premises incompatible with the logic of the UDHR. From the French academy, there emerged new wisdom on "authenticity." Tracts from the Sorbonne were often opaque enough to keep their practical effects ambiguous, but were unmistakably supportive of essentialist identity formation. By 1978, Edward Said's pioneering and eminently more readable work informed a new style of Western wariness when assessing the practice of other societies.[73]

Almost simultaneous to these trends, Islamic particularism and difference was revivified in both Sunni and Shia discourse.[74] Almost invisible from human rights discussions since Saudi Arabia's series of dissents to the UDHR, the Covenant, and almost every subsequent human rights instrument, Islamic exception, or the more subversive strategy of "Islamic Human Rights," would slowly become among the most potent criticisms of the 1990s and 2000s. At the 1968 World Conference on Human Rights, a book of conservative Islamic commentary, a considerable portion of which was corrosive to the core precepts of the UDHR, was unofficially circulated to every delegation from an Islamic majority country.[75] In 1975, Syed Abul A'la Mawdudi, a core founder of modern Islamic fundamentalist ideology, with an influence exceeded only by Qutb, turned his hand to human rights. His lecture, which left little of the UDHR intact, was extended into a published book.[76] Islam was the first and most vocal of the new human rights particularism, and had been expressed in the original Saudi abstention to the UDHR, but it would soon be joined by others, a process that would explode in the "Asian Values" controversies of the 1990s.

Breakthrough and breakup? The proliferation of "human rights" language

For NGO, state, and international organizational conversations on human rights in the key decades between 1948 and 1968, there was shared, albeit strained, recognition of the enabling place of the nation-state. This view began to change as the cumulative disappointments of postcolonial liberation became impossible to avoid. The responses polarized. Third World leaders doubled down on sovereignty as the road to freedom, with new schemes for its economic and cultural augmentation. By contrast, the rising NGO movement lost almost all of its residual belief in the state as a force for securing human rights.[77] Human rights NGOs like Amnesty International focused ever more exclusively on a more constrained vision of rights, with prime emphasis on torture and arbitrary detention, which asked for little more than diminished state malignancy. Third World states, and a whole tranche of scholarship, advocated massive inflationary innovations to the discourse – the so-called "structural" and "solidarity" generation of human rights language. A significant conceptual expanse separated each of these respective evolutions of "human rights" from the UDHR. The distance each had from the other was almost insuperably vast. This new milieu of the 1970s, the much-studied breakthrough decade, catalyzed the arrival of full-scale normative conflict, as these "human rights" species diverged.[78] Neither party, however, would abandon the term itself – the configuration was a struggle for custodianship of the language itself, not so much a criticism extrinsic to it.

Critical and well-publicized NGO reports, and outraged state response, were an exquisite means for revealing just how chasmic the delta within "human rights" had become. The second half of the 1970s, the dawn of mass NGO pressure, much of it now allocated to postcolonial states, was also the dawn of the most strident critiques of human rights. Perceptions of threat, or simple, intuitive irritation, sharpened the complex of arguments that had been coalescing across the preceding decade. Defensive reaction to human rights NGO action, and from 1977 onward, concern at revitalized US government human rights reporting was not exclusive to Asian, African, and Arab states. Leonid Brezhnev's Soviet Union, Jorge Videla's Argentina, P. W. Botha's South Africa, were all assiduous in denigrating their growing sets of human rights critics, and advancing their own "human rights" versions.[79] Among these, South Africa's extended published excursus on the illegitimacy of NGO attacks was arguably more faithful to the postcolonial, plurality of traditional values model than anything from an actual postcolonial state, or citizen.[80]

More proactive regimes launched elaborate projects of alternative "human rights." These were both an effort to preempt their critics, and to terraform the global human rights terrain in ways hospitable to their regimes. Shah Mohammed Reza Pahlavi's Iran was an early adopter, with a concerted effort to claim international human rights leadership from the mid-1960s, led by Princess Ashraf Pahlavi.[81] Aided by some vague degree of fidelity to elements of the UDHR on economic and social rights, and achievements in women's rights, it was more plausible than many similar exercises. Less convincing was the initiative from Erich Honecker's GDR, and its Human Rights Committee.[82] Saudi Arabia, a state that had, from 1948 onward, had mixed a policy of outright rejection, in the relativist mode, with more evasive diversionary tactics, sought to co-opt a human rights NGO into its defensive scheme in the early 1970s. The results were hilariously incoherent, and transparently dishonest, but the Kingdom's special joint conference series with the ICJ, and its ventriloquized reports offered at least some kind of shield.[83] Saudi human rights particularism, confidently stated almost every year from 1948, was more accepted than most. Only the People's Republic of China was more successful in avoiding the censorious moral spotlight, less out of its own defensive facilities, but simple inattention and lack of access from the Western NGO world, and strategic inconvenience for Western governments.[84]

Conclusions

After more than a decade of "dialogues of civilizations," rights against "the defamation of religion," and the pet project of the Russian Federation, "traditional values and the protection of human rights," it is now apparent that professed deepening and extension of human rights is not obviously less corruptive than critique. Those more crystalline criticisms of the 1960s, which through their clarity and specificity, preserved slightly more of the integrity of rights terminology, seemed almost preferable to the morass that originated in the late 1970s, and continues four decades later. Across this period of the late twentieth and early twenty-first century, the outer linguistic mold line of "human rights" was intact, or even strengthened by the endless invocations of rights. Internally its normative content was coming apart. Transition from postcolonial critique to postmodern subversion was less easily countered. The endless energy poured into proceduralist and bureaucratic forms, institutions, "plans of action," and mechanism delivered growth in verbiage without appreciable meaning in the enjoyment of human rights. While not without real successes, notably in the case of the Working Group on Disappearances, very often those subject to violations merely had those abuses rendered in more Baroque and technocratic phrase. Perversely, 60 years after the concerns and objections of Kabul, Dakar, and Nicosia, that kind of candid and specific speech, even if skeptical, would be a small increment closer to the UDHR.

Notes

1 Adamantia Pollis and Peter Schwab, "Human Rights: A Western Construct with Limited Applicability," in Pollis and Schwab (eds.) *Human Rights: Cultural and Ideological Perspectives*, New York: Praeger, 1979, pp. 1–18.

2 Perhaps the most historically oriented, with reference to the world outside of abstraction, is Reza Afshari, *Human Rights in Iran: the Abuse of Cultural Relativism*, Philadelphia: University of Pennsylvania Press, 2001. The history of anthropology's relationship with cultural relativism, and the discipline's critique of universal human rights, is also among the more fully analyzed, see Ellen Messer, "Anthropology and Human Rights," *Annual Review of Anthropology*, 1993, vol. 22, 221–49; and Wilcomb Washburn, "Cultural Relativism, Human Rights, and the AAA," *American Anthropologist*, 1987, vol. 89, 939–43.

3 This scholarship is immense, for the most substantial and paradigmatic example, see Makau Mutua, *Human Rights: A Political and Cultural Critique*, Philadelphia: University of Pennsylvania, 2002.

4 See, for instance, the case of Haile Mengistu's Ethiopia, and its series of tirades against Amnesty International's 1978 report, *Human Rights Violations in Ethiopia*, London: Amnesty International, 1978; and subsequently these documents: United Nations Economic and Social Council Papers, Preliminary Works of the Commission on Human Rights at its Thirty-Fifth Session, Tadesse Terrefe, Permanent Representative of Ethiopia, to Chairman of the Commission on Human Rights of the United Nations at Geneva, 14 March 1979, E/CN.4/1344, 15 March 1979; and Summary Records of the Commission, 1634th meeting, 10 March 1981, E/CN.4/SR.1634, para. 20. Terrefe's 1979 letter dismissed Amnesty International as little more than "a mouth-piece of international imperialism."

5 Patrick William Kelly, *Sovereign Emergencies: Latin America and the Making of Global Human Rights Politics*, Cambridge, UK: Cambridge University Press, 2018, pp. 272–303.

6 For late 1970s context, and pluralized human rights language, see Roland Burke, "'Human Rights Day After the 'Breakthrough': Celebrating the Universal Declaration of Human Rights at the United Nations in 1978 and 1988," *Journal of Global History*, 2015, vol. 10, 147–70.

7 The changing nature of human rights in this period is now a major area for historical inquiry, for representative state of the art, Jan Eckel, "The International League for the Rights of Man, Amnesty International, and the Changing Fate of Human Rights Activism from the 1940s Through the 1970s," *Humanity*, 2013, vol. 4, 183–214; Jan Eckel and Samuel Moyn (eds.), *The Breakthrough: Human Rights in the 1970s*, Philadelphia: University of Pennsylvania Press, 2013; Barbara Keys, *Reclaiming American Virtue: The Human Rights Revolution of the 1970s*, Cambridge, MA: Harvard University Press, 2014; and Bradley Simpson, "Self-Determination, Human Rights, and the End of Empire in the 1970s," *Humanity*, 2013, vol. 5, 239–60.

8 Burke, "'The Compelling Dialogue of Freedom': Human Rights at the 1955 Bandung Conference," *Human Rights Quarterly*, 2006, vol. 28, 947–65; and more recently, Steven Jensen, *The Making of International Human Rights: The 1960s, Decolonization, and the Reconstruction of Global Values*, Cambridge, UK: Cambridge University Press, 2016.

9 A. W. B. Simpson, *Human Rights and the End of Empire*, Oxford: Oxford University Press, 2001, p. 300; Reza Afshari, "On Historiography of Human Rights Reflections on Paul Gordon Lauren's 'The Evolution of International Human Rights: Visions Seen,'" *Human Rights Quarterly*, 2007, vol. 29, 1–67; and Samuel Moyn, *The Last Utopia: Human Rights in History*, Cambridge, MA: Harvard University Press, 2010.

10 There is substantial historiographic diversity on this topic, see the excellent precis from Jan Eckel, "Human Rights and Decolonization: New Perspectives and Open Questions," *Humanity*, 2010, vol. 1, 111–36. C.f. older survey account in Paul Gordon Lauren, *The Evolution of International Human Rights: Visions Seen*, Philadelphia: University of Pennsylvania Press, 1998. For more discrete, revealing episodes, see Meredith Terretta, "From Below and to the Left? Human Rights and Liberation Politics in Africa's Postcolonial Age," *Journal of World History*, 2013, vol. 24, 389–416.

11 Chike Obi, *Our Struggle: A Political Analysis of the Problems of the Negro Peoples Struggling for True Freedom*, 30 January 1955, University College, Ibadan, pamphlet reproduces original October 1953 mimeograph.

12 Obi, *Our Struggle*, pp. 9–10.

13 Obi, *Our Struggle*, pp. 25, 11.

14 Obi, *Our Struggle*, p. 16.

15 Obi, *Our Struggle*, p. 42.

16 Obi, *Our Struggle*, p. 36.

17 Obi, *Our Struggle*, pp. 30, 36 (capitalization in original).

18 Lee Kuan Yew, *From Third World to First*, New York: Harper Collins, 2000.

19 Lee, *From Third World to First*, p. 52.

20 Lee, *From Third World to First*, pp. 38, 47.

21 For perceptions of Obi, see Obi Nwakanma, *Christopher Okigbo, 1930–67*, Ibadan: HEBN, 2010, pp. 60, 66, 70, 85–93.

22 Richard Wright, *Black* Power, cited in Kwame Nkrumah, *Dark Days in Ghana*, New York: International Publishers, 1969, p. 7.

23 Wright, *Black Power*, cited in Nkrumah, *Dark Days*, p. 7.

24 "Ghana – Towards Dictatorship," *Bulletin of the International Commission of Jurists* 18, 1964, pp. 9–13.

25 Nkrumah, *Dark Days*, p. 67. The foreword is dated 24 August 1967.

26 Nkrumah, *Dark Days*, p. 64.

27 Office of the Press Secretary, Accra, Ghana: Head of State's Address to the Staff of the Ministry of Finance and Economic Planning, Monday 7 February 1972, p. 9, reproduced in Republic of Ghana, *Two Years in Office of Colonial Ignatius Kutu Acheampong, 13 January 1972–12 January 1974*, Accra, Ghana: Office of the Press Secretary to the National Redemption Council, [1974].

28 William Friedland and Carl Rosenberg Jr. (eds.), *African Socialism*, Stanford, CA: Stanford University Press 1964, p. 172. For further discussion of postcolonial governments arguing against ILO standards, see Daniel Maul, *Human Rights, Development, and Decolonization: The International Labour Organization, 1940–70*, New York: Palgrave, 2012, pp. 4–10, 114–21, 132–3, 210–11, 221–30, 278–80.

29 Sekou Touré, *Toward Full Re-Africanization*, Paris: Presence Africaine, 1959, pp. 46, 296 n. 32.

30 Touré, *The International Policy of the Democratic Party of Guinea: Extracts from the Report on Doctrine and Orientation submitted to the 3rd National Conference of the P.D.G.*, Cairo: Société Orientale de Publicité-Press, 1962, p. 56.

31 Ahmed Sékou Touré, "Message to the Nation Delivered by President Sékou Touré on the Occasion of the New Year, January 10 1962," in Ahmed Sékou Touré (ed.) *The International Policy and Diplomatic Action of the Democratic Party of Guinea. Extracts from the Report on Doctrine and Orientation submitted to the 3rd National Conference of the P.D.G.*, Cairo: S.O.P [Société Orientale de Publicité] Press, 1962, p. 185.

32 Sékou Touré, "Message to the Nation," p. 190.

33 GA Resolution 1710 (XVI), *United Nations Development Decade*, 19 December 1961; Julius Nyerere, "One Party Government," *Transition* 2, 1961, 9–11.
34 Nyerere, "One Party Government," 9.
35 Nyerere, "One Party Government," 10. On interdependence of rights, see Johannes Morsink, *The Universal Declaration of Human Rights: Origins, Drafting, and Intent*, Philadelphia: University of Pennsylvania Press, 1999, pp. 222–38.
36 Nyerere, "One Party Government," 10–11.
37 Nyerere, "One Party Government," 9–10.
38 Alex Quaison-Sackey, Nkrumah's ambassador, was an exemplar of the more modest expression. Reflecting on the particular question of Africa, Quaison-Sackey concluded that "Universal standards there must be … but those universal standards must be evolved by all nations." *Africa Unbound: Reflections of an African Statesman*, New York: Praeger, 1963, p. 166; see also pp. 55, 150–1, 162–3.
39 International Commission of Jurists perceived the relationship between economic development and the universal application of human rights in this manner. Its 1966 assessment, concluded that "what may be indefensible in a wealthy sophisticated society may become permissible in a society which is trying to fight against famine and hunger." Report of the Secretary-General (ICJ), Geneva, 30 September–2 October 1966, *Bulletin of the International Commission of Jurists*, 1966, vol. 28, 5.
40 In 1966, there was already an adequate corpus of examples for African scholars to study the patterns of rising authoritarianism. See UK National Archives, Kew, FCO 371/189948: *Seminar on Human Rights in Developing Countries, Dakar, Senegal 8–22 February 1966*, and specifically Ousmane Goundiam, "Background Paper A"; Mohamed Yousif Mudawi, "Background Paper B"; and Gaius Ezejiofor, "Background Paper C."
41 "Act of Athens," "The Congress of Athens," and "Resolutions of the Athens Congress," in *Bulletin of the International Commission of Jurists*, 1955, vol. 3, 3–14; "The Aftermath of the Athens Congress," *Bulletin of the International Commission of Jurists*, 1956, vol. 5, 5–6.
42 "Opening Plenary Proceedings," in Norman Marsh and Jean-Flavien Lalive (eds.) *The Rule of Law in a Free Society: A Report on the International Congress of Jurists, New Delhi, India, 5–10 January 1959*, n.p., 1959, p. 37.
43 See the elaboration of Khan's ideology, specifically its "Basic Democracy," in Mohammed Ayub Kahn, *Friends Not Masters: A Political Autobiography*, Oxford: Oxford University Press 1967.
44 *A Report on the International Congress of Jurists, New Delhi*, p. 42.
45 *A Report*, p. 42.
46 *A Report*, p. 41.
47 Lalive, "Foreword," in *A Report*, p. vii.
48 Vivian Bose, "Reflections on the Declaration of Delhi," *Journal of the International Commission of Jurists*, 1959, vol. 2, 42.
49 For contemporary commentary, see Laurence Lombard, "African Conference on the Rule of Law Held at Lagos, Nigeria," *American Bar Association Journal*, 1961, vol. 47, 563–7; and Charles Rhyne, "Law in Africa: A Report on the Lagos Conference," *American Bar Association Journal*, 1961, vol. 47, 685–8.
50 *African Conference on the Rule of Law Lagos, Nigeria, January 3–7, 1961: A Report on the Proceedings of the Conference*, Geneva: ICJ, 1961, 23–31; see also, "The African Conference on The Rule of Law," *Journal of the International Commission of Jurists*, 1961, vol. 3, 3–29.
51 Senghor's views of universalism and human rights were thoughtful, a reflection of his prior experience with the European Convention of Human Rights, and his philosophy, *Negritude*. See Leopold Senghor, *Nationhood and the African Road to Socialism*, Paris: Presence Africaine, 1961, pp. 68, 73, 83, 88, 103, 112–13.
52 Burke, "'Real Problems to Discuss': The Congress for Cultural Freedom's Asian and African Expeditions, 1951–1959," *Journal of World History*, 2016, vol. 27, 53–85.
53 *African Conference on the Rule of Law, Proceedings*, 7 January 1961, Closing Plenary, p. 166.
54 *African Conference*, p. 167.
55 *African Conference*, p. 167.
56 *African Conference*, p. 169.
57 *African Conference*, p. 169.

58 *African Conference*, p. 170.

59 Correspondence – Ghana, ILHR Papers, NYPL, Roger Baldwin, "A Few Observations on Ghana, November 1960"; ILHR Press Release, untitled, On Nkrumah and need for UN action, December 1961; The United Party of Ghana, "Open Letter to Nkrumah," 23 January 1962; K. A. Busia to Roger Baldwin, Correspondence on League and Ghana Human Rights Situation, 4 December 1961; Peter Benenson to Roger Baldwin, Regarding Letter from Parliamentarians, 21 November 1963.

60 Burke, "Challenging the Universal Declaration: Human Rights and the UN Advisory Services Program," *History Australia*, 2012, vol. 9, 27–42.

61 On indivisibility, see Daniel Whelan, *Indivisible Human Rights: A History*, Philadelphia: University of Pennsylvania Press, 2010.

62 United Nations. Online. Available at www.un.org/en/documents/index.html, ST/TAO/HR/21: *Seminar on Human Rights in Developing Countries, Kabul, Afghanistan, 12–25 May 1964*, New York: United Nations, 1964. See also the coverage in the *Kabul Times*, which was generally impressive in its complex handling of the nature of "trade-off" type arguments. See, notably, "Economic Planning Important for Promoting Rights," 13 May 1964, 1; and "Humans and Human Rights," 17 May 1964, 3. Further discussed by Burke, "Disseminating Discord and Discovering the World: UN Advisory Services on Human Rights and the Illusory Faith in Specialist Knowledge," *Journal of International Human Rights*, 2017, vol. 21, no. 5, 589–610.

63 Seminar on the Study of New Ways and Means for Promoting Human Rights with Special Attention to the Problems and Needs of Africa, Dar es Salaam, United Republic of Tanzania, 23 October–5 November 1973, ST/TAO/HR/48, para 20. For further brief note on the meeting, see UN, General Records of the Department of State, Subject Numeric Files, US mission, Dar es Salaam, "Tanzania Hosts UN Seminar on Human Rights," 9 November 1973, SOC 14 1970–3, Social, NACP.

64 Report of the Seminar on Human Rights in Developing Countries, Dakar, Senegal, 8–22 February 1966, ST/TAO/HR/25.l,

65 John Humphrey, Entry for Sunday, 20 February 1966, Humphrey and A. J. Hobbins, *On the Edge of Greatness*, vol. 5, Montreal: McGill/Fontanus, 1995, p. 188; Humphrey, *Human Rights & the United Nations: A Great Adventure*, Dobbs Ferry, NY: Transnational, 1984, p. 336. See also UN Archives, Humphrey to C.V. Narasimhan, Memorandum on Dakar, 16 February 1966, S-0198-003-09.

66 "Report of the Seminar on Special Problems Relating to Human Rights in Developing Countries, Nicosia, Cyprus, 26 June–9 July 1969," ST/TAO/HR/36, paras. 76–7.

67 "Report of the Seminar," para. 165.

68 American Anthropological Association, "Statement on Human Rights," *American Anthropologist* 49, 1947, 539–43; Mark Goodale, *Surrendering to Utopia. An Anthropology of Human Rights*, Stanford, CA: Stanford University Press, 2009, pp. 19–31.

69 Roland Burke, *Decolonization and the Evolution of International Human Rights*, Philadelphia: University of Pennsylvania Press, 2010, 126–9.

70 On colonial abuse of custom, see Mahmood Mamdani, *Citizen and Subject: Contemporary Africa and the Legacy of Late Colonialism*, Princeton, NJ: Princeton University Press, 1996; for National Party utilization of "tradition," see its classic exhibition, *The Transkei: A Progress Report and Multi-National Development*, Washington, DC: Department of Information, South African Embassy, 1968.

71 Seminar on the Establishment of Regional Commissions on Human Rights with Special Reference to Africa, Cairo, UAR, 2–15 September 1969, ST/TAO/HR/38, section A, para. 23.

72 Meeting of Experts on Cultural Rights as Human Rights, November 1968, Place de Fontenoy, UNESCO/SHC/120/1.

73 Edward Said, *Orientalism*, New York: Pantheon, 1978.

74 As one pro-Khomeini protestor was filmed as saying, "We don't want your human rights." Episode 5, "The State of the Union Is Not Good," *The Seventies* CNN, 16 July 2015. See the exceptional exchange in the Summary Records of the Human Rights Committee, 364–366th meetings, 15 July 1982, Geneva, CCPR/C/SR.364–366.

75 Sultanhussein Tabandeh, *A Muslim Commentary on the Universal Declaration of Human Rights*, London: Goulding, [1968], p. x.

76 Abul A'la Mawdudi, *Human Rights in Islam*, n.p., Islamic Foundation, 1980. The book is derived and extended from a 1975 lecture.

77 See also the related shift in *tiers-mondiste* thought, detailed by Eleanor Davey, *Idealism Beyond Borders*, Cambridge, UK: Cambridge University Press, 2015.

78 There were some exceptions, principally the ICJ, which devoted more effort to pursuing interaction with postcolonial states, rather than seeking to transcend them. For one of its more adventurous efforts, see *Human Rights in a One-Party State: International Seminar on Human Rights, Their Protection, and the Rule of Law in a One-Party State*, London: Search/ICJ, 1978, which collects the papers of the ICJ seminar, held 3–28 September 1976, in Dar es Salaam.

79 Many of these are assembled and excerpted in *AI in Quotes*, London: Amnesty International, 1976, Index NWS 50/001/1976; and *AI in Quotes*, London: Amnesty International, 1985, NWS 50/01/1985.

80 D. C. van der Spuy, *Amnesty for Terrorism*, Cape Town: South African Department of Information, March 1978.

81 For a notable example, circulated to British readers of the *Times*, see Statement by the Iranian Committee on Human Rights, "Continuing the Cyrus Tradition in Human Rights," *The Times* (Supplement), 21 May 1974, p. vii.

82 For representative texts, see Professor Bernhard Graefrath, *The Economic, Social and Cultural Human Rights in the German Democratic Republic*, Berlin: GDR Committee on Human Rights, 1970; and *Documentary Evidence of the Violation of Human Rights in the USA: Facts Bespeak Social Realities*, Berlin: Panorama DDR, [1978].

83 Saudi Ministry of Justice, *Proceedings of Conferences of Riyadh, Paris, Vatican City, Geneva, and Strasbourg, on Muslim Doctrine and Human Rights in Islam, Between Saudi Canonists and Eminent European Jurists and Intellectuals*, Riyadh: Ministry of Justice, [1975].

84 Roberta Cohen, "People's Republic of China: The Human Rights Exception," *Human Rights Quarterly*, 1987, vol. 9, 447–549.

13

"WHEN YOU ARE WEAK, YOU HAVE TO STICK TO PRINCIPLES"

Botswana and anticolonialism in human rights history

James Christian Kirby

Human rights historians have been divided in recent years on the question of whether anticolonialism was a human rights movement. Samuel Moyn's revisionist work *The Last Utopia* contends that the champions of national freedom in the 1950s and 1960s had no ambition to premise their sovereignty on observing individual freedoms.[1] Jan Eckel and Reza Afshari, similarly, argue that anticolonial activists in the global South merely evoked human rights principles as a tool to acquire state power.[2] Many postcolonial regimes violated the rights of citizens and used their newly gained sovereign status to shield against external scrutiny. This school of thought tends to marginalize non-Western actors and spotlight North American and Western European activists in international human rights history. At the same time as he recognizes how "Africa and Asia are deplorably under-researched regions," Jan Eckel asserts "that human rights did not acquire the same prominence there as in Western countries."[3]

New scholarship on the global South is challenging the supposed exclusivity between anticolonialism and human rights. The historian Meredith Terretta (see her essay in this volume), opens pathways for research into the trust territories of the United Nations (UN) Trusteeship Council. She shows in the British and French Cameroons that "many anti-colonial activists *did* consider collective liberation and individual rights to be interrelated."[4] Similarly, historian Steven Jensen surveys how larger Cold War powers were given a "master class" in human rights diplomacy and international lawmaking in the 1960s by Caribbean, African, and Asian diplomats.[5] These innovative studies recenter the narrative perspective away from a Western vantage point toward the institutions, lives, and localities of anticolonial triumph.[6]

This essay places Botswana at the center of the debate on human rights and anticolonialism. The country has been overlooked in human rights history, despite its position in Southern Africa at the crossroads of liberty, decolonization, development, race, and refugees. The first section begins by contextualizing Botswana within the history of race relations in Southern Africa and human rights on the continent. Next, the investigation traces the evolution of human rights ideas and terminology in Botswana from 1960, at the birth of its first major political parties, to 1980, at the death of its first president, Seretse Khama. Human rights became useful in resolving three interrelated challenges faced by Botswana: first, in securing a peaceful postcolonial transition; second, when the state desperately sought aid from the West; and third, as Botswana struggled for acceptance among fellow independent African states. The government's instrumental use of human rights idealism to maintain, and not merely attain, state sovereignty after independence shows how the decolonization and human rights movements were not necessarily inimical, but could intersect harmoniously and constructively. Botswana's leaders adopted multiple identities and postures on human rights, revealing there was more than just one human rights concept to address; the positions need not be contradictory nor hypocritical.[7] The country could find legitimacy among those especially, but not exclusively, in the West who championed political and civil rights. It could also gain the sympathy of other actors, principally in the global South, who prioritized national self-determination as "the first right."[8] Botswana's story is informative for revealing how the separation between national self-determination and individual human rights was not inevitable nor even as ubiquitous as currently thought. Such findings complicate the sweeping global narratives of human rights by revealing the intricacy of Third World politics and the variety of actors who engaged in human rights discourse.

To be sure, Botswana's case brings further evidence of human rights language deployed for strategic ends in the global South. The postcolonial leadership's chief priority was not international human rights, but state sovereignty. The use of human rights to advance political goals was common to all twentieth-century human rights movements, even those that claimed to be above politics. If political convenience does not automatically mean an absence of genuine ideological belief, then there is more room to include anticolonial actors in human rights history.[9] Indeed, anticolonial activists saw the removal of colonialism as a moral good. Botswana is an intriguing case given that its concern for state survival facilitated an embrace of human rights ideals. Quett Masire, Botswana's vice president under Seretse, summarized this outlook in his memoirs, stating, "When you are weak, you have to stick to principles."[10] Many non-Western actors during decolonization, in fact, did know and did care about human rights and these localities need to be researched and placed at the center of discussion to better understand the diversity of the anticolonial and human rights movements, as well as pinpoint where the two overlapped and deviated. Botswana is just one complex but compelling actor that defies simple categorization. Its history shows that at times agents of human rights were also agents of anticolonialism and state sovereignty.

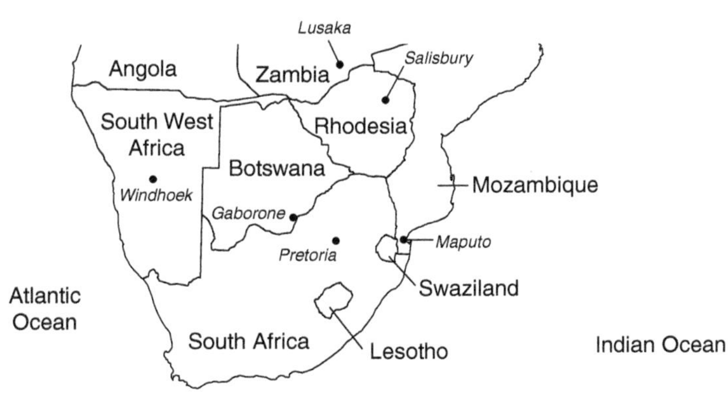

Figure 13.1 Southern Africa, ca. 1977.

The case of Botswana

Botswana was known as the Bechuanaland Protectorate under British rule between 1885 and 1966. The three South African High Commission Territories (HCTs) included Bechuanaland, Basutoland, and Swaziland. Bechuanaland was a landlocked territory that held no great strategic or economic interest for the British Empire, but provided a key access route within Southern Africa.[11] The 1909 Act to establish the Union of South Africa included a provision to eventually incorporate the HCTs. Pretoria requested the delivery of this promise from Britain for over 50 years, but its appeals were delayed and ultimately rejected. Traditional leaders in Bechuanaland abhorred the racialized policies of the Union government and British politicians expected international rebuke if they handed over the HCTs to an increasingly segregated South Africa.[12] The apartheid regime was consolidated in South Africa after the election of the National Party in 1948. It was guided by an ethno-nationalist ideology that entrenched the political and socioeconomic dominance of the white European population.

The year of apartheid coincided with the signing of the UN Universal Declaration of Human Rights (UDHR), at a time when international opinion began to rally against segregation.[13] Hendrik Verwoerd, the prime minister of South Africa, tried to obscure the oppressive nature of the apartheid system by shifting to the policy of "separate development" in 1959. The project sought the outright separation of African inhabitants by providing each ethnic group with a form of pseudo national self-determination in homelands or "Bantustans."[14] The 1955 Tomlinson Commission, an earlier study of the creation of African land reserves, envisaged Bechuanaland as a Bantu homeland.[15] These plans arose just as British colonial governments began to adopt a policy of multiracialism in the HCTs, which promoted greater social harmony between settlers and Africans. The creation of a republic in South Africa and South Africa's exit from the Commonwealth in 1961 signified the end of any realistic hope for the land transfer option.

The apartheid regime's racialist ideology deeply affected the life of Botswana's founding president, Seretse Khama. Seretse was the heir to the throne of the Bamangwato people, the largest chieftaincy in Bechuanaland. His marriage to a white British woman, Ruth Williams, in London on 29 September 1948 was controversial. South African leaders, who soon thereafter banned interracial marriage, were outraged that a prominent African leader on its doorstep had resisted racialist thinking. Pretoria made numerous threats, including the enforcement of Britain's earlier promise of a transfer. The British government attempted to ease tensions with South Africa by forcing Seretse into exile to England from 1950 to 1956. He was only allowed to return to Bechuanaland after abdicating his claim to the chiefdom.[16] Seretse would enter party politics in the early 1960s, leading the Bechuanaland Democratic Party to victory in the March 1965 elections for self-government and subsequently independence on 30 September 1966. Bechuanaland did not have a mass nationalist movement for colonial liberation. Rather, Seretse laid out a pathway to independence that involved a gradualist transition to self-government, political cooperation with the colonial authority, and an openness to economic cooperation with South Africa after independence. Botswana began with few anticolonial or pro-liberation credentials. Much of independent Africa initially regarded with skepticism the motivations of Seretse's government and doubted its support for human rights in Southern Africa.[17]

Botswana was geopolitically and economically vulnerable when it entered statehood. It was an African majority-ruled state surrounded by white minority regimes in South Africa, South-West Africa, and Rhodesia. The territory was sparsely populated, having fewer than 600,000 people situated in an area around the size of France. Botswana had only local police and, by 1977, a small defense force for security. It did not have the capacity to stop multiple incursions from South African and Rhodesian forces chasing suspected freedom fighters. Two key events typified the prolongation of white rule in the region and the exacerbation of racial conflict. The first was the apartheid regime's massacre of African protesters at Sharpeville in March 1960. This came only a few weeks after British prime minister Harold Macmillan's "wind of change" speech in Cape Town, which signified Britain's acceptance of the transfers of power sweeping the continent. The second was the announcement of a Unilateral Declaration of Independence by the white Rhodesian prime minister Ian Smith in November 1965. No country recognized this step and it was widely condemned. Despite such difficulties, Botswana became one of the most acclaimed success stories in Africa.[18] The risk of internal conflict was minimal because its eight principal chieftaincies originated from the same linguistic group. Botswana was severely underdeveloped by the British rulers and remained dependent on external financial and material assistance for many years. It began nationhood with little infrastructure and only a handful of university-educated citizens. Foreign aid made up 45 percent of total government spending in 1973 and 100 percent of development expenditure from 1967 to 1970.[19] A crucial asset came with the discovery of diamonds soon after independence, generating decades of income from vast mineral wealth. Botswana used the mining boom and generous foreign aid receipts to create one of the fastest growing economies in the world. In addition, there were very low levels of corruption under Seretse's leadership.

Botswana also became a model for human rights observance on the continent. The country is the only former British dependency in mainland Africa to have retained, largely intact, its independence constitution and bill of rights. Furthermore, it has Africa's longest running multiparty democracy. African nationalists elsewhere on the continent mostly came to power on a pledge to secure both freedom and unity. These two objectives sat in constant tension. Leaders regularly used the imperative for stability as an excuse to justify the abuse of human rights whenever disunity threatened civil conflict or a redistribution of political power. The one-party state became prevalent in sub-Saharan Africa by the mid-1960s, which involved the banning of rival political organizations. Well over 30 African states claimed single-party status at some point after colonial liberation either temporarily or permanently. Military rule was another common form of government, whereby a successful *coup d'état* resulted in an armed force taking control of the state. Over two-thirds of independent Africa had succumbed to military rule by the end of the 1970s.[20]

Many African regimes hoped to offset their poor record on individual freedoms by promising to alleviate chronic underdevelopment and deliver socioeconomic freedoms. The social scientist Rhoda Howard notes that African leaders generally subscribed to the "full-belly thesis" that political and civil rights could only be observed once a country has reached an adequate stage of development.[21] However, Seretse defied that thesis: He went further than most African leaders in presenting an unmistakable commitment to political liberties and individual protections before holding power. His stance not only undermined any potential argument for authoritarianism after independence; it became a key premise of Botswana's long-term viability and prosperity. The preservation of human rights under a nonracial democracy offered a unique identity for the country. This image of a small state projecting a beacon of hope in Southern Africa, formed the basis of Botswana's appeal to potential donors and allies. Even if human rights were easier to uphold in Botswana's specific geopolitical and economic conditions, that did not dilute its powerful message about the feasibility and desirability of such values on the continent. Botswana's experiences in human rights were an outstanding example of image-building in circumstances where survival was tied to international visibility.

Race and human rights in Bechuanaland

Human rights discourse was a prominent feature of Bechuanaland's lead-up to independence. The Legislative Council and Executive Council offered narrow representation for African people, but their establishment in 1961 encouraged the development of Bechuanaland's first major political parties. The postcolonial transition began in 1963, when the colonial authority held a conference to discuss the 1961 constitution and set out proposals for self-government under African majority rule. Bechuanaland would replace its segregated voter rolls and representation whereby Europeans held a commanding position in government with a common voter roll on the principle of one person, one vote. The rhetoric of human rights was useful at a time when the major parties were outlining their vision for the postcolonial era and the future of race relations in the country. Voices from a cross-section of society deliberated on the design of the democratic system, the protection of private property rights, and the enshrinement of individual freedoms. These topics were debated amid talks over the bill of rights and the hearings of the 1962–3 Select Committee on Racial Discrimination, a forum enacted by the Legislative Council to report on ways to improve race relations. Discussions of constitutional rights were of course a matter of domestic, not international, citizenship.[22] However, local and global rights claims intersected during these debates in various ways. The leading politicians appealed to universal human rights to support their national agendas and the ideals of nonracial democracy. These goals were enshrined in the state's founding document and became a philosophy of human rights applicable for all in Southern Africa.

The two major parties in Bechuanaland were the Democratic Party and the People's Party. The latter was the vanguard in Bechuanaland for anticolonialism, Pan-Africanism, and African socialism. The People's Party split into three separate factions before the 1965 elections for self-government. The party overwhelmingly lost the election, but it made a definitive contribution to the evolution of local human rights ideas and norms. Its postcolonial vision aimed to appeal to the concerns expressed by African witnesses at the Select Committee on Racial Discrimination, where disparities in standards of living and the distribution of government services were revealed.[23] The People's Party was the only political organization to detail a set of socioeconomic rights. Its election manifestos directly quoted from the UDHR, including Article 25 on the right to an adequate standard of living and Article 26 on the right to education.[24] Paired with this emphasis on socioeconomic rights was a racially exclusivist vision for the collective rights of Africans. White residents made up less than 1 percent of the population. Yet they occupied some of the most fertile land along the southeast and eastern border, and the Colonial Authority saw them as playing a pivotal economic role. White inhabitants, according to the People's Party, adhered to a foreign concept of private land ownership and had an illegitimate claim to property in Bechuanaland. The party proposed that "all land termed crown and/or European settlement in any part of our country … must be restored to the indigenous people," without compensation.[25] The Democratic Party was compelled to offer a convincing alternative that could compete with the People's Party's agenda. Different human rights could meet different political, economic, and social goals, favoring a range of internal interests. Bechuanaland's first democratic elections were not about whether to uphold human rights, but which rights to uphold in preference to others.

Seretse outlined a party platform a year before the vote based on a long-term commitment to democratic principles. His address was remarkable for its timing. It was given as a statement of values just as colonial officials and foreign observers questioned the country's prospects for achieving economic viability and autonomy from South Africa, and as Seretse came close to losing his life through illness. He prepared a speech to be presented to the Democratic Party's national congress in absentia, from his bed in Francistown Hospital. His health epitomized how Botswana's stance for human rights originated from a position of almost terminal weakness. Seretse watched multiple African colonial dependencies attain national freedom often with the loss of democratic freedoms. Seretse speculated whether Africans were aware of the challenges this freedom presents, especially how far "we may or may not maintain a free atmosphere in our free states." He promised that once in power the Democratic Party would encourage open political opposition and criticism in a multiparty state. "As regards freedom and basic human rights," Seretse declared, "we shall always endeavour to attach the same value to those concepts *for other people as we do for ourselves*."[26] The Democratic Party's manifesto outlined a commitment to elections "carried out on a one-man-one-vote basis" and a pledge to "uphold a democratic form of government and democratic institutions" once in power.[27] Seretse suggested that good governance was not just about serving the best interests of the people, but about being consistent regarding "universal basic human rights" and being tolerant of those with alternative political creeds who were seeking to keep the ruling party in check.[28] If the one-party state was adopted elsewhere due to fears over insecurity and underdevelopment, Seretse, facing similar problems, made a defiant pledge to preserve liberal-democratic rights.

The Democratic Party's ethos of political liberties included an emphasis on ensuring individual freedoms after independence.[29] Seretse crafted a philosophy of "nonracialism" in response to the People's Party's vision for African collective rights. Nonracialism sought to improve internal harmony by discarding the concept of race altogether and substituting a respect for individualism. "[I]t is quite possible for black and white," Seretse stated, "not only to live together, but to play together, to go to school together, and in fact form a real nation."[30] Dr. Silas M. Molema, a Democratic Party member, shared this idea. He emphasized how nonracialism was consistent with "this ideal of fundamental human rights."[31] However, in many former British dependencies with settler populations the notion of individual human rights in constitutional discussions served as an inconspicuous way of preserving white minority interests.[32] White residents needed further reassurance their economic interests would be safeguarded. The colonial authority prioritized the enshrinement of private property rights in the constitution to appease white settlers who threatened to leave. Peter Fawcus, the Resident Commissioner, noted that peaceful race relations were "conditional on a Bill of Rights to safeguard human rights."[33] Seretse acknowledged the advantages of retaining white capital, investment, and expertise in the country. It was essential "that we have an outlook above racial hate and dislikes."[34] The constitutional talks resulted in a clear provision for the protection of individual rights, with the final 1966 Independence Constitution outlining "[p]rotection from deprivation of property" without compensation, and "protection for privacy of home and other property."[35] Human rights principles in Bechuanaland could be used in both idealistic terms, for democracy and interracial unity, and for the practical politics of satisfying all major interest groups.

Seretse's advocacy of political liberties and individual protections made up a distinct philosophy of human rights under the label of "non-racial democracy." It was a principle that borrowed from international doctrines and Western liberal-democratic models, but applied to suit local conditions and regional circumstances. Different political actors in Bechuanaland identified with different sets of rights, thereby reflecting the variegated interpretations of human rights in global forums like the UN. This was a case of internationalist principles becoming provincialized within the politics of Bechuanaland's postcolonial transition, which featured a range of racial interests, party debates, and national concerns. Seretse reflected on his country's progress on Human Rights Day, 10 December 1975. "We have in the past nine years succeeded in laying the foundations for a non-racial society," he broadcast, "a society in which respect for human rights has become a national ideal." Quoting directly from the UDHR, he saw it as "a national vehicle through which we have been able to 'reaffirm our faith in the dignity and worth of the human person.'"[36] The president made this announcement in the middle of what historian Samuel Moyn has described as the "breakthrough" decade for human rights.[37] Yet this expression of commitment to human rights was not new for his country. The Democratic Party had been officially wedded to these principles since well before independence in 1966. Rights claims in the era of decolonization could be inspired by principles of universal human rights as well as targeted to the defense of national sovereignty. It is important to note that Botswana's experience actually confirms a political shift in the West: The country embraced human rights in the 1960s, but only earned its greatest rewards from the broader human rights movement in the 1970s.

Human rights idealism and the quest for foreign assistance

Seretse used human rights ideals to appeal to foreign donors and protect Botswana's territorial integrity. He deployed human rights rhetoric to serve the state's self-interest, without undermining Botswana's moral claim to be a champion of human rights. Human rights networks in North America and Western Europe became concerned with the mission to preserve Botswana's sovereignty. State interests and human rights ideals, as Botswana's experience shows, could be mutually tethered. Indeed, the state, by adhering to international standards of human rights and restricting its power over citizens, actually enhanced its legitimacy and security. The government's performative moralism was crucial for building an international image worthy of foreign aid, sympathy, and encouragement – all of which helped to safeguard Botswana's existence as a peaceful and viable country. The interests of the state were central in the leadership's calculations. The state, however, could not be separated from the principles that made it worth protecting. A commitment to human rights justified itself many times over for strategic, economic, and moral purposes.

Seretse's strategy for attracting prospective donors was to advertise Botswana's human rights credentials, exceptionality, and transformative potential in the region. Seretse sketched a bold mission statement for the territory in the lead-up to independence. "It has always been my belief," he sermonized at the 1966 Independence Conference in London, "that Bechuanaland, small country though it may be, has a role to play in Southern Africa and in the unnecessary conflicts between black and white."[38] Seretse told foreign media soon after winning the March 1965 elections that his country's intention was "to influence neighbouring states and other states to show that black and white people can live together quite harmoniously and work for the interests of their country."[39]

Seretse marked Botswana's ascendance on the world stage in his first address to the UN General Assembly on 24 September 1969. The president characterized Botswana as the antithesis of nearby societies based on racial separation. He located the biggest threat to Botswana's nonracialist ideals in those neighboring countries, "whose way of life is not our way of life and whose values are in most respects, the reverse of our own." He proclaimed Botswana's decisive strategic importance, whereby it could encourage an ideological transformation within Southern Africa. The greater the success of the multiracial project, the more it would expose the failures of apartheid and separate development. "Botswana as a thriving majority-ruled state," Seretse summed up, "will present an effective and serious challenge to the credibility of South Africa's racial policies," and to South Africa's attempts to develop independent Bantu homelands for its African population.[40] Seretse's efforts to sell Botswana as a worthy aid recipient spotlighted the merits of rewarding its exemplary behavior and the promise of promoting such values throughout the region by the strength of its example.

Seretse outlined the imperative of building a global reputation to the US African American Chamber of Commerce a day after his UN address. He argued that to continue on the path of development, "it is necessary to convince people and governments residing outside Africa that Botswana has a future and a role to play." His speech noted the stereotypical image of the continent, which depicted "dramatic failures," "lurid adventure stories," and "Africa's wildlife." The government needed "to create a recognisable identity," according to Seretse, for Botswana to stand out.[41] The president immediately attracted the United States, which became one of Botswana's most significant aid donors in the 1970s. Edward Brooke, an African American senator, brought Seretse's UN speech to the attention of the US Congress just over a week after its delivery. Brooke had met Seretse on a trip to Botswana in January 1968, where he was impressed by the country's leaders but wondered whether its territorial integrity and value system could survive in such a dangerous and oppressive region. After Seretse's convincing performance at the UN, Brooke found only inspiration and confidence in the country's endeavors. Botswana was fighting for "the rights which we ourselves have long proclaimed," Brooke acknowledged to his colleagues, and "deserves our fullest support and understanding." A respect for human rights, in Brooke's eyes, was pivotal for consolidating Botswana's nonracial democracy and offering a better future for race relations in Southern Africa. Brooke believed if Botswana could reach a state of prosperity with interracial unity, it would offer an influential model for the world on how to advance human rights, even from a position of geopolitical weakness. "Botswana, in some ways, more than any other nation," the senator exclaimed, "occupies a key position in the fight for human rights."[42] Powerful states like the United States identified with Seretse's campaign to advance human rights in a geographical context of troubled race relations. Botswana had a symbolic force that placed it at the center of this transnational concern and entitled it to a receptive audience looking for hope and solutions.

Seretse attracted American aid with a mixture of compatible strategic interests and common ideals. Washington saw Botswana as a symbolic asset that could help improve America's perception on the continent. The United States used its assistance to Botswana to show Washington's commitment to promoting human rights and independent African majority rule in Southern Africa. This offered a potential way to distance Washington from its links to the white minority regimes. Richard Rolfe, a South African journalist, quoted a US official in August 1971 who believed Botswana "gets more aid per head of population than any other country in the world, not excluding South Vietnam."[43] American officials and policymakers were also impressed by the substance behind the image. State Department reports on Botswana from 1976 onwards praised the country's respect for individual freedoms, the absence of political prisoners, and the provision of democratic rights under a multiparty system.[44] These conclusions were backed up by the views of independent human rights organizations such as Amnesty International and Freedom House.[45] The utility of this internal record was exemplified in a statement from one foreign diplomat in Botswana who told the *Washington Post* in December 1977, commenting on foreign aid, "You can't give this country enough, its human rights record is so good."[46] The United States committed over US$432 million in grants and loans between 1965 to 1980.[47] The hallmark project was a US$16.6 million loan package for the Bot-Zam road, a highway completed in January 1977 to develop transportation links between Botswana and Zambia on their tiny common border.[48] The human rights movement of the 1970s was not exclusively led from North America and Western Europe. Botswana, a small non-Western state, was so advanced in promoting human rights coming into the 1970s that it persuaded a global superpower to follow its lead and devote substantial resources to further its success.[49]

Botswana's experience shows that human rights could have strategic uses for postcolonial states and that the 1970s movement did not only include causes that were professedly above politics. State sovereignty and the imperatives of government were not automatically hostile to human rights. Human rights, far from merely a threat or hindrance to the state, could be treated as an asset for the fulfillment of security and development priorities. It could also be a survival strategy. A geopolitical situation, Steven Jensen argues, "can appear so critical and so dire that realism can only express itself meaningfully through an idealistic and transformative worldview" like human rights.[50] Seretse, in slight contrast, suggested the day after his 1969 UN speech that the only ideology followed in Botswana was "realism" with neither optimism nor cynicism. However, his definition offers an example of articulating immediate strategic priorities through a moralistic worldview, in this case, on political freedom, racial equality, and economic prosperity. For the president, it was "realistic," "pragmatic," and "moral" to accept that development could only be sustained under a nonracial democracy.[51] Seretse believed it was reasonable to assume that Botswana's nonracialism path would have an influential role to play in a region overshadowed by ideologies of racial separation. This was naive idealism at face value, but Seretse's grand vision was in fact a practical step in attracting external assistance. State survival, stability, and growth were pinned to a respect for human rights. Such small state actors, unlike many Western powers who enjoyed relative security and wealth, could inspire others through moral strength in the face of physical vulnerability. Botswana's leadership on upholding democratic freedoms and individual rights in a multiracial setting helped it to negotiate a difficult geopolitical predicament. However, there were other variants of human rights that commanded the attention of Seretse's government.

Botswana's movement for individual and national self-determination

Botswana's powerful message on the rights of the individual was interchangeable with another on the rights of aspiring and existing postcolonial entities. What mattered was the audience. Anticolonial and Third World circles sympathized with Botswana's struggle to preserve its own sovereignty and its limited measures for assisting those still oppressed under white minority rule. Botswana acquired this recognition in the anticolonial movement by the early 1970s, around the same moment when it developed close relations with human rights networks in the West. Yet the pathways to establish each connection and the ideas used to further each courtship were not the same. Botswana was met with animosity from the Organization of African Unity (OAU) in its early years. The Democratic Party did not lead a mass social movement to independence and, unlike the People's Party, failed to develop a bond with leading members of the OAU before independence. Icons of the OAU, like President Kwame Nkrumah of Ghana and President Julius Nyerere of Tanzania, initially regarded the Democratic Party with suspicion. The Democratic Party was embarrassed at its first OAU meeting in Accra, Ghana, in October 1965. Diallo Telli, secretary-general of the OAU, questioned the validity of Bechuanaland's 1965 elections and accused the Democratic Party of being financially backed by the apartheid regime.[52] All at once, Botswana needed to prove its legitimacy among Western partners in the human rights movement and African allies in the anticolonial movement. Seretse had to convince the OAU of Botswana's commitment, not to individual human rights, but to the collective right of self-determination.

Botswana had a very narrow space for developing ties to OAU members because of the country's delicate geopolitical situation. The state's dilemma was to somehow maintain vital economic relationships with neighboring white minority regimes while gaining political acceptance among African majority-ruled states further north. The two sides were generally antagonistic towards each other. The OAU militarily supported anti-apartheid forces, and white rule in Southern Africa represented the last remnants of colonial oppression on the continent. Botswana required the sympathy of the mass voting bloc of independent Africa at the UN. Without this support Botswana could count on only limited help in international forums to launch an effective protest and stir outrage if South Africa was to take aggressive action. However, Botswana could not build ties with the OAU through policies that would threaten South Africa and provoke retaliation (such as permitting suspected freedom fighters to launch attacks from Botswana's territory).[53] Seretse took productive steps to affirm Botswana's political standpoint by calling for the end of apartheid and maintaining an "open-door policy" on refugees. Both steps were justified on the basis of upholding international standards of human rights and the UDHR.[54] However, these measures on their own were insufficient for earning approval within the OAU. Botswana engaged in high-wire diplomacy whereby excess collaboration with either side risked isolating it from a vital source of political or economic cooperation.

Botswana could not rely on its outstanding record on individual human rights to affiliate with independent Africa. Its relations with Zambia and Tanzania exemplify the difficulties of diplomacy between states with philosophical differences regarding human rights. Seretse was disappointed by Zambian officials and government supporters who did not recognize the Democratic Party's long-standing commitment to multiparty democracy. Zambia became a one-party state in 1972 under the United National Independence Party (UNIP). Seretse was greeted awkwardly at Livingstone airfield by UNIP supporters in February 1972 to chants of "One Botswana: One Nation: One Leader: One Party State," in an adaption of a similar slogan in support of the Zambian government.[55] Seretse emphatically criticized the communitarian philosophy of African socialism at the same time as he reached out to states like Zambia and Tanzania that upheld their own versions of the concept.[56] Such statements of communitarianism were overshadowed by some African leaders' rejection of any responsibility to protect individual liberties after entering government. Julius Nyerere summarized his position on individual protections in August 1964, a year before Tanzania formally became a one-party state, stating that it was "better that ninety-nine innocent people should suffer temporary detention than that one possible traitor should wreck the nation."[57] Botswana's common ground with the West on individual human rights and democracy was not shared broadly in independent Africa.

Seretse focused instead on aligning Botswana with the OAU's emphasis on the right to national self-determination. To accomplish this goal, the Democratic Party aimed to become a more forceful advocate for liberation movements and it rewrote certain elements of its own history. It had supported a gradualist transition to independence in the early 1960s to accommodate Botswana's difficult geographic and economic circumstances. Seretse opposed violent means of achieving colonial liberation up until the late 1960s, based on lessons from "our own history."[58] His rhetoric shifted to a more typical anticolonial stance by the 1970s and became even more outspoken over the decade. He told a party conference in April 1973 that the Democratic Party "flatly refused to be influenced by the views of those who predicted a future of gloom and unmitigated poverty."[59] The government did not advocate the use of violence in principle, but voiced an understanding for the motivations of these groups to resort to desperate measures. The president characterized the guerrilla forces as "neither terrorists nor murderers," only as activists "fighting on behalf of humanity for their basic human rights."[60] "As a party we have always believed in the right to self-determination," Seretse proclaimed at a party conference in April 1977, "hence we cannot but support fully those who have been forced to take up arms to fight for this inalienable right."[61] Archibald Mogwe, Botswana's foreign minister, explained the main intent of such statements in July 1975 to David Bolen, the US ambassador. Mogwe described how "African states were preoccupied with human dignity, equality and self-determination in Southern Africa." These countries, according to Mogwe, "tended to judge issues and countries by the degree of support and interest demonstrated in resolving these problems."[62] Botswana hoped its affirmations of the right to national self-determination would be enough to build credibility within the OAU, because there was little else it could do without dangerously inflaming tensions with South Africa or Rhodesia.

Botswana's quest to gain acceptance of its foreign policy within the OAU was successful. This is seen clearly in July 1973 when Nzo Ekangaki, secretary-general of the OAU, visited Botswana. He commended Seretse's eloquent voice in opposition to the injustices of the apartheid regime. "The Liberation struggle has a military aspect and an economic aspect," Ekangaki remarked, "but also a spiritual aspect." The secretary-general agreed with Seretse that the greatest contribution the country could make was by upholding its nonracialist values in opposition to the doctrines of white supremacy.[63] Seretse confirmed to Radio Botswana in June 1974 that Botswana's position was understood and valued by the rest of independent Africa and the liberation movements themselves.[64] All African representatives supported Botswana when the government launched a complaint to the UN Security Council in January 1977 against increasing incursions from the Rhodesian regime.[65] Botswana found security in two movements that are usually presented in human rights historiography as mutually exclusive: human rights and anticolonialism. Seretse strategically aligned Botswana with the ideals of human rights activists in the West and with the fight for national self-determination in the colonial and postcolonial world. This shows that, to differing extents, there is space for authentic members of the anticolonial movement to be categorized within the human rights movement.

Conclusion

This essay has used the example of Botswana to illustrate the advantages of putting overlooked localities at the center of human rights history. Such narrative perspectives allow for a reassessment, and possibly a rethinking, of the wider history of human rights. Studies are needed particularly on the colonial and postcolonial world of the 1960s and 1970s. These regions lack sufficient archival investigation on the subject. The historians Samuel Moyn, Jan Eckel, and Reza Afshari, whose interpretations have permeated scholarly studies, prematurely declared that anticolonialism was not a human rights movement. They underestimated the range of political, economic, and social groups that engaged in the anticolonial struggle, and offered no space for existing research to add nuance to their sweeping claims. Larger geopolitical and economic powers are not the only valuable actors in human rights history. Small states like Botswana developed great symbolic currency via human rights idealism and proved immensely resourceful in using it for strategic ends. The country, like many forgotten non-Western actors, deserves to be integrated into international human rights history.

Whether such voices remain little known or gain broader exposure has consequences for broader debates in the literature. The concept and terminology of human rights in Bechuanaland emerged during the postcolonial transition and framed the party-political debates on freedom and racial justice, before the supposed "breakthrough" in the 1970s. Seretse, upon entering government, realized the usefulness of these values for building international visibility, attracting foreign aid, and ensuring state survival. Botswana's experience complicates the idea of there being only tension between human rights and state sovereignty. The country built ties with the movements of anticolonialism and human rights, finding legitimacy in the claims of both individual and national self-determination. A historiography that does not unearth fine-grained detail and account for domestic conditions limits the scope for analysis. Yet such cases as Botswana, together with others from colonial and postcolonial history that are found, for example, elsewhere in this volume, form a growing mosaic that will do much to clarify the place of decolonization in the evolution of human rights. This forms an important new trend in the scholarship towards a more intricate and inclusive historical understanding of human rights. To ask whether anticolonialism was a human rights movement is to assume, wrongly, that both are easily defined categories. The question for historians to consider is what the interweaving of anticolonialism and human rights, in places like Botswana, reveals about the diversity of actors in both movements and the various possibilities they envisaged for their own future and that of humanity.

Notes

1 Samuel Moyn, *The Last Utopia: Human Rights in History*, Cambridge, MA: Belknap Press of Harvard University Press, 2010, pp. 84–119. For critiques of *The Last Utopia*, see Christopher McCrudden, "Human Rights Histories," *Oxford Journal of Legal Studies*, 2015, vol. 35, 179–212; Robert Brier, "Beyond the Quest for a 'Breakthrough': Reflections on the Recent Historiography on Human Rights," in Sarah Panter (ed.) *Mobility and Biography*, Berlin: De Gruyter, 2015, pp. 155–73; Philip Alston, "Does the Past Matter? On the Origins of Human Rights," review of *The Slave Trade and the Origins of International Human Rights Law* by Jenny S. Martinez, *Harvard Law Review*, 2013, vol. 126, 2043–81; Seyla Benhabib, "Moving Beyond False Binarisms: On Samuel Moyn's *The Last Utopia*," *Qui Parle*, 2013, vol. 22, 81–93.

2 Jan Eckel, "Human Rights and Decolonization: New Perspectives and Open Questions," *Humanity: An International Journal of Human Rights, Humanitarianism, and Development*, 2010, vol. 1, 111–35; Reza Afshari, "On Historiography of Human Rights. Reflections on Paul Gordon Lauren's *The Evolution of International Human Rights: Visions Seen*," *Human Rights Quarterly*, 2007, vol. 29, 44–5. See also A. W. Brian Simpson, *Human Rights and the End of Empire: Britain and the Genesis of the European Convention*, New York: Oxford University Press, 2001, p. 300.

3 Jan Eckel, "The Rebirth of Politics from the Spirit of Morality: Explaining the Human Rights Revolution of the 1970s," in Jan Eckel and Samuel Moyn (eds.) *The Breakthrough: Human Rights in the 1970s*, Philadelphia: University of Pennsylvania Press, 2014, p. 238. A similar sentiment is expressed in Andreas Eckert, "African Nationalists and Human Rights, 1940s–1970s," in Stefan-Ludwig Hoffmann (ed.) *Human Rights in the Twentieth Century*, New York: Cambridge University Press, 2011, pp. 285–6.

4 Emphasis in original. Meredith Terretta, "'We Had Been Fooled into Thinking that the UN Watches Over the Entire World': Human Rights, UN Trust Territories, and Africa's Decolonization," *Human Rights Quarterly*, 2012, vol. 34, 329–60. On the League of Nation's mechanisms for petitioning, protesting, and reporting, see Susan Pedersen, *The Guardians: The League of Nations and The Crisis of Empire*, Oxford: Oxford University Press, 2015.

5 Steven L. B. Jensen, *The Making of International Human Rights: The 1960s, Decolonization and the Reconstruction of Global Values*, New York: Cambridge University Press, 2016, pp. 5–9, 277–80. The wars of independence in Algeria and Kenya also influenced international human rights discourse. See Fabian Klose, *Human Rights in the Shadow of Colonial Violence: The Wars of Independence in Kenya and Algeria*, Philadelphia: University of Pennsylvania Press, 2013.

6 For non-Western contributions to human rights in international forums, see Roland Burke, *Decolonization and the Evolution of International Human Rights*, Philadelphia: University of Pennsylvania Press, 2010; Susan Waltz, "Universalizing Human Rights: The Role of Small States in the Construction of the Universal Declaration of Human Rights," *Human Rights Quarterly*, 2001, vol. 23, 44–72; Lydia Liu, "Shadows of Universalism: The Untold Story of Human Rights around 1948," *Critical Inquiry*, 2014, vol. 40, 385–417.

7 On the multiplicity of human rights movements and actors, see Brad Simpson, "Self-determination, Human Rights, and the End of Empire in the 1970s," *Humanity: An International Journal of Human Rights, Humanitarianism, and Development*, 2013, vol. 4, 240–1.

8 On the placement of self-determination as "the first right" among postcolonial states, see Brad Simpson, "Denying the 'First Right': The United States, Indonesia, and the Ranking of Human Rights by the Carter Administration, 1976–1980," *International History Review*, 2009, vol. 31, 798–826.

9 Bonny Ibhawoh, *Human Rights in Africa*, Cambridge, UK: Cambridge University Press, 2018, p. 136; Bonny Ibhawoh, "Testing the Atlantic Charter: Linking Anticolonialism, Self-determination and Universal Human Rights," *International Journal of Human Rights*, 2014, vol. 18, 842–60, esp. 845; and Bonny Ibhawoh, "Human Rights and National Liberation: The Anticolonial Politics of Nnamdi Azikiwe," in Baba G. Jallow (ed.) *Leadership in Colonial Africa: Disruption of Traditional Frameworks and Patterns*, New York: Palgrave Macmillan, 2014, pp. 55–68.

10 Stephen R. Lewis Jr. (ed.), *Quett Ketumile Joni Masire: Very Brave or Very Foolish? Memoirs of an African Democrat*, Gaborone: Macmillan Botswana, 2006, p. 250.

11 Jackson Mutero Chirenje, *A History of Northern Botswana 1850–1910*, Cranbury, NJ: Associated University Presses, 1977.

12 Ronald Hyam, *The Failure of South African Expansion 1908–1948*, London: Macmillan, 1972.

13 Jan Smuts, the prime minister of South Africa, wrote the words "human rights" into the Charter of the United Nations. However, his notion of human rights was narrowly defined and hypocritical. Smuts, who presided over the discriminatory treatment of Indians living in South Africa, was later accused by India's UN delegation of violating international standards that he himself authored. See Christof Heyns and Willem Gravett, "'To Save Succeeding Generations from the Scourge of War': Jan Smuts and the Ideological Foundations of the United Nations," *Human Rights Quarterly*, 2017, vol. 39, 574–605.

14 Saul Dubow, *Apartheid: 1948–1994*, Oxford: Oxford University Press, 2014; Jamie Miller, *An African Volk: The Apartheid Regime and its Search for Survival*, New York: Oxford University Press, 2016.

15 Neil Parsons, Willie Henderson, and Thomas Tlou, *Seretse Khama: 1921–80*, Gaborone: Botswana Society and Braamfontein: Macmillan, 1995, p. 145.

16 Susan Williams, *Colour Bar: The Triumph of Seretse Khama and His Nation*, London: Penguin, 2007.

17 James Kirby, "'What Has Ghana Got That We Haven't?': Party Politics and the Right to National Self-Determination in Botswana, 1960–1966," *Journal of Imperial and Commonwealth History*, 2017, vol. 45, 1049–74.

18 For accounts of Botswana's success story, see Daron Acemoglu and James A. Robinson, *Why Nations Fail: The Origins of Power, Prosperity, and Poverty*, New York: Crown Business, 2012; James Clark Leith, *Why Botswana Prospered*, Montreal: McGill-Queen's University Press, 2005; Abdi Ismail Samatar, *An African Miracle: State and Class Leadership and Colonial Legacy in Botswana Development*, Portsmouth: Heinemann, 1999. For counter-arguments to the narrative of success, see Louis A. Picard, *The Politics of Development in Botswana: A Model for Success?* Boulder, CO: Lynne Rienner, 1987; Kenneth Good, "Interpreting the Exceptionality of Botswana," *Journal of Modern African Studies*, 1992, vol. 30, 69–95; Ørnulf Gulbrandsen, *The State and the Social: State Formation in Botswana and its Pre-Colonial and Colonial Genealogies*, New York: Berghahn, 2012; Ellen Hillbom, "Diamonds or Development? A Structural Assessment of Botswana's Forty Years of Success," *Journal of Modern African Studies*, 2008, vol. 46, 191–214.

19 Gervase S. Maipose, G. M. Somolekae, and Timothy Johnston, "Effective Aid Management: The Case of Botswana," in Jerker Carlsson, Gloria Somolekae, and Nicolas van de Walle (eds.) *Foreign Aid in Africa: Learning from Country Experiences*, Uppsala: Nordiska Afrikainstitutet, 1997, p. 19.

20 Nic Cheeseman, *Democracy in Africa: Successes, Failures, and the Struggle for Political Reform*, New York: Cambridge University Press, 2015. See also Frederick Cooper, *Africa Since 1940: The Past of the Present*, Cambridge, UK: Cambridge University Press, 2002 and the essay by Roland Burke in this volume.

21 Rhoda Howard, "The Full-Belly Thesis: Should Economic Rights Take Priority Over Civil and Political Rights? Evidence from Sub-Saharan Africa," *Human Rights Quarterly*, 1983, vol. 5, 467–90.

22 Moyn, *Last Utopia*, pp. 12–3, 20, 42–3.

23 Botswana National Archives and Records Services, Gaborone (hereafter BNARS) BNB 632, Legislative Council Report of the Select Committee on Racial Discrimination, November 1963.

24 The National Archives of the United Kingdom, London (hereafter TNA) CO 1048/531, Philip Matante's election manifesto, March 1965; BNARS BNB 1672, Botswana Independence Party election manifesto, 1965; TNA CO 1048/531, Kgaleman Motsete's election manifesto, 1965.

25 TNA CO 1048/113, Peter Maruping and J. L. Kgaboesele, People's Party resolutions, December 1962; TNA CO 1048/535, Motsamai Mpho and Emmanuel R. Mokobi to Harold Wilson, 6 November 1964.

26 Emphasis in original. Senate House Library, University of London (hereafter SHL) PP.BS.BDP, Seretse, address to Democratic Party National Congress, 28 March 1964.

27 SHL PP.BS.BDP, "This Is What We Stand For," Democratic Party election manifesto, January 1965.

28 SHL PP.BS.BDP, Seretse, address to Democratic Party National Congress, 28 March 1964.

29 James Kirby, "'Conditional on a Bill of Rights': Race and Human Rights in the Constitution of Botswana, 1960–66," *Law & History* [Journal of the Australian and New Zealand Law and History Society], 2017, vol. 4, 30–61.

30 Bechuanaland Legislative Council, *Official Report of the Debates of the First Meeting of the Second Session*, Mafeking: Bechuanaland Legislative Council, 1962, p. 120.
31 Bechuanaland Legislative Council, *Official Report of the Debates of the First Meeting of the First Session*, Mafeking: Bechuanaland Legislative Council, 1961, p. 29.
32 Stanley de Smith, *The New Commonwealth and Its Constitutions*, London: Stevens, 1964, p. 179. On bills of rights in former British dependencies, see Charles O. H. Parkinson, *Bills of Rights and Decolonization: The Emergence of Domestic Human Rights Instruments in Britain's Overseas Territories*, Oxford: Oxford University Press, 2007.
33 TNA CO 1048/404, Peter Fawcus to Courtenay Robert Latimer, 15 January 1963.
34 SHL PP.BS.BDP, Seretse, address to Democratic Party National Congress, 28 March 1964.
35 BNARS BNB 700, "Constitution of Botswana," 1966.
36 Seretse Khama, "Broadcast to the Nation on the Occasion of Human Rights Day, 10 December 1975," in Gwendolen M. Carter and E. Philip Morgan (eds.) *From the Frontline: Speeches of Sir Seretse Khama*, London: Rex Collings, 1980, pp. 201–3.
37 Jan Eckel and Samuel Moyn (eds.), *The Breakthrough: Human Rights in the 1970s*, Philadelphia: University of Pennsylvania Press, 2014.
38 BNARS BNB 5314, Seretse, speech at Bechuanaland Independence Conference, 14 February 1966.
39 Seretse, video interview by Adrian Porter, Independent Television News, 17 March 1965. Online. Available at URI>www.youtube.com/watch?v=C1iWS7BQlqc&t=44s (accessed 15 December 2018).
40 BNARS BNB 1392, Seretse, "Address to the General Assembly of the United Nations," September 1969.
41 TNA FCO 45/437, Seretse, speech to African American Chamber of Commerce, 25 September 1969.
42 US Congress, Senate, Senator Edward Brooke, 91st Congress, 1st Session, 8 October 1969, *Congressional Record*, vol. 115, part 21, pp. 29133–6.
43 Rhodes House Library, Oxford University, MMS Afr. s. 1681, Richard Rolfe, "Developing Mineral-based Wealth," *Financial Times*, 10 August 1971.
44 United States National Archives and Records Administration (NARA), Record Group 59: General Records of the Department of State, Central Foreign Policy Files, 1973–9 Electronic Telegrams, 1977STATE142614, Department of State to Embassy Gaborone, 20 June 1977; NARA, RG 59, Central Foreign Policy Files, 1973–9 Electronic Telegrams, 1978GABORO02964, Embassy Gaborone to Department of State, 28 September 1978.
45 NARA, RG 59, Central Foreign Policy Files, 1973–9 Electronic Telegrams, 1979STATE235933, Department of State to Embassy Addis Ababa, 7 September 1979.
46 J. Regan Kerney, "Texas-size Country in Southern Africa enjoys Tranquility and True Democracy: Letter from Botswana," *Washington Post*, 23 December 1977, A18. By the mid-1970s, the US Congress, with support from nongovernmental organizations, worked to pass legislation to link America's material and military aid with improvements in the human rights records of recipient states. See Sarah B. Snyder, *From Selma to Moscow: How Human Rights Activists Transformed U.S. Foreign Policy*, New York: Columbia University Press, 2018, pp. 148–67.
47 These figures are in constant dollars. See US Agency for International Development, "U.S. Overseas Loans and Grants: Obligations and Loan Authorizations," data from 1 July 1945 to 30 September 2014. Online. Available at https://explorer.usaid.gov/reports-greenbook.html (accessed 15 December 2018).
48 BNARS 5617, Botswana Ministry of Works and Communications, "Botswana-Zambia Road Project," final report, July 1978.
49 James Kirby, "'Our Bantustans are Better than Yours': Botswana, the United States, and Human Rights Idealism in the 1970s," *International History Review*, 2017, vol. 39, 860–84.
50 Jensen, *Making of International Human Rights*, p. 85.
51 TNA FCO 45/437, Seretse, speech to African American Chamber of Commerce, 25 September 1969.
52 TNA DO 216/50, Quett Masire, A. S. Mohale, and Makhosini Dlamini, "Joint Memorandum by the Leaders of the Elected Governments of Bechuanaland, Basotoland [*sic*] and Swaziland to the heads of African states in Accra," 25 October 1965.

53 Seretse, "Botswana's Policy of Non-alignment," 8–10 September 1970 in *Non-Aligned Conference: Lusaka, 1970*, Gaborone: Botswana Information Services, 1970, pp. 2–3.

54 TNA FCO 45/1698, Seretse, address to National Assembly, 24 November 1975; Seretse, "Speech Addressing the Sixteenth Annual Conference of the Botswana Democratic Party at Mochudi," 9 April 1977 in Carter and Morgan, *From the Frontline*, pp. 257–8; BNARS BNB 3899, Seretse, acceptance speech at the Nansen Award ceremony in Geneva, 22 May 1978; Richard Dale, *Botswana's Search for Autonomy in Southern Africa*, Westport, CT: Greenwood, 1995, pp. 44–5.

55 TNA FCO 45/1096, David Anderson to Peter Foster, 25 April 1972.

56 TNA FCO 45/439, Seretse, "Developing Democracy in Southern Africa," address at the Dag Hammarskjöld Centre, 11 November 1970.

57 Julius Nyerere, *Freedom and Unity*, London: Oxford University Press, 1966, p. 313.

58 TNA FCO 45/111, Seretse, address to National Assembly, 9 December 1968; TNA FCO 45/816, Seretse, "A Decade of Achievement – A Decade of Challenge," address to Botswana Democratic Party conference, 10 April 1971.

59 TNA FCO 45/1270, Seretse, address to Democratic Party conference, 21 April 1973.

60 Seretse, address to Council on Foreign Relations in New York, "The Liberation Struggle in Southern Africa and American Perceptions," 8 June 1976 in *Speeches by His Excellency the President, Sir Seretse Khama, on the Occasion of His Visits to India, United States of America, United Kingdom, Canada, China and North Korea*, Gaborone: Government Printer, 1976, p. 25.

61 Bechuanaland Democratic Party, *Laying the Foundation of Nationhood: Quotations from the Speeches of Sir Seretse Khama*, Gaborone: Bechuanaland Democratic Party, 1982, p. 26.

62 Hoover Institution Archives, Stanford University, David Benjamin Bolen Papers, Box 4, Folder 4, Embassy Gaborone to Department of State, 1 August 1975.

63 TNA FCO 45/1272, Nzo Ekangaki, speech at Gaborone agricultural and trade fair, 13 July 1973.

64 TNA FCO 45/1499, Seretse, interview with Radio Botswana and *Botswana Daily News*, 21 June 1974.

65 NARA, RG 59, Central Foreign Policy Files, 1973–9 Electronic Telegrams, 1977 USUNN00116, US Mission USUN to Department of State, 15 January 1977; BNARS MICRO 588, United Nations Security Council, "Assistance to Botswana," March 1977.

PART III

THE FORMATIVE UN ERA

C. Socialist and capitalist versions of human rights

14

THE INTERNATIONAL LABOUR ORGANIZATION AND THE GENDER OF ECONOMIC RIGHTS

Eileen Boris and Jill Jensen

As World War II ended, the Allied governments recommitted their allegiance to the International Labour Organization (ILO) – a specialized agency founded a quarter century earlier along with the League of Nations – that was responsible for formulating global standards for the world of work. Through the "Declaration of Philadelphia," representatives of the Allies assembled in that city asserted, "All human beings, irrespective of race, creed or sex, have the right to pursue both their material well-being and their spiritual development in conditions of freedom and dignity, of economic security and equal opportunity." They announced that "labor is not a commodity."[1] Thus, they upheld the ILO's interwar regulations for minimum wages, the eight-hour day, social security, collective bargaining, and child welfare. Women, like men, they affirmed, deserved basic economic and social rights – but women also required the unique right to maternity protection. This dual pledge – treating women in industry like all other workers, yet regarding them as needing special provisions to accommodate childbearing – persisted into the second half of the twentieth century and beyond.

This essay examines the postwar and Cold War period, the late 1940s to the mid 1970s, which saw both transformations in the nature of women's work and the expansion of human rights discourse. Despite growing acceptance of formal equality, the ILO came up against women's assumed responsibility for homes and families. The ILO's legacy for human rights, expressed in the right to decent work, reflected a basic contradiction: women were equal to men except when they were not. Including women in formal expressions of economic rights ran up against social and cultural definitions of gender difference. Women were mothers or potential mothers; they were the ones who left factories, fields, and offices for a second shift, the reproductive labors of housework and care work. Equal treatment on the job, including equal pay, non-discrimination, safe working conditions, and freedom to join a union, did nothing to relieve unequal burdens of what the ILO came to call "family responsibilities." Thus neither protection nor equality fully addressed the barriers to women's human rights.

Yet the daily unwaged labor of sustaining people continued to subsidize wage work more broadly as it interfered with women's right to earn. Women stretched inadequate wages to cover family needs, allowing employers to pay less to maintain their workforce.[2] ILO instruments, whether focused on equality or on special treatment, encouraged its member countries to deploy women's labor as needed – in the labor force or in the family. It wasn't that women-specific protections were wrong or counter to human rights, especially as linked with human dignity. Given most national legal instruments, labor feminists felt that they would help relieve class oppression until organized workers gained power in order to cover men under equivalent protections (against dangerous work or long hours, for example). It was that in championing wage labor in the formal sector, the ILO overlooked care as work and thus undermined conditions in the paid as well as unpaid care-work economy, where women dominated. In this regard, it reflected hegemonic understandings of trade unionists, governments, and even most feminists that reproductive labor was not work.

Universalizing the double day of women further obscured the burdens faced by women in the global South, especially subsistence producers. The ideal of "freedom from fear and want," as enshrined in several human rights instruments, remained all the more difficult to obtain. Not only did their informal sector and rural household labors sustain families and communities, but they also made cheap goods and raised future migrant workers, both of which lowered costs for industrialized areas. Geopolitical conflicts between the imperial North and decolonizing South and between state socialist and market economies helped to shape the possibility for economic rights regardless of sex, even as they reflected inequalities between men and women and between women whose "work and family" circumstances varied by class, region, and other demographic and social factors.

The ILO offers a unique arena for the study of human rights. It is the central deliberative body for generating worldwide labor standards as a means to secure human dignity. It has done so through research that generates knowledge about employment and working conditions, assisting governments with implementing labor law, and, most notably, setting treaty-like conventions and non-binding recommendations. But not all conventions pertained to all people or peoples; from the start, some measures applied to particular groups, defined by gender, geography, or occupation. These workers appeared to be subject to unique hazards, sometimes from the job, other times from their social or cultural position. For the ILO, women comprised such a group.

The reader will find an overview in the first section of the essay. The second section reinterprets ILO historiography through a gendered lens and introduces three approaches to labor standards as human rights: what we call the hidden gender paradigm, the equal treatment paradigm, and the special treatment paradigm. The third section discusses the hidden gender paradigm in universal instruments that have differential gender impacts. Examples of this paradigm include conventions promulgated as counterweights to Communism, such as "Freedom of Association," "Right to Organize," and "Abolition of Forced Labor." Some general conventions include distinct measures for women, such as "Plantations" and "Social Security." By discussing such measures in this section we highlight the multiple contours of hidden gender instruments. The fourth section takes up general conventions that directly codified the equal treatment of women and men. These included the conventions on "Equal Remuneration" and "Discrimination." It is important to note that the ILO's annual assembly, the International Labour Conference (ILC), passed both kinds of instruments simultaneously, that is, ones with differential gender impacts or distinct measures for women, and ones mandating equal treatment. The fifth section of the essay turns to measures intended to achieve equality through special treatment for women workers, which also continued during these years. Examples include the revision of an interwar convention on "Maternity Protection," a recommendation on "Women with Family Responsibilities," and measures for women as mothers in "developing countries." By focusing on specific conventions and recommendations, we introduce readers to the breadth of ILO concerns. The final section highlights the human rights legacy of the ILO in the years leading up to the first United Nations (UN) International Conference on Women, in 1975. In preparing for this landmark meeting, the ILO affirmed its unique place as the international arena where women's rights, labor rights, and human rights came together to define the world of work. Precisely because the ILO reflected the positions of member countries and strove for consensus, it would take decades for the vision of economic rights as human rights to account for women's family labor.

Overview

Knowing the structure of the ILO is imperative to understanding the passage of its conventions. Among international agencies, the Geneva-based ILO has a unique tripartite organization: workers, employers, and governments are formally represented in the governing body, all committees, and country delegations to the annual ILC. Representatives vote on various conventions, recommendations, and declarations annually at the ILC. The International Labour Office (the Office), staffed by global civil servants, runs the day-to-day activities of the organization, and is overseen by the elected director-general. The Office admits civil society organizations, such as international union federations, human rights groups, and international feminist nongovernmental organizations (NGOs), to the ILC as observers with limited participation rights. Even though the ILO constitution recommended women's presence as advisors to national delegations and to committees for industrial sectors like textiles whenever questions involving women as workers were on the agenda, a special place in the ILO's structure for women's issues was an afterthought. The status of a unit devoted to women workers has varied within the Office over the past century, ranging from a special assistant to the director-general to a distinct bureau. Women workers became more central to ILO policymaking as women's labor force participation rose during the last half of the twentieth century and the ILO itself turned to the problem of the informal economy in the global South.

It is important to note that the ILO has not necessarily been a feminist institution. The special treatment paradigm perpetuated unequal power relations among women and between men and women in the global North and South. Already during the interwar years (1919–39), when European colonial powers and social democratic trade unions dominated the ILO, the desire to protect motherhood led the ILO to reaffirm even older women-specific labor standards that had prohibited night work and exposure to hazardous substances. Many feminists in the interwar period condemned the ILO for upholding standards that they judged would backfire against women's equality; they argued that employers would discriminate against women if they had to abide by hour and safety restrictions for women that made women more costly to hire than men. Other feminists maintained that the achievement of equality for wage-earning women required measures targeted at women. Moreover, the ILO formulated distinct rules for workers in "non-metropolitan," i.e. colonial, territories that offered only limited protection to women relative to men. The rest of this essay concerns the gradual, difficult, and partial departure from the special treatment paradigm of the interwar era.

At mid-century, when the globally hegemonic United States had the most influence at the ILO, women staff, delegates, and advisors debated the optimum balance between special protection and equal treatment. The ILO began to edge away from protective labor legislation for women and toward promoting anti-discrimination and equal treatment with men, but it took decades to revise conventions and other instruments that targeted women as fundamentally different from men. Over the same years, treatment for the global South gradually shifted from colonial exceptionalism (that is, excepting colonial subjects from labor protections formulated for non-colonized peoples) to the embrace of world economic development – which, it must be noted, has avoided upending Western capitalist dominance.

The development of labor standards excluded the majority of the world's women who toiled in sectors expressly left out of such standard-setting, such as domestic service, subsistence agriculture, and home-based manufacturing. Only during the last decades of the twentieth century, when the ILO's membership had expanded to include more nations from the Third World, would it finally seek improved income generation for rural women in the global South. By then its dedication to worker rights seemed like a relic of an earlier era, next to the well-heeled World Bank and other international organizations promoting the neoliberal deregulation, privatization, and financialization that have weakened labor in relation to capital. The ILO nonetheless maintained its commitment to labor standards, especially for the Third World.

Even decades later, however, the ILO still exhibited a lingering adherence to gender and geographical difference, as in its declaration on the occasion of the International Women's Year in 1975. The ILO maintained an older labor feminist claim that equality for wage-earning women required targeted measures in the face of non-gendered human rights discourse and against the tide of equal rights feminism (that is, a feminism that insists on treating women the same as men even if other social factors like household and care work lead to unequal results). Here the ILO's champions were no longer the United States and other market economies, but rather non-aligned and state socialist nations. Likewise, the ILO sought to reduce UN efforts on women's rights from a binding convention to a non-binding declaration, although it did come to accept the UN's eventual Convention on the Elimination of All Forms of Discrimination Against Women (CEDAW, 1979). We see a complex situation in which the ILO sought to extend equality to women by using targeted labor standards covering women's employment and at the same time insisted on integrating economic rights into human rights. Not until preparing for its centennial in 2019 did the ILO begin to speak about care work at the center of decent work.

Gendered labor in human rights historiography

The historical literature on human rights has expanded exponentially since the 1990s. But the ILO is at best a footnote in it because the historiographies of labor standards and human rights generally stand apart from each other, reflecting the Cold War division between civil and political rights on the one hand, and economic, social, and cultural rights on the other hand, as embedded in UN covenants.[3] The ILO defied such dichotomies, as it saw economic and social rights as essential to the realization of human rights. Recent work on UN committees and programs for women perpetuates this scholarly lacuna; neither celebratory nor critical interpretations of the UN Conferences on Women consider ILO participation.[4]

Scholars of international feminism have mostly dismissed the ILO as protectionist and thus bad for women. Much of this literature replicates the historic debate between legal equality and social democratic or trade union feminists of the time. Women's historians tend to foreground legal equality groups like Open Door International and Woman's World Party and have suggested that the ILO aligned itself with governments and male trade unionists who sought to hold women back from full economic participation and occupational self-determination. These studies generally are North American or European in focus. A few works mention ILO protections for maternity pensions or for alleviating conditions in specific occupations.[5]

Initial ILO histories came from organizational insiders, but recent scholarship moves away from internalist documentation to address broad historiographical questions. Most studies focus on the institution without engaging in gender analysis or paying much attention to women when assessing development, social security, or specific conventions.[6] The major exception is *Social Justice for Women* (1990). Written by former ILO and UN staffers Carol Lubin and Ann Winslow, this account provides some basic facts on women employed within the agency and on ILO measures for women workers, but little interpretation.[7] Several additional works, most notably by Lourdes Benería and Maryse Gaudier, chronicle women staffers' direct experiences with the ILO and its affiliated International Institute for Labour Studies.[8] The new gendered ILO scholarship concentrates on either the interwar period or late 20th and early twenty-first century globalization. Susan Zimmermann's work is particularly noteworthy as she connects ILO instruments to larger geopolitical power relations and interrogates class and gender separately and together, showing the limits as well as promise of inter-war feminism.[9] Various case studies consider specific conventions, such as night-work restrictions, recent standard setting for home-based labor, and the gendered consequences of development.[10] Researchers are expanding beyond debates over women-only protective standards and women's right to employment to consider the impact of ILO policies in specific nations and regions and the Office's construction of social knowledge – the very data that other agencies and scholars use without questioning the politics of information assemblage. The pathbreaking collection *Women's ILO: Transnational Networks, Global Labour Standards, and Gender Equity* deploys intersectional and transnational approaches to assess the possibilities and limits of a century of ILO engagement with women's work, the gender of its legal instruments, and the role of transnational networks of women and their organizations. It further explores the ILO in relation to other global institutions, NGOs, and trade union federations in light of colonialism, imperialism, and decolonization; the Cold War and alternative visions of equality and social justice; and transformations in the nature of work itself. It considers national, international, and transnational scales of interaction, as is fitting for an organization that functions on all of these levels.[11] However, human rights are a secondary theme in that collection.

The hidden gender paradigm

Since World War II, the ILO's formal approach to human rights has combined attention to political freedom, civil liberties, economic progress, and social justice, considering them mutually dependent.[12] Universal rights, according to the Office, require dedication to broad policies supported by a multifaceted process of "education, promotion, inquiry, complaint, and assistance."[13] Nevertheless, in the early postwar years, conversations about full social and economic rights for women remained limited. The Declaration of Philadelphia set forth explicit aims to protect freedom of association as a right of speech and action – for workers and for employers – and the right to collective bargaining as essential for sustained socio-economic progress. "Freedom of Association" and "Protection of the Right to Organize" conventions became what the ILO now considers "core" standards.[14] The development of trade unions remains a priority for the ILO, both as social institutions supporting workers' economic interests and as part of the institutional structure of the ILO itself. Freedom of association and the right to collective bargaining were embedded as essential civil liberties in the International Covenant on Economic, Social and Cultural Rights (1966), yet states have continued to resist legalizing unions. Today more than half of the workers in ILO member states live under political regimes that have not ratified these ILO conventions.[15]

Freedom of association and the right to collective bargaining are not normally considered gendered issues, but they reflect important distinctions based on sex, and so exemplify rights whose gendered nature is hidden. Due to a multitude of sociocultural factors, such as traditional norms and persistent employment differentiations, women have faced greater obstacles than men in obtaining union rights. In Western industrialized nations, most women labor in sectors outside of union representation, making collective bargaining moot. State socialist nations have claimed that workers regardless of gender have a voice as members of society and thus *ipso facto* enjoy "freedom of association," though implementation has varied widely. The developing nations of the global South often lacked strong labor unions altogether. Balancing childrearing and other forms of household labor without state or union support, women have turned to self-employment, home-based work, and/or part-time employment. Such jobs usually placed them outside of labor standards. Meanwhile, women entering formal employment did so in lower-paid positions, often service oriented and, again, less unionized than industrial production. Rural women faced dire obstacles to gaining rights since they labored informally in the home and fields.

As early as the 1950s, the Office recognized this disadvantage, but hegemonic gender norms based on traditional conceptions of women's role in economic activity blocked treating women as workers like any other. Many ILO employment specialists regarded women merely as providers of "subsidiary sources of income." When women participated in labor unions, especially in less developed regions, they served as rank-and-file members, not as leaders. Their underrepresentation at the ILC as formal delegates representing workers reinforced the scant attention paid to women's issues.

Leadership programs for women unionists were limited, even though supported by the women's section of the ILO.[16] For example, when the Office recommended projects to strengthen women's participation in rural cooperatives, member governments resisted; in 1951, for example, the Indian Ministry of Labour was "not willing to accord a high priority" to a request made by women's groups for vocational training in agriculture.[17] In 1964, the Committee on Women Workers successfully added to the agenda of the annual ILC the issue of women's economic and social advancement and problems associated with women's part time work. The Committee on Women Workers also prioritized the traditional concerns of maternity protections and family responsibilities. But there was no mention of union representation for or by women, despite the goal of the 1964 conference of strengthening tripartism.[18] At decade's end, an ILO expert with the African Field Office still pondered "why women and girls [were] left out of development projects," including programs supporting collective action through cooperatives.[19]

The Cold War shaped another ILO human rights concern with hidden gender implications: forced labor. With the USSR rejoining the ILO in 1954, the United States supported a new forced labor convention so as to expose Eastern bloc violations. A 1956 panel of inquiry

> condemned … all systems of forced labor which are employed as a means of political coercion for punishment or for holding or expressing political views and are on such a scale as to constitute an important element in the economy of a given country.[20]

Such investigations, commissioned through the UN in association with the ILO, eventually generated the "Abolition of Forced Labour" Convention in 1957. Forced labor could not be used, the convention announced, as a form of political coercion or for "racial, social, national or religious discrimination"; as a mobilization of labor resources for economic development; as a means of discipline; or as a punishment for striking workers.[21] This convention revised an earlier 1930 measure that had allowed colonial governments to maintain the practice with regard to "native labor" if they adhered to specified labor standards.[22]

This 1950s discussion did not mention sex differences. Yet women activists had highlighted the gender-specific consequences of forced labor for decades. During the interwar years, the Office had garnered the support of major women's organizations for the 1930 Forced Labor Convention. The Women's International League for Peace and Freedom (WILPF) abhorred the practice of moving men away from their homes for long-term compulsory service because such removal disrupted family life. Even when women were "allowed or compelled to go with such gangs," that exposed them to sexual danger and prostitution. Exemption from forced labor still left women vulnerable to exploitation under contract labor.[23] During the 1950s, WILPF again conveyed to the ILO and UN its strong support for "energetic action."[24] Strict legal equality feminists like Open Door International, in contrast, protested treating "native" women differently than men; they believed that equal treatment for native women would be an opening wedge for enhanced rights for Western women in their own nations, no matter the consequences for women elsewhere.[25]

The ILO forced labor convention mentioned debt bondage and contract labor but ignored sexual divisions, including sexual exploitation. In the end, ILO scrutiny fell upon postcolonial regions rather than on the coerced work arrangements in the Soviet sphere of influence that Western advocates had expected. The existence of the UN Convention for the Suppression of the Traffic in Persons and of the Exploitation of the Prostitution of Others (1949) placed the question of sex trafficking with other agencies, though the ILO was also reluctant to tackle these issues.[26] Human rights specialist Virginia Leary, who worked with the ILO for years in the 1970s, noted that forced labor had both legal and economic dimensions and that "vulnerable populations are the most in danger."[27] ILO studies have since revealed that women and girls made up over half of the victims of forced labor, mostly in domestic work where they could face sexual harassment.[28]

The equal treatment paradigm

With the increased need for womanpower for national reconstruction and industrial development after World War II, the ILO shifted its emphasis from women-only protective labor laws to measures promoting equal treatment and non-discrimination, as exemplified by passage of the "Equal Remuneration Convention" (1951) and "Discrimination (Employment and Occupation) Convention" (1958). With 172 and 173 ratifications each as of 2016, these ILO conventions are among the most accepted worldwide.[29] For the Discrimination Convention, a number of member states, especially state socialist ones, enunciated their support by invoking the ILO's Declaration of Philadelphia as well as the authority of the UN Charter, the Universal Declaration of Human Rights (UDHR), and the UN Commission on Human Rights.[30] The UN Commission on the Status of Women (CSW) strongly supported advancing equal remuneration through these ILO instruments.[31]

The ILO has served as the UN agency meant to extend the reach of human rights to employment. It is obliged to respond to UN requests for information, including concerning human rights. In 1948, for example, the UN's Economic and Social Council asked the ILO to address equal remuneration at the same time that the UN added equal pay for men and women to the UDHR.[32] The ILO's governing body agreed, not least due to its rivalry with other UN units. While it carried out the research on equal remuneration, it relied on the UN's Sub-Committee for the Prevention of Discrimination and Protection of Minorities to guide work on discrimination.[33] This was one of many moments that reveal a curious intellectual division of labor concerning the significance of gender in what was seen as discrimination.

The equal treatment paradigm promoted conflicting agendas. Feminists wanted women to receive the same treatment as men. Employers accepted the principle but were uncomfortable with any interference with their ability to hire or set wages. Some of these same employers, however, wanted to appear fair. Male workers desired to maintain their working conditions and equal treatment seemed to be a way to do so. Newly independent states wanted equity. These varied "equal treatment" agendas played out in the deliberations over both equal remuneration and non-discrimination.

ILO administrators, whatever their personal beliefs about gender equality, believed that "non-discrimination should be achieved not only as a measure of social justice but to promote labour mobility and efficient utilization of the labour force."[34] Their embrace of equal remuneration belonged to a long history of attempts by organized male workers to protect the wage out of fear that employers would undercut the rate for the job by hiring women for less.[35] Women taking up men's work during World War II made the need for equal remuneration more pressing. However, most employer associations clung to the canard that "the overall value of the work is less … in the case of work done by women." Some employers incorporated into their costs of production the price of welfare amenities (e.g. toilet facilities), sex-based hours restrictions, and women's presumably greater absenteeism and turnover, using those expenses to justify a lower women's wage.[36]

Member states agreed that some international standard was appropriate but differed over whether it should take the form of a treaty-like convention or a non-binding recommendation. The Committee on Equal Remuneration recommended the stronger instrument of convention as well as a recommendation. Nations without robust labor inspectorates or capacity for enforcement balked at a convention. For example, India contended that it lacked "ordinary wage-fixing machinery," such as job classification boards, and the personnel qualified to make such determinations.[37] It further suggested exempting "family undertakings, domestic work, unorganized industries, and employment where the output of women was as a rule less than that of men," that is, the places where most women labored.[38] In formulating the convention, however, the ILC rejected the claims of formerly colonized nations like India that their underdevelopment interfered with enforcing the provisions of a binding convention. The resulting Equal Remuneration Convention would differ from pre-World War II instruments in that it no longer explicitly differentiated between metropolitan and "non-metropolitan," i.e. colonial, territories. However, it allowed member states to justify modification or even to declare the convention inapplicable for territories under their control.[39]

Member states also disagreed over definitions. They debated how to measure equal remuneration – whether through job evaluation to determine the rate for the job or by comparing jobs with skills of similar value – and whether to include the public sector or merely private enterprise. The final wording called for "objective appraisal of jobs on the basis of the work to be performed" rather than the sex of the worker, but allowed nations multiple paths for compliance – wage-fixing machinery, laws and regulations, and collective bargaining – that actually allowed for loopholes.[40] The accompanying recommendation suggested that governments, in consultation with worker and employer organizations, apply the principle to employees, public contracts, and entities under state control. All social partners were to work together to develop appraisal mechanisms and strive to equalize remuneration rates. Delegates placed measures that might interfere with ratification of the convention into the recommendation – a common tactic in such negotiations. These included equal access to vocational guidance and training, encouragement of women to use such facilities, and state financing of social services for women workers who had family responsibilities. In suggesting targeted efforts for women, the more detailed recommendation offered the possibility of special treatment as a means to secure equal remuneration.[41] Because government delegates voted with the worker delegates, the combination of a convention plus a recommendation passed at the 1951 ILC, despite opposition by most employers.

The growing Cold War became manifest during these deliberations. State socialist nations framed their support in terms of human rights, as these had been included in their bodies of law. The communist-led World Federation of Trade Unions (WFTU), Poland, and the Soviet Union deployed human rights as a wedge issue to distinguish their promises from those of market economies and to win over developing and other non-aligned nations to their side.[42] They first sought to move the question of equal pay away from the ILO to other UN entities. They used the UN Commission on the Status of Women (CSW) as a platform to point out how "some of the most pressing inequities were to be found in the most highly industrialized countries," chastising the United States and United Kingdom for the persistence of "flagrant discrimination" despite governmental acceptance of the equal remuneration principle. Pointing to the need to solve "important social problems of women," including childcare and training, they demanded a broader understanding of remedies than found with the ILO. The Russian delegate to the CSW charged that "the position taken by the ILO showed that it was acting not in the interests of workers but in the interests of those who exploit them."[43] At the ILO in 1949, Poland also enunciated skepticism toward the ILO. With other state socialist nations, it offered a broad conception of discrimination, based on the UDHR.[44] Czechoslovakia also linked its understanding of equal pay to anti-discrimination in terms of "sex, religion, race or political conviction."[45] For women to become more productive, they not only needed training, as proposed in the Office's draft recommendation, but also "social facilities which would enable the employment of women who take care of their households, especially of mothers."[46] State socialist nations later used discussions on the

Discrimination Convention to condemn obvious blemishes on the records of the United States, still in the grip of racial segregation, and colonial powers like France and Britain.[47]

While the ILO cast the question of equal remuneration as one of economic management and worker protection, feminists viewed it as a fundamental right. Like the ILO's own Office, most feminist organizations, notably the International Alliance of Women, preferred gender-neutral discourse, such as rates of remuneration, over phrases that referred to men and women.[48] The militant equal rights Open Door International voiced the most skepticism among women's groups:

> Until job classification systems are introduced everywhere the definition 'rates established on job content' has no practical meaning in countries where job classification is not introduced and thus many fictitious reasons can be given in order to delay for a long time the implementation of the principle 'the rate for the job.'

Board members Elizabeth Abbott and Ina Møller wrote to the ILO. Ultimately job classification depended on "the objectivity and integrity of the job classifiers." But they wondered, would not these assessors retain "traditional prejudices?" How could feminists be sure that the assessors would be "free from unproven erroneous conceptions of women's skill and abilities?" Rate for the job was the only way forward, but that could not succeed unless general social conditions improved that had "a direct bearing upon the position of women in the labour market and consequently upon their remuneration." Nonetheless, equal rates would entice women to improve their skills, reduce absenteeism, and become more efficient laborers, leading "to higher universal prosperity."[49] In other words, equal remuneration was a start but required a broader equality between the sexes to generate true equality.

In fact, discrimination instruments – formulated nearly a decade later – were more about race than sex. Drafted amid growing national liberation movements, they generated much controversy: some members wanted no mention of "dependent territories," while others, like India (which was leading the non-aligned movement) wanted a stronger statement of rights that extended to colonial entities.[50] Women's organizations did not send comments to the ILO as they had during discussions of equal remuneration. The 1950s were a transitional period: the older international feminist organizations were now less vocal at the ILO, and the new global feminism had yet to emerge. In the 1960s legal feminists would analogize sex discrimination to already won race discrimination, but the two forms of harm remained separate. The final text of the Discrimination Convention did reinstate the dualism of ILO constitutional principles when it came to women, namely: treatment like all other workers, except for sex-targeted measures to account or compensate for biological and social difference (i.e., women's reproductive labor). There were dissenting voices; Belgium observed, "such differences seem scarcely compatible with present day industrial and technical development."[51] Nevertheless, the dualism persisted.

The Discrimination Convention rejected "any distinction, exclusion, or preference made on the basis of race, colour, sex, religion, political opinion, national extraction or social origin, which has the effect of impairing or nullifying equality of opportunity or treatment in employment or occupation." ILC delegates agreed that distinctions "inherent" in the requirements for specific jobs could allow gender preference to be claimed as a "bona fide occupational qualification," the name subsequent US law gave to this loophole. Deliberators rejected calling such policy dualities contradictions, defining as non-discriminatory "special measures designed to meet the particular requirements of persons who, for reasons such as sex, age, disablement, family responsibilities or social or cultural status, are generally recognised to require special protection or assistance."[52] As a Czechoslovakian government advisor boasted, women in her country had both equality, including equal pay for equal work, and social security "better" than men, including coverage for maternity leave.[53] She saw no contradiction.

Normative understandings of gender encouraged most member states to treat sex discrimination apart from race, color, and ethnicity. They gave interestingly divergent reasons for such discrimination, interpreting sex discrimination as stemming from "social and economic" reasons while race discrimination arose from "hatred and prejudice."[54] Canada, for example, stressed how efforts other than legislation were appropriate for "promot[ing] equality of opportunity for women and men." Its representatives contended that the question of equality between the sexes required "special measures, separate from those designed to prevent discrimination on other grounds."[55] Given the Declaration of Philadelphia and the UDHR, however, its worker advisor demurred: "how could this International Labour Conference adopt a document [on discrimination] and exclude from the grounds of discrimination the question of sex?"[56]

These issues arose in varied ways during discussions. Some delegates who focused on race discrimination only gave a cursory nod to sex discrimination.[57] Others justified outright discriminatory practices on the basis of sex. Restrictions on women remained acceptable – and not only those justified as protective. During committee deliberations on the final amendment in 1958, the Irish government delegate admitted that his country, which would otherwise be willing to ratify the Convention, would be unable to do so because of "certain aspects of women's employment." To curb high unemployment, he explained, "women were required to retire from the public service on marriage and, in the private sector, some agreements provided that married women would not be employed." Hiring men, single women, and widows while barring married women "should not be termed discrimination."[58] Yet other nations privileged the male wage, or based responses to sex discrimination on women's status as wives and mothers. Netherlands accepted discrimination that "conform[ed] with national views regarding the contractual capacity of married women, minors and mental defectives," that is, discrimination did not apply to legal dependents.[59] Equality floundered when unable to accommodate entrenched notions of gender difference based on biology and social norms.

The special treatment paradigm

The idea that women's access to equal opportunity and non-discrimination required additional measures was a standard ILO refrain. In 1947, when stipulating the areas in which the ILO was to frame its deliberations on equal remuneration, the CSW flagged "provision of measures to lighten the tasks that arise from women's home responsibilities, as well as the tasks relating to maternity."[60] The ILO responded to that challenge throughout the 1950s. One of the first conventions in 1919 addressed maternity protection. This instrument excluded domestic service, home work, and agriculture until revision in 1952. Maternity protection stipulated not only specified leave but also medical care and job reinstatement and the ILO pushed for funding leaves through public monies rather than individual employers to militate against raising the costs of hiring women and discriminatory treatment of leave takers.[61] Though not framed initially in terms of human rights, maternity leave became a precondition for economic rights.

Women workers on plantations represented a special maternity case. ILO proposals on specific measures for these women reflected the centrality of their subsistence reproductive labor for the sustaining of plantation societies. With a long history associated with colonialism, plantations were considered a special form of economic activity, innately linked with conditions of mistreatment. Yet ILO definitions reflected Western and gender biases, even as the agency targeted plantation workers as a special group needing protection due to these vulnerabilities. It limited the term "plantation" to colonial and postcolonial regions, as production in tropical and subtropical areas utilizing "Western industrial methods," foreign capital, and foreign supervision. The plantation or "estate" represented exploitation of human labor for the benefit of an outsider who was eager to extract value in the form of commodities destined for international markets. Imperialist perceptions persisted. Yet the debate over workers on plantations also reflected post-World War II recalibrations of the geographic and gender division of global labor, underscoring how inequality in the division of labor persisted during decolonization and the subsequent restructuring of international economic relations.

Many plantations employed impoverished migrant labor brought from one region and settled specifically to work in another, essentially in captive circumstances. The family unit was the fulcrum of the system, as workers pooled resources. The biological and social reproduction of women sustained resident plantations, leading ILO experts to express great concern over the female body and maternal health. Nonetheless, domineering overlords consistently pushed the body and soul of the worker to the edge of survival.

The ILO undertook a rigorous study of plantation labor beginning in the late 1940s and continuing into the 1950s, with regional meetings in Indonesia and Cuba. Its Plantations Committee determined that an ILO convention could improve conditions for both productive and reproductive labor. It should require access to first aid services on plantations, mobile health staff for pre- and post-natal care, and medical exams for early detection of sickness.[62] The subsequent "Plantation Convention" (1958) included work relationships in the production of tea, coffee, bananas, rubber, jute, hemp, and, after a significant fight, sugar and cotton. It promoted improved living and working conditions for plantation residents. Its provisions encompassed rules overseeing the recruitment of migrant workers, maternity protections, standards for family housing, and medical care. It also included stipulations for ensuring freedom of association and the right to collective bargaining, the protection of wages, weekly periods for rest, and holidays with pay – certainly idealistic goals.[63]

The Plantation Convention embodied multidimensional aspirations, as had many other ILO instruments that aimed to promote decent standards in distinct economic environments around the world. It would advance human rights, combining gender equality with special treatment maternity and child protections, while also enhancing global development. The convention derived from one of the postwar ILO industrial committees (each of these committees focused on a specific industrial sector); it particularly benefited from consideration by Western labor feminists, who sought greater opportunities for working women.[64] Their attention to women's work and maternal welfare combined with ILO interests in steering the "developing" world into the fold of modernity, with the hope of mitigating dependencies. The goal was to make estate-based labor more like other forms of employment, with rising standards of living, social security, and even full employment. Yet these standards took on different form for women as mothers with family responsibilities.[65] In the end, only ten nations ratified the Plantation Convention. Had it gained greater traction it might have helped many women, children, and families, who into the 1970s were reported as dying of hunger when international market prices for commodities such as tea dropped dramatically.

During previous decades, the ILO had promoted more general measures to alleviate the "triple role of workers, mothers, and housewives" experienced by rising numbers of women employed outside of the home in industrialized regions.[66] State socialist nations offered their public services for employed mothers as a model. But other countries, including the United States and Britain, advocated part-time work, which the CSW asked the ILO to investigate at the same time as the ILO was reporting on handicraft and accepting home-based labor as a solution to the problem of combining family labor with income generation for women in the global South.

The ILO prefigured the critique of what feminist lawyers now call "family responsibility discrimination" as a barrier to women's equality.[67] By the 1960s, concern with labor power shortages of both men and women led it to consider reproductive labor as part of its overall initiative on "Women in a Changing World." In 1965, it passed a non-binding "Women with Family Responsibilities" recommendation that called for childcare facilities, services like vocational education and jobs counseling geared to the entry or re-entry of women into employment, coordination of transport and school hours with work schedules, and public facilities to lighten household tasks.[68] The coordinator of "Women, Youth, and Aging" explained that to maintain women with children in the workforce "society as a whole has to adapt realistically to a new pattern of needs in their work and life."[69] Women delegates at the ILC generally linked the recommendation to conventions on equal remuneration, the protection of maternity, and non-discrimination as necessary for real equality. Some representatives offered a broader equalitarian claim: "responsibility for the children and the family is, in general, the same for the man as for the woman," one Swedish Worker delegate declared.[70]

Nonetheless, this recommendation reinforced, even as it sought to relieve, the gendered division of labor. Assuming industrializing nations to be in transition from "a patriarchal, static society," a government delegate from Cyprus urged that women's entrance into the workforce occur "without too much disruption of the traditional family structures and without detriment to a woman's responsibilities and duties vis-à-vis her family and her children." A worker delegate from Italy expressed such sentiments more strongly: "In this developing world, development certainly should not mean the dissolution of the family." Against women's right to work, he posited the rights of families to women's labor and argued "for preparing and adopting efficient measures to lessen the economic necessity requiring women to seek work outside their homes." Though "the social emancipation" of women was a worthwhile goal, morality and social necessity should propel delegates to improve ILO instruments "with a view to defending the family in a developing world." The continuing emphasis on handicraft and cottage industry stood as a response to such attitudes among member states.[71] Some consultants on women's issues recognized the dual position of women in society, holding onto continued training of girls in "the elements of home-making and home management," even as they would "prepare themselves for economic activity outside the home."[72]

In 1981, reflecting the shift to the discourse of gender equality and the move to gender mainstreaming during the UN Decade for Women (1975–85), a new convention and recommendation spoke of "Workers with Family Responsibilities," including men's unpaid family work as well as women's. This articulation superseded the casting of family labor as only women's work – at least aspirationally. Despite claims to embrace "all categories of workers," it still concentrated on labor force participation in industry and commerce, excluding home-based and informal sector work.[73] Yet rather than wither away due to mechanization, family labors actually intensified with new norms for cleanliness and attentiveness, and so remained a drain on female employment.[74]

Women's rights as human rights

The ILC reflected consensus among its state members and employers and workers that sat as delegates. But the Office pushed the organization to embrace women's rights. By the 1960s, the ILC came to advocate more than freedom from discrimination for women: it called for incorporating women into the debate over international labor standards as human rights. "Women Workers in a Changing World," the 1963 Office report, offered an important normative text periodically reviewed and used as a "basis for discussion" over the next decade. It clarified problems associated with gendered distinctions: worldwide imbalances in women's integration in economic activity, societal discrimination against women's entry into certain fields of paid work, and implementation challenges to both equal pay and equal opportunity. Ever cautious, so not to upset its long-standing protocol, the Office opted for periodic review of ILO measures pertaining to women "in light of scientific and technological advances" rather than a "well-intentioned effort" to "de-protect," that is, eliminate sex-specific standards. Nonetheless, it was noted: "There will always remain a limited sphere in which women need protection: the sphere of maternity."[75]

Subsequent ILO strategy reinforced a new instrumentalist approach: women's labor became a vital means of economic and social development for nations and essential to alleviate worldwide poverty. But the transition from single sex protections was gradual. A 1972 ILC resolution requested that the director-general "bring up to date the report on women workers in a changing world, with particular reference to identifying the needs relating to equal opportunity and treatment and the problems arising from rapidly changing structures and conditions of work."[76] Two years later, the Consultants on Women Workers' Problems pressed for extension of economic opportunities to women, in keeping with feminist demands at the UN both to insert women into development and to end employment discrimination. Women workers faced broad challenges because socioeconomic and political structures still led to prejudice against their economic rights. In spite of intentions, they remained outside of UN development programs and access to "opportunity" varied, depending on what kinds of projects a nation requested technical assistance to pursue. The issue was "complex and delicate and any approach to it on a universal basis is bound to be fraught with very considerable difficulty,"[77] these ILO consultants concluded. Women needed an across-the-board strategy reflecting the idea of equity – a comprehensive vision of social justice that spoke to the problem of low pay, lesser status, and gaps in social security for working women. Social protections also required reconsideration; they should cover "all adult human beings … in their own right."[78]

For the 1975 World Conference of the International Women's Year, ILO experts prepared a "Declaration" on the topic of "equality of opportunity and treatment of women workers."[79] They asked whether women-only protective legislation remained "an obstacle to equality." They cited problems of equal treatment, education, and vocational training for women and girls. This Declaration reflected the ascension of gender equality discourse; it reaffirmed ILO commitment to "equality of opportunity, that is, non-discrimination in educational, training and employment policy and practice," and promoted equal pay and comparable worth. Maternity, however, was different, requiring "social protection of women." Though labeling restrictions on equality unacceptable, the Declaration then redefined discrimination: "Positive special treatment during a transitional period aimed at effective equality between the sexes shall not be regarded as discriminatory."[80]

The 1975 Declaration embodied the way that women's rights – indeed, the entire UN system – had become a terrain of anticolonial politics with Cold War valences. The Soviet Union supported anti-apartheid struggles and Palestinian rights and connected peace and development to anti-capitalist approaches to human rights. The Declaration explicitly reflected the growing influence of the non-aligned nations and their association of women's rights with the announcement of a New International Economic Order that "will contribute towards ensuring better employment, conditions of work and life for women, especially in developing countries," a concept added to the preamble of this declaration despite opposition from the United States, Canada, Great Britain, and employer delegates who saw the preamble as a direct attack on market economies.[81]

By the end of the twentieth century, the ILO approached gender, work, and human rights through gender mainstreaming, a process that infuses gender equality into all aspects of the institution's strategy and programming by considering each aspect in terms of its gender-specific impacts and the inclusion of women equally with men in decision-making. It assumed that improving women's status would require shifting the position of men in the family and the society. This perspective emerged in the wake of the Mexico City conference in 1975, where feminists discussed how development aid programs were disadvantaging women.[82] The Second World Conference on Women in Nairobi in 1985 endorsed gender mainstreaming programs and projects.[83] By the time of the Third Women's Conference in Beijing in 1995, the strategy included goals relating to education, health, decision-making, leadership, and economic relations. The ILO's Action Plan for Gender Equality (2010) belatedly echoed this "integrated approach" – much like broad conceptions of human rights – so as to utilize all tools available to support workers' rights (and women's rights) as human rights. Women-specific conventions belonged to the past, but in the 2000s the ILO recognized that women workers faced gender-specific issues stemming from sexual harassment, care responsibilities, or employment in low-waged women-dominated sectors uncovered by collective bargaining and labor law.

Through the example of the ILO, this essay has highlighted economic rights as an essential part of human rights. Mid-twentieth-century formulators of global labor standards saw the right to a job under decent conditions as foundational to the activation of civil, social, and political rights. But gaining such rights has required breaking through gender norms and questioning the sexual division of labor. Those processes were halting at best during the quarter century following World War II.

By categorizing ILO instruments in terms of their relationship to gender, we suggest the complexity of the task of accounting for social and cultural difference while promoting equal human rights. Hidden gender policies appeared to be without gender specificity but impacted women in negative ways, because of occupational segmentation by sex, women's position outside of trade unions, and the organization of family life. Legal equality, expressed through equal treatment conventions and recommendations, was the most legible way to promote human rights for women, but failed for its part to compensate for women's family responsibilities. Special treatment instruments, however, risked different and thus unequal treatment of those designated as deficient from a male norm. These formulas clashed and collided within the ILO even after its commitment to gender mainstreaming in the early twenty-first century. On the eve of its centennial in 2019, the ILO maintained its dual commitment to equal treatment and special treatment, while claiming that most conventions had nothing to do with gender at all, though as we have suggested many were subject to the hidden gender paradigm. It began to address the ways that characteristics of feminized labor – part-time, low-paid, temporary, and uncovered by labor standards – had spread to what were once thought of as good jobs: unionized with benefits and living wages, where workers had a voice in the conditions of their labor. Thus when the director-general spoke of gender equality being at the center of decent work in 2017, he was recognizing that without reorganizing family labor within the household and between the household and society, economic rights for women as well as for men would fall short.[84]

Future research needs to recognize the limits of basing international labor standards on a universal "woman," as doing so projects Western urban lives as the norm. It is time for a more robust intersectional analysis of all the dimensions of workers: their gender, race, religion, age, and other demographic and social factors. We need more studies of outcomes, of what happened when various stakeholders returned from Geneva and tried to change national policy using ILO conventions and recommendations. Such studies should look at the role of unions, women's organizations, human rights groups, churches, and local experts in making economic rights a reality. At a time when increasing numbers of workers are misclassified as independent contractors, self-employed, or own-account workers, the very employer–employee basis informing labor standards places more and more workers as outside of protection. In this context, the umbrella of human rights might very well provide the means to enhance social and economic rights, because its provisions are free from misclassifications stemming from employers' refusal to abide by wages, hours, and other labor provisions. The Declaration of Philadelphia, with its insistence that economic, civil, and social rights are interconnected, provides a powerful guide to the future by way of a usable past. However, neither women-specific protections nor legal equality alone can lead to gender justice without interrogating the gender division of labor at home as well as at work.

Notes

1 International Labour Office (hereafter ILO), *The Declaration of Philadelphia*, Geneva: ILO, 1944.
2 Silvia Federici, *Revolution at Point Zero: Housework, Reproduction, and Feminist Struggle*, Oakland, CA: PM Press, 2012.
3 An example from the time is Rita Falk Taubenfeld and Howard J. Taubenfeld, "Achieving the Human Rights of Women: The Base Line, the Challenge, the Search for a Strategy," *Human Rights*, 1975, vol. 4, no. 2, 125–69. General consideration of women at the UN has limited mention of the ILO. For example, Hilkka Pietilä and Jeanne Vickers, *Making Women Matter: The Role of the United Nations*, London: Zed Books, 1990, pp. 115, 116, 171, mentions the Equal Remuneration Convention; there are scattered references in Anne Winslow, *Women, Politics, and*

the United Nations, Westport, CT: Greenwood Press, 1995, with the most sustained discussion in Winslow's own chapter, "Specialized Agencies and the World Bank," p. 157. See also Lisa Baldez, *Defying Convention: U.S. Resistance to the UN Treaty on Women's Rights*, New York: Cambridge University Press, 2014, pp. 46–62, and Jean Quataert, *Advocating Dignity: Human Rights Mobilizations in Global Politics*, Philadelphia: University of Pennsylvania Press, 2009.

4 The exception is Eileen Boris' brief discussion in "Difference's Other: The ILO and 'Women in Developing Countries,'" in Jill Jensen and Nelson Lichtenstein (eds.) *The ILO from Geneva to the Pacific Rim: West Meets East*, New York and Geneva: Palgrave and ILO, 2016, pp. 149–50. For the earlier period, Marilyn Lake, "From Self-Determination via Protection to Equality via Non-Discrimination: Defining Women's Rights at the League of Nations and the United Nations," in Patricia Grimshaw, Katie Holmes, and Marilyn Lake (eds.) *Women's Rights and Human Rights: International Historical Perspectives*, New York: Palgrave, 2001, pp. 254–71. See also Arvonne S. Fraser, "Becoming Human: The Origins and Development of Women's Human Rights," *Human Rights Quarterly*, 1999, vol. 21, no. 4, 884–94; Roland Burke, "Competing for the Last Utopia? The NIEO, Human Rights, and the World Conference for the International Women's Year, Mexico City, June 1975," *Humanity*, 2015, vol. 6, no. 1, 47–61; Jocelyn Olcott, *International Women's Year: The Greatest Consciousness-Raising Event in History*, New York: Oxford University Press, 2017. This is also true for the historiography focused on state socialist activities: Kristen Ghodsee, "Revisiting the United Nations Decade for Women: Brief Reflections on Feminism, Capitalism and Cold War Politics in the Early Years of the International Women's Movement," *Women's Studies International Forum*, 2010, vol. 33, no. 1, 3–12; Celia Donert, "Whose Utopia? Gender, Ideology, and Human Rights at the 1975 World Congress of Women in East Berlin," in Jan Eckel and Samuel Moyn (eds.) *The Breakthrough: Human Rights in the 1970s*, Philadelphia: University of Pennsylvania Press, 2013, pp. 68–87.

5 Carol Miller, "'Geneva – the Key to Equality': Inter-War Feminists and the League of Nations," *Women's History Review*, 1994, vol. 3, no. 2, 219–45; Sandra Whitworth, *Feminism and International Relations*, London: Maclan Press, 1994; Nitza Berkovitch, *From Motherhood to Citizenship: Women's Rights and International Organizations*, Baltimore, MD: Johns Hopkins University Press, 1999; Suzanne Franzway and Mary Margaret Fonow, *Making Feminist Politics Transnational Alliances Between Women and Labor*, Urbana, IL: University of Illinois Press, 2011; Ann Therese Lotherington and Anne Britt Flemman, "Negotiating Gender: The Case of the International Labour Organization," in Kristi Anne Stølen and Mariken Vaa (eds.) *Gender and Change in Developing Countries*, New York: Oxford University Press, 1991, pp. 273–307.

6 Daniel Maul, *Human Rights, Development and Decolonization. The International Labour Organization, 1940–70*, New York and Geneva: Palgrave and the ILO, 2012; the majority of essays in Jasmien van Daele, Magaly Rodríquez Garcia, Geert van Goethem, and Marcel van der Linden (eds.), *ILO Histories: Essays on the International Labour Organization and its Impact on the World During the Twentieth Century*, New York: Peter Lang, 2010; and Gerry Rodgers, Eddy Lee, Lee Swepston, and Jasmien Van Daele, *The ILO and the Quest for Social Justice*, New York: Cornell University Press, 2009.

7 Carol Lubin and Anne Winslow, *Social Justice for Women: The International Labor Organization and Women*, Durham, NC: Duke University Press, 1990.

8 Lourdes Benería, *Gender, Development, and Globalization: Economics as if All People Mattered*, New York: Routledge, 2003; Maryse Gaudier, *La Question des Femmes à l'OIT et son Évolution 1919–1994*, Geneva: International Institute of Labour Studies, 1996; Maryse Gaudier, *The International Institute for Labour Studies: Its Research Function, Activities and Publications 1960–2001*, Geneva: ILO, 2001.

9 Susan Zimmermann, "'Special Circumstances' in Geneva: The ILO and the World of Non-Metropolitan Labour in the Interwar Years," in van Daele et al., *ILO Histories*, pp. 221–50; Susan Zimmermann, "Liaison Committees of International Women's Organizations and the Changing Landscape of Women's Internationalism, 1920s to 1945," in Kathryn Kish Sklar and Thomas Dublin (eds.) *Women and Social Movements, International, 1840 to Present*, Alexandria, VA: Alexander Street Press, 2012. Online. Available at https://alexanderstreet.com/products/women-and-social-movements-international (accessed 8 December 2018); Susan Zimmermann, "The International Labour Organization, Transnational Women's Networks, and the Question of Unpaid Work in the Interwar World," in Clare Midgley, Alison Twells, and Julie Carlier

(eds.) *Women in Transnational History: Gendering the Local and the Global*, New York: Routledge, 2016, pp. 33–53; Susan Zimmermann, "Night Work for White Women and Bonded Labour for 'Native' Women? Contentious Traditions and the Globalization of Gender-Specific Labour Protection and Legal Equality Politics, 1926 to 1939," in Sara Kimble and Marion Röwekamp (eds.) *New Perspectives on European Women's Legal History*, New York: Routledge, 2016, pp. 394–427; Susan Zimmermann, "Equality of Women's Economic Status? A Major Bone of Contention in the International Gender Politics Emerging During the Interwar Period," *International History Review*, 2017. Online. Available at https://doi.org/10.1080/07075332.2017.1395761 (accessed 8 December 2018); Susan Zimmermann, "Globalizing Gendered Labour Policy: International Labour Standards and the Global South, 1919–1947," in Eileen Boris, Dorothea Hoehtker, and Susan Zimmermann (eds.) *Women's ILO: Transnational Networks, Global Labour Standards and Gender Equity, 1919 to Present*, Leiden and Geneva: Brill and ILO, 2018, pp. 227–54.

10 For interwar discussions, see note 9 and Ulla Wikander, "Demands on the ILO by Internationally Organized Women in 1919," in van Daele et al., *ILO Histories*, pp. 67–89; Dorothy Sue Cobble, "Japan and the 1919 ILO: Debates Over Rights, Representation, and Global Labor Standards," in Jensen and Lichtenstein, *The ILO from Geneva to the Pacific Rim*, pp. 55–79; Françoise Thébaud, "Réseaux Réformateurs et Politiques du Travail Feminine: L'oit au Prisme de la Carrier et des Engagements de Marguerite Thibert," pp. 27–37 and Nora Natchkova and Céline Schoeni, "L'Organisation internationale du travail, les féministes et les réseaux d'expertes. Les enjeux d'une politique protectrice (1919–1934)," pp. 39–51, both in Isabelle Lespinet-Moret and Vincent Viet (eds.) *L'Organisation internationale du travail – Origine, Développement, Avenir*, Rennes: Presses Universitaires de Rennes, 2011, pp. 39–52; Nora Natchkova and Céline Schoeni, "The ILO, Feminists and Expert Networks: The Challenges of a Protective Policy, 1919–1934," in Sandrine Kott and Joëlle Droux (eds.) *Globalizing Social Rights: The International Labour Organization and Beyond*, New York and Geneva: Palgrave and ILO, 2013, pp. 49–64. See also Nora Natchkova, "Travail, Luttes et Inégalité: les Femmes au Cœur des Négociations de l'Organisation Internationale du Travail et de l'Horlogerie Suisse (1912–1931)," Université de Fribourg (Switzerland), PhD thesis, 2011. For labor standards, see note 9; Nora Natchkova and Céline Schoeni, "Qui a besoin de 'protéger' les femmes? La Convention sur le Travail de Nuit des Femmes (1919–1934)," *Travail, Genre et Sociétés*, 2008, vol. 20, 111–28; Eileen Boris, "'No Right to Layettes or Nursing Time:' Maternity Leave and the Question of United States Exceptionalism," in Leon Fink (ed.) *Workers Across the Americas: The Transnational Turn in Labor History*, New York: Oxford University Press, 2011, pp. 171–93; Paula Määttä, *The ILO Principle of Equal Pay and its Implementation*, Tampere, Finland: Tampere University Press, 2008; Elizabeth Prügl, *The Global Construction of Gender: Home-Based Work in the Political Economy of the 20th Century*, New York: Columbia University Press, 1999; Jennifer Fish and Jennifer Turner, "The Global Domestic: Mapping 'Decent Work' in International Dialogues" and Annie Delaney, Rosaria Burchielli, and Jane Tate, "Homeworkers Organizing for Recognition and Rights: Can International Standards Assist Them?" both in Jensen and Lichtenstein (eds.) *The ILO from Geneva to the Pacific Rim*; Eileen Boris and Jennifer Fish, "'Slaves No More': Making Global Labor Standards for Domestic Workers," *Feminist Studies*, 2014, vol. 40, no. 2, 411–43; Jennifer Fish, *Domestic Workers of the World Unite! A Global Movement for Dignity and Human Rights*, New York: New York University Press, 2017; and Leah Vosko, *Managing the Margins: Gender, Citizenship and the International Regulation of Precarious Employment*, New York: Oxford University Press, 2011.

11 Boris, Hoehtker, and Zimmermann, *Women's ILO*.

12 Based on the writing of C. Wilfred Jenks in "The ILO Approach to Human Rights," *ILO Panorama*, 1968, vol. 32, 2–3. For strategic reasons the ILO sometimes claimed economic rights as its portfolio, allowing other entities to be in charge of civil rights.

13 "The ILO Approach to Human Rights," 3.

14 Convention 87 "Freedom of Association and Protection of the Right to Organize," came into being in 1948 and Convention 98 "Right to Organize and Collective Bargaining" came into being 1949.

15 Clifford Donn and Minghua Zhao, "Freedom of Association: A Comparison of Chinese and US Approaches to ILO Standards," in Jensen and Lichtenstein, *The ILO from Geneva to the Pacific*

Rim, pp. 251–76, especially p. 252. While 153 states have ratified Convention 87, Brazil, China, India, Iran, and the United States have not.

16 For example, "Report on Workers' Education in Nigeria," Geneva: ILO, 1960, in ILO Archives, Geneva, Switzerland, ILO/OTA/Nigeria/R.2.

17 ILO Archives, Registry/229560, WN 8–4, "Women's Questions – Problems of Working Women in Special Occupations or Professions, Agriculture – General," letter from Albert Guigui to Mildred Fairchild, 15 October 1951.

18 "International Labor Organization," *International Organization*, 1965, vol. 19, no. 1, 132–3. See also ILO, *Official Bulletin*, 1964, vol. 47, no. 1, 1–25.

19 ILO Archives, Registry/229560, WN 8–4, J. B. Orizit to Elizabeth Johnstone, 28 April 1969.

20 ILO Archives, ILC 39–416, Report VI: Forced Labor, File: International Labour Conference, 9th Session, 1956, letter from Philippe Seynes of the ECOSOC to David Morse, 15 May 1956.

21 Article 1, Convention 105, Abolition of Forced Labour Convention, 1957. Online. Available at www.ilo.org/dyn/normlex/en/f?p=NORMLEXPUB:12100:0::NO::P12100_ILO_CODE:C105 (accessed 8 December 2018).

22 Maul, *Human Rights, Development and Decolonization*, pp. 23–7.

23 E. Unwin, "The Slavery Convention, and the Forthcoming Meeting of the ILO on Forced Labour," *Women's International League Monthly News Sheet* (British Section), 1927, vol. 18, no. 3, 3.

24 ILO Archives, "Resolution on the United Nations Report on Forced Labour," August 1953; Memo by Dr. A. R. Metail, 23 October 1953, FLC 1–1401, Jacket 1, 10/1953.

25 Zimmermann, "Globalizing Gendered Labour Policy."

26 Approval by the UN General Assembly in Resolution 317 (IV), 2 December 1949. Online. Available at www.ohchr.org/en/professionalinterest/pages/trafficinpersons.aspx (accessed 8 December 2018).

27 Virginia A. Leary, "The Paradox of Workers Rights and Human Rights," in Lance A. Compa and Stephen F. Diamond (eds.) *Human Rights, Labor Rights, and International Trade*, Philadelphia: University of Pennsylvania Press, 1996, p. 26.

28 ILO Press Release: "ILO Adopts New Protocol to Tackle Modern Forms of Forced Labour," 11 June 2014. Online. Available at www.ilo.org/global/about-the-ilo/newsroom/news/WCMS_246549/lang–en/index.htm (accessed 8 December 2018).

29 In contrast, by 2016 #102, "Social Security" had only 56, #103 "Maternity" had only 41, and #110 "Plantations" had only 12. Other "Fundamental Conventions" have about the same number of ratifications; these include forced labor, minimum age, and freedom of association. For ratifications of ILO Conventions, see the NORMLEX database. Online. Available at www.ilo.org/dyn/normlex/en/f?p=1000:1 (accessed 8 December 2018).

30 International Labour Conference, "Seventh Item on the Agenda: Discrimination in the Field of Employment and Occupation," *Report VII (2)*, Geneva: ILO, 1957, pp. 4, 8, 20, 23, 95; "Report of the Committee on Discrimination," in International Labour Conference, *Record of Proceedings, 42nd Session*, Geneva: ILO, 1958, pp. 402, 413.

31 Appendix VI, "Fourth Item on the Agenda," in International Labour Conference, *Record of Proceedings, 42nd Session*, p. 709.

32 National Archives at College Park, MD, RG 86 Records of the US Women's Bureau, Box 66, Office of the Director, General Correspondence of the Women's Bureau, 1948–1953, Folder "1949 Conference, Geneva," Frieda Miller to David Morse, 14 June 1948; Miller to Mrs. Nyswander, 14 June 1948.

33 ILO Archives, ILO 40–417, Jacket 1, Minute from R. M. Lyman to Mr. Rao, 23 May 1957.

34 International Labour Conference, "Equal Remuneration for Men and Women Workers for Work of Equal Value," Fifth Item on the Agenda for 33rd Session, *Report V (1)*, Geneva: ILO, 1949, p. 7.

35 Silke Neunsinger, "The Unobtainable Magic of Numbers: Equal Remuneration, the ILO, and the International Trade Union Movement 1950s–1980s," in Boris, Hoehtker, and Zimmermann, *Women's ILO*, pp. 121–48.

36 International Labour Conference, "Equal Remuneration for Men and Women Workers for Work of Equal Value," Fifth Item on the Agenda for 33rd Session, *Report V (1)*, Geneva: ILO, 1949, p. 16.

37 International Labour Conference, "Equal Remuneration for Men and Women Workers for Work of Equal Value," Fifth Item on the Agenda for 33rd Session, *Report V (2)*, Geneva: ILO, 1950, p. 4.
38 International Labour Conference, "Equal Remuneration for Men and Women Workers for Work of Equal Value," Fifth Item on the Agenda for 33rd Session, *Report V (2)*, Geneva: ILO, 1950, p. 16.
39 Equal Remuneration Convention (#100), Article 7. Online. Available at www.ilo.org/dyn/normlex/en/f?p=NORMLEXPUB:12100:0::NO::P12100_ILO_CODE:C100 (accessed 8 December 2018).
40 Equal Remuneration Convention (#100), Article 3. Online. Available at www.ilo.org/dyn/normlex/en/f?p=NORMLEXPUB:12100:0::NO::P12100_ILO_CODE:C100 (accessed 8 December 2018).
41 R090 Equal Remuneration Recommendation, 1951 (No. 90). Online. Available at www.ilo.org/dyn/normlex/en/f?p=NORMLEXPUB:12100:0::NO:12100:P12100_INSTRUMENT_ID:312428:NO (accessed 8 December 2018).
42 The WFTU was founded in London in 1945 to represent the international trade union movement. However, all non-communist unions disaffiliated to join the rival, Western-controlled International Confederation of Free Trade Unions (ICFTU) in 1950. Both union federations held NGO observer status at the UN and the ILO. See WFTU, *The World Federation of Trade Unions, 1945–1985*, Prague: WFTU in cooperation with Prace Czechoslovak Trade Unions, 1985.
43 ILO Archives, Unclassified, Commission on the Status of Women (94th and 95th Meetings), 10–12, Minutes Compiled by US State Department, ESC 1004–11-5.
44 International Labour Conference, "Equal Remuneration for Men and Women Workers for Work of Equal Value," Fifth Item on the Agenda for 33rd Session, *Report V (2)*, Geneva: ILO, 1950, p. 14.
45 International Labour Conference, "Equal Remuneration for Men and Women Workers for Work of Equal Value," Fifth Item on the Agenda for 33rd Session, *Report V (2)*, Geneva: ILO, 1950, p. 17.
46 International Labour Conference, "Equal Remuneration for Men and Women Workers for Work of Equal Value," Fifth Item on the Agenda for 33rd Session, *Report V (2)*, Geneva: ILO, 1950, p. 42.
47 Mr. Shkunaev, "Report of the Committee on Discrimination," in International Labour Conference, *Record of Proceedings, 42nd Session*, pp. 405–6.
48 ILO Archives, D634-412–01, Laurel Casinader, Chair of the Economic Committee, International Alliance of Women, "Proposed Recommendation Concerning Equal Remuneration for Men and Women Workers for Work of Equal Value," 22 May 1951.
49 ILO Archives, D633-415–0, Elizabeth Abbott and Ina Møller, "Memorandum on Equal Pay," June 1950, 7–8.
50 "Report of the Committee on Discrimination," in International Labour Conference, *Record of Proceedings, 42nd Session*, p. 403.
51 International Labour Conference, "Seventh Item on the Agenda: Discrimination," p. 33.
52 Discrimination (Employment and Occupation) Convention, 1958 (No. 111), Articles 1, 2, 5. Online. Available atwww.ilo.org/dyn/normlex/en/f?p=NORMLEXPUB:12100:0::NO:12100:P12100_INSTRUMENT_ID:312256:NO (accessed 8 December 2018). On "bona fide occupational qualification," see Title VII of the 1964 Civil Rights Act, SEC. 2000e-2 [Section 703 (e)]. Online. Available www.eeoc.gov/laws/statutes/titlevii.cfm (accessed 8 December 2018).
53 Mrs. Srnská, "Report of the Committee on Discrimination," in International Labour Conference, *Record of Proceedings, 42nd Session*, p. 409.
54 Appendix VI, "Fourth Item on the Agenda," in International Labour Conference, *Record of Proceedings, 42nd Session*, p. 709.
55 Mr. Carroll, Appendix VI, "Fourth Item on the Agenda," 408; International Labour Conference, "Seventh Item on the Agenda: Discrimination," p. 18.
56 Mr. Kaplansky, "Report of the Committee on Discrimination," in International Labour Conference, *Record of Proceedings, 42nd Session*, p. 414.

57 Mr. Nagler, "Report of the Committee on Discrimination," in International Labour Conference, *Record of Proceedings, 42nd Session*, pp. 403–5.
58 ILO Archives, Remarks by Mr. Agnew, "Corrigenda to C.D./RV.5, X/4," ILC, 42nd Session, Committee on Discrimination, 18 June 1958.
59 International Labour Conference, "Seventh Item on the Agenda: Discrimination," pp. 20, 27, 41.
60 ILO Archives, ECOSOC, Report on the Third Session of the CSW, Beirut, Lebanon, 21 March to 4 April 1949, E/1316, E/CN.6/124, 19 April 1949, "Equal Pay for Equal Work," 17–18.
61 Elizabeth Johnstone, "Women in Economic Life: Rights and Opportunities," *Annals of the American Academy of Political and Social Science*, 1968, vol. 375, no. 1, 103.
62 ILO Archives, "ILO Plantations Committee Second Meeting in Havana, Press Release ILO/681, 30 March 1953," Registry/196262, "Industrial Committees and Analogous Bodies," Plantations Committee – 2nd Session – Havana March 1953.
63 The final ILO Convention included "coffee, tea, sugarcane, rubber, bananas, cocoa, coconuts, groundnuts, cotton, tobacco, fibers (sisal, jute, and hemp), citrus, palm oil, cinchona, or pineapple." It also noted the ability of individual nations to include "rice, chicory, cardamom, geranium and pyrethrum, or any other crop." C110, Plantations Convention, 1958 (No. 110). The full text of Plantations Convention, 1958 (No. 110), is online. Available at www.ilo.org/dyn/normlex/en/f?p=NORMLEXPUB:12100:0::NO::P12100_INSTRUMENT_ID:312255</URI (accessed 8 December 2018).
64 See for example ILO Archives, "Mission Report: Conditions of Life and Work on Tea and Rubber Plantation in Ceylon with Special Reference to Women and Children," Registry/204329, DADG 13-6-17-3, "Luis Alvarado – Women and Young Workers' Division – Miss Erulkar's Mission Report to Ceylon, regarding Tea and Rubber Plantations."
65 *The First Session of the Committee on Work on Plantations*, Geneva: ILO, 1951, p. 16.
66 Miss Jedidi, in International Labour Conference, *Record of Proceedings, 49th Session*, Geneva: ILO, 1965, p. 373.
67 Joan C. Williams, *Unbending Gender: Why Family and Work Conflict and What to Do About It*, New York: Oxford University Press, 2000.
68 Employment (Women with Family Responsibilities) Recommendation, 1965 (No. 123). Online. Available at www.ilo.org/dyn/normlex/en/f?p=NORMLEXPUB:12100:0::NO:12100:P12100_INSTRUMENT_ID:312461:NO (accessed 8 December 2018).
69 Johnstone, "Women in Economic Life," 111.
70 International Labour Conference, *Record of Proceedings, 49th Session*, Geneva: ILO, 1965, p. 383.
71 International Labour Conference, *Record of Proceedings, 48th Session*, Geneva: ILO, 1964, p. 469, 465, 740.
72 ILO Archives, WN 2–1003-2, Jacket 1, ILO, Meeting of Consultants on Women Workers' Problems, Geneva, 20–28 September 1965, 20.
73 Workers with Family Responsibilities Recommendation, 1981 (No. 165). Online. Available at www.ilo.org/dyn/normlex/en/f?p=NORMLEXPUB:12100:0::NO::P12100_INSTRUMENT_ID:312503</URI (accessed 8 December 2018).
74 Ruth Cowan, *More Work for Mother: the Ironies of Household Technologies from the Open Hearth to the Microwave*, New York: Basic Books, 1983.
75 ILO, *Women Workers in a Changing World: Preliminary Report*, Geneva: ILO, 1973, pp. 22–3.
76 ILO, *Report VIII: Equality of Opportunity and Treatment for Women Workers*, Geneva: ILO, 1975, p. 1.
77 ILO Archives, MCWW/1974/D.2, "International Labour Office, Meeting of Consultants on Women Workers' Problems Geneva, May 1974, Draft for Discussion."
78 ILO, "Committee of Social Security Experts, Geneva, 26 November-3 December 1975. Social Security Issues Affecting Women. Working document prepared by Mrs. M. Grounin, ILO Consultant," Geneva: ILO, 1975), pp. 1–2.
79 ILO, *Report VIII: Equality of Opportunity and Treatment for Women Workers*, p. 2.
80 International Labour Conference, *Records of the Proceedings. 60th Session, 1975*, "Proposed Declaration on Equality of Opportunity and Treatment for Women Workers," Geneva: ILO, 1975, p. 781. The exact language was adopted in the final draft.

81 The Declaration also noted that its signers were "aware that the position of women cannot be changed without changing also the role of men in society and in the family." See International Labour Conference, *Records of the Proceedings. 60th Session*, 1975, "Declaration on Equality of Opportunity and Treatment for Women Workers," *ILO Official Bulletin*, 1975, vol. 58, Series A. no. 1, 96–100; ILO, *Report VIII: Equality of Opportunity and Treatment for Women Workers*, pp. 44–7.

82 Hilary Charlesworth, "Not Waving but Drowning: Gender Mainstreaming and Human Rights in the United Nations," *Harvard Human Rights Journal*, 2005, vol. 18, 2.

83 Quoted from "The Nairobi Forward-Looking Strategies for the Advancement of Women," 27 July 1985. Noted in Charlesworth, "Not Waving," 3.

84 Report of the Director-General, *The Women at Work Initiative: The Push for Equality*, Geneva: ILO, 2018.

15

HUMAN RIGHTS MOVEMENTS AND THE FALL OF THE BERLIN WALL

Explaining the peaceful revolution of 1989

Ned Richardson-Little

The image of crowds pouring through the newly opened Berlin Wall on 9 November 1989 has become one of the great symbolic triumphs of the human rights movement in Eastern Europe at the end of the Cold War.[1] Soon after this momentous event, the dictatorship of the Socialist Unity Party (Sozialistische Einheitspartei Deutschlands, SED) was swept away along with the very existence of East Germany as an independent state. Today, the German Democratic Republic (GDR) is synonymous with the abuse of human rights, ranging from arbitrary arrest to mass surveillance, the denial of political freedoms, the suppression of religious expression, and the rejection of freedom of movement. Ruled by a single party, without an independent judiciary, and subjected to the depredations of the Stasi, the East German secret police (Ministerium für Staatssicherheit, Ministry for State Security), East Germany was, by modern definitions, a state devoid of human rights.[2]

Even if – in retrospect – the collapse of the GDR seems inevitable, a year before the Berlin Wall came down the success of a human rights movement in East Germany would have appeared highly improbable. East Germans had begun to use the language of human rights to demand the right to leave the GDR in the 1970s, but there were no intellectuals or social movements pushing for political reform in the name of human rights until only a few years before the system as a whole dramatically collapsed.[3] The first independent human rights organization, the Initiative for Peace and Human Rights (Initiative für Frieden und Menschenrechte), was founded only in 1986 and half of its initial members were secret police informants.[4] Until spring 1989, the human rights movement in the GDR was limited to a few thousand hard-core activists in a country of 17 million. By contrast, the first human rights activism in the Soviet Union began in 1968, and Poland and Czechoslovakia had organized human rights movements beginning in the late 1970s.[5]

The people of East Germany were hardly unaware of human rights; the SED claimed to be their greatest champion. Beginning in the 1940s, the Party adopted the slogan "no human rights without socialism," and in 1959 it had even created the state-directed GDR Committee for Human Rights to campaign against abuses in the West.[6] In the 1960s, the SED developed a full-fledged philosophy of "socialist human rights" through which it claimed solidarity with Third World nations, who were also fighting for self-determination against Western oppression. East Germany gladly signed every United Nations (UN) human rights treaty, as well as, in 1975, the Helsinki Accords – a treaty with 34 other nations on both sides of the Iron Curtain that included the affirmation of human rights.[7] In contrast to the Soviet Union under Mikhail Gorbachev, which embraced the idea of human rights as a means of democratizing the USSR, the East German SED was so hard-line that it banned Soviet publications as a dangerous influence on the population in the late 1980s. Up until the fall of the Berlin Wall, the SED proclaimed that it was they who stood for human rights, not the hypocritical activists of the West who failed to challenge their own governments and who used human rights as a weapon in the ideological conflict of the Cold War.

How then did human rights become transformed from the advocacy of a handful of activists into hundreds of thousands in mass demonstrations within three years? Instead of acting as an explosive catalyst for revolution, at least in the GDR of the late 1980s, human rights were a discourse that helped bring together a diverse coalition to negotiate the end of dictatorship and the creation of a democratic system.[8] The small number of human rights activists who emerged a few years before the fall of the Berlin Wall used the language to link up multiple communities of disaffected East Germans from peace and environmental activists, and from conservative Christians to draft resisters. As the hard-line leadership of the SED refused to reform despite economic crisis and mass emigration, low-level party members came to join this coalition calling for increased freedom of speech and democratic participation as a means of improving society. Years of state propaganda about human rights meant that those who still believed in the cause of socialism could take on the language of human rights for the purpose of reform without needing to reject their ideology entirely. By the fall of 1989, mass demonstrations led in part by human rights activists gained momentum as the SED failed to produce viable alternatives to adapt to growing unrest. Ultimately, the security services refused to use mass violence to stem the spread of unrest, upon concluding that the people in the streets demanding human rights were not counter-revolutionaries, but citizens seeking to take part in the affairs of their own country. Human rights thus served as a tool for unifying the masses from below while eating away at the legitimacy of the SED's suppression of mass dissent.

Human rights and 1989 historiography

The role of human rights activism in the events of 1989 is a central question into the causes of the fall of the Berlin Wall and the collapse of state socialism. According to the historian Konrad Jarausch, in the case of East Germany the civic movement was the hero of 1989. The rebirth of civil society, in no small part due to the rise of human rights activism, fueled both mass emigration and street demonstrations that destabilized the SED and opened the Berlin Wall.[9] This interpretation complements similar claims that the idea of human rights was crucial to the collapse of state socialism and the end of the Cold War as a whole. According to this school of thought, it was the decision by Eastern bloc countries, including East Germany, to sign the 1975 Helsinki Accords (which contained promises to respect human rights), that sparked new transnational activist movements and networks that were crucial to the felling of the Soviet Empire.[10] Co-founder of Human Rights Watch Aryeh Neier has argued that while one can debate how large a part human rights played the events of 1989, "beyond a doubt, however, [human rights] was one of the causes, if not the most important cause, of that epic series of events."[11] According to Rosemary Foot, the triumph of human rights in 1989 "showed the dominance of the discourse on civil and political rights over that of economic, social, and cultural concerns."[12] The revolutions across Eastern Europe in 1989 have been used by some to promote the idea of human rights as a means of inducing liberal-democratic revolution, and sparked hopes in 2011 that the Arab Spring would repeat the same process of regional transformation through the power of ideas.[13]

Others have, however, challenged the centrality of the civic movement and the role of human rights as a catalyst for change in Eastern Europe in the 1980s. Stephen Kotkin has argued that it was not a renewed civil society that was responsible, but rather the "uncivil society" of the state socialist elite that caused the revolution of 1989 by bungling the planned economy and then crashing their own system through political incompetence.[14] First Gorbachev's reforms destabilized the system as whole and then the hard-liners, like East Germany's SED, failed to reestablish order allowed the system to collapse with a minimum of violence. Mark Kramer has argued that the Helsinki Accords were reduced to "insignificance" as the resultant wave of repression silenced, imprisoned, or exiled dissenters across the Eastern bloc.[15] Accordingly, it was the Soviet leadership throwing away its own empire, rather than plucky citizens reclaiming power from below that explains the extraordinary collapse of the system.

While critics are correct that the "explosive" power of human rights in driving change after the Helsinki Accords has been exaggerated, this does not mean that the idea of human rights did not play an important, even crucial, role in the revolution of 1989. In the case of East Germany, however, the "Helsinki narrative" is particularly problematic as the first independent human rights activist group in the GDR did not appear until the beginning of 1986. East Germans were motivated to dissent, to protest, and to take to the streets less by the idea of human rights than by tangible problems of political suppression, economic decline, and state incompetence. East Germans were not inspired by the concept of human rights that then led to political action, but rather the opposite: the act of taking part in active demonstrations led to the adoption of human rights as a unifying language that brought together a broad coalition of those who sought change, from there creating a movement, rather than a mass of individuals, to challenge the power of the SED.

From the international year for human rights to a human rights movement

For East Germans, the language of human rights began as a mild challenge to the state, taking years to radicalize. The first instances of GDR citizens employing human rights ideas for the purposes of protest came in 1968.[16] When the SED decided to create a new "socialist constitution" for East Germany that would supersede the less ideologically rigid founding document of the GDR, it organized mass consultations, and a plebiscite to ratify the final version. In order to reinforce the link between domestic reform and its international campaign with the Third World, the SED tied the constitutional referendum to the UN's International Year for Human Rights. In return, leaders from both the Catholic and Protestant churches in the GDR used this as an opportunity to reference the Universal Declaration of Human Rights (UDHR) and the UN's 1966 Human Rights Covenants, as part of an organized protest against the removal of protection for religious freedom from the list of rights recognized in the constitution.

Just as the SED had little success in using its human rights message to gain support from the Third World, East German human rights protests in 1968 did little to change the character of the constitution, aside from gaining one more section on religious freedom that meant little in practice. Nonetheless, this initial incident paved the way for those seeking to exit the GDR in the 1970s to cite human rights documents to support their case. Cut off by the Berlin Wall since 1961, East Germans, separated from family in the West, or simply wishing to travel abroad, became increasingly militant after ten years of isolation. When the SED signed a transit agreement with West Germany and then the Basic Treaty (which provided some mutual recognition between the two Germanies for the first time), hundreds of East Germans began to petition the state to allow them to travel or emigrate on the basis on human rights law. When the GDR officially joined the UN and became a signatory to the 1966 UN Covenants in 1973, the number of applications citing human rights spiked. This trend continued after the signing of the Helsinki Accords, as now thousands of citizens deployed new arguments and discourses to press their case in what was sometimes a fifth or sixth application for permission to leave.

The idea of human rights was not, however, used to demand political change within the GDR. Emerging from the intellectual and cultural elite in the 1970s, some dissidents began to press for greater pluralism under socialism. The physicist Robert Havemann repeatedly criticized the SED in Western publications from a Marxist standpoint, leading to his house arrest in 1977. Rudolf Bahro published his eco-utopian treatise *The Alternative in Eastern Europe* in West Germany, leading to his arrest and eventual expulsion from East Germany. Yet these dissidents did not align themselves with the emerging international human rights movement. Havemann supported the democratization of Eastern Europe, but in the context of completing the socialist revolution, and saw the international conflict over human rights as yet another iteration of unproductive Cold War propaganda from both sides.[17] Bahro summarily rejected the international human rights movement as a step backwards: "[T]he bulk of the oppositional elements have seen themselves pushed back to a program of purely liberal democratic demands, a human rights campaign, a position that is the most general, platitudinous, and inane possible."[18] The dissidents of East Germany were more likely to be idealistic socialists hoping to shed the ossified bureaucracy of SED rule than liberal democrats.

By the 1980s, the closest East Germany had to organized social movements outside of the control of the state were the independent peace and environmental movements, gathering in church basements, which had supplanted state-sponsored movements to address these problems. When the SED introduced compulsory military education in schools in 1977, it sparked the creation of an independent peace movement among pacifist Christians who already saw themselves as outsiders in an atheistic Marxist country. Environmentalism was also rapidly becoming a source of dissent as unrestricted industrial pollution from East Germany's chemical and heavy industries took an ecological toll, further exacerbated by a program to convert brown coal into oil to deal with shortages in Soviet deliveries.

At the beginning of the 1980s, however, none of these discontented and disgruntled GDR citizens sought to organize around the idea or language of human rights. The emergent peace and environmental movements were skeptical of human rights as a vehicle for change, viewing it as the discourse of Cold War tensions or anti-socialist propaganda. Human rights were thus a liability for East Germans who saw their own cause as apolitical and purely moral. Nonetheless, the SED and, in particular, the Stasi reacted harshly to these activists. In 1983 and 1984, a campaign against the movement destroyed half of the peace organizations in the country. The SED successfully pressured churches to evict activists; key figures such as Bärbel Bohley and Ulrike Poppe were jailed; Roland Jahn and others were involuntarily deported to West Germany; less prominent activists faced dismissal from work and educational institutions.[19]

While the state was ostensibly successful in suppressing these activist circles, the SED still faced the problems endemic to the East German centralized planning system, now exacerbated by global economic developments.[20] The GDR relied heavily on cheap Soviet oil, but by 1982, the Soviets had unilaterally cut deliveries by 10 percent and dramatically increased prices.[21] Huge investments in the microelectronic industry diverted funds from investment in existing profitable fields, but failed to deliver a globally competitive product.[22] Only through emergency loans from West Germany, orchestrated by minister-president of Bavaria Franz Josef Strauss, was the GDR saved from bankruptcy.

This economic decline threatened the implicit social contract of the GDR according to which the SED at the very least provided basic goods and services to the masses.[23] In response, the number of applications for emigration rose sharply in 1984.[24] Spikes had occurred in the past, but this time the surge did not subside. Hoping to simply rid the country of its most dissatisfied, the SED decided to allow the emigration of 37,000 "enemies, criminal elements, and incorrigibles."[25] First-time applicants quadrupled to more than 57,000. Mass emigration caused more demand to leave, in part because the SED had acceded to Helsinki Accords provisions allowing family reunification, instigating a process of chain migration. In spite of a strenuous crackdown by the Stasi, applications to exit the GDR would continue to rise every year until the borders finally opened in 1989.

Human rights for peace, the environment, and reform

The upsurge in applications to exit was accompanied by a revival of the peace movement, which now turned to the problem of human rights. Only in 1985 did the meaning of human rights for dissidents begin to move from the margins to the center. Many in the peace movement feared that the turn to human rights would be "political suicide" and sure to bring more Stasi repression. For others, it appeared as though they would always face repression without political reforms and the earlier tactic of claiming purely moral goals had already failed.[26] Frank Eigenfeld, a peace activist from Halle, later recalled:

> We realized that we were not at all accepted by the powers that be, and that we had little opportunity to articulate ourselves in public ... The focus changed from the arms race to human rights [but] only after we had begun to run into enormous organizing difficulties did our focus begin to change.[27]

Such sentiments were not universal and in shifting the conversation towards human rights, complications arose within the peace movement itself. Ulrike Poppe later explained,

> democratic freedoms were always seen in a capitalist context. This made the debate about them problematic ... I don't want to say that we used the theme of peace in order to actually work through human rights and bourgeois freedoms. At the least, however, the people were more open to the problem of human rights compared to just working on the problem of our own democratic deficits.[28]

The cause of peace was so important that it legitimized, at least for some, the venture into the world of human rights and political reform.

After months of infighting, in January 1986, Ralf Hirsch, Wolfgang Templin, and Peter Grimm, all longtime peace activists, issued a statement announcing the creation of the Initiative for Peace and Human Rights (IFM), the first dissident group to work outside of the protection of the church and to focus on human rights within the GDR.[29] Having determined that the "goals of peace initiatives depend upon the implementation of basic democratic rights and freedoms," they called for assistance from the various dissident communities as well as cooperation from the peace movement in developing the idea of human rights in relation to social justice, the right to work, protection of the environment, and the rejection of obligatory military service.[30] The human rights advocated by the IFM represented an important synthesis of political aims and ideologies. In their founding document, they sought to bring together activists to discuss such wide-ranging problems as education, religious freedom, the environment, the draft, workers' rights, and international peace. Instead of focusing on a single issue or grievance in the name of human rights, the IFM pulled together the concerns of the many disgruntled elements of East German society, from the peace movement, to religious believers, the growing environmental movement, draft resisters, and workers, all under the umbrella of human rights. Members of the IFM stressed the importance of legally guaranteed political and civil rights in the name of social well-being and harmony – but in contrast to the SED discourse of human rights – they also stressed the importance of a broad pluralism. In a letter to the 11th SED Party Congress, the IFM declared, "pluralism is an overarching value for the enforcement of fundamental human rights ... The essential tension between different approaches to human rights issues is productive and should not be destroyed by policy debates with the goal of unity."[31]

Finally, IFM members refused to side with the West in the human rights debate and presented themselves as part of a "third way" between state socialism and capitalism. In announcing the creation of the group they were careful to ascribe guilt to both sides of the Cold War:

> Over the heads of those affected, there is a tense continuation of the arms build-up in both political blocs, negotiations are being held behind closed doors, and peace movement activists are being prosecuted and sometimes criminalized. As far as these practices are concerned, the "Western democracies" are right up there with our governing leaders.[32]

The members did not connect human rights with the adoption of a Western system even if they saw elements of Western parliamentary democracy as admirable. As Gerd Poppe put it, "when we use ideas like democracy and human rights, they are connected to quite a different conception than in the West."[33] They rejected the theoretical split of capitalist versus socialist human rights and popular fears that freedom could only come at the cost of equality.

The following year, those trying to leave East Germany began to formally organize around the concept of claiming their rights. In September 1987, Günter Jeschonnek, an artist who had been blacklisted following his application to emigrate, formed the Working Group for State Citizenship Rights (Arbeitsgruppe Staatsbürgerschaftsrecht), the first formal effort to coordinate human rights demands by those trying to exit the GDR. Although controversial within the activist community, where those trying to exit were often seen as undermining the cause of reform, Wolfgang and Lotte Templin of the IFM assisted in the creation of the group and supported its activities. In turn, the public statements of Jeschonnek and the Working Group branched out from a single-minded focus on the right to leave to explicit criticisms of other human rights abuses in the GDR. In a manifesto delivered to the GDR Committee for Human Rights on 10 December 1987 – Human Rights Day – the group declared:

> The realization of human rights cannot be solely a matter of the state. In our view, it includes equal participation of all citizens, the unvarnished examination of existing problems, open dialogue with dissenters and free space in society for the unrestricted work of independent peace and human rights groups.[34]

Those who chose exit from the GDR were also using their voice on the way out.[35]

On a mass scale, those seeking to emigrate were also beginning to internalize that they had a human right to leave and that the SED simply had to respect that. Careful legalistic petitions were transforming into accusations of moral failing by the SED. According to a Ministry of the Interior report on applications to exit from 1988, almost all included "the slander against the politics of the GDR, especially accusations of massive human rights violations. The assertion that conflicts exist between international agreements and the domestic policies of the GDR plays a dominant role."[36] Jeschonnek recalled that he wanted to make clear that the right to leave the GDR was a "legitimate human right," and that "we are not supplicants but we have a right."[37] Gone was the polite language of begging permission to leave and the reminders that doing so could help with international opinion, replaced by a militant sense of entitlement based on the idea of human rights.

In December 1988, dissidents sought to appropriate Human Rights Day after decades of SED pageantry that had used the UN event to display the party-state's continuing commitment and fidelity to human rights. For the 40th anniversary of the UDHR, the human rights movement organized numerous church events to discuss human rights problems and deficits in the GDR. The Stasi estimated that 800 people took part in a Human Rights Day service at a church in Berlin-Treptow, including representatives from more than 200 groups and organizations. At another Berlin church 120 people discussed Article 19 of the UDHR on freedom of speech. At a third Berlin church, 50 attendees considered the role of the church in overcoming human rights abuses within the GDR. Demonstrations by those seeking to leave also took place in Berlin, Halle, and Erfurt.[38] Several human rights groups also issued their own declaration, pointing out the glaring contradictions between the regime's rhetoric and reality.[39]

Within the GDR itself, the SED's refusal to reform and its increasingly draconian reactions to criticism were driving previously loyal party members and civil servants towards dissent.[40] In September 1988, a group of students were expelled from the Carl von Ossietzky Gymnasium in Pankow (a school and a district favored by many of the leading members of the SED) for criticizing martial law in Poland and questioning the militarization of the GDR.[41] Such a punishment for students advocating peace at an elite high school was unnerving for those who thought that they could continue to work within the system. Party members complained of feeling "gagged," with one reporting, "I have been in the party a long time and cannot remember a time when I was so helpless and clueless."[42] The absence of the rule of law and freedom of expression was becoming increasingly visible in the daily lives even of East Germans committed to the regime.

1989 and the fall of the Berlin wall

In 1989, the SED was faced with a Soviet Union actively undermining the East German position on human rights, a rising activist movement from below, and a crumbling middle tier of disillusioned civil servants and party members. In January, the Vienna follow-up meeting for the Helsinki process concluded with a fresh round of compromises on human rights by the Eastern bloc led by Soviet representatives.[43] The agreement collapsed the distinction between the socialist and western blocs on the problem of human rights, and the Soviet concessions were so dramatic that Sarah Snyder has suggested that the document marks the end of the Cold War.[44] When Stasi Chief Erich Mielke met with his KGB counterpart following the meeting, he blamed the debacle on the lack of unity in the socialist camp. He blamed the USSR and railed at the Soviet rhetoric that "accused and defamed individual socialist states (the GDR and Czechoslovakia) as hostile to the Helsinki Process, hostile to reform and violators of human rights."[45] Mielke also wrote to the leaders of regional SED and Stasi offices warning that "those who think 'we must change our politics' no longer belong in our party."[46]

In an effort to deflect domestic and international criticism, the SED chose to allow some small-scale liberalization without accepting the possibility of broader reform that could actually threaten the primacy of the party. In May 1989, the Politburo decided that it would allow civic groups to monitor local elections. The electoral process in the GDR was always rigged insofar as candidates were all part of the National Front, constitutionally required to be led by the SED.[47] Citizens could cross out the names of National Front candidates, but doing so meant publicly dropping a ballot into a separate container, inhibiting many. The Politburo instructed local officials not to alter the results, still expecting a 90 percent approval rate. When some districts registered less than 50 percent approval, local officials took it upon themselves to rig the outcome anyway. Rather than acknowledging that some would refuse to acclaim the preselected candidates, local officials sought to erase dissent and present a picture of unanimity by showing a remarkable, even by GDR standards, 98.5 percent vote in favor of the official slate.[48] Even a symbolic vote against a panel of candidates guaranteed to retain power was now outlawed in the "socialist democracy."

Human rights organizations had tried to organize a boycott of the elections but the obvious fraud was far more useful: They demanded recounts in the presence of non-party observers, and organized protests, which prompted violent police reactions, creating new grounds for protest. Justifying their protests with reference to the GDR constitution's right to free expression (Article 27), human rights groups accused the SED of "violating the inner peace" of the country and declared that the police "must ask themselves whether the GDR is truly under the rule of law and if their actions are appropriate."[49] Human rights groups' documentation of the fraud was instrumental in convincing several church pastors to move protests out onto the streets, and demonstrations commemorated the fraudulent election on the 7th of every month thereafter.[50] Other citizens tried to use the legal system to punish SED officials involved in the count, alleging that the officials had violated their right to take part in the political system.[51]

In spring 1989, a brain trust of intellectuals from across the socialist world who had been called upon to refute Western human rights propaganda, instead called for reforms along the lines of the dissident movement. The group, led by the East German academic Rolf Reissig, identified a series of key errors in the thinking of the socialist bloc, including the idea that "social property and production methods and the political power of the working class meant that the problem of human rights had 'automatically' been solved in a qualitatively superior way." Such a misconception led to the "undervaluation of personal and political rights versus economic, social, and cultural rights and the undervaluation of the legal guarantees of personal rights of the citizen against state and society."[52] The intellectuals who were meant to be elucidating the harmony between the state socialist status quo and human rights had now broken from orthodoxy to join the dissidents on paper, if not in the streets.

After decades of resolving human rights criticism through ideological adaptation rather than actual change, the SED leadership was finally out of ideas on how to reconcile the realities of life in the GDR with the idea of human rights. In July, an internal SED report found widespread dissatisfaction among party members due to the leadership's failure to reverse the general economic decline and to address everyday problems like poor housing. In order to solve these problems, "more democracy and freedom is supported, and in this context the protection of human rights in the GDR is placed under criticism."[53] In August 1989, one teacher wrote to her local SED district office:

> The recognition of human rights for all citizens has been proclaimed by the state leadership of the GDR for years and years. In dealing with those who think differently politically, it appears as though, in my humble opinion, this principle has been repealed, or how else would you explain and justify the many actions of the police in front of the Nikolai Church in Leipzig? Students have been eyewitnesses and they have questions![54]

Functionaries who were supposed to be disseminating the values of the system to the next generation could not defend the charges of mass violations of human rights and they were getting no help from above.

Among youth, the loss of faith in the legitimacy of the state was growing rapidly: By spring 1989, more than half of SED members under 25 surveyed by the Leipzig Institute for Youth Research were willing to admit that they had lost confidence in the party's leadership.[55] In Leipzig, one such example was Katrin Walter, who quit her work as a secretary of her local Free German Youth chapter to become a human rights activist in 1989. She was from a loyal socialist family, raised with the stories of the "horrors of the evil imperialists," and had joined the state-run youth group to make her family proud: "But that quickly disillusioned me. My desire for justice and democracy could not be achieved there."[56] In order to live up to ideals they had been raised with, East Germans were now abandoning the SED and fighting for human rights with the opposition.

As officials, teachers, and party members began to defect to the cause of the dissidents, East Germans also continued to leave the country in record numbers. By the summer of 1989 the outflow of citizens had turned into a mass exodus and efforts to stem the tide by increasing the quota of those allowed to leave legally only provoked a greater number of applications to travel. East Germans began using West German embassies in Berlin and the rest of the Eastern bloc as places of sanctuary, while thousands took advantage of the newly open border between Austria and Hungary to flee en masse.[57] By September of that year, the SED had received 160,785 exit requests, of which 59,725 were from first-time applicants.[58]

As East Germans were flooding the exits, or at least applying to do so, they were also flooding into the streets. In Leipzig, peace demonstrations held every Monday since the early 1980s now transformed into massive marches for reform. Hartmut Zwahr described the atmosphere:

> Singing, the demonstrators encouraged each other. They began with the Internationale – learned in 7th and 8th grade music class at the polytechnic high schools of the GDR. Memorized, sullenly performed, never to be sung again, until this moment, when a chunk of the refrain suddenly fit, to sing out the protest with all the power of their voices: "people hear the signal/on to the last fight/the Internationale/wrests the human right!" Human rights. How they had been distorted! Now all felt the same. To go into the streets was a human right. In the call "Democracy Now!" and in the singing of "On to the last fight!" came together everything that this moment held. To dare. Now. Some only understood in this instant, in the pincer of state power, the loss of human rights, and that [they were] absolutely prepared to win them back.[59]

Zwahr's description illuminates how the discourse of human rights had become so essential to the dissident movement. First, in hijacking the "Internationale" as a song of protest rather than affirmation of SED rule, they reappropriated the state language of human rights. Second, the subjective shift: East Germans came to define their problems as human rights violations rather than as either material deprivations or political deficits. Third, the mass sense of empowerment that came with the internalization of the idea of human rights led citizens to act as though the right to speak, assemble, or leave was already a reality.

Political pluralism returned to the GDR in September 1989 as new organizations seeking mass membership formed. Some, like New Forum (Neues Forum), were concerned with opening dialogue and creating a participatory society, while others, such as the revived Social Democratic Party (Sozialdemokratische Partei, SDP), were organizations with definite policy objectives. Human rights appeared across the spectrum as both an end goal of their work and as a process for how to get there. The SDP program included the duty for all members to work towards the "protection of human rights and civil rights as contained in the Universal Declaration of Human Rights and the two human rights covenants (1966)."[60] At the same time, a splinter group of disillusioned officials from the SED and the Free German Trade Union Federation (Freier Deutscher Gewerkschaftsbund, the state trade union organization) formed the United Left (Vereinigte Linke). Its platform in early September 1989 demanded "political democracy, the rule of law, consistent implementation of the indivisible human rights and free expression of the individuality of each member of society."[61]

While left-wing political parties were calling for human rights, new opposition groups originating from within the church were doing the same. Founded on 14 September 1989,

Democratic Awakening (Demokratischer Aufbruch, DA), a group of Protestants focused on the creation of a "socialist society on a democratic basis." They called for the rule of law and argued that they did not expect "the state to grant human rights, but rather to respect them."[62] This meant both reforms from below and reforms from above with the goal of splitting apart party and state, developing a free and open public sphere, and the introduction of market mechanisms into the economy while maintaining a "society of solidarity."[63] In fighting for these causes, the DA sought to portray its cause as the outcome of "the realization of guaranteed human rights as found in the constitution and international agreements."[64]

While the Catholic Church had avoided political engagement in the GDR since the late 1970s, when it had sought narrowly to protect its own institutional interests, in the fall of 1989 it once again took up the problem of human rights, branching out into broader problems of freedom and political representation. In September, the Church made an official statement endorsing the right to travel and to emigrate. In October, this statement expanded to the right to free elections, the right to free speech, peaceful assembly, and free association. In a notice to all priests and deacons, the Bishops implored them to remember these rights "as contained in the UN Human Rights Declaration."[65]

Human rights as a broad concept and the institution of individual political and civil liberties along liberal democratic lines represented a baseline consensus among these groups even though they had very different ideological and religious beliefs. In early October 1989, most of the new opposition organizations, alongside many of the smaller dissident groups, came together to issue a joint declaration demanding free elections and democratization. In spite of differences among these dissidents, they could agree that their overall "goal is to end the situation in which citizens of this society lack the opportunity to enjoy political rights, as guaranteed in the human rights conventions of the UN and the CSCE documents."[66] Human rights symbolically represented the ideals of the opposition even if their programs for the realization of specific human rights were not always aligned.

Crucially for the opposition groups, reformers within the higher levels of the SED no longer saw the demands of the human rights activists as anti-socialist or anti-GDR. Hans Modrow, the most prominent reformer in the SED and head of the Dresden party office, entered into negotiations with the dissidents, reporting to East Berlin that "these groups recognize in their language the GDR and socialism, but demand changes and reforms … Participants explain that they are going into the streets because otherwise nothing about the acute problems in our development will be discussed."[67] In agreeing to talk with these groups as representatives of the people, the senior elements in the SED were effectively admitting that the party was failing in its task to represent the people and it was now reduced to negotiating with the representatives of a population whose interests it claimed to have fully realized for more than 40 years.

On 9 October 1989, as crowds at the weekly demonstration in Leipzig swelled to more than 80,000, security services ceased trying to contain the protesters. Rather than employ violence to suppress the demonstrators, the Stasi and the military simply withdrew. The demands for human rights from the crowds undermined rather than supported the claims of the Stasi that the protestors were nothing more than imperialist provocateurs.[68] Having heard the crowds singing the "Internationale" and demanding reform, General Major Raimund Kokott, a National People's Army officer sent to help restore order in Dresden, claimed to have reported that the demonstration "was no counterrevolution. The people wanted a better GDR."[69] When confronted with such crowds, many police and militia units were unwilling to do "the dirty work" of the party by stopping them.[70] Many worker militia units, which were formed to prevent such an event after the 1953 Berlin Uprising, were at half strength because members refused to muster. While many in the lower tiers of the security apparatus could justify defending socialism from counter-revolutionaries, they could not accept shooting peaceful demonstrators, many of whom were neighbors and colleagues, to prop up the SED. One might say that the dissidents had shifted the narrative lines and symbolically placed the East German state in the role of the fascistic state pointlessly brutalizing democracy-loving socialists seeking nothing more than human rights, and fewer and fewer police were willing to play that particular role.

After the retreat on 9 October, the SED abandoned plans to suppress the protests with force. As Hartmut Zwahr noted, "Something deep within broke that evening and in the end it all fell down like a house of cards."[71] The only people in the East German regime who did not realize that the SED's legitimacy and power had fatally cracked were those at the very top. By 11 October, with hundreds of thousands now protesting freely in the streets of Leipzig, Dresden, and Berlin, the SED's human rights rhetoric became more belligerent. The Politburo issued a statement saying,

> many of those who have turned their backs on our republic in recent months were victims of large-scale provocation. Once again, the imperialists of the FRG have confirmed that they will never come to terms with a socialist state on German soil; agreements have been broken and human rights have been violated.[72]

On 18 October, Egon Krenz, Erich Honecker's long-time right-hand man, deposed Honecker as the latter was recovering from surgery and announced that the GDR would begin a program of reform and that a turnaround – *Wende* – was at hand. The *Wende* would include political changes including free elections, the release of those imprisoned for the offence of "fleeing the republic" (*Republikflucht*) and immediate measures to stabilize the faltering economy. Such promises only increased the mass protests. Krenz had overseen the fraudulent elections in May 1989 and had publicly expressed support for the Chinese government following the Tiananmen Square massacre in June, giving him zero credibility with the dissidents and with much of the populace.[73] Krenz's decision to declare an amnesty for border violators and open the border to Czechoslovakia only inflamed protesters who demanded total freedom of movement and found the half-measures intolerable.[74] While he claimed to implement reforms, like Honecker before him, Krenz tried to paper over human rights violations with positive rhetoric. On 8 November, the Central Committee announced that its program was rooted in "the socialist rule of law [*sozialistischer Rechtsstaat*] emanating from the fundamental and human rights," but the street protests continued to grow.[75]

The fall of the Berlin Wall came not with a bang but with a whimper. In announcing that East Germans could begin traveling to the Federal Republic with the appropriate visa, Politburo member Günter Schabowski accidently reported that the liberalization of travel would take effect "immediately" rather than the following day. Word spread that the border was now open, the subtleties of Schabowski's announcement were ignored, and crowds gathered at checkpoints and border crossings. After a few tense hours, the guards stood aside and simply let the people pass, first stamping their identity cards to render them unusable, and after a while giving up on even that. Only a few years earlier, the SED and its security services were confident that the dictatorship they had built was the pinnacle of human rights achievement at the end point of a thousand-year history of struggle for social justice. The Berlin Wall was a tool in the realization of these human rights by preventing a counter-revolutionary invasion and maintaining the sovereignty of the socialist state. For nearly three decades, the border guards of the GDR had been willing to use deadly force against their fellow citizens and then on 9 November, they no longer were.

As Gareth Dale has argued, "it was only a willfully optimistic interpretation of the press conference by citizens" that could have led to such an unlikely event.[76] In this case, as Schabowski muddled the announcement of liberalized travel to West Germany, the interpretation of his message by East Germans to mean that the wall had already been opened created the conditions whereby it was. Spurred on by mistaken media reports, East Germans did not dismiss the announcement as an error but as the SED finally accepting what most of the population now saw as self-evident. This willful optimism was in many ways an extension of the mental revolution that had occurred within the GDR and the culmination of the evolution in human rights activism. More than 20 years earlier, East Germans had begun to claim a human right to free movement and travel, often at the risk of being fired or imprisoned. By 1989, hundreds of thousands had taken to the street demonstrating against the SED and in favor of human rights in spite of police brutality and intimidation. Among those seeking to emigrate, the presumption of a moral right to travel only increased. Mass emigration created mass activism in the streets, which in turn created the psychological condition in which the wall could fall. Without a universal sense of an unlimited human right to travel, Schabowski's announcement could very well have been dismissed as one more incremental reform rather than the end of the border between East and West Germany.

Conclusion

Human rights were crucial to the realization of a peaceful revolution in 1989, but the idea of human rights alone was not enough to have had such a powerful effect. The language of human rights was an effective means of linking together a broad coalition of activists with differing causes and goals ranging from free travel to the fulfillment of socialist ideals. East Germans decided to emigrate and take to the streets for a variety of reasons stemming from their diverse lived experiences, but they were able to work together through the shared language of human rights. The long-term commitment of the Socialist Unity Party to the rhetoric of human rights was a stabilizing factor for most of East Germany's existence, legitimizing one-party rule against claims for democratization. Once it was clear that the SED was unable to cope with multiple crises stemming from economic decline and political paralysis, citizens were able to claim the mantle of human rights in the name of fixing the broken status quo. Since human rights were also inherent to the cause of socialism, according to the SED itself, the mass demonstrations were able to invoke these principles to demand democratization. While this argument was rejected by the Politburo, the security services tasked with suppressing the demonstrators did not recognize in these demands for human rights the counter-revolutionary enemy they had been conditioned to fight, choosing instead to stand down.

Human rights did not serve as a bulldozer, so to speak, of the revolution knocking down the old order or the Berlin Wall, nor was the popularity of the discourse due to a total loss of faith in socialism.[77] While the revolution ultimately led to the introduction of a liberal market capitalist system in East Germany as the result of reunification, human rights were also more than just a stalking horse for the neoliberal international order.[78] Moreover, East German dissidents did not make use of human rights in order to appeal to a foreign, Western audience. Rather, they aimed at the SED through the co-optation of East German leaders' rhetoric. Although the human rights movement of the GDR was connected with the international rise of human rights activism, its effectiveness derived from its grounding in the lived realities of East German citizens and its capacity to speak in local dialect, not just universal morality. Only through the translation of human rights into a discourse that could appeal to both dissenters and disaffected members of the establishment, was this language able to bring together a movement powerful enough to end the East German dictatorship.

The example of the human rights movement and peaceful revolution of 1989 raises broader questions about the dynamics that lead groups and movements to adopt human rights as a language for change, and when such a turn is effective. What are the factors that are needed for such radical shifts in dominant discourses and regimes of human rights? To what extent are human rights politics effective only when local conditions align with global trends? Such questions are still relevant as several states that use human rights to legitimize dictatorships and deny political pluralism remain today. North Korea, Iran, Egypt, and several other countries with nondemocratic political systems have sought to employ human rights politics on their own terms and use similar tactics of creating illiberal state-sponsored nongovernmental organizations (NGOs) to campaign against abuses abroad and distract from violations at home. Although the human rights ideology of the SED is now gone, illiberal human rights remain.

Notes

1 On the fall of the Berlin Wall and the end of the GDR, see Charles Maier, *Dissolution: The Crisis of Communism and the End of East Germany*, Princeton, NJ: Princeton University Press, 1997, and Hans-Hermann Hertle, *Der Fall der Mauer: Die Unbeabsichtigte Selbstauflösung des SED-Staates*, Wiesbaden: VS Verlag für Sozialwissenschaften, 1999.

2 On human rights violations in East Germany, see Anja Mihr, *Amnesty International in der DDR: Der Einsatz für Menschenrechte im Visier der Stasi*, Berlin: Ch. Links, 2002. On the Stasi, see Jens Gieseke, *The History of the Stasi: East Germany's Secret Police, 1945–1990*, New York: Berghahn Books, 2014.

3 Patrick Major, *Behind the Berlin Wall: East Germany and the Frontiers of Power*, Oxford: Oxford University Press, 2010; John C. Torpey, *Intellectuals, Socialism, and Dissent: The East German Opposition and Its Legacy*, Minneapolis: University of Minnesota Press, 1995.

4 On the founding of the Initiative for Peace and Human Rights (IFM) and East German dissent in the 1980s, see Wolfgang Rüddenklau (ed.), *Störenfried: DDR-Opposition 1986–1989*, Berlin: BasisDruck, 1992.

5 On the emergence of human rights activism in the USSR, Poland, and Czechoslovakia, see Benjamin Nathans, "The Dictatorship of Reason: Aleksandr Vol'pin and the Idea of Rights under 'Developed Socialism,'" *Slavic Review*, 2007, vol. 66, no. 4, 630–63, and Jonathan Bolton, *Worlds of Dissent: Charter 77, the Plastic People of the Universe, and Czech Culture Under Communism*, Cambridge, MA: Harvard University Press, 2012.

6 The original use of human rights by the SED dates to 1946 with Karl Polak, "Gewaltteilung, Menschenrechte, Rechtsstaat: Begriffsformalismus und Demokratie," *Einheit*, 1946, vol. 7. On the GDR Committee for Human Rights, see the memoir of its Secretary, Siegfried Forberger, *Das DDR-Komitee für Menschenrechte: Erinnerungen an den Sozialismus-Versuch im 20. Jahrhundert; Einsichten und Irrtümer des Siegfried Forberger, Sekretär des DDR-Komitees für Menschenrechte von 1959 bis 1989*, Berlin: self-published, 2000. Also see Ned Richardson-Little, "Dictatorship and Dissent: Human Rights in East Germany in the 1970s," in Jan Eckel and Samuel Moyn (eds.)

The Breakthrough: Human Rights in the 1970s, Philadelphia: University of Pennsylvania Press, 2014, pp. 49–67.

7 The main work arguing for the centrality of the Helsinki Accords to the rise of human rights in the Cold War is Daniel Thomas, *The Helsinki Effect: International Norms, Human Rights, and the Demise of Communism*, Princeton, NJ: Princeton University Press, 2001. See also Sarah Snyder, *Human Rights Activism and the End of the Cold War: A Transnational History of the Helsinki Network*, Cambridge, UK: Cambridge University Press, 2011. On the role of the GDR in the Helsinki negotiations and its effects, see Hermann Wentker,"Pursuing Specific Interests Within the Warsaw Pact: The German Democratic Republic and the CSCE-Process," in Carla Meneguzzi Rostagni (ed.) *The Helsinki Process: A Historical Reappraisal*, Padova: CEDAM, 2005, pp. 13–28. See also Federica Caciagli, "The GDR's Targets in the Early CSCE Process: Another Missed Opportunity to Freeze the Division of Germany, 1969–73," in Vojtech Mastny, Christian Nünlist, and Andreas Wenger, *Origins of the European Security System: The Helsinki Process Revisited, 1965–75*, London: Routledge, 2008, p. 112 and Anja Hanisch, *Die DDR im KSZE-Prozess 1972–1985: Zwischen Ostabhängigkeit, Westabgrenzung und Ausreisebewegung*, Munich: Oldenbourg, 2012.

8 On the social dynamics of the revolution of 1989 in East Germany, see Steven Pfaff, *Exit-Voice Dynamics and the Collapse of East Germany: The Crisis of Leninism and the Revolution of 1989*, Durham NC: Duke University Press, 2006. On the translation of human rights in creating activist movements, see Sally Engle Merry, "Transnational Human Rights and Local Activism: Mapping the Middle," *American Anthropologist*, 2006, vol. 108, no. 1, 38–51.

9 Konrad Jarausch, *The Rush to German Unity*, Oxford: Oxford University Press, 1994. Later also Konrad Jarausch, "Kollaps des Kommunismus oder Aufbruch der Zivilgesellschaft?" in Eckart Conze (ed.) *Die demokratische Revolution 1989 in der DDR*, Cologne: Böhlau Verlag, 2009, pp. 25–45.

10 Thomas, *The Helsinki Effect*; Snyder, *Human Rights Activism and the End of the Cold War.*

11 Aryeh Neier, *The International Human Rights Movement: A History*, Princeton, NJ: Princeton University Press, 2012, 14.

12 Rosemary Foot, "The Cold War and Human Rights," in Melvyn P. Leffler and Odd Arne Westad (eds.) *The Cambridge History of the Cold War. Vol. 3*, Cambridge, UK: Cambridge University Press, 2010, p. 465.

13 Ned Richardson-Little, "Human Rights as Myth and History: Between the Revolutions of 1989 and the Arab Spring," *Journal of Contemporary Central and Eastern Europe*, 2015, vol. 23, no. 2–3, 151–66.

14 Stephen Kotkin, *Uncivil Society: 1989 and the Implosion of the Communist Establishment*, New York: Random House, 2009.

15 "Editor's Note," *Journal of Cold War Studies*, 2016, vol. 18, no. 3, 1–2.

16 In this analysis, I am drawing on Ehrhart Neubert's taxonomy, which delineates three separate types of oppositional behavior in East Germany: protest, challenging specific policies and actions without broad attacks on the system as a whole; resistance, the conscious use of illegal activity to oppose SED rule; opposition, the organization of groups to provide alternatives to the existing state socialist system. These definitions are fluid and their exact boundaries are at times unclear, but they provide a useful shorthand on the macro scale to distinguish the actions of East Germans in the aggregate. Ehrhart Neubert, *Geschichte der Opposition in der DDR: 1949–1989*, Berlin: Ch. Links, 1998, pp. 29–33.

17 See Havemann's exchange with Joachim Steffen in Jiří Pelikán and Manfred Wilke (eds.), *Menschenrechte: Ein Jahrbuch zu Osteuropa*, Reinbek bei Hamburg: Rowohlt, 1977, p. 476.

18 Rudolf Bahro, *Ich werde meinen Weg fortsetzen*, Frankfurt a.M: Europäische Verlagsanstalt, 1977, p. 13.

19 Steven Pfaff, "The Politics of Peace in the GDR: The Independent Peace Movement, the Church, and the Origins of the East German Opposition," *Peace & Change*, 2001, vol. 26, no. 3, 290.

20 André Steiner, *Von Plan zu Plan: eine Wirtschaftsgeschichte der DDR*, München: DVA, 2004; André Steiner, "The Globalisation Process and the Eastern Bloc Countries in the 1970s and 1980s," *European Review of History*, 2014, vol. 21, no. 2, 165–81.

21 Ray Stokes, "From *Schadenfreude* to Going-out-of-Business Sale: East Germany and the Oil Crises of the 1970s," in Hartmut Berghoff and Uta A. Balbier (eds.) *The East German Economy,*

1945–2010: Falling Behind or Catching Up? New York: Cambridge University Press, 2014, pp. 131–44.

22 Hans-Hermann Hertle, *Der Fall der Mauer: Die Unbeabsichtigte Selbstauflösung des SED-Staates*, Opladen: Westdeutscher Verlag, 1999; Charles Maier, *Dissolution: The Crisis of Communism and the End of East Germany*, Princeton, NJ: Princeton University Press, 1997.

23 On the interconnection between economic success and political legitimacy in the GDR, see Jeffrey Kopstein, *The Politics of Economic Decline in East Germany, 1945–1989*, Chapel Hill: University of North Carolina Press, 2000.

24 On the wave of applications to exit beginning in 1984, see Hermann Wentker, *Aussenpolitik in Engen Grenzen: Die DDR im Internationalen System, 1949–1989*, Munich: Oldenbourg, 2007, pp. 503–11.

25 Major, *Behind the Berlin Wall*, p. 215.

26 Marianne Schulz, *Von der Illegalität ins Parlament: Werdegang und Konzepte der neuen Bürgerbewegungen*, Berlin: Ch. Links, 1992, p. 150.

27 Dirk Philipsen, *We Were the People: Voices from East Germany's Revolutionary Autumn of 1989*, Durham, NC: Duke University Press, 1993, p. 54.

28 Hoover Institution Archive, Stanford, CA, Christian Joppke Collection (hereafter HIA Joppke Collection), Box 1, Interview mit Ulrike Poppe, 9 July 1991, p. 2.

29 Reprinted in Wolfgang Rüddenklau (ed.), *Störenfried: DDR-Opposition 1986–1989*, Berlin: Basis-Druck, 1992, p. 56.

30 Rüddenklau, *Störenfried*, p. 55.

31 Ferdinand Kroh (ed.), *"Freiheit ist immer Freiheit –": Die Andersdenkenden in der DDR*, Frankfurt a. M.: Ullstein, 1988, p. 226.

32 Reprinted in Rüddenkla, *Störenfried*, p. 56.

33 Christof Geisel, *Auf der Suche nach einem dritten Weg: Das politische Selbstverständnis der DDR-Opposition in den 80er Jahren*, Berlin: Ch. Links, 2005, p. 50.

34 Archiv der Robert Havemann Gesellschaft, Berlin, Germany (hereafter RHG), RG/B 12 Arbeitsgruppe Staatsbürgerschaftsrecht, Arbeitsgruppe Staatsbürgerschaftsrechte der DDR, Erklärung (10.12.1987), p. 4.

35 Pfaff dubs these activists "noisy exiters." Pfaff, *Exit-Voice Dynamics*, p. 80.

36 Bundesarchiv Lichterfelde, Berlin, Germany (hereafter BArch-Lichterfelde), DO 1/16491, Information über die Unterbindung und Zurückdrängung rechtswidriger Ersuchen auf Übersiedlung nach der BRD und nach Westberlin (June 1988), p. 4.

37 HIA Joppke Collection, Box 4, Interview with Guenter Jeschonnek, 12 September 1991, Q280, p. 2.

38 "Information Nr. 535/88 über Aktivitäten feindlich-negativer Kräfte in der DDR anlässlich des 40. Jahrestages der Annahme der, Allgemeinen Erklärung der Menschenrechte durch die UNO 10. Dezember 1988 (12.12.1988)," in Frank Joestel, Daniela Munkel, and Frank Giesecke (eds.) *Die DDR im Blick der Stasi 1988: Die Geheimen Berichte an die SED-Führung*, Göttingen: Vandenhoeck & Ruprecht, 2010, pp. 295–6.

39 See the open letters from organizations in RHG RG/Bra 02, RHG RG/B 10, RHG RHi 02, RHG SaGem 18, RHG GP 06 IFM (1), as well as *Samizdat* publications: RHG Samizdat PS 013/05, RHG Samizdat PS 041/12 Friedensnetz, RHG Samizdat PS 117/07 Wendezeit.

40 Dieter Segert, "The GDR Intelligentsia and Its Forgotten Political Role During the Wende of 1989," *Debatte: Journal of Contemporary Central and Eastern Europe*, 2009, vol. 17, no. 2, 143–57.

41 Thomas Klein, *"Frieden und Gerechtigkeit!": Die Politisierung der Unabhängigen Friedensbewegung in Ost-Berlin während der 80er Jahre*, Cologne: Böhlau, 2007, pp. 427–8.

42 Major, *Behind the Berlin Wall*, p. 233.

43 Hanisch, *Die DDR im KSZE-Prozess*, pp. 373–5; Wentker, *Aussenpolitik in Engen Grenzen*, p. 550.

44 Snyder, *Human Rights Activism and the End of the Cold War*, p. 2.

45 Walter Süss, *Staatssicherheit am Ende: Warum es den Mächtigen Nicht Gelang, 1989 eine Revolution zu Verhindern*, Berlin: Ch. Links, 1999, p. 97.

46 Mary Sarotte, *The Collapse: The Accidental Opening of the Berlin Wall*, New York: Basic Books, 2014, p. 18.

47 *Die Verfassung des sozialistischen Staates deutscher Nation*, Dresden: Verlag Zeit im Bild, 1968.

48 Maier, *Dissolution*, pp. 132–3.
49 RHG Samizdat PS 018/05 Ausblick Arbeitsgruppe Menschenrechte Leipzig. Offener Brief from Arbeitsgruppe Menschenrechte and Arbeitsgruppe Gerechtigkeit in Leipzig, 6 July 1989.
50 Jarausch, *Rush to German Unity*, p. 38.
51 Major, *Behind the Berlin Wall*, p. 238.
52 Rosa Luxemburg Stiftung Archiv Demokratischer Sozialismus (hereafter ADS), Bestand Reissig Berg, Band 1. Multilateraler Wissenschaftlicher Problemrat von Bruderparteien sozialistischer Länder zu Fragen der Menschenrechte: Konzeptionelle Grundlagen der gegenwärtigen Politik der Bruderparteien sozialistischer Länder auf dem Gebiet der Menschenrechte. Studie, April 1989, p. 13.
53 Quoted in Pfaff, *Exit-Voice Dynamics*, p. 181.
54 Barch-Lichterfelde, DY 30/5908, Dr. Micaela K. an Bezirksleitung der SED Leipzig, 30 August 1989, p. 2.
55 Walter Friedrich, Peter Förster, and Kurt Starke (eds.), *Das Zentralinstitut für Jugendforschung Leipzig 1966–1990: Geschichte, Methoden, Erkenntnisse*, Berlin: Edition Ost, 1999, p. 152.
56 HIA Joppke Collection, Box 1, Interview mit Katrin Walter (25 July 1991), p. 1.
57 Jarausch, *Rush to German Unity*, p. 19.
58 Barch-Lichterfelde, DO 1/16491, Information über die Unterbindung und Zurückdrängung rechtswidriger Ersuchen auf Übersiedlung nach der BRD und nach Westberlin, Berichtszeitraum 1 January 1989–30 September 1989, p. 1.
59 Hartmut Zwahr, *Ende einer Selbstzerstörung: Leipzig und die Revolution in der DDR*, Göttingen: Vandenhoeck & Ruprecht, 1993, pp. 42–3.
60 "Das vorläufige Statut der SDP," in Gerhard Rein (ed.) *Die Opposition in der DDR: Entwürfe für einen anderen Sozialismus*, Berlin: Wichern Verlag, 1989, p. 90.
61 Richard T. Gray and Sabine Wilke (eds. and trans.), *German Unification and Its Discontents: Documents from the Peaceful Revolution*, Seattle: University of Washington Press, 1996, p. 5.
62 "Aufruf zum 'Demokratischen Aufbruch – sozial, ökologisch,'" in Rein (ed.) *Die Opposition in der DDR*, p. 34.
63 Rein, *Die Opposition in der DDR*, pp. 35–6.
64 "Flugblatt für die Demokratie," in Rein, *Die Opposition in der DDR*, p. 46.
65 Ute Haese, *Katholische Kirche in der DDR: Geschichte einer politischen Abstinenz*, Düsseldorf: Patmos, 1998, pp. 93–4; Gerhard Lange, Ursula Pruss, and Franz Schrader (eds.), *Katholische Kirche – sozialistischer Staat DDR: Dokumente und öffentliche Äußerungen 1945–1990*, Berlin: Bischöfliches Ordinariat, 1993, pp. 362–8.
66 "Joint Declaration of the Civic Movement," in Konrad Jarausch and Volker Gransow (eds.) *Uniting Germany: Documents and Debates, 1944–1993*, New York: Berghahn, 1994, p. 50.
67 Quoted in Pfaff, *Exit-Voice Dynamics*, p. 185.
68 Pfaff, *Exit-Voice Dynamics*, p. 117.
69 Michael Richter, *Die Friedliche Revolution: Aufbruch zur Demokratie in Sachsen 1989/90*, Göttingen: Vandenhoeck & Ruprecht, 2010, p. 281.
70 Pfaff, *Exit-Voice Dynamics*, p. 178.
71 Zwahr, *Ende einer Selbstzerstörung*, p. 99.
72 "Politburo Declaration," 11 October 1989, in Jarausch and Gransow, *Uniting Germany*, p. 60.
73 Pfaff, *Exit-Voice Dynamics*, p. 225.
74 Jarausch, *Rush to German Unity*, p. 61.
75 Karl Wilhelm Fricke, *Der Wahrheit verpflichtet: Texte aus fünf Jahrzehnten zur Geschichte der DDR*, Berlin: Ch. Links, 2000, p. 168. Such language mirrored that of reform communists such as Uwe-Jens Heuer who had sought such reforms throughout the 1980s. See ADS, Bestand Heuer.
76 Gareth Dale, *The East German Revolution of 1989*, Manchester: Manchester University Press, 2006, p. 95.
77 On human rights as "a language to replace Marxism" in Eastern Europe, see Marci Shore, *The Taste of Ashes*, New York: Random House, 2013, p. 11. On the "bulldozer logic" of human rights, see Lynn Hunt, *Inventing Human Rights: A History*, New York: Norton, 2008, p. 160.
78 Samuel Moyn, "A Powerless Companion: Human Rights in the Age of Neoliberalism," *Law and Contemporary Problems*, 2015, vol. 77, 147–69.

16

HUMAN RIGHTS IN CHINA

Resisting orthodoxy

Pitman B. Potter

Introduction

This essay examines human rights in the People's Republic of China (PRC) in the context of historical norms and structures of governance orthodoxy and social resistance. Discussion of human rights in the PRC could easily follow the well-worn path of detailing abuses in various sectors of political and social life. The litany of abuse continues, with ongoing evidence of censorship, torture, extensive use of the death penalty, abuse of criminal process for political purposes, suppression of religious freedoms, and abuse of ethnic minorities, to name but a few.[1] In the socioeconomic sphere, corruption remains endemic while rising inequality undermines aspirations for improved living standards.[2] Environmental degradation continues.[3] Despite the availability of detailed reporting on abuses, however, more is needed to understand the conditions for human rights deprivation in China today.

A useful alternative involves examining human rights in the context of tensions between normative standards of governance officially articulated by the state and its agents and supporters (what might be termed "orthodoxy"[4]), and contending expectations emerging from non-orthodox sources in society. Much of the human rights narrative in China today can be understood in terms of a tension between orthodox ideals of benign rule and popular obedience on the one hand, and social resistance through calls for genuine rule of law and government accountability on the other. Whether on issues of civil and political rights, or social, economic, and cultural rights,[5] efforts to improve human rights protection necessarily involve engagement with existing government policies and practice, as efforts to improve the recognition and enforcement of human rights challenge established government orthodoxies of rule. Herein lies potential for comparative insight on global human rights conditions that combines detailed reporting on abuses with socio-legal analysis of norms and structures affecting human rights conditions.

This essay will examine human rights in the PRC today with reference to the tension between orthodoxy and resistance in historical and contemporary contexts, looking beyond doctrinal texts and recitations of abuse to build an understanding of underlying normative and structural dynamics. This will enable readers to understand human rights conditions in China more fully while inviting comparison with other essays in this volume. Focusing on norms and structures of law and governance, this essay relies on primary and secondary sources to explain the historical antecedents for contemporary discourse and behavior on human rights. This essay also invites consideration of human rights in China in light of basic questions about the transnational application of human rights norms and the local socio-legal contexts for their enforcement.

Orthodoxy and resistance in modern China's political tradition

Human rights were not part of the discourse of governance in traditional China, even though many of the conflicts that arose between state and society involved what we would now recognize as human rights issues. In Imperial China prior to the 1911 Republican Revolution, the orthodoxy of governance rested on interpretations of Confucian philosophy. Confucian classics extolled the role of hierarchy and stability and extended normative standards for family relations to dynamics of state governance and popular compliance.[6] Confucian governance was to mirror the great relationships of Confucianism (ruler to ruled, father to son, husband to wife, elder brother to younger brother, friend to friend), whose unequal hierarchy was buttressed by ideals of virtue intended to ensure harmony.[7] To the extent that Confucian norms depicted society by reference to relationships, the notion of formal rights challenged Confucian expectations about community.

The fabled "mandate of heaven" principle expressed ideals of Confucian governance and obedience, according to which rulers were called to be benign and society called to be obedient as matters of propriety and principle, with little room for formal rights claims.[8] Not surprisingly perhaps, processes akin to what Max Weber called the "routinization of charisma"[9] tended to entrench ideals of obedience to hierarchy more fully than ideals of wise rulership. Institutional relations between state and society tended to revolve around enforcement of obedience to authority, as law in traditional China imposed criminal punishments for violations of Confucian norms.[10] While mutuality of obligation was implied in Confucian principles of virtue and trust, in practice popular obedience to authority was not conditioned on benign leadership but, rather, was strictly enforced through a variety of penal mechanisms.[11] As the "mandate of heaven" ideal suggested that the authority of Confucian governance depended on the virtue of the rulers, challenges to established rule were not simply abstract questions about the proper mechanisms of governance, but rather challenge the personal virtue of imperial rulers, with punitive often brutal consequences.

China's history reveals a long-term dynamic of conflict between official norms of governance and resistance from across Chinese society from those seeking better conditions for political and social life.[12] In the course of China's long history of local violence, popular resistance to regime norms evinced dynamics of grievance that operated alongside a panoply of local parochial conflicts.[13] For all their wide variation and diversity in terms of participants, causes, and outcomes, these historical struggles tended to define a conflicted relationship between state orthodoxy and local popular resistance that resonates today.

Aside from popular resistance, intellectual resistance in traditional China posed a more serious challenge to orthodoxy, as more often than not it arose from within the ruling elite.[14] During the late nineteenth century, the continuing decline of the Qing dynasty (1644–1911) saw increased calls for governance reform in the face of imperialist intrusion from the West, economic decay, and more immediately in response to China's humiliating defeat in the Sino-Japanese war (1894–5). Reformist thinking by scholar officials like Kang Youwei (1858–1927) exemplified efforts at "reform from above" as Confucian intellectuals struggled to respond to the challenges posed by China's internal crises and external conflict.[15] Influenced in part by Buddhism as well as European enlightenment thinking, Kang's notion of the "great unity" (*Da Tong*//大同) reflected egalitarian principles that offered imposing alternatives to the rigid hierarchy of Confucian orthodoxy. Kang's reformist protégé Liang Qichao challenged Confucian norms through his writings on the virtues of liberalism and democracy (writings that remain widely influential in Taiwan and more recently in the PRC). These and other intellectuals challenged the orthodoxy of the imperial Qing state as unresponsive to local needs and inadequate to meet the crisis of China's engagement with the outside world. With support from the young emperor Guangxu and inspired by (failed) reform efforts in provinces such as Hunan, the Hundred Days of Reform in the summer of 1898 led by Kang and his adherents saw wide ranging proposals for reforms in economic, military, and educational institutions. The reform effort also included measures to strengthen the rights of criminal defendants.[16]

A key debate amongst both the reformers and their opponents involved questions about retaining the essence (*ti*//体) of Chinese traditional culture (as interpreted by the Qing state) while utilizing (*yong*//用) foreign technology and science. While the reformers claimed that a balance of *ti* and *yong* was both possible and desirable, most of the governing elite whose careers and stature were grounded in and dependent upon the Confucian orthodoxy of Qing rule were unable to accommodate reformist calls for economic liberalization, modernization of military organization and technology, and reliance on science-based education. The reform movement was ultimately suppressed by the forces of conservatism – most notably the Empress Dowager Zixi along with establishment officials whose worldview and personal interests remained bound to the Confucian orthodoxy of the Qing. Nonetheless, the reformers embodied a normative transformation that challenged Confucian authoritarianism and led ultimately to the rise of the Nationalist Party (Guomindang) of Sun Yat-sen and Chiang Kai-shek and the founding of the Republic of China (ROC) in 1911.

Tensions over orthodoxy and resistance were evident as well during the May 4th Movement of 1919, when students protested the ROC government's acquiescence to reparation decisions in the Treaty of Versailles awarding colonial holdings of defeated Germany to victorious ally Japan following the conclusion of World War I.[17] Inspired by the recently emergent "New Culture" discourse, students challenged a neotraditional orthodoxy that espoused state-controlled Confucian teaching in both education and political relations, urging instead greater reliance on science and democracy. While anti-imperialist at its core, the May 4th Movement nonetheless called for China to adopt foreign standards for education and governance. The May 4th Movement served as a crucible of sorts for the later emergence of the Communist Party of China (CPC) and highlighted yet again the dilemma of balancing Chinese tradition with (mostly foreign) standards of modernity that had characterized the *ti-yong* debates in 1898. Despite its successes, however, the May 4th Movement failed to institutionalize its ideals in the face of ongoing resistance from traditionalists opposed to reform and apprehensive about foreign influence.

The reform movements of the late nineteenth and early twentieth centuries represented a normative challenge to the orthodoxy of unfettered state power, and thus offer important historical antecedents for much of the human rights discourse of China today.[18] The *ti-yong* challenge of ensuring fealty to Chinese values claimed by the ruling regime in the face of foreign knowledge and technology continues to influence political discourse in China today, with implications for education, political and economic reform, and relations with the world political economy.[19] Recalling Confucianism's emphasis on popular obedience and the problems this raises for human rights,[20] efforts by the PRC regime to buttress its rule with claims to a Confucian legacy[21] make it all the more important to appreciate the normative and structural dynamics of resistance to governance orthodoxies of Confucian authoritarianism.

Human rights standards in China today

While rejecting the formal nomenclature of rights (including human rights) under the ideology of class struggle, the PRC after 1949 and its ruling CPC claimed in their early years of rule significant advances on issues that we would today classify as human rights matters. The Marriage Reform Law of 1950 improved gender equality over the patriarchal norms of Confucianism, while the Land Reform Law of 1950 and CPC-mandated labor regulations improved conditions for peasants and industrial workers.[22] Yet tensions between orthodoxy and resistance continued. Efforts to build a formal legal system in the 1950s were sidelined due to recurring political conflict. Proposals for political and legal reform solicited by the regime during the Hundred Flowers campaign of 1956 were met with state repression of proponents during the anti-Rightist campaign of 1957–8. The Cultural Revolution (1966–76) was characterized by widespread conflict over standards of orthodoxy and resistance in governance and socioeconomic relations. In 1978, two years after the death of Mao Zedong and the ending of the Cultural Revolution, the PRC began to rebuild its legal system, which has since become a contested domain where the orthodoxy of authoritarian rule confronts resistance expressed in part through human rights claims.

The governance orthodoxy of PRC today entrenches the leadership and authority of the CPC, through a dynamic of tradition and formalism.[23] The role of tradition is evident in CPC claims that it led the 1949 revolution and so should continue in power.[24] As the CPC anthem tells it, "without the Communist Party there would be no new China" (*Meiyou gongchandang jiu meiyou xin Zhongguo*//没有共产党就没有新中国).[25] Bolstering such traditionalism is a dynamic of formalism expressed through ritualistic references to the authority of the Constitution and laws under the leadership of the CPC.[26] The party-state claims to adhere to a "socialist rule of law," using the nomenclature of legality while still suppressing challenges to the regime's authority.[27] Whereas in traditional China there was no recognized nomenclature for "human rights," human rights have become an accepted if controversial subject of discourse in China today. And just as the reform movements of 1898 and 1919 were heavily influenced by international developments, so too does human rights discourse in the PRC today embody a complex process of interaction between ever-fluid international standards and local initiatives.[28] Echoing the *ti-yong* debates of earlier times, human rights discourse in the PRC today reflects a process of selective local adaptation of diverse international discourses of human rights.[29]

The PRC has ratified numerous international human rights treaties, including the International Covenant on Economic, Social, and Cultural Rights (ICESCR) and the Convention on Elimination of All Forms of Discrimination Against Women (CEDAW).[30]

The PRC has signed the International Convention on Civil and Political Rights (ICCPR), which carries an obligation to uphold its provisions even though Beijing has not yet ratified the agreement. The PRC's obligations under international human rights law require that it protect against human rights abuses by taking appropriate steps to prevent, investigate, punish, and redress such abuses through effective policies, legislation, regulations, and adjudication.[31] Yet China's ratification of the ICESCR was subject to reservations preserving the PRC's policy preferences prohibiting independent labor unions and collective bargaining. Similarly, China's performance of the CEDAW treaty has been compromised by enforcement of CPC policy imperatives repressing civil society and ethnic minorities.[32] Numerous PRC human rights White Papers and Action Plans, and responses to the Universal Periodic Review process of the UN Human Rights Council, reveal the extent of resistance to international human rights standards along with persistent efforts to adjust them to fit the policy preferences of the regime.[33] The PRC party-state deploys discourses of sovereignty to insulate itself from international human rights standards,[34] although such efforts are largely unsupported by current international law doctrine.[35]

Despite its international obligations, the governance orthodoxy of the PRC echoes traditional norms that privilege a hierarchical relationship of domination and compliance between state and society that marginalizes rights claims whether these be individual or collective. Thus, human rights are subordinated to the authority of the CPC. The Constitution of the PRC embraces the "Four Cardinal Principles" articulated by post-Mao leader Deng Xiaoping, which emphasize the importance of party leadership.[36] Article 33(4) of the Constitution requires that the exercise of legal rights is subject to compliance with "duties prescribed by the Constitution and the law,"[37] including the principle of subordination to the leadership of the CPC. The inclusion in 2004 of a Constitutional provision on respecting and ensuring human rights underscored the importance of party leadership as a condition for legal and constitutional rights claims.[38]

Principles of party leadership continue to dominate the PRC legal system, where human rights claims might ordinarily be expected to be heard. The 4th Plenum of the 18th Central Committee in October 2014, for example, expressly asserted the need for party leadership over the socialist legal system, both directly and through adherence to the principles of party rule that underpin the PRC Constitution.[39] Despite increased professionalism and autonomy among judicial personnel and institutions, party-led adjudication committees (*shenpan weiyuanhui*//审判委员会) in the People's Courts ensure CPC leadership over judicial decisions.[40] Courts are held to the standards of the so-called "three supremes" (*sange zhishang*//三个至上), which further emphasize subordination to the party.[41] Party dominance is also exercised through insertion of party organs (*Dang zu*//党组) into legislative, executive, and judicial institutions such as the National People's Congress (NPC) Standing Committee, the State Council, the Chinese People's Political Consultative Congress, the Supreme People's Court, and the Supreme People's Procuracy.[42] Chief Justice Zhou Qiang's critique of "Western" notions of judicial independence confirmed the extent to which the imperative of party leadership continues to dominate China's judiciary.[43] The PRC regime's imagery of fealty to the Constitution and the laws while retaining the substance of unfettered power brings to mind Max Weber's trenchant critique of "fake constitutionalism" regarding the 1905 Tsarist reforms in Russia, which failed to establish meaningful constitutional restraints on government authority even while trumpeting constitutional terminology.[44] Despite its own formalist language about the human rights and the rule of law, the PRC regime continues to embrace party domination as an ideological principle and a matter of governance organization and operation.

PRC governance orthodoxy also elevates socioeconomic rights over political and civil rights, under the discourse of the "right to development,"[45] as PRC human rights White Papers have consistently given priority to economic accumulation over political and civil rights.[46] The 2012 Human Rights Action Plan equated human rights with development and social harmony, while the 2016 plan specified that the party-state "puts the protection of people's rights to subsistence and development in the first place."[47] The party-state's focus on economic development works to crowd out and even to repress calls for political and civil rights, under the guise of maintaining the stability needed for economic development.[48] Yet even in the realm of economic, social, and cultural rights where it claims to excel, the PRC regime has underperformed other economies in Asia.[49] Indeed, the UN Special Rapporteur on extreme poverty and human rights commented following his 2016 inspection tour of the PRC that regime achievements on poverty alleviation are offset by increased inequality and undercut by institutional obstacles including the authoritarian role of the CPC.[50] Informed observers note the extent to which the authoritarianism of the party-state has contributed directly to problems of corruption and inequality that obstruct social and economic development.[51] Thus, the PRC's orthodoxy of governance has a demonstrable effect undermining human rights conditions in both the civil and political and the economic, social, and cultural rights sectors.

Forms of resistance in contemporary China

Even as PRC orthodoxy undermines human rights conditions, social resistance reminiscent of the late Qing and early Republican periods has emerged in many forms. Three are particularly significant, namely the intellectual resistance symbolized by the Charter 08 Movement, the professional challenge from "rights defenders," and popular resistance over matters of labor relations and the environment. While the continued presence of popular resistance echoes patterns of the past, activism by intellectuals not connected to the ruling regime and the emergence of professional groups such as lawyers reflect the importance of newly emerging actors in China's human rights landscape.

Intellectual resistance: the Charter 08 Movement[52]

In December 2008, the document labeled "Charter 08" was issued in China by a group of reformist intellectuals and community leaders to commemorate the 60th anniversary of the Universal Declaration of Human Rights.[53] Inspired by "Charter 77" published by the Czech reform movement of Vaclev Havel in January 1977, Charter 08 presented a series of proposals for political and legal reforms, of which human rights was listed as a fundamental requirement for legitimate governance. While recognizing general improvements in living conditions, as well as human rights achievements in accepting the standards of the ICESCR and the ICCPR, the Charter dismissed the human rights policies of the PRC party-state as paper formalities. Criticizing the regime's priority with maintaining its own power, the Charter listed a range of human rights abuses and depicted ineffective and corrupt institutions of the rule of law. The document proclaimed fundamental principles of freedom, human rights, and democracy while calling for a new constitution that would require compliance by the CPC itself.

The fundamental challenge posed by Charter 08 was the assertion that China's development requires dramatic and thorough-going reform of political and legal institutions and arrangements. Like the reformers of 1898 and the activists of the May 4th Movement, the authors and signatories of Charter 08 challenged regime orthodoxies of governance and offered proposals for reform through institutional change. Charter 08 represented resistance to orthodoxy by patriotic intellectuals in the mold of the 1898 reformers and the May 4th student rebels. As had Kang Youwei and his fellows, Liu Xiaobo and his colleagues presented a series of institutional reforms as necessary to save the ruling regime, even as their efforts also challenged the foundations for the regime's authority. Like the May 4th demonstrators, the proponents of Charter 08 asserted that existing institutional arrangements for governance and society were inadequate to meet the needs of China's development. Just as proposals for reform in education and governance in 1898 and 1919 challenged the authority of Confucian rule, so too has the CPC's monopoly on power been challenged by Charter 08's proposal that all organizations be subject to the authority of the rule of law and constitutional provisions for separation of powers, independence of the judiciary, and guarantees of human rights.

The apparent purity of the Charter's patriotic vision notwithstanding, the government's response to Charter 08 was harshly repressive. Activists who signed Charter 08, including Liu Xiaobo, Zhang Zuhua, and Pu Zhiqiang, were harassed and detained.[54] Liu was sentenced to 11 years imprisonment after a staged show trial that many considered unfair.[55] If anything, the regime's hostility to Liu and the Charter increased as a result of Liu being awarded the Nobel Peace Prize in October 2010.[56] Liu died in custody in July 2017 from liver cancer that apparently had been left untreated until it became terminal.[57] University students were directed to boycott Charter 08 while some professors associated with the Charter were reassigned or demoted.

While some of the proposals in Charter 08 were echoed by establishment political leaders such as then-premier Wen Jiabao,[58] the regime's harsh reaction reflected its rejection of calls for reform from outside the regime. The government's repression of other such reform efforts has been unremittingly harsh, as for example in jailing Xu Zhiyong who, with Teng Biao (also jailed), launched a "New Citizens' Movement" pushing for moderate reforms.[59] Nonetheless, by virtue of its support from intellectuals (a respected and privileged group in Chinese tradition) and in light of its avowed patriotic aims to reform and strengthen China, Charter 08 represented a powerful expression of resistance to the governance orthodoxy of the PRC party-state. Popular support for Charter 08 grew steadily from 303 signatures in December 2008, to nearly 10,000 by early 2009.[60]

Resistance from legal professionals: rights defenders

The PRC regime has invested significantly in constructing a socialist legal system that, subject to authority of the CPC, attempts to enforce legal standards and resolve disputes fairly and consistently. In contrast to internal party policy, which is not a matter for public debate, the expanded role of public law as an expression of authoritative norms has created opportunities for broader participation and engagement. Whereas official orthodox interpretation of party policy remains the province of CPC leading cadres, the interpretation of public law has become the province of professionals with legal training and institutional license. Thus, along with intellectuals, legal professionals have become a further site for resistance to orthodoxy.

Informed in part by an historical legacy of antipathy toward lawyers, referred to during the Qing as "litigation masters" (*songshi*//讼师) who were seen as abusing institutions for managing disputes and social order for personal gain,[61] the regime has devoted significant effort to controlling the conduct of lawyers. The CPC's United Front Work Department (*tongzhan bu*//统战部) oversees the All China Lawyers Association to ensure that lawyers conform to party policy. The Association's "Lawyers' Code of Conduct" requires lawyers to "support the Party's leadership" while also being "loyal to the motherland" and to the Constitution and the laws.[62] The PRC Lawyers Law requires that lawyers uphold the interests and authority of the party-state, even to the extent of constraining lawyers from advocating for their clients' legal rights.[63] Provisions of the PRC Criminal Law (Article 306) and Criminal Procedure Law (Article 38) prohibiting submission of false evidence (*weizao zhengju*//伪造证据) have been used to discourage defense counsel from introducing exculpatory evidence that might be disputed in court.[64]

Nonetheless, the emergence of a new category of legal advocates known as "rights defenders" (*weiquan*//维权) has challenged the party's nominal monopoly on legal interpretation.[65] Rights defenders use the PRC's own laws to advocate on behalf of rights claims not approved by the regime. The example of Chen Guangcheng, who took on sensitive cases involving China's (since cancelled) family planning policies, suggested the potential for courageous advocates to take on causes and clients against the wishes of local officials.[66] While Chen was not a licensed lawyer but rather an informal "legal advisor," his example was soon followed by prominent lawyers who challenged regime orthodoxy by pursuing human rights cases. Examples include Pu Zhiqiang, who defended sensitive free speech cases, including that of artist Ai Weiwei, and advocated abolishing China's administrative detention system.[67] Gao Zhisheng took on cases of administrative abuse, minority rights, and religious freedoms.[68] Cao Shunli called for government transparency in connection with China's submission to the UN Human Rights Council's Universal Periodic Review process.[69] Zhou Shifeng represented victims of the tainted Sanlu milk powder scandal and advocated free speech rights for Hong Kong's "Umbrella Movement."[70] Guo Feixiong challenged local corruption and called for an end to censorship and for China to ratify the International Convention on Civil and Political Rights.[71] Many other lawyers and activists have taken on the challenge of rights defense, but not surprisingly, the regime has responded with harassment and arrests.[72] Cao Shunli for example died in a military hospital in March 2014, while Guo Feixiong embarked on a hunger strike in prison to protest his abusive treatment. Xia Lin, who defended artist Ai Weiwei among others, was sentenced to 10 years' imprisonment (reduced on appeal from the original 12-year sentence).[73]

The "rights defenders" movement is noteworthy for many reasons, including the courage and commitment of its participants and the repression and violence with which the regime has responded. From the standpoint of the dynamic of orthodoxy and resistance, the movement signifies the importance of legal professionals in the articulation of resistance to regime norms. Whereas Charter 08 signified intellectual resistance over matters of normative principles and governance rules, the "rights defenders" movement poses a significant challenge from specialized professionals to the authority of the party-state. The resistance of rights defenders involves interpretation by professionals of the public laws on the basis of which the party-state claims authority, to assert rights that the regime doesn't like and advocate for the powerless whom the regime doesn't acknowledge. Much as the reform efforts of 1898 were personalized as attacks on the virtue of Qing rulers, the challenge to orthodoxy presented by "rights defenders" also poses a general affront to regime authority.

Popular resistance: unrest over labor and environmental conditions

Social resistance in the PRC today is not only a matter of intellectual debate and professional intervention, however. In contrast to the relatively organized patterns of intellectual and professional resistance, unorganized popular movements in resistance to regime orthodoxy have also emerged as rapid economic expansion of the past three decades has undermined labor conditions and the environment. One result has been increased popular unrest aimed at protesting these conditions, shaming local officials, and pleading for redress.[74]

In the labor area, despite the Ministry of Labor's regulatory regime for worker protection,[75] labor conditions in the PRC have deteriorated steadily over the past two decades.[76] The resulting number and severity of worker demonstrations over matters such as unpaid wages and working conditions reveals the extent to which the socialist market economy has apparently been unable to protect workers' rights and interests.[77] Moreover, while earlier protests focused on securing payment of agreed wages and other benefits, the causes of worker unrest seem to have shifted to more aspirational matters of fair wages and safe working conditions – a shift that reflects a transition from claiming what was agreed to specifically by employers, to claiming broader protections promised under generalized human rights norms for labor relations.[78]

Popular resistance over declining environmental conditions has also increased[79] as an ongoing and severe environmental crisis persists, despite lengthy efforts at national and regional legislation and policymaking by government and the CPC.[80] The tragic chemical explosion and fire in Tianjin in August 2015 revealed the extent to which environmental protection challenges are compounded – if not caused – by lax regulation, corruption, and lack of transparency in governance.[81] While labor protests have largely focused on contractual rights and expectations accruing to specific groups, environmental protests tend to be collective expressions of resistance against policies or actions that harm communities. Protests against construction of chemical plants for production of highly toxic paraxylene[82] or copper and molybdenum smelters,[83] for example, have joined together neighbors in affected communities and linked them through social media with concerned observers. But environmental protest also takes on a more prosaic form as local residents protest recurrent smog alerts[84] or the dumping of animal and chemical waste into local rivers.[85]

Popular resistance has also taken on a gendered aspect, as women have been active participants in labor and environmental demonstrations. However, despite rhetoric to the contrary, Chinese society remains deeply patriarchal, such that gendered dimensions of popular protest are generally confined to a small but vigorous women's rights movement.[86]

Like the intellectual resistance embodied in Charter 08 and challenges posed by legal professionals, popular resistance also has historical antecedents. Labor unrest has been a more or less constant feature of China's transition from imperial to modern rule and was an important source of support for the CPC revolution.[87] On the environment, while PRC development policy historically tended to diminish environmental concerns in pursuit of industrialization,[88] popular concern began to emerge beginning in the 1980s over environmental degradation and the health effects of rapid industrialization.[89] These examples of popular resistance pose important challenges for the PRC party-state, whose official ideology extols rights of the people to development and prosperity. Indeed, the prospects of popular unrest have become so grave that new measures were announced in March 2016 requiring local officials to prevent unrest or face removal.[90]

The seriousness of labor and environmental protests has led to some level of regime response. Enactment of a Labor Contract Law in 2007 imposed performance standards on employers aimed at curbing abuse of workers.[91] Revisions to the Environmental Protection Law in 2014 permitted for the first time public interest litigation to curb environmental abuses.[92] So far, however, the prospects are uncertain that these measures will respond effectively to the causes of popular resistance over labor and environmental conditions. The Labor Law of the PRC and its associated regulatory structures continue to subject workers to significant political controls through party-dominated unions and weak negotiation and dispute settlement provisions.[93] Legal mechanisms for achieving redress remain largely ineffective.[94] Similar obstacles emerge regarding popular resistance over environmental degradation. While the potential for public interest litigation inhibiting environmental abuse seems promising, earlier efforts to curb bureaucratic abuse through judicial review of administrative decisions were generally ineffective.[95] In both labor and environmental disputes, the continued dominance of the CPC over the judiciary inhibits judicial activism that might affirm rights of popular resistance to the authority of the party-state. Thus, the very mechanisms offered by the regime to redress the sources of popular resistance remain inadequate due to the continued refusal by the party-state to accept challenges to its authority.

Resting as it does on a combination of tradition and formalistic legal authority, the governance orthodoxy of the PRC party-state is challenged by human rights debates that question the ideals of authoritarian rule, demand accountability of political leaders, and examine social, economic, and cultural as well as civil and political conditions as indicators of regime performance. Most challenging for the PRC party-state is not that substantive disagreements emerge over the content and enforcement of human rights standards, but rather that human rights claims challenging governance orthodoxy come from individuals and groups who are outside the regime and thus are not considered legitimate sources of comment. That calls for human rights reform exist at all challenges Confucian and CPC norms prizing conformity and compliance. But that such calls emerge from outside the approved system of policy discourse makes it even more difficult (and unlikely) for the regime to accept them. Nonetheless, resistance continues.

Conclusion: resistance to orthodoxy and implications for the party-state

Human rights in the PRC may usefully be viewed by reference to the dynamic of orthodoxy and resistance that has infused state–society relations in China historically. The permitted space for individual rights in the PRC's governance orthodoxy remains highly constrained as the regime combines Confucian relational norms of hierarchy and submission with CPC tradition and legal formalism to justify its rule. Yet the examples of intellectual resistance through Charter 08, challenges from legal professionals embodied in the "rights defenders" movement, and popular protests over labor and environmental conditions, all suggest that regime efforts to ground its authority in the tradition of CPC rule combined with formalist recitations of constitutional and legal texts have had only partial success. Just as the legitimizing effects of Confucianism waned in the face of economic transformation and disruption in nineteenth and early twentieth century China, so too has the PRC party-state's reliance on traditional and formalistic authority proved increasingly inadequate. The history and ideology of the CPC no longer justifies its claims to authority, while resort to legal formality is similarly problematic as the regime ignores its own laws in suppression of its critics.[96] Problems of regime performance on living conditions, inequality, and corruption have in turn weakened the persuasiveness of governance orthodoxies that emphasize popular obedience and submission to supposedly benign governance from virtuous officials. Ultimately, this becomes an issue of popular trust.

Yet studies of popular opinion suggest that trust in government officials has waned steadily over the past decade. While popular trust in governance is stronger when applied to central governments,[97] the general pattern is that the more people interact with and experience governance and the legal system, the less trust they have.[98] This sends a poignant message to the PRC party-state, which has assiduously cultivated an aura of Confucian virtue in an effort to strengthen its authority.[99] For Confucius warned that absent trust, all would be lost:

> Confucius replied to his disciple Zigong on the needs of government, saying: "three things are needed for government: weapons, food and trust. If a ruler can't hold on to all three, he should give up the weapons first and the food next. Trust should be guarded to the end: without trust we cannot stand."[100]

Confucian admonitions that China's leaders should develop the trust of their subjects is ironic in light of human rights conditions in the PRC today. The PRC party-state has held on to its guns first and foremost, while also attempting secure public support though gradual (and vastly uneven) improvement of economic conditions.[101] But trust remains in short supply.

In the absence of public trust, human rights activism poses significant challenges for the governance orthodoxy of the party-state.[102] The breadth and reach of efforts by intellectuals, professionals, and ordinary citizens to challenge the power of the regime through rights-based discourses and actions echo efforts of years past to challenge the Confucian orthodoxy of Imperial and Republican governance. The human rights movements of today call for a fundamental reordering of relationships between state and society. The challenge for the regime's response lies in whether it can build trust in government and its ability to deliver sustainable prosperity, all without diminishing the power of the party-state. A tall order indeed, but one that invites research on a range of important issues.

Topics for future research might usefully focus on changing conditions for norms and structures of human rights in China. For example, how do variations in normative and structural aspects of human rights intersect? What are the long-term implications for governance legitimacy, economic prosperity, and social cohesion of China's current efforts to establish human rights doctrines that conflict with international human rights standards? How might China's changing economy and increased international engagement change popular and regime expectations about human rights? How does the PRC party-state inculcate its governance orthodoxy within the communities of officials upon which its rule depends, and in society? How are the communities of social actors engaged in human rights discourse changing? How might the dynamic of orthodoxy and resistance explain China's response to international standards on human rights? Research on questions such as these can build understanding not only of human rights in China, but also can encourage comparative and historical research on human rights elsewhere.

Acknowledgment

University of British Columbia doctoral students (now PhD alumnae) Liu Yue and Erika Cedillo-Corral and MA student Maia Berangere Parizeau provided research assistance in connection with this essay. This essay contains original research that is part of a broader research program on "Coordinating Performance of International Trade and Human Rights Standards" supported by the Major Collaborative Research Initiatives (MCRI) program of the Social Sciences and Humanities Research Council (SSHRC) of Canada, for which the author is deeply grateful.

Notes

1 Human Rights Watch, "China: Events of 2016" (2017). Online. Available at www.hrw.org/world-report/2017/country-chapters/china-and-tibet (accessed 22 December 2018). Congressional Executive Commission on China, *Annual Report 2017*. Online. Available at www.cecc.gov/media-center/press-releases/cecc-releases-2017-annual-report (accessed 22 December 2018).

2 Philip Alston, United Nations Special Rapporteur on Extreme Poverty and Human Rights, "End-of-Mission Statement on China," 23 August 2016. Online. Available at www.ohchr.org/EN/NewsEvents/Pages/DisplayNews.aspx? NewsID=20402&LangID=E (accessed 22 December 2018).

3 Eleanor Albert and Beina Xu, "China's Environmental Crisis," *Council on Foreign Relations Backgrounder*, 18 January 2016. Online. Available at www.cfr.org/china/chinas-environmental-crisis/p12608 (accessed 22 December 2018).

4 Just as canonical orthodoxy derives authority and a claim to obedience from the religious organization from which it emerges, normative standards of governance gain authority as orthodoxy through the authority of the ruling regime. See Max Weber, *Economy and Society*, Guenther Roth and Claus Wittich (trans. and eds.), Berkeley, CA: University of California Press, 1978, pp. 457–63, and John B. Henderson, *The Construction of Orthodoxy and Heresy: Neo-Confucian, Islamic, Jewish, and Early Christian Patterns*, Albany: State University of New York Press, 1998, pp. 39–84.

5 See generally US Human Rights Network, "ICCPR and ICESCR Summary." Online. Available at www.ushrnetwork.org/resources-media/iccpr-icescr-summary (accessed 22 December 2018).

6 T. Shi, *The Cultural Logic of Politics in Mainland China and Taiwan*, New York: Cambridge University Press, 2015, p. 49; B. Guo, "Political Legitimacy and China's Transition," *Journal of Chinese Political Science*, 2003, vol. 8, no. 1–2, 3–7.

7 Confucius, *The Analects of Confucius: Lun Yu*, Chichung Huang (trans. and ed.), Oxford: Oxford University Press, 1997, p. 51 (2.1).

8 Compare Yonglin Jiang, *The Mandate of Heaven and the Great Ming Code*, Seattle: University of Washington Press, 2011, esp. pp. 22–69, with William P. Alford, "The Inscrutable Occidental? Implications of Roberto Unger's Uses and Abuses of the Chinese Past," *Texas Law Review*, 1986, vol. 64, 915–46.

9 Weber, *Economy and Society*, pp. 246–54.

10 Derk Bodde and Clarence Morris, *Law in Imperial China*, Philadelphia: University of Pennsylvania Press, 1967, pp. 27–9.

11 Geoffrey MacCormack, *The Spirit of Traditional Chinese Law*, Athens: University of Georgia Press, 1996, p. 189. For discussion of the social constraints and local contexts for the

operation of law in traditional China, see Li Chen and Madeleine Zelin (eds.), *Chinese Law: Knowledge, Practice and Transformation*, Leiden: Brill, 2015.

12 See e.g., Elizabeth J. Perry, *Challenging the Mandate of Heaven*, Armonk, NY: M. E. Sharpe, 2002, and Elizabeth J. Perry, *Rebels and Revolutionaries in North China, 1845–1945*, Stanford, CA: Stanford University Press, 1980.

13 See generally, William T. Rowe, *Crimson Rain: Seven Centuries of Violence in a Chinese County*, Stanford, CA: Stanford University Press, 2007, esp. pp. 29–34 and 38–41.

14 Timothy Cheek, *The Intellectual in Modern Chinese History*, Cambridge, UK: Cambridge University Press, 2016.

15 See generally, H. Chang, "Intellectual Change and the Reform Movement: 1890–8," in John K. Fairbank and Kwang-Ching Liu (eds.) *The Cambridge History of China. Vol. 11. Late Ch'ing (1800–1911), Part 2*, Cambridge, UK: Cambridge University Press, 1980, 274–338; Timothy Cheek, "Part I – Reform: Making China Fit the World (1895–1915)," in Cheek, *The Intellectual*, pp. 29–66. But see Frank Ching, "New Finding: Foreign Aggression Didn't Trigger China's Decline," *Manila Times*, 18 July 2017. Online. Available at www.manilatimes.net/new-finding-foreign-aggression-didnt-trigger-chinas-decline/338990/ (accessed 22 December 2018).

16 Eva Pils, Human Rights in China. A Social Practice in the Shadows of Authoritarianism, Cambridge, UK: Polity Press, 2017, p. 18.

17 See generally, Jonathan Spence, *The Gate of Heavenly Peace: The Chinese and Their Revolution, 1895–1980*, New York: Viking Press, 1981, pp. 117–23; Benjamin I. Schwartz, "Themes of Intellectual History: May Fourth and After," in John K. Fairbank (ed.) *Cambridge History of Modern China. Vol. 12*, Cambridge, UK: Cambridge University Press, 1983, pp. 427–30; Leo Ou-fan Lee, "Literary Trends I: The Quest for Modernity, 1895–1927," in Fairbank, *Cambridge History of Modern China. Vol. 12*, pp. 464–504.

18 See generally, Robert Weatherly, *The Discourse of Human Rights in China: Historical and Ideological Perspectives*, New York: St. Martin's Press, 1999; D. Lary, "The Uses of the Past: History and Legitimacy," in Andre Laliberte and Marc Lanteigne (eds.) *The Chinese Party-State in the Twenty-First Century: Adaptation and the Reinvention of Legitimacy*, London: Routledge, 2009, pp. 130–45.

19 Eric Fish, "Why's Beijing So Worried About Western Values Infecting China's Youth?" *China File*, 4 February 2017. Online. Available at www.chinafile.com/features/whys-beijing-so-worried-about-western-values-infecting-chinas-youth (accessed 22 December 2018).

20 See e.g. Wm. Theodore De Bary and Weiming Tu (eds.), *Confucianism and Human Rights*, New York: Columbia University Press, 1998.

21 Jian Wang, "Xinhua Insight: Drawing on Confucian Wisdom for Better Governance," *New China News Agency*, 1 May 2016. Online. Available at http://news.xinhuanet.com/english/2016-01/05/c_134980261.htm (accessed 22 December 2018); Jeremy Page, "Why China Is Turning Back to Confucius," *Wall Street Journal*, 20 September 2015. Online. Available at www.wsj.com/articles/why-china-is-turning-back-to-confucius-1442754000 (accessed 22 December 2018).

22 See generally Pitman B. Potter, *China's Legal System*, Cambridge, UK: Polity Press, 2013, pp. 7–48.

23 Guoguang Wu, *China's Party Congress: Power, Legitimacy, and Institutional Manipulation*, Cambridge, UK: Cambridge University Press, 2015; Laliberte and Lanteigne, *The Chinese Party-State.*

24 "General Program, in "Full Text of the Constitution of the Communist Party of China," 29 March 2013, as "revised and adopted at the Eighteenth National Congress of the Communist Party of China on 14 November 2012." Online. Available at http://english.cpc.people.com.cn/206972/206981/8188065.html (accessed 22 December 2018); "Preamble," in "Constitution of the People's Republic of China," "after amendment on 14 March 2004." Online. Available at www.npc.gov.cn/englishnpc/Constitution/node_2825.htm (accessed 22 December 2018).

25 Kerry Brown, "Opinion: The Real Message for the World in China's First Global Congress," *South China Morning Post*, 21 October 2017. Online. Available at www.scmp.com/week-asia/opinion/article/2115953/real-message-world-chinas-first-global-congress (accessed 22 December 2018).

26 "Communique of the 4th Plenary Session of the 18th Central Committee of the Communist Party of China," 23 October 2014. Online. Available at www.china.org.cn/china/fourth_plenary_session/2014-12/02/content_34208801.htm (accessed 22 December 2018).

27 See Stanley Lubman, "Riding the Tiger: China's Struggle with Rule of Law," *China Real Time Report, Wall Street Journal*, 18 December 2013. Online. Available at https://blogs.wsj.com/chinarealtime/2013/12/18/riding-the-tiger-chinas-struggle-with-rule-of-law/ (accessed 22 December 2018).
28 See generally Pitman B. Potter, "China and the International Human Rights Regime: Orthodoxy, Resistance, and Legitimacy," in Jacques DeLisle and Avery Goldstein (eds.) *China's Global Engagement: Cooperation, Competition, and Influence in the twenty-first Century*, Washington, DC: Brookings Institution, 2017, pp. 291–324.
29 Pitman B. Potter, Assessing China's Treaty Performance: Trade and Human Rights, Vancouver: UBC Press, 2014.
30 UN Convention on Elimination of All Forms of Discrimination Against Women, with its ratification status regarding the PRC. Online. Available at www.umn.edu/humanrts/research/ratification-china.html (accessed 22 December 2018).
31 UN Office of the High Commissioner of Human Rights, *Guiding Principles on Business and Human Rights: Implementing the United Nations "Protect, Respect and Remedy" Framework*, New York: United Nations, 2011. HR/PUB/11/04. Online. Available at www.ohchr.org/Documents/Publications/GuidingPrinciplesBusinessHR_EN.pdf (accessed 22 December 2018).
32 Human Rights Watch, "China: Events of 2016"; Unrepresented Nations & Peoples Organization, "UNPO Alternative Report for CEDAW Documents Systematic Discrimination Endured by Uyghur and Tibetan Women in China," 27 October 2014. Online. Available at http://unpo.org/article/17645 (accessed 22 December 2018).
33 Human Rights in China, "The China Challenge to International Human Rights: What's at Stake?" November 2016. Online. Available at www.hrichina.org/sites/default/files/hric_upr_mid-term_assessment_11.06.2016.pdf (accessed 22 December 2018).
34 Stephanie Nebehay, "China Accuses U.N. Rights Envoy of 'Meddling' in its Judiciary," *Reuters*, 8 June 2017. Online. Available at www.reuters.com/article/us-china-un-rights/china-accuses-u-n-rights-envoy-of-meddling-in-its-judiciary-idUSKBN18Z23V (accessed 22 December 2018).
35 See generally, Roda Mushkat, "China's Multi-Layered Attitude towards State Sovereignty: Theory, Practice and Broad Implications," *Hong Kong Law Review*, 2017, vol. 47, no. 2, 659–88.
36 Zhen Peng, "Report on the Draft of the Revised Constitution of the People's Republic of China," *Beijing Review*, 1982, vol. 25, no. 50, 9–23, esp. pp. 10–11. Online. Available at www.marxists.org/subject/china/peking-review/1982/PR1982-50.pdf (accessed 22 December 2018). Also see X. Deng, "Jianchi sixiang jiben yuanze" [Uphold the Four Cardinal Principles], *Deng Xiaoping wenxuan 1975–1982* [Collected Works of Deng Xiaoping 1975–1982], Vol. 2, Beijing: People's Press, 1983, p. 144.
37 "Zhonghua renmin gongheguo xianfa" [Constitution of the People's Republic of China], rev. 2004. Online. Available at www.gov.cn/gongbao/content/2004/content_62714.htm (accessed 22 December 2018).
38 See C. Xin (vice chair, NPC Legislative Affairs Committee), "Zunzhong he baozhang renquan, shixian shehui quanmian jinbu" [Respect and Ensure Human Rights, Achieve Overall Progress in Society], in *Xianfa he xianfa xiuzhengan fudao duben* [Guidance Reader on the Constitution and Constitutional Amendments], Beijing: Legal System Press, 2004, pp. 218–30, esp. p. 230.
39 "Communique of the Fourth Plenary Session of the 18th Central Committee of the Communist Party of China," 23 October 2014. Online. Available at www.china.org.cn/china/fourth_plenary_session/2014-12/02/content_34208801.htm (accessed 22 December 2018).
40 Xin He, "Black Hole of Responsibility: The Adjudication Committee's Role in a Chinese Court," *Law and Society Review*, 2012, vol. 46, no. 4, 681–712.
41 The concept of *sange zhishang* requires courts to elevate the Party's cause, the interests of the people, and the constitution and laws above all else. See S. Wang, "Zhichi 'sange zhishang' tuidong renmin fayuan gongzuo kexue fazhan" [Uphold the Three Supremes in Promoting Scientific Development of Peoples' Court Work], *Fazhi wang* (Legal System Net), 14 December 2009. Online. Available at www.legaldaily.com.cn/index_article/content/2009-12/14/content_2004336.htm (accessed 22 December 2018).
42 "Zhengzhiju changweihui tingqu Renda Guowuyuan deng dangzu gongzuo huibao" [Politburo Standing Committee Hears Reports on Work of Party Organs at NPC, State Council, etc.],

Xinwen zhongxin (Sina), 16 January 2015. Online. Available at http://news.sina.com.cn/c/2015-01-16/195331409709.shtml (accessed 22 December 2018).

43 "Zhou Qiang: Yao ganyu xiang xifang 'xiangzheng minzhu,' 'sanqian fenli,' 'sifa duli' deng cuowu sichao liangjian" [Zhou Qiang: Dare to Excise Erroneous Western Notions of "Constitutional Democracy," "Separation of Powers," and "Judicial Independence"], *Caijing* [Finance], 14 January 2017. Online. Available at http://politics.caijing.com.cn/20170114/4224783.shtml (accessed 22 December 2018).

44 Iver B. Neumann, "Russia in International Society of the *longue duree*: Lessons from Early Rus' and Early Post-Soviet State Formation," in Raymond Taras, *Russia's Identity in International Relations: Images, Perceptions, Misperceptions*, London: Routledge, 2012, p. 36, and Werner Krawietz et al. (eds.), *Rule of Law: Political and Legal Systems in Transition*, Berlin: Duncker & Humblot, 1997, p. 79, both citing Max Weber, *Zur Russischen Revolution von 1905*, Wolfgang J. Mommsen (ed.), in Horst Baier et al. (eds.) *Max Weber-Gesamtausgabe*, Vol. I/10, Tübingen: J. C. B. Mohr, 1989, pp. 71–280.

45 United Nations General Assembly, "Declaration on the Right to Development," A/Res/41/128, 4 December 1986. Online. Available at www.un.org/documents/ga/res/41/a41r128.htm (accessed 22 December 2018). See also Roland Burke's essay in this volume.

46 See e.g., State Council Information Office, "Progress in China's Human Rights in 2014," June 2015. Online. Available at http://english.gov.cn/archive/white_paper/2015/06/08/content_281475123202380.htm (accessed 22 December 2018).

47 State Council Information Office, "National Human Rights Action Plan of China (2012–2015)," 11 June 2012. Online. Available at www.china.org.cn/government/whitepaper/2012-06/11/content_25619560.htm (accessed 22 December 2018); State Council Information Office, "Full Text: National Human Rights Action Plan of China (2016–2020)." Online. Available at http://news.xinhuanet.com/english/2016-09/29/c_135722183.htm (accessed 22 December 2018).

48 Sarah Biddulph, The Stability Imperative. Human Rights and Law in China, Vancouver: UBC Press, 2015.

49 For comparative assessment with other developing economies in Asia, see Stein Ringen, *The Perfect Dictatorship: China in the Twenty-First Century*, Hong Kong: Hong Kong University Press, 2016.

50 Alston, "End-of-Mission Statement on China." Professor Alston's report also questioned whether China's poverty alleviation efforts have been responsive to China's international human rights commitments.

51 Minxin Pei, *China's Crony Capitalism: The Dynamics of Regime Decay*, Cambridge, MA: Harvard University Press, 2016.

52 See generally, Pitman B. Potter, "International and Domestic Selective Adaptation: The Case of Charter 08," in John Gillespie and Pip Nicholson (eds.) *Law and Development and the Global Discourses of Legal Transfers*, Cambridge, UK: Cambridge University Press, 2012, pp. 56–81; Pitman B. Potter, and Sophia Woodman, "Boundaries of Tolerance: Charter 08 and Debates over Political Reform," in Jean-Philippe Béja, Hualing Fu, and Eva Pils (eds.) *Liu Xiaobo, Charter 08 and the Challenges of Political Reform in China*, Hong Kong: Hong Kong University Press, 2012, pp. 97–117; Pitman B. Potter, "4 June and Charter 08: Approaches to Remonstrance," *China Information*, 2011, vol. 25, no. 2, 121–38.

53 "China's Charter 08," Perry Link (trans. and commentator), *New York Review of Books*, 15 January 2009, 54–6.

54 Amnesty International, "Countdown for China: Charter 08's Legacy & China's Failure to Honor Human Rights Obligations." Online Available at www.amnesty.org.uk/blogs/countdown-china/charter-08's-legacy-china's-failure-honor-human-rights-obligations (accessed 22 December 2018).

55 Peter Foster, "China Upholds 11-Year Sentence for Dissident Liu Xiaobo," *Daily Telegraph*, 11 February 2010. Online. Available at www.telegraph.co.uk/news/worldnews/asia/china/7210857/China-upholds-11-year-sentence-for-dissident-Liu-Xiaobo.html (accessed 22 December 2018).

56 "Beijing Blasts Nobel Peace Prize Meddling," *People's Daily*, 9 October 2010. Online. Available at http://english.peopledaily.comcn/90001/90776/90882/7160366.html (accessed 22 December 2018).

57 Didi Tang and Mark Schiefelbein, "Questions Surround Nobel laureate Liu Xiaobo's Prison Medical Treatment," *Globe and Mail*, 27 June 2017. Online. Available at www.the

globeandmail.com/news/world/questions-surround-nobel-laureate-liu-xiaobos-prison-medical-treatment/article35474485/ (accessed 22 December 2018).

58 See e.g. "Transcript of Interview with Chinese Premier Wen Jiabao," 29 September 2008. Online. Available at www.cnn.com/2008/WORLD/asiapcf/09/29/chinese.premier.transcript/ (accessed 22 December 2018).

59 Tania Branigan, "China Jails Activist Xu Zhiyong for Four Years for 'Disturbing Public Order'," *Guardian*, 26 January 2014. Online. Available at www.theguardian.com/world/2014/jan/26/china-jails-activist-xu-zhiyong (accessed 22 December 2018).

60 Refugee Review Tribunal Australia, "RRTT Research Response, Charter 08," 12 November 2009. Online. Available at www.ecoi.net/file_upload/2107_1313059612_chn35725.pdf (accessed 22 December 2018).

61 See e.g., Melissa Ann Macauley, *Social Power and Legal Culture: Litigation Masters in Late Imperial China*, Stanford, CA: Stanford University Press, 1998, pp. 1–17 (esp. pp. 5–7) and 59–99.

62 "Lawyers Practice Code of Conduct (Draft Revisions)," *China Law Translate*, 18 June 2014. Online. Available at www.chinalawtranslate.com/lawyers-practice-code-of-conduct-draft-revisions/?lang=en (accessed 22 December 2018).

63 Human Rights Watch, "'Walking on Thin Ice': Control, Intimidation, and Harassment of Lawyers in China," April 2008. Online. Available at www.hrw.org/reports/2008/china0408/china0408web.pdf (accessed 22 December 2018).

64 "Editorial: 'Big Stick 306' and China's Contempt for Law," *New York Times*, 5 May 2011. Online. Available at www.nytimes.com/2011/05/06/opinion/06fri3.html?_r=0 (accessed 22 December 2018).

65 See e.g. Eva Pils, *China's Human Rights Lawyers: Advocacy and Resistance*, London: Routledge, 2014; Jonathan Benney, *Defending Rights in Contemporary China*, London: Routledge, 2012; Hualing Fu, and Richard Cullen, "Climbing the *weiquan* Ladder: A Radicalizing Process for Rights-Protection Lawyers," *China Quarterly*, 2011, vol. 205, 40–59.

66 "China Lacks Rule of Law, Chen Guangcheng Warns," *Guardian*, 20 May 2012. Online. Available at www.colombotelegraph.com/index.php/china-lacks-rule-of-law-chen-guangcheng-warns/ (accessed 22 December 2018).

67 Human Rights Watch, "China: Release Leading Rule of Law Activists," 22 January 2015. Online. Available at www.hrw.org/news/2015/01/22/china-release-leading-rule-law-activists (accessed 22 December 2018).

68 "Gao Zhisheng Fights On: A Chinese Dissident Exposes How Beijing Tried to Silence Him," *Wall Street Journal*, 15 June 2016. Online. Available at www.wsj.com/articles/gao-zhisheng-fights-on-1466006846 (accessed 22 December 2018).

69 Human Rights in China, "Cao Shunli." Online. Available at www.hrichina.org/en/defenders/cao-shunli (accessed 22 December 2018); Human Rights Watch, "China: Government Should Account for Activist's Detention, Death," 14 September 2015. Online. Available at www.hrw.org/news/2015/09/14/china-government-should-account-activists-detention-death (accessed 22 December 2018).

70 Human Rights in China, "Profiles: Gou Hongguo, Hu Shigen, Zhai Yanmin, and Zhou Shifen," 5 August 2016. Online. Available at www.hrichina.org/en/profiles-gou-hongguo-hu-shigen-zhai-yanmin-and-zhou-shifeng (accessed 22 December 2018).

71 Front Line Defenders, "Case History: Guo Feixiong," 2016. Online. Available at www.frontlinedefenders.org/en/case/case-history-guo-feixiong (accessed 22 December 2018).

72 Human Rights in China, "HRIC Urges Independent Observers at Upcoming Trials of Lawyers and Activists in China," 5 August 2016. Online. Available at www.hrichina.org/en/press-work/statement/hric-urges-independent-observers-upcoming-trials-lawyers-and-activists-china (accessed 22 December 2018).

73 Y. Lin, "Qiwei faxue xuezhe guanyu Xia Lin lushi bei kong zhaipian zui yi an de falu yijianshu" [Legal Opinion of Seven Legal Scholars on the False Fraud Case against Lawyer Xia Lin], *New Citizen Movement*, 23 September 2016. Online. Available at http://xgmyd.com/archives/27146 (accessed 22 December 2018).

74 Christian Goebel, and Lynette H. Ong, *Report on Social Unrest in China*, London: Europe China Research and Advice Network, 2012. Online. Available at file:///Users/wildenth/Downloads/ECRANSocialUnrestinChina_ChristianGobelandLynetteH.Ong.pdf (accessed 22 December 2018).

75 *Laodong falu wang* (Labor Law Net). Online. Available at www.laodong66.com (accessed 22 December 2018); *Falu jueche* (Lawtime), *Laodong fa* (Labor Law). Online. Available at www.lawtime.cn/info/laodong (accessed 22 December 2018); Cheng Liu, and Sean Cooney, "China's Legal Protection of Workers' Human Rights," in Colin Fenwick and Tonia Novitz (eds.) *Human Rights at Work: Perspectives on Law and Regulation*, Oxford: Hart, 2010, pp. 149–69.

76 US Department of State – Bureau of Democracy, Human Rights, and Labor, *Country Reports on Human Rights Practices – China (Includes Tibet, Hong Kong, and Macau)*, "Section 7: Workers' Rights." Online. Available at www.state.gov/j/drl/rls/hrrpt/humanrightsreport/index.htm?year=2015&dlid=252755 (accessed 22 December 2018).

77 "Protecting Workers' Rights in China: Q&A with Aaron Halegua," *China Real Time Report, Wall Street Journal*. Online. Available at http://blogs.wsj.com/chinarealtime/2016/10/19/protecting-workers-rights-in-china-qa-with-aaron-halegua/ (accessed 22 December 2018).

78 See e.g. Yiu Por Chen and Anita Chan, "Regular and Agency Workers, Attitudes and Resistance in Chinese Auto Joint Ventures," *China Quarterly*, 2018, vol. 233, 85–110. Online. Available at www.cambridge.org/core/journals/china-quarterly/article/regular-and-agency-workers-attitudes-and-resistance-in-chinese-auto-joint-ventures/999E3A616226B9ACD718642D34341ABE (accessed 22 December 2018); Manfred Elfstrom, and Sarosh Kuruvilla, "The Changing Nature of Labor Unrest in China," *Industrial & Labor Relations Review*, 2014, vol. 67, no. 2, 453–80. Online. Available at http://digitalcommons.ilr.cornell.edu/cgi/viewcontent.cgi?article=2014&context=articles (accessed 22 December 2018).

79 Yanhua Deng, and Guobin Yang, "Pollution and Protest in China: Environmental Mobilization in Context," *China Quarterly*, 2013, vol. 214, 321–36. Tianjie Ma, "Environmental Mass Incidents in Rural China: Examining Large-Scale Unrest in Dongyang, Zhejiang," in *China Environmental Series*, 2008/2009, no. 10, 33–49. Online. Available at www.wilsoncenter.org/sites/default/files/CES%2010%20Feature%20Article%2C%20pp.%2033-56.pdf (accessed 22 December 2018).

80 Tianjie Ma, "2016: The Changing Narratives of China's Environmental Story," *China Dialogue*, 30 December 2016. Online. Available at www.chinadialogue.net/article/show/single/en/9526-2-16-The-changing-narratives-of-China-s-environmental-story (accessed 22 December 2018); Albert, and Xu, "China's Environmental Crisis," *Qiongding zhi xia* (Under the Dome), dir. Chai Jing, PRC, 2015.

81 "China Explosions: What We Know About What Happened in Tianjin," *BBC News*, 17 August 2015. Online. Available at www.bbc.com/news/world-asia-china-33844084 (accessed 22 December 2018).

82 Samantha Hoffman, and Jonathan Sullivan, "Environmental Protests Expose Weakness in China's Leadership," *Forbes Asia*, 22 June 2015. Online. Available at www.forbes.com/sites/forbesasia/2015/06/22/environmental-protests-expose-weakness-in-chinas-leadership/#7b951ffb3241 (accessed 22 December 2018).

83 "Thousands Protest Planned Copper Smelting Plant in China's Heiliongjiang," *Radio Free Asia*, 20 September 2016. Online. Available at www.rfa.org/english/news/china/smelting-09202016104835.html (accessed 22 December 2018).

84 Benjamin Haas, "China Riot Police Seal Off City Centre after Smog Protesters Put Masks on Statues," *Guardian*, 12 December 2016. Online. Available at www.theguardian.com/world/2016/dec/12/china-riot-police-seal-off-city-centre-after-smog-protesters-put-masks-on-statues (accessed 22 December 2018).

85 Nicola Davison, "Rivers of Blood: The Dead Pigs Rotting in China's Water Supply," *Guardian*, 29 March 2013. Online. Available at www.theguardian.com/world/2013/mar/29/dead-pigs-china-water-supply (accessed 22 December 2018).

86 Alice C. Hu, "Half the Sky, But Not Yet Equal: China's Feminist Movement," *Harvard International Review*, 22 August 2016). Online. Available at http://hir.harvard.edu/china-womens-rights/ (accessed 22 December 2018); Jonathan Kaiman, "In China, Feminism Is Growing – and So Is the Backlash," *Los Angeles Times*, 15 June 2016. Online. Available at www.latimes.com/world/asia/la-fg-china-feminist-activists-20160614-snap-story.html (accessed 22 December 2018).

87 Mark Selden, "Labor Unrest in China, 1831–1990," *Review (Fernand Braudel Center)*, 1995, vol. 18, no. 1, 69–86.

88 Judith Shapiro, *Mao's War Against Nature: Politics and the Environment in Revolutionary China*, Cambridge, UK: Cambridge University Press, 2001.
89 See e.g., Daniel K. Gardner, "China's Environmental Awakening," *New York Times*, 14 September 2014. Online. Available at www.nytimes.com/2014/09/15/opinion/chinas-environmental-awakening.html (accessed 22 December 2018).
90 "Zhonggong zhongyang bangongting Guowuyuan bangingting yinfa 'Jianquan luoshi shehui zhian zonghe zhili lingdao zeren zhi guiding'" [General Office of CPC Central Committee and General Office of State Council Issue "Regulations on the leadership responsibility system for all round control of establishing and maintaining social order"], 23 March 2016. Online. Available at www.gov.cn/xinwen/2016-03/23/content_5056967.htm (accessed 22 December 2018).
91 "Labour Contract Law of the People's Republic of China (Order No. 65 of President of the People's Republic of China)," 29 June 2007. Online. Available at www.ilo.org/dyn/natlex/natlex4.detail?p_lang=en&p_isn=76384 (accessed 22 December 2018).
92 "Environmental Protection Law of the PRC," 24 April 2014, Article 58. Online. Available at www.chinadialogue.net/Environmental-Protection-Law-2014-eversion.pdf (accessed 22 December 2018).
93 Ruixue Bai, "The Role of the All China Federation of Trade Unions: Implications for Chinese Workers Today," *Working USA: The Journal of Labor and Society*, 2011, vol. 14, 19–39; Anita Chan, "Challenges and Possibilities for Democratic Grassroots Union Elections in China: A Case Study of Two Factory-Level Elections and their Aftermath," *Labor Studies Journal*, 2009, vol. 34, 293–317.
94 Aaron Halegna, *Who Will Represent China's Workers? Lawyers, Legal Aid, and the Enforcement of Labor Rights*, New York: New York University School of Law – US–Asia Law Institute, 2016. Online. Available at https://static1.squarespace.com/static/53960c86e4b010f46523d1fc/t/57f1cedd9de4bb8a69b0cfbd/1524770150399/Halegua%2C+Who+Will+Represent+China%27s+Workers%3F+%282016%29.pdf (accessed 22 December 2018).
95 Kevin J. O'Brien, and Lianjiang Li, "Suing the Local State: Administrative Litigation in Rural China," *China Journal*, 2004, vol. 51, 75–96; Minxin Pei, "Citizens v. Mandarins: Administrative Litigation in China," *China Quarterly*, 1997, vol. 152, 832–62.
96 Josh Chin, "China Lags Behind in Rule-of-Law Ranking," *China Real Time Report, Wall Street Journal*, 20 October 2016. Online. Available at http://blogs.wsj.com/chinarealtime/2016/10/20/china-lags-behind-in-rule-of-law-ranking/ (accessed 22 December 2018).
97 Tony Saich, "The Quality of Governance in China: The Citizens' View," *Harvard Kennedy School Faculty Research Working Paper Series*, November 2012 RWP 12–051. Online. Available at http://ash.harvard.edu/files/ash/files/quality_of_governance.pdf (accessed 22 December 2018).
98 Ethan Michelson and Benjamin L. Read, "Public Attitudes Toward Official Justice in Beijing and Rural China," in Margaret Y. K. Woo and Mary E. Gallagher (eds.) *Chinese Justice: Civil Dispute Resolution in Contemporary China*, Cambridge, UK: Cambridge University Press, 2011, pp. 169–203.
99 Pils, Human Rights in China, pp. 23–5.
100 Analects 12.7. Julia Tao, "Trust within Democracy: A Reconstructed Confucian Perspective," in Kam-por Yu, Julia Tao, and Philip J. Ivanhoe (eds.) *Taking Confucian Ethics Seriously: Contemporary Theories and Applications*, Albany: State University of New York Press, 2010, pp. 99–122.
101 Zhengxu Wang, "Before the Emergence of Critical Citizens: Economic Development and Political Trust in China," *International Journal of Sociology*, 2005, vol. 15, no. 1, 155–71.
102 See generally, Robert Weatherly, *Politics in China Since 1949: Legitimizing Authoritarian Rule*, London: Routledge, 2006; Zhenglai Deng and Sujian Guo (eds.), *Reviving Legitimacy: Lessons For and From China*, Plymouth, UK: Lexington, 2011; Thomas Heberer and Gunter Schubert (eds.), *Regime Legitimacy in Contemporary China. Institutional Change and Stability*, London: Routledge, 2009.

17

CONTINUITY AND CHANGE IN US HUMAN RIGHTS POLICY

Sarah B. Snyder

The degree to which US government officials should take human rights violations and protections into account as they formulate foreign policy has prompted considerable discussion, especially in the years since 1945. These debates have largely focused on civil and political rights that overlap with rights granted to US citizens by the Constitution, including the rights to due process and free speech and protections from religious persecution as well as from cruel and unusual punishment. Within the framework of a human rights policy, US policymakers may weigh the human rights records of other governments as they make decisions on military and economic support, formal and informal alliances, or high-level visits. Those decisions are premised on the idea that human rights are universal and thus not limited by citizenship or country of residence. Throughout its history, the US government has been largely consistent in minimizing attention to human rights concerns in its policy formulation. The two exceptions to this low level of interest took place when championing human rights aligned with the government's existing foreign policy priorities or when nongovernmental activists successfully pressured branches of the US government to take human rights violations into greater account. (Although the United States participates in international and regional organizations concerned with human rights, when it has engaged on human rights, it has done so largely unilaterally.)

This essay addresses US human rights policy in six distinct periods. First, it examines US efforts to create a human rights framework for the postwar world and the challenges the Cold War presented to a continued focus on human rights. Second, it outlines a new approach by US officials to human rights in the 1960s. Third, in the late 1960s and early 1970s, we see greater activism on human rights by members of Congress and nongovernmental organizations (NGOs). Fourth, in the mid- to late 1970s, we can identify the beginnings of a more broad-based movement for greater attention to human rights violations and efforts to address them through US power, a movement that culminated to some degree with, fourth, the end of the Cold War in Europe. Fifth, after the Cold War, the United States struggled to find a new organizing principle for its foreign policy agendas that would have a resonance similar to that of containment of the Soviet Union. Championing human rights presented one possibility, but it was not uniformly embraced between the end of the Cold War and the attacks on 11 September 2001. Sixth, the final section addresses how US policymakers struggled to balance human rights and security in the face of terror in the George W. Bush and Barack Obama years. I also highlight multiple examples in which the United States had no response to human rights violations.

Beginnings

As early as Thomas Jefferson's 1776 Declaration of Independence, Americans discussed their "rights" and those of others. Jefferson wrote that "all men are created equal, that they are endowed by their Creator with certain unalienable Rights, that among these are Life, Liberty and the pursuit of Happiness."[1] His declaration signaled a commitment to individual as opposed to group or collective rights and revealed an understanding of rights as "natural" rather than the province of governments to extend.

Concerns about human rights received greater, if uneven, attention after the establishment of the United Nations (UN) in 1945. Early in the post-World War II era, US officials were engaged in ensuring that human rights were a part of the UN and in shaping the organization's most significant articulation of those rights.[2] The 1945 UN Charter mentioned human rights in several places, and human rights became one element of the UN's mission. Historian Amanda McVety writes that US policymakers active in shaping the postwar world "had been taught that they should do something in the face of human suffering."[3] In the preceding years, President Franklin D. Roosevelt's speeches had served to popularize the concept of human rights. For example, Roosevelt said, "Freedom means the supremacy of human rights everywhere."[4] According to historian William Hitchcock, Roosevelt sought an order "based not only on individual liberties but also on collective responsibility for other human beings."[5] Roosevelt, along with allies in Latin America and the British Commonwealth, pressed for human rights to be included in the proposals for the Dumbarton Oaks conference that set up the UN.[6]

The United States played a significant role in shaping early practical UN human rights commitments. US officials had begun working on an international bill of rights as early as 1942.[7] In addition, through its delegate, former first lady Eleanor Roosevelt, the United States made a significant contribution to the development of an international human rights regime and the country's own acceptance of such a program. Legal scholar Mary Ann Glendon argues that Eleanor Roosevelt was essential to US acquiescence to the idea of including social and economic rights in the UN Universal Declaration of Human Rights.[8] Roosevelt played a substantial role as the UN Human Rights Commission worked to draft a document that outlined international human rights norms and protected individual freedoms. The United States committed a high-level figure who explicitly conjured Franklin Roosevelt's ideals because both the UN and the liberal postwar order that American officials hoped the UN could create were central to US foreign policy objectives in the late 1940s.

The primacy of the Cold War

Within the United States, attention to human rights questions was overtaken by worsening Soviet–American relations and the anticommunism that spread in the country in the aftermath of the war.[9] Dwight D. Eisenhower's administration argued it would pursue its human rights strategy through, as Secretary of State John Foster Dulles put it, "persuasion, education and example rather than formal undertaking" such as an international treaty.[10] The Bricker Amendment controversy ended US engagement with international human rights for several years. The Bricker Amendment, first proposed by Senator John

Bricker (R-OH) in September 1951, was intended to address concerns that the president might commit the United States to international treaties that would contravene the US Constitution. Bricker wanted to guard against international treaties being self-executing, or put another way, he wanted a requirement that the US Congress pass legislation implementing all international treaties and executive agreements. Explaining his rationale for the constitutional amendment, Bricker said in early 1952,

> I do not want any of the international groups, and especially the group headed by Mrs. Eleanor Roosevelt which has drafted the Covenant of Human Rights, to betray the fundamental, inalienable and God-given rights of American citizens enjoyed under the Constitution.[11]

Support for the Bricker Amendment was firmly rooted in opposition to human rights treaties and international institutions more broadly, a position shaped by Cold War politics and desires to maintain racial discrimination.[12] Proponents of the Bricker Amendment were concerned that executive agreements, international human rights treaties, and the entire UN structure might enable the spread of communism domestically as well as present threats to American sovereignty.[13] Despite a wide range of civic support for UN conventions, the treaties' opponents succeeded in labeling them "un-American." Although Bricker's amendment failed to gain the two-thirds support required, the United States did not prioritize human rights in any way during the Eisenhower years as the issue did not align with US interests, threatened executive branch power, and had limited support among activists.

A new approach to human rights

Signaling a rhetorical shift from the Eisenhower years, President John F. Kennedy included the term "human rights" in his 1961 inaugural address, declaring that a new generation of Americans were "unwilling to witness or permit the slow undoing of those human rights to which this nation has always been committed, and to which we are committed today at home and around the world."[14] Yet Kennedy's policies never fulfilled the broad promises of his speech. Ongoing struggles for civil rights at home and other factors limited US attention to human rights abroad. The high stakes of the Cold War also meant that human rights considerations were often overlooked in favor of pressing national security priorities.

In terms of appearances, Kennedy's approach differed significantly from Eisenhower's. Kennedy submitted three UN conventions to the Senate for ratification, paid attention to political prisoners in Cuba, put pressure on South Korea to end military rule, imposed an arms embargo against South Africa, and worked to avoid a declaration of independence by Rhodesia.[15] In these efforts, Kennedy was primarily motivated by Cold War considerations; in these cases supporting human rights claims aligned with broader US foreign policy goals. For example, US official William J. vanden Heuvel urged a greater focus on Cuban human rights violations:

> By concentrating the spotlight on the refugees and the 50,000 political prisoners in Castro jails, we would remind the world that another Police State has been created which is capable of all of the torture and brutality which this century has symbolized.[16]

As early as his 1960 presidential campaign, Kennedy took several steps to publicize the different approach he would bring to US policy toward Africa, including highly publicized meetings with African leaders and funding African students' travel to the United States. Kennedy wanted to gain liberal and African American support for his campaign, but he also had larger Cold War priorities: Africa could be a new opportunity for the expansion of US influence.[17] According to historian Roland Burke, "Decolonization initiated a global human rights debate," driving attention to apartheid, racial discrimination, and anticolonialism.[18] Given its trade and strategic interests, the Kennedy administration initially expressed its opposition to apartheid through rhetorical and symbolic measures, such as integrating social functions at American facilities in South Africa.[19] The government also came under external pressure to withdraw military and political support of the South African government.[20] In the middle of 1963, the US government decided to stop selling arms to South Africa to avoid damage to its relations with black African nations. Kennedy's attention to human rights in these cases demonstrates the public diplomacy considerations that shaped US policy as well as the readiness with which the United States incorporated human rights as a consideration when it aligned with other goals.

President Lyndon B. Johnson made great strides domestically with the Civil Rights Act and Voting Rights Act, but internationally his attention to Vietnam crowded nearly all other issues out of the picture, which meant that human rights rarely aligned with Johnson's policy agenda. One exception was the US response to the crisis over Rhodesia's unilateral declaration of independence from Great Britain in 1965, intended to ensure the continuation of white minority rule.[21] That event heightened American and international attention to human rights issues during Johnson's presidency. In response to white leader Ian Smith's unilateral declaration of independence, the United States withheld recognition of his government, recalled the American consul, shelved its US Information Agency activity, froze loans and credits to Smith, opposed American travel to Rhodesia, and demanded that those who did travel there have British visas. In addition, the United States imposed an embargo against shipments of military equipment and arms, encouraged American businesses to cease dealings with Rhodesia, and suspended sugar imports from the territory. Furthermore, the United States and Great Britain supported ending the shipment of oil and petroleum products to Rhodesia.[22] As with Kennedy, all of these efforts aligned with other national interests. Johnson's administration highlighted its stance on Rhodesia when it sought to appeal to newly independent African governments. Furthermore, American activists such as civil rights leader Martin Luther King, Jr. and Roy Wilkins, Executive Director of the National Association for the Advancement of Colored People (NAACP), pressed the administration to act against racial discrimination.[23] Their assessment of Johnson's domestic and foreign policy records was important to the president.

In the aftermath of the 1967 Greek *coup d'état*, the Johnson administration condemned the nature of the Greek regime, repeatedly inquired with the junta about the fate of political prisoners, and implemented an embargo against heavy military exports to Greece. However, it did not actively oppose the new leaders, despite their attack on Greek democracy. Even the selective embargo, implemented in May 1967, was later lifted due to Greece's place in the North Atlantic Treaty Organization (NATO) alliance, showing that when it came to human rights violations in Greece, broader Cold War foreign policy concerns carried more weight.[24] Activists outside of government and in the US Congress sought to toughen the US response; however, the Johnson and Nixon administrations stifled efforts to end military assistance to Greece.

Richard Nixon's administration confronted a series of human rights decisions in its first term due to growing congressional, diplomatic, and nongovernmental pressure. Yet championing human rights considerations over other priorities did not fit Nixon's conception of US foreign policy. Therefore, when the Nixon administration had to decide whether to continue the selective embargo Lyndon Johnson had implemented in May 1967, due to concerns that stemming the flow of military aid to Greece could weaken the NATO alliance, it resumed full military assistance. In formulating US policy toward Rhodesia, Nixon supported easing Johnson-era sanctions by allowing the import of chrome to the United States. Such a step aligned with Nixon's broader efforts to pursue what it regarded as a more balanced approach toward southern Africa but left the United States noncompliant with UN sanctions against Rhodesia.[25]

As Nixon devised his policy of détente toward the Soviet Union, he chose to minimize concerns about Soviet human rights abuses and privileged instead arms control, trade, and other agreements with the Soviets. According to Secretary of State Henry Kissinger, although "the United States always stands for human liberty, for individual rights, for freedom of movement, and for freedom of the person ... the United States has to conduct foreign policy with many nations around the world."[26] In Nixon's and Kissinger's views, interfering on behalf of Soviet Jews would be akin to the Soviets intervening in race relations in the United States. Speaking about Soviet dissident Andrei Sakharov in his confirmation hearings to become Secretary of State, Kissinger conceded that he may have been "moved as an individual" by the scientist, but questioned "whether the principal exercise of our foreign policy should be directed toward affecting the foreign policy of those societies."[27] Nixon's successor Gerald Ford would later come under increasing pressure to address the plight of Soviet Jews. Despite his continuing commitment to negotiating with the Soviets, he ultimately signed legislation that included the 1974 Jackson-Vanik Amendment, which had the effect of limiting Soviet–American trade.

Wide-scale repression in Chile in the wake of the September 1973 coup focused many Americans, if not always those in the White House, on human rights in the years that followed.[28] The Chilean case, which captured American attention in part due to the murder of two US citizens in the early days of the coup, fit within a broader framework of US leaders privileging right-wing violence over human rights in Latin America. In this context, Secretary of State Henry Kissinger maintained that human rights violations were internal matters in which the United States should not intervene. Given such priorities, he even admonished one ambassador, whom he viewed as pressing the issue too forcefully, to "cut out the political science lectures."[29] An alliance between members of Congress and nonstate actors, however, produced legislation that signaled Americans' concerns about human rights violations in Chile. For example, Senator Ted Kennedy (D-MA) attached an amendment to the 1976 International Security Assistance and Arms Export Control Act that banned any shipment of US manufactured weapons to Chile in effect ending all military assistance, credits, and cash sales of military equipment to Chile.[30]

In some ways, rather than discussing President Ford as having a human rights policy, it is more appropriate to talk about Secretary of State Henry Kissinger's policy, as he clearly was the architect of US human rights policy and the greatest obstacle to more significant executive branch activism on the issue.[31] Kissinger resisted pressure from many sides to take greater account of human rights violations in formulating US foreign policy. Whether from conservative democrats who disagreed that the pursuit of détente should trump the plight of Soviet Jews, or liberals in Congress who recoiled at US complicity in the coup in Chile, Kissinger's leadership was often questioned, yet he remained firm almost to the end of Ford's presidency that human rights were not a matter of concern in US foreign policy. The existing documentary record shows that the Ford administration, like the two that preceded it, was unwilling to incorporate concerns about human rights into foreign policy unless those concerns explicitly supported other foreign policy objectives. Such intransigence inspired growing activism among actors in the legislative branch and outside of government.

Democratization of US policymaking

In the late 1960s and early 1970s, two factors shaped growing American attentiveness to human rights in the formulation of US foreign policy during the late Cold War: congressional activism and the influence of nonstate actors such as organizations devoted to protecting human rights. The growing influence of these two constituencies, particularly on human rights, marked a meaningful shift in US foreign policy formulation. In Congress, a campaign for increased consideration of human rights in US foreign policy was led by Representative Donald M. Fraser, a Democrat from Minnesota who began publicly questioning the morality of US foreign policy in the 1960s.[32] Fraser believed the Cold War framework inhibited consistency between American morality and the government's foreign policy; his calls for greater attention to human rights were part of an effort to develop a new approach to relations with the wider world. As head of the House Foreign Affairs Subcommittee on International Organizations and Movements, Fraser organized a series of hearings in 1973 and ultimately pressed a number of measures that forced the US government to take greater account of human rights when formulating and executing its foreign policy. Explaining his support for human rights, Fraser suggests that by emphasizing the issue in foreign policy, the United States would be "consistent with [its] values."[33]

After 15 sessions in which more than 40 witnesses testified, the subcommittee drafted a report entitled "Human Rights in the World Community: A Call for US Leadership." The report made a series of suggestions, many of which were eventually implemented. First, the subcommittee formulated ideas about how Congress could enhance US support for human rights internationally. In its report, the subcommittee pressed the State Department to "treat human rights factors as a regular part of US foreign policy decision-making" and advocated greater US attention to human rights in its foreign policy.[34] In addition, it outlined a range of tactics the United States could use to influence governments to end abuse of human rights, such as discreet bilateral conversations, public efforts in international organizations, and ending military and economic assistance.

The subcommittee's report advocated reorganizing the State Department to better equip it to consider human rights as an element of US foreign relations. First, it suggested the establishment of an Office for Human Rights in the Bureau of International Organization Affairs. Second, it proposed designating a human rights officer in each regional bureau in the Department. Third, the subcommittee urged the Department to appoint an assistant legal adviser on human rights and form an Advisory Committee on Human Rights.[35] Despite its resistance to Fraser's hearings, the State Department tried to anticipate and blunt the subcommittee's suggestions by making administrative changes before the report's release. Within several months of the report the State Department had designated someone in the UN Political Affairs office to be in charge of human rights, appointed an assistant legal advisor for human rights, and selected human rights officers in three regional bureaus.[36] The next year State Department official James M. Wilson, Jr. became coordinator for humanitarian affairs.

There were several key consequences for US human rights policy following the subcommittee's report. First, members of Congress interested in human rights increasingly shifted their focus to curbing US military assistance to repressive governments. Congressional concern reached a decisive point in September 1974 when 104 members of Congress wrote to Kissinger, suggesting declining support in the House for military assistance to authoritarian regimes. They wrote:

> In the absence of extraordinary circumstances, we do not believe that long-term U.S. foreign policy interest are served by maintaining supportive relationships with oppressive governments, especially in the military field, since military power is directly associated with the exercise of governmental control over the civilian population.
>
> Unless U.S. foreign policies – especially military assistance policies – more accurately reflect the traditional commitment of the American people to promote human rights, we will find it increasingly difficult to justify support for foreign aid legislation to our constituents.[37]

In the aftermath of the subcommittee's hearings, Congress took incremental steps to try to curb assistance to repressive governments.[38] Congress passed Section 32 of the Foreign Assistance Act of 1973, which stated: "It is the sense of Congress that the President should deny any economic or military assistance to the government of any foreign country which practices the internment or imprisonment of that country's citizens for political purposes."[39] State Department officials criticized Section 32 as a "one-time thing" that did not allow the United States to maintain leverage with repressive governments and as unhelpful given the lack of definition of political imprisonment.[40] Congress therefore included far more specific language in the subsequent year's legislation. Section 502B of the 1974 Foreign Assistance Act stipulated:

> Except under extraordinary circumstances, the President shall substantially reduce or terminate security assistance to any government which engages in a consistent pattern of gross violations of internationally recognized human rights. Those violations are defined to include torture; cruel, inhuman or degrading treatment or punishment; prolonged detention without charges; or other flagrant denials of the right to life, liberty and security of person.[41]

The executive branch was able to circumvent 502B, however, by determining that human rights violations did not rise to the level of "gross violations" or that when there were significant human rights abuses, they did not constitute a "consistent pattern."[42] Between November 1974 and November 1975, no country had its military aid or sales stopped due to 502B.[43] As one scholar has put it, 502B is a "case study of executive frustration of congressionally mandated foreign policy."[44] As Fraser later wrote, "We might as well have opened the barn door and let the horses out right there! The Nixon-Ford administration walked right through that door."[45] US policy regarding human rights finally shifted because members of Congress, supported by nonstate actors, were committed to attention to the issue as a key component of US foreign policy.

The State Department began adopting a more proactive approach, including requesting in January 1975 reports on human rights violations from embassies abroad.[46] Yet the State Department under Ford and Kissinger did not send Congress individual reports on the human rights records of countries receiving military assistance in 1975, as members of Congress had been expecting.[47] Using language that particularly angered congressional supporters of human rights legislation, State Department officials declared: "We have found no adequately objective way to make distinctions of degree between nations."[48]

In response, Congress passed Section 301 of the International Security Assistance and Arms Export Control Act of 1976, which tightened the language in 502B to make the reporting mandatory. Ford vetoed the law, forcing Congress to pass a weakened version to secure a presidential signature.[49] Furthermore, the Harkin Amendment, or Section 116 of the International Development and Food Assistance language of the Foreign Assistance Act of 1961, prevented the extension of economic aid to governments that engaged in gross violations of human rights "unless such assistance will directly benefit the needy people of such country."[50] In the wake of stricter legislative language, the State Department and Congress worked together more successfully on monitoring human rights.

The beginning of a human rights movement

As human rights activist Aryeh Neier has put it, "the overwhelming majority of the world's national and local organizations promoting human rights have been established since the last half of the 1970s."[51] Within the United States, these include the Lawyers Committee for International Human Rights, now known as Human Rights First, which formed in 1976, and Helsinki Watch, the precursor to Human Rights Watch, established in 1979. Their proliferation was due in part to globalization. Ongoing innovations in telecommunications and information technology facilitated greater nongovernmental activism on human rights, and human rights violations were "more visible" in a globalized world.[52] Specifically, the lower cost of international travel facilitated human rights activists' ability to engage in contacts across national and East–West borders.[53] New trends in the dissemination of information domestically and transnationally also played an important role. Because ideally the information produced by human rights activism spurred government action to advance the human rights agenda, the collection of information about human rights abuses was a critical component of human rights campaigns.[54] In addition, private foundations such as the Ford Foundation increasingly supported human rights activism beginning in the 1970s, which put more resources at activists' disposal.[55] The power of these activists still was linked to the extent to which their concerns aligned with administration priorities.

Jimmy Carter's inauguration ushered in greater high-level attention to human rights. Carter championed human rights in his speeches and spoke out about human rights abuses in Argentina, the Soviet Union, and Uganda.[56] In addition to his rhetorical focus, Carter made personnel appointments that signaled a commitment to human rights, including naming civil rights activist Patricia Derian to be Assistant Secretary of State for Human Rights and Humanitarian Affairs. Most famously, Carter exchanged correspondence with the Soviet dissident Andrei Sakharov, but his actions did not stop there. His policy of publicly pointing out human rights violations, the issue's salience in Cold War competition with the Soviets, and an upsurge in Soviet repression meant the White House and State Department responded to many reports of abuses. Indeed, Carter's first months in office produced extensive administration commentary on Eastern European human rights cases. The United States responded to the arrest of Soviet dissident Yuri Orlov, to accusations that Jewish refusenik Anatoly Shcharansky had worked for the Central Intelligence Agency, and to the arrests and trials of Jewish refuseniks Ida Nudel and Vladimir Slepak.[57]

Soon after the election, the Carter administration commissioned a review of the role of human rights in US foreign policy, which would determine how the government responded to human rights abuses internationally. By July 1977, a Presidential Review Memorandum was drafted, delineating the administration's view of three types of human rights: freedom from government intervention such as wrongful arrest, torture, and false imprisonment; the right to food, shelter, medical care, and education; and civil and political rights. The administration's broad articulation of human rights is notable given that observers have suggested that Western leaders ignored social and economic rights during the Cold War.[58] It also outlined the US human rights strategy abroad: to emphasize American morals and virtue, spread the rule of law, and support and expand democratization efforts in the Soviet Union and Eastern Europe.[59] According to the memorandum's drafters, however, the Carter administration needed to be careful not to single out particular countries and instead to emphasize the global nature of its focus. The Presidential Review Memorandum signaled a shift in tactics and illustrates the administration's recognition that vocally supporting human rights was imperiling other significant priorities such as détente and arms control negotiations.

Despite policy advice that Carter adopt a balanced, global approach to human rights, many contemporary and subsequent observers have criticized inconsistencies in his approach. Similar to Kennedy, Johnson, Nixon, and Ford, Carter was episodic in his protection of human rights internationally and often prioritized Cold War concerns.[60] In particular, critics have charged that for geopolitical reasons that Carter administration did not subject the human rights records of, for example, Romania, Cambodia, Iran, South Africa, Indonesia, and China to sufficient scrutiny.[61] His complicated relations with the Shah in Iran and Anastasio Somoza in Nicaragua also raised questions about the consistency and consequences of Carter's policies.

Ronald Reagan criticized Carter's policy on human rights during the 1980 campaign, and upon taking office, his administration sought to transform the US approach to human rights.[62] It shifted emphasis to express concern about international terrorism. The Reagan administration charged that Carter's policy had not improved human rights and had neglected US national interests.[63] In his published memoirs and private diaries, Ronald Reagan said relatively little about human rights.[64] Yet, in the assessment of Kathryn Sikkink, "No human rights policy in U.S. history was more hotly contested in its time, or is more controversial today, than the practices and legacy of the Reagan administration."[65] In my view, this controversy is due to the strong influence of Reagan's anticommunism in shaping his approach to human rights. This was not inconsistent with previous presidents' approaches, but his willingness to overlook human rights abuses in Central America, South Africa, and the Philippines for Cold War aims frustrated many observers.

In some regions, such as Central America, the Reagan administration justified devastating human rights violations in the name of preventing the spread of communism.[66] In the assessment of Hauke Hartmann, the Reagan administration "hijacked" the Carter administration's emphasis on human rights to fit its conservative emphasis on "democratization."[67] In other spheres, particularly the Soviet Union and Poland, Reagan spoke forthrightly and repeatedly in defense of human rights activists and against repression in the Soviet bloc.[68] Finally, in a number of cases like South Africa, the Philippines, and Chile, the Reagan administration's stance evolved. The degree of credit that should be given to the US government for changes in those countries is often refracted through a political lens.[69] Those who attribute great significance to Reagan's support for human rights in these cases often overlook the degree to which Reagan came late or unwillingly to the cause.[70] Overall, however, Reagan's record is difficult to characterize neatly, which is one of the reasons his policy remains so contested today.

Human rights after the Cold War

As the political scientist John W. Dietrich wrote, at first "The end of the Cold War and other contemporaneous shifts appeared to finally remove all the long-standing limitations on U.S. human rights policy."[71] Early signals of a new US approach included heightened rhetoric, increased humanitarian interventions such as in the former Yugoslavia, greater participation in international treaties, and domestic legislation such as the Leahy Law, which prevents assistance to military units that commit gross violations of human rights. Yet trade, antiterrorism, and the weakness of nongovernmental actors all limited a transformation of US human rights policy.[72] The approach of the US government, which ignored human rights violations in China and Rwanda and only acted in Bosnia when its reputation was threatened, therefore was highly consistent regardless of the Cold War context.

George H. W. Bush and his aides were less concerned with reforming the human rights practices of communist regimes than their predecessors had been, prioritizing stability over transformation. This shift was likely due to individual preferences. For example, neither his published writings nor his diary entries suggest human rights violations were a significant concern.[73] In addition, Bush's chief foreign policy aide Brent Scowcroft had been skeptical of emphasizing human rights as a priority in US foreign policy since the 1976 election.[74]

Thus, it is not surprising that Bush and his advisers did not see ethnic cleansing in Bosnia as warranting US intervention. It is telling that there is no entry for Bosnia in Bush's co-written memoirs with Scowcroft. After the outbreak of civil war there in 1992, Secretary of State James Baker asserted that the United States did not "have a dog in this fight."[75] Political scientist Jon Western has argued that the first Bush administration intervened in Somalia due to mounting pressure on the United States to respond to the crises there and in Bosnia. In the midst of the 1992 presidential election, demands on the administration to act intensified, and officials made a tactical decision, as Western puts it, that "if the United States was going to intervene, it would be in Somalia – not in Bosnia" because the US military perceived the former as the easier operation.[76]

Bush was similarly reluctant to react to the brutal suppression of demonstrators in China's Tiananmen Square in June 1989. In the aftermath, his objective was to disavow Chinese actions without sacrificing the overall Sino–American relationship. Bush decided to target the Chinese army with his reprisals by suspending military sales and contacts.[77] Many members of the US Congress, the American public, and international leaders supported more far-reaching sanctions. Controversially, Scowcroft and Deputy Secretary of State Lawrence S. Eagleburger traveled to China the next month in secret, raising questions about the degree of the Bush administration's concern with the Chinese crackdown. Relations with China were controversial for the remainder of President Bush's term.

As Yugoslavia disintegrated in the early 1990s, nearly 300,000 people were killed. The new Clinton administration struggled to formulate an approach to Bosnia; Secretary of State Warren Christopher called it "the problem from hell."[78] US officials focused more closely on Bosnia in the wake of the murder of over 7,000 Muslims in the UN safe haven of Srebrenica in July 1995. The following month a devastating attack on a Sarajevo market further drew attention to Western inaction. The two attacks, which made the United States and NATO look impotent, finally led to more forceful action. The NATO bombardment, seen as essential to maintaining NATO and American credibility, pushed the warring parties to negotiate. On 21 November 1995, after 20 days of nonstop negotiations at Dayton Air Force Base in Ohio, all sides reached a peace agreement.

In the span of several months in the spring and summer of 1994, Rwanda, a small country in southern Africa, became the site of a staggering genocide. As many as 1 million Rwandans were killed. Although the United States, Italy, France, and Belgium undertook military operations to evacuate their foreign nationals, they did not intervene to stop the violence in Rwanda because acting to arrest the killings was not seen as in alignment with the Clinton administration's priorities. As Holly Burkhalter put it, "Washington was strangely silent" in the first weeks of the killings in Rwanda.[79] The US hesitation was shaped by the trauma of its recent intervention in Somalia, where 18 US soldiers had died. The United States subsequently outlined conditions for its future involvement in UN peacekeeping missions, and these conditions were not met in the case of Rwanda.

Human rights and the War on Terror

The terrorist attacks on 11 September 2001 shattered any remaining hopes that the end of the Cold War might usher in a new approach to human rights in US foreign policy. As the country confronted nearly 3,000 deaths, George W. Bush's administration developed a multipronged approach that included a willingness "to work sort of the dark side," as Vice President Dick Cheney put it the following week.[80] Not only did human rights considerations not figure prominently in US foreign policy under the second Bush administration, but the United States became a human rights violator as well. The Office of Legal Counsel determined that the Geneva Convention protections did not apply to Taliban, al Qaeda, or other terrorists held in captivity.[81] They were so-called unlawful enemy combatants and not prisoners of war. Later that year, the Office of Legal Counsel defined torture as an act that causes pain akin in "intensity to the pain accompanying serious physical injury, such as organ failure, impairment of bodily function, or even death."[82] Interrogators at the US detention facility in Guantanamo Bay, Cuba were given permission to use enhanced counter-resistance strategies that included the use of scenarios designed to convince the detainee that death or severely painful consequences were imminent for him and/or his family, exposure to cold weather or water, waterboarding or the use of a wet towel and dripping water to induce the perception of suffocation, and the use of mild, non-injurious physical contact such as grabbing, poking in the chest with the finger, and light pushing.[83] In addition, the United States subjected suspected terrorists to "extraordinary rendition," which transferred them to foreign governments, including those known to torture suspects and sent detainees to secret prisons, often referred to as "black sites."[84]

Over Bush's two terms, US human rights policy became increasingly controversial. Notably and in contrast to earlier administrations, in Bush's case it was US human rights abuses, rather than support for foreign governments engaging in human rights violations, that was of concern. The lack of due process accorded detainees, the use of torture against prisoners at Guantanamo, and the indefinite nature of detentions made the prison a target for human rights activists, legal scholars, and critics of the US war on terror. Furthermore, a 2014 Senate report determined that 39 detainees had been subject to torture, that the use of these interrogation techniques did not produce intelligence that averted terrorist attacks, and that torture had led instead to false confessions and inaccurate information.[85] Other observers have emphasized that US torture under the Bush administration weakened national security, including by serving as a recruiting tool for terrorists.[86]

Human Rights Watch Executive Director Kenneth Roth outlined a range of steps that the new Obama administration could take to signal a renewed American commitment to human rights, including closing CIA black sites, ending the use of torture, investigating human rights abuses by US personnel, and closing the prison at Guantanamo Bay.[87] Shortly after his inauguration, Obama and his aides pronounced new policies, many of which aligned with Roth's suggestions, including the closure of the CIA's secret prison system, an expressed commitment to the Geneva Convention, adherence to the military's interrogation rules, and a promise to close the detention center at Guantanamo Bay. Yet Obama did not succeed in closing the prison, and his failure to end detention at Guantanamo Bay was one of a number of elements of Obama's record that led some disappointed observers to charge that Obama's approach to human rights was more rhetorical than real.[88] To some, the president's commitment to "principled pragmatism" regarding human rights looked and sounded as if his administration did not prioritize commitment to human rights.[89] Furthermore, the expansion of the US drone warfare program led to the deaths of many innocent civilians over Obama's two terms.[90] Despite nongovernmental pressure, his administration did not modify its practices. Yet the Obama administration also broadened the definition of human rights championed by the United States. National Security Adviser Susan Rice asserted that the administration had supported LGBTQ activists internationally and worked to protect the rights of LGBTQ Americans, which were in line with Obama's enhanced attention to such rights in his second term.[91]

Examining the attention to human rights given by US foreign policy in the years since 1945 demonstrates a growing consideration of the issue. Largely fueled by external pressure from members of Congress, nongovernmental organizations, and concerned citizens, US presidents and their aides increasingly had to evaluate human rights considerations when making decisions about foreign assistance, rhetorical support or condemnation, or more forceful actions such as military intervention. Yet perhaps not surprisingly, the US government rarely prioritized human rights unless doing so aligned with other policy objectives. Studying US human rights policy formulation illuminates means by which activists can shape other governments' approaches.

Notes

1 Declaration of Independence, 4 July 1776. Online. Available at www.archives.gov/founding-docs/declaration-transcript (accessed 26 December 2018), and Michael Zuckert, "Natural Rights in the American Revolution," in Jeffrey N. Wassterstrom et al. (eds.) *Human Rights and Revolutions*, New York: Rowman & Littlefield, 2007, pp. 65–8.

2 Mary Ann Glendon, *A World Made New: Eleanor Roosevelt and the Universal Declaration of Human Rights*, New York: Random House, 2001, p. 17.

3 Amanda McVety, "The Internationalism of the Early Cold War," in Artemy M. Kalinovsky and Craig Daigle (eds.) *The Routledge Handbook of the Cold War*, New York: Routledge, 2014, p. 21.

4 Jan Herman Burgers, "The Road to San Francisco: The Revival of the Human Rights Idea in the Twentieth Century," *Human Rights Quarterly*, 1992, vol. 14, no. 4, 470, and Frank Costigliola, "Freedom from Fear," in Jeffrey A. Engel (ed.) *The Four Freedoms: Franklin D. Roosevelt and the Evolution of an American Idea*, New York: Oxford University Press, 2016, p172.

5 William Hitchcock, "'Everywhere in the World': The Strange Career of Four Freedoms since 1945," in Engel, *The Four Freedoms*, p. 217.

6 Glendon, *A World Made New*, p. 9, and Paul Gordon Lauren, *The Evolution of International Human Rights: Visions Seen*, 1st ed., Philadelphia: University of Pennsylvania Press, 1998, pp. 166–77.

7 Mark Bradley, *The World Reimagined: Americans and Human Rights in the Twentieth Century*, New York: Cambridge University Press, 2016, p. 44.

8 Glendon, *A World Made New*, p. 43.

9 Glendon, *A World Made New*, pp. 198–9.

10 Tony Evans, "Hegemony, Domestic Politics and the Project of Universal Human Rights," *Diplomacy and Statecraft*, 1995, vol. 6, no. 3, 636. This opposition in the 1950s had a long-lasting influence on Senate debates about ratifying human rights treaties. Natalie Hevener Kaufman, *Human Rights Treaties and the Senate: A History of Opposition*, Chapel Hill: University of North Carolina Press, 1990, pp. 2, 125. See also Elizabeth Borgwardt, "'Constitutionalizing' Human Rights: The Rise and Rise of the Nuremberg Principles," in Akira Iriye, Petra Goedde, and William Hitchcock (eds.) *The Human Rights Revolution. An International History*, New York: Oxford University Press, 2012, pp. 73–83.

11 Cathal J. Nolan, "The Last Hurrah of Conservative Isolationism: Eisenhower, Congress, and the Bricker Amendment," *Presidential Studies Quarterly*, 1992, vol. 22, no. 2, 342.

12 Natalie Hevener Kaufman and David Whiteman, "Opposition to Human Rights Treaties in the United States Senate: The Legacy of the Bricker Amendment," *Human Rights Quarterly*, 1988, vol. 10, 310, 318; Hanne Hagtvedt Vik, "The United States, the American Legal Community and the Vision of International Human Rights Protection," 1941–1953, PhD diss., University of Oslo, 2009, p. 10; Evans, "Hegemony," 626; and Kaufman, *Human Rights Treaties*, p. 24. Other scholars interpret the Bricker amendment controversy as rooted in isolationist tendencies rather than concerns about maintaining segregation or other conservative rationales for supporting the amendment. Nolan, "The Last Hurrah," 337; and Duane A. Tananbaum, "The Bricker Amendment Controversy: Its Origins and Eisenhower's Role," *Diplomatic History*, 1985, vol. 9, no. 1, 81.

13 Nolan, "The Last Hurrah," 338–9; Tananbaum, "The Bricker Amendment Controversy," 75, 79; and Kaufman, *Human Rights Treaties*, pp. 9, 38, 62, 112.

14 John F. Kennedy, "Inaugural Address," 20 January 1961, *The American Presidency Project*. Online. Available at www.presidency.ucsb.edu/documents/inaugural-address-2 (accessed 26 December 2018).

15 The three human rights conventions that Kennedy sent to the Senate for ratification were the Supplementary Convention on the Abolition of Slavery, the International Labour Organization's Abolition of Forced Labour Convention, and the United Nations Convention on the Political Rights of Women.

16 John F. Kennedy Library, Boston, Massachusetts, National Security Files Staff Files, Series I, Box 56A, Cuba, Subjects: Cuban Refugees, 8/61–3/63, William J. vanden Heuvel, "Cuba: Its Refugees and Its Liberation," 6 September 1962.

17 Thomas J. Noer, "New Frontiers and Old Priorities in Africa," in Thomas G. Paterson (ed.) *Kennedy's Quest for Victory: American Foreign Policy, 1961–1963*, New York: Oxford University Press, 1989, pp. 254, 256. See also Michael L. Krenn, *Black Diplomacy: African Americans and the*

State Department, 1945–1969, London: M. E. Sharpe, 1999, p. 116; Thomas Borstelmann, *The Cold War and the Color Line: American Race Relations in the Global Arena*, Cambridge, MA: Harvard University Press, 2001, pp. 138–9; and Mary Dudziak, *Cold War Civil Rights: Race and the Image of American Democracy*, Princeton, NJ: Princeton University Press, 2000, pp. 152–3.

18 Roland Burke, *Decolonization and the Evolution of International Human Rights*, Philadelphia: University of Pennsylvania Press, 2010, pp. 12, 147.

19 Noer, "New Frontiers," 275, 276.

20 Taylor Branch, *Parting the Waters: America in the King Years, 1954–63*, New York: Simon & Schuster, 1988, p. 684.

21 Only 6 percent of the Rhodesian population, or 220,000 of 4 million people, were white.

22 To embargo oil to Rhodesia required a considerable financial and logistical commitment, as it necessitated implementing an airlift to bring oil to Zambia due to the fact that Rhodesia blocked Zambia's sea access. Minnesota Historical Society, St. Paul, Minnesota, Donald M. Fraser Papers (hereafter MHS Fraser Papers), Box 151.H.3.7 (B), Press Release, 9 April 1966, Rhodesia, 1977 (3) and Thomas J. Noer, *Cold War and Black Liberation: The United States and White Rule in Africa, 1948–1968*, Columbia: University of Missouri Press, 1985, pp. 197–8, 203–4.

23 Comment by Martin Luther King, Jr., 25 October 1965 in Martin Luther King, Jr., *"In a Single Garment of Destiny": A Global Vision of Justice*, Boston: Beacon Press, 2012 and Lyndon B. Johnson Library, Austin, Texas, White House Central Files, CO Box 65, GEN CO 250 Rhodesia 11/22/63–1/5/66, Wilkins to Johnson, 4 May 1966.

24 Pauline Mian, "Infringement of Human Rights in Greece and the Response of the United States and the United Nations," *Congressional Research Service Report*, 1973; Effie G. H. Pedaliu, "Human Rights and Foreign Policy: Wilson and the Greek Dictators, 1967–1970," *Diplomacy and Statecraft*, 2007, vol. 18, 195; and Adam Garfinkle, "The Nadir of Greek Democracy," in Daniel Pipes and Adam Garfinkle (eds.) *Friendly Tyrants: An American Dilemma*, New York: St. Martin's Press, 1991, p. 73. For further discussion of the Johnson administration's response to human rights violations in Greece and Rhodesia, see Sarah B. Snyder, "The Rise of Human Rights During the Johnson Years," in Francis J. Gavin and Mark Atwood Lawrence (eds.) *Beyond the Cold War: Lyndon Johnson and the New Global Challenges of the 1960s*, New York: Oxford University Press, 2014, pp. 237–60.

25 Nixon Presidential Materials Project, College Park, Maryland, National Security Council Institutional Files, NSDM-38, Box H-213, Kissinger to Nixon, 15 January 1970.

26 Nomination of Henry A. Kissinger, Hearings before the Senate Committee on Foreign Relations, 93rd Congress, 1st Session, 11 September 1973, p. 116. Online. Available at https://babel.hathitrust.org/cgi/pt?id=uc1.b5148892;view=1up;seq=24 (accessed 26 December 2018).

27 Nomination of Henry A. Kissinger, Hearings before the Senate Committee on Foreign Relations, 93rd Congress, 1st Session, 7 September 1973, p. 40. Online. Available at https://babel.hathitrust.org/cgi/pt?id=uc1.b5148892;view=1up;seq=91 (accessed 26 December 2018).

28 The junta killed more than 3,000 Chileans while in power, and approximately 1,100 people were "disappeared" by the National Intelligence Directorate and other arms of the junta. In addition to the killings and arrests that are often noted in catalogues of the repression, Pinochet's Chile sent 200,000 people into exile, which represented about 2 percent of the country's population. Jan Eckel, "'Under a Magnifying Glass': The International Human Rights Campaign against Chile in the Seventies," in Stefan-Ludwig Hoffmann (ed.) *Human Rights in the Twentieth Century*, New York: Cambridge University Press, 2010, p. 324.

29 Seymour M. Hersh, "Kissinger Said to Rebuke U.S. Ambassador to Chile," *New York Times*, 27 September 1974.

30 PL 94–329, 30 June 1976. Online. Available at www.govinfo.gov/content/pkg/STATUTE-90/pdf/STATUTE-90-Pg729.pdf (accessed 26 December 2018); Kennedy Remarks, *Congressional Record*, 18 February 1976, 3598–9; Richard D. Lyons, "Senate Votes Overhaul of Military Aid," *New York Times*, 19 February 1976; Lars Schoultz, *Human Rights and United States Policy toward Latin America* (Princeton, NJ: Princeton University Press, 1981), pp. 255–6.

31 The Nixon administration may have been a degree less engaged on human rights because the Nixon Doctrine involved relying on second-tier, often authoritarian, powers to maintain regional security. Daniel J. Sargent, *A Superpower Transformed: The Remaking of American Foreign*

Relations in the 1970s, New York: Oxford University Press, 2015, p. 69. We can, however, identify some shifts in US policy over the Ford years. Whether the result of new legislation, the dynamics of a presidential campaign, or a different president in the White House, the Ford administration paid more attention to human rights than the Nixon administration had. According to David Forsythe, Ford, as a member of Congress, had "strongly supported human rights across the board." David P. Forsythe, *Human Rights and U.S. Foreign Policy: Congress Reconsidered*, Gainesville: University of Florida Press, 1988, p. 150.

32 For further discussion of Fraser's human rights activism, see Sarah B. Snyder, "'A Call for U.S. Leadership': Congressional Activism on Human Rights," *Diplomatic History*, 2013, vol. 37, no. 2, 372–97, on which this section is based.

33 Donald M. Fraser, "Freedom and Foreign Policy," *Foreign Policy*, 1977, vol. 26, 143.

34 "Human Rights in the World Community: A Call for U.S. Leadership," Report of the Subcommittee on International Organizations and Movements of the Committee on Foreign Affairs, House of Representatives, 27 March 1974.

35 "Human Rights in the World Community: A Call for U.S. Leadership."

36 University of Texas Libraries, the University of Texas at Austin, Austin, Texas, Benson Latin American Collection, George Lister Papers, Box 7, Folder 21, Fraser to Kissinger, 27 June 1974.

37 MHS Fraser Papers, Box 151.H.3.3 (B), Fraser to All Signatories, 18 September 1974, Dear Colleague – Kissinger, 1974, and Press Release, 22 September 1974.

38 Barbara Keys argues that Kissinger's intransigence on human rights forced Congress to pass increasingly restrictive legislation to force him to address the issue. Barbara J. Keys, "Congress, Kissinger, and the Origins of Human Rights Diplomacy," *Diplomatic History*, 2010, vol. 34, no. 5, 824, 850.

39 Foreign Assistance Act 1973, 93rd Congress, 1st Session. In April 1974, the State Department asked for widespread reporting on the treatment of political prisoners from its embassies.

40 University of South Dakota, Vermillion, South Dakota, University Libraries, Archives and Special Collections, James G. Abourezk Papers (hereafter USD UL Abourezk Papers), Box 312, Folder 5, Ingersoll to Morgan, 27 June 1974 and Ingersoll to Morgan, 28 July 1974; Department of State, *Foreign Relations of the United States, 1969–1976, Volume E-3, Documents on Global Issues, 1973–1976*, Washington, DC: Government Printing Office, 2009, Document 240; and Fiscal Year 1975 Foreign Assistance Request, 4, 5, 11, 12, 13, 18, 19, 20, 26 June and 1, 2, 10, 11 July 1974, 93rd Congress, 2nd Session. For further discussion of Abourezk and his amendments, see Barbara J. Keys, *Reclaiming American Virtue: The Human Rights Revolution of the 1970s*, Cambridge, MA: Harvard University Press, 2014, pp. 133–40. See also Clair Apodaca, *Understanding U.S. Human Rights Policy: A Paradoxical Legacy*, New York: Routledge, 2006, p. 35.

41 Foreign Assistance Act of 1974, 93rd Congress, 2nd Session. Clair Apodaca sees the language of "gross violations" as presenting a problem in definition, in that it was connected with the degree of violation as well as the number of people affected and for a significant duration of time. Apodaca, *Understanding U.S. Human Rights Policy*, p. 38.

42 Clair Apodaca, "U.S. Human Rights Policy and Foreign Assistance: A Short History," *Ritsumekian International Affairs*, 2005, vol. 3, 66, and Stephen B. Cohen, "Conditioning U.S. Security Assistance on Human Rights Practices," *American Journal of International Law*, 1982, vol. 76, no. 2, 268.

43 Cohen, "Conditioning U.S. Security Assistance," 252.

44 Cohen, "Conditioning U.S. Security Assistance," 277. Forsythe argues that general human rights legislation is not useful because "the votes are not there to force the executive to follow the letter – or indeed some times even the spirit – of the laws adopted." David P. Forsythe, "Congress and Human Rights in U.S. Foreign Policy: The Fate of General Legislation," *Human Rights Quarterly*, 1987, vol. 9, no. 3, 382.

45 Donald M. Fraser, "Human Rights and U.S. Foreign Policy: Some Basic Questions Regarding Principles and Practice," *International Studies Quarterly*, 1979, vol. 23, no. 2 179.

46 Department of State, *Foreign Relations of the United States, 1969–1976, Vol. E-3, Documents on Global Issues, 1973–1976*, Washington, DC: Government Printing Office, 2009, Document 247, SecState to AmEmbassy Nicosia, 20 February 1975.

47 James Wilson remembers that Kissinger insisted that Ronald Palmer write a general report, which sent members of Congress "through the roof." James M. Wilson, Jr. Oral History Interview, 31 March 1999, *The Foreign Affairs Oral History Collection of the Association for Diplomatic Studies and Training*, Library of Congress, Washington, District of Columbia. Bernard Gwertzman, "U.S. Blocks Rights Data On Nations Getting Arms," *New York Times*, 19 November 1975.

48 USD UL Abourezk Papers, Box 3, Folder 6, Report to the Congress on the Human Rights Situation in Countries Receiving U.S. Security Assistance, 14 November 1975.

49 Gerald R. Ford Library, Ann Arbor, Michigan, White House Records Office: Legislative Case Files, Box 44, Ford to Senate, 1976/05/07 S2662 International Security Assistance and Arms Export Control Act (vetoed) (3) and Box 48, Cannon to Ford, 30 June 1976, 6/30/76 HR12203 Foreign Assistance and Related Programs Appropriation Act of 1976 (1). Cohen, "Conditioning U.S. Security Assistance," 252–3.

50 Schoultz, *Human Rights and United States Policy Toward Latin America*, pp. 196–7, 208.

51 Aryeh Neier, *The International Human Rights Movement: A History*, Princeton, NJ: Princeton University Press, 2012, p. 250.

52 Shayne Weyker, "The Ironies of Information Technology," in Alison Brysk (ed.) *Globalization and Human Rights*, London: University of California Press, 2002, pp. 115, 118, 119; James N. Rosenau, "The Drama of Human Rights in a Turbulent, Globalized World," in Brysk, *Globalization and Human Rights*, p. 151; and Patrick William Kelly, *Sovereign Emergencies: Latin America and the Making of Global Human Rights Politics*, New York: Cambridge University Press, 2018.

53 Daniel Sargent, "Human Rights as a U.S. Foreign Policy Doctrine," paper presented at conference "A New Global Morality? The Politics of Human Rights and Humanitarianism in the 1970s," Freiburg Institute for Advanced Studies, Freiburg, Germany, June 2010; Margaret Keck and Kathryn Sikkink, *Activists Beyond Borders: Advocacy Networks in International Politics*, Ithaca, NY: Cornell University Press: 1998, p. 14.

54 Kenneth Cmiel, "The Emergence of Human Rights Politics in the United States," *Journal of American History*, 1999, vol. 86, no. 3, 1232, 1235–6, 1241.

55 Cmiel, "Emergence of Human Rights Politics," 1244, and Kathryn Sikkink, "Human Rights, Principled Issue-Networks, and Sovereignty in Latin America," *International Organization*, 1993, vol. 47, 420.

56 Keys argues convincingly that in Carter's statement in his inaugural address that "our commitment to human rights must be absolute" has been misunderstood. Carter was using the older definition of human rights as domestic civil rights and thus was committing the United States to a domestic rather than international project. Keys, *Reclaiming American Virtue*, p. 246.

57 Jimmy Carter Library, Atlanta, Georgia (hereafter JCL), National Security Adviser, Subject File, Brzezinski Material, Box 29, Human Rights, 4/79–4/80, Memorandum and Attachments, Bloomfield to Brzezinski; John Dumbrell, *The Carter Presidency. A Re-Evaluation*, 2nd ed., Manchester: Manchester University Press, 1995, p. 123; Rutgers University, New Brunswick, New Jersey, Alexander Library, Special Collections and University Archives, Millicent Fenwick Papers, Box 271, Helsinki/USSR, Starr to Fenwick, 23 June 1978; and Erwin C. Hargrove, *Jimmy Carter as President: Leadership and the Politics of the Public Good*, Baton Rouge: Louisiana State University Press, 1988, pp. 152–3.

58 For more on the history of this interpretation, see Daniel J. Whelan and Jack Donnelly, "The West, Economic and Social Rights, and the Global Human Rights Regime: Setting the Record Straight," *Human Rights Quarterly*, 2007, vol. 29, no. 4, 908–49.

59 JCL, Robert J. Lipshutz Files, Box 19, Presidential Review Memorandum/NSC-28: Human Rights, 7 July 1977, and Hauke Hartmann, "US Human Rights Policy Under Carter and Reagan, 1977–1981," *Human Rights Quarterly*, 2001, vol. 23, 410.

60 David Schmitz and Vanessa Walker have most effectively disputed this interpretation. David F. Schmitz, and Vanessa Walker, "Jimmy Carter and the Foreign Policy of Human Rights: The Development of a Post-Cold War Foreign Policy," *Diplomatic History*, 2004, vol. 28, 117.

61 Betty Glad, *An Outsider in the White House: Jimmy Carter, His Advisors, and the Making of American Foreign Policy*, Ithaca, NY: Cornell University Press, 2009, pp. 237–9; Luca Trenta, "The Champion of Human Rights Meets the King of Kings: Jimmy Carter, the Shah, and Iranian Illusions and Rage," *Diplomacy and Statecraft*, 2013, vol. 24, no. 3, 476–98; Kenton Clymer,

"Jimmy Carter, Human Rights, and Cambodia," *Diplomatic History*, 2003, vol. 27, no. 2, 245–77; Bradley R. Simpson, "Denying the 'First Right': The United States, Indonesia, and the Ranking of Human Rights by the Carter Administration, 1976–1980," *International History Review*, 2009, vol. 31, no. 4, 798–826; Simon Stevens, "'From the Viewpoint of a Southern Governor': The Carter Administration and Apartheid, 1977–81," *Diplomatic History*, 2012, vol. 36, 843–80; and Rosemary Foot, *Rights Beyond Borders: The Global Community and the Struggle over Human Rights in China*, New York: Oxford University Press, 2000, pp. 89–90. See also Scott Sidell, "The United States and Genocide in East Timor," *Journal of Contemporary Asia*, 1981, vol. 11, no. 1, 44–7.

62 David Carleton, and Michael Stohl, "The Foreign Policy of Human Rights: Rhetoric and Reality from Jimmy Carter to Ronald Reagan," *Human Rights Quarterly*, 1985, vol. 7, no. 2, 205.

63 Carleton, and Stohl, "The Foreign Policy of Human Rights," 208–9.

64 In his diaries, Reagan primarily noted his signing of annual human rights proclamations (the relevant index entries are Human Rights Commission, Human Rights Conference, Human Rights Day, Human Rights Week, and Human Rights Year) and delved into substance only on South Africa and a Soviet proposal to hold a human rights conference in Moscow. See Ronald Reagan, *An American Life*, New York: Pocket Books, 1990, pp. 299, 305, and Douglas Brinkley (ed.), *The Reagan Diaries*, New York: HarperCollins, 2007, pp. 286, 650, 728.

65 Kathryn Sikkink, *Mixed Signals. US Human Rights Policy and Latin America*, Ithaca, NY: Cornell University Press, 2004, p. 179.

66 Sikkink has argued that instances of human rights abuses increased in the first year of the Reagan administration as leaders in repressive countries took Reagan's election and his early policies as a signal that such practices were now permissible. Sikkink, *Mixed Signals*, p. 54.

67 Hartmann, "US Human Rights Policy Under Carter and Reagan," 403.

68 For more on Reagan's approach to human rights in the Soviet bloc, see Sarah B. Snyder, *Human Rights Activism and the End of the Cold War: A Transnational History of the Helsinki Network*, New York: Cambridge University Press, 2011, pp. 135–216, and Anatoly Adamishin and Richard Schifter, *Human Rights, Perestroika, and the End of the Cold War*, Washington, DC: United States Institute of Peace Press, 2009.

69 See for example Human Rights Watch Executive Director Aryeh Neier's criticism of the Reagan administration's record in difficult cases, "When the rewards were fewer and the costs were higher than those that followed from opposing Pinochet, the Reagan administration's practices … were generally not to serve as an advocate of human rights. Worse, it frequently defended the practices of such governments and, thereby, acted as an apologist for abuses." Aryeh Neier, "Human Rights in the Reagan Era: Acceptance in Principle," *Annals of the American Academy of Political and Social Science*, 1989, vol. 506, 34.

70 For more, see Sarah B. Snyder, "Compartmentalizing U.S. Foreign Policy: Human Rights in the Reagan Years," in Jonathan Hunt and Simon Miles (eds.) *Reagan's World: The Cold War and Beyond*, Ithaca, NY: Cornell University Press, in progress.

71 John W. Dietrich, "U.S. Human Rights Policy in the Post-Cold War Era," *Political Science Quarterly*, 2006, vol. 121, no. 2, 272.

72 Dietrich, "U.S. Human Rights Policy," 274–8, 288, 289, 293.

73 George Bush, *All the Best, George Bush: My Life in Letters and Other Writings*, New York: Simon & Schuster, 1999, p. 416, and Jeffrey A. Engel (ed.), *The China Diary of George H. W. Bush: The Making of a Global President*, Princeton, NJ: Princeton University Press, 2008, pp. 81, 251, 282.

74 David F. Schmitz, *Brent Scowcroft: Internationalism and Post-Vietnam War American Foreign Policy*, New York: Rowman & Littlefield, 2011, pp. 57, 63.

75 Richard Holbrooke, *To End a War*, rev. ed., New York: Modern Library 1999, p. 27.

76 Jon Western, "Sources of Humanitarian Intervention: Beliefs, Information, and Advocacy in the U.S. Decisions on Somalia and Bosnia," *International Security*, 2002, vol. 26, no. 4, 118, 123.

77 George Bush, and Brent Scowcroft, *A World Transformed*, New York: Vintage, 1998, pp. 86–9, 98–100.

78 Holbrooke, *To End a War*, p. 55.

79 Holly Burkhalter, "The Question of Genocide: The Clinton Administration and Rwanda," *World Policy Journal*, 1994–5, vol. 11. no. 4, 46.

80 Jane Mayer, *The Dark Side: The Inside Story of How the War on Terror Turned Into a War on American Ideals*, New York: Doubleday, 2008, p. 9.

81 Jay S. Bybee, Assistant Attorney General, Department of Justice to William J. Haynes II, General Counsel, Department of Defense, 13 March 2002. Online. Available at http://nsarchive.gwu.edu/torturingdemocracy/documents/20020313.pdf (accessed 26 December 2018).

82 Jay S. Bybee, Assistant Attorney General, Department of Justice to Alberto R. Gonzales, Counsel to the President, 1 August 2002. Online. Available at http://nsarchive.gwu.edu/NSAEBB/NSAEBB127/02.08.01.pdf (accessed 26 December 2018).

83 Memorandum, Jerald Phifer to Commander, Subject: Counter-Resistance Strategies, 11 October 2002. Online. Available at http://nsarchive.gwu.edu/torturingdemocracy/documents/20021011.pdf (accessed 26 December 2018). Two particularly powerful memoirs by Guantanamo Bay prisoners are: Mohamedou Ould Slahi, *Guantánamo Diary*, Larry Siems (ed.) New York: Back Bay Books, 2015, and Murat Kurnaz with Helmut Kuhn, *Five Years of My Life: An Innocent Man in Guantanamo*, Jefferson Chase (trans.) New York: St. Martin's Press, 2009.

84 Jane Mayer, "Outsourcing Torture," *New Yorker*, 14 February 2014, 2005, and Dana Priest, "CIA Holds Terror Suspects in Secret Prisons," *Washington Post*, 2 November 2005.

85 Senate Select Committee on Intelligence, Committee Study of the Central Intelligence Agency's Detention and Interrogation Program, 2012. Online. Available at www.feinstein.senate.gov/public/index.cfm/senate-intelligence-committee-study-on-cia-detention-and-interrogation-program (accessed 26 December 2018).

86 Douglas A. Johnson, Alberto Mora, and Averell Schmidt, "The Strategic Costs of Torture: How 'Enhanced Interrogation' Hurt America," *Foreign Affairs*, 2016, 121–32.

87 Kenneth Roth, "Taking Back the Initiative from the Human Rights Spoilers. World Report 2009 Introduction," in *Human Rights Watch World Report 2009*. Online. Available at www.hrw.org/world-report/2009/country-chapters/global (accessed 26 December 2018).

88 Kenneth Roth, "Empty Promises?" *Foreign Affairs*, 2010, vol. 89, no. 2, 10–16, and Kenneth Roth, "Obama's Hesitant Embrace of Human Rights," *New York Times*, 4 March 2010.

89 For an early articulation of "principled pragmatism," see Hillary Rodham Clinton, "Remarks on the Human Rights Agenda for the twenty-first Century," 14 December 2009, Online. Available at https://2009-2017.state.gov/secretary/20092013clinton/rm/2009a/12/133544.htm (accessed 26 December 2018).

90 For analysis of civilian deaths, see Reprieve, "You Never Die Twice: Multiple Kills in the US Drone Program," n.d. Online. Available at www.reprieve.org/wp-content/uploads/2014_11_24_PUB-You-Never-Die-Twice-Multiple-Kills-in-the-US-Drone-Program-1.pdf (accessed 26 December 2018).

91 Susan E. Rice, National Security Adviser, "Promoting and Protecting LGBT Rights," Remarks at American University, 26 October 2016. Online. Available at https://obamawhitehouse.archives.gov/the-press-office/2016/10/26/remarks-national-security-advisor-susan-e-rice-american-university (accessed 26 December 2018).

PART IV

AFTER FORMAL EMPIRE AND THE COLD WAR

How human rights are practiced around the globe (1980s–2001)

18

THE UNIVERSALITY OF HUMAN RIGHTS

Early NGO practices in the Arab world

Catherine Baylin Duryea

The debate over the universality of human rights has occupied scholars and activists since even before the advent of modern human rights law. Most explorations of the topic compare human rights laws to other religious, moral, and cultural texts. This approach tells us little about how the law is used. But 70 years have passed since the adoption of the Universal Declaration of Human Rights (UDHR) and 40 years since the coming into force of the International Covenant on Civil and Political Rights (ICCPR) and the International Covenant on Economic, Social and Cultural Rights (ICESCR). We now have a powerful way to think about whether human rights are universal, by looking at how human rights have been *practiced* around the world.

The experiences of Arab human rights activists provide new insights into how human rights have been put into practice. Arab human rights organizations occupied important spaces in the international movement. Their creation in Muslim-majority states positioned them as critical voices in the debate over the compatibility of religion and human rights. Their calls for adherence to international law in countries with complex legacies of colonial interference speak to whether human rights are uniquely Western. And their continued existence in countries with egregious violations highlight the role of human rights when international law is not respected.

Drawing on interviews as well as published material and organizational archives, this essay explores the practices of several Arab human rights nongovernmental organizations (NGOs) in Palestine, Morocco, and Kuwait, as well as a regional network of NGOs based in Cairo, from the late 1970s to the early 1990s. This was a formative time, when optimism and engagement were high. All of the organizations engaged in a range of activities that are familiar to any human rights NGO, including fact-finding, public education, and report-writing. Their common commitment to international law brought access to international funding, networks, and media. However, these similarities concealed great diversity. The organizations prioritized specific rights over others, targeted different audiences, had varying levels of involvement with foreign NGOs and the United Nations (UN), and made different choices regarding membership, funding, and leadership. They used international law and institutions in fundamentally different ways to pursue goals specific to their political context. These divergences reflected domestic and regional political constraints as well as the preferences and beliefs of early activists.

Two aspects of the emerging international human rights regime proved particularly beneficial. First, the UDHR and related treaties protected the rights of individuals regardless of citizenship or status. This made human rights law an attractive framework for populations denied rights under domestic law, either formally or in practice. Communities across the Arab world, from Palestinians, to non-citizens in Kuwait, to Moroccan political dissidents, could all claim protection under international law regardless of their legal status at home. Second, human rights were separate from partisan politics. Most human rights activism takes place within NGOs, intergovernmental organizations like the UN, and in state-to-state diplomacy. Human rights provided an alternative structure for political engagement at a time when political parties were, for various reasons, increasingly ineffective. These two features of human rights law – universal application and non-partisanship – were common threads linking Arab activists with vastly different goals and priorities. Arab NGOs were not mere "local collaborators in the civilizing mission," as non-Western human rights activists have been portrayed.[1] Through their activism, these organizations demonstrate how human rights became relevant throughout the Arab world.

Activism under occupation

Palestine occupies a unique position in the history of international law and human rights. Its status as occupied territory placed it in the center of debates over colonialism and internationalized any dispute over human rights. It is perhaps no surprise, then, that one of the region's earliest and most active human rights organizations was founded here. Al Haq, which translates from Arabic to "the right" in English, was established in 1979, 12 years after Israel occupied the Palestinian territories of the West Bank and Gaza.[2] The late 1960s and 1970s witnessed high levels of violence in the occupied territories, as Palestinians resisted Israel's consolidation of power.[3] Palestinian factions also carried out a number of well-known attacks against civilians, both inside Israel and abroad. Al Haq's founders – Raja Shehadeh, Jonathan Kuttab, and Charles Shamas – were Western-educated professionals experimenting with non-violent ways of opposing the occupation. Al Haq joined labor unions, student groups, and voluntary groups already active in Palestinian society. Some of these groups were increasingly influenced by Fatah, a nationalist political party that predominated in the Palestinian Liberation Organization, but Al Haq's founders were not partisan.[4] Non-partisanship was a foundational value to the organization, and it strove to be independent of existing political affiliations. Al Haq's goal was to end the occupation by exposing its logic and character.[5] They believed human rights and humanitarian law would be effective vehicles because they held Israelis and Palestinians to international neutral standards.

In the early years, the small organization relied on the volunteer efforts of its founders. They worked out of the Shehadeh law office in the evenings and weekends. In 1980, Al Haq and the International Commission of Jurists (ICJ) published a sweeping condemnation of Israeli practices entitled *The West Bank and the Rule of Law*.[6] The book marked a new era in which human rights became the dominant discourse for discussing the Israeli – Palestinian conflict. *The West Bank and the Rule of Law* launched Al Haq into international prominence. In the 1980s, Al Haq became the preeminent human rights organization in the West Bank, eventually moving into larger premises, welcoming foreign volunteers, and hiring fieldworkers and other staff.

International law provided a useful language for Al Haq because it was a globally accepted code that put Palestinians on the same footing as Israelis. As Shamas said,

> [W]hen we made an argument, we made it in the way that was compelling to the audience, that they couldn't say no to it. And that gave us increasing legitimacy because it wasn't [that] we were our version of a human rights organization but we were their version of a defender of human rights too.[7]

Israel used law and legalism to bolster its position in the West Bank.[8] Using Israel's own approach, the founders felt, would make it harder for Israel and the international community to dismiss Palestinian claims. Human rights reporting, with its universal standards and evidence-based documentation, would have to be believed.

The West Bank and the Rule of Law was Al Haq's first effort to apply these international standards to life under Israeli occupation. The report provided a holistic account of how Israel had transformed the justice system through a system of military orders. The UN and most countries agreed that Israel was a belligerent occupier, bound by the Geneva Conventions,[9] which prohibit an occupying power from altering local laws except when necessary for the security of its forces or to implement the Conventions themselves.[10] Israel did not accept that it was legally bound by the Conventions, but it agreed to follow their "humanitarian principles" in practice.[11] Al Haq argued that under both customary international law and the Fourth Geneva Convention of 1949, Jordanian law governed the West Bank at the time of Israeli occupation,[12] so any alteration of these laws would need to be justified by Israeli security needs. Al Haq alleged that Israel violated the Geneva Conventions by issuing military orders that altered local laws to suit its purposes. By using humanitarian law as the reference point, Al Haq showed that these military orders violated international law. Invoking international law was a way to reassert control over the rules of the game.

Al Haq also documented violations of what it referred to as "restrictions on basic rights." These encompassed civil, political, and economic rights: freedom of assembly, speech, and expression; academic freedom; property rights; the right to development; and freedom of movement. Al Haq addressed both individual and communal rights, noting that

> the military occupation itself places the greatest limitation on the rule of law. As long as it continues all essential requirements of a society under the rule of law such as the right to self-determination, representative government and an independent judiciary will continue to be denied.[13]

Violations of individual rights to property, development, and "adequate government services" had communal effects. For example, Palestinians were systematically denied permits to drill new wells, curtailing agricultural activity, while Israeli settlers were granted permits. This encouraged Palestinians to seek work as unskilled laborers, increasing their dependence on Israeli agricultural products.[14] The aggregate effects on Palestinians worked to Israel's economic advantage. Al Haq used documentation to change the way the international community – specifically the UN and human rights groups in the United States and Europe – understood the occupation.

Al Haq's approach to documentation was rigorous, systematic, and rare, even among larger and more established NGOs.[15] The organization established a fieldwork unit of investigators trained in taking affidavits and gathering evidence.[16] In its first six years, Al Haq collected more than 500 individual affidavits that provided the basis for several publications that followed *The West Bank and the Rule of Law*.[17] Al Haq systematically documented killings, house demolitions, deportations, and collective punishments, as well as torture and other violations.[18] It shared technical skills and information with researchers and organizations inside and outside of Palestine. Al Haq published or jointly published nearly 20 reports throughout the 1980s on human rights violations and legal developments.[19] Its prolific publications set a pattern of well-researched, detailed reports.

Documentation was important to Al Haq beyond its use in reports; it was a way of putting the process of colonization into the historical record and into Palestinian consciousness. Founder Raja Shehadeh articulated the particular value of this type of documentation for a colonized people:

> I always worried we would get to a point where we would not know how things have ... how things turned out. We would know how things turned out but we would not know how the process that brought us to this point happened. And we would feel perplexed and confused. How did the settlements happen? How did the land get taken over? How did the Israelis re-define and change the law and so on? I was concerned that we would be confused. And I think this confusion is a big part of colonization. A colonized people's will is taken, and their mind is taken.

Shehadeh saw a role for Al Haq's human rights documentation beyond the success or failure of individual cases or even of the effort to end the occupation:

> Maybe we cannot stop this, we cannot stop them from taking the land and building settlements on it, but at least we would know how they did it. And that would be very important. And we would know and we would be able to say to them you didn't do it legally, as you claim. And this is why.[20]

Human rights reporting was a form of communal memory, of setting down events in a way that preserved the narrative. This has perhaps been one of the most important legacies of Al Haq's work, even as greater transparency about the occupation has not led to an independent Palestine.

Documentation of violations was a large part of the work of the organization, but Al Haq also carried out public education, advocacy, research, and direct legal representation. Al Haq pursued a range of educational activities to inculcate a respect for human rights and the rule of law among Palestinians.[21] The organization regularly produced "Know Your Rights" pamphlets and authored weekly newspaper columns. Staff gave public lectures on specific rights and their work as a human rights organization. Al Haq also created the first public law library in Ramallah. The organization began circulating its responses to Israeli officials and commissioned translations of works related to human rights into Arabic. By 1985, Al Haq had grown to three full-time researchers, a secretary, four part-time fieldworkers, and one part-time lawyer. Their efforts were supported by volunteers and guided by two volunteer directors and a steering committee.[22] This expansion was supported by financial grants from the Ford Foundation, which maintained a close and productive relationship with Al Haq. Al Haq also intervened on behalf of individuals. These cases included a wide range of alleged violations, from denial of a travel permit to shootings by Israeli soldiers. In a few cases, Al Haq provided direct legal services. Staff chose specific cases that would raise new issues before the courts. By providing these services, even on a limited basis, Al Haq became both an advocacy and a legal service organization.

Al Haq's activities were guided by its goals of careful documentation, public education, and targeted direct legal aid. It used the media sparingly. In 1984, Al Haq issued only two press releases – one of which was to announce one of its own publications.[23] This was a conscious strategy. Shehadeh felt there was little point to publicly condemning violations without the careful fact-checking and legal analysis that would not be possible in immediate responses to current events. Instead, Al Haq prioritized long-term investigations and attempted to resolve issues through private means before turning to public censure.[24]

The eruption of the first *intifada* (uprising) in 1987 had profound implications for Al Haq and the practice of human rights in Palestine. The *intifada* was a mass uprising of Palestinians across the political spectrum, prompting a violent response from Israeli forces. The scope and urgency of rights violations increased. Many of Al Haq's fieldworkers were imprisoned. The organization rapidly expanded its research staff and adjusted priorities in response to the changing circumstances and increased media attention. Al Haq urged the international community to pressure Israel to follow humanitarian law. It also continued to pursue ongoing relationships with international organizations to disseminate information and provide protection for the organization itself, which faced greater repression. Documentation continued to be the centerpiece of Al Haq's activities; it doubled the number of full-time fieldworkers and hired new researchers to chronicle events in Gaza in 1988.[25]

Al Haq was able to expand because it had already earned trust within both international and Palestinian communities. Throughout the 1980s, Al Haq published reports with the International Commission of Jurists and worked with other international NGOs, including the World Council of Churches. Birzeit University in Palestine relied on the expertise of Al Haq fieldworkers documenting violence against its students in 1984.[26] These long-term relationships were the basis for Al Haq's credibility through the *intifada* and into the 1990s, when the organization struggled with internal conflicts that ultimately led to a restructuring and reemergence in the late 1990s. But the foundation of Al Haq – non-partisan engagement, rigorous documentation, and scrupulous attention to the needs of Palestinians – had been established in the 1980s.

By bringing the lived Palestinian experience of occupation into legal analysis, Al Haq was able to mobilize international law in new ways. The organization challenged common knowledge about the nature of the occupation; demonstrated that it was possible to advocate for Palestinians without engaging in partisan politics; documented the process of colonization; validated Palestinian experiences; and linked individual violations to broader systems of dispossession and occupation.

The struggle for non-partisanship in Morocco

Moroccan human rights activists operated in an entirely different political context from their Palestinian counterparts. After centuries of rule by independent monarchs, Morocco was subject to colonial domination by France and Spain from 1912–56. After independence, Morocco's political scene was dominated by King Hassan II, who reigned from 1961 until his death in 1999. Though Morocco boasted a long history of contentious politics and active political parties, the economic, judicial, and political spheres had strong ties to the palace. Hassan II was "both the master player and the referee."[27] Nevertheless, the king had to contend with various groups jockeying for influence and significant political opposition. In 1965, riots in Casablanca precipitated a political standoff between the king and several political parties; the king responded by bypassing them entirely and implementing direct rule until 1970. With the parties weakened, the king found it harder to work productively with different interest groups and faced a number of attempted coups, leading to an increase in political violence and state repression. In what became known as the "Years of Lead," as many as 50,000 people were victims of state violence between the 1960s and 1980s.[28]

The constant threat of violence constrained associational activity, which was largely built around political parties. Human rights activism was limited. The earliest post-World War II human rights association, the Moroccan League for the Defense of Human Rights (LMDDH), was founded in 1972 in affiliation with the Istiqlal (Independence) party.[29] The group observed political trials and published reports on unfair trials of opposition members.[30] When the Moroccan Association for Human Rights (AMDH) joined the scene in 1979, it was closely tied to a Socialist party with roots in Istiqlal.[31] AMDH's ability to operate was linked with the rising and falling fortunes of the party. AMDH was essentially shut down after 1983, when the state twice banned it from holding a general meeting and arrested the most active members.[32] Both AMDH and LMDDH had only modest accomplishments until the late 1980s because of the extent of government repression.

AMDH was not a typical human rights NGO. Unlike most national human rights organizations, which worked out of a headquarters in the capital city, AMDH created chapters around the country. In its early years, AMDH founded chapters in 13 cities. In contrast with Al Haq, many AMDH volunteers did not have legal training, and the organization relied on mass membership rather than elite staff. Though there were some parallels with Amnesty International, AMDH owes its organizational structure to the previous political and union experiences of its early members.[33] At this stage, AMDH focused on the rights of prisoners because many members had relatives in prison or were imprisoned themselves for political activity.[34] Founding members were also motivated by human rights abuses in Palestine, a politically safe topic which LMDDH and AMDH addressed more frequently than domestic events.[35] Self-determination was a central principle of AMDH from its early days. AMDH also organized some activities around the rights of women and supported women's groups. Even these limited activities stopped after the government crackdown in 1983.

The late 1980s and early 1990s were a time of great change in the Moroccan political scene. The interdependence between political parties and associations began to lessen. More organizations were formed that were not subjugated to a particular party.[36] With LMDDH and AMDH essentially defunct in the mid-1980s, the human rights space was wide open. Political elites came together to form the Moroccan Organization for Human Rights (OMDH), a new organization committed to human rights and non-partisan activism. Noting the limitations of AMDH and LMDDH because of their partisan connections, this group took pains to stress its independence. Members were recruited based on their commitment to the non-partisan advocacy of human rights.[37] In practice, this meant that OMDH balanced politically affiliated members with those who had no partisan ties. Non-partisanship was both an ideological commitment and a survival strategy, as the earlier organizations had been hindered by the political ties of their members.

Limiting party ties did not provide immunity from state interference, however. The state prohibited OMDH from hosting a public launch in May, June, and September 1988.[38] After negotiations with government officials, OMDH was finally permitted to hold its opening meeting on 10 December 1988, the anniversary of the adoption of the UDHR. OMDH began with a rush of activity and enthusiasm.[39] Within its first 100 days, the organization launched a number of projects to win the release of political prisoners, improve the status of prisons, and align legislation with international legal standards. OMDH leadership engaged the minister of justice repeatedly, asking for permission to visit prisoners and calling for action on specific cases.[40] The organization also began to prepare a list of all political prisoners so it could credibly counter the state's claim that Morocco held none.

From the outset, OMDH sought to publicize human rights violations in both the domestic and the international press. It forged connections with other human rights organizations through regional networks.[41] It quickly joined a regional network of national Arab NGOs and created a new North African network alongside groups in Tunisia and Algeria. The North African network proved fruitful, and the groups continued to meet and issue joint statements over the coming years. International ties, however, proved more problematic. The young organization quickly faced an internal conflict that threatened its ability to operate as a non-partisan force. In 1989, OMDH was considering affiliating with the International Federation of Human Rights (FIDH), a Paris-based association of human rights NGOs. FIDH and Madhi el Mandjra, OMDH's founding president, had irreconcilable differences. When the National Bureau of OMDH decided to join the network anyway, Mandjra resigned.[42] Mandjra's resignation necessitated changes in leadership and, with his departure, OMDH lost some of its non-partisan orientation. Realizing that this conflict constituted a crisis for the organization, the National Council called on members to prioritize internal questions over relations with international bodies to "safeguard the unity and cohesion of OMDH."[43]

After a slowdown in work resulting from this upheaval, OMDH continued to document human rights abuses and petition the government for their redress. Perhaps the most notable early accomplishment was the compilation of the list of political prisoners. In July 1989, only seven months after its opening meeting, OMDH published a list of 226 political prisoners with details of their locations and length of detention.[44] Through the 1990s, the organization continued to address political prisoners, torture, and violations of the right to assemble and freedom of the press. It took stances on international affairs, including executions in Sudan, the occupation of Palestine, and the American involvement in the first Gulf War (1990–1). It published press releases, issued short reports, held meetings with other NGOs, and organized occasional protests.

Though it was quite active, OMDH posed less of a threat to the monarchy than the earlier human rights organizations had in the 1970s. It was not overly combative in strategy, ideology, or membership. In general, OMDH did not oppose the legitimacy of the state.[45] Its members came from elite social classes, who were less likely to call for revolutionary change. Its primary activities – research, lobbying, and hosting conferences – did not engage with the bulk of the Moroccan population. Mass mobilization or political challenges to the monarchy were simply outside the scope of its work. In fact, OMDH worked in collaboration with the state from its early days. In 1990, the king created a governmental advisory council that became the National Human Rights Council

(CCDH). A representative of OMDH participated in the Council, a decision that the organization felt the need to justify publicly.[46]

The successful launch of OMDH signaled to the older human rights organizations that the political winds had shifted. Facing great internal and external pressure, King Hassan extended greater tolerance for domestic human rights NGOs. Some of the worst human rights violations were curtailed, and dozens of political prisoners were released. Serious human rights abuses continued, but there was meaningful change.[47] The revival in human rights activism owed a great deal to changes on the international scene. Increasingly oriented towards the West, King Hassan was invested in presenting a tolerant, pro-human rights stance towards his international allies.

In this new environment, AMDH and LMDDH reentered the public sphere. In 1989, AMDH held a small congress that established a new leadership and mobilized internally. In 1991, it held a much larger congress where the organization defined what would become its core values: commitment to human rights in their entirety and mass activism. This congress was the beginning of a new era for the organization. It reorganized to better reflect its values, including implementing quotas for the participation of women and young people.

AMDH's commitment to mass activism continued to set it apart from other human rights NGOs, in Morocco and internationally. This was a particular point of pride for its members. As one early member noted: "Human rights did not fall from the sky. Elites cannot assert human rights. It's the masses, and masses that are organized and trained."[48] In order to organize and train these masses, AMDH established a large, membership-based organization that could function around the country. As Abdelhamid Amine, former president of AMDH, stated:

> Human rights are first an action of … the people who suffer the most violation of human rights. So it is necessary to go to those people, endowed with the necessity of having an organization, a large organization … [with] many sections that represent all over Morocco.[49]

AMDH grew throughout the 1990s and 2000s until it consisted of dozens of chapters with thousands of members.

This structure gave AMDH a fundamentally different character from OMDH and from most other human rights organizations. Members paid dues and volunteered their time, so while AMDH has had outside funding for individual events like conferences, it was largely self-funded. Most did not make human rights work their profession. Rather than lead from above, AMDH strove to integrate human rights into the fabric of everyday life. Human rights education was a key element of the organization's work. It focused on domestic affairs, educating Moroccans and pressuring the Moroccan government for change. Unlike both OMDH and Al Haq, which often published material in Arabic and French or English, respectively, AMDH publications were primarily in Arabic with only a smattering of French. Individual activists were in contact with Amnesty International, the Tunisian League for Human Rights, and other NGOs, but it was not until the 1990s and into the 2000s that AMDH began to build robust official partnerships with foreign and international organizations. In some cases, this international engagement was in response to OMDH. Though the two organizations frequently worked together and issued joint letters, they often had different perspectives on human rights in Morocco. AMDH did not want OMDH to be the sole voice speaking for the country in international networks, so it stepped up its international engagement.[50]

In addition to mass activism, the other broad motivating principle for AMDH was the universality of human rights. For AMDH, this meant endorsing all principles of international human rights law. As a matter of ideology, AMDH did not pick and choose which rights were applicable to Morocco or, at the theoretical level at least, which rights deserved their focus. In practice, it was impossible to address every human rights issue at once. From its origins in activism for political prisoners, AMDH expanded into other civil and political rights and then eventually into economic and social rights. This commitment to embracing *all* of human rights law created both internal and external challenges. For example, in the early 1990s the central bureau learned that one of the section presidents had two wives. The leadership believed that polygamy violated the concept of equality between men and women, but they were divided about how to respond. Gender equality was a foundational pillar of the organization, and it had quotas to ensure representation of women in both membership and leadership. In the end, a compromise was reached where the section president was permitted to resign without being officially expelled, but this situation illustrated how the organization's commitment to all principles of international law – not just those widely endorsed in Morocco – could lead to disputes.[51]

Human rights activism looked quite different at OMDH and AMDH, but they took advantage of the rights framework for many of the same reasons. Human rights in Morocco served some of the same purposes as in Palestine. In theory, at least, human rights provided a non-partisan space for political engagement. NGOs, particularly AMDH because of its mass membership, presented a way to mobilize citizens outside of the ineffective party framework. But, unlike in Palestine, in Morocco the major players were members of political parties. Moroccan organizations struggled to maintain a non-partisan reputation and faced criticism for being political. The organizations took pains to distinguish their positions from those of political parties, but party affiliations hindered their ability to create independent identities and imported partisan disputes into the NGOs. The organizations struggle to this day to demonstrate that they are independent of party interests. Partisan ties also opened OMDH to issues of co-optation, as several members moved into government positions.

As in Palestine, the international human rights framework provided Moroccan NGOs with a common language readily understood by foreign audiences. International NGOs, foreign governments, and the foreign press all put pressure on the king to change state practices at a time when the king was trying to build his international reputation. The interest of the French press in Moroccan affairs assured that the monarch could not escape international attention. The Parisian newspaper *Le Monde* extensively covered OMDH's activities, and Amnesty International published a long report on imprisonment, disappearances, and torture in 1991.[52] This synergy between national and foreign organizations had significant impact on the king's decision to create the CCDH, close secret prisons, and reign in some egregious abuses. These steps towards expanding the public space to criticize the state reinforced the monarch's legitimacy internationally and domestically.[53]

Human rights filled an additional purpose in Morocco; they allowed activists to assert their identity as citizens, rather than subjects, in a way that did not directly call for overthrowing the king. The NGOs created a discourse around human rights that embraced democracy – and, in the case of AMDH, socialism – without explicitly calling for an end to the monarchy. Human rights, particularly the political and civil rights enshrined in the ICCPR, are most easily accommodated within a liberal democracy with strong legal protections for individual rights. But any regime can move closer to conformity with human rights law, particularly regarding prisoners and treatment of detainees. Imprisonment and torture, however, were integral to the monarchy's strategy for asserting control over opposition during the Years of Lead. Criticism of those strategies as human rights violations is not, on its face, a call for revolution, but it chipped away at the ability of the king to control his subjects and threatened his legitimacy on the international stage.

The Kuwait Society for Human Rights

The Kuwait Society for Human Rights (KSHR) illustrates another facet of the varied human rights landscape in the Arab World. The Kuwaiti organization was built around a charismatic founder, and it proved less radical than its Moroccan and Palestinian counterparts. Though the countries of the Arabian Peninsula are often perceived as despotic and autocratic, Kuwait is noted for its history of relatively open interactions between the government and society.[54] The constitution of 1963 called for legislative authority to be held jointly by an *amir*, drawn from the powerful al-Sabah family, and an elected National Assembly. The *amir* and the Assembly engaged in frequent power struggles throughout the 1970s and 1980s. The Assembly challenged the *amir* on government corruption, oil nationalization, and expenditures, leading the *amir* to repeatedly dissolve the constitutional body and exceed his constitutional authority.[55] The *amir* was often described as the head of the Kuwaiti family, distributing resources and commanding deference.[56] His considerable power was rooted in history, culture, and oil. Kuwait's economy revolved around oil revenue that funded subsidies to citizens, including free education, guaranteed employment, and generous social services.[57] These entitlements left Kuwaitis with bonds of loyalty to the state that were reinforced through the media and education.[58]

The state also supported the development of relatively independent organizations to organize, and arguably to better control, various segments of society.[59] Educated Kuwaitis were encouraged to create women's and professional associations in the 1960s.[60] Many of these early associations benefited from state subsidies, though they operated semi-autonomously. These organizations fostered the development of a national Kuwaiti identity through charity projects, social ties, and political activity. Though not part of the state apparatus, they often took a collaborative approach towards working with the government to solve problems.

Human rights organizations, however, were not among these state-sponsored groups. Human rights activism in Kuwait began in earnest in the 1980s under the umbrella of Amnesty International. Political scientist Ghanim al-Najjar joined the organization as a doctoral student in the United Kingdom and created a Kuwaiti branch when he returned home as a professor. At the time, local branches did not advocate for issues in their home countries, but the group held awareness-raising events such as art exhibits.[61] Amnesty International began expressing concern about Kuwaiti political prisoners and executions in the mid-1980s.[62] The local Amnesty branch faded away after the Iraqi invasion of Kuwait when al-Najjar decided to step away from a leadership position.

The oldest active Kuwaiti human rights NGO launched under the patronage of Jasim al-Qatami, the "godfather" of the Kuwaiti human rights movement.[63] Al-Qatami was a long-standing member of the political opposition and a staunch Arab nationalist. Arab pan-nationalism is a broad political ideology that recognizes the shared identity of Arabs across the region. Some Arab nationalists supported political unity of Arab states while others advanced cultural and social integration. Al-Qatami was part of a network that created the first regional umbrella organization for Arab human rights NGOs. The Arab Organization for Human Rights (AOHR) coordinated documentation, advocacy, and international relations. AOHR grew out of a meeting of pro-democracy Arab nationalists in Hammamat, Tunisia in 1983. At that meeting, 35 activists agreed to a short Declaration noting that democracy had been suppressed in the Arab world in the name of every other political goal – socialism, economic development, Arab unity, and opposition to Israel. They called for democracy as both a desirable end in itself and as a prerequisite for these goals. With the UDHR as their reference point, they focused primarily on civil and political rights but noted social and cultural repression. They specifically mentioned three concerning practices: political prisoners, extralegal courts and emergency laws, and secret police. With this Declaration as their guiding document, the group held another meeting in Cyprus after several Arab governments denied them permission to meet within their borders. Egypt eventually allowed AOHR to set up headquarters in Cairo. AOHR was a gathering place for political elites, and it focused on high-level organizing and documentation rather than grassroots mobilization or education. It organized conferences, published reports, and engaged with the UN. It brought together existing groups and encouraged the creation of new ones.

Several Kuwaitis attended the meeting in Cyprus, including al-Qatami and Suad al-Sabah, a member of the ruling family who became one of the patrons of AOHR. These individuals formed a local chapter, which eventually became the Kuwait Society for Human Rights. Though KSHR became an independent organization in 1993, it kept close ties with AOHR. Some Kuwaitis occupied leadership positions in both organizations. The relationship between AOHR and its Kuwaiti chapter was mutually beneficial. Financial support from Kuwaitis helped AOHR maintain its independence. The regional profile provided KSHR with some protection from repression by the *amir*. Al-Qatami's stature in Kuwait provided the most powerful shield, however. Unlike the Moroccan and Palestinian organizations, KSHR relied heavily on the stature of an individual founder.

KSHR's activities in the 1980s were limited. It held general meetings and promoted publications of AOHR.[64] The organization functioned more as a loose band of individuals who shared a political persuasion. Human rights, particularly under the auspices of a regional Arab umbrella organization, appealed to left-leaning elites after Arab nationalism suffered a blow with Israel's defeat of Egypt, Jordan, and Syria in the 1967 war. Membership in KSHR was effectively limited to those with a connection or similar political interests as the founders.[65] It did not develop a mass social base.

The 1980s saw a rise in human rights violations as the ruling family faced increasing political demands and economic pressures due to the oil price crash in 1986. The oil boom had led to the creation of a tiered society of citizens and non-citizens, which fundamentally altered the work of civil society organizations, sparked the creation of new NGOs, and became the basis for the major human rights issues of the next two decades. Benefits of citizenship did not extend to several categories of Kuwaiti residents: women, expatriate workers, and stateless residents (known as the Bedoon, which means "without" in Arabic).

Kuwaiti women did not have full citizenship rights. They could not vote, run for elected office, or pass their nationality down to their children. The children of Kuwaiti women married to non-citizens were not eligible for the social benefits afforded to Kuwaitis, and even their right to remain in the country was not protected. Kuwaiti women's organizations took up these issues. Though they largely reaffirmed patriarchal notions of women's roles, in a few instances they raised meaningful protest.[66] Their efforts were primarily based on the Kuwaiti constitution, not international law, though they worked in concert with the burgeoning human rights movement.[67]

Bedoons and expatriates could not rely on the constitution to guarantee their rights. Before the mid-1980s, Bedoons were eligible for education and employment like citizens. But beginning in 1986, the Bedoon were increasingly treated like expatriates, who made up a large percentage of the workforce in Kuwait.[68] Because of the subsidies provided to Kuwaiti citizens, much of the manual and technical labor in Kuwait is provided by third-party nationals. Bedoons and expatriates were often long-term residents who only knew life in Kuwait, but Bedoons were distinct because they had no other country of citizenship. Some Bedoon were children of Kuwaiti mothers and non-citizen fathers; others were from families who lived in Kuwait for generations but were excluded from citizen registration. By refusing to recognize them, Kuwait created a class of stateless people who fell outside many of the protections granted through Kuwaiti law. Expatriate workers also received only limited protections and were often subject to abusive work conditions. Bedoons and expatriates were particularly vulnerable to abuse after the Iraqi invasion of Kuwait in 1990. Iraq occupied Kuwait for seven months before being expelled by American forces. Some expatriates and Bedoon were suspected of collaborating with Iraqis during the occupation. After Iraqi forces were expelled, Kuwaiti security forces took revenge against members of these populations through extrajudicial killings, disappearances, torture, and expulsion, according to Human Rights Watch.[69]

A number of organizations, many of which had been formed to advocate for Kuwaitis detained by Iraq, took up the issue of mistreatment after the occupation. The Kuwaiti Association to Defend War Victims had become something of a home base for other human rights organizations. It had support from the government because it was working for Kuwaiti prisoners of war (POWs), but eventually the government faced criticism for its handling of POWs and retaliated against human rights organizations. In August 1993, the government shut down all unlicensed organizations, specifically targeting human rights groups that were either new or had been unable to register.[70]

The Association to Defend War Victims stepped back from public advocacy but continued to lobby behind the scenes.[71] KSHR was able to continue operations under the auspices of the Graduates Society, another NGO registered in the 1960s that was less subject to suppression by the government. In December 1992, KSHR established its own leadership, independent of AOHR. It called for addressing all human rights abuses against both Kuwaitis and foreigners.[72] KSHR engaged on both the national and international level. At the 1993 World Conference on Human Rights sponsored by the United Nations High Commissioner in Vienna, Austria, Al-Qatami and a delegation from Kuwait spoke about Indigenous people's rights, among other issues, and called for Iraq to release Kuwaiti prisoners of war.[73] Domestically, members of KSHR who were also elected officials worked to establish a permanent human rights committee within parliament. Al-Qatami advocated for rights education in schools, and the organization sponsored a number of exhibitions about human rights.[74] The organization published Kuwaiti legislation and commentary related to human rights.

Though it supported some controversial positions, KSHR took a collaborative approach towards working within existing systems. Like OMDH in Morocco, several of its leaders were well connected in the government and its elite membership did not pose a great threat to the regime. Nevertheless, KSHR does not fit the mold of "collaborator," nor could it be considered a neo-colonial organization or window dressing. Its funding was local, its (non-Arab) international connections were minimal, and it engaged in meaningful work that was controversial within some aspects of Kuwaiti society, particularly regarding Bedoons. Part of this is a product of the political culture in Kuwait, which is a small country where personal relationships and social ties are particularly important in political advocacy. As in Morocco and Palestine, human rights provided a non-partisan way for activists to challenge state action without necessarily posing an existential threat to the government.

Conclusion

This essay began by posing the question of whether human rights are universal. Taking the practice of human rights, rather than its foundational texts, as the object of inquiry allows us to use the lived experiences of human rights activists to reformulate this question. Instead of asking whether human rights are compatible with Islam, we can ask how and why Muslim activists, and other activists operating within Muslim-majority countries, understood, interpreted, and applied human rights in their political, religious, and cultural contexts. Instead of asking are human rights Western, we can explore how activists in non-Western countries have used human rights to advance specific political goals. And instead of asking are human rights universal, we can analyze how and why activists in vastly different contexts chose human rights law as an organizing principle. These questions reveal far more about the practice, relevance, and impact of human rights.

Palestine, Morocco, and Kuwait illustrate that human rights activism shared several common purposes. Forming a human rights NGO was a way to engage in politics without parties. Rights language made calls for equal treatment a matter of fundamental values, rather than political jockeying. Rejecting explicit partisan connections freed human rights activists to take positions consistent with international law that might be too unpopular for a party to endorse. They also allowed NGOs to criticize the parties themselves and to build coalitions among political opponents. Another value of the human rights framework, particularly for the Palestinians and non-citizens in Kuwait, lay in their ability to put all individuals on an equal playing field with equal claims to citizenship.

The legacy of Arab human rights organizations is complex. Israel still occupies Palestine. The Moroccan government is not democratic. The Bedoon have not obtained Kuwaiti citizenship. NGOs were not at the forefront of the protests across the Arab world in 2011.[75] With some exceptions (notably, AMDH in Morocco) Arab NGOs did not develop large social bases of support and struggled to achieve their most expansive goals.[76] But the continued prevalence of human rights violations does not suggest that human rights are inapplicable to the Arab world. Rather, the stories of Arab human rights activists illustrate that human rights can be made universally relevant through practice.

Acknowledgment

I would like to thank Hadil Mofadal of the American University in Kuwait for her very helpful research assistance. All translations, and errors, are my own.

Notes

1 Macau Mutua, *Human Rights: A Political and Cultural Critique*, Philadelphia: University of Pennsylvania Press, 2002, p. 38.

2 The organization was initially called Law in the Service of Man but later went by Al Haq. For clarity, I will refer to the organization as Al Haq throughout. For an excellent overview of the early years of Al Haq, see "The First Human Rights NGO: Al-Haq's Faith in Evidence," in Lori Allen (ed.) *The Rise and Fall of Human Rights: Cynicism and Politics in Occupied Palestine*, Stanford, CA: Stanford University Press, 2013, pp. 33–64.

3 Neve Gordan, *Israel's Occupation*, Berkeley: University of California Press, 2008, pp. 51–5.

4 Muhammad Muslih, "Palestinian Civil Society," *Middle East Journal*, 1993, vol. 47, 262.

5 Interview with Raja Shehadeh, Ramallah, 15 December 2015.

6 The ICJ is an international organization founded in the early 1950s to advance human rights and the rule of law with a particular focus on the role of judges. For a history of the ICJ, including its early ties to the CIA and early advocacy for social and economic rights, see Howard Tolley, *The International Commission of Jurists: Global Advocates for Human Rights*, Philadelphia: University of Pennsylvania Press, 1994, and Yves Dezalay and Bryant Garth, *The Internationalization of Palace Wars: Lawyers, Economists, and the Contest to Transform Latin American States*, Chicago: University of Chicago Press, 2002.

7 Interview with Charles Shamas, East Jerusalem, 22 December 2015.

8 "Legal Discourses and the Conflict in Israel/Palestine," in Lisa Hajjar (ed.) *Courting Conflict: The Israeli Military Court System in the West Bank and Gaza*, Berkeley: University of California Press, 2005, pp. 49–78.

9 This was first affirmed in Security Council Resolution 237 (1967), passed four days after the war, and reaffirmed several times since then.

10 Article 64 of the Fourth Geneva Convention reads:

"The penal laws of the occupied territory shall remain in force, with the exception that they may be repealed or suspended by the Occupying Power in cases where they constitute a threat to its security or an obstacle to the application of the present Convention.

Subject to the latter consideration and to the necessity for ensuring the effective administration of justice, the tribunals of the occupied territory shall continue to function in respect of all offences covered by the said laws.

The Occupying Power may, however, subject the population of the occupied territory to provisions that are essential to enable the Occupying Power to fulfil its obligations under the present Convention, to maintain the orderly government of the territory, and to ensure the security of the Occupying Power, of the members and property of the occupying forces or administration, and likewise of the establishments and lines of communication used by them."

11 The seminal position is that of Meir Shamgar, the architect of the legal system in the West Bank after the 1967 War and future Israeli attorney general and president of the Supreme Court. Shamgar, "The Observance of International Law in the Administered Territories," *Israel Yearbook on Human Rights*, 1971, vol. 1, 262–77. Further support is found in the proclamations of General Chaim Herzog towards the end of the war. Proclamation No. 2, the Law and Administration Ordinance, stated that existing laws would remain in force "subject to such modifications as may result from the establishment of the rule of the I.D.F. in the area." This statement conforms to the Fourth Geneva Convention, though it does not invoke it by name. For a full translation of the Proclamation, see Esther Rosalind Cohen, *Human Rights in the Israeli-Occupied Territories, 1967–1983*, Manchester: Manchester University Press, 1986, p. 93. Proclamation No. 3, Orders and Appointments of Israel Defense Forces in Judea and Samaria, initially stated that the Geneva Convention would take precedence over Israeli security legislation, but this provision was deleted via a further proclamation in October of 1967. Allan

Gerson, *Israel, the West Bank and International Law*, London: Frank Cass & Company, 1978, p. 111. For a more detailed discussion of the official Israeli position on the applicability of the Fourth Geneva Convention, see Adam Roberts, "Prolonged Military Occupation: The Israeli-Occupied Territories Since 1967," *American Journal of International Law*, 1990, vol. 84, 62–6.

12 This was not a universally accepted position within Israel. See Cohen, *Human Rights*, p. 94.

13 Raja Shehadeh, and Jonathan Kuttab, *The West Bank and the Rule of Law*, Geneva: International Commission of Jurists and Law in the Service of Man, 1980, p. 11.

14 Shehadeh and Kuttab, *The West Bank*, p. 66.

15 Diane Orentlicher, "Bearing Witness: The Art and Science of Human Rights Fact-Finding," *Harvard Human Rights Journal*, 1990, vol. 3, 85.

16 Fatih Samih Azzam, "Waiting for Justice: Al-Haq in 2004: A Twenty-Five Year Prospective," in Rouba Al-Salem (ed.) *Al-Haq: 25 Years Defending Human Rights (1979–2004): Waiting for Justice*, Ramallah: Al-Haq, 2005, p. 6.

17 Rockefeller Archive Center, in Sleepy Hollow, New York, USA (hereafter RAC), Ford Foundation Records, Law in the Service of Man, *Annual Report*, 1984, p. 3, Frames 001541–001548, Reel 7240.

18 Interview with Shawan Jabarin, Ramallah, 21 December 2015.

19 Law in the Service of Man, *Annual Report*, 1984, p. 3.

20 Interview with Shehadeh, 2015.

21 Interview with Shamas, 2015.

22 Law in the Service of Man, *Annual Report*, 1984, pp. 1–5.

23 Law in the Service of Man, *Annual Report*, 1984, p. 2.

24 Interview with Shehadeh, 2015.

25 RAC, Ford Foundation Records, Al Haq, *Summary of Program Strategy 1989–1990*, pp. 1–5, Frames 001390–001395, Reel 7240.

26 Law in the Service of Man, *Annual Report*, 1984, p. 3.

27 Susan Waltz, *Human Rights and Reform: Changing the Face of North African Politics*, Berkeley: University of California Press, 1995, p. 117.

28 Fadoua Loudly, *Transitional Justice and Human Rights in Morocco: Negotiating the Years of Lead*, New York: Routledge, 2014, p. 73.

29 Like most Moroccan organizations, LMDDH is known by the acronym for its French name, *La Ligue Marocaine de Défense des Droits de l'Homme.*

30 James Sater, *Civil Society and Political Change in Morocco*, New York: Routledge, 2007, p. 43.

31 El-Hussein A'boushi, "The Socialist Union of Popular Forces Party in Morocco," in Myriam Catusse and Karam Karam (eds.) *A Return to Partisan Politics? Partisan Logics and Political Transformations in the Arab World*, Beirut: Lebanese Center for Policy Studies, 2010, p. 145.

32 "Lamḥa ʿan Tārīkh al-Jamʿiyya" [About the History of the Organization], in *Wathāʾiq Marjiʿiyya* [*Reference Documents*], Salah, Morocco: The Moroccan Association for Human Rights, 2014, p. 14.

33 Interview with Abdelhamid Amine, Rabat, 1 October 2015; "About the History of the Organization," p. 14.

34 Interview with Amine, 2015.

35 Susan Waltz, "Making Waves: The Political Impact of Human Rights Groups in North Africa," *Journal of Modern African Studies*, 1991, vol. 29, 486.

36 Sater, *Civil Society*, pp. 52–3.

37 "Rapport de la Commission Preparatoire présenté au Congrès Constitutif de l'O. M. D. H. le 10 Décembre 1988," in *L'Organisation Marocaine des Droits de l'Homme à travers ses Communiqués et Déclarations: Mai 1988–Mars 1991*, Casablanca: Editions Imprimerie, 1991, p. 24.

38 "Pour la trosième [*sic*] fois … L'Assemblée est interdite" [For the Third Time … the Assembly is Prohibited], Preparatory Committee, Rabat, 16 September 1988, in *L'Organisation Marocaine des Droits de l'Homme à travers ses Communiqués et Déclarations*, p. 15.

39 Waltz, "Making Waves," 491.

40 "Baiyān bi-Munāsaba Murūr ١٠٠ Yaum ʿalā Taʾsīs al-Munaẓama" [Statement on the Occasion of 100 Days Since the Founding of the Organization], OMDH National Office, Rabat, 20 March 1989.

41 Email correspondence with Abdelaziz Bennani, 2016; "Affiliation à l'Organisation Arabe des Droits de l'Homme," and "Déclaration d'Algier sur le Maghreb des Droits de l'Homme" [Algiers Declaration on Human Rights in the Maghreb], in *L'Organisation Marocaine des Droits de l'Homme à travers ses Communiqués et Déclarations*, pp. 34–7.
42 Waltz, "Making Waves," 493.
43 "Le Conseil National Précise sa Position sur l'Affiliation à la FIDH et sur les Rencontres avec le Gouvernement," 7 October 1989, in *L'Organisation Marocaine des Droits de l'Homme à travers ses Communiqués et Déclarations*, p. 81.
44 "Présentation du Dossier de Presse relative aux Prisonniers Politiques," Preparatory Committee, Rabat, July 1989, in *L'Organisation Marocaine des Droits de l'Homme à travers ses Communiqués et Déclarations*, p. 68.
45 Sater, *Civil Society*, pp. 55–6.
46 "Poirquoi l'O. M. D. H. participe au Conseil Consultatif des Droits de l'Homme," 7 May 1990, in *L'Organisation Marocaine des Droits de l'Homme à travers ses Communiqués et Déclarations*, pp. 95–7.
47 "Human Rights in Morocco," *Human Rights Watch*, October 1995, vol. 7, no. 6, 8–9.
48 Interview with Esslemi Abdelhafid, Rabat, 7 September 2015.
49 Interview with Amine, 2015.
50 Interview with Khadija Riyadi, Rabat, 1 October 2015.
51 Interview with Amine, 2015.
52 Amnesty International, *Morocco: A Pattern of Imprisonment, Disappearances, and Torture*, 1 March 1991, Index No. MDE 29/001/1991. Online. Available at www.amnesty.org/en/documents/mde29/001/1991/en (accessed 15 January 2019).
53 Sater, *Civil Society*, p. 77.
54 Mary Ann Tétreault, *Stories of Democracy: Politics and Society in Contemporary Kuwait*, New York: Columbia University Press, 2000, pp. 59–75.
55 Tétreault, *Stories of Democracy*, p. 67; Neil Hicks and Ghanim al-Najjar, "The Utility of Tradition: Civil Society in Kuwait," in Augustus Richard Norton (ed.) *Civil Society in the Middle East*, vol. 1, Leiden: E. J. Brill, 1995, pp. 189–91.
56 Tétreault, *Stories of Democracy*, p. 67.
57 Mary Ann Tétreault and Haya al-Mughni, "Gender, Citizenship and Nationalism in Kuwait," *British Society for Middle Eastern Studies*, 1995, vol. 22, 70.
58 Jill Crystal, *Kuwait: The Transformation of an Oil State*, Boulder, CO: Westview Press, 1992, pp. 70–1.
59 Hicks and al-Najjar, "The Utility of Tradition," p. 187.
60 Interview with Lulwa al-Mullah, Kuwait, 23 February 2016.
61 Interview with Ghanim al-Najjar, Kuwait, 18 April 2016.
62 Crystal, *Kuwait*, p. 171.
63 Interview with Maha Alburges, Kuwait, 19 April 2016.
64 Al-Jam'iyya al-Kuwaitiyya li-Huqūq al-Insān far' al-Kuwait [Arab Organization for Human Rights – Kuwait Branch], *al-Taqrīr al-Sanawi* ١٩٩٣ (*Annual Report 1993*). Al Wazzan International Press, 1993, p. 6.
65 Interview with al-Najjar, 2016.
66 Haya al-Mughni, "Women's Movements and the Autonomy of Civil Society in Kuwait," in Robin L. Teske and Mary Ann Tétreault (eds.) *Conscious Acts and the Politics of Social Change*, Columbia: University of South Carolina Press, 2000, p. 173, 176.
67 Interview with Lulwa Al-Qatami, Kuwait, 24 February 2016.
68 Amnesty International, "The 'Withouts' of Kuwait: Nationality for Stateless Bidun Now," 16 September 2013. Online. Available at www.amnesty.org/en/documents/mde17/001/2013/en/ (accessed 15 January 2019).
69 Aziz Abu-Hamad, *A Victory Turned Sour: Human Rights in Kuwait Since Liberation*, New York: Human Rights Watch, 1991.
70 Aziz Abu-Hamad and Andrew Whitley, *Kuwait Closes All Human Rights Organizations*, New York: Middle East Watch, 1993.
71 Interview with al-Najjar, 2016.

72 "Al-Jam'iyya al-Kuwaitiyya li-Huqūq al-Insān Ta'qid Ijtamā'hā al-Ta'sīsī wa Tantakhib Jasim al-Qatami ra'īs" [The Kuwait Society for Human Rights Held Its Founding Meeting and Elected Jasim Al-Qatami President], *Al Amal Magazine*, 31 March 1993.
73 "Al-Qatami Yughādir ilā Vienna" [Al-Qatami Leaves for Vienna], *al Qabas*, 12 June 1993.
74 Faril Al-Ataar, "Aḥzābuna tunādī bi-l-dīmaqrāṭiyya ... wa tuṭabiq al-diktātūriyya" [Our Parties Call for Democracy ... and Apply Dictatorship], *al-Qabas*, 16 February 1994.
75 Mohamed Hussein El Naggar, "Human Rights Organizations and the Egyptian Revolution," *Institute of Development Studies Bulletin*, 2012, vol. 43, 83–4.
76 See generally Vickie Langohr, "Too Much Civil Society, Too Little Politics: Egypt and Liberalizing Arab Regimes," *Comparative Politics*, 2004, vol. 36, 181–204.

19

HOW WOMEN BECOME HUMAN

Chilean contributions to women's human rights from dictatorship to the twenty-first century

Jadwiga E. Pieper Mooney

In a recent memoir, Chilean domestic worker Aída Moreno recollects details of her life as a union leader. She campaigned for the rights of female domestic workers since the 1950s, first in Chile and later in other Latin American countries as well. Moreno dedicates her leadership "to the poor, those who have always been marginalized and deprived of their rights."[1] She recalls that the workers' movement made a breakthrough under the government of President Salvador Allende's Unidad Popular (Popular Unity, a coalition of Socialist, Communist, and other political parties of the left, 1970–3), which placed union leaders in significant management positions. From her perspective, the military that ousted Allende in 1973 resorted to excruciating violence not only "to silence and frighten these 'poor and ignorant' [workers]," but also because "many people did not accept that the 'rotos' [poor workers, literally "the broken ones"] had the audacity to feel human."[2] Moreno became part of an international network that united trade union leaders, feminist activists, and academics – and offers a glimpse of the complexities of women's collaboration in struggles for rights in the 1970s and 1980s. The experiences of individual women like Moreno, and their multiple collaborations with networks inside the state and transnationally, are vital for understanding women's interventions into human rights debates.

Universal claims about an individual's humanity have long been tied to claims of entitlements to rights.[3] Who deserves to be called human, and who is to say? Aída Moreno, cited above, emphasizes the less-than-human treatment of the poor in twentieth-century Chile and recalls that this changed under the Unidad Popular, only to reappear under military dictatorship. Moreno's work as a union leader for domestic workers, often rural or Indigenous women, showed her how gender, ethnicity, and class appeared to legitimize individuals' "natural" marginalization as people with fewer rights: There are those who think that those who are born poor have no alternative but to remain poor because they were born limited.

I place Chilean women's rights activism in the context of changing international human rights paradigms, evident in such markers as the 1948 Universal Declaration of Human Rights (UDHR) that promised equal rights between the sexes, and the 1979 Convention on the Elimination of All Forms of Discrimination against Women (CEDAW) that set the agenda of "achieving gender equality" and increased attention to gender norms and hierarchies as a distinct category of violation.[4] International legislation did not resolve the uncertainties about the relationship between women's rights and human rights, but it did create spaces for women's active contributions to new practices of rights.[5] The success of the UDHR and CEDAW, standard bearers on international level, hinged on effective human rights initiatives inside states, on national leaders who would ratify international conventions, and on strategies that would ensure accountability. In Chile, international human rights paradigms strengthened the legitimacy of human rights demands; women's interventions sought to expand such rights to make women human.

This essay traces Chilean women's interventions into human rights debates and presents evidence for three related claims: first, women's human rights activism in Chile arose from human rights violations by the military dictatorship. The restrictions of everyday life under dictatorship (1973–89) generated a sense of crisis, and thereby generated new discursive means for women to create identities for themselves. Women traded clandestine information, experiences, images, and texts; they produced strategic documents that not only challenged the authoritarian-patriarchal regime but also provided a new language of women's rights as human rights. Second, the unprecedented international attention to human rights violations in the Latin American Southern Cone created favorable conditions that allowed women to remake gendered understandings of rights. Solidarity organizations, human rights initiatives, international women's organizations, and the travels of political exiles spread news about and promoted understanding of Chilean human rights violations. Third, human rights protests within Chile as well as Chileans' transnational interactions legitimated women's grievances about their exclusion from the benefits of existing, internationally acknowledged human rights. Hence new international attention to women's rights as human rights had roots in so-called peripheral, non-hegemonic knowledge, previously excluded from the epistemic privilege of speaking and being heard under dictatorship.

International human rights initiatives and their discontents

In the second half of the twentieth century, deliberations over human rights became one of the most controversial international debates, and attention to women's rights only heightened the controversy. Specific declarations that asserted individual human rights – internationally and in national frameworks – often pretended to define the rights of two sexes yet excluded women by upholding men's rights as the default standard. This tension, evident in documents such as the UDHR, hindered the formation of a women's human rights language and practice internationally and sustained gender inequalities in national frameworks of rights.[6]

In 1948, when the United Nations (UN) General Assembly adopted the UDHR, that document presented the first international, cross-cultural consensus on a definition of human rights. The document still influences human rights practice, despite ongoing debates over its supposedly universal characteristics. The individuals whose rights were elevated to international attention remain gendered male, evident in the phrasing of Article 1, which declares that "all human beings … should act towards one another in a spirit of brotherhood." Article 2 appears to amend the gender bias that reduces all humans to "brothers" and moves away from the rights of man, asserting that the Declaration applies equally to women and men: "Everyone is entitled to all the rights and freedoms set forth in this Declaration, without distinction of any kind, such as race, colour, sex, language, religion, political or other opinion, national or social origin, property, birth or other status."[7] Yet in the decades since 1948, the human rights of women remained ignored around the world. Many nations had yet to enact rights declarations related to Article 2, including the right to be free of discrimination on grounds of sex.[8]

Women from many countries initiated human rights campaigns. After World War I and World War II, they fostered international collaborations to secure peace and to promote human rights. The Women's International League for Peace and Freedom (WILPF), founded in The Hague, Netherlands, in 1915, and the Women's International Democratic Federation (WIDF), established in 1945 in Paris, France, emphasized women's maternal responsibilities and the rights of mothers and children. These organizations amplified the visibility of women's political actions. They highlighted women's supposedly natural difference from men and justified their engagement by way of familial responsibilities. Such seemingly traditional responsibilities also extended to declaring peace initiatives to be a "women's issue," and women mobilized vast networks and resources for world disarmament and against the arms race in the Cold War.[9] The WIDF, arguably the most influential international women's organization in the Cold War, won the support of a wide range of political constituencies through its emphasis on mothers' and children's rights. WIDF delegates consulted at times with the UN Commission on the Status of Women (CSW) to support new projects for women's rights. The United Nations declared 1975 as International Women's Year because of WIDF interventions.[10]

UN-sponsored initiatives, such as the 1975 First World Conference on Women in Mexico City, showed that not all women agreed on which rights were needed most. Poor and Indigenous women who attended the Mexico City conference felt excluded by the priorities set by conference organizers. Bolivian activist Domitila Barrios de Chungara, long involved in the defense of the rights of mine workers and women in Bolivia, articulated this sentiment. She criticized some of the most vocal participants at the conference, who had declared men to be their enemies and who had expressed demands for rights that were irrelevant for her community in Bolivia. Barrios de Chungara voiced her dissatisfaction in a published account, in which she described her initial hope to "hear things that would make me get ahead in life, in the struggle, in my work [for the community]." She added,

> I'd left my *compañero* with the seven kids and him having to work in the mine every day. I'd left my country to let people know what my homeland's like, how it suffers, how in Bolivia the Charter of the United Nations isn't upheld.[11]

From her point of view, the fight for rights was not between the sexes, but rather a class struggle:

> I think that *machismo* is a weapon of imperialism just like feminism is. Therefore, I think that the basic fight isn't between the sexes; it's a struggle of the couple. And when I say couple, I also include children and grandchildren, who have to join the struggle for liberation from a class position.[12]

Barrios de Chungara's assessment confirmed that women did not set the same priorities in their struggles for rights. Quests for rights were neither universal nor self-explanatory.

Women deliberated over questions of human rights at other international UN-sponsored conferences and at regional meetings in Latin America. The 1975 Mexico conference ended with the drafting of a World Plan of Action and extended International Women's Year to a Decade for Women (1975–85). Delegates who joined subsequent UN conferences in Copenhagen (1980) and Nairobi (1985) debated which priorities should guide struggles for rights.[13] Women from Latin America participated in these international dialogues, and also established their own regional platform to address their priorities. The first regional meeting, organized by mostly middle-class, professional, and educated feminists, took place in Bogotá, Colombia in 1981, and more regional meetings were held in various Latin American cities roughly every two to three years thereafter.[14] Some participants saw these *Encuentros Feministas* (feminist encounters) as "springboards for the development of a common Latin American feminist political language and as staging grounds for often contentious political battles over what would constitute the most efficacious strategies for achieving gender equality in dependent, capitalist, and patriarchal states."[15] Others viewed the meetings as important sites for collective exchange and individual awareness raising.[16]

Many women – from Chile and from other countries under dictatorship, such as Argentina, Uruguay, and Brazil – experienced the first *Encuentro* in Bogotá in 1981 as a liberating space. The peaceful environment contrasted starkly with the daunting realities of human rights violations at home. Women talked about how they coped with the threat of political violence, arrest, and disappearance. They acknowledged that state-sponsored terror and family-sanctioned violence perpetuated male dominance and hurt women. Chilean feminist Julieta Kirkwood observed that "we began to assert that the family is authoritarian; that the socialization of children is authoritarian and rigid in the assignment of sexual roles; that education, factories, intermediating organizations and political parties are all constituted in an authoritarian manner."[17] For Kirkwood, Bogotá symbolized a conquest of spaces by and for women that included new access to an international realm.[18] *Encuentro* participants declared 25 November as the International Day for the Elimination of Violence against Women.[19] Kirkwood and other Chilean participants concluded that patriarchy, as a form of violence, linked private acts of domestic violence to public, gendered expressions of military violence. They translated this perspective into the motto that guided their active resistance to dictatorship back in Chile: "democracy in the country and democracy at home."[20]

Women's rights as human rights under Chilean dictatorship: confronting an authoritarian-patriarchal regime

Chilean women's campaigns to "make women human" formed in response to human rights violations under dictatorship. Authoritarian rule in Chile began with a military coup on 11 September 1973. The coup terminated the government of President Salvador Allende and the Unidad Popular coalition that had promised a peaceful and democratic road to socialism. Initially, the same four-man junta that led the takeover ruled the nation, but by 1974 General Augusto Pinochet controlled the dictatorship. The Pinochet dictatorship initiated years of political repression marked by a brutality that was entirely new in Chilean history. Arrests, political assassinations, and "disappearances" became everyday threats. A former agent of the security forces testified that

> the first cadavers began to arrive at the clandestine cemetery in November of 1973, a few months after the military coup. The first executed prisoners were from the National Stadium. In the early hours of the morning the army's … trucks would transfer their loads, covered with canvas, to the military installations in San Bernardo. … At first, due to the quantity of dead that were arriving, the graves were one meter deep. Later they gave orders that the graves be at least four meters deep.[21]

Although leftist politicians and civilians were the first victims of arrests, torture, and executions, state terror soon affected all members of Chilean society. An estimated 200,000 Chileans sought exile in foreign countries to save their lives.

Women framed their strategies of resistance in response to the military's contradictory claim to be defending family values. First Lady Lucía Hiriart de Pinochet proclaimed that "the family is the basic unit of society. It is the first school … the mold in which the moral character of each citizen is formed, [so that] the Nation is truly the reflection of the hearth."[22] Yet the dictatorship's public glorification of family values mocked the realities of women's lives under the regime. Surveillance, arrests, and incarcerations became everyday occurrences, together with concealed evidence of sexual torture, rape, and executions.[23] Some women who saw their families destroyed challenged the contradictions of gender-based doctrines that prevented them from acting as heads of households, even when male breadwinners could no longer fulfill their patriarchal duties. Others redefined traditional familial responsibilities, asserting that the authoritarian and patriarchal practices used by the regime to control the nation resembled those employed by men to control women at home. In the process, women exchanged clandestine information, experiences, images, and texts. Through protest actions and documents they challenged the authoritarian-patriarchal regime and tested a new language and practice of women's rights as human rights.

Self-help initiatives, solidarity art, and challenges to the master narrative

Right after the military coup, women dealt with political repression and economic need. In October 1973, after the military had converted Santiago's National Stadium into a prison and torture center, five friends founded the Agrupación de Mujeres Democráticas (Association of Democratic Women).[24] Olga Poblete, well-known for her role in the Chilean suffrage movement of the 1930s, was one of the founding members. Others joined when friends brought friends and helped transform spontaneous initiatives into organized survival strategies. The Agrupación assisted families of political prisoners, located missing relatives, and helped detainees after release from prison. Through underground information networks that braved censorship and curfews, they sheltered those who needed protection, often disguising them as family members. One woman recalled efforts to help victims of sudden arrests and detention:

> You never knew when someone was going to be released. Sometimes they would let someone out by 7 p.m … with no money and no way to get home. If they didn't get home before the 8 p.m. curfew, the police would arrest them

> again ... So we organized people with cars to be ready to pick up people at a moment's notice.[25]

Others remembered that communal kitchens and cottage industries helped address crises caused by poverty, fear, and hopelessness. Some women's self-help organizations became consumer cooperatives, which grew to over 300 groups in Santiago alone.[26]

Union leader Aída Moreno recalls the important role of the church in the protection of human rights in Chile. The church's efforts involved parish priests as well as high-level members of the church hierarchy. Cardinal Raúl Silva Henríquez founded the Vicariate of Solidarity to support those persecuted and marginalized by the dictatorship.[27] In 1975, the church, first through the Comité Pro Paz (Committee for Peace) and soon thereafter through the newly founded Vicariate of Solidarity, provided a protective umbrella for women's self-help and awareness-raising (*concientización*) activities. In meeting rooms provided by the church, women held sewing workshops and produced *arpilleras*, tapestry images made with scraps of cloth sewn onto rectangular pieces of fabric. These images gained meaning in the process of individual and collective awareness-raising. Sold in Chile and abroad, they presented visual depictions of violence and human rights abuses.[28]

Women's self-help initiatives, like the sewing of *arpilleras*, provided the *arpilleristas* or tapestry-makers with a small income and fostered collectivities for women to share experiences, ponder survival strategies, and explore new international relationships. *Arpilleras* depicted repression, violence, resistance, and economic hardship – all expressions of post-coup Chilean realities. These became key elements in what sociologist Jacqueline Adams terms a "solidarity art system."[29] This system worked through transnational networks of solidarity, which allowed artists to sell images that expressed their views of everyday Chilean realities. *Arpilleras* became tools of resistance not only in people's personal lives, but also in the international politics of resistance. This becomes clear as we trace the roads the pictures traveled from parishes, community centers, private homes, detention centers, or prison cells to international buyers, the latter helping the *arpilleristas* make a living.

A Chilean *arpillerista* we know as Cristina remembers meeting with other women and sharing personal experiences of trauma after the coup. She asserts that

> the *arpillera* really was a denunciation in its time. Yes, it really was a key to our existence; yes, it was a key to our subsistence. It was also something very, very much for denunciation, and that's what the *Vicaría* enabled us to do. We would not have been able to denounce if we had not had the protection of the *Vicaría*. Afterward, we organized ourselves really well.[30]

Her account reveals the vital components of women's production of *arpilleras*. While some sewed because of financial need, they also reflected about their lives in collective gatherings. Sewing and conversation became shared experiences that empowered some women to take pioneering action. Women created and joined new types of networks to tell alternative stories about everyday life under the military, challenging the dominant narrative imposed by the regime.

Women's storytelling that challenged the military's master narrative provoked official responses and threats. Neither church-based networks nor *arpillera* gatherings were immune to military interference. Nevertheless, some women responded to censorship in creative ways. When the military targeted *arpilleristas*, confiscated specific images, and threatened to arrest those who smuggled *arpilleras* across Chilean borders, the women tested alternative avenues to overcome censorship. Jacqueline Adams documents how *arpilleristas* who were political prisoners redesigned their depictions of soldiers in action. They avoided confiscation of their art by adding the green fabric that symbolized soldiers' uniforms only after they passed prison guards. Through these and other interventions, women denounced the dictatorship.[31] The *arpilleras* multiplied alternative narratives about human rights violations in Chile, and helped produce gendered social and political meaning.

The making of *arpilleras* contributed to a new discursive practice of women's human rights and also linked *arpilleristas* to a range of organizations and initiatives. It involved personal learning, new collective spaces, and a new awareness of rights. Individual women created pictures and related their lives to collective experiences of the painful everyday realities under military control. The pictures raised communal awareness and prompted collective action. They connected the personal to the (prohibited) political and social. And they permitted collective action by overcoming the barriers of curfew restrictions and laws against public gatherings. In the process of their making, and as traveling images, *arpilleras* connected people to each other and suggested new ways of thinking about realities of everyday life.[32] The *arpilleristas* invigorated knowledge-sharing, knowledge production, and new perspectives on the (gendered) details of human rights abuses. Some *arpilleristas* participated in parallel workshops dedicated to human rights and women's rights, such as those offered by the Círculo de Estudios de la Mujer (Women's Studies Circle), Mujeres de Chile (Women of Chile, MUDECHI), Mujeres por la Vida (Women for Life), and the Concertación Nacional de Mujeres por la Democracia (National Coalition of Women for Democracy).

Solidarity and the internationalization of women's rights

Chilean women's mobilization under dictatorship inspired, and was in turn inspired by, a process of the internationalization of human rights concern. At least three different yet entangled networks facilitated this process: first, international women's networks inspired by UN-sponsored conferences and the Latin American *Encuentros*; second, the Chilean exile communities throughout the world; and third, the transnational solidarity networks that increased their political weight in the midst of the Cold War. Chilean women at international conferences exchanged information and strengthened activist networks. Women in exile carried information about human rights abuses to local and national sites abroad. Women who had become victims of military violence testified at international human rights commissions. In the 1975 Helsinki Accords, a landmark international treaty intended to improve relations between the communist East and the capitalist West, included a human rights clause that proved influential in increasing attention to human rights generally.[33]

The initiatives of international organizations such as Amnesty International and WIDF helped produce worldwide responses to human rights abuses, including specifically the fate of political prisoners in Chile. Amnesty International publicly adopted "prisoners of conscience," a technique that shined a light on human rights violations while protecting victims. As a result of such campaigns, Coca Rudolphy, a Chilean actress who had been arrested and tortured after the coup, became the center of international attention and was able to leave Chile for Britain. She reported that she had been unaware of Amnesty International before it had picked up her case, and she had not understood how her life story gained international attention. Amnesty International strategies of "adopting" prisoners were complicated and delicate, but they did help victims of violence like Rudolphy exchange their prison cells for exile.[34] Individual women's initiatives also elicited responses from international networks. In January 1974, leftist activist Nieves Ayress, who was held captive in the torture center Villa Grimaldi, produced a personal testimony, a letter "for all women who were not able to speak," that described the sadistic details of her personal ordeal.[35] A fellow prisoner who left the torture center for exile in Argentina smuggled Ayress' letter out of the camp and across the border. In Buenos Aires, the letter reached Fanny Edelman, secretary-general of WIDF, who mobilized her organizational networks to support Ayress' act of empowerment and publicize what became a widely noted defense of women's rights.[36]

Using the details of Ayress' case, WIDF representatives lobbied the UN Commission on Human Rights in 1974 to send a telegram to the government of Chile.[37] They also supported international solidarity campaigns that addressed the gendered dimensions of human rights violations in Chile. In May 1974, the *Washington Post* published an account of the abuse Ayress had suffered. In the same month, the *New York Times* reported on "sexual assault," calling it "a common theme" in women's prisons and in the concentration camps run by the Chilean military regime.[38] As a result of petitions in Chile that gained strength through international pressure, Nieves Ayress was released into exile in December 1976 and found asylum in West Berlin, where she collaborated with existing Chile solidarity groups and exiles there.

In Berlin and other European cities such as Madrid, London, and Rome, Chilean women often joined forces with solidarity activists there who supported the vibrant exile communities. All contributed to ongoing awareness-raising and information campaigns intended to stop the abuses under dictatorship.[39] Spanish officials, for example, received 350 foreign delegations at a World Conference of Solidarity with Chile.[40] German activists brought together feminists and women of leftist political parties for awareness-raising and fundraising workshops in multiple West German cities. Women in London collected donations side by side with exiled Chilean women to support "their sisters in Chile."[41] And Italians, together with Chilean exiles in Rome, launched the serial publication *Chile-América* that published political commentary, academic research, and activist agendas.[42]

Argentine feminist Judith Astelarra summed up the sentiment of solidarity activists in one of her contributions to *Chile-América* in 1982, when public protest by Chilean women back in Chile entered a new, active, and public phase: "And today, when the battle for human rights has become the center of our activity, it will be important to assert that the problem of women's oppression is also a human rights problem."[43] Informal international solidarity networks helped pressure the Pinochet regime to stop human rights abuses, and more formal networks followed. International women's groups moved from the "logic of mutual solidarity" to the "logic of international advocacy," with which they pressured governments, including Chile's, to protect women's rights.[44] Some women, like the Chilean Cecilia Medina, who completed a law degree while exiled in the Netherlands in the 1980s, depicted women's rights as the natural outcome of the connection between democracy and feminism: "As a logical consequence of the fact that women's rights are human rights, feminism, in theory, is a movement to achieve a democratic society, without which human rights may not be fully enjoyed."[45]

Feminist awareness raising: knowledge production and actions

Back in Chile, the relationships among groups of women activists were often complicated, sometimes fruitful, and at times divided – yet they were overwhelmingly in agreement about the importance of women's rights. Disagreement over women's rights emerged and specific feminist positions became contentious when, for example, middle-class professionals led activities such as feminist literacy practice, or when they tried to teach women from poor neighborhoods how patriarchy caused inequality in Chilean society. The feminist focus on gender-based oppression depicted feminism as classless. This was, as historian Robert Austin documents, "anomalous for victims of the class system, particularly when emanating from those who were consistently class beneficiaries of the exploitation of *pobladoras* [women of poor neighborhoods]."[46] In the long years of dictatorship, women experimented with reading groups that did allow both middle-class and popular sectors to explore specific views on women's roles, to participate in collective processes of articulating women's rights, and to carve out spaces for interpretive and political power.[47]

Labor organizer Aída Moreno tells in her memoir of her own fruitful encounters with the Círculo de Estudios de la Mujer (Women's Studies Circle).[48] A group of professional women, all with ties to feminism and personal histories of political activism, founded the Círculo in 1979. Much like *arpilleristas*, the Círculo counted on church protection provided through the Vicaría (the Vicariate of Solidarity). The Círculo was founded when these feminists used their personal networks and word-of-mouth in order to invite women to a meeting "to discuss the situation of women" in Chile.[49] Even in the midst of a climate of violence, including sudden arrests and "disappearances" of suspected dissidents, approximately 300 women attended the first Círculo meeting. This exceeded the founders' expectations.[50]

Círculo members and guests met regularly and wrote about women's rights in Chile and elsewhere. They produced their own collective *Boletín* (Bulletin), as well as publications by individual members that challenged entrenched gender hierarchies in Chilean society.[51] Círculo participants identified cultural and legal mechanisms of gender-based oppression. The Chilean Civil Code displayed the patriarchal tradition of married women's legal subordination when it affirmed that "the husband has the right to oblige his wife to live with him and follow him wherever he moves" and that "the husband is the chief of the conjugal society, and as such may freely administer his property and that of his wife."[52] Círculo members contended that women ought to think critically about the legal and cultural constructions of their roles, and they agreed that change was possible, as "one is not born a woman, one learns to be a woman."[53]

Círculo initiatives made a difference: Awareness-raising inspired a new critical praxis of human rights. Discussion topics ranged from institutional discrimination in the legal system to women's personal internalization of repressive roles.[54] When meeting participants asked, "Where are the women who have disappeared?" they were challenging the military dictatorship and expressing the urgent need for action. They articulated new gendered perspectives on violence and state oppression. The disappearances, arrests, and brutal victimization of women required new forms of political participation and collective organizing to expose the military's hypocritical ideological exaltation of women's maternal roles and domestic responsibilities. Círculo women concluded that "we believe that it is our, and only our, responsibility to demand that women receive their rights. If we don't fight for ourselves, no one will fight for us."[55] Some women viewed their feminist political activism as an extension of their maternal responsibilities. Women's definitions of feminism and individuals' path to women's rights activism varied widely.

The details of Aída Moreno's encounters with the Círculo show that meeting participants did not share a uniform women's rights mission and that the meetings inspired different types of network building. Moreno sees the roots of her collaboration with feminist academics in Chile and the United States in her Círculo connections: "it all started with an invitation of women union activists to a Círculo gathering." She recalls that "professional women," Círculo academics, wanted to learn how domestic workers and union leaders had organized.[56] The group's *Boletín* featured a section on women domestic workers, including excerpts of interviews with children who spoke about their *nanas*, the domestic workers in their own homes. Most families in Chile relied on *nanas* for childcare and domestic work, yet their labor rights were unrecognized. Moreno considered these encounters and Círculo initiatives to be important contributions to an inclusive language of women's rights.[57] She built on these meetings to give domestic workers' rights a more prominent place in larger deliberations over women's rights.

Moreno's union activism fostered relationships with women's rights activists, such as Thelma Gálvez and Rosalba Todaro, academics whom she met at the Círculo. Gálvez and Todaro, founders of Santiago's Centro de Estudios de la Mujer (Women's Research Center, CEM), conducted research on Chilean domestic workers' lives. They invited Moreno and others to participate in CEM workshops. Those interactions culminated in the publication of a study of domestic workers that included testimonial accounts.[58] Moreno believed that the workshops empowered women union members. The union employed the scholarship on domestic workers' everyday lives in its campaigns for rights.[59] These relationships fostered yet others, such as Moreno's extended collaboration with US political scientist Elsa Chaney. Chaney invited Moreno to attend the Latin American Studies Association (LASA) Conference in Mexico City in 1983 and published some of the results of their collaboration. Moreno also helped to bring to fruition one of Chaney's seminal publications on domestic workers.[60]

Communication between scholars and union organizers as well as research publications strengthened organizational networks in support of women's labor rights, in Chile and elsewhere in the Americas. Elsa Chaney helped Moreno with grant applications, and in 1984, economic support through grants helped Moreno to revive regional union activity in Chile. For Chilean domestic workers, this entailed increased cooperation on a national level and closer connections to domestic workers elsewhere in Latin America and in the Caribbean. Moreno collaborated with union leaders from Peru and Colombia and invited domestic workers for meetings in Lima, Peru, in 1987. In 1988 they organized a congress in Bogotá, Colombia, where representatives of 11 countries founded the Confederation of Household Workers of Latin America and the Caribbean.[61]

Moreno's memoir recalls that her collaborations with *pobladoras*, activists in various political parties of the left, and academics and feminists all united, briefly, in one organization that sought to build cross-class alliances and overcome political disagreements. Mujeres de Chile (Women of Chile, MUDECHI) was founded in the meeting hall of Moreno's union building. Members were proud to build a non-partisan, inclusive organization. Moreno describes her collaboration with MUDECHI as a great learning experience. In 1986, she spent three months in Cuba on a grant paid for by MUDECHI and WIDF. In Moreno's words, these were "three months to gather new experiences and skills [including] learning about history from a different perspective, getting to know the history of women's movements."[62] Nevertheless, Moreno documents that many of the ambitions of MUDECHI remained illusions. MUDECHI was not able to maintain its non-partisan standing, having been, according to Moreno, "manipulated" by parties of the left early on.[63]

Meanwhile, *pobladoras* mobilized against class- and gender-based exploitation. Many poor women had a history of political mobilization quite different from academics with international ties, or from activists such as the founders of the Círculo, although they were equally dedicated to women's rights. One *pobladora* recalled: "We have always been organized, just like that. We had to, with our problems … we formed a committee to address unemployment. And we asked the Church for help."[64] Another *pobladora* activist made clear that many poor women agreed with middle-class and professional feminists' emphasis on gender inequality, but nevertheless saw things differently: "We could never count on the support of maids … we had to organize ourselves. Some women go to meetings with [all of] their children, I take just the younger ones."[65] Like the middle-class and academic feminists, they too engaged in awareness-raising about the condition of women, tested self-help strategies through collective organizing, and critiqued the double oppression of dictatorship and patriarchy.

In 1980, the Comité de Defensa de los Derechos de la Mujer (Committee for the Defense of Women's Rights, CODEM) became one of the most important organizations founded by *pobladoras*. Identifying with political parties on the left, CODEM aimed to increase women's active participation in politics. CODEM campaigns demanded greater rights for women such as access to healthcare and birth control. In 1981, it launched its own journal and documented changes in the healthcare system that were relevant to women's health. CODEM also analyzed teenage pregnancy, the lack of sex education, and gender-specific demands that some considered to be feminist critiques of Chilean society.[66] While many CODEM activists initially rejected feminist activism as a "divisive" tool of middle-class women, some reassessed their relationship with feminism over the course of their activist experience. In 1987, CODEM reversed its initial rejection of feminism and openly identified itself as a feminist organization.[67]

In other initiatives, *pobladoras* strengthened ties among the many organizations formed by women in poor neighborhoods. In May 1982, *pobladora* leaders brought together several smaller organizations under one central leadership, the Movimiento de Mujeres Pobladoras (Movement of Shantytown Women, MOMUPO). Clotilde Silva, one of the active members, explained that many women were reacting to the failure of male political leadership and felt that "it is terrible to see how children grow up without hope for the future [under dictatorship]."[68] MOMUPO members pointed out the double exploitation of women that justified the need for an autonomous women's organization. They simultaneously prioritized their working-class identity: "MOMUPO sees [itself] as part of the working class and understands that our class as a whole [including men] needs to confront … oppression."[69] We can better explain the wide reach that women's mobilizations had under the dictatorship when we note such diversity of perspectives and the multiple origins of women's activism.

Words, language, and knowledge production

> I remembered the phrase by a French provincial parish priest that I read in a novel and that had impressed me strongly: "And if they do not have words to express themselves, it is because we have taken away even those from them," he had said, referring to the impossibility of expression of the most miserable people of his parish. It was natural, then, to feel deeply and disconcertedly moved by [the condition of] those who had been deprived even of the word, which is the symbol and last stronghold of the attribute of humanity. Today I think, perhaps exaggeratedly, that those could also be us, the women, the same women who made it their task to insist that women's rights are met.[70]

Chilean feminists, activists, and academics engaged in national and transnational knowledge production through the creation of written texts. Their materials reached recipients in workshops, conferences, and transnational feminist and human rights networks. The sociologist and feminist Julieta Kirkwood, for example, played a critical role in rethinking the mechanisms of women's exclusion from political power in Chile. She emphasized gender-based mechanisms of oppression under authoritarianism. In her writings, she addresses the problem of women's conflicted status of "personhood" that was evident in the undisputed use of the term "human" as gendered male.[71] She uncovers shortcomings in women's rights by exploring the construction of women as human beings who exist only in relation to others: families, husbands, and children. In her analysis, removing women from their cultural and historical contexts and subjecting an abstraction of "woman" to unchanging laws of nature also restricts women's political participation and citizenship rights.

Kirkwood published many now-classic texts that unpacked the traditional world of Chilean party politics while the military was still in power. These document the language used by party militants, overwhelmingly male, and trace the discursive ways in which men control women through depictions of women as dependent. Kirkwood asserts that "the word 'women' is always qualified by the class, by popular, by the crisis, by the family. It is a term that can't be independent. They can't conceive of women alone."[72] The parties of the political left refused to acknowledge any "woman question." Female party members and leftist militants reproduced the silence about gendered hierarchies as they prioritized class-based inequalities in their political struggles. Kirkwood exposes tensions in women's activism that pitted the *políticas*, sectors that prioritized their leftist partisan militancy, against *feministas*, those who argued that any struggle for greater societal equality had to begin with the eradication of gender-based inequalities.[73]

Kirkwood's writings and her participation in conferences and workshops created alternative spaces for political action by women of different backgrounds. She invited critiques that challenged the regime's authoritarianism as well as specific manifestations of patriarchy in Chile. Kirkwood emphasized that research and the writing of history were political acts, and she encouraged women to seize interpretive power as they claimed citizenship rights equal to those of men. At a 1982 Women's Conference at the Mapocho Cultural Center in Santiago, she reminded the audience:

> We had to learn about all histories written about women through the pen and the lance of men ... they spoke to us of prostitutes, of witches, of mother-saints, and of martyrs ... never of real women, in real worlds.[74]

New research and writing were acts of reclaiming power and steps on the way to challenging the roles men had assigned women in history.

Women in exile contributed to feminist knowledge production and provided tools for awareness about gender equality and women's rights, often with a perspective that breached Chilean geographical boundaries. Adriana Santa Cruz and Viviana Erazo, exiled in Mexico, worked with local women's groups in collaborative research projects.[75] In the process, they identified themes of gender discrimination that affected women throughout Latin America and published *Compropolitan*, a book that became a standard of feminist education in the early 1980s.[76] Its title derived from the Spanish verb *comprar* (to buy) and the name of the well-known glamor magazine *Cosmopolitan*. *Compropolitan* provided a feminist critique of how the media reduced women to consumers and sex objects; it showed how advertisers manipulated Latin American women, teasing them into buying products for their supposed mission of conquering men.[77] Santa Cruz and Erazo also founded a new periodical, *Mujer/fempress*, as an alternative to mainstream magazines aimed at women.[78]

Even after exiles returned to Chile, many continued to work for women's rights across national borders. In 1986, Adriana Santa Cruz became editor of *Mujer/fempress* in Santiago. Published monthly, the periodical featured news and research from a feminist perspective. Santa Cruz and others followed the mandate of the UN Decade for Women: to document information about women and make it widely available. Historian Francesca Miller notes that "between 1980 and 1988, 153 women's periodicals with a feminist or women's liberationist perspective came into publication in Latin America."[79] Women's feminist publications spread a new language of women's rights as human rights and challenged the authoritarian-patriarchal regime in Chile.[80]

Las Protestas, the return to democracy, and the institutionalization of a women's rights agenda

> The aspiration, as women, to become relevant social actors has made us see the importance of developing an independent movement, which, although strengthened by [existing] ... political networks and organizations, allows us to express ourselves more clearly ... In this context we are ... convening all the women of Santiago at the National Stadium on 25 August. The motto "To conquer hope" seeks to bring together ... many [different] women who are dismayed by persistent injustices and violations of their rights as people.[81]

In December 1983, over 10,000 women of diverse political and class backgrounds came together at the Caupolicán Theatre in Santiago. It was the largest public gathering since the military coup, and had been organized by Mujeres por la Vida. In addition to agreeing on the unity motto above, participants proclaimed that "freedom has a woman's name."[82] In the public marches that followed, they protested the dictatorship's human rights violations and authoritarianism and demanded "*democracia en el país y en la casa*" (democracy in the country and at home).[83] These protests marked a new phase of public protest against dictatorship. Over the 1980s, the Chilean opposition's continued resistance, combined with pressure from international human rights initiatives, provoked reactions on the highest level. Pinochet, confident that the support of elite and middle sectors would keep him in power, scheduled a plebiscite in 1988. In this plebiscite, Chileans could vote "*Sí*," which would grant Pinochet another term, or "*No*," which would compel him to schedule elections.

Women asserted their presence in the 1988 plebiscite and their protests strengthened opposition to the dictatorship. A majority of Chileans voted "*No*," and the plebiscite thus led to Pinochet's removal from office. As military leaders began to transfer power to civilian politicians, women's groups helped the nation transition to democracy. The Concertación Nacional de Mujeres por la Democracia (National Coalition of Women for Democracy), founded in December 1988, developed a government program from a gendered perspective that emphasized women's rights. In the process, these women put forward moderate propositions, excluding "radical" demands such as changes in abortion and divorce legislation.[84] While such priorities alienated some women activists, they won the approval of a politically conservative opposition that had initially rejected their demands.

Other campaigns that were located outside the realm of party politics also picked up the issue of women's rights. In late 1988 and early 1989, feminists organized a massive campaign guided by the motto "*soy mujer, tengo derechos*" (I am a woman, I have rights).[85] Over the course of five months and 48 meetings, they afforded women from all walks of life the opportunity to listen to presentations, read documents, and discuss what they themselves perceived as major obstacles to women's rights. Campaigns reached far beyond the larger Santiago area; about 1,700 women from rural and urban backgrounds joined the meetings.[86] For these numerous women, conversations about women's rights and the formulation of gender-specific demands were no longer marginal or distant quests. Objectives included giving women spaces for individual expression, addressing problems that affected all women due to their roles in society, and identifying the violations of women's rights that needed the most urgent attention.[87]

Women aimed for gender equity in the spheres of politics, economics, and culture, and demanded equal rights with men in the realms of work and fair wages, health care, dignified housing, social security, and education, offering remarkable insights into the complexity of barriers to women's rights and creative proposals for solutions.[88] Outreach initiatives exemplified the tone and the content of their demands. For example, when 400 women participated in a protest march in the center of Santiago on 21 November 1989, they carried signs pointing to the problem of violence against women: "Violence against women is a crime, in the streets and at any time."[89] They depicted the power exerted by culture and education, and critically evoked their own role in the continuation of the gender system they rejected: "First we raise machos, and next we get scared of them."[90] Finally, they argued that a true democracy would take shape only with the inclusion of female citizens with equal rights: "If women are involved, then democracy evolves."[91]

In 1991, persevering women activists helped establish the Servicio Nacional de la Mujer (National Office for Women's Affairs, SERNAM), an institution dedicated to improving gender parity in Chile. While SERNAM's foundation signified a move forward, it also restricted some feminists' agendas from its inception. SERNAM pledged to safeguard the "traditional" family, the model of the dual-parent and heterosexual marriage that was officially recognized by the state. It subordinated women's citizenship rights to the maintenance of gendered traditions that relied on women-mothers to sustain the family as a key site of social reproduction. SERNAM's institutional mission promised "to collaborate with policymakers in the study and proposal of general plans and measures that lead women to enjoy equal rights and opportunities with respect to men," but it also maintained gender-based inequalities. In the same mission statement, SERNAM accepted "natural" differences and recreated biological determinism, setting the goal of "respecting the nature and specificity of the woman that emanates from the natural diversity of the sexes, including its adequate projection to the relations of the family."[92]

New leadership, persistent feminist critiques, and a changed political climate helped modify SERNAM's foundational emphasis on the fortification of the family. In the twenty-first century, SERNAM has promoted key policy changes, such as legislation on family violence that facilitates police intervention and preventive measures.[93] In 2006, 60 family courts with over 250 judges heard family violence cases.[94] In 2010, SERNAM also supported the penal code's modification and the Law No. 20.066, which introduced the term *femicidio* (femicide) and defined it as "homicide committed against a woman who is or has been a spouse or partner of the perpetrator of the crime."[95] The most visible signs that SERNAM has gone beyond its narrow founding mission are its reorganization as a ministry and the appointment of a leader who dared address sensitive subjects. SERNAM was renamed Servicio Nacional de la Mujer y de la Equidad de Género (National Office for Women's Affairs and Gender Equity) in 2015. It continues to function under the jurisdiction of the newly founded Ministerio de la Mujer y la Equidad de Género de Chile (Ministry for Women's Affairs and Gender Equity).[96] In 2016, President Michelle Bachelet appointed Claudia Pascual, Communist Party (PC) member and formerly the PC's national commissioner of women, as the first minister of women and gender equality. Pascual opened up a new public debate on the subject of reproductive rights, including support for legislation on the decriminalization of abortion. Illegal abortion is one of the leading causes of maternal mortality in Chile.[97]

The gains of state-led feminism have varied: SERNAM and the Ministry have remained vulnerable to the changing priorities of leading politicians, and political processes remain dominated by patriarchy. The legal measures regarding gender-based violence have brought both continuity and change. Activists and scholars agree that the new attention to family violence has introduced some important changes in the understandings of women's needs; however, the emphasis on the family, and a specific type of family, also limits the scope of demands that women can make. The legislation against violence focuses on the nuclear family unit with the goal of strengthening the family through therapeutic measures and achieving family reconciliation. While this legislation can potentially save lives, it fails to address some of the root causes of violence against women related to class, ethnicity, culture, geography, age, experience, ability, and other categories. Unequal power relations within the family unit and the larger community may lead to violence against women; those power relations remain interconnected with institutionalized gender-based inequalities in Chilean society and with a culture that ignores the links between gender inequality and violence. Furthermore, the neoliberal reorganization of Chilean society, one of the legacies of the dictatorship, has widened the gap between wealthy and poor Chileans. Patriarchal structures, in conjunction with the myth of a Chilean economic miracle, disproportionately affect women, who struggle with higher levels of poverty than men.

Conclusion: assessing the state of women's human rights

From Aída Moreno's perspective, the struggles for rights under dictatorship and for redemocratization have not yet garnered sufficient success. Moreno laments the absence of politicians who truly seek to make a difference, as did "the unforgettable deputy Laura Rodríguez, who one day came to our service to help improve the laws of the workers." She asserts that the dictatorship imposed an "inhuman system," evident in labor and pension reforms that eliminated the achievements workers had obtained through years of struggle; she adds that the *Concertación*, the governing coalition in charge of redemocratization, has maintained this inhuman system.[98] In short: legislators and politicians have not yet fully acknowledged the humanity of workers and women.[99]

I have traced "how women become human," in this essay, but I have not argued that this process represents a closed chapter of the recent past. On the contrary, the new attention to women's rights as human rights represents a paradigm shift that inspires continuing action. Chilean women's initiatives led to fresh attention to subjects such as women's empowerment, autonomy, and political representation. They created alternative frames of references in debates over women's roles and rights, different from those compromised by Cold War rivalries and dominated by political leaders' emphasis on economic development, fears of overpopulation, and anxieties about women's roles in the much-needed reproduction of human capital. Women's mobilizations in Chile have contributed to a shift in which a human rights approach to women's roles has gained international prominence. A women's human rights framework equips women with tools and networks useful for claiming "women's rights as human rights." However, this shift does not guarantee the protection of women's humanity for all women equally. The challenges of transforming cultural, economic, and political systems through collective critique of ensuring accountability for violations of the rights of all humans, and of testing vigorously the shortcomings of existing paradigms remain.[100]

New research must address the shortcomings of current rights paradigms, also in light of the dramatic increase of femicide, the gender-based murder of women by men. How can we identify and transform lasting symbolic representations, norms, and institutions that maintain sex–gender hierarchies and deny some individuals' humanity? Femicides have included rituals in which humans were mutilated, killed, and thrown away. They demonstrate literally and symbolically that public displays of individuals that have been transformed into sexually fetishized commodities still fit economic, political, and cultural systems that thrive in the absence of women's rights. Scholars and activists have linked gender-based violence to those legal systems and cultures that continue to assign unequal citizenship rights to women and men. Inequalities are legitimized through patriarchal performances that celebrate male privilege through acts of violence and that contribute to views of women as the waste products of patriarchal requirements – as disposable parts of a system in which they serve primarily to confirm power hierarchies among men.[101]

Patriarchal cultures matter, but we also have to ask new questions about the connections between ongoing violations of women's human rights, economic structures, and hiring practices that benefit from the image of the disposable woman worker. Alicia Schmidt Camacho and Melissa Wright document how economic globalization has long attracted a female industrial labor force, and that industries have used the actual vulnerabilities of women as well as the image of the disposable woman worker. Women migrant workers are exceptionally exposed due to the denial of citizenship rights in their workplaces. This is especially evident in the denationalized space of border industries in the Americas and elsewhere. Neoliberal economic practices in border regions (including both transnational and internal borders) permit the treatment of poor migrant women as "disposable non-citizens" who are valuable and much-desired workers precisely because of their lack of access to rights.[102]

This perpetuates the "myth of disposable women" that is part of a harsh reality in which globalization increases the vulnerability of workers. The myth is a script that employers and managers tell, repeat, and act, drawing upon it to normalize and maintain discriminatory labor practices that control "disposable" workers who can be replaced if they do not comply. Such employers and managers act as though that myth is an unchangeable reality.[103]

Notes

1 Aída Moreno Valenzuela, *Evidencias de una Líder: Memorias de una Trabajadora de Casa Particular*, Santiago de Chile: LOM Ediciónes, 2012, p. 43.

2 Moreno, *Evidencias*, p. 60.

3 In the Americas, European Christians referred to individuals as more or less human to justify conquest and domination. In 1550, in the now-famous exchange at Valladolid, Spain, Bartolomé de las Casas and Juan Ginés Sepúlveda deliberated over the humanity of American Indians. They used criteria such as Indians' ability to reason, possession of a soul, and capability of being saved from eternal damnation through conversion to Christianity. Daniel Brunstetter, "Sepúlveda, Las Casas, and the Other: Exploring the Tension between Moral Universalism and Alterity," *Review of Politics*, 2010, vol. 72, no. 3, 409–35. Not women's but native Americans' humanity remained at the forefront of colonial debates. Spanish colonial legislation, quite differently from Anglo-Saxon legislation, did not deny women juridical personhood. Elizabeth Dore and Maxine Molyneux, *Hidden Histories of Gender and the State in Latin America*, Durham, NC: Duke University Press, 2000, pp. 11–12.

4 For difficulties in quantifying gender (in)equality, see Debra J. Liebowitz and Susanne Zwingel, "Gender Equality Oversimplified: Using CEDAW to Counter the Measurement Obsession," *International Studies Review*, 2014, vol. 16, no. 3, 362–89.

5 See Karen Engle, "International Human Rights and Feminism: When Discourses Meet," *Michigan Journal of International Law*, 1992, vol. 13, no. 3, 517–610.

6 See also the essay by Regula Ludi in this volume.

7 United Nations, "Universal Declaration of Human Rights." Online. Available at www.un.org/en/udhrbook/pdf/udhr_booklet_en_web.pdf (accessed 5 January 2019).

8 United Nations High Commissioner of Human Rights, "Universal Declaration of Human Rights – In Six Cross-Cutting Themes." Online. Available at www.ohchr.org/EN/UDHR/Pages/CrossCuttingThemes.aspx (accessed 5 January 2019).

9 See Harriet Hyman Alonso, *Peace as a Women's Issue: A History of the US Movement for World Peace and Women's Rights*, Syracuse, NY: Syracuse University Press, 1993. See also the essay by Marie Sandell in this volume.

10 For the maternalist component of WIDF activism, see Jadwiga E. Pieper Mooney, "Fighting Fascism and Forging New Political Activism: The Women's International Democratic Federation (WIDF) in the Cold War," in Jadwiga E. Pieper Mooney and Fabio Lanza (eds.) *De-Centering Cold War History: Local and Global Change*, London: Routledge, 2013, pp. 52–72.

11 Domitila Barrios de Chungara and Moema Viezzer, *Let Me Speak! Testimony of Domitila, a Woman of the Bolivian Mines*, New York: Monthly Review Press, 1978, p. 198.

12 Barrios de Chungara and Viezzer, *Let Me Speak*! p. 234.

13 United Nations, *World Plan of Action for the Implementation of the Objectives of the International Women's Year. A Summarized Version*, New York: United Nations Center for Economic and

Social Information, 1976; Arvonne S. Fraser, "Becoming Human: The Origins and Development of Women's Human Rights," *Human Rights Quarterly*, 1999, vol. 21, no. 4, 853–906.

14 See Nancy Saporta Sternbach, Marysa Navarro, Patricia Chuchryk, and Sonia E. Alvarez, "Feminisms in Latin America: From Bogotá to San Bernardo," *Signs: Journal of Women in Culture and Society*, 1992, vol. 17, no. 2, 393–434.

15 Sternbach et al., "Feminisms," 396.

16 On the *Encuentros*, see Sonia Alvarez et al., "Encountering Latin American and Caribbean Feminisms," *Signs: Journal of Women in Culture and Society*, 2003, vol. 28, no. 2, 537–80.

17 Julieta Kirkwood, *Ser Política en Chile: Las Feministas y los Partidos*, Santiago: Facultad Latinoamericana de Ciencias Sociales (FLACSO), 1986, p. 180.

18 Julieta Kirkwood, *Ser Política en Chile: Los Nudos de la Sabiduría Feminista*, 2nd ed., Santiago: Editorial Cuarto Propio, 1990, 233–49; Marysa Navarro, "El Primer Encuentro Feminista de Latinoamérica y el Caribe," in Magdalena León (ed.) *Sociedad, subordinación y feminismo*, Bogotá: Asociación Colombiana para el Estudio de la Población, 1982, pp. 261–7.

19 "Testimonio," *Boletín Círculo de Estudios de la Mujer*, 1981, no. 6, 5.

20 On Chilean women's active role, see Irene Campos Can, "Second Feminist Conference of Latin America and the Caribbean: Two Reports," *Women's Studies International*, 1984, vol. 3, 26–9; see also Alicia Frohmann and Teresa Valdés, *Democracy in the Country and in the Home. The Women's Movement in Chile*, Santiago: Facultad Latinoamericana de Ciencias Sociales (FLACSO), 1993.

21 As cited in Mary Helen Spooner, *Soldiers in a Narrow Land: The Pinochet Regime in Chile*, Berkeley: University of California Press, 1994, p. 49.

22 Chile, Valores patrios y valores familiares. Cuadernos de Difusión No. 7, Santiago:: Secretaría Nacional de la Mujer, 1982, p. 11.

23 In 2004, the National Commission on Political Imprisonment and Torture documented that 94 percent of the military's detainees were tortured. 3,400 women testified, and nearly all suffered sexual torture. See Human Rights Watch, "Chile: Government Discloses Torture Was State Policy," 29 November 2004. Online. Available at www.hrw.org/news/2004/11/29/chile-government-discloses-torture-was-state-policy (accessed 5 January 2019).

24 For testimonial accounts, see Elisabet Prudant Soto (ed.), *Y Entonces Estaban Ellas: Memoria(s) de las Mujeres Democráticas durante la Dictadura*, Santiago: CEIBO Ediciónes, 2013.

25 As cited in Lisa Baldez, *Why Women Protest: Women's Movements in Chile*, New York: Cambridge University Press, 2002, p. 129.

26 Luis Razeto, *Las Organizaciones Económicas Populares. La experiencia de las Nuevas Organizaciones Económicas Populares en Chile. Situación y Perspectivas*, Santiago: Programa de Economía del Trabajo, Academia de Humanismo Cristiano, Arzobispado de Santiago, 1983.

27 Moreno, *Evidencias*, p. 67.

28 Marjorie Agosín, *Tapestries of Hope, Threads of Love: The Arpillera Movement in Chile*, Lanham, MD: Rowman & Littlefield, 2008.

29 Jacqueline Adams, *Art Against Dictatorship: Making and Exporting Arpilleras under Pinochet*, Austin: University of Texas Press, 2013, p. 13.

30 As cited in Adams, *Art Against Dictatorship*, p. 50.

31 Adams, *Art Against Dictatorship*, p. 86, 116–21.

32 Eliana Moya-Raggio, "'Arpilleras': Chilean Culture of Resistance," *Feminist Studies*, 1984, vol. 10, no. 2, 277–90; Baldez, *Why Women Protest*, p. 130.

33 On the Helsinki Commissions and the context of the Cold War, see Sarah B. Snyder, *Human Rights Activism and the End of the Cold War: A Transnational History of the Helsinki Network*, New York: Cambridge University Press, 2013.

34 Ann Marie Clark, *Diplomacy of Conscience: Amnesty International and Changing Human Rights Norms*, Princeton, NJ: Princeton University Press, 2001, pp. 49–51.

35 Jorge Ramos, *Lo que Vi: Experiencias de un Periodista Alrededor del Mundo*, Mexico City: Grijalbo, 1999, pp. 189–92. For a detailed account of Ayress' story, see Temma Kaplan, "Reversing the Shame and Gendering the Memory," *Signs*, 2002, vol. 28, no. 1, 179–99.

36 Kaplan, "Reversing the Shame," 186.

37 Bertrand G. Ramcharan, *The Concept and Present Status of the International Protection of Human Rights: Forty Years After the Universal Declaration*, Dordrecht: Martinus Nijhoff, 1989, pp. 90–1.

38 Anthony Lewis, "The Meaning of Torture," *New York Times*, 30 May 1974. Online. Available at www.nytimes.com/1974/05/30/archives/the-meaning-of-torture.html (accessed 5 January 2019).
39 Komitee Solidarität mit Chile, *Konterrevolution in Chile: Analysen und Dokumente zum Terror*, Reinbek: Rowohlt, 1973.
40 "La Conferencia Mundial de Solidaridad con Chile," *Chile-América* [Rome: Centro de Estudios y Documentación], 1978, no. 48, 20–2. On Chile solidarity in Spain, see also *Triunfo*, 1978, vol. 32, no. 825, 18 November 2026–8.
41 Catalina Palma, *Women in Chile Yesterday and Today*, London: Chile Solidarity Campaign, 1984, p. 1.
42 *Chile-América*, 1974–83, nos. 1–88/89.
43 Judith Astelarra, "El Feminismo como Perspectiva Teórica y como Práctica Política," *Chile-América*, 1982, no. 80/81, 117–18.
44 Sonia Alvarez located this shift in the 1990s in an unpublished paper presented at the University of California at Santa Cruz in 1999: Sonia Alvarez, "Thoughts on Distinctive Logics of Transnational Feminist Activism."
45 Cecilia Medina, "Women's Rights as Human Rights: Latin American Countries and the Organization of American States (OAS)," in Myriam Díaz-Diocaretz and Iris M. Zavala (eds.) *Women, Feminist Identity, and Society in the 1980s: Selected Papers*, Amsterdam: John Benjamins, 1985, p. 63.
46 Robert Austin, *The State, Literacy, and Popular Education in Chile, 1964–1990*, Lanham, MD: Lexington Books, 2003, 275–94.
47 Teresa Valdés and Marisa Weinstein, *Mujeres que Suenan las Organizaciones de Pobladoras en Chile 1973–1989*, Santiago: Facultad Latinoamericana de Ciencias Sociales (FLACSO), 1993.
48 Moreno, *Evidencias*, p. 120.
49 Rosa Bravo, María Isabel Cruzat, Elena Serrano, and Rosalba Todaro, "Y Así Va Creciendo … El Feminismo en Chile," in Isis Internacional (ed.) *Movimiento Feminista. Balance y Perspectivas. América Latina y el Caribe*, Santiago: Ediciónes Isis Internacional de las Mujeres, 1986, p. 26.
50 Bravo et al., "Y Así Va Creciendo," p. 26.
51 The *Boletín del Círculo de Estudios de la Mujer* was published between 1979 and 1983.
52 As cited in Mala Htun, *Sex and the State: Abortion, Divorce, and the Family under Latin American Dictatorships and Democracies*, Cambridge, UK: Cambridge University Press, 2003, p. 73.
53 Bravo et al., "Y Así Va Creciendo," p. 26.
54 See Annabel Ipsen, "The Women's Movement in Chile, From Grassroots to Nongovernmental Organization: A Case Study of La Casa de La Mujer, La Morada," MA thesis, University of New Mexico, 2000, pp. 96–7; Bravo et al., "Y Así Va Creciendo," p. 26.
55 Claudia Adriasola, *Algunas Ideas Respecto a la Condición de la Mujer*, Santiago: Academia de Humanismo Cristiano, 1979, p. 14.
56 Moreno, *Evidencias*, p. 217.
57 Moreno, *Evidencias*, p. 120; Isabel Undurraga, "La Nana," *Boletín del Círculo de Estudios de la Mujer*, 1981, no. 7.
58 Moreno, *Evidencias*, p. 70.
59 Moreno, *Evidencias*, p. 120.
60 See Elsa M. Chaney, Mary Garcia Castro, and Margo L. Smith (eds.), *Muchachas No More: Household Workers in Latin America and the Caribbean*, Philadelphia: Temple University Press, 1989, especially Aída Moreno Valenzuela, "History of the Household Workers' Movement in Chile, 1926–1983," in Chaney et al., *Muchachas No More*, pp. 407–16. For collaborative work, see Elsa M. Chaney and Aída Moreno Valenzuela, "The Difficult Path toward Organizing Household Workers: A Dialogue," in John Friedmann, Rebecca Abers, and Lilian Autler (eds.) *Emergences: Women's Struggles for Livelihood in Latin America*, Los Angeles: UCLA Latin American Center, 1996, pp. 107–36.
61 Moreno, *Evidencias*, pp. 121–2; Chaney et al., *Muchachas No More*, p. 6.
62 Moreno, *Evidencias*, p. 103.
63 Moreno, *Evidencias*, p. 100, 101.
64 Patricia López-Stewart and Elisabeth Gumberger, *Ich Bringe das Salz. Chilenische Frauen Berichten: Erfahrungen, Situationen, Positionen*, Bremen: Edition CON, 1985, p. 108.

65 Eda Cleary, *Frauen in der Politik Chiles. Zur Emanzipierung Chilenischer Frauen während der Militärdiktatur Pinochets*, Aachen: Alano, 1988, p. 225.
66 *Vamos mujer*, 1989, no. 3, 7–8, 10. *Vamos mujer* was CODEM's occasional journal.
67 Patricia M. Chuchryk makes this observation in "Subversive Mothers: The Women's Opposition to the Military Regime in Chile," in Sue Ellen Charlton, Jana Matson Everett, and Kathleen A. Staudt (eds.) *Women, the State, and Development*, Albany: State University of New York Press, 1989, pp. 130–51.
68 "Mujeres, volverémos a casa?" in Clotilde Silva and Movimiento de Mujeres Pobladoras, *Chile, No Estas Muerto*, Santiago: Centro Ecuménico Diego de Medellín, n.d., p. 34.
69 Cleary, *Frauen*, p. 221.
70 Chilean feminist Julieta Kirkwood in 1979. Julieta Kirkwood, *Tejiendo Rebeldías: Escritos Feministas*, Patricia Crispi (ed.), Santiago: Centro de Estudios de la Mujer and Casa de la Mujer La Morada, 1987, p. 39.
71 Julieta Kirkwood and Sonia Montecino Aguirre, *Feminarios*, Santiago: Ediciónes Documentas, 1987, pp. 18–19.
72 Kirkwood, *Ser Política en Chile: Las Feministas y los Partidos*; Kirkwood, *Ser Política en Chile: Los Nudos de la Sabiduría Feminista.*
73 Kirkwood, *Ser Política en Chile: Las Feministas y los Partidos*, p. 67.
74 Julieta Kirkwood, "Develemos NUESTRA Historia," in Kirkwood, *Tejiendo Rebeldías*, p. 26.
75 Adriana Santa Cruz and Viviana Erazo, *Mujer y Comunicación*, Mexico City: Unidad de Comunicación Alternativa de la Mujer del Instituto Latinoamericano de Estudios Transnacionales (ILET), 1982; Adriana Santa Cruz, Viviana Erazo, and Graciela Torricelli, *Mujer y Educación Formal*, Santiago: Unidad de Comunicación Alternativa de la Mujer del Instituto Latinoamericano de Estudios Transnacionales (ILET), 1985.
76 Gabriele Küppers, *Feministamente: Frauenbewegung in Lateinamerika*, Wuppertal: Peter Hammer, 1992, pp. 232–3; Adriana Santa Cruz and Viviana Erazo, *Compropolitan. El Orden Transnacional y su Modelo Femenino. Un Estudio de las Revistas Femeninas en América Latina*, Mexico City: Editorial Nueva Imagen, 1981.
77 Santa Cruz and Erazo, *Compropolitan*, pp. 100–1.
78 Berta Hiriart, "*Mujer/fempress*: Latin American Women's News Agency," in Gabriele Küppers (ed.) *Compañeras. Voices from the Latin American Women's Movement*, London: Latin American Bureau, 1994, pp. 163–6.
79 Francesca Miller, *Latin American Women and the Search for Social Justice*, Hanover, NH: University Press of New England, 1991, p. 227.
80 For a detailed discussion of these developments, see Jadwiga E. Pieper Mooney, *The Politics of Motherhood: Maternity and Women's Rights in Twentieth-Century Chile*, Philadelphia: University of Pittsburgh Press, 2009.
81 Letter from *Mujeres por la Vida* to Carmen Ramírez, Director of the Women's Section of the Chilean Christian Democratic Party, 1987. Facultad Latinoamericana de Ciencias Sociales (FLACSO), Santiago, Chile, Fondo Ruiz Tagle, B27 MxV 128, p. 2, Carta de Mujeres por la Vida a Carmen Ramírez, Directora Nacional del Departamento Femenino, Partido Demócrata Cristiano, Santiago, 19 de agosto de 1987.
82 Teresa Valdés, *Las Mujeres y la Dictadura Militar en Chile*, Santiago: FLACSO, 1987, p. 35.
83 Frohmann and Valdés, *Democracy in the Country and in the Home.*
84 Sonia Montecino and Josefina Rossetti, *Tramas para un Nuevo Destino: Propuestas de la Concertación de Mujeres por la Democracia*, n.p, 1990.
85 Coordinación de Organizaciones Sociales de Mujeres, *"Soy Mujer... Tengo Derechos." Campaña de Discusión*, Santiago: Facultad Latinoamericana de Ciencias Sociales (FLACSO)-SEPADE, 1991.
86 Coordinación de Organizaciones Sociales de Mujeres, *"Soy Mujer... Tengo Derechos,"* pp. 1–6.
87 Coordinación de Organizaciones Sociales de Mujeres, *"Soy Mujer... Tengo Derechos,"* p. 5.
88 Participants published their demands. See "Cuadro General" in Coordinación de Organizaciones Sociales de Mujeres, *"Soy Mujer... Tengo Derechos,"* pp. 47–9.
89 Anexo No. 6, "Consignas Utilizadas en el Acto del Paseo Ahumada (21/11/1989)," in Coordinación de Organizaciones Sociales de Mujeres, *"Soy Mujer... Tengo Derechos,"* pp. 47–9.
90 Anexo No. 6, "Consignas Utilizadas."

91 Anexo No. 6, "Consignas Utilizadas."

92 Ley 19.023, 1991, Article 2. Online. Available at www.leychile.cl/Navegar?idNorma=30390&buscar=Ley+19.023%2C+1991 (accessed 5 January 2019).

93 *El Mercurio* 22 July 2006 and 16 August 2006, 13–14. See also Research Directorate, Immigration and Refugee Board of Canada, Ottawa, "Chile: The Protection, Services and Recourse Available for Women Victims of Domestic Violence (2005–February 2007)," 13 March 2007. Online. Available at www.refworld.org/docid/469cd6a214.html (accessed 5 January 2019).

94 *El Mercurio*, 16 August 2006, 12. See also Research Directorate, "Chile: The Protection, Services and Recourse."

95 Chile, Ministerio de Justicia, "Modifica el Código Penal y la Ley No. 20.066 sobre Violencia Intrafamiliar, estableciendo el 'Femicidio'." Online. Available at www.leychile.cl/Navegar?idNorma=1021343 (accessed 5 January 2019).

96 "Chile Creates Ministry of Woman and Gender Equality," *San Diego Tribune*, 3 June 2016. Online. Available at www.sandiegouniontribune.com/hoy-san-diego/sdhoy-chile-creates-ministry-of-woman-and-gender-2016jun03-story.html (accessed 5 January 2019).

97 In 2017, Chile's constitutional court approved a bill that legalizes abortion under limited circumstances (if the pregnancy endangers the life of the woman, the fetus is not viable, or if the pregnancy resulted from rape). See Jadwiga E. Pieper Mooney, "The Long Road to Reproductive Rights in Chile," *NACLA* [North American Congress on Latin America] *Opinion and Analysis*, 19 September 2017. Online. Available at https://nacla.org/news/2017/09/27/long-road-reproductive-rights-chile (accessed 5 January 2019).

98 Moreno, *Evidencias*, p. 61.

99 Merike Blofield documents that while Aída Moreno spearheaded marches and political lobbying throughout the 1980s and 1990s, domestic workers' influence weakened. Merike Blofield, "Feudal Enclaves and Political Reforms: Domestic Workers in Latin America," *Latin American Research Review*, 2009, vol. 44, no. 1, 158–90.

100 For details see Cynthia Meillón with Charlotte Bunch (eds.), *Holding On To the Promise: Women's Human Rights and the Beijing + 5 Review*, New Brunswick, NJ: Center for Women's Global Leadership, 2001.

101 Rosa-Linda Fregoso and Cynthia Bejarano (eds.), *Terrorizing Women: Feminicide in the Americas*, Durham, NC: Duke University Press, 2010, p. 76.

102 Alicia Schmidt Camacho, "Ciudadana X: Gender Violence and the Denationalization of Women's Rights in Ciudad Juárez, Mexico," *CR: The New Centennial Review*, 2005, vol. 5, no. 1, 255–92.

103 Melissa W. Wright, *Disposable Women and Other Myths of Global Capitalism*, New York: Routledge, 2006.

20

THE MOTHERS OF THE PLAZA DE MAYO

From dictatorship to democracy

Jennifer Adair

Introduction

On the evening of 25 May 2010, the center of Buenos Aires filled with spectators gathered for a parade to mark the end of Argentina's bicentennial celebrations. The performance highlighted the popular heroes of national history, from the leaders of nineteenth-century independence to the immigrants who forged labor movements and built industries. The most talked about moments of the evening, however, were those that focused on Argentina's recent past, a period that began in 1976 with a vicious military coup and ended with defeat in the Malvinas (Falklands) War and the restoration of democracy in 1983.

At the center of the procession was a float representing the Mothers of the Plaza de Mayo, the human rights group formed in 1977 by women whose children were disappeared by the military regime. Members of a theatrical troupe dressed in long raincoats and the Mothers' signature white kerchiefs embroidered with their children's names walked in a circle as rain fell upon their headscarves. Under the street lamps that illuminated them, the kerchiefs gave off an iridescent and solemn glow.[1] As the float moved through the center of Buenos Aires, just a few blocks from where the organization began during the dictatorship, the performance recalled the history of the Mothers (*las Madres*) themselves, from their early origins as loosely coordinated groups of women to a robust social movement that fought to bring to justice those responsible for the crimes of state terror. More than 30 years after the organization's founding, the inclusion of the Mothers of the Plaza de Mayo in the bicentennial procession signaled that the women were protagonists in a sweeping national narrative that drew a direct link from the pain and sacrifice of their struggles to the ultimate triumph of democracy over authoritarianism.

Histories of the Mothers of the Plaza de Mayo tend to focus on the first two decades of the movement: from the Mothers' inception in the 1970s up through the disappointments of the transition to democracy, which culminated in the pardons of military leaders in the early 1990s.[2] This scholarship, whether focused on radical motherhood, the politicization of memory, or the performative aspects of the Mothers' activism, concludes with the steadfast heroism of the women in the face of state recalcitrance and the impunity of the armed forces.[3] Written in the wake of bitter reversals of justice, these works rightly highlight the "incomplete" and "open-ended" struggle of the Mothers. Yet, the place of the Mothers in the broader narrative of recent Argentine history and Latin American human rights movements has shifted since this first generation of scholarship. This essay reconstructs a history of the Mothers of the Plaza de Mayo with an eye to the present and future of the movement. As the analysis will show, the history of the Mothers of the Plaza de Mayo remains open-ended. However, that narrative is now framed by the new triumphs and challenges the movement has faced over the past decade.

The opening decades of this century have witnessed a transformation in Argentine and Latin American public life, as the trials of military leaders have been reopened throughout the region and as many states incorporated memory and human rights defense into official policy. The ascendance of human rights, combined with a willingness to address past abuses in countries emerging from periods of conflict and authoritarian rule, formed a regional transitional justice movement that gained momentum in the late 1990s.[4] In the Argentine case, the governments of Néstor Kirchner (2003–7) and Cristina Fernández de Kirchner (2007–15), which came to power in the wake of Argentina's 2001 economic crisis, incorporated human rights as part of a broad-based platform to address the social impact of over a decade's worth of neoliberal policies.

At rallies, public meetings, and government events, the Kirchners embraced the Mothers of the Plaza de Mayo in symbolic affirmation of the state's renewed commitment to dealing with the legacies of the past. In this political terrain, the Mothers of the Plaza de Mayo lent their support to a government that vindicated many of their long-term demands. The re-opening of trials represents an overwhelming achievement after long years of struggle. Many of the women will live to see their children's torturers and murderers sentenced to prison terms. But like other social movements before that have been recalibrated in the context of more favorable political settings, the Mothers of the Plaza de Mayo confronted new concerns in the midst of the often-factious public arena of the Kirchner years. Some chafed at the Mothers' association with the state, while others charged that the Mothers' relationship to the Kirchners opened the way for easy criticism of human rights and gender-based movements as a whole, particularly as the region sees a conservative resurgence. Internally, the activists have dealt with corruption scandals, in addition to the incorporation of an expanded list of social issues into their traditional repertoire.

As the Mothers entered the fourth decade of their activism, and as the women aged into their eighties and beyond, some asked: What will become of the Mothers of the Plaza de Mayo when they are no longer with us? What better culmination to over 30 years of unceasing labor than the concrete achievements of the Kirchner years? This was a compelling argument that many of the women and other human rights leaders considered and debated. To return to the bicentennial parade, the powerful rendering of the Mothers was indeed a highlight of national celebrations. However, it risked implying that the Mothers' struggle had ended in the context of a state willing to confront the past and demand accountability. That interpretation threatens to diminish the radical autonomy that has characterized and sustained the women's human rights movement for the majority of its existence. Beyond simple narratives of social movement co-optation, the recent history of the Mothers of the Plaza de Mayo builds on strategies evolved over decades of activism.

This essay will show how the Mothers of the Plaza de Mayo have consistently pushed the state and civil society to live up to the ideals that marked the end of authoritarianism in Argentina, shaping the values by which Argentine democracy has been measured and judged. Recent scholarship has begun to investigate the links between the ascendance of human rights in the "long 1970s" and the simultaneous rise of market fundamentalism.[5] The main concerns center on the question of a causal relationship between the two ideologies, and the extent to which they reinforce one another. At first glance, the history of Mothers of the Plaza de Mayo fits neatly into the timeline of this global phenomenon: the founding of the women's movement in the 1970s coincided with the military dictatorship's early experiments in free market liberalism, which reached their height under a democratically elected government in the 1990s. A closer look at the long-term history of the Mothers complicates any facile reading of the connection between the two concepts. For it was the Mothers who rejected any inherent relationship between the protection of individual human rights (for example, the protection of the body against torture and disappearance) and the individual freedoms promised by the proponents of neoliberalism. By linking past state terror to the economic and social injustices of the democratic present, the Mothers put forward the most powerful critique of Argentina's return to democracy. Read against the history of post-dictatorship Argentina, the Mothers' radicalism evolved not only in relation to their identity as mothers, but also through their politicization of the very concept and practice of human rights. Through the Mothers of the Plaza de Mayo, then, it is possible to read a history of the changing contours of modern Argentine democracy, which came together in the crucible of dictatorship and in the ongoing attempts to reconcile political and social justice, human rights, and memory.

In the crucible of state terror

A long-term social biography of the Mothers of the Plaza de Mayo begins with a singularly transformative period in Argentine public life. Though the women who make up the Mothers of the Plaza de Mayo bring unique personal histories from across class, geographic, and religious backgrounds to their activism, most of the women formed their families in the 1940s and 1950s. These decades saw the formal entrance of new protagonists into Argentine political life – most notably the industrial working class and organized labor – accompanied by the social changes inaugurated by the government of Juan Domingo Perón (1945–55). The coup that ended Perón's government initiated two decades of ever more violent clashes between the military right wing and an emboldened left that culminated in the 1976 military coup.

The women's children came of age during the heady years following Perón's ouster. Their political awakenings were framed by the national turmoil of the post-Perón era, the global anxieties of the Cold War, and the effervescent promise of a New Left sparked by the Cuban Revolution. For the most part, the women who founded the Mothers of the Plaza de Mayo did not actively participate in this changing world. Despite all of the vast transformations of the mid-twentieth century, the patriarchal structures of domestic life remained intact. While the world was altered around them, and as their children engaged in projects of social and revolutionary emancipation, many of the women's lives revolved around the home and the quotidian dramas of family life. Marta Ocampo Vásquez, whose daughter María Marta was disappeared in 1976, recalled how she had looked with both awe and concern at her daughter's growing political engagement, noting the distance between their lived realities, "She had these values that were so different from mine, but just look how my own values have changed."[6]

The women's lives were forever changed by the military dictatorship that came to power in March 1976. In the tumultuous months leading up to the coup, the overthrow of the government was widely anticipated by broad sectors of Argentine society and greeted with a sense of relief. This reaction was not surprising given the long history of military coups that dominated political life since the 1930s.[7] Immediately upon taking power, however, the junta made it clear that this time they intended a radical departure from earlier military interventions. The armed forces proposed to remake Argentina and Argentines through a mission they called the National Reorganization Process. With the military cast as the moral center of the nation, the junta vowed to stamp out "subversion," a sweeping category that included not only Marxist revolutionaries but also a wide range of others: "First we will kill all the subversives, then we will kill their collaborators, and after that … their sympathizers, and following that … those who remain indifferent, and finally we will kill the timid ones."[8] The junta leaders combined medieval, obscurantist, and messianic ideals with the language of modern rationality, systems, and bureaucratic coordination. Their ultimate goal was to restore Argentina to its rightful place in the pantheon of Western Christian nations. In practice, this translated into disappearances, torture, abductions, illegal adoptions, concentration camps, and thousands forced into exile or hiding. These steps, the military claimed, were the necessary and calculated sacrifices of a "dirty war" in the service of preparing Argentina for the eventual restoration of constitutional rule. Yet, as one junta leader after another lamented, "Argentines were not ready for democracy."

Paradoxically, within this period of overwhelming fear, loss, and exile, possibilities for democracy began to reemerge in ways that would eventually herald the end of the military's reign on Argentine public life. State terror sparked the birth of the contemporary human rights movement.[9] The Mothers of the Plaza de Mayo quickly became the most visible of the new organizations founded during this period. The women's collective movement began with the individual and deeply personal search for a child. In interviews and testimonies, the Mothers told familiar stories of how the disappearance of their sons and daughters began their own excruciating political initiation in the corridors of government buildings, law offices, hospitals, churches, and police stations.[10] Following a disappearance, many families exhausted the limited bureaucratic channels available to them in the midst of the dictatorship. They cleaned out savings accounts to pay lawyers, who filed ineffectual writs of habeas corpus. They returned daily to hospitals and police stations, waiting for hours on end, in the hopes of gaining information and the possible release of a loved one. Those with connections called in political favors. Often, these tasks fell to women – mothers, homemakers and spouses – who, unlike their employed husbands, "had the time." Other women balanced their jobs as teachers, shopkeepers, and factory workers as they looked for their children. Indicative of the calculated risks people made throughout that era, many believed that women faced less danger than did their male family members when going directly to the authorities. As the futile searches dragged on during the first year of the dictatorship (1976–7), the height of the worst violence, the women began to see familiar faces in their daily pursuits. Within a few months, they began to coordinate actions together.

The founding of the Mothers of the Plaza de Mayo has been told and retold, but the story still retains its potency. On 30 April 1977, 14 women gathered in the Plaza de Mayo, the center of state power in the heart of Buenos Aires, and the site of foundational moments in Argentine political history. At this point, the women believed that their children would be returned to them alive. The women's goal in meeting publicly was to break the stalemate of their searches. It was a Saturday, and the Plaza was empty of the weekly bustle of workers in the surrounding presidential palace and government buildings. The women decided to return during the workweek, and from these first gatherings, with the authorities urging the women to walk in a circle around the Plaza due to regime prohibitions on public gatherings of more than two people, the Mothers of the Plaza de Mayo grew. News of the women's presence in the Plaza spread through word of mouth, and soon they were joined by other mothers and relatives of the disappeared.[11] María del Rosario Cerruti, whose son Fernando was disappeared in 1976, noted that the main purpose of the early marches was to draw the attention of the authorities and the public to their plight:

> We wanted people to see us, to know we were there, so we began to walk in the center of the square, around the monument. Even if people supported us they stayed outside the square. It was very dangerous for them to approach us. We were very alone in the beginning.[12]

The Mothers' first innovation was the visible nature of their protests. Against the backdrop of clandestine state terror, which functioned through secret prisons, verbal obfuscation, and mendacity, the presence of the women in the Plaza de Mayo marked one of the first openly defiant confrontations of regime logic. While human rights organizations like the Center for Legal and Social Studies (CELS) and the Permanent Assembly for Human Rights (APDH) worked through legal channels, forging important connections to international solidarity networks, the Mothers complemented this broad strategy by becoming the public face of regime resistance. It would be a mistake, however, to read these efforts as part of a fully rendered plan against the junta. The Mothers of the Plaza de Mayo, and the contemporary human rights movement as a whole, evolved quickly through a balance of pragmatic calculation and direct action within the confines of authoritarianism. For example, the Mothers' decision to wear their iconic headscarves – fashioned out of their children's cloth diapers – resulted from the practical concern of being able recognize one another during a procession.[13] The Mothers' political education was born first of the loss of their children, and then of their frustration with regime lies, which led, as Maria del Rosario Cerruti's testimony implies, to no other alternative than public confrontation.

The political uses to which the women put their shared identity as mothers demonstrated the ethical and radical potential of their activism. According to the military leaders at the helm of the National Reorganization Process, all Argentines had a role to play in combating subversion. Mothers occupied a special place in the junta's domestic imagery and language. They were cast as the familial guardians of the nation and as a bulwark against the corrupting influences of Marxism, guerrilla warfare, and diffuse notions of an "anti-Argentine" menace. Within this context, the Mothers of the Plaza de Mayo used the rhetoric of the armed forces to expose and undermine the very premise of the regime. In one of their first public pronouncements, a full-page solicitation published in October 1977 in the newspaper *La Prensa*, the Mothers addressed the junta, the armed forces, and the ecclesiastical authorities on behalf of the "pain of hundreds of mothers and spouses of the Disappeared." They declared, "We can no longer endure the cruelest of tortures for a mother, which is the unknown fate of a child." The pronouncement concluded with a direct appeal to the image of the regime as composed of Christian men:

> We have exhausted all means to arrive at the Truth. That is why we are publicly imploring the help of decent men (*hombres de bien*), who genuinely love truth and peace, and who truly believe in God and Final Judgment, which no one can escape.[14]

The Mothers' collective protest, born of a private pain, converted maternal suffering into a national and international political imperative. In asking by what right the disappeared were taken, in calling for "truth," due legal process, and a list of those detained, the Mothers put in relief the illegality and immorality of state terror. For its part, the junta quickly tried to discredit the Mothers as "*locas*" or madwomen, and the women became targets of the regime. In December 1977, three of the founding Mothers were disappeared, along with nine other human rights activists, in an ambush at a church in Buenos Aires. While the loss struck a blow, it also fortified the women's resolve to grow their movement. In August 1979, the Association of the Mothers of the Plaza de Mayo was formally founded as an organization. During this period the organization took a leading role in gathering names of the disappeared and testimonies for the 1979 visit of the Inter-American Commission on Human Rights (IACHR).[15] By the end of the decade, the world came to know Argentina's Mothers. Emerging from the home to demand the return of their children, the mostly middle-aged women did not immediately conjure up images of radical protest. They were not attempting to upend the traditional structures of domesticity. Their radicalism took root in their public demands to restore a maternal promise of safety, private home life, and physical integrity, all of which had been suspended under the dictatorship.

In socializing motherhood beyond the domestic sphere, the Mothers of the Plaza de Mayo shaped expectations for what Argentine democracy should look like going forward. By the early 1980s the regime was in crisis, destabilized by its dismal international reputation and faltering under the weight of the impending regional debt crisis. Following defeat in the 1982 Malvinas War with Great Britain, the junta announced the transition to democratic rule.[16] By then, however, the Mothers had already solidified the maxim that any future constitutional government must protect the physical integrity of its citizens from state abuse. "Human rights" emerged as a rallying cry of the transition to democracy. Within six years of their first gatherings in the center of the nation, the Mothers had adopted the features of a formal organization, with offices, internal governance, and leadership. As they grew over the course of the dictatorship, they not only defined expectations for constitutional rule, but also prefigured the changing landscape of popular protest and new social movements at the end of the twentieth century. While many of their children embraced the promise of the revolutionary overthrow of state power, the Mothers of the Plaza de Mayo positioned themselves to pressure the state to bring to justice those responsible for the crimes of dictatorship. Their efforts came to define the "transition to democracy."

An incomplete transition

The democratic transition brought with it demands for accountability regarding the fate of thousands of disappeared. Human rights organizations and family members sought to position themselves for participation in the new system, seeking justice and information about loved ones. The initial measures taken by the government of Raúl Alfonsín

(1983–9), the first democratically elected president following the dictatorship, seemed to promise the realization of these goals. On 13 December 1983, three days after his inauguration, Alfonsín signed decrees ordering the prosecution of the three juntas that ruled during the dictatorship, in addition to leaders of the armed leftist group Ejército Revolucionario del Pueblo (People's Revolutionary Army, ERP) and Montoneros. He repealed a "Law of Pacification" – a self-amnesty issued by the military regime, which would have protected junta members from trials – and ordered the arrest of top military brass. He also authorized the creation of the National Commission on Disappeared Persons (CONADEP), the investigative efforts of which resulted in the publication of the *Nunca Más* report a year later.[17] These measures were among the most prominent first steps taken by the administration and boosted the moral authority of the new government.

The Mothers viewed the Alfonsín government with skeptical optimism. The human rights movement as a whole believed that Alfonsín had a popular mandate to take on the military.[18] It quickly became clear, however, that the government was both constrained by the ongoing power of the armed forces, and also disinclined to move forward with all of the movement's demands. By the one-year anniversary of the return to democracy, the Mothers openly criticized the limited scope of the investigations and upcoming trials, which would be confined to the upper ranks of military officials. An article in the organization's newspaper, launched in 1984, began, "The right to life, the pinnacle of all human rights, was violated by a nefarious force that remains in power ... Is the constitutional government unable to dominate this force? Or does it simply not want to?"[19] This criticism of the Alfonsín administration's obstruction of a more robust pursuit of justice grew louder over the course of the 1980s, especially as possibilities for prosecution diminished.

In 1985, as the trials led to inquiries into the actions of lower-ranking officers, sectors of the military threatened to boycott the proceedings, which increased fears of military revolt. In response to escalating military unrest, in December 1986 Alfonsín persuaded Congress to pass the "Full Stop Law," the first of two measures that placed limits on ongoing legal processes.[20] Then in April 1987, a contingent of lower-ranking soldiers calling themselves the *carapintadas* (painted faces) occupied the largest military garrison in Argentina and demanded an end to the trials. Alfonsín brokered the deal that ended the uprising, and in July Congress passed the "Due Obedience" law, which exempted from prosecution lower-ranking officers who tortured or murdered in fulfillment of orders. The Due Obedience Law effectively put an end to the trials and sparked condemnation throughout the country.[21]

By 1989, as the Alfonsín presidency drew to a close, the euphoria of democratic return had been displaced by fears of military insurrection, economic ruin, and the widespread recognition that the democratic transition had fallen far short of its initial promises.[22] In the midst of fiscal disarray and further military uprisings, many Argentines placed their hopes on the new government of Carlos Menem. Menem took office during a crisis of severe hyperinflation that had forced the early abdication of Raúl Alfonsín. Menem based his campaign on a pledge of a "productive revolution," in concert, at least rhetorically, with his Peronist roots. Yet upon taking office he almost immediately set out to undo the legacy of his party, launching a series of neoliberal reforms that dismantled what remained of the welfare state, and sparking the growth of massive inequalities over the course of the decade. Shortly after taking office, Menem also unveiled a platform to promote democratic stability, peace, and national "pacification." Among his first acts toward this goal was the pardon of officials prosecuted during the 1984–5 trials of the military juntas. The pardons, which freed over 400 by the end of 1990, represented the culmination of a gradual dismantling – from the mid-1980s on – of legal gains in accountability for the crimes of the dictatorship.

For the Mothers of the Plaza de Mayo, the first decade of democratic rule following the dictatorship etched a path from hope to disillusionment. At the same time, the constitutional return revealed deep fissures within the organization itself. During the dictatorship, the women formed a united front against the regime. With the return to democracy, however, unity gave way to tensions about the internal governance of the organization and the treatment of the past. One group of Mothers, led by Hebe de Bonafini, whose sons Jorge and Raúl and daughter-in-law María Elena were disappeared, objected to the state's exhumations of mass graves and to the CONADEP commission and trials, which they claimed did not sufficiently address the culpability of officials responsible for the specific deaths and disappearances. A second faction of mothers criticized the CONADEP commission and trials while still advocating participation in these state-led efforts. This latter group also objected to the leadership of de Bonafini, arguing that her style constrained democracy within the organization. In 1986, tensions came to a head and the organization split in two. Hebe de Bonafini assumed the leadership of the Association of the Mothers of the Plaza de Mayo. Another, smaller organization calling itself Mothers of the Plaza de Mayo – Founding Line rallied around the defense of the "founding principles" of the movement and "horizontal" leadership.[23]

Despite the organizational split and the political differences that emerged in the coming years, the Mothers as a whole never deviated from the protest repertoire that marked their entrance into public life during the first decade following constitutional return. They continued their weekly marches, occupying the Plaza de Mayo, which was by then indelibly associated as "belonging" to the Mothers. At the same time, the two groups each negotiated a complicated transition into a political force in its own right. The disappointments of the Alfonsín and Menem years helped solidify the Mothers of the Plaza de Mayo as a fiercely autonomous oppositional movement, located beyond specific party or ideological affiliation. The Mothers demanded truth and justice. These were not diffuse social ideals, but rather claims for investigations, concrete policies, and political institutions. While the Mothers never wavered in their commitment to constitutional rule as the principal guarantor against state terror, their efforts ultimately threw into relief the fact that democracy would remain an illusion without a full response to the past.

The politics of memory in a neoliberal age

The task of the Mothers of the Plaza de Mayo in the early 1990s was not so much to defend of the veracity of crimes of state terror, but rather to promote a historical narrative that presented the legal setbacks of the 1980s and 1990s as the product of authoritarianism that had not necessarily ended with the return to democracy. Emilio Mignone, co-founder of the human rights organization the Center for Legal and Social Studies, and a staunch ally of the Mothers, expressed the importance of memory for human rights organizations following pardons for military officials:

> [Our] role with respect to the past does not end with the conclusion of criminal trials. There exists another, equally important and never-ending task, which is

> the construction and consolidation of social memory. If legal justice will not sanction those responsible, then society has to do it.[24]

Legal pardons sanctioned by the Menem government might set military officers free, but remembrance would not. "Memory work" for the Mothers translated into concrete initiatives to raise awareness of the presence of the unfinished past in daily life. Evidence abounded – from pardoned military criminals encountering their victims in public, to the implementation of the dictatorship's neoliberal economic policies, to the absence of the disappeared. The women worked to change school curricula, among other initiatives, and the Mothers of the Plaza de Mayo – Founding Line participated in early discussions about ways to enshrine the memory of the period in memorials and museums.[25] As always, the women remained a public presence through their unfaltering weekly marches.

Social memory is closely linked to the notion of a "politics of memory" involving the struggle among groups to control and promote a specific vision of the past intended to inform and shape the present.[26] In the absence of legal recourse, promoting memory of the recent past proved a source of resilience for the Mothers' movement. Just as Alfonsín and Menem assessed recent Argentine history as a continuum of conflict, the Mothers of the Plaza de Mayo, along with other human rights organizations, identified a decades-long pattern of abuse, impunity, and permanent fiscal policies of structural adjustment. Even though the military had retreated as a political force by the early 1990s, other aspects of authoritarianism remained – even thrived – under the new democracy.

The Mothers of the Plaza de Mayo were instrumental in promoting what would become a prominent and convincing narrative of recent Argentine history that explicitly linked structural adjustment to political and social violence, whether during the dictatorship or after. In the early 1990s, the abuses of the recent past ranked lower in concern for wide swathes of Argentines than the more immediate problems facing the nation. In response, the Mothers expanded their protest repertoire to address the effects of neoliberalism, which they saw as intimately bound up with the forces that led to state terror. The women channeled their historic demands for truth and justice into a powerful reading of the neoliberal present, according to which the embrace of open market reforms exacerbated the same social injustices their children had fought against and sacrificed their lives for. Through this rendering of the recent past, the Mothers validated the activism of their children, not just as victims, but as righteous political militants. This shift accompanied the emergence of new social movements throughout Argentina that denounced structural adjustment and globalization.[27] The Association of the Mothers of the Plaza de Mayo, the larger of the two organizations and led by Hebe de Bonafini, was the more vocal in equating the economic struggles of the 1990s with the political battles of the 1970s. Yet both organizations frequently lent their support to progressive labor movements and community associations at the forefront of efforts to address the burdens of escalating debt and the fallout from deep inequalities sparked by the neoliberal era.[28]

The Mothers' work took on even greater urgency with the onset of the economic crisis that began in 2001. In late December of that year, Argentina defaulted on its debt, plunging half of the population into poverty. Several days of widespread popular uprisings against globalization and the political class met with state repression that resulted in an estimated 40 deaths. The resounding call of the protests was "*Que se vayan todos!*"

(They all must go!). As the center of Buenos Aires smoldered, then-president Fernando de la Rúa fled in a helicopter. He was followed in quick succession by four presidents in two months.

The Mothers stood at the center of the protests, their white kerchiefs gleaming in the Plaza de Mayo. The second day of the uprisings, 20 December, fell on a Thursday, the scheduled day of their weekly march. It seemed fitting that the Mothers should once again occupy the Plaza in defiance of a state of siege declared by the government. Once again, and mere steps away from where their movement began, the women found themselves confronting security forces and demanding information about the fate of young people dragged away violently by the police. Several suffered injuries from rubber bullets and police batons. One journalist described the violence against the Mothers that day as "the worst sin."[29] Photos of the women, arms linked, standing down riot police on horses circulated widely and brought to mind their formation at the height of state repression two decades earlier. The images placed in bitter relief their ongoing efforts to denounce and reverse the injustices of the authoritarian past and the democratic present.

La década ganada: an ambivalent triumph?

During the first two decades of their existence the Mothers of the Plaza de Mayo represented a fiercely oppositional political force. By contrast, the years following the 2001 crisis initiated an unprecedented era of alliances between the Mothers and government officials, and cooperation with the state. The governments of Néstor Kirchner (2003–7) and Cristina Fernández de Kirchner (2007–15) championed human rights and a willingness to address the past. Among other initiatives, they reopened trials of military officials. Events like these elevated the Mothers of the Plaza de Mayo as the nation's emblematic defenders of justice, memory, and due process. But while the Kirchner governments presented the Mothers of the Plaza de Mayo with new opportunities, the era also posed vexing challenges for the movement and the place of human rights in public life.

Néstor Kirchner assumed office in May 2003, in the midst of fiscal collapse, staggering rates of unemployment, and destitution. Within the first two years of his term, Kirchner successfully renegotiated Argentina's debt with the International Monetary Fund (IMF) and began to repair the economy. After a decade of punishing austerity measures, the expansion of progressive social policies improved the lives of many. By 2005, Argentina enjoyed growth rates of up to 7 percent a year.[30] As with other leaders associated with Latin America's "new left turn," Kirchner spoke out vehemently against the free-market recipes of the previous decade. He embraced the narrative articulated by the Mothers of the Plaza de Mayo and other social movement leaders, who had drawn a direct line from Latin America's Cold War authoritarian regimes to neoliberal ruin, and actively built upon it. In this context, a proper reckoning with the past became a political imperative and a matter of state policy.

On 24 March 2004, the 28th anniversary of the military coup, Kirchner designated the Navy Mechanics School (ESMA), the most infamous detention center of the dictatorship, as the official site of a future Museum of Memory. The Mothers of the Plaza de Mayo – Founding Line, among many other human rights groups, had long pushed for the creation of a museum dedicated to preserving the memory of state terrorism and the struggle against repression. As Kirchner addressed the crowds assembled at the site, he reserved special attention for "the mothers, grandmothers, and children" of those directly affected by state terror and asked "for forgiveness on behalf of the national state for the shame of having been silent about these atrocities during twenty years of democracy."[31] A widely circulated image of Kirchner ordering the removal of the portraits of military leaders at the ESMA was read by many as a groundbreaking change of the political guard: the arrival of a government finally willing to shatter the impunity of the armed forces. The symbolic gesture augured more concrete measures to come.

Néstor Kirchner and his wife Cristina, a senator who succeeded him in 2007, made human rights an organizing principle of their administrations. While efforts to reverse the Full Stop and Due Obedience laws of the 1980s had begun long before the Kirchners took office, events greatly accelerated after 2003, when Néstor Kirchner's presidency began. He immediately forced the retirement of military officials linked to repression and appointed new judges to the Supreme Court. Also in 2003, Congress declared the impunity laws unconstitutional. Two years later, the Supreme Court upheld the congressional decision, which paved the way for the reopening of trials across the country. As of December 2017, a total of 864 new sentences for military and police officials had been handed down.[32]

Throughout their political rise, the Kirchners purposefully identified themselves as members of the generation directly affected by the political violence of the last dictatorship. In their mid-fifties by the early 2000s, the Kirchners were the same age as many of their disappeared contemporaries. Despite their tenuous connections to left-wing movements during the years they spent as students at the University of La Plata, their carefully crafted autobiographies positioned them as taking up the political mantle of the disappeared members of their generation.

Thus began a close association with the Mothers of the Plaza de Mayo. In Cristina Kirchner's inaugural address in 2007, she emphasized the connection:

> My strength comes from the example of the women with the white kerchiefs who dared to do what nobody dared. This is the example of the Mothers and the Grandmothers, the Mothers and the Grandmothers of the *Patria* (fatherland). This is their example, and that of our forefathers, Mariano Moreno, San Martín, and Belgrano.[33]

In her speech, Kirchner made the case that justice and national sovereignty depended on the struggle of the Mothers, and, by association, her mandate as well. Throughout their presidencies, which spanned 12 years from 2003–15, the Kirchners relied on the presence of the Mothers, and often invoked them as a legitimizing force for their own initiatives. In the process, they converted the Mothers of the Plaza de Mayo into moral stateswomen on par with a pantheon of foundational national heroes.

For their part, the Mothers of the Plaza de Mayo gradually embraced the Kirchners as their symbolic *hijos*, or children. The Kirchners' pronouncements and policies on human rights solidified a political relationship that the Mothers expressed through the language of a maternal bond, one that connected the presidential couple to their own disappeared sons and daughters. Hebe de Bonafini, leader of the Association of the Mothers of the Plaza de Mayo, reversed her initial skepticism of Néstor Kirchner in April 2004, less than a year into his presidency. "I once said," she declared in an interview,

> that someday one of our children would cross the Plaza to sit in the presidential seat. Now [Néstor Kirchner] tells me that on 24 March 1976, he thought that he wanted to become president. I could never have dreamed that something like this would happen so fast.[34]

For the first time since the initial promise of the return to democracy, a government willing to challenge the cycle of impunity renewed the women's faith in Argentina's democratic institutions and the state as a legitimate space for their activism. Both groups of Mothers wholeheartedly championed the reopening of the trials as the culmination of their hard won battles for justice and a triumph. In 2008, when Cristina Kirchner's government came under fire during a bitter fight with agricultural producers, the Mothers stood by her side. When the powerful media conglomerate *Grupo Clarín* challenged a government-proposed media law, the Mothers offered their support. And when Néstor Kirchner died suddenly of a heart attack in 2010, the Mothers mourned him as their own son. Hebe de Bonafini wrote in an open letter, "Thank you, my son … for a life of such passion. I am proud of you and of that youthful generation of which you formed a part for a national popular project of liberation."[35]

Twelve years of government under the Kirchners saw closer collaboration between the Mothers and the state than ever before. The Association of the Mothers of the Plaza de Mayo was more explicitly aligned with the Kirchner government, but the Mothers of Plaza de Mayo – Founding Line also expressed their support for the presidential couple. Both groups moved towards public cooperation with a government that responded to and addressed their demands. Eventually, this relationship began to alter some of the women's most prominent public actions. In 2006, Hebe de Bonafini announced the end of the annual "March of Resistance," a yearly 24-hour vigil in the Plaza de Mayo first instituted in 1981. In explaining the decision to end the 25-year-old tradition, de Bonafini declared that the march would be ending because "there are no longer any enemies within the presidential palace."[36] The statement underscored the long history of the Mothers of the Plaza de Mayo as a steadfast oppositional force but also hinted at the end of the women's movement, given the new political moment.

In all of this, however, the Mothers courted controversy. The Kirchners oversaw the establishment of popular social policies and a significant reduction in inequality, but they also presided over one of the most divisive political landscapes since the return to democracy in 1983. Their opponents accused them of corruption, illicit enrichment, and crass populism, among other infractions. The close association with the Kirchners meant that the Mothers became linked to the more controversial aspects of their presidencies and governing style. In 2011, news broke that two of two associates of the Association of the Mothers of the Plaza de Mayo, the organization led by Hebe de Bonafini, had embezzled millions of pesos in public funds destined for a housing project sponsored by the Mothers' foundation. Though de Bonafini was found innocent of any knowledge or wrongdoing, the case opened up vociferous attacks against the human rights movement as a whole. Opponents seized upon the scandal as proof of the dishonesty of the Kirchners and their social agenda.[37] The case also emboldened critics of Hebe de Bonafini, who long considered her the most disruptive representative of the two Mothers organizations. Others pundits voiced dismay at what they saw as the politicization of human rights.[38] Such recriminations sometimes came from within the human rights movement itself, as with the Nobel Peace Prize winner Adolfo Pérez Esquivel, who accused the

Kirchners of using the legacy of the dictatorship as a way to avoid addressing the rights violations of the present.[39] These charges tended to cast the Mothers, by then elderly women, as pawns of a political project, seemingly unaware of the ways that their newfound affinity with the government might tarnish their prestige.

But these criticisms obscured more than they revealed. While the Mothers lauded the human rights advances ushered in by the Kirchner governments, the relationship was much more of a two-way process. The Mothers' support for the Kirchners was not automatic. It was granted only after concrete initiatives had begun to be put into place. In other words, if the Mothers relied on the Kirchners to advance their demands, the Kirchners also depended on the women to build consensus around a broad range of policies. The challenge was not necessarily social movement co-optation as some suggested, but rather historical memory. Supporters often described the Kirchner governments as the culmination of a long road to justice. When incorporated as part of this narrative, the history of the Mothers of the Plaza de Mayo as a radically autonomous political force risked falling victim to the very types of selective remembering that the movement long sought to combat within Argentine society.

Read against the long-term history of the movement, the women's alliance with the state drew upon many of the strategies of protest and contention that characterized their work over the course of decades of activism. During the clandestine terror of military rule, the Mothers publicly exposed the crimes of the armed forces. After the return to democracy, with all of its disappointments and reversals of justice, the women promoted a powerful politics of memory. And as neoliberal reforms threatened the most vulnerable sectors of Argentine society into the 1990s and beyond, the women made a case for the resonance of human rights as social justice. The Kirchner presidencies inaugurated a period of formidable gains for the Mothers' long-term demands. But even in the midst of this more auspicious political moment, the goals that drove the women's movement – the pursuit of truth, justice, and an end to impunity – remained unchanged. In this sense, the alliance with the Kirchners constituted a rational strategy to achieve their objectives – one more instance of the Mothers' ability to adapt to changing political opportunities throughout their history.

The 1980s are often referred to as a "lost decade," due to a combination of stalled fiscal reforms and the miscarriages of justice that defined the years immediately following the dictatorship. The first decade of this century has been termed *la década ganada* ("the won decade"), an era that witnessed advances in social justice and stunning reversals of impunity. The reopening of the trials and the convictions of military leaders are achievements to be celebrated for this is a reality that the Mothers of the Plaza de Mayo forged over several decades of labor beyond the bounds of national government. The "won decade" did not augur the end of the Mothers' work. It constituted one more chapter of a movement that has long shaped the values against which Argentine democracy has been judged and measured.

Conclusions

Forty years after their founding, the women who make up the Mothers of the Plaza de Mayo are still recognized nationally and internationally at the forefront of the Argentine human rights movement. With each passing year, as the number of Mothers who are able to attend their weekly marches dwindles, they are joined by younger activists and supporters, who parade around the white kerchiefs now painted in the center of the Plaza de Mayo, a testament to the longevity of a movement that began at the height of state terror. In the years since their beginnings, the Mothers have never deviated from their mission to bring to justice those responsible for the disappearance of their children. Looking beyond those beginnings, however, offers new insight into the place of the Mothers and human rights in post-dictatorship Argentina.

In the aftermath of Argentina's 2001 economic crisis, the governments of Néstor Kirchner and Cristina Fernández de Kirchner elevated to state policy a narrative that the Mothers had forged through their activism. The resumption of trials to convict those responsible for the most heinous crimes of the regime began to fulfill the women's long-term demands, as it solidified an emotional and political relationship with the presidential couple. This period begged the question: what happens to a social movement when its goals begin to be fulfilled? The advanced age of the women, many of them in their late eighties, added urgency to the matter. The longer-term history of the movement may offer some insights, as this essay has demonstrated how the women have been adept at expanding their protest repertoires and making clear the resonance of their demands in the context of ever-changing political realities. This most recent chapter of the Mothers' history is more than a story of simple co-optation. The women may have gotten closer to a state willing to address its demands, but this constituted one more instance of their political evolution, and perhaps an exceptional one at that. As of this writing, the Mothers of the Plaza de Mayo have returned to the more familiar role of an oppositional political force in the face of the government of Mauricio Macri, a conservative administration more openly critical of the human rights movement. Though trials to convict military officials have continued, human rights activists have faced new legal setbacks. In May 2017, for example, conservative Supreme Court judges appointed by Macri ruled in favor of early release for officials convicted of human rights abuses.[40] In response, the Mothers convened a march in the Plaza de Mayo. Tens of thousands of protesters gathered at the founding site of the women's movement and held high the Mothers' iconic kerchiefs in repudiation of the ruling, blanketing the Plaza in white.[41] As the Mothers of the Plaza de Mayo enter the fourth decade of their activism, their movement built from the loss of their children continues to serve as the political and moral compass of the democratic era re-inaugurated in 1983.

Notes

1 The theater group Fuerza Bruta represented the Mothers of the Plaza de Mayo in the bicentennial parade. For more on the celebrations, see "El desfile que deslumbró millones," *La Nación*, 26 May 2010. Online. Available atwww.lanacion.com.ar/1268722-el-desfile-que-deslumbro-a-millones (accessed 25 June 2018); "Toda es historia, en version multitudinaria," *Página 12*, 26 May 2016. Online. Avaialble atwww.pagina12.com.ar/diario/elpais/1-146377-2010-05-26.html (accessed 25 June 2018).

2 Select works on the history of the Mothers of the Plaza de Mayo are: Marguerite Bouvard, *Revolutionizing Motherhood: The Mothers of the Plaza de Mayo*, New York: Rowman & Littlefield, 1986; Marguerite Feitlowitz, *A Lexicon of Terror: Argentina and the Legacies of Torture*, New York: Oxford University Press, 1999; Jo Fisher, *Mothers of the Disappeared*, New York: South End Press, 1989; Ulises Gorini, *La rebelión de las madres: Historia de Las Madres de la Plaza de Mayo*, Buenos Aires: Grupo Editorial Norma, 2010; Maryssa Navaro, "The Personal Is Political: Las Madres de la Plaza de Mayo," in Susan Eckstein (ed.) *Power and Popular Protest: Latin American Social Movements*, Berkeley: University of California Press, 1989, pp. 241–58; and Diana Taylor,

Disappearing Acts: Spectacles of Gender and Nationalism in Argentina's Dirty War, Durham, NC: Duke University Press, 1997.

3 For more on Mothers' movements and their relationship to new social movements in Latin America at the end of the twentieth century see Sonia Alvarez, *Engendering Democracy in Brazil*, Princeton, NJ: Princeton University Press, 1990; Elsa Chaney, *Supermadre: Women in Politics in Latin America*, Austin: University of Texas Press, 1979; Elizabeth Dore and Maxine Molyneux, *Hidden Histories of Gender and the State in Latin America*, Durham, NC: Duke University Press, 2000; and Temma Kaplan, *Taking Back the Streets: Women, Youth, and Direct Democracy*, Berkeley: University of California Press, 2004.

4 For more on the rise of transitional justice movements in Latin America see Naomi Roht-Arriaza and Javier Mariecurrena (eds.), *Transitional Justice in the Twenty-first Century: Beyond Truth and Justice*, New York: Cambridge University Press, 2006; David Pion Berlin, "The Pinochet Case and Human Rights Progress in Chile: Was Europe a Catalyst, Cause, or Inconsequential?" *Journal of Latin American Studies*, 2004, vol. 36, no. 3, 479–505; Kathryn Sikkink, *The Justice Cascade: How Human Rights Prosecutions Are Changing the World*, New York: W.W. Norton, 2011; Winifred Tate, *Counting the Dead: The Culture and Politics of Human Rights Activism in Colombia*, Berkeley: University of California Press, 2007; Victoria Sanford, *Buried Secrets: Truth and Human Rights in Guatemala*, New York: Palgrave Macmillan, 2003.

5 For more on the emergence of human rights and neoliberalism see Samuel Moyn, "A Powerless Companion: Human Rights in the Age of Neoliberalism," *Law & Contemporary Problems*, 2014, vol. 77, 147–69.

6 Memoria Abierta, Archivo Oral, Video-recording: "Testimonio de María Marta Ocampo Vázquez," Buenos Aires, 2001.

7 For a more on the origins and history of the dictatorship see Federico Finchelstein, *The Ideological Origins of the Dirty War: Fascism, Populism, and Dictatorship in Twentieth Century Argentina*, New York: Oxford University Press, 2014.

8 The statement is attributed to the de facto military governor of Buenos Aires, General Ibérico Saint Jean in May 1977. In Spanish, the full quotation reads, "Primero mataremos a todos los subversivos, luego mataremos a sus colaboradores, después ... a sus simpatizantes, enseguida ... a aquellos que permanecen indiferentes, y finalmente mataremos a los tímidos." Quoted from Ministerio de Educación Argentina. Online. Available at www.me.gov.ar/efeme/24demarzo/frases.html (accessed 25 June 2018).

9 For a brief history of the modern Argentine human rights movement see Elizabeth Jelin, "Los derechos humanos: entre el estado y la sociedad," in Juan Suriano (ed.) *Nueva Historia Argentina*, vol. 10, *Dictadura y Democracia (1976–2001)*, Buenos Aires: Editorial Sudamericana, 2005, 507–57.

10 Memoria Abierta, Archivo Oral, Video-recording: "Testimonio de Lydia 'Taty' Stella Mercedes Miy Uranga de Almeida," Buenos Aires, 2001.

11 For example, women whose grandchildren were disappeared by the military regime also joined the weekly processions. They eventually founded their own organization, the Grandmothers of the Plaza de Mayo, which is dedicated to recuperating the children who were born in captivity and illegally adopted.

12 Quoted from Jo Fisher, *Mothers of the Disappeared*, Boston: South End Press, 1989, 54.

13 Memoria Abierta, Archivo Oral, Video-recording: "Testimonio de Carmen Lapacó," Buenos Aires, 2001.

14 "Madres y esposas de desaparecidos: Solo pedimos la verdad," *La Prensa*, 5 October 1977. Online. Available athttp://educacionymemoria.educ.ar/secundaria/wp-content/uploads/2011/03/fuentes-capitulo-2.-Pensar-la-dictadura.pdf (accessed 25 June 2018).

15 For the full results of the investigation see Inter-American Commission on Human Rights, "Report on the Situation in Argentina," December 1980. Online. Available at www.cidh.org/countryrep/Argentina80eng/toc.htm (accessed 25 June 2018).

16 Following Argentina's surrender to Great Britain in June 1982, it took close to six months to settle on the official date for democratic elections. Negotiations for the transfer of power from military to civilian rule continued throughout the early months of 1983, with presidential elections finally set for 30 October of that year.

17 Comisión Nacional sobre la Desaparación de Personas (CONADEP). *Nunca Más: The Report on the Argentine National Commission on the Disappeared*, trans. Writers and Scholars International, New York: Farrar Straus Giroux, 1986.

18 Memoria Abierta, Archivo Oral, Video-recording: "Testimonio de Lydia 'Taty' Stella Mercedes Miy Uranga de Almeida," Buenos Aires, 2001.

19 *Periódico de la Asociación Madres de Plaza de Mayo*, año I, N° 1. Buenos Aires, diciembre de 1984. Online. Available at http://archivohistorico.educ.ar/sites/default/files/IX_03.pdf (accessed 25 June 2018).

20 The law stipulated a 60-day statute of limitations, after which no further charges could be brought against military officers suspected of crimes. Though the government hoped Full Stop would appease the military, the strategy backfired: over 400 new cases were filed by the expiration in February 1987.

21 The only crimes exempted from the Due Obedience and Full Stop Laws were the thefts of babies stolen from mothers who were detained or disappeared.

22 From 1987 on, continued military unrest and fiscal turmoil steadily undermined the legitimacy of Alfonsín's government. Inflation had been on the rise since 1986, but it skyrocketed as the 1989 presidential elections drew near. Shortly before the elections in May 1989, international credit organizations cut off financing, sparking a run on the Argentine peso and a bout of hyperinflation that lasted for several months. Massive looting and riots engulfed the nation, leading to Alfonsín's resignation in July 1989, six months before his term was set to expire.

23 For more on the organizational split see Ulises Gorrini, *La otra lucha*, Buenos Aires: Grupo Editorial Norma, 2008.

24 Emilio Mignone, *Derechos Humanos y sociedad: El caso argentine*, Buenos Aires: Centro de Estudios Legales y Sociales, 1991, 169. See as well, Abuelas de Plaza de Mayo, Asamblea Permanente por los Derechos Humanos, Asociación de Ex-detenidos Desaparecidos, Centro de Estudios Legales y Sociales, Familiares de Desaparecidos Detenidos por Razones Políticas, Liga Argentina por los Derechos Humanos, Madres de Plaza de Mayo-Línea Fundadora, Movimiento Ecuménico por los Derechos Humanos, Movimiento Judío por los Derechos Humanos, and Servicio Paz y Justicia, *Culpables para la sociedad, impunes por la ley*, Buenos Aires: Centro de Estudios Legales y Sociales, 1988.

25 Memoria Abierta, Proceedings of "Primeras jornadas de debate interdisciplinario: Organización institucional y contenidos del futuro Museo de la Memoria," Conference held in Buenos Aires, 30 September–2 October 1999, Buenos Aires: Memoria Abierta, 1999.

26 Elizabeth Jelin, *State Repression and the Labors of Memory*, Minneapolis: University of Minnesota Press, 2003.

27 Maristella Svampa, *La sociedad excluyente: Argentina bajo el signo del neoliberalismo*, Buenos Aires: Taurus, 2005.

28 For more on the expanding work of the Association of the Mothers of the Plaza de Mayo in the 1990s, see *Historia de las Madres de la Plaza de Mayo*, Buenos Aires: Ediciones Madres de Plaza de Mayo, 2006; and Elizabeth Borland, "The Mature Resistance of Argentina's Mothers of the Plaza de Mayo," in Hank Johnston and Paul Almeida (eds.) *Latin American Social Movements: Globalization, Democratization, and Transnational Networks*, New York: Rowman & Littlefield, 2006.

29 Cristian Alarcón, "Crónica de una violenta represión que duró todo el día: La batalla de Plaza de Mayo," *Página 12*, December 2001. Online. Available at www.pagina12.com.ar/2001/01-12/01-12-21/pag13.htm (accessed 25 June 2018).

30 For more on the economic and social policies enacted in aftermath of the 2001 crisis see Cara Levey, Daniel Ozarow, and Christopher Wylde (eds.), *Argentina Since the 2001 Crisis: Recovering the Past, Reclaiming the Future*, New York: Palgrave Macmillan, 2014.

31 "Discurso del Presidente de la Nación Argentina, Dr. Néstor Kirchner, en el acto de firma del convenio de la creación del Museo de la Memoria, y para la promoción y defensa de los Derechos Humanos," 24 March 2004. Online. Available at https://es.wikisource.org/wiki/Discurso_de_N%C3%A9stor_Kirchner_por_la_creaci%C3%B3n_del_Museo_de_la_Memoria (accessed 25 June 2018).

32 For more information about the trials and convictions, see the data compilation covering 2005–16 by the Center for Legal and Social Studies (CELS). Online. Available at www.cels.org.ar/web/estadisticas-delitos-de-lesa-humanidad (accessed 12 November 2018).

33 Mariano Moreno, José de San Martín, and Manuel Belgrano led Argentina's independence movements in the nineteenth century. "Mensaje de la Presidenta a la Asamblea Legislativa del Congreso de la Nación en su asunción del mando, 10 de diciembre de 2007." Online. Available at www.cfkargentina.com/asuncion-de-cristina-kirchner-10-de-diciembre-de-2007 (accessed 25 June 2018).

34 "Reportaje a Hebe de Bonafini: 'La izquierda nunca entendió a las Madres'," 1 April 2004. Online. Available at www.lavaca.org/seccion/actualidad/0/912.shtml (accessed 25 June 2018).

35 "Carta a Néstor, mi hijo," Asociación Madres de la Plaza de Mayo, 28 October 2010. Online. Available at www.madres.org/navegar/nav.php?idsitio=5&idcat=33&pagina=4&idindex=173&b_frase (accessed 25 June 2018).

36 "La última Marcha de la Resistencia de Hebe," *Página 12*, 24 January 2006. Online. Available at www.pagina12.com.ar/diario/ultimas/20-62083-2006-01-24.html (accessed 25 June 2018).

37 Luis Gasulla, *El negocio de los derechos humanos*, Buenos Aires: Editorial Sudamericana, 2012.

38 "¿Son los Kirchner los dueños de los derechos humanos?" *La Nación*, 25 March 2010. Online. Available at www.lanacion.com.ar/1247001-son-los-kirchner-los-duenos-de-los-derechos-humanos (accessed 25 June 2018).

39 "Entrevista con Adolfo Pérez Esquivel. Nunca pudimos a sentar a hablar con la Presidente: no dialoga, monologa," 15 December 2014. Online. Available at www.infobae.com/2014/12/15/1615351-nunca-pudimos-sentarnos-hablar-la-presidente-no-dialoga-monologa (accessed 25 June 2018).

40 "Les están abriendo la puerta a los genocidas," *Página 12*, 3 May 2017. Online. Available at www.pagina12.com.ar/35399-les-estan-abriendo-la-puerta-a-los-genocidas (accessed 25 June 2018).

41 "'Mar de pañuelos,' la impactante foto de la marcha contra del 2x1 que emocionó a todos," *Los Andes*, 11 May 2017. Online. Available at https://losandes.com.ar/article/-mar-de-panuelos-la-impactante-foto-de-la-marcha-contra-el-2x1-que-emociono-a-todos (accessed 25 June 2018).

21

ASMA JAHANGIR

Personifying the human rights debate in Pakistan

Afiya Shehrbano Zia

Introduction

Asma Jahangir, the internationally acclaimed lawyer and activist, was a central figure in the debates, challenges, and achievements for women's and human rights in Pakistan. She was the founder of the independent Human Rights Commission of Pakistan, the country's preeminent human rights nongovernmental organization (NGO), which she chaired for several years. She also served as a United Nations (UN) Special Rapporteur on three occasions: on extrajudicial, summary, or arbitrary executions; on freedom of religion or belief; and on the human rights situation in Iran. She won an array of international awards, yet at home she was often a controversial figure, standing at the center of disputes between international women's rights norms and the complex, fragmented local gender regimes in Pakistan.

This essay discusses the dualisms that have shaped gender roles, relations, and rights in the Islamic Republic of Pakistan, including those of religious minorities. This duality includes, on the one hand, the liberal, individualized, secular, democratic, and rational underpinnings that are considered key to Western notions of human rights and, on the other hand, the values of collectivity, honor, complementarity of gender relations, and religious legal reasonings that are believed to characterize Islamic world views. This essay analyzes the criticisms, suspicions, and enmities that women's rights and human rights activism have faced since the 1980s, and that have escalated in the post-9/11 period. The hostility emanates not only from conservatives and Islamists, but also from several diasporic and Pakistani scholar-activists. In their criticism, a rights-based discourse has been taxonomized as "Western" and "Islamophobic," while feminists and human rights activists have been cast as imperialists, collaborators, and native informants. As Islam and nationalism have become increasingly intertwined in Pakistan, rights for religious minorities have come under sharper attack, leaving these groups vulnerable to majoritarianism. In this essay, all these contestations are framed by the person of Asma Jahangir, who came to symbolize human rights in Pakistan and was also made the principal target of nationalist, religious, majoritarian, and masculinist anxieties.

The rise of women's rights networks led to the emergence in the 1970s of a new system of global governance concerning women's rights, human rights, and gender equality. International principles, treaties, and other legal instruments with monitoring mechanisms were widely adopted. These carved out spaces for women's rights and human rights commissions in governments. However, it is considerably harder to estimate the impact of these steps across all societies and communities. Despite the international commitments made by states such as Pakistan, human rights have been subject to constant controversy over their interpretation, application, and impact for women.

For Pakistan and other Islamic contexts, the apparent conflict between Islam and women's rights has been an enduring topic of debate. In the post-9/11 period, these anxieties were heightened by a new set of critics, taking new directions. As religious militancy, terrorism, and the "War on Terror" were ravaging Afghanistan and Pakistan, the already embattled human rights discourse came under fresh scrutiny. Debates around cultural imperialism and the consequences of liberal rights in Muslim contexts were revived. Any criticism of Islamic laws and politics made by feminists was met by accusations of "Islamophobia." Already perceived as disloyal and "Westernized" by religio-nationalists, in the post-9/11 era activists were labeled "liberal fundamentalists," "native informants," and even "imperialist feminists."

Asma Jahangir's journey of human rights activism since the 1980s signifies the interplay, shifts, and conflicts involving these dualistic legal and normative rights regimes as they have clashed, converged, and sometimes settled at temporary stalemate in Pakistan. Her advocacy for democracy and the rights of workers, women, and religious minorities provoked contestations with the state, the military, and political parties. Looking at some of the causes she championed, this essay revisits core debates over the positioning of Islamic and Western value systems in women's and human rights movements in Pakistan over the past four decades.

This essay discusses the progress of women's human rights within Pakistan's legal, social, and cultural oppositional political context. It takes into account the interrelations of rights in both dictatorial and democratic regimes, and across theological and universalist arguments on women's human rights. It also focuses on key legal cases involving the two constituencies with which Asma was most intimately associated: women and religious minorities. Her involvement with cases of violence against women and the persecution of religious minorities through the blasphemy laws has altered the course of human rights in Pakistan.

Islamization of the 1980s: challenges to human rights

Pakistan presents a complicated, and often contradictory case, when it comes to the state's engagement with human rights. Pakistan was one of the 60 countries that voted on the Universal Declaration of Human Rights (UDHR) in 1948, bringing it into force – a commitment that is echoed in the chapter on "fundamental rights" in its constitution.[1] However, successive decades have seen a series of constitutional amendments and revocations of these rights, under military and civilian governments. These annulments of women's and religious minorities' rights have often rested on religious justifications, or pretexts of national security. The authors of these exceptions to rights have included conservatives, military dictators, and even avowedly secular, democratically elected leaders. The result of this desecularization of rights – where the question of gender has made unlikely allies of the religious right and self-proclaimed secularists – has been a "substantial confusion over where the lines are drawn between what is Islamic, what is codified tradition, and how (if at all) to delineate their separate jurisdictions."[2]

Women's participation in and contributions to state formation dominated the early years of Pakistan, and several progressive laws and policies "feminized" the republic. The period under General Ayub Khan (1958–69) saw the rise of many welfare-oriented women's associations under his benevolent, modernizing regime. The seeds of the contradictory relations between women's rights, opportunistic Islamic politics, and modern rights resulted in the progressive Muslim Family Law Ordinance (MFLO) of 1961.[3] Under Prime Minister Zulfiqar Ali Bhutto (1972–7) there was considerable progress for women, but the period was marked by consistent challenges from the orthodoxy and by compromises to which the civilian leadership acceded.[4]

Although several prior regimes used religion to compromise or undermine gender equality, it was in 1977, against the backdrop of a revolution brewing in Iran, that General Muhammad Zia ul Haq (1977–88) staged a coup and unleashed an aggressive campaign to "Islamize" Pakistan. Women and religious minorities were made exemplary symbols of this attempt and faced unprecedented reversals of their rights.[5] Women activists who had been politically active in their student years became the "anti-Islamic" nemeses of the Islamic Republic because of their dynamic struggles against the theocratic military dictatorship and their combined protest against a patriarchal regime defined by "Men, Money, Mullahs and the Military."[6] In 1981, many of them came together to form the Women's Action Forum – the lead organization that launched the strongest challenge to Zia ul Haq's dictatorship. Asma Jahangir was a member. When just 18, she petitioned against the military government of General Yahya Khan, challenging her father's political detention. The Supreme Court decided in her favor in 1972, after Yahya Khan's government had ended, with the judges declaring the military government illegal and finding General Yahya Khan to be a "usurper."[7] Asma was also part of street protests against the brutalities committed by West Pakistan's army in crushing the rebellion and the struggle for independence by East Pakistan/Bangladesh in 1971.

During General Zia ul Haq's dictatorship, the campaign around women's rights as human rights gained momentum. His regime effectively trumped several postcolonial lay[8] laws and replaced or compounded them with select Islamic laws, particularly the Hudood Ordinances of 1979. Under these Ordinances, the *zina* (adultery) law criminalized consensual sex (*zina*) while also covering broader sex crimes, including rape and abduction. The *zina* law carried a blatantly discriminatory bias, including the fact that testimony of four "upright Muslim men" of any rape or adulterous act was admissible as evidence. On the other hand, the inability of a rape victim to prove her abuse (absence of bruises, being of "loose character" or being "habitual" by way of sexual activity or even being pregnant as a result of the rape) carried the potential of converting rape complaints into adultery charges.[9] Since adultery and consensual sex was now made a cognizable crime against the state, the principle of presumption of innocence effectively stood dissolved.

Since the police was authorized to decide the nature of the offense,[10] the social repercussions meant that parents were able to annul their daughters' free-will marriages by accusing their daughters of *zina* if the police failed to find evidence of coercion. Husbands did the same, in order to take revenge on wives seeking divorce or as a pretext for contracting second marriages themselves.[11] As a tool of harassment, it enabled law enforcement officers to extort bribes from couples who could not prove their marital status. Activists were confronted by many allegations of physical abuse and rape during police custody of the women accused of committing *zina*.[12]

Parallel to the lay courts,[13] a new Federal Shariat Court was set up in order to decide whether laws and provisions were in accordance with Islam. The influence of the Shariat court on the notion of Islamic human rights and women's rights is a matter of ongoing debate in Pakistan.[14] Under Zia's regime, other discriminatory laws reduced the status and citizenship of Muslim women and all non-Muslims. These included laws such as the *Qanoon e Shahdat* (evidence) law of 1984, the *Qisas* and *Diyat* (retribution and compensation) laws, and amendments to the blasphemy law.

Women's struggles against a theocratic state

In 1980, Asma Jahangir set up the AGHS, the first all-women law firm that worked primarily on women's rights in family law.[15] The AGHS office was often used as a refuge by lawyers who were protesting against Zia ul Haq's military regime. On 12 February 1983, the Women's Action Forum held a public demonstration in Lahore against the discriminatory Hudood Ordinances. Asma and her sister Hina Jilani, also a lawyer, both joined the protest as members of the Punjab Women Lawyers Forum. It was the first open and public opposition to General Zia ul Haq's military regime of Islamization. The women were beaten, baton-charged and even arrested.[16] Activists recall anecdotally Asma's defiance in the police stations and how her status as a lawyer gave them the confidence that they would not be abandoned in jails. Since the language and narrative of human rights was relatively unknown at the time, it was legal constitutional rights that activists relied on. It was on this cusp of a postcolonial legal rights regime that was being heavily layered with Islamic laws and codes and, now, parallel Islamic courts, that certain cases become sites of contest and brought forward all the contradictions that defined this encounter.

During this time, Asma and members of Women's Action Forum pursued cases of gender-based violations as articulated through the *zina* law, honor crimes, and the persecution of religious minorities under the blasphemy laws. It was always by way of these laws and issues that the most contentious debates flared up concerning the place for human rights in the Islamic Republic of Pakistan. The *zina* law motivated women activists to launch an organized series of protests against its discriminatory intent and its facilitation of legal and social patriarchal collusion among men, the police, the judiciary, and social vigilantism in general. Several feminists and human rights activists have documented the abrogation of the rights of women and non-Muslims in this period.[17] The legacy of such violence has continued long after the Zia regime, to the extent that vigilantism under the cover of defending an abstraction called "Islam" operates with impunity in Pakistan society.

At societal levels, the construct of the "good Muslim" encouraged competitive public performativity of piety and orthopraxis by collectives in return for state patronage. General Zia ul Haq's campaign to put women into the "Chaddar and Chardewari" (the veil and the four walls, i.e. domesticity), a proposed dress code, prohibiting sportswomen's participation in national or regional games, and deterring women's participation in the performing arts were blatant threats to or violations of their fundamental rights. These attempts to enforce gender apartheid in Pakistan society has been the subject of feminist poetry and some fiction.[18]

Amina Jamal notes that after Haq's state-sponsored Islamization challenged urban, educated women's faith in the modern state, they found themselves struggling "against a confrontational rather than reformist state."[19] In 1988, the return to democracy under the liberal-leaning Benazir Bhutto, the first female prime minister of the Muslim world, held much promise for these women activists and other progressive forces. This hope was short-lived, as an adversarial military handicapped her government and her government did not dismantle many of the theocratic laws, bodies, and policies instituted by Zia ul Haq. It was during this democratic interregnum that human rights activism focused on reversing the Islamic laws and gained momentum by way of linking up with transnational human rights networks and becoming part of the regional and international rights community.

In the 1990s, several human rights, women's rights and nongovernmental organizations were born of the pro-democracy movement.[20] Asma, instinctively drawn to marginalized causes, moved beyond family law cases and took on the causes of bonded labor, child labor, and blasphemy accusations against minorities. At one point, under Zia ul Haq's regime, his handpicked parliament (Majlis e Shura) even accused her of blasphemy, but the inquiry was disposed of for lack of proof. At the same time, other activists were working on many other cases, concerning labor rights, enforced disappearances, and provincial autonomy, as well as initiating a people's peace talk series to mitigate historical hostilities with India. In particular, pro-democracy activists agitated against the systematic interventions of the Pakistan military in democratic processes.

To expand on a trust that she had cofounded for political prisoners, Asma Jahangir took the initiative to set up the Human Rights Commission of Pakistan (HRCP) in 1986. Several renowned lawyers endorsed the commission and Justice (retd) Dorab Patel, a former chief justice of the Sindh High Court who had refused to take a fresh oath as a judge of the Supreme Court under Zia's regime, was appointed its first chairperson. Human rights lawyer Saroop Ijaz notes that "[t]he most outstanding feature of the newly created HRCP was its overtly secular mandate" and its commitment to the rights of religious minorities in Pakistan.[21] Asma was part of the Women's Action Forum's decision, taken after many years of debate, to define its strategic political approach as secular, which eventually led the organization to ratify its status as a secular organization in 1994.

Activism over this period focused on reforms of discriminatory laws and attitudes in the justice system and on the relevance, interplay, and redefinition of culture, economics, and their relationships with Islam. Necessarily, groups disagreed on the role of Islam in organizing strategic resistance and on the framing of women's legal and sociocultural rights in a Muslim context. At the same time, international and regional debates over women's rights as human rights and the compatibility of Islam and universal rights influenced the narrative in Pakistan, too. This entanglement of Islam, human rights, and secular resistance has played an important role in the politics of rights-based activism and has influenced the broader legal and sociopolitical fabric of Pakistan, as discussed in the next section.

Global and local debates over human rights/Muslim rights for women

There is now considerable literature on the encounters between Islam and human rights discourses. The scholar of law and ethics Ann Mayer[22] points out how the historical path has not been a consistent one. She notes that prior to the global Islamic revivalism of the

1970s, there was considerable constructive input from Muslim states that were keen to influence and apply foundational UN human rights instruments. That was especially clear with reference to the first generation of international or universal "blue print" or negative rights that were largely protectionist in nature (civil-political freedoms) and the second-generation "red rights" or positive rights (social, economic, cultural, healthcare, employment). Mayer also mentions that no Muslim country initially voted against Article 18 of the UDHR, which states the right to change one's religion (apostasy is forbidden in many Islamic countries).[23] In that era of fervent decolonization and nationalism, Muslim countries supported and signed many human rights conventions. Sociologist David Johnston also notes the growing influence of Islam over UN resolutions, resulting in several declarations of human rights in Islam.[24]

It is the fourth generational set of rights (sexualities) that cause Muslim governments more anxieties, reservations, and reluctance to adopt. In 2004, Lisa Hajjar documented how the criticism of international human rights (as Western values) was steadily gaining momentum at international fora.[25] She notes that such defensiveness was based on a premise that prioritized collective relations and mutual duties over individual rights. She observes how women's rights became the "primary redoubts of anxieties about cultural imperialism."[26] Hajjar notes that Islamic resistance to international human rights law condensed specifically around women's rights and that most Muslim governments often present themselves as defenders of Islam and as building a "firewall" around Sharia. She questions though, whether such a stance "actually represent[s] a Muslim consensus?"[27]

It is around the issue of consensus that the debate thickens, and also divides the advocates of reform. Those who resist universalist modes and laws can range from orthodox members of the Ulema (clerical authorities) to postsecularist critics of (Western) liberal ideals or human rights. The prescription of reform pivots on the compatibility of Islam with human rights and refers to the flexible boundaries of the Sharia, its pragmatic resonance with Muslims, and the boundless possibilities in Islamic epistemology and painstaking restorative work of Islamic scholars towards this end. Hajjar questions such efforts to "reify religion," from the pragmatic point of view that religion is a reality for all Muslims, and she wonders whether this position would not simply "stifle and punish those offering dissenting views or alternative interpretations of religion."[28] It is also unclear as to which version would finally (and somehow consensually, in the eyes of billions of Muslims) be influential in deciding the dominant version of Islamic law or indeed, of national identity. The influence that women's voices could have on such a reform course is highly questionable, given that women's participation on panels of Ulemas around the Muslim world, like their voices on Islamic matters more generally, is marginal to nonexistent.

Pakistani feminists found themselves addressing the claim that UN human rights conventions were a disguised form of cultural imperialism and the claim, largely right-wing, that women's rights and feminism were aimed at undercutting and defaming Muslim cultures. Issues such as the veil have never been the focus of debate in Pakistan, but all through the 1980s and 1990s debates and contests over religious laws persisted.

Much of this controversy was put to an uneasy rest by the impact of the much-celebrated first Muslim woman leader of an Islamic country, the late prime minister Benazir Bhutto (in office 1988–91; 1993–6). In 1990 Pakistan became a State Party to the UN Convention on the Rights of the Child and signed the 1993 Vienna Declaration, which recognized women's rights as human rights. In 1994, despite fierce opposition from Islamist political parties and the conservative press, Bhutto attended the UN International Conference on Population and Development, held in Cairo, where she addressed the UN session and signed the Plan of Action. This was viewed as courageous defiance of Islamist lobbies that had contested the UN discourse on women's reproductive freedom and rights, and especially because other leaders from Muslim countries caved in to their countries' religious lobbies and made the pragmatic decision to abstain from participation. Bhutto did not intend any secular departure, however, and she emphasized Islamic tenets and opposed the legalization of abortion. In 1995, Bhutto led a strong delegation of women's rights activists to the Fourth UN Conference on Women (held in Beijing), and despite repeated opposition by the religious lobbies her government became a signatory and party to the UN Convention on the Elimination of Discrimination Against Women (CEDAW) in 1996. The Pakistani state thus turned its attention back to the issue of women's rights in the 1990s, but most of this attention came by way of treaty ratifications[29] rather than promoting legal reforms or enforcing new domestic policies.

In 1997 the government of Pakistan formed a Commission of Inquiry for Women (CIW), which in turn issued a report with radical recommendations. It was no coincidence that several prominent women's rights activists authored that report, including Asma Jahangir and Shahla Zia. The report identified key areas that were discriminatory toward women: laws, customs, practices, and criminal procedures. It made three important and controversial recommendations: to legalize abortion; to abolish the Federal Shariat Court, on the grounds that other courts could adjudicate the same issues and so it was redundant; and to repeal the Hudood laws, on the grounds that they had not achieved their objectives. The Report argued that the laws on *zina* and evidence contravened constitutional safeguards; it recommended that marital rape be made a penal offense "and to impose a severe punishment for rape on a minor wife."[30] It appealed to its readers with the claim that such reforms were inevitable if Pakistan's stature in the international arena were to be raised. Scholar Anita Weiss observes that recommendations such as these, which were made throughout the report, "drew the state further into the discourse of defining women's rights through the institutional structures it would support."[31] In any case, these recommendations were not implemented. The existing laws' bias and discriminatory thrust of the laws continued to push Pakistan toward the bottom of most international indices measuring progress on gender and human rights. The unsettled question of Muslim women's autonomy was the key issue of contention that prevented the implementation of such rights.

Women's autonomy as the key to human rights

The CIW report contested the role and identity of the *wali* (parent or guardian in Muslim tradition, and the figure who determined the boundaries of women's autonomy in Pakistan); Islamic laws; and continuing patriarchal collusion between Muslim men and the state. While the first was not a formal policy, the CIW raised it because it informed many policies and citizenship rules, and even influenced parliamentary deliberations on the value of the compensation to be made in the event of a woman's murder. The discriminatory bent of religious laws is based on the overarching principles of gender relations and gender division of roles and duties defined by Islamic ethos. The concept of a *wali* is indicative of an overall infantilizing of Muslim women, and binds their rights to protectionist, maternal, collective notions rather than autonomous ones. The CIW report objected to the *Qisas* and *Diyat* laws for how they converted criminal offenses into "a private matter rather than treating them as crimes against society."[32]

Although the *wali* is defined in gender-neutral terms, in both language and examples the *wali* is always male.[33] The concept of *wali* also underpins the rationale behind honor killings, when men murder women under the pretext of family honor. Historically, the state's prosecution of such crimes has been characterized by collusion between the patriarchal state and its male governing proxies.[34] Honor crimes have traditionally been shielded by Islamic laws of *Qisas* and *Diyat*, which have allowed forgiveness of the family member who has murdered the woman as part of a code for the restoration of the honor of the family/tribe.

These interrelated elements became apparent in 1997, when Asma Jahangir defended Saima Waheed. Saima, a 22-year-old woman, had married a man named Arshad Ahmad against the wishes of her conservative parents, who considered him beneath their class status.[35] When she broke the news of her elopement to her conservative family, Saima was beaten, drugged, and deprived of food until she managed to escape and avail herself of Asma Jahangir's services. By contracting Asma's legal support, living in a women's shelter, and publicizing her cause, Saima was perceived to be insulting the honor of the family. Her decision to exercise her legal rights was considered to be a transgression of her filial duties, which in turn were perceived to include deference in matters of sexual autonomy. Her family resorted to harassing her husband's family and filed a case that challenged the legality of her marriage – but not under *zina* law, as had been the norm in earlier cases. In the contentious legal battle that followed, Saima's father's counsel argued that her marriage was void *ab initio* because it lacked the father's – the *wali*'s – consent. Asma, in turn, petitioned the court seeking a declaration upholding the validity of Saima's marriage. Debates reverberated around the country about the notions of filial obedience and Islamic duty for women. As one critical observer noted, Asma's representation and feminists' support for Saima produced fears of the "loss of cultural purity caused by the combined influences of neo-imperial designs and the treachery of their local collaborators."[36]

Ultimately, the case pitted the requirement of the *wali*'s consent against the legal independence of adult Muslim women as based on statutory law inherited from the colonial era. The debate inside the lay court was anguished, as reflected in the judgement. It lamented the influence of Western liberalism in Pakistani society and concluded that the Sharia recognized women's full legal capacity and surpassed the rights of the common law. That is, the judgement resolved the dispute by appealing to the Sharia and by invoking a more "egalitarian" interpretation of Islam, instead of the word of law. A dissenting judgement entered by Justice Ihsan ul-Haq Chaudhary appealed to a protective Sharia, and would allow Muslim women only a limited legal capacity. Rejecting the contention that the Sharia allowed any Muslim to marry without the consent of a guardian, the judge invoked the role of national judges as the "custodians of the morals of Pakistan's citizens."[37] Justice Chaudhary appealed to the idea of an authentic or organic Islam, and argued for ranking cultural and communal values above Western individualism. While the Court's majority judgement concluded that ties of family and community could not deny Saima Waheed her right and freedom to marry a spouse of her own choosing, the commentary on this case revealed the paradoxical relationship of Islam and women's human rights.

Many celebrated the outcome of this case, but Asma Jahangir, Hina Jilani, and several rights activists were concerned by the supposedly progressive majority judgement. They pointed out that the judges may have upheld Saima's right to marry, but that they had also called for basic amendments to family laws to enforce parental authority and discourage courtships, extramarital relationships, and "secret" friendships and marriages. The majority judgment had gone so far as to recommend that "such like" relationships and marriages be made a penal offense and that courts should hold in abeyance decisions on such matters until laws were changed.[38] Asma Jahangir objected to how "Justice Ramday … expressed views and made recommendations which have added to the insecurity felt by Pakistani women, besides putting the legislature in a spot."[39] Hina Jilani likewise observed that Justice Ramday has "legislated for an interim period although he has no power to do so."[40] Justice Ramday denounced "husband shopping" as a "scheme" and disapproved of interfaith or other marriages based on "sheer momentary impulses which … are patently not in their interest and which are also a cause for shame and disgrace to the whole family."[41] He ruled that "the aggrieved person [i.e., a parent or brother] shall have a right to initiate proceedings in the competent Court seeking annulment of such a marriage."[42] The court not only overstepped its mandate, but also opined that jurists and superior courts were bound to issue progressive interpretations of Islamic laws and to shield society from the supposed Westernization of Muslim culture.

While that case revealed the power of a conservative religious morality, another case shows the emergence of a postsecular academic critique framing women's fundamental rights as neocolonial interference with Pakistani culture. In 1999 another of Asma's clients, Saima Sarwar, was murdered at the premises of Asma's office in Lahore by an assassin hired by her parents. She had exercised her legal right to divorce in order to remarry. Until Saima Sarwar's case, honor crimes had been commonly perceived as a rural and customary practice, but she was the daughter of an influential and urbane family. The family disapproved of her decision to disobey her guardian and to divorce, and decided to have her killed in order to restore the family honor. Women's rights groups lobbied and pressured the state for justice and for legal protection for women against honor crimes. In the post-9/11 period, by contrast, a revisionist and defensive academic commentary on this issue has emerged. For example, legal scholar Moeen Cheema is a strong supporter of the potential of Islamic legality and of the Federal Shariat Court that works in parallel to lay courts. He argues that Islamization has "introduced indigenous laws" against postcolonial ones and has encouraged a "public morality" fitting the larger project of Islamic egalitarianism and achievable through "a genuine Islamization of law" in the future.[43] He readily concedes that women's rights may be a casualty of such a project, as in the Saima Waheed free-will marriage case. There, he noted, "the court reached the correct decision but through reasoning reflecting judicial attitudes that would undermine women's rights in other contexts."[44]

It was during another period of military rule, under President-General Pervez Musharraf (1999–2008), that the tensions of the duality between Islamic duties and women's rights came to an uneasy settlement. Asma's untiring activism played a key role in this stalemate, which was complicated by the War on Terror in which Pakistan was embroiled. This created a whole host of new human rights concerns that preoccupied rights-based activists.

A "liberal" dictatorship and contradictions of rights

In 2002, a trial court in Kohat found Zafaran bibi guilty of *zina* and issued a sentence of death by stoning. Her pregnancy as a result of rape was taken as proof of her adultery. The Federal Shariat Court later overturned the sentence; in fact, a prescribed punishment of this nature has never been officially executed in Pakistan. The judgement prompted Asma to write a newspaper article recalling the historic miscarriages of justice enabled by the *zina* law, drawing upon all cases that she had been involved with since its enforcement.[45]

The Protection of Women (Criminal Laws Amendment) Act 2006, which finally reformed the *zina* law, was the culmination of nearly 30 years of women's rights activism that had begun soon after Zia's Islamization program in 1979. As signatory to CEDAW, Pakistan had made no progress on its commitments, but under General Musharraf's military regime women's empowerment became a defining feature of his purportedly liberal rule. The contradiction of Musharraf's support to Islamist parties on the one hand – on whom he depended for his regime – and women's rights on another led to conflicting social and political consequences.[46] Anita Weiss notes how "different constituencies become increasingly divided over what constitutes accepted roles and rights of women."[47] Musharraf authorized the reservation of an unprecedentedly high number of parliamentary seats for women; he revised the Hudood laws with reference to the new Protection of Women Act; and he placed the crimes of rape and adultery back into Pakistan's Penal Code. The government finally submitted and successfully defended Pakistan's CEDAW report before the UN Division for the Advancement of Women in 2007. It also introduced the Criminal Law (Amendment) Act of 2004 to tackle so-called honor killing. His government signed the pending UN Covenant on Economic, Social and Cultural Rights, as well as the International Labour Organization's Equal Remuneration Convention.

These actions by no means resulted in any kind of reconciliation or stitching together of the incongruities among religious laws, customary practices, and rights-based demands. Instead, an uneasy stalemate took hold between the religious lobbies and human rights groups over the Protection of Women Act of 2006. Islamist women actively resisted any reform. Once enacted, the Protection of Women Act was challenged in the Federal Shariat Court as a contradiction of Islamic law. Muhammed Taqi Usmani, former judge of the Sharia Court, summarized his and others' position over and against that of Asma and other human rights activists. His views resonate with those of postsecular scholars such as Moeen Cheema. Muhammed Taqi Usmani wrote:

> [T]he view that Hudud Laws should be scrapped merely because they have not produced the desired results so far is absurd. Rather, we should strive for reform in the system within which they operate. There is a need to avoid taking extreme positions and instead appreciate the efforts of Islamization in the context of this indigenous culture, the current situation and the challenges of modern times.[48]

While the reform of *zina* laws has relaxed the fierce regulation over women's sexual autonomy, the blasphemy laws[49] of Pakistan remain an instrument of persecution and even death. After General Zia amended the blasphemy law and criminalized offensive speech, the number of cases has risen exponentially, from a total of 14 recorded up until 1986, to 1,274 just up until 2010.[50] A total of 75 murders are estimated to have been committed in connection to blasphemy.[51]

Asma: the messiah for minorities

As controversial as Asma's determination to pursue cases of violence and discrimination against women and her efforts to commute death penalties imposed on women prisoners were, they were not half as controversial as her commitment to gain justice for religious minorities. In 1993, an 11-year-old Christian boy, Salamat Masih, and his uncles Manzoor Masih and Rehmat Masih were accused of writing blasphemous words on the wall of a mosque in a small town near Lahore. Manzoor Masih was later killed outside the district courts in Gujranwala, where the case was being heard. Asma Jahangir chose to represent Salamat and Rehmat Masih when they appealed against their conviction. Following intense political and religious tension, the Lahore High Court acquitted both the accused Christians in an unprecedented decision on 23 February 1995. One of the judges who had acquitted the two, Arif Iqbal Bhatti, was assassinated in 1997. His killer confessed that the motivation for the murder was that the judge had decided the case in favor of the accused.

Asma defended several more vulnerable victims who had been accused of blasphemy. She also took responsibility for relocating those whom she had managed to extricate from their legal binds. She lobbied hard for the repeal of the discriminatory blasphemy law. However, the climate for reform of this law dissipated after the Governor of Punjab, Salmaan Taseer, was murdered in 2011 by his own guard, Mumtaz Qadri, for pursuing the case of a poor Christian woman accused of blasphemy. Glorification and deification of the convicted murderer ensued. After a trial conducted amid opposition from Islamists and tremendous tension, and then his execution, religious leaders erected a shrine in the murderer's memory. More generally, there has been revived sympathy internationally for the supposed moral injury suffered by Muslims when confronted with perceived or actual blasphemy.[52]

The "Enlightened Moderation" regime of General Musharraf was repeatedly exposed for its paradoxical attempts to defend women's/human rights in some Sharia-compliant manner. Asma, as the representative of the combined causes of women's and religious minorities' rights, became the adversary in the eyes of Islamists and conservatives. For her critique of the military's interventions into democratic governance, she was painted as the traitor.[53] For her efforts at peace talks with Indian human rights groups, she was maligned an anti-Muslim Hindu-lover.[54] Her work and reports on violence against women in international fora earned her suspicion of behaving like a native informant.[55] For her support of religious minorities such as the Ahmedi sect, which was declared heretical by the state of Pakistan, she was cast as an apostate herself. Ahmedis are targets of blasphemy accusations, terrorist attacks, and ghettoized and excluded professionally and socially.[56] The Khatme Nabuwwat Lawyers Forum of Pakistan, which strongly opposes the Ahmedi sect, has been especially critical of Asma. The campaigns against her peaked when she contested and won the bar elections to become the first woman president of the Supreme Court Bar Association in 2010. The maligning of her reputation influenced people beyond Pakistan's borders: Asma was appointed in 2016 to serve as rapporteur for the human rights situation in Iran, and Iran's state-owned Islamic Republic of Iran

Broadcasting (IRIB) News and other outlets mimicked the accusations, accusing her of being a "heretic" and a "Qadiani" (i.e. follower of the Ahmadi sect, itself described as a "misguided cult created by the British, just like the Baha'i").[57]

Islamists have not been the only ones to issue condemnations of "elites," "liberal-secularists," feminists, and their perceived anti-Islam agendas. In a 2014 newspaper article, I criticized Pakistan's Council of Islamic Ideology, an advisory body tasked with screening all legislation so that it is not "repugnant to Islam," for defending child marriage.[58] Two internationally accredited Pakistani male scholars retorted vehemently to my critique. Abdul Rahman Mustafa argued that an overwhelming majority of Pakistanis favor Sharia and that liberals are fighting the will of that majoritarian consensus. Since Pakistan's constitution, he wrote, is "based on Islamic law principles … here's hoping Shehrbano's liberal friends do not ask the state to make an example of her the way they have done with others who have failed to respect our constitution."[59] Moeen Cheema, in his rejoinder to my article, dismissed Pakistani liberalism as insignificant and as doing nothing meaningful "beyond campaigns for the repeals of Islamisation era laws … and … earn[ing] points for CEDAW compliance." Arguing that the Council of Islamic Ideology has "always been an irrelevant institution," he focused his argument on how "Afiya Shehrbano can ignore all that with her rhetoric against Islam."[60] The entire spectrum of such characterizations against rights campaigners has made far more courageous activists, such as Asma, into targets of harassment and even death threats.

In 2005 Asma organized a marathon race in Lahore to raise awareness for the cause of violence against women. Groups such as the religious party of the Muthahida Majlis e Amal (MMA) strongly opposed the event because they considered mixed-gender events and women's mobility in public spaces to be un-Islamic. On the day of the marathon, these religious groups set out to obstruct it. The police then sought to thwart the event, forcing participants into police vans and in the process tearing the shirt off Asma's back. The image became a flashpoint and embarrassment for General Musharraf, who had pledged to turn Pakistan into an "Enlightened Moderate" Islamic republic. In true spirit, Asma refused to be embarrassed or intimidated, but rather converted the event into evidence of her very cause of violence against women. After the clash, another symbolic marathon-walk was held, this time peacefully, with Asma in the lead.

The importance of reclaiming public space cannot be underestimated. In 2016, the Punjab government held a "Women on Wheels" rally that donated motorcycles to women as part of a campaign to break down gender stereotypes and encourage women in public services. An official image of Asma riding with one of the women cyclists in the celebratory rally signifies her role in the expansion of public space by and for Pakistani women. After her death due to natural causes in early 2018, Asma was awarded the posthumous state award of the Nishan e Imtiaz in recognition of her services for the citizens of Pakistan. The path to this overdue acknowledgment had not been an easy one.

Human rights as the betrayal of Muslimness

By 2008, human rights violations were peaking in Pakistan under the War on Terror with its counterterrorism policies. Asma's work at international levels had gained her a reputation as an outspoken and fierce defender of democracy and of the human rights of the marginalized. However, within Pakistan she was viewed with suspicion as a "darling of the West" "working on a specifically anti-Islam agenda and … getting foreign funding to do that."[61]

Many progressives acknowledged how it was Asma's support for women's rights that caused fear among patriarchal forces, which those forces expressed with accusations that she was "Westernized," "morally bankrupt," and "depraved."[62] Yet even they, by 2012, seemed to be succumbing to the empire-anxiety that torments Islamists in Pakistan. In an essay entitled "Imperialist Feminism Redux," Saadia Toor associated several Pakistani feminists and human rights activists including Asma and Hina with "liberal hawks" like Salman Rushdie.[63] She bemoaned how rights activists supposedly were among those who "legitimize racist violence against Muslims" and who prevent the "genuine anti-imperialist and anti-racist work" of scholars and activists in the West.[64] This schism, and such suspicion of feminist activism again reflected the political divisions within rights-based discourse in Muslim contexts – except this time they came from some who claimed to be part of the progressive community.[65]

Many secular feminists in Pakistan have contended that national laws should comply with universal human rights, but others argue for a more ambivalent position that seeks a flexible "shifting back and forth from the legal arena to the realm of customary practices."[66] Asma's stated position was clear:

> Women's groups should not accept laws based on religion – whether they be family laws or Islamic criminal laws. It is now a foregone conclusion that a true liberal interpretation of Islam will never be widely accepted. On the other hand, the half-hearted liberalization of Islam will be more detrimental for women. Laws which violate the rights of women must be repealed. Those which give women no rights must be reformed.[67]

Transnational support in the post-9/11 period has become more ambiguous. Several international commentators have called on feminists to maintain a "strategic silence,"[68] to take a "break from feminism,"[69] or even to desist from "assigning culpability to the most visible actor"[70] when religious militants commit crimes against women.

Throughout the War on Terror, religio-nationalism in Pakistan in effect has served as a force to be tapped by militants and conservatives. The strategic use of religion as a source of empowerment for women has not translated into any tangible benefit or policy. Instead, women's religious practices and textual exegesis have led to a nationwide mobilization of women's piety movements.[71] Some of these mobilized women have held campaigns for the purpose of spreading religious conservatism, and their activism can even take the form of public vigilantism.[72] Meanwhile, any criticism of religious politics is easily interpreted as blasphemy and feminist struggles against religious patriarchy are often considered a betrayal to Muslimness. Once again, the incompatibility of Islamic and human rights seems to have surged forth. There is global pressure to iron out, accommodate, and fuse these different traditions.

New proposals for human rights in Muslim contexts

Islamic laws are perceived as being on one end of a spectrum, and human rights on the other end. Various proposals for a hybrid, accommodationist, and fusion approach claim to take a middle position.[73] Asifa Quraishi, for example, requests "both sides to tone it down a bit"[74] and appeals for "a significant paradigm shift." She writes:

> [S]pecifically, I ask internationally active women's rights advocates, especially those in or from the west, to eliminate any reference to Islamic law (positive or negative) from their advocacy and international pressure campaigns. I make this request both as a feminist and as a Muslim.[75]

The trouble with such appeals for a supposed truce is that they presume that lay laws and human rights do carry forward some uninterrupted linear legacy from the colonial era through the early postcolonial era and into the present day, and that conciliatory efforts are new in the post-9/11 moment. In fact, many Muslim-majority contexts have long since launched efforts at Quranic exegesis and hermeneutics.[76] Numerous academic and other efforts at strategic reinterpretion have aimed at disentangling outmoded cultural ideas and patriarchal practices from what can be considered authentic Quranic norms and divine messages of revelation. Since the 1980s, organizations such as Sisters in Islam and even more so the network called Women Living Under Muslim Laws have critically engaged with Islamic frameworks to pursue a gender equality agenda. More recently, the emergence of Islamic Feminism[77] has seen the development of new networks such as Karamah (Dignity, in Arabic) and Musawah (Equality, in Arabic). They work on issues of equality and justice in Muslim family laws rather than directly challenging Islamic statehood.

It has been suggested that the presence of intra-religious debates shows that reform of the *zina* law in Pakistan is possible. Yet we must note that reform happened because of an all-powerful, liberal-minded military dictator and a liberal political party that was in opposition in Parliament but still voted to reform the law – not because of the media campaign or any Sharia-minded strategy. That combination of circumstances was a historic anomaly and opportunity, unlikely to be repeated anytime soon.

Proposals that call for "a not-so-radical approach to human rights in Islam"[78] and appeal to "both sides to tone it down" and for "secular Western feminists to remember that they are part of a world of interconnected chess pieces in a continuing game"[79] reinforce the mistaken view that Muslims cannot be secular. They also fail to suggest how the activism of "Sharia-minded" women is to be analyzed in terms of whether it promotes patriarchal Islamist paradigms and agendas. Secular feminists are described as pawns in an imperialist game, yet the same observers do not seem to see Islamist women, Islamic feminists, and pietist movements as possible proxies for or as part of the male Islamist "game"; instead, they appear as authentic independent, agentive subjects.

The simple locational intersectionality of "Sharia-minded activists"[80] presumes a positive result for women's rights. Yet this has not been a convincing argument in many Muslim contexts. The pragmatic result of such proposals has been the rationalization of conservatism according to the gendered Islamic order. The renowned Pakistani Islamic scholar Khalid Masud maintains that enlisting the cooperation of clerics (*Ulema*) in development schemes or in policies related to rights serves to strengthen clerical authority "at the cost of development targets" and "has further politicized both religion and development in Pakistan."[81] Proposals for hybrid, accommodationist, fusion, or postsecular approaches serve to accommodate the creeping theocratization of formerly rights-based development and compromise other rights, especially sexual rights. Anthropologist Hania Sholkamy notes that in Egypt Sharia activism offers a "veneer for growing conservatism that is antithetical to change and reflection."[82]

Several postsecular Pakistani scholars argue that religious laws may be more culturally relevant than Pakistan's lay or colonial laws and can serve as a more appropriate buffer to the cruelties of the discriminatory customary laws. They are critical of the "forced diagnostic-prognostic couplings" of "equality-espousing human rights norms."[83] This post-9/11 postsecular turn invests hope in efforts beyond Quranic hermeneutics: in hybridity, Sharia-compliance accommodation, and even in a view of Islamic parties as secularizing forces.[84] Meanwhile, Pakistani human rights activists attempt to expand rights discourse in Pakistan and to call attention to failures and lapses in the government's commitments to international treaties.[85] Many continue to resist the limits of religious authority and to question the efficacy of Islamic laws and politics, despite the risks involved.[86]

The task of Asma's legacy

In November 2008, the Council of Islamic Ideology finally submitted some feeble recommendations to the government on the Muslim Family Law Ordinance of 1961. As soon as the recommendations were publicized, Islamist groups vehemently opposed even them. Weiss notes that thereafter "the legislation remained untouched: neither changed to empower women further, nor diminished to decrease the gains already made."[87] In 2010, the Federal Shariat Court declared the Protection of Women Act to be in violation of the Constitution, in response to petitioners who claimed the act was against Islam. The Supreme Court has issued a stay order on the Shariat Court's decision, and so the Protection of Women Act continues to be in effect. The legal debates over women's sexual autonomy are temporarily suspended. The adage about the more things change, the more they remain the same applies all too often when patriarchal content is challenged in laws or policies, particularly if reform threatens male privilege.

Strong state-backed support for human rights is more effective for women and minorities, making them part of a rights-based citizenry, than dependence on intermediaries, religious or otherwise. The appeal[88] for "middle-path" solutions is based on the acceptance of the idea that some moral injury is indeed inflicted on the faithful when Islamic laws are challenged. It rationalizes the need to gain consensus from Islamists and madrassa-educated students, rather than keeping the focus on using human rights to analyze potentially discriminatory law or policy and then seek reform. Given that the rationale for Islamic politics rests on controlling women's autonomy and on the unequal status of religious minorities, as well as a sense of security in a class-based economic system, it is naive to expect a genuine middle path. That expectation also ignores the manipulation of the blasphemy law to extend forgiveness to those who have the patronage of powerful Islamist groups. Those perceived as secular or Westernized lack that recourse to clemency or exoneration and are often murdered to ensure that they do not gain any relief from the courts – unlikely as that usually is – or through international assistance.

Yet other challenges are pending. Pakistan's compliance with CEDAW is in dispute with regard to coeducation, inheritance equality, and the status of legal witnesses. The government argues that coeducation is inapplicable because of cultural resistance to mixed gender education (even though primary schools and universities are mixed gender and private schools too can be mixed). On inheritance and the question of who has the status to give evidence or serve as a legal witness, the Quranic injunctions are considered immutable and the state's interpretation is that it cannot grant complete equality to men and women.

This essay has discussed some of the competing discourses and processes that influence the Pakistani state and its policies on human and women's rights. It has done so with a focus on the experiences and contributions of the leading human rights lawyer Asma Jahangir as she struggled to institute a democratic and secular rights regime in Pakistan. The Council of Islamic Ideology, religious groups, and lobbies strive to rescue Islam from the secular intentions of rights groups, feminists, human rights activists, and NGOs. Meanwhile, these continue to press for adherence to international human rights treaties and to monitor critically and to influence CEDAW reports and Universal Periodic Reviews.

Asma Jahangir's mass-attended funeral was held in Lahore on 13 February 2018. It encapsulated what she represented over the course of her lifelong commitment to human rights. In a show of radical departure from Muslim tradition (which does not observe mixed gender funerals), women activists, colleagues, lawyers, and well-wishers participated alongside men at Asma's funeral and last rites. The funeral sparked a posthumous controversy: right-wingers lashed out on social media at the mourners for warring against God; prominent clerics declared her funeral to be null and void; edicts were issued; and a legal petition was prepared that accused Asma's daughter and others who attended the funeral of blasphemy.[89] Political activist Ammar Rashid cautioned against using scriptural justifications for this defiant act, pointing to the "dubious interests" of Islamists whose "tenuous claims to gender justice" serve as a mask for their vested interest in gender segregation and who officiate as the "perpetual vanguard of patriarchy."[90]

Asma Jahangir's approach to human rights challenged precisely the cultural, nationalist, and faith-based values that threaten the lives of women and religious minorities. She refused to reify those values or look for a compromised, apologetic, patriarchy-boosting, and therefore ineffectual middle path. The notion of a variable Sharia may gain consensus among those who are not invested in a more accountable, human rights-based civil code, but the question remains whether that should be the legacy of Asma Jahangir's activism for Pakistan.

Notes

1 Constitution of the Islamic Republic of Pakistan, Chapter 1, "Fundamental Rights," including §8–28. Online. Available at www.constituteproject.org/constitution/Pakistan_2017?lang=en (accessed 5 January 2019).

2 Anita M. Weiss, *Interpreting Islam, Modernity, and Women's Rights in Pakistan*, New York: Palgrave Macmillan, 2014, p. 14.

3 Rubina Saigol, *Feminism and the Women's Movement in Pakistan: Actors, Debates and Strategies*, Islamabad: Friedrich-Ebert-Stiftung Pakistan Office, 2016.

4 Rubina Saigol, *The Pakistan Project: A Feminist Perspective on Nation and Identity*, New Delhi: Women Unlimited, 2013.

5 Saigol, *Pakistan Project* and Saigol, *Feminism and the Women's Movement in Pakistan*. See also Khawar Mumtaz and Farida Shaheed, *Women of Pakistan: Two Steps Forward, One Step Back*, London: Zed Books, 1987, and Asma Jahangir and Hina Jilani, *The Hudood Ordinances: A Divine Sanction?* Lahore: Rohtas, 1990.

6 Afiya Shehrbano Zia, *Faith and Feminism in Pakistan: Religious Agency or Secular Autonomy?* Brighton, UK: Sussex Academic Press, 2018.

7 *Miss Asma Jilani vs. Gov't of the Punjab*, PLD 1972 SC 139. Online. Available at https://pakistan constitutionlaw.com/pld-1972-sc-139-2/ (accessed 5 January 2019).

8 The reference to "lay" laws is only to distinguish this set of Pakistani penal laws from Islamic ones introduced in 1979 by General Zia ul Haq. It is not intended to suggest that the laws are stringently secular or void of religious ethos.

9 See Rahat Imran, "Legal Injustices: The Zina Hudood Ordinance of Pakistan and Its Implications for Women," *Journal of International Women's Studies*, 2005, vol. 7, no. 2, 78; Jahangir and Jilani, *Hudood Ordinances*; Moeen H. Cheema, "Beyond Beliefs: Deconstructing the Dominant Narratives of the Islamization of Pakistan's Law," *American Journal of Comparative Law*, 2012, vol. 60, no. 4, 875–918; Ruba Saboor, "Rape Laws in Pakistan: Will We Learn From Our Mistakes?" *Islamabad Law Review*, 2014, vol. 1, no. 1, 65–97; Afiya Shehrbano Zia, *Sex Crime in the Islamic Context: Rape, Class and Gender in Pakistan*, Lahore: ASR Publications, 1994.

10 Imran, "Legal Injustices."

11 Farida Shaheed, "Contested Identities: Gendered Politics, Gendered Religion in Pakistan," *Third World Quarterly*, 2010, vol. 31, no. 6, 851–67.

12 Commission of Inquiry for Women, *Report of the Commission of Inquiry for Women, Pakistan (CIW)*, Islamabad: Pakistan Law Commission, 1997.

13 The term "lay" courts simply differentiates from the Federal Shariat Court and Islamic Laws in Pakistan. The term "lay judges" does not mean that they are not versed in Islamic law or aloof from it; rather, the implication is that their judgments are not necessarily prescribed by religious laws and are guided more by the Pakistan Penal Code.

14 See the debate among Feisal Naqvi, Salman Akram Raja, and Afiya Shehrbano Zia in *The News International* (Pakistan): Feisal Naqvi, "The Curious Case of the Shariat Court," 10 January 2016; Salman Akram Raja, "An Act of Appeasement," 16 January 2016; and Afiya Shehrbano Zia, "The Gift of Zia – Keeps on Giving," 28 January 2016. Online. Available at www.thenews.com.pk (accessed 5 January 2019).

15 For information on the law firm, see www.aghslaw.net (accessed 8 September 2018).

16 Mumtaz and Shaheed, *Women of Pakistan*; Saigol, *Feminism and the Women's Movement in Pakistan*, p. 15.

17 Jahangir and Jilani, *Hudood Ordinances*; Mumtaz and Shaheed, *Women of Pakistan*; Saigol, *Feminism and the Women's Movement in Pakistan*; Zia, *Sex Crime*; Shahnaz Rouse, "Discourses on Gender in Pakistan," in Douglas Allen (ed.) *Religion and Political Conflict in South Asia: India, Pakistan, and Sri Lanka*, Westport, CT: Greenwood Press, 1992, pp. 87–112; Shahnaz Khan, *Zina, Transnational Feminism, and the Moral Regulation of Pakistani Women*, Vancouver: UBC Press, 2006; and Human Rights Commission of Pakistan, *Annual Reports*. Online. Available at http://hrcp-web.org/publication/book-genre/annual-reports (accessed 5 January 2019).

18 See the works put out by ASR Publications of Lahore, Pakistan. Online. Available at http://publications.asrresourcecentre.org (accessed 5 January 2019). See also the publications of the organization Shirkat Gah, associated with Women Living Under Muslim Laws. Online. Available at www.wluml.org/section/resource/latest (accessed 5 January 2019).

19 Amina Jamal, "Feminist 'Selves' and Feminism's 'Others': Feminist Representations of Jamaat-e-Islami Women in Pakistan," *Feminist Review*, 2005, no. 81, 67.

20 Saigol, *Feminism and the Women's Movement in Pakistan.*

21 Saroop Ijaz, "Asma the Street Fighter," originally published in *Herald* in September 2016; updated 11 February 2018. Online. Available at https://herald.dawn.com/news/1153540 (accessed 5 January 2018).

22 Ann Elizabeth Mayer, *Islam and Human Rights: Tradition and Politics*, Boulder, CO: Westview Press, 2013, p. 21, 24.

23 United Nations, "Universal Declaration of Human Rights." Online. Available at www.un.org/en/universal-declaration-human-rights/ (accessed 5 January 2019).

24 David L. Johnston, "Islam and Human Rights: A Growing Rapprochement?" *American Journal of Economics and Sociology*, 2015, vol. 74, no. 1, 121.

25 Lisa Hajjar, "Religion, State Power, and Domestic Violence in Muslim Societies: A Framework for Comparative Analysis," *Law and Social Inquiry*, 2004, vol. 29, no. 1, 1–38.

26 Hajjar, "Religion, State Power, and Domestic Violence," 15.

27 Hajjar, "Religion, State Power, and Domestic Violence," 18.

28 Hajjar, "Religion, State Power, and Domestic Violence."

29 Pakistan did not accede to the two major 1966 UN human rights conventions for over 30 years. It signed the International Covenant on Civil and Political Rights in 2008 and ratified it

in 2010, and signed the International Covenant on Economic, Social and Cultural Rights in 2004 and ratified it in 2008.

30 Commission of Inquiry for Women, *Report*, p. 75.

31 Weiss, *Interpreting Islam*, p. 31.

32 Commission of Inquiry for Women, *Report*, p. 56.

33 Weiss, *Interpreting Islam.*

34 Nafisa Shah, *Honor and Violence: Gender, Power, and Law in Southern Pakistan*, New York: Berghahn, 2016.

35 *Hafiz Abdul Waheed v. Asma Jahangir* PLD 1997 Lah 331, Criminal Miscellaneous No. 425-H of 1996, decided 10 March 1997.

36 Neelam Hussain, "The Narrative Appropriation of Saima: Coercion and Consent in Muslim Pakistan," in Neelam Hussain, Samiya Mumtaz, and Rubina Saigol (eds.) *Engendering the Nation-State*, Lahore: Simorgh Publications, 1997, pp. 199–242.

37 Beena Sarwar, "Pakistan: Saima Wins Case; But Judgement Threatens Women's Rights," *Inter-Press Service News Agency*, 17 March 1997. Online. Available at www.ipsnews.net/1997/03/pakistan-saima-wins-case-but-judgement-threatens-womens-rights (accessed 5 January 2019).

38 Sarwar, "Pakistan: Saima Wins Case."

39 Sarwar, "Pakistan: Saima Wins Case."

40 Sarwar, "Pakistan: Saima Wins Case."

41 Sarwar, "Pakistan: Saima Wins Case."

42 Sarwar, "Pakistan: Saima Wins Case."

43 Cheema, "Beyond Beliefs," 917.

44 Cheema, "Beyond Beliefs," 904.

45 Asma Jahangir, "A Law to Lament," *Dawn*, 5 June 2002. Online. Available at www.dawn.com/news/1063196 (accessed 5 January 2019).

46 Afiya Shehrbano Zia, "Faith-Based Challenges to the Women's Movement in Pakistan," in Huma Ahmed-Ghosh (ed.) *Contesting Feminisms: Gender and Islam in Asia*, Albany: State University of New York Press, 2015, pp. 181–206.

47 Weiss, *Interpreting Islam*, p. 36.

48 Muhammad Taqi Usmani, "The Islamization of Laws in Pakistan: The Case of Hudud Ordinances," *Muslim World*, 2006, vol. 96, no. 2, 287–304.

49 For a full text of the clauses, including the ones added by General Zia ul Haq that specified that the Ahmedi sect could not claim to be or worship as Muslims, see Pakistan, "Pakistan Penal Code (Act XLV of 1860)" with amendments, §298. Online. Available at www.pakistani.org/pakistan/legislation/1860/actXLVof1860.html (accessed 5 January 2019).

50 Madiha Afzal, *Pakistan under Siege: Extremism, Society, and the State*, Washington, DC: Brookings Institute Press, 2018, p. 55.

51 Madeeha Bakhsh, "More than 70% of Blasphemy Cases Spring from Punjab, Recent Report Says," *Christians in Pakistan. Voice of Pakistani Christians*, 21 March 2018. Online. Available at www.christiansinpakistan.com/more-than-70-of-blasphemy-cases-spring-up-from-punjab-recent-report-says/ (accessed 5 January 2019).

52 Talal Asad, Wendy Brown, Judith Butler, and Saba Mahmood, *Is Critique Secular? Blasphemy, Injury, and Free Speech*, Berkeley: University of California Press, 2009.

53 Sarwar, "Pakistan: Saima Wins Case."

54 Sarwar, "Pakistan: Saima Wins Case."

55 Asad Haroon, "Asma Jehangir Is Informant to External Forces: PTI," *Dispatch News Desk* (Pakistan), 21 February 2014. Online. Available at https://dnd.com.pk/pti-blasts-asma-jehangirs-statement-imran-khan/59235 (accessed 5 January 2019). Web Desk of *Express Tribune*, "Twitter Alert: Asma Jahangir a Target for Defamation," *Express Tribune* (Pakistan), 25 June 2012. Online. Available at https://tribune.com.pk/story/398938/twitter-alert-asma-jehangir-a-target-for-defamation (accessed 5 January 2019).

56 Ali Usman Qasmi, *The Ahmadis and the Politics of Religious Exclusion in Pakistan*, London: Anthem Press, 2014.

57 See the IRIB News Agency article at www.iribnews.ir/fa/news/1280530/تغییر-گزارشگر-ویژه-حقوق-بشر-سازمان-ملل-در-امور-ایران (accessed 5 January 2019). According to the authorities in Iran, the Baha'i are a suspect minority group.

58 Afiya Shehrbano Zia, "The Crisis of an Ideology," *The News International* (Pakistan), 16 March 2014. Online. Available at www.thenews.com.pk/print/88446-the-crisis-of-an-ideology (accessed 5 January 2019).
59 Abdul Rahman Mustafa, "Outside the Liberal Club," *The News International* (Pakistan), 27 March 2014. This article is no longer available on the *News* website, but can be viewed on another website. Online. Available at www.newageislam.com/islam-and-politics/abdul-rahman-mustafa/outside-the-liberal-club/d/66290 (accessed 5 January 2019).
60 Moeen H. Cheema, "The Crises of a Liberal Ideology," *News*, 22 March 2014. Online. Available at www.thenews.com.pk/archive/print/492174-the-crises-of-a-liberal-ideology (accessed 5 January 2019).
61 Ijaz, "Asma the Street Fighter."
62 Saadia Toor, "Gender, Sexuality, and Islam under the Shadow of Empire," *Scholar and Feminist Online*, 2011, vol. 9, no. 3. Online. Available at http://sfonline.barnard.edu/religion/print_toor.htm (accessed 5 January 2019).
63 Saadia Toor, "Imperialist Feminism Redux," *Dialectical Anthropology*, 2012, vol. 36, nos. 3–4, 152–3, n. 19.
64 Toor, "Imperialist Feminism Redux," 154.
65 Zia, "Faith-Based Challenges," and Zia, *Faith and Feminism in Pakistan.*
66 Farida Shaheed, "Engagements of Culture, Customs and Law: Women's Lives and Activism," in Farida Shaheed, Sohail Akbar Warraich, Cassandra Balchin, and Aisha Gazdar (eds.) *Shaping Women's Lives: Law, Practices and Strategies in Pakistan*, Lahore: Shirkat Gah, 1998, pp. 61–80.
67 Asma Jahangir, "The Origins of the MFLO: Reflections for Activism," in Shaheed et al., *Shaping Women's Lives*, pp. 93–106.
68 Nicola Pratt, "Weaponising Feminism for the 'War on Terror' Versus Employing Strategic Silence," *Critical Studies on Terrorism*, 2013, vol. 6, no. 2, 339.
69 Janet Halley, *Split Decisions: How and Why to Take a Break from Feminism.* Princeton, NJ: Princeton University Press, 2006.
70 For a debate on this, see Nivi Manchanda, "Out of Nowhere? The Taliban and Malala," *openDemocracy – openSecurity. Conflict and Peacebuilding*, 7 November 2012. Online. Available at www.opendemocracy.net/opensecurity/nivi-manchanda/out-of-nowhere-taliban-and-malala (accessed 5 January 2019), and Afiya Shehrbano Zia "Taliban: Agent or Victim," *openDemocracy – 50.50 Gender, Sexuality and Social Justice*, 30 November 2012. Online. Available at www.opendemocracy.net/5050/afiya-shehrbano-zia/taliban-agent-or-victim (accessed 5 January 2019).
71 Sadaf Ahmad, *Transforming Faith; The Story of Al-Huda and Islamic Revivalism Among Urban Pakistani Women*, New York: Syracuse University Press, 2009.
72 Fawzia Afzal-Khan, "What Lies Beneath: Dispatch from the Front Lines of the Burqa Brigade," *Social Identities*, 2008, vol. 14, no. 1, 3–11, and Zia, "Faith-Based Challenges."
73 Abadir M. Ibrahim, "A Not-So-Radical Approach to Human Rights in Islam," *Journal of Religion*, 2016, vol. 96, no. 3, 2016, 346–77, and Yefet Carmit Karin, "The Constitution and Female-Initiated Divorce in Pakistan: Western Liberalism in Islamic Garb," *Harvard Journal of Law and Gender*, 2011, vol. 34, no. 2, 553–615.
74 Asifa Quraishi, "What If Sharia Weren't the Enemy: Rethinking International Women's Rights Advocacy on Islamic Law," *Columbia Journal of Gender and Law*, 2011, vol. 22, no. 1, 247.
75 Quraishi, "What If Sharia Weren't the Enemy," 176.
76 John L. Esposito, *Women in Muslim Family Law*, Syracuse, NY: Syracuse University Press, 1982; Riffat Hassan, "On Human Rights and the Quranic Perspective," in Arlene Swidler (ed.) *Human Rights in Religious Traditions*, New York: Pilgrim Press, 1982; Asma Barlas, *Believing Women in Islam: Unreading Patriarchal Interpretations of the Qur'an*, Austin: University of Texas Press, 2002; and Amina Wadud, *Inside the Gender Jihad: Women's Reform in Islam*, Oxford: Oneworld, 2006.
77 Islamic Feminism is a discursive project that offers an against-the-grain reading of the Sharia and Quran. It developed in post-revolution Iran and is based on a specific feminist standpoint as well as its target of resistance. It became popular in the Muslim diaspora over the 1990s and seeks to offer Islamic alternatives to Western feminisms, as an authentic indigenous path to gender justice. See Ziba Mir-Hosseini, "Beyond 'Islam' vs. 'Feminism,'" *IDS [Institute of Development Studies] Bulletin*, 2011, vol. 42, no. 1, 67–77.

78 Ibrahim, "A Not-So-Radical Approach."
79 Quraishi, "What If Sharia Weren't the Enemy," 249.
80 Quraishi, "What If Sharia Weren't the Enemy," 249.
81 Muhammad Khalid Masud, "Religion and Development Challenges in Pakistan," in Anita M. Weiss and Saba Gul Khattak (eds.) *Development Challenges Confronting Pakistan*, West Hartford, CT: Kumarian Press, 2012, p. 192.
82 Hania Sholkamy, "Creating Conservatism or Emancipating Subjects? On the Narrative of Islamic Observance in Egypt," *IDS [Institute of Development Studies] Bulletin*, 2011, vol. 42, no. 1, 48.
83 Sadaf Aziz, "Beyond Petition and Redress: Mixed Legality and Consent in Marriage in Pakistan," *Bayan – Bi-Annual Socio-Legal Journal. Marital Law and Customary Practices* [Lahore], 2005, vol. 4, 58.
84 Humeira Iqtidar, *Secularizing Islamists? Jama'at-e-Islami and Jama'at-ud-Da'wa in Urban Pakistan*, Chicago: Chicago University Press, 2011.
85 Reema Omer, "Human Rights Review," *Dawn*, 10 November 2017. Online. Available at www.dawn.com/news/1369474 (accessed 5 January 2019).
86 Umer Ali, "Faking News: The Dark Side of News Media," *Herald*, 3 April 2018. Online. Available at https://herald.dawn.com/news/1154066 (accessed 5 January 2019), and Farieha Aziz, "Pakistan's Cybercrime Law: Boon or Bane?" *Heinrich-Böll- Stiftung – Islamabad, Pakistan*, 14 February 2018. Online. Available at www.boell.de/en/2018/02/07/pakistans-cybercrime-law-boon-or-bane (accessed 5 January 2019).
87 Weiss, *Interpreting Islam*, p. 41.
88 Tabinda M. Khan, "The Middle Path," *Dawn*, 6 April 2016. Online. Available at www.dawn.com/news/1250212 (accessed 5 January 2019).
89 Rabia Malik, "Lawyer Seeks FIR Against Participants of Asma Jahangir's Funeral," *Pakistan Today*, 20 February 2018. Online. Available at www.pakistantoday.com.pk/2018/02/20/lawyer-seeks-fir-against-participants-of-asma-jahangirs-funeral/ (accessed 5 January 2019).
90 Ammar Rashid, "Asma Jahangir's Funeral and the Ideology of Gender Segregation," *Dawn*, 5 March 2018. Online. Available at www.dawn.com/news/1393342> (accessed 5 January 2019).

PART V

THE UNIVERSAL HUMAN RIGHTS PANTHEON IN NATIONAL CONTEXTS

22

FREEDOM OF RELIGION AND THE NEW DIVERSITY

Case studies from Canada

Lori G. Beaman

Kławła Tukłułakʔis (Grizzly Bear Spirit) lives in Qat'muk, an area that if using a conventional colonial map would appear in the southeast corner of the Canadian province of British Columbia. Grizzly Bear Spirit is important to the people of the Ktunaxa Nation, and so when Glacier Resorts expressed interested in building a ski resort in Qat'muk the Ktunaxa were concerned. The consultation process with the Ktunaxa began in 1991 and after careful and lengthy reflection they concluded that such a project would drive Grizzly Bear Spirit from the area. The Ktunaxa's concern evolved into objection and the matter moved through the courts. A significant basis of the legal argument made by the Ktunaxa was that the decision to approve the ski hill development violated their constitutional right to freedom of religion.

Freedom of religion is the primary human rights protection related to religious belief and practice. Its form and interpretation varies from context to context, and it has been used both to protect[1] and to colonize.[2] It is contained in many constitutional documents (including the US and Canadian constitutions) as well as in international treaties, conventions and agreements (the Treaty of Westphalia and the European Convention on Human Rights, for example). As sociologist James Richardson notes, these documents "represent efforts to develop workable political compromises that would allow increasingly pluralistic societies to live together in peace."[3]

This chapter focuses on religious freedom as a human right drawing on the example of Canada as a case study. The issues that arise in Canada are common to other countries and although there are context-specific dimensions, the protection of religious belief and practice as a human rights issue has a long-standing history and remains a widespread matter of debate, with issues such as religious symbols in public spaces, forced conversion, and persecution for beliefs and practices retaining currency across time. The *Ktunaxa* case[4] illustrates some of the key challenges related to religious freedom, including its link to majoritarian conceptualizations of the concept of religion in Western democracies, the use of accommodation rather than equality as the goal of human rights responses and the shifting conceptualization of practices, symbols and places as religious, sacred, or cultural.

I begin below with a brief overview of the history of religious freedom and its location in a Christian imaginary of religion. I then turn to reasonable accommodation as a central theme in understanding human rights claims, and then return to the *Ktunaxa* case for a more detailed consideration of key issues.

Before the Canadian Charter of Rights and Freedoms (1982)

Religious freedom has been part of the Canadian lexicon from at least the 1760s,[5] including in provincial and federal legislation.[6] The Treaty of Paris (1763) was intended to extend protection to Roman Catholicism in a British (and therefore Anglican) dominated Canada. However, the definition of religion as interpreted by the courts was dogged by a narrow conceptualization that put Christianity at its center. That is not surprising given the dominance of Christianity as the majority religion in Canada. The early legislation (for example the Quebec Act [1774] and the Constitution Act [1867]) was primarily concerned with the two religious majorities, Roman Catholics and Protestants, and not with any other religious and Indigenous groups. Both were Christian religions and religious freedom was not really imagined to extend any further than these variations.

A key driver in the global development of religious freedom has been the Jehovah's Witnesses, who have tirelessly pursued the right to practice their religious commitments such as proselytization through door-to-door and public campaigns, refusal of blood transfusions, and military service. The Jehovah's Witnesses have, for example, "filed more religion-related cases than any other religious group before the European Court of Human Rights."[7] They have been instrumental in the pursuit of religious freedom in a wide range of countries, including Canada, the former Soviet Union, Turkey, and the United States. As Richardson notes, the Jehovah's Witnesses "have won over 50 US Supreme Court cases, which is far and away the most impressive record of any religious group in America."[8] The wins by the Jehovah's Witnesses are significant not only for the Witnesses, but for the evolution of human rights around religious freedom for all religious minorities.[9] This was especially the case in Canada in the 1950s, which was a critical phase in the development of freedom of religion and a precursor to more nuanced interpretations of religious freedom, which would expand to religions beyond Christianity and to include the nonreligious as well.

Two cases, both originating in Quebec, were especially path breaking. It is worth noting that of all the Canadian provinces Quebec had what might be described as the closest arrangement to an "establishment" in that the Roman Catholic Church was dominant and heavily intertwined with social services and the state.[10] This made it especially challenging for religions other than Roman Catholicism and mainstream Protestantism to express their beliefs publicly. In the *Saumur v. City of Quebec* case (1953)[11] Jehovah's Witnesses challenged an interpretation of a bylaw that prohibited them from distributing their pamphlets. These pamphlets were intended to evangelize, and also bluntly challenged the Catholic status quo, reading in part:

> Religion is the adulteress and idolatress that befriends and commits religious fornication with the political and commercial elements. She is the lover of this world and blesses the world from the balcony of the Vatican and in the pulpits. Religion, whose most powerful representative has ruled from Rome for sixteen centuries, traces her origin all the way back to Babylon of Nimrod's founding, and organized religion deservedly bears the name Babylon I will shew unto thee the judgment of the great whore (or idolatress) that sitteth upon many waters: with whom the kings of the earth have committed fornication, and the inhabitants of the earth have been made drunk with the wine of her fornication full of abominations and filthiness of her fornication; and upon her forehead was

a name written, MYSTERY, BABYLON THE GREAT, THE MOTHER OF HARLOTS AND ABOMINATIONS OF THE EARTH.[12]

In upholding their right to engage in such activities the Supreme Court of Canada noted the historic presence of religious freedom:

> From 1760, therefore, to the present moment religious freedom has, in our legal system, been recognized as a principle of fundamental character; and although we have nothing in the nature of an established church, that the untrammelled affirmations of religious belief and its propagation, personal or institutional, remain as of the greatest constitutional significance throughout the Dominion is unquestionable.[13]

The Court also said: "The Christian religion, its practices and profession, exhibiting in Europe and America an organic continuity, stands in the first rank of social, political and juristic importance."[14] *Saumur* is important because the court articulated the boundaries of religious freedom in Canada at that time, which were decidedly Christian. In many ways those "boundaries continue to be reproduced in contemporary legal decisions" as we will see in the later discussion of the *Ktunaxa* case.[15]

A second case, *Roncarelli v. Duplessis* (1959),[16] also brought before the courts by the Jehovah's Witnesses, involved the arbitrary cancelling of a liquor license for a Jehovah's Witness restaurant owner. He had provided bail for a number of members of his community who had been charged for distributing literature without the statutorily imposed mandatory license and he argued that the cancelling was retaliation. Despite the fact that the Supreme Court described the group as a "rather militant Christian religious sect"[17] and noted that the pamphlets it distributed were deliberately insulting and provocative,[18] the judges found that the liquor license had been wrongfully cancelled. These cases affirmed the place of freedom of religion in Canada, but did not conceptualize religion beyond Christianity, which was "in the first rank" of importance.

The discussion above is not intended to review the history of religious freedom in Canada in its entirety, but rather to signal a few key points: first, religious freedom has been part of human rights discussions in Canada since colonization; second, Jehovah's Witnesses, though not the only group active in pursuing human rights through religious freedom, played an important role in the evolution of judicial pronouncements on the meaning of religious freedom; and third, freedom of religion has often been understood in Christian terms. Then, in the 1980s a new era began.

After the Canadian Charter of Rights and Freedoms

A significant shift occurred with the enactment of the Constitution Act (1982) and specifically its Canadian Charter of Rights and Freedoms.[19] The Charter includes a number of provisions that touch on religious freedom, including section 2(a) which states that "everyone has the following fundamental freedoms: (a) freedom of conscience and religion." Section 15 also includes religion in its guarantee of equality: "Every individual is equal before and under the law and has the right to the equal protection and equal benefit of the law without discrimination, in particular, without discrimination based on race, national or ethnic origin, colour, religion." Though the meaning of the preamble is debated, it arguably contains resonances of the statements made in *Saumur* that preserve Christianity as the foundational religion of Canada (there is neither a formal separation of church and state in Canada nor an official state religion): "Canada is founded upon principles that recognize the supremacy of God and the rule of law." Section 27 of the Charter mentions multiculturalism, which arguably includes religion: "This Charter shall be interpreted in a manner consistent with the preservation and enhancement of the multicultural heritage of Canadians." Section 7 is also used in religion cases in relation to its reference to liberty: "Everyone has the right to life, liberty and security of the person and not to be deprived thereof except in accordance with the principles of fundamental justice." Section 29 repeats the denominational schools protection from section 93 of the Constitution Act (1867). All provinces now have human rights legislation that specifically mentions freedom of religion or creed.[20]

Like many Western democracies, Canada is experiencing what I refer to as a "new diversity" that when combined with human rights protections is posing new challenges. By new diversity I mean: a dramatic increase in numbers of people who self-describe as nonreligious;[21] an increasing presence through migration of minority religious groups who are not Christian;[22] a declining presence and influence of traditionally majoritarian Christian religions; and a recognition of the impact of colonialism on Indigenous peoples with a concomitant recognition of Indigenous spiritualities.[23] The credibility of human rights guarantees now depends on a willingness to protect religious practices outside of Christianity.[24]

There is evidence that this legal shift is well underway in Canada.[25] For example, in the *Amselem* (2004) case[26] the Supreme Court upheld the right of an Orthodox Jew to build his own *succah* on his balcony despite the fact that it contravened the co-ownership agreement for the building. The Court refused to privilege aesthetics over religious practice in which the claimant sincerely believed. In the *Multani* (2006) case[27] the Supreme Court found that a school board's prohibition of a Sikh schoolboy's *kirpan* unjustifiably infringed his freedom of religion. More recently the right of a Muslim woman to wear the *niqab* while swearing her citizenship was upheld in the *Ishaq* decision (2015).[28] In the *Ishaq* case, Zuneera Ishaq argued that denying her the right to wear her *niqab* infringed her freedom of religion and equality rights as protected by the Charter.

From religion to culture

Although these cases show promise for a more expansive approach to religious freedom, a simultaneous development has been the transformation of majoritarian religion into "culture." In the early post-Charter case of *Big M* (1985), which dealt with legislation requiring stores to close on Sunday, the Supreme Court found that such requirements effectively forced a particular (Christian) observance:

> What may appear good and true to a majoritarian religious group, or to the state acting at their behest, may not, for religious reasons, be imposed upon citizens who take a contrary view. The *Charter* safeguards religious minorities from the threat of "the tyranny of the majority."[29]

The approach of the Court in *Big M* was expansive and inclusive of everyone: "to accept that Parliament retains the right to compel universal observance of the day of rest preferred by one religion is not consistent with the preservation and enhancement of the multicultural heritage of Canadians."[30] However, in a subsequent similar Sunday closing case, *Edwards Books* (1986), the Court retreated to the discourse of culture, finding that the Sunday closing law was intended to provide "uniform holidays to retail workers" and that the Act was not a "surreptitious attempt to encourage religious worship." The Court found that the purpose of the legislation was "secular" rather than religious, despite the fact that its effect was essentially the same as that in *Big M*.[31] More recently in the *Saguenay* (2015) case the Supreme Court rejected the argument that Christian prayers at the beginning of municipal council meetings could be justified on the basis that they are part of culture and heritage. The Court noted that "if the state adheres to a form of religious expression under the guise of cultural or historical reality or heritage, it breaches its duty of neutrality."[32] However, the Court also left open the possibility that "cultural" practices that are religious in nature might be protected. It remained vague about what these might be, so it remains to be seen what might qualify. However, it is worth noting that Canada's parliament, for example, opens with a prayer, albeit before the doors are opened to the public:

> Almighty God, we give thanks for the great blessings which have been bestowed on Canada and its citizens, including the gifts of freedom, opportunity and peace that we enjoy. We pray for our Sovereign, Queen Elizabeth, and the Governor General. Guide us in our deliberations as Members of Parliament, and strengthen us in our awareness of our duties and responsibilities as Members. Grant us wisdom, knowledge, and understanding to preserve the blessings of this country for the benefit of all and to make good laws and wise decisions. Amen.[33]

I have argued that the reconstruction of symbols like the crucifix and practices such as prayer as "culture" effectively removes them from scrutiny as an imposition of religious practices and renders them acceptable as culture.[34] Along with the invocation of culture and heritage as a justification for protecting longstanding Christian symbols and practices, there also developed the notion of "reasonable accommodation" within human rights conversations as well as in civil society about religious diversity.

Reasonable accommodation

In the human rights context much of the evolution of the reasonable accommodation discourse has taken place in employment situations in which employees have sought to be able to practice their religions, either in terms of wearing clothing linked to their practice[35] or being able to observe holy days.[36] The idea that employers have a duty to accommodate religious employees emerged, tempered by the notion that employers should not suffer undue hardship and that accommodation does not need to be made if there was a bona fide occupational requirement, meaning that a particular skill, characteristic, or capability is necessary to do the work. There is much more nuance to the development of the law, but for the purposes here the notion is key that accommodation is the vehicle through which difference is to be managed. Legal scholars Shelagh Day and Gwen Brodsky, in their critical and insightful analysis of reasonable accommodation, note that accommodation was introduced to resolve the problem of "difference."[37]

As I have written elsewhere, reasonable accommodation inscribes inequality rather than its purported aim of achieving equality. In short, accommodation maintains a hierarchy that inevitably preserves the privilege of one group to bestow accommodation on another, who are cast as asking for (sometimes as demanding) "exemptions." Rather than achieving equality, it embeds inequality in its very structure. In Canada, the notion has migrated from a relatively narrow realm of law into public discourse, such that it now circulates in everyday use as a discursive organizer of difference.[38]

The reasons for this migration into public debate are complicated. One catalyst may have been the *Multani* (2006) case, for two reasons. First, some of the judges in that decision used the language of reasonable accommodation to discuss whether the request to wear the *kirpan* could be supported by the human rights protection of religious freedom. Although this move was explicitly rejected in a subsequent case, it did open the door for a broader use of the notion. The case also prompted a great deal of debate in Quebec about what some claimed was too much accommodation. The government response was to set up a public commission to study the matter, its mandate being to "take stock of accommodation practices in Quebec," to hold public consultations, and to prepare a report with recommendations that would bring accommodation practices in line with "Quebec's values as a pluralistic, democratic, egalitarian society."[39] The Commissioners traveled around Quebec for four months, holding public meetings to hear and receive submissions by members of the public about diversity in Quebec. The Commission received 900 submissions. Although the Commission's focus was broader than religion, it became the lightning rod for interventions that specifically identified religion as problematic. Anxiety over Muslims was a common theme. Ultimately, the commission report cautioned against the use of law to resolve disputes between citizens concerning matters such as religious symbols and practices, advocating instead "concerted adjustment" between individuals. It also attempted to navigate the "reasonable accommodation" terrain. The commission likely contributed to the more widespread use of the idea of reasonable accommodation in public discourse through the process of conducting hearings across the province that sparked debate about religious minorities and their "requests" or "demands" for accommodation.

It is difficult to know to what extent the proliferation of the language of accommodation is the result of law's shadow being cast over issues of diversity and inclusion. Legal scholar Winnifred Sullivan notes the power of law's "backstreaming effect," that is, the power of law to organize social life through its very presence.[40] In other words, the force of law shapes the ways in which people interact with each other even without law's direct intervention. Sullivan states that the "shaping of life to suit the law has backstream effects as well, beginning long before life enters the courts. One feature of the modern world is the thorough juridification of life in its very subjectivity."[41] A key challenge is to trace the ways in which law shapes people's decisions and practices in everyday life.

Legal scholar Effie Fokas picks up these themes of judicialization and the shadow effect of law in her Grassroots Moblise project in which she empirically measures the "radiating" effects of court decisions, focusing particularly in the European Court of Human Rights.[42] Fokas asks: "What is the aftermath of the Court's religion jurisprudence, in terms of its applications (beyond but also including its implementation) at the local and national level?"[43] She argues that "the Court has been setting, from above, certain parameters for religious pluralism in Europe."[44] Although it is important not to overestimate law's reach and influence, the ways in which law shapes possibilities on the ground warrant attention, Marc Galanter notes:

> [T]he impact of courts on disputes is accomplished largely by the dissemination of information. Courts produce not only decisions, but messages. These messages are resources that parties use in envisioning, devising, pursuing, negotiating, and vindicating claims (and in avoiding, defending, and defeating them).[45]

For religious freedom, law shapes not only the ways in which cases are constructed for legal process, but also sends powerful messages about who and what is included in the notion of religion as well as the appropriate language (such as reasonable accommodation) for framing claims.[46] These frameworks inevitably exclude other possibilities. Markus Dressler, for example, has studied the ways in which Alevis in Turkey are pressured through the state's notion of laicism (that is also legally implemented) to shape themselves as being within an Islamic-Turkish discourse. In Germany, by contrast, they are free to construct themselves outside of that discourse. As Dressler notes, "religio-secular discourses are always embodied in locally specific practices and in dialogue with the particular contexts in which they are embedded."[47] This is equally true of "reasonable accommodation," which has circulated to craft both minority and majority group identity and action.

The *Ktunaxa* case (2017)

The creation of Canada as a nation is intertwined with the history of Indigenous peoples who populated the land on the arrival of English and French settlers. In many cases settlers were dependent on Indigenous knowledge and resources for their very survival.[48] The Crown's promise of land to settlers could only be realized by displacing Aboriginal title through treaties. As a major human rights report summarized this history,

> prior to Confederation in 1867, the British government had negotiated numerous treaties with Aboriginal nations in eastern Canada. While the first of these treaties were concluded on the basis of one-time-only payments, later treaties included reserves (an area of often remote land set aside for specific bands of Aboriginal people) and annual payments.[49]

The treaties between Indigenous peoples and colonizers articulated and envisioned a nation-to-nation relationship, but this was gradually transformed into a relationship of assimilation, with the implementation of various measures to control the Indigenous population, including the residential school system. Under that system, Indigenous children were taken from their homes and families and sent to schools run by religious orders:[50]

> The purpose of the residential school system was to separate children from the influences of their parents and their community, so as to destroy their culture. The impact was devastating. Countless students emerged from the schools as lost souls, their lives soon to be cut short by drugs, alcohol, and violence.[51]

It was not only those students who were impacted, but future generations of Indigenous peoples.

The last residential school did not close until 1996. As evidence of the widespread harm done by the schools mounted, a commission known as the Truth and Reconciliation Commission was formed in 2008 to study the schools' impact and to make recommendations. The Commission was mandated to

> guide and inspire a process of truth and healing, leading toward reconciliation within Aboriginal families, and between Aboriginal peoples and non-Aboriginal communities, churches, governments, and Canadians generally. The process was to work to renew relationships on a basis of inclusion, mutual understanding, and respect.[52]

On 2 June 2015, the Truth and Reconciliation Commission of Canada released its final report and 94 Calls to Action, which set out a comprehensive plan for next steps. The key overarching theme was reconciliation.

The Calls to Action noted Canada's failure to support the United Nations (UN) Declaration on the Rights of Indigenous Peoples.[53] Adopted in 2007, it was supported by 144 countries and voted against by Australia, Canada, New Zealand, and the United States. As the Truth and Reconciliation Commission of Canada notes, the Declaration "calls upon member states to adopt and maintain its provisions as a set of 'minimum standards for the survival, dignity and well-being of the indigenous peoples of the world.'"[54] The Commission noted moreover that it was not a coincidence that the objecting countries "have a common history as part of the British Empire. The historical treatment of Aboriginal peoples in these other countries has strong parallels to what happened to Aboriginal peoples in Canada."[55] In 2016 Canada declared itself to be fully supportive of the UN Declaration. Bill C-262, *An Act to Ensure that the Laws of Canada Are in Harmony with the United Nations Declaration on the Rights of Indigenous Peoples*, remains before the Senate of Canada. It was not law at the time of the *Ktunaxa* case and is not yet law to date.[56] It is in this context that the *Ktunaxa* case (2017) was decided.

In its decision the Supreme Court concluded that the Ktunaxa claim did not fall within the section 2(a) parameters of the right to have and manifest religious beliefs. The Court interpreted the Ktunaxa claim as seeking the protection of the object of their belief – the territory of the Great Bear Spirit – rather than a belief or practice itself.

> This case is not concerned with either the freedom to hold a religious belief or to manifest that belief. The claim is rather that s. 2(a) of the Charter protects the presence of Grizzly Bear Spirit in Qat'muk. This is a novel claim and invites this Court to extend s. 2(a) beyond the scope recognized in our law.[57]

This the Court was unwilling to do.

> We would decline this invitation. The state's duty under s. 2(a) is not to protect the object of beliefs, such as Grizzly Bear Spirit. Rather, the state's duty is to protect everyone's freedom to hold such beliefs and to manifest them in worship and practice or by teaching and dissemination. In short, the Charter protects the freedom to worship, but does not protect the spiritual focal point of worship.[58]

The Court found that "the Ktunaxa's claim does not fall within the scope of s. 2 (a) because neither the Ktunaxa's freedom to hold their beliefs nor their freedom to manifest those beliefs is infringed by the Minister's decision to approve the project."[59] The fact that the Ktunaxa believe that the Grizzly Bear Spirit would go away should the development continue was not seen as preventing them from practicing or believing.

The Court mentioned reconciliation: "We arrive at these conclusions cognizant of the importance of protecting Indigenous religious beliefs and practices, and the place of such protection in achieving reconciliation between Indigenous peoples and non-Indigenous communities."[60] And later elaborated:

> [T]he best that can be achieved in the uncertain interim while claims are resolved is to follow a fair and respectful process and work in good faith toward reconciliation.
>
> For the Ktunaxa, this may seem unsatisfactory, indeed tragic. But in the difficult period between claim assertion and claim resolution, consultation and accommodation, imperfect as they may be, are the best available legal tools in the reconciliation basket.[61]

Key to the process of deciding was the Crown's duty to consult, which the Court found had been satisfied. It concluded: "While the goal of the process is reconciliation of the Aboriginal and state interest, in some cases this may not be possible. The process is one of "give and take," and outcomes are not guaranteed."[62] Given the long and sustained history of "take" by the Crown vis-à-vis Indigenous peoples, it would seem that the bulk of the "giving" had been done by the Ktunaxa and the "take" by the Crown. But the case raises the ongoing question of what counts as religion and how it is manifested. The consequence of a misinterpretation is serious in that those seeking human rights protection may be excluded. If the protection of religious beliefs and practices is especially concerned with minority groups, who may be particularly vulnerable to the "tyranny of the majority," this has implications for social inclusion in diverse societies. For historically oppressed groups who have suffered systemic discrimination the consequence is perhaps most profound.

Indigenous spiritualities have not always fit the category of religion that is imagined by law when it articulates freedom of religion.[63] Moreover, it is extremely difficult for a society whose culture has been profoundly shaped by a particular religion, here Christianity, to step outside of that model. Several issues arose in the *Ktunaxa* case. First, the connection of land – vast tracts of it – to religious practices and beliefs is not conceptually familiar to Christian religious models. It is important not to overstate this: churches are situated on land, there is the notion of the "Holy Land," we see pilgrimages such as the Camino de Santiago de Compostela, and so on. But Christianity, which is inherently portable, does not depend on them. Moreover, sacredness in the Christian model is created by humans (with divine help) and thus sites can be consecrated and deconsecrated. Ktunaxa religion is intimately connected with the land on which the Ktunaxa are situated. The Grizzly Bear Spirit is not everywhere, it is there, in the mountain territory occupied by the Ktunaxa people. The interweaving of human and non-human animal life and their shared ground is a fundamental component of Ktunaxa spirituality and indeed that of many Indigenous peoples. The disjuncture between a Christian portability model, arguably disconnected from place and non-human animals, and that of the Ktunaxa illustrates the challenge of defining religion for the purposes of human rights protections.

A second complication of the notion of religion also seems to have rendered the Ktunaxa claim on the basis of freedom of religion illegible for the Court. Catholic and Protestant proselytization with the goal of conversion translates into a toolkit of beliefs and practices that are part of that conversion repertoire and an outward-facing orientation. These tools are inherently knowable and accessible, and are to be put to use indiscriminately with the goal of conversion. At least in theory, all are worthy of knowing and using these tools. This seemingly democratic approach to access to religion is experienced by many as coercion rather than generosity, particularly within colonized Indigenous communities. Conversion is not a goal of Indigenous religions. This fundamental difference results in a profound disjuncture in approaches. Sophie Pierre, a Ktunaxa elder and legal activist, offers this insight:

> One of the very important things of the Ktunaxa culture is our spirituality. Now that is not something that you are going to open up a book and read the ten steps to Ktunaxa spirituality, neither are you going to see that, in that book, the ten steps to Haida spirituality, Anishinaabe spirituality, Haudenosaunee spirituality. Spirituality, again, is something that we have maintained as the Ktunaxa people and that has helped us. And we know, because we've been taught, that in order for us to continue to be Ktunaxa people, we must protect that culture, and part of that culture is the respect of all life amongst us. And one way that we express that, in English, to try to make it understood, is by talking about something like the Grizzly Bear Spirit.[64]

Much was made of the "secrecy" about the Ktunaxa approach to religion in the Court process:

> At meetings on June 9 and 10, however, the Ktunaxa took a very different and uncompromising position regarding the spiritual value of Qat'muk. They asserted that the consultation process was deficient, not because interest-based issues like money and land reserves had not been concluded, but because the process had not properly considered information that the Jumbo Valley was a sacred site. They advised the Minister that only certain members of the community, knowledge keepers, possessed information about these values. Elder Chris Luke Sr. was better placed to speak to the issue.[65]

Although the state representative (the minister) claimed to understand the need for "secrecy," that understanding went only so far:

> It emerged that the revelation that led to the position that permanent structures would desecrate and irrevocably devalue the sacred site came to Mr. Luke in 2004, but that health problems and secrecy concerns had prevented him from disclosing the revelation to others until 2009.[66]

The state representative also argued that he viewed the claim of the Ktunaxa as weak because of a

> lack of indication that the claimed right was part of an Aboriginal tradition, practice, or activity integral to the Ktunaxa culture, and the fact that details of the spiritual interest were not shared with or known to the general Ktunaxa population.[67]

The negative implications of secrecy and the contrast with the easy access to Christian truth combine to cast doubt on the revelations about the Great Bear Spirit and focused attention on the failure to share those immediately. The idea of spiritual worthiness, or that spiritual "news" should not be broadcast widely, leaves the Ktunaxa outside of the section 2(a) protection of religion.

Finally, courts have been reluctant to adjudicate the content of religious beliefs. Rather, they have developed a "sincerity" test as a threshold for claims to religious freedom. My contention is that sincerity is inextricably bound up with content and that courts inevitably deal with some content in any religious freedom claim. Interference with religious freedom inevitably requires some consideration of religion and its contents. The Supreme Court sidestepped the issue, stating:

> The extension of s. 2(a) proposed by the Ktunaxa would put deeply held personal beliefs under judicial scrutiny. Adjudicating how exactly a spirit is to be protected would require the state and its courts to assess the content and merits of religious beliefs.[68]

Yet the Court had already determined that the ability of the Ktunaxa to practice their religion (what the Ktunaxa, to be clear, had described as "spiritual practices," "spiritual interests," "spiritual beliefs," and "spiritual culture") was not prevented by the ski hill development.

Conclusions

This chapter has touched on only a few issues related to religion and human rights and has drawn only on the Canadian context. The intersection of human rights and religion includes an incredibly wide range of issues such as religious symbols in the public sphere, religious clothing, the right to proselytize, religious education and the right to control curriculum, the freedom not to believe, enforced religious observance, and so on. These issues are dynamic and context specific. In other words, laws and practices are continuously changing, as are social attitudes. The unique history of each country contributes to the shape of human rights protection practices. I refer to "practices" because legal protections often appear to be very similar from country to country. But the translation of those protections into practices is the most telling component of human rights protections.

At the same time, there is a global circulation of religious freedom discourse that is highly problematic. To be sure, it may offer some protection to persecuted minorities, but it can also flatten complex conflicts into "religious" conflicts, something that has been effectively articulated by Elizabeth Hurd:

> [T]o declare religion the cause of particular political conflicts reduces complex questions of causation and obscures the broader economic, historical, and political contexts in which discrimination and violence occur. Basic categories of social conflict and coexistence are framed in religious terms. Social tensions and

> conflicts with multiple contributing factors are depoliticized, their causes explained away through reference to intractable religious difference.[69]

Hurd calls for a more nuanced approach to religion and law that takes into account the local specificities and histories of religion in its social context. She criticizes the tendency of the media and state foreign policy makers to underestimate the complex vectors that shape conflict, and she argues that reducing these to "religious conflict" is often harmful to those caught up in such conflict by hardening lines of division.

Linked to Hurd's critique is the observation that religion has become something to be "managed" and that is being accomplished in part through human rights. As James Richardson observes, given the

> growth of religious diversity government officials and courts of law are evaluating religious groups on a regular basis to determine if they should be allowed to function, or what they can and cannot do. As distasteful as it may be to some, religiously pluralistic societies are being called on to 'manage' or 'regulate' religion, a development that by definition places limits on religious freedom.[70]

Inherent in such management is judgment about what religion looks like and which groups and practices should be protected. The *Ktunaxa* case offers just one example of this. Such adjudication is a persistent and often unarticulated feature of the management model of which human rights protections are a part.

As the religious landscape changes other issues will require attention and research. For example, the rapidly shifting diversity demographic means that symbols and practices affiliated with religious majorities and often taken for granted are increasingly coming under scrutiny. I have argued that the maintenance of power and privilege by claiming such practices and symbols as "heritage," "culture," or sanctioned by history threatens the credibility of human rights protections and that their place in the new diversity must be renegotiated create more inclusive societies.[71] The right not to be religious is quickly emerging as a core human rights issue on the horizon.[72] An increased awareness of the contemporary effects of historical harms to Indigenous peoples means that human rights protections must be responsive to the challenges posed by cases like *Ktunaxa*. Minority religious persons and groups are making human rights claims that require a reconceptualization of religious freedom.

Acknowledgments

I would like to acknowledge the ongoing financial support of my research through my Canada Research Chair in Religious Diversity and Social Change. I am also grateful to Cory Steele for his editorial and research assistance.

Notes

1 James T. Richardson, "Managing Religion and the Judicialization of Religious Freedom," *Journal for the Scientific Study of Religion*, 2015, vol. 54, no. 1, 5.

2 Elizabeth Shakman Hurd argues that "individuals or groups who resist or subvert the clean taxonomies and hierarchies of the secular-religious and religious-religious divides instantiated

through regimes of religious freedom are marginalized, falling between the cracks." Elizabeth Shakman Hurd, *Beyond Religious Freedom: The New Global Politics of Religion*, Princeton, NJ: Princeton University Press, 2015, p. 54.

3 Richardson, "Managing Religion," 1.

4 *Ktunaxa Nation v. British Columbia (Forests, Lands and Natural Resource Operations)*, 2017 SCC 54. Online. Available at https://scc-csc.lexum.com/scc-csc/scc-csc/en/item/16816/index.do (accessed 8 December 2018).

5 The Treaty of Paris (1763), allowed French settlers in British territory in Canada to practice Roman Catholicism "provided it did not contravene British law." Government of Canada, "Treaty of Paris," 2018. Online. Available at http://bataille.ccbn-nbc.gc.ca/en/traite-de-paris.php (accessed 8 December 2018).

6 For example, Ontario's Racial Discrimination Act (1944) states:

"No person shall,

(a) Publish or display or cause to be published or displayed; or
(b) Permit to be published or displayed on lands or premises or in a newspaper, through a radio broadcasting station or by means of any other medium which he owns or controls,

Any notice, sign, symbol, emblem or other representation indicating discrimination or an intention to discriminate against any person or any class of persons for any purpose because of the race or creed of such person or class of persons."

Section 1 of Racial Discrimination Act 1944 S.O. 1944, c. 51. Online. Available at https://archive.org/details/statutesofprovin1944onta (accessed 8 December 2018). The Saskatchewan Bill of Rights Act (1954) stipulates that "Every person and every class of persons shall enjoy the right to obtain the accommodation or facilities of any standard or other hotel, victualling house, theatre or other place to which the public is customarily admitted, regardless of the race, creed, religion, colour or ethnic or national origin of such persons or class of persons" (Saskatchewan Bill of Rights Act, 1954, section 11). Online. Available at www.publications.gov.sk.ca/freelaw/documents/english/statutes/historical/1953-CH-345.pdf (accessed 8 December 2018). The Canadian Bill of Rights also addresses religious freedom. In section 1 it states that "It is hereby recognized and declared that in Canada there have existed and shall continue to exist without discrimination by reason of race, national origin, colour, religion or sex, the following human rights and fundamental freedoms, namely … freedom of religion" (Canadian Bill of Rights, 1960, section 1). Online. Available at https://laws-lois.justice.gc.ca/eng/acts/c-12.3/page-1.html (accessed 8 December 2018).

7 James T. Richardson, "Update on Jehovah's Witness Cases Before the European Court of Human Rights: Implications of a Surprising Partnership," *Religion, State & Society*, 2017, vol. 45, nos. 3–4, 232.

8 Richardson, "Update on Jevhovah's Witness Cases," 242. See also Carolyn R. Wah, "Jehovah's Witnesses and the Responsibility of Religious Freedom: The European Experience," *Journal of Church and State*, 2001, vol. 43, no. 3, 579–601; Carolyn R. Wah, "Religious Freedom and the Best Interests of the Child: The Case of the Jehovah's Witnesses in Child Custody Litigation," in Pauline Côté (ed.) *Chercheurs de Dieux dans l'Espace Public* (Frontier Religions in Public Space), Ottawa: University of Ottawa Press, 2001, pp. 193–233; and Carolyn R. Wah, "Jehovah's Witnesses and the Empire of the Sun: A Clash of Faith and Religion during World War II," *Journal of Church and State*, 2002, vol. 44, no. 1, 45–73.

9 See Gary Botting, *Fundamental Freedoms and Jehovah's Witnesses*, Calgary: University of Calgary Press, 1993; William Kaplan, *State and Salvation*, Toronto: University of Toronto Press, 1989; Eric Michael Mazur, *The Americanization of Religious Minorities: Confronting the Constitutional Order*, Baltimore, MD: Johns Hopkins University Press, 1999; James T. Richardson and Alain Garay, "The European Court of Human Rights and Former Communist States," in Dinka Marinović Jerolimov, Siniša Zrinščak, and Irena Borowik (eds.) *Religion and Patterns of Social Transformation*, Zagreb: Institution for Social Research, 2004, pp. 223–34; and Chuck Smith, "The Persecution of West Virginia Jehovah's Witnesses and the Expansion of Legal Protection for Religious Liberty," *Journal of Church and State*, 2001, vol. 43, no. 3, 539–77.

10 See Jerzy Kłoczowski, *A History of Polish Christianity*, Cambridge, UK: Cambridge University Press, 2000; Brian Porter, "The Catholic Nation: Religion, Identity, and the Narratives of Polish History," *Slavic and East European Journal*, 2001, vol. 45, no. 2, 289–99; Brian Porter, *When Nationalism Began to Hate: Imagining Modern Politics in Nineteenth-Century Poland*, New York: Oxford University Press, 2000; and Geneviève Zubrzycki, *The Crosses of Auschwitz: Nationalism and Religion in Post-Communist Poland*, Chicago: University of Chicago Press, 2006.

11 *Saumur v. City of Quebec*, [1953] 2 S.C.R. 299. Hereafter "*Saumur*." Online. Available at https://scc-csc.lexum.com/scc-csc/scc-csc/en/item/2736/index.do (accessed 8 December 2018).

12 *Saumur*, 317.

13 Justice Rand, *Saumur*, 327.

14 Justice Rand, *Saumur*, 327.

15 Lori G. Beaman, *Defining Harm*, Vancouver: UBC Press, 2008, p. 23.

16 *Roncarelli v. Duplessis*, [1959] S.C.R. 121. Online. Available at https://scc-csc.lexum.com/scc-csc/scc-csc/en/item/2751/index.do (accessed 8 December 2018). Hereafter "*Roncarelli*."

17 Justice Rand, *Roncarelli*, 131.

18 Justice Fauteux, *Roncarelli*, 171.

19 The Canadian Charter of Rights and Freedoms is Part I of the Constitution Act. This act was enacted on 17 April 1982. Online. Available at http://laws-lois.justice.gc.ca/eng/const/page-15.html#h-38</URI (accessed 8 December 2018).

20 See Nancy Holmes, "Human Rights Legislation and the Charter: A Comparative Guide," 1992. Online. Available at http://publications.gc.ca/Collection-R/LoPBdP/MR/mr102-e.htm</URI (accessed 8 December 2018).

21 For a discussion on this new diversity in Canada see Lori G. Beaman, "Recognize the New Religious Diversity," *Canadian Diversity*, 2017, vol. 14, no. 4, 17–19. In Canada, for example, approximately 24 percent of the population identifies as having no religious affiliation. See Statistics Canada, "Two-Thirds of the Population Declare Christian as Their Religion," 2016. Online. Available at www.statcan.gc.ca/pub/91-003-x/2014001/section03/33-eng.htm (accessed 8 December 2018). In the United Kingdom the nonreligious account for roughly 50 percent of the population and in the United States they represent 19.6 percent. See Linda Woodhead, "The Rise of 'No Religion' in Britain: The Emergence of a New Cultural Majority," *Journal of the British Academy*, 2016, vol. 4, 245–61; and Pew Forum on Religion and Public Life, "'Nones' on the Rise: One-in-Five Adults Have No Religious Affiliation," 2012. Online. Available at www.pewforum.org/2012/10/09/nones-on-the-rise (accessed 8 December 2018). Clarke and Macdonald conclude that 55 percent of the Canadian population is de- and non-churched. See Brian Clarke and Stuart Macdonald, *Leaving Christianity: Changing Allegiances in Canada Since 1945*, Montreal and Kingston: McGill-Queen's University Press, 2017, p. 209. For a discussion of super-diversity, see Steven Vertovec, "Super-Diversity and Its Implications," *Ethnic and Racial Studies*, 2007, vol. 30, no. 6, 1024–54; Steven Vertovec, "Talking Around Super-Diversity," *Ethnic and Racial Studies*, 2017, vol. 42, no. 1, 125–39; and Marian Burchardt and Irene Becci, "Religion and Superdiversity: An Introduction," *New Diversities*, 2016, vol. 18, no. 1, 1–7.

22 In 2011, 1 percent of population the population identified as Jewish, 3.2 percent as Muslim, 1.5 percent as Hindu, and 1.4 percent as Sikh. See Statistics Canada, "Two-Thirds of the Population Declare Christian as their Religion." In 1981, 1.22 percent of the population was Jewish, 1.26 percent identified as belonging to "Eastern Non-Christian" traditions (Hinduism, Islam, and Sikhism) and 7.32 percent of the population identified as having "no religious preference." See Statistics Canada, "Canada, Provinces and Economic Regions: Population, Occupied Private Dwellings, Private Households and Census and Economic Families in Private Households," 1981. Online. Available at http://publications.gc.ca/collections/collection_2017/statcan/CS93-975-1981.pdf (accessed 8 December 2018). In comparison, in 1921 1.5 percent of the Canadian population identified as Jewish, and 0.45 percent as belonging to "Eastern Religions" (this includes Bahais, Buddhists, Confucians, Hindus, Muslims, Shintos, Sikhs, and Taoists). See Dominion Bureau of Statistics, *Sixth Census of Canada, 1921*, Ottawa: F. A. Acland, 1924, p. 568.

23 See Clarke and Macdonald, *Leaving Christianity*.

24 David Seljak, for example, writes that with respect to creed the Ontario Human Rights Code "was written largely to address religious discrimination suffered by members of minority religious groups at the hands of members of the majority, who were Christians (and almost all white). Today, the new ethno-racial and religious pluralism that has transformed Canadian society in the last five decades means that most complaints at Ontario's human rights tribunal citing a creed basis involve an intersection between faith-related and race-related grounds." David Seljak, "Post-Secularism, Multiculturalism, Human Rights, and Religion in Ontario," *Studies in Religion*, 2016, vol. 45, no. 4, 543.

25 Internationally this is also the case. See, for example: *Kokkinakis v. Greece* (1993); *Folgero v. Norway* (2007); *Religionsgemeinschaft der Zeugen Jehovas v. Austria* (2008); *Tsartsidze and Others v. Georgia* (2017); and *Bayatyan v. Armenia* (2011). All these cases can be located by searching the following European Court of Human Rights site. Online. Available at https://hudoc.echr.coe.int/eng#{%22documentcollectionid2%22:[%22GRANDCHAMBER%22,%22CHAMBER%22]} (accessed 8 December 2018).

26 *Syndicat Northcrest v. Amselem*, [2004] 2 S.C.R. 551, 2004 SCC 47. This and all following Supreme Court of Canada (SCC) cases can be located here: Online. Available at https://scc-csc.lexum.com/scc-csc/en/nav.do (accessed 8 December 2018).

27 *Multani v. Commission scolaire Marguerite-Bourgeoys*, [2006] 1 S.C.R. 256, 2006 SCC 6. Hereafter "*Multani*."

28 *Ishaq v. Canada (Citizenship and Immigration)*, [2015] 4 FCR 297, 2015 FC 156. Online. Available at www.canlii.org/en/ca/fct/doc/2015/2015fc156/2015fc156.pdf (accessed 8 December 2018).

29 *R. v. Big M Drug Mart Ltd.*, [1985] 1 S.C.R. 295 at para. 96. Hereafter "*Big M.*"

30 *Big M*, at para. 99. This is a Supreme Court of Canada case and can be located online as noted above (see note 26).

31 *R. v. Edwards Books and Art Ltd.*, [1986] 2 S.C.R. 713 at para. 62. Hereafter "*Edwards Books.*" This is a Supreme Court of Canada case and can be located online as noted above (see note 26).

32 Mouvement laïque québécois v. Saguenay (City), 2015 SCC 16, [2015] 2 S.C.R. 3, at para. 78. Hereafter "*Saguenay.*" This is a Supreme Court of Canada case and can be located online as noted above (see note 26) .

33 House of Commons Canada, *Compendium of Procedure*, n.d. Online. Available at www.ourcommons.ca/About/Compendium/TypicalSittingDay/c_d_prayer-e.htm (accessed 8 December 2018).

34 See Lori G. Beaman, "Battles over Symbols: The 'Religion' of the Minority Versus the 'Culture' of the Majority," *Journal of Law and Religion*, 2013, vol. 28, no. 1, 67–104; Lori G. Beaman, "Universal and Foundational: Law's Constitution of an Ethic of Belonging for Nones," in Roberto Cipriani and Franco Garelli (eds.) *Sociology of Atheism*, Leiden: Brill, 2016, pp. 17–35; and Lori G. Beaman, "Religious Diversity in the Public Sphere: The Canadian Case," *Religions*, 2017, vol. 8, no. 12, 1–18.

35 *Bhinder v. CN*, [1985] 2 SCR 561. This is a Supreme Court of Canada case and can be located online as noted above (see note 26).

36 *Central Alberta Dairy Pool v. Alberta (Human Rights Commission)*, [1990] 2 SCR 489 and *Ontario Human Rights Commission v. Simpsons-Sears*, [1985] 2 SCR 536. These are Supreme Court of Canada cases and can be located online as noted above (see note 26).

37 Shelagh Day and Gwen Brodsky, "The Duty to Accommodate: Who Will Benefit," *Canadian Bar Review*, 1996, vol. 75, no. 3, 462.

38 For a discussion of the conditions under which accommodation is used, see Richard Moon, "The Constitutional Protection of Religious Practices in Canada," in David M. Kirkham (ed.) *State Responses to Minority Religions*, London: Routledge, 2013, pp. 231–42.

39 Bouchard, Gérard, and Taylor, Charles, *Building the Future: A Time for Reconciliation*, Québec: Bibliothèque et Archives nationales du Québec, 2008, p. 17.

40 Winnifred F. Sullivan, "Law's Prayer: *Town of Greece v Galloway*," blog post for *SSRC Forum Reverberations: New Directions in the Study of Prayer*, 12 November 2013. Online. Available at http://forums.ssrc.org/ndsp/2013/11/05/laws-prayer-town-of-greece-v-galloway</URI (accessed 8 December 2018). See also Benjamin Berger, "The Aesthetics of Religious Freedom," in Winnifred F. Sullivan and Lori G. Beaman (eds.) *Varieties of Religious Establishment*, Farnham, UK: Ashgate, 2013, pp. 33–53.

41 See Sullivan, *Law's Prayer*.

42 "Scholars have observed a general increase in the judicialization of human rights as both individual and collective actors are more prone to seek redress, contest policies, and pursue social reform through courts." See Effie Fokas, "Directions in Religious Pluralism in Europe: Mobilizations in the Shadow of European Court of Human Rights Religious Freedom Jurisprudence," *Oxford Journal of Law and Religion*, 2015, vol. 4, no. 1, 73. Judicialization refers to a shift of power to courts that, based on a document of supreme legal status often encompassing a bill of rights, exercise review over governments and legislatures and adjudicate conflicts between states and individuals. See Matthias Koenig, "The Governance of Religious Diversity at the European Court of Human Rights," in Jane Boulden and Will Kymlicka (eds.) *International Approaches to Governing Ethnic Diversity*, Oxford: Oxford University Press, 2015, pp. 53–4. On Fokas' project: Online. Available at http://grassrootsmobilise.eu/ (accessed 8 December 2018).

43 Fokas, "Directions in Religious Pluralism," 56.

44 Effie Fokas, "The European Court of Human Rights at the Grassroots Level: Who Knows What About Religion at the ECtHR and to What Effects?" *Religion, State & Society*, 2017, vol. 45, nos. 3–4, 249–50.

45 Marc Galanter, "The Radiating Effects of Courts," in Keith O. Boyum and Lynn Mather (eds.) *Empirical Theories About Courts*, New York: Longman, 1983, p. 126.

46 "A single judicial action may radiate different messages to different audiences." Galanter, "The Radiating Effects of Courts," p. 126.

47 Markus Dressler, "Religio-Secular Metamorphoses: The Re-Making of Turkish Alevism," *Journal of the American Academy of Religion*, 2008, vol. 76, no. 2, 283.

48 As Kubik et al. note, the emergence of industrial capitalism and the wealth of resources in Canada meant that Indigenous people who resided in resource-rich areas came to be seen as a hindrance, rather than an asset, to the development of the industrial economy. See Wendee Kubik, Carrie Bourassa, and Mary Hampton, "Stolen Sisters, Second Class Citizens, Poor Health: The Legacy of Colonization in Canada," *Humanity & Society*, 2009, vol. 33, nos. 1–2, 19–20.

49 Truth and Reconciliation Commission of Canada, *They Came for the Children*, Winnipeg: Truth and Reconciliation Commission of Canada, 2012, p. 7.

50 Up to 60 percent of the schools were operated by the Roman Catholic Church, 25 percent by the Anglican Church, and roughly 2–3 percent by the Presbyterian Church. There was also a school run by a "US-based Baptist church" in the Yukon as well as three schools run by a Mennonite evangelical congregation in northwestern Ontario. See Truth and Reconciliation Commission of Canada, *They Came for the Children*, p. 15.

51 Truth and Reconciliation Commission of Canada, *They Came for the Children*, p. 1.

52 Truth and Reconciliation Commission of Canada, *Honouring the Truth, Reconciling for the Future: Summary of the Final Report of the Truth and Reconciliation Commission of Canada*, Canada: Truth and Reconciliation Commission of Canada, 2015, p. 23.

53 In the Truth and Reconciliation Commission of Canada's 94 Calls to Action, it calls on the governments of Canada to adopt and implement the United Nations Declaration on the Rights of Indigenous People:

43. We call upon federal, provincial, territorial, and municipal governments to fully adopt and implement the United Nations Declaration on the Rights of Indigenous Peoples as the framework for reconciliation.

44. We call upon the Government of Canada to develop a national action plan, strategies, and other concrete measures to achieve the goals of the United Nations Declaration on the Rights of Indigenous Peoples.

See Truth and Reconciliation Commission of Canada, *Truth and Reconciliation Commission of Canada: Calls to Action*, Winnipeg: Truth and Reconciliation Commission of Canada, 2015, p. 4. Further calls to include the UN's declaration in education, law and policy are also included in the Calls to Action.

54 Truth and Reconciliation Commission of Canada, *Honouring the Truth*, p. 187.

55 Truth and Reconciliation Commission of Canada, *Honouring the Truth*, p. 188.

56 See House of Commons (2018) *Private Member's Bill: C-262*, Canada. Online. Available at www.parl.ca/LegisInfo/BillDetails.aspx?billId=8160636&Language=E (accessed 8 February 2019).

57 *Ktunaxa Nation*, at para. 70.

58 *Ktunaxa Nation*, at para. 71.
59 *Ktunaxa Nation*, at para. 8.
60 *Ktunaxa Nation*, at para. 10.
61 *Ktunaxa Nation*, at para. 86.
62 *Ktunaxa Nation*, at para. 114.
63 See Nicholas D. Shrubsole, "Secularization, Dispossession, Forced Deprivatization: The Conditions of Public Religion and the Protection of First Nations' Sacred Space," *Studies in Religion*, 2016, vol. 45, no. 3, 335–59, and Dwight Newman, "Implications of the Ktunaxa Nation/ Jumbo Valley Case for Religious Freedom Jurisprudence," in Dwight Newman (ed.) *Religious Freedom and Communities*, Toronto: LexisNexis, 2016 [12 pages].
64 Sophie Pierre, "Defining the Nation to Nation Paradigm," 2017. Online. Available at www.victoriaforum.ca/videos-2017-victoria-forum (accessed 8 December 2018).
65 *Ktunaxa Nation*, at para. 35.
66 *Ktunaxa Nation*, at para. 36.
67 *Ktunaxa Nation*, at para. 46.
68 *Ktunaxa Nation*, at para. 72.
69 Hurd, *Beyond Religious Freedom*, p. 12.
70 Richardson, "Managing Religion," 2.
71 See Beaman, "Recognize the New Religious Diversity."
72 See Lori G. Beaman, Cory Steele, and Keelin Pringnitz, "The Inclusion of Nonreligion in Religion and Human Rights," *Social Compass*, 2018, vol. 65, no. 1, 43–61 and Marika McAdam, *Freedom from Religion and Human Rights Law: Strengthening the Right to Freedom of Religion and Belief for Non-Religious and Atheist Rights-Holders*, London: Routledge, 2018.

23

INDIGENOUS ACTIVISM FOR HUMAN RIGHTS

A case study from Australia

Rachel Standfield and Lynette Russell

Introduction

Indigenous peoples (including those people now living in settler-colonial contexts), although absent at the formulation of the Universal Declaration of Human Rights (UDHR), have been central to developments in conceptualizing human rights in the recent past. Indigenous people have helped shape a movement toward the recognition of group rights and also a movement away from the prominence of state or national rights in the United Nations (UN). In fact, the political scientist and former director of the Secretariat of the UN Permanent Forum on Indigenous Issues, Elsa Stamatopoulou, writes that the "gradual recognition of indigenous peoples' rights is one of the most pronounced examples" demonstrating the "dynamic" nature of human rights as it has been formulated by the UN.[1]

In addition to that activism on the contemporary global stage, Indigenous peoples have also struggled throughout colonial histories in diverse locations to attempt to protect their individual and collective rights. This they have done to signal to colonists their own understandings of their rights as First Peoples. Indigenous communities around the globe, with their histories of difficult and even traumatic relationships with national and local governments, have made clear use of human rights mechanisms in order to attempt to gain traction in recognition and protection of their human rights. This essay examines one case study from these long histories of struggle, focused on the activism of particular Aboriginal peoples in Victoria, Australia. We explore the histories of protests for the rights of Aboriginal communities, including the ways that these communities have used kin, political, and social networks to draw Aboriginal people together in order to survive dispossession and colonization and to agitate for rights. Examining examples of activism for civil, political, Indigenous, and land rights from the nineteenth through to the twenty-first centuries, we outline a history of sustained struggle. We call too for recognition of the distinctiveness of social organization and political systems of Indigenous peoples, in this case the specific nature of Victorian Indigenous politics, kin connections, and relationships to country.

Our approach responds to recent debates in the historiography of human rights which, in the search for specific moments that can function as a point of origin, have focused on European or American perspectives on rights and have highlighted the role of governments and institutions.[2] Yet alongside this search for supposed origins there is also scholarship that explores the ways that European definitions of rights have been complicit in colonization and how Indigenous peoples have used domestic and international mechanisms to attempt to manage colonial appropriation of land and protect people and culture.[3] Scholars should avoid teleological narratives of linear progress for all people, as well as approaches that suggest that perspectives on human rights espoused by European governments or institutions can stand in for the experiences of diverse peoples globally. Our approach does not see rights discourses as purely recent phenomena; they are part of a shifting arrangement of power and response with a multiplicity of manifestations in diverse contexts and for different peoples. We argue for attention to long histories, but also respect for difference in the ways that rights might be articulated, to the specific social structures and power relations that struggles for rights reflect, and we demonstrate that this fight has been based on distinctly Aboriginal forms of social organization and political systems.

Indeed, we argue that understanding the experiences of Indigenous peoples in relation to struggles for human rights is vitally important for students, indeed for non-Indigenous peoples in general, in order to understand the complexity of histories of human rights and the length of struggle by colonized peoples. Political theorist Jeff Spinner-Halev utilizes the concept of "enduring injustice" to help explain histories of oppression that span generations and that have proved exceptionally difficult for states to recognize and atone for.[4] Spinner-Halev argues that Indigenous peoples, sharing communal cultures, histories of injustice, and connection to land, are the archetypal examples of communities that qualify for the recognition of group rights.[5] As political scientists Duncan Ivison, Paul Patten, and Will Sanders have shown, the experiences of Indigenous people sorely test political theories that hold that liberal democracies and politics support justice. These authors have argued that one of the most important issues confronting political theory is the capacity to express a just relationship with Indigenous peoples, given the hierarchical relationships that underpin politics in the West:

> Western political thought has often embodied a set of culturally specific assumptions and judgments about the relative worth of other cultures, ways of life, value systems, social and political institutions, and ways of organizing property. As a result, egalitarian political theory has often ended up justifying explicitly inegalitarian institutions and practices.[6]

In the same vein, the human rights scholar Rhiannon Morgan has noted that contemporary recognition of Indigenous rights has "radically reformed international law."[7] Contemporary Indigenous activism on the international stage has thus led to the refashioning of the very body of law that was used to oppress and to colonize. The labor undertaken to refashion legal systems, to find a voice while confronting dominant depictions of inequality and oppression as "natural," and to resist the power imbalances of colonization, has been work taken on by Indigenous peoples over decades, responding in each generation to the issues of the time and the possibilities for actions available for each group of people.

Ravi de Costa – whose work has done much to draw attention to longer histories of Indigenous human rights struggles, both in Australia and elsewhere – has argued that with the development of world history as a field of historical research and the contemporary success of Indigenous activism for rights on the international stage, historians must turn to research the historical claims of Indigenous people and communities.[8] De Costa argues we should not be surprised by the "rapidity with which the indigenous movement became a global phenomenon in the last quarter of the twentieth century."[9] Long histories of Indigenous protest, fights for equality and rights, and engagement with the international community in order to put forward Indigenous claims are the forces that shape contemporary Indigenous activism. In the Australian context Indigenous leaders and scholars have echoed de Costa's arguments. Stan Grant, who has popularized the understanding of colonialism as an ongoing phenomenon, along with others including Larissa Behrendt, have stressed that there is a need for non-Indigenous people to understand that Indigenous people are engaged in colonial situations that span a period far longer than the post-World War II development of a modern human rights discourse.[10] Appreciating the context of colonial history provides a framework for understanding contemporary issues, and emphasizes that Indigenous communities have resisted colonization and agitated for their rights since the arrival of colonists on their land. In Australian historiography this history of activism is quite well documented by both Aboriginal and non-Aboriginal historians, and many specific examples of historical activism have been explored.[11]

In this essay, we follow a history of activism for rights over generations of Victorian Aboriginal communities, and trace the connections between specific individuals and groups of people over time since the first colonization of Victorian Aboriginal country. The human rights scholar and practitioner Philip Alston has argued that while understandings of human rights have changed over time, there is "a strong genealogical or ancestral component" through generations. In our case study we trace this specifically for particular groups of people.[12] Ravi de Costa shows that this continuity of resistance has an impact on contemporary Indigenous activism:

> Indigenous peoples were not pulled suddenly into international activism during the 1970s ... Indigenous activists were simply continuing with the political representation they had always undertaken, presenting their own claims for recognition and justice to authorities on the widest possible stage.[13]

Distinctive cultures, distinctive histories

Much of the enduring injustice that Indigenous people face throughout the world comes from non-Indigenous colonization of their land and the dispossession of Indigenous communities. Australia is a settler colony where Indigenous land rights were not recognized by the legal system or government from the initiation of colonization in 1788 until the final quarter of the twentieth century. As the former UN Special Rapporteur on the Rights of Indigenous Peoples and scholar James Anaya has demonstrated, after the Treaty of Westphalia (1648) legal theorists moved away from notions that there was a "universal moral code for humankind," dividing rights into those accruing to the individual and those rights enjoyed by states. The definition of what constituted a state, however, was "not alive to the rich variety of intermediate or alternative associational groupings actually found in human cultures," and hence treaties were far less likely to be negotiated with Indigenous peoples than previous acts of colonization.[14] Thus, Australian colonial governments did not seek Aboriginal or Torres Strait Islander consent for colonization and did not recognize Indigenous ownership of land. This legal history, combined with the absolute centrality of land (known as "country") to Aboriginal and Torres Strait cultures and identities, ensures that land looms large in terms of human rights in Australia, as it does for Indigenous people globally. Land has been central to Indigenous politics from the nineteenth century and continues to be so into the present day.

For Aboriginal and Torres Strait Islander peoples, land was and is, central to culture, identity, and spirituality. Land is not an economic resource as non-Indigenous people might imagine it to be. Country is life and the meaning of life – the basis of knowledges both everyday and religious that are embodied and inscribed onto land, the site of kin relations, and the basis of culture. The anthropologist Deborah Bird Rose speaks to the connection between people and land when she discusses country as a "nourishing terrain" that sustains both the individual and the group.[15] Each Indigenous nation, or language group, was and is intimately connected to a specific country from which springs a particular culture. While sustaining people both economically and culturally, country was not a commodity in the European sense. As the basis of culture, it was not bought and sold. Connection to specific areas determines obligations for caring for the land and everything on the land, including the people. The Australian anthropologist W. E. H. Stanner famoulsy described relationships to country and the incommensurability of Western and Indigenous understandings of country as follows:

> No English words are good enough to give a sense of the links between an Aboriginal group and its homeland. Our word "home," warm and suggestive though it be, does not match the Aboriginal word that may mean "camp," "hearth," "country," "everlasting home," "totem place," "life source," "spirit centre" and much else all in one … A different tradition leaves us tongueless and earless towards this other world of meaning and significance.[16]

Indigenous people have precise and extremely complex systems of land ownership that are different from the system that the British brought with them to Australia. These are systems that have lay at the heart of the populating of Australia for millennia – new archaeological research has discovered Aboriginal occupation in Australia spanning 65,000 years.

Each Indigenous nation also faces diversity in the demography of the non-Indigenous population that now lives on their country. Victorian peoples faced colonization of their respective countries from 1835, including a massive influx of non-Indigenous people due to the discovery of gold in Victoria in 1851. When colonization began the Victorian population was already severely reduced. Two smallpox epidemics sweeping from the north ahead of non-Indigenous settlement had reduced the population from an estimated 60,000 to 15,000.[17] During the early colonial period there was further significant population decline as disease, violence, and dispossession had a severe impact. By the late 1850s the Aboriginal population in Victoria was a little over 2,000 people.[18]

A particular feature of the Victorian colonial systems has been the prominence of policies and discourses of "protection." From the late 1830s until the end of the 1840s a number of Victorian Aboriginal communities had a British government-appointed protector sent to work among them, initiating policies that would in the mid-nineteenth century develop into a legislative regime. After the abolition of slavery, British humanitarians turned their attention to the treatment of Indigenous peoples throughout the British Empire, recommending regimes of "protection" as a response to the violent nature of colonization. As historians Alan Lester and Fae Dussart have outlined, there is a deep paradox at work here, where these modes of governing Indigenous peoples were driven by humanitarian concerns and yet were intrinsically connected to and indeed encouraged the invasion and occupation of Indigenous peoples' lands on "an unprecedentedly extensive scale." Lester and Dussart argue that "violent colonial conquest was foundational and intrinsic to the shared history of British humanitarianism and governmentality."[19] The complex and ambivalent nature of these humanitarian discourses and especially their complicity in colonial processes that dispossessed Indigenous peoples and attempted to impose significant cultural change all point to the need for research to examine not only the stated aims of human rights movement or humanitarian discourses but also their impacts.

The notion of "protection" would come to dominate the approach to Aboriginal affairs in the colony and later the state of Victoria. Legislation to protect, manage, and control Indigenous people was first developed in Victoria, and was later used as a model for other Australian colonies. The 1869 Aborigines Protection Act (Victoria) set up a Board of non-Indigenous people with the power to control Indigenous lives; there was "nothing similar in the other colonies until the 1880s."[20] Amended legislation in 1886 introduced strongly racialized categories and imposed government definitions of who was considered to be Aboriginal, and in the process caused the breaking up of communities and families. John Chesterman and Brian Galligan have described how the 1886 legislation "pioneered the sharp distinction made federally between 'aboriginal natives' and 'half-castes.'" People who were deemed "half-castes" were excluded from reserves: "Perversely, 'half-castes' were forcibly removed from stations and denied supporting benefits in the name of making them 'free and equal citizens,' a status denied to 'aboriginal natives.'"[21] Legislative categorization further undermined the size and cohesion of the population, as authorities deemed significant numbers of people to be "legally white" and broke families apart. Good intentions were often shaped by ideas of superiority over Indigenous and other non-European populations, and humanitarians' stated aims of "civilization" were ultimately about cultural destruction. These examples show the problematic nature of protection and the need to interrogate assumptions about humanitarianism.

In 1901 Australia's six separate colonies federated and formed the Commonwealth of Australia. Federation brought the explicit denial of civil and political rights to Aboriginal people, including the loss of voting rights that in some colonies had been allowed, the denial of citizenship, and exclusion from state support. In the early years of the twentieth century, while white Australians were seeing their own political and civil rights bolstered by governments and were garnering support from the development of an expansive government welfare system, the White Australia Policy[22] excluded those deemed to be non-white from entry while explicitly denying Indigenous people access to political and civil rights and state benefits.

As well as these policies designed to keep Indigenous people in poverty and exclude them from benefits that accrued to membership of a (white) Australian nation, Indigenous communities nationally faced the removal of their children to institutions and to white families. These removals, now described as the "Stolen Generations," were shaped by racialized thought and acted to formalize, extend, and harden earlier colonial practices that had intervened into Aboriginal family life. The removal of children was designed in particular to make children of mixed Indigenous and non-Indigenous heritage "white" and to facilitate the biological absorption of Aboriginal children into non-Aboriginal society. This was a policy with enormous and devastating repercussions for Aboriginal family life. In 1997 the Australian Human Rights Commission report into the separation of Aboriginal and Torres Strait Islander children from their families estimated that between 10 and 30 percent of Aboriginal children were removed from their families between 1910 and 1970.[23]

Gathering together: survival and land

It is vital to understand that Indigenous people have resisted these processes of invasion and cultural change. Resistance to colonization and to actions bringing the colonizers into the Aboriginal world was and is an ongoing exercise.

The first Europeans to settle in Victoria came from the southern island of Tasmania. The lead settler entrepreneur and explorer John Batman attempted to purchase, via treaty, the land of the present cities of Melbourne and Geelong. The document was almost immediately declared void and illegal by the Governor of New South Wales.[24] Recently historians have suggested that the Kulin Indigenous nations of the region saw the ill-fated Batman treaty as a *tanderrum*, a traditional ceremony that allows newcomers to pass through the country but attributes them no other rights.[25] This assertion certainly accords with our reading that Kulin nations responded in culturally appropriate ways, and fits with our previous contention that the historical struggle of Victorian Aboriginal communities should be seen as culturally derived and as an extension of traditional social political structures and conventions.

This pattern did not stop at the moment of settlement. Lynette Russell has argued elsewhere that what was read by early European colonists as "begging" in early Melbourne was an articulation of rights that stemmed from relationships to country.[26] Dja Dja Wurrung people, mining gold during the Victorian gold rush, refused to pay for a mining license, and instead asserted their rights to use the resources of country, stating "that the gold and land were theirs by right so why should they pay money to the Queen."[27] And Wayne Atkinson details how the Yorta Yorta nation from 1860

> demanded compensation from the Victorian authorities for the destruction of their natural fishing areas by paddle steamers. The demand was for a tax of 10 pounds (approximately $20) to be imposed on each steamer passing up and down the river, and to be expended in supplying food to the natives in lieu of fish which had been driven away.

Atkinson, an important contemporary Victorian Aboriginal leader, argues that these actions were claims for Indigenous rights, "[w]hile these demands were unsuccessful, they illustrate that as early as 1860, the Yorta Yorta ancestors were well aware of their natural indigenous rights and were quick to exercise them."[28]

During the 1850s, as the Victorian gold rush led to a settler population boom, Aboriginal people were increasingly dispossessed from their country, left to attempt to control processes of land loss to the best of their abilities. In July 1860 a deputation of Taungurung and Woiwurrung people visited William Thomas, previously protector and then "Guardian of Aborigines," asking for land to be "set apart for them."[29] Taungurung chose a site on the Acheron river, but the Protection Board ignored this site, setting aside another site on marginal farmland instead. This site became the Mohican station. This was not the first call for land to be kept for Indigenous people. Kulin people had been calling for their own land to be kept aside for them since Billibellary, the most senior Kulin *ngurungaeta* (clan head) asked William Thomas to arrange land from government in 1843.[30] Prior to the arrival of non-Indigenous invaders Indigenous peoples had regional alliances though they did not share a pan-Indigenous identity. In the area that is now southern and central Victoria different nations came together in the Kulin alliance, connected by kinship and political ties without living together on a permanent basis, each of the five nations being sustained by and responsible for their own country. In the face of dispossession from specific countries, these peoples made a strategic decision to petition for reserve land and to gather together as a larger group. A delegation of Woiwurrung people led by their *ngurungaeta* Simon Wonga and accompanied by John Green, the Protection Board's Inspector of Settlements and the official trusted by the Woiwurrung people, traveled to the Mohican Station.[31] Simon Wonga would later describe this journey to unite the communities:

> Mr. Green and all the Yarra blacks and me went through the mountains. We had no bread for four or five days. We did all this to let you [Goulburn blacks] know about the good word. Now you have come to the Yarra. I am glad.[32]

Kulin actions to campaign for their rights to land and to have land set aside for them while they were being rapidly dispossessed from their country demonstrates their agency in working within the systems set up by colonizers to attempt to protect their own rights. In the midst of rapid change – Wonga's reference to the "good word" suggests his adoption of Christianity, a central aspect of cultural change pressed by policies of "protection" – Victorian Aboriginal people were attempting to support each other and find a place on their traditional country where they could survive.

Following the journey, people began to gather at Coranderrk, a site on Woiwurrung country near present-day Healesville, about 60 kilometers from Melbourne. Forty people accompanied Wonga's delegation and "soon after another sixty, from six different parts of the Colony, were brought in."[33] During these migrations to Coranderrk we can see the explicit gathering together of a more broad-based community, finding support and community as the actions of government and settlers led to dispossession and dislocation. Among those who came from the Mohican station, for example, was William Barak, son of a Woiwurrung *ngurungaeta*, who as a young man had been present at the signing of the treaty.[34] In the coming years Barak, together with Simon Wonga, became central to the political leadership of Kulin peoples and to the articulation of rights for Victorian Aboriginal peoples.

This example of people from diverse Aboriginal nations coming together to survive through rapid processes of dispossession, illustrates Ravi de Costa's point that activism for justice and recognition of rights has been central to developing the very concept of being "Indigenous." He has traced a history of identity-making through Indigenous petitioning, arguing that the category of Indigenous itself has been shaped by calls for rights, in response to categories imposed from outside. This has been a process of effectively "indigenizing" imposed categories, by combining "traditional identities with the indigenized forms of identities imposed by colonial authorities."[35]

Having gathered community members together from central and southern Victoria, Coranderrk flourished as a community throughout the 1860s and 1870s. The community was financially independent, operating as a thriving farm, and community members were in demand as farm laborers in the district. From the early 1870s, however, Coranderrk came under increasing pressure from non-Indigenous settlers who demanded it be "more productively" used, that is, given over to non-Indigenous settlement.[36]

One of the most significant moments of coming together to create a pan-Indigenous community is observed in the example of the Kulin fight to save Coranderrk. Coranderrk is one of the best known historical examples of a campaign for rights by Aboriginal people; for example, the story has recently been commemorated in a play. The community coalesced around their leaders Simon Wonga and, after Wonga's death, William Barak. They wrote multiple petitions to the colonial Victorian government. Historian Penny van Toorn demonstrated through careful analysis of the writing on the petitions that the arrangement of signatures on the documents continued to demonstrate Kulin political structures and lines of authority. Authority earlier rested with Wonga and later with Barak, as *ngurungaeta* of the specific country on which the reserve stood. They were supported by a younger man, Thomas Dunnolly, who was proficient in writing English and acted as a scribe. On more than one occasion, a delegation of men including Barak, Robert Wandin (Barak's nephew), Robert Bamfield (a Taungurong man whose country was directly north of Coranderrk), and Thomas Dunnolly walked to Melbourne to deliver the petitions by hand. Barak later outlined the importance of these men: they were the men to whom a clan head "gave his words," "speakers" within Kulin forms of political organization; Dunnolly, van Toorn argues, although a young man not associated with Woiwurrung country, was cast in a similar role as a "writer."[37] Through their tireless efforts, the people of Coranderrk succeeded in having two parliamentary committees established to consider their claims. The final committee of 1881 set aside Coranderrk as a permanent reserve for Kulin peoples that could not be dissolved without parliamentary approval.

William Cooper: shared struggles, difference, and Indigenous rights in the twentieth century

William Cooper, one of the foremost Aboriginal activists of the twentieth century and himself belonging to the Yorta Yorta Aboriginal nation, was connected by relationships to this earlier history of Aboriginal activism, as well as being influenced by it. His sister's husband had been living at Maloga mission, which was on the Murray River on the border of New South Wales and Victoria, when Barak, the leader of the community at Coranderrk, had traveled there in 1880 to visit family and attempt to improve the health of his son. While there he had "thrilled the Maloga residents … with tales of the Kulin's struggles for land at Coranderrk and the residents' David and Goliath-like struggle against the Victorian Aborigines Protection Board."[38] In 1881, directly following Barak's visit, Maloga residents petitioned the government for land, and their petition was successful in 1883, when "the New South Wales government set aside 1,800 acres of land" to be named Cummeragunja, or "our home."[39]

William Cooper lived most of his life at Cummeragunja. In 1933, at the age of 72 years, he moved to Melbourne because if he continued to live on the reserve he would have been denied access to the age pension due to his Aboriginality. In his later life he became a well-known champion for Aboriginal rights, not just for the Victorian community, but across the country.[40] Along with other Aboriginal activists living in Melbourne, Cooper established an organization called the Australian Aborigines' League in 1934. Cooper and his compatriots agitated for change through the use of "written appeals in the press and to politicians, public meetings and demonstrations."[41] These included organizing a petition to King George V for Aboriginal representation in the federal parliament. Cooper also played a key role in organizing the 1938 Day of Mourning protest by southeastern Aboriginal activists to mark the sesquicentenary of non-Indigenous invasion of the country. He supported and publicized a walk-off from the Cummeragunja Aboriginal reserve over the poor treatment of the community there. Cooper was also particularly attentive to the experiences of oppressed peoples elsewhere. For example in 1938 he undertook a lone march to the German Consulate in South Melbourne to protest the treatment of Jewish people in Germany, "one of the first protests against the actions of the Nazis in the world."[42]

Cooper's activism demonstrates an important point made by historian Christopher McCrudden in relation to human rights historiography. When reviewing Samuel Moyn's *The Last Utopia*, McCrudden argued that Moyn's conclusion that international mechanisms alone constitute human rights ignored the complex interplay between domestic and international campaigns and remedies. William Cooper combined a strong international outlook and a keen attention to developments and issues elsewhere in the world with a deep commitment to and clear focus on Indigenous people domestically. He petitioned the British king, but he also campaigned to Australian politicians at both federal and state government levels and used domestic media channels to agitate for change. He also used comparisons with Indigenous peoples in New Zealand and Fiji to argue for Aboriginal rights in Australia. McCrudden suggests that this comparative methodology of using international comparison to campaign for rights domestically is an important point of continuity between historical and contemporary human rights campaigns.[43]

Cooper's organization, the Australian Aborigines' League (AAL), was "the first advocacy organisation with an entirely Aboriginal membership," providing a model for the next generation of Indigenous organizations. Membership, open to people "possessing some degree of Aboriginal blood," showed a clear rejection of the racialized categories of half-caste, quadroon, and so on that were utilized by Australian governments with extremely damaging impacts on individuals, families, and communities. The AAL set out a list of nine demands, the fourth of which called for "the ending of discrimination between Aborigines of full and part descent, and between Aborigines and Europeans."[44] Membership also ensured Aboriginal leadership and autonomy. While two white people were invited to join the organization, they only occupied honorary positions and supporting roles. One of these individuals acted as a scribe for Cooper, just as Thomas Dunnolly had done for Barak before him.[45] Their letters, it has been suggested, reflect the centrality of orality among Aboriginal people, and also illustrate kinship as the "dominant cultural code shaping relationships between people."[46] It may well be appropriate to consider this type of collaborative working as reflecting the Aboriginal political methodologies that earlier generations of Victorian Aboriginal political leaders had used, both within specifically Aboriginal contexts and in engaging with the white political system to call for recognition of rights.

William Cooper's activism in the 1930s shows an expanding concept of Aboriginality that confirms de Costa's contention that human rights activism helped develop the concept of being Indigenous. Cooper's activism was undertaken with people drawn together both by circumstances and kinship. Kinship between New South Wales and Victorian Aboriginal nations supported activism, the most notable example being the famous 1938 Day of Mourning demonstration for the sesquicentenary of non-Indigenous settlement.[47]

Cooper also argued for the right to be supported by the state by virtue of being First Peoples. While he asserted this right, he specifically chose not to claim it, believing that this would not be in Aboriginal people's best interests:

> We claim that the native has a right to live in the "Land of His Fathers." We claim he has the right to this without the need for working for it but we know this is not desirable and would do harm to the race. We therefore claim the right to work for our living under modern conditions. We want the right to full education, academic, cultural and industrial and to be able to take our place beside the white race in full equality and responsibility.[48]

Cooper was active not only on behalf of all Aboriginal people, his calls for rights explicitly articulated a common struggle under colonization. In 1933 in a letter to *The Age* newspaper, Cooper drew parallels between the contemporary situation of violence against Aboriginal people in Central Australia and histories of frontier violence elsewhere. "I wish to draw attention to the inhuman treatment of aborigines in Central Australia," Cooper wrote. These people were "not allowed to live in peace," he observed:

> When the first white settlers arrived 145 years ago there were hundreds of thousands of aborigines here. But brutal extermination followed, and the number of full-blooded natives was reduced to 17,000. The killing of natives is continuing today, and if it is not soon stopped the Australian aborigine will become extinct.[49]

Thus he protested against contemporary events affecting Indigenous people in different parts of the country and he used these events to highlight the local history of dispossession and oppression. In his inclusion of communities throughout Australia, Cooper shows an expansion of Indigenous solidarity beyond the borders of original precolonial alliances and beyond the connections among southeastern Australian communities in earlier colonial periods.

While Cooper wrote appeal after appeal to the non-Indigenous Australian population, he did not bow to non-Indigenous people in any way. He held the colonizing community to account for violence and for poor treatment of Aboriginal people: "instead of lifting our people up, the early comers to our country destroyed them." He believed that non-Indigenous people had been "destroying people better than themselves." As a result, "the white people of Australia must carry the bloodstains of the aborigines for evermore … and the tradition of cruelty was handed down from white generation to generation to the present day."[50] Cooper articulated the responsibility of non-Indigenous people for Indigenous depopulation, dispossession, and poverty, grounded in violence and cruelty, implying unflinchingly that the "white" population carried and carries a collective stain for its historical and contemporary treatment of Aboriginal people.

Historical lineages, contemporary struggles

Over the past 50 years the discourse of Indigenous rights has percolated through mainstream Australian society. Cooper and his colleagues became role models for a generation of activists to follow, and they shared kinship ties and mission backgrounds with activists like Marge Tucker and Doug Nicholls who followed on, working tirelessly through the mid-twentieth century. In 1967, after a decade of concerted campaigning by Aboriginal activists, the Australian Commonwealth government held a referendum to change the Australian Constitution. The constitution contained only two references to Indigenous people, both negative. After the success of the referendum, Aboriginal people were included in the census and the Commonwealth government was enabled to make laws for them. The extremely high "yes" vote in favor of these changes is widely regarded as the recognition of Aboriginal people as full Australian citizens.

The campaign for the referendum brought to public attention the fact that Aboriginal Australians were literally figured as second-class citizens, with all sorts of limitations – legislative and social – on their lives.[51] Two significant organizations, the Victorian Aborigines Advancement League (VAAL) and the Federal Council for the Advancement of Aborigines and Torres Strait Islanders (FCAATSI), played key roles in the referendum campaign. FCAATSI was a group of both Indigenous and non-Indigenous activists who had come together for the purpose of changing the Constitution. VAAL, by contrast, not only continued beyond the referendum but was also profoundly changed as a result of it, with an exclusively Aboriginal membership. These organizations were in many ways logical extensions of the early, pioneering work of Cooper and other activists. Indeed, many of his kin and community were part of their fabric. The members of VAAL and FCAATSI were deeply influenced by post-World War II human rights discourse, and in particular the emergence of the UN. William Cooper's protest against Germany and his clear understanding of the treatment of different "native" communities in an international context was significant.[52] In New South Wales Aboriginal activist Pearl Gibbs used the UDHR to frame her concerns. In an interview given in 1971, Gibbs produced her much-read copy of the

> book of Human Rights and read out the sonorous, beautiful words, slowly: "All human beings are born free and equal in dignity and rights. They are endowed with reason and conscience and should act towards one another in a spirit of brotherhood."

She went on to observe that as a mixed-race Aboriginal Australian she had "to be interested in citizenship rights. I'm not quite white enough to be able to ignore them."[53] These domestic campaigns thus were supported by developments in international human rights, and activists drew on global human rights discourses to support their domestic activism.

The key concern that runs through generations of Victorian Indigenous calls for rights – the struggle to have relationships to land recognized – has continued throughout postwar Indigenous activism and into the present. Australia was colonized on the basis of the legal fiction of *terra nullius*, the Latin term for a "land belonging to no one." This concept was reinscribed in Australian law in 1971 by Justice Blackburn in the Gove land rights case. Although challenged on three occasions, it was not until 1992 that the High Court of Australia ruled that the Meriam people (of the Torres Straits) were "entitled as against the whole world to possession, occupation, use and enjoyment of (most of) the lands of the Murray Islands."[54] The consequences of this judgement were felt across Australia and in the same year the federal government passed the first Commonwealth Native Title Act.[55]

The passing of this Act led Indigenous nations to pursue Native Title claims, in order to have their status as "traditional owners" recognized by under Australian law. The Yorta Yorta community were one of the first Indigenous peoples in Australia to make a Native Title claim through the Australian court system. Wayne Atkinson, a key claimant, has written of his indebtedness to William Cooper: "One can be assured … that Uncle William's words will continue to be the driving force of the Yorta Yorta struggle."[56] The experiences of Yorta Yorta people in their pursuit of land justice, however, was another scarring experience, in which the fact of Victorian Aboriginal dispossession was used to deny access to Native Title. In finding against their claim, the Federal Court relied on historical non-Indigenous perspectives on Indigenous relationships to land. A book published by a member of the Aboriginal Protection Board in the nineteenth century, Edward Curr, was used as evidence against the claims of the Yorta Yorta people. Curr denied Yorta Yorta attachment to country and forms of political and social organization. In prioritizing colonial documents rather than the evidence provided by the Yorta Yorta themselves, the presiding judge reinscribed discourses of protection that denied Victorian Aboriginal peoples' culture and ownership of country, a serious setback in the ongoing struggle for rights. The Australian High Court upheld the decision of the Federal Court in 2002. In response to the rejection of their Native Title claim through multiple court cases, the Yorta Yorta community announced their intention to go to the UN to have their rights recognized. Monica Morgan, a "Yorta Yorta member and coordinator of the native title claim," was quoted as stating "her people had run out of options under Australian law to address Aboriginal land rights" and that "[t]here's a whole raft of issues the Yorta Yorta people may need to look at because we're just not getting them looked at in domestic law."[57] This willingness to engage with international processes and appeal to the UN demonstrates the ways that Victorian Aboriginal histories of appeals to rights resonate into the contemporary period. The ways in which Indigenous peoples have used the UN strategically, particularly when Australian domestic rights advances prove inadequate and flawed, demonstrates again the relationship between international and domestic campaigns for rights and how contemporary leaders follow in the footsteps of their ancestors in their campaigns.

The Commonwealth government amended the Native Title Act in 1998, which resulted in a more complex and difficult process for Indigenous communities attempting to have rights in land recognized and respected. The changes included providing greater extinguishment of Native Title, which is a "significant diminution of the opportunity for indigenous peoples to pursue their claims to native title."[58] The United Nations Committee on the Elimination of Racial Discrimination (CERD) decided on 18 March 1998 that the Australian Commonwealth Government's Native Title Amendment Act "discriminated against Australian indigenous land title holders."[59] CERD called on Australia to address these issues as "a matter of urgency," to "suspend implementation of the 1998 amendments," and to negotiate with Indigenous representatives, but the Australian government "rejected the decision."[60] The difficulties encountered by Indigenous communities in attempting to achieve Native Title proved so great that many Victorian communities have subsequently turned to state-based negotiations when opportunities to work with the Victorian State government have arisen. In 2004 the Victorian State government negotiated a cooperative agreement with the Yorta Yorta community.[61] State-based processes have also led to Native Title settlements for Gunaikurnai, Dja Dja Wurrung, and Gunditjmara peoples. With these settlements come some guaranteed rights to access the country, employment for some community members, and a say in management of land. Where once the colony of Victoria was at the forefront of implementing the damaging policies of protection, Indigenous communities now choose to engage with the State of Victoria in order to secure greater recognition of their rights in land.[62]

Indigenous peoples globally are now recognized as important contributors to rights discourses and to rights activism in contemporary settings. Their articulations of rights and struggles for rights have a long history. Students, teachers, and scholars of human rights who engage with histories of human rights beyond the European or American story will be able to appreciate more fully the scope of struggles undertaken by those whose rights have been systematically violated by colonization. Scholarship should resist tendencies to see Indigenous people simply as engaging in models of or extensions of non-Indigenous systems of human rights that emanate from the West. Taking account of diverse cultures, political formations, and colonial experiences of Indigenous peoples in specific locations globally can help us to analyze not only the intent of developments in human rights but also the impact of particular discourses or policies. Struggles by communities, taking place over generations, can demonstrate the agency and the tenacity of colonized peoples to secure their rights.

Notes

1 Elsa Stamatopoulou, "Indigenous Peoples and the United Nations: Human Rights as a Developing Dynamic," *Human Rights Quarterly*, 1994, vol. 16, no. 1, 58–81.

2 See, for example, Jenny S. Martinez, *The Slave Trade and the Origins of International Human Rights Law*, Oxford: Oxford University Press, 2012, and Samuel Moyn, *The Last Utopia: Human Rights in History*, Cambridge, MA: Belknap Press at Harvard University Press, 2010. For critiques of these approaches see Philip Alston, "Does the Past Matter? On the Origins of Human Rights" (review of Martinez, *The Slave Trade and the Origins of International Human Rights Law*), *Harvard Law Review*, 2013, vol. 126, no. 7, 2043–81, and Christopher McCrudden, "Human Rights Histories," *Oxford Journal of Legal Studies*, 2015, vol. 35, no. 1, 179–212.

3 S. James Anaya, *Indigenous Peoples in International Law*, 2nd ed., Oxford: Oxford University Press, 2004; Mattias Åhrén, *Indigenous Peoples' Status in the International Legal System*, Oxford: Oxford University Press, 2016.

4 Jeff Spinner-Halev, "Land, Culture and Justice: A Framework for Group Rights and Recognition," *Journal of Political Philosophy*, 2000, vol. 8, no. 3, 319–42.

5 Jeff Spinner-Halev, "From Historical to Enduring Injustice," *Political Theory*, 2007, vol. 35, no. 5, 574–97.

6 Duncan Ivison, Paul Patton, and Will Sanders, *Political Theory and the Rights of Indigenous Peoples*, Cambridge, UK: Cambridge University Press, 2000, pp. 1–2.

7 Rhiannon Morgan, *Transforming Law and Institution: Indigenous Peoples, the United Nations and Human Rights*, Farnham, UK: Ashgate, 2011.

8 Ravi de Costa, "Identity, Authority, and the Moral Worlds of Indigenous Petitions," *Comparative Studies in Society and History*, 2006, vol. 48, no. 3, 669.

9 De Costa, "Identity, Authority, and the Moral Worlds," 693–4.

10 Larissa Behrendt, *Achieving Social Justice: Indigenous Rights and Australia's Future*, Sydney: Federation Press, 2003; Stan Grant, "The Australian Dream: Blood, History and Becoming," *Quarterly Essay*, 2016, no. 64.

11 See, for example, Ravi de Costa, *A Higher Authority: Indigenous Transnationalism and Australia*, Sydney: University of New South Wales Press, 2006; Marcia Langton, "Anthropology, Politics and the Changing World of Aboriginal Australians," *Anthropological Forum*, 2011, vol. 21, no. 1, 1–22; John Maynard, "'In the Interests of Our People': The Influence of Garveyism on the Rise of Australian Aboriginal Political Activism," *Aboriginal History*, 2005, vol. 29, 1–22; John Maynard, *Fight for Liberty and Freedom: The Origins of Australian Aboriginal Activism*, Canberra: Aboriginal Studies Press, 2007; Fiona Paisley, *The Lone Protestor: A. M. Fernando in Australia and Europe*, Canberra: Aboriginal Studies Press, 2012; Ann Curthoys and Jessie Mitchell, "'Bring this Paper to the Good Governor': Aboriginal Petitioning in Britain's Australian Colonies," in Saliha Belmessous (ed.) *Native Claims: Indigenous Law against Empire, 1500–1920*, Oxford: Oxford University Press, 2011; Bain Attwood and Andrew Markus, *Thinking Black: William Cooper and the Australian Aborigines' League*, Canberra: Aboriginal Studies Press, 2004; Bain Attwood, *Rights for Aborigines*, Crows Nest, New South Wales: Allen & Unwin, 2003; Diane Barwick, *Rebellion at Coranderrk*, Laura E. Barwick and Richard E. Barwick (eds.), Canberra: Aboriginal History, 1998; Jane Lydon, "The Experimental 1860s: Charles Walter's Images of Coranderrk Aboriginal Station, Victoria," *Aboriginal History*, 2002, vol. 26, 78–130; Jane Lydon, *The Flash of Recognition: Photography and the Emergence of Indigenous Rights*, Sydney: New South Books, 2012; Tracey Banivanua Mar, "Imperial Literacy and Indigenous Rights: Tracing Transoceanic Circuits of a Modern Discourse," *Aboriginal History*, 2013, vol. 37, 1–28; Henry Reynolds, *The Breaking of the Great Australian Silence: Aborigines in Australian Historiography 1955–1983*, London: University of London, Institute of Commonwealth Studies, Australian Studies Centre, 1984.

12 Alston, "Does the Past Matter?" 2052.

13 De Costa, "Identity, Authority, and the Moral Worlds," 693–4. See also Maynard, *Fight for Liberty and Freedom.*

14 Anaya, *Indigenous Peoples in International Law*, p. 14.

15 Deborah Bird Rose, *Nourishing Terrain: Australian Aboriginal Views on Landscape and Wilderness*, Canberra: Australian Heritage Commission, 1996.

16 W. E. H. Stanner, *After the Dreaming. Black and White Australians: An Anthropologist's View. The Boyer Lectures*, Sydney: Australian Broadcasting Commission, 1969.

17 Richard Broome, *Aboriginal Victorians: A History since 1800*, Crows Nest, New South Wales: Allen and Unwin, 2005, pp. 91–2.

18 Ann Curthoys and Jessie Mitchell, "How Different was Victoria? Aboriginal 'Protection' in a Comparative Context," in Leigh Boucher and Lynette Russell (eds.) *Settler Colonial Governance in Nineteenth-Century Victoria*, Canberra: Australian National University Press, 2015, p. 184.

19 Alan Lester and Fae Dussart, *Colonization and the Origins of Humanitarian Governance: Protecting Aborigines Across the Nineteenth-Century British Empire*, Cambridge, UK: Cambridge University Press, 2014, p. 1.

20 Curthoys and Mitchell, "How Different was Victoria?" 186.

21 John Chesterman and Brian Galligan, *Citizens Without Rights: Aborigines and Australian Citizenship*, Cambridge, UK: Cambridge University Press, 1997, p. 12.

22 The "White Australia Policy" is the colloquial name given to the Immigration Restriction Act of 1901. The policy was designed to make immigration to Australia only possible from certain countries. Its origins can be traced to the gold rushes of the 1850s, where white miners' hostility to the Chinese resulted in several violent encounters, and led the colonial governments of Victoria and New South Wales to introduce restrictions on Chinese immigration. Over the years these restrictions were extended to cover most non-European countries. While the Act was watered down during the 1950s and 1960s, it was not completely rescinded until the 1970s.

23 Human Rights and Equal Opportunity Commission, *Bringing them Home: Report of the National Inquiry into the Separation of Aboriginal and Torres Strait Islander Children from Their Families*, Sydney: Human Rights and Equal Opportunity Commission (HREOC), 1997.

24 Broome, *Aboriginal Victorians*, pp. 10–14.

25 Robert Kenny, "Tricks or Treats? A Case for Kulin Knowing in Batman's Treaty," *History Australia*, 2008, vol. 5, no. 2, 38.1–14; Penelope Edmonds, *Urbanizing Frontiers: Indigenous Peoples and Settlers in 19th-Century Pacific Rim Cities*, Vancouver: University of British Columbia Press,

2010. See also Bain Attwood, *Possession: Batman's Treaty and the Matter of History*, Carlton: Miegunyah Press, 2009.

26 Leigh Boucher and Lynette Russell, "'Soliciting Sixpences from Township to Township': Moral Dilemmas in Mid-Nineteenth-Century Melbourne," *Postcolonial Studies*, 2012, vol. 15 no. 2, 149–65.

27 David [Fred] Cahir and Ian Clark, "'Why Should They Pay Money to the Queen?' Aboriginal Miners and Land Claims," *Journal of Australian Colonial History*, 2008, vol. 10, no. 1, 123. See also Jessica Hodgens, "Colonisation, Violence and Ethics: Resisting Settler Colonial Erasure on Dja Dja Wurrung Country," PhD diss., Monash University, 2017, ch. 3.

28 Wayne Atkinson, "The Yorta Yorta Struggle for Justice Continues," in Greta Bird, Gary Martin, and Jennifer Nielson (eds.) *Majah: Indigenous Peoples and the Law*, Sydney: Federation Press, 1996, p. 284.

29 Aldo Massola, *Coranderrk: A History of the Aboriginal Station*, Kilmore: Lowden, 1975, p. 7.

30 Broome, *Aboriginal Victorians*, p. 123.

31 Massola, *Coranderrk*, p. 14.

32 Quoted in Massola, *Coranderrk*, p. 13.

33 Massola, *Coranderrk*, p. 14.

34 Gary Presland, *First People: The Eastern Kulin of Melbourne, Port Phillip and Central Victoria*, Melbourne: Museum Victoria Publishing, 2010, p. 110.

35 De Costa, "Identity, Authority, and the Moral Worlds," 669–70.

36 Penny Van Toorn, *Writing Never Arrives Naked: Early Aboriginal Cultures of Writing in Australia*, Canberra: Aboriginal Studies Press, 2006, p. 133.

37 Penny Van Toorn, "Authors, Scribes and Owners: The Sociology of Nineteenth-Century Aboriginal Writing on Coranderrk and Lake Condah Reserves," *Continuum*, 1999, vol. 13, no. 3, 333–43.

38 Richard Broome, *Fighting Hard: The Victorian Aborigines Advancement League*. Canberra: Aboriginal Studies Press, 2015, p. 3.

39 Broome, *Fighting Hard*, p. 4. See also *Victorian Indigenous Honour Roll*, Melbourne: Aboriginal Affairs Victoria, 2011, pp. 10–11.

40 *Victorian Indigenous Honour Roll*, pp. 10–11.

41 Andrew Markus, "William Cooper and the 1937 Petition to the King," *Aboriginal History*, 1983, vol. 7, nos. 1–2, 48.

42 *Victorian Indigenous Honour Roll*, p. 11.

43 McCrudden, "Human Rights Histories," 200.

44 Quoted in Markus, "William Cooper and the 1937 Petition," 48.

45 Bain Attwood and Andrew Markus, *Thinking Black: William Cooper and the Australian Aborigines' League*, Canberra: Aboriginal Studies Press, 2004, pp. 12–13.

46 Attwood and Markus, *Thinking Black*, p. 13.

47 Markus, "William Cooper and the 1937 Petition," 48.

48 "No. 78. William Cooper, Secretary, AAL, to T. Paterson, Minister for the Interior, 16 June 1937," in Bain Attwood and Andrew Markus (eds.) *The Struggle for Aboriginal Rights: A Documentary History*, St. Leonards, New South Wales: Allen & Unwin, 1999, p. 151.

49 Markus, "William Cooper and the 1937 Petition."

50 "No. 79. *Herald* (Melbourne), 7 August 1937, Aborigines Petition to the King, by Clive Turnbull," in Attwood and Markus, *Struggle for Aboriginal Rights*, p. 154, 153.

51 The constitution referred to Aboriginal people and did not explicitly include Torres Strait Islanders; the latter were at that time considered to fall under the term Aboriginal. Since the 1980s it has become increasingly common to refer to Aboriginal and Torres Strait Islanders as Australia's Indigenous peoples. National Museum Australia, "The Referendum, 1957–67." Online. Available at http://indigenousrights.net.au/civil_rights/the_referendum,1957-67 (accessed 5 January 2019); Bain Attwood, *The 1967 Referendum: Race, Power and the Australian Constitution*, Canberra: Aboriginal Studies Press, 2007; John Gardiner-Garden, *The 1967 Referendum: History and Myths*, Canberra: Parliamentary Library, 2007; Sue Taffe, "The Role of FCAATSI in the 1967 Referendum: Mythmaking about Citizenship or Political Strategy?" in Richard Nile and Tim Rowse (eds.) *Contesting Assimilation*, Perth: Network, 2005, pp. 285–98.

52 Attwood and Markus, *Thinking Black*; Richard Broome, "At the Grass Roots of White Support: Victorian Aboriginal Advancement League Branches 1957–1972," in Lynette Russell and John Arnold (eds.) *Indigenous Victorians: Repressed, Resourceful and Respected*, special edition of *La Trobe Journal*, 2010, 141–56; Sue Taffe, *Black and White Together. FCAATSI: The Federal Council for the Advancement of Aborigines and Torres Strait Islanders, 1958–1973*, St. Lucia, Queensland: University of Queensland Press, 2005; Broome, *Fighting Hard*, pp. 271–3.

53 "Stopping Off at Dubbo on the Track West …" *New Dawn*, 1971, vol. 19, no. 10, 7. Interview with Pearl Gibbs.

54 See *High Court of Australia, Mabo v. Queensland* (No. 2) [1992] HCA 23; (1992) 175 CLR 1 (3 June 1992). Online. Available at www.austlii.edu.au/cgi-bin/sinodisp/au/cases/cth/high_ct/175clr1.html?stem=0&synonyms=0&query=title+%28+%22mabo%22+%29 (accessed 5 January 2019).

55 Marc Gumbert, *Neither Justice nor Reason: A Legal and Anthropological Analysis of Aboriginal Land Rights*, St. Lucia: University of Queensland Press, 1984; John Hookey, "The Gove Land Rights Case: A Judicial Dispensation for the Taking of Aboriginal Lands in Australia," *Federal Law Review*, 1972, vol. 5, 85; David Mercer, "Terra Nullius, Aboriginal Sovereignty and Land Rights in Australia: The Debate Continues," *Political Geography*, 1993, vol. 12, no. 4, 299–318.

56 Wayne Atkinson, "'Not One Iota' of Land Justice: Reflections on the Yorta Yorta Native Title Claim 1994–2001," *Indigenous Law Bulletin*, 2001, vol. 5, no. 6, 23, quoted in Attwood and Markus, *Thinking Black*, p. 24.

57 "Yorta Yorta Take Land Rights Claim to UN," *The Age*, 13 February 2003. Online. Available at www.theage.com.au/articles/2003/02/13/1044927729801.html (accessed 5 January 2019).

58 Gillian Triggs, "Australia's Indigenous Peoples and International Law: Validity of the Native Title Amendment Act 1998 (Cth)," *Melbourne University Law Review*, 1999, vol. 23, no. 2, 372–415.

59 Triggs, "Australia's Indigenous Peoples and International Law."

60 Triggs, "Australia's Indigenous Peoples and International Law."

61 State Library of Victoria, "Native Title and the Yorta Yorta." Online. Available at http://ergo.slv.vic.gov.au/explore-history/fight-rights/indigenous-rights/native-title-yorta-yorta (accessed 5 January 2019).

62 The Victorian State government is currently pursuing a process of treaty negotiations with Victorian Aboriginal communities. See Victorian Government, "Treaty." Online. Available at www.vic.gov.au/aboriginalvictoria/treaty.html (accessed 5 January 2019).

24

THE INTERNATIONAL LGBT RIGHTS MOVEMENT

An introductory history

Laura A. Belmonte

The global landscape of international lesbian, gay, bisexual, and transgender (LGBT) rights is fraught with geopolitical complexities and stark contrasts. In 2017, 124 states have legalized same-sex sexual acts, but 72 countries criminalize such behavior, including 8 nations that impose the death penalty. While 22 countries have legalized same-sex marriage and 63 have nondiscrimination protections for gays and lesbians, 19 nations have "morality" laws that restrict freedom of expression relating to sexual orientation, usually under the guise of protecting youth, or "propaganda" laws modeled on Russia's June 2013 law banning pro-LGBT "propaganda" and advocacy for LGBT equality.[1] These triumphs and challenges reflect a long arc of transnational LGBT advocacy efforts dating from the mid-nineteenth century to the present day. It is a trajectory that has involved individuals, informal networks, nongovernmental organizations (NGOs), and states who have not always worked in concert and who often meet resistance from a similar constellation of actors determined to stop the global movement for LGBT equality. While progress toward LGBT equality has been marked in many nations, there are several others where LGBT people are brutally repressed. Although the global human rights community is working toward making LGBT rights an integral element of universal notions of human rights, its ability to enforce these norms and close dramatic disparities in the experiences of LGBT people around the world is so far limited. Using selected historical figures, organizations, and events to illuminate critical junctures in the global LGBT movement, this essay asks readers to contemplate whether global LGBT equality is possible, what such equality might look like, and what actions could be taken at the international level to facilitate that aim.

While there is an enormous body of work documenting gay rights movements in individual countries or regions,[2] the transnational connections among LGBT activists have only recently drawn sustained scholarly attention.[3] International relations experts are assessing how LGBT rights have become a norm in global human rights discourse, examining the interconnections between LGBT rights and other worldwide political struggles, and exploring why the trajectories toward legal recognition of marginalized peoples differ among states.[4] Historians of sexuality are addressing how sexual interactions shape transnational flows and inform legal structures, definitions of citizenship, power dynamics between individuals and the state, and global debates on liberalism, globalization, and Westernization.[5] Concurrently, scholars are documenting the history of the human rights revolution. They are providing cogent insights into the legal and philosophical underpinnings of human rights law, the roles of NGOs advocating for human rights, and the evolution of the international human rights agenda. But most of this scholarship pays insufficient attention to the myriad ways that LGBT rights intersect, enrich, and complicate this larger human rights history.[6]

In this essay, I draw on this work and provide a synthesis of transnational LGBT activism since the mid-nineteenth century. Although there were intellectual exchanges among early Japanese, Indian, European, and American sexologists,[7] I focus on American and European regions because the first individuals to articulate demands for full political and legal inclusion of LGBT citizens and to challenge notions of homosexuality as criminal or pathological were situated in these regions, as were the first transnational LGBT networks and organizations. The LGBT rights movement did not have fully global dimensions until the late twentieth century. I define advocacy as both informal and formal networks of individuals and organizations who exchange information; highlight the plight of marginalized people at risk of violence or who are being denied full civic equality; pressure states to use their economic, political, and legal power to champion a specific cause or issue; and hold states accountable for enforcing any protections that are enacted.[8] Interweaving historiography on the histories of human rights and sexuality as well as primary sources from US and international archives, this essay traces the history of the international LGBT rights movement and suggests pathways for future scholarly work.

The rise of transnational LGBT advocacy has rested on the historical context in which it originated. Attitudes about homosexuality changed dramatically from ancient times to the latter 1700s. Ancient Indians, Chinese, Egyptians, Greeks, and Romans tolerated homosexual practices. But with the rise of Christianity and Islam, codes making same-sex sexual activities crimes punishable by death or castration spread throughout Eurasia and into Africa. The legal definition of sodomy varied. Sometimes, it was limited to anal penetration of a man to the point of ejaculation. It did not always include oral sex, but some codes encompassed nonprocreative sex acts, regardless of the gender (and sometimes, the species) of those involved. However, many Indigenous societies in the Americas, sub-Saharan Africa, and the South Pacific accepted same-sex intimacy and in some cases, even celebrated those who defied gender norms.[9]

When the French, Spanish, Dutch, and English first settled in North America, virtually all of their colonies outlawed male same-sex sexual activity and attempted to impose European sexual norms upon Indigenous peoples as a means of "civilizing" them.[10] In the late seventeenth century, authorities in London, Paris, and Amsterdam periodically attempted to quash their emerging sodomitical subcultures through surveillance, arrests, and prosecutions. At the time, Catholic and Protestant reformers alike condemned sodomy, sex outside of marriage, masturbation, and oral sex. Those found to have engaged in these behaviors faced harsh penalties including fines, imprisonment, whipping, stoning, disfigurement, branding, pillorying, dismemberment, execution, and execution followed by dismemberment.[11]

In the eighteenth century, the Enlightenment triggered another shift in attitudes toward private sexual behavior. Frederick the Great of Prussia and Joseph II of Austria argued that "individuals should be free to believe, think, and even act as they wished, consistent with the rights of others, the maintenance of public order, and the ultimate authority of the state." Upon succeeding his father Frederick William I, for example, Frederick the Great – possibly because of his own sexual inclinations – ended anti-sodomy crackdowns on clubs, taverns, cruising areas, and male brothels in Berlin. He did not, however, repeal anti-sodomy laws. In France, Voltaire, Montesquieu, and other philosophes denounced sexual licentiousness and deviant practices like sodomy, adultery, and prostitution, but not on religious grounds. Bitterly critical of organized religion, the philosophes framed their objections to sexual deviance not in moral terms, but based on the view that sexual vice destabilized social order. In an age of frequent war and increasing economic competition, the philosophes deemed population growth essential to national prosperity and security. They therefore condemned nonprocreative sexual activities like sodomy. But they were even more critical of the state's harsh treatment of those convicted of sexual deviance.[12]

The Enlightenment's focus on individual rights and freedoms triggered change elsewhere. In the aftermath of the American Revolution, several states reformed their legal codes and opted to punish sodomy with imprisonment, not death.[13] In revolutionary France calls for liberalization also yielded major changes in anti-sodomy laws. In 1791, fueled by expansive notions of individual rights and no longer bound by prerevolutionary codes that fused religion and law, France became the first nation in modern Europe to decriminalize consensual homosexual acts between adults in private. As part of a larger trend toward eliminating penalties for victimless crimes, the French omitted sodomy from both the 1791 penal code and the Code Napoléon adopted in 1804.[14]

French reforms triggered change elsewhere. Belgium, Spain, Portugal, Scandinavia, China, and Japan all adopted similar codes. Though some of these nations temporarily deviated from the French model, "virtually none of the countries of the European empires, other than the British, ever imposed criminal sanctions specifically on same-sex consensual activity in private."[15] The divergence between states influenced by the French legal code and states influenced by the British model or Islamic Sharia law shaped the global landscape for LGBT rights in ways that resonate to the present day.

Economic as well as legal and political trends had major consequences for people's intimate lives. Industrialization dramatically changed preindustrial patterns of work and family life across much of Europe and North America. Infusions of job seekers leaving agricultural areas transformed dozens of cities from towns to sprawling metropolises. Middle- and upper-class families proclaimed a strict separation of work and home divided along gender lines. Houses were redesigned to create privacy. Sex, breastfeeding, and personal hygiene now occurred behind closed doors. But the divisions between urban and rural, the affluent and the working class, domestic servants and their employers also created new spaces for sexual attraction and deviation from expected norms. Despite the era's strong emphasis on marriage and domesticity, same-sex intimate friendships between men and between women flourished, though scholars disagree about how many such relationships were sexual. Urban life offered people interested in same-sex liaisons an escape from the close scrutiny of family and the ability to find people with similar inclinations.[16]

No one celebrated those newfound freedoms quite like Walt Whitman. Arriving in New York in 1841, he was electrified by the city. With a burgeoning population of 300,000, New York was as vibrant and diverse as any major European capital of the era. Whitman walked for hours, delighting in street life and cruising working-class men in public parks, the docks, ferries, streetcars, and the occasional bar. He kept detailed notes of his encounters with men. A few of these trysts blossomed into long-term love affairs.

Conflicted about his feelings for young men, Whitman turned to phrenology, then a trendy fad purporting to explain linkages between the shape of one's head and one's defining mental characteristics. In 1847, Whitman went to leading phrenologist Lorenzo Fowler to get his head read. Fowler concluded that Whitman had two very pronounced traits: amativeness (sexual love) and adhesiveness (comradeship). Whitman latched onto the concept of adhesiveness as a way to explain his intense attractions to men in a positive way. No longer conflicted about his feelings, he began to express them openly in his poetry. In 1860, Whitman added the Calamus poems to a new edition of *Leaves of Grass*, originally published five years earlier. Reflecting his embrace of adhesiveness, the poems boldly celebrated the "manly love of comrades." The poems incensed critics who objected to the "obscene" nature of Whitman's work. But they also made Whitman an international hero to same-sex attracted men seeking to define their sexual identity including the British cultural critic John Addington Symonds, the Irish playwright Oscar Wilde, and the French author André Gide.[17]

In an age of resurgent conservatism following the European political revolutions of 1848, the increasing visibility of men like Whitman alarmed legal authorities and medical scientists investigating the causes of social deviance. In 1857, French physician Bénédict A. Morel wrote *Treatise on Degenerations*, linking same-sex sexual attraction to degeneracy. That same year, Ambroise-Auguste Tardieu, France's leading forensic medical expert, published *Medicolegal Study of Assaults on Decency*. Based on his physical examinations of hundreds of men convicted of crimes, Tardieu claimed that he could identify "true pederasts" because frequent homosexual sex gave their anuses and penises distinctive shapes. Barring such examinations, Tardieu warned that such men could pass through society undetected, making their presence known only to their own kind. Accordingly, Tardieu called for the rigorous enforcement of laws against public indecency and the physical inspection of suspected pederasts in order to minimize the destabilizing impact they had on society. Identifying and classifying sexual deviants became powerful legal and medical weapons against those who defied sexual and gender norms.[18]

These attitudes were evident among authorities ruling British colonies throughout the world. Persuaded of their moral superiority, they imposed legal codes designed to police native peoples seen as especially prone to "vice."[19] Although there were variations among them, the codes shared a common condemnation of same-sex activity under British imperial law. In no case did subjugated peoples have input on the construction or imposition of these laws, regardless of their local cultures or traditions. Sodomy laws were undemocratically imposed by white imperial rulers intent on controlling sexual activities deemed corrupt.

The most widely imposed model was the Indian Penal Code of 1860, principally authored by Thomas Babington Macaulay. Its Paragraph 377 read:

> Whoever voluntarily has carnal intercourse against the order of nature with any man, woman, or animal, shall be punished with imprisonment for life, or with imprisonment … for a term which may extend to 10 years and shall also be liable to a fine.

Participants in these acts were equally condemned, regardless of assumption of the passive or active role, age, consent, or occurrence in public or private space. Adopted in over three dozen British territories across Asia, Africa, and the Pacific, Paragraph 377 was a blunt instrument that lumped together consensual private same-sex intimacy with violent sexual crimes like rape and pedophilia.[20] Having tacitly abandoned the use of the death penalty for sodomy offenses in 1836, Great Britain officially codified the change a year after implementation of Paragraph 377 in India. The Offenses against the Person Act of 1861 modified sodomy law in England and Wales, lessening the penalty from execution to imprisonment for ten years to life.[21]

Only one year later, German journalist Karl Heinrich Ulrichs penned a trenchant critique of sodomy laws and began articulating a theory about same-sex attracted men that had transnational ramifications. Drawing on the new field of embryology, Ulrichs' third-sex theory posited that "Urnings" had predominantly female personalities but predominately male bodies (or vice versa). Because these traits were innate, Ulrichs argued, persecution of Urnings was unjustified and misguided. In the 1860s, he became a controversial proponent of decriminalizing sodomy. Ulrichs gave up his crusade after 1871, when newly unified Germany adopted Paragraph 175, a statute outlawing "an unnatural sex act between persons of the male sex" that was not fully repealed until 1994.[22]

Although Ulrichs failed to secure any legal victories, his advocacy efforts inspired other gay rights pioneers like the Jewish German physician Magnus Hirschfeld. Early in his medical career, Hirschfeld was haunted by two episodes. The first was a lecture on "sexual degeneracy" at which a gay man who had been kept in an asylum for 30 years was paraded naked before his medical school class. The second was more personal. When Hirschfeld began treating people who expressed same-sex attractions, one of his patients was a German military officer who was engaged to a woman and trying to reconcile his homosexuality with his social status and the masculine ethos of German culture. On the eve of his wedding, the soldier shot himself in the head, leaving behind a suicide note calling homosexuality "a curse against human nature and the law." Hirschfeld was shattered. Although he maintained the impartiality expected of a scientist in his time and thus never discussed his own homosexuality publicly, he redoubled his efforts to help homosexuals accept themselves.

Hirschfeld began studying homosexuality and eventually wrote a pamphlet calling for the repeal of Paragraph 175. While some gay men flocked to his practice and were relieved when he told them they were perfectly healthy, other gays feared his calls for legal reforms would draw unwanted attention to them. In 1897, realizing he needed allies, Hirschfeld co-founded the Scientific Humanitarian Committee (SHC; Wissenschaftlich-Humanitäres Komitee), the world's first advocacy organization for gay and transgender rights. Adopting the motto "justice through science," SHC called for research to debunk anti-gay bias and started a petition calling for the decriminalization of homosexual conduct. Despite police surveillance, Hirschfeld campaigned vigorously and persuaded the German parliament to debate repealing Paragraph 175 just a year later. Although the effort failed, it catapulted gay rights into German political discourse and Hirschfeld continued his research on the nature and causes of homosexuality.

In 1919, Hirschfeld used his earnings from performing one of the world's first gender reassignment surgeries to establish the Institute for Sexual Science (ISS), nearly 30 years before Alfred Kinsey opened his famed institute for sex research in the United States. Some 20,000 people a year came to ISS for sex education, contraception, marital counseling, STD treatment, and advice on gay and transgender issues. In 1921, he organized the First Congress for Sexual Reform, which inspired the creation of the World League for Sexual Reform. Congresses were held in Copenhagen (1928), London (1929), Vienna

(1930), and Brno (1932). Hirschfeld began lecturing around the world, and American newspapers dubbed him "the Einstein of sex."

But Hirschfeld's work drew the ire of the Nazis. In 1933, while he was out of the country, Nazi Stormtroopers ransacked ISS and burned the over 20,000 documents and books in Hirschfeld's library, the largest collection on sexuality in the world at the time. They also seized Hirschfeld's client lists and the Gestapo used the information to track down and arrest gay men later sent to the concentration camps. Warned by friends not to return to Germany, Hirschfeld fled to France, where he died of a stroke in 1935.[23]

During his life, Hirschfeld's work inspired transnational organizing efforts. In 1911, after the Dutch government criminalized homosexual sex with men under the age of 21 (the age of consent for heterosexual relations was 16), activists led by Jacob Schorer, a jurist who had studied with Hirschfeld, and criminal anthropologist Arnold Aletrino launched the Dutch Scientific-Humanitarian Committee (Nederlandsch Wetenschappelijk Humanitair Komitee, NWHK), an offshoot of the SHC. Until it was disbanded when the Nazis occupied the Netherlands in 1940, NWHK ran a library and issued publications written in Dutch. Distributing thousands of free copies of its reports to students, legal authorities, and physicians, NWHK detailed how blackmailers used the anti-sodomy law to target gay men and denounced discrimination against homosexuals.[24] While working for the Allied Army of the Occupation in Germany in the aftermath of World War I, American Henry Gerber became enthralled with Hirschfeld's ideas and upon his return to Chicago, founded the Society for Human Rights, the first known – but short-lived – gay rights organization in the United States. In 1929, while living in Los Angeles, Henry Hay learned of the Society's existence from the partner of one of its former members. Some 21 years later, Hay co-founded the Mattachine Society, one of the most significant gay advocacy groups in US history.[25]

The rise of Nazi Germany and the eruption of World War II brought such transnational exchanges to a temporary halt, but also unleashed forces with long-ranging ramifications for the international LGBT rights movement. In 1933, the Nazis banned LGBT organizations, clubs, and publications. In 1935, they amended Paragraph 175 to outlaw a very broad and ambiguously defined array of interactions between men. Between 1933 and 1945, the Nazis arrested an estimated 100,000 German gay men, sentencing about 50,000 "convicted homosexuals" to prison terms, including 5,000 to 15,000 who were sent to concentration camps and singled out for especially harsh treatment by Nazi guards and fellow captives. At the same time, courts ordered the castration of hundreds of gay men living under Nazi occupation across Europe. When the war ended, gay concentration camp prisoners were not recognized as victims of Nazi persecution. Indeed, the Allied military government of Germany forced some of these men to finish out their prison sentences. In the post-Stonewall era as the stories of gay victims of the Holocaust were finally revealed, gay activists reclaimed the pink triangle gay men in the concentration camps were forced to wear, making it a sign of both liberation and survival.[26]

While World War II unleashed vicious anti-gay repression, it was also a time of discovery and self-realization. In the United States, for example, gays and lesbians found each other in same-sex environments on the home front and in the armed forces. Military psychiatrists – persuaded they could identify homosexuals – convinced the Department of War to revise its post-World War I policy of using courts martial and discharging or imprisoning soldiers accused of committing sodomy. Draft boards began screening suspected homosexual recruits with a number of "tests" that were easily evaded by gay men and women motivated to serve their nation in time of war. While many gay and lesbian soldiers successfully concealed their identities once on active duty, some were discovered by military authorities and given "blue" discharges (named because of the color of the paper on which they were printed) and subsequently denied benefits granted to other US veterans. These events helped gay and lesbian soldiers forge a sense of solidarity and inspired many to fight discrimination on the basis of sexual orientation in the postwar years. Some of the gay and lesbian soldiers expelled from the military chose not to return to unwelcoming hometowns and instead stayed where they had been discharged, thus leading to the emergence of strong and visible communities in port cities like Los Angeles, San Francisco, and New York.[27]

Despite wartime Nazi atrocities against homosexuals, sexual minorities were not explicitly included in the new international protections for human rights that arose in the postwar era. Indeed, German occupation authorities and the West German government continued to prosecute men for violating Paragraph 175 through the 1960s. When German men jailed for such offenses petitioned the newly established European Court of Human Rights, the European Commission on Human Rights in Strasbourg dismissed these complaints as "manifestly ill-founded" and justified under the "health and morals" exception to the protection granted in the European Convention on Human Rights to the right to private life.[28] This hostile climate inspired gay rights activists in Europe and the United States to organize. Taking cues from both prewar sexual reformers and newly emerging discourses and legal frameworks guarding human rights, they began building transnational relationships that provided a critical foundation for today's international LGBT rights movement.

After World War II ended, Dutch activists formed a new organization called the Shakespeare Club, later renamed the Cultuur en Ontspannings Centrum (Cultural and Recreational Center), better known as COC.[29] In 1951, COC organized the first International Congress for Sexual Equality, consciously modeling it on Hirschfeld's World League for Sexual Reform. Advocates from Denmark, Norway, Sweden, West Germany, Great Britain, Italy, France, and Switzerland gathered in Amsterdam. Inspired by the articulation of rights for all people "without distinction of any kind" in the Universal Declaration of Human Rights (UDHR),[30] they sent the United Nations (UN) a telegram requesting "steps towards granting [the] status of human, social, and legal equality to homosexual minorities throughout the world." They also created the International Committee for Sexual Equality (ICSE) to continue their efforts to connect homophile organizations seeking civil rights in a time fraught with Cold War tensions.

Over the next decade, ICSE linked homophile organizations in Europe and the United States through publications and international congresses. Its members included the Scandinavian group Forbundet af 1948, the French group Arcadie, the Swiss journal *Der Kreis* (The Circle), several German organizations, and the US homophile groups ONE and the Mattachine Society. In 1953, at the fifth annual ICSE meeting held in Frankfurt, Donald Webster Cory, author of the landmark 1951 book *The Homosexual in America*, gave the keynote address. Cory's work "was itself the product of transnational exchange and excavation," integrating sexology research conducted by Europeans. US homophile publications like *ONE Magazine* republished articles from European homophile publications and closely followed European gay culture and legal developments affecting European homosexuals.[31]

Beginning with the Danish group Alle for Een Klubben (All for One Club) in 1954, lesbian organizations also participated. The following year, the US-based Daughters of Bilitis became members and the male-dominated leadership of ICSE connected the American lesbians with other women's groups in England and Sweden. Individuals whose nations had no official homophile organizations also joined and throughout the 1950s, people from Australia, Austria, Greece, Indonesia, Italy, New Zealand, Portugal, Spain, and Syria attended ICSE congresses and social events.[32]

ICSE monitored political and legal developments and distributed information to its international network. They paid special attention to news of the Wolfenden Committee in Great Britain. Established by the Conservative government in 1954 following a wave of arrests and prosecutions of men charged with sodomy and other homosexual acts,[33] the committee released its report three years later. It called for the decriminalization of "homosexual behavior between consenting adults in private" and rejected the view that homosexuality was a mental illness. The news electrified US homophile activists seeking to legitimate their claims to legal protection. But it took Britain's Parliament another eight years to pass the Sexual Offenses Act of 1967 decriminalizing homosexuality for men over the age of 21 in England and Wales.[34]

ICSE's membership never became truly global and it proved short-lived. By the early 1960s, a lack of attendance, budgetary woes, and a failure to diversify its leadership killed ICSE. But in a challenging political climate that witnessed anti-gay repression such as the Lavender Scare that hit the United States and Great Britain,[35] the ICSE and national homophile organizations "created a network across national borders, nurtured a transnational homophile identity, and engaged in activism designed to change both laws and minds, aimed at both national governments and supranational bodies such as the UN."[36] In keeping with what historian John D'Emilio called "the retreat to respectability" characterizing the homophile movement, most ICSE members adopted an assimilationist philosophy and rejected prevailing views of homosexuality as pathological, criminal, and immoral, but relied on outside medical, scientific, legal, and religious experts to bolster their claims of normality.[37] Many homophiles also expressed discomfort with more flamboyant aspects of gay life such as drag shows.

Although ICSE disbanded years before the 1969 Stonewall uprising sparked the modern gay liberation movement, transnational contacts among homophile activists endured. They exchanged personal correspondence. American homophile publications included ads for foreign gay books and magazines. Foreigners read, wrote letters to, and subscribed to US homophile publications like *ONE Magazine*, *Mattachine Review*, and *The Ladder*. Members of ONE, Mattachine, and the Daughters of Bilitis made trips to Europe and connected with homophile activists there. In 1958, Rudolf Burkhardt, an editor for the Swiss magazine *Der Kreis*, made the first of several trips to Los Angeles to lecture on the pre-World War II homosexual movement.[38] In 1963, a newly founded British lesbian organization called the Minorities Research Group began forging ties with the Daughters of Bilitis.[39]

But logistical challenges and strategic differences often undermined transnational solidarity. In both written and live communications, activists struggled with language barriers. Many activists could not afford to travel internationally. While some homophiles wanted increased visibility and the creation of social spaces for gays, others feared more openness would trigger political backlash and intensified legal repression.

The June 1969 Stonewall riots thrust the LGBT movement squarely on the side of openness and ushered in a gay liberation movement that almost immediately took on transnational dimensions. In the 1970s, women's rights, environmental concerns, disability rights, and racial and ethnic equality became part of global human rights discourse and the timing was right for more visible and assertive types of international LGBT advocacy. In September 1970, UN secretary-general U Thant accepted a missive from the Homophile Youth Movement of the United States declaring that "the civil and legal rights of homosexuals should be insured under the legislation of every country and the world homophile movement should be assisted in its fight for pride, dignity, identity, and social and legal justice." Thant referred the letter to a subcommittee of the UN Commission on Human Rights.[40] Two years later, Swedish journalist Björn Vilson launched a one-man crusade to persuade the UN to investigate the status of gays around the world, to establish a public information campaign about the global persecution of sexual minorities, and to host an international conference on the legal and political challenges facing "millions existing in constant dread of having their homosexuality exposed." Vilson penned dozens of letters to UN officials and staged solo public demonstrations in Sweden.[41] Although neither of these actions inspired formal UN action, they portended a new phase of global LGBT advocacy, one in which activists once again demanded the protections accorded other minorities by international law and supranational bodies.

LGBT advocates also held international conferences and formed NGOs to define policy positions and to ensure representation in global human rights deliberations and decision-making. In 1974 two Scots, Ian C. Dunn and Derek Ogg, co-organized the first International Gay Rights Congress after realizing how many foreign activists were present at the first national meeting of the Campaign for Homosexual Equality (CHE), a British gay rights organization who rejected quiet assimilation and instead began organizing public demonstrations.[42] In December 1974, 200 delegates from ten different countries convened in Edinburgh, Scotland. They heard reports from Spain and Argentina detailing repression and imprisonment of gays and lesbians in both countries. A report from Australia offered more positive news about growing numbers of Australian gay organizations and gay activists lobbying Parliament to decriminalize consensual sex between male adults.[43]

The 1974 Congress contributed to the creation of the International Gay Association (IGA), the world's first NGO devoted to global LGBT equality. In August 1978, 30 men representing 17 organizations from 14 countries founded IGA during the conference of the Campaign for Homosexual Equality in Coventry, England. IGA's two major aims were to coordinate international political action for gay rights and to facilitate the exchange of information on the oppression of gay men and lesbian women throughout the world. The members agreed to meet again in Amsterdam the following year and set an ambitious list of priorities including asking the European Economic Community Commission to end employment discrimination on basis of sexual orientation; surveying candidates for the European Parliament on their views on gay rights; and having IGA members lobby their respective national Amnesty International (AI) organizations to expand the definition of "prisoners of conscience" to include individuals imprisoned solely because of their sexual orientation or consensual same-sex behavior between adults.[44] On 30 September 1978, IGA held its first worldwide protest as member organizations across Europe, Canada, and Australia coordinated actions against proposed anti-gay laws introduced in Greece. The demonstrations, press releases, and letters to Greek officials helped persuade the Athens government to withdraw the draft legislation.[45]

In 1981, international LGBT activists scored a major victory when the European Court of Human Rights (ECHR) ruled in favor of gay rights for the first time. In *Dudgeon v. the United Kingdom*, the court held that Section 11 of the Criminal Law Amendment Act (1885) that had criminalized male (but not female) homosexual acts in England, Wales, and Northern Ireland violated the European Convention on Human Rights. *Dudgeon v. the United Kingdom* led to legislation decriminalizing male homosexual sex in Northern Ireland, thus aligning its legal code with the rest of the United Kingdom.[46] The case served as a precedent for similar ECHR rulings in *Norris v. Ireland* (1988) and *Modinos v. Cyprus* (1993). US Supreme Court Justice Anthony Kennedy also cited *Dudgeon* in his majority opinion in *Lawrence v. Texas* (2003), the landmark ruling that struck down sodomy laws in 14 states and made same-sex sexual activities legal in all US states and territories.[47] In the wake of the *Dudgeon* ruling, LGBT advocates made litigation a critical element of their strategies for advancing gay rights worldwide.

Over the course of the 1980s, the emergence of the HIV epidemic added urgency and scope to global organizing efforts. In 1990, American activist Julie Dorf founded the International Gay and Lesbian Human Rights Commission (IGLHRC), a US-based NGO that first focused on human rights abuses in Russia but later incorporated other parts of the world in its work. In 1991, at the urgings of the International Lesbian and Gay Association (ILGA)[48] and Demet Demir, a Turkish transgender woman being harassed by the police, Amnesty International began including persecuted gays under its definition of "prisoners of conscience."[49] Other human rights groups like Human Rights Watch and Human Rights First also encompassed anti-LGBT abuses under their purview.

In 1993, ILGA became the first LGBT group to gain consultancy status at the UN, but lost that status after a controversy stemming from revelation of the North American Man-Boy Love Association's membership in ILGA. Although the ILGA quickly expelled the pedophile group, it did not regain its UN consultancy status until 2011. The previous year, the International Gay and Lesbian Human Rights Commission gained consultancy status, thereby securing the right to attend UN meetings, contribute statements, and collaborate with UN agencies.[50]

While US citizens have played leading roles in the establishment and governance of global LGBT advocacy organizations, the US government – despite its pretensions to global leadership on human rights – became an advocate for international LGBT rights only very recently. Indeed, as evidenced by the Lavender Scare in the early Cold War, expulsions of gays and lesbians from the US armed forces (which did not officially end until 2010), and interpretations of the US immigration laws that authorized the exclusion and deportation of homosexuals on the grounds of "psychopathic personality" or "sexual deviancy" – a practice upheld by the Supreme Court in *Boutilier v. INS* (1967) and not repealed until 1990, the US government has often actively repressed LGBT people. Despite the legalization of same-sex marriage in the United States in 2015, it remains legal to fire someone on the basis of sexual orientation in 29 states. Compared to many European and Latin American nations, the US domestic record on LGBT rights is incomplete and comparatively late.

Under the Clinton administration, the State Department took tentative steps toward improving America's record on international LGBT issues. In 1994, US Attorney General Janet Reno directed immigration officers and courts to treat as precedent a Board of Immigration Appeals decision that granted a gay Cuban man asylum on the basis that he faced persecution in his home country "simply because of his status as a homosexual," not because of conduct. *Matter of Toboso-Alfonso* was pivotal in establishing that a well-founded fear of persecution on the basis of sexual orientation is a valid basis for making a claim for asylum in the United States.

The Clinton years also witnessed openly LGBT individuals playing a more visible role in US diplomacy. In 1997, President Clinton nominated James Hormel, the openly gay philanthropist and heir to the meatpacking dynasty, as the US Ambassador to Luxembourg.[51] The nomination drew bipartisan support but died in the Senate in October 1998 after the Republican Majority Leader Trent Lott refused to let it go up for a full Senate vote. The same year, Lott had publicly declared that gays were sinners who, like kleptomaniacs or alcoholics, could overcome their affliction. The Traditional Values Coalition declared Hormel unacceptable to the predominantly Catholic Luxembourg after finding sexually explicit materials at a research center named for him at the San Francisco Public Library. However, these attempts to derail his nomination failed. The library explained that Hormel had provided a $500,000 donation to underwrite its LGBT collections, but had nothing to do with its acquisition process.[52] Luxembourg, which had abolished its laws against consensual same-sex conduct in the 1800s, said it would welcome Hormel as an envoy. Accordingly, Clinton re-nominated Hormel in early 1999 and then made a recess appointment. Sworn in in June 1999, Hormel became the first openly gay American to secure an ambassador post.[53]

Although LGBT diplomats remained visible during the presidency of George W. Bush, the administration did not champion LGBT rights globally. In 2001, diplomat Michael Guest became the first openly LGBT person confirmed by the Senate for an ambassadorial post and went on to serve for three years as US Ambassador to Romania. At a swearing-in ceremony six years later, Secretary of State Condoleezza Rice described the mother of the same-sex partner of a diplomat as his "mother-in-law." But such acceptance usually stopped at America's shores. For example, on 18 June 2006, Wan Kim, Assistant Attorney General for the Civil Rights Division of the Department of Justice, told the UN Human Rights Committee that the International Covenant on Civil and Political Rights (ratified by the United States in 1992) did not protect same-sex consensual relations – an assertion running counter to long-established precedents and refuted by members of the UN committee. Although the State Department's annual Human Rights Reports continued tracking LGBT concerns in dozens of countries (115 of the world's 186 nations in 2006), this reporting did not translate into significant US global action. In early 2007, when Nigeria threatened to criminalize same-sex relationships, the US Embassy there did not join a chorus of European embassies lambasting the bill before it died in the Nigerian legislature.[54]

Concurrently, activists recognized the need for a legal framework for stopping human rights abuses of LGBT people around the world. In November 2006, human rights experts gathered at a meeting of the International Commission of Jurists held at Gadjah Mada University in Yogyakarta, Java. Sonia Onufer Corrêa, Research Associate at the Brazilian Interdisciplinary AIDS Association, and Vitit Muntarbhorn, a law professor and UN Special Rapporteur on human rights for the Democratic People's Republic of Korea, co-chaired the sessions. Over the course of three days, they unanimously agreed on a set of 29 principles on sexual orientation and gender identity and named them after the city in which they convened. The Yogyakarta Principles identified pervasive patterns of discrimination and violence against LGBT people and made specific recommendations for actions that the UN, states, NGOs, the media, and human rights groups could take to ensure full equality for LGBT people everywhere. On 26 March 2007, the finalized version of the Yogyakarta Principles was released at the UN Human Rights Council in Geneva.[55] In December 2008, inspired by the Yogyakarta Principles, 66 mostly European and Latin American countries supported a French-sponsored UN declaration calling for the decriminalization of homosexuality, but the United States joined China, Russia, the Roman Catholic Church, and the Organization of the Islamic Conference in opposing the non-binding measure.[56]

Determined to rectify the disjuncture between US obstruction on international LGBT rights and American leadership on other human rights issues, Michael Guest, Mark Bromley, and others launched the Council for Global Equality (formerly the LGBT Foreign Policy Project), a coalition of human rights activists, foreign policy experts, LGBT organizations, and funders dedicated to ensuring that

> those in Congress, in the White House, in US embassies, and in US corporations use the diplomatic, political, and economic leverage available to them to oppose human rights abuses that are too often directed at individuals because of their sexual orientation, gender identity, or gender expression.[57]

Secretary of State Hillary Clinton soon became a strong advocate of this agenda. In May 2009, after receiving a petition in support of equal benefits for same-sex partners signed by more 2,200 Department of State employees, Clinton approved the policy change. Benefits include diplomatic passports, use of medical facilities at overseas posts, and emergency evacuation for same-sex partners in hazardous situations.[58]

In November 2009, on the eve of World AIDS Day, Clinton announced that the United States would not tolerate the criminalization of homosexuality in nations receiving US aid aimed at combatting HIV/AIDS. Her statement signaled an unprecedented level of commitment by a US administration to international LGBT issues. It coincided with weeks of private US diplomatic efforts to persuade Ugandan officials to drop pending legislation imposing the death penalty for those who repeatedly engaged in gay sex or exposed others to HIV.[59]

At a June 2010 State Department celebration of LGBT Month, Clinton emphasized that the US Department of State's Bureau for Democracy, Human Rights, and Labor tracked the treatment of LGBT people in its country-specific human rights reports and that it had begun offering emergency aid to human rights activists in Africa, South Asia, and the Middle East at risk because of their LGBT status or pro-LGBT advocacy. "Just as I was very proud to say the obvious more than 15 years ago in Beijing that human rights are women's rights and women's rights are human rights," Clinton declared, "well, let me say today that human rights are gay rights and gay rights are human rights."[60]

In June 2011, in contrast to the Bush administration's opposition to a similar resolution that failed in 2008, the Obama administration's UN envoys joined 85 nations in passing a South African-sponsored resolution condemning anti-LGBT violence and discrimination, a first for the UN Human Rights Council.[61] President Barack Obama spoke before the UN General Assembly three months later and asserted:

> No country should deny people their rights to freedom of speech and freedom of religion, but also no country should deny people their rights because of who they love, which is why we must stand up for the rights of gays and lesbians everywhere.[62]

No sitting US president had ever before offered such unequivocal support for global LGBT equality.

On 5 December 2011, Obama and Clinton formalized steps elevating international LGBT rights as a priority in US foreign policy. Obama issued a presidential memorandum "directing all agencies engaged abroad to ensure that US diplomacy and foreign assistance promote and protect the human rights of LGBT persons." Obama ordered intensified efforts to combat the criminalization of homosexual identity or conduct, to fight anti-LGBT discrimination, to protect LGBT refugees and asylum seekers, and to ensure "swift and meaningful US responses to human rights abuses of LGBT persons abroad." On the same day, Clinton addressed the UN Human Rights Council in Geneva and asserted, "Some have suggested that gay rights and human rights are separate and distinct, but in fact they are one and the same." She also announced the creation of a new $3 million Global Equality Fund to support the work of NGOs working on international LGBT issues. While neither Obama nor Clinton vowed to tie US foreign aid to a nation's record on LGBT equality, the symbolism of their statements was powerful.[63]

John Kerry, Clinton's successor as secretary of state, expanded America's global LGBT equality initiatives. In April 2013, USAID launched the LGBT Global Development Partnership, a $16 million public–private initiative that promoted LGBT rights around the world over four years.[64] In February 2015, Kerry appointed Randy Berry, an openly gay longtime foreign service officer, to be the first US special envoy to promote global gay rights.[65] Over the next year, he traveled to 42 countries.[66]

At the same time, the United States and several other nations continued pushing the UN to integrate LGBT rights into global human rights conventions and treaties. In August 2015, the UN Security Council received its first-ever briefing on LGBT issues at a meeting co-hosted by the United States and Chile. It followed the June 2015 release of a report by the UN Commissioner for Human Rights that found that thousands of people had been horrifically injured or killed worldwide because of their sexual orientation or gender identity. The briefers included UN deputy secretary-general Jan Eliasson, Jessica Stern of IGLHRC, a gay Iraqi refugee using the pseudonym "Adnan," and Subhi Nahas, a Syrian LGBT activist. Both "Adnan" and Nahas fled their nations after receiving death threats from Islamist extremists opposed to homosexuality. The key goal of the briefing was to highlight the Islamic State's brutality against gays as a means of winning support from member nations who might be ambivalent or even hostile to gay rights, but who strongly opposed Islamist extremist terrorism.[67]

The campaign is making steady progress. In June 2016, following a joint campaign led by 628 NGOs from 151 countries (about 70 percent from the global South), the UN Human Rights Council voted 23–18 (six abstentions) to create an independent expert charged with monitoring anti-LGBT violence and discrimination around the world. It was the UN's strongest demonstration to date of a commitment to integrating sexual orientation and gender identity into international human rights law.[68] In September 2016, Vitit Muntarbhorn of Thailand, the retired law professor and longtime UN official who had co-chaired the 2006 meeting at which the Yogyakarta Principles were drafted, was appointed to the post.[69]

Overall, however, the movement for international LGBT equality has had mixed success. In January 2014, Nigerian president Goodluck Jonathan signed a law that criminalizes same-sex relations, same-sex marriage, and pro-LGBT advocacy. Secretary of State John Kerry expressed "deep concern" over passage of the law, declaring "no one should face violence or discrimination for who they love." The statement did not dissuade Uganda president Yoweri Museveni from signing similar legislation a month later, a move that thwarted four years of international efforts to stop passage of the world's best-known anti-gay bill. After the Obama administration responded by cutting aid to Uganda, some Africans questioned why anti-LGBT activities seemed to be given primacy in a region rife with a host of human rights abuses. At the same time, American evangelicals like Lou Engle, Scott Lively, and Larry Jacobs escalated their international promotion of especially vitriolic anti-LGBT attitudes. The contradictions are not lost on foreign audiences or global LGBT rights activists and raise serious questions about the ability of the human rights community to curb international anti-gay discrimination.[70]

Universalized notions of rights based upon sexual orientation will remain hotly contested for the foreseeable future. Weak UN enforcement mechanisms and a strong reluctance to violate norms of national sovereignty compound the challenges of consistently applying human rights principles globally. If major global powers like the United States move beyond condemnatory rhetoric and backchannel diplomacy and begin using more forceful tactics like recalling ambassadors from nations that pass anti-gay laws, withdrawing foreign aid, or suspending visa privileges for officials responsible for such legislation, such moves risk further jeopardizing local activists already facing intense scrutiny, police harassment, and violence in these nations. Pressure from international LGBT advocacy groups also sparks anti-imperialist and nationalist resistance in many places. While the steps taken to forge a global consensus on LGBT equality are quite remarkable, it is clear there is much more to be done to ensure the safety and protection of LGBT people worldwide.

This short synthesis suggests multiple pathways for future research on the international LGBT rights movement and raises some key questions. Why did nations in the global South emerge as leaders in pro-LGBT initiatives at the UN earlier than many Western nations? How can we retrieve the LGBT histories of nations that have not yet been woven into the master narrative of global LGBT activism? Will international LGBT rights survive in a climate of rising authoritarianism? At a time of such fragility for human rights, it is critical that scholars pursue answers to such queries and keep telling the story of the courageous activists who have fought and are fighting for justice and inclusion around the globe.

Notes

1 International Lesbian, Gay, Bisexual, Trans and Intersex Association: Aengus Carroll and Lucas Ramón Mendos, *State Sponsored Homophobia 2017: A World Survey of Sexual Orientation Laws: Criminalisation, Protection and Recognition*, Geneva: ILGA, 2017. Online. Available at http://ilga.org/downloads/2017/ILGA_State_Sponsored_Homophobia_2017_WEB.pdf (accessed 8 December 2018).

2 See, for example, John D'Emilio, *Sexual Politics, Sexual Communities: The Making of a Homosexual Minority in the United States, 1940–1970*, Chicago: University of Chicago Press, 1983; Julian Jackson, *Living in Arcadia: Homosexuality, Politics, and Morality in France from the Liberation to AIDS*, Chicago: University of Chicago Press, 2009; Laurie Marhoefer, *Sex and the Weimar Republic: German Homosexual Emancipation and the Rise of the Nazis*, Toronto: University of Toronto Press, 2015; Jeffrey Weeks, *Coming Out: Homosexual Politics in Britain from the Nineteenth Century to the Present*, London: Quartet Books, 1977; Omar G. Encarnación, *Out in the Periphery: Latin America's Gay Rights Revolution*, New York: Oxford University Press, 2016; Jyoti Puri, *Sexual States: Governance and the Struggle over the Antisodomy Law in India*, Durham, NC: Duke University Press, 2016; and

Ashley Currier, *Out in Africa: LGBT Organizing in Namibia and South Africa*, Minneapolis: University of Minnesota Press, 2012.

3 David S. Campbell, "Transnationalism and Homophile Political Culture in the Postwar Decades," *GLQ: A Journal of Lesbian and Gay Studies*, 2009, vol. 15, no. 1, 31–65; Leila Rupp, "The Persistence of Transnational Organizing: The Case of the Homophile Movement," *American Historical Review*, 2011, vol. 116, no. 4, 1014–39; David Minto, "Special Relationships: Transnational Homophile Activism and Anglo-American Sexual Politics," PhD diss., Yale University, 2014.

4 Phillip M. Ayoub, *When States Come Out: Europe's Sexual Minorities and the Politics of Visibility*, Cambridge, UK: Cambridge University Press, 2016; Phillip Brett Remkus Britt, "LBGT Rights in Contemporary Global Politics: Norms, Identity, and the Politics of Rights," PhD diss., University of Delaware, 2015.

5 For a brilliant overview of these trends, see Joanne Meyerowitz, "AHR Forum: Transnational Sex and US History," *American Historical Review*, 2009, vol. 114, no. 5, 1273–86.

6 Examples of this body of work include: Kenneth Cmiel, "The Emergence of Human Rights Politics in the United States," *Journal of American History*, 1999, vol. 86, no. 3, 1231–50; Samuel Moyn, *The Last Utopia: Human Rights in History*, Cambridge, MA: Cambridge, MA: Belknap Press at Harvard University Press, 2010; Sarah B. Snyder, *Human Rights Activism and The End of the Cold War: A Transnational History of the Helsinki Network*, New York: Cambridge University Press, 2011; Barbara Keys, *Reclaiming American Virtue: The Human Rights Revolution of the 1970s*, Cambridge, MA: Harvard University Press, 2014; Elizabeth Borgwardt, *A New Deal for the World: America's Vision for Human Rights*, Cambridge, MA: Belknap Press at Harvard University Press, 2005; Akira Iriye, Petra Goedde, and William I. Hitchcock (eds.), *The Human Rights Revolution: An International History*, New York: Oxford University Press, 2012; Akira Iriye, *Global Community: The Role of the International Organizations in the Making of the Contemporary World*, Berkeley: University of California Press, 2002; Mark Philip Bradley, *The World Reimagined: Americans and Human Rights in the Twentieth-Century*, New York: Cambridge University Press, 2016. Ryan Thoreson's work on the International Lesbian and Gay Human Rights Commission (which was renamed OutRight Action International in September 2015) is an exception to the larger human rights literature's inattention to LGBT rights. See Ryan Thoreson, *Transnational LGBT Activism: Working for Sexual Rights Worldwide*, Minneapolis: University of Minnesota Press, 2014, and Michael K. Lavers, "Exclusive: IGLHRC to Change Its Name," *Washington Blade*, 28 September 2015. Online. Available at www.washingtonblade.com/2015/09/28/exclusive-iglhrc-to-change-its-name (accessed 8 December 2018).

7 On the transnational origins and evolution of sexology, see Veronika Fuechtner, Douglas E. Haynes, and Ryan M. Jones (eds.), *A Global History of Sexual Science, 1880–1960*, Berkeley: University of California Press, 2017.

8 For more on the definitions and components of advocacy, see Margaret E. Keck and Kathryn Sikkink, *Activists Beyond Borders: Advocacy Networks in International Politics*, Ithaca, NY: Cornell University Press, 1998.

9 For a brief overview, see Gay & Lesbian Vaishnava Association, "A Timeline of Gay World History," Online. Available at www.galva108.org/single-post/2014/05/08/A-Timeline-of-Gay-World-History (accessed 8 December 2018).

10 Thomas A. Foster (ed.), *Long Before Stonewall: Histories of Same-Sex Sexuality in Early America*, New York: New York University Press, 2007, pp. 5–6.

11 For an introduction to the vast literature on this history, see David F. Greenberg, *The Construction of Homosexuality*, Chicago: University of Chicago Press, 1988; Nicholas C. Edsall, *Toward Stonewall: Homosexuality in the Modern Western World*, Charlottesville: University of Virginia Press, 2003, pp. 17–32; and Colin Spencer, *Homosexuality in History*, New York: Harcourt Brace, 1995.

12 Edsall, *Toward Stonewall*, pp. 33–35; Bryant T. Ragan, "The Enlightenment Confronts Homosexuality," in Jeffrey Merrick and Bryant T. Ragan (eds.) *Homosexuality in Modern France*, New York: Oxford University Press, 1996, pp. 8–29.

13 Foster, *Long Before Stonewall*, p. 6.

14 Michael David Sibalis, "The Regulation of Male Homosexuality in Revolutionary and Napoleonic France, 1789–1815," in Merrick and Ragan, *Homosexuality in Modern France*, pp. 80–101.

15 Michael Kirby, "The Sodomy Offence: England's Least Lovely Criminal Law Export?" in Corinne Lennox and Matthew Waites (eds.) *Human Rights, Sexual Orientation, and Gender Identity in the Commonwealth: Struggles for Decriminalisation and Change*, London: University of London School of Advanced Study, Human Rights Consortium, Institute of Commonwealth Studies, 2013, p. 64. Online. Available at http://humanities-digital-library.org/index.php/hdl/catalog/view/commonwealth_lgtbi/51/150-1 (accessed 8 December 2018).

16 For a concise overview, see Annette F. Timm and Joshua A. Sanborn, *Gender, Sex, and the Shaping of Modern Europe*, 2nd ed., New York: Bloomsbury Academic, 2016, pp. 89–96.

17 Edsall, *Toward Stonewall*, pp. 69–80.

18 Edsall, *Toward Stonewall*, pp. 129–30.

19 On British efforts to impose their moral and sexual standards on colonized peoples, see Ann Laura Stoler, *Carnal Knowledge and Imperial Power: Race and the Intimate in Colonial Rule*, Berkeley: University of California Press, 2002.

20 Kirby, "The Sodomy Offence," pp. 64–7. Asian and Pacific colonies that instituted variants or replicates of Paragraph 377 included: Australia, Bangladesh, Bhutan, Brunei, Fiji, Hong Kong, India, Kiribati, Malaysia, Maldives, Marshall Islands, Myanmar (Burma), Nauru, New Zealand, Pakistan, Papua New Guinea, Singapore, Solomon Islands, Sri Lanka, Tonga, Tuvalu, and Western Samoa. In Africa, Paragraph 377 was imposed in Botswana, Gambia, Ghana, Kenya, Lesotho, Malawi, Mauritius, Nigeria, Seychelles, Sierra Leone, Somalia, Swaziland, Sudan, Tanzania, Uganda, and Zimbabwe. See Human Rights Watch, "This Alien Legacy: The Origins of 'Sodomy' Laws in British Colonialism," 17 December 2008. Online. Available at www.hrw.org/report/2008/12/17/alien-legacy/origins-sodomy-laws-british-colonialism (accessed 8 December 2018).

21 The full text of the act is online. Available at www.legislation.gov.uk/ukpga/Vict/24-25/100/contents (accessed 8 December 2018). In 1885, the British strengthened their sodomy law in ways that made it even harsher than Paragraph 377.

22 Edsall, *Toward Stonewall*, pp. 86–90.

23 Elena Mancini, *Hirschfeld and the Quest for Sexual Freedom: A History of the First International Sexual Freedom Movement*, London: Macmillan, 2010.

24 Rob Tielman, "Dutch Gay Emancipation History," *Journal of Homosexuality*, 1986, vol. 13, no. 2–3, 10–11; Edsall, *Toward Stonewall*, pp. 138–40.

25 Hayden L. Mora, "Henry Gerber's Bridge to the World," in Adrian Brooks (ed.) *The Right Side of History: 100 Years of LGBTQ Activism*, New York: Cleis Press, 2015, pp. 10–15.

26 The classic account is Richard Plant, *The Pink Triangle: The Nazi War against Homosexuals*, rev. ed., New York: Holt, 1988. See also Geoffrey J. Giles, "'The Most Unkindest Cut of All': Castration, Homosexuality, and Nazi Justice," *Journal of Contemporary History*, 1992, vol. 27, 41–61.

27 Allan Bérubé, *Coming Out Under Fire: The History of Gay Men and Women in World War Two*, New York: Penguin Books, 1990; Margot Canady, *The Straight State: Sexuality and Citizenship in Twentieth-Century America*, Princeton, NJ: Princeton University Press, 2009.

28 Nicole LaViolette and Sandra Whitworth, "No Safe Haven: Sexuality as a Universal Human Right and Gay and Lesbian Activism in International Politics," *Millennium: Journal of International Studies*, 1994, vol. 23, no. 3, 567.

29 Tielman, "Dutch Gay Emancipation History," 9–13.

30 On the homophile response to the Universal Declaration of Human Rights, see David S. Churchill, "Transnationalism and Homophile Political Culture in the Postwar Decades," *GLQ: A Journal of Gay and Lesbian Studies*, 2009, vol. 15, no. 1, 33–4.

31 Churchill, "Transnationalism and Homophile Political Culture," 36.

32 On the origins and evolution of the ICSE, see Rupp, "The Persistence of Transnational Organizing."

33 The Offenses Against the Person Act of 1861 outlawed sodomy. The 1885 Criminal Law Amendment Act (the Labouchère Amendment) outlawed all other homosexual acts.

34 Churchill, "Transnationalism and Homophile Political Culture," 47–8.

35 David Minto, "Cold War Open Secrets: Publicity and Diplomacy in the Anglo-American Lavender Scare," unpublished paper presented at SHAFR [Society for Historians of American Foreign Relations] annual meeting, June 2015; David K. Johnson, *The Lavender Scare: The Cold War Persecution of Gays and Lesbians in the Federal Government*, Chicago: University of Chicago, 2006.

36 Rupp, "The Persistence of Transnational Organizing," 1024.
37 D'Emilio, *Sexual Politics, Sexual Communities.*
38 Churchill, "Transnationalism and Homophile Political Culture," 43–8.
39 David Minto, "Mr. Grey Goes to Washington: The Homophile Internationalism of Britain's Homosexual Law Reform Society," in Brian Lewis (ed.) *British Queer History: New Approaches and Perspectives*, Oxford: Oxford University Press, 2013, p. 220.
40 "UN Commission to Study Request to Aid Homosexuals," *The Advocate*, 2–15 September 1970, 13.
41 "Swede Calls for UN Action for Homosexuals," *The Advocate*, 23 May 1973, 114.
42 In 1969, Ian Dunn organized the first meeting of what became the Scottish Minorities Group (SMG), the northern counterpart to CHE. See "First International Gay Rights Conference Set," *The Advocate*, 6 November 1974, 19. See also Peter Scott-Presland, *Amiable Warriors: A History of the Campaign for Homosexual Equality and Its Times. Vol. 1: A Space to Breathe, 1954–1973*, London: Paradise Press, 2015.
43 Jim Foster, "International Congress Report," *The Advocate*, 29 January 1975, 5 and 8–9.
44 Robert Mehl, "CHE Conference in Europe: International Gay Group Formed," *The Advocate*, 29 November 1978, 7, 11.
45 *IGA News*, 1978, vol. 1, no. 1, 3–4.
46 England and Wales decriminalized consensual male homosexual sex between adults in 1967. Scotland did so in 1980. Jeff Dudgeon was a shipping clerk in Belfast who also headed the Northern Ireland Gay Rights Association. In 1976, after he and 20 other gay men were rounded up by police and questioned for hours about their private sexual activities, four of the men signed statements attesting to illegal homosexual acts. Dudgeon, however, refused and appealed his case to the European Commission on Human Rights in Strasbourg. When the ECHR ruled in his favor, Northern Ireland faced a choice between decriminalizing male homosexual activities or being expelled from the Council of Europe. See "A Gay Activist in Ireland," *The Advocate*, 25 December 1980, 16, 23. *Dudgeon v. the United Kingdom* (1981) is online. Available at https://hudoc.echr.coe.int/eng#{%22itemid%22:[%22001-57473%22]} (accessed 8 December 2018).
47 For an overview of key ECHR rulings on LGBT issues, see European Court of Human Rights, Factsheet – Sexual Orientation Issues. Online. Available at www.echr.coe.int/Documents/FS_Sexual_orientation_ENG.pdf (accessed 8 December 2018). These ECHR cases may be located online. Available at https://hudoc.echr.coe.int/eng#{%22documentcollectionid2%22:[%22GRANDCHAMBER%22,%22CHAMBER%22]} (accessed 8 December 2018). See also Michael D. Goldhaber, *A People's History of the European Court of Human Rights*, New Brunswick, NJ: Rutgers University Press, 2009, pp. 37–41. For an assessment of the legal ramifications of *Dudgeon v. United Kingdom*, see Angioletta Sperti, *Constitutional Courts, Gay Rights, and Sexual Orientation Equality*, London: Hart, 2017, pp. 19–23.
48 In 1986, IGA changed its name to the International Lesbian and Gay Association (ILGA).
49 Laura A. Belmonte, "When Human Rights Were Straight: The Backstory of Amnesty International's Decision to Define Imprisoned Gays as Prisoners of Conscience," unpublished paper presented at the 2016 annual meeting of the Society for Historians of American Foreign Relations, University of San Diego, San Diego, California. This episode will be addressed in depth in Laura A. Belmonte, *The International LGBT Rights Movement: A History*, London: Bloomsbury Academic, forthcoming 2020.
50 In 2006, the Bush administration backed an Iranian resolution blocking ILGA's efforts to win back its UN consultative status based on ILGA's previous association with the North American Man-Boy Love Association (NAMBLA). See Warren Hoge, "Rights Groups Fault US Vote in UN on Gays," *New York Times*, 27 January 2006, A6. Online. Available at www.nytimes.com/2006/01/27/world/middleeast/rights-groups-fault-us-vote-in-un-on-gays.html (accessed 8 December 2018).
51 Philip Shenon, "Senators Keep Gay Nominee for Luxembourg Post in Limbo," *New York Times*, 8 March 1998, 11. Online. Available at www.nytimes.com/1998/03/08/world/senators-keep-gay-nominee-for-luxembourg-post-in-limbo.html (accessed 8 December 2018).
52 Philip Shenon, "Gay Philanthropist's Nomination to Become Ambassador to Luxembourg Dies in the Senate," *New York Times*, 20 October 1998, A12. Online. Available at www.nytimes.com/1998/10/20/world/gay-philanthropist-s-nomination-become-ambassador-luxembourg-dies-senate.html (accessed 8 December 2018).

53 Philip Shenon, "Clinton Renames Gay Philanthropist as Envoy," *New York Times*, 13 January 1999, A8 and Katharine Q. Seelye, "Clinton Appoints Gay Man as Ambassador as Congress Is Away," *New York Times*, 5 June 1999. Online. Available at www.nytimes.com/1999/01/13/world/clinton-renames-gay-philanthropist-as-envoy.html and www.nytimes.com/1999/06/05/us/clinton-appoints-gay-man-as-ambassador-as-congress-is-away.html (both accessed 8 December 2018).

54 Mark Bromley, "Building a Strategy for an LGBT-Inclusive US Foreign Policy," November 2007 Council for Global Equality discussion paper. Online. Available at http://globalequality.org/storage/documents/pdf/lgbt_foreign_policy_project-discussion_paper.pdf (accessed 8 December 2018).

55 The Yogyakarta Principles are published in their entirety in all six UN languages. Online. Available at www.yogyakartaprinciples.org (accessed 8 December 2018). See also Human Rights Watch, "'Yogyakarta Principles' A Milestone for Lesbian, Gay, Bisexual, and Transgender Rights," 26 March 2007. Online. Available at www.hrw.org/news/2007/03/26/yogyakarta-principles-milestone-lesbian-gay-bisexual-and-transgender-rights (accessed 8 December 2018).

56 Neil MacFarquhar, "In a First, Gay Rights Are Pressed at the UN," *New York Times* (19 December 2008), A22. Online. Available at www.nytimes.com/2008/12/19/world/19nations.html?mtrref=www.google.com&gwh=39D6CA467458D22BE4E8D7D43C7FF0E9&gwt=pay (accessed 8 December 2018). In June 2011, the Organization of the Islamic Conference formally changed its name to the Organization of Islamic Cooperation.

57 Bromley was a lawyer who had worked for the NGO International Human Rights Law Group, which later changed its name to Global Rights: Partners for Justice. The Council of Global Equality mission statement is online. Available at www.globalequality.org/who-we-are/our-mission (accessed 8 December 2018).

58 Mark Landler, "Diplomats' Same-Sex Partners to Get Benefits," *New York Times*, 24 May 2009, A24. Online. Available at www.nytimes.com/2009/05/24/us/24benefit.html?mtrref=www.google.com&gwh=B41A8E8B4BFE2AE117AA3C3687BB0E84&gwt=pay (accessed 8 December 2018).

59 Kerry Eleveld, "Clinton Condemns International Homophobia," *The Advocate*, 30 November 2009. Online. Available at www.advocate.com/news/daily-news/2009/11/30/clinton-condemns-international-homophobia (accessed 8 December 2018).

60 Hillary Rodham Clinton, Remarks at An Event Celebrating Lesbian, Gay, Bisexual, and Transgender (LGBT) Month, 22 June 2010. Online. Available at https://2009-2017.state.gov/secretary/20092013clinton/rm/2010/06/143517.htm (accessed 8 December 2018).

61 "UN Council: Gay Rights Are Human Rights," *The Advocate*, 17June 2011. Online. Available at www.advocate.com/news/daily-news/2011/06/17/un-gay-rights-are-human-rights (accessed 8 December 2018).

62 "Obama Addresses Global Gay Rights in UN Speech," *The Advocate*, 21 September 2011. Online. Available at www.advocate.com/news/daily-news/2011/09/21/obama-addresses-global-gay-rights-un-speech (accessed 8 December 2018).

63 Dan Robinson, "Obama Elevates Gay Rights as a Foreign Policy Priority," *Voice of America*, 5 December 2011. Online. Available at www.voanews.com/content/obama-elevates-gay-rights-as-a-foreign-policy-priority-135136743/174955.html (accessed 8 December 2018); Steven Lee Myers and Helene Cooper, "US to Aid Gay Rights Abroad, Obama and Clinton Say," *New York Times*, 6 December 2011. Online. Available at www.nytimes.com/2011/12/07/world/united-states-to-use-aid-to-promote-gay-rights-abroad.html?pagewanted=all&_r=0 (accessed 8 December 2018); Hillary Rodham Clinton, "Remarks in Recognition of International Human Rights Day," Palais des Nations, Geneva, Switzerland, 6 December 2011. Online. Available at https://photos.state.gov/libraries/belize/231771/PDFs/Remarks%20in%20Recognition%20of%20International%20Human%20Rights%20Day.pdf (accessed 8 December 2018); The White House; Office of the Press Secretary, "Presidential Memorandum – International Initiatives to Advance the Human Rights of Lesbian, Gay, Bisexual, and Transgender Persons," 6 December 2011. Online. Available at https://obamawhitehouse.archives.gov/the-press-office/2011/12/06/presidential-memorandum-international-initiatives-advance-human-rights-l (accessed 8 December 2018).

64 Michael K. Lavers, "Advocates Welcome US Efforts to Promote Global LGBT Rights," *Washington Blade*, 7 December 2014.

65 Randy Berry was consul general at the US Consulate in Auckland, New Zealand from 2009–12, deputy chief of mission at the US Embassy in Nepal from 2007–9, and had also served in Washington, DC, Bangladesh, Egypt, Uganda, and South Africa. See Michael K. Lavers, "State Department Names Randy Berry as LGBT Envoy," *Washington Blade*, 23 February 2015.

66 Michael K. Lavers, "Randy Berry Makes First Year as LGBT Envoy," *Washington Blade*, 25 April 2016.

67 Samantha Power, "Making History: The First UN Security Council Meeting on LGBT Rights," *Medium*, 24 August 2015. Online. Available at https://medium.com/@AmbassadorPower/making-history-the-first-un-security-council-meeting-on-lgbt-rights-f0ec18d216b (accessed 8 December 2018); Frank Bruni, "Gay and Marked for Death," *New York Times*, 21 August 2015. Online. Available at www.nytimes.com/2015/08/23/opinion/sunday/frank-bruni-gay-and-marked-for-death.html?_r=0 (accessed 8 December 2018).

68 J. Lester Feder, "The UN Votes to Create Its First LGBT Rights Watchdog," *Washington Blade*, 30 June 2016; Human Rights Watch, "UN Makes History on Sexual Orientation, Gender Identity," 30 June 2016.

69 Human Rights Campaign, "UN Appoints First-Ever Independent Expert on Sexual Orientation and Gender Identity," 30 September 2016. Online. Available at www.hrc.org/blog/un-appoints-first-ever-independent-expert-on-sexual-orientation-and-gender (accessed 8 December 2018). An effort to block the mandate for the independent expert, led by African and Islamic states, failed decisively in December 2016. See "New Attempt to Block United Nations Mandate on Sexual Orientation and Gender Identity Proves Unsuccessful," *ILGA Bulletin*, 19 December 2016, 69. Online. Available at www.ilga.org/new-attempts-to-block-un-sogi-mandate-unsuccessful (accessed 8 December 2018).

70 See, for example, "We Need to Talk About Colonialism Before We Criticize International Anti-LGBTQ Legislation," *Autostraddle*, 22 January 2014. Online. Available at www.autostraddle.com/we-need-to-talk-about-colonialism-before-we-criticize-international-anti-lgbtq-legislation-218306/ (accessed 8 December 2018); Norimitsu Onishi, "US Support of Gay Rights in Africa May Have Done More Harm than Good," *New York Times*, 20 December 2015. Online. Available at www.nytimes.com/2015/12/21/world/africa/us-support-of-gay-rights-in-africa-may-have-done-more-harm-than-good.html (accessed 8 December 2018); National Public Radio – Goats and Soda: Stories of Life in a Changing World, "When the US Back Gay and Lesbian Rights in Africa, Is There a Backlash?" 30 August 2016. Online. Available at www.npr.org/sections/goatsandsoda/2016/08/30/491818892/when-the-u-s-backs-gay-and-lesbian-rights-in-africa-is-there-a-backlash (accessed 8 December 2018).

25

RIGHTS IN ISOLATION

Lessons on public health and human rights from leprosy and HIV in the Pacific Islands

Adam R Houston

Introduction

The meeting of different cultures can alter the course of history, and these changes often have been catalyzed by diseases accompanying such encounters.[1] Perhaps most famously, smallpox and other infectious diseases transformed the New World as much as goods like potatoes and tobacco shaped the Old World as part of the so-called "Columbian Exchange" in the wake of European contact with the Americas.[2] By virtue of their remoteness, the Pacific Islands have historically been among the last to encounter diseases already familiar to the rest of the world. In turn, this remoteness has itself influenced the response to the arrival of novel afflictions. Nowhere has this been clearer than when it comes to the involuntary isolation of the infected away from the larger community.

Separating the sick from the healthy is the oldest tool in the public health toolkit. Although such measures may at times be necessary to protect the health of the community, they can also have serious ramifications for the rights and well-being of the isolated. Even if the conditions of isolation are themselves humane, it often means separation from friends and family, or the loss of income. While such separation may be a voluntary choice, it can also be imposed by the state or another authority. To strike the proper balance, scientifically justifiable measures to protect the wider populace must be carried out in a manner minimizing any negative impacts on the individual. The scales are more likely to tip to one side, however, when weighted down with stigma and fear. Most recently, the disease arriving in the Pacific Islands with such baggage in tow has been HIV.[3] Years earlier, the coming of leprosy was accompanied by a similar reaction.[4]

Parallels between the two diseases, and between the terror and stigma each evokes, have been drawn frequently all over the world since HIV emerged in the 1980s.[5] One result was the widespread suggestion that measures historically employed against leprosy, such as isolating the infected in colonies separate from the general population, should be resurrected against this new threat.[6] To dispel any uncertainty early in this essay, the fundamental flaw in the idea of reintroducing isolation colonies is that not only are they medically unnecessary in the case of HIV, but that they were never medically necessary to protect the public from leprosy in the first place. However, just as scientific understanding of these diseases has evolved over time, so too have other political and cultural influences that govern the response. As this essay will discuss, the emergence of human rights norms over the years between the arrivals of these two diseases in the Pacific has had a noticeable impact on responses to these diseases and the people they affect.

Despite considerable scholarship on the history and human rights implications of both diseases, the Pacific Islands have been largely overlooked. This oversight is unfortunate, as in few other regions has the basic public health tool of involuntary isolation occupied so central a role in response to the arrival of infectious disease. As illustrated in this essay, the Pacific Islands offer unique insights into the evolution of the balance between protecting the broader community through public health measures and safeguarding the human rights of each individual.

An isolated incident? An old approach to a new disease

There may be no more definitive image of involuntary isolation than being marooned on a deserted island. And if one wanted to isolate someone from other people, the Pacific Islands, with their many islets and atolls scattered over huge distances, would be one of the simplest places to do so. This conducive physical geography is itself one reason that leprosy colonies were more common here than elsewhere during the period of European colonization that followed upon explorers like Captain James Cook. As Rod Edmond notes in his history of leprosy and empire, "in most parts of Africa colonial governments lacked the resources to enforce segregation, and in India the scale of the problem defied any such policy."[7] In the Pacific Islands it was comparatively easy.

The relatively late consideration of HIV as a major threat in the region was followed by an even later acceptance of international human rights norms concerning the disease. In a particularly high profile incident at the 2008 Pacific Summit, Dr. Sitaleki Finau, the director of health of the host nation of Niue, proclaimed that persons with HIV "should

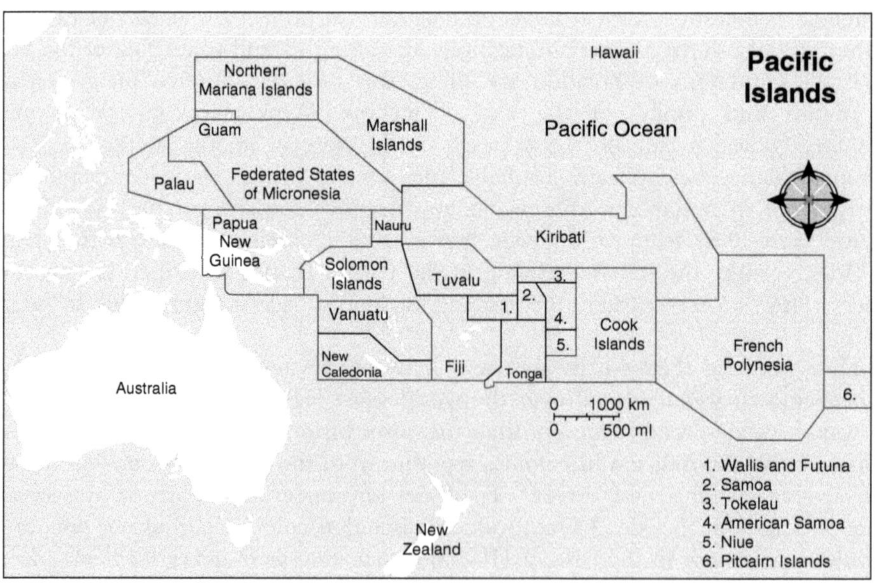

Figure 25.1 The Pacific Islands.

be locked up in a colony, where people living with the virus are looked after by their own peers, also people living with HIV/AIDS."[8] At the time, Niue was one of the few remaining countries in the world with zero recorded cases of HIV.[9] Anticipating that his approach would draw criticism for violating the human rights of people with HIV, Finau continued: "The emergence of human rights has impinged on the rights of people without the disease. Now people who have sinned have more rights than those who sin against them or prisoners have more rights than those they abuse."[10] He blamed a lack of political will for failure to enact such policies: "We have tried successfully with other infectious diseases like leprosy ... why not HIV/AIDS?"[11]

As this overt criticism of human rights norms suggests, this question had already been answered at the international level outside the region, where human rights, including the rejection of involuntary isolation, were an established component of the global HIV response. The United Nations (UN) had directly addressed isolation colonies in its then-current *International Guidelines on HIV/AIDS and Human Rights*:

> The right to liberty and security of person should, therefore, never be arbitrarily interfered with, based merely on HIV status by using measures such as quarantine, detention in special colonies, or isolation. There is no public health justification for such deprivation of liberty. Indeed, it has been shown that public health interests are served by integrating people living with HIV within communities and benefiting from their participation in economic and public life.[12]

Finau's remarks were criticized within the region as well.[13] Of particular note was the response from the Cook Islands' deputy prime minister Sir Terepai Maoate, who stated, "[T]o say something like this is very thoughtless, what does he hope to achieve by isolating people – this kind of attitude and approach is negative and does nothing for Pacific society."[14] Sir Terepai's response was informed by his own experiences visiting leprosy colonies as a young physician during the years such colonies were still active.[15] It appears the lessons the two men had learned from history regarding isolation colonies and human rights were very different.

The impact of isolation on public health and human rights

Historically, the isolation of the Pacific Islands inhibited the influx of foreign disease, but also left inhabitants particularly vulnerable to them upon arrival. This situation arose because few epidemic diseases were endemic (native) to the area. Small, scattered populations meant that many "crowd" diseases, which spread through the air (e.g. via coughing or sneezing) and require large numbers of potential hosts living in close proximity, were unable to sustain themselves in the region.[16] The dearth of epidemic diseases may also have impeded the development of local cultural responses to them.[17]

The introduction of outside diseases into populations with no immunity or history of exposure had serious consequences.[18] Highly contagious diseases that wreaked havoc in the region after European contact included dysentery, influenza, and smallpox.[19] An 1875 outbreak of measles in Fiji was reported to have resulted in 40,000 deaths, almost a third of the population, within a matter of weeks.[20] One consequence of introduced disease was considerable depopulation in the Pacific Islands.[21] As elsewhere in the world, this depopulation had destabilizing effects on Pacific societies, from fueling political turmoil to causing the loss of traditional knowledge as the result of the death of elders and other knowledge-holders.[22]

As the social anthropologist Epeli Hau'ofa observes, the parceling of the Pacific Islands into colonial states itself supported viewing them as isolated entities and ignoring expansive networks of trade and marriage that had long linked the region.[23] Nevertheless, the physical isolation of the islands could be capitalized upon by governments seeking to prevent the spread of highly infectious diseases.[24] For instance, while the global influenza pandemic of 1918 killed 20 percent of the population of Samoa, not a single case occurred in neighboring American Samoa thanks to the imposition of a naval blockade, making it the largest country in the world to escape the pandemic completely.[25] Indeed, a government's failure to take such measures could be viewed as dereliction of its duty to its populace at large, as belatedly reflected in New Zealand prime minister Helen Clark's apology more than eight decades later for permitting the ship that initially brought the flu to dock in Samoa, which was then under New Zealand's administration.[26]

States have long taken measures to prevent the introduction of disease from abroad. The term "quarantine" itself originates from the Italian "quaranta," referring to the length of the 40-day isolation period imposed on incoming ships by city-states like Venice to prevent the arrival of bubonic plague in the fifteenth century.[27] Modern states have similar duties, but also have human rights obligations towards individuals. Public health and human rights often reinforce each other, but can at times impose competing obligations. Involuntary isolation, for instance, conflicts with the right to liberty and security of the person under Article 9 of the International Covenant on Civil and Political Rights (ICCPR).[28] At the same time, it is explicitly acknowledged under international human rights law that public health is permissible grounds for laws restricting this right.[29]

The Siracusa Principles are the leading source of guidance on how rights under the ICCPR may be limited to protect public health, although they are not themselves legally binding. They state that such measures "must be specifically aimed at preventing disease or injury or providing care for the sick and injured."[30] International law scholar David Fidler outlines the factors that must be considered under the Siracusa Principles:

> Public health measures that infringe on civil and political rights must (1) be prescribed by law; (2) be applied in a non-discriminatory manner; (3) relate to a compelling public interest in the form of a significant infectious disease risk to the public's health; and (4) be necessary to achieve the protection of the public, meaning that the measure must be (a) based on scientific and public health information and principles; (b) proportional in its impact on individual rights to the infectious disease threat posed; and (c) the least restrictive measure possible to achieve protection against the infectious disease risk.[31]

More simply put, to be justifiable, public health measures that infringe upon human rights must actually be necessary, and not go beyond what is necessary, to protect public health.

Today it is understood that in contrast to other pathogens, like the flu of 1918 or the Ebola virus of recent headlines, leprosy and HIV are in fact ill-suited to isolation. Flu and Ebola are highly infectious through casual contact; there is no effective treatment once the disease has been contracted; the period between infection and illness is extremely short; and the disease quickly runs its course in weeks or even days, leaving the patient either recovering and immune to future attacks, or dead. In such cases, isolation – provided it is conducted humanely – may be both proportional and the least restrictive measure possible to protect the public from a significant risk. Virtually none of these attributes are shared by either HIV or leprosy. HIV and leprosy are each difficult to transmit, can be effectively treated (even if not cured, as is currently the case with HIV), and are chronic diseases whose symptoms may not be noticed until years after infection. Consequently, although isolation can be useful as a short-term tool for preventing the spread of highly contagious diseases during an acute public health crisis, advances in scientific knowledge have demonstrated it to be obsolete for both leprosy and HIV.

Medical efficacy is crucial, but it is not the only consideration. The bioethicists Bensimon and Upshur describe the effectiveness of public health measures like isolation as entailing more than empirical and scientific considerations. Effectiveness encompasses disparate perspectives that reflect the broader intellectual, institutional, and social contexts in which public health policies and interventions are made.[32] In their view, determining the effectiveness of involuntary isolation depends not only on scientific evidence but also on explicitly identifying and addressing the preferences and cultural considerations of affected communities.[33] These latter considerations thus involve not only universal human rights principles, but also the specific cultural context in which communities grapple with disease.

Imported diseases and imported responses

Newly arrived diseases have a long history of being negatively associated with foreign origins, regardless of accuracy. Today, the World Health Organization (WHO) even has guidelines on the naming of diseases to discourage potentially stigmatizing geographic appellations.[34] The Pacific Islands have been no exception. In Hawaii, for instance, leprosy was initially known as "Mai Pake," the Chinese disease, for the Chinese laborers were believed to have brought it there in the mid-nineteenth century.[35] This suspected provenance was echoed in local English-language documents with the term "Chinese leprosy."[36] The cycle of identifying leprosy with outsiders continued throughout the region; in Samoa, it was Hawaiians who were labeled as the source of the disease, leading to their deportation.[37] Hawaiians were also identified as the source in the northern Cook Islands, while the Chinese were blamed on the island of Rarotonga.[38] Meanwhile in Fiji, one early step taken to combat leprosy was to screen indentured Indian laborers and repatriate any found to be ill.[39]

Local responses to new diseases were also influenced by attitudes imported alongside them. It should be noted that the response to leprosy in the Pacific Islands cannot be treated as simply the passive acceptance across the region of values imposed from outside; as historian David Arnold notes, "even in a globalizing age, the history of leprosy is also a profoundly local history – of people, places, and cultures that cannot simply be absorbed and subsumed into an imperial grand narrative."[40] Nonetheless, some broad trends emerge relating to outside influence. Although other introduced pathogens may have been deadlier, they did not possess the same level of preexisting stigma as leprosy (or subsequently HIV). As the medical anthropologist Zachary Gussow puts it, "Of all the diseases known to have visited Hawaii from the early days of Western contact … leprosy alone elicited alarm among the Western residents of Hawaii, as in similar outposts of the colonial world."[41] Colonists also brought Christianity and its accompanying set of morals that took an especially negative view of leprosy, perhaps originating in the visible disfigurement and long duration that suggested a divine punishment for some earthly transgression.[42]

The Bible's Book of Leviticus strongly invokes isolation as the preferred recourse for leprosy: "All the days wherein the plague shall be in him he shall be defiled; he is unclean: he shall dwell alone; without the camp shall his habitation be."[43] While it is highly questionable whether leprosy is actually the disease described in the original Hebrew text, the fact remains that it has now become intimately associated with isolation, uncleanliness, and sin.[44] Indeed, Christianity's influence on the early development of law in many European states, and subsequently their colonies in the Pacific Islands and elsewhere, offered support to involuntary isolation as an appropriate public health law measure, particularly for leprosy. Thus, religious views and the stringent application of public health measures like involuntary isolation served to reinforce this stigma throughout the region.[45]

The word "taboo" itself originates from the Pacific Islands. Yet it was an imported Christian tradition that was to influence how HIV was addressed in the region, particularly in relation to sexual behavior. In many parts of the world, HIV's initial association with gay men – discussed later – contributed to suspicions not only of an outside disease, but also of sinful practices stemming from foreign corrupting influence. Press coverage in the Pacific frequently portrayed HIV as a foreign problem.[46] Legal scholar Anita Jowitt explains the situation in the Pacific as follows:

> Culture is not, of course, a static monolith in the Pacific region, but there has been a largely unified "official Pacific culture" presented in response to HIV. Features of it are that it is against Pacific island culture to talk about sex, and that practices such as homosexuality and prostitution contradict both traditional beliefs and Christianity, which, although introduced, has become an integral part of Pacific Island cultures.[47]

In this fashion, perceptions that were introduced from outside can spread much like the diseases they accompanied, eventually becoming endemic to the region.

Leprosy: the classic disease of isolation

Imported alongside attitudes toward disease were medical and legal measures to prevent their spread. The expansive colonialism of the nineteenth century was accompanied by huge advances in medicine. These two developments were directly linked: managing a colonial empire meant mitigating the risks of tropical diseases like yellow fever, as well as encountering diseases like leprosy that had largely vanished from Europe. At the same time, public health could also serve as a pretext for separating populations on racial or cultural grounds.

Colonization of the Pacific Islands provided legal and legislative frameworks allowing public health measures to be mandated and enforced.[48] Even where the government remained nominally Indigenous, foreign powers exerted increasing influence. Such was the case in the Kingdom of Hawaii, which passed *An Act to Prevent the Spread of Leprosy* in

1865.[49] This law sent ripples not only across the region, but also influenced the worldwide response to leprosy.

Under the Act, those found to have leprosy were forcibly removed to colonies. Such practices – both the shunning of infected individuals and their forced removal from the community – were not in keeping with traditional practices of the local population.[50] These measures had such an impact that even the name of the disease changed. What had once been the Chinese disease became "*mai ho'okawale*," the separating sickness; as such, "the agency used to name the disease … shifted from the supposed source of the infection … to the policy regulating its treatment."[51] Such discord between involuntary isolation and traditional culture was prevalent elsewhere in the region as well.[52]

The Act remained in force through Hawaii's annexation by the United States in 1898 and its ascension to statehood in 1959, before being repealed in 1969. In the interim, the island of Molokai became the site of one of the most notorious leprosy colonies in the world.[53] Its fame was linked to that of Father Damien, a Belgian priest who lived there for years before himself dying of leprosy in 1889. Canonized by the Catholic Church in 2009, Damien is now Patron Saint of both Hawaii and persons with leprosy. Damien's ministrations to those with a disease that made them outcasts from society would not be forgotten in the era of HIV. In response to his canonization, US president Barack Obama drew direct parallels between the two: "In our own time, as millions around the world suffer from disease, especially the pandemic of HIV/AIDS, we should draw on the example of Father Damien's resolve in answering the urgent call to heal and care for the sick."[54] At the same time, Damien's much publicized death had helped promote the message that not only was leprosy contagious, but that Europeans could catch it through contact with other races, combining fear of the nonwhite other with that of a dread disease.[55] Molokai was held up as a demonstration of how such a threat might be contained.

Molokai's fame was such that authors like Robert Louis Stevenson and Jack London visited and wrote about it.[56] The latter's story *Koolau the Leper* is a fictionalized account of a real historical figure who, resisting deportation, became an outlaw after killing the government agents sent to capture him.[57] The first paragraph is particularly evocative of the broader injustices promoted by the Act:

> Because we are sick they take away our liberty. We have obeyed the law. We have done no wrong. And yet they would put us in prison. Molokai is a prison. That you know. Niuli, there, his sister was sent to Molokai seven years ago. He has not seen her since. Nor will he ever see her. She must stay there until she dies. This is not her will. It is not Niuli's will. It is the will of the white men who rule the land.[58]

As this story hints, whatever the ostensible motives of the law, the disproportionate effect on Indigenous Hawaiians served as a method of shifting power towards white colonists.[59] Thus, "treatment of leprosy served as a focal lens for policies and statements aimed at marginalizing Hawaiians physically, discursively, and politically – out of sight, out of mind, out of power."[60] Things unfolded similarly elsewhere in the region, such as in Samoa under German colonial rule.[61] The political motivations behind these measures were at times explicit, with opposing parties adopting differing stances as they catered to different interests.[62]

Fear of leprosy could also disincentivize further colonization, as in this nineteenth-century commentary querying the wisdom of Hawaii's annexation by the United States as posing undue risk to (white) Americans:

> When it is considered that more than ten per cent of the Hawaiian race are affected with leprosy it becomes a serious question as to what will be the effect of the absorption of this tainted population upon the health interests of this country.[63]

Similar sentiments were expressed when New Zealand assumed control over the Cook Islands.[64]

Ironically, the development of germ theory – a massive advance in medical knowledge – would also contribute to the enforcement of more draconian measures for leprosy. Previously, prevailing views had ranged from leprosy being a hereditary condition to it being an environmental one. A 1867 report from the Royal College of Physicians and Surgeons, examining leprosy in Britain's colonies, concluded the evidence was "very greatly in favor of the non-contagiousness of leprosy" and as such there was "no evidence which … justifies any measures for the compulsory segregation of lepers."[65] However, in 1873, Gerhard Henrik Armauder Hansen identified the bacterium *mycobacterium leprae* as the causal agent of the illness now sometimes known as Hansen's Disease. Leprosy thus joined other diseases, such as the scourges of cholera and tuberculosis, whose cause had been identified even as its actual method of transmission remained unclear. In turn, science was seen as legitimizing prior religious views on isolation. This created "a double burden for people affected by leprosy – a widely accepted religious perspective that leprosy is divine punishment for immorality, and a scientific perspective that leprosy is an incurable infectious disease."[66]

Leprosy's causes and solutions were debated at the First International Leprosy Conference, held in Berlin in 1897 as one of a wave of international conferences on disease. The conference program lists an impressive roster of speakers comprised of many of the era's most prominent public health figures, including the Prussian physician Rudolf Virchow, the father of germ theory Robert Koch, and Hansen himself.[67] The conference ultimately endorsed the idea that leprosy was contagious; it also concluded that isolation was the best means of halting its spread. Hansen had already promoted a limited degree of enforced isolation in his home state of Norway, one of the few places where leprosy was still found in Europe.[68] In an era of mass European colonization, however, the scale tipped towards more stringent isolation for colonized, non-European, peoples.[69] The Conference thus called to mind another more famous Berlin Conference a decade earlier, which had formalized the carving of Africa into colonial territories.[70] Nor was the Leprosy Conference the only such public health meeting to yield measures with disproportionate impact on colonized peoples: A few years earlier, the world's first multilateral treaty relating to disease, the International Sanitary Convention of 1892, had focused entirely on protecting Europe from the introduction of cholera originating in the Indian subcontinent via the Suez Canal.[71]

Molokai had the highest profile as a natural isolation colony at the time of the Conference, but it was not the only island so used. South Africa's Robben Island – where Nelson Mandela would later be isolated for political rather than medical reasons – had been a leprosy colony since the mid-1800s, and its population increased dramatically after the Leprosy Repression Act of 1892 came into force.[72] In Canada, Chinese patients – but no others – were isolated with few amenities on D'Arcy Island off the west coast beginning in 1891.[73] The Leprosy Conference did mark a tipping point in leprosy policy at the international level. In some countries, like India, not much actually changed on the ground after the conference; the government paid lip service to segregation policies while in reality doing fairly little, ostensibly on financial grounds.[74] In the South Pacific, however, the Conference led to expanded action beyond Molokai.

The conference itself attracted public attention in the region.[75] Beginning with the Leper Ordinance of 1899, Fiji became a hub of the Pacific leprosy response outside Hawaii.[76] After a series of smaller sites had been tried, a leprosy colony on the Fijian island of Makogai was created in response to public demand in 1911.[77] This colony was host not only to Indigenous and Indo-Fijians, but eventually people from Tonga, Kiribati, Samoa, Niue, the Cook Islands, the Solomon Islands, and even New Zealand – a true cross-section of the Pacific community.[78] By the late 1920s, the practice of sending off to Makogai those cases who would have previously been isolated closer to home allowed places like Samoa and the Cook Islands to label themselves leprosy free.[79] A similar approach of consolidating cases from multiple sites in a single place was adopted in French and American territories. For instance, a few years after taking over Guam from the Spanish in 1898, the United States decided it would be cheaper and more effective to send all leprosy patients to Culion in the Philippines.[80] By 1959, at the tail end of the eras of both colonialism and leprosy isolation, a report shows cases from all around the Pacific Islands consolidated in a smaller number of colonies.[81]

The Fijian colony of Makogai closed in 1969. As elsewhere in the world, the development of effective drugs in the 1940s had shifted emphasis towards medical treatment and cure rather than isolation. As time wore on, the people who remained in leprosy colonies were increasingly those who had built a life there and had nowhere else to go. Despite the hardships of isolation, many residents had also found a sense of community within the colonies, free from outside prejudice; reintegration into the outside world could even renew such prejudice.[82] By the 1980s, even better treatment became available, provided free of charge by the WHO; these drugs have had a considerable impact on leprosy as a global public health issue.[83] In a twist of fate, this final shift towards treating leprosy like other medical conditions emerged just as HIV was beginning its worldwide conquest.

HIV: the first disease of the human rights era

The international response to HIV, like that to leprosy, originated in the West before spreading across the globe. The first cases of an unknown, untreatable disease were identified in the United States in the early 1980s, at a time when the WHO was still basking in the eradication of another of history's greatest killers, smallpox. That this new disease was initially associated with marginalized communities – gay men, then intravenous drug users and migrants from impoverished countries – furthered stigma around what would become known as HIV and whetted appetites for a firm public health response making full use of traditional tools like isolation.[84] Early public opinion surveys revealed considerable support for policies that would restrict civil liberties in the interests of stopping its spread.[85]

At the same time, HIV was also the first major disease to emerge after the creation of the UN human rights system, when increased prominence of human rights ideals meant that involuntary isolation was no longer so readily accepted, particularly by those directly affected. In the United States, HIV's emergence followed upon the heels of the Civil Rights and Gay Rights movements; consequently, American reflections on existing public health statutes found that these did not accurately reflect modern conceptions of the balance between individual rights and public health.[86] Western European countries, which shared similarities around both emerging human rights norms and the epidemiology of the epidemic itself, adopted comparable changes.[87] In this rebalancing of public health and individual rights, the argument for involuntary isolation was overpowered by the view that protecting the rights of infected people was not only valuable in its own right, but would actually benefit public health by encouraging the ill to seek out medical attention rather than pushing the epidemic underground where it would be harder to address.[88]

This approach was soon internationalized via the newly created WHO Global Program on AIDS. Its first head, Jonathan Mann, promoted human rights in the global response and refused to provide support for activities seen as discriminatory.[89] By 1987, nondiscrimination towards HIV-positive people was formally included in the first Global AIDS Strategy; this was a landmark for human rights in the context of infectious disease, as it marked the first time that the human rights of the infected became an integral part of an international strategy to control an epidemic.[90] It was this approach to HIV and human rights, propagated by the WHO, which became the de facto global norm; its spread has been described as "one of the most striking modern examples of globalization."[91]

At the same time, however, came growing awareness that the bulk of the HIV pandemic was in sub-Saharan Africa, where, in contrast to North America and Europe, the disease was spreading on a far greater scale through the general population. Under these circumstances, the transposition of a human rights approach built upon the civil and political rights of stigmatized minorities in wealthy countries onto impoverished postcolonial countries, where failure to realize economic and social rights was the primary driver of the epidemic, did not prove a perfect fit.[92] This mismatch was eventually recognized, and the resulting renewed attention to economic and social rights culminated in global recognition of universal access to antiretroviral medication as a human rights issue in the years after the mid-1990s, when effective treatment had first became available in wealthy countries.[93] Thus, human rights have long been a central pillar of the global response to HIV, even as the response evolved, and even where those rights have remained better realized on paper than in practice. As part of this process, involuntary isolation as a public health measure has been thoroughly rejected.

The sheer scale of the epidemic may also have contributed to the ultimate rejection of involuntary isolation. The disease simply affected too many people for isolation to be feasible, particularly given the fact that many of the countries most affected were also those with the fewest resources to enforce such measures. That leads to consideration of another island state, Cuba – the only country to deviate drastically from international norms around isolation.

Different lessons from another island: HIV and isolation in Cuba

Leprosy arrived in Cuba with European colonization, as it had in the Pacific Islands, and so too did stigma arise and a response emerge that was reliant on separating patients from the general population.[94] With HIV, however, Cuba went against global trends, implementing the world's only mass HIV isolation program in 1986, one year after the country's first documented case.[95] Under the program, seropositive persons were isolated in "controlled residential parks."[96]

Isolation was ultimately only one component of a broader response that Cuba had already been preparing prior to the first domestic case.[97] Cuba invested heavily in HIV care within the context of a strong healthcare system. These investments later included antiretroviral treatment, once it became available. Cuba's level of investment in isolation, providing treatment and care in comfortable surroundings, contrasts starkly with Finau's concern that, "If we have one case now, it will break our health budget to get it treated."[98]

Even in a communally oriented society, however, and despite reasonable living conditions in the residential parks, residents found separation from family, friends, and work to be difficult.[99] As both understanding of the disease and the ability to treat it improved, Cuba lifted its isolation policy in the early 1990s.[100] The Cuban experience took place under unique circumstances difficult to replicate elsewhere. Cuba's ability to infringe upon the rights of persons with HIV stemmed from the authoritarian nature of the Cuban state. This was compounded by Cuba's isolation from much of the world. That isolation was more political than geographical. Restrictions on freedom of movement ensured that few people entered or exited the country; indeed, sexual contact with foreigners – usually while serving the state abroad – was initially considered the single greatest risk factor for HIV.[101] Today, such restrictions would be less practicable, particularly given Cuba's popularity as a tourist destination. Tourists, even those arriving for the explicit purpose of sexual contact with locals, have never been subject to similar scrutiny.[102] Indeed, any attempt to target tourists with invasive measures would be less likely to protect public health than to encourage them to take their vacations, and their money, elsewhere. In many Pacific Islands, where tourism accounts for a sizable part of the economy – and where, unlike Cuba, locals are themselves permitted to come and go for recreational or economic reasons – there would likewise be substantial barriers to an invasive policy. Even in establishing the Makogai colony in Fiji at the turn of the twentieth century, the potential effects on tourism arose as a concern; a century later this is all the more the case.[103] The Cuban experience shows that even in a context where the human rights of individuals were not a high priority, isolation was both resource intensive and an impediment to income-generating activities such as tourism. It also shows that policies were changed once evidence showed such extreme measures were unnecessary.

A new disease and an old approach in the Pacific

The first cases of HIV in the Pacific Islands were recorded already in 1984 in the Marshall Islands.[104] Nonetheless, the global HIV narrative has largely overlooked this part of the world. The first major UN report focusing on the region was not released until 1996.[105] Even today, it is often lumped in with other regions such as Asia where epidemics take place under different circumstances and in far larger populations.[106] One of the first concerted regional engagements with the topic of HIV and human rights came in a special issue of *Pacific Health Dialogue* in 1995. The issue's editor was none other than Sitaleki Finau. At the time, only 13 of 22 countries in the region had reported any HIV cases.[107] A recurring theme throughout the issue was that the comparatively late emergence of HIV in the region had provided the opportunity to draw from experiences elsewhere and prepare for its arrival. This is best summed up by the Fijian minister of health, Apenisa Kuruisaqila, who concludes:

> Finally, as we have been blessed with the gift of time, and availing ourselves of our rich hoard of customs and traditions, let us demonstrate our leadership, by example to the world of how we provide care to those directly or indirectly affected by this condition – caring that is free from discrimination but full of understanding, compassion and love.[108]

Given the pattern of events elsewhere, it is unsurprising that a key theme is the need for legal reform. A review of the legal landscape in Fiji notes "our health legislation is a product of our colonial legacy with its primary focus being the control of infectious diseases through public health provisions. Its applicability to the situation today is questionable."[109] This theme is echoed in reviews from throughout the region, but in different ways. In Samoa's review, the "existing Health Ordinance from 1959" is acknowledged as a colonial inheritance whose modern applicability may be questionable; at the same time, it notes that the government added HIV under that ordinance in 1987, thus permitting the isolation of individuals in the interest of public health.[110] By contrast, the review from Vanuatu, written before any local cases were detected, explicitly highlights both a government commitment not to permit isolation and recognition that existing public health laws around infectious diseases were not appropriate for HIV.[111] And in the Solomon Islands, the conclusion was that reform was not yet necessary, as with only one identified case of HIV, it was not a high priority.[112]

The first regional meeting on HIV was held in 1999. The Fijian First Lady told delegates in her welcoming address: "The time has long passed when we can close our eyes and say 'It won't happen to us.'"[113] By 2005, the majority of cases in the Pacific Islands (outside Papua New Guinea) were concentrated in a handful of countries, such as French Polynesia, Kiribati, Guam, Fiji, and New Caledonia. Given that some states had populations best measured in the thousands, and that none save Papua New Guinea crested 1 million inhabitants, even a few cases could have an impact. The resulting regional plan, which was the one in place at the time of Finau's speech, does not explicitly address isolation but does emphasize human rights as a core theme.[114] Nevertheless, as a regional review of legislation in 2009 was to illustrate, many countries had still not updated their public health legislation well over a decade after the issue had been raised in 1995.[115]

Even with HIV squarely linked to human rights, the fact that certain rights within the pantheon of universal human rights have received different emphasis at different times and places in the global response is a reminder that "universal" rights may not be universally viewed or accepted in the same way. Legal scholar Anita Jowitt highlighted this issue in her review of the region's legal landscape concerning HIV:

> There are … numerous challenges for bodies that want to implement international best practice standards through the use of State law in the Pacific Islands region. These centre on the notion that external best practice standards lack authority due to their apparent lack of cultural continuity, and that this lack of authority is reinforced by a general distrust of potentially neo-colonial use of the law. It is not enough that best practice manuals are presented to

> lawmakers. Indeed, this may be counter-productive, creating a neo-colonial backlash. Instead reasons for adopting a human rights type of approach, which are clearly based on evidence which shows that it is the most effective way of containing the HIV epidemic, and not simply on ideological statements about the importance of human rights, must be presented. Best practices must also be repositioned as being within, or related to, traditional society, rather than being seen as an external force. The relationship between *evidence-based* best practice and cultural norms must also be addressed *before* presenting best practice standards [emphasis in original].[116]

Given the painful legacy of colonial-era leprosy programs that removed people from their communities, and at times served to collectively oppress local peoples, it is unsurprising that the imposition of outside approaches would not be accepted uncritically. Even though involuntary isolation had already been rejected from a rights-based perspective at the international level, it remains important to situate this evolving human rights approach within the Pacific context. Attention must be paid to local conditions and their influence rather than simply "Africanizing" the epidemic.[117]

Such themes emerge frequently in the Pacific Islands, where the importance of local ownership of the HIV response has been emphasized. For instance, one review remarks that "Fijians, like anybody else, do not want 'health initiatives' that affect them to be governed from outside, with their health needs determined by the perceptions of outsiders, including multi-lateral donors, researchers, and consultants, who, they feel, perceive them as 'diseased.'"[118] Such concerns are in turn reflected more recently in regional programs that have treated "traditional, cultural and religious values of Pacific communities that are based on compassion and reconciliation" as a key element of the HIV response on par with human rights.[119]

At the same time, there is little reason to believe that local values and international human rights norms are incompatible when it comes to involuntary isolation. In fact, as noted earlier in relation to the reaction of traditional cultures towards leprosy, and resistance towards the imported approach of isolation, there is little to suggest that the region's cultures – as opposed to the region's geographical attributes – are any more conducive to involuntary isolation than elsewhere. By contrast, there are numerous universal reasons to avoid involuntary isolation, starting with the fact that it is medically unnecessary for public health. Other approaches, such as ensuring access to treatment, ultimately require fewer resources while respecting the rights of both the individual and the community they are a part of. A more sensible approach to HIV colonies in the Pacific echoes that voiced by Dr. Dennie Iniakwala, Head of the HIV and STI Section at the Secretariat of the Pacific Community (SPC), in response to Finau's comments: "Why would we start introducing approaches that firstly we know don't work, and secondly that go against all the things we hold dear as Pacific people?"[120]

Conclusion

Even sensible plans built on a combination of local and international expertise and experience may nevertheless fall apart when an abstract threat becomes real, as subsequent events illustrated. The 1995 review of the Cook Islands' policy presciently remarked that adopting a human rights-sensitive approach was easier in the abstract than in practice: "Without a case of HIV infection, it may be difficult to deal with the issue realistically."[121] This was, after all, in a country whose Board of Tourism had once proudly advertised their country as "AIDS-free."[122] Then, in 2011, the country encountered what the media described as the first locally detected case of HIV.[123] Although the government had prepared for this long-anticipated event in accordance with international standards, the actual emergence of HIV in the country prompted a different reaction. When the news first emerged, members of the National Parliament advocated publicly identifying the infected individual.[124] Fortunately, this idea was dismissed after a few days.[125] By this time, however, the individual had already been reported as being a Fijian national, a fact not only rekindling concerns about HIV as a foreign disease, but one later reported to have contributed to an attack on two Fijians in the Cook Islands.[126] Although this latter report has been disputed, it remains a further warning of the potential consequences of departing from lessons learned at great cost elsewhere.[127]

Past experiences with disease and isolation should not be forgotten. In Hawaii there has been ongoing debate over what to do with the settlement on Molokai, where a handful of elderly residents remain voluntarily, decades after forced isolation ended in 1969.[128] In the Cook Islands, the tiny *motu* (islet) of Rapota in the Aitutaki lagoon was once used to isolate people with leprosy.[129] It is now a popular tourist spot; the last people isolated here were cast members of the television program *Survivor*.[130] At the same time, leprosy lingers on in a handful of Pacific Islands; in some, like Kiribati, it remains an important health consideration even as treatment becomes better integrated into the broader health system.[131] Meanwhile, familiarity is also bringing a sense of normalcy to the HIV response; while a serious disease, it is increasingly accepted that HIV can be treated, and that the rights of those affected should be respected. As such, it also appears that the statement at the Niue summit marked the last gasp of involuntary isolation for HIV as a matter of serious high-level consideration in the region.

Even though isolation has been discarded as a response to HIV and leprosy, the geography of the Pacific Islands will continue to affect public health. Costly and unreliable transportation, combined with limited human resources and poor economies of scale, complicate the implementation of health programs of all kinds, regardless of their effectiveness on paper. Today it is also widely recognized that the greatest threat currently facing the Pacific Islands is that of non-communicable diseases – frequently dubbed NCDs for short – like heart disease and diabetes. According to the WHO, the region has among the highest levels of obesity in the world; in some countries, up to 90 percent of the population are overweight.[132] In many ways, NCDs are outsider diseases as well; foreign habits and imported foods high in salt, sugar, and fat have displaced traditional lifestyles.[133] In some cases, the interests of more powerful countries directly influence these changes; Australia and New Zealand, for instance, have exported fatty cuts of meat that would not be sold for human consumption in their countries of origin but have become dietary staples in some Pacific Islands.[134]

Remaining isolated from unhealthy habits and products is increasingly difficult in a globalized world. NCDs also put a new twist on questions about state interference into an individual's autonomy and lifestyle choices for the sake of public health. There are also fewer effective public health responses to import from abroad: Former colonial states that pioneered approaches against infectious diseases are themselves struggling unsuccessfully with NCDs. The Pacific Islands are working to address the issue within the region.[135] Looking forward, the isolation of many Pacific Islands makes them a natural staging ground for innovation, particularly when it comes to restricting the arrival of unhealthy goods. This may once again grant them a unique voice to be integrated into, rather than isolated from, the global conversation around public health and human rights.

Acknowledgments

The author extends his thanks to Vicki Luker, Hilary Gorman, and his friends and colleagues at the Pacific Islands AIDS Foundation (PIAF).

Notes

1 Accessible introductions include: William H. McNeill, *Plagues and Peoples*, New York: Anchor Press, 1976; Jared M. Diamond, *Guns, Germs, and Steel: The Fates of Human Societies*, New York: W. W. Norton, 1997.
2 See e.g. Alfred W. Crosby, *The Columbian Exchange: Biological and Cultural Consequences of 1492*, Santa Barbara, CA: Greenwood, 1972.
3 On terminology: HIV (Human Immunodeficiency Virus) is the virus that causes AIDS (Acquired Immunodeficiency Syndrome). The outdated term HIV/AIDS appears in multiple cited sources. Despite the alternate name Hansen's Disease carrying less historical stigma, the term leprosy remains in widespread use, including by the World Health Organization (WHO). The offensive term "leper" appears only in historical sources. "Pacific Islands" in this essay refers to the Small Island States and Territories of Oceania (see Figure 25.1). Papua New Guinea, whose unique HIV epidemic merits its own discussion, is not covered here.
4 Vicki Luker, "The Lessons of Leprosy? Reflections on Hansen's Disease in the Response to HIV and AIDS in the Pacific," *Journal of Pacific History*, 2017, vol. 52, 385–406.
5 Douglas Shenson, "When Fear Conquers. A Doctor Learns about AIDS from Leprosy," *New York Times*, 28 February 1988; Susan Sontag, *AIDS and Its Metaphors*, New York: Farrar, Straus & Giroux, 1989.
6 Dorothy Rasinski Gregory, "AIDS – The Leprosy of the 1980s: Is There a Case for Quarantine?" *Journal of Legal Medicine*, 1988, vol. 9, 547–60.
7 Rod Edmond, *Leprosy and Empire: A Medical and Cultural History*, New York: Cambridge University Press, 2006, p. 143.
8 "Isolate People Living with HIV/AIDS," *Pacnews*, 19 August 2008.
9 Tim Sladden, "Twenty Years of HIV Surveillance in the Pacific – What Do the Data Tell Us and What Do We Still Need to Know?" *Pacific Health Dialog*, 2005, vol. 12, 23–37.
10 "Isolate People Living with HIV/AIDS."
11 "Isolate People Living with HIV/AIDS."
12 Joint United Nations Programme on HIV/AIDS and United Nations High Commissioner for Human Rights, *International Guidelines on HIV/AIDS and Human Rights. 2006 Consolidated Version*, Geneva: OHCHR, 2006.
13 Kerrie Ritchie, "Doctor under Fire Over HIV Quarantine Plan," *PM*, Radio National ABC, Australia, 2 September 2008. Online. Available at www.abc.net.au/pm/content/2008/s2353723.htm (accessed 8 December 2018).
14 "Proposal to Isolate People with HIV-AIDS Insensitive and Thoughtless – DPM," *Cook Islands Herald Weekly*, 23 August 2008.
15 "Proposal to Isolate People."
16 Richard Taylor, "History of Public Health in Pacific Island Countries," in Milton J. Lewis and Kerrie L. Macpherson (eds.) *Public Health in Asia and the Pacific*, London: Routledge, 2011, p. 276.
17 Paul Martin, "Emerging Infectious Diseases and the Depopulation of French Polynesia in the 19th Century," *Emerging Infectious Diseases*, 1996, vol. 2, 359–61.
18 G. Dennis Shanks and John F. Brundage, "Pacific Islands Which Escaped the 1918–1919 Influenza Pandemic and Their Subsequent Mortality Experiences," *Epidemiology and Infection*, 2013, vol. 141, 353–6.

19 Bridget S. Penman, Sunetra Gupta, and G. Dennis Shanks, "Rapid Mortality Transition of Pacific Islands in the 19th Century," *Epidemiology and Infection*, 2017, vol. 145, 1–11.
20 "Measles in Fiji," *Evening Star* (Otago, New Zealand), 12 August 1875.
21 Sylvester Maxwell Lambert, *The Depopulation of Pacific Races*, Honolulu: Bernice P. Bishop Museum, 1934.
22 G. Dennis Shanks, "Pacific Island Societies Destabilised by Infectious Diseases," *Journal of Military and Veterans'* Health, 2016, vol. 24, 71–4.
23 Epeli Hau'ofa, "Our Sea of Islands," *The Contemporary Pacific*, 1994, vol. 6, 147–61.
24 Hiroshi Nishiura, Nick Wilson, and Michael G. Baker, "Quarantine for Pandemic Influenza Control at the Borders of Small Island Nations," *BMC Infectious Diseases*, 2009, vol. 9, at 27.
25 John Ryan McLane, "Paradise Locked: The 1918 Influenza Pandemic in American Samoa," *Sites: A Journal of Social Anthropology and Cultural Studies*, 2013, vol. 10, 30–51.
26 Helen Clark, "Full Text: Helen Clark's Apology to Samoa," *New Zealand Herald* (Auckland), 4 June 2002. Online. Available at www.nzherald.co.nz/nz/news/article.cfm?c_id=1&objectid=2044857 (accessed 8 December 2018).
27 Eugenia Tognotti, "Lessons from the History of Quarantine, from Plague to Influenza A," *Emerging Infectious* Diseases, 2013, vol. 19, 254–9. To clarify two commonly confused terms: Quarantine is the separation of people suspected of possible infection as a temporary precautionary measure until their status is determined, and as such is generally of limited duration. Isolation can include quarantine but generally refers to the separation of people known to be infected or ill until they are deemed no longer a risk for spreading the disease. If there is no cure available, such a separation may be permanent.
28 *International Covenant on Civil and Political Rights (ICCPR)* Article 9(1), Geneva: Office of the High Commission for Human Rights, 1966. Also online. Available at www.ohchr.org/en/professionalinterest/pages/ccpr.aspx (accessed 8 December 2018).
29 ICCPR, Article 12(3).
30 UN Commission on Human Rights, *The Siracusa Principles on the Limitation and Derogation Provisions in the International Covenant on Civil and Political Rights*, 28 September 1984, E/CN.4/1985/4. Article 25. Also online. Available at http://hrlibrary.umn.edu/instree/siracusaprinciples.html (accessed 8 December 2018).
31 David P. Fidler, "SARS and International Law," *ASIL [American Society of International Law] Insights*, April 2003, vol. 8, no. 7, n.p. Online. Available at www.asil.org/insights/volume/8/issue/7/sars-and-international-law (accessed 8 December 2018).
32 Cecile M. Bensimon and Ross E. G. Upshur, "Evidence and Effectiveness in Decisionmaking for Quarantine," *American Journal of Public Health*, 2007, vol. 97, S44–8.
33 Bensimon and Upshur, "Evidence and Effectiveness."
34 World Health Organization, *World Health Organization Best Practices for the Naming of New Human Infectious Diseases*, Geneva: WHO, 2015. Online. Available at www.who.int/topics/infectious_diseases/naming-new-diseases/en/ (accessed 8 December 2018).
35 Arthur Albert St. M. Mouritz, *The Path of the Destroyer: A History of Leprosy in the Hawaiian Islands, and Thirty Years Research into the Means By Which It Has Been Spread*, Honolulu: Star Bulletin, 1916, p. 28.
36 Charles D. Bernholz, "Pestilence in Paradise: Leprosy Accounts in the Annual Reports of the Governor of the Territory of Hawaii," *Government Information Quarterly*, 2009, vol. 26, 407.
37 Safua Akeli, "Leprosy in Samoa 1890 to 1922: Race, Colonial Politics and Disempowerment," MA Thesis, University of Canterbury, Kent, 2007, p. 12.
38 Raeburn Lange, "Leprosy in the Cook Islands, 1890–1925," *Journal of Pacific History*, 2017, vol. 52, 302–24.
39 Mere Vakawaletabua and Iobi Batio, *A Short History of Leprosy Control in Fiji*, Suva: Pacific Health Voices, 2008, pp. 1–5. Some sources – e.g. Cyril J. Austin, "A Study of Leprosy in Fiji," *International Journal of Leprosy*, 1936, vol. 4, 55–70 – question whether leprosy was present in Fiji before European contact, but any effects on the post-contact narrative appear minimal.
40 David Arnold, "Leprosy: From 'Imperial Danger' to Postcolonial History – An Afterword," *Journal of Pacific* History, 2017, vol. 52, 407–19.
41 Zachary Gussow, *Leprosy, Racism, and Public Health: Social Policy in Chronic Disease Control*, Boulder, CO: Westview Press, 1989, p. 93.

42 Ilse J. Volinn, "Issues of Definitions and Their Implications: AIDS and Leprosy," *Social Science & Medicine*, 1989, vol. 29, 1157–62.
43 *King James Bible*, Leviticus 13:46. Online. Available at www.kingjamesbibleonline.org/Leviticus-Chapter-13 (accessed 8 December 2018).
44 Joseph Zias, "Lust and Leprosy: Confusion or Correlation?" *Bulletin of the American Schools of Oriental Research*, 1989, vol. 275, 27–31.
45 See generally, Dorothy McMenamin, "Leprosy and Stigma in the South Pacific: Camaraderie in Isolation," MA Thesis, University of Canterbury, Kent, 2009.
46 Trevor Cullen, "Press Coverage of AIDS/HIV in the South Pacific: Short-Term View of a Long-Term Problem," *Pacific Journalism Review*, 2003, vol. 9, 138–47.
47 Anita Jowitt, "Creating a Framework for HIV/AIDS Related Legal Reform in the South Pacific," *Journal of South Pacific Law*, 2004, vol. 8, n.p.
48 Taylor, "History of Public Health," 288.
49 *An Act to Prevent the Spread of* Leprosy, 1865. Online. Available at https://iiif.lib.harvard.edu/manifests/view/drs:8069466$8i (accessed 8 December 2018).
50 See Ron Amundson and Akira Oakaokalani Ruddle-Miyamoto, "A Wholesome Horror: The Stigmas of Leprosy in 19th Century Hawaii," *Disability Studies Quarterly*, 2010, vol. 30, n.p.
51 Edmond, *Leprosy and Empire*, p. 146.
52 Lange, "Leprosy in the Cook Islands."
53 John Tayman, *The Colony*, New York: Simon & Schuster, 2006.
54 Rachel Donadio, "Benedict Canonizes 5 New Saints," *New York Times*, 11 October 2009.
55 Kerri A. Inglis, "'One's Molokai Can Be Anywhere': Global Influence in the Twentieth-Century History of Hansen's Disease," *Journal of World History*, 2014, vol. 25, 611–27.
56 Tayman, *The Colony*, p. 3.
57 Pillani Kaluaikoolau and Frances N. Frazier, *The True Story of Kaluaikoolau*, Honolulu: Kauai Historical Society, 2001.
58 Jack London, *Koolau the Leper*, 1908. Online. Available at www.online-literature.com/london/72 (accessed December 2018).
59 Pennie Moblo, "Leprosy, Politics, and the Rise of Hawaii's Reform Party," *Journal of Pacific History*, 1999, vol. 34, 75–90.
60 R. Doug K. Herman, "Out of Sight, Out of Mind, Out of Power: Leprosy, Race, and Colonization in Hawaii," *Hülili: Multidisciplinary Research on Hawaiian Well-Being*, 2010, vol. 6, 271–301.
61 Safua Akeli, "Leprosy Control in Samoa from 1890 to 1914" in Measina a Sāmoa Conference (ed.), *5th Measina a Sāmoa Conference 2010: Papers Presented at the 5th Measina a Sāmoa Conference, 30th August–1 September 2010, National University of Sāmoa, Le Papaigalagala*, Apia, Samoa: Centre for Sāmoan Studies, 2011.
62 Moblo, "Leprosy, Politics."
63 Prince A. Morrow, "Leprosy and Hawaiian Annexation," *North American Review*, 1897, vol. 165, 582–590.
64 "A Leper Colony in New Zealand, More Work for the Health Department," *Otago Witness* (New Zealand), 24 October 1901.
65 Royal College of Physicians of London, *Report on Leprosy by the Royal College of Physicians, Prepared for Her Majesty's Secretary of State for the Colonies*, London: Edward Eyre & William Spottiswoode, 1867, p. vii.
66 Niyi Awofeso, "Leprosy Control, Public Health Paradigms and Stigma," *Australian and New Zealand Journal of Public Health*, 2011, vol. 35, 9–11.
67 William R. Day, "The Berlin Leprosy Conference," *Public Health Reports*, 1897, vol. 12, 686–89.
68 Shubhada S. Pandya, "The First International Leprosy Conference, Berlin, 1897: The Politics of Segregation," *História, Ciências, Saúde-Manguinhos*, 2003, vol. 10, 161–77.
69 Amundson and Ruddle-Miyamoto, "A Wholesome Horror."
70 See Stig Förster et al. (eds.), *Bismarck, Europe, and Africa: The Berlin Africa Conference 1884–1885 and the Onset of Partition*, London: Oxford University Press, 1988.
71 Valeska Huber, "The Unification of the Globe by Disease? The International Sanitary Conferences on Cholera, 1851–1894," *Historical Journal*, 2006, vol. 49, 453–76.

72 Samuel P. Impey, "Leprosy in South Africa," in *Prize Essays on Leprosy*, vol. 157, London: New Sydenham Society, 1895, pp. 189–206.
73 Chris J. Yorath, *A Measure of Value the Story of the D'Arcy Island Leper Colony*, Victoria, British Columbia: TouchWood Editions, 2009.
74 Kakar Sanjiv, "Leprosy in British India, 1860–1940: Colonial Politics and Missionary Medicine," *Medical History*, 1996, vol. 40, 215–30.
75 See "Berlin Leprosy Conference," *Samoa Weekly Herald*, 11 December 1897. Interestingly, this article highlights Virchow's dissenting view that leprosy is non-contagious.
76 Vakawaletabua and Batio, "A Short History."
77 Mary Stella, *Makogai – Image of Hope: A Brief History of the Care of Leprosy Patients in Fiji*, Christchurch, New Zealand: Pegasus Press, 1978, p. 29.
78 Cyril J. Austin, "Leprosy in Fiji and the South Seas," *International Journal of Leprosy*, 1949, vol. 17, 399–409.
79 "Free from Leprosy," *Evening Post* (Wellington, New Zealand), 29 May 1928.
80 Anne Perez Hattori, "Re-Membering the Past: Photography, Leprosy and the Chamorros of Guam, 1898–1924," *Journal of Pacific History*, 2011, vol. 46, 293–318.
81 David A. Lonie, *Trends in Leprosy in the Pacific: An Account of the Introduction and Spread of Leprosy in the Pacific and of its Importance in Pacific Health.* Noumea, New Caledonia: South Pacific Commission, 1959.
82 Jane Buckingham, "The Inclusivity of Exclusion: Isolation and Community among Leprosy-Affected People in the South Pacific," *Health and History*, 2011, vol. 13, 65–83.
83 Cairns S. Smith et al., "Multidrug Therapy for Leprosy: A Game Changer on the Path to Elimination," *The Lancet Infectious Diseases*, 2017, vol. 17, e293–7.
84 R. Bayer and A. Fairchild-Carrino, "AIDS and the Limits of Control: Public Health Orders, Quarantine, and Recalcitrant Behavior," *American Journal of Public Health*, 1993, vol. 83, 1471–6.
85 Gregory M. Herek, "AIDS and Stigma," *American Behavioral Scientist*, 1999, vol. 42, 1106–16.
86 Larry Gostin, "The Future of Communicable Disease Control: Toward a New Concept in Public Health Law," *Milbank Quarterly*, 1986, vol. 64, 79–96.
87 Rolf Rosenbrok et al., "The Normalization of AIDS in Western European Countries," *Social Science & Medicine*, 2000, vol. 50, 1607–29.
88 Gregory, "AIDS – The Leprosy of the 1980s."
89 Jonathan Mann and Kathleen Kay, "Confronting the Pandemic: The World Health Organization's Global Programme on AIDS, 1986–1989," *AIDS*, 1991, vol. 5, s221–9.
90 Sofia Gruskin, Jonathan Mann, and Daniel Tarantola, "Past, Present, and Future: AIDS and Human Rights," *Health and Human Rights Journal*, 1998, vol. 2, 1–3.
91 John Iliffe, *The African AIDS Epidemic: A History*, Athens: Ohio University Press, 2006, p. 69.
92 David Patterson and Leslie London, "International Law, Human Rights and HIV/AIDS," *Bulletin of the World Health Organization*, 2002, vol. 80, 964–9.
93 See Treatment Action Campaign, *Fighting for Our Lives: The History of the Treatment Action Campaign 1998–2010*, Cape Town: Treatment Action Campaign, 2010.
94 Enrique Beldarraín-Chaple, "Historical Overview of Leprosy Control in Cuba," *MEDICC Review. International Journal of Cuban Health and Medicine*, 2017, vol. 19, 23–30.
95 Helena Hanson and Nora Groce, "Human Immunodeficiency Virus and Quarantine in Cuba," *JAMA [Journal of the American Medical Association]*, 2003, vol. 290, 2875.
96 Eliseo J. Pérez-Stable, "Cuba's Response to the HIV Epidemic," *American Journal of Public Health*, 1991, vol. 81, 563–7.
97 Sarah Z. Hoffman, "HIV/AIDS in Cuba: A Model for Care or an Ethical Dilemma?" *African Health Sciences*, 2004, vol. 4, 208–9.
98 "Isolate People Living with HIV/AIDS."
99 Sarah Santana, Laura Faas, and K. Wald, "Human Immunodeficiency Virus in Cuba: The Public Health Response of a Third World Country," *International Journal of Health Services: Planning, Administration, Evaluation*, 1991, vol. 21, 511–37.
100 Hansen and Groce, "Human Immunodeficiency Virus and Quarantine."
101 Santana et al., "Human Immunodeficiency Virus in Cuba."
102 Helena Hansen and Nora Groce, "From Quarantine to Condoms: Shifting Policies and Problems of HIV Control in Cuba" *Medical Anthropology*, 2001, vol. 19, 259–92.

103 Stella, *Makogai*, p. 24.
104 Joint United Nations Programme on HIV/AIDS (ed.), *Turning the Tide: An Open Strategy for a Response to AIDS in the Pacific: Report of the Commission on AIDS in the Pacific Presented to Mr. Ban Ki-Moon, UN Secretary General, on 2 December 2009 in New York*, Geneva: UNAIDS, 2009.
105 United Nations (ed.), *Time to Act: The Pacific Response to HIV and AIDS*, Geneva: United Nations 1996.
106 See UNAIDS, "HIV in Asia and the Pacific," Geneva: UNAIDS, 2013. Online. Available at www.unaids.org/sites/default/files/media_asset/2013_HIV-Asia-Pacific_en_0.pdf (accessed 8 December 2018).
107 Vilimaina L. Rakaseta, "AIDS and Its Possible Impact on the Pacific," *Pacific Health Dialog*, 1995, vol. 2, 140–46.
108 Apenisa Kuruisaqila, "A Pacific Perspective on HIV/AIDS: Questions from 1990," *Pacific Health Dialog*, 1995, vol. 2, 75–7.
109 Daniel V. Fatiaki, "HIV/AIDS and Law Reform in the Pacific," *Pacific Health Dialog*, 1995, vol. 2, 84–7.
110 Fagaloa Tufuuga and Kamuta Seuseu, "HIV/AIDS in Western Samoa: The Legal Framework," *Pacific Health Dialog*, 1995, vol. 2, 65–7. Note that Western Samoa became known as Samoa in 1997.
111 Myriam Abel, "HIV/AIDS in Vanuatu," *Pacific Health Dialog*, 1995, vol. 2, 56–9.
112 Primo Afeau and Ezekial Nukuro, "Solomon Islands HIV/AIDS Programme," *Pacific Health Dialog*, 1995, vol. 2, 62–4.
113 Lisa Williams, "First Pacific Regional HIV/AIDS and STD Conference Opens at Nadi" *Pacific Islands Report*, 24 February 1999. Online. Available at www.pireport.org/articles/1999/02/24/first-pacific-regional-hivaids-and-std-conference-opens-nadi (accessed 8 December 2018).
114 Secretariat of the Pacific Community, *The Pacific Regional Strategy on HIV/AIDS 2004–2008*, Noumea, New Caledonia: Secretariat of the Pacific Community, 2005.
115 UNDP Pacific Centre, Regional Rights Resource Team SPC, and UNAIDS, "HIV, Ethics and Human Rights: Review of Legislation of Pacific Islands Countries. Regional Summary," 2009. Online. Available at www.asia-pacific.undp.org/content/dam/rbap/docs/Research%20&%20Publications/hiv_aids/Pacific_HIV_Review/Pacific_regional_summary_HIV_Ethics_and_HR_reviev.pdf (accessed 8 December 2018). See also individual country reports.
116 Jowitt, "Creating a Framework for HIV/AIDS."
117 Michael O'Keefe, "Contextualising the AIDS Epidemic in the South Pacific: Orthodoxies, Estimates and Evidence," *Australian Journal of International Affairs*, 2011, vol. 65, 185–202.
118 Lawrence J. Hammar, Jone Gucake, and Ferdinand Strobel, "Learning (at) Our Place: Qualitative Research Methods and Researchers Strengthen Fiji's National Response to HIV and AIDS," *Asia Pacific World*, 2013, vol. 4, 80–104.
119 See Secretariat of the Pacific Community, *The Pacific Regional Strategy on HIV and Other STIs for 2009–2013*, Noumea, New Caledonia: Secretariat for the Pacific Community, 2009.
120 Secretariat of the Pacific Community "Release – HIV and AIDS – No Room for Health Professions to Blame," 20 August 2008. Online. Available at http://lists.spc.int/pipermail/press-releases/2008-August/000153.html (accessed 8 December 2018).
121 Nati Tamarua Hermann and Tingika Elikana, "HIV/AIDS in the Cook Islands," *Pacific Health Dialog*, 1995, vol. 2, 54–5.
122 Hermann and Elikana, "HIV/AIDS in the Cook Islands."
123 "PM Voices Concerns Over HIV Case," *Cook Islands News*, 8 January 2011.
124 "HIV Name Advice Sought," *Cook Islands News*, 20 December 2010.
125 "Earlier Responses 'Flawed'," *Cook Islands News*, 27 January 2011.
126 "HIV Fijian Deported," *Fiji Times*, 12 April 2011.
127 "Fiji Times Misreports CI Case," *Cook Islands News*, 11 April 2011.
128 Mileka Lincoln, "Planning for Kalaupapa's Future Means Remembering Its Past," *Hawaii News Now*, 18 May 2015.
129 Lange, "Leprosy in the Cook Islands."
130 "US TV's 'Survivor': The Inside View from Paradise." Online. Available at www.cookislands.org.uk/survivor#.WTEc8hSOrbA (accessed 8 December 2018).

131 Roland Farrugia, "Sustainability of Leprosy Services in South Pacific Islands: The Kiribati Experience," *Leprosy Review*, 2010, vol. 81, 332–5.
132 "Pacific Islanders Pay Heavy Price for Abandoning Traditional Diet," *Bulletin of the World Health Organization*, 2010, vol. 88, 484.
133 United Nations Development Programme Pacific Centre, "Trade, Trade Agreement and Non-Communicable Diseases in the Pacific Islands," *Report of a Meeting Held in Nadi, Fiji. Feb. 11–14, 2013*. Suva: UNDP, 2013. Online. Available at www.undp.org/content/dam/undp/library/hivaids/English/Trade%20Agreements%20and%20NCDs%20in%20the%20Pacific%20Islands%202013.pdf (accessed 8 December 2018).
134 See Deborah B. Gewertz and Frederick Karl Errington, *Cheap Meat: Flap Food Nations in the Pacific Islands*, Berkeley: University of California Press, 2010.
135 See Pacific Community, *Pacific Noncommunicable Diseases Summit: Translating Global and Regional Commitments into Local Action (20–22 June 2016, Tonga). Summit Report*, Nuku'Alofa, Tonga: Pacific Community (SPC), 2016. Online. Available at www.wpro.who.int/southpacific/pic_meeting/2017/documents/12thphmm_session04_04_ncd_annex1_16aug.pdf (accessed 8 December 2018).

PART VI

NEW FORMS OF ACCOUNTABILITY IN A NATIONAL SECURITY WORLD (2001 TO THE PRESENT)

26

DECENTRALIZATION AND PUBLIC–PRIVATE DIPLOMACY IN THE BUSINESS AND HUMAN RIGHTS FIELD

Steven S. Nam

Transnational corporate accountability is a fixture of the business and human rights field. It has generated debate since its modern inception in Nuremberg's courtrooms following the international military tribunal of 1946. Transnational corporate accountability as developed there pointed to universal jurisdiction – the principle that any state could bring a case against an offender. In the United States, the Alien Tort Statute (ATS) had gone from being a little-used relic of the US Judiciary Act of 1789 to serving as a prominent vehicle for universal jurisdiction. It granted federal courts jurisdiction over civil actions "for a tort only, committed in violation of the law of nations."[1] Controversially, it had enabled victims of human rights violations anywhere in the world to sue non-US corporate tortfeasors in US federal courts. The ATS even reached where the much later International Criminal Court (ICC) could not, as Article 25(1) of the Rome Charter of the ICC limits the latter's jurisdiction to natural persons, and so excludes legal entities such as corporations. This essay will shed light on the factors that have sidelined universal jurisdiction in the United States with respect to achieving remedies for "foreign-cubed" matters of corporate accountability, that is, cases in which a foreign plaintiff sues a foreign defendant for acts committed in a foreign state. The essay will then trace the evolution of alternative avenues for redress that have been opened up by decentralized non-state actor participation and that thrive to this day.

Early corporate accountability at Nuremberg

In Nuremberg between 1947 and 1948, the United States tried before its military courts dozens of industrialists from the prominent German companies IG Farben, Flick, and Krupp for their heavy use of slave labor and plundering of businesses in formerly German-occupied territories.[2] The historic import of these industrialist trials seemingly has faded to an ancillary reminder that the American purge of the Nazi elite went beyond government and military leadership. At the time, British fears that the industrialist trials would be an ideological boon to Communism,[3] and the outpouring of criticism from Germans at the resulting convictions, led the United States to take a leading role at the trials.

Despite the political need for German industrial reconstruction and for German support against the Soviet Union, American authorities refused to soften their punitive stance as they strove to establish a liberal postwar international order. The political philosophy of liberalism is characterized by a commitment to citizens' juridical equality and civic rights, the recognition of private property rights, the shaping of economic decisions predominantly by market forces against a backdrop of multilateral institutions, and a representative government that derives its authority from a consenting electorate. It follows that under liberalism, a state and its constituents are subject neither to the external authority of other states nor to the internal authority of castes with special prerogatives, such as those held by the military.[4] A powerful military-industrial complex thrived in Germany after World War I largely because the Allies – out of respect for Germany's sovereignty – had left to it the trials of its own war instigators. Few trials and fewer convictions materialized, confounding prospects for a German transition into liberal democracy with accountable corporate governance. If "the tight network of factories and industries" in the Ruhr Valley managed by iron and steel magnates could be broken up, "then Germany, it was argued, would be prevented from unleashing another war of aggression."[5] Here accountability and liberalism were found to be linked in effect, and the notion that "failure of accountability signified the failure of liberalization"[6] after World War I meant that the United States was determined not to be complacent after that war's even bloodier sequel.

More than 70 years after the end of World War II, there are over 100 liberal states worldwide. This is a testament to the long-standing influence of the United States and its liberal allies. But gone are the days when American dominance could dictate liberalization with minimal regard for the liberal guarantee of respect between states. Varieties of capitalism and their diverse systems of corporate governance have come to trigger conflicting national responses to human rights pressures. Realist critics of the ATS – that is, those focused on the practical impact of actions on international relations – have come to include the US Supreme Court. Chief Justice John Roberts' majority opinion in *Kiobel v. Royal Dutch Petroleum* (2013) referenced "recent objections to extraterritorial applications of the ATS by Canada, Germany, Indonesia, Papua New Guinea, South Africa, Switzerland, and the United Kingdom" along with "diplomatic strife" precipitated by excessive jurisdiction.[7] The next year, Justice Ruth Bader Ginsburg and seven other justices in their opinion for *Daimler AG v. Bauman* (2014) stressed "risks to international comity" through the "expansive view of general jurisdiction posed [to foreign business enterprises]. Other nations do not share the uninhibited approach to personal jurisdiction advanced by the Court of Appeals in this case."[8] *Kiobel* and *Bauman* captured the contemporary reality that diverse systems of corporate governance in capitalism have come to trigger conflicting national responses to human rights pressures. The preponderance of Supreme Court justices across the ideological spectrum weighed in against what they saw as the judicial overreach of ATS litigation.

The Supreme Court decisions seemed to give credence to realist ATS criticisms of universal jurisdiction over foreign companies for its endangerment of international relations, trade, and investment. In fact, recent scholarship has pointed out the dearth of empirical evidence behind that realist criticism. At any rate, supporters of the ATS who had sought extraterritorial legal enforcement of human rights norms now faced a major setback. In spite of liberal aspirations for "the globalization of freedom" and the US human rights regime,[9] the pursuit of transnational corporate accountability unilaterally through the US judiciary proved inconsistent with a core tenet of liberalism itself – that a state and its constituents should not be subject to the external authority of other states. As we will see, even the most liberal of states (including stalwart American allies such as the UK and the Netherlands) protested the external authority of universal jurisdiction over their business enterprises and feared indefinite intervention.

Beginning in the late 1990s, the United States and Germany under the Clinton and Schröder administrations pioneered an inclusive public–private diplomacy model, inviting all stakeholders to the negotiating table including government representatives, culpable companies, and legal representatives for victims of their human rights abuses. After US district courts had dismissed as non-justiciable a pair of related class action lawsuits,[10] settlement talks in this mold regarding wartime forced labor produced a landmark compensation fund in 1999 for victims of the Third Reich. About a decade later the United Nations (UN) Guiding Principles on Business and Human Rights were drafted and adopted by a polycentric constellation of corporate accountability nongovernmental organizations (NGOs),[11] governments, and business enterprises. The Guiding Principles were not a panacea, as many victims of corporate human rights abuses struggled to access concrete remedies due to practical and legal barriers. The Accountability and Remedy Project under Office of the UN High Commissioner for Human Rights stewardship has sought to close this gap. Conventional liberalism views non-state actors as influential, yet only functional at the international level via the state agents allocated to them. Non-state actors' own transnational agency was either not considered or explicitly rejected. Yet these very alternatives presaged the development of a coherent global corporate accountability regime reliant on incentivized cooperation and coordination between stakeholders rather than extraterritorial unilateralism.

The downfall of US alien tort statute litigation

Discussion of critics and proponents of ATS litigation at the turn of the twenty-first century has assumed a simple binary – on the one hand, realist cost-benefit analysts who criticized universal jurisdiction for endangering US foreign policy, and on the other, liberal advocates who conflated the ATS with US leadership in developing a global human rights regime. Scholarship empirically assessing the extent to which ATS legislation against foreign corporations caused interstate friction has shown that actual US foreign policy implications were limited and short-lived.[12] Moreover, the historical record, while admittedly brief, does not support dire realist projections of economic downturns and exacerbated national security threats. The first ATS litigation against a multinational corporation for aiding and abetting human rights violations was filed in 1996 by Burmese citizens and human rights groups against the US oil company Unocal.[13] The *Kiobel* (2013) and *Bauman* (2014) decisions were game-changing, and so have precluded definitive answers as to whether those realist predictions would have been borne out – or if hindrances to US foreign policy would have proven superficial relative to the expected benefits of a strengthened global human rights regime.

The *Kiobel* plaintiffs were Nigerian citizens who alleged that Dutch, British, and Nigerian oil-exploration corporations aided and abetted the Nigerian government in property destruction, forced exile, and extrajudicial killings. The *Bauman* plaintiffs were Argentines who sued DaimlerChrysler AG for its Argentinian subsidiary's collaboration with a right-wing military junta that kidnapped, tortured, and murdered 22 labor leaders during the "Dirty War" of the 1970s. In neither case did the US Supreme Court find a sufficient nexus with the United States for jurisdiction. Per *Kiobel*'s majority opinion, claims against foreign business enterprises must "touch and concern the territory of the United States," and "do so with sufficient force to displace the presumption against extraterritorial application."[14] The *Bauman* majority opinion was backed by eight justices and asserted that *Kiobel* "rendered plaintiffs' ATS … claims infirm," thereby entrenching *Kiobel.*[15] Indeed, Professor John Ruggie, the special representative of the UN secretary-general on business and human rights, had feared in the runup to *Kiobel* that it would become an existential threat to ATS litigation, which he viewed positively as "an entire juridical edifice for redressing gross violations of human rights."[16]

The decisiveness of *Kiobel*'s rollback of the ATS and especially extraterritorial corporate liability, delivered in blunt judicial language that reappeared in *Bauman,* raised two questions that the conventional realist-versus-liberalist debate had not adequately addressed. Why were liberal stalwarts such as the United Kingdom, the Netherlands, and Germany – close US allies who would seem to favor an expansive global human rights regime over realist concerns – in fact among the most strident critics of universal jurisdiction over their culpable companies? Their governments, among many others, had supported the ICC (albeit sans jurisdiction over corporations), in contrast to the skeptical George W. Bush administration. And what compelled seven justices across the ideological spectrum to join Justice Ginsburg's *Bauman* opinion in rejecting the cosmopolitan argument that US federal courts have a "strong interest in adjudicating and redressing international human rights abuses,"[17] without so much as a mention of the potential benefits of those courts doing so? After all, the argument they denied did align with the liberal state's fundamental right for citizens to be treated and a duty to treat others as free individuals and ethical subjects, which might well outweigh the considerations of international rapport found in *Bauman.*

Effective accountability and liberalization are interwoven, and gradual expansion of the international liberal community has long been regarded as a preferable outcome for liberal states and peoples.[18] But to that end, the liberalizing force of universal jurisdiction over foreign business enterprises proved inconsistent with what prominent "liberal peace" theorist Michael W. Doyle deemed "the basic postulate of liberal international theory … that states have the right to be free from foreign intervention."[19] This precept is enshrined in the ideals of the UN Charter and has become a postwar truism despite a margin for certain sanctioned interventions:[20] In correlation with citizens' rights to liberty, the states that democratically represent them are entitled to political independence. Mutual respect for these rights forms in turn the cornerstone of international liberal theory. Thus, per economic liberalism, are economically interdependent states incentivized to resolve conflicts peacefully. Universal jurisdiction's judicial fiat over foreign companies ran contrary to a multilateral liberal framework under which individuals are free to establish private international ties without state interference, as "[p]rofitable exchanges between merchants … create a web of mutual advantages and commitments that bolsters sentiments of public respect."[21] At the state level, this interdependence of commerce has shaped "crosscutting transnational ties that serve as lobbies of mutual accommodation … ensur[ing] by their variety that no single conflict sours an entire relationship" and buttressing a global trade network of liberal as well as illiberal states.[22]

A discordance immediately developed between universal jurisdiction's unilateralism and the multilateral conduits through which many business enterprises operate. A web of cross-border contacts has helped sustain the contemporary liberal order. Stable expectations protect, in turn, the interdependent benefits of trade. Institutions have developed to reinforce that, and notwithstanding regular disputes, institutions such as "the

European Union, the North American Free Trade Agreement (NAFTA), and the Organization of American States … create a culture in which peace is expected and provide forums for negotiation."[23] It is true that these institutions are vulnerable to isolating trends, including from liberal quarters, as illustrated by the United Kingdom's vote to exit the European Union in 2016. Yet transnational consultations between state actors increasingly had welcomed non-state actor involvement. The use of related channels and tools had become customary in the international liberal community. Universal jurisdiction over foreign business enterprises bypassed intermediary multilateral institutions and disabled these consultations. In its extraterritorial push for greater accountability and liberalization, universal jurisdiction ironically disregarded channels and tools of the liberal international community. This was the crux of universal jurisdiction's mismatch with transnational corporate accountability and its rejection by many liberal states.

Of course, the case for nonintervention is much weaker where transnational business enterprises have abused economic interdependence at the expense of human rights and where oversight by host and home states has failed or is nonexistent. The preeminent political philosopher John Rawls asserted that the duty of nonintervention would "have to be qualified in the general case of … grave violations of human rights."[24] "[C]ondemnation by the world society" is merited when "domestic institutions violate human rights … [a] people's right to independence and self-determination is no shield from that condemnation nor even from coercive intervention by other peoples in grave cases."[25] Determining when and how to engage in an intervention is a challenging task for states, given the tension between justice and order as well as the array of options available, including military force. A proportionate, appropriate response is key to obtaining international backing. Disparate categories of human rights violators have warranted different types of intervention.

The liberal international community's general acceptance of intervention as a contingency tool has corresponded to its application in acute human rights crises. Since the 1990s, humanitarian interventions of limited duration in Somalia, Haiti, Bosnia, Kosovo, Liberia, and Sudan garnered significant international approval. By contrast, the use of universal jurisdiction to reach corporate human rights violators in order to punish them through civil lawsuits has drawn condemnation, as referenced in *Kiobel.* Realists have cited institutional competence arguments. These oppose inexpert and insulated judicial interference in issues with foreign policy implications. Yet these arguments do not explain past instances of the successful employment of universal jurisdiction over non-corporate human rights violators.[26]

To advocates of universal jurisdiction, litigation against companies that draws on the ATS offers a fairly even playing field and a fair chance of success. Advocates of universal jurisdiction offered compelling justifications for it, including limited capacity of victims, limited capability in the courts of the victims' home states, and questionable impartiality given strong government support for foreign investment. Yet it remains troubling that universal jurisdiction over transnational business enterprises required US courts to dictate unilaterally which claims foreign states should recognize against their own companies. Universal jurisdiction, contrary to its cosmopolitan intent, was capable of producing new strains of international law dressed in universality but in fact shaped by US domestic legal understandings. As a form of intervention, it could encroach upon foreign liberal and illiberal state regimes alike for an indefinite duration with little conventional precedent, giving rise to "fear of American international law 'hegemony,'"[27] in the words of Justice Stephen Breyer.

A lack of available standards complicated relief in US courts. There has been no framework of expectations or continuity built by cooperative liberal institutions across international borders. In 1999, Judge Dickinson Debevoise dismissed four civil lawsuits filed in New Jersey against German companies culpable of wartime forced labor, although "[e]very human instinct yearns to remediate in some way the immeasurable wrongs inflicted … in which corporate Germany unquestionably participated." He lamented the dearth of comparable domestic case law to guide a judicial ruling: Had his court attempted to design "appropriate reparations for the plaintiffs in the present case, it would lack any standards to apply … Wrongs were suffered not only by the classes of persons represented … but also by many other classes of persons in many lands." Such shortcomings in the actual execution of universal jurisdiction over foreign business enterprises stemmed from the difficult nature of universal jurisdiction's autonomy. These difficulties were arguably obfuscated by cosmopolitan intentions and presentation. Judge Debevoise asked, for instance: "What conceivable standard could a single court [use to] arrive at a fair allocation of resources among all the deserving groups? By what practical means could a single court acquire the information needed to fashion such a standard?" He referenced the importance of multilateral fora for the redress of forced labor in wartime instituted by German companies. Such redress

> was a task which the nations involved sought to perform as they negotiated the Potsdam Agreement, the Paris Agreement, the Transition Agreement and the 2+4 Treaty. It would be presumptuous for this court to attempt to do a better job.[28]

His observation was borne out when the German wartime forced labor issue did in fact find resolution away from US courts – through decentralized, public-private diplomacy.

Settling Nazi-era wartime forced labor: inclusive public–private diplomacy as an alternative to the courts

In December 1999, a settlement redressing German companies' use of forced labor under the Third Reich was reached via political negotiation in Berlin, during which all relevant stakeholders had direct representation at the table. It was a breakthrough for transnational corporate accountability. The settlement amounted to 10 billion marks, or approximately $5.2 billion, dwarfing later ATS lawsuit judgments and settlements. The contrasts between these successful negotiations designed by the Clinton and Schröder administrations and extraterritorial human rights litigation are instructive. First, the settlement saw a high level of acceptance among its parties, who lodged no subsequent challenges against its validity (although post-settlement disputes arose over peripheral issues such as accrued interest).[29] Second, the claims money was broadly allocated. Compensation went to forced laborers of the German companies sued in US courts, to surviving victims of defunct German firms,[30] and to forced laborers who had not been party to the independently dismissed district court civil lawsuits. This outcome arguably exceeded what would have been possible with even the most favorable ATS lawsuit outcomes against foreign business enterprises.

Over the two-plus decades since the end of the Cold War – roughly the same period as the Berlin settlement talks – decentralized diplomacy involving varied institutions (advocacy groups, businesses, consulting firms, philanthropic organizations) was rising in prominence. Such non-traditional political actors were addressing governance gaps between potent economic actors on the one hand, and the capacity of societies to hold them accountable, legally or otherwise, on the other. The emergence of these actors reflected the reality that international law's formal structure is limited to imposing human rights duties on states that ratify treaties.[31] Private companies cannot be so obligated. The interests of governmental and private entities clashed increasingly across transnational political economies rather than purely domestic ones. Without the direct participation of business as well as civil society, nuanced cross-border matters defied simple legal resolution. Corporate legal scholars Curtis Milhaupt and Katharina Pistor point out that political economy determines the "contestability" of the law, or "a measure of the extent to which law is subject to a process of creative destruction ... [by] private, social, as well as government actors as opposed to being an instrument exclusively in the hands of uncontested political authorities."[32] Creative (if temporary) destruction of corporate immunity under international law was precisely what occurred in Berlin. The talks' non-traditional actors complemented and cooperated with chief negotiators dispatched by the intermediary US and German governments, adding layers of feedback and calibration unavailable to the in any case aborted judicial route. The US camp regarded these non-traditional actors' overt participation as critical for this reason. The chief negotiator dispatched by the Clinton Administration, Stuart Eizenstat, persuaded the German side

> that to have an enduring agreement all stakeholders needed to be included – the class-action lawyers, Eastern European countries whose forced workers had never been paid, the state of Israel, and the [Holocaust] Claims Conference, which represented the interests of the Jewish slave laborers. This made for a messy and more complex negotiation ... But in the end I knew it would lead to a more satisfying result.[33]

The influence of private organizations and civil society groups on interstate relations has expanded, and inclusive public–private diplomacy, with its creative and democratic style, has continued to adapt to that expanded influence, accommodating both advocates and increasingly powerful multinational businesses. Its process does not depend on the legal protection of human rights in relationships between private actors, which is in fact a tenuous shield only indirectly guaranteed through positive state obligations. Instead, both state and non-state actors support direct negotiations among the concerned parties by helping to level the playing field. In the case of the Berlin negotiations, state efforts to convene representatives of the entire range of forced labor victims and of the culpable companies brought about a compromise tailored to their circumstances that both sides could accept with finality, without having to rely on unilateral judicial dicta. We now turn to the respective incentives of participant businesses, victims, and states in greater depth.

Restitution and relief from corporate transgressors via a negotiated settlement are the most visible results of inclusive public–private diplomacy. Yet Doyle's "lobbies of mutual accommodation" also offer restorative advantages. The culpable business enterprise is afforded opportunities to improve its reputation proactively, rather than having to react only, by defending against a lawsuit or settling out of court before a judgment is handed down, for purposes of damage control. In the case of the 1999 settlement, German companies that had collaborated with the Nazi regime saw marked improvement in their public image due to the public's perception of their willingness to acknowledge and make amends for forced labor. By contrast, their Japanese counterparts have no such settlement for wartime transgressions and have continued to suffer negative headlines with reputational effects on their products. Stuart Eizenstat, the chief US negotiator at the Berlin talks, noted that victory in court would not necessarily have been satisfactory outcome enough for the German companies. According to Eizenstat, the companies "had never given much credence to the legal case against them. What they really wanted was to remove the threat of economic sanctions, boycotts, and other recriminations … that would haunt them even if they were victorious in court."[34] Indeed, the companies insisted on "legal peace" in the Berlin negotiations, that is, plaintiffs' dismissal of any pending Holocaust-era lawsuit against German corporate defendants and the promise of US government Statements of Interest to discourage future litigation, and this was accepted by all parties to the negotiations. Such incorporation of legal peace into a restitution scheme closes the door to the potential for new litigation. By contrast, even after *Kiobel* there have been fresh lawsuits in various fora against Royal Dutch Shell for damage done in Nigeria, and lawsuits continue to be initiated to this day.[35]

There are advantages of inclusive public–private diplomacy for victims of corporate human rights violations (and for their advocates) as well, and these advantages are unavailable in extraterritorial human rights litigation. The Berlin settlement was transnational: it covered victims of wartime forced labor across nation-state borders, providing them a uniform resolution. Their advocates would have been hard-pressed to achieve that by way of separate domestic plaintiff classes. Furthermore, a settlement can be structured so that it does not fixate solely on monetary compensation for each harmed individual, but rather takes "due account of the harm inflicted on groups of people, ethnic groups, and communities … and incorporates a collective dimension" for posterity.[36] Appropriately, the German law that created the foundation for distributing settlement compensation began with a preamble acknowledging responsibility for corporate abuses under the Third Reich and pledging to sustain the memory of those injustices. Corporations entangled in litigation, by contrast, are loath to admit any sort of responsibility for fear that it could be used against them in future lawsuits. A decentralized and inclusive settlement process can furthermore preclude the possibility of appeals by would-be corporate defendants, and so victims can avoid the risk of a higher court reversing a victory and denying them redress.

Speedy compensation for victims can be another advantage of circumventing judicial proceedings in favor of public–private diplomacy. A binding international treaty or legislative reform in Congress regarding corporate accountability are worthy goals, but it should be noted that they require extensive deliberations without any guarantee of tangible result even after new norms are in place. Former UN High Commissioner for Human Rights Louise Arbour noted that dependence on future binding norms "would be frankly very ambitious … considering how long this would take and how much damage could be done in the meantime."[37] The German settlement, by contrast, resulted in payouts that reached victims in a shorter period of time than would be possible under US class action litigation rules.[38]

Inter-state relations can be improved through the proxy of big business in a setting of inclusive public–private diplomacy to strengthen transnational corporate accountability. In July 2015, Mitsubishi Materials Corporation issued a formal apology at the Simon Wiesenthal Center's Museum of Tolerance for the nearly 900 US prisoners of war who had been used as slave laborers by its predecessor company Mitsubishi Mining Corporation. The few remaining survivors and victims' families welcomed the apology; a former advisor to Japanese prime minister Shinzō Abe who was in attendance "expressed regret that it had taken so long" to deliver.[39] The apology presumably strengthened Japan's alliance with the United States in June 2016, Mitsubishi Materials announced an initial settlement regarding thousands of Chinese forced laborers. Offered were a formal apology and compensation of up to $56 million depending on the number of victims' claims. The announcement has been described as a catalyst for improved ties between Beijing and Tokyo.

Decentralized, inclusive public–private diplomacy may be applicable to other kinds of situations, as well. The US and other countries allocate considerable resources to their own institutions for international development and trade. Many multilateral development banks and other state-based international financial institutions already have, or are currently developing, so-called independent accountability mechanisms (IAMs). These are internal institutional processes for resolving grievances that can be formally lodged by communities and individuals who have suffered harm from institution-financed projects. The Organization for Economic Cooperation and Development (OECD), which is comprised of developed liberal economies seeking to stimulate economic progress and international trade, has followed suit. In 2000, newly established National Contact Points in each member state began accepting complaints about the failure of some companies to comply with the OECD Guidelines for Multinational Enterprises.[40]

These are all noteworthy actual or potential successes of inclusive public–private diplomacy. It has also has revealed its share of limitations. States plagued by poor relations with other states or by conflicting national interests may find it difficult to embark upon negotiating corporate accountability matters with the non-state stakeholders in tow. The US government could have reprised its intermediary role of 1999 in more than one instance of large-scale corporate human rights violations, yet failed to act. The calculus of US government interests did not favor South African Apartheid victims adversely impacted by foreign companies' conduct[41] or Korean wartime forced laborers.[42] Human rights harms on a smaller scale often fail to attract governments' notice at all, and victims can at best hope that NGOs in the area of business and human rights take up their neglected cases.[43] States also have hindered their own image-conscious corporations from moving for reconciliation and redress if that would clash with states' own political aims. For instance, even though the Japanese government approved of Mitsubishi's settlement with Chinese forced laborers, it allegedly opposed Mitsubishi regarding the company's wish to pursue settlement negotiations with Korean forced laborers.[44] Given such state neglect and governance gaps in transnational corporate accountability, the importance of non-state stakeholders is all the greater.

Proliferation of the UN guiding principles on business and human rights

John Ruggie, special representative of the UN secretary-general on business and human rights, commissioned a comprehensive study of the varied uses of extraterritorial jurisdiction in advance of the June 2011 launch of his brainchild, the *UN Guiding Principles on*

Business and Human Rights (UNGPs). The study concluded that "multilateral measures are likely to be seen as more acceptable than unilateral measures; principles-based approaches are less problematic than prescriptive rules-based approaches."[45] Ruggie's UNGPs have indeed thrived on multilateral, principles-based guidance regarding transnational corporate accountability. In comparison to such multilateral negotiations, universal jurisdiction can be a quagmire. The General Principles call for:

> (a) States' existing obligations to respect, protect and fulfil human rights and fundamental freedoms; (b) The role of business enterprises as specialized organs of society performing specialized functions, required to comply with all applicable laws and to respect human rights; (c) The need for rights and obligations to be matched to appropriate and effective remedies when breached. These Guiding Principles apply to all States and to all business enterprises, both transnational and others … contributing to a socially sustainable globalization. Nothing in these Guiding Principles should be read as creating new international law obligations, or as limiting or undermining any legal obligations a State may have undertaken or be subject to under international law with regard to human rights.[46]

UNGPs are both aspirational and pragmatic, as this language illustrates. They are a rare example of an international "soft law" instrument with great impact that was not negotiated by national governments. The UNGPs have quickly gained widespread acceptance as a reference point for public actors such as states, state-created institutions, and the UN, and for private actors such as corporations and NGOs.

The UNGPs depart from conventional perceptions of adversarial relationships among states, businesses, and civil society. They herald a polycentric governance for corporate accountability that depends on the coordinated efforts of all three groups to prevent, navigate, and redress corporate human rights violations.[47] Even as the UNGPs were welcomed in the global liberal community for their emphasis on improving multilateral grievance mechanisms and on voluntary initiatives (unlike ATS lawsuits that threatened universal jurisdiction over corporations), they were in fact challenging state sovereignty – or more precisely, working around it. Focusing on the United States, international law scholar Peter Spiro sees a shift:

> Existing models of international law and international relations are ill-equipped to project the more complete assimilation of the United States into international norm regimes. On the one hand, norm-driven theories fail to explain how international actors will overcome entrenched US resistance to international lawmaking … On the other hand, rationalist theories systematically underestimate the incentives that the United States may have for buying into international regimes. By segregating interests and actors along national lines, these models miss transnational accelerants of international norms … Transnationality affords nondomestic actors enhanced leverage in pressing US participation in international regimes.[48]

The UNGPs' promise is predicated on such ongoing deconstruction and transnational dispersion of the traditional liberal framework based on discrete states.

Corporate accountability NGOs pierce the veil of statehood regularly: Human Rights Watch, the Centre for Research on Multinational Organizations (SOMO), the Center for International Environmental Law (CIEL), and other civil society leaders advise governments regarding policy while rallying public opinion into a form of leverage. Unconstrained by a state-hegemonic concept of international human rights law and with their newfound tool of the UNGPs, they have pressured transnational business enterprises on human rights due diligence, especially regarding the improvement of self-enforcement mechanisms. Respect for sovereignty binds the global liberal community, yet these NGOs continue to advocate changes in domestic and foreign state institutions' accountability practices. The NGOs often refer to the UNGPs as they do so; the UNGPs are serving as a needed "authoritative focal point around which the expectations and behavior of the relevant actors can converge."[49] Some 41 leading domestic and international NGOs and advocates highlighted the UNGPs' non-judicial mechanism effectiveness criteria in a recent joint letter to the chairman and president of the Export-Import Bank of the United States. The bank's grievance mechanism was created to handle claims from individuals and communities harmed by overseas bank-funded corporate projects. The letter both praised the bank's grievance mechanism and offered recommendations for its further development.[50] It detailed metrics for the mechanism's efficacy, such as legitimacy, accessibility, predictability, equitability, and transparency. In cyclical and polycentric fashion, civil society input, informed by the UNGPs and directed at domestic institutions, can thus reach transnational corporate activity and heighten accountability standards, without disrupting state sovereignty.

The UNGPs have permeated the governance structures of representative global institutions, especially with respect to their universality and clarity, to the benefit of states. Many of the multilateral, principles-based concepts were integrated into institutional language, from the human rights chapter of the OECD Guidelines for Multinational Enterprises, to provisions in the International Finance Corporation's new funding standards, to the social responsibility standard issued by the International Standards Organization. By conditioning project approval and/or funding on compliance with the UNGPs, states and their institutions have been able to lessen the likelihood of becoming implicated in overseas corporate abuse due to having supported culpable firms. Liberal states' calls to their business enterprises to adhere to the UNGPs has translated into "much-needed support to host states that lack the capacity to implement fully and effectively regulatory environments on their own."[51] States and their transnational businesses have been navigating disparate patchworks of corporate governance regimes across different host governments; in the long term, an increasingly uniform regulatory playing field worldwide could reduce costs for them.

In the context of the UNGPs, business enterprises have become actors rather than mere objects of the carrot and stick approach. Their participation has been key to multi-stakeholder initiatives (MSIs), which are industry-wide initiatives designed by a polycentric and transnational array of government, corporate, and civil society stakeholders to encourage voluntary standards and verification schemes. The UNGPs note that in complex operating contexts, business enterprises would do well to engage not only with "expertise and cross-functional consultation within the enterprise, but also to consult externally with credible, independent experts, including from … multi-stakeholder initiatives" in their respective industries.[52] The Extractive Industries Transparency Initiative (EITI) is an example of a MSI whose global membership and credibility among liberal states has grown even as it is subject to ongoing constructive criticism from civil society.[53] EITI invites greater scrutiny and accountability for the once largely opaque extractive industries sector. Overseen by a polycentric and international board including representatives from corporations, civil society, and government, it is prominent among a growing number of MSIs. Each is adapted to the distinct circumstances of a given industry. These MSIs have the common objective of incentivizing every stakeholder to cooperate for their respective economic, reputational, ethical, and moral interests. To the extent an MSI's legitimacy is strengthened via polycentric feedback and checks, it can counteract adversarial zero-sum attitudes concerning transnational corporate accountability in the relevant industry.

Joint development and implementation of the accountability and remedy project

The liberal community has come to rely more and more on the UNGPs. A pillar of these UNGPs is effective state-based judicial mechanisms that ensure access to remedy for transnational corporate human rights abuses. However, these have yet to coalesce. Under a mandate from the Human Rights Council, the Office of the UN High Commissioner for Human Rights launched the Accountability and Remedy Project in November 2014,[54] requesting and receiving input from a wide range of state, corporate, and NGO stakeholder groups. This project received submissions from states (including the United States and the European Union), from the International Organisation of Employers, from leading corporate accountability NGOs (including the Centre for Research on Multinational Corporations or SOMO,[55] the International Corporate Accountability Roundtable (ICAR), and other business and human rights nonprofit organizations, and from individual attorneys, law firms, and academia. The project drew upon all this feedback for its own independent study.[56] The project's study noted that improving access to remedy in practice will require "concerted and multifaceted efforts from all states … and closer international cooperation,"[57] especially with respect to challenges "exacerbated in cross-border cases."[58]

Improvements in state-based judicial mechanisms for victims in transnational cases would address two problem areas. First, awareness and effective use of non-judicial grievance mechanisms at the disposal of workers and affected communities have lagged, in spite of NGOs' assistance worldwide. Many of these workers and communities fear that these non-judicial grievance mechanisms "reflect the power imbalance between companies and rights-holders and … might become substitutes for judicial processes."[59] Second, domestic legal regimes have left undeveloped their systems for redressing transnational corporate human rights abuses, as they have tended to focus on business activities and impacts within their own territories.[60] Years before the UNGPs, there were suggestions for creating domestic pathways for states to "strengthen judicial capacity to hear complaints and enforce remedies against all corporations operating or based in their territory, while also protecting against frivolous claims,"[61] yet any such pathway would have had to operate in a unilateral vacuum with respect to cross-border cases. The impediments to extraterritorial jurisdiction over business enterprises that this essay has discussed, along with the perennial and troublesome requirement of "reasonableness" for extraterritorial jurisdiction,[62] require greater coordination among countries to develop complementary transnational judicial mechanisms.

The Accountability and Remedy Project has benefited from polycentric input and the legitimacy that comes with that as it has provided a guidance for "cross-border cooperation between relevant state agencies and judicial bodies, tailored to the contexts of both public law enforcement and private law claims."[63] The project's scope is realistic, and it notes the varied contexts in which these efforts must operate:

> There are many differences between jurisdictions in terms of legal structures, cultures, traditions, resources and stages of development, all of which have implications for the issues covered by the guidance. For instance, some legal systems are highly codified, whereas others place more reliance on legal development through judicial decisions and precedent. Some domestic legal systems are adversarial, whereas others are inquisitorial, and some contain elements of both. Some legal systems are federal, or devolved in nature, whereas others are unitary. Some legal systems provide for corporate criminal liability, and some do not. The guidance is therefore necessarily flexible and anticipates the need for adaptation to local needs and contexts. Identifying areas where improvement is needed in domestic legal regimes may be a complex task, and in some jurisdictions a formal legal review may be necessary.[64]

The project has recommended facilitating "detection, investigation, prosecution, and enforcement of cross-border cases concerning business involvement in severe human rights abuses" with reference to new normative frameworks. In such frameworks, requests for interstate legal assistance and collaboration would be recognized under "appropriate bilateral and multilateral arrangements," and joint investigation teams would be a viable prospect.[65] The project envisions mutually negotiated agreements and initiatives that draw upon multiple states' domestic judicial mechanisms in tandem to produce rapid responses, in contrast to universal jurisdiction's threat of forcing unilateral judgments upon the business enterprises of averse states. The project also admonished negotiating states to recognize "patterns of inward and outward foreign direct investment" so as to avoid self-interested biases and favoritism,[66] and urged judicial bodies to impose restitution upon companies that takes into account the companies' human rights due diligence (this reflects input from businesses at the time of the project's development).[67] The project has also recommended accessible information repositories for points of contact and outstanding requests and the involvement of judicial and enforcement agency personnel in multilateral networks for exchange of know-how.[68] Such collaborative elements are not new to international arrangements in the area of law enforcement.[69] Yet there is little precedent for extending such collaborative elements to relevant judicial bodies.

More radical concepts for judicial mechanisms involving binding legal instruments, such as the creation of a new jurisdiction over business enterprises appear impractical and are very unlikely to be adopted, due to a lack of control on the enterprises' parts as well as any assurance of high-level representation for state and non-state stakeholders. At the 2016 American Society of International Law Roundtable on Business and Human Rights, further ideas for innovative judicial mechanisms were discussed, including national mechanisms overseen by regional human rights commissioners to be appointed by the UN Human Rights Commission, or by regional human rights courts where applicable; specialized permanent tribunals at a regional level; the extension of the ICC's Rome Statute to apply to corporate, as well as natural persons; and the establishment of a corporate human rights chamber at the International Court of Justice (ICJ) in the Hague. National mechanisms and regional tribunals would require impartial institutional oversight and clear governing guidelines for the sake of convergence in enforcement and to avoid deterioration into arbitrary silos. Expansion of the ICC's jurisdiction to include corporations or the formation of a separate corporate human rights chamber at the ICJ would depend on the international community's buy-in, which would be difficult to achieve without diluting high standards for enforcement. National systems of corporate governance, including the attitudes of business toward human rights, cannot be expected to cohere on their own amidst clashing political interests and varieties of capitalism that have disincentivized their convergence. The more that polycentric elements can be introduced into the development and implementation of the above proposals, the greater their chances of coming to fruition.

The Accountability and Remedy Project, tapping into the liberal internationalism characteristic of the UNGPs, has called for state-based judicial mechanisms to transcend conventional bounds of comity with respect to transnational corporate abuses. Their proactive cross-border coordination is intended to shape mutually acceptable resolutions ending in concrete remedy. Whether the project can gain the kind of polycentric traction enjoyed by the UNGPs remains to be seen. Its success would represent the latest contribution to a nascent, coherent global corporate accountability regime driven by stakeholder cooperation as opposed to extraterritorial unilateralism.

Conclusion

The continuing failure of corporations to converge on a most efficient form of corporate governance underscores the importance of the evolution of the field of business and human rights. Legal scholars Henry Hansmann and Reinier Kraakman famously predicted that international competition would drive business enterprises, as well as their host states, to converge on a set of corporate governance best practices.[70] In reality, however, "the continuance of states' ability to regulate (alongside corporations' ability to influence states' policy)" has fostered "continued differentiation in regulatory regimes,"[71] while market forces remain subject to distortion by protectionist governments and to national silos in competition enforcement.[72] These are unfavorable global conditions, and state and business interests continue to leave governance gaps. The business and human rights field has adapted to these realities by providing tools and lessons for the polycentric resolution of these governance gaps.

Notes

1 The Alien Tort Statute (ATS) is a provision of the 1789 Judiciary Act that enables federal courts jurisdiction over civil actions for torts committed in violation of, as noted, "the law of nations." It is also known as 28 US Code §1350. Online. Available awww.govinfo.gov/content/pkg/USCODE-2009-title28/pdf/USCODE-2009-title28-partIV-chap85-sec1350.pdf (accessed 22 December 2018).

2 See International Military Tribunal, *Trial of the Major War Criminals Before the International Military Tribunal in Nuremberg*, Nuremberg: Secretariat of the Tribunal, 1947–9. The convictions from a fourth trial before a French military tribunal, that of Saar magnate Hermann Roechling and several associates, were reversed on appeal in 1949. Grietje Baars, "Capitalism's Victor's Justice? The Hidden Stories Behind the Prosecution of Industrialists Post-WWII," in Kevin

J. Heller and Gerry Simpson (eds.) *The Hidden Histories of War Crimes Trials*, Oxford: Oxford University Press, 2013, p. 188.

3 Tom Bower, *The Pledge Betrayed: America and Britain and the Denazification of Post-War Germany*, New York: Doubleday, 1982, pp. 287–354.

4 Michael W. Doyle, "Liberalism and Foreign Policy," in Steve Smith, Amelia Hadfield, and Tim Dunne (eds.) *Foreign Policy: Theories, Actors, Cases*, Oxford: Oxford University Press, 2012, pp. 55–6.

5 S. Jonathan Wiesen, *West German Industry and the Challenge of the Nazi Past*, Chapel Hill: University of North Carolina Press, 2001, p. 54.

6 Rudi Teitel, "Transitional Jurisprudence: The Role of Law in Political Transformation," *Yale Law Journal*, 1997, vol. 106, 2039.

7 *Kiobel v. Royal Dutch Petroleum*, 133 S. Ct. 1659 at 1669 (2013). Online. Available at https://supreme.justia.com/cases/federal/us/569/108 (accessed 22 December 2018). Per *Kiobel*, foreign tortfeasors including corporate human rights violators may no longer be sued in US courts by their foreign victims via the Alien Tort Statute (ATS) without a sufficient nexus to US territory.

8 *Daimler AG v. Bauman*, 134 S. Ct. 763 (2014). Online. Available at www.supremecourt.gov/opinions/13pdf/11-965_1qm2.pdf (accessed 22 December 2018).

9 Harold H. Koh, "The Globalization of Freedom," *Yale Journal of International Law*, 2001, vol. 26, 305.

10 Michael J. Bazyler, *Holocaust Justice: The Battle for Restitution in America's Courts*, New York: New York University Press, 1982, pp. 59–83.

11 UN Office of the High Commissioner of Human Rights, *Guiding Principles on Business and Human Rights: Implementing the United Nations "Protect, Respect and Remedy" Framework*, New York: United Nations, 2011. HR/PUB/11/04. Online. Available at www.ohchr.org/Documents/Publications/GuidingPrinciplesBusinessHR_EN.pdf (accessed 22 December 2018). Hereafter *Guiding Principles*.

12 Robert Knowles, "A Realist Defense of the Alien Tort Statute," *Washington University Law Review*, 2011, vol. 88, 1173.

13 *Doe I v. Unocal Corp.*, 963 F. Supp 880, 883–4 (C.D. Cal. 1997). ATS lawsuits targeting foreign corporations began arising shortly thereafter. See, e.g., *Wiwa v. Royal Dutch Petroleum Co.*, No. 96 Civ. 8386 (KMW) (HBP), 1998 US Dist. LEXIS 23064 (S.D.N.Y. 25 September 1998); *Sarei v. Rio Tinto*, 221 F. Supp.2d 1116 (C.D. Cal. 2002); In re South Africa Apartheid Litigation, 346 F. Supp. 2d 538 (S.D.N.Y. 2004).

14 *Kiobel*, 133 S. Ct. at 1669.

15 *Bauman*, 134 S. Ct. at 763. Whereas *Kiobel* limited subject matter jurisdiction in transnational human rights cases using the ATS, *Bauman* limited the ability of courts to assert personal general jurisdiction over foreign corporations in transnational cases.

16 John Ruggie, "Kiobel and Corporate Social Responsibility," Issues Brief, Harvard Kennedy School, 2012, 6. Online. Available at sites.hks.harvard.edu/m-rcbg/CSRI/KIOBEL_AND_-CORPORATE_SOCIAL_RESPONSIBILITY%20(3).pdf (accessed 30 September 2018). *Kiobel* restricted the ATS but did not apply to other statutes authorizing federal human rights litigation. The Torture Victim Protection Act, the Anti-Terrorism Act, the Trafficking Victims Protection Act, and the "state sponsors of terrorism" exception to the Foreign Sovereign Immunities Act remain unaffected.

17 *Bauman*, 134 S. Ct. at 763.

18 John Rawls, *The Law of Peoples*, Cambridge, MA: Harvard University Press, 1999, p. 82.

19 Michael W. Doyle, "Kant, Liberal Legacies, and Foreign Affairs," *Philosophy and Public Affairs*, 1983, vol. 12, 213. See also General Assembly Resolution 2625 (XXV), "Declaration on Principles of International Law Concerning Friendly Relations and Cooperation Among States in Accordance with the Charter of the United Nations" (24 October 1970) ("No State or group of States has the right to intervene, directly or indirectly, for any reason whatever, in the internal or external affairs of any other state."). Online. Available at https://documents-dds-ny.un.org/doc/RESOLUTION/GEN/NR0/348/90/IMG/NR034890.pdf?OpenElement (accessed 22 December 2018).

20 UN Charter, Article 2. Online. Available at www.un.org/en/charter-united-nations/ (accessed 22 December 2018).
21 Doyle, "Kant, Liberal Legacies, and Foreign Affairs," 213.
22 Doyle, "Kant, Liberal Legacies, and Foreign Affairs," 231–2.
23 Joseph S. Nye, Jr. and David A. Welch, *Understanding Global Conflict and Cooperation*, London: Pearson, 2013, p. 209.
24 Rawls, *The Law of Peoples*, p. 37.
25 Rawls, *The Law of Peoples*, p. 38.
26 Special tribunals other than at Nuremberg have prosecuted criminal cases against individuals for business activities that abetted war crimes. See, e.g., *Prosecutor v. Nahimana, Barayagwiza, and Ngeze (the Media Case)*, Case No. ICTR-99-52-T (International Criminal Tribunal for Rwanda Trial Chamber I, 3 December 2003).
27 Stephen Breyer, *The Court and the World: American Law and the New Global Realities*, New York: Alfred A. Knopf, 2015, p. 148.
28 Burger-Fischer v. Degussa AG, 65 F. Supp. 2d. 248 (D.N.J. 1999).
29 Stuart E. Eizenstat, *Imperfect Justice: Looted Assets, Slave Labor, and the Unfinished Business of World War II*, New York: PublicAffairs, 2003. According to Eizenstat, the chief negotiator of the German forced labor settlement talks, "in a negotiation, a lasting result is more likely to emerge by including everyone with a stake in the outcome rather than by freezing out people who may be left resentful. It is a way of neutralizing adversaries." Eizenstat, *Imperfect Justice*, p. 217.
30 Approximately 1.25 million victims received funds from the settlement. Michael J. Bazyler, "The Holocaust Restitution Movement in Comparative Perspective," *Berkeley Journal of International Law*, 2002, vol. 20, 24–5.
31 John Ruggie, *Just Business: Multinational Corporations and Human Rights*, New York: W. W. Norton, 2013, p. 47.
32 Curtis J. Milhaupt and Katharina Pistor, *Law and Capitalism: What Corporate Crises Reveal about Legal Systems and Economic Development around the World*, Chicago: University of Chicago Press, 2008, p. 11.
33 Eizenstat, *Imperfect Justice*, pp. 217–8.
34 Eizenstat, *Imperfect Justice*, p. 246.
35 "Shell Faces Fresh Nigeria Pollution Claims in London," *Vanguard*, 2 March 2016, Online. Available at www.vanguardngr.com/2016/03/shell-faces-fresh-nigeria-pollution-claims-in-london/ (accessed 22 December 2018): "Oil giant Royal Dutch Shell came under renewed scrutiny on Wednesday over its environmental record in Nigeria after lawyers brought fresh claims of damage caused by spills to a London court … Shell agreed in January 2015 to pay more than $80 million to the Nigerian fishing community of Bodo for two serious oil spills in 2008, following a three-year legal battle … A Dutch court also ruled in December that four Nigerian farmers demanding compensation and a clean-up in four heavily-polluted Niger Delta villages can bring a case against the energy giant in the Netherlands."
36 Clara Sandoval and Gill Surfelet, "Corporations and Redress in Transitional Justice Processes," in Sabine Michalowski (ed.) *Corporate Accountability in the Context of Transitional Justice*, New York: Routledge, 2013, p. 106.
37 "Interview: Louise Arbour," *Financial Times*, 8 January 2008.
38 Bazyler, *Holocaust Justice*, pp. 100–1.
39 "Japanese Firms and Their Wartime Crimes: Mitsubishi Shows Some Remorse," *The Economist*, 20 July 2015.
40 OECD Guidelines for Multinational Enterprises, *National Contact Points*, Online. Available at mneguidelines.oecd.org/ncps (accessed 30 September 2018).
41 *Khulumani v. Barclay National Bank, Ltd.*, 504 F.3d 254, 259 (2d Cir. 2007) (*per curiam*). South Africa's government requested the dismissal of a representative ATS lawsuit for "interfering 'with a foreign sovereign's efforts to address matters in which it has predominant interest'," while the obliging US government asserted that continuing the case would "risk potentially serious adverse consequences for significant interests of the United States." Tara L. Van Ho, "Transnational Civil and Criminal Litigation," in Michalowski, *Corporate Accountability in the Context of Transitional Justice*, p. 66.

42 John Haberstroh, "In Re World War II Era Japanese Forced Labor Litigation and Obstacles to International Human Rights Claims in US Courts," *Asian Law Journal*, 2003, vol. 10, 253. Lack of US support was cited as a key chilling factor leading to the 2000 and 2001 dismissals of *In Re World War II Era Japanese Forced Labor Litigation* by the Northern District Court of California and the Ninth Circuit Court of Appeals. In that case, wartime forced labor claims were brought by allied POWs, US civilians, and Korean, Chinese, and Filipino plaintiffs.

43 For updated summaries of business and human rights lawsuits around the world, refer to "The Case Map," a project of the Business and Human Rights Resource Centre. Online. Available at https://business-humanrights.org/en/corporate-legal-accountability/case-profiles/legal-case-map (accessed 30 September 2018).

44 "Mitsubishi to Compensate Chinese Wartime Laborers, Ignores Korean Victims," *The Dong-A Ilbo*, 25 July 2015. See also Steven S. Nam, "From Individual to Collective Restitution: Recasting Corporate Accountability for Korean Forced Labor in the Second World War," *UC Davis Journal of International Law and Policy*, 2015, vol. 22, 1–19.

45 Ruggie, *Just Business*, p. 141.

46 *Guiding Principles*, p. 1.

47 John Ruggie, "Just Business: Multinational Corporations and Human Rights," 2013 Raymond and Beverly Sackler Distinguished Lecture at the Thomas J. Dodd Research Center, University of Connecticut, 28 February 2013. Online. Available at http://mediasite.dl.uconn.edu/Mediasite/Play/76c132b67e3e4aa0ad91295b041cbf381d (accessed 30 September 2018): "For states, the focus is on the legal obligations they have under the international human rights regime to protect human rights abuses by third parties, including business, as well as policy rationales that are consistent with, and supportive of, meeting those obligations. For businesses, beyond compliance with legal obligations that may vary across countries … the Guiding Principles focus on the need to manage the risk of involvement in human rights abuses, which requires acting with due diligence to avoid infringing on the rights of others, and to address harm where it does occur. For affected individuals and communities, the Guiding Principles provide a basis for the further realization of their right to remedy, both judicial and non-judicial."

48 Peter J. Spiro, "Disaggregating US Interests in International Law," *Law and Contemporary Problems*, 2004, vol. 67, 218.

49 Ruggie, *Just Business*, p. 78: "One reason that existing initiatives, public and private, do not add up to a more coherent system capable of truly moving markets is the lack of an authoritative focal point around which the expectations and behavior of the relevant actors can converge. Thus, my immediate objective was to develop and obtain agreement on a normative framework and corresponding policy guidance for the business and human rights domain, establishing both its parameters and its perimeters."

50 Letter from Accountability Counsel et al. to Fred Hochberg, Chairman and President, Export-Import Bank of the United States, 4 January 2016. Online. Available at www.accountabilitycounsel.org/wp-content/uploads/2017/08/1.4.15-Ex-Im-Grievance-Mechanism-Sign-on-Letter.pdf (accessed 30 September 2018). Note that while the date in the URL is in error, the date on the document itself is correct. The sign-ons transcended borders and included Accountability Counsel, Action Contre l'impunité pour les Droits Humains, EarthRights International, Friends of the Earth, La Fundación para el Desarrollo de Políticas Sustentables, Uganda Land Alliance, and Urgewald.

51 Ruggie, *Just Business*, p. 85.

52 *Guiding Principles*, p. 26.

53 Extractive Industries Transparency Initiative, "Multi-Stakeholder Governance. The Power of Three." Online. Available at https://eiti.org/oversight (accessed 30 September 2018). This document describes EITI's approach: "In each implementing country, a multi-stakeholder group (MSG) comprised of representatives from government, companies and civil society is established to oversee EITI implementation. Although the mandate of the MSG varies across countries, the MSG is the main decision-making body responsible for setting objectives for EITI implementation linked to wider national priorities in the extractive sector, producing EITI Reports, and ensuring that the findings contribute to public debate and get turned into reforms. While the MSG has a mandate to determine the scope of the EITI in its country, the

EITI Standard contains some minimum requirements including those related to the role, rights and responsibilities of the MSG."

54 UN High Commissioner for Human Rights, "Improving Accountability and Access to Remedy for Victims of Business-Related Human Rights Abuse," UN Doc A/HRC/32/19, 2016, 10. Online. Available at https://documents-dds-ny.un.org/doc/UNDOC/GEN/G16/093/78/PDF/G1609378.pdf?OpenElement (accessed 22 December 2018). Hereafter "Improving Accountability and Access to Remedy."

55 SOMO stands for its Dutch name Stichting Onderzoek Multinationale Ondernemingen.

56 Jennifer Zerk, *Business and Human Rights: Enhancing Accountability and Access to Remedy*, Office of the United Nations High Commissioner for Human Rights, 2014, pp. 2–3, Online. Availible at www.ohchr.org/Documents/Issues/Business/DomesticLawRemedies/RemedyProject1.pdf (accessed 22 December 2018).

57 "Improving Accountability and Access to Remedy," 10.

58 "Improving Accountability and Access to Remedy," 5. A "cross-border" case is defined as "one where the relevant facts have taken place in, the relevant actors are located in order the evidence needed to prove a case is located in more than one State."

59 Ruggie, *Just Business*, p. 121.

60 "Improving Accountability and Access to Remedy," 5.

61 John Ruggie (Special Representative on Business and Human Rights), *Protect, Respect and Remedy: A Framework for Business and Human Rights*, A/HRC/8/5, 2008, 89–90.

62 Zerk, *Business and Human Rights*, p. 10. ("International law places limits on the use of direct extraterritorial jurisdiction. As well as having to rely on one or more established jurisdictional principles (i.e. relevant territorial connections, nationality connections, or the more controversial passive personality, protective or universality principles), it is generally agreed that the use of direct extraterritorial jurisdiction is subject to an overarching 'reasonableness' requirement. This requirement is only vaguely defined in international legal discourse.")

63 "Improving Accountability and Access to Remedy," 28.

64 "Improving Accountability and Access to Remedy: Explanatory Notes," 5.

65 "Improving Accountability and Access to Remedy," 9 and 9.2–3.

66 "Improving Accountability and Access to Remedy," 9.7.

67 "Improving Accountability and Access to Remedy," 11.2.

68 "Improving Accountability and Access to Remedy," 9.5–6.

69 "Improving Accountability and Access to Remedy: Explanatory Notes," 36.

70 Henry Hansmann and Reinier Kraakman, "The End of History for Corporate Law," *Georgetown Law Journal*, 2001, vol. 89, 439–68.

71 Christopher May, *Global Corporations in Global Governance*, New York: Routledge, 2015, p. 79.

72 Steven S. Nam, "Our Country, Right or Wrong: The FTC Act's Influence on National Silos in Antitrust Enforcement," *University of Pennsylvania Journal of Business Law*, 2017, vol. 20, 210–46.

27

THE SELECTIVITY OF UNIVERSAL JURISDICTION

The history of transnational human rights prosecutions in Latin America and Spain

Ulrike Capdepón

Introduction

From the beginning of its application in the 1990s, the foundation of universal jurisdiction was the "fight against impunity" in an effort to bring those accused of having committed horrendous human rights violations to trial in domestic courts of another country. Since the extradition warrant and arrest in London of Chilean ex-dictator Augusto Pinochet in October 1998, the Spanish judiciary has played an important role in its application. For victims of human rights crimes, especially in Latin American countries after the civil wars and dictatorship experiences that had shaped the continent in the second half of the last century, Spain seemed to be the last option and resort for victims demanding justice in the courts.

This essay analyzes the challenges and contradictions in the application of universal jurisdiction as a mechanism for coming to terms with a repressive past, particularly in different constellations in South American countries and Spain. It aims to interrogate the tensions between the increasing international determination of criminal justice policies and the obstacles and ambivalences toward its local implementation. The essay moves from the "Pinochet case," the extradition request against the former Chilean dictator in Madrid's National Court, to the example of the current complaints in Argentina, investigating human rights violations in the Spanish Civil War (1936–9) and the Franco dictatorship (1939–75). The latter case study is highly significant as it inverts the original relationship between global South and North, with human rights organizations using the transnational proceedings to try to extend the practice of universal jurisdiction to continents in the global South, namely Latin American and African countries. Taking the Pinochet case as a starting point, this contribution focuses on the cross-border consequences of the Spanish transnational investigations into the crimes of the Chilean and Argentine military for local memory processes in Spain. It discusses the discursive entanglements of the transnational prosecutions, particularly focusing on how legal categories that have emerged from Latin American post-dictatorship experiences, such as the three basic transitional justice principles of truth, justice, and reparation, have been adopted by the civil society memory movement in Spain by framing the Francoist repression within an international human rights discourse.

With the Pinochet precedent, a legal complaint investigating human rights crimes related to the Spanish Civil War and the Franco regime was initiated in 2010 in Buenos Aires, Argentina by relatives of victims, which called for the investigation of acts of Francoist repression as "crimes against humanity." That initiative has evolved into an important transnational accountability effort. The ongoing complaint was presented by human rights and civil society memory organizations invoking the principle of universal jurisdiction, in response to the suspension of the contested Spanish magistrate Baltasar Garzón at the center of the Pinochet decision. In February 2012, he was removed from his post in the Audiencia Nacional (AN), Spain's National Court. The judge, who had become internationally renowned also for investigating grave human rights violations committed during the Chilean dictatorship (1973–90), was barred from holding his office for 11 years.

When Pinochet was arrested in London on the basis of an extradition request issued by Judge Garzón, the impact on the process of coming to terms with the human rights violations of the dictatorships in both Chile and in Spain was enormous. The Pinochet case has revealed the international dimensions at work in how a dictatorial past is handled in the public realm, when the host country fails to act. Spanish legal actions to end impunity in Chile and Argentina triggered a powerful "boomerang effect" that has, in turn, had a decisive impact on the discursive confrontation with the country's own Francoist past.

While the Spanish legal system became involved in the process of coming to terms with the Chilean and Argentine dictatorship's past, the legal and administrative treatment of military personnel and officials associated with the Franco dictatorship was determined by immunity from criminal proceedings under the 1977 amnesty law. Because the Spanish-negotiated transition process was marked by an official reconciliation discourse, there have been no prosecutions of those responsible for crimes attributable to the Franco dictatorship. The Spanish example reflects a "double standard" evidencing the challenges and ambiguities surrounding universal jurisdiction as a mechanism for dealing with a repressive past since the Pinochet case. Yet, the principle of universal jurisdiction applied in third-party state national courts, was ultimately to support the judicial investigations of Spain's Franco dictatorship in Buenos Aires.

The essay addresses the domestic significance of efforts to achieve transnational accountability. As a political scientist, I am interested in the social and political consequences in the application of universal jurisdiction from an international as well as domestic and local perspective. I seek to evaluate the circumstances under which the extraterritorial human rights prosecutions have had a catalytic effect on investigations and prosecutions in the home state, changing historical narratives and activating local processes of coming to terms with a repressive past, and thus increasing domestic accountability claims.[1] In so doing, I also examine what transforms the application of universal jurisdiction into a contested and selective mechanism, dependent on asymmetrical international and domestic political power relations. The political tension is the interface between domestic amnesty laws, seen as the main legal barrier for criminal prosecutions at a national level, and international pressure in bringing accused military personnel, former dictators, or government leaders to trial.

After proposing a definition of universal jurisdiction, I provide a short overview of the legal concept, its origins and its evolution and present the current thinking with regard to the analysis of universal jurisdiction as a transitional justice mechanism. The next section is devoted to the history of attempts to achieve transnational accountability through the application of universal jurisdiction before Spain's National Court, focusing on the Pinochet case and the most prominent prosecutions of Argentine military personnel. The specific case study in the section that follows explores how the transnational proceedings in Buenos Aires have drawn attention to Francoist repression in Spain by increasing the visibility of accountability claims in the public arena. The essay concludes by reflecting on the scope and selectivity of universal jurisdiction more broadly.

By analyzing the legal proceedings as a "boomerang effect," following on from the proceedings against the Argentine military junta before Spain's National Court from 1996 onwards, the intention is to examine the extent to which universal jurisdiction can also be applied in the opposite transatlantic direction from the southern into the northern hemisphere with a view to facilitating its application in a non-discriminatory manner.[2]

Universal jurisdiction: definition, scope, and limits

In the context of growing globalization and "domestication" of international norms, universal jurisdiction remains a controversial topic, in bilateral relations between states and at the international level, as well as in local public debates. Over the past 20 years, despite much criticism from various quarters, a remarkable practice of applying universal jurisdiction has evolved. After the end of the East–West conflict, judicial efforts aimed at coming to terms with a violent or dictatorial past via international judicial bodies, or indeed national courts belonging to other states, seemed a viable option as a complement to domestic trials.[3] The rapid development of international criminal jurisdiction raises the question of what role externalized human rights trials play when a society is coming to terms with a dictatorial past.

Here, my analysis is restricted to trials based on universal jurisdiction in foreign national courts in Latin America and Spain. According to the non-binding Princeton Principles developed by a group of international legal scholars, universal jurisdiction can be defined as the right to prosecute the perpetrators of serious international crimes "based solely on the nature of the crime without regard to where the crime was committed, the nationality of the alleged or convicted perpetrator, the nationality of the victim, or any other connection to the state exercising such jurisdiction."[4] The principle is based on the notion that the fight against impunity allows states to act in the name of the international community by prosecuting perpetrators of "core international crimes," genocide, crimes against humanity, torture, or war crimes, before its national courts.[5]

In the aftermath of the Pinochet case, the controversy over universal jurisdiction has persisted and countries in the global South, notably, have reproached European states for applying "double standards" with regard to such attempts at transnational accountability. The selectivity of the prosecutions has contributed to the repeated criticism (mostly on the part of African states) that the globalization of justice is biased, showing that its application cannot be separated from diplomatic tensions and asymmetry in international power relations. Critics claim that its underlying rationale operates within a universalistic framework that pays insufficient attention to particular local, national, and international contexts.

The link of the application of universal jurisdiction to the field of human rights advocacy as a negotiation process between global human rights ideas, and how they translate in local space becomes manifest in the proliferation of the increasingly interconnected transnational human rights movement. This pattern is one of the most striking developments to have resulted from the increased "anti-impunity discourse."[6] It has played a decisive part in the public treatment of repressive pasts, when efforts to address the crimes of dictatorships seemed to be blocked nationally. Within this field, the international human rights and local civil society movement in Argentina and Chile have become crucial exemplars for the struggle against impunity.[7] They serve as models for the important role played by non-state actors in norm diffusion across borders. In both countries, the struggle to combat impunity succeeded in bringing about legal proceedings, thereby making an important contribution towards a further development of universal jurisdiction.

From a long-term perspective, I focus on the crossing-border consequences of the Spanish judicial investigations into the crimes of the Chilean and Argentinian military for transnational memory and accountability processes in the countries implied. Taking into consideration the controversies and difficulties in the application of universal jurisdiction, the essay analyzes the role and scope of the principle as well as the dynamism it triggers at a local level, followed by one specific qualitative in-depth case study limited to Spain and Argentina. The suits presented in Buenos Aires challenge the recurring criticisms of selectivity, neo-colonialism, and paternalism raised against the principle of universal jurisdiction. In addition, the extradition proceedings initiated at the behest of Belgium against Chad's former dictator Hissène Habré, described as "Africa's Pinochet," is significant.[8] The Habré case is highly relevant because, as with the process of coming to terms with the Franco dictatorship in Buenos Aires, human rights organizations are actually using the proceedings to try to extend the practice of universal jurisdiction to continents in the global South, in this case in an inter-African collaboration. As Kaleck states, this demonstrates "the potential of transnational prosecutions to trigger the ending of [...] impunity in societies that have suffered from mass violence in the past – the Pinochet Videla effect has reached Africa."[9]

Evolution of international accountability: universal jurisdiction as a transitional justice mechanism

After a long time when impunity had been the rule following war, dictatorship, and mass violence, in recent years human rights prosecutions have advanced in cases of Latin American military officials, political leaders, and heads of state charged with responsibility for major human rights violations.[10] Justice in the courts has become one of the most prominent mechanisms to obtain accountability in processes of dealing with the past.

Although over the past two decades Spain, together with several other European states, have begun to prosecute former heads of state or government from Latin American countries accused of "crimes against humanity," in the existing literature on transitional justice the application of universal jurisdiction in foreign tribunals is hardly mentioned as a legal option for coming to terms with a violent or dictatorial past.[11]

The global trend to hold perpetrators accountable for human rights crimes has led to a burgeoning corpus of interdisciplinary studies in the field of the politics of accountability, human rights, and what has come to be known as transitional justice – a field that investigates the transition process from authoritarian regimes to democracies including instruments such as truth commissions, reparations and, above all, prosecutions in trials.[12] One of the main contributions about the consequences of domestic and international human rights trials is the concept of "justice cascade," addressing the increase of criminal accountability for human rights violations worldwide.[13] The political scientist Kathryn Sikkink has acknowledged and documented the growing deployment of trials for mass atrocities in diverse countries. This scholar perceives a growing normative international consensus away from blanket amnesty or impunity and toward the inclusion of some dimensions of international judicialization. Although the debate about the "internationalization of transitional justice" and the aforementioned global diffusion of anti-impunity and human rights discourses in post-conflict situations is directly linked to the application of universal jurisdiction, the relationship between them has yet to be studied in depth.[14] Besides the politics of universal jurisdiction, further research needs to be done on the impact of transnational accountability efforts on victims, judiciaries, and societies as a whole in the target, as well as in the forum state, where the trials are taking place.

The Nuremberg Trials are often seen as the starting point of the global proliferation of human rights ideas about and demands for transnational accountability. Although the Nuremberg Charter did not specifically refer to universality, the trials of high-ranking officials and Nazi collaborators before the International Military Tribunal (IMT) that handed down its judgments in 1946, established a precedent for international accountability, as these were the first ever prosecutions for "crimes against humanity."[15]

Following the establishment of the Nuremberg Principles, more recent examples of prosecutions for war crimes and human rights violations include, in the 1990s, the efforts of the International Criminal Tribunal for Rwanda (ICTR), the International Criminal Tribunal for the former Yugoslavia (ICTY), the Special Court for Sierra Leone (SCSL), and other special tribunals. These judicial proceedings only became possible after the end of the Cold War, which had such a polarizing effect on international relations. The most significant symbol of this trend was the establishment of the permanent International Criminal Court (ICC) in 1998 – not coincidental in the same year in which the Pinochet case evolved – and entered into force in 2002. Through the adoption of the Rome Statute, the ICC's mandate authorizes it to apply the prevailing international consensus regarding the obligation to prosecute the "most serious" international crimes, based on the principle of complementarity. The contemporaneous arrest of and extradition request for the former Chilean dictator Augusto Pinochet is also widely perceived as an important step toward universal human rights, although concerns have been raised about the potentially arbitrary proliferation and selective application of the principle of universal jurisdiction.

The history of universal jurisdiction in Latin America and Spain: complaints before the Spanish national court

The cases pursued in Spanish courts in the mid-1990s concerning crimes committed during the military dictatorships in Argentina and Chile introduced a significant new dynamism to the transnational prosecution of international crimes. These cases, which reflect unprecedented interpretations of the law on the part of the Spanish investigative judge Baltasar Garzón and the human rights movement, were set in motion on 28 March 1996, by a criminal complaint issued by Carlos Castresana, a Spanish public prosecutor and the president of the Spanish Union of Progressive Prosecutors (UPF). The resulting network formed by lawyers, human rights associations, and activists from the Argentine exile community, began collecting information, looking for witnesses and victims, building cases and finally bringing them before the courts in Spain. On the basis of these investigations and the testimony of over 200 witnesses, Garzón issued numerous arrest warrants for Argentine military officers.

As a consequence, three months later, the Catalan lawyer Joan Garcés, who had been the Chilean president Salvador Allende's political advisor until the military coup in September 1973, filed a similar complaint against Pinochet and a number of high-ranking junta members. The political climate in Spain at the time was conducive to such cases, and the nation's *acusación* or *acción popular* (popular action) principle established in the Spanish Constitution of 1978 provides the possibility to pursue criminal cases brought by ordinary third-party citizens. Moreover, Spain's universal jurisdiction statute, established in 1985 in Article 23(4) of the post-Franco Organic Law of the Judiciary (LOPJ), covered particularly grave international crimes (including genocide, terrorism, and torture) even when neither the accused nor the victim was a Spanish citizen.

The Pinochet case

When the former Chilean dictator Augusto Pinochet traveled to the United Kingdom on 17 October 1998, to undergo back surgery, he was arrested in a London private hospital.[16] The arrest warrant and extradition request was issued by Spanish judge Baltasar Garzón for the crimes of genocide, terrorism, torture, and enforced disappearance committed against Spanish and Chilean citizens during the dictatorship. In Chile, the blanket self-amnesty of 1978 protected the security forces from prosecution for human rights violations that occurred between 1973 and 1978, the period of the worst repression under the Pinochet dictatorship. Transnational contacts of actors' coalitions between Spanish and Chilean human rights organizations, lawyers, and local victim groups created the preconditions for the cross-border collaborations required to overcome immunity from criminal proceedings in Chile. During the extradition hearings, the British House of Lords twice approved Pinochet's extradition to Spain on charges of torture.

After 503 days of his house arrest in London, during which time serious diplomatic tensions poisoned the bilateral relationships of the countries involved, the British authorities allowed Pinochet to return to Chile on grounds of his health. However, the events in Europe had important political repercussions in Chile. Criminal complaints against Pinochet had been admitted for the first time in a Chilean court in early 1998, but the number of these complaints increased drastically during the former dictator's unexpected detention. Once back in the country, Pinochet remained under several indictments until his death in December 2006. In May 2000, he was stripped of parliamentary immunity, making a trial possible. Although the arrest of the ex-dictator did not result in sentencing under criminal law abroad, it did influence the Chilean courts' legal approach to human rights violations by the dictatorship and also impacted the international application of global jurisdiction. In Chile, it sparked a renewed debate over the legacy of the Pinochet dictatorship, and repressed memories were set free, generating intense discussion.

The outcome in Chile was a considerable increase in the sentencing of members of the military who were brought before the courts; in addition, the validity of the amnesty law was called into question and came to be largely circumvented. This was partly the result of changes in political power relations within the country; however, decisive roles were played by the transnational activities of relatives' associations and human rights organizations and the increasing impact of international law, in particular with regard to the extradition process against Pinochet.

Despite the failure to extradite Pinochet, due to the high impact of the case new suits were filed for the prosecution of crimes committed in other dictatorial regimes such as Argentina, El Salvador, and Guatemala for the genocide of Indigenous groups in the 1980s. Naomi Roht-Arriaza interprets the Pinochet case as the end product of the activities of an alliance consisting of national and international human rights activists, members of victims' families, lawyers, journalists, and scientists on the one side and judges and governments on the other.[17] In her view, this interplay of institutional and non-institutional protagonists led first to Pinochet's arrest and then to what she describes as the "Pinochet effect." An increasingly transnationally organized civil society ensured that another country's jurisdiction could become a "catalyst of domestic change."[18] This catalytic effect had expressed itself in a reaction from the international discussions and the efforts to commence investigations and criminal prosecution activities in Chile, but also in the accelerated judicial prosecuting of human rights abuses in other countries. In the process, the "Pinochet effect" came to symbolize a trend toward global jurisdiction aimed at combating immunity from punishment following dictatorships. It not only advanced the debate about international criminal jurisdiction, but also served simultaneously as a precedent, so that former dictators did not benefit from immunity in foreign countries. The chain reactions that followed from this momentous step manifested themselves in various attempts to hold amnestied dictators or incriminated military officers responsible before courts in another country for the human rights abuses committed under their rule.

In effect, Pinochet's arrest, detention, and the subsequent legal interpretation of these events have set a precedent in the realm of international law and human rights, clarifying that certain international crimes are not subject to immunity – even when former heads of state or government officials are involved. Not only did these developments strengthen the hope for global justice among prominent scholars, they also set a precedent for human rights nongovernmental organizations (NGOs) and victims' associations, motivating them to file more complaints before different domestic courts, including in France, Germany, and Belgium, concerning serious crimes committed outside of Europe. In the light of the catalytic impact of the paradigmatic Pinochet case, the following proceedings brought before Spain's National Court against high-ranking members of the Chilean and Argentine military juntas, as well and those responsible for the Guatemalan genocide, had repercussions for the local discourse of remembrance and the domestic ways of dealing with the repressive past, as well as the prevalence of international human rights imperatives and proceedings in the domestic courts.

The Cavallo and Scilingo cases

Collectively, Baltasar Garzón – based on the investigation proceedings that were initiated before the Spanish National Court in October 1999 – charged a total of 186 military officers as a result of the human rights abuses that were committed during the Argentinian military dictatorship and, shortly afterwards, submitted requests for extradition against 98 of them. The defendants included the former military rulers Jorge Rafael Videla and Emilio Eduardo Massera, the former marine captain Alfredo Astiz, and Domingo Bussi, an ex-general and former governor of the Tucumán province. As a consequence of the Pinochet case and the crumbling immunity for former heads of state and high-ranking military officers, the Argentinian corvette captain Miguel Angel

Cavallo was arrested on 24 August 2000 during an attempt to escape from the airport in the Mexican town of Cancún and, following two years of negotiations based on extradition treaties originating in 1978, was handed over to the Spanish judiciary on 29 June 2003 in order to be charged with genocide and terrorism before the Spanish National Court. This was the first time that a state – Mexico – extradited a defendant on grounds of human rights violations in a third country – Spain – for crimes committed in another country. Cavallo was accused, among other crimes, of involvement in the kidnapping of 16 babies whose mothers had been "disappeared" into confinement and approving of the illegal adoption of these babies. In Spain, the AN did not want to take the case in December 2006, referring to the jurisdiction of Argentinian courts – where upon the Argentinian public prosecutors submitted a request for extradition. In February 2008, a Spanish court consented to an Argentinian application for extradition in which Cavallo had to answer for crimes against humanity. Then, in October 2011 within the scope of the ESMA proceedings (Escuela de Mecánica de la Armada, the most notorious torture and detention center located in Buenos Aires), he was sentenced to life imprisonment alongside 17 further principal defendants.

The Argentinian ex-military officer Adolfo Francisco Scilingo, one of the defendants, also was arrested in Madrid. Like Cavallo, he was involved in the human rights violations committed during the Argentinian military dictatorship at the illegal imprisonment and torture center set up in the ESMA military school.[19] Having testified in 1997 before the AN, and subsequently arrested by Judge Garzón, in April 2005, Scilingo was additionally sentenced to a total of 640 years' imprisonment. He was convicted of the so-called "death flights," in which anaesthetized political prisoners were thrown alive from helicopters into the Río de la Plata, of crimes against humanity, as well as of enforced disappearance of persons in 30 cases. In July 2007, the court of justice increased the sentence symbolically to 1,084 years, as it had been proven also that Scilingo was involved in 255 further cases of unlawful imprisonment. This was the first time that a foreign court, namely the Spanish Audiencia Nacional, was able to convict with legally binding force the perpetrators of human rights abuses such as genocide, torture, and enforced disappearance that were committed in other countries – on the grounds of universal jurisdiction.

Initial efforts to secure domestic investigations and prosecutions were spearheaded mainly by local memory associations. The Mothers of the Plaza de Mayo in Argentina are an example of this powerful local action. At first, none of the regional human rights organizations from Argentina, Chile, or Guatemala managed to overcome without external support the impunity for the crimes committed by their countries in the 1970s and 1980s. The situation only began to improve once the local groups linked up with transnational human rights organization, such as AI or Human Rights Watch referring to the principle of universal jurisdiction. As a consequence of mounting international pressure by local victims and pro-accountability organizations such as associations of survivors and relatives of the "disappeared" through applications for extradition, the Argentine parliament countermanded the amnesty regulations in August 2003. The annulment of these laws was confirmed by the Supreme Court in June 2005, accompanied by the ratification of international norms in criminal law.

Since then, the "Pinochet model" has constituted a central point of reference in the international debate about how to deal with human rights crimes, the universalization of justice and the influence of international law on the impunity of perpetrators protected by domestic amnesties, and consequently national processes of dealing with a repressive past. The arrest warrants and requests for extradition submitted by Spanish public prosecutors and courts had a considerable impact on criminal prosecution in the original countries, both in Chile and in Argentina. In the process, the "Pinochet effect" initially highlighted a trend toward universal jurisdiction, with a view to combating the impunity enjoyed by state terrorism and human rights abuses at national level.

Victims of the Franco dictatorship seeking justice in Argentina

The widespread attention and discussion of Chile's and Argentina's dictatorial past in Spanish public debate by the end of the 1990s triggered by the application of universal jurisdiction brought the Franco dictatorship, previously a subject that was taboo, back onto the political agenda, and with that human rights and anti-impunity discourses started to proliferate in Spanish public debates.[20] The final consequence of the Pinochet affair was to re-politicize the local politics of memory in Spain. While changing political forces and generational change were influential, developments in international criminal and human rights law as well as the growing international rejection of national impunity laws have helped to give impetus to demands of accountability and justice arising within the Spanish local memory movement.[21]

On 14 April 2010, two exiled relatives of Spanish citizens who were killed at the beginning of the Civil War and lay in unmarked mass graves, lodged a complaint in Argentina against the crimes of the Franco dictatorship. The unprecedented legal actions were symbolically charged, having been announced on the anniversary of the proclamation of Spain's Second Republic (1931). The (still ongoing) complaints in Buenos Aires were filed by victims of the Franco dictatorship as a reaction first to the memory law passed by the Socialist government under Prime Minister José Luis Rodriguez Zapatero in 2007, which was perceived as insufficient by many victims' and human rights groups,[22] and second to the suspension of the Spanish magistrate Baltasar Garzón (in 2010) following his initiation of investigations into Francoist crimes. For the victims of the Franco dictatorship, once Garzón had been removed from office, the investigations abroad appeared to represent the last opportunity to prosecute Francoist agents for crimes of Enforced Disappearance of the Civil War and also less-publicized cases of repression in the later years of the Franco regime, such as the "stolen children" and acts of torture, which in the complaint are categorized as "crimes against humanity."

This step was supported initially by a total of ten Argentine human rights organizations, and included Nobel Peace Prize laureate Adolfo Pérez Esquivel, and human rights lawyers Ana Messuti and Carlos Slepoy, who died in April 2017 – both residents of Spain following their exile from Argentina's last dictatorship and former initiators of the universal jurisdiction-cases in Madrid.[23] Their initiative aimed at a legal examination of and discursive confrontation with the Franco dictatorship by applying universal jurisdiction principles in Argentinian courts to prompt and accelerate investigations and prosecutions in Spain.

In May 2013, as the number of complaints filed in Buenos Aires continued to increase, Spanish civil society associations created the National Coordination Network in Support of Legal Actions Against the Crimes of Francoism (Coordinadora Estatal de Apoyo a la Querella contra Crímenes del Franquismo, CEAQUA). This organization with several regional offices has been very active in Spain and abroad, establishing transnational links to victims and human rights organizations in Argentina and taking its cause to institutions including the Spanish Congress and the European Parliament, in addition to organizing trips to Buenos Aires to hear victim testimony. At present, there are approximately 600 lawsuits underway, and a widespread transnational movement of more than 150 social and political organizations has emerged.[24]

While Garzón's failed order in October 2008 sought to investigate the crimes committed in Spain between 1936 and 1951, including the postwar repression; the time frame of the Argentine complaint is much wider, encompassing the period between the uprising led by Franco's troops on 17 July 1936, the beginning of the Spanish Civil War, and 15 June 1977, when the first democratic elections were held during the transition process. Its remit thus covered not only the late Franco regime but also the first years after his death in November 1975. While Garzón's order was restricted to the violence perpetrated in the Civil War and the to postwar period, the complaint in Argentina also placed special emphasis on the repression during the late Francoist regime to which hardly any attention had been paid until then. After the annulment of the amnesty and due obedience law in 2003, the conditions in Argentina seemed to be favorable for the successful prosecution of human rights trials.[25]

The complaint, however, was blocked from the outset by the Spanish government and legal system: In response to the complaint presented to the Argentinian first Federal Court (Juzgado Nacional Criminal y Correcional Federal No. 1), Judge Servini de Cubría issued a formal petition asking the Spanish government to declare whether its own courts were investigating cases of torture, murder, and the disappearance of Franco's political opponents. It took ten months for the state prosecutor (*fiscalia general del estado*) to answer, responding affirmatively in July 2011 and claiming that numerous complaints were being investigated at the territorial courts corresponding to the locations of the respective mass graves, where victims could bring their cases. However, as was obvious, one of the Amnesty International (AI) reports entitled "Closed Cases, Open Wounds," points out that such courts continue to be closed without investigation.[26] A trip to Spain planned by Argentine judge Servini in order to obtain testimony was not supported by the Spanish government. Instead, the victims had to travel to Buenos Aires, or testify via video-conference from the Argentinian embassy in Madrid, efforts that Spanish diplomats severely criticized and tried to prevent.[27]

A first international arrest order was issued in September 2013 by the Argentine court against two former Spanish officials, including members of the police: an officer of the civil guard (*guardia civil*) and an agent of the former secret police, the Brigada Político Social (BPS). Both stood accused of torture during the later years of the Franco dictatorship and were ordered to appear before the AN in December 2013. Although they are being pursued by Interpol, Spanish government officials and the majority of Spanish judges and prosecutors refused to cooperate, referring to the Spanish amnesty law of 1977. Consequently, on 24 April 2014, the Spanish National Court rejected the extradition request. Indeed, the Spanish government in that context de facto abolished the principle of universal jurisdiction in Spanish legislation in February 2014.[28] Following several failed attempts, Judge Servini finally visited Spain in May 2014 to obtain oral testimony from victims (as plaintiffs) in various parts of the country.[29]

In October 2014, notwithstanding the previous court's decision, Investigating Judge Servini issued detention orders against 19 accused former Spanish officials, ex-ministers, and former members of the police forces, in order to request their extradition to

Argentina. She thus renewed the effort to pursue cases of human rights abuses beyond Spain's borders. Two of the most notorious suspects were José Utrera Molina, the minister of housing during the last years of the Franco regime, who was accused of signing the death sentence of Salvador Puig Antich, an anarchist executed in 1974, and Rodolfo Martin Villa, a politician who served in various cabinets under the dictatorship and was minister of the interior between 1976 and 1979. Villa was accused of ordering the Victoria massacre of 1976, in which the police suppressed a general strike, killing five demonstrators and injuring dozens of others.

While Spanish authorities promptly rejected the extradition request, and justice minister Rafael Catalá argued that the acts during the Franco era were not considered crimes by the Criminal Code in effect at that time the request for the extradition of these alleged perpetrators has focused a spotlight on the plights of the victims and their relatives.[30] A growing number of associations representing victims and relatives have since joined the first plaintiffs, magnifying the significance of the Argentinian complaint. In a process that anthropologist Francisco Ferrándiz describes as "legal download," the civil society and victim groups arising from the local memory movement are increasingly framing the experience of political repression during the Civil War and the (late) Franco regime within human rights discourses invoked by the Latin American human rights movement, adopting terms such as "impunity," "enforced disappearance," and "universal jurisdiction" in their local idioms.[31] Thus, they are demanding truth, justice, and reparation for the victims of the Francoist repression. These legal discourses invoked by victims groups re-emerged with the complaint in Argentina, reinforced by international organizations (e.g. AI and the United Nations), creating and supporting historical counter narratives about the Civil War, the Franco dictatorship, and the transition process.

In the light of the decision by the Spanish Supreme Court to put Garzón on trial for his attempts to judicialize Francoist crimes, the complaint in Argentina can be considered a response by the memory movement in Spain to the legal obstacles standing in the way of an effective official investigation, since Spain appears unwilling and unable to try these crimes itself. In an interesting twist and reversal of roles, notably, Argentina is the first Latin American country to apply the principle of universal jurisdiction to prosecute "crimes against humanity" committed not merely outside its borders, but also within those of its former European colonial power. Although the results of this legal action cannot yet be predicted, its very existence illustrates how impulses to confront past human rights violations and repression are increasingly coming from the Latin American Southern Cone into Spain.

In the recent *Mendieta Case*, an 88-year-old woman had testified to Judge Servini in 2013, demanding to recover the human remains of her father, unionist Timoteo Mendieta, who was arrested in November 1939, shortly after Franco's Civil War victory, and dumped in a mass grave on the Guadalajara cemetery. After her attempts to locate and identify the remains through the local government had failed, she sought legal support elsewhere in her quest to rebury her father's body. The case became the first foreign-court-ordered exhumation in Spain. The remains were successfully located on orders of Judge Servini, and reburied in June 2017, setting an important precedent.[32] Moreover, recent changes in the local city councils have breathed new life into the victims' fight against impunity. A growing number of city governments – including Barcelona,

Pamplona, Zaragoza, and Cádiz – have joined the Argentine complaint and are filing their own with Spanish courts.

Conclusions: the selective application of a contested global norm

Although controversies over the internationalization of justice persist, marked by criticisms of double standards and neo-colonialism made by countries in the global South against the European states on grounds of selective application, the legal actions described in this essay reveal that the application of universal jurisdiction principles may be beginning to change direction. The Argentine complaint facilitated the expanding role of international law through the application of universal jurisdiction in the strategic discourse of the movement for the recovery of historical memory, serving as a powerful tool for victim claims.

The universal jurisdiction-based complaint in Argentina, therefore, has been central in uniting a range of international human rights and local memory actors and pooling their efforts, in turn lending the wider civil society movement new impetus. It is these internal catalytic effects, as shown in the cases of the Argentine and Chilean transnational trials before the Spanish National Court by the end of the 1990s, that may prove to be the greatest argument in favor of universal jurisdiction. The strength of universal jurisdiction lies in its ability to prompt the local process of coming to terms with the past at home and change local memory discourses, in both the home and target states.[33] In the countries studied, the influence of increasingly interconnected human rights movements across borders played a decisive part in this transformation in public dealings with dictatorial pasts. Both in Chile and in Argentina the human rights movements have made increasing use of international instruments against impunity, thereby adding to the further development of universal jurisdiction. Transnational pursuit of grave infringements of human rights turned out to be significant for the fight against impunity in those two countries, increasing the efforts of national prosecutors to bring those crimes before a domestic court. From the viewpoint of the international human rights community, it initially signified a remarkable victory and success for international law. While the accountability demands of the victims and their relatives in Chile – supported by international human rights organizations – invoked universal human rights norms, the recently established Spanish memory movement is oriented toward the internationally established paradigmatic triad of transitional justice comprising truth, justice, and reparation, which at the local level provides a powerful reference framework for coming to terms with the dictatorial past, and which has been adopted from the former experience of the Latin American human rights movement.

It remains, however, doubtful whether an optimistic assessment regarding the international assertion of human rights and universal justice norms for the purpose of coming to terms with the dictatorial past is justified. While there was optimism about the establishment of an international human rights regime in the 1990s, the initial idealism concerning the application of universal jurisdiction has in the meantime given way to a more critical standpoint: Although gains in the past few years have also been considerable, the era of impunity is far from being over. This means that an effective, workable system of universal jurisdiction is still, at best, in the development stage and is frequently rejected as more than just an unacceptable restriction of national sovereignty. Similarly, the problem of selectivity, i.e. the existing double standards between rich and powerful states and poor states in the global South is a repeated criticism. The limitation of universal jurisdiction by the Spanish parliament in May 2009 and its virtual removal from the Spanish constitution in February 2014 confirms this negative trend and reflects the fact that the application of universal jurisdiction in a third country is capable of plunging the governments involved – as the Pinochet case and the legal action for coming to terms with the crimes of the Franco dictatorship in Buenos Aires illustrate – into severe bilateral diplomatic crises. A consistent global universal prosecution of human rights crimes is still not guaranteed as it continues to be dominated by geopolitical interests, embedded in asymmetrical global and local power relations.

However, while it remains open whether the emergence of new actors within the historical memory groupings in Spain – which have established transnational links to victims' and human rights organizations in Argentina – will serve as an example for the successful extension of the application of universal justice in global South countries, it already illustrates that the creative transnational adoption of international human rights discourses can be a powerful strategic and mobilizing tool. The emergence of new actors, combined with the acceptance of a legal discourse that has been successful in boosting the legitimacy of anti-impunity struggles of the Southern Cone human rights movement, has advanced the cause of the Spanish memory and human rights associations and growing judicial demands on a domestic level.

The outcome of the Pinochet case as well as the ongoing prosecutions in Buenos Aires to investigate the crimes of the Franco dictatorship, which are constantly blocked by Spanish government officials, demonstrate at the same time that the application of universal jurisdiction as an instrument to confront "crimes against humanity" in a foreign court is highly contested and selective and its implementation across borders is dependent on asymmetrical international and domestic political power relations.

Notes

1 The term "catalyst" is used in the context of the consequences from the Pinochet affair in Chile by, among others, David Pion-Berlin, "The Pinochet Case and Human Rights Progress in Chile: Was Europe a Catalyst, Cause or Inconsequential?," *Journal of Latin American Studies*, 2004, vol. 36, 479–505.

2 Margaret E. Keck and Kathryn Sikkink, *Activists Beyond Borders: Advocacy Networks in International Politics*, Ithaca, NY: Cornell University Press, 1998, p. 156; Sikkink, *The Justice Cascade: How Human Rights Prosecutions are Changing World Politics*, New York: Norton, 2011, p. 77.

3 Interest in universal jurisdiction grew significantly in the 1990s, when several European states passed legislation extending their domestic criminal laws on the prosecution and punishment of certain particularly heinous crimes. International tribunals substituted the national prosecutions in countries which were not able, or willing, to carry out adjudication. For the historical development of the principle, see Cherif Bassiouni, "The History of Universal Jurisdiction and Its Place in International Law," in Stephen Macedo (ed.) *Universal Jurisdiction: National Courts and the Prosecution of Serious Crimes Under International Law*, Philadelphia: University of Pennsylvania Press, pp. 39–63; Luc Reydams, "The Rise and Fall of Universal Jurisdiction," in William A. Schabas (ed.) *Handbook of International Criminal Law*, London: Routledge, 2010, pp. 338–54, here 310; Magdalena Kmack, *The Scope and Application of the Principle of Universal Jurisdiction*, Helsinki: Erik Castrén Institute Research Reports, 2011, pp. 11–66.

4 For a detailed definition of the concept, see Program in Law and Public Affairs (2001), *Princeton Principles on Universal Jurisdiction*, Princeton, NJ: Princeton University Press, esp.

p. 28. Online. Available at https://lapa.princeton.edu/hosteddocs/unive_jur.pdf (accessed 15 August 2018).

5 Maximo Langer, "The Diplomacy Of Universal Jurisdiction: The Political Branches and The Transnational Prosecutions of International Crimes," *American Journal of International Law*, 2011, vol. 5, 1.

6 Stephanie Golob, *Evolution or Revolution? Transnational Justice Culture Across Borders*, Madrid: Instituto de Politicas y Bienes Públicos, CSIC, 2010.

7 María Luisa Bartolomei, "Universal Jurisdiction vs. National Sovereignty – the Cases of Argentina and Chile," *Iberoamericana. Nordic Journal of Latin American and Caribbean Studies*, 2007, vol. 37, 107–47.

8 Reed Brody, *Autumn of the Patriarch*, Human Rights Watch, 2006, Online. Available at www.hrw.org/en/news/2006/12/18/autumn-patriarch (accessed 15 August 2018). The Senegalese government initially rebuffed a Belgian request for his extradition, but eventually agreed to the African Union's recommendation that Senegal amend its laws and prosecute the former dictator itself. Finally, the inauguration of a Special Court in Senegal in February 2013 and Habré's arrest in July 2013 marked a turning point for the human rights organizations involved, in the long campaign to bring the former Chadian dictator to justice with the application of universal jurisdiction for the first time in a domestic African court, the Extraordinary African Chambers inaugurated in Dakar. On 30 May 2016, Habré was convicted of crimes against humanity, war crimes, and torture, including rape and sexual violence, and sentenced to life in prison. See Mbacké Fall, "The Extraordinary African Chambers: The Case of Hissène Habré," in Gerhard Werle et al. (eds.) *Africa and the International Criminal Court*, New York: Springer, 2014, pp. 117–31.

9 Wolfgang Kaleck, *Double Standards. International Criminal Law and the West*, Berlin: Wagenbach/Torkel Opsahl, 2015, p. 68.

10 Elin Skaar, Jemima García-Godos and Cath Collins (eds.), *Transitional Justice in Latin America: The Uneven Road from Impunity Towards Accountability*, London: Routledge, 2016, p. 7.

11 Ellen L. Lutz and Caitlin Reiger (eds.), *Prosecuting Heads of State*, New York: Cambridge University Press, 2009. The key interrelationship between transitional justice and International Criminal Law in general is the subject of a special issue of the *International Journal for Transitional Justice*, but without any particular focus on universal jurisdiction in a third-state country. See Naomi Roht-Arriaza, "Editorial Note," *The International Journal of Transitional Justice*, 2013, vol. 1, 1–10. Generally, handbooks on transitional justice focus more on the *International Criminal Court* (ICC) and hybrid and national courts as the established standard toolkit of judicial mechanisms for coping with the past than on the highly contested application of universal jurisdiction in national courts outside the country where the crimes were committed. For a critical but constructive view on the application of universal jurisdiction, see for example the work by Wolfgang Kaleck, *Double Standards. International Criminal Law and the West*, Berlin: Torkel Ophsal, 2015.

12 The term transitional justice, which is relatively new in the discourse of socio-legal studies, has been defined as a "conception of justice associated with periods of political change, characterized by legal responses to confront the wrongdoings of repressive predecessor regimes," Ruti Teitel, "Transitional Justice Genealogy," *Harvard Human Rights Journal*, 2003, vol. 16, 69–94.

13 See Kathryn Sikkink and Caitlin Booth Walling, "The Impact of Human Rights Trials in Latin America," *Journal of Peace Research*, 2007, vol. 44, 427–45; Kathryn Sikkink, *The Justice Cascade: How Human Rights Prosecutions are Changing World Politics*, New York: Norton, 2011.

14 Mark Arenhövel, "Democratization and Transitional Justice," *Democratization*, 2008, vol. 15, 570–87.

15 Christoph Safferling and Herbert R. Reginbogen (eds.), *Die Nürnberger Prozesse: Völkerstrafrecht seit 1945*, Munich: Saur, 2006.

16 An extensive literature analyzing the Pinochet case has developed in its aftermath: See Roger Burbach, *The Pinochet Affair: State Terrorism and Global Justice*, New York: Zed Books, 2003; Antonio Ramiro Brotóns, *El caso Pinochet. Los límites de la impunidad*, Madrid: Biblioteca Nueva, 1999; Ariel Dorfman, *Exorcising Terror: The Incredible Unending Trial of General Augusto Pinochet*, London: Seven Stories Press, 2000; Richard J. Wilson, "Prosecuting Pinochet: International Crimes in Spanish Domestic Law," *Human Rights Quarterly*, 1999, vol. 4, 927–79.

17 Naomi Roht-Arriaza, *The Pinochet Effect. Transnational Justice in the Age of Human Rights*, Philadelphia: University of Pennsylvania Press, 2005.
18 Roht-Arriaza, *The Pinochet Effect*, p. 92.
19 See Ellen L. Lutz and Caitin Reiger (eds.), *Prosecuting Heads of State*, New York: Cambridge University Press, 2009.
20 Ulrike Capdepón, *From the Pinochet Case to the desaparecidos of the Spanish Civil War: Coming to Terms with the Dictatorships' Past and Human Rights Violations in Chile and Spain* (in German), Bielefeld: Transcript, 2015, pp. 210–32; Omar G. Encarnación, *Democracy without Justice in Spain. The Politics of Forgetting*, Philadelphia: University of Pennsylvania Press, 2014, pp. 132–56.
21 As a direct consequence of the debates on universal jurisdiction and the so-called Pinochet effect more than 60 years after the end of the Spanish Civil War the victims association Amicale de Mauthausen, an association of Republican survivors of the Nazi concentration camp, in April of 2002 prepared an indictment against Serrano Suñer, the first foreign minister of the Franco regime. They accused him for being responsible for the deportation of republican refugees from France to the Austrian concentration camp. With this legal action they wanted to extradite him from Spain to sentence him in Paris. Although Serrano Suñer died in 2003, the aim was to draw public attention to the system of impunity in Spain.
22 While the importance of the memory law lies in its symbolic and reparative effects, one of the many shortcomings criticized by victims' groups is its refusal to nullify sentences handed down by Francoist tribunals, declaring them "illegitimate" rather than "illegal," as well as the fact that the amnesty law from 1977 was not called into question.
23 The indictment is supported by the following Argentine human rights organizations: Abuelas de Plaza de Mayo, Liga Argentina por los Derechos del Hombre, Comisión Provincial por la Memoria, Asamblea Permanente por los Derechos Humanos, Centro de Estudios Legales y Sociales (CELS), Asociación de Ex-Detenidos Desaparecidos, Federación de Asociaciones Gallegas de la República de Argentina, Instituto de Estudios Comparados en Ciencias Penales y Sociales, Comité de Acción Jurídica, and Madres de Plaza de Mayo Línea fundadora, s. Querella, 14 April 2010, at pp. 1–2, Online. Available at www.scribd.com/doc/30169670/querella-argentina-franquismo (accessed 15 August 2018).
24 The victims can be differentiated as follows: (1) relatives of desaparecidos who to this day remain buried in Civil War mass graves; (2) convicts sentenced to death or lengthy prison sentences in Francoist drumhead trials without even minimum legal standards; (3) relatives of children abducted from Republican prisoners during the war, a practice that had been applied throughout the Franco dictatorship; (4) victims of torture, most of which was applied in confinement; and (5) former forced laborers. See Ana Messuti, "La querella argentina. La aplicación del principio de la justicia universal al caso de las deapariciones forzadas," in Rafael Escudero Alday and Carmenn Pérez Gonzalez (eds.) *Desapariciones Forzadas, represión política y crímenes del Franquismo*, Madrid: Trotta, pp. 112–40, here 129.
25 In this context, Sikkink has described the normative agency for Argentina under the Kircher government with regard to accountability processes as a "global human rights protagonist" from the Global South. Kathryn Sikkink: "From Pariah to Global Protagonist: Argentina and the Struggle for International Human Rights," *Latin American Politics and Society*, 2008, vol. 50, 1–29.
26 AI Spanish division significantly chose Buenos Aires to release this report, now and again outlining how the Spanish state is not complying with its international obligations. Amnistía Internacional, Sección Española, *Casos cerrados, heridas abiertas: El desemparo de las víctimas de la Guerra Civil y del franquismo en España*, Online. Available at https://doc.es.amnesty.org/ms-opac/doc?q=mssearch_fld41:"justiciauniversal"&start=20&rows=1&sort=fecha desc&fq=norm&fv=*&fo=and&fq=mssearch_mlt98&fv=gseg01&fo=and (accessed 15 August 2018).
27 "El gobierno español frenó la declaración de víctimas del franquismo ante la jueza María Servini de Cubría," *La Nación*, 8 May 2013.
28 The severe restriction of universal jurisdiction was triggered after a Spanish court ordered the detention of several Chinese political leaders for the repression in Tibet. See Cambio 16, *España da la espalda a la Justicia Universal* 22, March, 2014. Like the first limitations of the universal jurisdiction principle in Spanish legislation under the PSOE (Partido Socialista Obrero Español, Spanish Socialist Workers Party) government in spring 2009, this demonstrates that the main reason for its reduction

and partial abolition is external pressure from powerful nations, in that case from the United States and Israel, and the resulting diplomatic tensions in asymmetrical, international power relations. Stephanie S. Golob, "Windows on the World: Spanish Courts and the Location of Universal Jurisdiction," Paper presented at the *51st Annual Meeting of the International Studies Association*, ISA (New Orleans, 17–20 February 2010), Online. Available at http://politicasdelamemoria.org/es/publicaciones-equipo/publicaciones-enpdf/cat_view/43-publicaciones-del-equipo/64-publicaciones-del-2010.html (accessed 30 November 2017).

29 "La juez argentina que investiga el franquismo recoge pruebas en España," *El País*, 19 May 2014.

30 "El Gobierno deniega la extradición de ocho ministros franquistas," *El País*, 14 March 2015.

31 Francisco Ferrándiz Martín, "De las fosas comunes a los derechos humanos: El descubrimiento de las desapariciones forzadas en la España contemporánea," *Revista de Antropología Social*, 2010, vol. 19, 161–89.

32 "Asunción Mendieta halla por fin a su padre. Identifican los restos de Timoteo Mendieta entre los exhumados en Guadalajara," *Público*, 9 June 2017.

33 Naomi Roht-Arriaza, "The Pinochet Effect and the Spanish Contribution to Universal Jurisdiction," in Wolfgang Kaleck, Michael Ratner, Tobias Singelstein, and Peter Weiss (eds.) *International Prosecution of Human Rights Crimes*, New York: Springer, 2007, pp. 113–23.

28

MILITARIZED SEXUAL VIOLENCE AND CAMPAIGNS FOR REDRESS

Vera Mackie

In 2018, the Nobel Peace Prize was awarded to physician Denis Mukwege and sexual violence survivor Nadia Murad for their advocacy for victims of militarized sexual violence in the Democratic Republic of the Congo.[1] As Murad comments in an account of her experiences, it is only in the early twenty-first century that we have seen systematic prosecutions for crimes of sexual violence committed in wartime.[2]

In this essay, I trace how the issue of militarized sexual violence came to be embedded in international legal institutions. In the late twentieth and early twenty-first century, global advocacy movements pushed the matter of accountability, inserting the issue of militarized sexual violence in the ad hoc tribunals of the International Criminal Tribunal for Yugoslavia (ICTY, 1993–2017) and the International Criminal Tribunal for Rwanda (ICTR, 1994–2015). The Rome Statute of the International Criminal Court was adopted in 1998 and entered into force in 2002 when the International Criminal Court was formally established in The Hague. The Rome Statute explicitly mentions rape, sexual slavery, enforced prostitution, forced pregnancy, and enforced sterilization as crimes against humanity.[3] The United Nations (UN) Security Council Resolution 1325 in October 2000 reinforces recognition of sexual violence and rape as crimes against humanity and further strengthens provisions under the earlier Geneva Conventions. The UN Security Council Resolution 1820 in June 2008 focuses on women, peace, and security and the prevention of sexual violence.[4]

What was the legal situation before the Rome Statutes and the UN Security Council Resolutions? To answer this question, I range widely, for issues of sexual violence, enforced sexual labor, enforced labor migration (known by some as "trafficking"), and militarized sexual violence are often hard to clearly separate out in practice. My sources include publications from movements for redress, legal documents, official and unofficial war crimes tribunals, archival sources, and testimonies collected by redress movements.[5]

The early twentieth century

In the late nineteenth and early twentieth centuries, trans-Atlantic Anglophone women's reform movements focused on what was then known as the "White Slave Trade," or the "White Slave Traffic." In these debates, there was anxiety that white women were allegedly being forced into sexual slavery by entrepreneurs in the Eastern European and Asian regions. In fact, though, most of the enforced labor migration and enforced migration for sexual labor was inflicted on women from the Asian region.[6] In the early twentieth century, the

International Agreement for the Suppression of the "White Slave Traffic" was signed on 18 May 1904 and entered into force on 18 July 1905. The International Convention for the Suppression of the White Slave Traffic was signed in Paris on 4 May 1910.[7]

Complementing these efforts, the first Hague Conventions on the laws of war dealt with unacceptable behavior in wartime, although they did not explicitly name crimes of sexual violence, as Christoph Schiessl explains:

> The two Hague Conventions in 1899 and 1907 featured a unique approach, unprecedented in international law regarding war. The so-called Martens Clause stipulated that: "[t]he inhabitants and the belligerents remain under the protection and the rule of the principles of the law of nations, as they result from the usages established among civilized peoples, from the law of humanity, and the dictates of the public conscience" ... It therefore acknowledged the existence of certain basic principles of humanity, which have to be respected under all circumstances, even if they are not put in treaty form. The antecedent of what would later be called humanitarian law, which stands above national law, can be seen here. It was to be used during the post-World War II Nuremberg Tribunal helping to establish the "crimes against humanity" clause. More specifically, Article 46 reads: "[f]amily honor and rights, the lives of persons ... as well as religious convictions and practice, must be respected." The term "family honor" can be read to include violence against women. Interestingly, in this approach the rape would be targeted not at women in particular, but at their families, meaning male members, as well. Rape becomes a crime of honor in this interpretation, not so much a crime of violence against women.[8]

After World War I, the League of Nations was founded at the Paris Peace Conference of 1919. The Commission on Responsibilities of the Paris Peace Commission listed enforced prostitution and rape as war crimes, specifically mentioning "[a]bduction of girls and women for the purpose of enforced prostitution," although the crime was not pursued.[9] This suggests that the practice of enforced military prostitution (allegedly by Germany in this case) well predated the Japanese military's practices that came to light at the end of World War II.

The Slavery Convention, signed at Geneva on 25 September 1926 and entered into force on 9 March 1927, was largely focused on chattel slavery.[10] The International Labour Organization (ILO) was established in 1919 in the wake of World War I. It sponsored the Convention Concerning Forced or Compulsory Labour signed on 28 June 1930, which entered into force on 1 May 1932.[11] In 1932 the League of Nations Commission of Enquiry into Traffic in Women and Children in the East conducted an investigation into the issue of enforced labor and enforced migration of women and children.[12] After World War II, the issue of militarized sexual violence received limited attention in some of the military tribunals. First, though, some background is needed.

The military management of sexuality in the Asia-Pacific War (1937–45)

Japanese military forces were stationed on the Asian mainland from the late nineteenth century in order to protect Japanese trading interests after the Sino-Japanese War of 1894–5, the annexation of Taiwan in 1895, the Russo-Japanese War of 1904–5 and the annexation of Korea in 1910. Over the following years the Japanese military gained control of more and more Chinese territory, including the creation of the puppet state of Manzhouguo (Manchukuo) in 1932, unleashing the Nanjing (Nanking) Massacre of 1937 and subsequent war with China. By 1945, the Japanese military had captured territory in the Pacific, South Asia, Southeast Asia, and East Asia, setting up military brothels wherever they advanced.

From the 1870s, entrepreneurs traveled overseas to organize brothels where they profited from the sexual labor of emigrant Japanese women.[13] A system of licensed prostitution also was established in Japan and its colonies. Soldiers, sailors, traders, and laborers had access to these forms of prostitution, as well as brothels run by locals. Although each of these systems is distinct from the military brothels, many argue that the long decades of involvement in various aspects of the prostitution industry in Japan and neighboring countries facilitated the creation of the military wartime facilities.[14]

Some brothels were directly managed by the military; some were managed by private entrepreneurs but regulated by the military; and some were private but catered to soldiers. The first directly military-run brothels were set up in the 1930s.[15] Military doctors conducted medical inspections and distributed prophylactics, while the military issued regulations concerning the brothels. In colonial and military situations the practices of state-sanctioned licensed prostitution and enforced military prostitution reinforced racialized hierarchies, and reinforced the conceptual divisions between "us" and "them," which made militarism and colonialism possible.[16] Military training fostered aggression, with an intimate relationship between masculinity, violence, and sexuality.[17]

Perhaps 100,000, 200,000, or even more women were coerced into military prostitution. As far as we know, the majority were from Korea (a Japanese colony from 1910 to 1945) and the occupied Chinese territories. Japanese women could also be found in the brothels.[18] Women were captured and enslaved wherever the military advanced. Some were indentured; some were misled into thinking they were being recruited for other work; some may have known what they were initially recruited for but were then forcibly transported from one battlefield to another. The women were referred to in Japanese by the offensive euphemism "*ianfu*" (comfort women), a term that has now been translated into several languages.[19] Survivors were discovered by the Allied troops throughout Asia and the Pacific towards the end of the war.[20]

Post-World War II military tribunals

War crimes trials were held against Germany in 1945 and 1946. The Charter of the International Military Tribunal in London in 1945 defines "crimes against peace" and "crimes against humanity." These new categories were necessary to capture those situations where human rights violations went beyond The Hague-codified war crimes committed in military conflicts between nation-states.[21]

After its surrender, Japan was occupied by the Allies from 1945 to 1952. The International Military Tribunal for the Far East (IMTFE, or the Tokyo Trial) was held from April 1946 to November 1948. Interrogation records included reference to the army and navy setting up military brothels, asking local leaders to provide women, the kidnapping of local women, or instances of sexual assault.[22] Sexual enslavement and forced prostitution were barely mentioned during the Tokyo Tribunal, despite extensive knowledge and documentation. Charges were, however, brought against Japanese defendants for war crimes committed during the Nanjing invasion under the 1907 Hague Convention IV and the 1929 Geneva Convention. The Nanjing Massacre – also known as the Rape of Nanjing – involved violence, torture, and sexual assaults. Although there were no specific prosecutions for the sexual enslavement of women in the Tokyo Tribunal, this issue was mentioned in some of the regional tribunals.[23]

In February 1948, managers of such facilities received sentences of 5 to 20 years in the Dutch War Crimes Tribunal in Batavia.[24] They were indicted for forcing European and what were then known as "Eurasian" women into prostitution in the Javanese city of Semarang.[25] Later critics have pointed out that the Dutch tribunals did not address the situation of the many Indonesian women who also were enslaved. Although the Tokyo Tribunal did not prosecute the issue, the interrogation records have provided resources for later generations of scholars, activists, and lawyers.

Further advances came with the Fourth Geneva Convention of 1949, which included the following stipulations:

Article 12: "Women shall be treated with all consideration due to their sex."
Article 14: "Women shall be treated with all the regard due to their sex and shall in all cases benefit by treatment as favourable as that granted to men."
Article 25: "In any camps in which women prisoners of war, as well as men, are accommodated, separate dormitories shall be provided for them."
Article 27: "Women shall be especially protected against any attack on their honour, in particular against rape, enforced prostitution, or any form of indecent assault."[26]

The UN Convention for the Suppression of the Traffic in Persons and of the Exploitation of the Prostitution of Others entered into force in 1949.

At the end of the Allied Occupation in 1952, Japan paid reparations to some former combatant nations and provided development assistance to neighboring countries. In these agreements, there was no further reflection on the question of what crimes had or had not been prosecuted in the post-World War II tribunals. The president of the Philippines pardoned Japanese war criminals and their Philippine collaborators in 1953.[27] Relations with Indonesia were normalized in 1958, with war debts deemed to be settled at this time. In 1965, Japan and South Korea signed the Treaty on Basic Relations between Japan and the Republic of Korea (ROK). Under the normalization treaty the grants and loans provided at this time foreclosed any future claims against the Japanese government. When relations were normalized with the People's Republic of China in 1972, the Chinese government also waived claims for reparations.[28]

The Korean War and its aftermath

At the end of World War II, the Korean peninsula was split between the Russian-affiliated North and the US-affiliated South. War broke out from 1950 to 1953. The North–South conflict is still unresolved, with the two sides in an uneasy truce to the present day.

In May 1951, a delegation from the Women's International Democratic Federation (WIDF) visited Korea and reported on allegations of atrocities by the "UN" troops (US, UK, South Korea, and their allies). The report includes accounts of sexual violence and reports of setting up brothels for the military, with differentiation made between those serving US and UK and South Korean troops.[29]

During and after the Korean War, a sexual service industry developed in South Korea to service the US and other Allied soldiers. In Japan, prostitution was officially prohibited from 1958 (while continuing tacitly), but in South Korea exceptions were made in specific areas around military bases and in tourism precincts. The policy of regulation allowed for medical examinations and testing for sexually transmissible diseases.[30] Because South Korea was seen by the US forces as a "hardship" post where troops needed to be on continuous alert, soldiers (until recently) tended not to be accompanied by families, and were deployed for a relatively short time. This means that there was limited meaningful contact with the local population, and a greater demand for commercialized sexual services. A distinction developed between "respectable" Korean women, who were seen to be worthy of protection, and the stigmatized women who provided sexual services. Different establishments serviced Korean soldiers and "UN" soldiers (the US and its allies), with further distinctions between white and African American clientele.[31]

For some of the post-Korean War period, sex workers around bases were referred to as *wianbu* (*ianfu*, comfort women) and brothels were referred to as *wianso* (*ianjo*, comfort stations), suggesting an association between the Japanese army's military brothels and the sexual service industry for the US and Allied soldiers in South Korea. In the early 1970s, violent incidents erupted in the camptowns, building on African American troops' resentment at their exclusion from some establishments, and local peoples' resentment at the continued presence of US troops.[32] The US army and the South Korean government cooperated in encouraging businesses and camptown workers to provide sexual services to African American soldiers, a not unusual example of government-to-government discussion of the provision of sexual services for troops. At the same time, the US military and the South Korean government cooperated in a program of inspection for sexually transmissible diseases, despite the official US policy of not condoning prostitution.[33]

The continued presence of US troops in South Korea means the perpetuation of this sexual service industry. With democratization in South Korea since the 1980s, it has become easier for survivors of the militarized sex industry and their advocates to speak out about sexual exploitation. In 1992, the brutal murder of a Korean woman by a US soldier prompted the creation of the National Campaign for Eradication of Crimes by US Troops in Korea. In 2009, a group of women called for apology and compensation from the South Korean and US governments that had facilitated the sexual service industry around US bases since the 1950s. These elderly former sex workers gained inspiration from the campaigns by the survivors of enforced military prostitution in the Asia-Pacific War.[34] Their campaigns brought together two issues that had hitherto been kept separate: the wartime militarized sexual violence perpetrated by the Japanese military and the commercialized sexual service industry that had developed around military bases with the collusion of the South Korean and US governments. The campaigners refused to see the military sexual service industry as different from the enforced sexual service in the Asia-Pacific War. They also sought solidarity with other countries that hosted military bases and the associated sexual service industries. In Okinawa, too, incidents of sexual violence by US military personnel prompted political activism.[35]

Feminist campaigns

In Anglophone circles, a heightened awareness of sexual violence came from the "consciousness raising" groups of the women's liberation movement of the 1970s, where women shared their reflections on the sexual politics of everyday life. Once women had shared private experiences of sexual assault with other women, they brought this issue into public spheres of discussion. Susan Brownmiller's 1975 book *Against Our Will* turned international attention to rape as a political issue. Brownmiller's book also included extensive discussion of militarized sexual violence, including the military brothels run by the German and Japanese military forces during World War II and the sexual violence perpetrated by US soldiers in the Vietnam War.[36] In the UK, the group Women Against Rape (WAR) was formed in 1976.[37] In Australia, groups with the name "Women Against Rape in War" were formed in several major cities. They protested against rape in war on ANZAC Day, the national day of military commemoration.[38]

While commentators often refer to decades of "silence" about the abovementioned militarized prostitution/sexual slavery system in the Asia-Pacific War, there was in fact widespread knowledge of the system in Japan and its wartime occupied territories. The encounters in the military "brothels" lived on in the memories of the military personnel and the enslaved women, not to mention the officers, doctors, bureaucrats, pimps, and entrepreneurs who facilitated the system. Early postwar memoirs and literary works mention the system and, as noted above, ample evidence appeared in interrogation reports prepared for various military tribunals. Several books on the issue appeared in the Japanese language in the 1970s.[39] In Anglophone literature, too, there are casual references to so-called "comfort girls" in the early post-World War II years, suggesting tacit knowledge of the system.[40]

Nonetheless, a changed understanding of the issue of militarized sexual violence was necessary before this issue could become the subject of international human rights discourse. The feminist movements of the 1970s and beyond were vital to this changed understanding as were coalitions between feminists in different countries.[41] In the early post-World War II years, the existence of military "brothels" was not really problematized and the question of coercion was rarely raised. By the late twentieth century, however, feminist commentators were talking about the issue in terms of a "war crime" and a "crime against humanity."[42]

From the 1970s, feminists from South Korea, Japan, and Southeast Asian nations collaborated in protests against contemporary forms of prostitution, in particular the purchase of sexual services by tourists in East and Southeast Asia. They then connected this issue with the provision of sexual services for the US military stationed in South Korea, Japan, and other places, as noted above.[43] They also put these issues into historical perspective by exploring the history of enforced military prostitution/sexual slavery.[44] In April 1988 at the International Conference on Women and Tourism at Jejudo in South Korea, Yun Chung-ok of Ewha University presented a paper on the wartime system. In January 1989 women staged a demonstration in Seoul, protesting plans to send a Korean representative to the funeral of Emperor Hirohito (1901–89), for they held the wartime Emperor ultimately responsible for the actions of the Japanese military. In May 1990, when then-president of South Korea Roh Tae Woo was planning a state visit to Japan, women's organizations wrote to him, demanding that he raise the issue with the Japanese government. At a state banquet in honor of Roh's visit, Japan's Emperor Akihito expressed regret for the suffering of Koreans under Japanese colonial rule. At this stage the official Japanese government position was that military brothels had been privately run. Korean women's organizations wrote to then-prime minister of Japan Kaifu Toshiki prior to his visit to South Korea in October 1990, demanding an admission, an apology, and compensation.

The Korean Council for the Women Drafted for Military Sexual Slavery (Chongsindae munje taech'aek hyopuhoe) was founded in November 1990 as an umbrella group for several feminist organizations in South Korea. It was also allied with feminist groups in Japan, Taiwan, Burma, the Philippines, and North Korea. The Council has been at the forefront of research on the issue and in campaigns for redress for Korean survivors. In Japan, the Asian Women's Association and the Violence Against Women in War Network (VAWW-Net-Japan) have been important.[45] In the early stages of campaigns on this issue, it tended to be framed as an issue between the Japanese state and its former colony of Korea. As more and more women from other countries came forward, though, it could no longer be framed as a bilateral issue. The issue was also complicated by the division of the Korean peninsula into North and South.

Until the 1990s very few individual survivors had provided public testimony of their experiences. A Japanese woman, Yoshie Mihara (1921–93), published an autobiography under the pseudonym Shirota Suzuko in 1971. In 1979, filmmaker Yamatani Tetsuo made a documentary and published a book about a Korean survivor, Pae Pong-gi (1914–91), who lived out the post-World War II years in Okinawa.[46] On 14 August 1991, a Korean survivor, Kim Hak Sun (1924–97) held a press conference to tell of her wartime experiences. The date was significant, as it was one day before the anniversary of Japan's surrender in World War II, 15 August. She was soon joined by other survivors. Dutch-Australian Jan Ruff O'Herne came forward in 1992 and published her autobiography in 1994. Maria Rosa Henson (1927–97) from the Philippines also came forward in 1992 and published her autobiography in 1996. Taiwanese survivor Liu Huang A-tao (1923–2011) told her story in 1992.[47]

On 4 March 1992 the Korean Council for the Women Drafted for Military Sexual Slavery submitted a petition to the UN Human Rights Commission (UNHRC), requesting that it investigate atrocities committed against women during World War II and pressure the Japanese government to pay reparations. The UNHRC placed the issue on the agenda for its August 1992 meeting. The UNHRC's Subcommission for the Protection of Minorities described the system as a "crime against humanity that violated the human rights of Asian women and the international agreement against forced labor that Japan signed in 1932."[48]

Nongovernmental organizations (NGOs) conducted a fundraising campaign to support the survivors. The South Korean government of then-president Kim Young Sam (1921–2015) chose not to bring claims against the Japanese government, but did pass a special bill in August 1993 to support the survivors. Each survivor was to receive a one-time payment of 5 million *won* (about US $6,250 at that time) and monthly support of 250,000 *won*.[49] In Taiwan, the government pays monthly social welfare payments and medical insurance for the survivors and provides financial support for the Taipei Women's Rescue Foundation.

The initial response of the Japanese government was to deny direct military involvement. In January 1992, however, historian Yoshimi Yoshiaki went public with documents he had found in official archives. The "Taiwan Army Telegram 602" of 12 March 1942 contains the following passage:

> In regard to the Secret Telegram of Army No 63, we've been asked by the Southern Army General Command to dispatch as soon as possible 50 native comfort women to "Borneo." On the basis of Secret Telegram of Army No 623,

> we request travel permits for the 3 operators named below [names deleted by Japanese authorities], who have been investigated and selected by the military police.[50]

Yoshimi revealed six documents in all from the military archives that incriminated the Japanese government. After the release of these documents, the Japanese government initially issued a statement by then chief cabinet secretary Kōno Yōhei, which admitted government involvement. The government investigated the issue and released a report in 1993 acknowledging that there had been military "comfort stations" in "Japan, China, the Philippines, Indonesia, the then Malaya, Thailand, the then Burma, the then New Guinea, Hong Kong, Macao, and the then French Indochina."[51]

With respect to compensation, the Japanese government maintained that all claims for reparation had been settled in the treaties with former combatant nations. Rather than acknowledge responsibility by providing compensation or reparations, it facilitated the creation of a private organization generally known as the "Asian Women's Fund."[52] The Fund sought donations from private individuals, and in July 1996 it announced it would pay US$18,500 to each of around 300 survivors in Korea, Taiwan, and the Philippines.[53] This has been contentious among the survivors and their supporters, with many seeing the money as tainted.[54]

In 1996, UN Special Rapporteur Radhika Coomaraswamy described the system as "military sexual slavery" and recommended that the Japanese government pay compensation. This strong call prompted another wave of denials from public figures on the political right.[55] Although there have been fears that ultraconservative prime minister Abe Shinzō would retract the Kōno Statement, for the moment this statement still stands. Abe's statement on the 70th anniversary of the end of World War II in 2015 stopped short of repudiating the Kōno Statement, although it has been criticized as historically inaccurate in other ways.[56]

Litigation and international political pressure

In December 1991 Kim Hak Sun was part of a class action against the government of Japan sponsored by the Association of Pacific War Victims and Bereaved Families. A separate suit was filed by four women at the Shimonoseki branch of the Yamaguchi District Court. In the late 1990s, 16 women from Yu County in China sued the Japanese state for compensation and an apology, supported by a team of Japanese and Chinese lawyers. Their claims were denied, due to the statute of limitations and to the individuals' lack of standing to sue the state.[57] In August 1999, nine Taiwanese women brought a suit in the Tokyo District Court, which turned down the case. Appeals were subsequently lost in the Tokyo High Court in February 2004 and the Tokyo Supreme Court in February 2005.[58] Another case was brought in the United States in September 2000 by 18 survivors. The US court system allows litigation where human rights abuses have occurred, even if the events did not occur in the United States.[59] This case went as far the Supreme Court, but was unsuccessful.

Democratic Congressional representative Mike Honda from California submitted a nonbinding resolution to the Congressional Committee on Foreign Relations on 12 January 2007. The resolution called on the government of Japan to apologize formally and accept historical responsibility "in a clear and unequivocal manner for … the coercion of young women into military sexual slavery."[60] The House Subcommittee on Asia, the Pacific, and the Global Environment held a public hearing where Korean survivors Yi Yong-su and Kim Kun-ja and Dutch-Australian Jan Ruff O'Herne testified. The US House of Representatives approved House Resolution 121 in July 2007. Similar resolutions have been passed in the Netherlands, Canada, and the European Parliament. There was a related campaign in Australia, with a few local governments passing resolutions, but none passed at the national government level.[61] In each of these places, diasporic communities played an important role. In parallel with these transnational campaigns, local activities in support of the survivors continued in each country.

Women's International War Crimes Tribunal on Japan's Military Sexual Slavery

The movement for redress in the Asia-Pacific region has also been supported by research. A team in South Korea has been collecting survivor testimonies since 1993.[62] At an Asian Women's Solidarity Conference in Seoul in 1998, members of VAWW-Net Japan proposed holding a People's Tribunal.[63] The South Korean team conducting research for the Tribunal was formed in April 1999, with similar teams based in other countries.[64] Planning for the Tribunal took two and a half years and involved preparatory meetings in Seoul, Tokyo, Shanghai, Manila, and Taipei, and a judges' meeting in The Hague. North and South Korean teams cooperated in preparing a joint indictment, which also included mention of ethnically Korean survivors living in China and Japan. Survivors from the newly independent nation of Timor-Leste also participated.[65] The Women's International War Crimes Tribunal on Japan's Military Sexual Slavery was held in Tokyo on 8–12 December 2000. This was a people's tribunal with no legal force, but it did follow international legal protocols. The judges had experience in International Criminal Tribunals; professional lawyers prosecuted the case, and amici curiae (friends of the court) presented defenses on behalf of the Japanese government, which did not send representatives. Some 64 survivors attended from South Korea, North Korea, the People's Republic of China, Taiwan, the Philippines, the Netherlands, Indonesia, Timor-Leste, and Japan; 20 survivors testified. Expert witnesses and former military personnel also testified.[66] The tribunal indicted the Emperor of Japan, high military officials, and the Japanese government for crimes against humanity.

The Women's Tribunal drew on the papers of the International Military Tribunal for the Far East and on research carried out by historians, lawyers, and activists. The judgment was handed down one year later in December 2001. It found that the Japanese Emperor, the Japanese government, and the other accused individuals were liable for criminal responsibility for crimes against humanity committed through the system of sexual slavery.[67]

The move for the Women's Tribunal was led by activists in Japan in collaboration with teams from the countries whose nationals were represented at the tribunal. The historian and activist Kim Puja has commented:

> The efforts of all those involved serve, I believe, as a model of how the power of women and citizenry can create a tribunal for the investigation and prosecution of war crimes. Moreover, as the result of a cooperative alliance between women from both perpetrator and victimized countries, the realization of the Tribunal

offers one model for a form of feminism that transcends national borders. By foregrounding the concepts of *gender* and *people's* justice, this historic event also contributed to the development of international law, which has traditionally been male dominant and Eurocentric in orientation (and had therefore neglected the crime of the "comfort women" system).[68]

The Wednesday demonstration

In South Korea, Buddhist organizations and other NGOs conducted fundraising campaigns to support the survivors. From 1992, a group of elderly survivors shared a rented house in Seoul, known as the House of Sharing (the Korean name *Nanum-ui Jip* literally means "our house"). The House of Sharing moved to the suburbs of Seoul in 1995. As well as housing the survivors, the complex also includes a museum, a gallery of paintings by the survivors, and memorial statues to those who have passed away.[69] Similar support activities are carried out for survivors in other countries, although there are no doubt countless other survivors who have not come forward with their stories of wartime abuse.[70]

In January 1992, then-prime minister of Japan Miyazawa Kiichi visited South Korea. On Wednesday, 8 January 1992, survivors and their supporters gathered in front of the Japanese Embassy in downtown Seoul. They demanded that the Japanese government make an official apology and provide compensation, chanting "Apologize!" "Punish!" "Compensate!" There has been a "Wednesday demonstration" every week since then. Demonstrators hold placards in Japanese, Korean, or English. The elderly survivors sit on portable stools facing the Japanese Embassy, flanked by their younger supporters. When international supporters visit Seoul, they often join in the demonstrations.[71] Their placards show that they are addressing multiple audiences: the South Korean government and the South Korean public, the Japanese government and the Japanese public, and an international community that often communicates in the English language.

To mark the 1,000th Wednesday demonstration on 14 December 2011, a commemorative statue was erected on the site of the demonstrations. It depicts a young woman in Korean ethnic dress and bobbed hair seated on a chair, facing the Embassy, with an empty chair beside her. On the platform beside the statue is a plaque, with an inscription in Korean, Japanese, and English:

> 14 December 2011 marks the 1,000th Wednesday demonstration for the solution of Japanese military sexual slavery issue after its first rally on 8 January 1992 in front of the Japanese Embassy. This peace monument stands to commemorate the spirit and the deep history of the Wednesday demonstration.[72]

The figure wears Korean ethnic dress (*hanbok*, or *chima jeogori*); her bobbed hair suggests that she is a young unmarried woman. Her fists are clenched on her lap; and she has bare feet. She does not smile, but rather stares steadfastly ahead. A small bird is perched on one shoulder. Behind her, at pavement level, is a mosaic, suggesting the shadow of an old woman. The mosaic also includes a butterfly. The statue and its "shadow" suggest the different stages of life of the survivor: the young woman before her ordeal and the old woman who refuses to forget. The bird is an icon of peace and of escape, while the butterfly has spiritual connotations. The empty seat suggests those who are missing, but also provides a site for participation in the installation, as demonstrators or visitors have their photographs taken beside the statue.

The statue does not simply commemorate the suffering of the thousands and thousands of women who suffered from militarized sexual violence. It also commemorates the determination of those demonstrators and supporters who keep the issue alive. Placed at the site where these demonstrations have now occurred for over 25 years, the statue is a form of petition to the Japanese government and its diplomatic representatives. The statue has been reproduced in several sites, including the War and Women's Human Rights Museum in Seoul, and several international sites. These commemorative statues have prompted international controversies and crises in international relations. The statue, its replicas, and the museums that have been dedicated to the issue of militarized sexual violence underline the importance of cultural representations and cultural politics in political campaigns.[73]

Japan–South Korea joint communiqué

In December 2015, the South Korean and Japanese governments issued a joint communiqué. Then-foreign minister of Japan Kishida Fumio stated that Prime Minister Abe Shinzō "expresses anew his most sincere apologies and remorse to all the women who underwent immeasurable and painful experiences and suffered incurable physical and psychological wounds as comfort women." Kishida stated that the Japanese government would provide the South Korean government with funds for the establishment of a foundation for the care of the survivors and that "this issue is resolved finally and irreversibly." The statement was met with hostility by the South Korean survivors, who felt that as a basic principle of restorative justice they should have been consulted before any government-to-government agreement was reached. Then-South Korean foreign minister Yun Byung Se confirmed that the issue is "resolved finally and irreversibly" and that the ROK and Japan would "refrain from accusing or criticizing each other regarding this issue in the international community." The statue was not mentioned in the Japanese statement, but the South Korean statement included an acknowledgment that "the Government of Japan is concerned about the statue built in front of the Embassy of Japan in Seoul" and that the South Korean government would "strive to solve this issue in an agreeable manner through taking measures such as consulting with related organizations about possible ways of addressing this issue."[74] The agreement also returned the issue to a bilateral one between Japan and South Korea. Survivors from other countries, though, demanded similar recognition. The Japan-ROK joint communiqué was a matter of geopolitics, an attempt to forge a closer alliance between the governments of the United States, Japan, and South Korea against China. The agreement was brought into question by Park Geun-Hye's successor as president, Moon Jae-In, who in 2018 announced plans to dissolve the foundation set up with Japanese funds. The South Korean government has proposed a research centre on the issue and a national day of commemoration.[75] In November 2018, the UN Committee on Enforced Disappearances "voiced its concerns about the fact that Japan had not provided adequate compensation to the victims."[76]

While the victims of militarized sexual abuse in the Asia-Pacific war have not received redress in courts of law,[77] their campaigns have contributed to the visibility of the issue of wartime sexual abuse in conflict situations and the necessity of dealing with such situations in international law.

Sexual violence and international law

Although the issue of rape in war and the issue of enforced prostitution had garnered some attention before the World War II, it was the conjunction of two issues – the history of the militarized sexual abuse perpetrated by the Japanese military in the Asia-Pacific War and the revelations of militarized sexual abuse in conflicts in the former Yugoslavia and in Rwanda – which turned the world's attention to sexual violence in the 1990s. The situations in Yugoslavia and Rwanda involved conflict between ethnic groups in a civil war rather than conflict between nation-states (although the former Yugoslavia would later break up into several independent states). Two UN-sponsored ad hoc Tribunals were set up: the International Criminal Tribunal for the former Yugoslavia (ICTY) from 1993 and the International Criminal Court for Rwanda (ICTR) from 1994. They initiated pathfinding judgments in criminalizing sexual violence in international law.

The International Criminal Tribunal for Rwanda (ICTR) brought down its judgment in 1998. In *Prosecutor v. Akayesu*, Akayesu was sentenced to life imprisonment for the crime of genocide and 15 years for rape and torture as crimes against humanity.[78] On 22 February 2001 the International Criminal Tribunal for Yuglosavia handed down its judgment in *Prosecutor v. Kunarac, Kovac and Vukovic*. They were found guilty as principals and accessories of rape, enslavement, and outrages on personal dignity.[79] They were found to have committed war crimes and crimes against humanity. As legal scholar Rosalind Dixon explains,

> The verdict in *Kunarac* was the first time a commanding officer, and all the defendants in an indictment, were convicted as primary actors ("rapists") rather than "simply" having command responsibility for or being accessories to rape … It was the first time that a custodial sentence for crimes of sexual violence was rendered visible from the obscurity of "lesser" concurrent sentences. *Kunarac* was also the first indictment in which the crime of sexual enslavement was charged as enslavement – either as a war crime under Article 27 of the Fourth Geneva Convention, or as a crime against humanity. It was the first time the objectification of women as live pornography was prosecuted as a war crime before the ICTY, following the lead of the International Criminal Tribunal for Rwanda (ICTR) in *Akayesu*. In Kunarac, the Trial Chamber also expanded the definition of rape adopted in *Akayesu* and *Furundzija*, to encompass all situations in which consent is not "freely" and "voluntarily" given.[80]

Bosnian plaintiffs also made use of the US Alien Torts Claims Act, which, as we have seen above, had also been attempted by survivors of the sexual abuse perpetrated by the Japanese military in the Asia-Pacific War. The plaintiffs sued Bosnian Serb leader Radovan Karadzic on behalf of Bosnian "women and men who suffered genocide, war crimes, summary execution, wrongful death, torture, cruel, inhuman or degrading treatment, assault, battery, rape and intentional infliction of emotional harm." They were awarded compensation by the Court, but this is unlikely to be paid.[81] The cases concerning the former Yugoslavia also brought out that men, too, could be victims of sexual violence and sexualized forms of torture in wartime.

The ICTR and ICTY judged genocidal rape to be a crime against humanity and "brought the issue of gendered violence to the center of the international community's attention."[82] These were ad hoc Tribunals established to deal with specific conflicts. The next development was the establishment of the International Criminal Court. The Rome Statute of the International Criminal Court was adopted in on 17 July 1998 and entered into force on 1 July 2002, when the International Criminal Court was formally established in The Hague. The Rome Statute explicitly mentions rape, sexual slavery, enforced prostitution, forced pregnancy, enforced sterilization, and sexual violence as crimes against humanity.[83] The International Criminal Court has several investigations and preliminary investigations in progress and has convicted 39 individuals. Among the investigations that have concluded, the decision in the trial of Jean-Pierre Bemba, former vice president of the Central African Republic in 2016 was the first time the International Criminal Court convicted someone of sexual violence.[84]

The UN Security Council Resolution 1325 in October 2000 reinforces recognition of sexual violence and rape as crimes against humanity and further strengthens provisions under the earlier Geneva Conventions. The UN Security Council Resolution 1820 in June 2008 focuses on women, peace and security, and the prevention of sexual violence.[85]

Conclusions

Recent years have seen the issue of militarized sexual violence become a matter of concern for international law through the institutions of the UN, the UN Security Council, the International Criminal Court, and the ad hoc military tribunals in Rwanda and the former Yugoslavia. The issue of sexual violence in military conflict situations has long been acknowledged, but was not usually prosecuted as a war crime. One factor in bringing this issue to international attention was feminist campaigns that focused on a changed understanding of rape and other forms of sexual violence as a political issue that should be spoken about, rather than treated as a shameful secret. Before the prosecutions in Rwanda and the former Yugoslavia, decades of political work helped bring the issue of militarized sexual violence to light: mining historical records, collecting and publishing testimonies, and conducting people's tribunals. NGOs interacted with the UN and its committees, resulting in statements by the relevant committees and special rapporteurs. We still hear regular reports of sexual violence in conflict situations. Thanks to the efforts of scholars, activists, survivors, and their legal advocates, there is now a more robust system for prosecuting cases of militarized sexual violence. Further research is needed to track how the International Criminal Court will deal with the issue in the future.

Notes

1 This essay draws on research completed as part of the Australian Research Council-funded Future Fellowship project "From Human Rights to Human Security: Changing Paradigms for Dealing with Inequality in the Asia-Pacific Region" (FT0992328). East Asian name order is used in this essay except where an author's name is recorded differently in an English-language publication.

2 Nadia Murad, "I Was An Isis Sex Slave. I Tell My Story Because It Is The Only Weapon I Have," *Guardian*, 7 October 2018; "Nobel Peace Prize Awarded to Denis Mukwege and Nadia Murad for Efforts to End Sexual Violence in War," *ABC News*, 5 October 2018). Online. Available at www.abc.net.au/news/2018-10-05/nobel-peace-prize-awarded-for-efforts-to-end-sexual-violence-war/10344706 (accessed 5 January 2019). See also Anna Maedl, "Rape as Weapon of War in the Eastern DRC: The Victims' Perspective," *Human Rights Quarterly*, 2011, vol. 33, 128–47.

3 Amy Barrow, "UN Security Council Resolutions 1325 and 1820: Constructing Gender in Armed Conflict and International Humanitarian Law," *International Review of the Red Cross*, 2010, no. 877, 227. Online. Available at www.icrc.org/en/international-review/article/un-security-council-resolutions-1325-and-1820-constructing-gender-armed (accessed 5 January 2019).

4 Barrow, "UN Security Council Resolutions 1325 and 1820," 230–3.

5 See also Vera Mackie, "Sexual Violence, Silence, and Human Rights Discourse: The Emergence of the Military Prostitution Issue," in Anne-Marie Hilsdon, Martha Macintyre, Vera Mackie, and Maila Stivens (eds.) *Human Rights and Gender Politics: Asia-Pacific Perspectives*, London: Routledge, 2000, pp. 37–59; Vera Mackie, "In Search of Innocence: Feminist Historians Debate the Legacy of Wartime Japan," *Australian Feminist Studies*, 2005, vol. 20, 207–17; Vera Mackie, "Gender, Geopolitics and Gaps in the Records: Women Glimpsed in the Military Archives," in Kirsty Reid and Fiona Paisley (eds.) *Sources and Methods in Histories of Colonialism: Approaching the Imperial Archive*, Oxford: Routledge, 2017, pp. 129–53; Vera Mackie, "One Thousand Wednesdays: Transnational Activism from Seoul to Glendale," in Barbara Molony and Jennifer Nelson (eds.) *Women's Activism and "Second Wave" Feminism: Transnational Histories*, London: Bloomsbury, 2017, pp. 249–71; Sharon Crozier-De Rosa and Vera Mackie, *Remembering Women's Activism*, Oxford: Routledge, 2019, pp. 161–99; and Vera Mackie and Miyume Tanji, "Militarised Sexualities in East Asia," in Mark McLelland and Vera Mackie (eds.) *The Routledge Handbook of Sexuality Studies in East Asia*, Oxford: Routledge, 2015, pp. 60–73.

6 Julia Martìnez, "Mapping the Trafficking of Women Across Colonial Southeast Asia, 1600s–1930s," *Journal of Global Slavery*, 2016, vol. 1, 224–47.

7 *The International Convention for the Suppression of the White Slave Traffic, Paris, 4 May 1910*, London: His Majesty's Stationary Office, 1912.

8 Christoph Schiessl, "An Element of Genocide: Rape, Total War and International Law in the Twentieth Century," *Journal of Genocide Research*, 2002, vol. 4, no. 2, 203–4. Regarding Article 46, see "Fourth Hague Convention of 1907 on Respecting the Laws and Customs of War on Land" and its "Annex: Regulations Concerning the Laws and Customs of War on Land, The Hague, 18 October 1907." Online. Available at https://ihl-databases.icrc.org/ihl/INTRO/195 (accessed 5 January 2019). For more on humanitarian law, see Kimberly Lowe's essay in this volume.

9 "Commission on the Responsibility of the Authors of the War and on Enforcement of Penalties. Report Presented to the Preliminary Peace Conference, 29 March 1919," *American Journal of International Law*, 1920, vol. 14, nos. 1–2, 114–15; Harry M. Rheah, "The Commission on the Responsibility of the Authors of the War and on Enforcement of Penalties and its Contribution to International Criminal Justice after World War II," *Criminal Law Forum*, 2014, vol. 25, 147–69.

10 League of Nations, "Slavery Convention, Signed at Geneva on 25 September 1926; entered into force 9 March 1927." Online. Available at https://treaties.un.org/doc/Treaties/1926/09/19260925%2003-12%20AM/Ch_XVIII_3p.pdf (accessed 5 January 2019).

11 "Convention Concerning Forced or Compulsory Labour," 28 June 1930; entered into force 1 May 1932. Online. Available at www.ilo.org/dyn/normlex/en/f?p=NORMLEXPUB:12100:0::NO::P12100_ILO_CODE:C029 (accessed 5 January 2019). For more details on the ILO, see Eileen Boris and Jill Jensen's essay in this volume.

12 League of Nations, *Commission of Enquiry into Traffic in Women and Children in the East: Report to the Council*, Geneva: League of Nations, 1932.

13 Bill Mihalopoulos, *Sex in Japan's Globalization, 1870–1930: Prostitutes, Emigration and Nation Building*, London: Pickering & Chatto, 2011.

14 Hyunah Yang, "Revisiting the Issue of Korean 'Military Comfort Women': The Question of Truth and Positionality," *positions*, 1997, vol. 5, no. 1, 7, 59.

15 Mark Driscoll, "Seeds and (Nest) Eggs of Empire: Sexology Manuals/Manual Sexology," in Barbara Molony and Kathleen Uno (eds.) *Gendering Modern Japanese History*, Cambridge, MA: Harvard Asia Center, 2008, pp. 191–225.

16 Vera Mackie, *Feminism in Modern Japan: Citizenship, Embodiment and Sexuality*, Cambridge, UK: Cambridge University Press, 2003, p. 111; Mackie and Tanji, "Militarised Sexualities in East Asia."

17 Suzuki Masahiro, "Sensō ni okeru dansei sekushuariti" [Men's Sexuality During Wartime], in Asai Haruo, Itō Satoru, and Murase Yukihiro (eds.) *Nihon no otoko wa doko kara kite doku e iku?* [Where Have Japanese Men Come From? Where Are They Going?],Tokyo: Jūgatsusha, 2001, pp. 98–111.

18 See, however, a recent book that mentions a figure of 400,000 women, "at least half of whom were Chinese." Peipei Qiu with Su Zhiliang and Chen Lifei, *Chinese Comfort Women: Testimonies from Imperial Japan's Sex Slaves*, Vancouver: UBC Press, 2013, p. 6.

19 Words equivalent to *ianfu* (comfort woman) or *jūgun ianfu* (military comfort woman) appear in several languages. Chinese, Japanese, and Korean use versions of the term with the same Chinese characters: *ianfu* in Japanese, *wianbu* in Korean, and *wèiānfù* in Chinese. Indonesian takes the term *jugun ianfu* directly from the Japanese, while English and Dutch use the direct translations "comfort women" and "*troost meisjes*," respectively. Contemporary writers use these terms reluctantly, for they are offensive to the survivors, but "comfort woman" (or its equivalent in other languages) is the most easily recognized term.

20 Yuki Tanaka, *Japan's Comfort Women: Sexual Slavery and Prostitution during World War II and the US Occupation*, Oxford: Routledge, 2002; Yoshimi Yoshiaki, *Comfort Women: Sexual Slavery in the Japanese Military During World War II*, Suzanne O'Brien (trans.), New York: Columbia University Press, 2002; C. Sarah Soh, *The Comfort Women: Sexual Violence and Postcolonial Memory in Korea and Japan*, Chicago: University of Chicago Press, 2008; and Mackie, "Gender, Geopolitics and Gaps in the Records."

21 Schiessl, "An Element of Genocide," 204.

22 US National Archives and Records Administration (NARA), Record Group 208, Box 226, US Office of War Information, Japanese Prisoner of War Interrogation Report No. 49, Psychological Warfare Team attached to US Army Forces India-Burma Theater, 1944; National Archives of Australia (NAA), C10/7, 8392, Summary Examination of Jose Augusto Gomes, 25 June 1946 and 8385, Summary of Examination of Francisco Tilman de Ataide, 29 June 1946. See also Tessa Morris-Suzuki, "You Don't Want to Know About the Girls? The 'Comfort Women,' the Japanese Military and Allied Forces in the Asia-Pacific War," *Asia-Pacific Journal: Japan Focus*, 2015, vol. 13, no. 31. Online. Available at www.japanfocus.org/-Tessa-Morris_Suzuki/4352/article.html (accessed 5 January 2019).

23 Nicola Henry, "Memory of an Injustice: The 'Comfort Women' and the Legacy of the Tokyo Trial," *Asian Studies Review*, 2013, vol. 37, no. 3, 362–80.

24 Tanaka, *Japan's Comfort Women*, p. 76; William Bradley Horton, "Comfort Women," in Peter Post (ed.) *Encyclopedia of Indonesia in the Pacific War*, Leiden: Brill, 2010, pp. 184–96.

25 As Robert Cribb points out, the attribution of ethnicity and nationality was complex in the Dutch East Indies: "The term 'Dutch' in this context is ambiguous. The Netherlands Indies used a legal system of racial classification which divided the population into 'Europeans,' 'Natives' and 'Foreign Orientals.' The system depended mainly on the paternal line of descent, meaning that some 'Europeans' had a high proportion of indigenous ancestry and some 'Natives' had significant European ancestry. It was also possible for Natives and Foreign Orientals to be legally assimilated to European status. During the occupation, however, the Japanese authorities had generally been influenced in their treatment of people by their physical appearance, rather than their official ethnic status." Robert Cribb, "Avoiding Clemency: The Trial and Transfer of Japanese War Criminals in Indonesia, 1946–1949," *Japanese Studies*, 2011, vol. 31, no. 2, 156–62. In English-language newspaper reports on the discovery of survivors of the enforced military prostitution system in Indonesia and Timor at the end of World War II, the term "Eurasian" is used for those of mixed descent. Mackie, "Gender, Geopolitics and Gaps in the Records."

26 "Convention (IV) relative to the Protection of Civilian Persons in Time of War. Geneva, 12 August 1949." Online. Available at https://ihl-databases.icrc.org/ihl/385ec082b509e76c41256739003e636d/6756482d86146898c125641e004aa3c5 (accessed 5 January 2019).

27 "Jap. [*sic*] Prisoners Pardoned," *Canberra Times*, 7 July 1953. Online. Available at https://trove.nla.gov.au/newspaper/article/2885859/701444; Ronron Calunsod, "Former 'Comfort Women,' Leftists Protest Growing Philippines-Japan Military Ties," *Japan Times*, 30 June 2015. Online. Available at www.japantimes.co.jp/news/2015/06/30/national/wartime-sex-victims-leftists-protest-growing-philippines-japan-military-ties/#.XEM5Ec9KjBI; Ronron Calunsod, "Relatives of Philippine Leader Quirino Recall 1953 Act of Forgiveness Toward Japan," *Japan*

Times, 21 April 2015. Online. Available at www.japantimes.co.jp/news/2015/04/21/national/history/relatives-philippine-leader-quirino-recall-1953-act-forgiveness-toward-japan#Vq0cQa88ah8 (all accessed 5 January 2019).

28 Katharine McGregor. "Emotions and Activism for Former So-Called 'Comfort Women' of the Japanese Occupation of the Netherlands East Indies," *Women's Studies International Forum*, 2016, vol. 54, 67–78; Lucy Hornby, "China's 'Comfort Women,'" *Financial Times*, 20 March 2015. Online. Available at www.ft.com/intl/cms/s/2/b44ae604-cdc1-11e4-8760-00144feab7de.html#axzz3rR25UkHS (accessed 5 January 2019).

29 Women's International Democratic Federation, *We Accuse! Report of the Commission of the Women's International Democratic Federation in Korea, May 16 to 27, 1951*, Berlin: Women's International Democratic Federation, 1951. On the WIDF, see Francisca de Haan, "Eugénie Cotton, Pak Ching-ae and Claudia Jones: Rethinking Transnational Feminism and I International Politics," *Journal of Women's History*, 2013, vol. 25, no. 4, 174–89.

30 Seungsook Moon, "Regulating Desire, Managing the Empire: US Military Prostitution in South Korea," in Maria Höhn and Seungsook Moon (eds.) *Over There: Living with the U.S. Military Empire from World War Two to the Present*, Durham, NC: Duke University Press, 2010, pp. 49–50.

31 Moon, "Regulating Desire," p. 51.

32 The areas close to military bases where various retail, entertainment, and service businesses are clustered are known as "camptowns."

33 Maria Höhn, "The Racial Crisis of 1971 in the US Military: Finding Solutions in West Germany and South Korea," in Höhn and Moon, *Over There*, pp. 326–330.

34 Sang-Hun Choe, "Ex-Prostitutes Say South Korea and US Enabled Sex Trade Near Bases," *New York Times*, 7 January 2009. Online. Available at www.nytimes.com/2009/01/08/world/asia/08korea.html (accessed 5 January 2019).

35 Mackie and Tanji, "Militarised Sexualities in East Asia," pp. 69–70.

36 See the discussion of women's liberationists' "speak-outs" on rape in Susan Brownmiller, *Against Our Will: Men, Women and Rape*, New York: Simon & Schuster, 1975, pp. 396–7. Kate Millett's *Sexual Politics*, New York: Doubleday, 1970, and Germaine Greer's *The Female Eunuch*, London: MacGibbon & Kee, 1970, each included discussion of literary representations of sexual violence.

37 "Panel Discussion on Women against Rape," *History Workshop Online*, 13 January 2017. Online. Available at www.historyworkshop.org.uk/panel-discussion-on-women-against-rape (accessed 5 January 2019); Adrian Williamson, "The Law and Politics of Marital Rape in England, 1945–1994," *Women's History Review*, 2016, vol. 26, no. 3, 2016, 392–3. The UK group focused on the issue of marital rape rather than militarized sexual violence.

38 Adrian Howe, "Anzac Day: Who Owns the Means of Resistance?" *Scarlet Woman*, 1984, no. 19, 22–6; Christina Twomey, "Trauma and the Reinvigoration of Anzac: An Argument," *History Australia*, 2013, vol. 10, no. 3, 85–108; Crozier-De Rosa and Mackie, *Remembering Women's Activism*, pp. 162–5.

39 As Erik Ropers has noted, these were not obscure titles; many were mass market paperback books. Erik Ropers, "Mutable History: Japanese Language Historiographies of Wartime Korean Enforced Labor and Enforced Military Prostitution, 1965–2008," PhD diss., University of Melbourne, 2011, p. 150. See Tomita Kunihiko (ed.), *Senjō Ianfu* [Battlefield Comfort Women], Tokyo: Fuji Shobō, 1953; Shirota Suzuko, *Mariya no Sanka* [Maria's Hymn], Tokyo: Nihon Kirisuto Kyō Shuppankyoku, 1971; Senda Kakō, *Jūgun Ianfu: "Koe naki onna" Hachiman nin no kokuhatsu* [Military Comfort Women: The Grievances of 80,000 Voiceless Women], Tokyo: Futabasha, 1973; Hirota Kazuko, *Shōgen kiroku jūgun ianfu, kangofu: Senjō ni ikita onna no dōkoku* [Testimonies and Records of Military Comfort Women and Nurses: Lamentations of Women Who Went to the Battlefront], Tokyo: Shin Jinbutsu Ōraisha, 1975; Kim Il-Myon, *Tennō no Guntai to Chōsenjin Ianfu* [The Emperor's Army and Korean Comfort Women], Tokyo: San'ichi Shobō, 1976; Yamatani Tetsuo, *Okinawa no Harumoni: Dai Nihon Baishun Shi* [An Old Woman in Okinawa: A History of Prostitution in Greater Japan], Tokyo: Banseisha, 1979. On early post-World War II knowledge of the system, see Kanō Mikiyo, "The Problem with the 'Comfort Women Problem,'" *Ampo: Japan-Asia Quarterly Review*, 1993, vol. 24, no. 2, 40–3; H. Eleanor Kerkham, "Pleading for the Body: Tamura Taijirō's 1947 Korean Comfort

Woman Story, *Biography of a Prostitute*," in Marlene J. Mayo and Thomas J. Rimer, with H. Eleanor Kerkham (eds.) *War, Occupation, and Creativity: Japan and East Asia, 1920–1960*, Honolulu: University of Hawai'i Press, 2001, pp. 310–59.

40 Ralph E. Lapp, *The Voyage of the Lucky Dragon: The True Story of the Japanese Fishermen Who Were the First Victims of the H-Bomb*, Harmondsworth: Penguin, 1957, pp. 80, 85; Anthony H. Johns, "Towards a Modern Indonesian Literature," *Meanjin*, 1960, 385; John Ashmead, *The Mountain and the Feather*, Boston: Houghton Mifflin, 1961, pp. 166, 205, and 293.

41 Mackie, "Sexual Violence, Silence, and Human Rights Discourse"; Mackie, "In Search of Innocence," 207–17; Jungmin Seo, "Politics of Memory in Korea and China: Remembering the Comfort Women and the Nanjing Massacre," *New Political Science*, 2008, vol. 30, no. 3, 369–92; Ropers, "Mutable History."

42 The terms "crime against humanity" and "crime against peace" were used in the judgments in the Nuremberg Trials. The terms were not used in the Tokyo Tribunal.

43 Katherine H. S. Moon, *Sex Among Allies: Military Prostitution in US-Korea Relations*, New York: Columbia University Press, 1997; Katharine H. S. Moon, "Military Prostitution and the US Military in Asia," *Asia-Pacific Journal: Japan Focus*, 2009, vol. 7, no. 3. Online. Available at https://apjjf.org/-Katharine-H.S.-Moon/3019/article.html (accessed 5 January 2019); Höhn and Moon (eds.), *Over There: Living with the U.S. Military Empire from World War Two to the Present*; Jin-Kyung Lee, *Service Economies: Militarism, Sex Work and Migrant Labor in South Korea*, Minneapolis: University of Minnesota Press, 2010.

44 The following discussion draws on Mackie, "Sexual Violence, Silence, and Human Rights Discourse" and Chunghee Sarah Soh, "The Korean 'Comfort Women' Movement for Redress," *Asian Survey*, 1996, vol. 36, no. 12, 1996, 1226–40.

45 Yang, "Revisiting the Issue," 51–71. Both the Asian Women's Association and VAWW-Net-Japan have had name changes since then.

46 Shirota, *Mariya no Sanka*; Soh, *The Comfort Women*, p. 198; Yamatani, *Okinawa no Harumoni: Dai Nihon Baishun Shi*; Ropers, "Mutable History," p. 194.

47 Yang, "Revisiting the Issue," 68, n. 2; Maria Rosa Henson, *Comfort Woman: Slave of Destiny*, Manila: Philippine Centre for Investigative Journalism, 1996; Jan Ruff O'Herne, *Fifty Years of Silence*, Sydney: Editions Tom Thompson, 1994; Graceia Lai, Wu Hui-ling, and Yu Ju-fen (eds.), *Silent Scars: History of Sexual Slavery by the Japanese Military*, Sheng-mei Ma (trans.), Taipei: Shanzhou, 2005; Floyd Whaley, "In Philippines, World War II's Lesser-Known Sex Slaves Speak Out," *New York Times*, 29 January 2016. Online. Available at www.nytimes.com/2016/01/30/world/asia/japan-philippines-comfort-women-emperor-akihito.html?_r=0 (accessed 5 January 2019).

48 Soh, "The Korean 'Comfort Women' Movement for Redress," 1235. This refers to the Convention Concerning Forced or Compulsory Labour; see above.

49 Soh, "The Korean 'Comfort Women' Movement for Redress," 1236.

50 "Taiwan Army Telegram 602," 12 March 1942, translated and excerpted in Gabrielle Kirk McDonald et al., *The Judgement of the Women's International War Crimes Tribunal for the Trial of Japan's Military Sexual Slavery*, Case No PT-2000-1-T, The Hague, 4 December 2001 (corrected 31 January 2002), 25. Online. Available at http://vawwrac.org/war_crimes_tribunal (accessed 15 January 2019).

51 McDonald et al., *The Judgement of the Women's International War Crimes Tribunal*, 29–30.

52 The full title is the Asian Women's Friendship and Peace People's Foundation (Josei no tame no Ajia Heiwa Kokumin Kikin).

53 Chungmoo Choi, "Guest Editor's Introduction," *positions*, 1997, vol. 5, no. 1, vi.

54 On the Asian Women's Fund and associated controversies, see Soh, *The Comfort Women*, p. 44, and the Digital Museum: The Comfort Women Issue and the Asian Women's Fund. Online. Available at www.awf.or.jp/index.html (accessed 5 January 2019).

55 Radhika Coomaraswamy, "Report on the Mission to the Democratic People's Republic of Korea, the Republic Korea and Japan on the Issue of Military Sexual Slavery in Wartime," UN Doc.E/CN.4/1996/53/Add.1, 4 January 1996. Online. Available at https://digitallibrary.un.org/record/228137 (accessed 5 January 2019).

56 For criticism of the Abe Statement, see Tessa Morris-Suzuki, "Abe's WWII Statement Fails History 101," *East Asia Forum*, 18 August 2015. Online. Available at www.eastasiaforum.org/2015/08/18/abes-wwii-statement-fails-history-101 (accessed 5 January 2019).

57 Soh, "The Korean 'Comfort Women' Movement for Redress," 1233; Hornby, "China's 'Comfort Women.'" The Yamaguchi Prefectural Court Shimonoseki Branch found in favor of the plaintiffs in 1998, but this was overturned by the High Court in 2001. See "Japan Court Rules against 'Comfort Women,'" *CNN*, 29 March 2001. Online. Available at http://edition.cnn.com/2001/WORLD/asiapcf/east/03/29/japan.comfort.women/index.html (accessed 5 January 2019).
58 Lai et al., *Silent Scars*, p. 107.
59 This takes place via the Alien Tort Statute (ATS), also known as 28 US Code §1350, which grants federal courts jurisdiction over civil actions for torts committed in violation of "the law of nations": "The district courts shall have original jurisdiction of any civil action by an alien for a tort only, committed in violation of the law of nations or a treaty of the United States." Online. Available at www.govinfo.gov/content/pkg/USCODE-2009-title28/pdf/USCODE-2009-title28-partIV-chap85-sec1350.pdf (accessed 5 January 2019). On the Alien Tort Statute, see also Steven S. Nam's essay in this volume.
60 Michael Honda, "House Resolution 121 110th" Online. Available at www.govtrack.us/congress/bills/110/hres121/text/ih (accessed 5 January 2019).
61 Soh, *The Comfort Women*, pp. 66–8; Anna Song, "The Task of an Activist: 'Imagined Communities and the 'Comfort Women' Campaigns in Australia," *Asian Studies Review*, 2013, vol. 37, no. 3, 381–95.
62 Hyunah Yang, "'Finding the Map of Memory': Testimony of the Military Sexual Slavery Survivors," *positions*, 2008, vol. 16, no. 1, 82; Keith Howard (ed.), *True Stories of the Korean Comfort Women*, Young Joo Lee (trans.), London: Cassell, 1995. For other collections of testimonies and documents, see Dai Sil Kim-Gibson, *Silence Broken: Korean Comfort Women*, Parkersburg, IA: Mid-Prairie Books, 1999; Sangmie Choi Schellstede (ed.), *Comfort Women Speak: Testimony by Sex Slaves of the Japanese Military*, New York: Holmes & Meier, 2000; Yoshimi Yoshiaki, *Jūgun Ianfu Shiryōshū* [Collection of Documents on Military Comfort Women], Tokyo: Ôtsuki Shoten, 1992; Yoshimi Yoshiaki, *Jūgun Ianfu* [Comfort Women], Tokyo: Iwanami Shoten, 1995; Yoshimi Yoshiaki, *Comfort Women: Sexual Slavery in the Japanese Military During World War II*, Suzanne O'Brien (trans.), New York: Columbia University Press, 2000; Lai, et al., *Silent Scars*.
63 This form of People's Tribunal can be traced back to Bertrand Russell and Jean-Paul Sartre's People's Tribunal on the Vietnam War in 1967. See International War Crimes Tribunal and John Duffett (eds.), *Against the Crime of Silence: Proceedings of the Russell International War Crimes Tribunal. Stockholm – Copenhagen.* New York: Bertrand Russell Peace Foundation, 1968.
64 Yang, "Finding the Map of Memory," 84.
65 Kim Puja, "Global Civil Society Remakes History: The 'Women's International War Crimes Tribunal 2000,'" Hideko Mitsui (trans.), *positions*, 2001, vol. 9, no. 3, 616.
66 Kim, "Global Civil Society Remakes History," 612. A one-day public hearing was also held at the Women's Caucus for Gender Justice in New York on 11 December 2000, where 15 survivors of militarized sexual violence from around the world testified.
67 McDonald et al., *The Judgement of the Women's International War Crimes Tribunal.*
68 Kim, "Global Civil Society Remakes History," 614. Emphasis in original.
69 See "House of Sharing," n.d. Online. Available at www.nanum.org/eng/sub1/sub1.php (accessed 5 January 2019); Crozier-De Rosa and Mackie, *Remembering Women's Activism*, p. 171.
70 Survivors in the Philippines are supported by Lilas Pilipinas (League of Filipino Grandmothers) and Friends of Lolas; see "Friends of Lolas." Online. Available at http://labanforthelolas.blogspot.com (accessed 5 January 2019); "Lolas' House," *IMDiversity*, 20 October 2012. Online. Available at https://imdiversity.com/villages/asian/lolas-house-women-living-with-war/ (accessed 5 January 2019). Survivors in Taiwan are supported by the Taiwan Women's Rescue Foundation; see "Painful Memories," *Taiwan Today*, 1 October 1995. Online. Available at https://taiwantoday.tw/news.php?post=3967&unit=4,20,29,31,35,45 (accessed 5 January 2019). For activities in support of the Indonesian survivors, see McGregor, "Emotions and Activism"; for support of Chinese survivors, see Hornby, "China's 'Comfort Women.'"
71 Soh, "The Korean 'Comfort Women' Movement for Redress," 1235; Tae-ick Kim, "Former 'Comfort Women' Hold 1,000th Protest at Japanese Embassy," *Chosun Ilbo* [Chosun Daily], 14 December 2011. Online. Available at http://english.chosun.com/site/data/html_dir/2011/12/14/2011121401645.html (accessed 5 January 2019). Kim reports that they skipped a protest only once, during the Kobe earthquake of 1995, and that they marked the

Fukushima disaster of March 2011 by holding their protest in silence. Demonstrations have been carried out in other places, too. Ronron Calunsod, "Former 'Comfort Women,' Leftists Protest"; CGTN America, "Former Sex Slaves Protest in Manila during Emperor Visit," 27 January 2016. Online. Available at https://m.youtube.com/watch?v=gZx_K7rOdoY (accessed 5 January 2019); Lai, et al., *Silent Scars*, p. 100; Mackie, "One Thousand Wednesdays"; Vera Mackie, "An Avatar of Peace: Commemorating Human Rights Activism," in Jane Lydon (ed.) *Visualising Human Rights*, Crawley: University of Western Australia Press, 2018, pp. 131–2.

72 Mackie, "One Thousand Wednesdays."

73 Mackie, "One Thousand Wednesdays," and also Crozier-De Rosa and Mackie, *Remembering Women's Activism*, pp. 172–88.

74 "Full Text: Japan-South Korea Statement on 'Comfort Women,'" *Wall Street Journal*, 28 December 2015. Online. Available at https://blogs.wsj.com/japanrealtime/2015/12/28/full-text-japan-south-korea-statement-on-comfort-women (accessed 5 January 2019).

75 Steve Miller, "Questions Remain over Comfort Women Foundation Future as Protests Continue," *VOA News*, 1 October 2018. Online. Available at www.voanews.com/a/comfort-women-reconciliation-in-question/4594210.html</URI (accessed 5 January 2019). Civil society activists in several countries have for some years marked 14 August as the "International Memorial Day for the 'Comfort Women.'" This date is the anniversary of Kim Hak Sun's 1991 press conference where she related her wartime experiences, and the day before the anniversary of Japan's surrender, which brought the Asia-Pacific War to a close. See Crozier-De Rosa and Mackie, *Remembering Women's Activism*, p. 181.

76 "UN Declares Japan's Compensation to Comfort Women as Inadequate," *Hankyoreh* 21 November 2018. Online Available at http://english.hani.co.kr/arti/english_edition/e_international/871186.html (accessed 5 January 2019).

77 As noted above, an exception is the Dutch Tribunal at the end of World War II.

78 ICTR, *Prosecutor v. Akayesu*, Case No ICTR-96-4-T, Sentencing Judgment, 2 September 1998. Online. Available at http://unictr.irmct.org/sites/unictr.org/files/case-documents/ictr-96-4/trial-judgements/en/980902.pdf (accessed 5 January 2019).

79 ICTY, *Prosecutor v. Kunarac, Kovac and Vukovic*, Case No IT-96-23T, Judgment, 22 February 2001. Online. Available at www.icty.org/x/cases/kunarac/tjug/en/kun-tj010222e.pdf (accessed 5 January 2019).

80 Rosalind Dixon, "Rape as a Crime in International Criminal Law: Where To From Here?" *European Journal of International Law*, 2012, vol. 13, no 3, 699–700.

81 Dixon, "Rape as a Crime in International Law," 706; *Kadic v. Karadzic* and *Doe I, Doe II v. Karadzic*, 70F 3d 232, US CA Second Circuit 1996. Online. Available at file:///Users/wildenth/Downloads/Doe%20&%20Kadic%20v.%20Karadzic%20-%20Decision%20of%2013%20October%201995.pdf (accessed 5 January 2019).

82 Debra B. Bergoffen, "From Genocide to Justice: Women's Bodies as a Legal Writing Pad," *Feminist Studies*, 2006, vol. 32, no. 1, 12.

83 Barrow, "UN Security Council Resolutions 1325 and 1820," 227.

84 Kevin Sieff, "In Historical Ruling, International Court Cites Rape in War Crimes Conviction in War Crimes Conviction of Ex-Congo Official," *Washington Post*, 21 March 2016. Online. Available at www.washingtonpost.com/world/africa/international-court-adds-rape-to-war-crimes-list-in-congo-conviction/2016/03/21/2e7f4320-ef72-11e5-85a6-2132cf446d0a_story.html?utm_term=.becf1db94d66 (accessed 5 January 2019).

85 Barrow, "UN Security Council Resolutions 1325 and 1820," 230–3. An update: United Nations Resolution 2467, passed on 23 April 2019, permits the Security Council to use sanctions against countries which perpetrate sexual violence in conflict; affirms a survivor-centered approach in all actions; calls for the provision of reparations and livelihood support to survivors; and affirms that empowering women is necessary to counter the root cause of sexual violence in conflict. The Resolution is available at https://www.un.org/sexualviolenceinconflict/wp-content/uploads/2019/04/resolution/resolution-2467-2019/S_RES_24672019_E.pdf (accessed 2 August 2019).

29

SOLIDARITY RIGHTS AND THE COMMON HERITAGE OF HUMANITY

Anca Claudia Prodan

Introduction

Solidarity rights, also known as the rights of peoples, new human rights, or third generation of human rights, are a category that emerged in the 1970s and include rights to development, to a healthy environment, to communicate, and to the common heritage of mankind.[1] Solidarity rights emerged at a time when international law was developing toward what some have called a "law of humankind," that is, exhibiting a tendency toward being less state-oriented, with humankind emerging as a subject of law.[2] This tendency resulted from the increased interdependence of the world that followed the dissolution of the colonial empires and the emergence of newly independent states. Solidarity rights were illustrative of those developments.[3] They particularly addressed imbalances between developed and developing countries in areas such as the economy, technology, and communications, and were predicated on notions of equity, sovereign equality, interdependence, common interest, and cooperation among all states.

As many have noted, solidarity rights did not emerge in order to replace already established human rights, but rather "to meet certain pressing needs which the international community, at a given time in its historical development, [saw as] being basic or vital and which states should be legally obliged to provide."[4] Solidarity rights reflected a shift in thinking toward global justice, and a key aim was an equitable international order.[5] Opinion has been split as to whether solidarity rights can be considered "real" human rights. The strongest criticism has concerned solidarity rights' applicability to collectivities rather than to individuals, which runs counter to human rights that address the individual.[6] Another criticism has been that they create confusion about rights holders by failing to distinguish clearly among such categories as states, nations, groups, and peoples. Due to the way solidarity rights have been conceptualized, they have not fitted smoothly into human rights discourse and have not achieved the level of acceptance of other human rights.[7] Their importance has been correspondingly overlooked.

The "pressing needs" that solidarity rights addressed at the time they first emerged have not faded away. On the contrary, the subject matter of various solidarity rights – development, environmental protection, global communications, heritage – is becoming more and more important, especially in a world heavily marked by the processes of globalization that have brought people closer together. We should therefore reopen the discussion about solidarity rights and reflect on their relevance as human rights. To that end, in this essay I turn for illustration to the concept of the "common heritage of humanity," a solidarity right that is present in international normative tools concerning heritage protection.[8] The common heritage of humanity as a legal principle and solidarity rights generally are rooted in the samc historical context, and the same philosophy underpins them. While the common heritage of humanity has not managed to gain a foothold in human rights discourse, it has evolved as a legal principle. In this essay I draw on consequences stemming from the common heritage of humanity, as it has been applied in various legal contexts, to illustrate solidarity rights' underlying gist and potential implications. This topic has so far been discussed primarily from the perspective of legal theory and legal philosophy, and so in the present essay I rely mainly on these areas to develop my interpretations.

As a first step, I provide a conceptual clarification of solidarity rights, emphasizing solidarity as a key characteristic. Human rights scholarship has not properly emphasized the characteristic of solidarity, focusing instead, as suggested above, on the question of whether solidarity rights apply to individuals or groups. Yet solidarity in fact marked the development of heritage protection into a matter of international law, as is reflected in the evolution of the concept of a common heritage of humanity. As a second step, I introduce the common heritage of humanity as framed in international law, in relation to both international spaces and cultural resources. This overview, which draws on the theoretical study of various international normative tools, is followed by a section that illustrates some practical implications. The practical examples are related to the United Nations Educational, Scientific and Cultural Organization (UNESCO) Convention Concerning the Protection of the World Cultural and Natural Heritage (1972), popularly known as the World Heritage Convention. The final section will recapitulate the key points concerning the common heritage of humanity in order to provide some final reflections and suggestions for further research into the relevance of solidarity rights to an increasingly interconnected world.

Solidarity rights

In order to clarify the concept of solidarity rights, I would like to sketch the context in which they emerged. The process of decolonization and its consequences, in particular the formation of new states in the 1950 and 1960s and the ensuing processes of globalization that increased the interdependence of the world, have played a significant role. These events triggered a growing awareness that there were issues that were important to the world as a collective that could no longer be treated in isolation by states' governments, or treated as if they were matters of national importance only. In an interdependent world, decisions taken in one part of the world have an effect on the other parts.[9] Consequently, there was a need in international law to move beyond approaches focusing on states, as had been the case up to that point. The analysis of Antônio Augusto Cançado Trindade, professor of law and judge at the International Court of Justice, offers a useful example. Cançado Trindade traces the shift from internationalization to globalization in the area of environmental law, and explains that regulations initially focused on sectors, areas, or concrete situations such as oceans, the atmosphere, or wildlife. People then observed that the problems that were initially addressed separately were in fact interrelated, and that issues addressed at a national level and then at an international level were in fact global.[10] According to Cançado Trindade, this finding caused international law no longer to be seen as exclusively state-oriented; "reiterated references to 'mankind' [are] pointing towards an international law of mankind," which, in the environmental field, appears in concepts such as "common concern of humankind" or "the common good of mankind."[11] While some have claimed that these concepts evolved from the concept of the common heritage of mankind,[12] Cançado Trindade argues convincingly that, despite semantic variations, "when referring to mankind, a common denominator underlying them all appears to be the common interest of mankind."[13]

I detail the implications of this in the next section, but for now, it is necessary to note only that the same historical context marked the emergence of solidarity rights. Both are intertwined with the need to address the common interest of humankind, but scholarship has not emphasized this aspect sufficiently. Instead, most scholars approach them as collective rights, group rights, or peoples' rights.[14] Although these notions have not been used consistently, a distinction has been made between the individual as rights holder and the group as rights holder, in this case the group being taken as one entity and equivalent to the individual. Solidarity rights have become mired in the controversial discussion of the individual as opposed to collective dimensions of human rights. Yet some scholars have argued against that very dichotomy, as for example the philosopher David Makinson, who argues that some rights may have both an individual and a collective dimension,[15] or Gillian Triggs, former president of the Australian Human Rights Commission, who argues that the dichotomy is false because many individual rights are balanced with the interests of a democratic society, which by definition implies a collective dimension, such that they are subject to the just requirements of the general welfare in a democratic society and to the rights and freedoms of others.[16]

The scholarship focusing on group rights provides plenty of insights for reflection on the individual and collective dimensions of human rights, allowing us to study how the two dimensions are linked and how they have been reflected in discussions of Indigenous peoples, minorities of all kinds, or in relation to cultural rights more broadly.[17] Nevertheless, this scholarship is less pertinent for understanding the content and implications of solidarity rights, due to its focus on rights holders. It is solidarity itself that is a very important characteristic, in fact, so important that it was chosen to name the rights under discussion. Those who use solidarity rights instead of other designations prefer it because solidarity expresses "the recognition of our common destiny and the desire to enable each individual to exercise his rights and assume his share of responsibility for safeguarding and improving the future of mankind."[18] I argue that it is precisely solidarity that must be brought to the fore in order to understand the scope and content of these rights. However, to avoid confusion, I should note that scholars have rarely discussed solidarity rights under that exact label. I have extracted my interpretations from the results of a series of UNESCO workshops that were held to identify and clarify this category of rights. The authors of those documents concede that a minimum of solidarity is needed for the observance of all rights. However, while established human rights are preoccupied with the individual and the individual's place in society, solidarity rights are

> predicated essentially on the notion of solidarity among people. Such rights, in that they reflect a particularly human conception of community life, can as a result be achieved only through the joint efforts of all those representing the social interests involved: individuals, States and other public and private entities and bodies.[19]

An example will illustrate. Air – and air pollution, to stay with the environmental law analysis of Cançado Trindade – does not know borders. If I pollute the air, my neighbors cannot exercise their right to a healthy environment, and the opposite is also true. Exercising the right to a healthy environment, or to any other solidarity right, requires cooperation, ultimately on a global scale. This is not necessarily needed in the case of established human rights, whose observance depends primarily on the negative or positive obligations of states.[20]

The notion of solidarity is crucial because it draws attention away from the holders of rights while emphasizing a type of relationship between them – a certain way of acting and behaving. This is not to deny the importance of the rights holders – after all, human rights are for them, regardless of how we conceptualize them – but to emphasize that the sharing of responsibility, the obligation of solidarity, acquires a pivotal role here. Unless there is acceptance and active pursuit of joint responsibilities, these rights cannot be observed on a global basis.[21] Thus, when talking about solidarity rights (as opposed to group rights or peoples' rights), the question is not whether they apply to individuals or groups, but how individuals and groups should behave toward each other and toward specific resources of crucial importance for humanity. This interpretation is compatible with legal theorists' emphasis on solidarity rights as a manifestation of natural law triggering *erga omnes* obligations, i.e. pertaining to everyone without exception.[22] According to Kemal Baslar, solidarity rights are a "new interpretation and exploration of the human rights doctrine in the sense that the world community owes a moral duty to safeguard the continued existence of mankind."[23] Thus, Baslar argues, solidarity rights, as a manifestation of natural law theory, and as being fundamental, peremptory, inalienable, intertemporal, and universal, are even a prerequisite for other human rights.[24]

The fact that solidarity rights ended up in the controversy surrounding the dichotomy between collective and individual rights has acted as an obstacle to their proper understanding and has not done justice to their importance. In essence, solidarity rights are about resources that are crucial for all humanity and therefore entail specific actions and behavior that are the same for everyone, regardless whether we speak of individuals, peoples, or other human groupings. Solidarity rights have been rarely discussed from this perspective or under this precise designation. Thus, we do not have much research to rely upon for a better understanding of their content, scope, or implications. The common heritage of humanity is, however, both a solidarity right and also a principle of international law. As a principle of international law, it has been regulating and guiding behavior and action. A focus on the common heritage of humanity can therefore bring us closer to understanding solidarity rights.

The common heritage of humanity in international law

In this section, I introduce the common heritage of humanity as framed in international law. I start by defining it and, in order to illustrate its relations to the notion of solidarity, I focus on the World Heritage Convention, discussing its history and main features. Then, to further clarify the content of the common heritage of humanity, I discuss provisions from selected normative tools that protect international spaces and cultural resources. I emphasize that the benefit of humankind is the core of the common heritage of humanity. To grasp the practical implications of the common heritage of humanity, I show how legal scholarship has interpreted the notion.

Since its establishment in 1945, UNESCO adopted many normative tools for heritage protection, covering resources as varied as buildings, natural areas, documents, submerged shipwrecks, dances, and songs.[25] Despite protecting different resources, all normative tools draw on the idea that heritage refers to

> an inheritance received from the past, to be held "in trust" by the current generation (that may enjoy its value in the present) to be handed down in at least as good a state as it was received to the next generation.[26]

Many normative tools refer to a common heritage of humanity, or use alternative names such as, for example, the universal heritage of humanity, the heritage of humankind, or world heritage. The Convention for the Protection of Cultural Property in the Event of Armed Conflict, adopted at The Hague in 1954, mentioned this notion for the first time. Its preamble states that "damage to cultural property belonging to any people whatsoever means damage to the cultural heritage of all mankind, since each people makes its contribution to the culture of the world."[27] The view that there is a common world cultural heritage was crystallized later in the World Heritage Convention (1972) whose preamble indicates that "parts of the cultural and natural heritage are of outstanding interest and therefore need to be preserved as part of the world heritage of mankind as a whole."[28] Many subsequent heritage-related normative tools of UNESCO restate this idea.[29] However, for the purposes of this essay, I will focus on the history of the World Heritage Convention.

Perhaps the most illustrative example from that history is the campaign to safeguard the Abu Simbel temples built under the Egyptian Pharaoh Ramesses the Great. Due to population growth in the Nile Valley in Egypt and Sudan in the 1950s, the need emerged for more cropland and hydroelectric power. The optimal solution was to build a dam and create an artificial lake. The problem was that the lake could only be established in the very spot where the Abu Simbel temples were situated. The water would have flooded the temples, along with 2,000 years of human history. The director-general of UNESCO explained in a message that the authorities charged with developing the Nile Valley stood before a dilemma: "how are they to choose between the needs and welfare of their people and the treasures which belong not only to their country but to humanity as a whole?"[30] The governments of Egypt and Sudan decided to build the dam, but at the same time they did not turn their back on history. They appealed to UNESCO, which replied by launching an international campaign to save the temples by removing them from the site. They were literally cut into pieces and reassembled a few hundred meters away from the water – a giant jigsaw puzzle of over 1,000 massive pieces of stone.

This international safeguarding campaign was the first of its kind and size, attracting support from more than 50 countries, various organizations, and countless people. Most important for this essay, it was a milestone in international cooperation. Solidarity underscored the entire action, inspiring the concept of a world heritage and the World Heritage Convention. The World Heritage List became the heart of the effort: a list featuring some of the most fascinating places of the world, whose value is thought to exceed temporal and spatial boundaries and that are thought to be (potentially) relevant for humankind as a whole. Examples of the 1,073 properties inscribed on the list at the time of this writing include the temples of Abu Simbel, the pyramids of Machu Picchu, the Taj

Mahal, Stonehenge, Venice, and Palmyra. The global significance of these places, that is, their status as belonging to the heritage of the world, is what entails the need for special protection. An assessment of the meaning of the common heritage of humanity as a principle of law, which I will carry out next, serves to illustrate what this means. Kemal Baslar observes that in international law the common heritage of humanity has in fact referred to two different doctrines: the property of all mankind and the public trust.[31] These concepts suitably illustrate the range of approaches that exist in international law, and I use them to structure my own arguments and examples.

The doctrine of a property of all mankind is related to international spaces and resources, such as the high seas or the moon, and arises outside the context of UNESCO. In the context of UNESCO, reference is made strictly to the "common heritage of mankind," and a legal regime was developed to establish norms and rules for how to treat specific resources declared common heritage. It is important to note that as a legal regime, the common heritage of mankind has its roots in the international developments that marked the 1950 and 1960s, as do solidarity rights. The background of the United Nations Convention on the Law of the Sea (UNCLOS, 1982), an international treaty regulating the use of waters, illustrates the pairing of the common heritage of mankind and solidarity rights. In brief, at the time when the common heritage principle was introduced, developed countries were the ones capable of benefiting from the use of international spaces due to their advanced technology, and indeed they were controlling and benefiting from them. Developing countries lacking technological facilities could not take advantage of them. The legal regime developed under the common heritage principle was designed to enable the equitable sharing of common resources. In UNCLOS, this includes principles such as non-appropriation and non-sovereignty over those resources (as all the rights are vested in mankind); the mandate to use them for the benefit of mankind, with special consideration of the needs of developing countries and those that have not attained self-governing status; and the duty to protect and conserve the natural resources and the marine environment.[32] International resources belong to no one in particular yet equally to all, so the principles of non-sovereignty and non-appropriation follow logically, reflecting the doctrine of the property of all mankind.

However, the same principles of non-sovereignty and non-appropriation do not apply as obviously to cultural heritage or other resources situated within the territorial sovereignty of states. These are already in someone's ownership, so the common heritage of humanity in the realm of culture has a different normative character. The juridical status of a heritage property continues to rest with its rightful owner, but the concept indicates that the international community has an interest in the property's protection and enjoyment that is distinct from proprietary titles.[33] In the field of culture we therefore move away from the property of mankind idea, and move toward a public trust doctrine. The implication is that owners are expected to behave as stewards or trustees who preserve the heritage not simply for themselves but also for another beneficiary, namely humankind.[34] Law professor Francesco Francioni's explanation is revealing:

> The expression "heritage of mankind" in the World Heritage Convention is therefore to be understood not in the sense of establishing the international community as a titleholder, but rather in the sense of a common international commitment to its preservation and protection.[35]

Indeed, in practice the World Heritage Convention imposes obligations on States Parties[36] not only to protect the heritage situated within their territories but also to set up a system of international cooperation and assistance and support each other in cases where protection at the national level is insufficient.

A careful analysis of how the common heritage of humanity has been approached in various normative tools inside and outside of UNESCO allows us to infer that, of all principles deriving from the concept, and regardless of doctrine, the benefit of humankind represents its heart. However, more specific implications depend on how humankind is understood, and I will briefly clarify this, staying with the example of a normative tool I have already introduced, namely UNCLOS. Craig Forrest, an academic who has written extensively on cultural heritage law, distinguishes between interpretations of humankind in terms of natural or positive law.[37] Forrest observes: "[Humankind] has … been interpreted in a positive legal framework to mean 'all States,' while in a natural law context it may pertain to all human beings, including future generations," and he notes that the former is the dominant framework in international law.[38] A statist view does indeed dominate international law, and so Forrest's analysis may be correct. However, reducing mankind to states would ignore that a "law of humankind" stretching beyond the boundaries of states is emerging. Thus, it seems more appropriate to interpret humankind in a natural law context, and for this we find support in the analyses of other legal scholars.

Rüdiger Wolfrum, an academic who wrote a comprehensive study of the concept of mankind, emphasizes that in the context of UNCLOS, mankind cannot be interpreted as an active subject in, for example, deep sea-bed mining activities. Yet at the same time, and paradoxically, mankind's interests must be taken into account.[39] Despite uncertainties about how to interpret "mankind," Wolfrum manages to find a feasible explanation in the relationship between mankind and heritage. Relating mankind to the notion of heritage, he says,

> at least indicates that the interests of future generations have to be respected in making use of the sea-bed. More substantively, it requires that deep sea-bed activities should avoid undue waste of resources and provides for the protection of the environment.[40]

Scholars such as international law expert Sabine von Schorlemer interpret the common heritage of humanity in its cultural dimension similarly, concluding that it implies both transmission to future generations and the idea of handling resources carefully.[41] By studying relevant normative tools, we can bring in supporting evidence for these observations. The benefit of humankind is often operationalized through further provisions and principles such as the equitable sharing of resources, solidarity, cooperation, and common but differentiated responsibility. If humankind is taken in its temporal dimension, that is, as including future generations, then the benefit of humankind translates into principles of intergenerational equity, sustainability, and precaution.

The analysis carried out above shows that the common heritage of humanity entails measures that address the protection, use, and sharing of certain resources of importance for humanity, some of which are subject to solidarity rights. These measures trigger commitments toward everyone, including future generations. The benefit of humankind is ever present, although its content may differ from resource to resource. It requires the commitment of transcending our personal interests, of seeing ourselves as part of a greater unit – humankind itself – and of developing a sense of responsibility, which entails an active involvement in the well-being of others. Precisely this is the message that solidarity rights seek to transmit, and that can be highlighted with the concept of common heritage of humanity.

The common heritage of humanity: the World Heritage Convention and practical implications

In order to illustrate implications of the common heritage of humanity, in this section I give examples of provisions and case law related to the World Heritage Convention. It must be noted at the outset that this subject is marked by disagreement. Nobody contests that in UNCLOS the common heritage of mankind is a binding principle of law,[42] but not everyone agrees on the implications that has in the field of cultural heritage. International law researcher Roger O'Keefe, for example, analyzes relevant normative tools as well as state practice and asserts that the international community or other states may protest to a state that fails to care for the common heritage of humanity, but that the international community or other states cannot enforce preservation through judicial measures. The common heritage is the proper concern of the international community as a whole, he holds, but it is not the object of obligations owed to that community.[43] He argues that it triggers obligations exclusively to other States Parties to the convention, but not to the international community as a whole, and so excludes everyone who is not party to the convention.

The question of whether obligations are owed to the international community or only to States Parties to the convention is less important today than at the time of Roger O'Keefe's writing because only three member states of UNESCO have not yet ratified the convention (Nauru, Somalia, and Tuvalu), and few countries in the world are not member states of UNESCO. O'Keefe's opinion is relevant here for another reason, however: It illustrates vividly Craig Forrest's distinction between the meaning of humankind in a positive law context and its meaning in a natural law context. Obviously, O'Keefe interprets the notion of humankind in a positive law sense, and in so doing shows the limits of that perspective. That perspective does not accurately reflect the obligations of solidarity that underpin normative tools like the World Heritage Convention, especially the obligation to transmit the common heritage of humanity to future generations, which requires approaching humankind in terms of natural law. Consequently, I tend to agree with those scholars who see practical implications arising in relation to cultural resources and who anchor this with the connection that exists between heritage protection and human rights.

Judge Cançado Trindade analyzes the relationship between heritage protection and human rights in a book in which he discusses the basis for a law of humankind, and concludes that,

> Recourse to the very notion of humankind as subject of International Law brings into the fore, or places the whole discussion within, the human rights framework, and this should be properly emphasized, it should not be left implicit or neglected as allegedly redundant. Just as law, or the rule of law itself, does not operate in a vacuum, humankind is neither a social nor a legal abstraction: it is composed of human collectivities, of all human beings of flesh and bone, living in human societies and extended in time.[44]

Cançado Trindade is not alone with his observation. The heritage lawyer Francesco Francioni also believes that references to the cultural heritage of humanity underscore its connection to human rights and foreshadow "the idea of an integral obligation owed to the international community as a whole (*erga omnes*) rather than to individual states on a contractual basis."[45] Whether in a positive law or a natural law context, states become accountable to the world community through references to humankind. The experience of the World Heritage Convention, which I will describe next, highlights this.

From the perspective of natural law, the obligations that arise are due to the "trusteeship" status, which everyone acquires when it comes to duties of the present generations toward future generations, that is, the obligation we have to safeguard the future of humankind. From the positive law perspective, the trusteeship status does not disappear; the states that ratified the World Heritage Convention are the trustees who act on behalf of humankind. This has prompted legal scholars to conclude that the common heritage of humanity

> must be protected even against the wishes of the territorial State. This new form of protection entails that, today, States are bound to tolerate scrutiny and intervention ... when they wilfully engage in, or intentionally fail to prevent, the destruction of, or serious damage to, cultural heritage of significant value for humanity.[46]

For Francioni, the common heritage of humanity becomes a tool to counterbalance sovereignty, understood as the complete and undisturbed dominion over a territorial space. By inscribing sites on the World Heritage List, states accept several limitations within their own territories and accord priority not to their own interests but to those of the international community.[47] Indeed, a closer look at the implementation of the World Heritage Convention shows that we can consider the common heritage of humanity a normative concept that produces effects on the behavior of states.

Against states that fail to fulfill their obligations under the convention, there is a provision for removal of the property from the World Heritage List. One could argue that this is not a strong provision, and in fact it has been applied only twice.[48] This is the case not because all the properties have been protected accordingly, but because the intention of the convention is to protect them, which implies keeping them on the World Heritage List. There are, therefore, other methods for remedying the situation before reaching the point of deciding to remove a site. For example, apart from the World Heritage List, there is a so-called List of World Heritage in Danger for properties that require urgent protection. Intended as a tool for prioritizing resources and action, it has turned out to have the unintended effect of pressuring states to act in accordance with the convention. In cases where damage is not due to natural or other unpreventable disasters, having a property inscribed on the List of World Heritage in Danger is seen as an indication that a State Party has failed to fulfill its obligations. This has a shaming effect. For that reason, States Parties have tried to avoid having sites placed on that list.[49] Nevertheless, the decision-making committee of the convention has the power to place a site on the World Heritage List in Danger, in exceptional circumstances even against the will of the State Party concerned.[50] This has already happened in a few cases, confirming Francioni's opinion that states must tolerate intervention.[51]

The common heritage of humanity not only creates obligations that hold states accountable to the world community; it also triggers individual criminal responsibility. Even if the convention has not always managed to enforce the correct measures for the protection of properties inscribed on the World Heritage List, it has contributed to the development of international heritage law as a separate branch of international law and as an evolving dimension of other areas such as international humanitarian law.[52] Relevant provisions exist in the statutes of the International Criminal Tribunal for the Former Yugoslavia (ICTY)[53] and the International Criminal Court (ICC)[54] regarding the willful destruction of buildings dedicated to religion, charity, education, arts, sciences, historic monuments, works of art and science – all of which are heritage – as a violation of the laws or customs of war. I will use the jurisprudence of the two courts to illustrate how this provision has been applied.

The ICTY has charged several individuals for the willful destruction of cultural heritage during the Balkan Wars.[55] The idea of a common heritage of humanity played an important role in the case concerning the shelling of the Old Town of Dubrovnik, which had been inscribed on the World Heritage List since 1979. Documents on the case state that the Old Town was "legally distinct from the rest of the wider city because the Old Town, in its entirety including the medieval walls, enjoys a World Heritage listing and the protections and immunities that are consequent on that listing."[56] The Trial Chamber also observed that the site was of great importance to the cultural heritage of every people, and "it therefore considers that, even though the victim of the offence at issue is to be understood broadly as 'people,' rather than any particular individual, the offence can be said to involve grave consequences for the victim."[57] International law professor Federico Lenzerini commented on the case, saying that the recognition of the collective character of the crime's victim, namely people, was a very significant feature of this finding. In his view,

> the Chamber thus transcends the traditional vision of human rights as enforceable and justiciable only when their breach affects one or more individuals specifically … No member of the community concerned is thus specially affected, and – at the same time – all such members are affected.[58]

The Chamber even stated that "it is a serious violation of international humanitarian law to attack civilian buildings" (invoking another case), but that "it is a crime of even greater seriousness to direct an attack on an especially protected site, such as the Old Town."[59]

The first case adjudicated by the International Criminal Court was recent – in 2016 – and involved the destruction of the mausoleums in Timbuktu, Mali. The Chamber accused Ahmad al-Faqi Al-Mahdi, who ordered the destruction of the mausoleums, not of crimes against people but of crimes against property. The fact that the destroyed sites were inscribed on the World Heritage List made a difference. Trial Chamber III of the ICC remarked in its sentence that

> all the sites but one (the Sheikh Mohamed Mahmoud Al Arawani Mausoleum) were UNESCO World Heritage sites and, as such, their attack appears to be of particular gravity as their destruction does not only affect the direct victims of the crimes, namely the faithful and inhabitants of Timbuktu, but also people throughout Mali and the international community.[60]

Such court cases created precedents that are extremely important today, when the destruction of heritage around the world has intensified due to becoming a main target of terrorist attacks. The tragic destruction and looting of almost all World Heritage properties in Syria and Iraq by the Islamic State of Iraq and the Levant (known as ISIL or ISIS) and the attacks on Timbuktu by the radical Islamist militia Ansar Dine are recent examples. Such cases have prompted the international community to adopt normative tools that increasingly connect heritage to human rights. In 2003 UNESCO adopted the Declaration on the Intentional Destruction of Cultural Heritage, the first normative tool to spell out the link between heritage and human rights. Its preamble states: "cultural heritage is an important component of the cultural identities of communities, groups and individuals, and of social cohesion, so that its intentional destruction may have adverse consequences on human dignity and human rights."[61] Even more recently, in 2017, the United Nations (UN) Security Council acknowledged the importance of heritage for peace and security by adopting its first resolution on heritage protection.[62] As Irina Bokova, former director-general of UNESCO, explained,

> the deliberate destruction of heritage is a war crime. It is also a tactic of war to accelerate the long-term degradation of societies, as part of a strategy of cultural cleansing. That is why defending cultural heritage is more than a cultural issue; it is a security imperative that cannot be separated from the protection of human lives.[63]

These developments in international law illustrate the growing recognition that heritage protection is a human rights issue. This essay contends that heritage protection pertains just as much to solidarity rights, and the reflections in the next section are intended to crystallize that.

Solidarity, rights, and heritage: final reflections

The aim of this essay has been to contribute to the understanding of solidarity rights and their importance in a globalized world. Solidarity rights, due to the way they have been conceptualized, have not fitted easily into human rights discourse, and their core message has not been clearly understood. This has caused solidarity rights not to develop significantly, even as the subjects they address become ever more important. There is a need to reopen the discussion of solidarity rights and reflect again on their relevance. In so doing, the focus should be on the notion of solidarity, rather than on rights holders, because these rights emerged as a response to the interdependence of the world and the recognition that some contemporary issues can only be addressed through global solidarity. It is surprising how little attention the notion of solidarity itself has received from scholarship, although it is crucial to both the field of heritage and to the observance of some human rights.

Solidarity is a principle with strong ethical connotations. Some scholars have remarked that solidarity introduces moral concerns into the international legal system and thereby blurs the boundary between law and morality.[64] This may also be why many consider solidarity, or for that matter solidarity rights and the actions entailed by them, to be mere lofty ideals. However, I agree with the philosopher George Khushf, who wrote in 1999 that "solidarity seems to have a special resonance with the needs of our day. For many it provides a moral and political principle that counters the individualism, atomism, and fragmentation of human life."[65] The salience of that statement has only increased over time, and solidarity has now become the subject of debate concerning its role as a structural and constitutional principle.[66] It is now also the focus of normative tools such as the "Draft Declaration on the Right of Peoples and Individuals to International Solidarity," which is in preparation at the UN Human Rights Council.[67] Solidarity has not been properly acknowledged by human rights scholarship, but is in fact an important principle for humankind today and research is needed to gain a better understanding of the role solidarity plays in the enforcement or observance of human rights.

In this essay, I have approached solidarity more modestly, seeking to shift our perspective toward reconceptualizing solidarity rights in terms of the actions and behaviors entailed. The common heritage of humanity as a principle of law has aided me in this regard, due to its similarities to solidarity rights. They have similar roots and are driven by principles such as equity, cooperation, common concern, and joint responsibility. As Kemal Baslar notes, the common heritage of humanity was the least developed and accepted of the solidarity rights. If the right to the common heritage of humanity were accepted, he argues, states would have to cooperate to materialize it. This would require reassessing many principles of international law, such as the principle of sovereignty, the principle of nonintervention, and the role of *erga omnes* obligations.[68] The common heritage of humanity, while not formally accepted as a solidarity right, fits Baslar's argument well because of the duties of solidarity that it entails and the pressure it can bring to bear to treat common heritage resources in specific ways. The common heritage of humanity represents a manifestation of natural law and an illustration of an emerging law of humankind, and so it drives human rights discourse toward transcending the state. My research shows that states continue to be active in the World Heritage Convention, even though that sometimes implies having to tolerate intervention and give up some sovereignty. This shows us that states' reluctance to engage with solidarity rights cannot be explained exclusively through such implications. Again, research would be welcome to gain a comprehensive overview of the reasons that have led to the marginalization of solidarity rights in human rights discourse and scholarship.

Scholarship to date has also failed to pay proper attention to the relationship between the common heritage of humanity and human rights. Although scholarship has provided important perspectives on heritage as a human right,[69] human rights as a framework for heritage protection,[70] and human rights as heritage,[71] it has focused on heritage, not on the common heritage of humanity. The distinction is crucial, and emerges clearly in another UNESCO normative tool: the Convention for the Safeguarding of the Intangible Cultural Heritage (2003). This convention concentrates on the role of heritage – in the form of traditions, rituals, knowledge systems, and performances – for cultural identity and small-scale community building. It does not deal with the heritage of the world, but with heritage that exists within communities that create, practice, and maintain it for the sake of their own continuity. This understanding is incompatible with the idea that there is a global heritage common to all humanity, and indeed the full concept of a common heritage of humanity was intentionally avoided, as the drafting history of the Convention for the Safeguarding of the Intangible Cultural Heritage shows. Instead, the notion of a "common concern" appears there.[72] Obviously, the concepts of cultural heritage and common heritage of humanity can have different practical implications, and we know little so far about the implications of the common heritage of humanity. For example, the implementation of the World Heritage Convention shows that while heritage protection and human rights protection can reinforce each other, there are also cases of human rights violations in the name of heritage protection. Thus, further research is needed to have a more informed understanding of whether indeed heritage and human rights protect each other and if so, in what circumstances.

Scholarship has also tended to approach heritage as a cultural right, not as a solidarity right. This, too, triggers different implications. It is undeniable that the common heritage of humanity, if related to culture, falls within the remit of cultural rights. Relevant provisions exist in Article 27 of the Universal Declaration on Human Rights (1948): "everyone has the right freely to participate in the cultural life of the community."[73] Article 15 of the International Covenant on Economic, Social and Cultural Rights (1966) is even more specific, providing that the States Parties recognize the right of everyone to take part in cultural life, and that the steps for "the full realization of this right shall include those necessary for the conservation, the development and the diffusion of science and culture."[74] These provisions and others[75] have led scholars to suggest that human rights provide a "network of standards, a safety net" supporting the right to heritage.[76] However, to approach the common heritage of humanity as a cultural right and through the notion of culture would lead us back either to small-scale community building or to the controversial discussion of individual and collective dimensions of human rights. It is the concept of the common heritage of humanity, rooted as it is in the recognition of the unity of humankind, of common interests and concerns, and of the need to take joint action when resources crucial for humankind are at stake, that is best positioned to help us gain a closer understanding of solidarity rights. This essay has offered some glimpses of its potential and, I hope, some motivation for further research and reflection.

Notes

1 The notions of humankind and humanity are preferred today because they are gender-neutral, but in the 1970s mankind was the most frequent designation. In this essay, I use the notion of mankind when referring to sources where its exact use is important.

2 A. A. Cançado Trindade, "The Contribution of International Human Rights Law to Environmental Protection, with Special Reference to Global Environmental Change," in Edith Brown Weiss (ed.) *Environmental Change and International Law: New Challenges and Dimensions*, Tokyo: United Nations University Press, 1992. Online. Available at http://archive.unu.edu/unupress/unupbooks/uu25ee/uu25ee00.htm (accessed 29 December 2018). See also A. A. Cançado Trindade, *International Law for Humankind: Towards a New Jus Gentium*, Leiden: Martinus Nijhoff, 2010.

3 For an analysis of how human rights discourse reflected those events, see Antony Anghie, "International Human Rights Law and a Developing World Perspective," in Scott Sheeran and Sir Nigel Rodley (eds.) *Routledge Handbook of International Human Rights Law*, London: Routledge, 2013, pp. 109–25.

4 E.g. UNESCO, *UNESCO and Peoples' Rights. Conclusions of the International Symposium of Experts on Rights of Solidarity and Peoples' Rights, Republic of San Marion, 4–8 October 1982*, Paris: UNESCO, 1982, p. 5. See also UNESCO, *The Rights of Solidarity: An Attempt at Conceptual Analysis. Symposium on the Study of New Human Rights: The "Rights of Solidarity," Mexico, 12–15 August 1980*, UNESCO Doc. SS-80/CONF.806/6, 1980. Online. Available at https://unesdoc.unesco.org/ark:/48223/pf0000040770 (accessed 29 December 2018). See also Ian Brownlie, "The Rights of

Peoples in Modern International Law," in James Crawford (ed.) *The Rights of Peoples*, Oxford: Clarendon Press, 1988, p. 11.
5 Janet Blake, "Taking a Human Rights Approach to Cultural Heritage Protection," *Heritage and Society*, 2011, vol. 4, no. 2, 229.
6 On this, see Anghie, "International Human Rights Law."
7 Blake, "Taking a Human Rights Approach." Makinson notes several problems in relation to the rights of peoples: David Makinson, "Rights of Peoples: A Logician's Point of View," in Crawford, *The Rights of Peoples*, pp. 69–92.
8 I use "normative tools" to refer to the international conventions, recommendations, declaration, charters, and programs of UNESCO that provide obligations, principles, or guidelines for action.
9 UNESCO, *Expert Meeting on Human Rights, Human Needs and the Establishment of a New International Economic Order, Paris, June 1978*, UNESCO Doc. SS.78/CONF.630/12, p. 77. Online. Available at https://unesdoc.unesco.org/ark:/48223/pf0000032647 (accessed 29 December 2018).
10 Cançado Trindade, "Contribution of International Human Rights Law."
11 Cançado Trindade, "Contribution of International Human Rights Law."
12 E.g. Kemal Baslar, *The Concept of the Common Heritage of Mankind in International Law*, Leiden: Martinus Nijhoff, 1998.
13 Cançado Trindade, "Contribution of International Human Rights."
14 For an analysis of the distinction between these concepts, see Peter Jones, "Human Rights, Group Rights and Peoples' Rights," *Human Rights Quarterly*, 1999, vol. 21, no. 1, 80–107.
15 Makinson, "Rights of Peoples," p. 72.
16 Gillian Triggs, "The Right of Peoples and Individual Rights: Conflict or Harmony?," in Crawford, *The Rights of Peoples*, pp. 141–57.
17 A comprehensive overview can be found in Crawford, *The Rights of Peoples*.
18 UNESCO, *The Rights of Solidarity: An Attempt at Conceptual Analysis*.
19 UNESCO, *Expert Meeting on Human Rights;* See also Karel Vasak, "A 30-Year Struggle: The Sustained Efforts to Give Force of Law to the Universal Declaration of Human Rights," *UNESCO Courier*, 1977, vol. 30, 29–32. Online. Available at https://unesdoc.unesco.org/ark:/48223/pf0000048063 (accessed 29 December 2018).
20 In the field of human rights, a positive obligation refers to an obligation of states to take active measures for the observance of human rights, while a negative obligation requires states to refrain from taking actions that violate human rights.
21 UNESCO, *Expert Meeting on Human Rights*, p. 91.
22 See Cançado Trindade, "Contribution of International Human Rights," and Baslar, *Concept of the Common Heritage*.
23 Baslar, *Concept of the Common Heritage*, p. 320. See also Cançado Trindade, "Contribution of International Human Rights."
24 Baslar, *Concept of the Common Heritage*, p. 231.
25 Modern international heritage law has been very much driven by UNESCO, now recognized internationally as the most important organization setting standards in the field of heritage.
26 Janet Blake, *International Cultural Heritage Law*, Oxford: Oxford University Press, 2015, p. 7. She drew this conclusion after analyzing relevant normative tools.
27 UNESCO, "Convention for the Protection of Cultural Property in the Event of Armed Conflict," 1954. Online. Available at http://portal.unesco.org/en/ev.php-URL_ID=13637&URL_DO=DO_TOPIC&URL_SECTION=201.html (accessed 29 December 2018).
28 UNESCO, "World Heritage Convention," 1972. Online. Available at https://whc.unesco.org/archive/convention-en.pdf (accessed 29 December 2018).
29 E.g. UNESCO, "The Convention on the Protection of the Underwater Cultural Heritage," 2001. Online. Available at https://unesdoc.unesco.org/ark:/48223/pf0000126065 (accessed 29 December 2018).
30 Vittorino Veronese, "A Message from the Director General of UNESCO," 1960, vol. 13, *UNESCO Courier*, 3. Online. Available at https://unesdoc.unesco.org/ark:/48223/pf0000064522 (accessed 29 December 2018).
31 Baslar, *Concept of the Common Heritage*, p. 371.

32 United Nations, "United Nations Convention on the Law of the Sea," 1982, Part XI, Section 2, Articles 136–49. Online. Available at www.un.org/depts/los/convention_agreements/convention_overview_convention.htm (accessed 29 December 2018).

33 E.g. Francesco Francioni, "Beyond State Sovereignty: The Protection of Cultural Heritage as a Shared Interest of Humanity," *Michigan Journal of International Law*, 2004, vol. 25, no. 4., 1209–28. See also Sabine von Schorlemer, *Internationaler Kulturgüterschutz: Ansätze zur Prävention im Frieden sowie im bewaffneten Konflikt*, Berlin: Duncker & Humblot, 1992, and Craig Forrest, *International Law and the Protection of Cultural Heritage*, London: Routledge, 2010.

34 Forrest, *International Law and the Protection of Cultural Heritage*, p. 412.

35 Francesco Francioni, "A Dynamic Evolution of Concept and Scope: From Cultural Property to Cultural Heritage," in Abdulqawi A. Yusuf (ed.) *Standard-Setting in UNESCO. Vol. I: Normative Action in Education, Science and Culture*, Leiden and Boston: UNESCO Publishing/Martinus Nijhoff, 2007, p. 230.

36 This phrase is the official designation for states that have ratified this or other international conventions.

37 Natural law has been held to be the "permanent underlying basis of all law … a kind of perfect justice given to man by nature," and it "is distinguished from positive law, which is the body of law imposed by the state." See Jonathan Law and Elizabeth A. Martin (eds.), *A Dictionary of Law*, 6th ed., Oxford: Oxford University Press, 2006, p. 351.

38 Forrest, *International Law and the Protection of Cultural Heritage*, p. 412. See also UNESCO, *Colloquium on the New Human Rights, Matias Romero Institute of Diplomatic Studies of the Secretariat for External Affairs of Mexico, Mexico City, 12–15 August 1980, Final Report, 1980*, UNESCO Doc. SS.80/CONF.806/4, p. 27. Online. Available at https://unesdoc.unesco.org/ark:/48223/pf0000045394?posInSet=1&queryId=95fe11b2-8148-4ab3-8af7-ed6f3e051660 (accessed 29 December 2018).

39 Rüdiger Wolfrum, "The Principle of the Common Heritage of Mankind," *Zeitschrift für ausländisches öffentliches Recht und Völkerrecht*, 1983, no. 43, 312–37.

40 Wolfrum, "Principle of the Common Heritage of Mankind," 319.

41 Von Schorlemer, *Internationaler Kulturgüterschutz*, pp. 564–6.

42 UNCLOS even establishes "the Authority," an organization of states comprised of all States Parties, to represent the world community. United Nations, *United Nations Convention on the Law of the Sea*, 1982, Part XI, Section 4, Article 156.

43 Roger O'Keefe, "World Cultural Heritage: Obligations to the International Community as a Whole," *International and Comparative Law Quarterly*, 2004, vol. 53, 189–209.

44 Cançado Trindade, *International Law for Humankind*, p. 286.

45 Francesco Francioni, "The Human Dimension of International Cultural Heritage Law: An Introduction," *European Journal of International Law*, 2011, vol. 22, no. 1, 13.

46 Francioni, "Beyond State Sovereignty," 12.

47 Francioni, "Beyond State Sovereignty," 12.

48 These cases are the Arabian Oryx Sanctuary in Oman and the Dresden Elbe Valley in Germany.

49 At the time of this writing (March 2018), 54 properties are inscribed on the List of World Heritage in Danger.

50 UNESCO, "World Heritage Convention," Article 11(4).

51 An example is the Kakadu National Park in Australia. It concerns mining activities within the perimeter of the site, which the convention usually prohibits. For a discussion see Sam Litton, "The World Heritage 'In Danger' Listing as a Taking," *International Law and Politics*, 2011, vol. 44, 219–65.

52 Francesco Francioni and James Gordley, "Introduction," in Francioni and Gordley (eds.) *Enforcing International Cultural Heritage Law*, Oxford: Oxford University Press, 2013, p. 1.

53 United Nations, "Statute of the International Criminal Tribunal for the Former Yugoslavia," 1993, Article 3(d). Online. Available at www.icty.org/en/documents/statute-tribunal (accessed 29 December 2018).

54 United Nations, "Rome Statute of the International Criminal Court," 1998, Article 8 2(b)(ix). Online. Available at www.ohchr.org/EN/ProfessionalInterest/Pages/InternationalCriminalCourt.aspx (accessed 29 December 2018).

55 See Federico Lenzerini, "The Role of International and Mixed Criminal Courts in the Enforcement of International Norms Concerning the Protection of Cultural Heritage," in Francioni and Gordley, *Enforcing International Cultural Heritage Law*, p. 48.
56 ICTY, Prosecutor v. Strugar, Case IT-01-42-T, Trial Chamber II, Judgement of 31 January 2005, §279. Online. Available at www.icty.org/x/cases/strugar/tjug/en/str-tj050131e.pdf (accessed 29 December 2018). See p. 122 of this document for the quotation.
57 ICTY, Prosecutor v. Strugar, Case IT-01-42-T, Trial Chamber II, Judgement of 31 January 2005, §232. Online. Available at www.icty.org/x/cases/strugar/tjug/en/str-tj050131e.pdf (accessed 29 December 2018). See p. 106 of this document for the quotation.
58 Lenzerini, "The Role of International and Mixed Criminal Courts," p. 53.
59 ICTY, Prosecutor v. Jokic, Case IT-01-42/1-S, Trial Chamber I, Judgement of 18 March 2004, §53. Online. Available at www.icty.org/x/cases/miodrag_jokic/tjug/en/jok-sj040318e.pdf (accessed 29 December 2018). See p. 14 of this document for the quotation.
60 International Criminal Court (ICC), Prosecutor v. Ahmad Al Faqi Al Mahdi, Case ICC-01/12-01/15, Trial Chamber VIII, Summary of the Judgment and Sentence 17 August 2017, §51. Online. Available at www.icc-cpi.int/CourtRecords/CR2017_05117.PDF (accessed 29 December 2018). See p. 20 of this document for the quotation.
61 UNESCO, "Declaration on the Intentional Destruction of Cultural Heritage," 2003. Online. Available at https://unesdoc.unesco.org/ark:/48223/pf0000133874?posInSet=4&queryId=37a39801-f9db-4cba-8e26-3e97e94663e7 (accessed 29 December 2018). See p. 1 of this document for the quotation.
62 United Nations Security Council, "Resolution 2347," 24 March 2017. UN Document S/RES/2347 (2017). Online. Available at http://undocs.org/S/RES/2347(2017) (accessed 29 December 2018).
63 Irina Bokova, Director-General of UNESCO, cited in "UN Security Council Adopts Historic Resolution for the Protection of Heritage," *UNESCO News*, 24 March 2017. Online. Available at http://en.unesco.org/news/security-council-adopts-historic-resolution-protection-heritage (accessed 29 December 2018).
64 Karel Wellens, "Revisiting Solidarity as a (Re-)Emerging Constitutional Principle: Some Further Reflections," in Rüdiger Wolfrum and Chie Kojima (eds.) *Solidarity: A Structural Principle of International Law*, Heidelberg: Springer, 2010, p. 5.
65 George Khushf, "Solidarity as a Moral and Political Concept: Beyond the Liberal/Communitarian Impasse," in Kurt Bayertz (ed.) *Solidarity*, Dordrecht: Kluwer Academic, 1999, p. 57.
66 Wolfrum and Kojima, *Solidarity: A Structural Principle.*
67 United Nations Human Rights Council, "Report of the Independent Expert on Human Rights and International Solidarity," 25 April 2017. United Nations Document A/HRC/35/35 Online. Available at http://docstore.ohchr.org/SelfServices/FilesHandler.ashx?enc=dtYoAzPhJ4NMy4Lu1TOebEemUbRcMKMVNIMH7cp7iH94yyIADDIBsX%2BMCV1KWb4Gmj5DrJLk1ivxGlyFlrmBDhNNi7uHg8xhsexTYsDVzc%2FVGEUkN1upZzZuBvbp0igv (accessed 29 December 2018).
68 Baslar, *Concept of the Common Heritage*, p. 330.
69 Hilary Charlesworth, "Human Rights and the UNESCO Memory of the World Programme," in Michele Langfield, William Logan, and Mairead Nic Craith (eds.) *Cultural Diversity, Heritage and Human Rights: Intersections in Theory and Practice*, New York: Routledge, 2010, pp. 21–30. See also Helaine Silverman and D. Fairchild Ruggles, "Cultural Heritage and Human Rights," in Silverman and Fairchild Ruggles (eds.) *Cultural Heritage and Human Rights*, New York: Springer, 2007, pp. 3–22.
70 William Logan and Michele Langfield, "Intersecting Concepts and Practices," in Langfield, Logan, and Craith, *Cultural Diversity, Heritage and Human Rights*, pp. 3–20; Charlesworth, "Human Rights and the UNESCO Memory of the World Programme"; and Blake, *International Cultural Heritage Law.*
71 Charlesworth, "Human Rights and the UNESCO Memory of the World Programme."
72 UNESCO, "Final Report, International Round Table on 'Intangible Cultural Heritage – Working Definitions,' 14–17 March 2001, Turin, Italy," 2001. Online, Available at www.unesco.org/culture/ich/doc/src/00077-EN.pdf (accessed 29 December 2018). See p. 14 of this document for the phrase "common concern."

73 United Nations, "Universal Declaration of Human Rights," 1948, Article 27. Online. Available at www.un.org/en/universal-declaration-human-rights/ (accessed 29 December 2018).

74 United Nations, "International Covenant on Economic, Social and Cultural Rights," 1966, Article 15. Online. Available at www.ohchr.org/en/professionalinterest/pages/cescr.aspx (accessed 29 December 2018).

75 A comprehensive overview is in Blake, *International Cultural Heritage Law.*

76 Charlesworth, "Human Rights and the UNESCO Memory of the World Programme," p. 28.

30

INTELLECTUAL PROPERTY LAW AND HUMAN RIGHTS

Steven Wilf

This essay tells the story of a relationship with more than its share of complications. Two legal frameworks – intellectual property and human rights – are domains that emerged separately despite sharing a common rights language. How has their interaction unfolded over time? These regimes share similar historical trajectories and exert an ever-more powerful impact on global governance. Their modern, rather limited incarnation emerged in the period of the major eighteenth-century North Atlantic revolutions. In the course of the nineteenth and early twentieth centuries their foundational concepts evolved into a dense legal skein that was subsequently repurposed for the needs of industrial societies. Over time, especially with the emergence of the knowledge economy in recent decades, they have become important transnational legal actors in an ever-more globalizing contemporary world.

Intellectual property in its early modern beginnings was a metropolitan law, simply operating within a country's geographic boundaries. It extended no further than the signposts marking a territorial frontier. Patents and copyrights were used to foster the creation of domestic creative classes such as artisan inventors and writers. In its formative years, human rights as a legal architecture was often imposed in limited fashion upon colonial subjects or within foreign contexts. At least in the long nineteenth century, an external demand to comply with basic rights-based norms was rarely applied to Great Powers, especially those possessing significant political and economic ballast of their own. Few anticipated that such modest, even marginal beginnings for both regimes ultimately would come to embody an entire realm of legal rules. Yet these two rights-based areas of law now routinely project their norms across territorial borders. Indeed, they define two realms absolutely critical to human flourishing across the globe: human rights – which often begins at the fulcrum point of protecting the body – and intellectual property, with its asserting guardianship for the mind's expression and invention.

What happens at moments of encounter when intellectual property and human rights must contend with each other? What legal and political responses are prompted by this particular *pas de deux*? The prevailing narrative is that the problem is new, largely appearing in the 1990s. This essay offers a different story. It argues that intellectual property's fraught interface with human rights must be understood as a historical phenomenon. Looking at intellectual property over the course of several centuries, we can see how it assumed aspects of a rights regime over time, launched ambitious experiments in international governance, and – this is most salient – came to envision creativity in art and invention in technology as an essential predicate for human flourishing.

To understand intellectual property as human rights we must decenter existing historical commonplaces. This means departing from the traditional intellectual property narrative that concentrates on the shaping of law to meet the challenge of new technologies.[1] Nor does our account focus on the customary human rights story of the struggle to implement norms despite uneven enforcement mechanisms. Instead, the subject of this historical essay is the interaction, even jostling, of these two regimes. While both intellectual property and human rights claim a pedigree grounded in natural rights, there are differences in how rights are articulated. For example, there are competing rights to free expression – protection of creator versus user rights, access to knowledge, the right to genetic and biometric information, the right to be forgotten, moral rights for artists, right to health – particularly pertaining to pharmaceutical patent protection, or the right of farmers to seed reproduction. The Universal Declaration of Human Rights (UDHR), Article 27(2) itself recognizes a right to intellectual property by requiring the protection of "the moral and material interests resulting from any scientific, literary, or artistic production of which he is the author."[2]

A story of two legal regimes divided by a common rights language

These illustrative points of intersection suggest the complexity of the linkage between intellectual property and human rights. Much of the existing literature remains preoccupied with whether their relationship might be characterized as a conflict or as two compatible legal systems. Proponents emphasizing conflict assert that a fundamental rift exists between intellectual property's protections of private rights versus human rights' concern with public welfare. Those arguing for a more harmonious understanding of their interaction point out that both are founded on rights discourse even if many intellectual property rules tilt towards property rights. Intellectual property law, by deploying rights language as part of its pervasive concern with public use, suggests an overlap with human rights. Perhaps the most apt metaphor is mutual, even if wary, encounter. According to lawyer Laurence R. Helfer, human rights are "intellectual property's new frontier."[3]

As a historical investigation, this essay interrogates the past development of the complex, often fraught interactions between these two regimes. More broadly, it raises historiographical questions about the very nature of human rights. Human rights have been identified largely through their past embodiments. They focused on the human body as the situs of pain, power, torture, and physical abuse. They have relied upon the body politic, the state, to regulate its use of violence and prevent the actions of others. As Max Weber commented, territoriality with state control establishes fixed boundaries whereby the state can operate to pursue legitimate aims intended to protect rights for both citizens and non-citizens.[4] And, of course, human rights have been embodied in broad international legal instruments such as charters and conventions. Intellectual property deconstructs these commonplace categories. Intellectual property's emphasis is on intangible forms of expression rather than the body. Digital intellectual property, in the forms of electronic reproductions of expression or the ideas behind inventions, readily and often circulate across formal national boundaries. Moreover, intellectual property is generally grounded in a normative thicket of detailed rules, not directed by broad overarching principles like human rights.

Intellectual property is what the postmodernist theorist Michel Foucault refers to as *hétérotopie*.[5] It is layered, complex, and often maddeningly hard to situate within the classic contours of human rights. To a certain extent, the problem of intellectual property's vexed place within human rights mirrors a broad debate in the humanities over the origins of human rights themselves. The literary scholar Elaine Scarry has underscored the connection to the body[6] and historian Samuel Moyn has pointed to the search in the 1970s for a reinvigorated body politic.[7] This pattern developed, he argues, in Europe from the search for a post-Cold War identity. According to Moyn, the United States particularly after the Vietnam War sought a newly recalibrated moral compass. But it is Lynn Hunt's scholarship that most closely links intellectual property and human rights from their very beginnings.[8] She situates the origin of human rights in the emergence of new compelling notions of sympathy that arise with the invention of the modern novel. The emergence of a broad republic of letters composed of such disparate works as political tracts and epistolary fiction is significant for both the establishing of the empathy needed to ground human rights and a growing need to protect the interests of authors. Hunt's portrayal underscores the shared historical genealogy of human rights and intellectual property.

The debate over the compatibility of human rights and intellectual property rights presumes that there is a unified normative solution to resolving their differences. It might be that different instances of potential interaction at the intellectual property/human rights interface are subject to different sorts of resolutions. Only by examining their encounters over time can we hope to fashion mechanisms to negotiate between the regimes. This essay, therefore, insistently asserts the salience of historical analysis. It maps the emerging historical pattern of the many points of overlap to see how alternative jurisprudential approaches jostled for the attention of courts and legislatures, and to ask how those implementing international legal rules seek to balance competing claims. It begins with a brief history of the development of these two legal spheres, underscores the points of intersection between human rights and knowledge production, and, ultimately, addresses the question of how we mediate a growing number of conflicts.

This essay's argument is deceptively simple. Although the discord between human rights and intellectual property as normative regimes only appears when global governance insists that rights must be absolute and trumping, the seeds of this conflict are long in the making. This essay will follow the narrative arc of intellectual property from its beginnings in the early modern period when conceptions of property were first insistently deployed. It will show how property claims increasingly were garbed in rights language by the early nineteenth century. During this period, intellectual property was transformed from an agent of a republic of letters to a formal doctrinal satrap of law's empire. A normative thicket was fashioned as authors and inventors, readers, and those improving or utilizing new technologies, came to clash as they pressed their claims ever-more vociferously in the framework of intellectual property and human rights law.

Over time, intellectual property's regulation of the products of the mind entailed designing tools for balancing the demands of competing creator and user stakeholders. By contrast, human rights' focus on the body in pain demanded the invention of a powerful language of trumping rights. How as these regimes evolved have we negotiated the divergent approaches of balancing and trumping?

The age of ateliers: from monarchical privilege to the uncertain beginnings of creator rights

While various forms of intellectual property protection, such as control over esoteric knowledge in traditional societies, have existed from ancient times, our legacy of legal regulation in a familiar codified form is an early modern European invention. In part, this is due to the rise of centralized nation-states with an interest in distributing privileges over knowledge within a patronage system. Eventually, these crown privileges were transformed into general rules. In 1474, Venice established an early form of patent protection by enacting a statute that granted a monopoly to "any new and ingenious contrivances not made heretofore."[9] Similarly, the English Statute of Monopolies (1624) evolved from an earlier practice of letters of patent whereby monopolies were granted by the monarch as a matter of crown favor.[10] It regularized the assignment and provided patents for new inventions during a term of 14 years. The patent must be novel and not cause harm to the public. English copyright underwent a parallel progress. Prior to the passage of the Statute of Anne (1710), a guild of printers, the Stationers' Company, retained the exclusive power to print and censor books. As the first copyright statute, the Statute of Anne transformed a private corporate privilege into a public statutory right.[11] Its provisions resembled later copyright legislation by creating a registration system and setting a limited term – in its case a duration of 14 years.

The Statute of Anne vested rights in authors. By the beginning of the eighteenth century, England established intellectual property legal regimes that although rooted originally in patronage ultimately pivoted towards independence for the creators of knowledge. Inventors and authors were granted rights allowing them access to capital, markets, and audiences directly without having to seek patrons. Consumers of new technologies and book readers supported a new creative class. In the case of authors, for example, what historian Robert Darnton has called a literary underground emerged by the mid-eighteenth century that was freed of the constraints imposed by the earlier patronage system. Not surprisingly, this period, poised on the cusp of revolution and when artisan tinkerers and Grub Street scribblers came into their own, became the seedtime of intellectual property.

Early modern English law transformed patent and copyright from a pastiche of discretionary monopoly privileges granted by the crown into statutory law. Various justifications were made for this shift. The Statute of Anne, for example, stated that it was intended to prevent publication without the consent of authors and to encourage the production of books. Yet were these rights? The English justification for copyright remained mostly utilitarian and poorly unpacked. Indeed, it was US law after Independence that began the process of transforming intellectual property into a panoply of rights. It did so in three ways. First, America constitutionalized intellectual property protection by granting Congress the power "to promote the progress of science and useful arts, by securing for limited times to authors and inventors the exclusive right to their respective writings and discoveries."[12] We know very little from Philadelphia Constitutional Convention notes about this remarkable decision to embed an embryonic legal field in a foundational document. Ironically, this Copyright and Patent Clause seems to be merely utilitarian. The only Constitutional provision including a stated purpose, its aim is to construct incentives for the production of knowledge. The granting of power over copyright and patent to Congress may have simply been an echo of a response to Crown privileges, a gesture towards anti-monopoly sentiment, or a recognition of the importance of writing and invention to the new republic – and therefore calling for the establishing of a single federal system rather than a bricolage of state protections. Nothing in the clause suggests that it should serve as the grounding for the assignment of rights. Nevertheless, James Madison in "Federalist No. 43" set forth a syllogism: patent privileges are the equivalent of copyright protection, and copyright is grounded in common law even if no statute existed to extend authorial control.[13] At the end of the eighteenth century, common law was often seen as equivalent to establishing rights via natural law.

Second, the Constitutional clause was understood as linking copyright and patent even though the term intellectual property would not be introduced until the mid-1840s. By grounding intellectual property in the Constitution, the Early Republic surfaced its rights dimension. Indeed, almost immediately after ratification in 1790 Congress passed parallel though different statutes for the two regimes. During the end of the eighteenth and early nineteenth century, a debate arose about whether copyright and patent were common law rights, that is, inherent human rights apart from any legislative or judicial construction, or not. In England, over the course of what historians have called the Battle of the Booksellers, the House of Lords decision *Donaldson v. Beckett* (1774) determined that the Statute of Anne superseded the doctrine of common law copyright and authorial rights could not extend in perpetuity, unlike other forms of property.[14] Similarly, the US Supreme Court in *Wheaton v. Peters* (1834) found that inherent common law rights were exhausted by the first publication.[15]

Third, the identification of rights in the products of the mind was grounded on the theory that these were just another form of property. Yet the analogy of intellectual property to material possessions posed all sorts of difficulties. When is there occupancy of an intangible form of expression? How can we consider intellectual property as exclusive, when it can so easily be copied? And is the labor of the mind really similar to the kind of physical labor that John Locke theorized as forming the basis of tangible property ownership? Although the limitations placed upon inherent rights in literary works and technological inventions circumscribed what today would be considered rights-based claims, they did not dampen the recourse to rights language that became increasingly important through the nineteenth century. Even if copyright and patent as property was a bit of an analytical stretch, it became commonplace by the middle of the nineteenth century. Intellectual property law routinely gestured to Lockean conceptions of property rights. Authorial rights were often intertwined with romantic notions of authorial creation. The Statute of Anne and the earliest US Copyright Act (1790) initially vested rights in authors. Moreover, in common law countries this burgeoning recognition of authorial rights was balanced in pragmatic fashion against the claims of other stakeholders such as publishers and the public at large – though often these were not expressed in rights language.

Describing intellectual property rights as property rights drew significantly on the late eighteenth-century Anglo-American identification of property ownership with civic liberty. William Murray, a Maryland Congressman in 1793 distinguished between patent rights in England granted "by grace of the monarch" and the republican United States where "a citizen has a *right* in the inventions he may make."[16] Around nearly the same time, Revolutionary France embraced a natural rights theory of *droit d'auteur*. With the abolishing of Old Regime print privileges in August 1789 and the ending of the Paris book guild in 1791, there was no legal mechanism for organizing the book trade. A new

Copyright Act was introduced in 1793 reflecting revolutionary currents. The general Enlightenment French notion of an author's unequivocal natural right in his or her own creations is deeply connected the assertion of autonomous self-mastery that also animates the beginnings of human rights. In this sense, French thinkers asserted the products of the mind had a greater connection to individual genius than conventional real or moveable property. Yet, as historian Carla Hesse has shown, the author was supposed to be a public-directed citizen.[17] For this reason, early French copyright law eschewed posthumous authorial rights and permitted works to be available more readily to the public.

All three nascent eighteenth-century North Atlantic intellectual property regimes – those of Britain, the United States, and France – developed a rights language crystallizing around the creation of intangible property. But the invention of intellectual property as a foundational right was complicated. How did the definition of such a right differ from one legal culture to another? Should noncitizens as well be provided rights to printed books and technological inventions? And, ultimately, are authors and inventors the only rights holders? Almost inevitably the rights forged to govern human knowledge in an age of workshops would lead to multiple competing stakeholders in an industrial society. Creators and their many intermediaries – such as publishers and industrial corporations – would have to contend with rights claims from users and the public at large. This led to a fundamental conundrum. How might the legal system balance the competing rights of different stakeholders?

Age of international dreamers: from reciprocal rights to universal rights

The territoriality of intellectual property law, which varied so much from one country to another in its substantive and procedural rules, was visibly at odds with its justification founded upon inherent human rights. England granted patents to inventions newly introduced from elsewhere into the kingdom even if these were not original. While the United States in the 1830s upheld a standard of novelty for patents through a rigorous examination procedure and kept fees low in order to encourage innovation by ordinary citizens, it established discriminatory higher patent fees for noncitizens. France's denial of posthumous copyright protection was anomalous compared to Anglo-American law. Different countries had different notions of the substantive and procedural laws relating to both copyright and patent. Most striking were the dissimilar rights in intellectual property rights afforded citizens as opposed to noncitizens.

Between the 1790 beginnings of federal copyright and the Chace Act of 1891 (international copyright), the United States failed to recognize foreign copyrights or to assign protection to foreign authors.[18] Indeed, the 1790 Federal Copyright Act explicitly stated that it would not constrain the importation, sale, or publishing of any works by noncitizens. By 1820, one contemporary commentator estimated that some 70 percent of the American book trade consisted of unauthorized copying of British works. Jacksonian America political figures asserted that by reprinting English works without the payment of royalties US publishers allowed for the dissemination of cheap books – and therefore furthered the public policy goal of promoting knowledge among citizens. Moreover, mid-nineteenth-century advocates of free trade criticized the limits placed on exchange by granting monopolies in copyright and patent. Through much of the century, America was the Barbary States of book piracy.

A growing number of critics nevertheless came to oppose American book piracy. According to the eminent nineteenth-century American legal scholar Francis Lieber, the United States betrayed its obligation to the law of nations through such nonrecognition.[19] Calling copyright in 1840 a "spontaneous right," he flatly stated that only "barbarous or degenerate nations" would retreat from granting such rights to foreign authors.[20] Born in Germany, Lieber (who also authored the groundbreaking code introducing legal norms for the conduct of war) conceived of copyright as a universal right. The first brush with the United States providing protection to foreign authors in the late 1830s might be seen in the limited reciprocal rights proposed for French and British authors by Henry Clay.[21] Although this proposal was a far cry from Lieber's vision of universal rights law, and was based on what Clay called "reciprocal justice," it was rejected by Congress.

In 1883, the American Copyright League was formed in order to prod the United States to provide copyright protection for foreign authors. By this time, the situation had changed from earlier attempts in the 1830s. Throughout much of the nineteenth century, publishers had arranged for an informal system called "courtesy of the trade," whereby only the first publisher to introduce a book from Britain would reprint it in the United States. The rise of the new industrial book based on the technology of printing from plates during this period allowed for the emergence of large publishing houses as intermediaries – and provided for the effectiveness of such agreements. Yet the system was breaking down at the time of the American Copyright League's founding. "Print capitalism," the term that literary scholar Trish Loughran has borrowed from Benedict Anderson to discuss this phenomenon, became increasingly rough and tumble, with small presses producing their own reprints of British books.[22] Large publishers lessened their resistance to international copyright. Nevertheless, the League's call for extending copyright protection was an uphill battle. It required various forms of mobilization: petitions to Congress, public readings and protests, the enlistment of well-known literary figures from the United States and abroad to clamor for change, producing pamphlets for the cause, bolstering the League, and, particularly, enlisting other stakeholders. Agitation for protecting the rights of foreign authors was a social movement. Addressing ever-broadening audiences, including publishers, journeymen printers, and the reading public, the Copyright League needed to be cognizant of more than simply authorial rights. The Chace Act (1891) and 1905 Copyright Act recognized these varied groups as stakeholders.

The situation was very different in Europe. In 1852, Napoleon III envisioned a Francophone print market encompassing France, Belgium, and Switzerland. A decree was issued criminalizing copying the works of foreign authors even absent the willingness of other countries to similarly protect French literary production. France was heading towards the principle that natural rights demanded international governance. Britain favored reciprocity fashioned through negotiated bilateral treaties. In order to comply with the obligations of the Anglo-French Copyright Convention providing reciprocal protection, Britain also passed a statute in 1852 extending copyright protection to translations.[23] This watershed year marked a recognition by two major powers of an obligation towards international standards for intellectual property rights.

Even if one agreed that creators – authors and inventors – must receive a right in the products of their minds, such an argument becomes less compelling when those claiming rights are not creators, but intermediaries or non-creator owners. Industrial age intellectual property often entailed the transfer of rights to those who best could capitalize upon knowledge assets, such as large-scale publishing houses, newspaper associations, advertising agencies, and the vast research and development apparatus of a corporate laboratory. A second late nineteenth-century US social movement highlighted the possibility of expanding intellectual property rights beyond creators to user stakeholders. An anti-patent movement emerged in the Great Plains in the 1880s, as patent holders largely from other states harassed agriculturalists over the use of patented agricultural technology such as barbed wire or certain kinds of wells. Patent holders canvassed the countryside, threatening ordinary farmers with crippling lawsuits. Again, Americans were prompted to mobilize over intellectual property rights. Activists deluged Congress with petitions, proposed legislation to limit the ability of patent holders to sue, and created legal defense funds. Since many of the contested patents concerned barbed wire, the call was raised for Free Wire. Drawing on the politics of the broader populist movement, this prairie uprising against the assertion of patent rights countered with its own notion that users, especially innocent users, had their own bundle of rights.

Not only America experienced political agitation to curb patent rights. By the middle of the nineteenth century, a number of European countries saw a backlash against patents. German economists proposed the abolition of the patent system. Holland's legislature repealed that country's 1817 patent law in 1869, and, claiming that the abolition of patent was conducive to free trade, did not reestablish a patent system until 1910. In 1866 and 1882, the Swiss public voted down the passage of federal legislation to protect industrial property. Victorian England had more than its share of anti-patent agitators, many of whom called for patent abolition. The lessons from tumultuous late nineteenth-century intellectual property politics became increasingly clear. Creator rights operating within a single jurisdiction were fragile. They failed to adequately address the rights of foreign creators. Authors and inventors were challenged by competing stakeholders. And – as the American and European anti-patent movements suggested – intellectual property ownership might be rolled back at the behest of political forces. Only international norms grounded in rights could ensure domestic protection for the products of the mind.

Both domestic difficulties and the failure to protect intellectual property beyond political borders prompted a shift to the international arena. Victor Hugo and other writers in 1858 met in Brussels to call for international copyright protection. This first genuine international intellectual property organization was unofficial. It was the nineteenth century's version of a nongovernmental organization (NGO) – an association of authors relying on persuasion rather than the force of law. Founded at a Paris gathering in 1878 with Hugo as its honorary president, the International Literary and Artistic Association (Association Littéraire et Artistique Internationale) promoted transborder authorial rights. The goal was to establish a uniform international copyright statute. By the early 1880s, however the Association had abandoned the demand for a universal copyright law that would apply across the globe, and instead sought a copyright union to establish rights to be enforced by different countries.

Discussions of such a union ultimately culminated in the Berne Convention for the Protection of Literary and Artistic Works (1886). With the adoption of Berne for copyright and the Paris Convention for the Protection of Industrial Property (1883) setting rules for the international protection of patents, advocates sought to unite their common goals in 1893 under an umbrella organization, the United International Bureaux for the

Protection of Intellectual Property (Bureaux Internationaux réunis pour la protection de la propriété intellectuel, BIRPI) as a particularly early form of global governance. BIRPI was ahead of its time as a transnational institution precisely because of the degree of domestic discord about the scope of intellectual property. Historians have underestimated the significance of the parallel emergence of internal dissension over intellectual property in the last decades of the nineteenth century and the growing clamor for international protection of creator rights.

The United States remained aloof from BIRPI. Indeed, it would not become a signatory of the Berne Convention until 1988, nearly a century after its founding. The major reason for America's reluctance to join was its resistance to a copyright system without formalities such as registration. The automatic acquisition of copyright simply by creating a work was favored by Continental European countries. The very terms used, *Urheberrecht* or *droit d'auteur*, suggest inherent human rights. Yet the absence of the United States ironically fostered the objective of establishing Berne as a rights-based regime. In the 1928 Rome Conference, BIRPI member states adopted a system of moral rights, which might not have happened if America was present to oppose this provision.

Moral rights are a quintessential example of an author-based rights system. They provide a legal claim for artists against the removal of attribution or violation of the integrity of the art work, even after a work is sold. Although moral rights vary from country to country both in terms of the scope of what constitutes art and the nature of the rights, the importance of establishing moral rights as a requirement of the Berne Convention under Article 6(b) is that it unequivocally identifies the importance for creators of human rights (rather than simply economic rights).[24] As historian Peter Baldwin has shown, moral rights have a checkered past.[25] The notion was based on a 1925 Italian act that Mussolini wanted to showcase during the conference on the Berne Convention held in Rome in 1928, and reflected fascist Italy's particular concern with the corrosive effect of artistic commodification on the honor of artists themselves. Moral rights exemplify the assertion that creator dignity is at its core human rights.

When newly independent nations joined BIRPI after World War II, their leaders were less concerned with an intellectual property framework organized around human rights. None of the former colonies of European powers had a part in shaping the major postwar intellectual property international legal frameworks. These laws were focused on protecting private creator rights. Even some of the most important post-World War II human rights documents, which did have broader input from countries, echoed the objective of promoting the interests of creators. Perhaps the best examples of this are the provisions of the UDHR (1948). Its Article 27(1) guarantees the "right freely to participate in the cultural life of the community, to enjoy the arts and to share in scientific advancement and its benefits." In Article 27(2) creators are promised a "right to the protection of the moral and material interests resulting from any scientific, literary or artistic production of which he is the author." Human rights language was deployed to prevent the deprivation experienced by creators if they should lose control of their inventive output or be unable to enter the broader intellectual endeavors of others.

By the mid-1960s, there was growing disenchantment with the international ordering of intellectual property. Multinational corporations as rights holders and Northern hemisphere countries often engaged in asymmetrical market exchanges with less well-to-do trading partners. Signatory states were obligated to grant a certain level of protection to creators and owners. The major conventions imposed legal norms from the outside that often proved disadvantageous. Intellectual property rights appeared as dolled-up claims to monopoly. In the words of open-source activist Richard Stallman, BIRPI was an institution of legislative colonization whereby wealthy countries imposed norms that extracted wealth from less fortunate countries.

This critique made little headway until the 1967 Stockholm Conference when the decision was made to formalize BIRPI and to transform it in 1974 into a specialized agency of the United Nations (UN), the World Intellectual Property Organization (WIPO) headquartered in Geneva. The founding of WIPO meant that developing nations had a more prominent role while the link to the UN placed it within the orbit of larger international political trends. Behind its façade as a technocratic, seemingly apolitical institution, WIPO's stated mission of promoting intellectual property protection emerged as an issue. At the urging of non-Northern hemisphere countries such as Argentina, Brazil, and South Africa, and after three years of rancorous debate, WIPO adopted the Development Agenda in 2007. It specified that promotion of intellectual property must accord with the wider aims of the UN system.[26] For many of the countries supporting the Development Agenda, the interest was largely economic. Yet at the core of UN goals, from the UDHR adopted immediately after World War II on, was the furthering of human rights.

The age of global governance: collective and personal rights

Neither the Paris nor Berne Conventions made explicit reference to human rights. Indeed, deontological justifications (justifications based on obligations) took a back seat to the express purpose of international accords to protect economic interests in valuable intangible property across geopolitical borders. Nevertheless, the very enlisting of support for internationalization fostered a turn towards justifying rights. The traditional Anglo-American Lockean grounding that creators should benefit from the products of their labor was supplemented by continental European Kantian justifications identifying autonomous authority over property with human flourishing. Even if not overtly asserted, the major intellectual property international agreements such as Paris and Berne – unlike the reciprocal treaties that were their forebears – implicitly relied upon the proposition that intellectual property constitutes a fundamental human right.

In light of the Development Agenda, the hurdles erected by the bureaucratic and the troublesome consensus approach of WIPO, and the immense problem of harmonization (when after every attempt to unify intellectual property rules, another divergence in legal norms was always just a bit further down the road), wealthier countries found the large umbrella international treaties less attractive. Enforcement proved the most notable frustration. Concerned with widespread global piracy, the United States led a shift away from WIPO. Although the United States was an intellectual property pirate economy for almost the entirety of the nineteenth century, it showed little patience with the infringement of copyright and patent by other countries. A combination of diplomatic bluster and economic threats, however, proved unsuccessful in pressuring rapidly industrializing countries such as China to stop turning a blind eye to widespread intellectual property piracy.

The adoption of the Trade Related Aspects of Intellectual Property Rights (TRIPS) Agreement in 1995 marked the apotheosis of this disenchantment.[27] By linking policing to trade agreements, the hope was that there finally would emerge an effective enforcement mechanism. TRIPS upped the ante for enforcement. While TRIPS required policing minimums, Article 1 set the stage for signatory countries to heighten intellectual property protection, often under the umbrella of separately negotiated Free Trade Agreements (FTAs).[28] TRIPS Article 61 demanded the imposition of criminal sanctions for counterfeiting. Redress for intellectual piracy could be sought through trade sanctions imposed by the World Trade Organization (WTO).[29]

Instead of connecting intellectual property to the Development Agenda's contested call for economic redistribution, the trend in the new millennium has been to extend rights to other rights holders beyond creators and owners. Two sets of human rights have been particularly notable. The first set concerns collective rights. WIPO initiated a negotiating framework to provide developing countries with their own bundle of rights through traditional knowledge. Traditional knowledge was defined as knowledge, know-how, skills and practices that are developed, sustained, and passed on from generation to generation within a community, often forming part of its cultural or spiritual identity. Discussions are also underway in the area of knowledge rights in biodiversity. Collective rights in culture and the environment were largely promoted by developing countries. The second set emerged from increasingly savvy digital citizens and NGOs in economically advanced nations supporting individual human rights regarding such core constructs as privacy, access to knowledge, and concern with the increasingly propertization of the information commons. Both of these sets of new human rights interventions will be discussed below.

Intellectual property as a collective human right

Traditional knowledge was part of a broader turn towards recognizing collective rights as well as individual rights. It borrowed from rights language emerging in the course of decolonization, particularly in India and French sub-Saharan Africa (1947–60). Its rights-based genealogy could be traced through the Convention Concerning the Protection and the Integration of Indigenous and other Tribal and Semi-Tribal Populations in Independent Countries (1957) that recognizes the right of ownership for the populations over their traditional territories,[30] the establishment of the UN Working Group on Indigenous Populations (1982) that became the major forum dedicated to protection of Indigenous populations' human rights, and the founding of the Permanent UN Forum on Indigenous Issues (2000).

A major purpose of traditional knowledge was to prevent the commodification of Indigenous heritage by outsiders – although this has resulted at times in the fabrication of ersatz, often exoticized, versions of culture. On one hand, traditional knowledge promoted a proprietary norm in which the right of a people to claim its entire culture is recognized. A First Nation entity might determine the stewardship of ritual artifacts even if owned by outsiders; limit performance of customary dance; or prohibit activities on a sacred mountain. On the other hand, some proponents of traditional knowledge have stressed the importance of access to world cultures. This position valorizes a principle of cultural diffusion, based on the idea that cultures are part of a global intellectual commons to which all humans have some rights. As an intellectual property system, traditional knowledge was teeming with problems from its beginning. What was not authentic traditional knowledge in a society deeply rooted in its own history? Who has the authority to speak for the collective and seek to vindicate legal claims? And, in the end, does not the very notion of traditional knowledge favor conservative definitions of culture, privileging preservation over innovation? If traditional knowledge was a means of sidestepping the asymmetry between industrialized and less-industrialized societies, it created a new asymmetry between the past and the future.

Since 2009 WIPO has been trying unsuccessfully to draft international legal instruments that can shift traditional knowledge from theoretical considerations of human rights to a bundle of rights that might be recognized by courts across the globe. Definitional conundrums and the absence of international consensus have stymied this project. Nevertheless, the very existence of rights language concerning traditional knowledge has been important in domestic legal systems, especially in countries such as Australia and Canada, where there is a growing awareness of a government role in fostering Indigenous culture analogous to other intellectual property systems. In the United States, the 1990 passage of the Native American Graves Protection & Repatriation Act (NAGPRA) was a milestone in recognizing a collective right to cultural property.[31] NAGPRA provided for the protection of Native American graves, funerary objects, and sacred objects – specific ceremonial objects needed for the practice of their traditional religion. The statute identified the rights holder for this cultural patrimony as a collective that could establish shared identity through affiliation or kinship. However, NAGPRA remained tethered to the neocolonial apparatus of American legalism. Identification of rights holders generally relied upon a listing in the registry of the Bureau of Indian Affairs. A special agency, the Indian Claims Commission, was established to process any legal entitlements emerging under the statute. NAGPRA required that those holding Native American patrimony must make an inventory of these objects, notify the appropriate Indigenous group, and possibly repatriate their holdings. In practice, NAGPRA has led to negotiations between museums and other repositories and rights holders, rather than to mass repatriation.

NAGPRA proved that circumscribed traditional knowledge statutes might work as domestic law. Geographic Indications (GIs) demonstrated that cultural patrimony might be protected at the international level, at least when there is a constituency promoting such an agenda coming from established international powers. A particular concern of French legal culture, GIs embrace the idea that *terroir* – the territorial site and artisanal method of production – are essential features of certain products, and these products cannot be produced elsewhere utilizing the same appellation or trademark. Champagne, for example, can only be labeled as such if the grapes are grown and fermented in that particular region of France using customary forms of viniculture. The right is purely a privilege granted traditional Indigenous European culture. Called linkage (*le lien*), this right made an early transnational appearance in the Paris Convention (1883).[32] Nevertheless, only the regional harmonization of the European Union and in particular TRIPS (1995) provided traction for GIs in international law. Article 22 of TRIPS provides this right for a GI where "a given quality, reputation or other characteristic of the good is essentially attributable to its geographic origin." In Article 23, additional protection is provided for wine and spirits. The focus on wine, mushrooms, and cheese suggests a Eurocentric core to this right.

Article 3 of the UN 1992 Convention on Biological Diversity, adopted in Rio de Janeiro, reflected the concerns of mostly southern hemisphere countries.[33] It recognizes the rights of sovereign states to establish control over genetic resources within their territory. Nonetheless, Article 8 obligates states to

> respect, preserve and maintain knowledge, innovations and practices of indigenous and local communities embodying traditional lifestyles relevant for the conservation and sustainable use of biological diversity and promote their wider application with the approval and involvement of the holders of such knowledge, innovations and practices and encourage the equitable sharing of the benefits arising from the utilization of such knowledge, innovations and practices.

Both provisions were nonbinding. Their capacious wording rooted in general principles borrowed more from human rights than intellectual property law. How would preservation of Indigenous knowledge practices be enacted? Clearly, the Convention left the matter up to signatory states – and many of these had a long history of ignoring the needs of First Peoples.

Intellectual property as personal human right

If southern hemisphere countries lobbied for collective human rights such as protection of traditional knowledge and biodiversity, citizens and NGOs in northern hemisphere nations have become increasingly preoccupied with personal rights. Such an interest, of course, did not begin in our times. With its privileged protection of artist moral rights even after the sale of the artwork to another party, the Berne Convention had long recognized a personal right. Moral rights presumed that a painting, for example, is the embodiment of an individual artist's persona. But what about other representations of the self? How do we know what constitutes a person? Is it the Borgesian library of chromosomal genetic material inherited from progenitors or epigenetic regulation, or even its ultimate somatic expression, that constitutes a unique persona? Whatever it might be, there is certainly a human rights perspective endowing the persona with particular dignity rights.

Biometric information, for example, controlled by conventional intellectual property holders in databases, may violate fundamental rights to control one's self. A sea change is currently taking place in intellectual property law as it accommodates the gaze of human rights doctrine. Perhaps one of the best examples of this might be the shift in less than a decade from the United Kingdom's Criminal Justice Act (2003), which mandated the collection of DNA from suspects arrested for all but the most minor offenses to the Protection of Freedoms Act (2012), which obligates the government to remove the DNA information of innocent individuals from this database.[34] Architects in this emergent area of law are struggling to make meaningful distinctions. Are certain bodily tissues or secretions – such as blood or milk – less personal than those laden with revealing genetic information – such as sperm and ova? For the purposes of utilizing data, might we consider anonymized information a *res communes omnium*, a public knowledge commons, which should be readily available for scientific research?

Two well-known US cases illustrate how biometric material collected through genetic testing websites such as 23andMe, Fitbit, or routine medical laboratory analysis might implicate simultaneously both intellectual property and human rights law. In *Moore v. Regents of the University of California* (1990), George Moore entered hospital for leukemia treatment.[35] Later, tissue from his spleen was used to develop a commercially marketed cell line. The California Supreme Court found against Moore. It decided Moore lacked an absolute property right to his body. There was no privacy right since he had provided informed consent for the procedure. The court denied the tortious conversion claim because as a matter of public policy it might chill research.

A similar story with a different outcome involved the case of Henrietta Lacks who died of cervical cancer in 1951. Although her tissue was collected without informed consent about its research use, a cell line derived from it, the HeLa cell line, proved quite valuable for oncological researchers. In 2013, the US National Institute of Health negotiated an agreement with Lacks' family. Lacks would receive attribution in scientific papers highlighting her contribution when the HeLa cell line is used. Moreover, the family would participate in a panel regulating access to her genetic code. The difference between the results of the Moore and Lacks disputes reflects shifting attitudes about how to balance the rights of legal proprietors of biometric data, the public, and the dignity rights of experimental subjects. So much biometric information is now circulating that European courts are currently insisting upon a human rights intervention. In the 2015 *Willems* case, the Court of Justice of the European Union (CJEU) required a guarantee that when collecting biometric data used for authenticating passports, member states were to apply a purpose limitation rule that such information could only be used for an articulated original purpose.[36] As we shall see below, privacy concerns have increasingly become a site of interaction between competing intellectual property rights and human rights norms.

The second wave of intellectual property protests and human rights: digital citizen movements

By the end of the twentieth century, the very success of constructing a global regulatory infrastructure emanating from Geneva suggested a hegemonic cast to the harmonization project. As WIPO's development agenda conceded, fundamental asymmetries existed in the control of copyright, patent, and other intellectual property. The push for enforcement provisions by intellectual property rights holders disillusioned with WIPO suggested that they were using the international system to acquire protections that could never pass muster in democratically elected domestic legislatures. Moreover, the seeming endless extension of the copyright term in Europe with the Copyright Duration Directive (1993)[37] and in the United States through the Copyright Term Extension Act (1998)[38] spotlighted the erosion of the public domain. Some critics spoke darkly of a new enclosure movement similar to the seizure of landed property in seventeenth-century England.

The irony was that both the greater capacity to appropriate intellectual property and the ever-more capacious rules to protect that property, once appropriated, led to a sense that only by asserting human rights could law construct a sufficient counter to intellectual property rights. In the digital age the focus was now on the difficulties users in the United States and Europe encountered when seeking access to information on the internet. Digital citizens, as they often styled themselves, launched what might be considered the second wave of intellectual property movements.

Emerging at the end of the twentieth century, the second wave of unrest was prompted by a number of salient changes in intellectual property law. Perhaps the most significant change in the status of intellectual property rights came with the introduction of private ordering through the invention of digital rights management (DRM) systems. The bolstering of new tracing technologies such as encryption with legal protections marked a significant change. Hacking could result in criminal penalties even if the information guarded by a digital lockbox included material belonging to the public domain. When the United States shifted away from WIPO and sought to forge plurilateral trade-linked treaties like the now defunct Trans-Pacific Partnership (TPP), it sought to create enhanced requirements for policing intellectual property. Internally, within the Europe, the EU Copyright Directive demanded greater policing of copyright infringement.

In the wake of heightened European enforcement, pirate parties sprung up across Europe. The first of these, Sweden's *Piratpartiet*, was founded in 2006. This political movement was characterized by a fundamental contradiction. On one hand, its members promoted access to information as a core human right. Not just authors and inventors, but also consumers of knowledge were said to be vested with rights. On the other hand, the group also promoted the human right of privacy. How would these competing rights be balanced? And how might they become an obligatory set of rights with the capacity to challenge the assertion of knowledge property rights?

Proponents of access drafted a proposed A2K (Access to Knowledge) treaty.[39] Completed in 2005, its foundational principles were to protect and enhance access to knowledge, to facilitate the transfer of technology to developing countries, to protect and expand the knowledge commons, and to protect the public domain against restrictions by technological measures. Perhaps the most notable aspect of the A2K treaty was the way in which it was drafted. Provisions were placed on a website where crowdsourced comments could be posted and alterations made. There was no official body behind the treaty's composition, no legislature, and no self-appointed law professors under an umbrella organization such as the American Law Institute or even a UN commission. It was simply the product of concerned individuals. A2K was a salient example of knowledge users clamoring for the legal recognition of their rights. Yet as with all social movements it was difficult to sustain mobilizing for rights against the unrelenting lobbying of corporate stakeholders. Access movements often splintered. HIV/AIDs activists called for A2M (Access to Medicine). Musicians feeling stymied by legal bars to sampling promoted A2C (Access to Copyrighted Material) in a bid for creating a culture of music exchange. The most successful example of this sort of mobilization was the software Open Source Movement.

The demand for increased privacy protection resulted in national statutes such as Germany's Federal Data Protection Law (Bundesdatenschutzgesetz, 2017),[40] which places limits on the collection and use of personal data, and the new European Union General Data Protection Regulation (GDPR).[41] Coming into effect in 2018, the GDPR sets out guidelines for the anonymization of data, requires informed consent to collect personal data, and establishes a right to view retained data. Perhaps the most striking result of digital citizenry's mobilization is the emergence of a new right to be forgotten (*le droit d'oubli*). In *Google Spain v. AEPD and Mario Costeja González* (2014), the CJEU found that individuals could seek to have deleted any information that is no longer ongoing.[42] This particular case decided that an individual might compel search engines to remove past bankruptcy records.

As with a right to access, the right to privacy was seen as a fundamental human right. Proponents argued that it was included in the ambit of the European Convention on Human Rights (1953), Article 8, which extended protection to a person's "private and family life, his home and his correspondence." The European Court of Human Rights (ECtHR) has applied this protection to personal identity, images such as photographs, and private information, claiming that this protection trumps intellectual property law. Clearly, the stage has been set for a clash between intellectual property rights to collect, retain, and disseminate information and opposing claims to human rights of access to knowledge and privacy.

The struggle over rights versus intellectual property in a time of crisis

With the rise of the late twentieth- and early twenty-first-century knowledge economy, intellectual property had simply become too important. It was no longer just a system to provide incentives for the creation and mechanisms for the dissemination of writings and inventions. It had become the basis for exerting economic leverage across the globe. Yet all these competing rights – claimed by creators, intermediaries, and users, by citizens, nations, and international actors – have created new points of contention.

The problem of access became a matter for competing national economic claims when it came to access to pharmaceuticals (A2P). TRIPS fortified intellectual property rights in medicines. Pharmaceutical companies argued that high prices were necessary to support research budgets necessary for developing new medications. Yet the steep price of pharmaceuticals proved daunting to developing countries, imposing immense costs on already burdened public health systems. Poor countries without their own domestic pharmaceutical industries blamed patent law. They argued that the right to health was grounded in the right to human dignity. According to the UDHR's Article 25(a), every individual "has the right to a standard of living adequate for the health and well-being of himself and of his family, including food, clothing, housing and medical care and necessary social services." Not surprisingly, wealthier states resisted the extension of human rights when that extension clashed with economic rights.

TRIPS Articles 7 and 8 provided for an exception to patent law in cases where there was a national health emergency. But what constitutes such an emergency? In TRIPS, the matter was intentionally left vague and ill-defined. On one hand, this might allow for a rapid response to an epidemic. There was no need to surmount a series of procedural hurdles. On the other hand, such ambiguity set the stage for contestation. Drug-producing countries could claim that those seeking to produce pharmaceuticals off-patent were simply looking for an excuse to appropriate intellectual property. The Doha Declaration (2001)[43] emerged from petitions to clarify the flexibility of TRIPS, though it only provided the thinnest resolution of TRIPS' uncertainty. Paragraph 6 allowed for a waiver that enables the export of generic medication to countries with deficient pharmaceutical production capabilities in the case of "national emergency" and "extreme urgency." Nevertheless, it left these terms undefined.

From a historical point of view, what is interesting about the battle between public health rights and the rights of patent holders is that it takes place largely between countries. To a large extent, such contention reflects asymmetrical development and underscores how difficult states endowed with intellectual property find negotiating in international forums. The Trans-Pacific Partnership, recently scuttled by President Trump's administration, reflected a knowledge internationalism more reminiscent of late medieval trading networks like the Hanseatic League than the grand internationalism of early twentieth-century figures such as the international lawyer Hersch Lauterpacht. Intended simply for countries who were willing to adopt pro-intellectual property rules within a broader trade treaty, it provided such patent-friendly provisions as term extension when the patent was delayed, data exclusivity for pharmaceuticals, and, directly addressing the issues arising in the wake of Doha, WTO dispute resolution when a country issued compulsory licenses for patents.

Public health depends upon food security in addition to medications. Seeds, stored, traded, and often altered by the practices of traditional agriculturalists, have been since earliest times considered part of a common heritage of mankind. Selection of seed was based on desirable traits such as drought resistance, frost tolerance, and pest resistance. With the rise of national governments, seeds were often distributed to foster agricultural development in new regions, as the US Patent Office did in the early nineteenth century with Westward expansion, or transported to far-off continents, as part of a colonial project. The legacy of a colonial bio-commons has now been taken up by multinational corporations working with governmental development agencies. With the post-World War II Green Revolution new industrial seed production, seen in industrial forms including Wallace's Hi-Bred Corn and Pioneer Hi-Bred, shifted the site of production from field to laboratory. Instead of slow methods of selective breeding, genetic manipulation quickly created hybrids. The advantages were palpable: high yield (through greater nitrogen absorption), pest resistance, and increasing nutritional value.

In 1961, WIPO adopted the International Convention for the Protection of New Varieties of Plants (Union Internationale pour la Protection des Obtentions Végétales, UPOV).[44] UPOV established a particular intellectual property regime for plant breeding. Plant Breeders' Rights granted rights to creators of new, homogeneous, and stable varieties over time. UPOV's Articles 14 and 15 provide for control over seed. Developing countries were particularly irked by the inclusion of so-called terminator genes in seeds, which prevent the seeds' reuse during the next agricultural season. The national laws of India and Brazil ban terminator genes as a violation of a fundamental human right to the bio-commons. By ca. 2000, nearly every subject matter of intellectual property had developed its own human rights dimension. Databases, biometrics, traditional folk choreography, pharmaceuticals, and plant seeds are only a few examples of the emerging interface of intellectual property and human rights.

Conclusion

This essay has argued that the complex interaction of intellectual property and human rights did not simply emerge in the 1990s. It is the result of a lengthy historical process extending from the very origins of these two regimes. Intellectual property and human rights both sought their justification in rights – whether it be property rights in intangible knowledge or rights to integrity for an all-too real, and vulnerable, body. Proponents of both areas of law expanded into the international arena as they recognized the limitations imposed by the straitjacket of national boundaries. These similarities – a kind of cousinhood of legalism – might suggest that they would or should work closely in tandem. Instead, ironically, rights claims were shaped by the demands of social movements – digital citizens' concerns, postcolonial aspirations, and the issues encapsulated by various NGOs – which led to creating rights thickets.

Such rights thickets have proved very difficult to resolve. Even within the framework of a public-directed sense of rights, competing interests emerge. How do we square privacy with public safety, access to information with the right to have it erased, the demand for pharmaceuticals to meet health emergencies with the need for funding to create new drugs, or preservation of traditional knowledge with the notion that culture is a global resource to be shared with others as well? Even the pirate parties find their agenda riven with contradictions. And who should resolve these contradictions? Trade tribunals such as the WTO, human rights panels, or domestic courts?

Future research must examine underlying contradictions embedded in the past while also pivoting towards the future. For too long the focus has been on human rights as a welcome (or unwelcome) corrective to an ascendancy of intellectual property. Yet the real difference between intellectual property and human rights has been grounded in how, precisely, contradictions and contention might be addressed. Human rights contribute a focus on human flourishing. Yet human rights advocates often assert them as an absolute, trumping system. Intellectual property has been sometimes overly responsive to stakeholders. Yet it has practiced the art of balancing their competing demands. It routinely manages rival policies, often admitting the need to revise legal norms to meet the demands of new technologies or changing social circumstances. How can flourishing be paired with the delicate tightrope walk of the balancing of demands? And is not this precisely what human rights might need in what might be called the Age of Rights Thickets?

Acknowledgments

I would like to thank Molly Land, Willajeanne McLean, Guy Pessach, and Zeynep Sasmazel for their suggestions. Lora Wildenthal and Jean Quataert provided astute editorial comments mixed with remarkable patience. Some of the themes identified in my essay were elaborated in a series of lectures on intellectual property law and human rights at the Law Faculty of the Interdisciplinary Center in Herzliya, Israel. I especially want to thank the skilled, gracious, and committed attorneys at the US Copyright Office in Washington where I wrote the essay. The views expressed in this chapter are my own and do not represent those of the Government.

Notes

1 Steven Wilf, "Intellectual Property," in Sally E. Hadden and Alfred L. Brophy (eds.) *A Companion to American Legal History*, New York: Wiley-Blackwell, 2013, pp. 441–59.

2 Universal Declaration of Human Rights, Article 27(2), 1948. Online. Available at www.un.org/en/universal-declaration-human-rights/ (accessed 26 December 2018).

3 Laurence R. Helfer, "The New Innovation Frontier? Intellectual Property and the European Court of Human Rights," *Harvard International Law Journal*, 2008, vol. 49, 1.

4 Charles Maier, *Once Within Borders: Territories of Power, Wealth, and Belonging Since 1500*, Cambridge, MA: Harvard University Press, 2016, pp. 3–13.

5 Michel Foucault, "Des Espaces Autres," *Architecture/Mouvement/Continuité*, 1984, vol. 5, 1984, 46–9.

6 Elaine Scarry, *The Body in Pain: The Making and Unmaking of the World*. Oxford: Oxford University Press, 1987.

7 Samuel Moyn, *The Last Utopia: Human Rights in History*, Cambridge, MA: Belknap Press at Harvard University Press, 2010, pp. 7–10.

8 Lynn Hunt, *Inventing Human Rights: A History*, New York: W. W. Norton, 2007, pp. 25–50.

9 Venetian Statute on Industrial Brevets, Venice (1474). Lionel Bently and Martin Kretschmer (eds.), *Primary Sources on Copyright (1450–1900)*, n.d. Online. Available at www.copyrighthistory.org/cam/tools/request/showRecord?id=record_i_1474 (accessed 26 December 2018).

10 Statute of Monopolies, 21 Jac. 1 c. 3, 1624. Bently and Kretschmer, *Primary Sources on Copyright*. Online. Available at www.copyrighthistory.org/cam/tools/request/showRecord.php?id=record_uk_1624 (accessed 26 December 2018).

11 Statute of Anne, 8 Ann. c. 21, 1710. Bently and Kretschmer, *Primary Sources on Copyright.* Online. Available at www.copyrighthistory.org/cam/tools/request/showRecord.php?id=record_uk_1710 (accessed 26 December 2018).
12 U.S. Const. Article I, Section 8, Cl. 8. Online. Available at www.law.cornell.edu/constitution (accessed 26 December 2018).
13 James Madison, "The Same Subject Continued: The Powers Conferred by the Constitution Further Considered," *Federalist No. 43*, 1788. Online. Available at www.congress.gov/resources/display/content/The+Federalist+Papers#TheFederalistPapers-43 (accessed 26 December 2018).
14 *Donaldson v. Beckett*, 4 Burr. 2408, 1774. Bently and Kretschmer, *Primary Sources on Copyright.* Online. Available at www.copyrighthistory.org/cam/tools/request/showRecord.php?id=record_uk_1774 (accessed 26 December 2018).
15 *Wheaton v. Peters*, 33 U.S. 591, 1834. Online. Available at https://supreme.justia.com/cases/federal/us/33/591/ (accessed 26 December 2018).
16 Annals of Congress 855 (2d Cong. 2d Sess.), 30 January 1793. Online. Available at https://memory.loc.gov/ammem/amlaw/lwaclink.html (accessed 26 December 2018). Jump to image 855 for quotation.
17 Carla Hesse, "The Rise of Intellectual Property 700 B.C.–2000 A.D.: An Idea in the Balance," *Daedalus*, 2002, vol. 131, 26–45.
18 International Copyright Act of 1891, 26 Stat. 1106. Bently and Kretschmer, *Primary Sources on Copyright.* Online. Available at www.copyrighthistory.org/cam/tools/request/showRecord.php?id=record_us_1891a (accessed 26 December 2018).
19 Francis Lieber, *On International Copyright.* New York: William C. Preston, 1840.
20 Steven Wilf, "Copyright and Social Movements in Late Nineteenth-Century America," *Theoretical Inquiries in Law*, 2011, vol. 12, 134.
21 Wilf, "Copyright and Social Movements," 123–37.
22 Trish Loughran, *The Republic in Print. Print Culture in the Age of U.S. Nation-Building, 1770–1870*, New York: Columbia University Press, 2007, pp. 5–6.
23 International Copyright Act, London, c. 12 s. III (1852). Bently and Kretschmer, *Primary Sources on Copyright.* Online. Available at www.copyrighthistory.org/cam/tools/request/showRecord.php?id=record_uk_1852 (accessed 26 December 2018).
24 Berne Convention for the Protection of Literary and Artistic Works, Article 6*bis*, 1979. Online. Available at www.wipo.int/treaties/en/text.jsp?file_id=283698 (accessed 26 December 2018).
25 Peter Baldwin, *The Copyright Wars: Three Centuries of Trans-Atlantic Battle*, Princeton, NJ: Princeton University Press, 2014.
26 Christopher May, *The World Intellectual Property Organization: Resurgence and Development Agenda*, London: Routledge, 2007, pp. 75–93.
27 Agreement on Trade-Related Aspects of Intellectual Property Rights (TRIPS), 15 April 1994, Marrakesh Agreement Establishing the World Trade Organization, Annex 1C, 1869 U.N.T.S. 299, 33 I.L.M. 1197 (1994). Online. Available at www.wto.org/english/docs_e/legal_e/27-trips.pdf (accessed 26 December 2018).
28 TRIPS, Article 1.
29 TRIPS, Article 61.
30 International Labour Organization, Convention 107, 1957. Online. Available at www.ilo.org/dyn/normlex/en/f?p=NORMLEXPUB:12100:0::NO::P12100_ILO_CODE:C107 (accessed 26 December 2018).
31 Native American Graves Protection & Repatriation Act, 25 U.S.C. 32. Online. Available at www.law.cornell.edu/uscode/text/25/chapter-32 (accessed 26 December 2018).
32 World Intellectual Property Organization, *Paris Convention for the Protection of Industrial Property*, 1883. Online. Available at https://wipolex.wipo.int/en/treaties/textdetails/12995 (accessed 26 December 2018).
33 United Nations, *Convention on Biological Diversity*, Article 3, 1992. Online. Available at https://treaties.un.org/pages/ViewDetails.aspx?src=IND&mtdsg_no=XXVII-8&chapter=27&clang=_en (accessed 26 December 2018).
34 Criminal Justice Act, 2003 c. 44. Online. Available at www.legislation.gov.uk/ukpga/2003/44/contents; Protection of Freedoms Act, 2012 c. 9. Online. Available at www.legislation.gov.uk/ukpga/2012/9/contents/enacted (both accessed 26 December 2018).

35 *Moore v. Regents of the University of California*, 51 Cal. 3d 120, 1990. Online. Available at https://scocal.stanford.edu/opinion/moore-v-regents-university-california-31115 (accessed 26 December 2018).
36 *Willems v. Burgemeester van Nuth*, Case C-446/12, 2015. Online. Available at http://curia.europa.eu/juris/liste.jsf?num=C-446/12 (accessed 26 December 2018).
37 European Union, Council Directive 93/98/EEC, 1992. Online. Available at https://wipolex.wipo.int/en/legislation/details/1427 (accessed 26 December 2018).
38 112 Stat. 2827. Online. Available at www.govinfo.gov/app/details/STATUTE-112/STATUTE-112-Pg2827/context (accessed 26 December 2018).
39 Consumer Project on Technology, A2K Treaty, 2005. Online. Available at www.keionline.org/book/proposalfortreatyofaccesstoknowledgemay102005draft (accessed 26 December 2018).
40 Federal Republic of Germany, Federal Data Protection Law (Bundesdatenschutzgesetz, BDSG), 2017. Online. Available at www.gesetze-im-internet.de/englisch_bdsg/ (accessed 26 December 2018).
41 European Union, Regulation 2016/679. Online. Available at https://eur-lex.europa.eu/legal-content/EN/TXT/HTML/?uri=CELEX:32016R0679&from=EN (accessed 26 December 2018).
42 *Google Spain v. AEPD and Mario Costeja González*, Case C-131/12, 2014. Online. Available at https://eur-lex.europa.eu/legal-content/EN/TXT/HTML/?uri=CELEX:62012CJ0131&from=EN (accessed 26 December 2018).
43 World Trade Organization, Doha Declaration, 2001. Online. Available at www.wto.org/english/res_e/booksp_e/ddec_e.pdf (accessed 26 December 2018).
44 World Intellectual Property Organization, International Convention for the Protection of New Varieties of Plants (Union Internationale pour la Protection des Obtentions Végétales, UPOV), 1961. Online. Available at www.upov.int/edocs/pubdocs/en/upov_pub_221.pdf (accessed 26 December 2018).

31

CAGED AT THE BORDER

Immigration detention and the denial of human rights to asylum seekers and other migrants

Stephanie J. Silverman and Petra Molnar

Introduction: if you come, we will take your children

After 14 years in the United States, Elvira, 17, finds herself in a cage.[1] The Immigration and Customs Enforcement Agency (ICE) has apprehended the teenager and her mother while they were trying to regularize their immigration status. When Elvira was 3 years old, her mother, then only 19 years old, fled with her from El Salvador to the United States due to gang violence. After months of dangerous travel, the pair was apprehended when attempting to cross the United States–Mexico border by floating across the Rio Grande. They were eventually allowed to meet Elvira's maternal grandfather in Dallas. The family settled in Detroit, where Elvira goes to school and plans to become a pediatrician – until the specter of detention and deportation reared its head again and ICE came calling.

After apprehension and in the middle of their immigration proceedings and a deportation order, Elvira and her mother were deported to El Salvador, a country Elvira had not seen for 14 years as it was still plagued by rampant gang violence. Unable to find schooling and a job, Elvira's mother made the desperate suggestion of trying to re-enter the United States and rejoin their Detroit lives. Elvira was on board. She missed her friends and her old life, and was desperate to attend junior prom.

With the help of "coyotes," or human smugglers, Elvira and her mother traveled to the border and were apprehended in a trailer with 25 other people:

> They took fingerprints and photos and gave me a form that said I had two options: I could see a counselor and present myself in front of a judge, or I could decline and return to my country. The officer suggested I check the bottom one, but I was like, "Wait, wait, wait." I know my rights because I took a civics class in school.

During the course of the proceedings, Elvira was separated from her mother, unsure if she would ever see her again:

> Honestly, I thought this was going to be the last time I saw her because the officer told me she was going to be deported. I started crying. My mom told me to trust in God that everything was going to be fine and to never lose faith. I told her, "I love you, I love you so much," and she said, "I love you too."[2]

Elvira's story is one of thousands. Migrants are detained in violent systems that separate children from their parents, incarcerate individuals without allowing them to exercise their basic rights, and exacerbate mental health issues and preexisting vulnerabilities. Under the Trump Administration "zero tolerance" policy, babies are put in cages[3] and unequivocally desperate people kill themselves rather than face deportation to violence and despair.[4] In our own refugee and immigration practice,[5] we have seen countless examples of how immigration detention destroys human lives and violates core rights and values in liberal-identified societies. In theory, all people have the right to liberty, a right which encompasses protection from arbitrary arrest and detention. This basic principle of liberalism applies to every resident of any liberal-identifying country, regardless of his or her immigration or citizenship status. However, immigration detention practices, policies, laws, and architectures are proliferating around the world. In their midst, fundamental human rights are revealed to be fragile lifeboats upon which asylum seekers and other migrants are clinging. Detention also reveals how liberal societies use immigration status as a differentiator on a very steep hierarchy of rights created and enforced by state actors. Immigration detention regimes illustrate both contemporary trends towards the degradation of human rights such as privatization, securitization, and racialization, and also older, more normative notions outlining who is captured and demobilized as a detainable migrant.

The idea of the state wanting to control Others is older than modernity, even though its expansion is modern. The importance of securing freedom from arbitrary arrest and detention was inscribed in several of the foundational liberal texts from Europe, including the Magna Carta, the Habeas Corpus Acts of England, and the French Declaration of the Rights of Man and the Citizen. Modern international law first inscribed this principle in Article 9 of the Universal Declaration of Human Rights (UDHR), and it was subsequently enshrined in various widely promulgated treaties and conventions.[6] Incarceration, as a fundamental deprivation of liberty, is so serious that the onus usually falls on the state to rebut the presumption that most individuals have the right to live freely in the community. Hence, most liberal countries have bail hearings in the criminal justice context, where a government representative is called upon to justify the prisoner's ongoing incarceration. However, immigration detention is situated in the realm of administrative law, governed by opaque and discretionary policies and norms, and presided over by tribunals and decision-makers who arbitrate virtually without oversight and are often not subject to appeals procedures.

Immigration detention is thus an aberration from the central norms and ethics animating liberal political communities. It is extrajudicial in almost every way: it operates outside of, parallel to, and often overlapping with, judicial incarceration in the criminal justice context, with fewer checks and balances or rights protections. No warrants are needed to arrest an immigration detainee, and often no bail hearings or readings of rights are provided.[7] Detention operates with virtual impunity in every state around the world. It is only when a moral tipping point is reached – when children are put in Texan cages without their parents, or a London grandmother is thrown into a detention center and threatened with removal to Jamaica, or terrorism suspects are held without charges for years (as in Guantanamo Bay) – that the world pays attention to it.

International human rights law clearly states the differences between lawful and unlawful immigration detention. Detention is always to be non-punitive, non-arbitrary, and inapplicable to vulnerable persons. Like other modes of incarceration, detention should be a measure of last resort. Non-custodial measures such as bail, sureties, community supervision, or reporting mechanisms should be considered, weighed, and ruled against before making the decision to incarcerate a non-citizen for migration-related reasons. At least in theory, there is always a presumption against immigration detention and it is a measure of last resort. In reality, as this essay will show, detention is cemented into immigration, asylum, and border control apparatuses to a dangerous degree. The normalization of detention around the world, taking place mostly out of sight and definitely out of mind, has proceeded with little foresight and in the margins of domestic immigration legislation.[8]

Significant racial, gender, and other discrepancies characterize the differences between detained populations and greater migrant populations, as will be explained below. Answers to who gets detained, why, where, and for how long, are often arbitrary and reflect biased tendencies handed down through history. US policies such as Japanese internment, or the decades-long crusade to root out undocumented Latinx residents in American cities and farmlands, are both implicated in the rise of detention and continue to lend opaque justifications to the sequestration and incarceration of minority and racialized groups.

Despite the invention of the "nation-state" and its sovereign borders, migration is natural and inevitable, both within and across territorial borders. People have always traveled and always will. Families will always seek opportunities to better their livelihoods. The sociologist Douglas Massey observes a paradox that "while the global economy unleashes powerful forces that produce larger and more diverse flows of migrants from developing to developed countries, it simultaneously produces conditions within developed countries that promote the implementation of restrictive immigration."[9] If detention is meant to stop, deter, or reroute people, that effort will most likely be futile. Instead, immigration detention drives up the costs and risks of migration and closes off the preferred circular routes of temporary stay and return, forcing people to stay longer to recoup their costs.[10] Detention has been, and will continue to be, a socially and financially costly mistake with grave consequences for realizing the human rights of migrants.

This essay argues that normalizing detention inevitably and unjustifiably produces grave human rights infringements, particularly when used as a mechanism of deterrence. By highlighting case studies like Elvira's and other anonymized individuals from our own legal practice mentioned below, we orient the reader to the real-world ramifications of these policies, especially concerning how people are stymied when seeking to exercise their human rights. We focus on a branch of non-derogable human rights – fundamental rights that are not suspendable by governments and other actors – such as the right to liberty and security of the person. Detention shows how irregular immigration status can erode these rights, too.

We begin the main part of this essay by exploring the roots of the idea that people can be incarcerated based on their immigration, refugee, or citizenship status. Where is the seed for this spreading ideology planted, and why does it matter? Following Benedict Anderson and others, we argue that it is rooted in the double-body idea: a territorial community of nationals linked to a particular set of borders and embodied in a particular kind of person. We then offer a brief, comparative history of the early development of modern detention regimes in the United States and the United Kingdom. We also add examples from jurisdictions where detention also proliferates, such as Australia and frontier European countries. We place particular emphasis on the Obama

Administration's escalation and rollback of detention and the Trump Administration's uptake of some of the cruelest detention practices. Responding especially to the misplaced motivation behind the "zero tolerance" policy of separating children from parents, we then unpack and analyze governments' uptake of detention as a deterrent – a strategy to dissuade certain categories of migrants from coming. We conclude the essay with the contention that this instrumentalization of detention tramples on migrants' human rights, and is immoral and illegal.

On behalf of an imagined community: the roots of the idea of detaining migrants and asylum seekers

> I was taken to a huge, huge cage inside a detention center. They had other cages for the boys, men, and women. It was prison.[11]

"Immigration detention" is an imprecise term that refers to a range of practices to incarcerate noncitizens in an administrative capacity. States construct detention regimes in order to exert more forceful control over their borders, immigration, and asylum systems, and the mobilities of the people traversing their territory. It is important to note that immigration detainees (or "detainees") are not being imprisoned for any crime they have committed. While the immigration detention (or "detention") regime resembles the criminal system – and there is literal overlap, with detainees being held in correctional facilities where they commingle with criminal convicts – they are meant to be separate streams of incarceration. Immigration detention does not require a warrant, unlike the criminal system. Detainees often have less access to judicial oversight, legal representation, interpretation, bail, and rights' protections than do criminal prisoners. In the United Kingdom, United States, and elsewhere, there is no upper time limit on a given period of detention, creating a regime that is both discretionary and indefinite.

Elvira's detention leads us to ask about the motivations for detaining in secure, peaceful states. Criminal prisoners are incarcerated in order to realize policy-prescribed goals: to punish, rehabilitate, or exact restitution. By contrast, asylum seekers like Elvira are being caged to facilitate the smoother or more efficient functioning of the administrative state apparatus of migration control. Specifically, detention is meant to facilitate deportation. Yet this justification is confounded by facts such as that in the United Kingdom over half of detainees are released and not deported.[12] States also construe detention as a deterrent for other migrants, which contravenes international law. Detention is a site of tension concerning both state power to decide the composition of its population and the opportunity for people claim their universal human rights in the face of this extreme power.[13]

> Why us? Why does immigration think that we can be placed in cells, treated like animals? I work hard to contribute, and take care of my children. After all that we have been through … All I want is a safe home and a happy life. Not to be treated like a criminal.[14]

Nancy suffers from frequent episodes of depression and post-traumatic stress disorder as a result of being placed in immigration detention and separated from her children for weeks during the course of regularizing her residence status in Canada.[15]

The modern liberal community is rooted in respect for civil liberties and social order. The modern liberal state is grounded in principles of sovereignty and national self-determination. Benedict Anderson's well-known formulation of the "imagined community" is instructive. The theory is that legitimacy for the modern state takes shape through a shared history of generating and supporting the significance of a national community, and the creation and enforcement of territorial borders that bound this community in space and place. As Rainer Bauböck argues, the

> primary function of a political border is to demarcate the jurisdiction of a political authority. Its secondary function is as a site of control over flows of goods or people. A border that is completely open in the sense of being uncontrolled still clearly [identifies] the territory within which the laws of a particular government apply. Internal borders in liberal democracies are all open in this way.[16]

This prevailing conception of borders can be characterized as "hard on the outside and soft on the inside." The "hard" borders demarcate the state's jurisdiction, while the "soft" inside is where people can move freely. The law professor Linda Bosniak explains this conception as follows:

> This conception of membership based on jurisdictional splitting between border and interior – whereby anti-caste values apply within the community, while the community possesses the right to limit the ingress of outsiders into the community – is widespread among liberals and progressives in and out of the immigration debate. The inclusive universalism of territorialism is commonly understood to be framed, and enabled, by a hard or hard-ish shell around the territorial perimeter.[17]

The permanent members of the state's national community possess citizenship. Citizenship can be earned, usually in a multistep process, but more often it is inherited or transmitted through close family members. In a memorable passage, political scientist Joseph H. Carens analogizes citizenship to historic feudalism: "Citizenship in Western liberal democracies is the modern equivalent of feudal privilege – an inherited status that greatly enhances one's life chances. Like feudal birthright privilege, restrictive citizenship is hard to justify when one thinks about it closely."[18] Citizens are accorded exclusive access to a bundle of social, political, and economic rights. While adhering to principles of equality, democracy, and a collective good, in truth the state streamlines the realization of these rights into a path available only to citizens. While many long-term residents conduct lives that bear striking resemblance to those of citizens, they are not accorded two key rights: the right to vote, and the right to freedom from removal or deportation as well as the right to exit and return at will.

Detention festers in this blurry zone between rights for some but not for all, and rights on paper versus rights in practice. Detention casts some people as "perpetual foreigners, as outside the 'we' of the 'imagined community' of the nation."[19] Since certain people are detainable, they are less rights-bearing than citizens, and since they are less rights-bearing, they become always-detainable.

An unbalanced international system

An asymmetry crystallizes in liberal internationalism: while the right of entry, exit, and return is limited to members of the nation, the right of exit is universal. People are generally free to leave their countries but they are not free to settle wherever they please.[20] Sovereignty imparts to states the monopoly on decision-making regarding who can come and who can stay as citizens or guests (and conversely, who must leave). Since only totalitarian regimes deny people the ability to opt out of a political community, the right to exit and return is seen as a hallmark of liberal societies. International law codifies this right in Article 13(1) of the UDHR, for example, and in Article 21(1) of the International Covenant on Civil and Political Rights. Yet every land mass in the globe is parceled into sovereign states, and each state reserves from international law its own power over immigration and borders, including arrest, detention, and removal. As such, there is an asymmetry not only between democratic principles and the realization of rights for citizens only, but between individuals' universal human right to exit and the national monopoly over the right of entry and residence.[21] There is no corresponding duty or responsibility to take in those persons who have exercised their right to exit and have left their states of origin. Some people who leave are not allowed back, and they join the ranks of the undeportable in their countries of residence. These are people who have no right to stay, but no other country will admit them.

A "sedentarist bias" animates the liberal view of state and society.[22] This ingrained notion that people are "rooted" to a place – that we are happier when we have a permanent home that we can "grow from – leads to a pathology of migrants and all noncitizens as alien to the community."[23] Indeed, until very recently, many key pieces of immigration rulemaking referred to noncitizens as "aliens," as in for instance the British Aliens Act of 1905 and the American Aliens Act of 1798. This sedentarist bias allows migrants to be subjected to treatment that would not be tolerated among citizens, such as indefinite detention under threat of deportation. Policies resting on this bias negate a state's duty to admit individuals exercising their human rights. Yet such policies are supported by a gamut of progressives from liberal to conservative, many of whom cite fears of too many newcomers overwhelming the welfare state, taking too many scarce resources, and changing the overall face of the citizenry.[24] As the political philosopher Hannah Arendt famously pointed out, and as we will endeavor to demonstrate below, in practice things transpire such that human rights are not all persons' rights, but rather belong to the domain of citizens' rights. People lose their "right to have rights" when they lose their citizenship, and must endure "the abstract nakedness of being human and nothing but human."[25]

Immigration detention is the apotheosis of various asymmetries that dispossess migrants of their human rights or block migrants from accessing them. What is missing is the counterpart in international law for the right to exit, namely the right to enter. This means that people can be stopped at the border, arrested, and detained on their way to return or expulsion. Binary thinking means that the "soft" inside of an inclusive, egalitarian community necessitates a "hard" border to keep out the unwanted foreigners. The violence that takes place at the shifting border is swept under the rug or explained away by pointing to the rights and privileges enjoyed by citizens. Thus, paying attention to detention means confronting a number of pressing, interrelated issues for human rights that are inherent to the contemporary regulation of immigration control.[26]

A brief history of immigration detention

Immigration detention is insidious because it positions itself as normal, ahistorical, and unassailable. In fact, the normalization of detaining asylum seekers and other migrants is wholly abnormal. It is always legislated into existence, as opposed to being controlled through legislation like the majority of subjects of law. This is because Anglo-American law and ethics require the strongest possible justifications for deprivations of liberty, enshrined, as noted above, in foundational human rights documents.

Detention was, then, based on the state's power to inspect or screen noncitizens seeking entry, and courts and public officials made much of the supposed distinction between immigration detention and punishment. Accordingly, detention was an administrative tool from the start, and authorities in the United States and United Kingdom used it for the selective screening of newcomers in the 1800s and early 1900s. At that time, there were some detention cases based on flight risk – today, the most common justification for detaining asylum seekers and other migrants – but most of those early detention cases were for screening for disease, the probability of becoming a public charge, and other factors for admission.[27]

While there were sporadic and war-related bursts of "enemy alien" internment, supplemented by the detention and geographic segregation of Indigenous peoples, regular detention was long considered a step too far. Much of the legislation regulating detention dates to either slightly before or immediately following the 11 September 2001 terrorist attacks on the United States, and therefore most histories begin there. We look at earlier, precedent-setting policies to unpack some of the narratives that allow states to rationalize detention as serving and legitimizing border control, migration management, and national security.

Canada, the United States, and the United Kingdom contain a multitude of immigration histories along with ways to interpret those histories. On the one hand, there are events and traditions that connote and promote welcome, integration, and hopes for better lives and livelihoods. These include progressive immigration policies and orders, such as amnesties for irregular migrants and the lifting of ethnicity-based visa restrictions. On the other hand, there are clear expressions of xenophobia, or at the very least, an unwarranted fear of outsiders as threats to the community. These expressions take the forms of "racist exclusionary laws, fundamentally unfair enforcement of immigration laws, and the repeated scapegoating of immigrants for a variety of problems."[28] Racialized associations in the public discourse figuring Mexicans as unwanted immigrants, Muslims as potential terrorists, and borders as conduits for danger that predate 9/11 show the larger construction of immigration as a national security issue with poor respect for human rights.

Wartime internment

The historical antecedent for normalizing the detention of migrants can be found in wartime internment. The US Administration and the Canadian government interned families of Japanese citizens and Japanese immigrants during World War I and World War II. The UK government also practiced the detention of "enemy aliens" and revived the practice of selective internment of "enemy aliens" during the Gulf War (1990–1). Internment and detention remained available due to earlier wartime legislation: for example, the UK Parliament annually renewed the Aliens Restriction (Amendment) Act of 1919, and so the government continued practicing administrative immigration detention throughout the 1920s and 1930s, although on a small scale.[29] This startling practice was normalized in national contexts of threat and paranoia. It also developed outside of the public eye and away from legal scrutiny of violations of human rights.

It is also during the early period that important court decisions were handed down that established that detention was not a punishment. These court decisions narrowed the scope of those human rights that could possibly be violated and made future legal challenges more difficult. US Supreme Court decisions in the wake of the US Chinese Exclusion Act (1882) provide the clearest articulation of the influential idea that, as detention was not punishment, officials had carte blanche to expand administrative detention. In the case of *Chae Chan Ping v. United States* (1889), the US Supreme Court formulated the "plenary power doctrine," which held that US sovereignty was pre-eminent over virtually all other political concerns. The case of *Fong Yue Ting v. United States* (1893) confirmed Congress' absolute discretion in deciding who could enter and remain in the United States. It also concluded that removal, or deportation, was an administrative process for returning noncitizens. The case *Wong Wing v. United States* (1896) found that immigration detention is valid so long as it "[gives] effect to the provisions for the exclusion or expulsion of aliens." In the eyes of the Supreme Court, the detention of Chinese immigrants was therefore not punishment but a bureaucratic act in pursuit of their deportations (on racist, though legally acceptable, grounds).[30]

A number of the powers of detention extant today in Western liberal countries were introduced during the lead-up to World War I, World War II, or the Gulf War. These powers are concentrated in the executive branch of government, that powerful and largely discretionary branch of the state, and executive branch has moved to expand detention. Since that time, "these emergency powers have been regularized and repackaged as commonplace aspects of immigration law and policy," demonstrating that "in an atmosphere of fear, distrust, and xenophobia, an official appeal to national security concerns can override [migrants'] enjoyment of core individual rights."[31]

Legislative foundations, 1950s–70s

Much of the legislative foundation for contemporary detention regimes was built in the 1950s and 1970s, and legislation accelerated around the time of the 9/11 attacks on the United States. In the United Kingdom, the 1971 Immigration Act is the first formal statutory basis for immigration detention there, and remains in place. The Act legislates for administrative immigration detention pending completion of an examination or a decision for removal, or for the execution of removal directions or deportation orders. There is no specified upper time limit. The Act is accompanied by non-statutory immigration rules that provide structure for the discretionary powers bequeathed to immigration officers.[32] The first designated facility for immigration detention for five days or more opened in 1976; the facility, known now as the Harmondsworth Immigration Removal Centre, is still in use. Its parliamentary architects never intended for detention to be used routinely, particularly to arrest and hold asylum seekers.[33]

In the United States, Congress passed the Immigration and Nationality Act (INA) in 1952, and it remains the basis of current US immigration law. The INA regulated the conditions under which noncitizens may enter the United States by setting forth a list of grounds for deportability, and a list of grounds for inadmissibility (formerly known as "excludability"). If a removal order could not be executed, the INA gave the US attorney general special permission to detain the removable noncitizen for more than 90 days. Again, we see that the law does not indicate a maximum length for detention. Section 1226 of the Act creates a presumption of detention for people apprehended at the border without admission documents, such as a visa, and without regard for whether or not they would otherwise abscond. In effect, Section 1226 creates a mandatory detention provision for "asylum seekers, torture survivors, victims of human trafficking, longtime lawful permanent residents, and the parents of US children."[34]

The US detention system remained minimal and out of sight from 1952 until 1970. In 1970, the federal government responded to a large-scale migration of Cubans and Haitians by reviving and expanding dormant practices. The "Freedom Flotilla" or the "Mariel Boatlift" brought roughly 125,000 Cubans to Florida between spring 1979 and autumn 1980. Cuban president Fidel Castro refused to take back most of the Flotilla arrivals, most of whom had arrived without documents and were thus "excludable" and subject to detention. The attorney general, acting through the Immigration and Naturalization Service (precursor agency to ICE), detained the Cuban asylum seekers at camps in Florida, Arkansas, Pennsylvania, and the Atlanta Penitentiary in Georgia for varying lengths of time. But, by August 1981, the attorney general had "paroled" around 123,000 detainees. Parole meant that they were released from detention, but not formally admitted to the United States, a "legal fiction" that compromises enjoyment of constitutional and human rights.[35] An additional 25,000 Haitians and 1 million Salvadoran, Guatemalan, and Nicaraguan asylum seekers also entered the United States during this decade, all fleeing political upheaval and violence.[36] The American public was given the false and prejudiced impression that the newcomers were criminals, ideologically left-wing, racially different, and diseased.[37] The Reagan Administration ordered the interdiction and mandatory detention of all arriving Haitians. Then-attorney general, William French Smith, said of the decision: "Detention of aliens seeking asylum was necessary to *discourage* people like the Haitians from setting sail in the first place."[38] The US Coast Guard brought the detainees to the US naval base in Guantánamo Bay, Cuba, where they were pre-screened for asylum and detained until a decision was handed down.[39] Krome Avenue Detention Center, also called Krome Service Processing Center, was built in 1979 on a 15-acre former Nike missile site on the edges of the Florida Everglades and 20 miles from downtown Miami. Krome is still in use as an immigration detention facility, and one of a number of detention sites that are either structurally unsound or present grave physical risks in the event of a natural disaster.[40]

In the late 1990s, the United States and the United Kingdom rapidly and quietly expanded their detention practices without concurrently bolstering oversight and legal, welfare, or other much-needed mechanisms of support for detainees and their communities. In 1996, the Clinton Administration passed a raft of legislation that combined the mandatory detention provision with a retroactive expansion of the categories of deportable offenses. The result was dramatic expansion of the numbers of people affected by detention. In 1994, the United States held roughly 5,500 detainees in custody. This number rose to 16,000 in 1997, representing a tripling over a period of four years. During the 2000 fiscal year, the United States detained almost 190,000 noncitizens; and, by 2001, there were on average 19,500 noncitizens in detention on any given day.[41]

The United Kingdom implemented an accelerated appeals process in 1993 for groups of asylum seekers whose cases were "without foundation," "frivolous," or "vexatious," or whose detention did not otherwise violate Refugee Convention obligations. The United Kingdom also created, in 1996, a so-called White List of safe countries of origin suitable for rapid repatriation with few avenues for appeal. The Detention Centre Rules were promulgated in 2001, as a statutory instrument that governs administrative, everyday processes in detention facilities. The Nationality, Immigration and Asylum Act (2002) repealed a policy of mandatory bail hearings and thereby set the stage for the indefinite incarceration that characterizes the UK detention landscape today for a majority of detainees.

Current conditions

Not counting the combined efforts of the European Union immigration enforcement agency Frontex, the United Kingdom now operates the largest immigration detention system in Europe. From 2009 until the end of 2017, between 2,250 and 3,500 migrants have been in detention at any given time, with a total of approximately 27,300 people entering detention in 2017. Most people are held for less than two months, but a significant minority of one-fifth of detainees are incarcerated for longer. The estimated financial cost for detention is £86 per day.[42]

There have been some positive steps in the United Kingdom towards recognizing and realizing immigration detainees' human rights. The Home Office has paid £21.2 million in compensation payments for unlawful detention between 2012 and 2017.[43] In legislative terms, we can characterize progress as "one step forward, two steps back," with the example of pregnant detainees as illustrative. Pregnant noncitizens are rarely deported, but the experience of immigration detention puts them under avoidable maternal health risk. A coalition of lobbying groups in the United Kingdom and the recommendations of the official Shaw Report (2016) successfully challenged Home Office policy on detaining pregnant women. While the Shaw Report recommended a total exclusion from detention of pregnant women, the government policy of July 2016 guaranteed only that detention for this group would be limited to a maximum of 72 hours (three days), or up to one week with the agreement of a minister. Currently, around 50 pregnant women are detained annually for administrative immigration purposes, again not on criminal grounds.[44]

The United States bears the inglorious distinction of being the liberal democratic state that detains the greatest number of asylum seekers and other migrants, with the most elaborate legal and infrastructural architecture for arresting, demobilizing, and ejecting noncitizens. President Barack Obama was pejoratively known as the "Deporter-in-Chief."[45] Indeed, the Obama Administration was highly complicit in the criminalization of migration, that is, the importation of criminal norms and regulations into administrative immigration law, but without the accompanying rights and protections enjoyed by criminal justice suspects, such as Miranda rights, the right to a lawyer, or the right to family visits. Scholars in the United States, the United Kingdom and other major immigrant-receiving countries around the world are documenting how media depictions and political discourse are sustaining the punitive turn of labeling and treating asylum seekers and other migrants as criminals. They are also demonstrating how bureaucratic systems of mass detention and deportation informed by private for-profit interests have proliferated in response to and in support of the criminalization of migration.[46]

What is the situation regarding detention and human rights on the ground now in the United States? Between 1997 and 2015, the United States deported 5 million people, more than twice the number of all deportations prior to 1997. This has led to widespread insecurity, stigma, poverty, and vulnerability across the United States and Latin America.[47] ICE averaged 25,473 arrests per month between 2008 and 2012.[48] In 2009, the first full year of the Obama Presidency, more people entered federal prison for immigration offenses than for violent, weapons, and property offenses combined. In fiscal year 2013, US courts prosecuted 97,384 people for federal immigration offenses, an increase of 367 percent over the number in 2003. In the same year, US Customs and Border Protection referred more cases for federal criminal prosecution than did the FBI.[49]

The criminalization of migration presents a fundamental challenge to the human rights of asylum seekers and other migrants. The civil offense of crossing the border has been magicked into a federal crime that carries a criminal record, imprisonment, and even then results in deportation. "Crimmigration" invariably results in human rights violations for detainees such as commingling with the criminal population, overcrowding, inadequate access to legal representation, and prohibition from earning wages and from reuniting with family members. "Crimmigration" takes concrete form when ICE assumes custody of individuals that had been held by another US law enforcement agency. One program, the now-shuttered "Secure Communities," encapsulates this interagency cooperation and its problematic nature regarding human rights. Secure Communities called for taking the fingerprints of every arrestee in the United States and running them through a Department of Homeland Security (DHS) database to identify immigration violators. Unsurprisingly, perhaps, analysis found that Secure Communities had no positive effects on public safety, and that it appeared to have prioritized jurisdictions with large Latino populations.[50] Interagency cooperation means that there is now a pipeline from prison or jail, where an asylum seeker or other migrant is serving a sentence for a criminal conviction, to detention. This pipeline accounts for more than seven out of every ten ICE arrests in fiscal year 2017.[51]

"Crimmigration" has also promoted the obscene idea that the United States should maintain a minimum number of detainees. In 2006, conservative lawmakers insisted that ICE was not deporting enough people, and so Congress passed a directive for a "mandated minimum" of detention beds. This "bed quota" becomes part of contracts with prisons, many of which are privately held, prominent among them those owned and run by Corrections Corporation of America or by GEO Group. These prisons are paid to incarcerate immigration detainees, whether or not there are people sleeping in those beds. The "bed quota" has risen to 34,000 mandated beds as of 2018. In 2013, the "bed quota" cost US taxpayers $2 billion.[52]

"Crimmigration" should concern all human rights advocates. The Congressional directive that drives detention expansion via mandated minimums also stunts efforts to enact penal reform for all prisoners.[53] Since the DHS is an administrative body with its own mandate, it can contract with as many or as few private firms as it wishes, without public feedback or oversight. Over the last nine years, an increasing percentage of immigration detention has been privatized (from 25 percent in 2008 to 49 percent in 2009, to 73 percent in 2016); the majority of DHS detention contracts now go to private firms. The DHS now employs more outside contractors than actual federal employees. Private prison firms spent at least $3 million on lobbying, and contributed $500,000 to President Trump's inauguration ceremony.[54]

President Obama, facing the ire of immigration activists and the Latino community, had rolled back detention and deportation overall in his last years in Office. He also took measures to create safe spaces for asylum seekers and other migrants in so-called sensitive locations where ICE was not allowed to look for irregularly resident people, including hospitals, courthouses, churches, and schools. President Obama also issued an executive order giving a renewable two-year period of "deferred action" to individuals who immigrated to the United States as children. This legislated protection from detention and deportation, known as the Deferred Action for Childhood Arrivals (DACA) program, authorized these persons to stay, work, and attend school. There are now nearly 2 million registered Dreamers, including an estimated 75,000 LGBTQ Dreamers who would face unique risks and harms if detained and/or deported.[55] One harm is vulnerability to sexual abuse and assault in ICE detention: LGBTQ people make up fewer than 1 percent of detainees, but account for a shocking 12 percent of reported victims. In other words, LGBTQ people are 97 times more likely to report being sexually abused in detention than non-LGBTQ people in the same conditions.[56]

The Obama Administration constructed, as one of us has written elsewhere, a

> pyramid of deportability for irregular residents: the "bad hombres" were at the top, including often-single men who had committed felony crimes, people who posed terrorist threats, and new irregular entrants. Near the bottom, and those who were often granted leaves to stay pending annual check-ins, were youth with no criminal records, and women who had American citizen children, were married to or were themselves veterans, looked after a disabled family member, or otherwise could document a longstanding presence in the country that featured cooperation with ICE.[57]

Many people were technically in "removal proceedings," especially those with children or with longstanding ties to the United States, but only a subset were detained.

In August 2016, Trump called the Dream Act an "unconstitutional executive amnesty" in a speech that also included the following passage:

> According to federal data, there are at least 2 million, 2 million, think of it, criminal aliens now inside of our country, 2 million people criminal aliens [sic]. We will begin moving them out day one. As soon as I take office. Day one. In joint operation with local, state, and federal law enforcement.
>
> They live with these people. They get mocked by these people. They can't do anything about these people, and they want to. They know who these people are. Day one, my first hour in office, those people are gone.[58]

By March 2017, DHS had begun creating capacity for 20,000 more detention beds so as to indefinitely incarcerate women and children migrating from Central America.[59] The plan was to separate mothers from their children, thereby striking fear and provoking them to consider a different site for protection claims.[60]

This plan morphed into the "zero tolerance" policy that netted Elvira, her mother, and thousands of other asylum-seeking families. This policy separated more than 2,500 children from their parents at the border in May and June 2018; after a court found the policy illegal, the Administration was ordered to reunite all families. It has been revealed that ICE also arrested some of the immigrants who came forward to shelter the children separated from their parents[61] and that immigration officials pressured parents to sign forms waiving their reunification rights in a "coercive and misleading manner."[62] As of September 2018, nearly 200 traumatized children are still alone in federal custody, including many under the age of 5 years, and no Administration official has been held accountable for this "humanitarian disaster."[63]

ICE arrests "appear to have stabilized and are no longer increasing" under the Trump Administration, with an average of 13,318 arrests per month between February and September 2017.[64] Yet the new Administration's policies are being experienced as more cruel, because they are. Beyond the horrific "zero tolerance" family separation policy, the Trump Administration is reviving Secure Communities and the bed mandate. With irregular border crossings from Mexico falling to their lowest levels since the early 1970s, ICE is turning to "interior enforcement" tactics. It is looking more closely at court records to find foreign-born but legal US residents whose convictions (no matter how old) render them deportable. In 2017, ICE arrested more than 28,000 "non-criminal immigration violators," the fastest-growing category of detainees.[65] ICE is no longer respecting the Obama-era policy of sensitive locations, and people are being profiled, arrested, and detained at various checkpoints, including children as they are rushed to the hospital.[66] The Agency is also targeting dissenters and activists for punishment through surveillance and detention.[67] Former US attorney general Jeff Sessions intervened to make domestic abuse survivors ineligible for asylum claims and protection in the United States.[68] Dawn raids on worksites have continued to wreak havoc and fear for immigrants and their children in both rural and urban settings.[69] ICE is using regularly scheduled immigration check-ins to threaten asylum seekers and other migrants. Advocates name this tactic as "silent raids."[70]

Detention as deterrence: a human rights violation

> My mom and I have talked about what it will be like if I get to stay and she's forced to leave. She says, "Honey, you'll be able to study. At least your future is going to be set. If you have the opportunity, then why waste it?" I tell her I'm going to miss her, but she tells me sometimes we have to make sacrifices. I don't like talking about it because it makes me really sad just to think about my mom not being here.[71]

> Will they take my children? What will happen to them? I am still breastfeeding and my babies need me.[72]

What can explain the transformation of detention into a multi-sited instrument? One possibility is its use by politicians concerned to deter certain groups of unwanted immigrants. Indeed, British politicians drew upon this justification for detention as early as 1906.[73] Since then, it has been invoked repeatedly: in the Canadian context by the Conservative government of Stephen Harper;[74] in the United States context by the Obama Administration in response to the 2014 surge of Central American families seeking asylum[75] and by the Trump Administration (Executive Order 2017) when it aimed to keep out "undesirable" classes of migrants by explicitly linking them to terrorism, Islamophobia, and national security concerns.

Despite its popularity, detention as deterrence contravenes international law. Arriving at the border of another state is the legally enshrined way to request asylum. As such, attempting to deter refugees from reaching the border infringes on their basic right to seek asylum. Accordingly, and in line with Kantian principles of respect for individual human dignity, detention cannot legally be used as a deterrence mechanism to dissuade future migrants from coming.[76] The use of detention as a deterrent strategy can be understood as yet another way that detention is a "politically successful policy failure."[77] Detention is a "spectacle" that encourages populations to believe that the state is protecting them by imprisoning migrants who allegedly prove a threat or risk to them and their livelihoods.[78]

Deterrence mechanisms can take forms other than detention. They can include measures limiting arrival, admission, offshore processing, and extraterritorialization, as well as indirect measures such as disincentivization by way of making family reunification very difficult and the broader trend of the criminalization of migration. Research makes clear that detention-as-deterrence does not work in the long term. Restrictive or punitive border control measures like detention may succeed at rerouting migrants in the short term, but this is often along more dangerous corridors and sometimes with smugglers or traffickers. Attempting to deter migration using undifferentiated mechanisms such as the threat or enforcement of detention is futile because migration, particularly forced migration, is a complex, multilevel, natural phenomenon whose social, economic, and political determinants far outweigh any domestic immigration policy.[79] As sociologists Douglas Massey, Karen A. Pren, and Jorge Durand argue, expansive detention regimes form part of larger border enforcement efforts that will inevitably "backfire," with new arrivals continuing to come and the existing undocumented populations opting to settle "both to cover the increased costs of border crossing and also to put off the physical risks of clandestine crossings in the future."[80]

While the historical record is mixed, there are indications that effective strategies for managing global flows include development and other policies aimed at preventing or diverting migration, not deterring people. These migration management tools that better respect human rights address root causes of forced displacement and open up safe passages for migration, including modes of transport.[81] Walls and closed borders are "known to lead to greater permanence in migration, as the possibility of 'circular migration' which enables people to move back and forth and retain strong links with their families, is removed."[82]

A key example here is the current "zero tolerance" policy of using detention to deter Central Americans from seeking asylum in the United States. This policy assumes that the women and children share a single cause or motivation – to get to the United States – and that, by disrupting them through detention, they will be dissuaded from trying. However, scholarship indicates that the complexity of the mix of push and pull factors leading to the increase in asylum claims cannot be resolved by as simple a solution as mass incarceration.[83] Even the Australian government – the progenitor of detention-as-deterrence with its "Stop the Boats" campaign – acknowledges that even the harshest form of detention, mandatory incarceration, does not deter new arrivals. As early as 2010, the Australian minister for immigration acknowledged: "We already have the toughest mandatory detention regime in the Western developed world, yet people still come to Australia … So I don't think mandatory detention should be seen as a deterrent."[84]

Unfortunately, restriction of movement and deterrence, as opposed to a commitment to rights protection, have become the go-to response of Western liberal nations.[85] How does this trend square with the status of deterrence in international legal norms? International refugee law extends various individual protections to refugees. Article 14(1) of the UDHR makes it clear that the fundamental right to seek and enjoy asylum inherently belongs to everyone. Various instruments also prohibit the use of deterrence, and clearly state the prohibition on expelling or returning asylum seekers to a country or territory where one's life or freedom would be threatened. This latter norm is known as the principle of nonrefoulement and is enshrined in Article 33(1) of the UN Refugee Convention (1951). Countries that routinely practice extraterritorial detention and interdiction of migrants have been called out for infringing these rights, such as in the Australian High Court decision of *Al-Kateb v. Godwin* (2004).[86] Using detention as deterrence has elicited significant resistance from both courts and civil society resistance in countries such as the United States and Israel.[87] There are also a number of current court challenges to the US practices of automatic detention[88] and the separation of children from their families.[89]

Freedom of movement and the right not to be returned to the site of persecution are fundamental, non-derogable rights. Detention-as-deterrence derogates from these rights and undermines this paradigm by concretizing the primacy of the sovereign nation's ability to control its borders and handpick the population that is allowed to enter. Liberal nations mark certain classes of migrants as detainable and rationalize their increasingly repressive policies as matters of national security and protection of the rights of its bona fide citizens. Detention-as-deterrence has the ability to shift and expand the border apparatus of the nation beyond its political boundaries.[90] As the international law scholar Michael Kagan cogently reminds us, detention-as-deterrence presents a key human rights problem of "how far can a government go to infringe the rights of person A in order to send a message to person B."[91] That is, in the state's conceptualization, to what extent can detainees be used to serve as proxies for sending messages of deterrence to far-off migrants waiting and ready to take advantage of a state's generosity or porous borders?

Perhaps most importantly, detention-as-deterrence cements the trend of importing criminal law norms into administrative immigration proceedings. It unfairly and unjustly punishes migrants for daring to migrate. By preventing migrants from being able to exercise their fundamental right to seek asylum and limiting their freedom of movement as if they were criminals, the state effectively extends its criminal apparatus beyond its borders and reifies citizenship as the only sure way to have the ability to exercise one's basic rights. We contend that detention-as-deterrence places state sovereignty and border control above and beyond commitments to upholding basic rights and freedoms, in a wrong and troubling manner.

Conclusion: the persistent violence of immigration detention

> The nightmares don't stop. I don't understand why I was detained when I came to Canada. Don't they know my story? Don't they know I was jailed at home? Every time I see an officer, I want to die.[92]

> Wearing this orange jumpsuit makes me feel like an outlaw, a criminal. Why am I in prison? My refugee hearing hasn't even been decided and already they shove me in this hole to die.[93]

Immigration detention harms thousands of people and infringes on fundamental human rights. Yet recent years have seen an increased use of administrative detention in countries like the United States, United Kingdom, Canada, and Australia. Liberal states are increasingly turning to the incarceration of migrants in the name of border enforcement and national security. It is not surprising that many of these practices take place at borders between richer and poorer states and reinforce a global hierarchy that the geographer Joseph Nevins has termed a "global apartheid" based on racist discrimination.[94] Repressive policies like the separation of children from their families, denial of counsel, denial of psychosocial supports, and the specter of indefinite detention are used as mechanisms of deterrence to stop migrants from exercising their right to seek asylum from violence and persecution. Administrative detention at the border, in country, or before deportation affords fewer rights protections and presents significant concerns regarding access to justice for an already vulnerable group.

This essay has briefly traced the history of immigration detention policies in liberal states and spotlighted real-life examples to indicate their human impact. Detention has become a multi-sited instrument that shows the limitations on exercising one's right to liberty and security. Access to citizenship is the great differentiator here: Without citizenship status, a person remains detainable and deportable at the mercy of the nation-state, no matter what rhetoric is employed to justify incarceration. The very existence of "baby jails" shows the extent to which the modern liberal state is willing to justify the incarceration of migrants. Detention affects populations that are already marginalized and easily reduced to an "us vs. them" formulation. The rise in populism and xenophobia in the Western world has normalized the detention of migrants and made very clear that human rights are simply not exercisable in the same way by everyone. Further research on how states justify the derogation of human rights of migrants and how state practices normalize detention is necessary for grasping immigration detention's very real as well as symbolic violence.[95] Detention rips apart communities, traumatizes generations,[96] and calls into question the core liberal values that we claim to hold and that underwrite respect for human rights. Elvira, Nancy, Anna, Almaz, James, and tens of thousands of others are left to face an increasingly violent system that clearly shows just how steep the hierarchy of rights has become.

Notes

1 The name has been changed. Elvira's story was first published in "The Immigration Issue," a special issue of the magazine *Marie Claire*. Kayla Webley Adler, "'I Was Taken to a Huge Cage': One Salvadoran Teenager Recounts being Separated from Her Mother at the U.S.–Mexico Border in June," *Marie Claire*, September 2018. Online. Available at www.marieclaire.com/politics/a22700754/immigrant-child-cage-true-story (accessed 22 December 2018). It is used throughout this essay to highlight the human impact of immigration detention policies.

2 Adler, "'I Was Taken to a Huge Cage.'"

3 Online. Available at www.cnn.com/2018/06/20/politics/immigration-border-separations-tender-age-shelters/index.html (accessed 22 December 2018).

4 On the United States, see this source: Online. Available at www.cnn.com/2018/06/20/health/immigrant-detainee-deaths-medical-care-bn/index.html (accessed 22 December 2018). On Canada, see this source: Online. Available at https://theconversation.com/migrants-are-dying-in-detention-centres-when-will-canada-act-87237 (accessed 22 December 2018).

5 The examples of Nancy, Anna, Almaz, and James in this essay serve to illustrate the actual human impact of detention policies and help the reader grasp these issues beyond the level of

a merely theoretical inquiry. All names and identifying features have been changed to protect the identity of the informants, and all quotations attributed to them are drawn from our refugee and immigration practice in Toronto, Canada, in 2016.

6 See, for example, the following documents: Universal Declaration of Human Rights, Articles 3, 7, and 9. Online. Available at www.un.org/en/universal-declaration-human-rights; International Covenant on Civil and Political Rights, Article 9(1). Online. Available at www.ohchr.org/en/professionalinterest/pages/ccpr.aspx; UN Human Rights Committee's General Comment 35. Online. Available at www.ohchr.org/EN/HRBodies/CCPR/Pages/GC35-Article9Libertyand Securityofperson.aspx; UN General Assembly's Body of Principles for the Protection of All Persons under Any Form of Detention or Imprisonment, Principle 2. Online. Available at www.ohchr.org/Documents/ProfessionalInterest/bodyprinciples.pdf; European Convention on Human Rights, Article 5(1). Online. Available at www.echr.coe.int/Documents/Convention_ENG.pdf; UN Refugee Convention, Article 31. Online. Available at www.ohchr.org/en/professionalinterest/pages/statusofrefugees.aspx; Migrant Worker Convention, Article 16(1) Online. Available at www.ohchr.org/en/professionalinterest/pages/cmw.aspx; UN Declaration on the Human Rights of Individuals Who Are Not Nationals of the Country in Which They Live, Article 5(1)(a). Online. Available at www.un.org/documents/ga/res/40/a40r144.htm; Organization of African Unity, African Charter on Human and Peoples' Rights, also known as the Banjul Charter, Article 6. Online. Available at www.achpr.org/instruments/achpr; Organization of American States, American Convention on Human Rights, Article 7(1). Online. Available at www.cidh.oas.org/basicos/english/basic3.american%20convention.htm; Organization of American States, American Declaration on the Rights and Duties of Man, Article 1. Online. Available at www.cidh.oas.org/Basicos/English/Basic2.american%20Declaration.htm; Council of the League of Arab States, Arab Charter on Human Rights, Article 14. Online. Available at http://hrlibrary.umn.edu/instree/loas2005.html; UN High Commissioner for Refugees, Detention Guidelines, "Introduction." Online. Available at www.unhcr.org/en-us/publications/legal/505b10ee9/unhcr-detention-guidelines.html. See also Amnesty International UK Section, "A Matter of Routine: The Use of Immigration Detention in the UK," 2017. Available at www.amnesty.org.uk/files/2017-12/A%20Matter%20Of%20Routine%20ADVANCE%20COPY.PDF?ya06n1Z2uH6J0bP8HmO7R2Pn7nabDymO= (all accessed 22 December 2018).

7 Stephanie J. Silverman and Amy Nethery, "Understanding Immigration Detention and its Human Impact," in Amy Nethery and Stephanie J. Silverman (eds.) *Immigration Detention: The Journey of a Policy and Its Human Impact*, London: Routledge, 2015, pp. 1–12.

8 Alison Mountz et al., "Conceptualizing Detention: Mobility, Containment, Bordering, and Exclusion," *Progress in Human Geography*, 2013, vol. 37, no. 4, 522–41; Stephanie J. Silverman, "Return to the Isle of Man: The Implications of Internment for Understanding Immigration Detention in the UK," University of Oxford, Centre on Migration, Policy and Society Working Paper No. 102, 2012, 19; Stephanie J. Silverman, "'Regrettable But Necessary'? A Historical Study of the UK Immigration Detention Estate and Its Opposition," *Politics and Policy*, 2012, vol. 40, no. 6, 1131–57.

9 Douglas S. Massey, "Political Economy of Migration in the Era of Globalization," in Samuel Martínez (ed.) *International Migration and Human Rights: The Global Repercussions of US Policy*, Berkeley: University of California Press, 2009, p. 33.

10 Douglas S. Massey, Karen A. Pren, and Jorge Durand, "Why Border Enforcement Backfired," *American Journal of Sociology*, 2016, vol. 121, no. 5, 1557–600.

11 Elvira, age 17, 2018. Adler, "'I Was Taken to a Huge Cage.'"

12 Jerome Phelps, "Alternatives to Detention in the UK: From Enforcement to Engagement?" *Forced Migration Review*, 2013, no. 44, 47.

13 Silverman and Nethery, "Understanding Immigration Detention."

14 Nancy, a mother of two from Nigeria in her late thirties, 2016. See n. 5.

15 See n. 5.

16 Rainer Bauböck, "Global Justice, Freedom of Movement and Democratic Citizenship," *European Journal of Sociology/Archives Européennes de Sociologie*, 2009, vol. 50, no. 1, 10.

17 Linda Bosniak, "Being Here: Ethical Territoriality and the Rights of Immigrants," *Theoretical Inquiries in Law*, 2007, vol. 8, no. 2, 396.

18 Joseph H. Carens, "Aliens and Citizens: The Case for Open Borders," *Review of Politics*, 1987, vol. 49, no. 2, 252.
19 Leo R. Chavez, "Mexicans of Mass Destruction: National Security and Mexican Immigration in a Pre- and Post-9/11 World," in Martínez, *International Migration and Human Rights*, p. 89.
20 Jane McAdam, "An Intellectual History of Freedom of Movement in International Law: The Right to Leave as a Personal Liberty," *Melbourne Journal of International Law*, 2011, vol. 12, no. 1, 27–56.
21 See Philip Cole, "Towards a Symmetrical World: Migration and International Law," *Éthique et économique/Ethics and Economics*, 2006, vol. 4, no. 1, 1–7 and Lea Ypi, "Justice in Migration: A Closed Borders Utopia?" *Journal of Political Philosophy*, 2008, vol. 16, no. 4, 391–418.
22 See Jennifer Hyndman, "The Geopolitics of Migration and Mobility," *Geopolitics*, 2012, vol. 17, no. 2, 243–55, and Liisa Malkki, "National Geographic: The Rooting of Peoples and the Territorialization of National Identity among Scholars and Refugees," *Cultural Anthropology*, 1992, vol. 7, no. 1, 24–44.
23 See Bosniak, "Being Here," and Bridget Anderson, *Us and Them? The Dangerous Politics of Immigration Control*, Oxford: Oxford University Press, 2013.
24 An erudite articulation of the liberal-nationalist position is provided by David Miller, "Border Regimes and Human Rights," *Law and Ethics of Human Rights*, 2013, vol. 7, no. 1, 1–23. Miller takes up the question of whether a liberal state that denies freedom to enter is trespassing migrants' human rights. In a rather unsatisfactory move, he finds that states do not owe them entry because they do not exercise authority over them and, moreover, there is no right to enter since migrants have lots of states to choose among and so can always go elsewhere: "In order to fix the scope of particular human rights such as freedom of movement, we have to make judgments about the dangers that may follow from the misuse of state power. Permitting states to control the inward movement of people across their borders does not appear to present similar dangers, because the state's power to oppress outsiders is limited by the fact that these outsiders can choose which states they attempt to enter. There are not long queues of people seeking to enter North Korea or Burma under the generals. Miller, "Border Regimes and Human Rights," 9.
25 Hannah Arendt, *The Origins of Totalitarianism*, London: Harcourt, Brace, 1951, pp. 296–7.
26 Stephanie J. Silverman and Evelyne Massa, "Why Immigration Detention is Unique," *Population, Space and Place*, 2012, vol. 18, no. 6, 678.
27 Alina Das, "Immigration Detention: Information Gaps and Institutional Barriers to Reform." *University of Chicago Law Review*, 2013, vol. 80, no. 1, 137–64.
28 J. C. Salyer, "The Treatment of Noncitizens after September 11 in Historical Context," in Martínez, *International Migration and Human Rights*, p. 65.
29 Stephanie J. Silverman, "The Normative Ethics of Immigration Detention in Liberal States," University of Oxford, DPhil thesis, 2013, p. 76.
30 *Chae Chan Ping v. United States*, 130 US 581 (1889). Online. Available at https://supreme.justia.com/cases/federal/us/130/581/; *Fong Yue Ting v. United States*, 149 US 698 (1893). Online. Available at https://supreme.justia.com/cases/federal/us/149/698/; *Wong Wing v. United States*, 163 US 228, 235 (1896). Online. Available at https://supreme.justia.com/cases/federal/us/163/228/ (all accessed 22 December 2018). See also Stephanie J. Silverman, "Immigration Detention in America: A History of Its Expansion and a Study of its Significance," COMPAS Working Paper 80, Oxford: Centre on Migration, Policy and Society, 2010.
31 Silverman, "Return to the Isle of Man," 19.
32 Silverman, "The Normative Ethics," p. 77.
33 Christine Bacon, "The Evolution of Immigration Detention in the UK: The Involvement of Private Prison Companies," RSC Working Paper No. 27, Oxford, Refugee Studies Centre, 2005; Silverman, "Regrettable but Necessary?"
34 Anshu Budhrani, "Regardless of My Status, I Am a Human Being: Immigrant detainees and Recourse to the Alien Tort Statute," *University of Pennsylvania Journal of Constitutional Law*, 2012, vol. 14, no. 3, 787.
35 Mark D. Kemple, "Legal Fictions Mask Human Suffering: The Detention of the Mariel Cubans. Constitutional, Statutory, International Law, and Human Considerations," *Southern California Law Review*, 1989, vol. 62, no. 6, 1733–804; see 1736 and throughout.

36 Silverman, "Immigration Detention in America," 8–9.
37 David Manuel Hernández, "Pursuant to Deportation: Latinos and Immigrant Detention," *Latino Studies*, 2008, vol. 6, 35–63.
38 Mark Dow, *American Gulag: Inside US Immigration Prisons*. Berkeley: University of California Press, 2004, p. 7. Emphasis added.
39 Despite becoming host to terrorist suspects after 11 September 2001, Guantánamo Bay never ceased functioning as an offshore immigration detention facility for migrants interdicted at sea. The Haitians were detained for longer periods than the Cubans, leading to accusations of a racially informed double standard by minority leaders, including the Congressional Black Caucus. Silverman, "Immigration Detention in America," 10.
40 Silverman, "Immigration Detention in America," 10. Another detention facility that should be shut down due to its risks to human safety is the Northwest Detention Center in Tacoma, Washington. This detention center officially holds 1,500 immigrant detainees. When the next tsunami strikes the area, the detention center will fill with as much as two meters of water in fewer than eight minutes. Lael Henterly, "The Disaster Waiting to Happen at the Northwest Detention Center," *Seattle Globalist*, 18 March 2015. Online. Available at www.seattleglobalist.com/2015/03/18/northwest-detention-center-tsunami-disaster-evacuation-tacoma/34981 (accessed 22 December 2018).
41 Teresa A. Miller, "The Impact of Mass Incarceration on Immigration Policy," in Marc Mauer and Meda Chesney-Lind (eds.) *Invisible Punishment: The Collateral Consequences of Mass Imprisonment*, New York, New Press, 2002, p. 214.
42 Stephanie J. Silverman and Melanie Griffiths, "Immigration Detention in the UK," Migration Observatory briefing, COMPAS, University of Oxford, UK, May 2018. Online. Available at http://migrationobservatory.ox.ac.uk/resources/briefings/immigration-detention-in-the-uk (accessed 22 December 2018).
43 "Detainees. Compensation. Written question – 132374," *Parliamentary Written Questions and Answers and Written Statements*. Online. Available at www.parliament.uk/business/publications/written-questions-answers-statements/written-question/Commons/2018-03-13/132374 (accessed 22 December 2018).
44 Joanne Vincett, "Three Days Is Still Too Long to Hold Pregnant Women in Immigration Detention," *The Conversation*, UK Edition, 17 September 2018. Online. Available at https://theconversation.com/three-days-is-still-too-long-to-hold-pregnant-women-in-immigration-detention-100352 (accessed 22 December 2018). See also Stephen Shaw, "Review into the Welfare in Detention of Vulnerable Persons: A Report to the Home Office," January 2016. Online. Available at www.gov.uk/government/uploads/system/uploads/attachment_data/file/490782/52532_Shaw_Review_Accessible.pdf (accessed 22 December 2018).
45 Matt Welch, "Trump May Have Bad Intentions, But Obama Was a Deporter-in-Chief Too," *Los Angeles Times*, 17 February 2017. Online. Available at www.latimes.com/opinion/op-ed/la-oe-welch-immigration-enforcement-obama-trump-20170216-story.html (accessed 22 December 2018).
46 Cecilia Menjívar, Andrea Gómez Cervantes, and Daniel Alvord, "The Expansion of 'Crimmigration,' Mass Detention, and Deportation" *Sociology Compass*, 2018, vol. 12, no. 4, 8.
47 Tanya M. Golash-Bazo, "The Racial Injustices of Mass Deportation," *CounterPunch*, 20 March 2015. Online. Available at www.counterpunch.org/2015/03/20/the-racial-injustices-of-mass-deportation (accessed 22 December 2018).
48 Transactional Records Access Clearinghouse (TRAC), "ICE Apprehensions Half Levels of Five Years Ago," 12 June 2018. Online. Available at http://trac.syr.edu/immigration/reports/517 (accessed 22 December 2018).
49 American Civil Liberties Union and American Civil Liberties Union of Texas, "Warehoused and Forgotten: Immigrants Trapped in Our Shadow Private Prison System," 22 June 2014. Online. Available at www.aclu.org/other/warehoused-and-forgotten-immigrants-trapped-our-shadow-private-prison-system (accessed 22 December 2018).
50 Jennifer M. Chacón, "Immigration and the Bully Pulpit," *Harvard Law Review*, 2017, vol. 130, no. 7, 250.
51 Transactional Records Access Clearinghouse (TRAC), "ICE Apprehensions Half Levels."

52 William Selway and Margaret Newkirk, "Congress's Illegal-Immigration Detention Quota Costs $2 Billion a Year," *Bloomberg Business Week*, 26 September 2013. Online. Available at www.bloomberg.com/news/articles/2013-09-26/congresss-illegal-immigration-detention-quota-costs-2-billion-a-year (accessed 22 December 2018).

53 The private firms Corrections Corporation of America (CCA) and GEO Group hired 20 lobbyists in 2015 at $1.6 million; in October 2016, GEO hired three new lobbying firms, including David Stewart and Ryan Robichaux of Bradley Arant Boult Cummings, both of whom are former staff of US Attorney Jeff Sessions. In 2015, CCA lobbied against the Justice Is Not For Sale Act, which would have banned private prisons at the federal, state, and local levels, and the Private Prison Information Act, which would have removed the exemption that allows private prison companies to avoid disclosing details of their contracts or information about what goes on inside its facilities. Mary Small, *A Toxic Relationship: Private Prisons and US Immigration Detention*, Washington: Detention Watch Network, December 2016, 11. Online. Available at www.detentionwatchnetwork.org/sites/default/files/reports/A%20Toxic%20Relationship_DWN.pdf (accessed 22 December 2018).

54 Franklin Foer, "How Trump Radicalized ICE," *Atlantic*, September 2018. Online. Available at www.theatlantic.com/magazine/archive/2018/09/trump-ice/565772 (accessed 22 December 2018).

55 Charlotte Clymer, "One Year After Trump Gave Order to Discriminate Against Dreamers, We Need Action," *Human Rights Campaign*, 5 September 2018. Online. Available at www.hrc.org/blog/one-year-after-trump-gave-order-to-discriminate-against-dreamers-we-need-ac (accessed 22 December 2018).

56 Viet Tran, "HRC Calls On DHS to Address Alarming Rate of Sexual Abuse LGBTQ Detainees Face in ICE Detention," 24 September 2018, Online. Available at www.hrc.org/blog/hrc-calls-on-dhs-to-address-rate-of-sexual-abuse-lgbtq-detainees-face-in-ic (accessed 22 December 2018).

57 Stephanie J. Silverman, "The Illegalization of Maribel Trujillo-Diaz," in Canadian Association for Refugee and Forced Migration Studies/L'Association Canadienne d'Etudes sur les Refugiés et la Migration Forcée (CARFMS), *CARFMS Blog*, 27 April and 25 May 2017. Online. Available at http://carfms.org/blog/the-illegalization-of-maribel-trujillo-diaz-12-by-stephanie-j-silverman (accessed 22 December 2018).

58 Rishi Iyengar, "Read Donald Trump's Speech on Immigration," *Time*, 1 September 2016. Online. Available at http://time.com/4475349/donald-trumps-speech-immigration-transcript (accessed 22 December 2018).

59 Chris Hayes and Brian Montopoli, "Exclusive: Trump Admininistration Plans Expanded Immigrant Detention," *MSNBC*, 3 March 2017. Online. Available at www.msnbc.com/all-in/exclusive-trump-admin-plans-expanded-immigrant-detention?cid=sm_tw_allin (accessed 22 December 2018).

60 Julia Edwards Ainsley, "Exclusive: Trump Administration Considering Separating Women, Children at Mexico Border," *Reuters*, 4 March 2017. Online. Available at www.reuters.com/article/us-usa-immigration-children/exclusive-trump-administration-considering-separating-women-children-at-mexico-border-idUSKBN16A2ES (accessed 22 December 2018).

61 Tal Kopan, "ICE Arrested Undocumented Immigrants Who Came Forward to Take in Undocumented Children," *CNN*, 20 September 2018. Online. Available at www.cnn.com/2018/09/20/politics/ice-arrested-immigrants-sponsor-children/index.html (accessed 22 December 2018).

62 Joshua Barajas, "Separated Parents Unknowingly Gave Up Reunification Rights, Lawyers Say," *NPR Nation*, 26 July 2018. Online. Available at www.pbs.org/newshour/nation/separated-parents-unknowingly-gave-up-reunification-rights-lawyers-say (accessed 22 December 2018).

63 Jess Morales Rocketto, "Trump's Deadline to Reunite Families Has Passed. Why Are So Many Terrified Children Still Alone?" *Newsweek*, 26 September 2018. Online. Available at www.newsweek.com/trumps-deadline-reunite-families-passed-why-are-so-many-terrified-children-1138926 (accessed 22 December 2018).

64 Transactional Records Access Clearinghouse (TRAC), "ICE Apprehensions Half Levels."

65 Tina Vasquez, "The New ICE Age: An Agency Unleashed," *New York Review of Books*, 2 May 2018. Online. Available at www.nybooks.com/daily/2018/05/02/the-new-ice-age-an-agency-unleashed (accessed 22 December 2018).

66 In October 2017, ICE agents in Laredo, Texas apprehended an undocumented 10-year-old girl named Rosa Maria Hernandez as she was on the way to the hospital for emergency gallstone surgery. Five armed agents accompanied her to the operating theater and tried to prevent her attorney from seeing her. Hernandez has cerebral palsy. Liz Posner, "6 ICE Horror Stories: Astonishing Levels of Taxpayer-Funded Cruelty Against Undocumented Immigrants," *Salon/AlterNet*, 4 November 2017. Online. Available at www.salon.com/2017/11/04/6-ice-horror-stories-astonishing-levels-of-taxpayer-funded-cruelty-against-undocumented-immigrants_partner (accessed 22 December 2018).

67 Emily Pope-Obeda, "Expelling Dissent," *Jacobin Magazine*, 3 February 2018. Online. Available at www.jacobinmag.com/2018/02/deportation-united-states-immigrants-activists (accessed 22 December 2018).

68 University of California Hastings College of the Law Center for Refugee and Gender Studies, *Backgrounder and Briefing on Matter of A-B-*, 20 June 2018. Online. Available at https://cgrs.uchastings.edu/matter-b/backgrounder-and-briefing-matter-b (accessed 22 December 2018).

69 Ryan Devereaux and Alice Speri, "The Day After Trump's ICE Raid in a Small Tennessee Town, 550 Kids Stayed Home From School," *Intercept*, 10 April 2018. Online. Available at https://theintercept.com/2018/04/10/ice-raids-tennessee-meatpacking-plant (accessed 22 December 2018).

70 Vasquez, "The New ICE Age." See also the reporting in Foer, "How Trump Radicalized ICE."

71 Elvira, age 17, 2018. Adler, "'I Was Taken to a Huge Cage.'"

72 Anna, single mother of three from Uganda, age 32, 2016. Anna fled her abusive husband and gave birth to twin girls in Canada. She was placed in detention upon arrival and separated from her toddler son. She fears the same will happen now to her twins, and that she will never see her babies again. See n. 5.

73 Silverman, "Regrettable but Necessary?"

74 Karl Nerenberg, "Bill C-31: Empowering Jason Kenney, Endangering Refugees," *Rabble.ca*, 12 June 2012. Online. Available at http://rabble.ca/blogs/bloggers/karl-nerenberg/2012/06/bill-c-31-empowering-jason-kenney-endangering-refugees (accessed 22 December 2018); Stephanie J. Silverman, "In the Wake of Irregular Arrivals: Changes to the Canadian Immigration Detention System," *Refuge: Canada's Periodical on Refugees*, 2014, vol. 30, no. 2, 27–34.

75 Claudia Morales, "Families Crossing the Border: 'We are not Criminals,'" *CNN*, 2 November 2016. Online. Available at www.cnn.com/2016/11/02/us/family-immigration-detention-centers (accessed 22 December 2018); Stephanie J. Silverman and Ben Lewis, "Families in US Immigration Detention: What Does It Mean to Do 'The Right Thing'?" *Contemporary Readings in Law and Social Justice*, 2017, vol. 9, no. 2, 95–115.

76 International Detention Coalition [Australia], "Briefing Paper: Does Detention Deter?" 2015. Online. Available at https://idcoalition.org/wp-content/uploads/2015/04/Briefing-Paper_Does-Detention-Deter_April-2015-A4_web.pdf (accessed 22 December 2018).

77 Peter Andreas, "A Tale of Two Borders: The US-Mexico and US-Canada Lines after 9–11," in Peter Andreas and Thomas Biersteker (eds.) *The Rebordering of North America: Integration and Exclusion in a New Security Context*, New York: Routledge, 2003, p. 33.

78 Cetta Mainwaring and Stephanie J. Silverman, "Detention-as-Spectacle," *International Political Sociology*, 2017, vol. 11, no. 1, 21–38.

79 International Detention Coalition, "Briefing Paper: Does Detention Deter?"

80 Massey et al., "Why Border Enforcement Backfired," 1565.

81 Mary Crock and Daniel Ghezelbash, "Do Loose Lips Bring Ships?" *Griffith Law Review*, 2010, vol. 19, 238–87.

82 Heaven Crawley, Franck Düvell, Katharine Jones, Simon McMahon, and Nando Sigona, "Destination Europe? Understanding the Dynamics and Drivers of Mediterranean Migration in 2015," *MEDMIG* [Unravelling the Mediterranean Migration Crisis] *Final Report*, 2016, 73. Online. Available at www.medmig.info/research-brief-destination-europe/#more-762 (accessed 22 December 2018).

83 As Muzaffar Chishti and Faye Hipsman put it: "In reality, there is no single cause. Instead, a confluence of different pull and push factors has contributed to the upsurge. Recent US policies toward unaccompanied children, faltering economies and rising crime and gang activity in Central American countries, the desire for family reunification, and changing operations of

smuggling networks have all converged ... Ultimately, only improved national and regional economic and security conditions in the children's countries of origin can stem the flow. All of these solutions – whether immediate, mid, or long term – are uphill battles that are costly to undertake and politically difficult to execute." Muzaffar Chishti and Faye Hipsman, "Dramatic Surge in the Arrival of Unaccompanied Children Has Deep Roots and No Simple Solutions," *Migration Policy Institute Policy Beat*, 13 June 2014. Online. Available at http://migrationpolicy.org/article/dramatic-surge-arrival-unaccompanied-children-has-deep-roots-and-no-simple-solutions (accessed 22 December 2018).

84 International Detention Coalition, "Briefing Paper: Does Detention Deter?" 3.

85 Thomas Gammeltoft-Hansen and Nikolas F. Tan, "The End of the Deterrence Paradigm? Future Directions for Global Refugee Policy," *Journal on Migration and Human Security*, 2017, vol. 5, no. 1, 28–56.

86 *Al-Kateb v. Godwin* (2004) 219 CLR 562, (Austl). Online. Available at http://eresources.hcourt.gov.au/showCase/2004/HCA/37 (accessed 22 December 2018). In this case, non-refoulement was preserved, but the lawfulness of indefinite detention of a stateless person was affirmed.

87 Michael Kagan, "Limiting Deterrence: Judicial Resistance to Detention of Asylum-Seekers in Israel and the United States," *Texas International Law Journal*, 2016, vol. 51, 191–211.

88 Miriam Jordan, "Court Blocks Trump Administration From Blanket Detention of Asylum Seekers," *New York Times*, 2 July 2018. Online. Available at www.nytimes.com/2018/07/02/us/asylum-court-ruling-detention.html (accessed 22 December 2018).

89 Meredith Mandell, "Lawsuit Challenges 'Jail-like' Detention of Migrant Children," *NBC News*, 30 June 2018. Online. Available at www.nbcnews.com/storyline/immigration-border-crisis/lawsuit-challenges-jail-detention-migrant-children-n887981 (accessed 22 December 2018).

90 Nancy A. Hiemstra, "Geopolitical Reverberations of US Migrant Detention and Deportation: The View from Ecuador," *Geopolitics*, 2012, vol. 17, no. 2, 239–311.

91 Kagan, "Limiting Deterrence," 198.

92 Almaz, age 45, 2016. Almaz was detained while protesting in Eritrea. She was raped by a prison guard and relives the trauma during every appointment with Canadian Border Services Agency. The Agency placed her in detention for failing to appear for a call-in interview in the course of her application for permanent residence granted on humanitarian and compassionate grounds.

93 James, age 25, 2014. James fled gang violence in the Caribbean. He has been placed in the Central East Correctional Facility in Lindsay, Ontario, Canada, a medium-risk prison where some immigration detainees are housed. They commingle with convicted criminals and have very few supports available as they await decisions on their refugee claims. For more information on access to justice in Canada's immigration detention, see Stephanie Silverman and Petra Molnar, "Everyday Injustices: Barriers to Access to Justice for Immigration Detainees in Canada," *Refugee Survey Quarterly*, 2016, vol. 35, no. 1, 109–27.

94 Joseph Nevins, "Policing Mobility: Maintaining Global Apartheid from South Africa to the United States," in Jenna M. Loyd, Matt Mitchelson, and Andrew Burridge (eds.) *Beyond Walls and Cages: Prisons, Borders, and Global Crisis*, Athens: University of Georgia Press, 2012, pp. 19–26.

95 Pierre Bourdieu, *Language and Symbolic Power*, John Thompson (ed.), Gino Raymond (trans.), Cambridge, MA: Harvard University Press, 1993.

96 Stephanie J. Silverman and Petra Molnar, "How Canada's Immigration Detention System Spurs Violence Against Women," *The Conversation*, US edition, 15 September 2018. Online. Available at https://theconversation.com/how-canadas-immigration-detention-system-spurs-violence-against-women-95009 (accessed 22 December 2018).

PART VII

THE TRANSFORMATIVE IMPACT OF HUMAN RIGHTS ON KNOWLEDGE

32

ARCHIVING HUMAN RIGHTS IN LATIN AMERICA

Transitional justice and shifting visions of political change

Michelle Carmody

In the 1980s, as civilian regimes started replacing the Cold War-era dictatorships of Latin America, state leaders developed a new formula for how to facilitate this political change and ensure a durable democratization. Transitional justice, as this practice became known, promised to overcome the divisions and clashes of the past and establish stable social and political relations by addressing the human rights violations of the previous regime. Criminal and reparative justice measures had been implemented previously in Europe to deal with the legacy of the Nazi regime, but during the Latin American transitions from authoritarian rule these and other measures were developed into a more comprehensive set of policy recommendations attached to new ideas about democratization. Transitional justice, as it appeared in the 1980s, married political conceptions of liberalizing change with the kinds of justice and redress measures that were being discussed in human rights circles at the time. These policies sought to foster a political and cultural commitment to the rule of law and create a state that upheld rather than violated human rights.

A central element of these transitional justice programs was the production and collection of information about past human rights violations. Often this took the form of state-sponsored investigations, known as truth commissions, which aimed to provide an official version of the past that would allow the society to move forward.[1] Other initiatives focused on the collection of existing documentation relating to past human rights violations. The collected documentation formed an archive that could be used to support judicial investigations, reparations, or even continued efforts at shaping collective national memory of the past. While truth commissions were temporary events, these archives became permanent features of the political landscape in the countries that established them. Established initially in Paraguay following the discovery of a cache of dictatorship-era police files in the early 1990s, human rights archives have proliferated across Latin America and indeed in other parts of the post-authoritarian world. Their permanent nature allows scholars to use them as windows onto the evolution of transitional justice practices in the decades following the end of the late Cold War-era dictatorships and, by extension, the evolving relationships among human rights, ideas about justice, and the search for political order.

While action around human rights has always sought to bring about political change, the ways in which this change has been understood and pursued has shifted over time.

In the context of transitional justice, the law has played a particular role as a conduit for change. When in 1989 Paraguayan judge José Augustín Fernandez searched a suburban police station for documentation relating to past human rights violations, declaring in front of numerous news cameras that he was acting with the authority vested in him by the national constitution, he reflected the enthusiasm within human rights circles for the law and its power to produce both institutional and cultural change. The documentation that he uncovered that day became the basis for the Paraguayan human rights archive, constructed under the auspices of the Supreme Court. But this particular understanding of law and justice, which performed its work at the level of society rather than for individuals or groups, came to be challenged by new conceptions of justice and redress that were being developed within human rights circles during the 1990s. These new conceptions emphasized memory and culture as essential to reshaping the current political order and providing a bulwark against future violations. By the year 2003, when neighboring Argentina created its official human rights archive, memory had assumed a central role in conceptions of how justice could be achieved and maintained. In this essay, I chart the creation and operation of the Paraguayan and Argentine archives as a way of examining developments within transitional justice and human rights more broadly.

The historiography of human rights has yet to pay due attention to transitional justice. Emerging as a historical phenomenon in the late 1980s, it falls out of the remit of investigations focused on the debate around the 1970s "breakthrough" and is also overlooked in light of the scholarly attention to humanitarian intervention when the focus is on the 1990s.[2] Perhaps because of its intimate connection with democratization, explicit engagements with transitional justice itself have mainly been the concern of legal scholars and political scientists. While this literature often has a strong normative character, seeking to identify best practices, there are also some important critical contributions that examine democratization efforts and global governance patterns in the context of neoliberalism, demonstrating the interactions between these themes and human rights.[3] An important historical examination comes from political historian Paige Arthur who explored the making of transitional justice by a group of transitional technocrats who, during the late 1980s and early 1990s, tied policies designed to address past human rights violations to the goal of building stable democratic order.[4] Like Arthur, I look at the role of individuals and groups in developing and shaping transitional justice. But while she concentrates on the breakthrough moment, I place transitional justice in a longer-term perspective, identifying how people's ideas about justice changed over time, and how these ideas in turn shaped approaches to democratization. I concentrate the analysis on the archives as examples of information politics, the mobilization of information about human rights violations in order to achieve a particular goal. The influential political scientists Margaret Keck and Kathryn Sikkink identify information politics as "*the* human rights methodology ... promoting change by reporting facts."[5] I look at the way information has been used to promote democratizing change within the context of Paraguayan and Argentine transitional justice.

The essay briefly examines the origins of transitional justice; it centers, however, on the creation and development of the human rights archives in Paraguay and Argentina as a way of exploring the shift from ideas about justice as law, with its implicit emphasis on institutional democratization, to justice as memory, which emphasizes culture as a central democratizing mechanism. I open with the Paraguay example. In March 1993, the country's Supreme Court officially created the Centro de Documentación y Archivo para la Defensa de los Derechos Humanos (Center for Documentation and Archive for the Defense of Human Rights, CDyA), making it the first human rights archive in Latin America. The CDyA houses documents produced by the Paraguayan security forces during the dictatorship of Alfredo Stroessner (1954–89), the majority of them found during Fernandez's raid on the police station in outer Asunción. While the CDyA's initial creation reflected the enthusiasm for pursuing human rights-related goals through judicial means characteristic of the late 1980s early post-transitional period, this enthusiasm ran up against deep distrust of the state on the part of certain human rights activists, especially those that identified as or with the victims of the regime. This distrust led them to challenge the judiciary's ownership of the dictatorship-era documentation and argue that the material should be understood primarily as a tool for constructing collective memory and be located within the public domain.

I then move to looking at Argentina where in 2003 President Nestor Kirchner created the Archivo Nacional de Memoria (National Memory Archive). The Argentine archive is an aggregate of documents produced by the state in the course of previous transitional justice initiatives such as the 1984 truth commission, documents from domestic and international human rights organizations and individual activists, documents produced by the armed forces during the dictatorship of 1976–83, as well as materials generated by the archive itself like oral histories and historical research. Kirchner's decision to explicitly frame the archive in terms of memory, although the documents it contains do serve judicial purposes, reflected the fundamental shift within human rights towards an understanding of justice that prioritizes memory and the experience of the victims of state-sponsored violence.

This essay is, then, a political history of transitional justice through the lens of these two human rights archives, looking at how ideas about justice have developed and how these ideas have shaped concrete initiatives like the collection and use of information about human rights violations. This history is based on semi-structured interviews with key actors involved in the establishment of each archive and a reading of key documents and newspaper accounts, paying attention to the ways a range of individuals and groups interacted with others both internationally and domestically to pursue their goals.

Human rights activism, information politics, and the precursors to transitional justice

From the 1980s onwards, government authorities across Latin American began to develop transitional justice programs, drawing on practices that had been developed in the 1970s to oppose the violation of human rights on the part of military governments in the region and transforming them into initiatives designed to create a social understanding and institutional framework for the new democratic order.[6] Many of these earlier practices had involved the mobilization of information about human rights violations and its funneling through transnational and international activist and diplomacy networks. During the 1970s, for example, many human rights advocacy groups such as the Centro de Estudios Legales y Sociales (Center for Legal and Social Studies) in Argentina and the exile group Comisión Argentina de Derechos Humanos (Argentine Human Rights Commission, based in Madrid, Paris and Washington, DC), worked to provide information through these networks to the US Congress in order to shape foreign policy towards violating regimes in the region.[7] Domestically, activists also mobilized information to discredit the regimes they were living under and to try and carve out some political space for resistance.[8] But domestic opportunities to shape the military government's policy or to pursue legal redress were limited, and local activists found more opportunities in the human rights developments of the 1970s in the United States, at the United Nations (UN), or with international human rights organizations like Amnesty International. They helped these international actors gather information and produce reports on what was occurring, and these reports were, in turn, used to shape policy towards the region and to pressure the military regimes for reform.

In the 1980s the authoritarian regimes across Latin America began to give way to civilian governments. The reasons for the transitions varied, and while transnational pressure over the human rights issue did not single-handedly bring about regime change, many of the activities that had been developed by transnational activists and organizations to exert this pressure did provide a model for transitional justice policymakers looking to formulate a kind of justice that would facilitate democratization. While criminal justice had been relatively marginal within human rights networks during the previous decade, the practice of gathering information and reporting on the human rights situation had functioned as a form of historical justice, establishing the historical record in the face of military regime denials and clandestine activities. Information gathering and reporting, then, provided a model for these policymakers to develop truth commissions, investigations into the events of the recent past that aimed to construct an official version of that past as a form of historical justice. Accounting for the past was considered a prerequisite for the creation of a new political order as the 1990 decree authorizing the creation of the Chilean National Commission for Truth and Reconciliation reveals: "only upon the foundations of truth will it be possible to satisfy the demands for justice and to create the conditions necessary to achieve an effective national reconciliation."[9] Operating much like the fact-finding missions run by human rights activists and organizations during the dictatorships, truth commissions gathered information about human rights violations and presented it to the public as a way of drawing a line between the human rights-violating past and the human rights-respecting present and future.

The transitions to democracy brought new possibilities and new debates within the realm of human rights. As demonstrated by the shift to engaging in information gathering and reporting to *legitimize* rather than to *delegitimize* a regime, human rights were becoming a central part of new forms of political order. In 1993 US assistant secretary of state for inter-American affairs Bernard Aronson summed up the prevailing mood around transitional justice in the region when, at a meeting in El Salvador, he declared that democratizing nations had the chance to create an order "where human rights are respected and protected, where tolerance and the rule of law reign, where differences are fought out in the political arena but ultimately compromise and consensus and the good of the nation prevail."[10] But despite the triumphant tone there was actually a high level of contention between policymakers themselves on the "ideal" form of justice to facilitate transition. The issue of criminal justice was particularly controversial. The transitions allowed scholars and policymakers within international law to imagine actually implementing many of the ideas that they had been developing over recent years about advancing the protections of international law. These ideas, which challenged national sovereignty, were resisted by the democratization technocrats as threatening domestic stability.[11]

One participant in these debates, US legal scholar Diane Orentlicher, conveyed many of these new ideas when she argued that international law dictated that victims had the right to justice and governments a duty to either engage in criminal prosecution or to investigate the crimes in question. Argentine policy advisor Carlos Nino countered that these governments also had to contend with domestic laws and norms, not to mention the need to maintain fragile democratic stability, making the "ideal" judicial response almost impossible to implement.[12] He argued for limiting criminal justice as a way of generating stability and accord between different interest groups. Orentlicher's view was echoed in forums like the Inter-American Court of Human Rights, which increasingly ordered states to take judicial action, and the UN, which in 1991 authorized French legal scholar Louis Joinet to investigate and establish a protocol around the issue of impunity for perpetrators of civil and political human rights violations.[13] By the beginning of the 1990s the idea of seeking justice within the courts had evolved within the broader international human rights field, which in turn shaped the way that policymakers and other democratizing elites operated domestically. It was within this context that the collection of documents relating to past human rights violations was uncovered in Paraguay.

Paraguay: the judicialization of transitional justice

In 1989 Paraguayan president General Alfredo Stroessner was removed from power via an internal coup, resulting in the military replacing him with a transitional government to oversee the process of liberalization and democratization.[14] New president General Andrés Rodriguez focused on institutional and administrative reform, rather than transitional justice per se, as the main vehicle for the democratization of the Paraguayan political order. There was, therefore, no truth commission investigation into the Stroessner period or any other government policy aimed at dealing with past human rights violations. Instead the government focused on modernizing Paraguayan democracy with initiatives like institutional reforms.

Past repression was, however, being discussed and debated within the newly opened public sphere. Activists had been demanding information about their own and their family members' incarceration since the fall of the regime, and the media reported regularly on accusations that documentation belonging to the security forces existed in police stations and ex-clandestine detention centers across the city of Asunción.[15] At the same time, a number of grassroots efforts used testimony to produce truth commission-style information about past violence.[16] While the government itself was largely unresponsive to demands around the past, Rodriguez did not actively prevent others engaging in transitional justice-style initiatives, including judicial action.

One month after the fall of the dictatorship a woman brought a criminal case against a group of high-ranking officials within the regime, including Stroessner himself, over the disappearance of her partner at the hands of the regime. This case, known as the Schaerer Prono case, came to trial in March 1992, leading to 25-year sentences for many of the accused and a verdict of aggravated and cruel homicide. The judge presiding in the Schaerer Prono case, Luís María Benitez, was also active in discussions with other jurists about ways they could facilitate both the modernization of the judiciary and the provision of justice within the democratization process. Connected to the development of human rights judicial thinking internationally and regionally, across Latin America there was a trend towards an emphasis on constitutional law and a belief in the centrality of human rights for constitutional rule; the Paraguayan jurists' discussions were influenced by these trends.[17] Working within the Interdisciplinary

Center for Social Law and Political Economy at the Catholic University in Asunción they developed a proposal for the agenda of the 1992 Constitutional Convention that included the constitutionalization of a series of fundamental rights.[18] Influenced by similar provisions inserted into the constitutions of Brazil and Colombia in recent years, they proposed establishment of habeas data, the "right to access information and details about oneself ... in either official or private records of a public nature" through petition before a magistrate.[19] They also advocated for constitutional guarantees of judicial independence, such as security of tenure for judges and independence from executive pressure.[20] Both these proposals were accepted, strengthening both human rights legal protections and the judiciary itself, setting the stage for the judicialization of transitional politics.[21]

Soon after, activist Martín Almada lodged a habeas data petition for the release of police records pertaining to his detention. He had been pursuing this information since his period in exile in Paris, where he had worked as a consultant for UN Educational, Scientific and Cultural Organization (UNESCO). His petition was assigned to the judge on duty who happened to be José Agustin Fernandez, assistant to Benítez Riera in the Schaerer Prono case. Fernandez led the expedition out to the suburban police station on 22 December 1992 where they forced access to a locked basement that turned out to be full of documents produced by the Investigations Department of the police force, the main source of repressive intelligence during the Stroessner period. The documentation was then removed from the basement and transported immediately to the Palacio de Justicia (High Court) in Asunción.

The uncovered police archive was rapidly transformed into a judicial archive as the files were taken into the custody of the court. Fernandez's central aim in requisitioning the material was to protect it as evidence. The status of the documents first and foremost as evidence led inadvertently to the implementation of a key archival protocol, maintaining chain of custody, with a literal human chain created to safely transport the documents to their new home. The documentation then needed to be processed and catalogued in order to be useful. The Supreme Court gave Fernandez approval to spend his time on the project, a decision he explains as motivated by the opportunity the documents presented to expand the judicial sphere of action:

> There were many cases already in which there was the version of the victims, but there was no documentation. There were a few [of these] cases already initiated. And logic dictated that we could then open more ... And so precisely for this reason we decided that they needed to be studied, revised, that they needed to be processed.[22]

Pursuing the organization of the information also provided a way for the Court to distance itself from the Stroessner period. Like other institutional actors the judiciary remained largely the same as under the dictatorship. By engaging in trials they were able to distance themselves from the past and lay blame for its excesses on a relatively small number of individuals.[23] The documents provided the Court with the chance to strengthen its position within the newly democratic order, a position it then used to challenge the government. While the president requested that the information in the documents not come to light, Fernandez defied his orders and allowed journalists, activists, and family members to access the materials resulting in widespread media coverage and allowing activists and victims to engage with the documents. The judiciary also pursued the further collection of information. Two days after the execution of Almada's warrant Benitez Riera authorized a raid on the premises of the Dirección Nacional de Asuntos Técnicos (National Technical Division, known as La Técnica), the Stroessner-era police department responsible for monitoring suspected communist activities. The raid did not respond to a habeas data writ but instead was undertaken to support a case against Antonio Campus Alum, the ex-director of La Técnica. The uncovered files were again taken into judicial custody, confirming the Palacio de Justicia as the central repository for information relating to past repression.

While the documents provided the Court with an opportunity to strengthen its institutional position, it could not perform the work required to organize the documentation without the help of others, and Fernandez worked on them alongside volunteers from the court, donating their own time to the project, and from civil society. This came about largely due to practical necessity: while the Court provided an institutional home for the documents, it did not provide staffing costs. Everything, then, says Fernandez, "depended on our own good will [to give our own time]. But there was always support, and in this the intervention of the private sector [volunteers] was fundamental." Soon after the discovery of the documents the Court signed an agreement with the civil society organization Centro de Documentación y Estudios (Center for Documentation and Study, CDE) by which the latter would provide assistance in inventorying the material. Individuals from the CDE assisted in sorting through the documents alongside representatives from the UN Human Rights Program, the Paraguayan Chamber of Deputies, the Attorney General's office, and victims and their family members. They worked to organize the material guided by the end goal of facilitating potential future judicial cases, using Fernandez's office as a workspace. As they worked, "it was clear that the documents had a logic, for example a letter, and this letter correlated with others, and so it was that we [reconstructed] the same logic that the police had for archiving."[24] Despite not being trained archivists, then, their broad remit of organizing the documents to facilitate the greatest number of possible future judicial actions led them to replicate another central element of archival practice, original order, producing an archive that details not only individual violations but also the way the police understood and operated within Paraguayan society. Recapturing the original order of the documents meant that they could be used to provide historical justice as well as criminal justice. This potential other use for the material intersected with a deep institutional distrust on the part of victims and some activists, sparking a debate over its use and ownership.

Institutionalization and its discontents

While the Court relied on civil society collaboration, not all activists accepted the judiciary's possession of the documents and, by extension, the designation of the information as legal evidence. This came to the fore when, several days after the discovery, Fernandez restricted access to the room with the files in order to safeguard the privacy of the victims. This move provoked widespread expressions of distrust among activists. One group immediately requested that the Court move the documents out of Fernandez's office, arguing that they were "insulted that people unconnected to the documents are making them their own just because they are part of this unjust structure known as the judiciary."[25] In January 1993 the National Commission for Human Rights, a civil society group, demanded that President Rodriguez provide more security for the documents and to move them out of the custody of the Court. The documents, they claimed, were "national heritage and not government property."[26] The conflict over the fate of the documents raised the attention of the international human rights community, and in February the nongovernmental organization (NGO) Americas Watch visited Paraguay to investigate the situation.[27] What they found when they arrived was that civil society groups were arguing for a new designation of the documents, emphasizing their role in "the conservation of the historical memory of our *pueblo* [which] is fundamental for saying never again to repression, to torture, to exile, to the violation of human rights."[28] Paraguayan activists did not oppose judicial processes, per se, but argued that they should not be seen as the primary vehicle for resolving human rights issues and reimagined them as elements within a broader, multilateral approach to dealing with the past. In March 1993 human rights activists, supported by two leftist presidential candidates, took their struggle to reclassify the documentation to the Congress, requesting that the archive be declared National Heritage, which would allow it to be used to "cure wounds and scars, to achieve trial and punishment of all the guilty of crimes against humanity, to reconstruct the social fabric and to serve as invaluable testimony for the generations to come."[29] They spoke to the documents' social rather than legal uses and, by extension, the social rather than strictly legal elements of transitional justice. Furthermore, they challenged the ownership of the documents, and, by extension, ownership over the transitional justice process. In their view, the nation should be the key protagonist in transitional justice, rather than the state and its institutions.

Fernandez responded to this challenge by emphasizing the need to accept and work within the authority of the law:

> At the beginning [the activists and family members] were present because I authorized it. But this is something extra-judicial and I did it because many of them said that they were political prisoners and that they'd suffered under the previous regime. But they weren't able to maintain harmony and dialogue and they went around complaining, distrusting the work of the prosecutor's office.[30]

While he echoed the need for compromise and cooperation that characterized transitional justice thinking more broadly, Fernandez was anxious to establish the institutional authority of the Court, and to have that authority recognized and respected by others. For its part, the Paraguayan government, which was happy to play a minimal role in rebuilding democratic order, supported the judicialization of the transition. In March 1993 they even decided to recognize the competency of the Inter-American Court for Human Rights, expanding the judicialization of human rights while also signaling Paraguay's democratic modernization. As the diplomatic representative had remarked when signing the order submitting to the jurisdiction of the Inter-Regional court,

> the triumph of democracy in my country through institutional mechanisms ... has opened new perspectives for Paraguayans, demonstrating to us that we are advancing towards the reestablishment of a civilized existence that seeks to ensure liberty, justice and respect for human rights.[31]

But many activists did not share this emphasis on the institutional path to change. Reflecting a strong institutional distrust particularly on the part of victims and their families they charged that the Court displayed "incomprehension and a lack of respect" towards their concerns.[32] Indeed, figures like Fernandez were not activists, and their interest in judicial processing for the crime of the dictatorship sprung from a sense of legal rather than social justice. As activists felt unable to see themselves represented by the understanding of justice promoted by the court, they turned to memory as a way of asserting their own version of justice.

Memory, democratization, and the voice of the victim

The Paraguayan human rights activists' emphasis on memory was part of a growing use of the concept across the region. Throughout the early 1990s bodies such as the Inter-American Commission for Human Rights, the Inter-American Court, and the UN spoke increasingly about impunity, a concept developed to describe the absence of criminal prosecutions for past human rights violations, prosecutions they themselves had been recommending to states to very little avail. Discussions on how to address this impunity, however, went beyond simply continuing to recommend criminal justice, and included other types of justice such as historical justice, the provision of information and truth.[33] Historical justice measures already constituted a central part of transitional justice polices, with truth commissions being used across the region and worldwide to establish an official national version of the past since the 1980s. This new understanding of historical justice was different in that it conflated history with memory, emphasizing the revelation of information about victim experiences and understanding truth as told from the perspective of the victim. A key moment in the development of this victim-centered approach was the 1993 release of a UN report on the right to restitution for victims of gross human rights violations, which introduced the idea of satisfaction alongside compensation and assurances of non-repetition.[34] At the same time, grassroots mobilizations against impunity in places like neighboring Argentina, Chile, and Uruguay invoked the concept of memory as a way of resisting the "forgetting" that impunity, the lack of criminal justice, represented. Memory, an active awareness of and appreciation for the voice and experience of the victims, became a way of staking a claim in the debate over transitional justice and of challenging institutional forms of justice that had in many cases proven disappointing due to their subordination to the drive for democratic stability. In Paraguay, while there were no amnesties or other explicit impediments to criminal justice as there had been in neighboring countries, the demand that the documents be used to build memory challenged the dominance of the judiciary, which the activists deeply distrusted, and became a way for them to propose new forms of non-institutional justice.

Rosa Palau, the head archivist at the CDyA, came from an activist and civil society background, having joined Fernandez's team through her involvement with the CDE. She was sympathetic to the claims that activists made over the documentation, but insisted that without an appropriate institutional structure, the material's potential for building memory could not be exploited. In 1997 Congress passed a law mandating the transfer of official documents, including the documentation held by the CDyA, to the National Archive.[35] For Palau, this measure ran counter to the activists' professed desire to use the documents to build memory. As she saw it, the aim of building memory calls for a separate archive for human rights since "the need to know [what happened] is much more immediate than the need to investigate on the part of historians." She called for different investigative and analytical techniques and different archives, noting that

> a human rights archive needs to be temporary. A museum of human rights needs to be temporary. Afterwards it has to be united with everything that relates to the history of the country, it should be in what's called a national archive.[36]

Palau's insistence on the ability of memory to be built from within an institutional structure reflected the fact that the CDyA itself was not strictly a judicial body. While it had been created by the Court the involvement of civil society had been central to its foundation and operation, as evidenced by the central role played by Palau herself. In her view, the open nature of the CDyA, where any victims or family member was welcome to come and see the original documents relating to their own experiences, made it a potential memory archive.

Palau's openness to the reimagining of the documents as foundations of memory, albeit still in the possession of the Court, reflected the rise of memory within international human rights circles throughout the 1990s and the filtering of these ideas into the realm of those interested in democratization.[37] These ideas motivated the French sociologist Alain Touraine's visit to Paraguay as part of a UNESCO delegation in June 2000, invited by Palau to help prepare an application to list the CDyA's documents on UNESCO's Memory of the World register.[38] Touraine, who had long been interested in processes of social change at the popular level, had developed an interest during the 1990s in Latin American post-dictatorial societies and their processes of transitional justice and democratization. He saw the Paraguayan documents as vitally important for constructing democracy in the region. Adopting the language of anti-impunity activists, he argued that while some thought that forgetting was the way to move forward, "a country or individual that fails to face up to the past is unable, in general, to face up to the future. Democracy cannot be built if the motives and working of dictatorship are not understood."[39] Two years later he returned to Paraguay to lead a workshop on Historical Memory and the Archives of Repression, arguing that "it is necessary to listen more and more often to the voices of the victims. These voices can tell us more about the future."[40]

The idea that memory and the voice of the victim could prevent future recurrence continued to shape developing international norms and frameworks. In 2003 the UN entrusted Diane Orentlicher to update its principles on impunity, originally elaborated by Louis Joinet in 1997. While some 15 years earlier she had been one of the most forceful advocates of the state's responsibility to pursue criminal justice within international law, her analysis of how best to bring about democratizing change had evolved along with what she characterized as "the broadening and deepening of global experience," notably her reflections on the international criminal processes dealing with the former Yugoslavia and Rwanda. She now had "a deeper appreciation of the multifaceted nature of transitional justice and the special contribution that non-judicial measures, when effective, can make to a broader process of political and social transition." While law was important, she now argued that "an effective program for combating impunity requires … the broad participation of citizens, including victims."[41] She updated the UN principles to include "the duty to preserve memory" based on the idea that "a people's knowledge of its oppression is part of its heritage and, as such, must be ensured by appropriate measures in fulfillment of the State's duty to preserve archives and other evidence concerning the violations of human rights."[42] Her emphasis on memory and heritage stemmed from her insistence that victims' agency be prioritized, resulting in an approach to transitional justice that followed what the victims wanted, rather than what international law dictated.[43] Orentlicher's own transformation reflected the evolution within transitional justice towards an understanding of democratization as a cultural rather than an exclusively institutional process.[44]

Transitional justice in the twenty-first century: beyond law as justice

Orentlicher's revised principles on impunity were released in 2005 but the ideas behind them had already begun to filter into national contexts. The idea that memory was an essential part of a multi-pronged transitional justice program was shaping policy in Argentina, where new president Nestor Kirchner, elected in 2003, embraced the trilogy of truth, justice, and memory as the defining slogan of his government. This was not the first transitional justice initiative in the country; in the 1980s the Argentine government had been one of the first to experiment with the new ideas about transition, justice, and democratization, authorizing both a truth commission and criminal trials. During the 1990s, however, under a different president the government had shifted to seeing criminal justice as a threat to democratization rather than a tool for it, leading to a series of amnesties for perpetrators. But in the year 2001 a deep economic and political crisis engulfed the Argentine state allowing Kirchner, who was elected in the shadow of this crisis, to break with all aspects of his predecessor's policies, including the approach to transitional justice.

One of the first measures that Kirchner took was the creation of the Archivo Nacional de Memoria (National Archive of Memory) to assist "in the search for truth, justice and reparation."[45] Kirchner's creation of the archive was a direct attempt to conform to the developing international consensus around justice, in particular the state's obligation to facilitate memory.[46] The decree establishing the archive mentioned Orentlicher's revision of the Joinet Principles, as well as the declarations on eradicating impunity that had come out of the 1993 Vienna World Conference on Human Rights.

Kirchner's creation of the archive also responded to domestic pressures, which themselves dovetailed with Orentlicher's entreaty to recover the memory of oppression. As activists had embraced memory during the 1990s as a way of opposing the amnesties that prevented criminal processing of past human rights violations, they had engaged in the creation of popular memorials and commemorations to the victims of these violations. In an attempt to develop a memorializing form of information politics, in 1997 activists within the Congress proposed the creation of a national human rights archive that would be used to guarantee the right to truth and to safeguard national memory, but the proposal failed to gather enough political support to make it a reality.[47] The economic crisis of 2001, however, and the subsequent political crisis it sparked, created the conditions for activist demands around transitional justice to be taken up by the new government. Announcing the archive's creation in 2003 Kirchner declared that he believed the country to be "at a critical juncture in the difficult task of restoring, consolidating and reforming our identity, our values." Argentina, he added, needed to "move decisively in the construction of our truth, in the construction of our reality, in the construction of justice and the breakdown of impunity."[48] Democratization was understood in terms of identity as well as institutional strength, and could be achieved by addressing the past in arenas beyond the courtroom. Furthermore, it was "the responsibility of the state to promote, respect and guarantee [these] human rights."[49] After many years of being the object of human rights developments, on the receiving end of numerous directives from the Inter-American Commission and opposition protests domestically, the Argentine state would now be the protagonist of human rights action.

Unlike the CDyA, which was created after the unexpected discovery of documentation, the National Archive of Memory's collections were constructed out of documents already held within other parts of the state bureaucracy, such as the documentation produced during the 1984 truth commission and other testimonies that had been collected in the interim.[50] This documentation served administrative functions such as providing advice regarding decisions on promotions, extra-territorial postings and other issues within the armed forces, and facilitating claims for reparations. Now included in the archive it would continue to serve these functions, as well as provide evidence for possible future criminal trials.[51] Guidelines were also developed to ensure the preservation and transfer of relevant material from the executive, the legislative and the judicial branches, and agreements of cooperation and exchange were signed with both international and domestic nongovernmental entities soon after.[52] This power to actively requisition documents from other institutional bodies put the new National Archive of Memory into conflict with the Archivo General de la Nación (General Archive of the Nation), in theory the institutional home of all state documents. The General Archive enjoyed low levels of support among activists, who in the past had claimed that to send the documents to the national archives "was tantamount to killing the victims all over again, since the archive was a place for dead people."[53] The distrust of state institutions that had been evident in Paraguay was also on display in Argentina, both in the attitude towards the General Archive and in the events of the 2001 crisis. Kirchner's establishment of a memory archive circumvented this distrust and aligned his government's transitional justice policy with the trend towards a deinstitutionalized, victim-centered understanding of justice.

In line with ideas shared by Touraine and Orentlicher, the National Archive of Memory was to mobilize information about past human rights violations to pursue democratization in the cultural rather than structural arena. In 2004 the archive's director Carlos Lafforgue explained that the institution was aiming to "engage in the systematization of a type of information that will allow the formation of a culture that promotes the existence of human rights."[54] To this end the archive was authorized to collect materials from private individuals, and to produce new materials. Collection policy focused on written documents as well as the creation of an audio-visual archive, an oral history archive, and a photographic archive. It was these artifacts that were to be the most important in pursuing the archive's aim of promoting culture. As Judith Said, former executive coordinator of the archive, explained, "the idea [motivating the decree] was to work with photos, audiovisual, different elements that could be preserved that were historically connected to the topic [of violations], but that added context to it."[55] The archive aimed to go beyond the documentation of human rights violations, as earlier information practices had done, and towards the documentation of a human rights movement.

Rather than providing critical historical context, however, the archive's materials would tell the story of the past from the contemporary point of view of the victims, their family, and activists who worked in their name. As Said explained, the archive was to be a space "which centralizes the struggle of the [human rights] organizations ... There was an important debate going on amongst the human rights organizations and we wanted to show that the state was present alongside those demands."[56] This debate focused on recuperating the political identity of the victims and valorizing the political activism of the 1970s. While this was not the only debate occurring under the umbrella of human rights activism in Argentina, with a number of other groups using the concept of human rights to animate their struggles for an expansion of citizenship rights, among other things, it was only the groups with this perspective on the victims of the regime that were brought into partnership with the state.[57] The contextualizing information in the archive, then, was to be "based on the point of view of those who were victims of state terrorism, and the politics that motivated activists to join various organizations, both armed and unarmed, but to join in pursuit of a political vision."[58] The archive itself was a sign to these activists that the Kirchner government was different to the previous one, and that they could trust it to protect their interests.[59] Archive staff conducted oral history interviews with victims and activists as well as trade unionists, professionals, and politicians; they collected documentation from dictatorship-era human rights groups as well as transnational human rights organizations like Amnesty International, and they collected photographs from activists, lawyers, politicians, and press agencies. While the archive's holdings did contain significant amounts of material detailing the violations themselves, these other materials documented the struggles against these violations and against the dictatorship itself.

A similar process of centering the perspective of the victim and reconstructing their social world was occurring in Paraguay, where the court itself was embracing the role of the documents in allowing the victims' voices and experiences to be heard and drawing a link between this and the construction of a new political culture. In 2007 the court launched the program Proyecto Conmemoria (Project Commemoration/With Memory), which linked "the recuperation of historical memory" with the creation of an awareness of the importance of human rights and institutional order.[60] The CDyA was included under the umbrella of this program, which saw it moved to a new space on the ground floor of the High Court alongside the newly created Museo de la Justicia Paraguaya (Museum of Paraguayan Justice). A visitor to the relocated archive first encounters the museum, a small room with panels describing the history of the justice system in Paraguay from the pre-Colombian period until today. "Today" is represented by material from the CDyA collection that illustrates not just the repressive system and political project of the Stroessner period but also the values and political ideals of the victims and their generation. Palau explains that

> if we don't [allow the voices of this material to be heard] we are not going to be able to advance, we are not going to be able to realize that the things they were demanding 40 years ago are the things that continue being demanded today.[61]

Like in Argentina, the oppositional struggles of the past were being invoked by the state and its institutions in the face of widespread distrust of and discontent with these very institutions. Memory, which had emerged as a way for victims' groups to claim a form of justice when they were dissatisfied with the institutional form on offer, was used by the state to build democratic stability and cohesion.

The valorization of the struggle against dictatorship and the conflating of memory and history was not without its critics. As well-known Argentine cultural critic, Beatriz Sarlo, commented,

> I was a militant in those years and I know that I did not merely have humanitarian and generous dreams but also authoritarian and violent ones; I know that the very idea of "human rights" was completely foreign to me.[62]

Sarlo's comments reminded people that the historical justice provided by the memory archive was partial, incomplete, and prone to error. The partial nature of these memories was emphasized by others who expressed concern that memory initiatives like the archive were becoming less about the memory of the dictatorship and more of a political platform for groups aligned with the government.[63] For the Kirchner government and those connected to it, however, the archive represented "the historical and social memory of both the violations of human rights and fundamental freedoms … and the actions of institutions and civil society for humanitarian defense, justice and solidarity."[64] The heroic actions in the name of human rights did not necessarily need to have been understood as such by participants at the time, what mattered was the ability to mobilize them in pursuit of political order in the present.

Conclusion: memory and the instrumentalization of information about human rights violations

While judicial processes were still considered an important component of twenty-first-century transitional justice, as seen particularly in Argentina where trials of dictatorship-era perpetrators recommenced in 2005, by the turn of the century institutional channels such as the law were no longer considered to be sufficient in the democratization process. The memory of the victims, what they suffered and the type of society they had struggled for had become central to post-1990s conceptions of post-conflict democratization. This development was linked to an evolution of thinking about justice within human rights. During the 1980s and early 1990s individuals working within international and regional human rights structures like the Inter-American system or the UN emphasized an institutional understanding of justice and were focused on thinking about the relationship between international law and state sovereignty and the best ways to promote and enforce international rights protection. These ideas were shaped by the changing political context brought about by the end of authoritarian regimes in Latin America and beyond and the new possibilities for redress that this opened up. But this judicialization of human rights did not satisfy everybody, and throughout the 1990s critiques began to appear that presented criminal justice as partial justice, arguing for a new form of historical justice that centered the experience and perspective of the victim in the form of "memory." These ideas about memory were shaped by a deep institutional distrust on the part of many victims and activists, as well as by a dissatisfaction with the experience of retributive criminal justice within transitional programs. By the turn of the century the idea of justice as victim-led and victim-centered had taken center stage within human rights.

Information politics, a central part of human rights methodologies since at least the 1970s, were also transformed by this evolution in thinking about justice. The judicialization of human rights politics turned information about human rights violations into evidence, while the resurgence of demands for historical justice turned information into building blocks for memory. But history and memory are not the same thing, and the historical justice that is pursed through the mobilization of information as memory will always be partial and particular. This is something common to all iterations of justice within human rights and transitional justice, from the earlier versions of historical justice represented by the official truth commissions, which were criticized for not sufficiently including the victims' perspective, to criminal justice and its burden of proof and its need to differentiate levels of responsibility and grades of involvement. As seen in the case of human rights archives, the information they contain is used specifically to counter the perceived deficiencies of other forms of justice, namely to place the victims at the center of narratives about the past. Human rights archives are the product of historical struggles over justice and over the use of information in the provision of this justice. As such they tell the history of these struggles, rather than the history of other, prior struggles against dictatorship and against human rights violations.

Looking at these changes in the use of information about human rights violations and the attendant evolution of human rights conceptions of justice enhances our understanding of the history of human rights more broadly. Transitional justice is a key site where human rights ideas were married with ideas about democratization and put into practice in the form of policy. This process saw ideas about human rights and justice applied in concrete contexts; it also saw the reality of these contexts produce shifts in thinking about human rights and justice. This process was initiated in the 1980s and continued to develop throughout the 1990s and into the twenty-first century. By bringing transitional justice into the picture we gain an insight into how human rights thinking and practice evolved beyond the 1970s breakthrough, highlighting the important connections between the thickening of international human rights and the political developments of the end of the Cold War in Latin America and beyond.

Notes

1 For a foundational contribution to the study of truth commissions, see Priscilla Hayner, *Unspeakable Truths: Confronting State Terror and Atrocity*, London: Routledge, 2000.

2 Stefan-Ludwig Hoffmann, "Human Rights and History," *Past & Present*, 2016, vol. 232, 279–310.

3 Nicolas Guilhot, *The Democracy Makers: Human Rights and International Order*, New York: Colombia University Press, 2005; Yves Dezalay and Bryant Garth, *The Internationalization of Palace Wars: Lawyers, Economists and the Contest to Transform Latin American States*, Chicago: University of Chicago Press, 2002; Karen Engle, Zinaida Miller and D. M. Davis (eds.), *Anti-Impunity and the Human Rights Agenda*, Cambridge, UK: Cambridge University Press, 2016. For an overview of transitional justice scholarship and developments within the political science literature, see Michelle Carmody, "From Transitional to Post-transitional Justice: Continuity and Change after Democratization," *Latin American Perspectives*, 2017, vol. 44, 210–15.

4 Paige Arthur, "How 'Transitions' Reshaped Human Rights: A Conceptual History of Transitional Justice," *Human Rights Quarterly*, 2009, vol. 31, 321–67.

5 Margaret Keck and Kathryn Sikkink, *Activists Beyond Borders: Advocacy Networks in International Politics*, Ithaca, NY: Cornell University Press, 1998.

6 See Michelle Carmody, *Human Rights, Transitional Justice and the Reconstruction of Political Order in Latin America*, New York: Palgrave, 2018.

7 For the reimagining of US political identity, its place in the world, and foreign policy, see Barbara J. Keys, *Reclaiming American Virtue: The Human Rights Revolution of the 1970s*, Cambridge, MA: Harvard University Press, 2014; Mark Philip Bradley, *The World Reimagined:*

Americans and Human Rights in the Twentieth Century, Cambridge, UK: Cambridge University Press, 2016.

8 In Argentina, for example, activists seeking information about the whereabouts and fate of the victims had placed an advertisement in a major newspaper that asked the regime "Where are our children? All we ask is the truth!" alongside the names of 136 disappeared family members. *La Nación*, 10 December 1977.

9 Decreto Supremo no. 355 (Chile), "Crea Comisión de Verdad y Reconciliación," 25 April 1990.

10 Project on Justice in Times of Transition, "Reconciliation in Times of Transition" conference report, San Salvador, 11–12 January 1993.

11 For the milieu centered on ideas about transition and the "third wave" democratization theory, see Arthur, "How Transitions Shaped Human Rights," 343–8, and Guilhot, *The Democracy Makers*, pp. 134–65.

12 This debate began at a 1988 conference sponsored by the Aspen Institute and continued in the pages of the *Yale Law Journal* in 1991 and at a larger conference sponsored by the Charter 77 Foundation in 1992. The main results of the second conference were subsequently published in Kritz, *Transitional Justice*.

13 Karen Engle, "Anti-Impunity and the Turn to Criminal Law in Human Rights," *Cornell Law Review*, 2015, vol. 100, 1080–4.

14 See Peter Lambert and Andrew Nickson (eds.), *The Transition to Democracy in Paraguay*, New York: Palgrave, 1997.

15 "Archivos y calabazos aún se encuentran igual que antaño," *ABC Color*, 17 December 1992, 8; "Informes indican que aún se espía a la ciudadanía," *ABC Color*, 18 December 1992, 3.

16 Comité de Iglesias, *Serie Nunca Mas: Testimonio de la represión política en Paraguay 1954–1974* (1990–1); Centro de Estudios Paraguayos Antonio Guasch (CEPAG), *El Precio de la Paz* (1991).

17 Javier Couso, "The Transformation of Constitutionalist Discourse and the Judicialization of Politics in Latin America," in Javier Couso, Alexandra Huneeus, and Rachel Sieder (eds.) *Cultures of Legality: Judicialization and Political Activism in Latin America*, Cambridge, UK: Cambridge University Press, 2010, pp. 146–8; Jose Augustín Fernandez, interview with author, 6 July 2016, Asunción.

18 Luis María Benítez, "La Acción de Hábeas Data en el Derecho Paraguayo," *Ius et Praxis*, 1997, vol. 3, 108; CIDSEP, *Hacía una Constitución Democrática para le Paraguay. Proyectos y Fundamentos*, Asunción, 1992.

19 Benítez, "La Acción de Hábeas Data," 108; Article 136, Chapter IV, Constitution of Paraguay, 1992.

20 Andrew Nickson, "Corruption and the Transition," in Lambert and Nickson, *The Transition to Democracy in Paraguay*, p. 33.

21 The "judicialization of politics" has been identified by scholars of Latin American legal cultures, and refers to "the expansion of judicial power into domains formerly left to the executive and legislative branches." Couso, "The Transformation of Constitutionalist Discourse," p. 142.

22 Fernandez, interview.

23 Peter Lambert, "Assessing the Transition," in Lambert and Nickson, *The Transition to Democracy in Paraguay*, p. 208.

24 Fernandez, interview.

25 Quoted in Myrian González Vera, "Los Archivos del Terror del Paraguay: La historia oculta de la repression," in Ludmila da Silva Catela and Elizabeth Jelín (eds.) *Los Archivos de la Represión: Documentos, memoria y verdad*, Buenos Aires: Siglo XXI, 2002, p. 99.

26 "Demandan al Gobierno garantías para los 'archivos del horror,'" *ABC Color*, 5 January 1993.

27 "Vendrá una commission de DD.HH," *ABC Color*, 29 January 1993.

28 Comisión Permanente de Defensa de los Derechos Humanos, quoted in González Vera, "Los Archivos del Terror del Paraguay," 100.

29 "Piden que se declare patrimonio nacional al 'archivo del terror,'" *ABC Color*, 5 March 1993.

30 Quoted in Myrian González Vera, "Archivos del Terror del Paraguay: velos que desnudan la dictadura stronista," in María Graciela Acuña F. et al. (eds.) *Archivos y memoria de la represión en América Latina (1973–90)*, Santiago: LOM Ediciones, 2016, p. 80.

31 "Paraguay aceptó jurisdicción de la Corte Interamericana de DD.HH," *ABC Color*, 3 January 1993.
32 "Vendrá una commission de DD.HH," *ABC Color*, 29 January 1993.
33 In 1986 the Inter-American Commission for Human Rights stated in its annual report that families of victims had "an inalienable right to know the truth about past events ... in order to prevent the repetition of such acts in the future," while two years later the Inter-American Court found that it was the state's responsibility to investigate in order to provide families with this information. Interamerican Commission on Human Rights, *Annual Report 1985–1986*, OEA/Ser.L/V/II.68 Doc. 8 rev. 1, 26 September 1986, p. 205; Inter-American Court of Human Rights, Velasquez Rodriguez case, Judgement of 29 July 1988 (Ser. C) n. 4 (1988). For the rise of impunity as a concern see Engle, "Anti-Impunity and the Turn to Criminal Law."
34 Subcommission on the Prevention of Discrimination and Protection of Minorities, United Nations Commission on Human Rights, "Study Concerning the Right to Restitution, Compensation and Rehabilitation for Victims of Gross Violations of Human Rights and Fundamental Freedoms," E/CN.4/Sub.2/1993/8, 2 July 1993.
35 Ley 1.099/97 "Que establece la obligatoriedad del depósito de los Documentos Oficiales en el Archivo General de la Nación," 25 August 1997. Article 7 reads: "The documents in the use of the Judicial Branch known as the 'Archive of Terror,' previously ordered and classified, shall be transferred to the National Archive."
36 Rosa Palau, Interview with author, 8 June 2016, Asunción.
37 While criminal justice remained important, as reflected in the 1998 arrest of former Chilean dictator Augusto Pinochet in London, this form of justice was no longer seen as sufficient to prevent recurrence.
38 Alain Touraine, "Democracy in the Light of Dictatorship," *UNESCO Courier*, July/August 2000, vol. 53, 11.
39 Ibid.
40 "Touraine y la memoria histórica," *BBC World*, 30 October 2002.
41 Diane Orentlicher, "'Settling Accounts' Revisited: Reconciling Global Norms with Local Agency," *International Journal of Transitional Justice*, 2007, vol. 1, 16, 19; See also *Independent Study on Best Practices, Including Recommendations, to Assist States in Strengthening their Domestic Capacity to Combat all Aspects of Impunity, By Professor Diane Orentlicher*, UN Doc. E/CN.4/2004/88, 27 February 2004.
42 *Report of the Independent Expert to Update the Set of Principles to Combat Impunity, Diane Orentlicher*, UN Doc. E/CN.4/2005/102/Add.1, 8 February 2005, p. 7.
43 Orentlicher, "'Settling Accounts' Revisited," 18–19.
44 See for example Naomi Roht-Arraza and Javier Mariezcurrena (eds.), *Transitional Justice in the Twenty-First Century: Beyond Truth versus Justice*, Cambridge, UK: Cambridge University Press, 2006.
45 Decreto 1259/2003 (Argentina), "Archivo Nacional de la Memoria. Creación. Objetivos. Actividades fundamentales," *Boletín Oficial* 17 December 2003.
46 Archivo Nacional de Memoria, Fondo Institutional, Secretaría de Derechos Humanos, "Informe de Gestión. 2003–2005," 11.
47 See Proyecto de Ley, El Senado y Cámara de Diputados de la Nación Argentina, "Crease el 'Archivo Nacional de Documentos para la Defensa y el Resguardo del Derecho a la Verdad," 5 November 1997, Ref. 5565-D-97.
48 "Palabras del Presidente Néstor Kirchner en el Acto de Presentación del Archivo de la Memoria, 16 December 2003," *Discursos del Señor Presidente de la Nación, Dr. Néstor Kirchner*, Buenos Aires: Ministerio del Interior, 2003.
49 Decreto 1259/2003 (Argentina), "Archivo Nacional de la Memoria. Creación. Objetivos. Actividades fundamentales," *Boletín Oficial* 17/12/2003.
50 In addition to the files from the truth commission, the Human Rights Secretariat held other testimonies that it had received following the end of the Commission's work, as well as the documentation belonging to the Comisión Nacional por el Derecho a la Identidad (National Commission on the Right to Identity, CONADI), the deaths registry from during the dictatorship, and the documentation produced by the reparations program. All of this material was passed on to the Archivo Nacional de Memoria, which was itself a dependency of the Secretariat.

51 The amnesties preventing criminal prosecution were still in effect when Kirchner came to the presidency, but he encouraged the Supreme Court to overturn them as unconstitutional, which they did in 2005.
52 "El Archivo de Nunca Más (Interview with Carlos Lafforgue and Judith Said)," *Puentes*, 2004, vol. 12, 7.
53 Mariana Nazar, Interview with author, Buenos Aires, June 2016.
54 "El Archivo de Nunca Más (Interview with Carlos Lafforgue and Judith Said)," *Puentes*, 2004, vol. 12, 9.
55 Said, Interview.
56 Ibid.
57 Karen Faulk, *In the Wake of Neoliberalism: Citizenship and Human Rights in Argentina*, Palo Alto, CA: Stanford University Press, 2012.
58 Said, Interview.
59 Ibid.
60 Corte Suprema de Justicia (Paraguay), Resolución n. 1097, 24 April 2007.
61 Palau, interview
62 "Nunca más el discurso único," *Pagina 12*, 28 March 2004.
63 Archivo Nacional de Memoria, Mabel Gutierrez Collection, Box 2, Minutes, Ad Hoc Committee.
64 Archives for Truth, Justice and Memory in the Struggle Against State Terrorism, Archivo Nacional de Memoria, Institutional collection, "Human Rights Documentary Heritage 1976–83," Argentine submission to UNESCO Memory of the World register, Ref. 2006–40.

33

EMOTION IN THE HISTORY OF HUMAN RIGHTS

A case study of the Canadian Museum for Human Rights

Christine Lavrence

Introduction

The Canadian Museum for Human Rights (CMHR) opened in the fall of 2014 in the prairie city of Winnipeg and claims to be the first museum in the world to make the meaning, history, and practice of human rights its primary object. While there have been other museums that thematize specific historical instances where human rights have been violated, such as slavery or the Holocaust, or that use specific historical examples to facilitate broader discussions about the importance of human rights, the CMHR is unique in its mandate. Contrast, for example, the World Centre for Peace, Freedom and Human Rights. It thematizes Verdun as a symbol of French–German reconciliation, memorializes World War I and explores the impact of war and conflict more generally on human rights. The mandate of the CMHR is broader and more ambitious: it explores human rights as a historical construct that has become the world's primary and guiding model of justice, both as it relates to the Canadian context and globally. In its own words, the CMHR describes itself as "the first museum solely dedicated to the evolution, celebration and future of human rights. Our aim is to build not only a national hub for human rights learning and discovery, but a new era of global human rights leadership."[1]

While the CMHR aims to educate visitors about the development of the concept of human rights and its transnational and Canadian applications, it also provides visitors with an "experience" designed to "inspire" and produce deeper, emotional levels of identification with and commitment to the human rights project. The CMHR aims to instruct through emotion and as such, raises questions about the new genre of human rights museums that has emerged in recent decades, focusing on specific examples of human rights violations – slavery, war, genocide – and in some cases using these examples to generate broader discussions about human rights. These human rights museums play an important, custodial role in cultivating what Terence Duffy argues can be described as "a human rights culture" that has emerged and been consolidated in the last few decades.[2] Moreover, the CMHR and human rights museums more generally raise questions about how human rights have transformed museological practice and are linked to what has been called the "new museology."[3] While traditional museology focused on the display and preservation of artifacts of the past, the new museum has a more activist orientation, focuses less on objects and more on ideas, and aims to "inspire" actors rather than inform them, and as such, to build moral capacity in addition to historical knowledge.[4] Reflecting this new paradigm of museology are key terms such as "hope," "empowerment," and emotions; historical ambiguities become heightened and human subjects are understood as "vulnerable" and "self-reflective."[5] The mandate of the human rights museum therefore is to teach us to invest in human rights through an appeal to emotions, and is reflected in these new museological methods.

Given that the new museum offers its visitors an "experience" instead of merely information, historiographical methodologies that are more closely aligned with non-official forms of memory become more common. This museology is less confident of its own institutional practices and will often question the "epistemological status of artifacts" and how its own practices of display and evidence are situated in broader historical and institutional relations of power.[6] As such, museums increasingly foreground survivor testimonials, personal experiences, and belongings, in the attempt to animate and personalize abstract historical data. History on display is driven by a pedagogical and curatorial sensibility that encourages visitors to develop affective investments in the information. The emphasis on experience and empathy is motivated by the activist mission of human rights museums and the awareness that "mere knowledge about the past might not suffice to prevent violent histories from happening again."[7] As such, the new museum has become "the harbinger of the new" rather than the guardian of the past.[8] Rather than preserving a lost past, the concern is crafting a better future. It is within this context that the human rights museum as a new genre and a distinctive museological practice has emerged and become popularized since the 1980s.

This essay argues that the CMHR instructs through an appeal to emotion as much as it does through historical knowledge. Historian Lynn Hunt has attempted to link the history of the human rights framework as it has emerged in the North Atlantic with a social history of emotions, in particular with emotions like Christian pity, compassion, and empathy.[9] The CMHR maps out a version of human rights culture that is deeply resonant in contemporary Canada, emphasizing individual autonomy, empathy, and suffering, which are central to the emotional norms of Western culture. In the North Atlantic context, where personal suffering has become increasingly generative of legal and political entitlements, and rights-based claims are often made through a language of psychological recognition and trauma, transnational practices of human rights advocacy and culture increasingly emphasize suffering and emotions, particularly empathy. This essay explores how the human rights framework presented in the CMHR reflects this shift and is articulated through narrative structures of empathy. The CMHR provides a case study for thinking about how the new genre of human rights museums emphasizes experience and emotion over historical knowledge, reflecting contemporary human rights culture. While, as Larissa Wodtke points out, the narratives of hope articulated at the CMHR pose the risk of "defusing" critique, there is also the possibility according to Angela Failler for a "version of hope" where "the future is held open to change through critical and unsettling engagements."[10] The narrative of empathy that underpins the human rights project at the CMHR will be explored in what follows.

This essay is based on two key sociological methodologies: textual analysis of written materials and observations visiting the museum. First, it undertakes a textual analysis of the materials within the museum. It examines the texts, artifacts, and digital materials presented in the exhibitions in order to identify their dominant terms, themes, and patterns. The essay also examines the official materials produced for public consumption beyond what is found in the museum, such as its website, the report that was issued by the museum after consultations with the Canadian public about the museum's content, the public activities that the CMHR facilitates, the blogs it produces, and the archives that it is developing. The purpose of focusing on the official discourse of the museum is to understand how the museum understands itself and its mission, how it constructs a broader narrative about human rights, and how it positions Canada within this narrative.

The second empirical layer of this study is observation undertaken during several visits to the museum between 2015 and 2017, in order to think about what it is like to visit the museum, experience the exhibitions, and participate in its guided tours and interactive activities. If, as previously mentioned, the mandate of the museum is experiential rather than merely educational, this methodological approach adds an important layer to this study. In addition to the content of the exhibits, I explore the architectural design of the CMHR, because the architecture is not merely functional or aesthetic but an active part of the narrative produced about human rights and the overall experience generated for visitors. The combination therefore of textual and experiential methodologies provides the empirical basis for this study and allows us to probe the museum's mission and its relationship to human rights culture and advocacy. These two modes of analysis allow us to consider both the official version of the museum – that is, how the museum understands its mission – and the experiential. This essay will begin with an exploration of the history of the CMHR and the historically charged debates that it triggered, and then turn to an analysis of the content, self-representation, and architectural design of the museum.

Designing the Canadian Museum for Human Rights: debates and context

The Canadian Museum for Human Rights was the idea of Israel (Izzy) Asper, a wealthy Canadian philanthropist based in the city of Winnipeg, who initially had the idea of creating a museum that explored the Holocaust in the Canadian context. Asper had been involved with a program that sent Canadian youth to the Holocaust Memorial Museum in Washington, and was keen to develop a similar initiative relevant to the Canadian context. Dating back to the 1990s there had been discussions about creating a national Holocaust museum that ultimately lost momentum because the government at the time had concerns about the divisiveness the plan had unleashed. Many immigrant groups, notably Canadian Ukrainians and Armenians, immediately opposed the idea of a Holocaust museum; they favored a broader genocide museum that emphasized many examples of genocide in a comparative and horizontal fashion. In time, the vision shifted: while it was to include a gallery on the Holocaust, the CMHR indeed became transformed into something "well beyond a genocide museum."[11] As the project developed through fundraising initiatives and public debate, the formal mandate of the museum became more ambitious. It rejected the idea of serving only to commemorate human rights violations and developed instead future-oriented, aspirational goals. In its final version, in its own words, the CMHR offered an exploration of "the issue of human rights with special but not exclusive reference to Canada" and sought to "contribute to the sense of collective memory and national identity of all Canadians."[12] The initiative to build the museum was announced to the public on 17 April 2003, the 21st anniversary of the Canadian Charter of Rights and Freedoms, a gesture that solidified this new direction.

The construction of the museum was funded through a combination of private donation and support from federal, provincial and municipal levels of government. As the project grew in scale, so did its costs, and it was finally decided that annual operating costs were to be funded by the federal government. In 2008 the Canadian parliament passed a bill that formally transformed the CMHR into a national museum – which raised questions about the museum's ability to fulfill its human rights mandate, given that close alignment with the federal government. For instance, as a national museum, its chair of the board is appointed by the prime minister, at the time Stephen Harper. Moreover, as a publicly funded institution, the importance of public opinion is magnified so that as Canadian heritage minister James Moore declared, the museum came to be tasked with being a "forum for unity and conversation" because "taxpayers are not going to pump in $21 million a year to operate this museum if they see it as a perpetual source of division for … the people of Canada."[13] The museum therefore came to be at risk of reproducing familiar national narratives rather than unsettling them. It is a site where consensus is sought, such that many of the pressing and deeply rooted issues that trouble Canada's settler-colonial and deeply multicultural landscape remain off limits. In the genocide gallery for instance, content is limited to state-sanctioned understandings of genocides, such that the five genocides that are officially recognized by the Canadian government are the only ones featured: the Holocaust and the Rwandan, Armenian, and Bosnian (Srebrenica) genocides, as well as the Ukrainian Holomodor.[14]

The tensions between the museum's state and activist purposes were inscribed into the governance and funding structures of the museum, and discussions about the design and content of the museum were especially fractious. In 2009, a Content Advisory Committee formed to consult with the Canadian public on what a Canadian human rights museum should cover. The committee, consisting of human rights activists and lawyers, traveled across Canada and conducted roundtable discussions, collected video testimony of individuals, held open meetings in public forums across Canada, such as libraries and community centers, and targeted specific communities by invitation that the committee felt were especially important to Canadian history. The meetings were held in urban centers across Canada; people living in rural and remote locations, many of whom are Indigenous, were invited to contribute by phone or email, although the report admits that the vast majority of input came from the face-to-face process. In total, the committee held 357 meetings and consulted with a total of 1,222 people.[15] The result was a 100-page document summarizing the findings. It was clear from this process that Canadians preferred a museum of social history instead of elite and institutional versions, and that there was considerable disagreement regarding what should be included in the museum, how space should be parceled out, how decisions should be made, and whether communities donating funds to the museum should be able to influence the content of the exhibits.[16] The process of designing the museum unleashed a fractious debate, resulting in what one critic described as an "unseemly competition" among communities regarding who had suffered the most and whose suffering deserved the most recognition as well as space and prestige in the design of the museum.[17]

Controversy over the museum's content followed two main fault lines. First, a protracted and historically charged debate between Jewish Canadian and Ukrainian Canadian associations was triggered by discussions of museum designs.[18] As Ira Basen has pointed out, the "roots" of this conflict refer to the end of World War Two when the Canadian government allegedly allowed hundreds of Ukrainians who had been part of the Ukrainian Division of the Waffen SS to immigrate to Canada.[19] In 1985, the government established the Deschênes Commission to investigate possible Nazi criminals who had received Canadian citizenship after the end of the war. Given the advanced age and in many cases poor health of suspects, lack of international cooperation, and rigorous evidentiary standards, the process did not result in any convictions and left a wound between Jewish Canadian and Ukrainian–Canadian communities that was reopened in the CMHR consultation process. Historian Dirk Moses has pointed out that the Ukrainian immigrant communities in the CMHR debate reflected the "double-genocide thesis," which claims that the Jewish and Slavic peoples of the region were subjected to Nazi and Soviet violence in equal measures, and that has animated the memory politics in recent years in the Baltics and east-central Europe.[20] This thesis has mobilized the Ukrainian Canadian community in recent years, leading it to push for more recognition of Soviet crimes not just in reference to the CMHR but also the construction of a national memorial to the victims of communism.

Ukrainian associations strongly opposed the centrality of the Holocaust to the original design and conceptualization of the museum. Ukrainian associations' responses aligned themselves with two positions: one advocated a Holodomor gallery of equal size to the Holocaust gallery, and another proposed a series of galleries that would present a cross section of genocides comparatively and horizontally.[21] Ukrainian groups were accused of inflating the numbers of the Holodomor victims and minimizing Ukraine's involvement in the Holocaust. A broader debate emerged about the uniqueness of the Holocaust, its role in the formation of the human rights frameworks, and its usefulness as a paradigmatic example of state-sponsored violence.[22] In the spirit of compromise, the size and importance of the Holocaust gallery gradually shrank, but the narrative of the Holocaust as catalyst for the contemporary global human rights system was preserved in the final version of the museum. The museum arguably never recovered from these bitter debates. These divisions illustrate the fractious nature of Canadian multicultural memory that is arguably mitigated or managed through a Canadian human rights narrative that focuses more on individual rights instead of group grievances.

The second fault line was in relation to the settler-colonialism of Canada. Most tellingly, First Nation voices, whose grievances are so deeply fused with the legitimacy of the Canadian state, were absent from these debates about the Holocaust gallery and more generally from debates about the treatment of multiple, sometimes competing, historical grievances in the context of the multicultural nation that is Canada. As a museum of human rights located in the Canadian context, the CMHR must grapple with what the 1996 Royal Commission on Aboriginal Peoples called the "fundamental contradiction at the heart of Canada."[23] Canada's global reputation as a human rights leader is difficult to reconcile with its founding and ongoing colonial violence towards its Indigenous peoples. While there was discussion with Indigenous elders and a general commitment to "decoloniz[ing] the way Indigenous peoples are consulted with and represented in the museum,"[24] the museum has been controversial among Indigenous peoples for several reasons. The location of the museum itself, at the intersection of the Assiniboine and the Red rivers, a site in Winnipeg known as "The Forks," is on Treaty I Territory. It is a historically important site for Canada's Indigenous people, a sacred space that has traditionally been the site for peace meetings and trade for 6,000 years.[25] During the period of colonial settlement, "The Forks" was central site of the fur trade. In recent years the site has been reinvented as the tourist and commercial center of the city. In the rush to appropriate this site and its symbolic value as a "national metaphor" of trade and intercultural contact, fuller discussions about the appropriateness of the site were foreclosed.[26] Considered one of the most significant and densely concentrated archaeological sites in the province of Manitoba and the nation, with estimates that it contains over 1 million artifacts, exploratory archaeological digs undertaken between 2008 and 2012 produced highly significant findings.[27] Despite these findings, the plans to build the museum on the site went ahead. The CMHR website explains that after consulting Indigenous Elders, with "their advice, medicine bags were deposited into holes dug for concrete piles and caissons, to show respect and honour the earth."[28] While Indigenous activists protested the opening of the museum in Winnipeg in 2014, they were often focused on current living conditions rather than the representation of historical issues in the museum. For example, a critical issue for Indigenous peoples in Canada continues to be access to clean drinking water. Shoal Lake 40 First Nation provides drinking water for the city of Winnipeg, including the CMHR, but has been on a boil-water advisory since 1997. To protest the opening of the museum, Shoal Lake 40 organized guided tours to the reserve as a "Living Museum" dedicated to current human rights violations.[29]

The CMHR opened in 2014, as the last phase of the Truth and Reconciliation Commission of Canada (TRC) was being completed. The TRC began in 2008. It was mandated by the Indian Residential Schools Settlements Agreement to document what happened during the residential school system and the impact on Indigenous communities and children who were taken away from their cultures and homes, including the abuse to which they were subjected. The Commission gathered evidence from 6,000 survivors over the course of six years, has generated an archive of testimonials, and issued a final report in 2015, naming the Indian Residential Schools system an instrument of "cultural genocide." The report mapped out a series of recommendations in order to facilitate a process of "reconciliation" between Indigenous and non-Indigenous peoples as well as the Canadian state, with the United Nations (UN) Declaration on the Rights of Indigenous Peoples (2007) as its guiding framework. The TRC's 94 guiding principles and "Calls to Action" emphasize human rights, the status of Indigenous people as the original peoples of Canada, the right to self-determination, socioeconomic and health equity, and respect for treaties, to name a few key themes.[30] The Calls to Action also discuss memorial practices and recommend a review of museum and archival policies to bring them into line with the UN Declaration on the Rights of Indigenous Peoples and the UN Joinet-Orentlicher Principles. The 150th anniversary of Canada was celebrated in 2017, which was branded by the federal government as "Canada150," and the memory was articulated and organized around this notion of "reconciliation" and Canada's commitment as a global human rights leader. The Calls to Action recommended that in anticipation of the 150th anniversary of Canada in 2017 a fund be established for commemorative projects on the theme of reconciliation. The Calls to Action issuing from the TRC also addressed the CMHR specifically and asked that the museum "not simply tell one party's version of the past" but instead represent "the history of residential schools and Aboriginal peoples in ways that invite multiple, sometimes conflicting, perspectives, yet ultimately facilitate empathy, mutual respect and a desire for reconciliation that is rooted in justice."[31]

As a result of the TRC, the negotiation of the legacy of Canada's settler-colonialism between Indigenous peoples and the state has been framed in terms of "reconciliation," that is, through an affective and therapeutic language. As expressed in the TRC Final

Report, "Reconciliation is a process of healing of relationships that requires public truth sharing, apology, and commemoration that acknowledge and redress past harms."[32] The emphasis on "reconciliation" is implicitly therapeutic in orientation, organized around a notion of "healing," which Indigenous scholars and critics point out poses the risk of historicizing the Indian Residential School system, such that colonial violence is positioned in the past rather than continuing, and is understood as isolated events rather than as part of a broader system of assimilation. Moreover, framing injuries to the Indigenous community in psychological terms produces solutions that are articulated through a "politics of recognition" and understood as a therapeutic encounter, which Glen Coulthard and others have criticized as symbolic and affective in nature and lacking deeper, structural reach.[33] Indigenous scholar Dian Million argues that this approach produces a "wounded subjectivity," whereby Indigenous peoples are "thickly ensconced in the intensities, logics and languages of trauma, particularly now as they are called on to speak as subjects of 'truth and reconciliation.'"[34] Million argues that "healing" is a political practice situated both in Indigenous practices of justice but also in a neoliberal biopolitics that medicalizes the process and positions the trauma victim as in need of management, a strategy has the capacity to both help and hinder Indigenous self-determination. The CHMR opened its doors at a moment when Canada's global rights record arguably has been in decline. This has been signaled through events such as the boycott of the 2001 World Conference on Racism in Durbin, South Africa, and the passage of the Anti-Terrorism Act (2015), which broadens the powers of the Canadian Security Intelligence Service and facilitates information sharing among security agencies. The UN Human Rights Council and Canadian civil rights organizations criticized its passage. Altogether, the political context of the CMHR is rife with complexity at both the national and international level.

Inside the museum

When the CMHR finally opened its doors on 20 September 2014, the Can$350 million building met mixed reviews, largely because of its architectural monumentality and the relentless use of metaphor in its design. The building is imposing and as ambitious as the idea of the human rights project itself. On the exterior of the building are four large stone structures serving as roots, symbolizing a connection with the earth and with Indigenous grasses planted throughout to represent all "children of the earth."[35] The museum takes the visitor on "journey" of the history of human rights, through a series of ascending galleries and moving toward the highest point of the museum. There is only one way to travel through all the galleries, so that the architecture reflects the idea that there is only one human rights journey. As such, a teleological narrative about human rights unfolds in the gallery. The journey from a "dark, cavernous" origin takes visitors upwards toward a glass structure called the "Tower of Hope," a 100-meter glass structure at the building's apex.[36] The tower was the explicit wish of Izzy Asper and resisted by many of the architects because of its clichéd symbolism. From the exterior of the building, through "The Cloud," a glass façade designed to resemble a peace dove from some outside perspectives is visible.[37] The journey through the museum is physically and emotionally demanding. It consists of a long walk through the galleries on a gradual upward slope through a series of events that help visitors understand what human rights are, how human rights formed, and what is at stake in their violation.

In addition to the historical story produced in the museum, there are affective and emotional undertones that arguably foreground a narrative of empathy and hope that has become highly salient in Canadian political and human rights discourse.[38] This is not necessarily a new development; human rights ideology has a long history of being linked with forms of compassion. For example, historian Lynn Hunt links American and French rights-based declarations in 1776 and 1789, European penal reform, anti-torture efforts, and slavery abolitionism with the emergence of new aesthetic literary forms in the eighteenth-century Atlantic context that, she argues, reflected an expanding capacity for empathy. She links this new rights sensibility with the contemporaneous popularity of epistolary novels in Europe that thematized the interior lives of female protagonists and allowed people to develop more imaginative forms of sympathy and an enhanced appreciation of personal and bodily autonomy.[39] Hunt's work flags the historical relationship between empathy and human rights ideology, and offers some context for the ways in which the CMHR engages the broader public through an affective vocabulary.

In its own words, the CMHR describes its mandate in experiential and affective terms, taking visitors on a "journey of inspiration" where they will be "moved by the power of human rights."[40] It aims to create a "safe and engaging space to cultivate respect, gratitude, understanding and ongoing improvement of this human rights inheritance."[41] Visitors are addressed as the ethical and "compassionate Canadians" they believe themselves to be, confirming comforting notions of national identity that are typical of a national museum.[42] The goal is to produce an emotional connection between visitors and the material, and to facilitate what Jennifer Carter has called the "empathetic communities" at the heart of the museum's mission.[43] Empathy, as cultural studies scholar Carolyn Pedwell has pointed out, has recently begun to be understood as a political practice in the North Atlantic, and has become instrumentalized in that it is understood as a tool for social and political transformation.[44] In other words, the assumption is that empathy is what is needed in order to build support of human rights. This helps to account for why the CMHR appeals to emotion as well as building historical knowledge.

The alabaster ramp leads visitors through a narrative arc that begins with stories of suffering, violence and violation and passes through to stories of emerging philosophical and political structures of human rights advocacy, intervention, resistance, and personal agency. The CMHR describes the architectural design as symbolizing the journey from "darkness to light" and describes "the brightness of enlightenment" [as] the goal of the human rights journey, reminding the visitor of "the power and necessity of hope and tolerance."[45] The architecture and design of the galleries leads visitors through a journey of ascension that is supposed to be enlightening, educational, therapeutic, and morally transformative.[46] A Eurocentric and teleological story of progress and Western enlightenment becomes difficult to avoid.[47] As Christopher Powell has written, the journey begins in the Indigenous Gallery "in the earth, in darkness and savagery, and proceeds up into the sky and light and hope" towards the apex of Western civilization, where "human rights appear as a mark of superior cultural achievement."[48]

After entering the dark and cavernous ground floor of the museum, visitors begin the journey through the ten main galleries featured in the museum. The journey through the galleries follows a series of alabaster ramps that are lit from within. As the website indicates, the "ramps of glowing alabaster that criss-cross galleries are designed to challenge, motivate and uplift."[49] During a guided tour in the winter of 2017, the museum guide explained to the group that alabaster was selected as the primary material for the ramps because in addition to its aesthetic appeal, the stone is considered to have healing and therapeutic properties. The translucent appearance of alabaster is said to represent purity. As the museum path moves along the trajectory toward hope, the first gallery begins with the general question "What are human rights?" It features a loose chronology of 100 human rights "moments" from across the globe. Collectively, these avoid making any stronger claims that could trigger academic debates about the term "human rights." The "Indigenous Perspectives" gallery follows and explores how Indigenous peoples of Canada conceptualize rights within their own frameworks. Mirroring the ways in which the Canadian state has issued reparations for Indian Residential School survivors, official apologies, and organized the TRC under the broader umbrella of "reconciliation," since the 1990s attention has been paid to Indigenous people in Canadian museums. As Tricia Logan has argued, the representation of Indigenous peoples has been traditionally dominated by the "salvage paradigm," in which museums display the objects and artifacts of "dying race[s]" "plundered" from the colonies, as fragments of an "authentic" and "pre-modern" past.[50] The Indigenous Perspectives gallery is a departure from that mode of representation, in that it attempts to explore Indigenous perspectives on rights, the diversity of Indigenous cultures, and the work of Indigenous artists. The emphasis therefore is on Indigenous resilience and the "profiling [of] Indigenous perspectives as living, breathing, contemporary ways of knowing and being."[51] There is a 360-degree film featuring the oral tradition of some Indigenous-centered notions of rights, and there is also a window and the only terrace in the museum, off the Indigenous gallery, which symbolizes the link to land. The window faces the distant Saint Boniface Cathedral, an important site in Canadian historical memory that signals Indigenous resistance, as it is the burial place of Louis Riel, who led the Métis rebellions against the Canadian state after confederation in 1867.

While the Indigenous gallery aims to celebrate Indigenous resilience, it stops short of fully recognizing the violence and oppression still experienced by Indigenous peoples, and it does not position this violence as systemic and intrinsic to the broader logic of settler-colonialism. Rather, the human rights violations that are singled out in the exhibitions on the Indian Residential School system, or the thousands of Indigenous women who are missing or whose murders remain unsolved, are presented as anomalous tragedies rather than systemic and reflective of the broader, ongoing power relations constitutive of colonialism.[52] Deeper, more critical questions remain unasked because of the museum's refusal to address Canada's treatment of Indigenous peoples through what Rita Kaur Dhamoon has called an "ontology of genocide."[53] Reflecting this limitation, the word "genocide" was banned from Indigenous exhibits. This caused one of the most contentious debates, and involved First Nations advocating the use of this term. CMHR spokesperson Angela Cassie's response reflected the conservatism of a federally funded museum when she stated, "We are not a court. We are not an academic institution. We rely on those sources for information to inform our exhibits."[54] The museum announced in May 2019 however that they have reconsidered their position on the use of the term: Louise Waldman, the CMHR's manager of marketing stated "we recognize as a museum that our lack of clear acknowledgement of the genocide against Indigenous Peoples has caused hurt, and we've listened and we are working to do better."[55]

The narrative continues in a third gallery called "Canadian Journeys." It is a large circular room featuring interactive digital exhibits on a variety of historical and contemporary cases of human rights violations in Canada, such as the internment of Japanese Canadians in World War II, the conditions of migrant farm workers in the Canadian agricultural sector, and the exploitation of Chinese workers in the building of the Canadian Pacific Railway, to name a few. The visitor walks around the perimeter of the circular space and engages with these various small exhibits. These cases of rights violations are treated as "missteps on the road to greater rights for everyone in Canada,"[56] that is, as anomalous moments in the Canadian story of human rights. How these events might be linked with systemic inequities related to race, economic structures, imperialism, and colonialism, rather than moments where Canada, so to speak, dropped the ball, is not articulated in the museum. Instead, and in keeping with the liberal humanism underpinning human rights ideology, the emphasis is on Canadian law as the foundation of human rights and individual rights. Law is represented in one gallery through the metaphor of a tree – hence a continuously evolving and organic entity.

Consistent with the new museological practices that characterize the human rights museum genre, including instruction through an appeal to emotion, there are very few actual historical artifacts at the CMHR. Instead, the museum foregrounds survivor narratives that are communicated through digital media, much of it interactive, and in the idiom of contemporary culture. At a moment in Canada when interest in historical modes of memory transmission is low and enrollment in history programs in Canadian universities has dropped dramatically, the attempt to generate identification with and emotional investment in human rights history relies on the use of digital storytelling techniques. These reflect dominant narrative practices in contemporary culture. The CMHR does not conceptualize itself as having a memorializing function, nor does it conceive of itself as a "museum," despite its name, but rather understands itself as an "educational hub."[57] The CMHR animates the past rather than documenting it, through the interactive digital storytelling and also video recordings of personal testimonials. These comprise a significant portion of the gallery content. Rather than looking at artifacts and data, the visitor experiences the personal stories of other ordinary people, allowing the cultivation of the emotional identifications that are at the heart of the CMHR's mission. There are exhibits in which personal testimonials of human rights advocates are showcased on life-sized screens. The person is filmed standing, blinking, breathing, shifting his or her weight from time to time, and waiting for the visitor to press the button that begins the video testimonial. This creates the illusion that the person is standing in front you, telling his or her story, and allows for the humanization of their stories.

The American philosopher Richard Rorty has argued that in the absence of universal moral codes to underpin human rights, an "astonishingly rapid progress of sentiments" in the last two centuries has driven the emergence of rights-based frameworks.[58] The consolidation of the modern human rights system depends on the cultivation of individuals who can respond empathetically to the "sad and sentimental stories" of distant others,[59] primarily through exposure to narratives of suffering in the form of personal testimonials, which is increasingly the medium of human rights advocacy. Sympathy, Rorty claims, is a privilege afforded to those with adequate physical and material security to allow for imagining the suffering of others, such that human rights can only be based on "condescension," where the powerful "ceas[e] to oppress others … out of mere niceness."[60] Emotion, and specifically the empathy of the privileged, is understood here as the primary tool of political change and poses the risk of leaving economic and structural causes of these inequities and human rights violations unquestioned.

The use of metaphor organized around giving the visitor an inspiring, therapeutic, and redemptive experience is encoded throughout the museum's architectural design. After exploring the room devoted to the rule of law in relation to human rights, visitors can spend a few moments in the "Garden of Contemplation," an indoor water garden with reflective pools of water and surrounded by pieces of "Mongolian basalt."[61] The pause in the garden prepares the visitors for the horrors that continue ahead, as the genocide galleries follow.

The Holocaust gallery, "Examining the Holocaust," is, as noted earlier, smaller than originally planned due to the bitter conflicts that emerged. It includes personal narratives, a small selection of artifacts, and a film that illustrates some of the Canadian government's complicity with anti-Semitism during World War II. Following it is a gallery on genocide called "Breaking the Silence," which features interactive digital exhibitions on the five genocides that are formally recognized by the Canadian government: the Armenian genocide, the Holocaust, the Rwandan genocide, Srebrenica, and the Holodomor. Following the narrative arc of the museum, from this point on many of the exhibits turn their attention to the development of the modern political system of human rights, as well as to stories of personal resistance and agency. The CMHR signals this balancing act by explaining that "the struggles and progression of human rights must be expressed with respect for the past, and optimism for the future."[62] The museum now shifts attention to the emergence of the modern human rights system in a gallery called "Turning Points of Humanity," which features a chronology of human rights declarations starting with the 1948 Declaration of Human Rights. Large monitors designed in the form of "open books" present people who have worked to address human rights violations in a variety of contexts. The journey from this point on as visitors ascend is up through the Cloud and the Tower of Hope. Embedded in these parts of the museum is a commitment to the individual as the fundamental holder of rights and agent of change. The next gallery, called "Actions Count," features an interactive game aimed at younger visitors designed to prompt "reflection on how the choices we make in everyday life affect others."[63] The final galleries thematize a variety of contemporary global human rights issues and successes, and a final interactive exhibit invites visitors to "contemplate their our own role in building a better worlds for all people" and to write their parting impressions on a card for others to read.[64]

In the fall of 2015 a traveling interactive exhibit was in the lower gallery of the museum entitled "Experience XOXO: An Exhibit About Love and Forgiveness." It focused on "feelings" designed to foster "a deeper understanding of love and forgiveness and their connection to human rights." The exhibit included a series of activities that encourage children to express themselves, build friendships, show gratitude, and forgive. These activities focused on things like gift-giving, writing letters of gratitude to veterans, doing yoga to develop "self-dignity," and exploring the idea of "masks" and of masking and revealing emotions when engaging with others. The exhibition overall sought to develop emotional literacy and made explicit how, in the Canadian context, emotions are understood as foundational to the human rights project. The CMHR explains motivations behind the exhibition:

> If our children are to become human rights defenders, then we need to teach them compassion. We need to teach them to recognize their feelings and the feelings of others. The intersection of love, forgiveness and human rights is

> crucial for children, and the basic concepts of inclusion, fairness, respect and empathy are the building blocks of human rights.[65]

This statement indicates the centrality of emotions as building blocks of human rights. Indeed, a questionnaire administered by the CMHR to 500 visitors about how the museum impacted their feelings shows that the mission has been accomplished. Some 90 percent of visitors "felt moved" by the content of the museum and 70 percent "left the CMHR feeling more empathy towards others."[66] Measuring and showcasing these results demonstrates that building empathy is a deliberate, core mission of the museum. While linking human rights with emotion is not necessarily new, the emphasis on emotion in contemporary human rights culture can be said to reflect the blurring of humanitarianism and human rights (on both conceptual and concrete levels) in recent decades.[67]

Recent attempts to link human rights history with cultural practices of emotions may partly be understood in the context of epistemological shifts, which complicate the traditional binary between affect and reason. This resonates with neuropsychological research, which has been increasingly locating cognitive and affective processes in shared functions of the brain.[68] The historian Samuel Moyn's argument that the crystallization of human rights ideology in the 1970s replaced revolutionary politics with morally transcendent principles of individual dignity is relevant here.[69] Arguably as human rights frameworks moved away from substantive and collective claims, they began to employ a vernacular of suffering and more explicit reference to emotional and psychological rights, such that in 2011 the UN adopted a resolution making happiness a "fundamental human goal," along with self-esteem, self-respect, personal empowerment, and memory.[70]

Conclusion

The purpose of this essay has been to explore the role of emotion in the CMHR. Not only does the CMHR use emotion to instruct about human rights in order to inspire visitors, it also reflects the greater emphasis on empathy in Canadian political culture and beyond. A reflective emotional literacy is currently seen as foundational to the human rights project. While historians have long attempted to map out the trajectory of rights-based ideologies as they emerged through Western liberal thought and were consolidated through a series of declarations and legal structures, the role of emotion in human rights history has been less explored. This essay argues that contemporary human rights culture, epitomized in the CMHR, dovetails with contemporary forms of museum practice that understand their mandates as providing visitors with an emotionally transformative experience rather than simply displaying evidence of the past. This shift in museum practice, and the emergence of the human rights museum as a distinct museological phenomenon around the same time, should be situated in the context of the popularization of human rights ideology since the late 1970s and, more generally, in the context of the emergence of the therapeutic ethos in Western society.

Not surprisingly, the content of the CMHR's galleries is largely celebratory of the key categories of Western liberalism. Personal choice and agency are highlighted, individual actors and their capacity to make a difference are showcased, and the law is presented as the cornerstone of social justice. Indeed, the emphasis on emotion demonstrates how contemporary liberalism's commitment to individualism underpins the museum's narrative.

Human rights are celebrated as an enlightened and ethical response to suffering, reflecting the assumption that building a culture of empathy is the primary goal and tool of social and political change.[71] Politics is often framed here as a therapeutic encounter between victims and perpetrators (whether as individuals or as states), and political goals are understood in terms of "healing," "reconciliation," and catharsis, and expressed in symbolic gestures that have become popular in Canada, such as formal state apologies, truth and reconciliation commissions, and a booming memorial culture since the 1980s.[72] This is a political ethos that emphasizes the overcoming of personal suffering and trauma. It is replicated in a variety of ways throughout the Canadian human rights system: in how rights are advocated and claimed, how damages are measured and repaired, and how the goal and tools of change are understood and employed. The CMHR is illustrative of this wider national culture.

If, as Richard Rorty argues, contemporary human rights ideology issues out of hope instead of knowledge, then it is not surprising that a human rights museum would be saturated in emotionality. Human rights are a utopic and hopeful practice. Nations and states are deeply grounded in affective experiences of pride, home, and belonging. They build hopeful futures by referencing mythologized pasts, so that national museums dedicated to human rights are doubly implicated in emotionally charged narrative forms. As Failler has argued, striking the right balance between the utopic values implicit to nation-building and the human rights project, the recognition of the scale of suffering and failures, and retaining the critical thinking essential to social change are deep challenges for the CMHR.[73] As one commentator said about the CMHR, "No one wanted a superficial story of redemption and happy endings, because that would be a lie. No one wanted a big house of horrors, either."[74] Avoiding sentimentalizing, monumentalizing, and teleological accounts of human rights remains a central challenge to the ambitious project of writing and commemorating human rights history.

Future research could explore the role of emotion in contemporary human rights culture cross-culturally, tracing more closely and comparatively the cultural practices of emotion as they have developed in relation to human rights museology. The extent to which the link between emotion and human rights in the CMHR reflects a specifically Canadian or Anglo-American therapeutic culture or is reflective of more global trends needs to be explored. Critical questions emerge about framing human rights through empathy: For example, does empathy activate action? Or does it become a substitute for action? Does the emphasis on individual stories and the personal agency of actors within the museology of human rights – however moving, instructive and important – pose the risk of obscuring the historical and structural conditions and systemic colonial practices that rendered these human rights violations possible in the first place? Attending to these tensions and questions is important for mapping out a thoughtful and critical human rights museology, in the CMHR and in the genre more broadly.

Notes

1 "About the Museum." Online. Available at https://humanrights.ca/about (accessed 13 December 2018).

2 Terence Duffy, "Museums of 'Human Suffering' and the Struggle for Human Rights," *Museum International*, 2001, vol. 53, no. 1, 10.

3 Vikki McCall and Clive Gray, "Museums and the 'New Museology': Theory, Practice and Organisational Change," *Museum Management and Curatorship*, 2014, vol. 29, no. 1, 19–35.

4 Stephen Weil, *Rethinking the Museum and Other Meditations*, Washington, DC: Smithsonian Press, 1990.
5 Julia Harrison, "Ideas of Museums in the 1990s," *Museum Management and Curatorship*, 1994, vol. 13, 171.
6 McCall and Clive Gray, "Museums and the 'New Museology'," 20.
7 Jens Andermann and Silke Arnold-de Simine, "Introduction: Memory, Community and the New Museum," *Theory, Culture and Society*, 2012, vol. 29, no. 1, 8.
8 Andermann and Arnold-de Simine, "Introduction," 5.
9 Lynn Hunt, *Inventing Human Rights: A History*, New York: W. W. Norton, 2007.
10 Larissa Wodtke, "A Lovely Building for Difficult Knowledge: The Architecture of the Canadian Museum for Human Rights," *Review of Education, Pedagogy and Cultural Studies*, 2015, vol. 37, no. 2–3, 207–26; Angela Failler, "Hope Without Consolation: Prospects for Critical Learning at the Canadian Museum for Human Rights," *Review of Education, Pedagogy and Cultural Studies*, 2015, vol 37, no. 2–3, 228.
11 See Dirk Moses, "The Canadian Museum for Human Rights: The 'Uniqueness of the Holocaust' and the Question of Genocide," *Journal of Genocide Research*, 2012, vol. 12, no. 2, 224.
12 "About the Museum."
13 James Adams, "Inside the Canadian Museum for Human Rights, the Labyrinth of Conscience," *Globe and Mail*, 19 September 2014. Online. Available at www.theglobeandmail.com/arts/art-and-architecture/inside-the-canadian-museum-for-human-rights-the-labyrinth-of-conscience/article20701809/ (accessed 13 December 2018).
14 Canadian parliament passed the Holocaust Memorial Day Act in 2003. The following year, the government passed a resolution recognizing the extermination of 1.5 million Armenians by the Ottomans. The Armenians were a Christian minority threatened by increasing Turkish homogeneity as the Ottoman Empire was collapsing due to Christian Balkan nations' moves toward independence. The Rwandan genocide was recognized by Canadian parliament in 2008. In the spring of 1994 in Rwanda, the Hutu majority government, working with the Rwandan army and a network of militia organizations massacred 800,000 Tutsi. The Canadian parliament passed the Srebrenica genocide motion in 2015. In July of 1995, 8,000 Bosniak Muslim men and boys were massacred by the Bosnian Serbian Army in the attempt to build an ethnically homogenous Serbian territory during the Bosnian War. Srebrenica had been deemed a UN "safe area" in 2003, under protection by Dutch soldiers. The events there were formally labeled "genocide" by the International Criminal Tribunal for the Former Yugoslavia in 2004. Canada formally recognized the Holodomor as genocide in 2008. This memorialized the death by starvation of between 3 and 8 million Ukrainians in 1932–3. Scholars debate the extent to which mass starvation was the result of a genocidal campaign by Stalin to curb Ukrainian independence or of Stalin's forced agricultural collectivization process.
15 "Content Advisory Committee Final Report to the Canadian Museum for Human Rights," 25 May 2010, p. 9. Online. Available at http://publications.gc.ca/pub?id=9.693794&sl=0 (accessed 13 December 2018).
16 "How Will the Canadian Museum for Human Rights Represent Genocide?" *Armenian Weekly*, 19 February 2012. Online. Available at https://armenianweekly.com/2012/02/19/how-will-the-canadian-museum-for-human-rights-represent-genocide/ (accessed 13 December 2018).
17 Kate Taylor, "Ideas under Glass: As Museums Turn from Artifacts to Stories, Cultural Tensions Arise," *Literary Review of Canada*, 2013. Online. Available at http://reviewcanada.ca/magazine/2013/04/ideas-under-glass/ (accessed 13 December 2018).
18 See Catherine Chatterley, "Canada's Struggle with Holocaust Memorialization: The War Museum Controversy, Ethnic Identity Politics and the Canadian Museum for Human Rights," *Holocaust and Genocide Studies*, 2015, vol. 29, no. 2, 189–211.
19 Ira Basen, "Memory Becomes a Minefield at Canada's Museum for Human Rights," *The Globe and Mail*, 20 August 2011. Online. Available at www.theglobeandmail.com/news/national/memory-becomes-a-minefield-at-canadas-museum-for-human-rights/article555660/?page=all (accessed 13 December 2018).
20 Moses, "The Canadian Museum for Human Rights," 217.
21 Moses, "The Canadian Museum for Human Rights," 229.

22 "Content Advisory Committee Final Report to the Canadian Museum for Human Rights," (25 May 2010), as cited in Moses, "The Canadian Museum for Human Rights," 228.
23 Royal Commission on Aboriginal Peoples, *Report of the Royal Commission on Aboriginal Peoples*, 1996. Online. Available at www.bac-lac.gc.ca/eng/discover/aboriginal-heritage/royal-commission-aboriginal-peoples/Pages/final-report.aspx (accessed 13 December 2018).
24 Tricia Logan, "National Memory and Museums: Remembering Settler Colonial Genocide of Indigenous Peoples in Canada," in Nigel Eltringham and Pam Maclean (eds.) *Remembering Genocide*: New York, Routledge, 2014, p. 122.
25 Logan, "National Memory and Museums," p. 123.
26 Adele Weder, "Faulty Tower: The Canadian Museum for Human Rights as Tourist Trap, Failed Memorial and White Elephant," 29 October 2014. Online. Available at https://thewalrus.ca/faulty-tower/ (accessed 13 December 2013).
27 "CMHR Releases Important Archaeology Findings: New Light Cast on Historical Role of the Forks," 28 August 2013. Online. Available at https://humanrights.ca/about-museum/news/cmhr-releases-important-archaeology-findings-new-light-cast-historic-role-forks (accessed 13 December 2018).
28 Canadian Museum for Human Rights, "Unique Construction." Online. Available at https://humanrights.ca/explore/architecture/unique-construction (accessed 13 December 2018). At the time of going to press, the museum was launching a new website, but the old website, where this text is located, was still available.
29 Erwin Redsky and Cathy Merrick, "For Our First Nations, New Museum a Monument to Hypocrisy," *Globe and Mail*, 25 September 2014. Online. Available at www.theglobeandmail.com/opinion/for-our-first-nations-new-museum-a-monument-to-hypocrisy/article20784499 (accessed 13 December 2018).
30 Truth and Reconciliation Commission of Canada, *Truth and Reconciliation Commission of Canada: Calls to Action*, Winnipeg: Truth and Reconciliation Commission of Canada, 2015. Online. Available at www.trc.ca/websites/trcinstitution/File/2015/Findings/Calls_to_Action_English2.pdf (accessed 13 December 2018).
31 Canadian Museum for Human Rights, "What Every Canadian Should Know About Truth and Reconciliation," 10 November 2015. Online. Available at https://humanrights.ca/blogue/ce-que-tous-les-canadiens-et-toutes-les-canadiennes-doivent-savoir-sur-la-verite-et-la (accessed 13 December 2018).
32 Truth and Reconciliation Commission of Canada, *What We Have Learned: Principles of Truth and Reconciliation*, Winnipeg: Truth and Reconciliation Commission of Canada, 2015. Online. Available at www.trc.ca/websites/trcinstitution/File/2015/Findings/Principles_2015_05_31_web_o.pdf (accessed 13 December 2018).
33 Glen Coulthard, *Red Skins, White Masks: Rejecting the Colonial Politics of Recognition*, Minneapolis: University of Minnesota Press, 2014.
34 Dian Million, *Therapeutic Nations: Healing in an Age of Indigenous Human Rights*, Tucson: University of Arizona Press, 2013, pp. 3, 6.
35 Karen Busby, Adam Muller, and Andrew Woolford, "Introduction," in Karen Busby, Adam Muller, and Andrew Woolford (eds.) *The Idea of a Human Rights Museum*, Winnipeg: University of Manitoba Press, 2015, p. 5.
36 Steve Lambert, "At This Museum, Even the Building Structure is About a Journey to Hope," Winnepeg News, 9 April 2018, www.chrisd.ca/2018/04/09/indigenous-perspectives-canadian-museum-for-human-rights/#.XPq3WyMwiu0 (accessed 6 June 2019).
37 Lambert, "At This Museum, Even the Building Structure is About a Journey to Hope."
38 For more on the metaphor of hope in the architecture of the museum see Larissa Wodtke, "A Lovely Building for Difficult Knowledge: The Architecture of the Canadian Museum for Human Rights," *Review of Education, Pedagogy and Cultural Studies*, 2015, vol. 37, no. 2–3, 207–26.
39 Hunt, *Inventing Human Rights*, p. 39.
40 Canadian Museum for Human Rights, "Mandate and Museum Experience." Online. Available at https://humanrights.ca/about/mandate-and-museum-experience (accessed 13 December 2018).
41 Canadian Museum for Human Rights, "Mandate and Museum Experience."
42 Dirk Moses, "Protecting Human Rights and Preventing Genocide: The Canadian Museum for Human Rights and the Will to Intervene," in Busby, Muller, and Woolford, *The Idea of a Human Rights Museum*, p. 42.

43 Jennifer Carter, "The Museology of Human Rights," in Busby, Muller, and Woolford, *The Idea of a Human Rights Museum*, p. 219.
44 Carolyn Pedwell, *Affective Relations: The Transnational Politics of Sympathy*, London: Palgrave Macmillan, 2014.
45 Canadian Museum for Human Rights, "From Darkness to Light," 18 December 2012. Online. Available at https://humanrights.ca/blog/darkness-light (accessed 13 December 2018).
46 Christopher Powell, "Transcendence or Struggle? Top-Down and Bottom-Up Narratives of Human Rights," in Busby, Muller, and Woolford, *The Idea of a Human Rights Museum*, pp. 128–44.
47 David Petrasek, "Illusion and the Human Rights Museum," in Busby, Muller, and Woolford, *The Idea of a Human Rights Museum*, pp. 87–100. See also Alex Bozikovic, "Canadian Museum for Human Rights: An Anticipated Work of Architecture but Not One of Our Best," Globe and Mail, 26 September 2014. Online. Available at www.theglobeandmail.com/arts/art-and-architecture/canadian-museum-for-human-rights-ananticipated-work-of-architecture-but-not-one-of-our-best/article20801763 (accessed 13 December 2018).
48 Powell, "Transcendence or Struggle?" p.131.
49 Canadian Museum for Human Rights, "Mandate and Museum Experience."
50 Logan, "National Memory and Museums," p. 116.
51 Canadian Museum for Human Rights, "Indigenous Perspectives." Online. Available at https://humanrights.ca/exhibit/indigenous-perspectives (accessed 13 December 2018).
52 Logan, "National Memory and Museums."
53 Rita Kaur Dhamoon, "Re-presenting Genocide: The Canadian Museum of Human Rights and Settler Colonial Power," *Journal of Race, Ethnicity, and Politics*, 2016, vol. 1, no. 1, 25.
54 "Human Rights Museum Sparks Debate Over Term 'Genocide,'" CBC [Canadian Broadcasting Corporation] News, 26 July 2013. Online. Available at www.cbc.ca/news/canada/manitoba/human-rights-museum-sparks-debate-over-term-genocide-1.1400154 (accessed 13 December 2018).
55 Lenard Monkman, "Genocide Against Indigenous Peoples Recognized by Canadian Museum for Human Rights," CBC, May 17 2019. Online. Available at www.cbc.ca/news/indigenous/cmhr-colonialism-genocide-indigenous-peoples-1.5141078 (accessed June 6 2019).
56 Canadian Museum for Human Rights, "Canadian Journeys." Online. Available at https://humanrights.ca/exhibit/canadian-journeys (accessed 13 December 2018).
57 Canadian Museum for Human Rights, "Built on Education: The Canadian Museum for Human Rights Will Be a National Educational Hub for Teachers." Online. Available at https://humanrights.ca/sites/default/files/attachments/built_on_education.pdf (accessed 13 December 2018).
58 Richard Rorty, "Human Rights, Rationality and Sentimentality," in Richard Rorty, *Truth and Progress. Philosophical Papers*, Vol. 3, Cambridge, UK: Cambridge University Press, 1998, p. 185.
59 Rorty, "Human Rights, Rationality and Sentimentality," p. 172.
60 Rorty, "Human Rights, Rationality and Sentimentality," p. 181.
61 Bozikovic, "Canadian Museum for Human Rights."
62 Canadian Museum for Human Rights, "Human Rights and Design Thinking," 9 July 2013. Online. Available at https://humanrights.ca/blog/human-rights-and-design-thinking?pedisable=false (accessed 13 December 2018).
63 Canadian Museum for Human Rights, "Actions Count." Online. Available at https://humanrights.ca/exhibit/actions-count (accessed 13 December 2018).
64 Canadian Museum for Human Rights, "Facts about the Museum." Online. Available at https://humanrights.ca/sites/default/files/media/cmhr_facts_2017.pdf (accessed 13 December 2018).
65 Canadian Museum for Human Rights, "XOXO: An Exhibit About Love and Forgiveness," 6 October 2015. Online Available at https://humanrights.ca/blogue/xoxo-une-exposition-sur-lamour-et-le-pardon (accessed 13 December 2018).
66 Canadian Museum for Human Rights, "New National Museum an Inspiration that Must Be Seen: Visitor Survey." Online. Available at https://humanrights.ca/about-museum/news/new-national-museum-inspiration-must-be-seen-visitor-survey (accessed 13 December 2018).
67 See Moyn, *The Last Utopia.*
68 Antonio Damasio, *Descartes Error: Emotion, Reason and the Human Brain*, New York: Harper Collins, 1994.
69 Samuel Moyn, *The Last Utopia. Human Rights in History*, Cambridge, MA: Belknap Press at Harvard University Press, 2012, p. 76.

70 UN House in Ukraine, "The Pursuit of Happiness Is a Fundamental Human Goal." Online. Available at www.un.org.ua/en/information-centre/news/1584-2013-03-20-12-40-59 (accessed 13 December 2018).

71 Pedwell, *Affective Relations.*

72 Andreas Huyssen, *Twilight Memories: Marking Time in a Culture of Amnesia*, New York: Routledge, 1995.

73 See Angela Failler, "Hope Without Consolation: Prospects for Critical Learning at the Canadian Museum for Human Rights," *Review of Education, Pedagogy and Cultural Studies*, 2015, vol. 37, no. 2–3 2015, 227–50.

74 Pearl Eliadis, "CMHR a Symbol of Dissent and Protest," *Winnipeg Free Press*, 24 September 2014. Online. Available at www.winnipegfreepress.com/opinion/analysis/cmhr-a-symbol-for-dissent-and-protest-276885241.html (accessed 13 December 2018).

34

FROM THE CLASSROOM TO THE PUBLIC

Engaging students in human rights history

Jessica M. Frazier

What do undergraduate students expect to learn in a course on human rights? Judging from students' chosen research topics: human rights atrocities, violations, and shortcomings. But I research (and therefore often teach about) social movements – sometimes formed in response to human rights violations. Perhaps to the disappointment of my students (but arguably to their psychological benefit) inhumane acts themselves are not a central feature of what I teach. Instead, one of the primary objectives of the course is to trace the recent history of human rights thought, implementation, and activism. Through the assigned readings and discussion, students identify limits to the definition of human rights and problems with past responses to violations, but they also see transformative change in terms of the expansion of protective measures and of the category of "human."[1] Students enter the human rights classroom with a host of present-day examples of perceived human "rights" and "wrongs." I try to use students' contemporary knowledge and interests to engage them in discussion while contextualizing their understanding of the human rights system. I do this through presenting material on key events, social movements, and individual activists who grappled with strengths and weaknesses in the human rights system as they knew it. Despite the documented perpetuation of social injustices, my hope is that by taking a social movements approach, the course can inspire students to make the changes that they see fit while helping them hone analytical skills so that they can be critical of the status quo.

The students I teach are primarily non-history majors, and they are enrolled in an interdisciplinary honors program at a public university in the United States. Many of them are unfamiliar with the history of human rights, of the United Nations (UN), and of twentieth-century international affairs more broadly, but they often have some knowledge of current world events; civil rights, women's rights, and gay rights movements in the United States; and the US role in the world. Adding historical context to their understanding of current world events and a global component to their knowledge of US history, without bogging them down in details, is one task of this course. The assignments – writing a paper, leading discussion, responding to readings, and creating a video – signal that understanding the material is primary, and memorizing facts is secondary. The structure of the course is loosely chronological and loosely thematic, and I try to balance learning about key events with asking some of the major questions posed by interdisciplinary scholarship on human rights and with analyzing important concepts.

The entrée into the course belies the size of the endeavor the students have agreed to undertake. We begin our conversation on human rights on a small scale, with analysis of the Universal Declaration of Human Rights (UDHR), signed in 1948. As part of an icebreaker exercise on the first day of class, I ask each student to name a human right without having read the document. Most name political or civil rights and very few think of economic or social rights. The odd student also assumes sexuality rights or some form of environmental justice should appear on the list. The assignment for the next class is to read the UDHR and consider which rights are missing by today's standards, which rights could be interpreted in potentially problematic ways, which rights the US government fails to uphold, as well as which rights unexpectedly appear in the UDHR. Having forced students to guess human rights on the first day of class, they are better primed to analyze the reality of a normative list of human rights on the second day of class.[2]

I also call attention to the constructed nature of human rights through a 1947 passage by political thinker Jacques Maritain and a 1993 statement by UN secretary-general Boutros Boutros-Ghali during his opening address to the World Conference on Human Rights in Vienna. Maritain's piece explains his role in conducting a survey of human rights traditions and legal precedents that sought to "crystallize this body of common practical convictions,"[3] making clear that the UDHR was an agreed-upon list of human rights open to interpretation. Some 45 years later, Boutros-Ghali envisioned human rights as both timeless and fluid when he stated,

> Human rights should be viewed not only as the absolute yardstick which they are, but also as a synthesis resulting from a long historical process. As an absolute yardstick, human rights constitute the common language of humanity. Adopting this language allows all peoples to understand others and to be the authors of their own history. Human rights, by definition, are the ultimate norm of all politics. As an historical synthesis, human rights are, in their essence, in constant movement. By that I mean that human rights have a dual nature. They should express absolute, timeless injunctions, yet simultaneously reflect a moment in the development of history. Human rights are both absolute and historically defined.[4]

My hope is that through an evaluation of this quote alongside a reflection on the fact that the UDHR is an imperfect document, the class has laid the groundwork for future conversations to analyze why human rights have been interpreted in the ways they have and how human rights definitions have changed since the 1940s.

Examining the context of the creation of the UDHR further allows for insight on its limits, complexities, and contradictions. G. Daniel Cohen's chapter in the edited volume *The Human Rights Revolution* argues that the Holocaust was simultaneously central to and invisible in postwar human rights discourse.[5] He analyzes articles in the UDHR, pointing out that some directly related to the recent Holocaust while others did not, and he follows three Jewish survivors of the Holocaust who promoted human rights and the new UN organization to see how their experiences may have influenced their views of universal human rights. He concludes that even for these three men, the Holocaust both directly and indirectly impacted their approaches to human rights.

Some students doggedly disagree that the Holocaust could be anything but central to the newfound human rights system, but Jean Quataert's *Advocating Dignity* offers an alternative explanation as to why the UDHR was created when it was.[6] Quataert's work examines the competing forces of transnational social movements crossing geopolitical boundaries and international laws upholding state sovereignty in the first half of the twentieth century. While transnational social movements pushed for universal recognition of human dignity, international law reinforced a principle of non-intervention as it sought to regulate matters of mutual concern. Voices of contemporary activists capture some of the hopes and frustrations prevalent in the late 1940s and early 1950s in regard to the power of transnational social movements following the formation of the UN.[7] In 1947, African American W. E. B. Du Bois, founding member of the National Association for the Advancement of Colored People in the United States, wrote "An Appeal to the World" in which he declared that human rights were regularly denied to African Americans, and he asked the "peoples of the world" to step in.[8] Similarly, in a 1951 petition to the UN titled "We Charge Genocide," an American civil rights group recorded the "cruel and inhuman" treatment of African Americans at the hands of the US government.[9] These civil rights activists looked to the UN as an alternative means to gain "justice." But because the UN had no ability to enforce human rights and it upheld national sovereignty – flaws that students quickly point out – both appeals would remain solely normative. Although these activists seemed to hope that in evoking a common human race past wrongs would be righted, they could not but be aware of potential conflicts and limits imposed upon the fledgling UN.

W. E. B. Du Bois' appeal and the civil rights petition also lend themselves to a conversation on the development of a "Third World" identity. Both pieces describe the lived experiences of African Americans in the United States in reference to a transnational racial identity that connected people of color across the globe – from the Jim Crow South in the United States to the apartheid state of South Africa – through their common oppression.[10] At the 1955 Bandung Conference in Indonesia, leaders of African and Asian nations similarly created a common racial identity as they discussed what freedom and self-determination would mean to recently decolonized and decolonizing nations.[11] Determined to achieve more than "liberation from foreign rule,"[12] some leaders expressed a desire for "a complete democratic reformation."[13] In a way, the Bandung conference allows the course to take a step away from centering the story solely on the West and the United States. Our narrator, however, is African American Richard Wright, a contemporary observer and writer, who published an account of the conference. I call attention to Wright's identity and ask students how his perspective as both an insider (as a man of color) and an outsider (as an American) may have shaped the story he told. We think about his audience – likely white Westerners – and his motive – to explain the purpose of the conference and the development of a "Third World" consciousness in a celebratory, but critical, way.

In his piece, Wright argues that despite differences in religion and ideology, people who "had the same background of colonial experience, of subjection, of color consciousness,"[14] came together based on their sense of belonging to a "'colored' nation."[15] In response, according to Wright, attendees created a "color curtain" behind which they formed a non-aligned movement during the Cold War.[16] Wright admitted, however, that some posturing occurred in the first few days – namely, Chinese prime minister Zhou Enlai decried the UDHR as a document that he and leaders in other nations had no voice in, and he urged his fellow delegates to look to the Eastern bloc for succor. To students, I ask whether it matters if nations had had no part in the writing of the UDHR – were they still bound by it? To which students reply both "yes" and "no." Some argue that as a document created by people, the UDHR cannot be forced upon those who did not have a hand in making it; others point out that many of the articles relate to seemingly inherent and necessary rights for all humans, and all should abide by it.

Another issue Wright's piece notes is the possibility that elite factions in decolonized nations would undermine progress toward self-determination by continuing colonial practices and policies.[17] Afro-Caribbean philosopher Frantz Fanon echoed Wright's concern in *The Wretched of the Earth* published in 1963.[18] In it, Fanon described the process of decolonization as one that would not actually deconstruct the colonial system; rather, it would "simply … transfer into native hands … those unfair advantages which are a legacy of the colonial period."[19] In short, although there may be new rulers, an oppressive regime would remain intact as those with newfound power would seek to maintain it. According to Fanon, neo-colonialism would prevail – one formalized around the export of resources to the "former mother country" for too little in exchange.[20] In a classroom where students tend to blame the "West" for all the ills in the "Third World," Fanon's piece calls attention to class distinctions within decolonized nations that complicate depictions of a monolithic and passive Third World.

By 1968, which was a year of reflection as it marked the 20th anniversary of the signing of the UDHR, Fanon's fears that leaders in underdeveloped and recently decolonized nations would undermine calls for social justice and civil rights seemed realized with the growing prevalence of "developmental dictatorships."[21] Historian Roland Burke argues that many leaders prioritized development over human rights, as apparent at the first UN International Conference on Human Rights in Tehran in 1968.[22] The setting of the conference, in the heart of an autocratic regime, did not bode well for human rights advocacy; neither did the fact that the majority of countries represented in Tehran had undemocratic governments.[23] In their addresses to the conference, the shah of Iran and his twin sister, Princess Ashraf Pahlavi, declared the 1948 UDHR a relic and hoped to create a new worldview for the Third World – one that placed nations' development goals above individual freedoms.[24] American diplomat Morris Abram described this new trend in a 1969 piece he wrote for *Foreign Affairs* magazine.[25] He explained,

> These new nations were concerned with raising their people from the depths of poverty, with holding together diverse racial, tribal and religious elements, with eradicating massive illiteracy, with acquiring an elementary technology … [t]he immensity of their problems inclined them to favor a strong role for the state … many of them were *not* interested in the agenda of the dominant Western members, which emphasized the 'traditional' liberties.[26]

Abram also mentioned the ideological differences of the Cold War as a reason for continued disagreement over the UDHR – the preference for political and civil rights in the West or economic and social rights in the East shaped conversations surrounding the UDHR since the 1940s. Here, we pause, just as those in attendance at the Tehran conference did, to reflect on how the UDHR had served the peoples of the world in its first 20 years of existence. For students, these pieces beg the question of whether certain rights should be prioritized, and if so, which rights. Although some students agree with

Tehran participants that economic needs should be met first, others lament the outcome of the Tehran conference, which reinforced a hierarchy of rights.

Following the Tehran conference, we turn to what some scholars have termed the "breakthrough" decade in human rights, the 1970s. Returning our attention to activism, we hone in on the newfound ability of nongovernmental organizations (NGOs) to call attention to human rights violations thanks to a 1975 conference in Helsinki, which brought together leaders of European nations along with the United States, Canada, and the Soviet Union. The Helsinki Final Act "gave rise to a host of citizens' initiatives and NGO watchdog groups,"[27] according to Jean Quataert, as it also repositioned political and civil rights as those of utmost concern to monitoring networks.[28] Her work provides two examples of human rights activism gaining international visibility following the Helsinki Final Act: the case of Soviet dissidents, specifically the Belgrade Six, who were arrested because of their participation in a "free university" – intellectual gatherings in people's apartments that allowed for uncensored discussion; and the Mothers of the Plaza de Mayo, a group of Argentinian mothers who held (and still hold) weekly vigils to call attention to state-sanctioned disappearances of their children.[29]

For many students, the topics of Soviet dissidents and disappearances are new, and I assign primary sources alongside both readings to help better illustrate the context. Accompanying the reading on the Belgrade Six, students read *New York Times* articles on the trial and a statement by Charter 77 – a dissident group in Czechoslovakia in the 1970s – that pointed to international covenants and agreements coming out of the Tehran and Helsinki conferences, which were signed by Czechoslovakia, as a basis upon which to declare human rights violations within their nation.[30] As a class we identify the kinds of freedoms and liberties sought, the perceived responsibilities of people and the government in upholding rights, and the role of actors outside the nation-state in framing conversations surrounding human rights violations.

These questions come up again when we discuss disappearances in Argentina. Quataert examines this topic through the lens of the Mothers of the Plaza de Mayo, which formed in response to the disappearances of family members. I also assign excerpts from Marguerite Guzmán Bouvard's *Revolutionizing Motherhood: The Mothers of the Plaza de Mayo* and Eric Stener Carlson's *I Remember Julia: Voices of the Disappeared* that provide insight into the possible emotional consequences of these tactics of terror, which were meant to silence witnesses and relatives.[31] Instead, mothers (and other relatives) spoke out. Quataert reports that up to the present day, Mothers "have remained a consistent witness to the horrors and have fed the understanding of how important memory is to the human rights culture of justice and truth."[32] To this end, I ask students to review the webpage of the Mothers today to show that indeed they continue to push for truth and justice.[33] We then discuss why the memory of human rights violations is important, what kinds of narratives may be most compelling, and what the Mothers might hope to gain by continuing their weekly vigils. By featuring stories of the Mothers, the conversation moves beyond asking how states and people could be complicit in such acts of violence – questions that students raise regardless of the material I assign – to showing how people make a space for themselves to speak out against such abuse despite the possible repercussions. In the Mothers, students identify bravery.

In addition to the increased ability of groups to bring attention to local abuses, some began to measure the effects of development policies in decolonizing nations. In the 1970s, studies revealed that the benefits of economic growth did not reach people on the ground as intended.[34] To combat growing disparities, human rights strategists worked to center "dignity, security, and welfare" in economic development plans.[35] Participants at the 1975 World Conference of International Women's Year in Mexico City joined emerging conversations on women, gender, and development. White American financier Michaela Walsh drew inspiration from stories she heard at the Mexico City conference and, following the conference, helped to found Women's World Banking (WWB), which provided women access to credit and financial services. Using her experience in the for-profit banking sector, Walsh turned WWB into "an independent, global financial institution," but one that put women at the center and enhanced their economic independence.[36] In the mid-1970s, Indian economist Devaki Jain too became involved in conversations on women, gender, and development through her work on a book, *Indian Women*, solicited and published in time for International Women's Year. As she came to recognize the invisibility of women's work and bumped up against assumptions about the family unit, she challenged social scientists to pay attention to gender in their analyses of the poor. Taking what she termed a "Gandhian feminist perspective on development," Jain also urged a rethinking of policies in such a way that did not ask women to "catch up with men";[37] instead, she wanted "men to join us [women], not the other way around."[38] I highlight this quote in class as an example of a critique of development principles that implied that there was only one path to economic prosperity, but we also discuss it in terms of what "human rights," "women's rights," and "men's rights" mean. Thus, Walsh's and Jain's work moves us into a discussion of how people tried to intertwine human rights thought and action with development programs.

These initiatives to reorient the UN in a way that would place conversations on development within a human rights framework had to contend with global economic pressures. In the wake of recessions worldwide in the 1970s, the World Bank and International Monetary Fund pressed for structural adjustment programs that reduced social welfare programs in the global South in order to free up money to pay off loans and interest due in the North. One observer described the 1980s as "the 'lost decade' for development" because "more money in 1980 flowed South to North … than North to South."[39] By the late 1990s, Amnesty International cited statistics that just over half of the world's largest 100 economies were multinational corporations, not countries (these numbers particularly strike students); these corporations could make decisions that affected human rights and laborers worldwide, but they were not beholden to constituents.[40] Undercutting structural adjustment program arguments that education, health care, and social welfare systems were "luxuries" ill afforded by developing nations, in 1999 economist Amartya Sen proposed a redefinition of development that viewed the expansion of freedom as both the primary means and the desired end of development.[41] Therefore, nation-states should not cut social welfare programs or forgo political rights in order to achieve economic goals, according to Sen. Here, we return to a conversation on whether certain rights should and can take priority; it is interesting to note that by this point in the course, a number of students argue that economic and social rights need to be prioritized, in contrast to students' initial assumptions that human rights meant political and civil rights.

Students' reasoning seems confirmed when we turn to the ethnic violence in the 1990s that stemmed in part from economic and social strife of the 1970s and 1980s. Jean Quataert states that both the Rwandan and Bosnian genocides could "easily [be] framed in ethnic and religious terms, [but] these conflicts were equally about the maintenance of elite power and growing frustrations at the structural poverty and misallocation of resources that followed economic and social exploitation."[42] The atrocities that occurred in the 1990s have been well documented, but my goal is to bring attention to the voices of survivors of violence and to advances in international law that came out of these conflicts. The episode "I Came to Testify," in the *Women, War, and Peace* PBS documentary series about the International War Crimes Tribunal for Yugoslavia does both as it portrays the act of testifying as an act of defiance. The tribunal charged rape as a crime against humanity – a significant departure from the precedent of the Nuremberg trials. Women in the documentary reclaimed their dignity by standing up in court and facing their abusers, and students recognize the strength of the women and see them as survivors, not passive victims. Instead of highlighting atrocious behavior or pitying victims, this course draws attention to the tenacity of survivors. At the same time, the documentary makes clear that many perpetrators of sexual violence were still at large – one woman stated that she still saw her abuser walking free in her hometown. Thus, the limits of what the UN or international tribunals could do also comes through.

Nevertheless, these tribunals show the accomplishments of transnational feminist activism since the UN Decade for Women (1975–85), which brought explicit attention to women's human rights issues. During the Decade, feminist analyses of the human rights system increasingly identified underlying assumptions about who was worthy of protection and from what. Women involved in the Decade recognized that human rights victims were often coded as male and the abusers assumed to be nation-states – political prisoners were the quintessential victims and only women who fit this description were seen as having their human rights violated. By the 1995 Beijing Women's Conference, which assessed the progress made in implementing policies promoting women's human rights since the Decade, human rights organizations such as Amnesty International had taken steps to address feminists' concerns regarding the absence of women's perspectives and experiences in human rights discourses. In the early 1990s, Amnesty International released reports on unique human rights violations faced by women that pushed past previous assumptions of what human rights abuse looked like. Literary scholar Saba Bahar analyzed Amnesty International's statements and noted improvements in its attention to gendered abuses, but she also noticed that the organization most often described women as passive victims. Thus, men, she presumed, needed to rescue women from other men's violence.[43] Juxtaposed against the recent example of the survivors of abuse in Yugoslavia, Amnesty International's depiction of women rings false, and students are able to identify examples of women taking matters into their own hands.

Participants at UN Decade conferences also made breakthroughs in recognizing abuses faced by women on a day-to-day basis within the privacy of their homes and workplaces, forcing a reimagining of the human rights system. The assumed patriarchal structure of family life came under fire as the complicated nature of whose rights took precedence – male heads of households or female (or male) dependents – came into focus. Mobilizations against domestic violence, female genital mutilation (FGM), and other abuses in the "private" realm gained momentum amid reinvigorated transnational feminist fervor.[44] Kelly Shannon's chapter, "The Right to Bodily Integrity," in *The Human Rights Revolution* is a favorite for students because it provides a comprehensible overview of transnational and feminist discussions regarding FGM from the 1970s through the early 1990s.[45] She describes disagreements between women in the global North and global South, a move toward decrying FGM as a public health issue, and some of the complex reasons for the continued practice of FGM in many societies. Shannon's chapter also raises questions about cultural authenticity and universal rights – two major themes that continue into the next set of readings.[46]

The 1990s saw renewed discussion in activist and intellectual circles around the issues of cultural imperialism, universalism, and cultural authenticity – a conversation that still seems salient to many students as they try to conceptualize their own role in the world. I assign an excerpt from philosopher Martha Nussbaum's *Sex and Social Justice* that forwards her conception of the "capabilities approach" to human rights; a piece by political scientist Chandra Muzaffar that criticizes Western notions of human rights as limited to individual political and civil rights; and activist Mallika Dutt's analysis of reflections by American activists of color on the 1995 Beijing Women's Conference.[47] While the first two pieces are theoretical, Dutt's work shows how cross-cultural dialogues led American women to a more complex perception of their positions within US society and the world. Together, the three works comment on tensions that arose when activists tried to work across geopolitical and cultural boundaries. Students themselves are torn as they try to come up with ways to best implement human rights policies without obliterating cultures. Nussbaum's work, however, throws a wrench in the process as it begs the question: who gets to define a culture in the first place? Once again, conflicting human rights, which often have gendered undertones, come to the fore.

Malala Yousafzai's memoir, *I Am Malala*, grapples with Nussbaum's question as it also brings together threads from previous lesson plans on women's and girls' rights, development, war, internal conflict, and so much more. Malala's memoir contextualizes life under Taliban rule in the Swat Valley of Pakistan, providing historical information on the region and describing the local Pashtun culture. It also destabilizes monolithic portrayals of Islam by briefly explaining distinctions between religious sects to a Western, non-Islamic audience and by describing contemporary debates about how to interpret the Quran. The book is ostensibly about the right to an education for girls; yet, read in a course on human rights, students identify many more freedoms necessary to live a healthy, productive, and secure life.[48] The freedom of expression and the freedom of information, the freedom of religion and the right to leisure, the freedom from inhumane punishment and from arbitrary interference – these rights also came under attack during Taliban rule. Malala also explains why the Taliban attracted followers. Some rights and freedoms had not been met by the government – inadequate sanitation, corruption, and illiteracy plagued many communities in the Swat Valley before Taliban rule. Malala's memoir seamlessly incorporates these aspects of the human rights system alongside her argument for the right to an education.

As a contemporary young woman, Malala's example speaks to students in ways that previous stories did not. Her youth – she is about the same age as many college students today – and her innocence – she simply stood up for what she believed in and seemingly held no ill will against those who hurt her and her family – particularly strike students. Malala's text also opens up a conversation on what we mean by an education. Students quickly discern that to Malala an education is something more than a means to get a job, as it is often understood in the United States today. Malala and her classmates risked their safety and security to attend school, and I ask students to put themselves in Malala's place. What does one give up as a human rights activist, I ask, and what would you say to Malala if you met her?[49] These questions bring human rights activism into the classroom in a new way as the material we have learned becomes more tangible.

Continuing to reflect on human rights movements today, the course ends with gay and lesbian rights activism. We watch the 2012 documentary *Call Me Kuchu*, which follows members of the kuchu (meaning LGBTQI) community in Uganda who brought international attention to harassment and violence they faced. The activists worked with members of the UN to claim gay and lesbian rights to be human rights as they also organized local opposition to a proposed Anti-Homosexuality Bill. The bill would not only make it a crime to be involved in homosexual activity, but would also penalize those – including parents, doctors, and peers – who failed to report suspected gays or lesbians. The bill has since been passed and annulled, and the fight against it continues, making the success of the social movement unknown. The inability to wrap up this last segment of the course as an undeniable success is disconcerting for students as is the fact that during the filming of the documentary, David Kato, one of the key activists fighting antigay sentiment in Uganda, was killed. The shock of this violence comes through in responses students write about the film. Following the in-class screening of *Call Me Kuchu*, we read a piece by scholar Rachel Lewis, "Deportable Subjects," on the difficulties lesbians face when seeking asylum from just such violence as faced by Kato and other activists in the film.[50] Lewis argues that adjudicators in asylum cases often have preconceived ideas of appropriate lesbian behavior and seek proof of women's sexuality through the presence of these characteristics. If women do not act like lesbians – in one case this meant that a woman had to subscribe to lesbian periodicals – their applications for refuge could be denied under the premise that even if they were lesbians they could be "discreet" in their home country to avoid violence. Circling back to *Call Me Kuchu*, students argue the impossibility of people living such a discreet lifestyle and having their full human rights intact.

At this point in the course, students are generally upset about the seeming impossibility of the human rights situation. The final piece of the course, however, allows students to take part in a potential form of activism to raise awareness, at the very least, about some of the issues we have covered. In groups of two or three, students produce a five-minute video on a human rights topic of their choice, and they team up with a member of the media services department, which provides technical support by editing the films. Students in the course provide the content: they interview one or two experts on their topic; sometimes they survey the student body; and they use "found footage" for visuals (video clips that are openly available for use). Such videos have focused on genocide, human trafficking, human rights violations within the United States, and a number of other themes. At the end of the semester, I host a film screening to which I invite anyone who has participated in their making, including interviewees.

As a professor, I find multiple aspects of the video project, as compared to a final exam or final paper (which I do assign alongside the videos), are attractive. First, between the found footage, interviews conducted, and other possible content, students have an overwhelming amount of information to fit into five short minutes. The challenge of editing down everything they have gathered contrasts starkly with their usual problem of dragging out information in order to fill an allotted page count for a research paper. In conversations following the film screening, students have commented that for the first time, they have had to decide what to tell their audience first, what information is most significant, and how best to make their case. These are all skills I try to teach students when I assign papers, but this new format makes it more necessary for students to employ these skills. Second, the students are not producing the videos with just me in mind as the sole audience; I post the videos to my website, and the students often post these videos online themselves. Knowing in advance that the videos will be made public increases the incentive for students to produce something of quality that is well researched. Third, because students are working with a member of the media services team, they have to explain their content to someone who has little to no knowledge of the course material. Thus, students are forced to take ownership outside of the classroom over what they are learning in the classroom. Interviewing one or two experts for the videos further enforces the need to understand the topic of their films thoroughly in order to ask questions that will lead to informative and useful responses.

The films also answer the question: Why is human rights education important in the academy? When I ask students at the end of the semester what they learned in the course, some respond with factual information – they had never heard of disappearances or FGM, for example. Others claim a new knowledge of their own human rights, which, in conversations and on social media outlets, they refer to in an informed manner. They may also claim to have become cynics of our geopolitical or economic system because of the course. But, in reality, it is clear that they have learned to be critical of the status quo. The subject of human rights forces students to grapple with complex social, economic, and cultural issues of the day. Students consider the nature of rights and rights language – do human rights, development, culture, and security hold the same meaning across time and space? What do we mean when we refer to human rights? When it comes to conflicting rights, how do we decide whose rights or which rights should be prioritized? Students may actually leave the course with more questions than answers. For me, the uncertainty that students may still have points to an accomplishment rather than a failure of the course. I do not have answers to many of these questions myself, and, as a historian, I would likely say, it depends on the context. Despite their disappointment in the flaws in the current human rights system, I believe many of my students would agree with historian Kelly Shannon's statement that "the story of human rights in the twentieth century is that of the continuous expansion of rights, increasingly due to the efforts of grassroots activists and NGOs rather than governments or the United Nations."[51] Most importantly, they have started to consider what their role should be in forwarding human rights causes, and they have proved their ability to think of themselves within a global and historical context.

Acknowledgments

I would like to thank the participants at the May 2017 Human Rights Workshop at Rice University, many of whom read and commented on this piece. I would especially like to thank Jean Quataert and Lora Wildenthal as well as Ulrike Capdepon, Nandini Deo, Rachel George, Mairi MacDonald, Jadwiga Pieper Mooney, and Caroline Shaw.

Notes

1 When I have assigned the chapter "Are Women 'Human'?" the question in the title has stopped students and made them confront the idea of the mythical norm – i.e. human rights (and other rules or legislation within nations) have been written with white, elite, heterosexual, male, able-bodied persons in mind. Allida Black, "Are Women 'Human'? The UN and the Struggle to Recognize Women's Rights as Human Rights," in Akira Iriye, Petra Goedde, and

William I. Hitchcock (eds.) *The Human Rights Revolution: An International History*, New York: Oxford University Press, 2012, pp. 133–55.

2 We also spend time during the second class period talking about what it means for human rights to be universal, we begin a conversation on underlying assumptions about who needed protection from what, and we discuss some of the contradictory aspects of the UDHR; we return to these topics at a number of junctures over the course of the semester. In addition to the Universal Declaration of Human Rights, in some semesters, I have also assigned Shashi Tharoor, "Are Human Rights Universal?" *World Policy Journal*, 1999/2000, vol. 16, 1–6; Carola Sachse and Atina Grossman, "Human Rights, Utopias, and Gender in Twentieth-Century Europe," *Central European History*, 2001, vol. 44, 1–12; "Human Rights," in Susan C. Mapp, *Human Rights and Social Justice in a Global Perspective: An Introduction to International Social Work*, New York: Oxford University Press, 2014; the introduction in Jean H. Quataert, *Advocating Dignity: Human Rights Mobilizations in Global Politics*, Philadelphia: University of Pennsylvania Press, 2009; and Jacques Maritain, "'The Grounds for an International Declaration of Human Rights' (1947)," in Micheline Ishay (ed.) *The Human Rights Reader: Major Political Essays, Speeches and Documents From Ancient Times to the Present*, 2nd ed., New York: Routledge, 2007, pp. 2–6.

3 Maritain, "The Grounds for an International Declaration of Human Rights," p. 2.

4 Quoted in: Steven L. B. Jensen, *The Making of International Human Rights: The 1960s, Decolonization, and the Reconstruction of Global Values*, New York: Cambridge University Press, 2016, p. 1.

5 G. Daniel Cohen, "The Holocaust and the 'Human Rights Revolution,'" in Iriye, Goedde, and Hitchcock, *The Human Rights Revolution*, pp. 53–71.

6 Quataert, *Advocating Dignity*, esp. chapter 1.

7 W. E. B. Du Bois, "An Appeal to the World: A Statement of Denial of Human Rights to Minorities in the Case of Citizens of Negro Descent in the United States of America and an Appeal to the United Nations for Redress," 1947. Online. Available at www.blackpast.org/1947-w-e-b-dubois-appeal-world-statement-denial-human-rights-minorities-case-citizens-n (accessed 10 November 2018).

8 Du Bois, "An Appeal."

9 Civil Rights Congress, *We Charge Genocide: The Historic Petition to the United Nations for Relief From a Crime of the United States Government Against the Negro People*, New York: Civil Rights Congress, 1951, pp. xi–xiii, 3–10. Online. Available at www.blackpast.org/we-charge-genocide-historic-petition-united-nations-relief-crime-united-states-government-against#sthash.oG8Trj8o.dpuf (accessed 6 April 2017).

10 I also assign Jean Quataert's chapter on apartheid alongside these pieces. Quataert, *Advocating Dignity*, chap. 2.

11 Roland Burke, "'The Compelling Dialogue of Freedom': Human Rights at the Bandung Conference," *Human Rights Quarterly*, 2006, vol. 28, 947–65.

12 Charles Malik, quoted in Burke, "'The Compelling Dialogue of Freedom,'" 959.

13 Burke, "'The Compelling Dialogue of Freedom,'" 959.

14 Richard Wright, *Black Power: Three Books from Exile: Black Power; The Color Curtain; and White Man, Listen!*, New York: Harper Perennial Modern Classics, 2008, quote on p. 572. I assign parts two and four of *The Color Curtain.*

15 Wright, *Black Power*, p. 573.

16 This term plays on the Iron Curtain separating East from West during the Cold War; Burke, "'The Compelling Dialogue of Freedom,'" 953. Nations belonging to the non-aligned movement refused to ally with either the East or the West in the global conflict.

17 Wright, *Black Power*, p. 588.

18 I assign an excerpt from the text available in Ishay, *The Human Rights Reader*, pp. 326–32.

19 Frantz Fanon, *The Wretched of the Earth*, New York: Grove Press, 1963, p. 331.

20 Fanon, *Wretched*, p. 331.

21 Roland Burke, "From Individual Rights to National Development: The First UN International Conference on Human Rights, Tehran, 1968," *Journal of World History*, 2008, vol. 19, 275–96, quote on p. 286. See also Roland Burke's essay in this volume.

22 Burke, "From Individual Rights." See also Jensen, *The Making of International Human Rights.*

23 Burke, "From Individual Rights," 283.

24 Burke, "From Individual Rights," 285.

25 Morris Abram, "The U.N. and Human Rights," *Foreign Affairs*, 1969, vol. 47, 363–74.
26 Emphasis in the original. Abram, "The U.N. and Human Rights," 364–5.
27 Quataert, *Advocating Dignity*, pp. 94–5.
28 Quataert, *Advocating Dignity*, p. 94.
29 Quataert, *Advocating Dignity*, chaps. 2 and 3.
30 Charter 77, "Declaration of Charter 77," *Making the History of 1989*, Item #628. Online. Available at http://chnm.gmu.edu/1989/items/show/628; "Subverting Titoism," *New York Times*, 7 January 1985. Online. Available at www.nytimes.com/1985/01/07/opinion/subverting-titoism.html; "Topics: Louder Than Words," *New York Times*, 8 February 1985. Online. Available at www.nytimes.com/1985/02/08/opinion/topics-louder-than-words.html; "Topics: Supportive Voices; Not Just Academic," *New York Times*, 11 December 1986. Online. Available at www.nytimes.com/1986/12/11/opinion/topics-supportive-voices-not-just-academic.html (all accessed 10 November 2018).
31 Marguerite Guzmán Bouvard, *Revolutionizing Motherhood: The Mothers of the Plaza de Mayo*, Wilmington, DE: SR Books, 1994, pp. 24–7, 256; Eric Stener Carlson, *I Remember Julia: Voices of the Disappeared*, Philadelphia, PA: Temple University Press, 1996. I have assigned the introduction and chaps. 1, 2, and 3.
32 Quataert, *Advocating Dignity*, p. 135.
33 The webpage is in Spanish, but with new web translation technology, this is not too much of a hindrance for most students. Online. Available at http://madres.org (accessed 10 November 2018).
34 Quataert, *Advocating Dignity*, chap. 5.
35 Quataert, *Advocating Dignity*, p. 183.
36 Michaela Walsh, "Women's World Banking," in Arvonne S. Fraser and Irene Tinker (eds.) *Developing Power: How Women Transformed International Development*, New York: Feminist Press at CUNY, 2004, pp. 115–27, quote on p. 118.
37 Devaki Jain, "A View from the South: A Story of Intersections," in Fraser and Tinker, *Developing Power*, pp. 128–37; quote on p. 135.
38 Jain, "A View," p. 131.
39 Quotes in Quataert, *Advocating Dignity*, pp. 185, 184.
40 Amnesty International, "On Human Rights and Labor Rights (1998)," in Ishay, *The Human Rights Reader*, pp. 353–6.
41 I assign an excerpt from *Development as Freedom*. See Amartya Sen, "Development as Freedom (1999)," in Ishay, *The Human Rights Reader*, pp. 356–9, quote on p. 359.
42 Quataert, *Advocating Dignity*, p. 229.
43 Saba Bahar, "Human Rights Are Women's Right: Amnesty International and the Family," in Bonnie G. Smith (ed.) *Global Feminisms since 1945*, New York: Routledge, 2000, pp. 265–89.
44 Bahar, "Human Rights"; Kelly Shannon, "The Right to Bodily Integrity: Women's Rights as Human Rights and the International Movement to End Female Genital Mutilation," in Iriye, Goedde, and Hitchcock, *The Human Rights Revolution*, pp. 285–310. See also chap. 4 in Quataert, *Advocating Dignity*.
45 Shannon, "The Right to Bodily Integrity."
46 Quataert's fourth chapter in *Advocating Dignity* explicitly poses these questions.
47 Martha Nussbaum, "Women and Cultural Universals," in Ishay, *The Human Rights Reader*, pp. 422–30; Chandra Muzaffar, "On Western Imperialism and Human Rights ('From Human Rights to Human Dignity,' 1999)," in Ishay, *The Human Rights Reader*, pp. 414–18; Mallika Dutt, "Some Reflections on United States Women of Color and the United Nations Fourth World Conference on Women and NGO Forum in Beijing, China," in Smith, *Global Feminisms Since 1945*, pp. 305–13.
48 Malala Yousafzai and Christina Lamb, *I Am Malala: The Girl Who Stood Up for Education and Was Shot by the Taliban*, New York: Little, Brown & Company, 2013.
49 Actually, one of my students first asked these questions during discussion, and I encouraged all of my students to write a reflection answering them.
50 Rachel Lewis, "Deportable Subjects: Lesbians and Political Asylum," *Feminist Formations*, 2013, vol. 25, 174–94.
51 Shannon, "The Right to Bodily Integrity," p. 301.

SELECTED BIBLIOGRAPHY

The editors have asked the authors of the essays in this volume to name the works that have been the most influential and important for them, whether or not the works were related to their essays. This bibliography, with some annotations, is the result. This bibliography serves to point teachers and students to texts that are highly valued by the experts in the fields represented in this volume. It is by no means a complete record of all works consulted in this volume.

Afshari, Reza, "On Historiography of Human Rights: Reflections on Paul Gordon Lauren's *The Evolution of International Human Rights: Visions Seen*," *Human Rights Quarterly*, 2007, vol. 29, no. 1, 1–67.

Agamben, Giorgio, *Homo Sacer: Sovereign Power and Bare Life*, Stanford, CA: Stanford University Press, 1998.

Allen, Lori, *The Rise and Fall of Human Rights: Cynicism and Politics in Occupied Palestine*, Stanford, CA: Stanford University Press, 2013.

Alston, Philip, "Does the Past Matter? On the Origins of Human Rights. Review of *The Slave Trade and the Origins of International Human Rights Law* by Jenny S. Martinez," *Harvard Law Review*, 2013, vol. 126, no. 7, 2043–81.

Alston, Philip, and Ryan Goodman, *International Human Rights*, 2nd, rev. ed., Oxford: Oxford University Press, 2012.

Anaya, S. James, *Indigenous Peoples in International Law*, 2nd ed., Oxford: Oxford University Press, 2004.

Anderson, Bridget, *Us and Them? The Dangerous Politics of Immigration Control*, Oxford: Oxford University Press, 2013.

Anderson, Carol, *Eyes Off the Prize: The United Nations and the African American Struggle for Human Rights, 1944–1955*, Cambridge, UK: Cambridge University Press, 2003.

Anghie, Antony, *Imperialism, Sovereignty, and the Making of International Law*, Cambridge, UK: Cambridge University Press, 2005.

Arendt, Hannah, *Eichmann in Jerusalem: A Report on the Banality of Evil*. New York: Viking, 1963.

No list of timeless works on human rights – including the impetus for the Genocide Convention – is complete without Arendt. This short book merits inclusion for raising so many of the important questions about human complicity in, and (rare) resistance to, atrocity that underlie the post-World War II discussion about human "rights" and how best to protect them.

Arendt, Hannah, *The Origins of Totalitarianism. New Edition with Added Prefaces*, Orlando: Harcourt, 1985.

Arthur, Paige, "How 'Transitions' Reshaped Human Rights: A Conceptual History of Transitional Justice," *Human Rights Quarterly*, 2009, vol. 31, 321–67.

An example of historical sociology looking at human rights "top-down."

Atkinson, Wayne, "The Yorta Yorta Struggle for Justice Continues," in Greta Bird, Gary Martin, and Jennifer Nielson (eds.) *Majah: Indigenous Peoples and the Law*, Sydney: Federation Press, 1996, pp. 281–89.

Attwood, Bain, and Andrew Markus, *Thinking Black: William Cooper and the Australian Aborigines' League*, Canberra: Aboriginal Studies Press, 2004.

Ayoub, Phillip M., *When States Come Out: Europe's Sexual Minorities and the Politics of Visibility*, Cambridge, UK: Cambridge University Press, 2016.

Bashford, Alison, and Jane McAdam, "The Right to Asylum: Britain's 1905 Aliens Act and the Evolution of Refugee Law," *Law and History Review*, 2014, vol. 32, no. 2, 309–50.

A universal ethos made its way into law in perhaps unexpected areas. Britain's 1905 Aliens Act was further-reaching in terms of a right to refuge than international or other domestic law until the 1960s. Catherine Shaw came to this point looking forward from the nineteenth century to the 1905 Act; Bashford and McAdam come to this point looking from the 1905 Act on into the twentieth century.

Baslar, Kemal, *The Concept of the Common Heritage of Mankind in International Law*, The Hague: Martinus Nijhoff, 1998.

Bass, Gary J., *Freedom's Battle: The Origins of Humanitarian Intervention*, New York: Vintage, 2009.

Bayertz, Kurt (ed.) *Solidarity*, Dordrecht: Kluwer Academic, 1999.

Beaumont, Catriona, "Citizens Not Feminists: The Boundary Negotiated Between Citizenship and Feminism by Mainstream Women's Organizations in England, 1928–39," *Women's History Review*, 2000, vol. 9, no. 2, 411–29.

Bazyler, Michael J., *Holocaust Justice: The Battle for Restitution in America's Courts*, New York: New York University Press, 1982.

Behrendt, Larissa, *Achieving Social Justice: Indigenous Rights and Australia's Future*, Sydney: Federation Press, 2003.

Beinin, Joel, and Frédéric Vairel, *Social Movements, Mobilization, and Contestation in the Middle East and North Africa*, Stanford, CA: Stanford University Press, 2011.

Birke, Roman, and Carola Sachse (eds.) *Menschenrechte und Geschlecht im 20. Jahrhundert. Historische Studien*, Göttingen: Wallstein Verlag, 2018.

Blake, Janet, *International Cultural Heritage Law*, Oxford: Oxford University Press, 2015.

Bolt, Christine, *Sisterhood Questioned? Race, Class and Internationalism in the American and British Women's Movements, c.1880s–1970s*, London: Routledge, 2004.

Borgwardt, Elizabeth, *A New Deal for the World: America's Vision for Human Rights*, Cambridge, MA: Belknap Press at Harvard University Press, 2005.

Bosworth, Mary, *Inside Immigration Detention*, Oxford: Oxford University Press, 2014.

Bradley, Mark Philip, *The World Reimagined: Americans and Human Rights in the Twentieth Century*, New York: Cambridge University Press, 2016.

Broome, Richard, *Aboriginal Victorians: A History Since 1800*, Crows Nest, New South Wales: Allen & Unwin, 2005.

Browning, Christopher, *Ordinary Men: Reserve Police Battalion 101 and the Final Solution in Poland*, rev. ed., New York: Harper Collins, 2017.

Bruey, Alison, *Bread, Justice, and Liberty: Grassroots Activism and Human Rights in Pinochet's Chile*, Madison: University of Wisconsin Press, 2018.

Buchanan, Tom, "'The Truth Will Set You Free': The Making of Amnesty International," *Journal of Contemporary History*, 2002, vol. 37, no. 4, 575–97.

Burgers, Jan Herman, "The Road to San Francisco: The Revival of the Human Rights Idea in the Twentieth Century," *Human Rights Quarterly*, 1992, vol. 14, no. 4, 447–77.

Burke, Roland, *Decolonization and the Evolution of International Human Rights*, Philadelphia: University of Pennsylvania Press, 2010.

Cabanes, Bruno, *The Great War and the Origins of Humanitarianism, 1918–1924*, Cambridge, UK: Cambridge University Press, 2014.

Calhoun, Craig, "The Imperative to Reduce Suffering: Charity, Progress, and Emergencies in the Field of Humanitarian Action," in Michael Barnett and Thomas G. Weiss (eds.) *Humanitarianism in Question: Politics, Power, Ethics*, Ithaca, NY: Cornell University Press, 2008, pp. 73–97.

Nuanced and seminal for thinking through the relationship between humanitarianism and human rights issues.

Campbell, David S. "Transnationalism and Homophile Political Culture in the Postwar Decades," *GLQ: A Journal of Lesbian and Gay Studies*, 2009, vol. 15, no. 1, 31–65.

Cançado Trindade, A. A., *International Law for Humankind: Towards a New Jus Gentium*, Leiden: Martinus Nijhoff, 2010.

Cangemi, Michael, "Announcement: Guatemala Police Archive Under Threat," *H-Diplo*, 14 August 2018. Online. Available at https://networks.h-net.org/node/28443/discussions/2201579/guatemala-police-archive-under-threat (accessed 10 February 2019).

Carens, Joseph H., "Aliens and Citizens. The Case for Open Borders," in Will Kymlicka (ed.) *The Rights of Minority Cultures*, New York: Oxford University Press, 1995, pp. 331–49.

Carlson, Eric Stener, *I Remember Julia: Voices of the Disappeared*, Philadelphia: Temple University Press, 1996.

Chase, Anthony, and Amr Hamzawy (eds.) *Human Rights in the Arab World*, Philadelphia: University of Pennsylvania Press, 2006.

Cheah, Pheng, *Inhuman Conditions: On Cosmopolitanism and Human Rights*, Cambridge, MA: Harvard University Press, 2006.

Chirwa, Vera, *Fearless Fighter: The Life of Vera Chirwa*, London: Zed Books, 2007.

Chirwa was the first African woman to qualify as a barrister in London, which she did in the 1950s when her homeland, Malawi, was still part of the Central African Federation. Her memoir is a vivid testament to the connection between human rights, as an abstract concept, and the requirement of access to a functioning, independent judiciary in order to make human rights real. She testifies to the difficulty of claiming rights from both the colonial and the postcolonial state. Chirwa also talks about her involvement in theater as a way to publicize human rights in postcolonial Malawi.

Cmiel, Kenneth, "The Emergence of Human Rights Politics in the United States," *Journal of American History*, 1999, vol. 86, no. 3, 1231–50.

Cook, Rebecca J. (ed.) *Human Rights of Women: National and International Perspectives*, Philadelphia: University of Pennsylvania Press, 1994.

Costa, Ravi de, *A Higher Authority: Indigenous Transnationalism and Australia*, Sydney: University of New South Wales Press, 2006.

Crawford, James (ed.) *The Rights of Peoples*, Oxford: Clarendon Press, 1988.

Crosby, Alfred W., *The Columbian Exchange: Biological and Cultural Consequences of 1492*, Westport, CT: Greenwood, 1972.

Currier, Ashley, *Out in Africa: LGBT Organizing in Namibia and South Africa*, Minneapolis: University of Minnesota Press, 2012.

Daoud, Kamel, *The Meursault Investigation*, John Cullen (trans.), New York: Other Press, 2015.

D'Emilio, John, *Sexual Politics, Sexual Communities: The Making of a Homosexual Minority in the United States, 1940–1970*, Chicago: University of Chicago Press, 1983.

Diamond, Jared M., *Guns, Germs and Steel: A Short History of Everybody in the Last 13,000 Years*, London: Vintage, 2005.

Dietrich, John W., "U.S. Human Rights Policy in the Post-Cold War Era," *Political Science Quarterly*, 2006, vol. 121, no. 2, 269–94.

Duranti, Marco, *The Conservative Human Rights Revolution. European Identity, Transnational Politics, and the Origins of the European Convention*, New York: Oxford University Press, 2017.

Dodson, Michael, "Linking International Standards with the Contemporary Concerns of Aboriginal and Torres Strait Islander Peoples," in Sarah Pritchard (ed.) *Indigenous Peoples, the United Nations and Human Rights*, London; Sydney: Zed Books; Federation Press, 1998, pp. 18–29.

Donnelly, Jack, "The Relative Universality of Human Rights," *Human Rights Quarterly*, 2007, vol. 29, no. 2, 281–306.

DuBois, Ellen C., "Internationalizing Married Women's Nationality: The Hague Campaign of 1930," in Karen Offen (ed.) *Globalizing Feminisms, 1789–1945*, London: Routledge, 2010, pp. 204–16.

Dudziak, Mary L., *Cold War Civil Rights*, Princeton, NJ: Princeton University Press, 2000.

Durbach, Andrea, and Lucas Lixinski (eds.) *Heritage, Culture and Rights: Challenging Legal Discourses*, Oxford: Hart, 2017.

Eagly, Ingrid, Steven Shafer, and Jana Whalley, "Detaining Families: A Study of Asylum Adjudication in Family Detention," *California Law Review*, 2018, vol. 106, no. 3, 785–868.

Eckel, Jan, and Samuel Moyn (eds.) *The Breakthrough: Human Rights in the 1970s*, Philadelphia: University of Pennsylvania Press, 2013.

Edmond, Rod, *Leprosy and Empire: A Medical and Cultural History*, Cambridge, UK: Cambridge University Press, 2006.

Eisenberg, Jaci, "The Status of Women: A Bridge from the League of Nations to the United Nations," *Journal of International Organizations*, 2013, vol. 4, no. 2, 8–24.

Eizenstat, Stuart E., *Imperfect Justice: Looted Assets, Slave Labor, and the Unfinished Business of World War II*, New York: PublicAffairs, 2003.

Encarnación, Omar G., *Out in the Periphery: Latin America's Gay Rights Revolution*, New York: Oxford University Press, 2016.

Englund, Harri, *Prisoners of Freedom: Human Rights and the African Poor*, Berkeley: University of California Press, 2006.

Ferree, Myra Marx, and Aili Mari Tripp (eds.) *Global Feminism: Transnational Women's Activism, Organizing, and Human Rights*, New York: NYU Press, 2006.

Finau, Sitaleki (ed.) "AIDS, STD and Sexuality in the Pacific," Special Issue of *Pacific Health Dialog*, 1995, vol. 2 no. 2, 4–167.

Fink, Carole, *Defending the Rights of Others. The Great Powers, the Jews, and International Minority Protection, 1878–1938*, Cambridge, UK: Cambridge University Press, 2004.

Forrest, Craig, *International Law and the Protection of Cultural Heritage*, London: Routledge, 2010.

Foster, Catherine, *Women for All Seasons: The Story of the Women's International League for Peace and Freedom*, Athens: University of Georgia Press, 1989.

Francioni, Francesco, and James Gordley (eds.) *Enforcing International Cultural Heritage Law*, Oxford: Oxford University Press, 2013.

Francioni, Francesco, and Martin Scheinin (eds.) *Cultural Human Rights*, Leiden: Martinus Nijhoff, 2008.

Fraser, Arvonne S., and Irene Tinker (eds.) *Developing Power: How Women Transformed International Development*, New York: Feminist Press at CUNY, 2004.

Friedman, Elisabeth Jay, "Re(gion)alizing Women's Human Rights in Latin America," *Politics and Gender*, 2009, vol. 5, no. 3, 349–75.

Garner, Karen, *Shaping a Global Women's Agenda. Women's NGOs and Global Governance, 1925–1985*, Manchester: Manchester University Press, 2010.

Goldsmith, Jack L., and Eric A. Posner, *The Limits of International Human Rights Law*, New York: Oxford University Press, 2005.

Gordon, Linda, *Woman's Body, Woman's Right: A Social History of Birth Control in America*, New York: Grossman/Viking, 1976.

Gostin, Larry, "The Future of Communicable Disease Control: Toward a New Concept in Public Health Law," *Milbank Quarterly*, 1986, vol. 64, 79–96.

Gourevitch, Philip, *We Wish to Inform You That Tomorrow We Will Be Killed with Our Families: Stories from Rwanda*, New York: Farrar, Straus & Giroux, 1998.

Graf, Philipp, *Die Bernheim-Petition 1933. Jüdische Politik in der Zwischenkriegszeit*, Göttingen: Vandenhoeck & Ruprecht, 2008.

Grant, Stan, "The Australian Dream: Blood, History and Becoming," *Quarterly Essay*, 2016, no. 64, 1–80.

Grimshaw, Patricia, Katie Holmes, and Marilyn Lake (eds.) *Women's Rights and Human Rights: International Feminist Perspectives*, Basingstoke, UK: Palgrave, 2001.

Guilhot, Nicolas, *The Democracy Makers: Human Rights and the Politics of Global Order*, New York: Columbia University Press, 2005.

An example of historical sociology looking at human rights "top-down."

Gussow, Zachary, *Leprosy, Racism, and Public Health: Social Policy in Chronic Disease Control*, Boulder, CO: Westview, 1989.

Hafner-Burton, Emilie M., *Forced to Be Good: Why Trade Agreements Boost Human Rights*, Ithaca, NY: Cornell University Press, 2009.

Heerten, Lasse, *The Biafran War and Postcolonial Humanitarianism: Spectacles of Suffering*, Cambridge, UK: Cambridge University Press, 2017.

Henkin, Louis, Sarah Cleveland, Laurence Helfer, Gerald Neuman, and Diane Orentlicher, *Human Rights*, 2nd ed., New York: Foundation Press, 2009.

Hilsdon, Anne-Marie, Martha Macintyre, Vera Mackie, and Maila Stivens (eds.) *Human Rights and Gender Politics: Asia-Pacific Perspectives*, London: Routledge, 2000.

Hopgood, Stephen, *The Endtimes of Human Rights*, Ithaca, NY: Cornell University Press, 2013.

Hopgood, Stephen, *Keepers of the Flame: Understanding Amnesty International*, Ithaca, NY: Cornell University Press, 2006.

Howard, Rhoda, "The Full-Belly Thesis: Should Economic Rights Take Priority Over Civil and Political Rights? Evidence from Sub-Saharan Africa," *Human Rights Quarterly*, 1983, vol. 5, no. 4, 467–90.

This analysis of the debate over the "full-belly thesis" – over political and civil rights on the one hand and economic and social rights on the other – is memorable. The article is also impressive as an early comparative study of human rights in post-colonial Africa. It has been influential for its examination of the justifications used by political leaders for abusing human rights.

Hunt, Lynn, *Inventing Human Rights: A History*, New York: W. W. Norton, 2007.

Hutchinson, John F., *Champions of Charity: War and the Rise of the Red Cross*, Boulder, CO: Westview Press, 1996.

Huzzey, Richard, *Freedom Burning: Anti-Slavery and Empire in Victorian Britain*, Ithaca, NY: Cornell University Press, 2012.

Explains how a humanitarian ideal became central to British foreign policy and imperialism in the nineteenth century by exploring how antislavery became a norm and a central part of British self-image. The process can be seen as analogous to how twentieth- and twenty-first-century societies (and states) have used the language of international human rights. Perceiving this process can help turn shallow and sterile debates about "true" vs. "hypocritical" adherence to the belief that all humans have inherent rights into a more nuanced understanding of how such a norm functions in the world.

Ibhawoh, Bonny, *Human Rights in Africa*, Cambridge, UK: Cambridge University Press, 2018.

Ibhawoh, Bonny, *Imperialism and Human Rights: Colonial Discourses of Rights and Liberties in African History*, Albany: State University of New York Press, 2007.

Ignatieff, Michael, *Human Rights as Politics and Idolatry*, Amy Gutmann (ed.), Princeton, NJ: Princeton University Press, 2001.

Iliffe, John, *The African AIDS Epidemic: A History*, Athens: Ohio University Press, 2006.

Ingram, James D., "What Is a 'Right to Have Rights'? Three Images of the Politics of Human Rights," *American Political Science Review*, 2008, vol. 102, no. 4, 401–16.

Lucid overview article of different ways of interpreting Hannah Arendt's remarks on human rights politics in *The Origins of Totalitarianism*. While this may sound narrow at first, Ingram actually offers an excellent introduction to the central ways of thinking about what it means to promote the realization of human rights.

Iriye, Akira, Petra Goedde, and William I. Hitchcock (eds.) *The Human Rights Revolution: An International History*, New York: Oxford University Press, 2012.

Irvine, William D., *Between Justice and Politics. The Ligue des Droits de l'Homme 1898–1945*, Stanford, CA: Stanford University Press, 2007.

Ishay, Micheline (ed.) *The Human Rights Reader: Major Political Essays, Speeches and Documents from Ancient Times to the Present* (2nd ed.), New York: Routledge, 2007.

Jackson, Julian, *Living in Arcadia: Homosexuality, Politics, and Morality in France from the Liberation to AIDS*, Chicago: University of Chicago Press, 2009.

Jahangir, Asma, "The Origins of the MFLO: Reflections for Activism," in Farida Shaheed et al. (eds.) *Shaping Women's Lives: Law, Practices and Strategies in Pakistan*, Lahore: Shirkat Gah, 1998, pp. 93–106.

Jahangir, Asma, and Hina Jilani, *The Hudood Ordinances: A Divine Sanction?* Lahore: Rohtas, 1990.

Jelin, Elizabeth, *State Repression and the Labors of Memory*, Minneapolis: University of Minnesota Press, 2003.

Jelin, Elizabeth, and Eric Hershberg (eds.) *Constructing Democracy: Human Rights, Citizenship, and Society in Latin America*, Boulder, CO: Westview Press, 1996.

Looks at how human rights demands have shaped the construction of collective identities in the post-authoritarian period in the Southern Cone of Latin America.

Jensen, Steven L. B., *The Making of International Human Rights: The 1960s, Decolonization and the Reconstruction of Global Values*, New York: Cambridge University Press, 2016.

Jowitt, Anita, "Creating a Framework for HIV/AIDS Related Legal Reform in the South Pacific," *Journal of South Pacific Law*, 2004, vol. 8, n.p.

Kaplan, Temma, "Women's Rights Are Human Rights," *Studies in Practical Philosophy*, 2000, vol. 2, no. 1, 50–63.

Keck, Margaret E., and Kathryn Sikkink, *Activists Beyond Borders: Advocacy Networks in International Politics*, Ithaca, NY: Cornell University Press, 1998.

Kennedy, David, *The Rights of Spring: A Memoir of Innocence Abroad*, Princeton, NJ: Princeton University Press, 2009.

Kévonian, Dzovinar, "André Mandelstam and the Internationalization of Human Rights (1869–1949)," in Pamela Slotte and Miia Halme-Tuomisaari (eds.) *Revisiting the Origins of Human Rights*, Cambridge, UK: Cambridge University Press, 2015, pp. 239–66.

Keys, Barbara J., "Congress, Kissinger, and the Origins of Human Rights Diplomacy," *Diplomatic History*, 2010, vol. 34, no. 5, 823–51.

Keys, Barbara J., *Reclaiming American Virtue: The Human Rights Revolution of the 1970s*, Cambridge, MA: Harvard University Press, 2014.

Klenner, Hermann, *Marxismus und Menschenrechte: Studien zur Rechtsphilosophie*, Berlin: Akademie Verlag, 1982.

Klose, Fabian, *Human Rights in the Shadow of Colonial Violence: The Wars of Independence in Kenya and Algeria*, Philadelphia: University of Pennsylvania Press, 2013.

Koskenniemi, Martti, *The Gentle Civilizer of Nations. The Rise and Fall of International Law 1870–1960*, Cambridge, UK: Cambridge University Press, 2002.

Lake, Marilyn, "From Self-Determination via Protection to Equality via Non-Discrimination: Defining Women's Rights at the League of Nations and the United Nations," in Patricia Grimshaw, Katie Holmes, and Marilyn Lake (eds.) *Women's Rights and Human Rights. International Historical Perspectives*, Basingstoke: Palgrave, 2001, pp. 254–71.

Langfield, Michele, William Logan, and Máiréad Nic Craith (eds.) *Cultural Diversity, Heritage and Human Rights: Intersections in Theory and Practice*, London: Routledge, 2010.

Lauren, Paul Gordon, *The Evolution of International Human Rights: Visions Seen*, 3rd ed., Philadelphia: University of Pennsylvania Press, 2011.

Lee, Erika, and Judy Yung, *Angel Island: Immigrant Gateway to America*, New York: Oxford University Press, 2010.

Levy, Daniel, and Natan Sznaider, *Human Rights and Memories*, University Park, PA: Penn State University Press, 2010.

Liu, Lydia, "Shadows of Universalism: The Untold Story of Human Rights around 1948," *Critical Inquiry*, 2014, vol. 40, 385–417.

Ludi, Regula, "Geschlechtergleichheit als Menschenrecht? Überlegungen zur Bedeutung der Menschenrechtssprache im Völkerbund," in Roman Birke and Carola Sachse (eds.) *Menschenrechte und Geschlecht im 20. Jahrhundert*, Göttingen: Wallstein Verlag 2018, pp. 46–71.

Luker, Vicki and Jane Buckingham (eds.) "Leprosy in the Pacific," Special Issue of *Journal of Pacific History*, 2017, vol. 52, no. 3, 265–419.

Mackie, Vera (ed.) *Ways of Knowing About Human Rights in Asia*, Oxford: Routledge, 2014.

Mann, Jonathan M., Sofia Gruskin, Michael A. Grodin, and George J. Annas (eds.) *Health and Human Rights: A Reader*, New York: Routledge, 1999.

Marhoefer, Laurie, *Sex and the Weimar Republic: German Homosexual Emancipation and the Rise of the Nazis*, Toronto: University of Toronto Press, 2015.

Markarian, Vania, *Left in Transformation: Uruguayan Exiles and the Latin American Human Rights Networks, 1967–1984*, New York: Routledge, 2005.

Focusing on the experience of Uruguayan leftists in exile, Markarian argues that activists did not adopt human rights language to replace a comprehensive framework for radical political action, but as a means for demanding very concrete goals in response to developments in the region, in addition to protecting the physical integrity of those still in the country. The study demonstrates how liberal democratic and socialist principles could sustain critiques of – and challenges to – new democracies during the early years of the Latin American transitions from authoritarian rule in the 1980s.

Martinez, Jenny S., *The Slave Trade and the Origins of International Human Rights Law*, Oxford: Oxford University Press, 2012.

Matera, Marc, and Susan Kingsley Kent, *The Global 1930s: The International Decade*, New York: Routledge, 2017.

Maul, Daniel R., *Human Rights, Development and Decolonisation: The International Labour Organisation, 1940–70*, Basingstoke, UK: Palgrave Macmillan, 2012.

Maynard, John, *Fight for Liberty and Freedom: The Origins of Australian Aboriginal Activism*, Canberra: Aboriginal Studies Press, 2007.

McNeill, William H., *Plagues and Peoples*, Garden City, NY: Anchor Press, 1976.

Merry, Sally Engle, *Human Rights and Gender Violence. Translating International Law into Local Justice*, Chicago: University of Chicago Press, 2006.

Merry, Sally Engle, *The Seductions of Quantification. Measuring Human Rights, Gender Violence, and Sex Trafficking*, Chicago: University of Chicago Press, 2016.

Miller, Carol, "'Geneva – The Key to Equality': Inter-War Feminists and the League of Nations," *Women's History Review*, 1994, vol. 3, no. 2, 219–45.

Minto, David, "Special Relationships: Transnational Homophile Activism and Anglo-American Sexual Politics," PhD diss., Yale University, 2014.

Moeckli, Daniel, Sangeeta Shah, and Sandesh Sivakumaran (eds.) *International Human Rights Law*, Oxford: Oxford University Press, 2018.

Mora, Claudia (ed.) *Desigualdad en Chile: La Continua Relevancia del Género*, Santiago: Ediciónes Universidad Alberto Hurtado, 2013.

Moyn, Samuel, *The Last Utopia: Human Rights in History*, Cambridge, MA: Belknap Press of Harvard University Press, 2010.

Moyn, Samuel, *Not Enough: Human Rights in an Unequal World*, Cambridge, MA: Belknap Press of Harvard University Press, 2018.

Mutua, Macau, *Human Rights: A Political and Cultural Critique*, Philadelphia: University of Pennsylvania Press, 2002.

Nethery, Amy, and Stephanie J. Silverman (eds.) *Immigration Detention: The Journey of a Policy and Its Human Impact*, London: Routledge, 2015.

Normand, Roger, and Sarah Zaidi, *Human Rights at the UN: The Political History of Universal Justice*, Bloomington: Indiana University Press, 2008.

Offen, Karen, *European Feminisms 1700–1950. A Political History*, Stanford, CA: Stanford University Press, 2000.

Office of the High Commissioner on Human Rights and the Joint United Nations Programme on HIV/AIDS, *International Guidelines on HIV/AIDS and Human Rights Consolidated Version*, Geneva: Joint United Nations Programme on HIV/AIDS (UNAIDS), 2006.

Ondaatje, Michael, *Anil's Ghost*, New York: Knopf, 2000.

Parkinson, Charles O. H., *Bills of Rights and Decolonization: The Emergence of Domestic Human Rights Instruments in Britain's Overseas Territories*, Oxford: Oxford University Press, 2007.

Parkinson surveys the constitutional debates over bills of rights in the run-up to independence in almost all former British dependencies. His monograph is important as a sweeping legal history of human rights and decolonization in the British Empire. The view of human rights from the Colonial Office exposes the political and economic interests that have informed rights debates, especially those regarding private property rights.

Pedersen, Susan, *The Guardians: The League of Nations and the Crisis of Empire*, Oxford: Oxford University Press, 2015.

Pedersen's book empirically demonstrates both the colonial origins of international governance and decolonization's potential to mortgage the economic sovereignty of newly independent weak states to their former colonial powers. Explains how interwar Jewish settlement of Palestine became the only instance of settler colonialism that the Permanent Mandates Commission of the League of Nations did not impede.

Pepin, Jacques, *The Origins of AIDS*, Cambridge, UK: Cambridge University Press, 2011.

Peters, Julie, and Andrea Wolper (eds.) *Women's Rights, Human Rights: International Feminist Perspectives*, London: Routledge 1995.

Pogge, Thomas, "Poverty, Human Rights and Cosmetic Progress," in Malcolm Langford, Andy Sumner, and Alicia Ely Yamin (eds.) *Millennium Development Goals and Human Rights: Past, Present, and Future*, New York: Cambridge University Press, 2013, pp. 209–231.

Pouligny, Béatrice, *Peace Operations Seen from Below: UN Missions and Local People*, Bloomfield, CT: Kumarian Press, 2006.

Pritchard, Sarah (ed.) *Indigenous Peoples, the United Nations and Human Rights*, London; Sydney: Zed Books; Federation Press, 1998.

Puri, Jyoti, *Sexual States: Governance and the Struggle over the Antisodomy Law in India*, Durham, NC: Duke University Press, 2016.

Pyle, Christopher, *Extradition, Politics, and Human Rights*, Philadelphia: Temple University Press, 2001.

Quataert, Jean H., *Advocating Dignity: Human Rights Mobilizations in Global Politics*. Philadelphia: University of Pennsylvania Press, 2010.

Quataert, Jean H., *The Gendering of Human Rights in the International Systems of Law in the Twentieth Century*, Washington, DC: American Historical Association, 2006.

Rawls, John, *The Law of Peoples*, Cambridge, MA: Harvard University Press, 1999.

Richards, Patricia, *Pobladoras, Indigenas, and the State: Conflicts over Women's Rights in Chile*, New Brunswick, NJ: Rutgers University Press, 2004.

Risse, Thomas, Stephen C. Ropp, and Kathryn Sikkink (eds.) *The Power of Human Rights: International Norms and Domestic Change*, Cambridge, UK: Cambridge University Press, 1999.

This book expanded on the boomerang model that Keck and Sikkink had introduced previously and develops a "spiral model."

Rodogno, Davide, *Against Massacre: Humanitarian Interventions in the Ottoman Empire 1815–1914*, Princeton, NJ: Princeton University Press, 2011.

Roht-Arriaza, Naomi, *The Pinochet Effect: Transnational Justice in the Age of Human Rights*, Philadelphia: University of Pennsylvania Press, 2005.

Roniger, Luis, and Mario Sznajder, *The Legacy of Human Rights Violations in the Southern Cone: Argentina, Chile and Uruguay*, Oxford: Oxford University Press, 1999.

Looks at how human rights demands have shaped the construction of collective identities in the post-authoritarian period in the Southern Cone of Latin America.

Ruggie, John, *Just Business: Multinational Corporations and Human Rights*, New York: W. W. Norton, 2013.

Rupp, Leila J., "The Persistence of Transnational Organizing: The Case of the Homophile Movement," *American Historical Review*, 2011, vol. 116, no. 4, 1014–39.

Rupp, Leila J., *Worlds of Women: The Making of an International Women's Movement*, Princeton, NJ: Princeton University Press, 1997.

Schmitz, David F., and Vanessa Walker, "Jimmy Carter and the Foreign Policy of Human Rights: The Development of a Post-Cold War Foreign Policy," *Diplomatic History*, 2004, vol. 28, 113–43.

Schreiber, Adele, and Margaret Mathieson, *Journey Towards Freedom: Written for the Golden Jubilee of the International Alliance of Women*, Copenhagen: International Alliance of Women, 1955.

Shah, Nafisa, *Honor and Violence: Gender, Power, and Law in Southern Pakistan*, New York: Berghahn, 2016.

Shah, Nafisa, *Honour Unmasked: Gender Violence, Law, and Power in Pakistan*, Karachi: Oxford University Press, 2016.

Shah, Zulfiqar, *Decline of Pakistan: Essays on Federalism, Ethnic-Nationalism, Minorities and Human Rights in Pakistan*, Scotts Valley, CA: Createspace Independent Publishing Platform, 2014.

Shaheed, Farida, Sohail Akbar Warraich, Cassandra Balchin, and Aisha Gazdar (eds.) *Shaping Women's Lives: Law, Practices and Strategies in Pakistan*, Lahore: Shirkat Gah, 1998.

Sheeran, Scott, and Sir Nigel Rodley (eds.) *Routledge Handbook of International Human Rights Law*, London: Routledge, 2013.

Shehadeh, Raja, and Jonathan Kuttab *The West Bank and the Rule of Law*, Geneva: International Commission of Jurists and Law in the Service of Man, 1980.

Shelton, Dinah (ed.) *Oxford Handbook of International Human Rights Law*, Oxford: Oxford University Press, 2013.

Sikkink, Kathryn, *Evidence for Hope. Making Human Rights Work in the 21st Century*, Princeton, NJ: Princeton University Press, 2017.

Sikkink, Kathryn, *The Justice Cascade: How Human Rights Prosecutions Are Changing World Politics*, New York: W. W. Norton, 2011.

Sikkink, Kathryn, *Mixed Signals: US Human Rights Policy and Latin America*, Ithaca, NY: Cornell University Press, 2004.

Silverman, Helaine, and D. Fairchild Ruggles (eds.), *Cultural Heritage and Human Rights*, New York: Springer, 2007.

Silverman, Stephanie J., and Petra Molnar, "Everyday Injustices: Barriers to Access to Justice for Immigration Detainees in Canada," *Refugee Survey Quarterly*, 2016, vol. 35, no. 1, 109–27.

Simmons, Beth A., *Mobilizing for Human Rights. International Law and Domestic Politics*, New York: Cambridge University Press, 2009.

Simms, Brendan, and D. J. B. Trim (eds.) *Humanitarian Intervention: A History*, New York: Cambridge University Press, 2011.

Simpson, Brian A. W., *Human Rights and the End of Empire: Britain and the Genesis of the European Convention*, New York: Oxford University Press, 2001.

Simpson, Brad, "Denying the 'First Right': The United States, Indonesia, and the Ranking of Human Rights by the Carter Administration, 1976–1980," *International History Review*, 2009, vol. 31, no. 4, 798–826.

Simpson, Brad, "Self-Determination, Human Rights, and the End of Empire in the 1970s," *Humanity: An International Journal of Human Rights, Humanitarianism, and Development*, 2013, vol. 4, no. 2, 239–60.

Simpson's article is at the vanguard of the scholarship on human rights and decolonization. It forces us to consider the multiple definitions, debates, and usages of the right to national self-determination. It informs us that we are only just beginning to recognize the complexity of the relationship between self-determination and human rights. It also calls for human rights histories that study the priorities and interests of actors in the global South.

Slotte, Pamela, and Miia Halme-Tuomisaari (eds.) *Revisiting the Origins of Human Rights*. Cambridge, UK: Cambridge University Press, 2015.

Slovic, Paul, and Daniel Västfjäll, "The More Who Die, the Less We Care: Psychic Numbing and Genocide," in Susanne Kaul and David Kim (eds.) *Imagining Human Rights*, Berlin: Walter de Gruyter, 2015, pp. 55–69.

Sluga, Glenda, *Internationalism in the Age of Nationalism*, Philadelphia: University of Pennsylvania Press, 2013.

Sluga, Glenda, and Patricia Clavin, "Rethinking the History of Internationalism," in Glenda Sluga and Patricia Clavin (eds.) *Internationalisms: A Twentieth-Century History*, Cambridge, UK: Cambridge University Press, 2017, pp. 3–14.

Snyder, Sarah B., *From Selma to Moscow: How Human Rights Activists Transformed US Foreign Policy*, New York: Columbia University Press, 2018.

Snyder, Sarah B., *Human Rights Activism and the End of the Cold War: A Transnational History of the Helsinki Network*, New York: Cambridge University Press, 2011.

Stamatopoulou, Elsa, "Indigenous Peoples and the United Nations: Human Rights as a Developing Dynamic," *Human Rights Quarterly*, 1994, vol. 16, no. 1, 58–81.

Stanner, W. E. H., *After the Dreaming: Black and White Australians: An Anthropologist's View. The Boyer Lectures*, Sydney: Australian Broadcasting Commission, 1969.

Steiner, Zara, *The Triumph of the Dark. European International History 1933–1939*, Oxford: Oxford University Press, 2011.

Stella, Mary, *Makogai – Image of Hope: A Brief History of the Care of Leprosy Patients in Fiji*, Christchurch: Pegasus Press, 1978.

Stienstra, Deborah, *Women's Movements and International Organizations*, London: Macmillan, 1994.

Stites Mor, Jessica, *Human Rights and Transnational Solidarity in Cold War Latin America*, Madison: University of Wisconsin Press, 2013.

Stuurman, Siep, *The Invention of Humanity: Equality and Cultural Difference in World History*, Cambridge, MA: Harvard University Press, 2017.

With the "frontier" as guiding conceptual propulsion, Stuurman examines how the world's thinkers grappled with the dialectical tensions in the articulation of the notion of a common humanity and with cultural difference over two millennia.

Taffe, Sue, *Black and White Together: FCAATSI: The Federal Council for the Advancement of Aborigines and Torres Strait Islanders, 1958–1973*, St. Lucia, Queensland: University of Queensland Press, 2005.

Tanaka, Yuki, *Japan's Comfort Women: Sexual Slavery and Prostitution During World War II*, London: Routledge, 2002.

Tate, Winifred, *Counting the Dead: The Culture and Politics of Human Rights Activism in Colombia*, Berkeley: University of California Press, 2007.

Tayman, John, *The Colony: The Harrowing True Story of the Exiles of Molokai*, New York: Simon & Schuster, 2006.

Terretta, Meredith, "From Below and to the Left? Human Rights and Liberation Politics in Africa's Postcolonial Age," *Journal of World History*, 2013, vol. 24, no. 2, 389–416.

Terretta, Meredith, "'We Had Been Fooled into Thinking that the UN Watches Over the Entire World': Human Rights, UN Trust Territories, and Africa's Decolonization," *Human Rights Quarterly*, 2012, vol. 34, 329–60.

Thoreson, Ryan, *Transnational LGBT Activism: Working for Sexual Rights Worldwide*, Minneapolis: University of Minnesota Press, 2014.

Treatment Action Campaign, *Fighting for Our Lives: The History of the Treatment Action Campaign 1998–2010*, Cape Town: Treatment Action Campaign, 2010.

UN Office of the High Commissioner of Human Rights, *Guiding Principles on Business and Human Rights: Implementing the United Nations "Protect, Respect and Remedy" Framework*, New York: United Nations, 2011. HR/PUB/11/04. Online. Available at www.ohchr.org/Documents/Publications/GuidingPrinciplesBusinessHR_EN.pdf (accessed 22 December 2018).

van Toorn, Penny, *Writing Never Arrives Naked: Early Aboriginal Cultures of Writing in Australia*, Canberra: Aboriginal Studies Press, 2006.

Vick, Brian, *The Congress of Vienna: Power and Politics after Napoleon*, Cambridge, MA: Harvard University Press, 2014.

Waltz, Susan, *Human Rights and Reform: Changing the Face of North African Politics*, Berkeley: University of California Press, 1995.

Waltz, Susan, "Universalizing Human Rights: The Role of Small States in the Construction of the Universal Declaration of Human Rights," *Human Rights Quarterly*, 2001, vol. 23, 144–72.

Wasserstrom, Jeffrey N., Greg Grandin, Lynn Hunt, and Marilyn Young (eds.) *Human Rights and Revolutions*, 2nd ed., Lanham, MD: Rowman & Littlefield, 2007.

Comprehensive volume that looks closely at the relationship between revolutionary moments of upheaval and human rights discourse and practice.

Webster, Andrew, "The League of Nations, Disarmament and Internationalism," in Glenda Sluga and Patricia Clavin (eds.) *Internationalisms: A Twentieth-Century History*, Cambridge, UK: Cambridge University Press, 2017, pp. 139–69.

Weiss, Anita M., *Interpreting Islam, Modernity, and Women's Rights in Pakistan*, New York: Palgrave Macmillan, 2014.

Weschler, Lawrence, *A Miracle, A Universe*, Chicago: University of Chicago Press, 1998.

Witt, John Fabian, *Lincoln's Code: The Laws of War in American History*, New York: Free Press, 2013.

Wolfrum, Rüdiger, and Chie Kojima (eds.), *Solidarity: A Structural Principle of International Law*, Heidelberg: Springer, 2009.

Wong, Tom K., *Rights, Deportation, and Detention in the Age of Immigration Control*, Stanford, CA: Stanford University Press, 2015.

Wright, Richard, *Black Power: Three Books from Exile – Black Power; the Color Curtain; and White Man, Listen!* New York: Harper Perennial Modern Classics, 2008.

Yoshimi, Yoshiaki, *Comfort Women: Sexual Slavery in the Japanese Military during World War II*, Suzanne O'Brien (trans.), New York: Columbia University Press, 2000.

Yousafzai, Malala, and Christina Lamb, *I Am Malala: The Girl Who Stood Up for Education and Was Shot by the Taliban*, New York: Little, Brown, 2013.

Zia, Afiya Shehrbano, *Faith and Feminism in Pakistan: Religious Agency or Secular Autonomy?* Brighton, UK: Academic Press, 2018.

INDEX

9/11 attacks 326–327, 393

abolitionism, John Anderson case 23, 25, 26, 28–30
Aboriginal peoples, Australia 432–444
Aboriginality 440–441
Abram, Morris 641–642
access to pharmaceuticals (A2P) 574–575
accountability; Accountability and Remedy Project 500–502; downfall of US alien tort statute litigation 491–494; early corporate accountability at Nuremberg 489–491; national security 11–12; Nazi-era wartime forced labor 494–497; transnational corporate accountability 489; *UN Guiding Principles on Business and Human Rights (UNGPs)* 497–500
activism; colonial Africa 205–208, 217; democratization of US policymaking 321; indigenous activism for human rights 432–444; Kuwait Society for Human Rights 346–347; language of 22–24; Morocco's struggle for non-partisanship 345; Palestinian occupation 338–341; peace activism methods 104–106; prior to universal declaration 203–204; students of human rights history 642; transitional justice 605–607; *see also* women activists
advocacy; Congo reform (early twentieth century) 57; LGBTQ rights 449, 456; as a practice of persuasion 70–72; transnational rights 14, 99–100, 114–115
Afghanistan; soldier recruitment 192; treaty ratification 168–169
Africa; civil rights 213–217; expropriated lands 212–213; history of human rights 203–204; legalism in Africa's internationally mandated territories 204–209; LGBTQ rights 460–461; political rights 213–217; racial discrimination 210–212; universal human rights in UN trust territories 209–217; US human rights policy 319, 326; *see also individually named countries*; Middle East and North Africa
Afshari, Reza 241
Aidos commission of inquiry 45–50
air pollution 545
Al Haq 338–341
Alfonsín, Raúl 380–382
Alien Tort Statute (ATS) 489, 490–494
'aliens', migration control 584, 585–586
Almada, Martín 608
Al-Qatami, Jasin 347–349
American Convention on Human Rights 148–149
American Red Cross 81
Amnesty International; Chile 360–361; Moroccan NGOs 342, 344–346; prisoners of conscience 360–361, 457; state courts 516; Third World 223, 224, 225
amnesty laws 508, 511, 512, 516
Anaya, James 434
Anderson, John 21–33
antecedents to human rights 22
anticolonial human rights critique 222–224, 228–231, 235–236
anticolonialism as a human rights movement 241–242, 250–252
anti-impunity 510
apartheid; Botswana 243, 245–247, 250–251; global hierarchy 594; South Africa 223, 243, 248; Universal Declaration of Human Rights 232, 243
Arab Organization for Human Rights (AOHR) 347
Arab world; diplomatic dialogues with UN 172–179; human rights treaty ratification 163–164, 165–172; Kuwait Society for Human Rights 346–349; Morocco's struggle for non-partisanship 341–346; NGO practices 337–349; Palestinian occupation 338–341
Arendt, Hannah 208, 584

Argentina; democratization 613–616; Mothers of the Plaza de Mayo 375–388, 642; universal jurisdiction 515–518
arpilleras production 359–360
Asia-Pacific War 524–525
Asma Jahangir 392, 395–396, 398–407
Asper, Israel 623
Association to Defend War Victims 348–349
asylum seekers 579–594
Australia, indigenous activism for human rights 432–444
authoritarianism; Chile 357–358; women's rights 357
Ayress, Nieves 361

Bahrain, treaty ratification 171–172
Balkan Wars 551
Balkans, international commissions of inquiry (1876–80) 37–38, 50–52; Eastern Roumelia 45–50; 'Great Eastern Crisis' 38–39; Russo-Turkish War 39–45
Bandung Conference 640
Barrios de Chungara, Domitila 356
Bechuanaland, race and human rights 243, 245–247
Bedoons 348
Berlin Act 66
Berlin Wall, fall of 281–282, 288–293
Berne Convention 566–567
Bernheim petition 127
biological diversity 570–571
biometric information 571–572
blasphemy law 401–402
books, intellectual property law 563–568
borders, and migration 584
Bosnia, Cold War context 325
Bosnia-Herzegovina 39, 40, 51
Botswana 250–252; anticolonialism as a human rights movement 241–242, 250–252; foreign assistance 248–249; history of 243–245; human rights idealism 247–249; individual and national self-determination 250–252
Boutros-Ghali, Boutros 639
Bricker Amendment 317–318
Britain; Congo reform (early twentieth century) 67–69; 'Great Eastern Crisis' (1876) 38–40; immigration detention 587–588; Women's Peace Crusade 111
British Africa 206–207, 212–213, 226
British Empire; John Anderson case 21–33; language of activism 22–24; sovereignty and intra-imperial politics 28–32
British Six Point Group 131
Brownmiller, Susan 529
Brussels Act 66–67
Bulgaria; Ottoman abuses 51; Russo-Turkish War 39–45
Bunche, Ralph 209–210
Burke, Roland 641
Bush, George H. W. administration 325–326
Bush, George W. administration 326–327, 458
business *see* corporate accountability

Canada; freedom of religion 416–421; John Anderson case 21, 25–33; *Ktunaxa* case 415, 421–425; social and economic rights 152–154
Canadian Charter of Rights and Freedoms 417–418
Canadian Museum for Human Rights 13, 621–633
Cançado Trindade, Antônio Augusto 543–544, 549–550
Carter administration 323–324
Casement, Roger 57, 58–72
Catholic Church; advocacy for human rights 291; Damien, Patron Saint of persons with leprosy 473; freedom of religion 416–417
Cavallo, Miguel Angel 513–514
Center for Documentation and Archive for the Defense of Human Rights (CDyA) 605, 611–613, 614, 615
Charter 08 Movement 303–304, 305–306
child rights *see* Convention on the Rights of the Child (CRC)
childcare, International Labour Organization 271
Chile; authoritarian-patriarchal regime 357–358; democracy and the institutionalization of a women's rights agenda 366–368; feminism and language 365–366; feminist awareness raising 362–364; gender equality 354–355, 357–369; Pinochet case 512–513, 514–515; self-help initiatives, solidarity art, and challenges to the master narrative 358–360; solidarity and the internationalization of women's rights 360–361
China 298–299; contemporary human rights standards 301–303; leprosy cases 471, 473; orthodoxy and resistance 299–301, 303–309; Sino-American relationship 325–326
Christianity; advocacy for human rights 291; freedom of religion 416–421; 'Great Eastern Crisis' (1876) 38–40; leprosy 472, 473
Círculo de Estudios de la Mujer 362
citizenship; equal treatment of women 112, 130, 348; Kuwait 347–348, 349; Malagasy citizenship campaign 206, 216; and migration 583, 584; New York Declaration 126; veterans' rights movement 206
civil rights; colonial contexts 213–217; human rights history 640; International Labour

Organization 263–264; migration 584; nineteenth century 22
Civil Rights Act 319
civilian hostages 89
civilians; Red Cross/Red Crescent movement 75; violence against wounded soldiers, POWs and civilians 77, 82–83
Clinton, Hillary 459
Clinton administration 326
Cold War; Berlin Wall, fall of 281–282, 288–293; human rights as movement 323–325; human rights historiography 282–283; International Labour Organization 265, 267; US human rights policy 317–318
collective bargaining rights 264
collective rights; intellectual property law 568–572; solidarity 544
colonial contexts 8–9; Africa universal human rights claims 203–204, 209–217; Al Haq in Palestine 340; anticolonial human rights critique 222–224, 228–231, 235–236; Brussels Act 66–67; Congo reform (early twentieth century) 58, 64–65, 70–71; development as a human rights exception 225–228; human rights against and after Empire 224–225; indigenous activism in Australia 434–437; legalism in Africa's internationally mandated territories 205–208; leprosy 472–474, 479; Morocco's struggle for non-partisanship 341–346; postcolonial human rights critique 231–232; proliferation of human rights language 234–235; universal particularism 233–234
Commission on the Status of Women (CSW) 266, 267, 356
commissions *see* international commission of inquiry in the Congo international commissions of inquiry in the Balkans (1876–80)
Committee for the Defense of Women's Rights (CODEM) 364
Committee on Economic, Social and Cultural Rights 143–144
Committee on the Elimination of Racial Discrimination (CERD) 443–444
common heritage of humanity 545–551, 553–554
common law 563
conflicts *see* military war victims
Confucianism 299, 300–301, 308
Congo 7
Congo reform (early twentieth century) 57–58; advocacy as a practice of persuasion 70–72; evidence for inquiry 58–63, 69–70; legal framework 63–68
congressional activism 319
consensus on human rights; child rights 191, 194; international context 180; Islam 397
Constantinople Congress 39–40, 44
constitutionalism; China 302–303; intellectual property law 563; US human rights policy 317–318
Convention Against Torture (CAT) 163, 168, 171–175
Convention on Biological Diversity 570–571
Convention on the Elimination of all forms of Discrimination Against Women (CEDAW); China 301–302; Middle East and North Africa 163, 168, 170, 175–177; Pakistan's human rights debate 398
Convention on the Rights of the Child (CRC); age limit 184, 191–192, 195–196; Article 38 183–186, 194, 196–198; drafting mistake 191–195; establishment of 183–186; Middle East and North Africa 163, 168, 177–179; negotiations and drafting 186–191; Optional Protocol 196
Cook Islands 469, 474, 475, 479–480
Cooper, William 439–442
copyright law 563–564; *see also* intellectual property law
corporate accountability; Accountability and Remedy Project 500–502; Nuremberg 489–491; transnational context 489, 490–494; *UN Guiding Principles on Business and Human Rights (UNGPs)* 497–500
Coulson, Noel 166
Council of Europe, establishment of 147–148
"crimmigration" 589
Cuba; HIV isolation program 476–477; immigration detention 587
Cuban Red Cross 81
cultural context, common heritage of humanity 545–549, 554
cultural rights; China 301–302, 303; freedom of religion 418–419; indigenous activism for human rights 434–444; international law 141–147; universal particularism 233–234
Damien, Patron Saint of persons with leprosy 473
data protection 573–574
de Costa, Ravi 433–434, 438, 440–441
Declaration of Independence 317
Declaration of Philadelphia 259, 263–264, 274
decolonization; anticolonial human rights critique 222–224, 228–231, 235–236; development as a human rights exception 225–228, 232; human rights against and after Empire 224–225; postcolonial human rights critique 231–232; proliferation of human rights language 234–235; solidarity rights 543–544; universal particularism 233–234, 235

Deferred Action for Childhood Arrivals (DACA) program 590
democracy; development as a human rights exception 225–226; institutionalization of a women's rights agenda in Chile 366–368; Mothers of the Plaza de Mayo movement 375, 380–382, 386–387; transitional justice 606, 611–613
democratization of policymaking 321–323
Deng Xiaoping 302
depopulation, Congo 60
detention; immigration 579–594; political 86–87
deterrence, immigration detention 591–593
development; China 303; colonial contexts 211; gender equality and labor 271; as a human rights exception 225–228, 232; students of human rights history 642–643
Development Agenda 568–569
digital citizen movements 572–574
digital rights management (DRM) systems 572–573
disarmament, women activists for 102, 106–108, 111–112, 114–115
discrimination; colonial policies 210–212; equal treatment paradigm 265–269; immigration detention 581, 594; LGBTQ 458–459; sex equality as a human rights norm 122–124, 128–132; special treatment paradigm 269–272
Discrimination Convention 266, 268–269
diseases, quarantine and public health 467–481
Dja Dja Wurrung people 437
domestic jurisprudence 149–154
Donnelly, Jack 180
Du Bois, W. E. B. 208–209, 640

Ebola virus 470–471
Eckel, Jan 241
economic rights; China 301–302, 303; colonial contexts 211; definition 141; domestic jurisprudence 149–154; equal treatment paradigm 265–269; international law 141–147; justiciability 146–154; regional developments 147–149; *see also* development
education; colonial policies 211; human rights history 638–647
Egypt, treaty ratification 170
Eisenhower administration 317
Emachoua, Chrestine 214–215
emotion, history of human rights 621–633
Empire, age of 21–22; human rights against and after Empire 224–225; intra-imperial politics 28–32; John Anderson case 21–33; language of activism 21–22
enlightenment, as human rights narrative 628
environment; biological diversity 570–571; resistance in China 306–307; solidarity rights 543–544, 545
Equal Remuneration Convention 266
Equal Rights International (ERI) 111
Equal Rights Treaty 113
equal treatment paradigm 265–269
Erazo, Viviano 366
European Convention on Human Rights, establishment of 148
European Court of Human Rights (ECHR); establishment of 148; General Data Protection Regulation 573–574; LGBTQ rights 457
expropriated lands 212–213
Extractive Industries Transparency Initiative (EITI) 499–500

Fanon, Frantz 641
Federal Council for the Advancement of Aborigines and Torres Strait Islanders (FCAATSI) 442
female genital mutilation (FGM) 644–645
feminism 9; awareness raising in Chile 362–364; equal treatment paradigm 267–268; as label 110; language and knowledge production 365–366; militarized sexual violence 527–530; Pakistan's human rights debate 397–398, 403–404; 'rights of man' 129–130; sex equality as a human rights norm 122–124, 128–132, 272–273; students of human rights history 644–645; UN Decade for Women 366, 644
Fernandez, José Agustin 608–609
Fiji; HIV response 478–479; leprosy response 475
Finau, Sitaleki 468–470
First World Conference on Women 356
forced labor 265, 494–496
Ford administration 320–321, 323
Four Freedoms 133, 209
Franco dictatorship 508
Fraser, Donald M. 321–323
freedom; development as a human rights exception 225–226; LGBTQ rights 448, 459–460
freedom of association 264
freedom of movement 593
freedom of religion 415–417, 425–426; Canadian Charter of Rights and Freedoms 417–418; cultural rights 418–419; *Ktunaxa* case 415, 421–425; reasonable accommodation 419–421
Full Stop and Due Obedience laws 385

Gálvez, Thelma 363
gay rights *see* LGBTQ rights
gender equality 9, 14; Chilean contributions 354–355, 357–369; equal pay 266; equal treatment paradigm 265–269; human rights historiography 262–263; International Labour Organization 130, 259–261, 263–265; Kuwait Society for Human Rights 348; Middle East and North Africa 163, 165, 168, 170, 175–177; Moroccan Association for Human Rights 345; Muslim rights for women 396–398, 404–406, 407; Pakistani women's autonomy 398–400; Pakistani women's struggles against a theocratic state 395–396; Pakistan's human rights debate 393–394; popular resistance in China 306; Red Cross 80; sex equality as a human rights norm 122–124, 128–132, 272–273; women's rights as human rights 272–274; women's rights as human rights 357; *see also* Convention on the Elimination of all forms of Discrimination Against Women (CEDAW)
General Data Protection Regulation (GDPR) 573–574
Geneva Convention; child rights 188, 189, 193; civilian hostages 89; constraints on state behavior 76–77, 78–79, 82, 88; War on Terror 326–327; World War II 90
Geographic Indications (GIs) 570
germ theory 474
German Democratic Republic (GDR); Berlin Wall, fall of 281–282, 288–293; human rights as movement 283–288; human rights historiography 282–283
German Red Cross 85
Ghana 226–228, 231
government *see* nation-state
'Great Eastern Crisis' (1876) 38–39
Great Powers, international commissions of inquiry in the Balkans (1876–80) 38–39, 40, 49, 50, 51
Greece, human rights violations 319
group rights 544
Guantanamo Bay 327

habeas corpus 207
Hague Codification Conference 113
Hague conference, women activists 100–102
Hague Conventions; civilian hostages 89; constraints on state behavior 76, 78–79, 82, 86; incorporation into Geneva Convention 90; militarized sexual violence 524
Hajjar, Lisa 397
Hansen's Disease 474
Hassan II, King of Morocco 341–342
Hawaii, leprosy cases 471–474
health rights; India 151–152; leprosy and HIV in the Pacific Islands 467–481; quarantine 467–481
Helsinki Accords 360
Helsinki Final Act 642
Helsinki Watch (later Human Rights Watch) 323
heritage in international law 546–549
Hirschfeld, Magnus 452–453
historians in human rights 3–4
"historicization" 2
Hitler, Adolf 126–127
HIV/AIDS 459; the first disease of the human rights era 475–476; isolation in Cuba 476–477; Pacific Islands 477–479; parallels with leprosy 467–481
Holocaust; museum 623, 631; Universal Declaration of Human Rights 639–640
homophile organizations 454–455
homosexuality *see* LGBTQ rights
honor killings 398–399, 401
human dignity 592
human rights; antecedents 22; distinction from humanitarianism 75–76, 91–92; "historicization" 2; as movement 283–288, 323–323
Human Rights Commission of Pakistan (HRCP) 396
Human Rights Day 287
Human Rights First 323
human rights historiography 262–263, 282–283
human rights museum, Canada 13
human rights treaty ratification, Middle East and Islam 163–164, 165–172
Human Rights Watch 223, 323, 327
humanitarianism; child rights 186, 187, 190–195, 196–197; distinction from human rights 75–76, 91–92
humanity in international law 545–551, 553–554
Hurd, Elizabeth 425–426

ICS *see* Congo
Immigration and Customs Enforcement Agency (ICE) 579
Immigration and Nationality Act (INA) 586–587
immigration detention 579–594
independent accountability mechanisms (IAMs) 497
India, social and economic rights 151–152
indigenous activism for human rights 432–444
indigenous peoples; Canadian activism 415, 421–425; Canadian Museum for Human Rights 629; intellectual property law 569–571
individual self-determination 250–252

infectious diseases, medical understanding 474; *see also* HIV/AIDS; leprosy
information politics 605–607, 616–617
Initiative for Peace and Human Rights (IFM) 286
Institute for Sexual Science (ISS) 452–453
institutional capacity 146
institutionalization 609–611
intellectual property law 559–561, 575–576; collective and personal rights 568–572; contemporary struggles over 574–575; digital citizen movements 572–574; from monarchical privilege to creator rights 562–564; from reciprocal rights to universal rights 564–568
intellectual resistance, China 303–304
international accountability 510–511
International Alliance of Women *see* International Woman Suffrage Alliance (IWSA)
International Catholic Child Bureau and Defence for Children International 188
international commission of inquiry in the Congo (early twentieth century) 57–58; advocacy as a practice of persuasion 70–72; evidence for inquiry 58–63, 69–70; legal framework 63–68
International Commission of Jurists (ICJ) 229–230, 231
international commissions of inquiry in the Balkans (1876–80) 37–38, 50–52; Eastern Roumelia 45–50; 'Great Eastern Crisis' 38–39; Russo-Turkish War 39–45
International Committee for Sexual Equality (ICSE) 454–455
International Committee of the Red Cross (ICRC) 75–79; absence of sacred respect 85–89; child rights 184–185, 189, 191–195; gender 80; international legal revisions (1945-9) 90–91, 92; superior laws of humanity 83–85; violence against wounded soldiers, POWs and civilians 82–83
International Convention for the Protection of New Varieties of Plants (UPOV) 575
International Council of Women (ICW) 99, 100–104, 106–108, 109–111
International Court of Justice (ICJ); corporate accountability 502; solidarity rights 543
International Covenant on Civil and Political Rights (ECCPR); China 302; public health 470
International Covenant on Economic, Social and Cultural Rights 141–145, 146–154, 301–302
International Criminal Court (ICC); Alien Tort Statute 489; child soldiers 196; corporate accountability 501–502; establishment of 511
International Criminal Tribunal for Rwanda (ICTR) 534–535
International Criminal Tribunal for the Former Yugoslavia (ICTY) 534–535, 551
International Gay Association (IGA) 456
International Labor Office 261
International Labour Organization (ILO); equal treatment paradigm 265–269; gender equality 130, 259–261, 263–265; post-World War II 259; special treatment paradigm 269–272; structure of 261–262; women's rights as human rights 272–274
international law 13–14; common heritage of humanity 545–551, 553–554; declaration of the rights of man 124–126; domestic jurisprudence 149–154; economic and social rights 141–147; human rights' entry into 126–128; human rights treaty ratification 163–164; immigration detention 584; sex equality 130; sexual violence 534–535; transnational corporate accountability 489, 490–494, 501–502; *see also* legal context
International Law Institute (ILI) 125–126
International League of the Rights of Man (ILRM) 215
International Lesbian and Gay Association (ILGA) 457–458
international peace movement 104–106
International Security Assistance and Arms Export Control Act 323
International Woman Suffrage Alliance (IWSA) 99, 100–104, 106–108, 109–111, 114–115, 268
International Year for Human Rights 283–284
internationalisms; challenges to 114–115; women activists 99, 102–104, 114–115; *see also* transnational rights advocacy
intersectionality, Muslim rights for women 405
intervention/nonintervention 493
intra-imperial politics, British Empire 28–32
Iran; Asma Jahangir 402–403; children in the military 189–190; treaty ratification 170
Islam; diplomatic dialogues between Middle East-UN 172–179; human rights as the betrayal of Muslimness 403–404; human rights treaty ratification in the Middle East 163–164, 165–172; international commissions of inquiry in the Balkans (1876–80) 39–42, 45–51; Muslim rights for women 396–398, 404–406, 407; new proposals for human rights in Muslim contexts 404–406; Pakistan's Islamization of the 1980s 392, 393–395
Israel 338–341
Italo-Abyssinian (Ethiopian) War 88

Japan; Asia-Pacific War 524–525; feminism 528–530; joint communiqué with South Korea 533; post-World War II tribunals 524–525
Jefferson, Thomas 317
Jehovah's Witnesses 416, 417
Jewish Canadians 624–625
Jews, Nazi Germany 126–127
jobs *see* labor
Johnson administration 319
Joinet, Louis 607, 612, 613
Jordan, treaty ratification 169, 176
justiciability; economic rights 146–154; social rights 146–154

Kang Youwei 300
Kato, David 646
Kennedy administration 318–319
Kenyon, Dorothy 122, 123
Kirchner, Cristina Fernández de 376, 384–387
Kirchner, Néstor 376, 384–387, 605, 613–616
Kirdjali commission of inquiry 45–50
Kirkwood, Julieta 357, 365–366
Kissinger, Henry 320–321, 323
knowledge creation 12–13, 365–366
Korean War 526–527
Krenz, Egon 292
Ktunaxa case 415, 421–425
Kuwait; citizenship 347–348, 349; treaty ratification 169, 170–171, 174–175
Kuwait Society for Human Rights 346–349

labor; equal treatment paradigm 265–269; gender equality 130, 259–261; resistance in China 306–307; special treatment paradigm 269–272; standards and laws 261–262; work-life balance 269–272; *see also* International Labour Organization
Lacks, Henrietta 572
land ownership, colonial contexts 212–213
language; of activism 22–24; Arab world human rights framework 338–339, 345; feminism 365–366; human rights 124, 125; proliferation of human rights language 234–235; reasonable accommodation of religion 420; 'rights of man' 124, 128–132
Las Protestas 366–367
Latin America; transitional justice and shifting visions of political change 376, 603–617; universal jurisdiction 509, 510–519
Lauterpacht, Hersh 122–123
Lawyers Committee for International Human Rights (later Human Rights First) 323
League of Nations 7; creation of 125; human rights' entry into international arena 126–128; militarized sexual violence 524; Permanent Mandates Commission 204–205; replacement of 209; sex equality 129–130; women activists 100, 106, 112–114
League of the Rights of Man 206
legal context 2; Al Haq in Palestine 338–341; Chinese legal professionals' resistance to human rights 304–306; colonial contexts 8–9; Congo reform (early twentieth century) 63–68; domestic jurisprudence 149–154; economic and social rights 146–154; equal rights through peace 112–114; immigration detention 586–587; labor 261–262; legalism in Africa's internationally mandated territories 204–209; prisoners of war (POWs), civilians and wounded soldiers 83–85, 89, 90–91; sex equality 130; Sharia 165–175, 177, 395, 397; US human rights policy 316–317; *see also* international law
legalism, Africa's internationally mandated territories 204–209
legitimacy; economic and social rights 146; Socialist Unity Party 289–290
Leopold II, king-sovereign of the Congo 57, 58, 60–61, 63, 65, 68–70
leprosy, health rights in the Pacific Islands 467–481
Leprosy Conference 474–475
lesbian rights *see* LGBTQ rights
LGBTQ rights; immigration detention 590; as international movement 448–461; Obama administration 327; students of human rights history 646
'liberal' dictatorship 401–402
liberalism; immigration detention 580, 582–583; transnational corporate accountability 489–490, 492
Liu, Lydia 207–208
Liu Xiaobo 304
Lopatka, Adam 192–194

Machel, Graça 195–196
Malagasy citizenship campaign 206, 216
Malala Yousafzai 645
'mandate of heaven' principle 299
mandate system, colonial Africa 204–209
Mandelstam, André 125–126
Maritain, Jacques 639
marriage; Middle East and North Africa 176; Sharia law 399–400
Masih, Manzoor 402
Masih, Rehmat 402
Masih, Salamat 402
Massey, Douglas 581

maternity protection 269–270, 273
May 4th Movement 300, 304
memory; importance for Mothers of the Plaza de Mayo 382–383; transitional justice 611–613
metaphor, Canadian Museum for Human Rights 630–631
Middle East and North Africa (MENA) 164; diplomatic dialogues with UN 172–179; human rights treaty ratification 163–164, 165–172
military; Mothers of the Plaza de Mayo 375–388; protection of children from military recruitment 183–191, 188, 196–198; Red Cross/Red Crescent movement 78–82; sexual violence and international law 534–535; sexual violence campaigns and responses 527–534; sexual violence cases 523–527; violence against wounded soldiers, POWs and civilians 77, 82–83
Mirkine-Guetzevitch, Boris 124
Missouri Compromise 24
Molokai island 473, 474–475
monarchical privilege 562–564
Moreno, Aida 354, 359, 362–364, 369
Moroccan Association for Human Rights (AMDH) 342–346
Moroccan League for the Defense of Human Rights (LMDDH) 342–346
Moroccan Organization for Human Rights (OMDH) 342–346
Morocco; NGO practices 337, 341–346; treaty ratification 178–179
Mothers of the Plaza de Mayo 375–388, 642
Moyn, Samuel 14, 58, 75, 142, 217, 241, 561, 632
Mujeres de Chile (Women of Chile, MUDECHI) 363–364
multistakeholder initiatives (MSIs) 499–500
museums; Canadian Museum for Human Rights 13, 621–633; Center for Documentation and Archive for the Defense of Human Rights 605, 611–613, 614, 615; Holocaust 623–625, 631
Muslims *see* Islam

nation-state; Argentina and the Mothers of the Plaza de Mayo movement 375–388; constraints on state behavior 76, 78–79; obedience to the state 78–82; role in controlling migration 580, 583, 584
national security 11–12
national self-determination, Botswana 250–252
national sovereignty; British Empire 28–32; constraints on state behavior 76–77
Native American Graves Protection & Repatriation Act (NAGPRA) 570–571
Native Title Act 443
Nazi Germany; forced labor 494–496; League of Nations 126–127; LGBTQ rights 453–454; military tribunals 525–526; Nuremberg Trials 511; transnational corporate accountability 489–490
Nehru, Jawaharlal 229–230
neoliberalism, importance of for Mothers of the Plaza de Mayo 382–384
new human rights (solidarity rights) 542–554
New International Economic Order 223–224
New International Order 111
New Internationalism 6, 101–102
New York Declaration 125–126, 128
Nigeria 226
Nixon administration 320
Nkrumah, Kwame 226–228, 231
non-appropriation 547
nongovernmental organizations (NGOs) 4; 1980s era of optimism 10–11; anticolonial human rights critique 223, 229–230; Arab world 337–349; child rights 188–189; corporate accountability 499–500; economic and social rights 143–144; militarized sexual violence 529; 'post-optimism' world 15; proliferation of human rights language 234–235; students of human rights history 642
nonintervention 493
non-sovereignty 547
North Atlantic Treaty Organization (NATO) 319–320
Nuremberg Principles 511
Nuremberg Trials 511

Obama administration; immigration detention 581–582, 588, 590, 591; LGBTQ rights 327, 459–460
Obi, Chike 225–226
Oman, treaty ratification 177
Open Door International (ODI); equal treatment paradigm 268; feminism 111; sex equality 132
Orentlicher, Diane 606–607, 612–613
Organization for Economic Cooperation and Development (OECD) 497
Organization of African Unity (OAU) 250–252
Ottoman Empire; 'Great Eastern Crisis' (1876) 38–40; Red Crescent movement 79, 85

Pacific Islands, public health and human rights 467–481
Pakistan's human rights debate 392–393; Asma Jahangir 392, 395–396, 398–407; human rights as the betrayal of Muslimness 403–404; Islamization of the 1980s 392, 393–395;

'liberal' dictatorship 401–402; Muslim rights for women 396–398, 404–406, 407; women's autonomy 398–400; women's struggles against a theocratic state 395–396
Palau, Rosa 611–612
Palestine, NGO practices 337, 338–341
Pan-American Union 130
Paraguay, transitional justice 607–613, 615
Paris Convention 568
patriarchy, Chile 357–358, 369
peace; 1989 revolution 283, 290–292, 293; cooperation for peace and disarmament 106–108; equal rights through 112–114; revival of movement 285–288; as a unifying goal in the 1920s 102–104
Permanent Mandates Commission 204–205
Perón, Juan Domingo 377
personal rights, intellectual property law 571–572
personal sovereignty, British Empire 28–32
pharmaceuticals access (A2P) 574–575
Phipps, E. Constantine 65–66, 70
phrenology 450–451
Pinochet, Augusto 508, 509, 512–513, 514–515
Plantation Convention 270–271
policy *see* international law legal context
political detainees 86–87
political prisoners 86–87
political rights, colonial contexts 213–217
postcolonial human rights critique 231–232
pregnant women, immigration detention 588
Presidential Review Memorandum 324
Princeton Principles 509
prisoners of war (POWs); absence of sacred respect 85–89; superior laws of humanity 83–85; violence against wounded soldiers, POWs and civilians 77, 82–83
privacy; biometric information 571–572; digital citizen movements 572–573
progressive realization 143–144
property rights *see* intellectual property law
Protection of Women (Criminal Laws Amendment) Act 2006 401
Protestantism, advocacy for human rights 291
Protocol of San Salvador 148–149
public opinion, resistance in China 306–307

Qatar, treaty ratification 168, 173–174
Qing dynasty 299–300
quarantine and public health 467–481
Quataert, Jean 643–644

racial discrimination; Bechuanaland 245–247; colonial policies 210–212; human rights history 640; immigration detention 581, 594; indigenous activism in Australia 443–444; Johnson administration 319; labor 268–269; Third World 232
Rädda Barnen 188–189, 192
rape; campaigns and responses 527–534; international law 534–535; military cases 523–527; Sharia law 401
Rawls, John 493
Reagan administration 324–325
reciprocal rights, intellectual property law 564–568
Red Crescent movement; absence of sacred respect 85–90; child rights 191–192; humanitarianism 75–77, 91–92; international legal revisions (1945-9) 90–91; obedience to the state 78–82; origins 79; superior laws of humanity 83–85; violence against wounded soldiers, POWs and civilians 77, 82–83
Red Cross movement; absence of sacred respect 85–90; child rights 191–192; humanitarianism 75–77, 91–92; international legal revisions (1945-9) 90–91; obedience to the state 78–82; origins 78; superior laws of humanity 83–85; violence against wounded soldiers, POWs and civilians 77, 82–83
refugees; immigration detention 579–594; John Anderson case 21–33
religion *see* Catholic Church Christianity Islam
religious freedom *see* freedom of religion
Reservations, Understandings and Declarations (RUDs) 163–164, 167–172
Rhodope Mountains Commission 42–44, *43*, 51
right to collective bargaining 264
'rights defenders' movement 305–306
'rights of man' 124, 128–132; colonial context 208, 215; League of the Rights of Man 206; *see also* human rights
rights of peoples (solidarity rights) 542–554
Roman Catholicism *see* Catholic Church
Roosevelt, Eleanor 317
Roosevelt administration 317
Rorty, Richard 630, 633
Roumelia, international commissions of inquiry 45–50
Rudolphy, Coca 360–361
Ruggie, John 497–498
Rukeba, François 211–212, 214
Russian Red Cross 85
Russo-Turkish War, European commission following 39–45
Rwanda 326

Said, Judith 614–616
Saima Sarwar 400
Santa Cruz, Adriana 366

Sarlo, Beatriz 616
Saudi Arabia; treaty ratification 167, 171–173, 175, 176–177, 178; universal particularism 235
Schaerer Prono case 607–608
scholarship; overview of human rights scholarship 1–5; students of human rights history 638–647
Scilingo, Adolfo Francisco 514
Scott, James Brown 129
self-determination 250–252
self-help initiatives, gender equality 358–360
Sen, Amartya 643
Seretse Khama 243–244, 246–252
Servicio Nacional de la Mujer (SERNAM) 367–368
'sex' 124; *see also* gender equality
sex equality as a human rights norm 122–124, 128–132, 272–273
sexual violence; campaigns and responses 527–534; immigration detention 590; international law 534–535; military cases 523–527; Sharia law 401
shadow reporting 176–177
Sharia law 165–175, 177, 395, 397; blasphemy law 401–402; marriage 399–400; rape and adultery 401
Siracusa Principles 470
slavery; John Anderson case 24–33; militarized sexual violence 523–525
social class, women's rights 356–357
social rights; definition 141; domestic jurisprudence 149–154; international law 141–147; justiciability 146–154; regional developments 147–149
socialism; equal treatment paradigm 267–268; German Democratic Republic 281–283
socialist human rights 9–10
Socialist Unity Party (SED); Berlin Wall, fall of 281–282, 288–293; human rights as movement 283–288; human rights historiography 282–283
sodomy laws 449–450, 451–452
soldiers *see* military prisoners of war (POWs)
solidarity; art system 359–360; Chile 359–361; as concept 544, 551–552; internationalization of women's rights 360–361
solidarity rights 542–554
South Africa; apartheid 223, 243, 248; Permanent Mandates Commission 205; social and economic rights 149–150
South Korea; feminism 528–530; joint communiqué with Japan 533; sex industry 527; Wednesday demonstration 532–533
sovereignty, British Empire 28–32
Soviet Union 282, 323–324
Spain, Franco dictatorship and universal jurisdiction 507–519
Spanish Civil War 89, 111
special treatment paradigm 269–272
state *see* nation-state
Statute of Anne 562–563
Stonewall riots 456
students of human rights history 638–647

Tehran conference 641–642
terrorism, US human rights policy 326–327
theocracy, Pakistan's human rights debate 395–396
third generation of human rights (solidarity rights) 542–554
Third World; anticolonial human rights critique 222–224, 223–224, 228–231, 235–236; development as a human rights exception 225–228, 232; postcolonial human rights critique 231–232; proliferation of human rights language 234–235; universal particularism 233–234
Todaro, Rosalba 363
Torres Strait Islanders 435
torture, Convention Against Torture (CAT) 163, 168, 171–175
Trade Related Aspects of Intellectual Property Rights (TRIPS) 568–569, 574
tradition, importance in China 301
traditional knowledge 569–571
transitional justice; Latin America 376, 603–617; universal jurisdiction 510–511
transnational corporate accountability 489, 490–494, 501–502
transnational public 6–7
transnational rights advocacy 14; challenges to internationalisms 114–115; women activists 99–100; *see also* internationalisms
Treaty of Versailles 300
Trump administration, immigration detention 580, 582, 590–591
Truth and Reconciliation Commission of Canada (TRC) 626–627
Tunisia, treaty ratification 170
Twelvetrees, Harper 24–25

Ukrainian Canadians 624–625
Ulrichs, Karl Heinrich 452
UN Decade for Women 366, 644
UN Guiding Principles on Business and Human Rights (UNGPs) 497–500
UNESCO Memory of the World register 612
UNESCO world heritage 546–552
United Arab Emirates (UAE), treaty ratification 169, 171–172, 177–178

United International Bureaux for the Protection of Intellectual Property (BIRPI) 566–568
United Kingdom *see* Britain
United Nations; establishment of 141; freedom and equality 122; overview of role 7–8
United States; Alien Tort Statute 491–494; Bush, George H. W. administration 325–326; Bush, George W. administration 326–327, 458; Carter administration 323–324; Clinton administration 326; Cold War 317–318; after the Cold War 325–326; democratization of policymaking 321–323; Ford/Kissinger era 320–321, 323; historical overview of human rights policy 316–317; human rights movement 323–325; immigration detention 580, 586–587, 588–591, 592; intellectual property law 563–572; Johnson administration 319; Kennedy's new approach 318–319; Nixon administration 320; Obama administration 327, 459–460, 581–582, 588, 590, 591; Reagan administration 324–325; Trump administration 580, 582, 590–591; War on Terror 326–327
Universal Declaration of Human Rights (UDHR); activism prior to 203–204; Africa 203–204, 207–209; anticolonial human rights critique 223–224, 228–231; Arab world 337–338; economic and social rights 142–145; establishment of 141; gender equality 123, 355–357; immigration detention 593; indigenous activism for human rights 432; Pakistan's human rights debate 393; postcolonial human rights critique 231–232; students of human rights history 639–641; types of rights 142; universal particularism 233–234
universal human rights 6; Africa's UN trust territories 209–217; anticolonial human rights renovation 228–231; Arab world NGO practices 337–349; British Empire 22–33; indigenous activism in Australia 434–437; intellectual property law 564–568; LGBTQ 461; national settings 11; regional developments 147–149; sex equality 128–129
universal jurisdiction; Alien Tort Statute 489, 490–492; application and history of 507–509; definition, scope, and limits 509–510; Franco dictatorship 515–518; international community 492–493; Latin America and Spain 511–515; selective application of a contested global norm 518–519; as a transitional justice mechanism 510–511
universal particularism 233–234, 235
Uruguay 81–82, 646

veterans' rights movement 206
Victorian Aborigines Advancement League (VAAL) 442
Vienna conference, women activists 104
Vienna Convention on the Law of Treaties (VCLT) 167–168
voice of the victim 611–613
Voting Rights Act 319

wali 398–399
Walsh, Michaela 643
War on Terror 326–327, 393
war victims; absence of sacred respect 85–90; international legal revisions (1945-9) 90–91; Kuwait Society for Human Rights 348–349; Mothers of the Plaza de Mayo 375–388; non-combatants/combatants distinction 75, 79; obedience to the state 78–82; Red Cross/Red Crescent movement 75–76; superior laws of humanity 83–85; violence against wounded soldiers, POWs and civilians 82–83; *see also* military
wartime internment 585–586
Webster-Ashburton Treaty 21
Westlake, John 67–68
Whitman, Walt 450–451
women activists; Asma Jahangir 392, 395–396, 398–407; challenges to internationalisms 114–115; Chile 354–366; cooperation for peace and disarmament 106–108; equal rights through peace 112–114; the Hague 100–102; internationalism 99, 102–104, 114–115; militarized sexual violence 523–525; Mothers of the Plaza de Mayo 375–388; peace activism methods 104–106; peace as a unifying goal in the 1920s 102–104; students of human rights history 644–645; UN Decade for Women 366, 644; Women's International League for Peace and Freedom 100–102; between the World Wars 99–116; *see also* Convention on the Elimination of all forms of Discrimination Against Women (CEDAW)
Women's Consultative Committee on Nationality 112
Women's International Democratic Federation (WIDF) 356, 360–361
Women's International League for Peace and Freedom (WILPF) 100–111, 113–115, 356
Women's International War Crimes Tribunal 531–532
Women's Peace Crusade 111
women's rights as human rights 272–274
Women's World Banking (WWB) 643
work-life balance 269–272
World Federation of Trade Unions (WFTU) 267

World Health Organization (WHO) 471, 475, 476
World Heritage Convention 549–550
World Intellectual Property Organization (WIPO) 568–572, 572–573, 575
World War I, Red Cross/Red Crescent movement 83
World War II; Geneva Convention 90; Holocaust museum 623, 631; LGBTQ rights 453–454; military tribunals 525–526
Wright, Richard 226–227, 640–641

Yogyakarta Principles 458–459
Yorta Yorta nation 437, 443
Yugoslavia 326

Zia ul Haq 394–395
zina 401–402, 405
Zubaida, Sami 165–170

For Product Safety Concerns and Information please contact our EU
representative GPSR@taylorandfrancis.com
Taylor & Francis Verlag GmbH, Kaufingerstraße 24, 80331 München, Germany

www.ingramcontent.com/pod-product-compliance
Ingram Content Group UK Ltd.
Pitfield, Milton Keynes, MK11 3LW, UK
UKHW050052200926
475702UK00019B/2799
9781032089669